Artificial Intelligence

**PRENTICE HALL SERIES
IN ARTIFICIAL INTELLIGENCE**
Stuart Russell and Peter Norvig, Editors

Artificial Intelligence
A Modern Approach

Stuart J. Russell and Peter Norvig

Contributing writers:
John F. Canny, Jitendra M. Malik, Douglas D. Edwards

Prentice-Hall International, Inc.

© 1995 by Prentice Hall, Inc.
Upper Saddle River, NJ 07458

The author and publisher of this book have used their best efforts in preparing this book. These efforts include the development, research, and testing of the theories and programs to determine their effectiveness. The author and publisher shall not be liable in any event for incidental or consequential damages in connection with, or arising out of, the furnishing, performance, or use of these programs.

Printed in the United States of America

10   9   8   7

ISBN   0-13-360124-2

Prentice-Hall International (UK) Limited, *London*
Prentice-Hall of Australia Pty. Limited, *Sydney*
Prentice-Hall of Canada, Inc., *Toronto*
Prentice-Hall Hispanoamericana, S. A., *Mexico*
Prentice-Hall of India Private Limited, *New Delhi*
Prentice-Hall of Japan, Inc., *Tokyo*
Pearson Education Asia Pte. Ltd., *Singapore*
Editora Prentice-Hall do Brasil, Ltda., *Rio de Janeiro*

For my parents — S.J.R.

For Isabella — P.N.

Preface

There are many textbooks that offer an introduction to artificial intelligence (AI). This text has five principal features that together distinguish it from other texts.

1. *Unified presentation of the field.*
   Some texts are organized from a historical perspective, describing each of the major problems and solutions that have been uncovered in 40 years of AI research. Although there is value to this perspective, the result is to give the impression of a dozen or so barely related subfields, each with its own techniques and problems. We have chosen to present AI as a unified field, working on a common problem in various guises. This has entailed some reinterpretation of past research, showing how it fits within a common framework and how it relates to other work that was historically separate. It has also led us to include material not normally covered in AI texts.

2. *Intelligent agent design.*
   The unifying theme of the book is the concept of an *intelligent agent.* In this view, the problem of AI is to describe and build agents that receive percepts from the environment and perform actions. Each such agent is implemented by a function that maps percepts to actions, and we cover different ways to represent these functions, such as production systems, reactive agents, logical planners, neural networks, and decision-theoretic systems. We explain the role of learning as extending the reach of the designer into unknown environments, and show how it constrains agent design, favoring explicit knowledge representation and reasoning. We treat robotics and vision not as independently defined problems, but as occurring in the service of goal achievement. We stress the importance of the task environment characteristics in determining the appropriate agent design.

3. *Comprehensive and up-to-date coverage.*
   We cover areas that are sometimes underemphasized, including reasoning under uncertainty, learning, neural networks, natural language, vision, robotics, and philosophical foundations. We cover many of the more recent ideas in the field, including simulated annealing, memory-bounded search, global ontologies, dynamic and adaptive probabilistic (Bayesian) networks, computational learning theory, and reinforcement learning. We also provide extensive notes and references on the historical sources and current literature for the main ideas in each chapter.

4. *Equal emphasis on theory and practice.*
   Theory and practice are given equal emphasis. All material is grounded in first principles with rigorous theoretical analysis where appropriate, but the point of the theory is to get the concepts across and explain how they are used in actual, fielded systems. The reader of this book will come away with an appreciation for the basic concepts and mathematical methods of AI, and also with an idea of what can and cannot be done with today's technology, at what cost, and using what techniques.

5. *Understanding through implementation.*
   The principles of intelligent agent design are clarified by using them to actually build agents. Chapter 2 provides an overview of agent design, including a basic agent and environment

project. Subsequent chapters include programming exercises that ask the student to add capabilities to the agent, making it behave more and more interestingly and (we hope) intelligently. Algorithms are presented at three levels of detail: prose descriptions and pseudo-code in the text, and complete Common Lisp programs available on the Internet or on floppy disk. All the agent programs are interoperable and work in a uniform framework for simulated environments.

This book is primarily intended for use in an undergraduate course or course sequence. It can also be used in a graduate-level course (perhaps with the addition of some of the primary sources suggested in the bibliographical notes). Because of its comprehensive coverage and the large number of detailed algorithms, it is useful as a primary reference volume for AI graduate students and professionals wishing to branch out beyond their own subfield. We also hope that AI researchers could benefit from thinking about the unifying approach we advocate.

The only prerequisite is familiarity with basic concepts of computer science (algorithms, data structures, complexity) at a sophomore level. Freshman calculus is useful for understanding neural networks and adaptive probabilistic networks in detail. Some experience with nonnumeric programming is desirable, but can be picked up in a few weeks study. We provide implementations of all algorithms in Common Lisp (see Appendix B), but other languages such as Scheme, Prolog, Smalltalk, C++, or ML could be used instead.

Overview of the book

The book is divided into eight parts. Part I, "Artificial Intelligence," sets the stage for all the others, and offers a view of the AI enterprise based around the idea of intelligent agents—systems that can decide what to do and do it. Part II, "Problem Solving," concentrates on methods for deciding what to do when one needs to think ahead several steps, for example in navigating across country or playing chess. Part III, "Knowledge and Reasoning," discusses ways to represent knowledge about the world—how it works, what it is currently like, what one's actions might do—and how to reason logically with that knowledge. Part IV, "Acting Logically," then discusses how to use these reasoning methods to decide what to do, particularly by constructing *plans*. Part V, "Uncertain Knowledge and Reasoning," is analogous to Parts III and IV, but it concentrates on reasoning and decision-making in the presence of *uncertainty* about the world, as might be faced, for example, by a system for medical diagnosis and treatment.

Together, Parts II to V describe that part of the intelligent agent responsible for reaching decisions. Part VI, "Learning," describes methods for generating the knowledge required by these decision-making components; it also introduces a new kind of component, the *neural network*, and its associated learning procedures. Part VII, "Communicating, Perceiving, and Acting," describes ways in which an intelligent agent can perceive its environment so as to know what is going on, whether by vision, touch, hearing, or understanding language; and ways in which it can turn its plans into real actions, either as robot motion or as natural language utterances. Finally, Part VIII, "Conclusions," analyses the past and future of AI, and provides some light amusement by discussing what AI really is and why it has already succeeded to some degree, and airing the views of those philosophers who believe that AI can never succeed at all.

Using this book

This is a big book; covering *all* the chapters and the projects would take two semesters. You will notice that the book is divided into 27 chapters, which makes it easy to select the appropriate material for any chosen course of study. Each chapter can be covered in approximately one week. Some reasonable choices for a variety of quarter and semester courses are as follows:

- *One-quarter general introductory course*:
  Chapters 1, 2, 3, 6, 7, 9, 11, 14, 15, 18, 22.
- *One-semester general introductory course*:
  Chapters 1, 2, 3, 4, 6, 7, 9, 11, 13, 14, 15, 18, 19, 22, 24, 26, 27.
- *One-quarter course with concentration on search and planning*:
  Chapters 1, 2, 3, 4, 5, 6, 7, 9, 11, 12, 13.
- *One-quarter course with concentration on reasoning and expert systems*:
  Chapters 1, 2, 3, 6, 7, 8, 9, 10, 11, 14, 15, 16.
- *One-quarter course with concentration on natural language*:
  Chapters 1, 2, 3, 6, 7, 8, 9, 14, 15, 22, 23, 26, 27.
- *One-semester course with concentration on learning and neural networks*:
  Chapters 1, 2, 3, 4, 6, 7, 9, 14, 15, 16, 17, 18, 19, 20, 21.
- *One-semester course with concentration on vision and robotics*:
  Chapters 1, 2, 3, 4, 6, 7, 11, 13, 14, 15, 16, 17, 24, 25, 20.

These sequences could be used for both undergraduate and graduate courses. The relevant parts of the book could also be used to provide the first phase of graduate specialty courses. For example, Part VI could be used in conjunction with readings from the literature in a course on machine learning.

We have decided *not* to designate certain sections as "optional" or certain exercises as "difficult," as individual tastes and backgrounds vary widely. Exercises requiring significant programming are marked with a keyboard icon, and those requiring some investigation of the literature are marked with a book icon. Altogether, over 300 exercises are included. Some of them are large enough to be considered term projects. Many of the exercises can best be solved by taking advantage of the code repository, which is described in Appendix B. Throughout the book, important points are marked with a *pointing icon*.

If you have any comments on the book, we'd like to hear from you. Appendix B includes information on how to contact us.

Acknowledgements

Jitendra Malik wrote most of Chapter 24 (Vision) and John Canny wrote most of Chapter 25 (Robotics). Doug Edwards researched the Historical Notes sections for all chapters and wrote much of them. Tim Huang helped with formatting of the diagrams and algorithms. Maryann Simmons prepared the 3-D model from which the cover illustration was produced, and Lisa Marie Sardegna did the postprocessing for the final image. Alan Apt, Mona Pompili, and Sondra Chavez at Prentice Hall tried their best to keep us on schedule and made many helpful suggestions on design and content.

Stuart would like to thank his parents, brother, and sister for their encouragement and their patience at his extended absence. He hopes to be home for Christmas. He would also like to thank Loy Sheflott for her patience and support. He hopes to be home some time tomorrow afternoon. His intellectual debt to his Ph.D. advisor, Michael Genesereth, is evident throughout the book. RUGS (Russell's Unusual Group of Students) have been unusually helpful.

Peter would like to thank his parents (Torsten and Gerda) for getting him started, his advisor (Bob Wilensky), supervisors (Bill Woods and Bob Sproull) and employer (Sun Microsystems) for supporting his work in AI, and his wife (Kris) and friends for encouraging and tolerating him through the long hours of writing.

Before publication, drafts of this book were used in 26 courses by about 1000 students. Both of us deeply appreciate the many comments of these students and instructors (and other reviewers). We can't thank them all individually, but we would like to acknowledge the especially helpful comments of these people:

Tony Barrett, Howard Beck, John Binder, Larry Bookman, Chris Brown, Lauren Burka, Murray Campbell, Anil Chakravarthy, Roberto Cipolla, Doug Edwards, Kutluhan Erol, Jeffrey Forbes, John Fosler, Bob Futrelle, Sabine Glesner, Barbara Grosz, Steve Hanks, Othar Hansson, Jim Hendler, Tim Huang, Seth Hutchinson, Dan Jurafsky, Leslie Pack Kaelbling, Keiji Kanazawa, Surekha Kasibhatla, Simon Kasif, Daphne Koller, Rich Korf, James Kurien, John Lazzaro, Jason Leatherman, Jon LeBlanc, Jim Martin, Andy Mayer, Steve Minton, Leora Morgenstern, Ron Musick, Stuart Nelson, Steve Omohundro, Ron Parr, Tony Passera, Michael Pazzani, Ira Pohl, Martha Pollack, Bruce Porter, Malcolm Pradhan, Lorraine Prior, Greg Provan, Philip Resnik, Richard Scherl, Daniel Sleator, Robert Sproull, Lynn Stein, Devika Subramanian, Rich Sutton, Jonathan Tash, Austin Tate, Mark Torrance, Randall Upham, Jim Waldo, Bonnie Webber, Michael Wellman, Dan Weld, Richard Yen, Shlomo Zilberstein.

Summary of Contents

Contents

Part I

ARTIFICIAL INTELLIGENCE

The two chapters in this part introduce the subject of Artificial Intelligence or AI and our approach to the subject: that AI is the study of *agents* that exist in an environment and perceive and act.

1 INTRODUCTION

In which we try to explain why we consider artificial intelligence to be a subject most worthy of study, and in which we try to decide what exactly it is, this being a good thing to decide before embarking.

ARTIFICIAL
INTELLIGENCE

Humankind has given itself the scientific name **homo sapiens**—man the wise—because our mental capacities are so important to our everyday lives and our sense of self. The field of **artificial intelligence**, or AI, attempts to understand intelligent entities. Thus, one reason to study it is to learn more about ourselves. But unlike philosophy and psychology, which are also concerned with intelligence, AI strives to *build* intelligent entities as well as understand them. Another reason to study AI is that these constructed intelligent entities are interesting and useful in their own right. AI has produced many significant and impressive products even at this early stage in its development. Although no one can predict the future in detail, it is clear that computers with human-level intelligence (or better) would have a huge impact on our everyday lives and on the future course of civilization.

AI addresses one of the ultimate puzzles. How is it possible for a slow, tiny brain, whether biological or electronic, to perceive, understand, predict, and manipulate a world far larger and more complicated than itself? How do we go about making something with those properties? These are hard questions, but unlike the search for faster-than-light travel or an antigravity device, the researcher in AI has solid evidence that the quest is possible. All the researcher has to do is look in the mirror to see an example of an intelligent system.

AI is one of the newest disciplines. It was formally initiated in 1956, when the name was coined, although at that point work had been under way for about five years. Along with modern genetics, it is regularly cited as the "field I would most like to be in" by scientists in other disciplines. A student in physics might reasonably feel that all the good ideas have already been taken by Galileo, Newton, Einstein, and the rest, and that it takes many years of study before one can contribute new ideas. AI, on the other hand, still has openings for a full-time Einstein.

The study of intelligence is also one of the oldest disciplines. For over 2000 years, philosophers have tried to understand how seeing, learning, remembering, and reasoning could, or should,

3

be done.[1] The advent of usable computers in the early 1950s turned the learned but armchair speculation concerning these mental faculties into a real experimental and theoretical discipline. Many felt that the new "Electronic Super-Brains" had unlimited potential for intelligence. "Faster Than Einstein" was a typical headline. But as well as providing a vehicle for creating artificially intelligent entities, the computer provides a tool for testing theories of intelligence, and many theories failed to withstand the test—a case of "out of the armchair, into the fire." AI has turned out to be more difficult than many at first imagined, and modern ideas are much richer, more subtle, and more interesting as a result.

AI currently encompasses a huge variety of subfields, from general-purpose areas such as perception and logical reasoning, to specific tasks such as playing chess, proving mathematical theorems, writing poetry, and diagnosing diseases. Often, scientists in other fields move gradually into artificial intelligence, where they find the tools and vocabulary to systematize and automate the intellectual tasks on which they have been working all their lives. Similarly, workers in AI can choose to apply their methods to any area of human intellectual endeavor. In this sense, it is truly a universal field.

1.1   WHAT IS AI?

We have now explained why AI is exciting, but we have not said what it *is*. We could just say, "Well, it has to do with smart programs, so let's get on and write some." But the history of science shows that it is helpful to aim at the right goals. Early alchemists, looking for a potion for eternal life and a method to turn lead into gold, were probably off on the wrong foot. Only when the aim changed, to that of finding explicit theories that gave accurate predictions of the terrestrial world, in the same way that early astronomy predicted the apparent motions of the stars and planets, could the scientific method emerge and productive science take place.

Definitions of artificial intelligence according to eight recent textbooks are shown in Figure 1.1. These definitions vary along two main dimensions. The ones on top are concerned with *thought processes* and *reasoning*, whereas the ones on the bottom address *behavior*. Also, the definitions on the left measure success in terms of *human* performance, whereas the ones

RATIONALITY

on the right measure against an *ideal* concept of intelligence, which we will call **rationality**. A system is rational if it does the right thing. This gives us four possible goals to pursue in artificial intelligence, as seen in the caption of Figure 1.1.

Historically, all four approaches have been followed. As one might expect, a tension exists between approaches centered around humans and approaches centered around rationality.[2] A human-centered approach must be an empirical science, involving hypothesis and experimental

---

[1] A more recent branch of philosophy is concerned with proving that AI is impossible. We will return to this interesting viewpoint in Chapter 26.

[2] We should point out that by distinguishing between *human* and *rational* behavior, we are not suggesting that humans are necessarily "irrational" in the sense of "emotionally unstable" or "insane." One merely note that we often make mistakes; we are not all chess grandmasters even though we may know all the rules of chess; and unfortunately, not everyone gets an A on the exam. Some systematic errors in human reasoning are cataloged by Kahneman *et al.* (1982).

"The exciting new effort to make computers think ... *machines with minds*, in the full and literal sense" (Haugeland, 1985)	"The study of mental faculties through the use of computational models" (Charniak and McDermott, 1985)
"[The automation of] activities that we associate with human thinking, activities such as decision-making, problem solving, learning ..." (Bellman, 1978)	"The study of the computations that make it possible to perceive, reason, and act" (Winston, 1992)
"The art of creating machines that perform functions that require intelligence when performed by people" (Kurzweil, 1990)	"A field of study that seeks to explain and emulate intelligent behavior in terms of computational processes" (Schalkoff, 1990)
"The study of how to make computers do things at which, at the moment, people are better" (Rich and Knight, 1991)	"The branch of computer science that is concerned with the automation of intelligent behavior" (Luger and Stubblefield, 1993)

Figure 1.1   Some definitions of AI. They are organized into four categories:

Systems that think like humans.	Systems that think rationally.
Systems that act like humans.	Systems that act rationally.

confirmation. A rationalist approach involves a combination of mathematics and engineering. People in each group sometimes cast aspersions on work done in the other groups, but the truth is that each direction has yielded valuable insights. Let us look at each in more detail.

Acting humanly: The Turing Test approach

TURING TEST

The **Turing Test**, proposed by Alan Turing (1950), was designed to provide a satisfactory operational definition of intelligence. Turing defined intelligent behavior as the ability to achieve human-level performance in all cognitive tasks, sufficient to fool an interrogator. Roughly speaking, the test he proposed is that the computer should be interrogated by a human via a teletype, and passes the test if the interrogator cannot tell if there is a computer or a human at the other end. Chapter 26 discusses the details of the test, and whether or not a computer is really intelligent if it passes. For now, programming a computer to pass the test provides plenty to work on. The computer would need to possess the following capabilities:

NATURAL LANGUAGE PROCESSING

◇ **natural language processing** to enable it to communicate successfully in English (or some other human language);

KNOWLEDGE REPRESENTATION

◇ **knowledge representation** to store information provided before or during the interrogation;

AUTOMATED REASONING

◇ **automated reasoning** to use the stored information to answer questions and to draw new conclusions;

MACHINE LEARNING

◇ **machine learning** to adapt to new circumstances and to detect and extrapolate patterns.

Turing's test deliberately avoided direct physical interaction between the interrogator and the computer, because *physical* simulation of a person is unnecessary for intelligence. However,

TOTAL TURING TEST   the so-called **total Turing Test** includes a video signal so that the interrogator can test the subject's perceptual abilities, as well as the opportunity for the interrogator to pass physical objects "through the hatch." To pass the total Turing Test, the computer will need

COMPUTER VISION   ◇ **computer vision** to perceive objects, and

ROBOTICS   ◇ **robotics** to move them about.

Within AI, there has not been a big effort to try to pass the Turing test. The issue of acting like a human comes up primarily when AI programs have to interact with people, as when an expert system explains how it came to its diagnosis, or a natural language processing system has a dialogue with a user. These programs must behave according to certain normal conventions of human interaction in order to make themselves understood. The underlying representation and reasoning in such a system may or may not be based on a human model.

Thinking humanly: The cognitive modelling approach

If we are going to say that a given program thinks like a human, we must have some way of determining how humans think. We need to get *inside* the actual workings of human minds. There are two ways to do this: through introspection—trying to catch our own thoughts as they go by—or through psychological experiments. Once we have a sufficiently precise theory of the mind, it becomes possible to express the theory as a computer program. If the program's input/output and timing behavior matches human behavior, that is evidence that some of the program's mechanisms may also be operating in humans. For example, Newell and Simon, who developed GPS, the "General Problem Solver" (Newell and Simon, 1961), were not content to have their program correctly solve problems. They were more concerned with comparing the trace of its reasoning steps to traces of human subjects solving the same problems. This is in contrast to other researchers of the same time (such as Wang (1960)), who were concerned with getting the right answers regardless of how humans might do it. The interdisciplinary field of

COGNITIVE SCIENCE   **cognitive science** brings together computer models from AI and experimental techniques from psychology to try to construct precise and testable theories of the workings of the human mind.

Although cognitive science is a fascinating field in itself, we are not going to be discussing it all that much in this book. We will occasionally comment on similarities or differences between AI techniques and human cognition. Real cognitive science, however, is necessarily based on experimental investigation of actual humans or animals, and we assume that the reader only has access to a computer for experimentation. We will simply note that AI and cognitive science continue to fertilize each other, especially in the areas of vision, natural language, and learning. The history of psychological theories of cognition is briefly covered on page 12.

Thinking rationally: The laws of thought approach

The Greek philosopher Aristotle was one of the first to attempt to codify "right thinking," that is,

SYLLOGISMS   irrefutable reasoning processes. His famous **syllogisms** provided patterns for argument structures that always gave correct conclusions given correct premises. For example, "Socrates is a man;

LOGIC

all men are mortal; therefore Socrates is mortal." These laws of thought were supposed to govern the operation of the mind, and initiated the field of **logic**.

The development of formal logic in the late nineteenth and early twentieth centuries, which we describe in more detail in Chapter 6, provided a precise notation for statements about all kinds of things in the world and the relations between them. (Contrast this with ordinary arithmetic notation, which provides mainly for equality and inequality statements about numbers.) By 1965, programs existed that could, given enough time and memory, take a description of a problem in logical notation and find the solution to the problem, if one exists. (If there is no solution,

LOGICIST

the program might never stop looking for it.) The so-called **logicist** tradition within artificial intelligence hopes to build on such programs to create intelligent systems.

There are two main obstacles to this approach. First, it is not easy to take informal knowledge and state it in the formal terms required by logical notation, particularly when the knowledge is less than 100% certain. Second, there is a big difference between being able to solve a problem "in principle" and doing so in practice. Even problems with just a few dozen facts can exhaust the computational resources of any computer unless it has some guidance as to which reasoning steps to try first. Although both of these obstacles apply to *any* attempt to build computational reasoning systems, they appeared first in the logicist tradition because the power of the representation and reasoning systems are well-defined and fairly well understood.

Acting rationally: The rational agent approach

AGENT

Acting rationally means acting so as to achieve one's goals, given one's beliefs. An **agent** is just something that perceives and acts. (This may be an unusual use of the word, but you will get used to it.) In this approach, AI is viewed as the study and construction of rational agents.

In the "laws of thought" approach to AI, the whole emphasis was on correct inferences. Making correct inferences is sometimes *part* of being a rational agent, because one way to act rationally is to reason logically to the conclusion that a given action will achieve one's goals, and then to act on that conclusion. On the other hand, correct inference is not *all* of rationality, because there are often situations where there is no provably correct thing to do, yet something must still be done. There are also ways of acting rationally that cannot be reasonably said to involve inference. For example, pulling one's hand off of a hot stove is a reflex action that is more successful than a slower action taken after careful deliberation.

All the "cognitive skills" needed for the Turing Test are there to allow rational actions. Thus, we need the ability to represent knowledge and reason with it because this enables us to reach good decisions in a wide variety of situations. We need to be able to generate comprehensible sentences in natural language because saying those sentences helps us get by in a complex society. We need learning not just for erudition, but because having a better idea of how the world works enables us to generate more effective strategies for dealing with it. We need visual perception not just because seeing is fun, but in order to get a better idea of what an action might achieve—for example, being able to see a tasty morsel helps one to move toward it.

The study of AI as rational agent design therefore has two advantages. First, it is more general than the "laws of thought" approach, because correct inference is only a useful mechanism for achieving rationality, and not a necessary one. Second, it is more amenable to scientific development than approaches based on human behavior or human thought, because the standard of rationality is clearly defined and completely general. Human behavior, on the other hand, is well-adapted for one specific environment and is the product, in part, of a complicated and largely unknown evolutionary process that still may be far from achieving perfection. *This book will therefore concentrate on general principles of rational agents, and on components for constructing them.* We will see that despite the apparent simplicity with which the problem can be stated, an enormous variety of issues come up when we try to solve it. Chapter 2 outlines some of these issues in more detail.

One important point to keep in mind: we will see before too long that achieving perfect rationality—always doing the right thing—is not possible in complicated environments. The computational demands are just too high. However, for most of the book, we will adopt the working hypothesis that understanding perfect decision making is a good place to start. It simplifies the problem and provides the appropriate setting for most of the foundational material

LIMITED
RATIONALITY
in the field. Chapters 5 and 17 deal explicitly with the issue of **limited rationality**—acting appropriately when there is not enough time to do all the computations one might like.

1.2   THE FOUNDATIONS OF ARTIFICIAL INTELLIGENCE

In this section and the next, we provide a brief history of AI. Although AI itself is a young field, it has inherited many ideas, viewpoints, and techniques from other disciplines. From over 2000 years of tradition in philosophy, theories of reasoning and learning have emerged, along with the viewpoint that the mind is constituted by the operation of a physical system. From over 400 years of mathematics, we have formal theories of logic, probability, decision making, and computation. From psychology, we have the tools with which to investigate the human mind, and a scientific language within which to express the resulting theories. From linguistics, we have theories of the structure and meaning of language. Finally, from computer science, we have the tools with which to make AI a reality.

Like any history, this one is forced to concentrate on a small number of people and events, and ignore others that were also important. We choose to arrange events to tell the story of how the various intellectual components of modern AI came into being. We certainly would not wish to give the impression, however, that the disciplines from which the components came have all been working toward AI as their ultimate fruition.

Philosophy (428 B.C.–present)

> The safest characterization of the European philosophical tradition is that it consists of a series
> of footnotes to Plato.
> —Alfred North Whitehead

We begin with the birth of Plato in 428 B.C. His writings range across politics, mathematics, physics, astronomy, and several branches of philosophy. Together, Plato, his teacher Socrates, and his student Aristotle laid the foundation for much of western thought and culture. The philosopher Hubert Dreyfus (1979, p. 67) says that "The story of artificial intelligence might well begin around 450 B.C." when Plato reported a dialogue in which Socrates asks Euthyphro,[3] "I want to know what is characteristic of piety which makes all actions pious . . . that I may have it to turn to, and to use as a standard whereby to judge your actions and those of other men."[4] In other words, Socrates was asking for an *algorithm* to distinguish piety from non-piety. Aristotle went on to try to formulate more precisely the laws governing the rational part of the mind. He developed an informal system of syllogisms for proper reasoning, which in principle allowed one to mechanically generate conclusions, given initial premises. Aristotle did not believe all parts of the mind were governed by logical processes; he also had a notion of intuitive reason.

Now that we have the idea of a set of rules that can describe the working of (at least part of) the mind, the next step is to consider the mind as a physical system. We have to wait for René Descartes (1596–1650) for a clear discussion of the distinction between mind and matter, and the problems that arise. One problem with a purely physical conception of the mind is that it seems to leave little room for free will: if the mind is governed entirely by physical laws, then it has no more free will than a rock "deciding" to fall toward the center of the earth. Although a

DUALISM

strong advocate of the power of reasoning, Descartes was also a proponent of **dualism**. He held that there is a part of the mind (or soul or spirit) that is outside of nature, exempt from physical laws. On the other hand, he felt that animals did not possess this dualist quality; they could be considered as if they were machines.

MATERIALISM

An alternative to dualism is **materialism**, which holds that all the world (including the brain and mind) operate according to physical law.[5] Wilhelm Leibniz (1646–1716) was probably the first to take the materialist position to its logical conclusion and build a mechanical device intended to carry out mental operations. Unfortunately, his formulation of logic was so weak that his mechanical concept generator could not produce interesting results.

It is also possible to adopt an intermediate position, in which one accepts that the mind has a physical basis, but denies that it can be *explained* by a reduction to ordinary physical processes. Mental processes and consciousness are therefore part of the physical world, but inherently unknowable; they are beyond rational understanding. Some philosophers critical of AI have adopted exactly this position, as we discuss in Chapter 26.

Barring these possible objections to the aims of AI, philosophy had thus established a tradition in which the mind was conceived of as a physical device operating principally by reasoning with the knowledge that it contained. The next problem is then to establish the

EMPIRICIST

source of knowledge. The **empiricist** movement, starting with Francis Bacon's (1561–1626) *Novum Organum*,[6] is characterized by the dictum of John Locke (1632–1704): "Nothing is in the understanding, which was not first in the senses." David Hume's (1711–1776) *A Treatise*

INDUCTION

of Human Nature (Hume, 1978) proposed what is now known as the principle of **induction**:

---

[3] The *Euthyphro* describes the events just before the trial of Socrates in 399 B.C. Dreyfus has clearly erred in placing it 51 years earlier.

[4] Note that other translations have "goodness/good" instead of "piety/pious."

[5] In this view, the perception of "free will" arises because the deterministic generation of behavior is constituted by the operation of the mind selecting among what appear to be the possible courses of action. They remain "possible" because the brain does not have access to its own future states.

[6] An update of Aristotle's *organon*, or instrument of thought.

that general rules are acquired by exposure to repeated associations between their elements. The theory was given more formal shape by Bertrand Russell (1872–1970) who introduced **logical positivism**. This doctrine holds that all knowledge can be characterized by logical theories connected, ultimately, to **observation sentences** that correspond to sensory inputs.[7] The **confirmation theory** of Rudolf Carnap and Carl Hempel attempted to establish the nature of the connection between the observation sentences and the more general theories—in other words, to understand how knowledge can be acquired from experience.

LOGICAL POSITIVISM
OBSERVATION
SENTENCES
CONFIRMATION
THEORY

The final element in the philosophical picture of the mind is the connection between knowledge and action. What form should this connection take, and how can particular actions be justified? These questions are vital to AI, because only by understanding how actions are justified can we understand how to build an agent whose actions are justifiable, or rational. Aristotle provides an elegant answer in the *Nicomachean Ethics* (Book III. 3, 1112b):

> We deliberate not about ends, but about means. For a doctor does not deliberate whether he shall heal, nor an orator whether he shall persuade, nor a statesman whether he shall produce law and order, nor does any one else deliberate about his end. They assume the end and consider how and by what means it is attained, and if it seems easily and best produced thereby; while if it is achieved by one means only they consider *how* it will be achieved by this and by what means *this* will be achieved, till they come to the first cause, which in the order of discovery is last ... and what is last in the order of analysis seems to be first in the order of becoming. And if we come on an impossibility, we give up the search, e.g. if we need money and this cannot be got; but if a thing appears possible we try to do it.

Aristotle's approach (with a few minor refinements) was implemented 2300 years later by Newell and Simon in their GPS program, about which they write (Newell and Simon, 1972):

MEANS–ENDS
ANALYSIS

> The main methods of GPS jointly embody the heuristic of **means–ends analysis**. Means–ends analysis is typified by the following kind of common-sense argument:
>
> > I want to take my son to nursery school. What's the difference between what I have and what I want? One of distance. What changes distance? My automobile. My automobile won't work. What is needed to make it work? A new battery. What has new batteries? An auto repair shop. I want the repair shop to put in a new battery; but the shop doesn't know I need one. What is the difficulty? One of communication. What allows communication? A telephone ... and so on.
>
> This kind of analysis—classifying things in terms of the functions they serve and oscillating among ends, functions required, and means that perform them—forms the basic system of heuristic of GPS.

Means–ends analysis is useful, but does not say what to do when several actions will achieve the goal, or when no action will completely achieve it. Arnauld, a follower of Descartes, correctly described a quantitative formula for deciding what action to take in cases like this (see Chapter 16). John Stuart Mill's (1806–1873) book *Utilitarianism* (Mill, 1863) amplifies on this idea. The more formal theory of decisions is discussed in the following section.

---

[7] In this picture, all meaningful statements can be verified or falsified either by analyzing the meaning of the words or by carrying out experiments. Because this rules out most of metaphysics, as was the intention, logical positivism was unpopular in some circles.

Mathematics (c. 800–present)

ALGORITHM

Philosophers staked out most of the important ideas of AI, but to make the leap to a formal science required a level of mathematical formalization in three main areas: computation, logic, and probability. The notion of expressing a computation as a formal **algorithm** goes back to al-Khowarazmi, an Arab mathematician of the ninth century, whose writings also introduced Europe to Arabic numerals and algebra.

Logic goes back at least to Aristotle, but it was a philosophical rather than mathematical subject until George Boole (1815–1864) introduced his formal language for making logical inference in 1847. Boole's approach was incomplete, but good enough that others filled in the gaps. In 1879, Gottlob Frege (1848–1925) produced a logic that, except for some notational changes, forms the first-order logic that is used today as the most basic knowledge representation system.[8] Alfred Tarski (1902–1983) introduced a theory of reference that shows how to relate the objects in a logic to objects in the real world. The next step was to determine the limits of what could be done with logic and computation.

David Hilbert (1862–1943), a great mathematician in his own right, is most remembered for the problems he did not solve. In 1900, he presented a list of 23 problems that he correctly predicted would occupy mathematicians for the bulk of the century. The final problem asks if there is an algorithm for deciding the truth of any logical proposition involving the natural numbers—the famous *Entscheidungsproblem*, or decision problem. Essentially, Hilbert was asking if there were fundamental limits to the power of effective proof procedures. In 1930, Kurt Gödel (1906–1978) showed that there exists an effective procedure to prove any true statement in the first-order logic of Frege and Russell; but first-order logic could not capture the principle of mathematical induction needed to characterize the natural numbers. In 1931, he showed that real

INCOMPLETENESS
THEOREM

limits do exist. His **incompleteness theorem** showed that in any language expressive enough to describe the properties of the natural numbers, there are true statements that are undecidable: their truth cannot be established by any algorithm.

This fundamental result can also be interpreted as showing that there are some functions on the integers that cannot be represented by an algorithm—that is, they cannot be computed. This motivated Alan Turing (1912–1954) to try to characterize exactly which functions *are* capable of being computed. This notion is actually slightly problematic, because the notion of a computation or effective procedure really cannot be given a formal definition. However, the Church–Turing thesis, which states that the Turing machine (Turing, 1936) is capable of computing any computable function, is generally accepted as providing a sufficient definition. Turing also showed that there were some functions that no Turing machine can compute. For example, no machine can tell *in general* whether a given program will return an answer on a given input, or run forever.

INTRACTABILITY

Although undecidability and noncomputability are important to an understanding of computation, the notion of **intractability** has had a much greater impact. Roughly speaking, a class of problems is called intractable if the time required to solve instances of the class grows at least exponentially with the size of the instances. The distinction between polynomial and exponential growth in complexity was first emphasized in the mid-1960s (Cobham, 1964; Edmonds, 1965). It is important because exponential growth means that even moderate-sized in-

---

[8]   To understand why Frege's notation was not universally adopted, see the cover of this book.

stances cannot be solved in any reasonable time. Therefore, one should strive to divide the overall problem of generating intelligent behavior into tractable subproblems rather than intractable ones. REDUCTION The second important concept in the theory of complexity is **reduction**, which also emerged in the 1960s (Dantzig, 1960; Edmonds, 1962). A reduction is a general transformation from one class of problems to another, such that solutions to the first class can be found by reducing them to problems of the second class and solving the latter problems.

How can one recognize an intractable problem? The theory of **NP-completeness**, pioneered by Steven Cook (1971) and Richard Karp (1972), provides a method. Cook and Karp showed the existence of large classes of canonical combinatorial search and reasoning problems that are NP-complete. Any problem class to which an NP-complete problem class can be reduced is likely to be intractable. (Although it has not yet been proved that NP-complete problems are necessarily intractable, few theoreticians believe otherwise.) These results contrast sharply with the "Electronic Super-Brain" enthusiasm accompanying the advent of computers. Despite the ever-increasing speed of computers, subtlety and careful use of resources will characterize intelligent systems. Put crudely, the world is an *extremely* large problem instance!

Besides logic and computation, the third great contribution of mathematics to AI is the theory of probability. The Italian Gerolamo Cardano (1501–1576) first framed the idea of probability, describing it in terms of the possible outcomes of gambling events. Before his time, the outcomes of gambling games were seen as the will of the gods rather than the whim of chance. Probability quickly became an invaluable part of all the quantitative sciences, helping to deal with uncertain measurements and incomplete theories. Pierre Fermat (1601–1665), Blaise Pascal (1623–1662), James Bernoulli (1654–1705), Pierre Laplace (1749–1827), and others advanced the theory and introduced new statistical methods. Bernoulli also framed an alternative view of probability, as a subjective "degree of belief" rather than an objective ratio of outcomes. Subjective probabilities therefore can be updated as new evidence is obtained. Thomas Bayes (1702–1761) proposed a rule for updating subjective probabilities in the light of new evidence (published posthumously in 1763). Bayes' rule, and the subsequent field of Bayesian analysis, form the basis of the modern approach to uncertain reasoning in AI systems. Debate still rages between supporters of the objective and subjective views of probability, but it is not clear if the difference has great significance for AI. Both versions obey the same set of axioms. Savage's (1954) *Foundations of Statistics* gives a good introduction to the field.

As with logic, a connection must be made between probabilistic reasoning and action. DECISION THEORY **Decision theory**, pioneered by John Von Neumann and Oskar Morgenstern (1944), combines probability theory with utility theory (which provides a formal and complete framework for specifying the preferences of an agent) to give the first general theory that can distinguish good actions from bad ones. Decision theory is the mathematical successor to utilitarianism, and provides the theoretical basis for many of the agent designs in this book.

Psychology (1879–present)

Scientific psychology can be said to have begun with the work of the German physicist Hermann von Helmholtz (1821–1894) and his student Wilhelm Wundt (1832–1920). Helmholtz applied the scientific method to the study of human vision, and his *Handbook of Physiological Optics* is even now described as "the single most important treatise on the physics and physiology of human vision to this day" (Nalwa, 1993, p.15). In 1879, the same year that Frege launched first-order logic, Wundt opened the first laboratory of experimental psychology at the University of Leipzig. Wundt insisted on carefully controlled experiments in which his workers would perform a perceptual or associative task while introspecting on their thought processes. The careful controls went a long way to make psychology a science, but as the methodology spread, a curious phenomenon arose: each laboratory would report introspective data that just happened to match the theories that were popular in that laboratory. The **behaviorism** movement of John Watson (1878–1958) and Edward Lee Thorndike (1874–1949) rebelled against this subjectivism, rejecting *any* theory involving mental processes on the grounds that introspection could not provide reliable evidence. Behaviorists insisted on studying only objective measures of the percepts (or *stimulus*) given to an animal and its resulting actions (or *response*). Mental constructs such as knowledge, beliefs, goals, and reasoning steps were dismissed as unscientific "folk psychology." Behaviorism discovered a lot about rats and pigeons, but had less success understanding humans. Nevertheless, it had a strong hold on psychology (especially in the United States) from about 1920 to 1960.

BEHAVIORISM

COGNITIVE
PSYCHOLOGY

The view that the brain possesses and processes information, which is the principal characteristic of **cognitive psychology**, can be traced back at least to the works of William James[9] (1842–1910). Helmholtz also insisted that perception involved a form of unconscious logical inference. The cognitive viewpoint was largely eclipsed by behaviorism until 1943, when Kenneth Craik published *The Nature of Explanation*. Craik put back the missing mental step between stimulus and response. He claimed that beliefs, goals, and reasoning steps could be useful valid components of a theory of human behavior, and are just as scientific as, say, using pressure and temperature to talk about gases, despite their being made of molecules that have neither. Craik specified the three key steps of a knowledge-based agent: (1) the stimulus must be translated into an internal representation, (2) the representation is manipulated by cognitive processes to derive new internal representations, and (3) these are in turn retranslated back into action. He clearly explained why this was a good design for an agent:

> If the organism carries a "small-scale model" of external reality and of its own possible actions within its head, it is able to try out various alternatives, conclude which is the best of them, react to future situations before they arise, utilize the knowledge of past events in dealing with the present and future, and in every way to react in a much fuller, safer, and more competent manner to the emergencies which face it. (Craik, 1943)

An agent designed this way can, for example, plan a long trip by considering various possible routes, comparing them, and choosing the best one, all before starting the journey. Since the 1960s, the information-processing view has dominated psychology. It it now almost taken for granted among many psychologists that "a cognitive theory should be like a computer program" (Anderson, 1980). By this it is meant that the theory should describe cognition as consisting of well-defined transformation processes operating at the level of the information carried by the input signals.

For most of the early history of AI and cognitive science, no significant distinction was drawn between the two fields, and it was common to see AI programs described as psychological

---

[9] William James was the brother of novelist Henry James. It is said that Henry wrote fiction as if it were psychology and William wrote psychology as if it were fiction.

results without any claim as to the exact human behavior they were modelling. In the last decade or so, however, the methodological distinctions have become clearer, and most work now falls into one field or the other.

Computer engineering (1940–present)

For artificial intelligence to succeed, we need two things: intelligence and an artifact. The computer has been unanimously acclaimed as the artifact with the best chance of demonstrating intelligence. The modern digital electronic computer was invented independently and almost simultaneously by scientists in three countries embattled in World War II. The first operational modern computer was the Heath Robinson,[10] built in 1940 by Alan Turing's team for the single purpose of deciphering German messages. When the Germans switched to a more sophisticated code, the electromechanical relays in the Robinson proved to be too slow, and a new machine called the Colossus was built from vacuum tubes. It was completed in 1943, and by the end of the war, ten Colossus machines were in everyday use.

The first operational *programmable* computer was the Z-3, the invention of Konrad Zuse in Germany in 1941. Zuse invented floating-point numbers for the Z-3, and went on in 1945 to develop Plankalkul, the first high-level programming language. Although Zuse received some support from the Third Reich to apply his machine to aircraft design, the military hierarchy did not attach as much importance to computing as did its counterpart in Britain.

In the United States, the first *electronic* computer, the ABC, was assembled by John Atanasoff and his graduate student Clifford Berry between 1940 and 1942 at Iowa State University. The project received little support and was abandoned after Atanasoff became involved in military research in Washington. Two other computer projects were started as secret military research: the Mark I, II, and III computers were developed at Harvard by a team under Howard Aiken; and the ENIAC was developed at the University of Pennsylvania by a team including John Mauchly and John Eckert. ENIAC was the first general-purpose, electronic, digital computer. One of its first applications was computing artillery firing tables. A successor, the EDVAC, followed John Von Neumann's suggestion to use a stored program, so that technicians would not have to scurry about changing patch cords to run a new program.

But perhaps the most critical breakthrough was the IBM 701, built in 1952 by Nathaniel Rochester and his group. This was the first computer to yield a profit for its manufacturer. IBM went on to become one of the world's largest corporations, and sales of computers have grown to $150 billion/year. In the United States, the computer industry (including software and services) now accounts for about 10% of the gross national product.

Each generation of computer hardware has brought an increase in speed and capacity, and a decrease in price. Computer engineering has been remarkably successful, regularly doubling performance every two years, with no immediate end in sight for this rate of increase. Massively parallel machines promise to add several more zeros to the overall throughput achievable.

Of course, there were calculating devices before the electronic computer. The abacus is roughly 7000 years old. In the mid-17th century, Blaise Pascal built a mechanical adding

---

[10] Heath Robinson was a cartoonist famous for his depictions of whimsical and absurdly complicated contraptions for everyday tasks such as buttering toast.

and subtracting machine called the Pascaline. Leibniz improved on this in 1694, building a mechanical device that multiplied by doing repeated addition. Progress stalled for over a century until Charles Babbage (1792–1871) dreamed that logarithm tables could be computed by machine. He designed a machine for this task, but never completed the project. Instead, he turned to the design of the Analytical Engine, for which Babbage invented the ideas of addressable memory, stored programs, and conditional jumps. Although the idea of programmable machines was not new—in 1805, Joseph Marie Jacquard invented a loom that could be programmed using punched cards—Babbage's machine was the first artifact possessing the characteristics necessary for universal computation. Babbage's colleague Ada Lovelace, daughter of the poet Lord Byron, wrote programs for the Analytical Engine and even speculated that the machine could play chess or compose music. Lovelace was the world's first programmer, and the first of many to endure massive cost overruns and to have an ambitious project ultimately abandoned.[11] Babbage's basic design was proven viable by Doron Swade and his colleagues, who built a working model using only the mechanical techniques available at Babbage's time (Swade, 1993). Babbage had the right idea, but lacked the organizational skills to get his machine built.

AI also owes a debt to the software side of computer science, which has supplied the operating systems, programming languages, and tools needed to write modern programs (and papers about them). But this is one area where the debt has been repaid: work in AI has pioneered many ideas that have made their way back to "mainstream" computer science, including time sharing, interactive interpreters, the linked list data type, automatic storage management, and some of the key concepts of object-oriented programming and integrated program development environments with graphical user interfaces.

Linguistics (1957–present)

In 1957, B. F. Skinner published *Verbal Behavior*. This was a comprehensive, detailed account of the behaviorist approach to language learning, written by the foremost expert in the field. But curiously, a review of the book became as well-known as the book itself, and served to almost kill off interest in behaviorism. The author of the review was Noam Chomsky, who had just published a book on his own theory, *Syntactic Structures*. Chomsky showed how the behaviorist theory did not address the notion of creativity in language—it did not explain how a child could understand and make up sentences that he or she had never heard before. Chomsky's theory—based on syntactic models going back to the Indian linguist Panini (c. 350 B.C.)—could explain this, and unlike previous theories, it was formal enough that it could in principle be programmed.

Later developments in linguistics showed the problem to be considerably more complex than it seemed in 1957. Language is ambiguous and leaves much unsaid. This means that understanding language requires an understanding of the subject matter and context, not just an understanding of the structure of sentences. This may seem obvious, but it was not appreciated until the early 1960s. Much of the early work in **knowledge representation** (the study of how to put knowledge into a form that a computer can reason with) was tied to language and informed by research in linguistics, which was connected in turn to decades of work on the philosophical analysis of language.

---

[11] She also gave her name to Ada, the U.S. Department of Defense's all-purpose programming language.

Modern linguistics and AI were "born" at about the same time, so linguistics does not play a large foundational role in the growth of AI. Instead, the two grew up together, intersecting in a hybrid field called **computational linguistics** or **natural language processing**, which concentrates on the problem of language use.

1.3   THE HISTORY OF ARTIFICIAL INTELLIGENCE

With the background material behind us, we are now ready to outline the development of AI proper. We could do this by identifying loosely defined and overlapping phases in its development, or by chronicling the various different and intertwined conceptual threads that make up the field. In this section, we will take the former approach, at the risk of doing some degree of violence to the real relationships among subfields. The history of each subfield is covered in individual chapters later in the book.

The gestation of artificial intelligence (1943–1956)

The first work that is now generally recognized as AI was done by Warren McCulloch and Walter Pitts (1943). They drew on three sources: knowledge of the basic physiology and function of neurons in the brain; the formal analysis of propositional logic due to Russell and Whitehead; and Turing's theory of computation. They proposed a model of artificial neurons in which each neuron is characterized as being "on" or "off," with a switch to "on" occurring in response to stimulation by a sufficient number of neighboring neurons. The state of a neuron was conceived of as "factually equivalent to a proposition which proposed its adequate stimulus." They showed, for example, that any computable function could be computed by some network of connected neurons, and that all the logical connectives could be implemented by simple net structures. McCulloch and Pitts also suggested that suitably defined networks could learn. Donald Hebb (1949) demonstrated a simple updating rule for modifying the connection strengths between neurons, such that learning could take place.

The work of McCulloch and Pitts was arguably the forerunner of both the logicist tradition in AI and the connectionist tradition. In the early 1950s, Claude Shannon (1950) and Alan Turing (1953) were writing chess programs for von Neumann-style conventional computers.[12] At the same time, two graduate students in the Princeton mathematics department, Marvin Minsky and Dean Edmonds, built the first neural network computer in 1951. The SNARC, as it was called, used 3000 vacuum tubes and a surplus automatic pilot mechanism from a B-24 bomber to simulate a network of 40 neurons. Minsky's Ph.D. committee was skeptical whether this kind of work should be considered mathematics, but von Neumann was on the committee and reportedly said, "If it isn't now it will be someday." Ironically, Minsky was later to prove theorems that contributed to the demise of much of neural network research during the 1970s.

---

[12] Shannon actually had no real computer to work with, and Turing was eventually denied access to his own team's computers by the British government, on the grounds that research into artificial intelligence was surely frivolous.

Princeton was home to another influential figure in AI, John McCarthy. After graduation, McCarthy moved to Dartmouth College, which was to become the official birthplace of the field. McCarthy convinced Minsky, Claude Shannon, and Nathaniel Rochester to help him bring together U.S. researchers interested in automata theory, neural nets, and the study of intelligence. They organized a two-month workshop at Dartmouth in the summer of 1956. All together there were ten attendees, including Trenchard More from Princeton, Arthur Samuel from IBM, and Ray Solomonoff and Oliver Selfridge from MIT.

Two researchers from Carnegie Tech,[13] Allen Newell and Herbert Simon, rather stole the show. Although the others had ideas and in some cases programs for particular applications such as checkers, Newell and Simon already had a reasoning program, the Logic Theorist (LT), about which Simon claimed, "We have invented a computer program capable of thinking non-numerically, and thereby solved the venerable mind–body problem."[14] Soon after the workshop, the program was able to prove most of the theorems in Chapter 2 of Russell and Whitehead's *Principia Mathematica*. Russell was reportedly delighted when Simon showed him that the program had come up with a proof for one theorem that was shorter than the one in *Principia*. The editors of the *Journal of Symbolic Logic* were less impressed; they rejected a paper coauthored by Newell, Simon, and Logic Theorist.

The Dartmouth workshop did not lead to any new breakthroughs, but it did introduce all the major figures to each other. For the next 20 years, the field would be dominated by these people and their students and colleagues at MIT, CMU, Stanford, and IBM. Perhaps the most lasting thing to come out of the workshop was an agreement to adopt McCarthy's new name for the field: **artificial intelligence**.

Early enthusiasm, great expectations (1952–1969)

The early years of AI were full of successes—in a limited way. Given the primitive computers and programming tools of the time, and the fact that only a few years earlier computers were seen as things that could do arithmetic and no more, it was astonishing whenever a computer did anything remotely clever. The intellectual establishment, by and large, preferred to believe that "a machine can never do X" (see Chapter 26 for a long list of X's gathered by Turing). AI researchers naturally responded by demonstrating one X after another. Some modern AI researchers refer to this period as the "Look, Ma, no hands!" era.

Newell and Simon's early success was followed up with the General Problem Solver, or GPS. Unlike Logic Theorist, this program was designed from the start to imitate human problem-solving protocols. Within the limited class of puzzles it could handle, it turned out that the order in which the program considered subgoals and possible actions was similar to the way humans approached the same problems. Thus, GPS was probably the first program to embody the "thinking humanly" approach. The combination of AI and cognitive science has continued at CMU up to the present day.

---

[13] Now Carnegie Mellon University (CMU).

[14] Newell and Simon also invented a list-processing language, IPL, to write LT. They had no compiler, and translated it into machine code by hand. To avoid errors, they worked in parallel, calling out binary numbers to each other as they wrote each instruction to make sure they agreed.

At IBM, Nathaniel Rochester and his colleagues produced some of the first AI programs. Herbert Gelernter (1959) constructed the Geometry Theorem Prover. Like the Logic Theorist, it proved theorems using explicitly represented axioms. Gelernter soon found that there were too many possible reasoning paths to follow, most of which turned out to be dead ends. To help focus the search, he added the capability to create a numerical representation of a diagram—a particular case of the general theorem to be proved. Before the program tried to prove something, it could first check the diagram to see if it was true in the particular case.

Starting in 1952, Arthur Samuel wrote a series of programs for checkers (draughts) that eventually learned to play tournament-level checkers. Along the way, he disproved the idea that computers can only do what they are told to, as his program quickly learned to play a better game than its creator. The program was demonstrated on television in February 1956, creating a very strong impression. Like Turing, Samuel had trouble finding computer time. Working at night, he used machines that were still on the testing floor at IBM's manufacturing plant. Chapter 5 covers game playing, and Chapter 20 describes and expands on the learning techniques used by Samuel.

John McCarthy moved from Dartmouth to MIT and there made three crucial contributions in one historic year: 1958. In MIT AI Lab Memo No. 1, McCarthy defined the high-level language **Lisp**, which was to become the dominant AI programming language. Lisp is the second-oldest language in current use.[15] With Lisp, McCarthy had the tool he needed, but access to scarce and expensive computing resources was also a serious problem. Thus, he and others at MIT invented time sharing. After getting an experimental time-sharing system up at MIT, McCarthy eventually attracted the interest of a group of MIT grads who formed Digital Equipment Corporation, which was to become the world's second largest computer manufacturer, thanks to their time-sharing minicomputers. Also in 1958, McCarthy published a paper entitled *Programs with Common Sense*, in which he described the Advice Taker, a hypothetical program that can be seen as the first complete AI system. Like the Logic Theorist and Geometry Theorem Prover, McCarthy's program was designed to use knowledge to search for solutions to problems. But unlike the others, it was to embody general knowledge of the world. For example, he showed how some simple axioms would enable the program to generate a plan to drive to the airport to catch a plane. The program was also designed so that it could accept new axioms in the normal course of operation, thereby allowing it to achieve competence in new areas *without being reprogrammed*. The Advice Taker thus embodied the central principles of knowledge representation and reasoning: that it is useful to have a formal, explicit representation of the world and the way an agent's actions affect the world, and to be able to manipulate these representations with deductive processes. It is remarkable how much of the 1958 paper remains relevant after more than 35 years.

1958 also marked the year that Marvin Minsky moved to MIT. For years he and McCarthy were inseparable as they defined the field together. But they grew apart as McCarthy stressed representation and reasoning in formal logic, whereas Minsky was more interested in getting programs to work, and eventually developed an anti-logical outlook. In 1963, McCarthy took the opportunity to go to Stanford and start the AI lab there. His research agenda of using logic to build the ultimate Advice Taker was advanced by J. A. Robinson's discovery of the resolution method (a complete theorem-proving algorithm for first-order logic; see Section 9.6). Work at Stanford emphasized general-purpose methods for logical reasoning. Applications of

LISP

---

[15] FORTRAN is one year older than Lisp.

logic included Cordell Green's question answering and planning systems (Green, 1969b), and the Shakey robotics project at the new Stanford Research Institute (SRI). The latter project, discussed further in Chapter 25, was the first to demonstrate the complete integration of logical reasoning and physical activity.

MICROWORLDS

Minsky supervised a series of students who chose limited problems that appeared to require intelligence to solve. These limited domains became known as **microworlds**. James Slagle's SAINT program (1963a) was able to solve closed-form integration problems typical of first-year college calculus courses. Tom Evans's ANALOGY program (1968) solved geometric analogy problems that appear in IQ tests, such as the one in Figure 1.2. Bertram Raphael's (1968) SIR (Semantic Information Retrieval) was able to accept input statements in a very restricted subset of English and answer questions thereon. Daniel Bobrow's STUDENT program (1967) solved algebra story problems such as

> If the number of customers Tom gets is twice the square of 20 percent of the number of advertisements he runs, and the number of advertisements he runs is 45, what is the number of customers Tom gets?

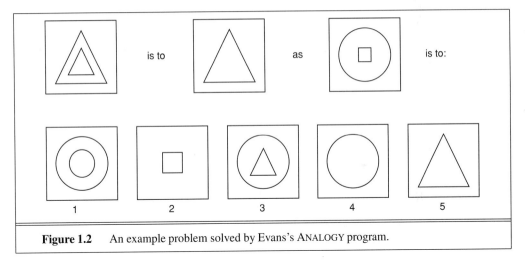

Figure 1.2   An example problem solved by Evans's ANALOGY program.

The most famous microworld was the blocks world, which consists of a set of solid blocks placed on a tabletop (or more often, a simulation of a tabletop), as shown in Figure 1.3. A task in this world is to rearrange the blocks in a certain way, using a robot hand that can pick up one block at a time. The blocks world was home to the vision project of David Huffman (1971), the vision and constraint-propagation work of David Waltz (1975), the learning theory of Patrick Winston (1970), the natural language understanding program of Terry Winograd (1972), and the planner of Scott Fahlman (1974).

Early work building on the neural networks of McCulloch and Pitts also flourished. The work of Winograd and Cowan (1963) showed how a large number of elements could collectively represent an individual concept, with a corresponding increase in robustness and parallelism. Hebb's learning methods were enhanced by Bernie Widrow (Widrow and Hoff, 1960; Widrow, 1962), who called his networks **adalines**, and by Frank Rosenblatt (1962) with his **perceptrons**.

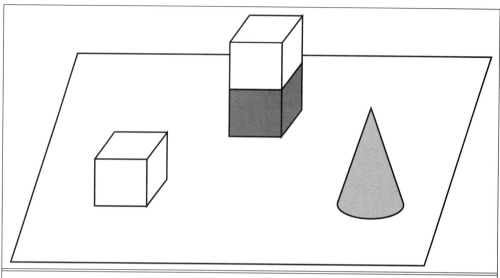

Figure 1.3   A scene from the blocks world. A task for the robot might be "Pick up a big red block," expressed either in natural language or in a formal notation.

Rosenblatt proved the famous **perceptron convergence theorem**, showing that his learning algorithm could adjust the connection strengths of a perceptron to match any input data, provided such a match existed. These topics are covered in Section 19.3.

A dose of reality (1966–1974)

From the beginning, AI researchers were not shy in making predictions of their coming successes. The following statement by Herbert Simon in 1957 is often quoted:

> It is not my aim to surprise or shock you—but the simplest way I can summarize is to say that there are now in the world machines that think, that learn and that create. Moreover, their ability to do these things is going to increase rapidly until—in a visible future—the range of problems they can handle will be coextensive with the range to which human mind has been applied.

Although one might argue that terms such as "visible future" can be interpreted in various ways, some of Simon's predictions were more concrete. In 1958, he predicted that within 10 years a computer would be chess champion, and an important new mathematical theorem would be proved by machine. Claims such as these turned out to be wildly optimistic. The barrier that faced almost all AI research projects was that methods that sufficed for demonstrations on one or two simple examples turned out to fail miserably when tried out on wider selections of problems and on more difficult problems.

The first kind of difficulty arose because early programs often contained little or no knowledge of their subject matter, and succeeded by means of simple syntactic manipulations. Weizenbaum's ELIZA program (1965), which could apparently engage in serious conversation on any topic, actually just borrowed and manipulated the sentences typed into it by a human. A typical story occurred in early machine translation efforts, which were generously funded by the National Research Council in an attempt to speed up the translation of Russian scientific papers in the wake of the Sputnik launch in 1957. It was thought initially that simple syntactic transformations based on the grammars of Russian and English, and word replacement using an electronic dictionary, would suffice to preserve the exact meanings of sentences. In fact, translation requires general knowledge of the subject matter in order to resolve ambiguity and establish the content of the sentence. The famous retranslation of "the spirit is willing but the flesh is weak" as "the vodka is good but the meat is rotten" illustrates the difficulties encountered. In 1966, a report by an advisory committee found that "there has been no machine translation of general scientific text, and none is in immediate prospect." All U.S. government funding for academic translation projects was cancelled.

The second kind of difficulty was the intractability of many of the problems that AI was attempting to solve. Most of the early AI programs worked by representing the basic facts about a problem and trying out a series of steps to solve it, combining different combinations of steps until the right one was found. The early programs were feasible only because microworlds contained very few objects. Before the theory of NP-completeness was developed, it was widely thought that "scaling up" to larger problems was simply a matter of faster hardware and larger memories. The optimism that accompanied the development of resolution theorem proving, for example, was soon dampened when researchers failed to prove theorems involving more than a few dozen facts. *The fact that a program can find a solution in principle does not mean that the program contains any of the mechanisms needed to find it in practice.*

MACHINE EVOLUTION

The illusion of unlimited computational power was not confined to problem-solving programs. Early experiments in **machine evolution** (now called **genetic algorithms**) (Friedberg, 1958; Friedberg *et al.*, 1959) were based on the undoubtedly correct belief that by making an appropriate series of small mutations to a machine code program, one can generate a program with good performance for any particular simple task. The idea, then, was to try random mutations and then apply a selection process to preserve mutations that seemed to improve behavior. Despite thousands of hours of CPU time, almost no progress was demonstrated.

Failure to come to grips with the "combinatorial explosion" was one of the main criticisms of AI contained in the Lighthill report (Lighthill, 1973), which formed the basis for the decision by the British government to end support for AI research in all but two universities. (Oral tradition paints a somewhat different and more colorful picture, with political ambitions and personal animosities that cannot be put in print.)

A third difficulty arose because of some fundamental limitations on the basic structures being used to generate intelligent behavior. For example, in 1969, Minsky and Papert's book *Perceptrons* (1969) proved that although perceptrons could be shown to learn anything they were capable of representing, they could represent very little. In particular, a two-input perceptron could not be trained to recognize when its two inputs were different. Although their results did not apply to more complex, multilayer networks, research funding for neural net research soon dwindled to almost nothing. Ironically, the new back-propagation learning algorithms for multilayer networks that were to cause an enormous resurgence in neural net research in the late 1980s were actually discovered first in 1969 (Bryson and Ho, 1969).

Knowledge-based systems: The key to power? (1969–1979)

The picture of problem solving that had arisen during the first decade of AI research was of a general-purpose search mechanism trying to string together elementary reasoning steps to find complete solutions. Such approaches have been called **weak methods**, because they use weak information about the domain. For many complex domains, it turns out that their performance is also weak. The only way around this is to use knowledge more suited to making larger reasoning steps and to solving typically occurring cases in narrow areas of expertise. One might say that to solve a hard problem, you almost have to know the answer already.

WEAK METHODS

The DENDRAL program (Buchanan *et al.*, 1969) was an early example of this approach. It was developed at Stanford, where Ed Feigenbaum (a former student of Herbert Simon), Bruce Buchanan (a philosopher turned computer scientist), and Joshua Lederberg (a Nobel laureate geneticist) teamed up to solve the problem of inferring molecular structure from the information provided by a mass spectrometer. The input to the program consists of the elementary formula of the molecule (e.g., $C_6H_{13}NO_2$), and the mass spectrum giving the masses of the various fragments of the molecule generated when it is bombarded by an electron beam. For example, the mass spectrum might contain a peak at $m = 15$ corresponding to the mass of a methyl (CH_3) fragment.

The naive version of the program generated all possible structures consistent with the formula, and then predicted what mass spectrum would be observed for each, comparing this with the actual spectrum. As one might expect, this rapidly became intractable for decent-sized molecules. The DENDRAL researchers consulted analytical chemists and found that they worked by looking for well-known patterns of peaks in the spectrum that suggested common substructures in the molecule. For example, the following rule is used to recognize a ketone (C=O) subgroup:

> **if** there are two peaks at x_1 and x_2 such that
> (a) $x_1 + x_2 = M + 28$ (M is the mass of the whole molecule);
> (b) $x_1 - 28$ is a high peak;
> (c) $x_2 - 28$ is a high peak;
> (d) At least one of x_1 and x_2 is high.
> **then** there is a ketone subgroup

Having recognized that the molecule contains a particular substructure, the number of possible candidates is enormously reduced. The DENDRAL team concluded that the new system was powerful because

> All the relevant theoretical knowledge to solve these problems has been mapped over from its general form in the [spectrum prediction component] ("first principles") to efficient special forms ("cookbook recipes"). (Feigenbaum *et al.*, 1971)

The significance of DENDRAL was that it was arguably the first successful *knowledge-intensive* system: its expertise derived from large numbers of special-purpose rules. Later systems also incorporated the main theme of McCarthy's Advice Taker approach— the clean separation of the knowledge (in the form of rules) and the reasoning component.

With this lesson in mind, Feigenbaum and others at Stanford began the Heuristic Programming Project (HPP), to investigate the extent to which the new methodology of **expert systems** could be applied to other areas of human expertise. The next major effort was in the area of medical diagnosis. Feigenbaum, Buchanan, and Dr. Edward Shortliffe developed MYCIN to diagnose blood infections. With about 450 rules, MYCIN was able to perform as well as some

EXPERT SYSTEMS

experts, and considerably better than junior doctors. It also contained two major differences from DENDRAL. First, unlike the DENDRAL rules, no general theoretical model existed from which the MYCIN rules could be deduced. They had to be acquired from extensive interviewing of experts, who in turn acquired them from direct experience of cases. Second, the rules had to reflect the uncertainty associated with medical knowledge. MYCIN incorporated a calculus of uncertainty called **certainty factors** (see Chapter 14), which seemed (at the time) to fit well with how doctors assessed the impact of evidence on the diagnosis.

Other approaches to medical diagnosis were also followed. At Rutgers University, Saul Amarel's *Computers in Biomedicine* project began an ambitious attempt to diagnose diseases based on explicit knowledge of the causal mechanisms of the disease process. Meanwhile, large groups at MIT and the New England Medical Center were pursuing an approach to diagnosis and treatment based on the theories of probability and utility. Their aim was to build systems that gave provably optimal medical recommendations. In medicine, the Stanford approach using rules provided by doctors proved more popular at first. But another probabilistic reasoning system, PROSPECTOR (Duda *et al.*, 1979), generated enormous publicity by recommending exploratory drilling at a geological site that proved to contain a large molybdenum deposit.

The importance of domain knowledge was also apparent in the area of understanding natural language. Although Winograd's SHRDLU system for understanding natural language had engendered a good deal of excitement, its dependence on syntactic analysis caused some of the same problems as occurred in the early machine translation work. It was able to overcome ambiguity and understand pronoun references, but this was mainly because it was designed specifically for one area—the blocks world. Several researchers, including Eugene Charniak, a fellow graduate student of Winograd's at MIT, suggested that robust language understanding would require general knowledge about the world and a general method for using that knowledge.

At Yale, the linguist-turned-AI-researcher Roger Schank emphasized this point by claiming, "There is no such thing as syntax," which upset a lot of linguists, but did serve to start a useful discussion. Schank and his students built a series of programs (Schank and Abelson, 1977; Schank and Riesbeck, 1981; Dyer, 1983) that all had the task of understanding natural language. The emphasis, however, was less on language *per se* and more on the problems of representing and reasoning with the knowledge required for language understanding. The problems included representing stereotypical situations (Cullingford, 1981), describing human memory organization (Rieger, 1976; Kolodner, 1983), and understanding plans and goals (Wilensky, 1983). William Woods (1973) built the LUNAR system, which allowed geologists to ask questions in English about the rock samples brought back by the Apollo moon mission. LUNAR was the first natural language program that was used by people other than the system's author to get real work done. Since then, many natural language programs have been used as interfaces to databases.

The widespread growth of applications to real-world problems caused a concomitant increase in the demands for workable knowledge representation schemes. A large number of different representation languages were developed. Some were based on logic—for example, the Prolog language became popular in Europe, and the PLANNER family in the United States. Others, following Minsky's idea of **frames** (1975), adopted a rather more structured approach, collecting together facts about particular object and event types, and arranging the types into a large taxonomic hierarchy analogous to a biological taxonomy.

FRAMES

AI becomes an industry (1980-1988)

The first successful commercial expert system, R1, began operation at Digital Equipment Corporation (McDermott, 1982). The program helped configure orders for new computer systems, and by 1986, it was saving the company an estimated $40 million a year. By 1988, DEC's AI group had 40 deployed expert systems, with more on the way. Du Pont had 100 in use and 500 in development, saving an estimated $10 million a year. Nearly every major U.S. corporation had its own AI group and was either using or investigating expert system technology.

In 1981, the Japanese announced the "Fifth Generation" project, a 10-year plan to build intelligent computers running Prolog in much the same way that ordinary computers run machine code. The idea was that with the ability to make millions of inferences per second, computers would be able to take advantage of vast stores of rules. The project proposed to achieve full-scale natural language understanding, among other ambitious goals.

The Fifth Generation project fueled interest in AI, and by taking advantage of fears of Japanese domination, researchers and corporations were able to generate support for a similar investment in the United States. The Microelectronics and Computer Technology Corporation (MCC) was formed as a research consortium to counter the Japanese project. In Britain, the Alvey report reinstated the funding that was cut by the Lighthill report.[16] In both cases, AI was part of a broad effort, including chip design and human-interface research.

The booming AI industry also included companies such as Carnegie Group, Inference, Intellicorp, and Teknowledge that offered the software tools to build expert systems, and hardware companies such as Lisp Machines Inc., Texas Instruments, Symbolics, and Xerox that were building workstations optimized for the development of Lisp programs. Over a hundred companies built industrial robotic vision systems. Overall, the industry went from a few million in sales in 1980 to $2 billion in 1988.

The return of neural networks (1986–present)

Although computer science had neglected the field of neural networks after Minsky and Papert's *Perceptrons* book, work had continued in other fields, particularly physics. Large collections of simple neurons could be understood in much the same way as large collections of atoms in solids. Physicists such as Hopfield (1982) used techniques from statistical mechanics to analyze the storage and optimization properties of networks, leading to significant cross-fertilization of ideas. Psychologists including David Rumelhart and Geoff Hinton continued the study of neural net models of memory. As we discuss in Chapter 19, the real impetus came in the mid-1980s when at least four different groups reinvented the back-propagation learning algorithm first found in 1969 by Bryson and Ho. The algorithm was applied to many learning problems in computer science and psychology, and the widespread dissemination of the results in the collection *Parallel Distributed Processing* (Rumelhart and McClelland, 1986) caused great excitement.

At about the same time, some disillusionment was occurring concerning the applicability of the expert system technology derived from MYCIN-type systems. Many corporations and

---

[16] To save embarrassment, a new field called IKBS (Intelligent Knowledge-Based Systems) was defined because Artificial Intelligence had been officially cancelled.

research groups found that building a successful expert system involved much more than simply buying a reasoning system and filling it with rules. Some predicted an "AI Winter" in which AI funding would be squeezed severely. It was perhaps this fear, and the historical factors on the neural network side, that led to a period in which neural networks and traditional AI were seen as rival fields, rather than as mutually supporting approaches to the same problem.

Recent events (1987–present)

Recent years have seen a sea change in both the content and the methodology of research in artificial intelligence.[17] It is now more common to build on existing theories than to propose brand new ones, to base claims on rigorous theorems or hard experimental evidence rather than on intuition, and to show relevance to real-world applications rather than toy examples.

The field of speech recognition illustrates the pattern. In the 1970s, a wide variety of different architectures and approaches were tried. Many of these were rather *ad hoc* and fragile, and were demonstrated on a few specially selected examples. In recent years, approaches based on **hidden Markov models** (HMMs) have come to dominate the area. Two aspects of HMMs are relevant to the present discussion. First, they are based on a rigorous mathematical theory. This has allowed speech researchers to build on several decades of mathematical results developed in other fields. Second, they are generated by a process of training on a large corpus of real speech data. This ensures that the performance is robust, and in rigorous blind tests the HMMs have been steadily improving their scores. Speech technology and the related field of handwritten character recognition are already making the transition to widespread industrial and consumer applications.

Another area that seems to have benefitted from formalization is planning. Early work by Austin Tate (1977), followed up by David Chapman (1987), has resulted in an elegant synthesis of existing planning programs into a simple framework. There have been a number of advances that built upon each other rather than starting from scratch each time. The result is that planning systems that were only good for microworlds in the 1970s are now used for scheduling of factory work and space missions, among other things. See Chapters 11 and 12 for more details.

Judea Pearl's (1988) *Probabilistic Reasoning in Intelligent Systems* marked a new acceptance of probability and decision theory in AI, following a resurgence of interest epitomized by Peter Cheeseman's (1985) article "In Defense of Probability." The **belief network** formalism was invented to allow efficient reasoning about the combination of uncertain evidence. This approach largely overcomes the problems with probabilistic reasoning systems of the 1960s and 1970s, and has come to dominate AI research on uncertain reasoning and expert systems. Work by Judea Pearl (1982a) and by Eric Horvitz and David Heckerman (Horvitz and Heckerman, 1986; Horvitz *et al.*, 1986) promoted the idea of *normative* expert systems: ones that act rationally according to the laws of decision theory and do not try to imitate human experts. Chapters 14 to 16 cover this area.

---

17 Some have characterized this change as a victory of the **neats**—those who think that AI theories should be grounded in mathematical rigor—over the **scruffies**—those who would rather try out lots of ideas, write some programs, and then assess what seems to be working. Both approaches are important. A shift toward increased neatness implies that the field has reached a level of stability and maturity. (Whether that stability will be disrupted by a new scruffy idea is another question.)

Similar gentle revolutions have occurred in robotics, computer vision, machine learning (including neural networks), and knowledge representation. A better understanding of the problems and their complexity properties, combined with increased mathematical sophistication, has led to workable research agendas and robust methods. Perhaps encouraged by the progress in solving the subproblems of AI, researchers have also started to look at the "whole agent" problem again. The work of Allen Newell, John Laird, and Paul Rosenbloom on SOAR (Newell, 1990; Laird *et al.*, 1987) is the best-known example of a complete agent architecture in AI. The so-called "situated" movement aims to understand the workings of agents embedded in real environments with continuous sensory inputs. Many interesting results are coming out of such work, including the realization that the previously isolated subfields of AI may need to be reorganized somewhat when their results are to be tied together into a single agent design.

1.4   THE STATE OF THE ART

International grandmaster Arnold Denker studies the pieces on the board in front of him. He realizes there is no hope; he must resign the game. His opponent, HITECH, becomes the first computer program to defeat a grandmaster in a game of chess (Berliner, 1989).

"I want to go from Boston to San Francisco," the traveller says into the microphone. "What date will you be travelling on?" is the reply. The traveller explains she wants to go October 20th, nonstop, on the cheapest available fare, returning on Sunday. A speech understanding program named PEGASUS handles the whole transaction, which results in a confirmed reservation that saves the traveller $894 over the regular coach fare. Even though the speech recognizer gets one out of ten words wrong,[18] it is able to recover from these errors because of its understanding of how dialogs are put together (Zue *et al.*, 1994).

An analyst in the Mission Operations room of the Jet Propulsion Laboratory suddenly starts paying attention. A red message has flashed onto the screen indicating an "anomaly" with the Voyager spacecraft, which is somewhere in the vicinity of Neptune. Fortunately, the analyst is able to correct the problem from the ground. Operations personnel believe the problem might have been overlooked had it not been for MARVEL, a real-time expert system that monitors the massive stream of data transmitted by the spacecraft, handling routine tasks and alerting the analysts to more serious problems (Schwuttke, 1992).

Cruising the highway outside of Pittsburgh at a comfortable 55 mph, the man in the driver's seat seems relaxed. He should be—for the past 90 miles, he has not had to touch the steering wheel, brake, or accelerator. The real driver is a robotic system that gathers input from video cameras, sonar, and laser range finders attached to the van. It combines these inputs with experience learned from training runs and succesfully computes how to steer the vehicle (Pomerleau, 1993).

A leading expert on lymph-node pathology describes a fiendishly difficult case to the expert system, and examines the system's diagnosis. He scoffs at the system's response. Only slightly worried, the creators of the system suggest he ask the computer for an explanation of

---

[18] Some other existing systems err only half as often on this task.

the diagnosis. The machine points out the major factors influencing its decision, and explains the subtle interaction of several of the symptoms in this case. The expert admits his error, eventually (Heckerman, 1991).

From a camera perched on a street light above the crossroads, the traffic monitor watches the scene. If any humans were awake to read the main screen, they would see "Citröen 2CV turning from Place de la Concorde into Champs Elysées," "Large truck of unknown make stopped on Place de la Concorde," and so on into the night. And occasionally, "Major incident on Place de la Concorde, speeding van collided with motorcyclist," and an automatic call to the emergency services (King *et al.*, 1993; Koller *et al.*, 1994).

These are just a few examples of artificial intelligence systems that exist today. Not magic or science fiction—but rather science, engineering, and mathematics, to which this book provides an introduction.

1.5 SUMMARY

This chapter defines AI and establishes the cultural background against which it has developed. Some of the important points are as follows:

- Different people think of AI differently. Two important questions to ask are: Are you concerned with thinking or behavior? Do you want to model humans, or work from an ideal standard?

- In this book, we adopt the view that intelligence is concerned mainly with **rational action**. Ideally, an **intelligent agent** takes the best possible action in a situation. We will study the problem of building agents that are intelligent in this sense.

- Philosophers (going back to 400 B.C.) made AI conceivable by considering the ideas that the mind is in some ways like a machine, that it operates on knowledge encoded in some internal language, and that thought can be used to help arrive at the right actions to take.

- Mathematicians provided the tools to manipulate statements of logical certainty as well as uncertain, probabilistic statements. They also set the groundwork for reasoning about algorithms.

- Psychologists strengthened the idea that humans and other animals can be considered information processing machines. Linguists showed that language use fits into this model.

- Computer engineering provided the artifact that makes AI applications possible. AI programs tend to be large, and they could not work without the great advances in speed and memory that the computer industry has provided.

- The history of AI has had cycles of success, misplaced optimism, and resulting cutbacks in enthusiasm and funding. There have also been cycles of introducing new creative approaches and systematically refining the best ones.

- Recent progress in understanding the theoretical basis for intelligence has gone hand in hand with improvements in the capabilities of real systems.

BIBLIOGRAPHICAL AND HISTORICAL NOTES

Daniel Crevier's (1993) *Artificial Intelligence* gives a complete history of the field, and Raymond Kurzweil's (1990) *Age of Intelligent Machines* situates AI in the broader context of computer science and intellectual history in general. Dianne Martin (1993) documents the degree to which early computers were endowed by the media with mythical powers of intelligence.

The methodological status of artificial intelligence is discussed in *The Sciences of the Artificial*, by Herb Simon (1981), which discusses research areas concerned with complex artifacts. It explains how AI can be viewed as both science and mathematics.

Artificial Intelligence: The Very Idea, by John Haugeland (1985) gives a readable account of the philosophical and practical problems of AI. Cognitive science is well-described by Johnson-Laird's *The Computer and the Mind: An Introduction to Cognitive Science*. Baker (1989) covers the syntactic part of modern linguistics, and Chierchia and McConnell-Ginet (1990) cover semantics. Allen (1995) covers linguistics from the AI point of view.

Early AI work is covered in Feigenbaum and Feldman's *Computers and Thought*, Minsky's *Semantic Information Processing*, and the *Machine Intelligence* series edited by Donald Michie. A large number of influential papers are collected in *Readings in Artificial Intelligence* (Webber and Nilsson, 1981). Early papers on neural networks are collected in *Neurocomputing* (Anderson and Rosenfeld, 1988). The *Encyclopedia of AI* (Shapiro, 1992) contains survey articles on almost every topic in AI. These articles usually provide a good entry point into the research literature on each topic. The four-volume *Handbook of Artificial Intelligence* (Barr and Feigenbaum, 1981) contains descriptions of almost every major AI system published before 1981.

The most recent work appears in the proceedings of the major AI conferences: the biennial International Joint Conference on AI (IJCAI), and the annual National Conference on AI, more often known as AAAI, after its sponsoring organization. The major journals for general AI are *Artificial Intelligence*, *Computational Intelligence*, the IEEE *Transactions on Pattern Analysis and Machine Intelligence*, and the electronic *Journal of Artificial Intelligence Research*. There are also many journals devoted to specific areas, which we cover in the appropriate chapters. Commercial products are covered in the magazines *AI Expert* and *PC AI*. The main professional societies for AI are the American Association for Artificial Intelligence (AAAI), the ACM Special Interest Group in Artificial Intelligence (SIGART), and the Society for Artificial Intelligence and Simulation of Behaviour (AISB). AAAI's *AI Magazine* and the *SIGART Bulletin* contain many topical and tutorial articles as well as announcements of conferences and workshops.

EXERCISES

These exercises are intended to stimulate discussion, and some might be set as term projects. Alternatively, preliminary attempts can be made now, and these attempts can be reviewed after completing the book.

1.1   Read Turing's original paper on AI (Turing, 1950). In the paper, he discusses several potential objections to his proposed enterprise and his test for intelligence. Which objections still carry some weight? Are his refutations valid? Can you think of new objections arising from developments since he wrote the paper? In the paper, he predicts that by the year 2000, a computer will have a 30% chance of passing a five-minute Turing Test with an unskilled interrogator. Do you think this is reasonable?

1.2   We characterized the definitions of AI along two dimensions, human vs. ideal and thought vs. action. But there are other dimensions that are worth considering. One dimension is whether we are interested in theoretical results or in practical applications. Another is whether we intend our intelligent computers to be conscious or not. Philosophers have had a lot to say about this issue, and although most AI researchers are happy to leave the questions to the philosophers, there has been heated debate. The claim that machines can be conscious is called the **strong AI** claim; the **weak AI** position makes no such claim. Characterize the eight definitions on page 5 and the seven following definitions according to the four dimensions we have mentioned and whatever other ones you feel are helpful.

STRONG A
WEAK AI

> Artificial intelligence is . . .

a. "a collection of algorithms that are computationally tractable, adequate approximations of intractably specified problems" (Partridge, 1991)

b. "the enterprise of constructing a physical symbol system that can reliably pass the Turing Test" (Ginsberg, 1993)

c. "the field of computer science that studies how machines can be made to act intelligently" (Jackson, 1986)

d. "a field of study that encompasses computational techniques for performing tasks that apparently require intelligence when performed by humans" (Tanimoto, 1990)

e. "a very general investigation of the nature of intelligence and the principles and mechanisms required for understanding or replicating it" (Sharples *et al.*, 1989)

f. "the getting of computers to do things that seem to be intelligent" (Rowe, 1988).

1.3   There are well-known classes of problems that are intractably difficult for computers, and other classes that are provably undecidable by any computer. Does this mean that AI is impossible?

1.4   Suppose we extend Evans's ANALOGY program so that it can score 200 on a standard IQ test. Would we then have a program more intelligent than a human? Explain.

1.5   Examine the AI literature to discover whether or not the following tasks can currently be solved by computers:

a. Playing a decent game of table tennis (ping-pong).

b. Driving in the center of Cairo.

c. Playing a decent game of bridge at a competitive level.

d. Discovering and proving new mathematical theorems.

e. Writing an intentionally funny story.

f. Giving competent legal advice in a specialized area of law.

g. Translating spoken English into spoken Swedish in real time.

For the currently infeasible tasks, try to find out what the difficulties are and estimate when they will be overcome.

1.6   Find an article written by a lay person in a reputable newspaper or magazine claiming the achievement of some intelligent capacity by a machine, where the claim is either wildly exaggerated or false.

1.7   Fact, fiction, and forecast:

    a. Find a claim in print by a reputable philosopher or scientist to the effect that a certain capacity will never be exhibited by computers, where that capacity has now been exhibited.

    b. Find a claim by a reputable computer scientist to the effect that a certain capacity would be exhibited by a date that has since passed, without the appearance of that capacity.

    c. Compare the accuracy of these predictions to predictions in other fields such as biomedicine, fusion power, nanotechnology, transportation, or home electronics.

1.8   Some authors have claimed that perception and motor skills are the most important part of intelligence, and that "higher-level" capacities are necessarily parasitic—simple add-ons to these underlying facilities. Certainly, most of evolution and a large part of the brain have been devoted to perception and motor skills, whereas AI has found tasks such as game playing and logical inference to be easier, in many ways, than perceiving and acting in the real world. Do you think that AI's traditional focus on higher-level cognitive abilities is misplaced?

1.9   "Surely computers cannot be intelligent—they can only do what their programmers tell them." Is the latter statement true, and does it imply the former?

1.10   "Surely animals cannot be intelligent—they can only do what their genes tell them." Is the latter statement true, and does it imply the former?

2 INTELLIGENT AGENTS

In which we discuss what an intelligent agent does, how it is related to its environment, how it is evaluated, and how we might go about building one.

2.1 INTRODUCTION

An **agent** is anything that can be viewed as **perceiving** its environment through **sensors** and **acting** upon that environment through **effectors**. A human agent has eyes, ears, and other organs for sensors, and hands, legs, mouth, and other body parts for effectors. A robotic agent substitutes cameras and infrared range finders for the sensors and various motors for the effectors. A software agent has encoded bit strings as its percepts and actions. A generic agent is diagrammed in Figure 2.1.

Our aim in this book is to design agents that do a good job of acting on their environment. First, we will be a little more precise about what we mean by a good job. Then we will talk about different designs for successful agents—filling in the question mark in Figure 2.1. We discuss some of the general principles used in the design of agents throughout the book, chief among which is the principle that agents should *know* things. Finally, we show how to couple an agent to an environment and describe several kinds of environments.

2.2 HOW AGENTS SHOULD ACT

RATIONAL AGENT A **rational agent** is one that does the right thing. Obviously, this is better than doing the wrong thing, but what does it mean? As a first approximation, we will say that the right action is the one that will cause the agent to be most successful. That leaves us with the problem of deciding *how* and *when* to evaluate the agent's success.

31

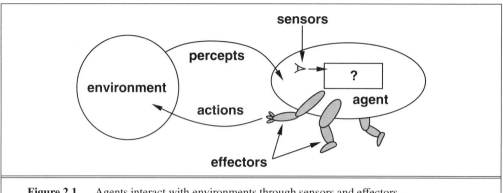

Figure 2.1   Agents interact with environments through sensors and effectors.

PERFORMANCE
MEASURE   We use the term **performance measure** for the *how*—the criteria that determine how successful an agent is. Obviously, there is not one fixed measure suitable for all agents. We could ask the agent for a subjective opinion of how happy it is with its own performance, but some agents would be unable to answer, and others would delude themselves. (Human agents in particular are notorious for "sour grapes"—saying they did not really want something after they are unsuccessful at getting it.) Therefore, we will insist on an objective performance measure imposed by some authority. In other words, we as outside observers establish a standard of what it means to be successful in an environment and use it to measure the performance of agents.

As an example, consider the case of an agent that is supposed to vacuum a dirty floor. A plausible performance measure would be the amount of dirt cleaned up in a single eight-hour shift. A more sophisticated performance measure would factor in the amount of electricity consumed and the amount of noise generated as well. A third performance measure might give highest marks to an agent that not only cleans the floor quietly and efficiently, but also finds time to go windsurfing at the weekend.[1]

The *when* of evaluating performance is also important. If we measured how much dirt the agent had cleaned up in the first hour of the day, we would be rewarding those agents that start fast (even if they do little or no work later on), and punishing those that work consistently. Thus, we want to measure performance over the long run, be it an eight-hour shift or a lifetime.

OMNISCIENCE   We need to be careful to distinguish between rationality and **omniscience**. An omniscient agent knows the *actual* outcome of its actions, and can act accordingly; but omniscience is impossible in reality. Consider the following example: I am walking along the Champs Elysées one day and I see an old friend across the street. There is no traffic nearby and I'm not otherwise engaged, so, being rational, I start to cross the street. Meanwhile, at 33,000 feet, a cargo door falls off a passing airliner,[2] and before I make it to the other side of the street I am flattened. Was I irrational to cross the street? It is unlikely that my obituary would read "Idiot attempts to cross

---

[1] There is a danger here for those who establish performance measures: you often get what you ask for. That is, if you measure success by the amount of dirt cleaned up, then some clever agent is bound to bring in a load of dirt each morning, quickly clean it up, and get a good performance score. What you really want to measure is how clean the floor is, but determining that is more difficult than just weighing the dirt cleaned up.

[2] See N. Henderson, "New door latches urged for Boeing 747 jumbo jets," *Washington Post*, 8/24/89.

street." Rather, this points out that rationality is concerned with *expected* success *given what has been perceived*. Crossing the street was rational because most of the time the crossing would be successful, and there was no way I could have foreseen the falling door. Note that another agent that was equipped with radar for detecting falling doors or a steel cage strong enough to repel them would be more successful, but it would not be any more rational.

In other words, we cannot blame an agent for failing to take into account something it could not perceive, or for failing to take an action (such as repelling the cargo door) that it is incapable of taking. But relaxing the requirement of perfection is not just a question of being fair to agents. The point is that if we specify that an intelligent agent should always do what is *actually* the right thing, it will be impossible to design an agent to fulfill this specification—unless we improve the performance of crystal balls.

In summary, what is rational at any given time depends on four things:

- The performance measure that defines degree of success.
- Everything that the agent has perceived so far. We will call this complete perceptual history the **percept sequence**.

 PERCEPT SEQUENCE

- What the agent knows about the environment.
- The actions that the agent can perform.

 IDEAL RATIONAL AGENT

This leads to a definition of an **ideal rational agent**: *For each possible percept sequence, an ideal rational agent should do whatever action is expected to maximize its performance measure, on the basis of the evidence provided by the percept sequence and whatever built-in knowledge the agent has.*

We need to look carefully at this definition. At first glance, it might appear to allow an agent to indulge in some decidedly underintelligent activities. For example, if an agent does not look both ways before crossing a busy road, then its percept sequence will not tell it that there is a large truck approaching at high speed. The definition seems to say that it would be OK for it to cross the road. In fact, this interpretation is wrong on two counts. First, it would not be rational to cross the road: the risk of crossing without looking is too great. Second, an ideal rational agent would have chosen the "looking" action before stepping into the street, because looking helps maximize the expected performance. Doing actions *in order to obtain useful information* is an important part of rationality and is covered in depth in Chapter 16.

The notion of an agent is meant to be a tool for analyzing systems, not an absolute characterization that divides the world into agents and non-agents. Consider a clock. It can be thought of as just an inanimate object, or it can be thought of as a simple agent. As an agent, most clocks always do the right action: moving their hands (or displaying digits) in the proper fashion. Clocks are a kind of degenerate agent in that their percept sequence is empty; no matter what happens outside, the clock's action should be unaffected.

Well, this is not quite true. If the clock and its owner take a trip from California to Australia, the right thing for the clock to do would be to turn itself back six hours. We do not get upset at our clocks for failing to do this because we realize that they are acting rationally, given their lack of perceptual equipment.[3]

---

[3]   One of the authors still gets a small thrill when his computer successfully resets itself at daylight savings time.

The ideal mapping from percept sequences to actions

Once we realize that an agent's behavior depends only on its percept sequence to date, then we can describe any particular agent by making a table of the action it takes in response to each possible percept sequence. (For most agents, this would be a very long list—infinite, in fact, unless we place a bound on the length of percept sequences we want to consider.) Such a list is called

MAPPING   a **mapping** from percept sequences to actions. We can, in principle, find out which mapping correctly describes an agent by trying out all possible percept sequences and recording which actions the agent does in response. (If the agent uses some randomization in its computations, then we would have to try some percept sequences several times to get a good idea of the agent's average behavior.) And if mappings describe agents, then **ideal mappings** describe ideal agents.

IDEAL MAPPINGS   *Specifying which action an agent ought to take in response to any given percept sequence provides a design for an ideal agent.*

This does not mean, of course, that we have to create an explicit table with an entry for every possible percept sequence. It is possible to define a specification of the mapping without exhaustively enumerating it. Consider a very simple agent: the square-root function on a calculator. The percept sequence for this agent is a sequence of keystrokes representing a number, and the action is to display a number on the display screen. The ideal mapping is that when the percept is a positive number x, the right action is to display a positive number z such that $z^2 \approx x$, accurate to, say, 15 decimal places. This specification of the ideal mapping does not require the designer to actually construct a table of square roots. Nor does the square-root function have to use a table to behave correctly: Figure 2.2 shows part of the ideal mapping and a simple program that implements the mapping using Newton's method.

The square-root example illustrates the relationship between the ideal mapping and an ideal agent design, for a very restricted task. Whereas the table is very large, the agent is a nice, compact program. It turns out that it is possible to design nice, compact agents that implement

Percept x	Action z
1.0	1.000000000000000
1.1	1.048808848170152
1.2	1.095445115010332
1.3	1.140175425099138
1.4	1.183215956619923
1.5	1.224744871391589
1.6	1.264911064067352
1.7	1.303840481040530
1.8	1.341640786499874
1.9	1.378404875209022
$\vdots$	$\vdots$

```
function SQRT(x)
    z ← 1.0                 / * initial guess * /
    repeat until |z² − x| < 10⁻¹⁵
            z ← z − (z² − x)/(2z)
    end
    return z
```

Figure 2.2   Part of the ideal mapping for the square-root problem (accurate to 15 digits), and a corresponding program that implements the ideal mapping.

the ideal mapping for much more general situations: agents that can solve a limitless variety of tasks in a limitless variety of environments. Before we discuss how to do this, we need to look at one more requirement that an intelligent agent ought to satisfy.

Autonomy

AUTONOMY

There is one more thing to deal with in the definition of an ideal rational agent: the "built-in knowledge" part. If the agent's actions are based completely on built-in knowledge, such that it need pay no attention to its percepts, then we say that the agent lacks **autonomy**. For example, if the clock manufacturer was prescient enough to know that the clock's owner would be going to Australia at some particular date, then a mechanism could be built in to adjust the hands automatically by six hours at just the right time. This would certainly be successful behavior, but the intelligence seems to belong to the clock's designer rather than to the clock itself.

An agent's behavior can be based on both its own experience and the built-in knowledge used in constructing the agent for the particular environment in which it operates. *A system is autonomous[4] to the extent that its behavior is determined by its own experience.* It would be too stringent, though, to require complete autonomy from the word go: when the agent has had little or no experience, it would have to act randomly unless the designer gave some assistance. So, just as evolution provides animals with enough built-in reflexes so that they can survive long enough to learn for themselves, it would be reasonable to provide an artificial intelligent agent with some initial knowledge as well as an ability to learn.

Autonomy not only fits in with our intuition, but it is an example of sound engineering practices. An agent that operates on the basis of built-in assumptions will only operate success-fully when those assumptions hold, and thus lacks flexibility. Consider, for example, the lowly dung beetle. After digging its nest and laying its eggs, it fetches a ball of dung from a nearby heap to plug the entrance; if the ball of dung is removed from its grasp *en route*, the beetle continues on and pantomimes plugging the nest with the nonexistent dung ball, never noticing that it is missing. Evolution has built an assumption into the beetle's behavior, and when it is violated, unsuccessful behavior results. A truly autonomous intelligent agent should be able to operate successfully in a wide variety of environments, given sufficient time to adapt.

2.3   STRUCTURE OF INTELLIGENT AGENTS

AGENT PROGRAM

ARCHITECTURE

So far we have talked about agents by describing their *behavior*—the action that is performed after any given sequence of percepts. Now, we will have to bite the bullet and talk about how the insides work. The job of AI is to design the **agent program**: a function that implements the agent mapping from percepts to actions. We assume this program will run on some sort of computing device, which we will call the **architecture**. Obviously, the program we choose has

_____

4   The word "autonomous" has also come to mean something like "not under the immediate control of a human," as in "autonomous land vehicle." We are using it in a stronger sense.

to be one that the architecture will accept and run. The architecture might be a plain computer, or it might include special-purpose hardware for certain tasks, such as processing camera images or filtering audio input. It might also include software that provides a degree of insulation between the raw computer and the agent program, so that we can program at a higher level. In general, the architecture makes the percepts from the sensors available to the program, runs the program, and feeds the program's action choices to the effectors as they are generated. The relationship among agents, architectures, and programs can be summed up as follows:

$$agent = architecture + program$$

Most of this book is about designing agent programs, although Chapters 24 and 25 deal directly with the architecture.

Before we design an agent program, we must have a pretty good idea of the possible percepts and actions, what goals or performance measure the agent is supposed to achieve, and what sort of environment it will operate in.[5] These come in a wide variety. Figure 2.3 shows the basic elements for a selection of agent types.

It may come as a surprise to some readers that we include in our list of agent types some programs that seem to operate in the entirely artificial environment defined by keyboard input and character output on a screen. "Surely," one might say, "this is not a real environment, is it?" In fact, what matters is not the distinction between "real" and "artificial" environments, but the complexity of the relationship among the behavior of the agent, the percept sequence generated by the environment, and the goals that the agent is supposed to achieve. Some "real" environments are actually quite simple. For example, a robot designed to inspect parts as they come by on a conveyer belt can make use of a number of simplifying assumptions: that the lighting is always just so, that the only thing on the conveyer belt will be parts of a certain kind, and that there are only two actions—accept the part or mark it as a reject.

SOFTWARE AGENTS

SOFTBOTS

In contrast, some **software agents** (or software robots or **softbots**) exist in rich, unlimited domains. Imagine a softbot designed to fly a flight simulator for a 747. The simulator is a very detailed, complex environment, and the software agent must choose from a wide variety of actions in real time. Or imagine a softbot designed to scan online news sources and show the interesting items to its customers. To do well, it will need some natural language processing abilities, it will need to learn what each customer is interested in, and it will need to dynamically change its plans when, for example, the connection for one news source crashes or a new one comes online.

Some environments blur the distinction between "real" and "artificial." In the ALIVE environment (Maes *et al.*, 1994), software agents are given as percepts a digitized camera image of a room where a human walks about. The agent processes the camera image and chooses an action. The environment also displays the camera image on a large display screen that the human can watch, and superimposes on the image a computer graphics rendering of the software agent. One such image is a cartoon dog, which has been programmed to move toward the human (unless he points to send the dog away) and to shake hands or jump up eagerly when the human makes certain gestures.

---

[5] For the acronymically minded, we call this the PAGE (Percepts, Actions, Goals, Environment) description. Note that the goals do *not* necessarily have to be represented within the agent; they simply describe the performance measure by which the agent design will be judged.

Agent Type	Percepts	Actions	Goals	Environment
Medical diagnosis system	Symptoms, findings, patient's answers	Questions, tests, treatments	Healthy patient, minimize costs	Patient, hospital
Satellite image analysis system	Pixels of varying intensity, color	Print a categorization of scene	Correct categorization	Images from orbiting satellite
Part-picking robot	Pixels of varying intensity	Pick up parts and sort into bins	Place parts in correct bins	Conveyor belt with parts
Refinery controller	Temperature, pressure readings	Open, close valves; adjust temperature	Maximize purity, yield, safety	Refinery
Interactive English tutor	Typed words	Print exercises, suggestions, corrections	Maximize student's score on test	Set of students

Figure 2.3   Examples of agent types and their PAGE descriptions.

The most famous artificial environment is the Turing Test environment, in which the whole point is that real and artificial agents are on equal footing, but the environment is challenging enough that it is very difficult for a software agent to do as well as a human. Section 2.4 describes in more detail the factors that make some environments more demanding than others.

Agent programs

We will be building intelligent agents throughout the book. They will all have the same skeleton, namely, accepting percepts from an environment and generating actions. The early versions of agent programs will have a very simple form (Figure 2.4). Each will use some internal data structures that will be updated as new percepts arrive. These data structures are operated on by the agent's decision-making procedures to generate an action choice, which is then passed to the architecture to be executed.

There are two things to note about this skeleton program. First, even though we defined the agent mapping as a function from percept *sequences* to actions, the agent program receives only a single percept as its input. It is up to the agent to build up the percept sequence in memory, if it so desires. In some environments, it is possible to be quite successful without storing the percept sequence, and in complex domains, it is infeasible to store the complete sequence.

---

function SKELETON-AGENT(*percept*) **returns** action
   static: *memory*, the agent's memory of the world

   memory ← UPDATE-MEMORY(*memory, percept*)
   action ← CHOOSE-BEST-ACTION(*memory*)
   memory ← UPDATE-MEMORY(*memory, action*)
   return *action*

Figure 2.4   A skeleton agent. On each invocation, the agent's memory is updated to reflect the new percept, the best action is chosen, and the fact that the action was taken is also stored in memory. The memory persists from one invocation to the next.

Second, the goal or performance measure is *not* part of the skeleton program. This is because the performance measure is applied externally to judge the behavior of the agent, and it is often possible to achieve high performance without explicit knowledge of the performance measure (see, e.g., the square-root agent).

Why not just look up the answers?

Let us start with the simplest possible way we can think of to write the agent program—a lookup table. Figure 2.5 shows the agent program. It operates by keeping in memory its entire percept sequence, and using it to index into *table*, which contains the appropriate action for all possible percept sequences.

   It is instructive to consider why this proposal is doomed to failure:

1. The table needed for something as simple as an agent that can only play chess would be about 35^{100} entries.
2. It would take quite a long time for the designer to build the table.
3. The agent has no autonomy at all, because the calculation of best actions is entirely built-in. So if the environment changed in some unexpected way, the agent would be lost.

---

function TABLE-DRIVEN-AGENT(*percept*) **returns** *action*
   static: *percepts*, a sequence, initially empty
         table, a table, indexed by percept sequences, initially fully specified

   append *percept* to the end of *percepts*
   action ← LOOKUP(*percepts, table*)
   return *action*

Figure 2.5   An agent based on a prespecified lookup table. It keeps track of the percept sequence and just looks up the best action.

4. Even if we gave the agent a learning mechanism as well, so that it could have a degree of autonomy, it would take forever to learn the right value for all the table entries.

Despite all this, TABLE-DRIVEN-AGENT *does* do what we want: it implements the desired agent mapping. It is not enough to say, "It can't be intelligent;" the point is to understand why an agent that *reasons* (as opposed to looking things up in a table) can do even better by avoiding the four drawbacks listed here.

An example

At this point, it will be helpful to consider a particular environment, so that our discussion can become more concrete. Mainly because of its familiarity, and because it involves a broad range of skills, we will look at the job of designing an automated taxi driver. We should point out, before the reader becomes alarmed, that such a system is currently somewhat beyond the capabilities of existing technology, although most of the components are available in some form.[6] The full driving task is extremely *open-ended*—there is no limit to the novel combinations of circumstances that can arise (which is another reason why we chose it as a focus for discussion).

We must first think about the percepts, actions, goals and environment for the taxi. They are summarized in Figure 2.6 and discussed in turn.

Agent Type	Percepts	Actions	Goals	Environment
Taxi driver	Cameras, speedometer, GPS, sonar, microphone	Steer, accelerate, brake, talk to passenger	Safe, fast, legal, comfortable trip, maximize profits	Roads, other traffic, pedestrians, customers

Figure 2.6   The taxi driver agent type.

The taxi will need to know where it is, what else is on the road, and how fast it is going. This information can be obtained from the **percepts** provided by one or more controllable TV cameras, the speedometer, and odometer. To control the vehicle properly, especially on curves, it should have an accelerometer; it will also need to know the mechanical state of the vehicle, so it will need the usual array of engine and electrical system sensors. It might have instruments that are not available to the average human driver: a satellite global positioning system (GPS) to give it accurate position information with respect to an electronic map; or infrared or sonar sensors to detect distances to other cars and obstacles. Finally, it will need a microphone or keyboard for the passengers to tell it their destination.

The **actions** available to a taxi driver will be more or less the same ones available to a human driver: control over the engine through the gas pedal and control over steering and braking. In addition, it will need output to a screen or voice synthesizer to talk back to the passengers, and perhaps some way to communicate with other vehicles.

---

[6] See page 26 for a description of an existing driving robot, or look at the conference proceedings on Intelligent Vehicle and Highway Systems (IVHS).

What **performance measure** would we like our automated driver to aspire to? Desirable qualities include getting to the correct destination; minimizing fuel consumption and wear and tear; minimizing the trip time and/or cost; minimizing violations of traffic laws and disturbances to other drivers; maximizing safety and passenger comfort; maximizing profits. Obviously, some of these goals conflict, so there will be trade-offs involved.

Finally, were this a real project, we would need to decide what kind of driving **environment** the taxi will face. Should it operate on local roads, or also on freeways? Will it be in Southern California, where snow is seldom a problem, or in Alaska, where it seldom is not? Will it always be driving on the right, or might we want it to be flexible enough to drive on the left in case we want to operate taxis in Britain or Japan? Obviously, the more restricted the environment, the easier the design problem.

Now we have to decide how to build a real program to implement the mapping from percepts to action. We will find that different aspects of driving suggest different types of agent program. We will consider four types of agent program:

- Simple reflex agents
- Agents that keep track of the world
- Goal-based agents
- Utility-based agents

Simple reflex agents

The option of constructing an explicit lookup table is out of the question. The visual input from a single camera comes in at the rate of 50 megabytes per second (25 frames per second, 1000×1000 pixels with 8 bits of color and 8 bits of intensity information). So the lookup table for an hour would be $2^{60 \times 60 \times 50M}$ entries.

However, we can summarize portions of the table by noting certain commonly occurring input/output associations. For example, if the car in front brakes, and its brake lights come on, then the driver should notice this and initiate braking. In other words, some processing is done on the visual input to establish the condition we call "The car in front is braking"; then this triggers some established connection in the agent program to the action "initiate braking". We call such
CONDITION–ACTION RULE
a connection a **condition–action rule**[7] written as

> **if** *car-in-front-is-braking* **then** *initiate-braking*

Humans also have many such connections, some of which are learned responses (as for driving) and some of which are innate reflexes (such as blinking when something approaches the eye). In the course of the book, we will see several different ways in which such connections can be learned and implemented.

Figure 2.7 gives the structure of a simple reflex agent in schematic form, showing how the condition–action rules allow the agent to make the connection from percept to action. (Do not worry if this seems trivial; it gets more interesting shortly.) We use rectangles to denote

---

[7] Also called **situation–action rules**, **productions**, or **if–then rules**. The last term is also used by some authors for logical implications, so we will avoid it altogether.

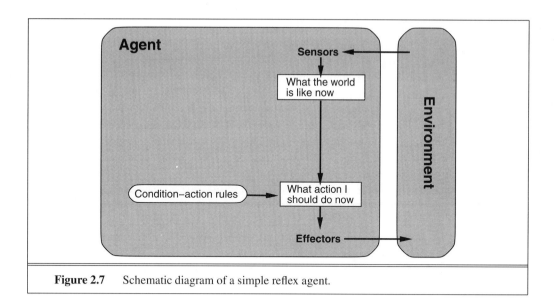

Figure 2.7   Schematic diagram of a simple reflex agent.

function SIMPLE-REFLEX-AGENT(*percept*) **returns** *action*
   static: *rules*, a set of condition-action rules

   state ← INTERPRET-INPUT(*percept*)
   rule ← RULE-MATCH(*state, rules*)
   action ← RULE-ACTION[*rule*]
   return *action*

Figure 2.8   A simple reflex agent. It works by finding a rule whose condition matches the current situation (as defined by the percept) and then doing the action associated with that rule.

the current internal state of the agent's decision process, and ovals to represent the background information used in the process. The agent program, which is also very simple, is shown in Figure 2.8. The INTERPRET-INPUT function generates an abstracted description of the current state from the percept, and the RULE-MATCH function returns the first rule in the set of rules that matches the given state description. Although such agents can be implemented very efficiently (see Chapter 10), their range of applicability is very narrow, as we shall see.

Agents that keep track of the world

The simple reflex agent described before will work only if the correct decision can be made on the basis of the current percept. If the car in front is a recent model, and has the centrally mounted brake light now required in the United States, then it will be possible to tell if it is braking from a single image. Unfortunately, older models have different configurations of tail

INTERNAL STATE

lights, brake lights, and turn-signal lights, and it is not always possible to tell if the car is braking. Thus, even for the simple braking rule, our driver will have to maintain some sort of **internal state** in order to choose an action. Here, the internal state is not too extensive—it just needs the previous frame from the camera to detect when two red lights at the edge of the vehicle go on or off simultaneously.

Consider the following more obvious case: from time to time, the driver looks in the rear-view mirror to check on the locations of nearby vehicles. When the driver is not looking in the mirror, the vehicles in the next lane are invisible (i.e., the states in which they are present and absent are indistinguishable); but in order to decide on a lane-change maneuver, the driver needs to know whether or not they are there.

The problem illustrated by this example arises because the sensors do not provide access to the complete state of the world. In such cases, the agent may need to maintain some internal state information in order to distinguish between world states that generate the same perceptual input but nonetheless are significantly different. Here, "significantly different" means that different actions are appropriate in the two states.

Updating this internal state information as time goes by requires two kinds of knowledge to be encoded in the agent program. First, we need some information about how the world evolves independently of the agent—for example, that an overtaking car generally will be closer behind than it was a moment ago. Second, we need some information about how the agent's own actions affect the world—for example, that when the agent changes lanes to the right, there is a gap (at least temporarily) in the lane it was in before, or that after driving for five minutes northbound on the freeway one is usually about five miles north of where one was five minutes ago.

Figure 2.9 gives the structure of the reflex agent, showing how the current percept is combined with the old internal state to generate the updated description of the current state. The agent program is shown in Figure 2.10. The interesting part is the function UPDATE-STATE, which is responsible for creating the new internal state description. As well as interpreting the new percept in the light of existing knowledge about the state, it uses information about how the world evolves to keep track of the unseen parts of the world, and also must know about what the agent's actions do to the state of the world. Detailed examples appear in Chapters 7 and 17.

Goal-based agents

GOAL

SEARCH

PLANNING

Knowing about the current state of the environment is not always enough to decide what to do. For example, at a road junction, the taxi can turn left, right, or go straight on. The right decision depends on where the taxi is trying to get to. In other words, as well as a current state description, the agent needs some sort of **goal** information, which describes situations that are desirable— for example, being at the passenger's destination. The agent program can combine this with information about the results of possible actions (the same information as was used to update internal state in the reflex agent) in order to choose actions that achieve the goal. Sometimes this will be simple, when goal satisfaction results immediately from a single action; sometimes, it will be more tricky, when the agent has to consider long sequences of twists and turns to find a way to achieve the goal. **Search** (Chapters 3 to 5) and **planning** (Chapters 11 to 13) are the subfields of AI devoted to finding action sequences that do achieve the agent's goals.

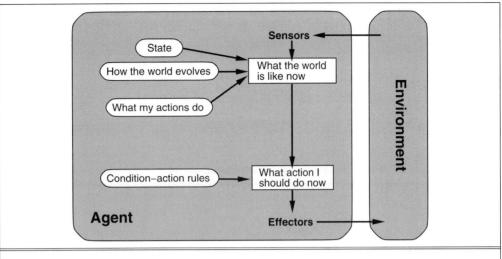

Figure 2.9   A reflex agent with internal state.

---

function REFLEX-AGENT-WITH-STATE(*percept*) **returns** *action*
  static: *state*, a description of the current world state
        rules, a set of condition-action rules

  state ← UPDATE-STATE(*state, percept*)
  rule ← RULE-MATCH(*state, rules*)
  action ← RULE-ACTION[*rule*]
  state ← UPDATE-STATE(*state, action*)
  return *action*

Figure 2.10   A reflex agent with internal state. It works by finding a rule whose condition matches the current situation (as defined by the percept and the stored internal state) and then doing the action associated with that rule.

Notice that decision–making of this kind is fundamentally different from the condition–action rules described earlier, in that it involves consideration of the future—both "What will happen if I do such-and-such?" and "Will that make me happy?" In the reflex agent designs, this information is not explicitly used, because the designer has precomputed the correct action for various cases. The reflex agent brakes when it sees brake lights. A goal-based agent, in principle, could reason that if the car in front has its brake lights on, it will slow down. From the way the world usually evolves, the only action that will achieve the goal of not hitting other cars is to brake. Although the goal-based agent appears less efficient, it is far more flexible. If it starts to rain, the agent can update its knowledge of how effectively its brakes will operate; this will automatically cause all of the relevant behaviors to be altered to suit the new conditions. For the reflex agent, on the other hand, we would have to rewrite a large number of condition–action rules. Of course, the goal-based agent is also more flexible with respect to reaching different destinations. Simply by specifying a new destination, we can get the goal-based agent to come up with a new behavior. The reflex agent's rules for when to turn and when to go straight will only work for a single destination; they must all be replaced to go somewhere new.

Figure 2.11 shows the goal-based agent's structure. Chapter 13 contains detailed agent programs for goal-based agents.

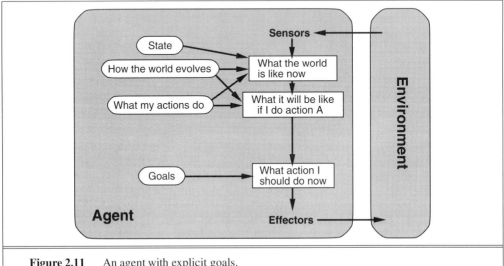

Figure 2.11   An agent with explicit goals.

Utility-based agents

Goals alone are not really enough to generate high-quality behavior. For example, there are many action sequences that will get the taxi to its destination, thereby achieving the goal, but some are quicker, safer, more reliable, or cheaper than others. Goals just provide a crude distinction between "happy" and "unhappy" states, whereas a more general performance measure should allow a comparison of different world states (or sequences of states) according to exactly how happy they would make the agent if they could be achieved. Because "happy" does not sound very scientific, the customary terminology is to say that if one world state is preferred to another, then it has higher **utility** for the agent.[8]

UTILITY

Utility is therefore a function that maps a state[9] onto a real number, which describes the associated degree of happiness. A complete specification of the utility function allows rational decisions in two kinds of cases where goals have trouble. First, when there are conflicting goals, only some of which can be achieved (for example, speed and safety), the utility function specifies the appropriate trade-off. Second, when there are several goals that the agent can aim for, none

---

[8] The word "utility" here refers to "the quality of being useful," not to the electric company or water works.

[9] Or sequence of states, if we are measuring the utility of an agent over the long run.

of which can be achieved with certainty, utility provides a way in which the likelihood of success can be weighed up against the importance of the goals.

In Chapter 16, we show that any rational agent can be described as possessing a utility function. An agent that possesses an *explicit* utility function therefore can make rational decisions, but may have to compare the utilities achieved by different courses of actions. Goals, although cruder, enable the agent to pick an action right away if it satisfies the goal. In some cases, moreover, a utility function can be translated into a set of goals, such that the decisions made by a goal-based agent using those goals are identical to those made by the utility-based agent.

The overall utility-based agent structure appears in Figure 2.12. Actual utility-based agent programs appear in Chapter 5, where we examine game-playing programs that must make fine distinctions among various board positions; and in Chapter 17, where we tackle the general problem of designing decision-making agents.

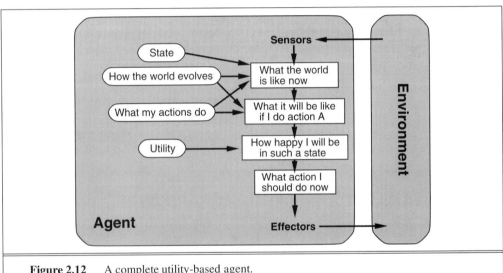

Figure 2.12   A complete utility-based agent.

2.4   ENVIRONMENTS

In this section and in the exercises at the end of the chapter, you will see how to couple an agent to an environment. Section 2.3 introduced several different kinds of agents and environments. In all cases, however, the nature of the connection between them is the same: actions are done by the agent on the environment, which in turn provides percepts to the agent. First, we will describe the different types of environments and how they affect the design of agents. Then we will describe environment programs that can be used as testbeds for agent programs.

Properties of environments

Environments come in several flavors. The principal distinctions to be made are as follows:

ACCESSIBLE

◇ **Accessible** vs. **inaccessible**.

If an agent's sensory apparatus gives it access to the complete state of the environment, then we say that the environment is accessible to that agent. An environment is effectively accessible if the sensors detect all aspects that are relevant to the choice of action. An accessible environment is convenient because the agent need not maintain any internal state to keep track of the world.

DETERMINISTIC

◇ **Deterministic** vs. **nondeterministic**.

If the next state of the environment is completely determined by the current state and the actions selected by the agents, then we say the environment is deterministic. In principle, an agent need not worry about uncertainty in an accessible, deterministic environment. If the environment is inaccessible, however, then it may *appear* to be nondeterministic. This is particularly true if the environment is complex, making it hard to keep track of all the inaccessible aspects. Thus, it is often better to think of an environment as deterministic or nondeterministic *from the point of view of the agent*.

EPISODIC

◇ **Episodic** vs. **nonepisodic**.

In an episodic environment, the agent's experience is divided into "episodes." Each episode consists of the agent perceiving and then acting. The quality of its action depends just on the episode itself, because subsequent episodes do not depend on what actions occur in previous episodes. Episodic environments are much simpler because the agent does not need to think ahead.

STATIC

◇ **Static** vs. **dynamic**.

If the environment can change while an agent is deliberating, then we say the environment is dynamic for that agent; otherwise it is static. Static environments are easy to deal with because the agent need not keep looking at the world while it is deciding on an action, nor need it worry about the passage of time. If the environment does not change with the passage of time but the agent's performance score does, then we say the environment is

SEMIDYNAMIC

semidynamic.

DISCRETE

◇ **Discrete** vs. **continuous**.

If there are a limited number of distinct, clearly defined percepts and actions we say that the environment is discrete. Chess is discrete—there are a fixed number of possible moves on each turn. Taxi driving is continuous—the speed and location of the taxi and the other vehicles sweep through a range of continuous values.[10]

We will see that different environment types require somewhat different agent programs to deal with them effectively. It will turn out, as you might expect, that the hardest case is *inaccessible*, *nonepisodic*, *dynamic*, and *continuous*. It also turns out that most real situations are so complex that whether they are *really* deterministic is a moot point; for practical purposes, they must be treated as nondeterministic.

---

[10] At a fine enough level of granularity, even the taxi driving environment is discrete, because the camera image is digitized to yield discrete pixel values. But any sensible agent program would have to abstract above this level, up to a level of granularity that is continuous.

Figure 2.13 lists the properties of a number of familiar environments. Note that the answers can change depending on how you conceptualize the environments and agents. For example, poker is deterministic if the agent can keep track of the order of cards in the deck, but it is nondeterministic if it cannot. Also, many environments are episodic at higher levels than the agent's individual actions. For example, a chess tournament consists of a sequence of games; each game is an episode, because (by and large) the contribution of the moves in one game to the agent's overall performance is not affected by the moves in its next game. On the other hand, moves within a single game certainly interact, so the agent needs to look ahead several moves.

Environment	Accessible	Deterministic	Episodic	Static	Discrete
Chess with a clock	Yes	Yes	No	Semi	Yes
Chess without a clock	Yes	Yes	No	Yes	Yes
Poker	No	No	No	Yes	Yes
Backgammon	Yes	No	No	Yes	Yes
Taxi driving	No	No	No	No	No
Medical diagnosis system	No	No	No	No	No
Image-analysis system	Yes	Yes	Yes	Semi	No
Part-picking robot	No	No	Yes	No	No
Refinery controller	No	No	No	No	No
Interactive English tutor	No	No	No	No	Yes

Figure 2.13   Examples of environments and their characteristics.

Environment programs

The generic environment program in Figure 2.14 illustrates the basic relationship between agents and environments. In this book, we will find it convenient for many of the examples and exercises to use an environment simulator that follows this program structure. The simulator takes one or more agents as input and arranges to repeatedly give each agent the right percepts and receive back an action. The simulator then updates the environment based on the actions, and possibly other dynamic processes in the environment that are not considered to be agents (rain, for example). The environment is therefore defined by the initial state and the update function. Of course, an agent that works in a simulator ought also to work in a real environment that provides the same kinds of percepts and accepts the same kinds of actions.

The RUN-ENVIRONMENT procedure correctly exercises the agents in an environment. For some kinds of agents, such as those that engage in natural language dialogue, it may be sufficient simply to observe their behavior. To get more detailed information about agent performance, we insert some performance measurement code. The function RUN-EVAL-ENVIRONMENT, shown in Figure 2.15, does this; it applies a performance measure to each agent and returns a list of the resulting scores. The *scores* variable keeps track of each agent's score.

In general, the performance measure can depend on the entire sequence of environment states generated during the operation of the program. Usually, however, the performance measure

---

procedure RUN-ENVIRONMENT(*state,* UPDATE-FN, *agents, termination*)
    inputs: *state*, the initial state of the environment
            UPDATE-FN, function to modify the environment
            agents, a set of agents
            termination, a predicate to test when we are done

    repeat
        for each *agent* **in** *agents* **do**
            PERCEPT[*agent*] ← GET-PERCEPT(*agent, state*)
        end
        for each *agent* **in** *agents* **do**
            ACTION[*agent*] ← PROGRAM[*agent*](PERCEPT[*agent*])
        end
        state ← UPDATE-FN(*actions, agents, state*)
    until *termination*(*state*)

Figure 2.14   The basic environment simulator program. It gives each agent its percept, gets an action from each agent, and then updates the environment.

---

function RUN-EVAL-ENVIRONMENT(*state,* UPDATE-FN, *agents,*
                              termination, PERFORMANCE-FN) **returns** *scores*
    local variables: *scores*, a vector the same size as *agents*, all 0

    repeat
        for each *agent* **in** *agents* **do**
            PERCEPT[*agent*] ← GET-PERCEPT(*agent, state*)
        end
        for each *agent* **in** *agents* **do**
            ACTION[*agent*] ← PROGRAM[*agent*](PERCEPT[*agent*])
        end
        state ← UPDATE-FN(*actions, agents, state*)
        scores ← PERFORMANCE-FN(*scores, agents, state*)
    until *termination*(*state*)
    return *scores*   */ * change * /*

Figure 2.15   An environment simulator program that keeps track of the performance measure for each agent.

---

works by a simple accumulation using either summation, averaging, or taking a maximum. For example, if the performance measure for a vacuum-cleaning agent is the total amount of dirt cleaned in a shift, *scores* will just keep track of how much dirt has been cleaned up so far.

    RUN-EVAL-ENVIRONMENT returns the performance measure for a a single environment, defined by a single initial state and a particular update function. Usually, an agent is designed to

ENVIRONMENT
CLASS

work in an **environment class**, a whole set of different environments. For example, we design a chess program to play against any of a wide collection of human and machine opponents. If we designed it for a single opponent, we might be able to take advantage of specific weaknesses in that opponent, but that would not give us a good program for general play. Strictly speaking, in order to measure the performance of an agent, we need to have an environment generator that selects particular environments (with certain likelihoods) in which to run the agent. We are then interested in the agent's average performance over the environment class. This is fairly straightforward to implement for a simulated environment, and Exercises 2.5 to 2.11 take you through the entire development of an environment and the associated measurement process.

A possible confusion arises between the state variable in the environment simulator and the state variable in the agent itself (see REFLEX-AGENT-WITH-STATE). As a programmer implementing both the environment simulator and the agent, it is tempting to allow the agent to peek at the environment simulator's state variable. This temptation must be resisted at all costs! The agent's version of the state must be constructed from its percepts alone, without access to the complete state information.

2.5 SUMMARY

This chapter has been something of a whirlwind tour of AI, which we have conceived of as the science of agent design. The major points to recall are as follows:

- An **agent** is something that perceives and acts in an environment. We split an agent into an architecture and an agent program.

- An **ideal agent** is one that always takes the action that is expected to maximize its performance measure, given the percept sequence it has seen so far.

- An agent is **autonomous** to the extent that its action choices depend on its own experience, rather than on knowledge of the environment that has been built-in by the designer.

- An **agent program** maps from a percept to an action, while updating an internal state.

- There exists a variety of basic agent program designs, depending on the kind of information made explicit and used in the decision process. The designs vary in efficiency, compactness, and flexibility. The appropriate design of the agent program depends on the percepts, actions, goals, and environment.

- **Reflex agents** respond immediately to percepts, **goal-based agents** act so that they will achieve their goal(s), and **utility-based agents** try to maximize their own "happiness."

- The process of making decisions by reasoning with knowledge is central to AI and to successful agent design. This means that representing knowledge is important.

- Some environments are more demanding than others. Environments that are inaccessible, nondeterministic, nonepisodic, dynamic, and continuous are the most challenging.

BIBLIOGRAPHICAL AND HISTORICAL NOTES

The analysis of rational agency as a mapping from percept sequences to actions probably stems ultimately from the effort to identify rational behavior in the realm of economics and other forms of reasoning under uncertainty (covered in later chapters) and from the efforts of psychological behaviorists such as Skinner (1953) to reduce the psychology of organisms strictly to input/output or stimulus/response mappings. The advance from behaviorism to functionalism in psychology, which was at least partly driven by the application of the computer metaphor to agents (Putnam, 1960; Lewis, 1966), introduced the internal state of the agent into the picture. The philosopher Daniel Dennett (1969; 1978b) helped to synthesize these viewpoints into a coherent "intentional stance" toward agents. A high-level, abstract perspective on agency is also taken within the world of AI in (McCarthy and Hayes, 1969). Jon Doyle (1983) proposed that rational agent design is the core of AI, and would remain as its mission while other topics in AI would spin off to form new disciplines. Horvitz *et al.* (1988) specifically suggest the use of rationality conceived as the maximization of expected utility as a basis for AI.

The AI researcher and Nobel-prize-winning economist Herb Simon drew a clear distinction between rationality under resource limitations (procedural rationality) and rationality as making the objectively rational choice (substantive rationality) (Simon, 1958). Cherniak (1986) explores the minimal level of rationality needed to qualify an entity as an agent. Russell and Wefald (1991) deal explicitly with the possibility of using a variety of agent architectures. *Dung Beetle Ecology* (Hanski and Cambefort, 1991) provides a wealth of interesting information on the behavior of dung beetles.

EXERCISES

2.1   What is the difference between a performance measure and a utility function?

2.2   For each of the environments in Figure 2.3, determine what type of agent architecture is most appropriate (table lookup, simple reflex, goal-based or utility-based).

2.3   Choose a domain that you are familiar with, and write a PAGE description of an agent for the environment. Characterize the environment as being accessible, deterministic, episodic, static, and continuous or not. What agent architecture is best for this domain?

2.4   While driving, which is the best policy?

  a. Always put your directional blinker on before turning,

  b. Never use your blinker,

  c. Look in your mirrors and use your blinker only if you observe a car that can observe you?

What kind of reasoning did you need to do to arrive at this policy (logical, goal-based, or utility-based)? What kind of agent design is necessary to carry out the policy (reflex, goal-based, or utility-based)?

The following exercises all concern the implementation of an environment and set of agents in the vacuum-cleaner world.

2.5   Implement a performance-measuring environment simulator for the vacuum-cleaner world. This world can be described as follows:

◇ **Percepts**: Each vacuum-cleaner agent gets a three-element percept vector on each turn. The first element, a touch sensor, should be a 1 if the machine has bumped into something and a 0 otherwise. The second comes from a photosensor under the machine, which emits a 1 if there is dirt there and a 0 otherwise. The third comes from an infrared sensor, which emits a 1 when the agent is in its home location, and a 0 otherwise.

◇ **Actions**: There are five actions available: go forward, turn right by 90°, turn left by 90°, suck up dirt, and turn off.

◇ **Goals**: The goal for each agent is to clean up and go home. To be precise, the performance measure will be 100 points for each piece of dirt vacuumed up, minus 1 point for each action taken, and minus 1000 points if it is not in the home location when it turns itself off.

◇ **Environment**: The environment consists of a grid of squares. Some squares contain obstacles (walls and furniture) and other squares are open space. Some of the open squares contain dirt. Each "go forward" action moves one square unless there is an obstacle in that square, in which case the agent stays where it is, but the touch sensor goes on. A "suck up dirt" action always cleans up the dirt. A "turn off" command ends the simulation.

We can vary the complexity of the environment along three dimensions:

◇ **Room shape**: In the simplest case, the room is an $n \times n$ square, for some fixed n. We can make it more difficult by changing to a rectangular, L-shaped, or irregularly shaped room, or a series of rooms connected by corridors.

◇ **Furniture**: Placing furniture in the room makes it more complex than an empty room. To the vacuum-cleaning agent, a piece of furniture cannot be distinguished from a wall by perception; both appear as a 1 on the touch sensor.

◇ **Dirt placement**: In the simplest case, dirt is distributed uniformly around the room. But it is more realistic for the dirt to predominate in certain locations, such as along a heavily travelled path to the next room, or in front of the couch.

2.6   Implement a table-lookup agent for the special case of the vacuum-cleaner world consisting of a 2×2 grid of open squares, in which at most two squares will contain dirt. The agent starts in the upper left corner, facing to the right. Recall that a table-lookup agent consists of a table of actions indexed by a percept sequence. In this environment, the agent can always complete its task in nine or fewer actions (four moves, three turns, and two suck-ups), so the table only needs entries for percept sequences up to length nine. At each turn, there are eight possible percept vectors, so the table will be of size $8^9 = 134,217,728$. Fortunately, we can cut this down by realizing that the touch sensor and home sensor inputs are not needed; we can arrange so that the agent never bumps into a wall and knows when it has returned home. Then there are only two relevant percept vectors, ?0? and ?1?, and the size of the table is at most $2^9 = 512$. Run the environment simulator on the table-lookup agent in all possible worlds (how many are there?). Record its performance score for each world and its overall average score.

2.7   Implement an environment for a $n \times m$ rectangular room, where each square has a 5% chance of containing dirt, and n and m are chosen at random from the range 8 to 15, inclusive.

2.8   Design and implement a pure reflex agent for the environment of Exercise 2.7, ignoring the requirement of returning home, and measure its performance. Explain why it is impossible to have a reflex agent that returns home and shuts itself off. Speculate on what the best possible reflex agent could do. What prevents a reflex agent from doing very well?

2.9   Design and implement several agents with internal state. Measure their performance. How close do they come to the ideal agent for this environment?

2.10   Calculate the size of the table for a table-lookup agent in the domain of Exercise 2.7. Explain your calculation. You need not fill in the entries for the table.

2.11   Experiment with changing the shape and dirt placement of the room, and with adding furniture. Measure your agents in these new environments. Discuss how their performance might be improved to handle more complex geographies.

Part II

PROBLEM-SOLVING

In this part we show how an agent can act by establishing *goals* and considering sequences of actions that might achieve those goals. A goal and a set of means for achieving the goal is called a *problem*, and the process of exploring what the means can do is called *search*. We show what search can do, how it must be modified to account for adversaries, and what its limitations are.

3 SOLVING PROBLEMS BY SEARCHING

In which we look at how an agent can decide what to do by systematically considering the outcomes of various sequences of actions that it might take.

In Chapter 2, we saw that simple reflex agents are unable to plan ahead. They are limited in what they can do because their actions are determined only by the current percept. Furthermore, they have no knowledge of what their actions do nor of what they are trying to achieve.

PROBLEM-SOLVING AGENT

In this chapter, we describe one kind of goal-based agent called a **problem-solving agent**. Problem-solving agents decide what to do by finding sequences of actions that lead to desirable states. We discuss informally how the agent can formulate an appropriate view of the problem it faces. The problem type that results from the formulation process will depend on the knowledge available to the agent: principally, whether it knows the current state and the outcomes of actions. We then define more precisely the elements that constitute a "problem" and its "solution," and give several examples to illustrate these definitions. Given precise definitions of problems, it is relatively straightforward to construct a search process for finding solutions. We cover six different search strategies and show how they can be applied to a variety of problems. Chapter 4 will then cover search strategies that make use of more information about the problem to improve the efficiency of the search process.

This chapter uses concepts from the analysis of algorithms. Readers unfamiliar with the concepts of asymptotic complexity and NP-completeness should consult Appendix A.

3.1 PROBLEM-SOLVING AGENTS

Intelligent agents are supposed to act in such a way that the environment goes through a sequence of states that maximizes the performance measure. In its full generality, this specification is difficult to translate into a successful agent design. As we mentioned in Chapter 2, the task is somewhat simplified if the agent can adopt a **goal** and aim to satisfy it. Let us first look at how and why an agent might do this.

Imagine our agent in the city of Arad, Romania, toward the end of a touring holiday. The agent has a ticket to fly out of Bucharest the following day. The ticket is nonrefundable, the agent's visa is about to expire, and after tomorrow, there are no seats available for six weeks. Now the agent's performance measure contains many other factors besides the cost of the ticket and the undesirability of being arrested and deported. For example, it wants to improve its suntan, improve its Romanian, take in the sights, and so on. All these factors might suggest any of a vast array of possible actions. Given the seriousness of the situation, however, it should adopt the **goal** of driving to Bucharest. Actions that result in a failure to reach Bucharest on time can be rejected without further consideration. Goals such as this help organize behavior by limiting the

GOAL FORMULATION   objectives that the agent is trying to achieve. **Goal formulation**, based on the current situation, is the first step in problem solving. As well as formulating a goal, the agent may wish to decide on some other factors that affect the desirability of different ways of achieving the goal.

For the purposes of this chapter, we will consider a goal to be a set of world states—just those states in which the goal is satisfied. Actions can be viewed as causing transitions between world states, so obviously the agent has to find out which actions will get it to a goal state. Before it can do this, it needs to decide what sorts of actions and states to consider. If it were to try to consider actions at the level of "move the left foot forward 18 inches" or "turn the steering wheel six degrees left," it would never find its way out of the parking lot, let alone to Bucharest, because constructing a solution at that level of detail would be an intractable problem. **Problem**

PROBLEM
FORMULATION   **formulation** is the process of deciding what actions and states to consider, and follows goal formulation. We will discuss this process in more detail. For now, let us assume that the agent will consider actions at the level of driving from one major town to another. The states it will consider therefore correspond to being in a particular town.[1]

Our agent has now adopted the goal of driving to Bucharest, and is considering which town to drive to from Arad. There are three roads out of Arad, one toward Sibiu, one to Timisoara, and one to Zerind. None of these achieves the goal, so unless the agent is very familiar with the geography of Romania, it will not know which road to follow.[2] In other words, the agent will not know which of its possible actions is best, because it does not know enough about the state that results from taking each action. If the agent has no additional knowledge, then it is stuck. The best it can do is choose one of the actions at random.

But suppose the agent has a map of Romania, either on paper or in its memory. The point of a map is to provide the agent with information about the states it might get itself into, and the actions it can take. The agent can use this information to consider subsequent stages of a hypothetical journey through each of the three towns, to try to find a journey that eventually gets to Bucharest. Once it has found a path on the map from Arad to Bucharest, it can achieve its goal by carrying out the driving actions that correspond to the legs of the journey. In general, then, an agent with several immediate options of unknown value can decide what to do by first examining different possible *sequences* of actions that lead to states of known value, and then choosing the

SEARCH   best one. This process of looking for such a sequence is called **search**. A search algorithm takes
SOLUTION   a problem as input and returns a **solution** in the form of an action sequence. Once a solution is

---

[1] Notice that these states actually correspond to large *sets* of world states, because a world state specifies every aspect of reality. It is important to keep in mind the distinction between states in problem solving and world states.

[2] We are assuming that most readers are in the same position, and can easily imagine themselves as clueless as our agent. We apologize to Romanian readers who are unable to take advantage of this pedagogical device.

EXECUTION

found, the actions it recommends can be carried out. This is called the **execution** phase. Thus, we have a simple "formulate, search, execute" design for the agent, as shown in Figure 3.1. After formulating a goal and a problem to solve, the agent calls a search procedure to solve it. It then uses the solution to guide its actions, doing whatever the solution recommends as the next thing to do, and then removing that step from the sequence. Once the solution has been executed, the agent will find a new goal.

---

function SIMPLE-PROBLEM-SOLVING-AGENT(p) **returns** an action
   inputs: p, a percept
   static: s, an action sequence, initially empty
          state, some description of the current world state
          g, a goal, initially null
          problem, a problem formulation

   state ← UPDATE-STATE(*state*, p)
   if s is empty **then**
      g ← FORMULATE-GOAL(*state*)
      problem ← FORMULATE-PROBLEM(*state*, g)
      s ← SEARCH(*problem*)
   action ← RECOMMENDATION(s, *state*)
   s ← REMAINDER(s, *state*)
   return *action*

Figure 3.1   A simple problem-solving agent.

We will not discuss the UPDATE-STATE and FORMULATE-GOAL functions further in this chapter. The next two sections describe the process of problem formulation, and then the remainder of the chapter is devoted to various versions of the SEARCH function. The execution phase is usually straightforward for a simple problem-solving agent: RECOMMENDATION just takes the first action in the sequence, and REMAINDER returns the rest.

3.2 FORMULATING PROBLEMS

In this section, we will consider the problem formulation process in more detail. First, we will look at the different amounts of knowledge that an agent can have concerning its actions and the state that it is in. This depends on how the agent is connected to its environment through its percepts and actions. We find that there are four essentially different types of problems—single-state problems, multiple-state problems, contingency problems, and exploration problems. We will define these types precisely, in preparation for later sections that address the solution process.

Knowledge and problem types

Let us consider an environment somewhat different from Romania: the vacuum world from
Exercises 2.5 to 2.11 in Chapter 2. We will simplify it even further for the sake of exposition. Let
the world contain just two locations. Each location may or may not contain dirt, and the agent
may be in one location or the other. There are 8 possible world states, as shown in Figure 3.2.
The agent has three possible actions in this version of the vacuum world: *Left*, *Right*, and *Suck*.
Assume, for the moment, that sucking is 100% effective. The goal is to clean up all the dirt. That
is, the goal is equivalent to the state set $\{7, 8\}$.

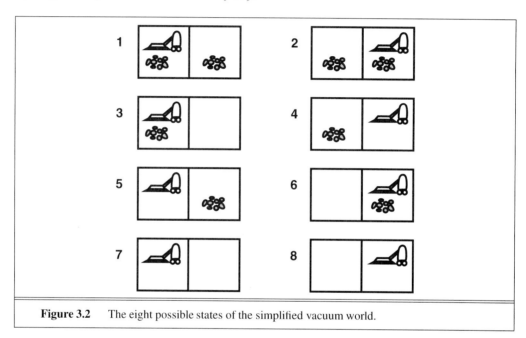

Figure 3.2   The eight possible states of the simplified vacuum world.

First, suppose that the agent's sensors give it enough information to tell exactly which state
it is in (i.e., the world is accessible); and suppose that it knows exactly what each of its actions
does. Then it can calculate exactly which state it will be in after any sequence of actions. For
example, if its initial state is 5, then it can calculate that the action sequence [*Right,Suck*] will get
to a goal state. This is the simplest case, which we call a **single-state problem**.

SINGLE-STATE
PROBLEM

Second, suppose that the agent knows all the effects of its actions, but has limited access
to the world state. For example, in the extreme case, it may have no sensors at all. In that case,
it knows only that its initial state is one of the set $\{1, 2, 3, 4, 5, 6, 7, 8\}$. One might suppose that
the agent's predicament is hopeless, but in fact it can do quite well. Because it knows what its
actions do, it can, for example, calculate that the action *Right* will cause it to be in one of the
states $\{2, 4, 6, 8\}$. In fact, the agent can discover that the action sequence [*Right,Suck,Left,Suck*]
is guaranteed to reach a goal state no matter what the start state. To summarize: when the world
is not fully accessible, the agent must reason about sets of states that it might get to, rather than

MULTIPLE-STATE
PROBLEM

single states. We call this a **multiple-state problem**.

Although it might seem different, the case of ignorance about the effects of actions can be treated similarly. Suppose, for example, that the environment appears to be nondeterministic in that it obeys Murphy's Law: the so-called *Suck* action *sometimes* deposits dirt on the carpet *but only if there is no dirt there already*.[3] For example, if the agent knows it is in state 4, then it knows that if it sucks, it will reach one of the states $\{2, 4\}$. For any *known* initial state, however, there is an action sequence that is guaranteed to reach a goal state (see Exercise 3.2).

Sometimes ignorance prevents the agent from finding a guaranteed solution sequence. Suppose, for example, that the agent is in the Murphy's Law world, and that it has a position sensor and a local dirt sensor, but no sensor capable of detecting dirt in other squares. Suppose further that the sensors tell it that it is in one of the states $\{1, 3\}$. The agent might formulate the action sequence [*Suck,Right,Suck*]. Sucking would change the state to one of $\{5, 7\}$, and moving right would then change the state to one of $\{6, 8\}$. If it is in fact state 6, then the action sequence will succeed, but if it is state 8, the plan will fail. If the agent had chosen the simpler action sequence [*Suck*], it would also succeed some of the time, but not always. It turns out there is no fixed action sequence that guarantees a solution to this problem.

Obviously, the agent *does* have a way to solve the problem starting from one of $\{1, 3\}$: first suck, then move right, then suck *only if there is dirt there*. Thus, solving this problem requires sensing *during the execution phase*. Notice that the agent must now calculate a whole tree of actions, rather than a single action sequence. In general, each branch of the tree deals with a possible contingency that might arise. For this reason, we call this a **contingency problem**. Many problems in the real, physical world are contingency problems, because exact prediction is impossible. For this reason, many people keep their eyes open while walking around or driving.

CONTINGENCY PROBLEM

Single-state and multiple-state problems can be handled by similar search techniques, which are covered in this chapter and the next. Contingency problems, on the other hand, require more complex algorithms, which we cover in Chapter 13. They also lend themselves to a somewhat different agent design, in which the agent can act *before* it has found a guaranteed plan. This is useful because rather than considering in advance every possible contingency that might arise during execution, it is often better to actually start executing and see which contingencies *do* arise. The agent can then continue to solve the problem given the additional information. This type of **interleaving** of search and execution is also covered in Chapter 13, and for the limited case of two-player games, in Chapter 5. For the remainder of this chapter, we will only consider cases where guaranteed solutions consist of a single sequence of actions.

INTERLEAVING

Finally, consider the plight of an agent that has no information about the effects of its actions. This is somewhat equivalent to being lost in a strange country with no map at all, and is the hardest task faced by an intelligent agent.[4] The agent must *experiment*, gradually discovering what its actions do and what sorts of states exist. This is a kind of search, but a search in the real world rather than in a model thereof. Taking a step in the real world, rather than in a model, may involve significant danger for an ignorant agent. If it survives, the agent learns a "map" of the environment, which it can then use to solve subsequent problems. We discuss this kind of **exploration problem** in Chapter 20.

EXPLORATION PROBLEM

---

[3] We assume that most readers face similar problems, and can imagine themselves as frustrated as our agent. We apologize to owners of modern, efficient home appliances who cannot take advantage of this pedagogical device.

[4] It is also the task faced by newborn babies.

Well-defined problems and solutions

PROBLEM

A **problem** is really a collection of information that the agent will use to decide what to do. We will begin by specifying the information needed to define a single-state problem.

We have seen that the basic elements of a problem definition are the states and actions. To capture these formally, we need the following:

INITIAL STATE
- The **initial state** that the agent knows itself to be in.

OPERATOR
- The set of possible actions available to the agent. The term **operator** is used to denote the description of an action in terms of which state will be reached by carrying out the

SUCCESSOR
FUNCTION
action in a particular state. (An alternate formulation uses a **successor function** S. Given a particular state x, $S(x)$ returns the set of states reachable from x by any single action.)

STATE SPACE

PATH

Together, these define the **state space** of the problem: the set of all states reachable from the initial state by any sequence of actions. A **path** in the state space is simply any sequence of actions leading from one state to another. The next element of a problem is the following:

GOAL TEST
- The **goal test**, which the agent can apply to a single state description to determine if it is a goal state. Sometimes there is an explicit set of possible goal states, and the test simply checks to see if we have reached one of them. Sometimes the goal is specified by an abstract property rather than an explicitly enumerated set of states. For example, in chess, the goal is to reach a state called "checkmate," where the opponent's king can be captured on the next move no matter what the opponent does.

Finally, it may be the case that one solution is preferable to another, even though they both reach the goal. For example, we might prefer paths with fewer or less costly actions.

PATH COST
- A **path cost** function is a function that assigns a cost to a path. In all cases we will consider, the cost of a path is the sum of the costs of the individual actions along the path. The path cost function is often denoted by g.

Together, the initial state, operator set, goal test, and path cost function define a problem. Naturally, we can then define a datatype with which to represent problems:

---

datatype PROBLEM
    components: INITIAL-STATE, OPERATORS, GOAL-TEST, PATH-COST-FUNCTION

SOLUTION

Instances of this datatype will be the input to our search algorithms. The output of a search algorithm is a **solution**, that is, a path from the initial state to a state that satisfies the goal test.

To deal with multiple-state problems, we need to make only minor modifications: a problem consists of an initial state *set*; a set of operators specifying for each action the *set* of states reached from any given state; and a goal test and path cost function as before. An operator is applied to a state set by unioning the results of applying the operator to each state in the set. A path now connects *sets* of states, and a solution is now a path that leads to a set of states *all of which* are

STATE SET SPACE
goal states. The state space is replaced by the **state set space** (see Figure 3.7 for an example). Problems of both types are illustrated in Section 3.3.

Measuring problem-solving performance

SEARCH COST

TOTAL COST

The effectiveness of a search can be measured in at least three ways. First, does it find a solution at all? Second, is it a good solution (one with a low path cost)? Third, what is the **search cost** associated with the time and memory required to find a solution? The **total cost** of the search is the sum of the path cost and the search cost.[5]

For the problem of finding a route from Arad to Bucharest, the path cost might be proportional to the total mileage of the path, perhaps with something thrown in for wear and tear on different road surfaces. The search cost will depend on the circumstances. In a static environment, it will be zero because the performance measure is independent of time. If there is some urgency to get to Bucharest, the environment is semidynamic because deliberating longer will cost more. In this case, the search cost might vary approximately linearly with computation time (at least for small amounts of time). Thus, to compute the total cost, it would appear that we have to add miles and milliseconds. This is not always easy, because there is no "official exchange rate" between the two. The agent must somehow decide what resources to devote to search and what resources to devote to execution. For problems with very small state spaces, it is easy to find the solution with the lowest path cost. But for large, complicated problems, there is a trade-off to be made—the agent can search for a very long time to get an optimal solution, or the agent can search for a shorter time and get a solution with a slightly larger path cost. The issue of allocating resources will be taken up again in Chapter 16; for now, we concentrate on the search itself.

Choosing states and actions

Now that we have the definitions out of the way, let us start our investigation of problems with an easy one: "Drive from Arad to Bucharest using the roads in the map in Figure 3.3." An appropriate state space has 20 states, where each state is defined solely by location, specified as a city. Thus, the initial state is "in Arad" and the goal test is "is this Bucharest?" The operators correspond to driving along the roads between cities.

One solution is the path Arad to Sibiu to Rimnicu Vilcea to Pitesti to Bucharest. There are lots of other paths that are also solutions, for example, via Lugoj and Craiova. To decide which of these solutions is better, we need to know what the path cost function is measuring: it could be the total mileage, or the expected travel time. Because our current map does not specify either of these, we will use the number of steps as the cost function. That means that the path through Sibiu and Fagaras, with a path cost of 3, is the best possible solution.

The real art of problem solving is in deciding what goes into the description of the states and operators and what is left out. Compare the simple state description we have chosen, "in Arad," to an actual cross-country trip, where the state of the world includes so many things: the travelling companions, what is on the radio, what there is to look at out of the window, the vehicle being used for the trip, how fast it is going, whether there are any law enforcement officers nearby, what time it is, whether the driver is hungry or tired or running out of gas, how far it is to the next

---

[5] In theoretical computer science and in robotics, the search cost (the part you do before interacting with the environment) is called the **offline** cost and the path cost is called the **online** cost.

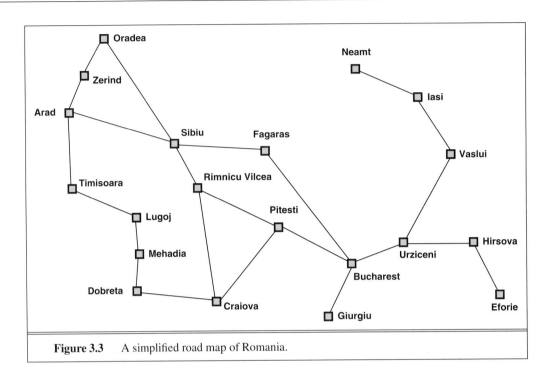

Figure 3.3   A simplified road map of Romania.

ABSTRACTION

rest stop, the condition of the road, the weather, and so on. All these considerations are left out of state descriptions because they are irrelevant to the problem of finding a route to Bucharest. The process of removing detail from a representation is called **abstraction**.

As well as abstracting the state description, we must abstract the actions themselves. An action—let us say a car trip from Arad to Zerind—has many effects. Besides changing the location of the vehicle and its occupants, it takes up time, consumes fuel, generates pollution, and changes the agent (as they say, travel is broadening). In our formulation, we take into account only the change in location. Also, there are many actions that we will omit altogether: turning on the radio, looking out of the window, slowing down for law enforcement officers, and so on.

Can we be more precise about defining the appropriate level of abstraction? Think of the states and actions we have chosen as corresponding to sets of detailed world states and sets of detailed action sequences. Now consider a solution to the abstract problem: for example, the path Arad to Sibiu to Rimnicu Vilcea to Pitesti to Bucharest. This solution corresponds to a large number of more detailed paths. For example, we could drive with the radio on between Sibiu and Rimnicu Vilcea, and then switch it off for the rest of the trip. Each of these more detailed paths is still a solution to the goal, so the abstraction is valid. The abstraction is also useful, because carrying out each of the actions in the solution, such as driving from Pitesti to Bucharest, is somewhat easier than the original problem. The choice of a good abstraction thus involves removing as much detail as possible while retaining validity and ensuring that the abstract actions are easy to carry out. Were it not for the ability to construct useful abstractions, intelligent agents would be completely swamped by the real world.

3.3   EXAMPLE PROBLEMS

TOY PROBLEMS
REAL-WORLD
PROBLEMS

The range of task environments that can be characterized by well-defined problems is vast. We can distinguish between so-called **toy problems**, which are intended to illustrate or exercise various problem-solving methods, and so-called **real-world problems**, which tend to be more difficult and whose solutions people actually care about. In this section, we will give examples of both. By nature, toy problems can be given a concise, exact description. This means that they can be easily used by different researchers to compare the performance of algorithms. Real-world problems, on the other hand, tend not to have a single agreed-upon description, but we will attempt to give the general flavor of their formulations.

Toy problems

The 8-puzzle

8-PUZZLE

The **8-puzzle**, an instance of which is shown in Figure 3.4, consists of a 3×3 board with eight numbered tiles and a blank space. A tile adjacent to the blank space can slide into the space. The object is to reach the configuration shown on the right of the figure. One important trick is to notice that rather than use operators such as "move the 4 tile into the blank space," it is more sensible to have operators such as "the blank space changes places with the tile to its left." This is because there are fewer of the latter kind of operator. This leads us to the following formulation:

◊ **States**: a state description specifies the location of each of the eight tiles in one of the nine squares. For efficiency, it is useful to include the location of the blank.
◊ **Operators**: blank moves left, right, up, or down.
◊ **Goal test**: state matches the goal configuration shown in Figure 3.4.
◊ **Path cost**: each step costs 1, so the path cost is just the length of the path.

SLIDING-BLOCK
PUZZLES

The 8-puzzle belongs to the family of **sliding-block puzzles**. This general class is known to be NP-complete, so one does not expect to find methods significantly better than the search

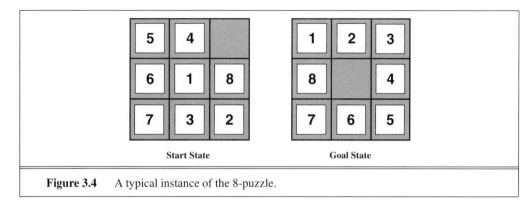

Start State   **Goal State**

Figure 3.4   A typical instance of the 8-puzzle.

algorithms described in this chapter and the next. The 8-puzzle and its larger cousin, the 15-puzzle, are the standard test problems for new search algorithms in AI.

The 8-queens problem

The goal of the 8-queens problem is to place eight queens on a chessboard such that no queen attacks any other. (A queen attacks any piece in the same row, column or diagonal.) Figure 3.5 shows an attempted solution that fails: the queen in the rightmost column is attacked by the queen at top left.

Figure 3.5   Almost a solution to the 8-queens problem. (Solution is left as an exercise.)

Although efficient special-purpose algorithms exist for this problem and the whole *n*-queens family, it remains an interesting test problem for search algorithms. There are two main kinds of formulation. The *incremental* formulation involves placing queens one by one, whereas the *complete-state* formulation starts with all 8 queens on the board and moves them around. In either case, the path cost is of no interest because only the final state counts; algorithms are thus compared only on search cost. Thus, we have the following goal test and path cost:

◇ **Goal test**: 8 queens on board, none attacked.

◇ **Path cost**: zero.

There are also different possible states and operators. Consider the following simple-minded formulation:

◇ **States**: any arrangement of 0 to 8 queens on board.

◇ **Operators**: add a queen to any square.

In this formulation, we have 64^8 possible sequences to investigate. A more sensible choice would use the fact that placing a queen where it is already attacked cannot work, because subsequent placings of other queens will not undo the attack. So we might try the following:

◇ **States**: arrangements of 0 to 8 queens with none attacked.

◇ **Operators**: place a queen in the left-most empty column such that it is not attacked by any other queen.

It is easy to see that the actions given can generate only states with no attacks; but sometimes no actions will be possible. For example, after making the first seven choices (left-to-right) in Figure 3.5, there is no action available in this formulation. The search process must try another choice. A quick calculation shows that there are only 2057 possible sequences to investigate. *The right formulation makes a big difference to the size of the search space.* Similar considerations apply for a complete-state formulation. For example, we could set the problem up as follows:

◇ **States**: arrangements of 8 queens, one in each column.

◇ **Operators**: move any attacked queen to another square in the same column.

This formulation would allow the algorithm to find a solution eventually, but it would be better to move to an unattacked square if possible.

Cryptarithmetic

In cryptarithmetic problems, letters stand for digits and the aim is to find a substitution of digits for letters such that the resulting sum is arithmetically correct. Usually, each letter must stand for a different digit. The following is a well-known example:

```
    FORTY       Solution:   29786       F=2, O=9, R=7, etc.
  +   TEN                     850
  +   TEN                     850
    -----                   -----
    SIXTY                   31486
```

The following formulation is probably the simplest:

◇ **States**: a cryptarithmetic puzzle with some letters replaced by digits.

◇ **Operators**: replace all occurrences of a letter with a digit not already appearing in the puzzle.

◇ **Goal test**: puzzle contains only digits, and represents a correct sum.

◇ **Path cost**: zero. All solutions equally valid.

A moment's thought shows that replacing E by 6 then F by 7 is the same thing as replacing F by 7 then E by 6—order does not matter to correctness, so we want to avoid trying permutations of the same substitutions. One way to do this is to adopt a fixed order, e.g., alphabetical order. A better choice is to do whichever is the most *constrained* substitution, that is, the letter that has the fewest legal possibilities given the constraints of the puzzle.

The vacuum world

Here we will define the simplified vacuum world from Figure 3.2, rather than the full version from Chapter 2. The latter is dealt with in Exercise 3.17.

First, let us review the single-state case with complete information. We assume that the agent knows its location and the locations of all the pieces of dirt, and that the suction is still in good working order.

◇ **States**: one of the eight states shown in Figure 3.2 (or Figure 3.6).

◇ **Operators**: move left, move right, suck.

◇ **Goal test**: no dirt left in any square.

◇ **Path cost**: each action costs 1.

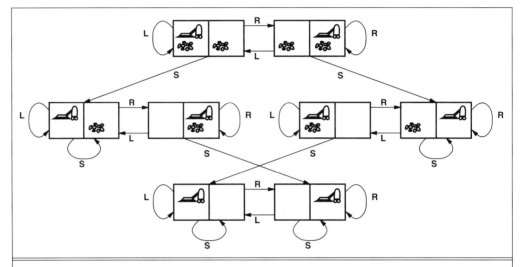

Figure 3.6   Diagram of the simplified vacuum state space. Arcs denote actions. L = move left, R = move right, S = suck.

Figure 3.6 shows the complete state space showing all the possible paths. Solving the problem from any starting state is simply a matter of following arrows to a goal state. This is the case for all problems, of course, but in most, the state space is vastly larger and more tangled.

Now let us consider the case where the agent has no sensors, but still has to clean up all the dirt. Because this is a multiple-state problem, we will have the following:

◇ **State sets**: subsets of states 1–8 shown in Figure 3.2 (or Figure 3.6).

◇ **Operators**: move left, move right, suck.

◇ **Goal test**: all states in state set have no dirt.

◇ **Path cost**: each action costs 1.

The start state set is the set of all states, because the agent has no sensors. A solution is any sequence leading from the start state set to a set of states with no dirt (see Figure 3.7). Similar state set spaces can be constructed for the case of uncertainty about actions and uncertainty about both states and actions.

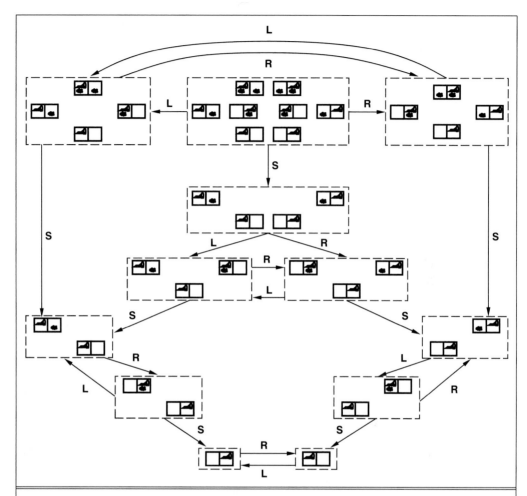

Figure 3.7   State set space for the simplified vacuum world with no sensors. Each dashed-line box encloses a set of states. At any given point, the agent is within a state set but does not know which state of that set it is in. The initial state set (complete ignorance) is the top center box. Actions are represented by labelled arcs. Self-loops are omitted for clarity.

Missionaries and cannibals

The missionaries and cannibals problem is usually stated as follows. Three missionaries and three cannibals are on one side of a river, along with a boat that can hold one or two people. Find a way to get everyone to the other side, without ever leaving a group of missionaries in one place outnumbered by the cannibals in that place.

    This problem is famous in AI because it was the subject of the first paper that approached problem formulation from an analytical viewpoint (Amarel, 1968). As with travelling in Romania, the real-life problem must be greatly abstracted before we can apply a problem-solving strategy.

Imagine the scene in real life: three members of the Arawaskan tribe, Alice, Bob, and Charles, stand at the edge of the crocodile-infested Amazon river with their new-found friends, Xavier, Yolanda, and Zelda. All around them birds cry, a rain storm beats down, Tarzan yodels, and so on. The missionaries Xavier, Yolanda, and Zelda are a little worried about what might happen if one of them were caught alone with two or three of the others, and Alice, Bob, and Charles are concerned that they might be in for a long sermon that they might find equally unpleasant. Both parties are not quite sure if the small boat they find tied up by the side of the river is up to making the crossing with two aboard.

To formalize the problem, the first step is to forget about the rain, the crocodiles, and all the other details that have no bearing in the solution. The next step is to decide what the right operator set is. We know that the operators will involve taking one or two people across the river in the boat, but we have to decide if we need a state to represent the time when they are in the boat, or just when they get to the other side. Because the boat holds only two people, no "outnumbering" can occur in it; hence, only the endpoints of the crossing are important. Next, we need to abstract over the individuals. Surely, each of the six is a unique human being, but for the purposes of the solution, when it comes time for a cannibal to get into the boat, it does not matter if it is Alice, Bob, or Charles. Any permutation of the three missionaries or the three cannibals leads to the same outcome. These considerations lead to the following formal definition of the problem:

◇ **States**: a state consists of an ordered sequence of three numbers representing the number of missionaries, cannibals, and boats on the bank of the river from which they started. Thus, the start state is (3,3,1).

◇ **Operators**: from each state the possible operators are to take either one missionary, one cannibal, two missionaries, two cannibals, or one of each across in the boat. Thus, there are at most five operators, although most states have fewer because it is necessary to avoid illegal states. Note that if we had chosen to distinguish between individual people then there would be 27 operators instead of just 5.

◇ **Goal test**: reached state (0,0,0).

◇ **Path cost**: number of crossings.

This state space is small enough to make it a trivial problem for a computer to solve. People have a hard time, however, because some of the necessary moves appear retrograde. Presumably, humans use some notion of "progress" to guide their search. We will see how such notions are used in the next chapter.

Real-world problems

Route finding

We have already seen how route finding is defined in terms of specified locations and transitions along links between them. Route-finding algorithms are used in a variety of applications, such as routing in computer networks, automated travel advisory systems, and airline travel planning systems. The last application is somewhat more complicated, because airline travel has a very complex path cost, in terms of money, seat quality, time of day, type of airplane, frequent-flyer mileage awards, and so on. Furthermore, the actions in the problem do not have completely known outcomes: flights can be late or overbooked, connections can be missed, and fog or emergency maintenance can cause delays.

Touring and travelling salesperson problems

Consider the problem, "Visit every city in Figure 3.3 at least once, starting and ending in Bucharest." This seems very similar to route finding, because the operators still correspond to trips between adjacent cities. But for this problem, the state space must record more information. In addition to the agent's location, each state must keep track of the set of cities the agent has visited. So the initial state would be "In Bucharest; visited {Bucharest}," a typical intermediate state would be "In Vaslui; visited {Bucharest,Urziceni,Vaslui}," and the goal test would check if the agent is in Bucharest and that all 20 cities have been visited.

TRAVELLING
SALESPERSON
PROBLEM

The **travelling salesperson problem** (TSP) is a famous touring problem in which each city must be visited exactly once. The aim is to find the *shortest* tour.[6] The problem is NP-hard (Karp, 1972), but an enormous amount of effort has been expended to improve the capabilities of TSP algorithms. In addition to planning trips for travelling salespersons, these algorithms have been used for tasks such as planning movements of automatic circuit board drills.

VLSI layout

The design of silicon chips is one of the most complex engineering design tasks currently undertaken, and we can give only a brief sketch here. A typical VLSI chip can have as many as a million gates, and the positioning and connections of every gate are crucial to the successful operation of the chip. Computer-aided design tools are used in every phase of the process. Two of the most difficult tasks are **cell layout** and **channel routing**. These come after the components and connections of the circuit have been fixed; the purpose is to lay out the circuit on the chip so as to minimize area and connection lengths, thereby maximizing speed. In cell layout, the primitive components of the circuit are grouped into cells, each of which performs some recognized function. Each cell has a fixed footprint (size and shape) and requires a certain number of connections to each of the other cells. The aim is to place the cells on the chip so that they do not overlap and so that there is room for the connecting wires to be placed between the cells. Channel routing finds a specific route for each wire using the gaps between the cells. These search problems are extremely complex, but definitely worth solving. In Chapter 4, we will see some algorithms capable of solving them.

Robot navigation

Robot navigation is a generalization of the route-finding problem described earlier. Rather than a discrete set of routes, a robot can move in a continuous space with (in principle) an infinite set of possible actions and states. For a simple, circular robot moving on a flat surface, the space

---

6   Strictly speaking, this is the travelling salesperson optimization problem; the TSP itself asks if a tour exists with cost less than some constant.

is essentially two-dimensional. When the robot has arms and legs that must also be controlled, the search space becomes many-dimensional. Advanced techniques are required just to make the search space finite. We examine some of these methods in Chapter 25. In addition to the complexity of the problem, real robots must also deal with errors in their sensor readings and motor controls.

Assembly sequencing

Automatic assembly of complex objects by a robot was first demonstrated by FREDDY the robot (Michie, 1972). Progress since then has been slow but sure, to the point where assembly of objects such as electric motors is economically feasible. In assembly problems, the problem is to find an order in which to assemble the parts of some object. If the wrong order is chosen, there will be no way to add some part later in the sequence without undoing some of the work already done. Checking a step in the sequence for feasibility is a complex geometrical search problem closely related to robot navigation. Thus, the generation of legal successors is the expensive part of assembly sequencing, and the use of informed algorithms to reduce search is essential.

3.4   SEARCHING FOR SOLUTIONS

We have seen how to define a problem, and how to recognize a solution. The remaining part—finding a solution—is done by a search through the state space. The idea is to maintain and extend a set of partial solution sequences. In this section, we show how to generate these sequences and how to keep track of them using suitable data structures.

Generating action sequences

To solve the route-finding problem from Arad to Bucharest, for example, we start off with just the initial state, Arad. The first step is to test if this is a goal state. Clearly it is not, but it is important to check so that we can solve trick problems like "starting in Arad, get to Arad." Because this is not a goal state, we need to consider some other states. This is done by applying the operators to the current state, thereby **generating** a new set of states. The process is called **expanding** the state. In this case, we get three new states, "in Sibiu," "in Timisoara," and "in Zerind," because there is a direct one-step route from Arad to these three cities. If there were only one possibility, we would just take it and continue. But whenever there are multiple possibilities, we must make a choice about which one to consider further.

This is the essence of search—choosing one option and putting the others aside for later, in case the first choice does not lead to a solution. Suppose we choose Zerind. We check to see if it is a goal state (it is not), and then expand it to get "in Arad" and "in Oradea." We can then choose any of these two, or go back and choose Sibiu or Timisoara. We continue choosing, testing, and expanding until a solution is found, or until there are no more states to be expanded. The choice of which state to expand first is determined by the **search strategy**.

GENERATING
EXPANDING

SEARCH STRATEGY

It is helpful to think of the search process as building up a **search tree** that is superimposed over the state space. The root of the search tree is a **search node** corresponding to the initial state. The leaf nodes of the tree correspond to states that do not have successors in the tree, either because they have not been expanded yet, or because they were expanded, but generated the empty set. At each step, the search algorithm chooses one leaf node to expand. Figure 3.8 shows some of the expansions in the search tree for route finding from Arad to Bucharest. The general search algorithm is described informally in Figure 3.9.

It is important to distinguish between the state space and the search tree. For the route-finding problem, there are only 20 states in the state space, one for each city. But there are an

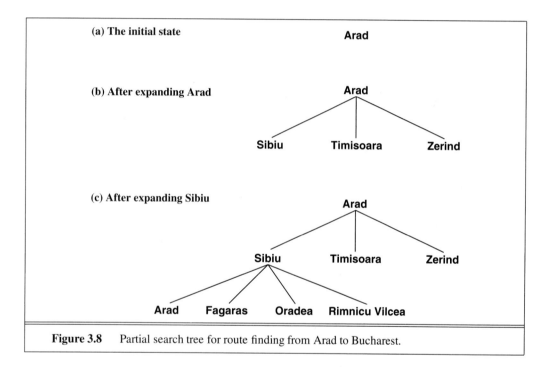

Figure 3.8   Partial search tree for route finding from Arad to Bucharest.

function GENERAL-SEARCH(*problem, strategy*) **returns** a solution, or failure
    initialize the search tree using the initial state of *problem*
    loop do
        if there are no candidates for expansion **then return** failure
        choose a leaf node for expansion according to *strategy*
        if the node contains a goal state **then return** the corresponding solution
        else expand the node and add the resulting nodes to the search tree
    end

Figure 3.9   An informal description of the general search algorithm.

infinite number of paths in this state space, so the search tree has an infinite number of nodes. For example, in Figure 3.8, the branch Arad–Sibiu–Arad continues Arad–Sibiu–Arad–Sibiu– Arad, and so on, indefinitely. Obviously, a good search algorithm avoids following such paths. Techniques for doing this are discussed in Section 3.6.

Data structures for search trees

There are many ways to represent nodes, but in this chapter, we will assume a node is a data structure with five components:

- the state in the state space to which the node corresponds;

PARENT NODE

- the node in the search tree that generated this node (this is called the **parent node**);
- the operator that was applied to generate the node;

DEPTH

- the number of nodes on the path from the root to this node (the **depth** of the node);
- the path cost of the path from the initial state to the node.

The node data type is thus:

---

datatype node
    components: STATE, PARENT-NODE, OPERATOR, DEPTH, PATH-COST

It is important to remember the distinction between nodes and states. A node is a bookkeeping data structure used to represent the search tree for a particular problem instance as generated by a particular algorithm. A state represents a configuration (or set of configurations) of the world. Thus, nodes have depths and parents, whereas states do not. (Furthermore, it is quite possible for two different nodes to contain the same state, if that state is generated via two different sequences of actions.) The EXPAND function is responsible for calculating each of the components of the nodes it generates.

FRINGE

FRONTIER

We also need to represent the collection of nodes that are waiting to be expanded—this collection is called the **fringe** or **frontier**. The simplest representation would be a set of nodes. The search strategy then would be a function that selects the next node to be expanded from this set. Although this is conceptually straightforward, it could be computationally expensive, because the strategy function might have to look at every element of the set to choose the best

QUEUE

one. Therefore, we will assume that the collection of nodes is a implemented as a **queue**. The operations on a queue are as follows:

- MAKE-QUEUE(*Elements*) creates a queue with the given elements.
- EMPTY?(*Queue*) returns true only if there are no more elements in the queue.
- REMOVE-FRONT(*Queue*) removes the element at the front of the queue and returns it.
- QUEUING-FN(*Elements*,*Queue*) inserts a set of elements into the queue. Different varieties of the queuing function produce different varieties of the search algorithm.

With these definitions, we can write a more formal version of the general search algorithm. This is shown in Figure 3.10.

---

function GENERAL-SEARCH(*problem,* QUEUING-FN) **returns** a solution, or failure

    nodes ← MAKE-QUEUE(MAKE-NODE(INITIAL-STATE[*problem*]))
    loop do
        if *nodes* is empty **then return** failure
        node ← REMOVE-FRONT(*nodes*)
        if GOAL-TEST[*problem*] applied to STATE(*node*) succeeds **then return** *node*
        nodes ← QUEUING-FN(*nodes*, EXPAND(*node*, OPERATORS[*problem*]))
    end

Figure 3.10   The general search algorithm. (Note that QUEUING-FN is a variable whose value will be a function.)

3.5   SEARCH STRATEGIES

The majority of work in the area of search has gone into finding the right **search strategy** for a problem. In our study of the field we will evaluate strategies in terms of four criteria:

COMPLETENESS

◇ **Completeness**: is the strategy guaranteed to find a solution when there is one?

TIME COMPLEXITY

◇ **Time complexity**: how long does it take to find a solution?

SPACE COMPLEXITY

◇ **Space complexity**: how much memory does it need to perform the search?

OPTIMALITY

◇ **Optimality**: does the strategy find the highest-quality solution when there are several different solutions?[7]

UNINFORMED SEARCH

This section covers six search strategies that come under the heading of **uninformed search**. The term means that they have no information about the number of steps or the path cost from the current state to the goal—all they can do is distinguish a goal state from a nongoal state.

BLIND SEARCH

Uninformed search is also sometimes called **blind search**.

Consider again the route-finding problem. From the initial state in Arad, there are three actions leading to three new states: Sibiu, Timisoara, and Zerind. An uninformed search has no preference among these, but a more clever agent might notice that the goal, Bucharest, is southeast of Arad, and that only Sibiu is in that direction, so it is likely to be the best choice.

INFORMED SEARCH

HEURISTIC SEARCH

Strategies that use such considerations are called **informed search** strategies or **heuristic search** strategies, and they will be covered in Chapter 4. Not surprisingly, uninformed search is less effective than informed search. Uninformed search is still important, however, because there are many problems for which there is no additional information to consider.

The six uninformed search strategies are distinguished by the *order* in which nodes are expanded. It turns out that this difference can matter a great deal, as we shall shortly see.

---

[7] This is the way "optimality" is used in the theoretical computer science literature. Some AI authors use "optimality" to refer to time of execution and "admissibility" to refer to solution optimality.

Breadth-first search

One simple search strategy is a **breadth-first search**. In this strategy, the root node is expanded first, then all the nodes generated by the root node are expanded next, and then *their* successors, and so on. In general, all the nodes at depth d in the search tree are expanded before the nodes at depth $d + 1$. Breadth-first search can be implemented by calling the GENERAL-SEARCH algorithm with a queuing function that puts the newly generated states at the end of the queue, after all the previously generated states:

---

function BREADTH-FIRST-SEARCH(*problem*) **returns** a solution or failure
    return GENERAL-SEARCH(*problem*,ENQUEUE-AT-END)

Breadth-first search is a very systematic strategy because it considers all the paths of length 1 first, then all those of length 2, and so on. Figure 3.11 shows the progress of the search on a simple binary tree. If there is a solution, breadth-first search is guaranteed to find it, and if there are several solutions, breadth-first search will always find the shallowest goal state first. In terms of the four criteria, breadth-first search is complete, and it is optimal *provided the path cost is a nondecreasing function of the depth of the node.* (This condition is usually satisfied only when all operators have the same cost. For the general case, see the next section.)

So far, the news about breadth-first search has been good. To see why it is not always the strategy of choice, we have to consider the amount of time and memory it takes to complete a search. To do this, we consider a hypothetical state space where every state can be expanded to yield b new states. We say that the **branching factor** of these states (and of the search tree) is b.
The root of the search tree generates b nodes at the first level, each of which generates b more nodes, for a total of b^2 at the second level. Each of *these* generates b more nodes, yielding b^3 nodes at the third level, and so on. Now suppose that the solution for this problem has a path length of d. Then the maximum number of nodes expanded before finding a solution is

$$1 + b + b^2 + b^3 + \cdots + b^d$$

This is the maximum number, but the solution could be found at any point on the dth level. In the best case, therefore, the number would be smaller.

Those who do complexity analysis get nervous (or excited, if they are the sort of people who like a challenge) whenever they see an exponential complexity bound like $O(b^d)$. Figure 3.12 shows why. It shows the time and memory required for a breadth-first search with branching factor $b = 10$ and for various values of the solution depth d. The space complexity is the same as the time complexity, because all the leaf nodes of the tree must be maintained in memory

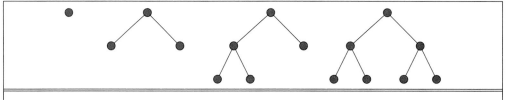

Figure 3.11   Breadth-first search trees after 0, 1, 2, and 3 node expansions.

at the same time. Figure 3.12 assumes that 1000 nodes can be goal-checked and expanded per second, and that a node requires 100 bytes of storage. Many puzzle-like problems fit roughly within these assumptions (give or take a factor of 100) when run on a modern personal computer or workstation.

Depth	Nodes	Time		Memory	
0	1	1	millisecond	100	bytes
2	111	.1	seconds	11	kilobytes
4	11,111	11	seconds	1	megabyte
6	10^6	18	minutes	111	megabytes
8	10^8	31	hours	11	gigabytes
10	10^{10}	128	days	1	terabyte
12	10^{12}	35	years	111	terabytes
14	10^{14}	3500	years	11,111	terabytes

Figure 3.12   Time and memory requirements for breadth-first search. The figures shown assume branching factor $b = 10$; 1000 nodes/second; 100 bytes/node.

There are two lessons to be learned from Figure 3.12. First, *the memory requirements are a bigger problem for breadth-first search than the execution time.* Most people have the patience to wait 18 minutes for a depth 6 search to complete, assuming they care about the answer, but not so many have the 111 megabytes of memory that are required. And although 31 hours would not be too long to wait for the solution to an important problem of depth 8, very few people indeed have access to the 11 gigabytes of memory it would take. Fortunately, there are other search strategies that require less memory.

The second lesson is that the time requirements are still a major factor. If your problem has a solution at depth 12, then (given our assumptions) it will take 35 years for an uninformed search to find it. Of course, if trends continue then in 10 years, you will be able to buy a computer that is 100 times faster for the same price as your current one. Even with that computer, however, it will still take 128 days to find a solution at depth 12—and 35 years for a solution at depth 14. Moreover, there are no other uninformed search strategies that fare any better. *In general, exponential complexity search problems cannot be solved for any but the smallest instances.*

Uniform cost search

Breadth-first search finds the *shallowest* goal state, but this may not always be the least-cost solution for a general path cost function. **Uniform cost search** modifies the breadth-first strategy by always expanding the lowest-cost node on the fringe (as measured by the path cost $g(n)$), rather than the lowest-depth node. It is easy to see that breadth-first search is just uniform cost search with $g(n) = \text{DEPTH}(n)$.

When certain conditions are met, the first solution that is found is guaranteed to be the cheapest solution, because if there were a cheaper path that was a solution, it would have been expanded earlier, and thus would have been found first. A look at the strategy in action will help explain. Consider the route-finding problem in Figure 3.13. The problem is to get from S to G, and the cost of each operator is marked. The strategy first expands the initial state, yielding paths to *A*, *B*, and *C*. Because the path to *A* is cheapest, it is expanded next, generating the path *SAG*, which is in fact a solution, though not the optimal one. However, the algorithm does not yet recognize this as a solution, because it has cost 11, and thus is buried in the queue below the path *SB*, which has cost 5. It seems a shame to generate a solution just to bury it deep in the queue, but it is necessary if we want to find the optimal solution rather than just any solution. The next step is to expand *SB*, generating *SBG*, which is now the cheapest path remaining in the queue, so it is goal-checked and returned as the solution.

Uniform cost search finds the cheapest solution provided a simple requirement is met: the cost of a path must never decrease as we go along the path. In other words, we insist that

$$g(\text{SUCCESSOR}(n)) \geq g(n)$$

for every node *n*.

The restriction to nondecreasing path cost makes sense if the path cost of a node is taken to be the sum of the costs of the operators that make up the path. If every operator has a nonnegative cost, then the cost of a path can never decrease as we go along the path, and uniform-cost search can find the cheapest path without exploring the whole search tree. But if some operator had a negative cost, then nothing but an exhaustive search of all nodes would find the optimal solution, because we would never know when a path, no matter how long and expensive, is about to run into a step with high negative cost and thus become the best path overall. (See Exercise 3.5.)

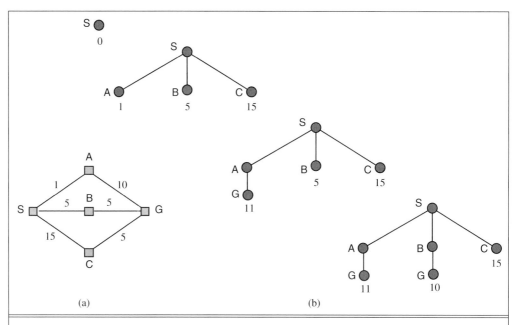

Figure 3.13   A route-finding problem. (a) The state space, showing the cost for each operator. (b) Progression of the search. Each node is labelled with $g(n)$. At the next step, the goal node with $g = 10$ will be selected.

Depth-first search

DEPTH-FIRST
SEARCH

Depth-first search always expands one of the nodes at the deepest level of the tree. Only when the search hits a dead end (a nongoal node with no expansion) does the search go back and expand nodes at shallower levels. This strategy can be implemented by GENERAL-SEARCH with a queuing function that always puts the newly generated states at the front of the queue. Because the expanded node was the deepest, its successors will be even deeper and are therefore now the deepest. The progress of the search is illustrated in Figure 3.14.

Depth-first search has very modest memory requirements. As the figure shows, it needs to store only a single path from the root to a leaf node, along with the remaining unexpanded sibling nodes for each node on the path. For a state space with branching factor b and maximum depth m, depth-first search requires storage of only bm nodes, in contrast to the b^d that would be required by breadth-first search in the case where the shallowest goal is at depth d. Using the same assumptions as Figure 3.12, depth-first search would require 12 kilobytes instead of 111 terabytes at depth $d = 12$, a factor of 10 billion times less space.

The time complexity for depth-first search is $O(b^m)$. For problems that have very many solutions, depth-first may actually be faster than breadth-first, because it has a good chance of

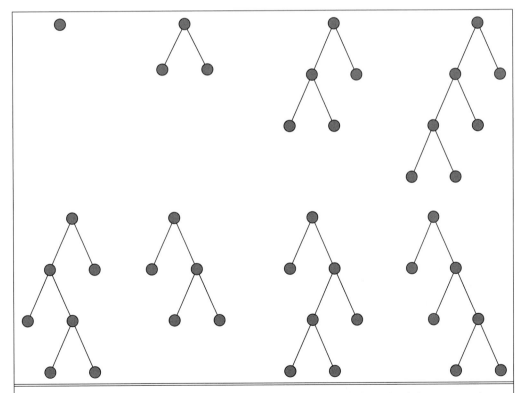

Figure 3.14   Depth-first search trees for a binary search tree. Nodes at depth 3 are assumed to have no successors.

finding a solution after exploring only a small portion of the whole space. Breadth-first search would still have to look at all the paths of length $d - 1$ before considering any of length d. Depth-first search is still $O(b^m)$ in the worst case.

The drawback of depth-first search is that it can get stuck going down the wrong path. Many problems have very deep or even infinite search trees, so depth-first search will never be able to recover from an unlucky choice at one of the nodes near the top of the tree. The search will always continue downward without backing up, even when a shallow solution exists. Thus, on these problems depth-first search will either get stuck in an infinite loop and never return a solution, or it may eventually find a solution path that is longer than the optimal solution. That means depth-first search is neither complete nor optimal. Because of this, *depth-first search should be avoided for search trees with large or infinite maximum depths.*

It is trivial to implement depth-first search with GENERAL-SEARCH:

---

function DEPTH-FIRST-SEARCH(*problem*) **returns** a solution, or failure
        GENERAL-SEARCH(*problem*,ENQUEUE-AT-FRONT)

It is also common to implement depth-first search with a recursive function that calls itself on each of its children in turn. In this case, the queue is stored implicitly in the local state of each invocation on the calling stack.

Depth-limited search

DEPTH-LIMITED
SEARCH

Depth-limited search avoids the pitfalls of depth-first search by imposing a cutoff on the maximum depth of a path. This cutoff can be implemented with a special depth-limited search algorithm, or by using the general search algorithm with operators that keep track of the depth. For example, on the map of Romania, there are 20 cities, so we know that if there is a solution, then it must be of length 19 at the longest. We can implement the depth cutoff using operators of the form "If you are in city A and have travelled a path of less than 19 steps, then generate a new state in city B with a path length that is one greater." With this new operator set, we are guaranteed to find the solution if it exists, but we are still not guaranteed to find the shortest solution first: depth-limited search is complete but not optimal. If we choose a depth limit that is too small, then depth-limited search is not even complete. The time and space complexity of depth-limited search is similar to depth-first search. It takes $O(b^l)$ time and $O(bl)$ space, where l is the depth limit.

Iterative deepening search

The hard part about depth-limited search is picking a good limit. We picked 19 as an "obvious" depth limit for the Romania problem, but in fact if we studied the map carefully, we would discover that any city can be reached from any other city in at most 9 steps. This number, known DIAMETER as the **diameter** of the state space, gives us a better depth limit, which leads to a more efficient depth-limited search. However, for most problems, we will not know a good depth limit until we have solved the problem.

Iterative deepening search is a strategy that sidesteps the issue of choosing the best depth
limit by trying all possible depth limits: first depth 0, then depth 1, then depth 2, and so on.
The algorithm is shown in Figure 3.15. In effect, iterative deepening combines the benefits of
depth-first and breadth-first search. It is optimal and complete, like breadth-first search, but has
only the modest memory requirements of depth-first search. The order of expansion of states is
similar to breadth-first, except that some states are expanded multiple times. Figure 3.16 shows
the first four iterations of ITERATIVE-DEEPENING-SEARCH on a binary search tree.

Iterative deepening search may seem wasteful, because so many states are expanded
multiple times. For most problems, however, the overhead of this multiple expansion is actually

---

function ITERATIVE-DEEPENING-SEARCH(*problem*) **returns** a solution sequence
    inputs: *problem*, a problem

    for *depth* ← 0 **to** ∞ **do**
        if DEPTH-LIMITED-SEARCH(*problem*, *depth*) succeeds **then return** its result
    end
    return failure

Figure 3.15   The iterative deepening search algorithm.

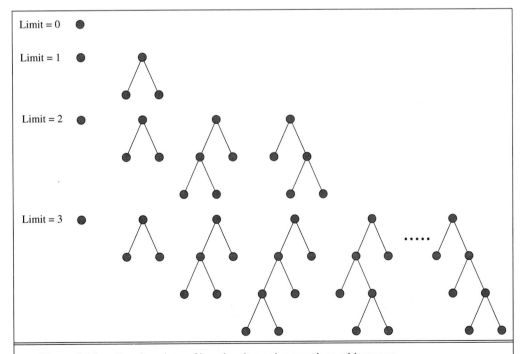

Figure 3.16   Four iterations of iterative deepening search on a binary tree.

rather small. Intuitively, the reason is that in an exponential search tree, almost all of the nodes are in the bottom level, so it does not matter much that the upper levels are expanded multiple times. Recall that the number of expansions in a depth-limited search to depth d with branching factor b is

$$1 + b + b^2 + \cdots + b^{d-2} + b^{d-1} + b^d$$

To make this concrete, for $b = 10$ and $d = 5$, the number is

$$1 + 10 + 100 + 1,000 + 10,000 + 100,000 = 111,111$$

In an iterative deepening search, the nodes on the bottom level are expanded once, those on the next to bottom level are expanded twice, and so on, up to the root of the search tree, which is expanded $d + 1$ times. So the total number of expansions in an iterative deepening search is

$$(d + 1)1 + (d)b + (d - 1)b^2 + \cdots + 3b^{d-2} + 2b^{d-1} + 1b^d$$

Again, for $b = 10$ and $d = 5$ the number is

$$6 + 50 + 400 + 3,000 + 20,000 + 100,000 = 123,456$$

All together, an iterative deepening search from depth 1 all the way down to depth d expands only about 11% more nodes than a single breadth-first or depth-limited search to depth d, when $b = 10$. The higher the branching factor, the lower the overhead of repeatedly expanded states, but even when the branching factor is 2, iterative deepening search only takes about twice as long as a complete breadth-first search. This means that the time complexity of iterative deepening is still $O(b^d)$, and the space complexity is $O(bd)$. *In general, iterative deepening is the preferred search method when there is a large search space and the depth of the solution is not known.*

Bidirectional search

The idea behind bidirectional search is to simultaneously search both forward from the initial state and backward from the goal, and stop when the two searches meet in the middle (Figure 3.17). For problems where the branching factor is b in both directions, bidirectional search can make a big difference. If we assume as usual that there is a solution of depth d, then the solution will be found in $O(2b^{d/2}) = O(b^{d/2})$ steps, because the forward and backward searches each have to go only half way. To make this concrete: for $b = 10$ and $d = 6$, breadth-first search generates 1,111,111 nodes, whereas bidirectional search succeeds when each direction is at depth 3, at which point 2,222 nodes have been generated. This sounds great in theory. Several issues need to be addressed before the algorithm can be implemented.

- The main question is, what does it mean to search backwards from the goal? We define
PREDECESSORS
  the **predecessors** of a node n to be all those nodes that have n as a successor. Searching backwards means generating predecessors successively starting from the goal node.
- When all operators are reversible, the predecessor and successor sets are identical; for some problems, however, calculating predecessors can be very difficult.
- What can be done if there are many possible goal states? If there is an *explicit* list of goal states, such as the two goal states in Figure 3.2, then we can apply a predecessor function to the state set just as we apply the successor function in multiple-state search. If we only

Figure 3.17   A schematic view of a bidirectional breadth-first search that is about to succeed, when a branch from the start node meets a branch from the goal node.

have a *description* of the set, it may be possible to figure out the possible descriptions of "sets of states that would generate the goal set," but this is a very tricky thing to do. For example, what are the states that are the predecessors of the checkmate goal in chess?

- There must be an efficient way to check each new node to see if it already appears in the search tree of the other half of the search.
- We need to decide what kind of search is going to take place in each half. For example, Figure 3.17 shows two breadth-first searches. Is this the best choice?

The $O(b^{d/2})$ complexity figure assumes that the process of testing for intersection of the two frontiers can be done in constant time (that is, is independent of the number of states). This often can be achieved with a hash table. In order for the two searches to meet at all, the nodes of at least one of them must all be retained in memory (as with breadth-first search). This means that the space complexity of uninformed bidirectional search is $O(b^{d/2})$.

Comparing search strategies

Figure 3.18 compares the six search strategies in terms of the four evaluation criteria set forth in Section 3.5.

Criterion	Breadth-First	Uniform-Cost	Depth-First	Depth-Limited	Iterative Deepening	Bidirectional (if applicable)
Time	b^d	b^d	b^m	b^l	b^d	$b^{d/2}$
Space	b^d	b^d	bm	bl	bd	$b^{d/2}$
Optimal?	Yes	Yes	No	No	Yes	Yes
Complete?	Yes	Yes	No	Yes, if $l \geq d$	Yes	Yes

Figure 3.18   Evaluation of search strategies. b is the branching factor; d is the depth of solution; m is the maximum depth of the search tree; l is the depth limit.

3.6   AVOIDING REPEATED STATES

Up to this point, we have all but ignored one of the most important complications to the search process: the possibility of wasting time by expanding states that have already been encountered and expanded before on some other path. For some problems, this possibility never comes up; each state can only be reached one way. The efficient formulation of the 8-queens problem is efficient in large part because of this—each state can only be derived through one path.

For many problems, repeated states are unavoidable. This includes all problems where the operators are reversible, such as route-finding problems and the missionaries and cannibals problem. The search trees for these problems are infinite, but if we prune some of the repeated states, we can cut the search tree down to finite size, generating only the portion of the tree that spans the state space graph. Even when the tree is finite, avoiding repeated states can yield an exponential reduction in search cost. The classic example is shown in Figure 3.19. The space contains only $m + 1$ states, where m is the maximum depth. Because the tree includes each possible path through the space, it has 2^m branches.

There are three ways to deal with repeated states, in increasing order of effectiveness and computational overhead:

- Do not return to the state you just came from. Have the expand function (or the operator set) refuse to generate any successor that is the same state as the node's parent.
- Do not create paths with cycles in them. Have the expand function (or the operator set) refuse to generate any successor of a node that is the same as any of the node's ancestors.
- Do not generate any state that was ever generated before. This requires every state that is generated to be kept in memory, resulting in a space complexity of $O(b^d)$, potentially. It is better to think of this as $O(s)$, where s is the number of states in the entire state space.

To implement this last option, search algorithms often make use of a hash table that stores all the nodes that are generated. This makes checking for repeated states reasonably efficient. The trade-off between the cost of storing and checking and the cost of extra search depends on the problem: the "loopier" the state space, the more likely it is that checking will pay off.

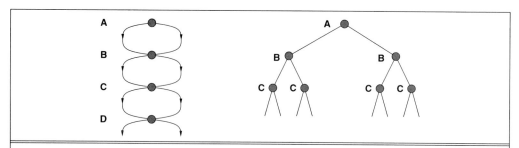

Figure 3.19   A state space that generates an exponentially larger search tree. The left-hand side shows the state space, in which there are two possible actions leading from A to B, two from B to C, and so on. The right-hand side shows the corresponding search tree.

3.7   CONSTRAINT SATISFACTION SEARCH

CONSTRAINT
SATISFACTION
PROBLEM

VARIABLES

CONSTRAINTS

A **constraint satisfaction problem** (or CSP) is a special kind of problem that satisfies some additional structural properties beyond the basic requirements for problems in general. In a CSP, the states are defined by the values of a set of **variables** and the goal test specifies a set of **constraints** that the values must obey. For example, the 8-queens problem can be viewed as a CSP in which the variables are the locations of each of the eight queens; the possible values are squares on the board; and the constraints state that no two queens can be in the same row, column or diagonal. A solution to a CSP specifies values for all the variables such that the constraints are satisfied. Cryptarithmetic and VLSI layout can also be described as CSPs (Exercise 3.20). Many kinds of design and scheduling problems can be expressed as CSPs, so they form a very important subclass. CSPs can be solved by general-purpose search algorithms, but because of their special structure, algorithms designed specifically for CSPs generally perform much better.

Constraints come in several varieties. Unary constraints concern the value of a single variable. For example, the variables corresponding to the leftmost digit on any row of a cryptarithmetic puzzle are constrained not to have the value 0. Binary constraints relate pairs of variables. The constraints in the 8-queens problem are all binary constraints. Higher-order constraints involve three or more variables—for example, the columns in the cryptarithmetic problem must obey an addition constraint and can involve several variables. Finally, constraints can be *absolute* constraints, violation of which rules out a potential solution, or *preference* constraints that say which solutions are preferred.

DOMAIN

Each variable V_i in a CSP has a **domain** D_i, which is the set of possible values that the variable can take on. The domain can be *discrete* or *continuous*. In designing a car, for instance, the variables might include component weights (continuous) and component manufacturers (discrete). A unary constraint specifies the allowable subset of the domain, and a binary constraint between two variables specifies the allowable subset of the cross-product of the two domains. In discrete CSPs where the domains are finite, constraints can be represented simply by enumerating the allowable combinations of values. For example, in the 8-queens problem, let V_1 be the row that the first queen occupies in the first column, and let V_2 be the row occupied by the second queen in the second column. The domains of V_1 and V_2 are $\{1, 2, 3, 4, 5, 6, 7, 8\}$. The no-attack constraint linking V_1 and V_2 can be represented by a set of pairs of allowable values for V_1 and V_2: $\{\langle 1, 3\rangle, \langle 1, 4\rangle, \langle 1, 5\rangle, \ldots, \langle 2, 4\rangle, \langle 2, 5\rangle, \ldots\}$ and so on. Altogether, the no-attack constraint between V_1 and V_2 rules out 22 of the 64 possible combinations. Using this idea of enumeration, any discrete CSP can be reduced to a binary CSP.

Constraints involving continuous variables cannot be enumerated in this way, and solving continuous CSPs involves sophisticated algebra. In this chapter, we will handle only discrete, absolute, binary (or unary) constraints. Such constraints are still sufficiently expressive to handle a wide variety of problems and to introduce most of the interesting solution methods.

Let us first consider how we might apply a general-purpose search algorithm to a CSP. The initial state will be the state in which all the variables are unassigned. Operators will assign a value to a variable from the set of possible values. The goal test will check if all variables are assigned and all constraints satisfied. Notice that the maximum depth of the search tree is fixed at n, the number of variables, and that all solutions are at depth n. We are therefore safe in using depth-first search, as there is no danger of going too deep and no arbitrary depth limit is needed.

In the most naive implementation, any unassigned variable in a given state can be assigned a value by an operator, in which case the branching factor would be as high as $\sum_i |D_i|$, or 64 in the 8-queens problem. A better approach is to take advantage of the fact that the order of variable assignments makes no difference to the final solution. Almost all CSP algorithms therefore generate successors by choosing values for only a single variable at each node. For example, in the 8-queens problem, one can assign a square for the first queen at level 0, for the second queen at level 1, and so on. This results in a search space of size $\prod_i |D_i|$, or 8^8 in the 8-queens problem. A straightforward depth-first search will examine all of these possibilities. Because CSPs include as special cases some well-known NP-complete problems such as 3SAT (see Exercise 6.15 on page 182), we cannot expect to do better than exponential complexity in the worst case. In most real problems, however, we can take advantage of the problem structure to eliminate a large fraction of the search space. The principal source of structure in the problem space is that, *in CSPs, the goal test is decomposed into a set of constraints on variables rather than being a "black box."*

Depth-first search on a CSP wastes time searching when constraints have already been violated. Because of the way that the operators have been defined, an operator can never redeem a constraint that has already been violated. For example, suppose that we put the first two queens in the top row. Depth-first search will examine all 8^6 possible positions for the remaining six queens before discovering that no solution exists in that subtree. Our first improvement is therefore to insert a test before the successor generation step to check whether any constraint has been violated by the variable assignments made up to this point. The resulting algorithm, called **backtracking search**, then backtracks to try something else.

BACKTRACKING
SEARCH

Backtracking also has some obvious failings. Suppose that the squares chosen for the first six queens make it impossible to place the eighth queen, because they attack all eight squares in the last column. Backtracking will try all possible placings for the seventh queen, even though the problem is already rendered unsolvable, given the first six choices. **Forward checking** avoids this problem by looking ahead to detect unsolvability. Each time a variable is instantiated, forward checking deletes from the domains of the as-yet-uninstantiated variables all of those values that conflict with the variables assigned so far. If any of the domains becomes empty, then the search backtracks immediately. Forward checking often runs far faster than backtracking and is very simple to implement (see Exercise 3.21).

FORWARD
CHECKING

Forward checking is a special case of **arc consistency** checking. A state is arc-consistent if every variable has a value in its domain that is consistent with each of the constraints on that variable. Arc consistency can be achieved by successive deletion of values that are inconsistent with some constraint. As values are deleted, other values may become inconsistent because they relied on the deleted values. Arc consistency therefore exhibits a form of **constraint propagation**, as choices are gradually narrowed down. In some cases, achieving arc consistency is enough to solve the problem completely because the domains of all variables are reduced to singletons. Arc consistency is often used as a preprocessing step, but can also be used during the search.

ARC CONSISTENCY

CONSTRAINT
PROPAGATION

Much better results can often be obtained by careful choice of which variable to instantiate and which value to try. We examine such methods in the next chapter.

3.8 SUMMARY

This chapter has introduced methods that an agent can use when it is not clear which immediate action is best. In such cases, the agent can consider possible sequences of actions; this process is called **search**.

- Before an agent can start searching for solutions, it must formulate a goal and then use the goal to formulate a problem.

- A **problem** consists of four parts: the **initial state**, a set of **operators**, a **goal test** function, and a **path cost** function. The environment of the problem is represented by a **state space**. A **path** through the state space from the initial state to a goal state is a **solution**.

- In real life most problems are ill-defined; but with some analysis, many problems can fit into the state space model.

- A single **general search** algorithm can be used to solve any problem; specific variants of the algorithm embody different strategies.

- Search algorithms are judged on the basis of **completeness**, **optimality**, **time complexity**, and **space complexity**. Complexity depends on b, the branching factor in the state space, and d, the depth of the shallowest solution.

- **Breadth-first search** expands the shallowest node in the search tree first. It is complete, optimal for unit-cost operators, and has time and space complexity of $O(b^d)$. The space complexity makes it impractical in most cases.

- **Uniform-cost search** expands the least-cost leaf node first. It is complete, and unlike breadth-first search is optimal even when operators have differing costs. Its space and time complexity are the same as for breadth-first search.

- **Depth-first search** expands the deepest node in the search tree first. It is neither complete nor optimal, and has time complexity of $O(b^m)$ and space complexity of $O(bm)$, where m is the maximum depth. In search trees of large or infinite depth, the time complexity makes this impractical.

- **Depth-limited search** places a limit on how deep a depth-first search can go. If the limit happens to be equal to the depth of shallowest goal state, then time and space complexity are minimized.

- **Iterative deepening search** calls depth-limited search with increasing limits until a goal is found. It is complete and optimal, and has time complexity of $O(b^d)$ and space complexity of $O(bd)$.

- **Bidirectional search** can enormously reduce time complexity, but is not always applicable. Its memory requirements may be impractical.

BIBLIOGRAPHICAL AND HISTORICAL NOTES

Most of the state-space search problems analyzed in this chapter have a long history in the literature, and are far less trivial than they may seem. The missionaries and cannibals problem was analyzed in detail from an artificial intelligence perspective by Amarel (1968), although Amarel's treatment was by no means the first; it had been considered earlier in AI by Simon and Newell (1961), and elsewhere in computer science and operations research by Bellman and Dreyfus (1962). Studies such as these led to the establishment of search algorithms as perhaps the primary tools in the armory of early AI researchers, and the establishment of problem solving as the canonical AI task. (Of course, one might well claim that the latter resulted from the former.)

Amarel's treatment of the missionaries and cannibals problem is particularly noteworthy because it is a classic example of formal analysis of a problem stated informally in natural language. Amarel gives careful attention to *abstracting* from the informal problem statement precisely those features that are necessary or useful in solving the problem, and selecting a formal problem representation that represents only those features. A more recent treatment of problem representation and abstraction, including AI programs that themselves perform these tasks (in part), is to be found in Knoblock (1990).

The 8-queens problem was first published anonymously in the German chess magazine *Schach* in 1848; it was later attributed to one Max Bezzel. It was republished in 1850, and at that time drew the attention of the eminent mathematician Carl Friedrich Gauss, who attempted to enumerate all possible solutions. Even Gauss was able to find only 72 of the 92 possible solutions offhand, which gives some indication of the difficulty of this apparently simple problem. (Nauck, who had republished the puzzle, published all 92 solutions later in 1850.) Netto (1901) generalized the problem to "n-queens" (on an $n \times n$ chessboard).

The 8-puzzle initially appeared as the more complex 4×4 version, called the 15-puzzle. It was invented by the famous American game designer Sam Loyd (1959) in the 1870s and quickly achieved immense popularity in the United States, comparable to the more recent sensation caused by the introduction of Rubik's Cube. It also quickly attracted the attention of mathematicians (Johnson and Story, 1879; Tait, 1880). The popular reception of the puzzle was so enthusiastic that the Johnson and Story article was accompanied by a note in which the editors of the *American Journal of Mathematics* felt it necessary to state that "The '15' puzzle for the last few weeks has been prominently before the American public, and may safely be said to have engaged the attention of nine out of ten persons of both sexes and all ages and conditions of the community. But this would not have weighed with the editors to induce them to insert articles upon such a subject in the American Journal of Mathematics, but for the fact that . . ." (there follows a brief summary of the reasons for the mathematical interest of the 15-puzzle). The 8-puzzle has often been used in AI research in place of the 15-puzzle because the search space is smaller and thus more easily subjected to exhaustive analysis or experimentation. An exhaustive analysis was carried out with computer aid by P. D. A. Schofield (1967). Although very time-consuming, this analysis allowed other, faster search methods to be compared against theoretical perfection for the quality of the solutions found. An in-depth analysis of the 8-puzzle, using heuristic search methods of the kind described in Chapter 4, was carried out by Doran and Michie (1966). The 15-puzzle, like the 8-queens problem, has been generalized to the $n \times n$ case. Ratner and

Warmuth (1986) showed that finding the shortest solution in the generalized $n \times n$ version belongs to the class of NP-complete problems.

"Uninformed" search algorithms for finding shortest paths that rely on current path cost alone, rather than an estimate of the distance to the goal, are a central topic of classical computer science, applied mathematics, and a related field known as *operations research*. Uniform-cost search as a way of finding shortest paths was invented by Dijkstra (1959). A survey of early work in uninformed search methods for shortest paths can be found in Dreyfus (1969); Deo and Pang (1982) give a more recent survey. For the variant of the uninformed shortest-paths problem that asks for shortest paths between *all* pairs of nodes in a graph, the techniques of *dynamic programming* and *memoization* can be used. For a problem to be solved by these techniques, it must be capable of being divided repeatedly into subproblems in such a way that identical subproblems arise again and again. Then dynamic programming or memoization involves systematically recording the solutions to subproblems in a table so that they can be looked up when needed and do not have to be recomputed repeatedly during the process of solving the problem. An efficient dynamic programming algorithm for the all-pairs shortest-paths problem was found by Bob Floyd (1962a; 1962b), and improved upon by Karger *et al.* (1993). Bidirectional search was introduced by Pohl (1969; 1971); it is often used with heuristic guidance techniques of the kind discussed in Chapter 4. Iterative deepening was first used by Slate and Atkin (1977) in the CHESS 4.5 game-playing program.

The textbooks by Nilsson (1971; 1980) are good general sources of information about classical search algorithms, although they are now somewhat dated. A comprehensive, and much more up-to-date, survey can be found in (Korf, 1988).

EXERCISES

3.1   Explain why problem formulation must follow goal formulation.

3.2   Consider the accessible, two-location vacuum world under Murphy's Law. Show that for each initial state, there is a sequence of actions that is guaranteed to reach a goal state.

3.3   Give the initial state, goal test, operators, and path cost function for each of the following. There are several possible formulations for each problem, with varying levels of detail. The main thing is that your formulations should be precise and "hang together" so that they could be implemented.

-   **a**. You want to find the telephone number of Mr. Jimwill Zollicoffer, who lives in Alameda, given a stack of directories alphabetically ordered by city.
-   **b**. As for part (a), but you have forgotten Jimwill's last name.
-   **c**. You are lost in the Amazon jungle, and have to reach the sea. There is a stream nearby.
-   **d**. You have to color a complex planar map using only four colors, with no two adjacent regions to have the same color.

    e. A monkey is in a room with a crate, with bananas suspended just out of reach on the ceiling. He would like to get the bananas.

    f. You are lost in a small country town, and must find a drug store before your hay fever becomes intolerable. There are no maps, and the natives are all locked indoors.

3.4   Implement the missionaries and cannibals problem and use breadth-first search to find the shortest solution. Is it a good idea to check for repeated states? Draw a diagram of the complete state space to help you decide.

3.5   On page 76, we said that we would not consider problems with negative path costs. In this exercise, we explore this in more depth.

    a. Suppose that a negative lower bound c is placed on the cost of any given step—that is, negative costs are allowed, but the cost of a step cannot be less than c. Does this allow uniform-cost search to avoid searching the whole tree?

    b. Suppose that there is a set of operators that form a loop, so that executing the set in some order results in no net change to the state. If all of these operators have negative cost, what does this imply about the optimal behavior for an agent in such an environment?

    c. One can easily imagine operators with high negative cost, even in domains such as route-finding. For example, some stretches of road might have such beautiful scenery as to far outweigh the normal costs in terms of time and fuel. Explain, in precise terms, why humans do not drive round scenic loops indefinitely, and explain how to define the state space and operators for route-finding so that artificial agents can also avoid looping.

    d. Can you think of a real domain in which step costs are such as to cause looping?

3.6   The GENERAL-SEARCH algorithm consists of three steps: goal test, generate, and ordering function, in that order. It seems a shame to generate a node that is in fact a solution, but to fail to recognize it because the ordering function fails to place it first.

    a. Write a version of GENERAL-SEARCH that tests each node as soon as it is generated and stops immediately if it has found a goal.

    b. Show how the GENERAL-SEARCH algorithm can be used unchanged to do this by giving it the proper ordering function.

3.7   The formulation of problem, solution, and search algorithm given in this chapter explicitly mentions the path to a goal state. This is because the path is important in many problems. For other problems, the path is irrelevant, and only the goal state matters. Consider the problem "Find the square root of 123454321." A search through the space of numbers may pass through many states, but the only one that matters is the goal state, the number 11111. Of course, from a theoretical point of view, it is easy to run the general search algorithm and then ignore all of the path except the goal state. But as a programmer, you may realize an efficiency gain by coding a version of the search algorithm that does not keep track of paths. Consider a version of problem solving where there are no paths and only the states matter. Write definitions of problem and solution, and the general search algorithm. Which of the problems in Section 3.3 would best use this algorithm, and which should use the version that keeps track of paths?

3.8   Given a pathless search algorithm such as the one called for in Exercise 3.7, explain how you can modify the operators to keep track of the paths as part of the information in a state. Show the operators needed to solve the route-finding and touring problems.

3.9   Describe a search space in which iterative deepening search performs much worse than depth-first search.

3.10   Figure 3.17 shows a schematic view of bidirectional search. Why do you think we chose to show trees growing outward from the start and goal states, rather than two search trees growing horizontally toward each other?

3.11   Write down the algorithm for bidirectional search, in pseudo-code or in a programming language. Assume that each search will be a breadth-first search, and that the forward and backward searches take turns expanding a node at a time. Be careful to avoid checking each node in the forward search against each node in the backward search!

3.12   Give the time complexity of bidirectional search when the test for connecting the two searches is done by comparing a newly generated state in the forward direction against all the states generated in the backward direction, one at a time.

3.13   We said that at least one direction of a bidirectional search must be a breadth-first search. What would be a good choice for the other direction? Why?

3.14   Consider the following operator for the 8-queens problem: place a queen in the column with the fewest unattacked squares, in such a way that it does not attack any other queens. How many nodes does this expand before it finds a solution? (You may wish to have a program calculate this for you.)

3.15   The **chain problem** (Figure 3.20) consists of various lengths of chain that must be reconfigured into new arrangements. Operators can open one link and close one link. In the standard form of the problem, the initial state contains four chains, each with three links. The goal state consists of a single chain of 12 links in a circle. Set this up as a formal search problem and find the shortest solution.

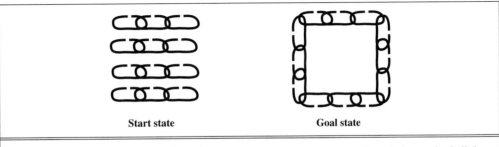

Start state   **Goal state**

Figure 3.20   The chain problem. Operators can open, remove, reattach, and close a single link at a time.

3.16   Tests of human intelligence often contain **sequence prediction** problems. The aim in such problems is to predict the next member of a sequence of integers, assuming that the number in position n of the sequence is generated using some sequence function $s(n)$, where the first element of the sequence corresponds to $n = 0$. For example, the function $s(n) = 2^n$ generates the sequence $[1, 2, 4, 8, 16, \ldots]$.

In this exercise, you will design a problem-solving system capable of solving such prediction problems. The system will search the space of possible functions until it finds one that matches the observed sequence. The space of sequence functions that we will consider consists of all possible expressions built from the elements 1 and n, and the functions $+$, $\times$, $-$, $/$, and exponentiation. For example, the function 2^n becomes $(1 + 1)^n$ in this language. It will be useful to think of function expressions as binary trees, with operators at the internal nodes and 1's and n's at the leaves.

- **a.** First, write the goal test function. Its argument will be a candidate sequence function s. It will contain the observed sequence of numbers as local state.

- **b.** Now write the successor function. Given a function expression s, it should generate all expressions one step more complex than s. This can be done by replacing any leaf of the expression with a two-leaf binary tree.

- **c.** Which of the algorithms discussed in this chapter would be suitable for this problem? Implement it and use it to find sequence expressions for the sequences $[1, 2, 3, 4, 5]$, $[1, 2, 4, 8, 16, \ldots]$, and $[0.5, 2, 4.5, 8]$.

- **d.** If level d of the search space contains all expressions of complexity $d+1$, where complexity is measured by the number of leaf nodes (e.g., $n + (1 \times n)$ has complexity 3), prove by induction that there are roughly $20^d (d + 1)!$ expressions at level d.

- **e.** Comment on the suitability of uninformed search algorithms for solving this problem. Can you suggest other approaches?

3.17   The full vacuum world from the exercises in Chapter 2 can be viewed as a search problem in the sense we have defined, provided we assume that the initial state is completely known.

- **a.** Define the initial state, operators, goal test function, and path cost function.

- **b.** Which of the algorithms defined in this chapter would be appropriate for this problem?

- **c.** Apply one of them to compute an optimal sequence of actions for a 3×3 world with dirt in the center and home squares.

- **d.** Construct a search agent for the vacuum world, and evaluate its performance in a set of 3×3 worlds with probability 0.2 of dirt in each square. Include the search cost as well as path cost in the performance measure, using a reasonable exchange rate.

- **e.** Compare the performance of your search agent with the performance of the agents constructed for the exercises in Chapter 2. What happens if you include computation time in the performance measure, at various "exchange rates" with respect to the cost of taking a step in the environment?

- **f.** Consider what would happen if the world was enlarged to $n \times n$. How does the performance of the search agent vary with n? Of the reflex agents?

3.18   The search agents we have discussed make use of a complete model of the world to construct a solution that they then execute. Modify the depth-first search algorithm with repeated state checking so that an agent can use it to explore an arbitrary vacuum world even without a model of the locations of walls and dirt. It should not get stuck even with loops or dead ends. You may also wish to have your agent construct an environment description of the type used by the standard search algorithms.

3.19   In discussing the cryptarithmetic problem, we proposed that an operator should assign a value to whichever letter has the least remaining possible values. Is this rule guaranteed to produce the smallest possible search space? Why (not)?

3.20   Define each of the following as constraint satisfaction problems:

   a. The cryptarithmetic problem.

   b. The channel-routing problem in VLSI layout.

MAP-COLORING   **c**. The **map-coloring** problem. In map-coloring, the aim is to color countries on a map using a given set of colors, such that no two adjacent countries are the same color.

FLOOR-PLANNING   **d**. The rectilinear **floor-planning** problem, which involves finding nonoverlapping places in a large rectangle for a number of smaller rectangles.

3.21   Implement a constraint satisfaction system as follows:

   a. Define a datatype for CSPs with finite, discrete domains. You will need to find a way to represent domains and constraints.

   b. Implement operators that assign values to variables, where the variables are assigned in a fixed order at each level of the tree.

   c. Implement a goal test that checks a complete state for satisfaction of all the constraints.

   d. Implement backtracking by modifying DEPTH-FIRST-SEARCH.

   e. Add forward checking to your backtracking algorithm.

   f. Run the three algorithms on some sample problems and compare their performance.

4 INFORMED SEARCH METHODS

In which we see how information about the state space can prevent algorithms from blundering about in the dark.

Chapter 3 showed that uninformed search strategies can find solutions to problems by systematically generating new states and testing them against the goal. Unfortunately, these strategies are incredibly inefficient in most cases. This chapter shows how an informed search strategy—one that uses problem-specific knowledge—can find solutions more efficiently. It also shows how optimization problems can be solved.

4.1 BEST-FIRST SEARCH

In Chapter 3, we found several ways to apply knowledge to the process of formulating a problem in terms of states and operators. Once we are given a well-defined problem, however, our options are more limited. If we plan to use the GENERAL-SEARCH algorithm from Chapter 3, then the only place where knowledge can be applied is in the queuing function, which determines the node to expand next. Usually, the knowledge to make this determination is provided by an **evaluation function** that returns a number purporting to describe the desirability (or lack thereof) of expanding the node. When the nodes are ordered so that the one with the best evaluation is expanded first, the resulting strategy is called **best-first search**. It can be implemented directly with GENERAL-SEARCH, as shown in Figure 4.1.

EVALUATION FUNCTION

BEST-FIRST SEARCH

The name "best-first search" is a venerable but inaccurate one. After all, if we could really expand the best node first, it would not be a search at all; it would be a straight march to the goal. All we can do is choose the node that *appears* to be best according to the evaluation function. If the evaluation function is omniscient, then this will indeed be the best node; in reality, the evaluation function will sometimes be off, and can lead the search astray. Nevertheless, we will stick with the name "best-first search," because "seemingly-best-first search" is a little awkward.

Just as there is a whole family of GENERAL-SEARCH algorithms with different ordering functions, there is also a whole family of BEST-FIRST-SEARCH algorithms with different evaluation

---

function BEST-FIRST-SEARCH(*problem*, EVAL-FN) **returns** a solution sequence
    inputs: *problem*, a problem
               Eval-Fn, an evaluation function

    Queueing-Fn ← a function that orders nodes by EVAL-FN
    return GENERAL-SEARCH(*problem, Queueing-Fn*)

Figure 4.1   An implementation of best-first search using the general search algorithm.

---

functions. Because they aim to find low-cost solutions, these algorithms typically use some estimated measure of the cost of the solution and try to minimize it. We have already seen one such measure: the use of the path cost g to decide which path to extend. This measure, however, does not direct search *toward the goal. In order to focus the search, the measure must incorporate some estimate of the cost of the path from a state to the closest goal state.* We look at two basic approaches. The first tries to expand the node closest to the goal. The second tries to expand the node on the least-cost solution path.

Minimize estimated cost to reach a goal: Greedy search

One of the simplest best-first search strategies is to minimize the estimated cost to reach the goal. That is, the node whose state is judged to be closest to the goal state is always expanded first. For most problems, the cost of reaching the goal from a particular state can be estimated but cannot be determined exactly. A function that calculates such cost estimates is called a **heuristic**

HEURISTIC
FUNCTION
function, and is usually denoted by the letter h:

    $h(n) =$ estimated cost of the cheapest path from the state at node n to a goal state.

GREEDY SEARCH
A best-first search that uses h to select the next node to expand is called **greedy search**, for reasons that will become clear. Given a heuristic function h, the code for greedy search is just the following:

---

function GREEDY-SEARCH(*problem*) **returns** a solution or failure
    return BEST-FIRST-SEARCH(*problem, h*)

Formally speaking, h can be any function at all. We will require only that $h(n) = 0$ if n is a goal.
    To get an idea of what a heuristic function looks like, we need to choose a particular problem, because heuristic functions are problem-specific. Let us return to the route-finding problem from Arad to Bucharest. The map for that problem is repeated in Figure 4.2.

STRAIGHT-LINE
DISTANCE
    A good heuristic function for route-finding problems like this is the **straight-line distance** to the goal. That is,

    $h_{SLD}(n) =$ straight-line distance between n and the goal location.

HISTORY OF "HEURISTIC"

> By now the space aliens had mastered my own language, but they still made
> simple mistakes like using "hermeneutic" when they meant "heuristic."
> — a Louisiana factory worker in Woody Allen's *The UFO Menace*

The word "heuristic" is derived from the Greek verb *heuriskein*, meaning "to find" or "to discover." Archimedes is said to have run naked down the street shouting "*Heureka*" (I have found it) after discovering the principle of flotation in his bath. Later generations converted this to Eureka.

The technical meaning of "heuristic" has undergone several changes in the history of AI. In 1957, George Polya wrote an influential book called *How to Solve It* that used "heuristic" to refer to the study of methods for discovering and inventing problem-solving techniques, particularly for the problem of coming up with mathematical proofs. Such methods had often been deemed not amenable to explication.

Some people use heuristic as the opposite of algorithmic. For example, Newell, Shaw, and Simon stated in 1963, "A process that may solve a given problem, but offers no guarantees of doing so, is called a heuristic for that problem." But note that there is nothing random or nondeterministic about a heuristic search algorithm: it proceeds by algorithmic steps toward its result. In some cases, there is no guarantee how long the search will take, and in some cases, the quality of the solution is not guaranteed either. Nonetheless, it is important to distinguish between "nonalgorithmic" and "not precisely characterizable."

Heuristic techniques dominated early applications of artificial intelligence. The first "expert systems" laboratory, started by Ed Feigenbaum, Bruce Buchanan, and Joshua Lederberg at Stanford University, was called the Heuristic Programming Project (HPP). Heuristics were viewed as "rules of thumb" that domain experts could use to generate good solutions without exhaustive search. Heuristics were initially incorporated directly into the structure of programs, but this proved too inflexible when a large number of heuristics were needed. Gradually, systems were designed that could accept heuristic information expressed as "rules," and rule-based systems were born.

Currently, heuristic is most often used as an adjective, referring to any technique that improves the average-case performance on a problem-solving task, but does not necessarily improve the worst-case performance. In the specific area of search algorithms, it refers to a function that provides an estimate of solution cost.

A good article on heuristics (and one on hermeneutics!) appears in the *Encyclopedia of AI* (Shapiro, 1992).

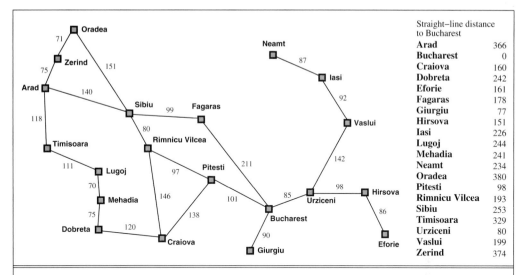

Straight–line distance
to Bucharest

Arad	366
Bucharest	0
Craiova	160
Dobreta	242
Eforie	161
Fagaras	178
Giurgiu	77
Hirsova	151
Iasi	226
Lugoj	244
Mehadia	241
Neamt	234
Oradea	380
Pitesti	98
Rimnicu Vilcea	193
Sibiu	253
Timisoara	329
Urziceni	80
Vaslui	199
Zerind	374

Figure 4.2   Map of Romania with road distances in km, and straight-line distances to Bucharest.

Notice that we can only calculate the values of h_{SLD} if we know the map coordinates of the cities in Romania. Furthermore, h_{SLD} is only useful because a road from A to B usually tends to head in more or less the right direction. This is the sort of extra information that allows heuristics to help in reducing search cost.

Figure 4.3 shows the progress of a greedy search to find a path from Arad to Bucharest. With the straight-line-distance heuristic, the first node to be expanded from Arad will be Sibiu, because it is closer to Bucharest than either Zerind or Timisoara. The next node to be expanded will be Fagaras, because it is closest. Fagaras in turn generates Bucharest, which is the goal. For this particular problem, the heuristic leads to minimal search cost: it finds a solution without ever expanding a node that is not on the solution path. However, it is not perfectly optimal: the path it found via Sibiu and Fagaras to Bucharest is 32 kilometers longer than the path through Rimnicu Vilcea and Pitesti. This path was not found because Fagaras is closer to Bucharest in straight-line distance than Rimnicu Vilcea, so it was expanded first. The strategy prefers to take the biggest bite possible out of the remaining cost to reach the goal, without worrying about whether this will be best in the long run—hence the name "greedy search." Although greed is considered one of the seven deadly sins, it turns out that greedy algorithms often perform quite well. They tend to find solutions quickly, although as shown in this example, they do not always find the optimal solutions: that would take a more careful analysis of the long-term options, not just the immediate best choice.

Greedy search is susceptible to false starts. Consider the problem of getting from Iasi to Fagaras. The heuristic suggests that Neamt be expanded first, but it is a dead end. The solution is to go first to Vaslui—a step that is actually farther from the goal according to the heuristic—and then to continue to Urziceni, Bucharest, and Fagaras. Hence, in this case, the heuristic causes unnecessary nodes to be expanded. Furthermore, if we are not careful to detect repeated states, the solution will never be found—the search will oscillate between Neamt and Iasi.

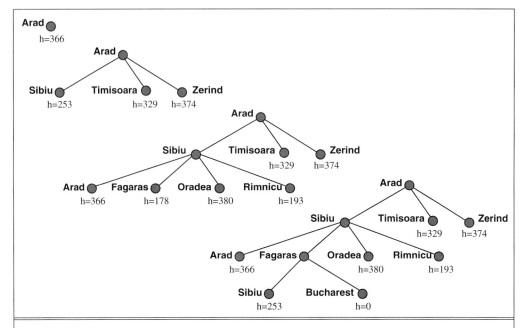

Figure 4.3   Stages in a greedy search for Bucharest, using the straight-line distance to Bucharest as the heuristic function h_{SLD}. Nodes are labelled with their h-values.

Greedy search resembles depth-first search in the way it prefers to follow a single path all the way to the goal, but will back up when it hits a dead end. It suffers from the same defects as depth-first search—it is not optimal, and it is incomplete because it can start down an infinite path and never return to try other possibilities. The worst-case time complexity for greedy search is $O(b^m)$, where m is the maximum depth of the search space. Because greedy search retains all nodes in memory, its space complexity is the same as its time complexity. With a good heuristic function, the space and time complexity can be reduced substantially. The amount of the reduction depends on the particular problem and quality of the h function.

Minimizing the total path cost: A* search

Greedy search minimizes the estimated cost to the goal, $h(n)$, and thereby cuts the search cost considerably. Unfortunately, it is neither optimal nor complete. Uniform-cost search, on the other hand, minimizes the cost of the path so far, $g(n)$; it is optimal and complete, but can be very inefficient. It would be nice if we could combine these two strategies to get the advantages of both. Fortunately, we can do exactly that, combining the two evaluation functions simply by summing them:

$$f(n) = g(n) + h(n).$$

Since $g(n)$ gives the path cost from the start node to node n, and $h(n)$ is the estimated cost of the cheapest path from n to the goal, we have

$f(n) =$ estimated cost of the cheapest solution through n

Thus, if we are trying to find the cheapest solution, a reasonable thing to try first is the node with the lowest value of f. The pleasant thing about this strategy is that it is more than just reasonable. We can actually prove that it is complete and optimal, given a simple restriction on the h function.

ADMISSIBLE HEURISTIC

A* SEARCH

The restriction is to choose an h function that *never overestimates* the cost to reach the goal. Such an h is called an **admissible heuristic**. Admissible heuristics are by nature optimistic, because they think the cost of solving the problem is less than it actually is. This optimism transfers to the f function as well: *If h is admissible, $f(n)$ never overestimates the actual cost of the best solution through n.* Best-first search using f as the evaluation function and an admissible h function is known as **A* search**

---

function A*-SEARCH(*problem*) **returns** a solution or failure
   return BEST-FIRST-SEARCH(*problem*,$g + h$)

Perhaps the most obvious example of an admissible heuristic is the straight-line distance h_{SLD} that we used in getting to Bucharest. Straight-line distance is admissible because the shortest path between any two points is a straight line. In Figure 4.4, we show the first few steps of an A* search for Bucharest using the h_{SLD} heuristic. Notice that the A* search prefers to expand from Rimnicu Vilcea rather than from Fagaras. Even though Fagaras is closer to Bucharest, the path taken to get to Fagaras is not as *efficient* in getting close to Bucharest as the path taken to get to Rimnicu. The reader may wish to continue this example to see what happens next.

The behavior of A* search

Before we prove the completeness and optimality of A*, it will be useful to present an intuitive picture of how it works. A picture is not a substitute for a proof, but it is often easier to remember and can be used to generate the proof on demand. First, a preliminary observation: if you examine the search trees in Figure 4.4, you will notice an interesting phenomenon. Along any path from the root, the f-cost never decreases. This is no accident. It holds true for almost all admissible heuristics. A heuristic for which it holds is said to exhibit **monotonicity**.[1]

MONOTONICITY

If the heuristic is one of those odd ones that is not monotonic, it turns out we can make a minor correction that restores monotonicity. Let us consider two nodes n and n', where n is the parent of n'. Now suppose, for example, that $g(n) = 3$ and $h(n) = 4$. Then $f(n) = g(n)+h(n) = 7$—that is, we know that the true cost of a solution path through n is at least 7. Suppose also that $g(n') = 4$ and $h(n') = 2$, so that $f(n') = 6$. Clearly, this is an example of a nonmonotonic heuristic. Fortunately, from the fact that *any path through n' is also a path through n*, we can see that the value of 6 is meaningless, because we already know the true cost is at least 7. Thus, we should

---

[1] It can be proved (Pearl, 1984) that a heuristic is monotonic if and only if it obeys the triangle inequality. The triangle inequality says that two sides of a triangle cannot add up to less than the third side (see Exercise 4.7). Of course, straight-line distance obeys the triangle inequality and is therefore monotonic.

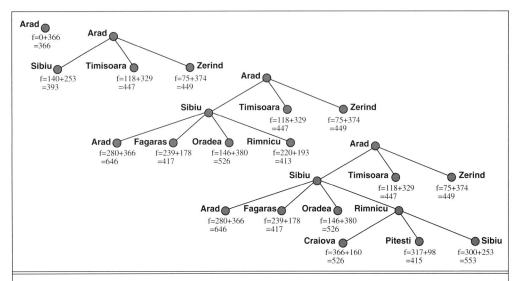

Figure 4.4   Stages in an A* search for Bucharest. Nodes are labelled with $f = g + h$. The h values are the straight-line distances to Bucharest taken from Figure 4.1.

check, each time we generate a new node, to see if its f-cost is less than its parent's f-cost; if it is, we use the parent's f-cost instead:

$$f(n') = max(f(n), g(n') + h(n')).$$

PATHMAX

In this way, we ignore the misleading values that may occur with a nonmonotonic heuristic. This equation is called the **pathmax** equation. If we use it, then f will always be nondecreasing along any path from the root, provided h is admissible.

CONTOURS

The purpose of making this observation is to legitimize a certain picture of what A* does. If f never decreases along any path out from the root, we can conceptually draw **contours** in the state space. Figure 4.5 shows an example. Inside the contour labelled 400, all nodes have $f(n)$ less than or equal to 400, and so on. Then, because A* expands the leaf node of lowest f, we can see that an A* search fans out from the start node, adding nodes in concentric bands of increasing f-cost.

With uniform-cost search (A* search using $h = 0$), the bands will be "circular" around the start state. With more accurate heuristics, the bands will stretch toward the goal state and become more narrowly focused around the optimal path. If we define f^* to be the cost of the optimal solution path, then we can say the following:

- A* expands all nodes with $f(n) < f^*$.
- A* may then expand some of the nodes right on the "goal contour," for which $f(n) = f^*$, before selecting a goal node.

Intuitively, it is obvious that the first solution found must be the optimal one, because nodes in all subsequent contours will have higher f-cost, and thus higher g-cost (because all goal states have $h(n) = 0$). Intuitively, it is also obvious that A* search is complete. As we add bands of

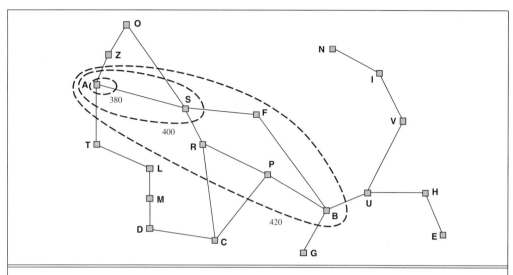

Figure 4.5   Map of Romania showing contours at $f = 380, f = 400$ and $f = 420$, with Arad as the start state. Nodes inside a given contour have f-costs lower than the contour value.

increasing f, we must eventually reach a band where f is equal to the cost of the path to a goal state. We will turn these intuitions into proofs in the next subsection.

OPTIMALLY
EFFICIENT

One final observation is that among optimal algorithms of this type—algorithms that extend search paths from the root—A* is **optimally efficient** for any given heuristic function. That is, no other optimal algorithm is guaranteed to expand fewer nodes than A*. We can explain this as follows: any algorithm that *does not* expand all nodes in the contours between the root and the goal contour runs the risk of missing the optimal solution. A long and detailed proof of this result appears in Dechter and Pearl (1985).

Proof of the optimality of A*

Let G be an optimal goal state, with path cost f^*. Let G_2 be a suboptimal goal state, that is, a goal state with path cost $g(G_2) > f^*$. The situation we imagine is that A* has selected G_2 from the queue. Because G_2 is a goal state, this would terminate the search with a suboptimal solution (Figure 4.6). We will show that this is not possible.

Consider a node n that is currently a leaf node on an optimal path to G (there must be some such node, unless the path has been completely expanded—in which case the algorithm would have returned G). Because h is admissible, we must have

$$f^* \geq f(n).$$

Furthermore, if n is not chosen for expansion over G_2, we must have

$$f(n) \geq f(G_2).$$

Combining these two together, we get

$$f^* \geq f(G_2).$$

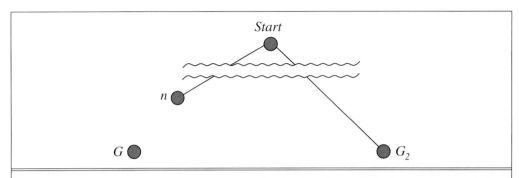

Figure 4.6   Situation at the point where a suboptimal goal state G_2 is about to be expanded. Node n is a leaf node on an optimal path from the start node to the optimal goal state G.

But because G_2 is a goal state, we have $h(G_2) = 0$; hence $f(G_2) = g(G_2)$. Thus, we have proved, from our assumptions, that

$$f^* \geq g(G_2).$$

This contradicts the assumption that G_2 is suboptimal, so it must be the case that A* never selects a suboptimal goal for expansion. Hence, because it only returns a solution after selecting it for expansion, A* is an optimal algorithm.

Proof of the completeness of A*

We said before that because A* expands nodes in order of increasing f, it must eventually expand to reach a goal state. This is true, of course, unless there are infinitely many nodes with $f(n) < f^*$. The only way there could be an infinite number of nodes is either (a) there is a node with an infinite branching factor, or (b) there is a path with a finite path cost but an infinite number of nodes along it.[2]

Thus, the correct statement is that A* is complete on **locally finite graphs** (graphs with a finite branching factor) provided there is some positive constant δ such that every operator costs at least δ.

Complexity of A*

That A* search is complete, optimal, and optimally efficient among all such algorithms is rather satisfying. Unfortunately, it does not mean that A* is the answer to all our searching needs. The catch is that, for most problems, the number of nodes within the goal contour search space is still exponential in the length of the solution. Although the proof of the result is beyond the scope of this book, it has been shown that exponential growth will occur unless the error in the heuristic

---

[2] Zeno's paradox, which purports to show that a rock thrown at a tree will never reach it, provides an example that violates condition (b). The paradox is created by imagining that the trajectory is divided into a series of phases, each of which covers half the remaining distance to the tree; this yields an infinite sequence of steps with a finite total cost.

function grows no faster than the logarithm of the actual path cost. In mathematical notation, the condition for subexponential growth is that

$$|h(n) - h^*(n)| \leq O(\log h^*(n)),$$

where $h^*(n)$ is the *true* cost of getting from n to the goal. For almost all heuristics in practical use, the error is at least proportional to the path cost, and the resulting exponential growth eventually overtakes any computer. Of course, the use of a good heuristic still provides enormous savings compared to an uninformed search. In the next section, we will look at the question of designing good heuristics.

Computation time is not, however, A*'s main drawback. Because it keeps all generated nodes in memory, A* usually runs out of space long before it runs out of time. Recently developed algorithms have overcome the space problem without sacrificing optimality or completeness. These are discussed in Section 4.3.

4.2   HEURISTIC FUNCTIONS

So far we have seen just one example of a heuristic: straight-line distance for route-finding problems. In this section, we will look at heuristics for the 8-puzzle. This will shed light on the nature of heuristics in general.

The 8-puzzle was one of the earliest heuristic search problems. As mentioned in Section 3.3, the object of the puzzle is to slide the tiles horizontally or vertically into the empty space until the configuration matches the goal configuration (Figure 4.7).

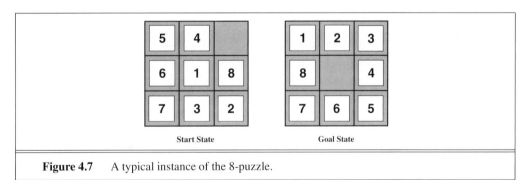

Start State   **Goal State**

Figure 4.7   A typical instance of the 8-puzzle.

The 8-puzzle is just the right level of difficulty to be interesting. A typical solution is about 20 steps, although this of course varies depending on the initial state. The branching factor is about 3 (when the empty tile is in the middle, there are four possible moves; when it is in a corner there are two; and when it is along an edge there are three). This means that an exhaustive search to depth 20 would look at about $3^{20} = 3.5 \times 10^9$ states. By keeping track of repeated states, we could cut this down drastically, because there are only $9! = 362,880$ different arrangements of 9 squares. This is still a large number of states, so the next order of business is to find a good heuristic function. If we want to find the shortest solutions, we need a heuristic function that never overestimates the number of steps to the goal. Here are two candidates:

- h_1 = the number of tiles that are in the wrong position. For Figure 4.7, seven of the eight tiles are out of position, so the start state would have $h_1 = 7$. h_1 is an admissible heuristic, because it is clear that any tile that is out of place must be moved at least once.

- h_2 = the sum of the distances of the tiles from their goal positions. Because tiles cannot move along diagonals, the distance we will count is the sum of the horizontal and vertical distances. This is sometimes called the **city block distance** or **Manhattan distance**. h_2 is also admissible, because any move can only move one tile one step closer to the goal. Tiles 1 to 8 in the start state give a Manhattan distance of

$$h_2 = 2 + 3 + 3 + 2 + 4 + 2 + 0 + 2 = 18$$

**MANHATTAN
DISTANCE**

The effect of heuristic accuracy on performance

**EFFECTIVE
BRANCHING FACTOR**

One way to characterize the quality of a heuristic is the **effective branching factor** b^*. If the total number of nodes expanded by A* for a particular problem is N, and the solution depth is d, then b^* is the branching factor that a uniform tree of depth d would have to have in order to contain N nodes. Thus,

$$N = 1 + b^* + (b^*)^2 + \cdots + (b^*)^d.$$

For example, if A* finds a solution at depth 5 using 52 nodes, then the effective branching factor is 1.91. Usually, the effective branching factor exhibited by a given heuristic is fairly constant over a large range of problem instances, and therefore experimental measurements of b^* on a small set of problems can provide a good guide to the heuristic's overall usefulness. A well-designed heuristic would have a value of b^* close to 1, allowing fairly large problems to be solved. To test the heuristic functions h_1 and h_2, we randomly generated 100 problems each with solution lengths $2, 4, \ldots, 20$, and solved them using A* search with h_1 and h_2, as well as with uninformed iterative deepening search. Figure 4.8 gives the average number of nodes expanded by each strategy, and the effective branching factor. The results show that h_2 is better than h_1, and that uninformed search is much worse.

DOMINATES

One might ask if h_2 is *always* better than h_1. The answer is yes. It is easy to see from the definitions of the two heuristics that for any node n, $h_2(n) \geq h_1(n)$. We say that h_2 **dominates** h_1. Domination translates directly into efficiency: A* using h_2 will expand fewer nodes, on average, than A* using h_1. We can show this using the following simple argument. Recall the observation on page 98 that every node with $f(n) < f^*$ will be expanded. This is the same as saying that every node with $h(n) < f^* - g(n)$ will be expanded. But because h_2 is at least as big as h_1 for all nodes, every node that is expanded by A* search with h_2 will also be expanded with h_1, and h_1 may also cause other nodes to be expanded as well. *Hence, it is always better to use a heuristic function with higher values, as long as it does not overestimate.*

	Search Cost			Effective Branching Factor		
d	IDS	A*(h_1)	A*(h_2)	IDS	A*(h_1)	A*(h_2)
2	10	6	6	2.45	1.79	1.79
4	112	13	12	2.87	1.48	1.45
6	680	20	18	2.73	1.34	1.30
8	6384	39	25	2.80	1.33	1.24
10	47127	93	39	2.79	1.38	1.22
12	364404	227	73	2.78	1.42	1.24
14	3473941	539	113	2.83	1.44	1.23
16	–	1301	211	–	1.45	1.25
18	–	3056	363	–	1.46	1.26
20	–	7276	676	–	1.47	1.27
22	–	18094	1219	–	1.48	1.28
24	–	39135	1641	–	1.48	1.26

Figure 4.8   Comparison of the search costs and effective branching factors for the ITERATIVE-DEEPENING-SEARCH and A* algorithms with h_1, h_2. Data are averaged over 100 instances of the 8-puzzle, for various solution lengths.

Inventing heuristic functions

We have seen that both h_1 and h_2 are fairly good heuristics for the 8-puzzle, and that h_2 is better. But we do not know how to invent a heuristic function. How might one have come up with h_2? Is it possible for a computer to mechanically invent such a heuristic?

h_1 and h_2 are estimates to the remaining path length for the 8-puzzle, but they can also be considered to be perfectly accurate path lengths for simplified versions of the puzzle. If the rules of the puzzle were changed so that a tile could move anywhere, instead of just to the adjacent empty square, then h_1 would accurately give the number of steps to the shortest solution. Similarly, if a tile could move one square in any direction, even onto an occupied square, then h_2 would give the exact number of steps in the shortest solution. A problem with less restrictions on the operators is called a **relaxed problem**. *It is often the case that the cost of an exact solution to a relaxed problem is a good heuristic for the original problem.*

RELAXED PROBLEM

If a problem definition is written down in a formal language, it is possible to construct relaxed problems automatically.[3] For example, if the 8-puzzle operators are described as

A tile can move from square A to square B if A is adjacent to B and B is blank,

we can generate three relaxed problems by removing one or more of the conditions:

(a) A tile can move from square A to square B if A is adjacent to B.
(b) A tile can move from square A to square B if B is blank.
(c) A tile can move from square A to square B.

Recently, a program called ABSOLVER was written that can generate heuristics automatically from problem definitions, using the "relaxed problem" method and various other techniques (Prieditis, 1993). ABSOLVER generated a new heuristic for the 8-puzzle better than any existing heuristic, and found the first useful heuristic for the famous Rubik's cube puzzle.

---

[3]   In Chapters 7 and 11, we will describe formal languages suitable for this task. For now, we will use English.

One problem with generating new heuristic functions is that one often fails to get one "clearly best" heuristic. If a collection of admissible heuristics $h_1 \ldots h_m$ is available for a problem, and none of them dominates any of the others, which should we choose? As it turns out, we need not make a choice. We can have the best of all worlds, by defining

$$h(n) = max(h_1(n), \ldots, h_m(n)).$$

This composite heuristic uses whichever function is most accurate on the node in question. Because the component heuristics are admissible, h is also admissible. Furthermore, h dominates all of the individual heuristics from which it is composed.

Another way to invent a good heuristic is to use statistical information. This can be gathered by running a search over a number of training problems, such as the 100 randomly chosen 8-puzzle configurations, and gathering statistics. For example, we might find that when $h_2(n) = 14$, it turns out that 90% of the time the real distance to the goal is 18. Then when faced with the "real" problem, we can use 18 as the value whenever $h_2(n)$ reports 14. Of course, if we use probabilistic information like this, we are giving up on the guarantee of admissibility, but we are likely to expand fewer nodes on average.

FEATURES   Often it is possible to pick out **features** of a state that contribute to its heuristic evaluation function, even if it is hard to say exactly what the contribution should be. For example, the goal in chess is to checkmate the opponent, and relevant features include the number of pieces of each kind belonging to each side, the number of pieces that are attacked by opponent pieces, and so on. Usually, the evaluation function is assumed to be a linear combination of the feature values. Even if we have no idea how important each feature is, or even if a feature is good or bad, it is still possible to use a learning algorithm to acquire reasonable coefficients for each feature, as demonstrated in Chapter 18. In chess, for example, a program could learn that one's own queen should have a large positive coefficient, whereas an opponent's pawn should have a small negative coefficient.

Another factor that we have not considered so far is the search cost of actually running the heuristic function on a node. We have been assuming that the cost of computing the heuristic function is about the same as the cost of expanding a node, so that minimizing the number of nodes expanded is a good thing. But if the heuristic function is so complex that computing its value for one node takes as long as expanding hundreds of nodes, then we need to reconsider. After all, it is easy to have a heuristic that is perfectly accurate—if we allow the heuristic to do, say, a full breadth-first search "on the sly." That would minimize the number of nodes expanded by the real search, but it would not minimize the overall search cost. A good heuristic function must be efficient as well as accurate.

Heuristics for constraint satisfaction problems

In Section 3.7, we examined a class of problems called **constraint satisfaction problems** (CSPs). A constraint satisfaction problem consists of a set of variables that can take on values from a given domain, together with a set of constraints that specify properties of the solution. Section 3.7 examined uninformed search methods for CSPs, mostly variants of depth-first search. Here, we extend the analysis by considering heuristics for selecting a variable to instantiate and for choosing a value for the variable.

To illustrate the basic idea, we will use the map-coloring problem shown in Figure 4.9. (The idea of map coloring is to avoid coloring adjacent countries with the same color.) Suppose that we can use at most three colors (red, green, and blue), and that we have chosen green for country A and red for country B. Intuitively, it seems obvious that we should color E next, because the only possible color for E is blue. All the other countries have a choice of colors, and we might make the wrong choice and have to backtrack. In fact, once we have colored E blue, then we are forced to color C red and F green. After that, coloring D either blue or red results in a solution. In other words, we have solved the problem with no search at all.

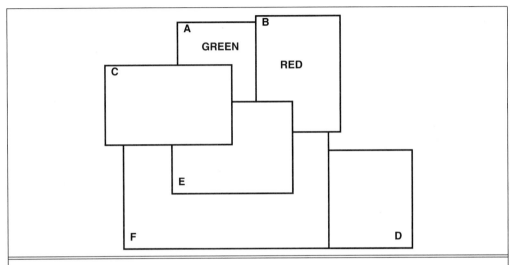

Figure 4.9   A map-coloring problem after the first two variables (A and B) have been selected. Which country should we color next?

MOST-
CONSTRAINED-
VARIABLE
This intuitive idea is called the **most-constrained-variable** heuristic. It is used with forward checking (see Section 3.7), which keeps track of which values are still allowed for each variable, given the choices made so far. At each point in the search, the variable with the *fewest* possible values is chosen to have a value assigned. In this way, the branching factor in the search tends to be minimized. For example, when this heuristic is used in solving n-queens problems, the feasible problem size is increased from around 30 for forward checking to approximately

MOST-
CONSTRAINING-
VARIABLE
100. The **most-constraining-variable** heuristic is similarly effective. It attempts to reduce the branching factor on future choices by assigning a value to the variable that is involved in the largest number of constraints on other unassigned variables.

Once a variable has been selected, we still need to choose a value for it. Suppose that we decide to assign a value to country C after A and B. One's intuition is that red is a better choice than blue, because it leaves more freedom for future choices. This intuition is the

LEAST-
CONSTRAINING-
VALUE
least-constraining-value heuristic—choose a value that rules out the smallest number of values in variables connected to the current variable by constraints. When applied to the n-queens problem, it allows problems up to $n=1000$ to be solved.

4.3   MEMORY BOUNDED SEARCH

Despite all the clever search algorithms that have been invented, the fact remains that some problems are intrinsically difficult, by the nature of the problem. When we run up against these exponentially complex problems, something has to give. Figure 3.12 shows that *the first thing to give is usually the available memory.* In this section, we investigate two algorithms that are designed to conserve memory. The first, IDA*, is a logical extension of ITERATIVE-DEEPENING-SEARCH to use heuristic information. The second, SMA*, is similar to A*, but restricts the queue size to fit into the available memory.

Iterative deepening A* search (IDA*)

IDA*

In Chapter 3, we showed that iterative deepening is a useful technique for reducing memory requirements. We can try the same trick again, turning A* search into iterative deepening A*, or **IDA*** (see Figure 4.10). In this algorithm, each iteration is a depth-first search, just as in regular iterative deepening. The depth-first search is modified to use an f-cost limit rather than a depth limit. Thus, each iteration expands all nodes inside the contour for the current f-cost, peeping over the contour to find out where the next contour lies. (See the DFS-CONTOUR function in Figure 4.10.) Once the search inside a given contour has been completed, a new iteration is started using a new f-cost for the next contour.

IDA* is complete and optimal with the same caveats as A* search, but because it is depth-first, it only requires space proportional to the longest path that it explores. If δ is the smallest operator cost and f^* the optimal solution cost, then in the worst case, IDA* will require bf^*/δ nodes of storage. In most cases, bd is a good estimate of the storage requirements.

The time complexity of IDA* depends strongly on the number of different values that the heuristic function can take on. The Manhattan distance heuristic used in the 8-puzzle takes on one of a small number of integer values. Typically, f only increases two or three times along any solution path. Thus, IDA* only goes through two or three iterations, and its efficiency is similar to that of A*—in fact, the last iteration of IDA* usually expands roughly the same number of nodes as A*. Furthermore, because IDA* does not need to insert and delete nodes on a priority queue, its overhead per node can be much less than that for A*. Optimal solutions for many practical problems were first found by IDA*, which for several years was the only optimal, memory-bounded, heuristic algorithm.

Unfortunately, IDA* has difficulty in more complex domains. In the travelling salesperson problem, for example, the heuristic value is different for every state. This means that each contour only includes one more state than the previous contour. If A* expands N nodes, IDA* will have to go through N iterations and will therefore expand $1 + 2 + \cdots + N = O(N^2)$ nodes. Now if N is too large for the computer's memory, then N^2 is almost certainly too long to wait!

One way around this is to increase the f-cost limit by a fixed amount ϵ on each iteration, so that the total number of iterations is proportional to $1/\epsilon$. This can reduce the search cost, at the expense of returning solutions that can be worse than optimal by at most ϵ. Such an algorithm is

ϵ-ADMISSIBLE   called ϵ-**admissible**.

---

function IDA*(*problem*) **returns** a solution sequence
  inputs: *problem*, a problem
  local variables: *f-limit*, the current *f*- COST limit
                                root, a node

  root ← MAKE-NODE(INITIAL-STATE[*problem*])
  f-limit ← *f*- COST(*root*)
  loop do
        solution, f-limit ← DFS-CONTOUR(*root, f-limit*)
        if *solution* is non-null **then return** *solution*
        if *f-limit* = ∞ **then return** failure; **end**

---

function DFS-CONTOUR(*node, f-limit*) **returns** a solution sequence and a new *f*- COST limit
  inputs: *node*, a node
                  f-limit, the current *f*- COST limit
  local variables: *next-f*, the *f*- COST limit for the next contour, initially ∞

  if *f*- COST[*node*] > *f-limit* **then return** null, *f*- COST[*node*]
  if GOAL-TEST[*problem*](STATE[*node*]) **then return** *node, f-limit*
  for each node *s* **in** SUCCESSORS(*node*) **do**
        solution, new-f ← DFS-CONTOUR(*s, f-limit*)
        if *solution* is non-null **then return** *solution, f-limit*
        next-f ← MIN(*next-f, new-f*); **end**
  return null, *next-f*

Figure 4.10   The IDA* (Iterative Deepening A*) search algorithm.

SMA* search

IDA*'s difficulties in certain problem spaces can be traced to using *too little* memory. Between iterations, it retains only a single number, the current f-cost limit. Because it cannot remember its history, IDA* is doomed to repeat it. This is doubly true in state spaces that are graphs rather than trees (see Section 3.6). IDA* can be modified to check the current path for repeated states, but is unable to avoid repeated states generated by alternative paths.

SMA*   In this section, we describe the **SMA*** (Simplified Memory-Bounded A*) algorithm, which can make use of all available memory to carry out the search. Using more memory can only improve search efficiency—one could always ignore the additional space, but usually it is better to remember a node than to have to regenerate it when needed. SMA* has the following properties:

- It will utilize whatever memory is made available to it.
- It avoids repeated states as far as its memory allows.
- It is complete if the available memory is sufficient to store the *shallowest* solution path.
- It is optimal if enough memory is available to store the shallowest optimal solution path. Otherwise, it returns the best solution that can be reached with the available memory.
- When enough memory is available for the entire search tree, the search is optimally efficient.

The one unresolved question is whether SMA* is always optimally efficient among all algorithms given the same heuristic information and the same memory allocation.

The design of SMA* is simple, at least in overview. When it needs to generate a successor but has no memory left, it will need to make space on the queue. To do this, it drops a node from the queue. Nodes that are dropped from the queue in this way are called **forgotten nodes**. It prefers to drop nodes that are unpromising—that is, nodes with high f-cost. To avoid reexploring subtrees that it has dropped from memory, it retains in the ancestor nodes information about the quality of the best path in the forgotten subtree. In this way, it *only* regenerates the subtree when *all other paths* have been shown to look worse than the path it has forgotten. Another way of saying this is that if all the descendants of a node n are forgotten, then we will not know which way to go from n, but we will still have an idea of how worthwhile it is to go anywhere from n.

SMA* is best explained by an example, which is illustrated in Figure 4.11. The top of the figure shows the search space. Each node is labelled with $g + h = f$ values, and the goal nodes (D, F, I, J) are shown in squares. The aim is to find the lowest-cost goal node with enough memory for only *three* nodes. The stages of the search are shown in order, left to right, with each stage numbered according to the explanation that follows. Each node is labelled with its current f-cost, which is continuously maintained to reflect the least f-cost of any of its descendants.[4] Values in parentheses show the value of the best forgotten descendant. The algorithm proceeds as follows:

1. At each stage, one successor is added to the deepest lowest-f-cost node that has some successors not currently in the tree. The left child B is added to the root A.

2. Now $f(A)$ is still 12, so we add the right child G ($f = 13$). Now that we have seen all the children of A, we can update its f-cost to the minimum of its children, that is, 13. The memory is now full.

3. G is now designated for expansion, but we must first drop a node to make room. We drop the shallowest highest-f-cost leaf, that is, B. When we have done this, we note that A's best forgotten descendant has $f = 15$, as shown in parentheses. We then add H, with $f(H) = 18$. Unfortunately, H is not a goal node, but the path to H uses up all the available memory. Hence, there is no way to find a solution through H, so we set $f(H) = \infty$.

4. G is expanded again. We drop H, and add I, with $f(I) = 24$. Now we have seen both successors of G, with values of ∞ and 24, so $f(G)$ becomes 24. $f(A)$ becomes 15, the minimum of 15 (forgotten successor value) and 24. Notice that I is a goal node, but it might not be the best solution because A's f-cost is only 15.

5. A is once again the most promising node, so B is generated for the second time. We have found that the path through G was not so great after all.

6. C, the first successor of B, is a nongoal node at the maximum depth, so $f(C) = \infty$.

7. To look at the second successor, D, we first drop C. Then $f(D) = 20$, and this value is inherited by B and A.

8. Now the deepest, lowest-f-cost node is D. D is therefore selected, and because it is a goal node, the search terminates.

---

[4] Values computed in this way are called **backed-up values**. Because $f(n)$ is supposed to be an estimate of the least-cost solution path through n, and a solution path through n is bound to go through one of n's descendants, backing up the least f-cost among the descendants is a sound policy.

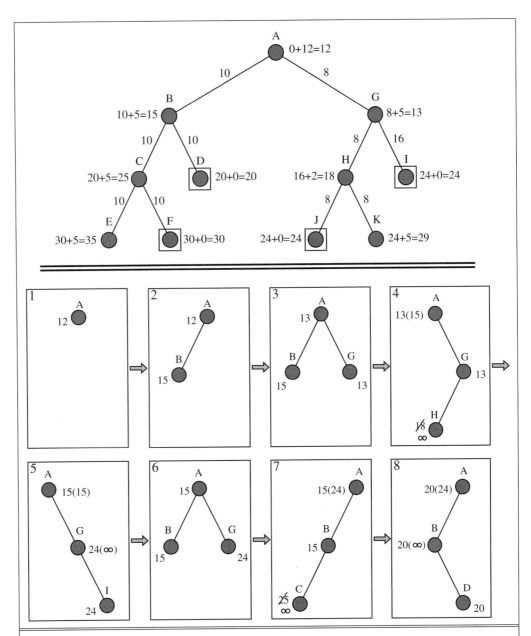

Figure 4.11   Progress of an SMA* search with a memory size of three nodes, on the state space shown at the top. Each node is labelled with its *current f*-cost. Values in parentheses show the value of the best forgotten descendant.

In this case, there is enough memory for the shallowest optimal solution path. If J had had a cost of 19 instead of 24, however, SMA* still would not have been able to find it because the solution path contains four nodes. In this case, SMA* would have returned D, which would be the best reachable solution. It is a simple matter to have the algorithm signal that the solution found may not be optimal.

A rough sketch of SMA* is shown in Figure 4.12. In the actual program, some gymnastics are necessary to deal with the fact that nodes sometimes end up with some successors in memory and some forgotten. When we need to check for repeated nodes, things get even more complicated. SMA* is the most complicated search algorithm we have seen yet.

---

function SMA*(*problem*) **returns** a solution sequence
   inputs: *problem*, a problem
   local variables: *Queue*, a queue of nodes ordered by *f*-cost

   Queue ← MAKE-QUEUE({MAKE-NODE(INITIAL-STATE[*problem*])})
   loop do
      if *Queue* is empty **then return** failure
      n ← deepest least-f-cost node in *Queue*
      if GOAL-TEST(*n*) **then return** success
      s ← NEXT-SUCCESSOR(*n*)
      if *s* is not a goal and is at maximum depth **then**
         f(*s*) ← ∞
      else
         f(*s*) ← MAX(f(*n*), g(*s*)+h(*s*))
      if all of *n*'s successors have been generated **then**
         update *n*'s *f*-cost and those of its ancestors if necessary
      if SUCCESSORS(*n*) all in memory **then** remove *n* from *Queue*
      if memory is full **then**
         delete shallowest, highest-f-cost node in *Queue*
         remove it from its parent's successor list
         insert its parent on *Queue* if necessary
      insert *s* on *Queue*
   end

Figure 4.12   Sketch of the SMA* algorithm. Note that numerous details have been omitted in the interests of clarity.

Given a reasonable amount of memory, SMA* can solve significantly more difficult problems than A* without incurring significant overhead in terms of extra nodes generated. It performs well on problems with highly connected state spaces and real-valued heuristics, on which IDA* has difficulty. On very hard problems, however, it will often be the case that SMA* is forced to continually switch back and forth between a set of candidate solution paths. Then the extra time required for repeated regeneration of the same nodes means that problems that would be practically solvable by A*, given unlimited memory, become intractable for SMA*. That is to say, memory limitations can make a problem intractable from the point of view of computation time. Although there is no theory to explain the trade-off between time and memory, it seems that this is an inescapable problem. The only way out is to drop the optimality requirement.

4.4   ITERATIVE IMPROVEMENT ALGORITHMS

ITERATIVE
IMPROVEMENT

We saw in Chapter 3 that several well-known problems (for example, 8-queens and VLSI layout) have the property that the state description itself contains all the information needed for a solution. The path by which the solution is reached is irrelevant. In such cases, **iterative improvement** algorithms often provide the most practical approach. For example, we start with all 8 queens on the board, or all wires routed through particular channels. Then, we might move queens around trying to reduce the number of attacks; or we might move a wire from one channel to another to reduce congestion. *The general idea is to start with a complete configuration and to make modifications to improve its quality.*

The best way to understand iterative improvement algorithms is to consider all the states laid out on the surface of a landscape. The height of any point on the landscape corresponds to the evaluation function of the state at that point (Figure 4.13). The idea of iterative improvement is to move around the landscape trying to find the highest peaks, which are the optimal solutions. Iterative improvement algorithms usually keep track of only the current state, and do not look ahead beyond the immediate neighbors of that state. This resembles trying to find the top of Mount Everest in a thick fog while suffering from amnesia. Nonetheless, sometimes iterative improvement is the method of choice for hard, practical problems. We will see several applications in later chapters, particularly to neural network learning in Chapter 19.

HILL-CLIMBING

GRADIENT DESCENT

SIMULATED
ANNEALING

Iterative improvement algorithms divide into two major classes. **Hill-climbing** (or, alternatively, **gradient descent** if we view the evaluation function as a cost rather than a quality) algorithms always try to make changes that improve the current state. **Simulated annealing** algorithms can sometimes make changes that make things worse, at least temporarily.

Hill-climbing search

The hill-climbing search algorithm is shown in Figure 4.14. It is simply a loop that continually moves in the direction of increasing value. The algorithm does not maintain a search tree, so the node data structure need only record the state and its evaluation, which we denote by VALUE. One important refinement is that when there is more than one best successor to choose from, the algorithm can select among them at random. This simple policy has three well-known drawbacks:

◇ **Local maxima**: a local maximum, as opposed to a global maximum, is a peak that is lower than the highest peak in the state space. Once on a local maximum, the algorithm will halt even though the solution may be far from satisfactory.

◇ **Plateaux**: a plateau is an area of the state space where the evaluation function is essentially flat. The search will conduct a random walk.

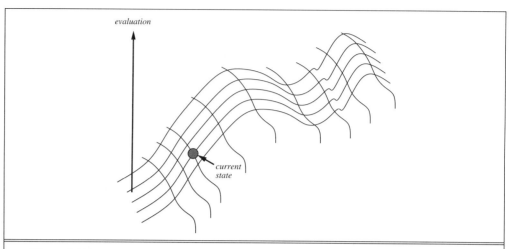

Figure 4.13   Iterative improvement algorithms try to find peaks on a surface of states where height is defined by the evaluation function.

---

function HILL-CLIMBING(*problem*) **returns** a solution state
    inputs: *problem*, a problem
    local variables: *current*, a node
                     next, a node

    current ← MAKE-NODE(INITIAL-STATE[*problem*])
    loop do
        next ← a highest-valued successor of *current*
        if VALUE[next] < VALUE[current] **then return** *current*
        current ← *next*
    end

Figure 4.14   The hill-climbing search algorithm.

◇ **Ridges**: a ridge may have steeply sloping sides, so that the search reaches the top of the ridge with ease, but the top may slope only very gently toward a peak. Unless there happen to be operators that move directly along the top of the ridge, the search may oscillate from side to side, making little progress.

RANDOM-RESTART
HILL-CLIMBING In each case, the algorithm reaches a point at which no progress is being made. If this happens, an obvious thing to do is start again from a different starting point. **Random-restart hill-climbing** does just this: it conducts a series of hill-climbing searches from randomly generated initial states, running each until it halts or makes no discernible progress. It saves the best result found so far from any of the searches. It can use a fixed number of iterations, or can continue until the best saved result has not been improved for a certain number of iterations.

Clearly, if enough iterations are allowed, random-restart hill-climbing will eventually find the optimal solution. The success of hill-climbing depends very much on the shape of the state-space "surface": if there are only a few local maxima, random-restart hill-climbing will find a good solution very quickly. A realistic problem has a surface that looks more like a porcupine. If the problem is NP-complete, then in all likelihood we cannot do better than exponential time. It follows that there must be an exponential number of local maxima to get stuck on. Usually, however, a reasonably good solution can be found after a small number of iterations.

Simulated annealing

Instead of starting again randomly when stuck on a local maximum, we could allow the search to take some downhill steps to escape the local maximum. This is roughly the idea of **simulated annealing** (Figure 4.15). The innermost loop of simulated annealing is quite similar to hill-climbing. Instead of picking the *best* move, however, it picks a *random* move. If the move actually improves the situation, it is always executed. Otherwise, the algorithm makes the move with some probability less than 1. The probability decreases exponentially with the "badness" of the move—the amount ΔE by which the evaluation is worsened.

A second parameter T is also used to determine the probability. At higher values of T, "bad" moves are more likely to be allowed. As T tends to zero, they become more and more unlikely, until the algorithm behaves more or less like hill-climbing. The *schedule* input determines the value of T as a function of how many cycles already have been completed.

The reader by now may have guessed that the name "simulated annealing" and the parameter names ΔE and T were chosen for a good reason. The algorithm was developed from an explicit analogy with **annealing**—the process of gradually cooling a liquid until it freezes. The VALUE function corresponds to the total energy of the atoms in the material, and T corresponds to the

---

function SIMULATED-ANNEALING(*problem, schedule*) **returns** a solution state
    inputs: *problem*, a problem
            schedule, a mapping from time to "temperature"
    local variables: *current*, a node
                next, a node
                T, a "temperature" controlling the probability of downward steps

    current ← MAKE-NODE(INITIAL-STATE[*problem*])
    for $t \leftarrow$ 1 **to** ∞ **do**
        $T \leftarrow schedule[t]$
        if T=0 **then return** *current*
        next ← a randomly selected successor of *current*
        $\Delta E \leftarrow$ VALUE[*next*] – VALUE[*current*]
        if $\Delta E > 0$ **then** *current* ← *next*
        else *current* ← *next* only with probability $e^{\Delta E/T}$

Figure 4.15   The simulated annealing search algorithm.

temperature. The *schedule* determines the rate at which the temperature is lowered. Individual moves in the state space correspond to random fluctuations due to thermal noise. One can prove that if the temperature is lowered sufficiently slowly, the material will attain a lowest-energy (perfectly ordered) configuration. This corresponds to the statement that if *schedule* lowers T slowly enough, the algorithm will find a global optimum.

Simulated annealing was first used extensively to solve VLSI layout problems in the early 1980s. Since then, it has been applied widely to factory scheduling and other large-scale optimization tasks. In Exercise 4.12, you are asked to compare its performance to that of random-restart hill-climbing on the *n*-queens puzzle.

Applications in constraint satisfaction problems

Constraint satisfaction problems (CSPs) can be solved by iterative improvement methods by first assigning values to all the variables, and then applying modification operators to move the configuration toward a solution. Modification operators simply assign a different value to a variable. For example, in the 8-queens problem, an initial state has all eight queens on the board, and an operator moves a queen from one square to another.

HEURISTIC REPAIR

Algorithms that solve CSPs in this fashion are often called **heuristic repair** methods, because they repair inconsistencies in the current configuration. In choosing a new value for a variable, the most obvious heuristic is to select the value that results in the minimum number of

MIN-CONFLICTS

conflicts with other variables—the **min-conflicts** heuristic. This is illustrated in Figure 4.16 for an 8-queens problem, which it solves in two steps.

Min-conflicts is surprisingly effective for many CSPs, and is able to solve the million-queens problem in an average of less than 50 steps. It has also been used to schedule observations for the Hubble space telescope, reducing the time taken to schedule a week of observations from three weeks (!) to around ten minutes. Min-conflicts is closely related to the GSAT algorithm described on page 182, which solves problems in propositional logic.

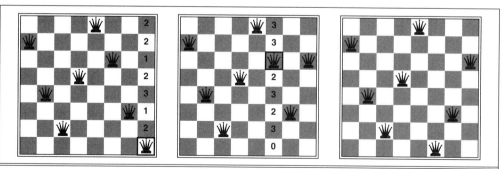

Figure 4.16   A two-step solution for an 8-queens problem using min-conflicts. At each stage, a queen is chosen for reassignment in its column. The number of conflicts (in this case, the number of attacking queens) is shown in each square. The algorithm moves the queen to the min-conflict square, breaking ties randomly.

4.5 SUMMARY

This chapter has examined the application of **heuristics** to reduce search costs. We have looked at number of algorithms that use heuristics, and found that optimality comes at a stiff price in terms of search cost, even with good heuristics.

- **Best-first search** is just GENERAL-SEARCH where the minimum-cost nodes (according to some measure) are expanded first.

- If we minimize the estimated cost to reach the goal, $h(n)$, we get **greedy search**. The search time is usually decreased compared to an uninformed algorithm, but the algorithm is neither optimal nor complete.

- Minimizing $f(n) = g(n) + h(n)$ combines the the advantages of uniform-cost search and greedy search. If we handle repeated states and guarantee that $h(n)$ never overestimates, we get **A* search**.

- A* is complete, optimal, and optimally efficient among all optimal search algorithms. Its space complexity is still prohibitive.

- The time complexity of heuristic algorithms depends on the quality of the heuristic function. Good heuristics can sometimes be constructed by examining the problem definition or by generalizing from experience with the problem class.

- We can reduce the space requirement of A* with memory-bounded algorithms such as IDA* (iterative deepening A*) and SMA* (simplified memory-bounded A*).

- **Iterative improvement** algorithms keep only a single state in memory, but can get stuck on local maxima. Simulated annealing provides a way to escape local maxima, and is complete and optimal given a long enough cooling schedule.

- For constraint satisfaction problems, variable and value ordering heuristics can provide huge performance gains. Current algorithms often solve very large problems very quickly.

BIBLIOGRAPHICAL AND HISTORICAL NOTES

The same paper that introduced the phrase "heuristic search" (Newell and Ernst, 1965) also introduced the concept of an evaluation function, understood as an estimate of the distance to the goal, to guide search; this concept was also proposed in the same year by Lin (1965). Doran and Michie (1966) did extensive experimental studies of heuristic search as applied to a number of problems, especially the 8-puzzle and the 15-puzzle. Although Doran and Michie carried out theoretical analyses of path length and "penetrance" (the ratio of path length to the total number of nodes examined so far) in heuristic search, they appear to have used their heuristic functions as the sole guiding element in the search, ignoring the information provided by current path length that is used by uniform-cost search and by A*.

The A* algorithm, incorporating the current path length into heuristic search, was developed by Hart, Nilsson, and Raphael (1968). Certain subtle technical errors in the original presentation of A* were corrected in a later paper (Hart *et al.*, 1972). An excellent summary of early work in search is provided by Nilsson (1971).

The original A* paper introduced a property of heuristics called "consistency." The monotonicity property of heuristics was introduced by Pohl (1977) as a simpler replacement for the consistency property. Pearl (1984) showed that consistency and monotonicity were equivalent properties. The pathmax equation was first used in A* search by Mero (1984).

Pohl (1970; 1977) pioneered the study of the relationship between the error in A*'s heuristic function and the time complexity of A*. The proof that A* runs in linear time if the error in the heuristic function is bounded by a constant can be found in Pohl (1977) and in Gaschnig (1979). Pearl (1984) strengthened this result to allow a logarithmic growth in the error. The "effective branching factor" measure of the efficiency of heuristic search was proposed by Nilsson (1971).

A* and other state-space search algorithms are closely related to the *branch-and-bound* techniques that are widely used in operations research. An early survey of branch-and-bound techniques is given by Lawler and Wood (1966). The seminal paper by Held and Karp (1970) considers the use of the minimum-spanning-tree heuristic (see Exercise 4.11) for the travelling salesperson problem, showing how such admissible heuristics can be derived by examining relaxed problems. Generation of effective new heuristics by problem relaxation was successfully implemented by Prieditis (1993), building on earlier work with Jack Mostow (Mostow and Prieditis, 1989). The probabilistic interpretation of heuristics was investigated in depth by Hansson and Mayer (1989).

The relationships between state-space search and branch-and-bound have been investigated in depth by Dana Nau, Laveen Kanal, and Vipin Kumar (Kumar and Kanal, 1983; Nau *et al.*, 1984; Kumar *et al.*, 1988). Martelli and Montanari (1978) demonstrate a connection between dynamic programming (see Chapter 17) and certain types of state-space search. Kumar and Kanal (1988) attempt a "grand unification" of heuristic search, dynamic programming, and branch-and-bound techniques under the name of CDP—the "composite decision process." More material along these lines is found in Kumar (1991).

There are a large number of minor and major variations on the A* algorithm. Pohl (1973) proposed the use of *dynamic weighting*, which uses a weighted sum $f_w(n) = w_g g(n) + w_h h(n)$ of the current path length and the heuristic function as an evaluation function, rather than the simple sum $f(n) = g(n) + h(n)$ used in A*, and dynamically adjusts the weights w_g and w_h according to certain criteria as the search progresses. Dynamic weighting usually cannot guarantee that optimal solutions will be found, as A* can, but under certain circumstances dynamic weighting can find solutions much more efficiently than A*.

The most-constrained-variable heuristic was introduced by Bitner and Reingold (1975), and further investigated by Purdom (1983). Empirical results on the *n*-queens problem were obtained by Stone and Stone (1986). Brelaz (1979) used the most-constraining-variable heuristic as a tie-breaker after applying the most-constrained-variable heuristic. The resulting algorithm, despite its simplicity, is still the best method for *k*-coloring arbitrary graphs. The least-constraining-value heuristic was developed and analyzed in Haralick and Elliot (1980). The min-conflicts heuristic was first proposed by Gu (1989), and was developed independently by Steve Minton (Minton *et al.*, 1992). Minton explains the remarkable performance of min-conflicts by modelling the search process as a random walk that is biased to move toward solutions. The effectiveness of algorithms such as min-conflicts and the related GSAT algorithm (see Exercise 6.15) in solving randomly generated problems almost "instantaneously," despite the NP-completeness of the associated problem classes, has prompted an intensive investigation. It turns out that almost all randomly generated problems are either trivially easy or have no solutions. Only if the parameters of the problem generator are set in a certain narrow range, within which roughly half of the problems are solvable, do we find "hard" problem instances (Kirkpatrick and Selman, 1994).

Because computers in the late 1950s and early 1960s had at most a few thousand words of main memory, memory-bounded heuristic search was an early research topic. Doran and Michie's (1966) Graph Traverser, one of the earliest search programs, commits to an operator after searching best-first up to the memory limit. As with other "staged search" algorithms, optimality cannot be ensured because until the best path has been found the optimality of the first step remains in doubt. IDA* was the first widely used optimal, memory-bounded, heuristic search algorithm, and a large number of variants have been developed. The first reasonably public paper dealing specifically with IDA* was Korf's (1985b), although Korf credits the initial idea to a personal communication from Judea Pearl and also mentions Berliner and Goetsch's (1984) technical report describing their implementation of IDA* concurrently with Korf's own work. A more comprehensive exposition of IDA* can be found in Korf (1985a). A thorough analysis of the efficiency of IDA*, and its difficulties with real-valued heuristics, appears in Patrick *et al.* (1992). The SMA* algorithm described in the text was based on an earlier algorithm called MA* (Chakrabarti *et al.*, 1989), and first appeared in Russell (1992). The latter paper also introduced the "contour" representation of search spaces. Kaindl and Khorsand (1994) apply SMA* to produce a bidirectional search algorithm that exhibits significant performance improvements over previous algorithms.

Three other memory-bounded algorithms deserve mention. RBFS (Korf, 1993) and IE (Russell, 1992) are two very similar algorithms that use linear space and a simple recursive formulation, like IDA*, but retain information from pruned branches to improve efficiency. Particularly in tree-structured search spaces with discrete-valued heuristics, they appear to be competitive with SMA* because of their reduced overhead. RBFS is also able to carry out a best-first search when the heuristic is inadmissible. Finally, **tabu search** algorithms (Glover, 1989), which maintain a bounded list of states that must not be revisited, have proved effective for optimization problems in operations research.

TABU SEARCH

Simulated annealing was first described by Kirkpatrick, Gelatt, and Vecchi (1983), who borrowed the algorithm directly from the **Metropolis algorithm** used to simulate complex systems in statistical physics (Metropolis *et al.*, 1953). Simulated annealing is now a subfield in itself, with several hundred papers published every year.

PARALLEL SEARCH

The topic of **parallel search** algorithms was not covered in the chapter, partly because it requires a lengthy discussion of parallel architectures. As parallel computers are becoming widely available, parallel search is becoming an important topic in both AI and theoretical computer science. A brief introduction to the AI literature can be found in Mahanti and Daniels (1993).

By far the most comprehensive source on heuristic search algorithms is Pearl's (1984) *Heuristics* text. This book provides especially good coverage of the wide variety of offshoots and variations of A*, including rigorous proofs of their formal properties. Kanal and Kumar (1988) present an anthology of substantive and important articles on heuristic search. New results on search algorithms appear regularly in the journal *Artificial Intelligence*.

4.1   Suppose that we run a greedy search algorithm with $h(n) = -g(n)$. What sort of search will the greedy search emulate?

4.2   Come up with heuristics for the following problems. Explain whether they are admissible, and whether the state spaces contain local maxima with your heuristic:

  a. The general case of the chain problem (i.e., with an arbitrary goal state) from Exercise 3.15.
  b. Algebraic equation solving (e.g., "solve $x^2 y^3 = 3 - xy$ for x").
  c. Path planning in the plane with rectangular obstacles (see also Exercise 4.13).
  d. Maze problems, as defined in Chapter 3.

4.3   Consider the problem of constructing crossword puzzles: fitting words into a grid of intersecting horizontal and vertical squares. Assume that a list of words (i.e., a dictionary) is provided, and that the task is to fill in the squares using any subset of this list. Go through a complete goal and problem formulation for this domain, and choose a search strategy to solve it. Specify the heuristic function, if you think one is needed.

4.4   Sometimes there is no good evaluation function for a problem, but there is a good comparison method: a way to tell if one node is better than another, without assigning numerical values to either. Show that this is enough to do a best-first search. What properties of best-first search do we give up if we only have a comparison method?

4.5   We saw on page 95 that the straight-line distance heuristic is misleading on the problem of going from Iasi to Fagaras. However, the heuristic is perfect on the opposite problem: going from Fagaras to Iasi. Are there problems for which the heuristic is misleading in both directions?

4.6   Invent a heuristic function for the 8-puzzle that sometimes overestimates, and show how it can lead to a suboptimal solution on a particular problem.

4.7   Prove that if the heuristic function h obeys the triangle inequality, then the f-cost along any path in the search tree is nondecreasing. (The triangle inequality says that the sum of the costs from A to B and B to C must not be less than the cost from A to C directly.)

4.8   We showed in the chapter that an admissible heuristic heuristic (when combined with pathmax) leads to monotonically nondecreasing f values along any path (i.e., $f(successor(n)) \geq f(n)$). Does the implication go the other way? That is, does monotonicity in f imply admissibility of the associated h?

4.9   We gave two simple heuristics for the 8-puzzle: Manhattan distance and misplaced tiles. Several heuristics in the literature purport to be better than either of these. (See, for example, Nilsson (1971) for additional improvements on Manhattan distance, and Mostow and Prieditis (1989) for heuristics derived by semimechanical methods.) Test these claims by implementing the heuristics and comparing the performance of the resulting algorithms.

4.10   Would a bidirectional A* search be a good idea? Under what conditions would it be applicable? Describe how the algorithm would work.

4.11   The travelling salesperson problem (TSP) can be solved using the minimum spanning tree (MST) heuristic, which is used to estimate the cost of completing a tour, given that a partial tour has already been constructed. The MST cost of a set of cities is the smallest sum of the link costs of any tree that connects all the cities.

   a. Show how this heuristic can be derived using a relaxed version of the TSP.
   b. Show that the MST heuristic dominates straight-line distance.
   c. Write a problem generator for instances of the TSP where cities are represented by random points in the unit square.
   d. Find an efficient algorithm in the literature for constructing the MST, and use it with an admissible search algorithm to solve instances of the TSP.

4.12   Implement the *n*-queens problem and solve it using hill-climbing, hill-climbing with random restart, and simulated annealing. Measure the search cost and percentage of solved problems using randomly generated start states. Graph these against the difficulty of the problems (as measured by the optimal solution length). Comment on your results.

4.13   Consider the problem of finding the shortest path between two points on a plane that has convex polygonal obstacles as shown in Figure 4.17. This is an idealization of the problem that a robot has to solve to navigate its way around a crowded environment.

   a. Suppose the state space consists of all positions (x,y) in the plane. How many states are there? How many paths are there to the goal?
   b. Explain briefly why the shortest path from one polygon vertex to any other in the scene must consist of straight-line segments joining some of the vertices of the polygons. Define a good state space now. How large is this state space?
   c. Define the necessary functions to implement the search problem, including a successor function that takes a vertex as input and returns the set of vertices that can be reached in a straight line from the given vertex. (Do not forget the neighbors on the same polygon.) Use the straight-line distance for the heuristic function.
   d. Implement any of the admissible algorithms discussed in the chapter. Keep the implementation of the algorithm *completely* independent of the specific domain. Then apply it to solve various problem instances in the domain.

4.14   In this question, we will turn the geometric scene from a simple data structure into a complete environment. Then we will put the agent in the environment and have it find its way to the goal.

   a. Implement an evaluation environment as described in Chapter 2. The environment should behave as follows:

   • The percept at each cycle provides the agent with a list of the places that it can see from its current location. Each place is a position vector (with an x and y component) giving the coordinates of the place *relative to the agent*. Thus, if the agent is at (1,1) and there is a visible vertex at (7,3), the percept will include the position vector (6,2). (It therefore will be up to the agent to find out where it is! It can assume that all locations have a different "view.")

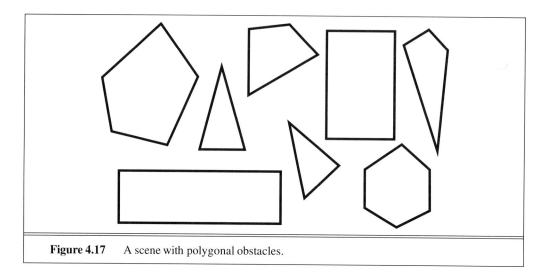

Figure 4.17   A scene with polygonal obstacles.

- The action returned by the agent will be the vector describing the straight-line path it wishes to follow (thus, the relative coordinates of the place it wishes to go). If the move does not bump into anything, the environment should "move" the agent and give it the percept appropriate to the next place; otherwise it stays put. If the agent wants to move (0,0) and is at the goal, then the environment should move the agent to a *random vertex in the scene.* (First pick a random polygon, and then a random vertex on that polygon.)

b. Implement an agent function that operates in this environment as follows:

- If it does not know where it is, it will need to calculate that from the percept.
- If it knows where it is and does not have a plan, it must calculate a plan to get home to the goal, using a search algorithm.
- Once it knows where it is and has a plan, it should output the appropriate action from the plan. It should say (0,0) once it gets to the goal.

c. Show the environment and agent operating together. The environment should print out some useful messages for the user showing what is going on.

d. Modify the environment so that 30% of the time the agent ends up at an unintended destination (chosen randomly from the other visible vertices if any, otherwise no move at all). This is a crude model of the actual motion errors from which both humans and robots suffer. Modify the agent so that it always tries to get back on track when this happens. What it should do is this: if such an error is detected, first find out where it is and then modify its plan to first go back to where it was and resume the old plan. Remember that sometimes getting back to where it was may fail also! Show an example of the agent successfully overcoming two successive motion errors and still reaching the goal.

e. Now try two different recovery schemes after an error: head for the closest vertex on the original route; and replan a route to the goal from the new location. Compare the performance of the three recovery schemes using a variety of exchange rates between search cost and path cost.

4.15   In this exercise, we will examine hill-climbing in the context of robot navigation, using the environment in Figure 4.17 as an example.

    a. Repeat Exercise 4.14 using hill-climbing. Does your agent ever get stuck on a local maximum? Is it *possible* for it to get stuck with convex obstacles?

    b. Construct a nonconvex polygonal environment in which the agent gets stuck.

    c. Modify the hill-climbing algorithm so that instead of doing a depth-1 search to decide where to go next, it does a depth-k search. It should find the best k-step path and do one step along it, and then repeat the process.

    d. Is there some k for which the new algorithm is guaranteed to escape from local maxima?

4.16   Prove that IDA* returns optimal solutions whenever there is sufficient memory for the longest path with cost $\leq f^*$. Could it be modified along the lines of SMA* to succeed even with enough memory for only the shortest solution path?

4.17   Compare the performance of A*, SMA*, and IDA* on a set of randomly generated problems in the 8-puzzle (with Manhattan distance) and TSP (with minimum spanning tree) domains. Discuss your results. What happens to the performance of IDA* when a small random number is added to the heuristic values in the 8-puzzle domain?

4.18   Proofs of properties of SMA*:

    a. SMA* abandons paths that fill up memory by themselves but do not contain a solution. Show that without this check, SMA* will get stuck in an infinite loop whenever it does not have enough memory for the shortest solution path.

    b. Prove that SMA* terminates in a finite space or if there is a finite path to a goal. The proof will work by showing that it can never generate the same tree twice. This follows from the fact that between any two expansions of the same node, the node's parent must increase its f-cost. We will prove this fact by a downward induction on the depth of the node.

        (i) Show that the property holds for any node at depth $d = MAX$.

        (ii) Show that if it holds for all nodes at depth $d + 1$ or more, it must also hold for all nodes at depth d.

5 GAME PLAYING

In which we examine the problems that arise when we try to plan ahead in a world that includes a hostile agent.

5.1 INTRODUCTION: GAMES AS SEARCH PROBLEMS

Games have engaged the intellectual faculties of humans—sometimes to an alarming degree—for as long as civilization has existed. Board games such as chess and Go are interesting in part because they offer pure, abstract competition, without the fuss and bother of mustering up two armies and going to war. It is this abstraction that makes game playing an appealing target of AI research. The state of a game is easy to represent, and agents are usually restricted to a fairly small number of well-defined actions. *That makes game playing an idealization of worlds in which hostile agents act so as to diminish one's well-being.* Less abstract games, such as croquet or football, have not attracted much interest in the AI community.

Game playing is also one of the oldest areas of endeavor in artificial intelligence. In 1950, almost as soon as computers became programmable, the first chess programs were written by Claude Shannon (the inventor of information theory) and by Alan Turing. Since then, there has been steady progress in the standard of play, to the point where current systems can challenge the human world champion without fear of gross embarrassment.

Early researchers chose chess for several reasons. A chess-playing computer would be an existence proof of a machine doing something thought to require intelligence. Furthermore, the simplicity of the rules, and the fact that the world state is fully accessible to the program[1] means that it is easy to represent the game as a search through a space of possible game positions. The computer representation of the game actually can be correct in every relevant detail—unlike the representation of the problem of fighting a war, for example.

---

[1] Recall from Chapter 2 that **accessible** means that the agent can perceive everything there is to know about the environment. In game theory, chess is called a game of **perfect information**.

122

The presence of an opponent makes the decision problem somewhat more complicated than the search problems discussed in Chapter 3. The opponent introduces *uncertainty*, because one never knows what he or she is going to do. In essence, all game-playing programs must deal with the **contingency problem** defined in Chapter 3. The uncertainty is not like that introduced, say, by throwing dice or by the weather. The opponent will try as far as possible to make the least benign move, whereas the dice and the weather are assumed (perhaps wrongly!) to be indifferent to the goals of the agent. This complication is discussed in Section 5.2.

But what makes games *really* different is that they are usually much too hard to solve. Chess, for example, has an average branching factor of about 35, and games often go to 50 moves by each player, so the search tree has about 35^{100} nodes (although there are "only" about 10^{40} *different* legal positions). Tic-Tac-Toe (noughts and crosses) is boring for adults precisely because it is easy to determine the right move. The complexity of games introduces a completely new kind of uncertainty that we have not seen so far; the uncertainty arises not because there is missing information, but because one does not have time to calculate the exact consequences of any move. Instead, one has to make one's best guess based on past experience, and act before one is sure of what action to take. In this respect, *games are much more like the real world than the standard search problems we have looked at so far.*

Because they usually have time limits, games also penalize inefficiency very severely. Whereas an implementation of A* search that is 10% less efficient will simply cost a little bit extra to run to completion, a chess program that is 10% less effective in using its available time probably will be beaten into the ground, other things being equal. Game-playing research has therefore spawned a number of interesting ideas on how to make the best use of time to reach good decisions, when reaching optimal decisions is impossible. These ideas should be kept in mind throughout the rest of the book, because the problems of complexity arise in every area of AI. We will return to them in more detail in Chapter 16.

We begin our discussion by analyzing how to find the theoretically best move. We then look at techniques for choosing a good move when time is limited. **Pruning** allows us to ignore portions of the search tree that make no difference to the final choice, and heuristic **evaluation functions** allow us to approximate the true utility of a state without doing a complete search. Section 5.5 discusses games such as backgammon that include an element of chance. Finally, we look at how state-of-the-art game-playing programs succeed against strong human opposition.

5.2   PERFECT DECISIONS IN TWO-PERSON GAMES

We will consider the general case of a game with two players, whom we will call MAX and MIN, for reasons that will soon become obvious. MAX moves first, and then they take turns moving until the game is over. At the end of the game, points are awarded to the winning player (or sometimes penalties are given to the loser). A game can be formally defined as a kind of search problem with the following components:

- The **initial state**, which includes the board position and an indication of whose move it is.
- A set of **operators**, which define the legal moves that a player can make.

TERMINAL TEST
- A **terminal test**, which determines when the game is over. States where the game has ended are called **terminal states**.

PAYOFF FUNCTION
- A **utility function** (also called a **payoff function**), which gives a numeric value for the outcome of a game. In chess, the outcome is a win, loss, or draw, which we can represent by the values +1, −1, or 0. Some games have a wider variety of possible outcomes; for example, the payoffs in backgammon range from +192 to −192.

If this were a normal search problem, then all MAX would have to do is search for a sequence of moves that leads to a terminal state that is a winner (according to the utility function), and then go ahead and make the first move in the sequence. Unfortunately, MIN has something to say about it. MAX therefore must find a **strategy** that will lead to a winning terminal state regardless of what MIN does, where the strategy includes the correct move for MAX for each possible move by MIN. We will begin by showing how to find the optimal (or rational) strategy, even though normally we will not have enough time to compute it.

STRATEGY

Figure 5.1 shows part of the search tree for the game of Tic-Tac-Toe. From the initial state, MAX has a choice of nine possible moves. Play alternates between MAX placing X's and MIN placing O's until we reach leaf nodes corresponding to terminal states: states where one player has three in a row or all the squares are filled. The number on each leaf node indicates the utility value of the terminal state from the point of view of MAX; high values are assumed to be good for MAX and bad for MIN (which is how the players get their names). It is MAX's job to use the search tree (particularly the utility of terminal states) to determine the best move.

Even a simple game like Tic-Tac-Toe is too complex to show the whole search tree, so we will switch to the absolutely trivial game in Figure 5.2. The possible moves for MAX are labelled A_1, A_2, and A_3. The possible replies to A_1 for MIN are A_{11}, A_{12}, A_{13}, and so on. This particular game ends after one move each by MAX and MIN. (In game parlance, we say this tree is one move deep, consisting of two half-moves or two **ply**.) The utilities of the terminal states in this game range from 2 to 14.

PLY

MINIMAX

The **minimax** algorithm is designed to determine the optimal strategy for MAX, and thus to decide what the best first move is. The algorithm consists of five steps:

- Generate the whole game tree, all the way down to the terminal states.
- Apply the utility function to each terminal state to get its value.
- Use the utility of the terminal states to determine the utility of the nodes one level higher up in the search tree. Consider the leftmost three leaf nodes in Figure 5.2. In the $\bigtriangledown$ node above it, MIN has the option to move, and the best MIN can do is choose A_{11}, which leads to the minimal outcome, 3. Thus, even though the utility function is not immediately applicable to this $\bigtriangledown$ node, we can assign it the utility value 3, under the assumption that MIN will do the right thing. By similar reasoning, the other two $\bigtriangledown$ nodes are assigned the utility value 2.
- Continue backing up the values from the leaf nodes toward the root, one layer at a time.
- Eventually, the backed-up values reach the top of the tree; at that point, MAX chooses the move that leads to the highest value. In the topmost $\bigtriangleup$ node of Figure 5.2, MAX has a choice of three moves that will lead to states with utility 3, 2, and 2, respectively. Thus, MAX's best opening move is A_1. This is called the **minimax decision**, because it maximizes the utility under the assumption that the opponent will play perfectly to minimize it.

MINIMAX DECISION

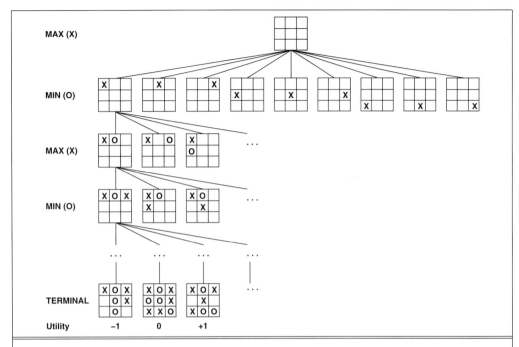

Figure 5.1   A (partial) search tree for the game of Tic-Tac-Toe. The top node is the initial state, and MAX moves first, placing an X in some square. We show part of the search tree, giving alternating moves by MIN (O) and MAX, until we eventually reach terminal states, which can be assigned utilities according to the rules of the game.

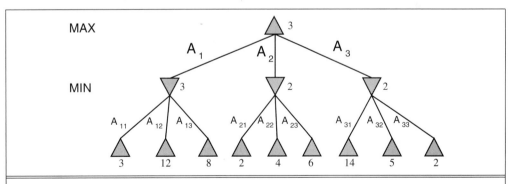

Figure 5.2   A two-ply game tree as generated by the minimax algorithm. The △ nodes are moves by MAX and the ▽ nodes are moves by MIN. The terminal nodes show the utility value for MAX computed by the utility function (i.e., by the rules of the game), whereas the utilities of the other nodes are computed by the minimax algorithm from the utilities of their successors. MAX's best move is A_1, and MIN's best reply is A_{11}.

Figure 5.3 shows a more formal description of the minimax algorithm. The top level function, MINIMAX-DECISION, selects from the available moves, which are evaluated in turn by the MINIMAX-VALUE function.

If the maximum depth of the tree is m, and there are b legal moves at each point, then the time complexity of the minimax algorithm is $O(b^m)$. The algorithm is a depth-first search (although here the implementation is through recursion rather than using a queue of nodes), so its space requirements are only linear in m and b. For real games, of course, the time cost is totally impractical, but this algorithm serves as the basis for more realistic methods and for the mathematical analysis of games.

---

function MINIMAX-DECISION(*game*) **returns** *an operator*

   for each *op* **in** OPERATORS[*game*] **do**
      VALUE[*op*] ← MINIMAX-VALUE(APPLY(*op*, *game*), *game*)
   end
   return the *op* with the highest VALUE[*op*]

---

function MINIMAX-VALUE(*state, game*) **returns** *a utility value*

   if TERMINAL-TEST[*game*](*state*) **then**
      return UTILITY[*game*](*state*)
   else if MAX is to move in *state* **then**
      return the highest MINIMAX-VALUE of SUCCESSORS(*state*)
   else
      return the lowest MINIMAX-VALUE of SUCCESSORS(*state*)

Figure 5.3   An algorithm for calculating minimax decisions. It returns the operator that corresponding to the best possible move, that is, the move that leads to the outcome with the best utility, under the assumption that the opponent plays to minimize utility. The function MINIMAX-VALUE goes through the whole game tree, all the way to the leaves, to determine the backed-up value of a state.

5.3   IMPERFECT DECISIONS

The minimax algorithm assumes that the program has time to search all the way to terminal states, which is usually not practical. Shannon's original paper on chess proposed that instead of going all the way to terminal states and using the utility function, the program should cut off the search earlier and apply a heuristic **evaluation function** to the leaves of the tree. In other words, the suggestion is to alter minimax in two ways: the utility function is replaced by an evaluation function EVAL, and the terminal test is replaced by a cutoff test CUTOFF-TEST.

Evaluation functions

An evaluation function returns an *estimate* of the expected utility of the game from a given position. The idea was not new when Shannon proposed it. For centuries, chess players (and, of course, aficionados of other games) have developed ways of judging the winning chances of each side based on easily calculated features of a position. For example, introductory chess books give an approximate **material value** for each piece: each pawn is worth 1, a knight or bishop is worth 3, a rook 5, and the queen 9. Other features such as "good pawn structure" and "king safety" might be worth half a pawn, say. All other things being equal, a side that has a secure material advantage of a pawn or more will probably win the game, and a 3-point advantage is sufficient for near-certain victory. Figure 5.4 shows four positions with their evaluations.

MATERIAL VALUE

It should be clear that the performance of a game-playing program is extremely dependent on the quality of its evaluation function. If it is inaccurate, then it will guide the program toward positions that are apparently "good," but in fact disastrous. How exactly do we measure quality?

First, the evaluation function must agree with the utility function on terminal states. Second, it must not take too long! (As mentioned in Chapter 4, if we did not limit its complexity, then it could call minimax as a subroutine and calculate the exact value of the position.) Hence, there is a trade-off between the accuracy of the evaluation function and its time cost. Third, an evaluation function should accurately reflect the actual chances of winning.

One might well wonder about the phrase "chances of winning." After all, chess is not a game of chance. But if we have cut off the search at a particular nonterminal state, then we do not know what will happen in subsequent moves. For concreteness, assume the evaluation function counts only material value. Then, in the opening position, the evaluation is 0, because both sides have the same material. All the positions up to the first capture will also have an evaluation of 0. If MAX manages to capture a bishop without losing a piece, then the resulting position will have an evaluation value of 3. The important point is that a given evaluation value covers many different positions—all the positions where MAX is up by a bishop are grouped together into a *category* that is given the label "3." Now we can see how the word "chance" makes sense: the evaluation function should reflect the chance that a position chosen at random from such a category leads to a win (or draw or loss), based on previous experience.[2]

This suggests that the evaluation function should be specified by the rules of probability: if position A has a 100% chance of winning, it should have the evaluation 1.00, and if position B has a 50% chance of winning, 25% of losing, and 25% of being a draw, its evaluation should be $+1 \times .50 + -1 \times .25 + 0 \times .25 = .25$. But in fact, we need not be this precise; the actual numeric values of the evaluation function are not important, as long as A is rated higher than B.

The material advantage evaluation function assumes that the value of a piece can be judged independently of the other pieces present on the board. This kind of evaluation function is called a **weighted linear function**, because it can be expressed as

$$w_1f_1 + w_2f_2 + \cdots + w_nf_n$$

where the w's are the weights, and the f's are the features of the particular position. The w's would be the values of the pieces (1 for pawn, 3 for bishop, etc.), and the f's would be the numbers

---

[2] Techniques for automatically constructing evaluation functions with this property are discussed in Chapter 18. In assessing the value of a category, more normally occurring positions should be given more weight.

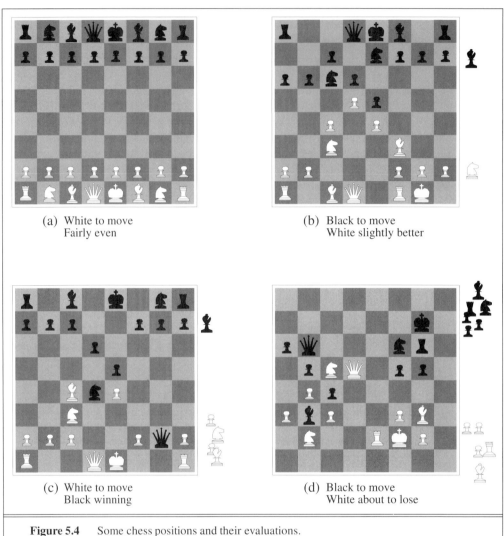

(a) White to move
     Fairly even

(b) Black to move
     White slightly better

(c) White to move
     Black winning

(d) Black to move
     White about to lose

Figure 5.4   Some chess positions and their evaluations.

of each kind of piece on the board. Now we can see where the particular piece values come from:
they give the best approximation to the likelihood of winning in the individual categories.

Most game-playing programs use a linear evaluation function, although recently nonlinear
functions have had a good deal of success. (Chapter 19 gives an example of a neural network that
is trained to learn a nonlinear evaluation function for backgammon.) In constructing the linear
formula, one has to first pick the features, and then adjust the weights until the program plays
well. The latter task can be automated by having the program play lots of games against itself,
but at the moment, no one has a good idea of how to pick good features automatically.

Cutting off search

The most straightforward approach to controlling the amount of search is to set a fixed depth limit, so that the cutoff test succeeds for all nodes at or below depth d. The depth is chosen so that the amount of time used will not exceed what the rules of the game allow. A slightly more robust approach is to apply iterative deepening, as defined in Chapter 3. When time runs out, the program returns the move selected by the deepest completed search.

These approaches can have some disastrous consequences because of the approximate nature of the evaluation function. Consider again the simple evaluation function for chess based on material advantage. Suppose the program searches to the depth limit, reaching the position shown in Figure 5.4(d). According to the material function, white is ahead by a knight and therefore almost certain to win. However, because it is black's move, white's queen is lost because the black knight can capture it without any recompense for white. Thus, in reality the position is won for black, but this can only be seen by looking ahead one more ply.

QUIESCENT

QUIESCENCE
SEARCH

HORIZON PROBLEM

Obviously, a more sophisticated cutoff test is needed. The evaluation function should only be applied to positions that are **quiescent**, that is, unlikely to exhibit wild swings in value in the near future. In chess, for example, positions in which favorable captures can be made are not quiescent for an evaluation function that just counts material. Nonquiescent positions can be expanded further until quiescent positions are reached. This extra search is called a **quiescence search**; sometimes it is restricted to consider only certain types of moves, such as capture moves, that will quickly resolve the uncertainties in the position.

The **horizon problem** is more difficult to eliminate. It arises when the program is facing a move by the opponent that causes serious damage and is ultimately unavoidable. Consider the chess game in Figure 5.5. Black is slightly ahead in material, but if white can advance its pawn from the seventh row to the eighth, it will become a queen and be an easy win for white. Black can forestall this for a dozen or so ply by checking white with the rook, but inevitably the pawn will become a queen. The problem with fixed-depth search is that it believes that these stalling moves have avoided the queening move—we say that the stalling moves push the inevitable queening move "over the horizon" to a place where it cannot be detected. At present, no general solution has been found for the horizon problem.

5.4   ALPHA-BETA PRUNING

Let us assume we have implemented a minimax search with a reasonable evaluation function for chess, and a reasonable cutoff test with a quiescence search. With a well-written program on an ordinary computer, one can probably search about 1000 positions a second. How well will our program play? In tournament chess, one gets about 150 seconds per move, so we can look at 150,000 positions. In chess, the branching factor is about 35, so our program will be able to look ahead only three or four ply, and will play at the level of a complete novice! Even average human players can make plans six or eight ply ahead, so our program will be easily fooled.

Fortunately, it is possible to compute the correct minimax decision without looking at every node in the search tree. The process of eliminating a branch of the search tree from consideration

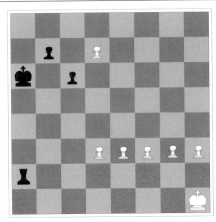

Black to move

Figure 5.5   The horizon problem. A series of checks by the black rook forces the inevitable queening move by white "over the horizon" and makes this position look like a slight advantage for black, when it is really a sure win for white.

PRUNING
ALPHA-BETA
PRUNING

without examining it is called **pruning** the search tree. The particular technique we will examine is called **alpha-beta pruning**. When applied to a standard minimax tree, it returns the same move as minimax would, but prunes away branches that cannot possibly influence the final decision.

Consider the two-ply game tree from Figure 5.2, shown again in Figure 5.6. The search proceeds as before: A_1, then A_{11}, A_{12}, A_{13}, and the node under A_1 gets minimax value 3. Now we follow A_2, and A_{21}, which has value 2. At this point, we realize that if MAX plays A_2, MIN has the option of reaching a position worth 2, and some other options besides. Therefore, we can say already that move A_2 is worth *at most 2* to MAX. Because we already know that move A_1 is worth 3, there is no point at looking further under A_2. In other words, we can prune the search tree at this point and be confident that the pruning will have no effect on the outcome.

The general principle is this. Consider a node n somewhere in the tree (see Figure 5.7), such that Player has a choice of moving to that node. If Player has a better choice m either at the parent node of n, or at any choice point further up, then n *will never be reached in actual play*. So once we have found out enough about n (by examining some of its descendants) to reach this conclusion, we can prune it.

Remember that minimax search is depth-first, so at any one time we just have to consider the nodes along a single path in the tree. Let α be the value of the best choice we have found so far at any choice point along the path for MAX, and β be the value of the best (i.e., lowest-value) choice we have found so far at any choice point along the path for MIN. Alpha-beta search updates the value of α and β as it goes along, and prunes a subtree (i.e., terminates the recursive call) as soon as it is known to be worse than the current α or β value.

The algorithm description in Figure 5.8 is divided into a MAX-VALUE function and a MIN-VALUE function. These apply to MAX nodes and MIN nodes, respectively, but each does the same thing: return the minimax value of the node, except for nodes that are to be pruned (in

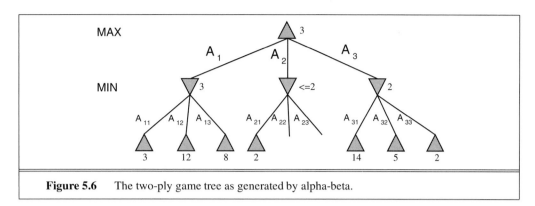

Figure 5.6   The two-ply game tree as generated by alpha-beta.

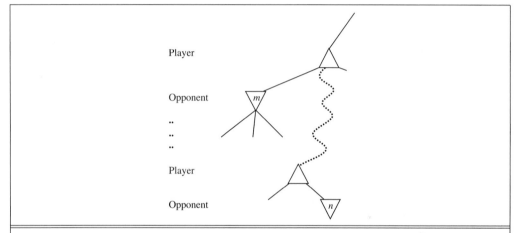

Figure 5.7   Alpha-beta pruning: the general case. If m is better than n for Player, we will never get to n in play.

which case the returned value is ignored anyway). The alpha-beta search function itself is just a copy of the MAX-VALUE function with extra code to remember and return the best move found.

Effectiveness of alpha-beta pruning

The effectiveness of alpha-beta depends on the ordering in which the successors are examined. This is clear from Figure 5.6, where we could not prune A_3 at all because A_{31} and A_{32} (the worst moves from the point of view of MIN) were generated first. This suggests it might be worthwhile to try to examine first the successors that are likely to be best.

If we assume that this can be done,[3] then it turns out that alpha-beta only needs to examine $O(b^{d/2})$ nodes to pick the best move, instead of $O(b^d)$ with minimax. This means that the effective branching factor is $\sqrt{b}$ instead of b—for chess, 6 instead of 35. Put another way, this means

[3] Obviously, it cannot be done perfectly, otherwise the ordering function could be used to play a perfect game!

---

function MAX-VALUE(*state, game,* α, β) **returns** the minimax value of *state*
   inputs: *state*, current state in game
          game, game description
          α, the best score for MAX along the path to *state*
          β, the best score for MIN along the path to *state*

   if CUTOFF-TEST(*state*) **then return** EVAL(*state*)
   for each *s* **in** SUCCESSORS(*state*) **do**
      $\alpha \leftarrow$ MAX(α, MIN-VALUE(*s, game,* α, β))
      if $\alpha \geq \beta$ **then return** β
   end
   return α

---

function MIN-VALUE(*state, game,* α, β) **returns** the minimax value of *state*

   if CUTOFF-TEST(*state*) **then return** EVAL(*state*)
   for each *s* **in** SUCCESSORS(*state*) **do**
      $\beta \leftarrow$ MIN(β, MAX-VALUE(*s, game,* α, β))
      if $\beta \leq \alpha$ **then return** α
   end
   return β

Figure 5.8   The alpha-beta search algorithm.   It does the same computation as a normal minimax, but prunes the search tree.

that alpha-beta can look ahead twice as far as minimax for the same cost. Thus, by generating 150,000 nodes in the time allotment, a program can look ahead eight ply instead of four. By thinking carefully about *which computations actually affect the decision*, we are able to transform a program from a novice into an expert.

The effectiveness of alpha-beta pruning was first analyzed in depth by Knuth and Moore (1975). As well as the best case described in the previous paragraph, they analyzed the case in which successors are ordered randomly. It turns out that the asymptotic complexity is $O((b/\log b)^d)$, which seems rather dismal because the effective branching factor $b/\log b$ is not much less than b itself. On the other hand, the asymptotic formula is only accurate for $b > 1000$ or so—in other words, not for any games we can reasonably play using these techniques. For reasonable b, the total number of nodes examined will be roughly $O(b^{3d/4})$. In practice, a fairly simple ordering function (such as trying captures first, then threats, then forward moves, then backward moves) gets you fairly close to the best-case result rather than the random result. Another popular approach is to do an iterative deepening search, and use the backed-up values from one iteration to determine the ordering of successors in the next iteration.

It is also worth noting that all complexity results on games (and, in fact, on search problems in general) have to assume an idealized **tree model** in order to obtain their results. For example, the model used for the alpha-beta result in the previous paragraph assumes that all nodes have the same branching factor b; that all paths reach the fixed depth limit d; and that the leaf evaluations

TREE MODEL

are randomly distributed across the last layer of the tree. This last assumption is seriously flawed: for example, if a move higher up the tree is a disastrous blunder, then most of its descendants will look bad for the player who made the blunder. The value of a node is therefore likely to be highly correlated with the values of its siblings. The amount of correlation depends very much on the particular game and indeed the particular position at the root. Hence, there is an unavoidable component of *empirical science* involved in game-playing research, eluding the power of mathematical analysis.

5.5   GAMES THAT INCLUDE AN ELEMENT OF CHANCE

In real life, unlike chess, there are many unpredictable external events that put us into unforeseen situations. Many games mirror this unpredictability by including a random element such as throwing dice. In this way, they take us a step nearer reality, and it is worthwhile to see how this affects the decision-making process.

Backgammon is a typical game that combines luck and skill. Dice are rolled at the beginning of a player's turn to determine the set of legal moves that is available to the player. In the backgammon position of Figure 5.9, white has rolled a 6-5, and has four possible moves.

Although white knows what his or her own legal moves are, white does not know what black is going to roll, and thus does not know what black's legal moves will be. That means white cannot construct a complete game tree of the sort we saw in chess and Tic-Tac-Toe. A game tree in backgammon must include **chance nodes** in addition to MAX and MIN nodes. Chance nodes are shown as circles in Figure 5.10. The branches leading from each chance node denote the possible dice rolls, and each is labelled with the roll and the chance that it will occur. There are 36 ways to roll two dice, each equally likely; but because a 6-5 is the same as a 5-6, there are only 21 distinct rolls. The six doubles (1-1 through 6-6) have a 1/36 chance of coming up, the other fifteen distinct rolls a 1/18 chance.

CHANCE NODES

The next step is to understand how to make correct decisions. Obviously, we still want to pick the move from $A_1, \ldots, A_n$ that leads to the best position. However, each of the possible positions no longer has a definite minimax value (which in deterministic games was the utility of the leaf reached by best play). Instead, we can only calculate an average or **expected value**, where the average is taken over all the possible dice rolls that could occur.

EXPECTED VALUE

It is straightforward to calculate expected values of nodes. For terminal nodes, we use the utility function, just like in deterministic games. Going one step up in the search tree, we hit a chance node. In Figure 5.10, the chance nodes are circles; we will consider the one labelled C. Let d_i be a possible dice roll, and $P(d_i)$ be the chance or probability of obtaining that roll. For each dice roll, we calculate the utility of the best move for MIN, and then add up the utilities, weighted by the chance that the particular dice roll is obtained. If we let $S(C, d_i)$ denote the set of positions generated by applying the legal moves for dice roll $P(d_i)$ to the position at C, then we can calculate the so-called **expectimax value** of C using the formula

EXPECTIMAX VALUE

$$expectimax(C) = \sum_i P(d_i) \max_{s \in S(C,d_i)}(utility(s))$$

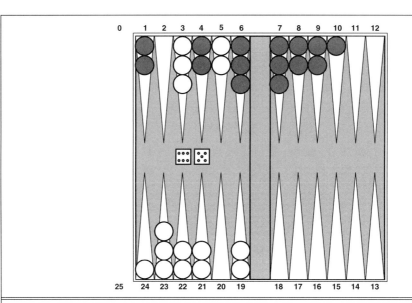

Figure 5.9   A typical backgammon position. The aim of the game is to move all one's pieces off the board. White moves clockwise toward 25, and black moves counterclockwise toward 0. A piece can move to any position except one where there are two or more of the opponent's pieces. If it moves to a position with one opponent piece, that piece is captured and has to start its journey again from the beginning. In this position, white has just rolled 6-5 and has four legal moves: (5-10,5-11), (5-11,19-24), (5-10,10-16), and (5-11,11-16).

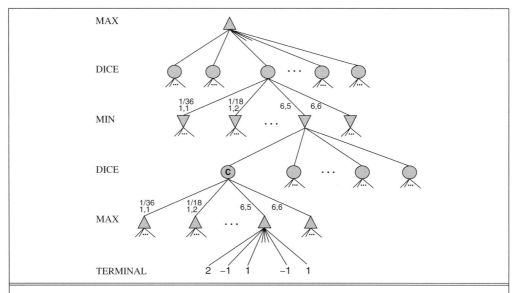

Figure 5.10   Schematic game tree for a backgammon position.

This gives us the expected utility of the position at C assuming best play. Going up one more level to the MIN nodes ($\bigtriangledown$ in Figure 5.10), we can now apply the normal minimax-value formula, because we have assigned utility values to all the chance nodes. We then move up to chance node B, where we can compute the **expectimin value** using a formula that is analogous to expectimax.

EXPECTIMIN VALUE

This process can be applied recursively all the way up the tree, except at the top level where the dice roll is already known. To calculate the best move, then, we simply replace MINIMAX-VALUE in Figure 5.3 by EXPECTIMINIMAX-VALUE, the implementation of which we leave as an exercise.

Position evaluation in games with chance nodes

As with minimax, the obvious approximation to make with expectiminimax is to cut off search at some point and apply an evaluation function to the leaves. One might think that evaluation functions for games such as backgammon are no different, in principle, from evaluation functions for chess—they should just give higher scores to better positions.

In fact, the presence of chance nodes means one has to be more careful about what the evaluation values mean. Remember that for minimax, any order-preserving transformation of the leaf values does not affect the choice of move. Thus, we can use either the values 1, 2, 3, 4 or the values 1, 20, 30, 400, and get the same decision. This gives us a good deal of freedom in designing the evaluation function: it will work fine as long as positions with higher evaluations lead to wins more often, on average.

With chance nodes, we lose this freedom. Figure 5.11 shows what happens: with leaf values 1, 2, 3, 4, move A_1 is best; with leaf values 1, 20, 30, 400, move A_2 is best. Hence, the program behaves totally differently if we make a change in the scale of evaluation values! It turns out that to avoid this sensitivity, the evaluation function can be only a *positive linear* transformation of the likelihood of winning from a position (or, more generally, of the expected utility of the position). This is an important and general property of situations in which uncertainty is involved, and we discuss it further in Chapter 16.

Complexity of expectiminimax

If the program knew in advance all the dice rolls that would occur for the rest of the game, solving a game with dice would be just like solving a game without dice, which minimax does in $O(b^m)$ time. Because expectiminimax is also considering all the possible dice-roll sequences, it will take $O(b^m n^m)$, where n is the number of distinct rolls.

Even if the depth of the tree is limited to some small depth d, the extra cost compared to minimax makes it unrealistic to consider looking ahead very far in games such as backgammon, where n is 21 and b is usually around 20, but in some situations can be as high as 4000. Two ply is probably all we could manage.

Another way to think about the problem is this: the advantage of alpha-beta is that it ignores future developments that just are not going to happen, given best play. Thus, it concentrates on likely occurrences. In games with dice, there are *no* likely sequences of moves, because for those moves to take place, the dice would first have to come out the right way to make them legal.

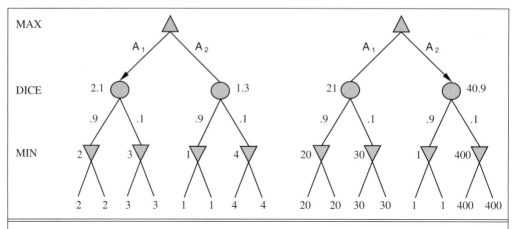

Figure 5.11   An order-preserving transformation on leaf values changes the best move.

This is a general problem whenever uncertainty enters the picture: the possibilities are multiplied enormously, and forming detailed plans of action becomes pointless because the world probably will not play along.

No doubt it will have occurred to the reader that perhaps something like alpha-beta pruning could be applied to game trees with chance nodes. It turns out that it can, with a bit of ingenuity. Consider the chance node C in Figure 5.10, and what happens to its value as we examine and evaluate its children; the question is, is it possible to find an upper bound on the value of C before we have looked at all its children? (Recall that this is what alpha-beta needs in order to prune a node and its subtree.) At first sight, it might seem impossible, because the value of C is the *average* of its children's values, and until we have looked at all the dice rolls, this average could be anything, because the unexamined children might have any value at all. But if we put boundaries on the possible values of the utility function, then we can arrive at boundaries for the average. For example, if we say that all utility values are between +1 and −1, then the value of leaf nodes is bounded, and in turn we *can* place an upper bound on the value of a chance node without looking at all its children. Designing the pruning process is a little bit more complicated than for alpha-beta, and we leave it as an exercise.

5.6   STATE-OF-THE-ART GAME PROGRAMS

Designing game-playing programs has a dual purpose: both to better understand how to choose actions in complex domains with uncertain outcomes and to develop high-performance systems for the particular game studied. In this section, we examine progress toward the latter goal.

Chess

Chess has received by far the largest share of attention in game playing. Although not meeting the promise made by Simon in 1957 that within 10 years, computers would beat the human world champion, they are now within reach of that goal. In speed chess, computers have defeated the world champion, Gary Kasparov, in both 5-minute and 25-minute games, but in full tournament games are only ranked among the top 100 players worldwide at the time of writing. Figure 5.12 shows the ratings of human and computer champions over the years. It is tempting to try to extrapolate and see where the lines will cross.

Progress beyond a mediocre level was initially very slow: some programs in the early 1970s became extremely complicated, with various kinds of tricks for eliminating some branches of search, generating plausible moves, and so on, but the programs that won the ACM North American Computer Chess Championships (initiated in 1970) tended to use straightforward alpha-beta search, augmented with book openings and infallible endgame algorithms. (This offers an interesting example of how high performance requires a hybrid decision-making architecture to implement the agent function.)

The first real jump in performance came not from better algorithms or evaluation functions, but from hardware. Belle, the first special-purpose chess computer (Condon and Thompson, 1982), used custom integrated circuits to implement move generation and position evaluation, enabling it to search several million positions to make a single move. Belle's rating was around 2250, on a scale where beginning humans are 1000 and the world champion around 2750; it became the first master-level program.

The HITECH system, also a special-purpose computer, was designed by former world correspondence champion Hans Berliner and his student Carl Ebeling to allow rapid calculation of very sophisticated evaluation functions. Generating about 10 million positions per move and using probably the most accurate evaluation of positions yet developed, HITECH became

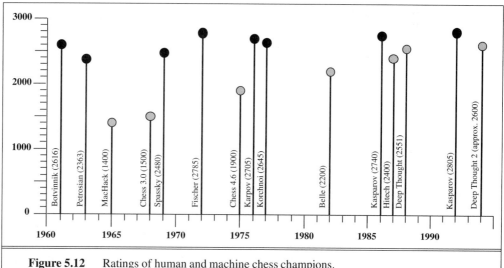

Figure 5.12   Ratings of human and machine chess champions.

computer world champion in 1985, and was the first program to defeat a human grandmaster, Arnold Denker, in 1987. At the time it ranked among the top 800 human players in the world.

The best current system is Deep Thought 2. It is sponsored by IBM, which hired part of the team that built the Deep Thought system at Carnegie Mellon University. Although Deep Thought 2 uses a simple evaluation function, it examines about half a billion positions per move, allowing it to reach depth 10 or 11, with a special provision to follow lines of forced moves still further (it once found a 37-move checkmate). In February 1993, Deep Thought 2 competed against the Danish Olympic team and won, 3–1, beating one grandmaster and drawing against another. Its FIDE rating is around 2600, placing it among the top 100 human players.

The next version of the system, Deep Blue, will use a parallel array of 1024 custom VLSI chips. This will enable it to search the equivalent of one billion positions per second (100–200 billion per move) and to reach depth 14. A 10-processor version is due to play the Israeli national team (one of the strongest in the world) in May 1995, and the full-scale system will challenge the world champion shortly thereafter.

Checkers or Draughts

Beginning in 1952, Arthur Samuel of IBM, working in his spare time, developed a checkers program that learned its own evaluation function by playing itself thousands of times. We describe this idea in more detail in Chapter 20. Samuel's program began as a novice, but after only a few days' self-play was able to compete on equal terms in some very strong human tournaments. When one considers that Samuel's computing equipment (an IBM 704) had 10,000 words of main memory, magnetic tape for long-term storage, and a cycle time of almost a millisecond, this remains one of the great feats of AI.

Few other people attempted to do better until Jonathan Schaeffer and colleagues developed Chinook, which runs on ordinary computers using alpha-beta search, but uses several techniques, including perfect solution databases for all six-piece positions, that make its endgame play devastating. Chinook won the 1992 U.S. Open, and became the first program to officially challenge for a real world championship. It then ran up against a problem, in the form of Marion Tinsley. Dr. Tinsley had been world champion for over 40 years, losing only three games in all that time. In the first match against Chinook, Tinsley suffered his fourth and fifth losses, but won the match 21.5–18.5. More recently, the world championship match in August 1994 between Tinsley and Chinook ended prematurely when Tinsley had to withdraw for health reasons. Chinook became the official world champion.

Othello

Othello, also called Reversi, is probably more popular as a computer game than as a board game. It has a smaller search space than chess, usually 5 to 15 legal moves, but evaluation expertise had to be developed from scratch. Even so, Othello programs on normal computers are far better than humans, who generally refuse direct challenges in tournaments.

Backgammon

As mentioned before, the inclusion of uncertainty from dice rolls makes search an expensive luxury in backgammon. The first program to make a serious impact, BKG, used only a one-ply search but a very complicated evaluation function. In an informal match in 1980, it defeated the human world champion 5–1, but was quite lucky with the dice. Generally, it plays at a strong amateur level.

More recently, Gerry Tesauro (1992) combined Samuel's learning method with neural network techniques (Chapter 19) to develop a new evaluation function. His program is reliably ranked among the top three players in the world.

Go

Go is the most popular board game in Japan, requiring at least as much discipline from its professionals as chess. The branching factor approaches 360, so that regular search methods are totally lost. Systems based on large knowledge bases of rules for suggesting plausible moves seem to have some hope, but still play very poorly. Particularly given the $2,000,000 prize for the first program to defeat a top-level player, Go seems like an area likely to benefit from intensive investigation using more sophisticated reasoning methods.

5.7   DISCUSSION

Because calculating optimal decisions in games is intractable in most cases, all algorithms must make some assumptions and approximations. The standard approach, based on minimax, evaluation functions, and alpha-beta, is just one way to do this. Probably because it was proposed so early on, it has been developed intensively and dominates other methods in tournament play. Some in the field believe that this has caused game playing to become divorced from the mainstream of AI research, because the standard approach no longer provides much room for new insight into general questions of decision making. In this section, we look at the alternatives, considering how to relax the assumptions and perhaps derive new insights.

First, let us consider minimax. Minimax is an optimal method for selecting a move from a given search tree *provided the leaf node evaluations are exactly correct*. In reality, evaluations are usually crude estimates of the value of a position, and can be considered to have large errors associated with them. Figure 5.13 shows a two-ply game tree for which minimax seems inappropriate. Minimax suggests taking the right-hand branch, whereas it is quite likely that true value of the left-hand branch is higher. The minimax choice relies on the assumption that *all* of the nodes labelled with values 100, 101, 102, and 100 are *actually* better than the node labelled with value 99. One way to deal with this problem is to have an evaluation that returns a *probability distribution* over possible values. Then one can calculate the probability distribution for the parent's value using standard statistical techniques. Unfortunately, the values of sibling nodes are usually highly correlated, so this can be an expensive calculation and may require detailed correlation information that is hard to obtain.

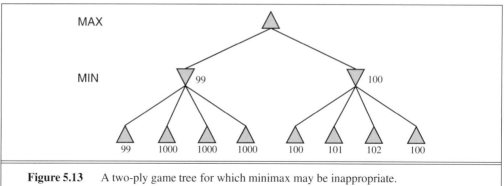

Figure 5.13   A two-ply game tree for which minimax may be inappropriate.

Next, we consider the search algorithm that generates the tree. The aim of an algorithm designer is to specify a computation that completes in a timely manner and results in a good move choice. The most obvious problem with the alpha-beta algorithm is that it is designed not just to select a good move, but also to calculate the values of all the legal moves. To see why this extra information is unnecessary, consider a position in which there is only one legal move. Alpha-beta search still will generate and evaluate a large, and totally useless, search tree. Of course, we can insert a test into the algorithm, but this merely hides the underlying problem—many of the calculations done by alpha-beta are largely irrelevant. Having only one legal move is not much different from having several legal moves, one of which is fine and the rest of which are obviously disastrous. In a "clear-favorite" situation like this, it would be better to reach a quick decision after a small amount of search than to waste time that could be better used later for a more problematic position. This leads to the idea of the *utility of a node expansion*. A good search algorithm should select node expansions of high utility—that is, ones that are likely to lead to the discovery of a significantly better move. If there are no node expansions whose utility is higher than their cost (in terms of time), then the algorithm should stop searching and make a move. Notice that this works not only for clear-favorite situations, but also for the case of *symmetrical* moves, where no amount of search will show that one move is better than another.

METAREASONING   This kind of reasoning about what computations to do is called **metareasoning** (reasoning about reasoning). It applies not just to game playing, but to any kind of reasoning at all. All computations are done in the service of trying to reach better decisions, all have costs, and all have some likelihood of resulting in a certain improvement in decision quality. Alpha-beta incorporates the simplest kind of metareasoning, namely, a theorem to the effect that certain branches of the tree can be ignored without loss. It is possible to do much better. In Chapter 16, we will see how these ideas can be made precise and implementable.

Finally, let us reexamine the nature of search itself. Algorithms for heuristic search and for game playing work by generating sequences of concrete states starting from the initial state and then applying an evaluation function. Clearly, this is not how humans play games. In chess, one often has a particular goal in mind—for example, trapping the opponent's queen—and can use this to *selectively* generate plausible plans for achieving it. This kind of **goal-directed reasoning** or **planning** sometimes eliminates combinatorial search altogether (see Part IV). David Wilkins' (1980) PARADISE is the only program to have used goal-directed reasoning successfully in chess: it was capable of solving some chess problems requiring an 18-move combination. As yet, however, there is no good understanding of how to *combine* the two kinds of algorithm into a robust and efficient system. Such a system would be a significant achievement not just for game-playing research, but also for AI research in general, because it would be much more likely to apply to the problem faced by a general intelligent agent.

5.8   SUMMARY

Games are fascinating, and writing game-playing programs perhaps even more so. We might say that game playing is to AI as Grand Prix motor racing is to the car industry: although the specialized task and extreme competitive pressure lead one to design systems that do not look much like your garden-variety, general-purpose intelligent system, a lot of leading-edge concepts and engineering ideas come out of it. On the other hand, just as you would not expect a Grand Prix racing car to perform well on a bumpy dirt road, you should not expect advances in game playing to translate immediately into advances in less abstract domains.

The most important ideas are as follows:

- A game can be defined by the initial state (how the board is set up), the operators (which define the legal moves), a terminal test (which says when the game is over), and a utility or payoff function (which says who won, and by how much).
- In two-player games with perfect information, the **minimax** algorithm can determine the best move for a player (assuming the opponent plays perfectly) by enumerating the entire game tree.
- The **alpha-beta** algorithm does the same calculation as minimax, but is more efficient because it prunes away branches of the search tree that it can prove are irrelevant to the final outcome.
- Usually, it is not feasible to consider the whole game tree (even with alpha-beta), so we need to cut off the search at some point and apply an evaluation function that gives an estimate of the utility of a state.
- Games of chance can be handled by an extension to the minimax algorithm that evaluates chance nodes by taking the average utility of all its children nodes, weighted by the probability of the child.

BIBLIOGRAPHICAL AND HISTORICAL NOTES

The early history of mechanical game playing was marred by numerous frauds. The most notorious of these was Baron Wolfgang von Kempelen's "Turk," exhibited in 1769, a supposed chess-playing automaton whose cabinet actually concealed a diminutive human chess expert during play. The Turk is described in Harkness and Battell (1947). In 1846, Charles Babbage appears to have contributed the first serious discussion of the feasibility of computer game playing

(Morrison and Morrison, 1961). He believed that if his most ambitious design for a mechanical digital computer, the Analytical Engine, were ever completed, it could be programmed to play checkers and chess. He also designed, but did not build, a special-purpose machine for playing Tic-Tac-Toe. Ernst Zermelo, the designer of modern axiomatic set theory, later speculated on the rather quixotic possibility of searching the entire game tree for chess in order to determine a perfect strategy (Zermelo, 1976). The first functioning (and nonfraudulent) game-playing machine was designed and built around 1890 by the Spanish engineer Leonardo Torrès y Quevedo. It specialized in the "KRK" chess endgame (king and rook vs. king), playing the side with the king and rook against a human opponent attempting to defend with the lone king. Its play was correct and it was capable of forcing mate from any starting position (with the machine moving first). The "Nimotron" (Condon *et al.*, 1940) demonstrated perfect play for the very simple game of Nim. Significantly, a completely optimal strategy for Nim and an adequate strategy for the KRK chess endgame (i.e., one which will always win when given the first move, although not necessarily in the minimal number of moves) are both simple enough to be memorized and executed algorithmically by humans.

Torrès y Quevedo's achievement, and even Babbage's and Zermelo's speculations, remained relatively isolated until the mid-1940s—the era when programmable electronic digital computers were first being developed. The comprehensive theoretical analysis of game strategy in *Theory of Games and Economic Behavior* (Von Neumann and Morgenstern, 1944) placed emphasis on minimaxing (without any depth cutoff) as a way to define mathematically the game-theoretic value of a position in a game. Konrad Zuse (1945), the first person to design a programmable computer, developed ideas as to how mechanical chess play might be accomplished. Adriaan de Groot (1946) carried out in-depth psychological analysis of human chess strategy, which was useful to designers of computer chess programs. Norbert Wiener's (1948) book *Cybernetics* included a brief sketch of the functioning of a possible computer chess-playing program, including the idea of using minimax search with a depth cutoff and an evaluation function to select a move. Claude Shannon (1950) wrote a highly influential article that laid out the basic principles underlying modern computer game-playing programs, although the article did not actually include a program of his own. Shannon described minimaxing with a depth cutoff and evaluation function more clearly and in more detail than had Wiener, and introduced the notion of quiescence of a position. Shannon also described the possibility of using nonexhaustive ("type B") as opposed to exhaustive ("type A") minimaxing. Slater (1950) and the commentators on his article in the same volume also explored the possibilities for computer chess play. In particular, Good (1950) developed the notion of quiescence independently of Shannon.

In 1951, Alan Turing wrote the first actual computer program capable of playing a full game of chess. (The program was published in Turing (1953).) But Turing's program never actually ran on a computer; it was tested by hand simulation against a very weak human player, who defeated it. Meanwhile D. G. Prinz (1952) had written, and actually run, a program that solved chess problems, although it did not play a full game.

Checkers, rather than chess, was the first of the classic games for which a program actually running on a computer was capable of playing out a full game. Christopher Strachey (1952) was the first to publish such research, although Slagle (1971) mentions a checkers program written by Arthur Samuel as early as 1947. Chinook, the checkers program that recently took over the world title from Marion Tinsley, is described by Schaeffer et al. (1992).

A group working at Los Alamos (Kister *et al.*, 1957) designed and ran a program that played a full game of a variant of chess using a 6×6 board. Alex Bernstein wrote the first program to play a full game of standard chess (Bernstein and Roberts, 1958; Bernstein *et al.*, 1958), unless possibly this feat was accomplished by the Russian BESM program mentioned in Newell *et al.* (1958), about which little information is available.

John McCarthy conceived the idea of alpha-beta search in 1956, although he did not publish it. The NSS chess program (Newell *et al.*, 1958) used a simplified version of alpha-beta; it was the first chess program to do so. According to Nilsson (1971), Arthur Samuel's checkers program (Samuel, 1959; Samuel, 1967) also used alpha-beta, although Samuel did not mention it in the published reports on the system. Papers describing alpha-beta were published in the early 1960s (Hart and Edwards, 1961; Brudno, 1963; Slagle, 1963b). An implementation of full alpha-beta is described by Slagle and Dixon (1969) in a program for playing the game of kalah. Alpha-beta was also used by the "Kotok-McCarthy" chess program written by a student of John McCarthy (Kotok, 1962) and by the MacHack 6 chess program (Greenblatt *et al.*, 1967). MacHack 6 was the first chess program to compete successfully with humans, although it fell considerably short of Herb Simon's prediction in 1957 that a computer program would be world chess champion within 10 years (Simon and Newell, 1958). Knuth and Moore (1975) provide a history of alpha-beta, along with a proof of its correctness and a time complexity analysis. Further analysis of the effective branching factor and time complexity of alpha-beta is given by Pearl (1982b). Pearl shows alpha-beta to be asymptotically optimal among all game-searching algorithms.

It would be a mistake to infer that alpha-beta's asymptotic optimality has completely suppressed interest in other game-searching algorithms. The best-known alternatives are probably the B* algorithm (Berliner, 1979), which attempts to maintain interval bounds on the possible value of a node in the game tree, rather than giving it a single point-valued estimate as minimax and alpha-beta do, and SSS* (Stockman, 1979), which dominates alpha-beta in the sense that the set of nodes in the tree that it examines is a (sometimes proper) subset of those examined by alpha-beta. Palay (1985) uses probability distributions in place of the point values of alpha-beta or the intervals of B*. David McAllester's (1988) conspiracy number search is an interesting generalization of alpha-beta. MGSS* (Russell and Wefald, 1989) uses the advanced decision-theoretic techniques of Chapter 16 to decide which nodes to examine next, and was able to outplay an alpha-beta algorithm at Othello despite searching an order of magnitude fewer nodes. Individual games are subject to ad hoc mathematical analysis; a fascinating study of a huge number of games is given by Berlekamp et al. (1982).

D. F. Beal (1980) and Dana Nau (1980; 1983) independently and simultaneously showed that under certain assumptions about the game being analyzed, any form of minimaxing, including alpha-beta, using an evaluation function, yields estimates that are actually *less* reliable than the direct use of the evaluation function, without any search at all! *Heuristics* (Pearl, 1984) gives a thorough analysis of alpha-beta and describes B*, SSS*, and other alternative game search algorithms. It also explores the reasons for the Beal/Nau paradox, and why it does not apply to chess and other games commonly approached via automated game-tree search. Pearl also describes AND/OR graphs (Slagle, 1963a), which generalize game-tree search but can be applied to other types of problems as well, and the AO* algorithm (Martelli and Montanari, 1973; Martelli and Montanari, 1978) for searching them. Kaindl (1990) gives another survey of sophisticated search algorithms.

The first two computer chess programs to play a match against each other were the Kotok-McCarthy program and the "ITEP" program written at Moscow's Institute of Theoretical and Experimental Physics (Adelson-Velsky et al., 1970). This intercontinental match was played by telegraph. It ended in 1967 with a 3–1 victory for the ITEP program. The first ACM North American Computer Chess Championship tournament was held in New York City in 1970. The first World Computer Chess Championship was held in 1974 in Stockholm (Hayes and Levy, 1976). It was won by Kaissa (Adelson-Velsky et al., 1975), another program from ITEP.

A later version of Greenblatt's MacHack 6 was the first chess program to run on custom hardware designed specifically for chess (Moussouris et al., 1979), but the first program to achieve notable success through the use of custom hardware was Belle (Condon and Thompson, 1982). Most of the strongest recent programs, such as HITECH (Ebeling, 1987; Berliner and Ebeling, 1989) and Deep Thought (Hsu et al., 1990) have run on custom hardware. Major exceptions are Cray Blitz (Hyatt et al., 1986), which runs on a general-purpose Cray supercomputer, and Socrates II, winner of the 23rd ACM North American Computer Chess Championship in 1993, which runs on an Intel 486-based microcomputer. It should be noted that Deep Thought was not there to defend its title. Deep Thought 2 regained the championship in 1994. It should also be noted that even custom-hardware machines can benefit greatly from improvements purely at the software level (Berliner, 1989).

The Fredkin Prize, established in 1980, offered $5000 to the first program to achieve a Master rating, $10,000 to the first program to achieve a USCF (United States Chess Federation) rating of 2500 (near the grandmaster level), and $100,000 for the first program to defeat the human world champion. The $5000 prize was claimed by Belle in 1983, and the $10,000 prize by Deep Thought in 1989. The $100,000 prize remains unclaimed, in view of convincing wins in extended play by world champion Gary Kasparov over Deep Thought (Hsu et al., 1990).

The literature for computer chess is far better developed than for any other game played by computer programs. Aside from the tournaments already mentioned, the rather misleadingly named conference proceedings *Heuristic Programming in Artificial Intelligence* report on the Computer Chess Olympiads. The International Computer Chess Association (ICCA), founded in 1977, publishes the quarterly *ICCA Journal*. Important papers have been published in the numbered serial anthology *Advances in Computer Chess*, starting with (Clarke, 1977). Some early general AI textbooks (Nilsson, 1971; Slagle, 1971) include extensive material on game-playing programs, including chess programs. David Levy's *Computer Chess Compendium* (Levy, 1988a) anthologizes many of the most important historical papers in the field, together with the scores of important games played by computer programs. The edited volume by Marsland and Schaeffer (1990) contains interesting historical and theoretical papers on chess and Go along with descriptions of Cray Blitz, HITECH, and Deep Thought. Several important papers on chess, along with material on almost all games for which computer game-playing programs have been written (including checkers, backgammon, Go, Othello, and several card games) can be found in Levy (1988b). There is even a textbook on how to write a computer game-playing program, by one of the major figures in computer chess (Levy, 1983).

The expectimax algorithm described in the text was proposed by Donald Michie (1966), although of course it follows directly from the principles of game-tree evaluation due to Von Neumann and Morgenstern. Bruce Ballard (1983) extended alpha-beta pruning to cover trees with chance nodes. The backgammon program BKG (Berliner, 1977; Berliner, 1980b) was the first program to defeat a human world champion at a major classic game (Berliner, 1980a), although Berliner was the first to acknowledge that this was a very short exhibition match (not a world championship match) and that BKG was very lucky with the dice.

The first Go-playing programs were developed somewhat later than those for checkers and chess (Lefkovitz, 1960; Remus, 1962) and have progressed more slowly. Ryder (1971) used a search-based approach similar to that taken by most chess programs but with more selectivity to overcome the enormous branching factor. Zobrist (1970) used a pattern-recognition approach. Reitman and Wilcox (1979) used condition–action rules based on complex patterns, combined with highly selective localized search. The Go Explorer and its successors (Kierulf *et al.*, 1990) continue to evolve along these lines. YUGO (Shirayanagi, 1990) places heavy emphasis on knowledge representation and pattern knowledge. The *Computer Go Newsletter*, published by the Computer Go Association, describes current developments.

EXERCISES

5.1 This problem exercises the basic concepts of game-playing using Tic-Tac-Toe (noughts and crosses) as an example. We define X_n as the number of rows, columns, or diagonals with exactly n X's and no O's. Similarly, O_n is the number of rows, columns, or diagonals with just n O's. The utility function thus assigns +1 to any position with $X_3 = 1$ and -1 to any position with $O_3 = 1$. All other terminal positions have utility 0. We will use a linear evaluation function defined as

$$Eval = 3X_2 + X_1 - (3O_2 + O_1)$$

    a. Approximately how many possible games of Tic-Tac-Toe are there?

    b. Show the whole game tree starting from an empty board down to depth 2, (i.e., one X and one O on the board), taking symmetry into account. You should have 3 positions at level 1 and 12 at level 2.

    c. Mark on your tree the evaluations of all the positions at level 2.

    d. Mark on your tree the backed-up values for the positions at levels 1 and 0, using the minimax algorithm, and use them to choose the best starting move.

    e. Circle the nodes at level 2 that would *not* be evaluated if alpha-beta pruning were applied, assuming the nodes are generated *in the optimal order for alpha-beta pruning*.

5.2 Implement a general game-playing agent for two-player deterministic games, using alpha-beta search. You can assume the game is accessible, so the input to the agent is a complete description of the state.

5.3 Implement move generators and evaluation functions for one or more of the following games: kalah, Othello, checkers, chess. Exercise your game-playing agent using the implementation. Compare the effect of increasing search depth, improving move ordering, and improving the evaluation function. How close does your effective branching factor come to the ideal case of perfect move ordering?

5.4   The algorithms described in this chapter construct a search tree for each move from scratch. Discuss the advantages and disadvantages of retaining the search tree from one move to the next and extending the appropriate portion. How would tree retention interact with the use of selective search to examine "useful" branches of the tree?

5.5   Develop a formal proof of correctness of alpha-beta pruning. To do this, consider the situation shown in Figure 5.14. The question is whether to prune node n_j, which is a max-node and a descendant of node n_1. The basic idea is to prune it if and only if the minimax value of n_1 can be shown to be independent of the value of n_j.

a. The value of n_1 is given by

$$n_1 = \min(n_2, n_{21}, \dots, n_{2b_2})$$

By writing a similar expression for the value of n_2, find an expression for n_1 in terms of n_j.

b. Let l_i be the minimum (or maximum) of the node values to the left of node n_i at depth i. These are the nodes whose minimax value is already known. Similarly, let r_i be the minimum (or maximum) of the node values to the right of n_i at depth i. These nodes have not yet been explored. Rewrite your expression for n_1 in terms of the l_i and r_i values.

c. Now reformulate the expression to show that in order to affect n_1, n_j must not exceed a certain bound derived from the l_i values.

d. Repeat the process for the case where n_j is a min-node.

You might want to consult Wand (1980), who shows how the alpha-beta algorithm can be automatically synthesized from the minimax algorithm, using some general program-transformation techniques.

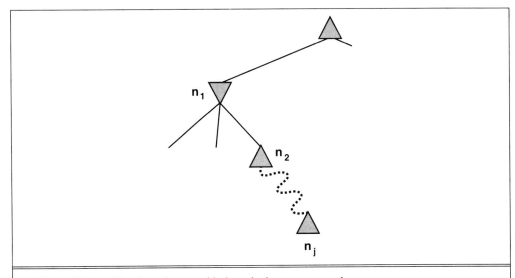

Figure 5.14   Situation when considering whether to prune node n_j.

5.6 Prove that with a positive linear transformation of leaf values, the move choice remains unchanged in a game tree with chance nodes.

5.7 Consider the following procedure for choosing moves in games with chance nodes:

- Generate a suitable number (say, 50) dice-roll sequences down to a suitable depth (say, 8).
- With known dice rolls, the game tree becomes deterministic. For each dice-roll sequence, solve the resulting deterministic game tree using alpha-beta.
- Use the results to estimate the value of each move and choose the best.

Will this procedure work correctly? Why (not)?

5.8 Let us consider the problem of search in a *three-player* game. (You can assume no alliances are allowed for now.) We will call the players 0, 1, and 2 for convenience. The first change is that the evaluation function will return a list of three values, indicating (say) the likelihood of winning for players 0, 1, and 2, respectively.

a. Complete the following game tree by filling in the backed-up value triples for all remaining nodes, including the root:

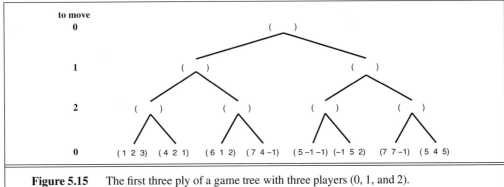

Figure 5.15   The first three ply of a game tree with three players (0, 1, and 2).

b. Rewrite MINIMAX-DECISION and MINIMAX-VALUE so that they work correctly for the three-player game.

c. Discuss the problems that might arise if players could form and terminate alliances as well as make moves "on the board." Indicate briefly how these problems might be addressed.

5.9 Describe and implement a general game-playing environment for an arbitrary number of players. Remember that time is part of the environment state, as well as the board position.

5.10 Suppose we play a variant of Tic-Tac-Toe in which each player sees only his or her own moves. If the player makes a move on a square occupied by an opponent, the board "beeps" and the player gets another try. Would the backgammon model suffice for this game, or would we need something more sophisticated? Why?

5.11   Describe and/or implement state descriptions, move generators, and evaluation functions for one or more of the following games: backgammon, Monopoly, Scrabble, bridge (declarer play is easiest).

5.12   Consider carefully the interplay of chance events and partial information in each of the games in Exercise 5.11.

   a. For which is the standard expectiminimax model appropriate? Implement the algorithm and run it in your game-playing agent, with appropriate modifications to the game-playing environment.

   b. For which would the scheme described in Exercise 5.7 be appropriate?

   c. Discuss how you might deal with the fact that in some of the games, the players do not have the same knowledge of the current state.

5.13   The Chinook checkers program makes extensive use of endgame databases, which provide exact values for every position within 6 moves of the end of the game. How might such databases be generated efficiently?

5.14   Discuss how well the standard approach to game playing would apply to games such as tennis, pool, and croquet, which take place in a continuous, physical state space.

5.15   For a game with which you are familiar, describe how an agent could be defined with condition-action rules, subgoals (and their conditions for generation), and action-utility rules, instead of by minimax search.

5.16   The minimax algorithm returns the best move for MAX under the assumption that MIN plays optimally. What happens when MIN plays suboptimally?

5.17   We have assumed that the rules of each game define a utility function that is used by both players, and that a utility of x for MAX means a utility of $-x$ for MIN. Games with this property are called **zero-sum** games. Describe how the minimax and alpha-beta algorithms change when we have nonzero-sum games—that is, when each player has his or her own utility function. You may assume that each player knows the other's utility function.

Part III

KNOWLEDGE AND REASONING

In Part II, we showed that an agent that has goals and searches for solutions to the goals can do better than one that just reacts to its environment. We focused mainly on the question of how to carry out the search, leaving aside the question of general methods for describing states and actions.

In this part, we extend the capabilities of our agents by endowing them with the capacity for general logical reasoning. A logical, knowledge-based agent begins with some knowledge of the world and of its own actions. It uses logical reasoning to maintain a description of the world as new percepts arrive, and to deduce a course of action that will achieve its goals.

In Chapter 6, we introduce the basic design for a knowledge-based agent. We then present a simple logical language for expressing knowledge, and show how it can be used to draw conclusions about the world and to decide what to do. In Chapter 7, we augment the language to make it capable of expressing a wide variety of knowledge about complex worlds. In Chapter 8, we exercise this capability by expressing a significant fragment of commonsense knowledge about the real world, including time, change, objects, categories, events, substances, and of course money. In Chapters 9 and 10 we discuss the theory and practice of computer systems for logical reasoning.

6 AGENTS THAT REASON LOGICALLY

In which we design agents that can form representations of the world, use a process of inference to derive new representations about the world, and use these new representations to deduce what to do.

In this chapter, we introduce the basic design for a knowledge-based agent. As we discussed in Part I (see, for example, the statement by Craik on page 13), the knowledge-based approach is a particularly powerful way of constructing an agent program. It aims to implement a view of agents in which they can be seen as *knowing* about their world, and *reasoning* about their possible courses of action. Knowledge-based agents are able to accept new tasks in the form of explicitly described goals; they can achieve competence quickly by being told or learning new knowledge about the environment; and they can adapt to changes in the environment by updating the relevant knowledge. A knowledge-based agent needs to know many things: the current state of the world; how to infer unseen properties of the world from percepts; how the world evolves over time; what it wants to achieve; and what its own actions do in various circumstances.

We begin in Section 6.1 with the overall agent design. Section 6.2 introduces a simple new environment, the wumpus world, where a knowledge-based agent can easily attain a competence that would be extremely difficult to obtain by other means. Section 6.3 discusses the basic elements of the agent design: a formal language in which knowledge can be expressed, and a means of carrying out reasoning in such a language. These two elements constitute what we LOGIC call a **logic**. Section 6.4 gives an example of how these basic elements work in a logic called **propositional logic**, and Section 6.5 illustrates the use of propositional logic to build a logical agent for the wumpus world.

6.1 A KNOWLEDGE-BASED AGENT

KNOWLEDGE BASE The central component of a knowledge-based agent is its **knowledge base**, or KB. Informally, a knowledge base is a set of representations of facts about the world. Each individual representation SENTENCE is called a **sentence**. (Here "sentence" is used as a technical term. It is related to the sentences

151

KNOWLEDGE
REPRESENTATION
LANGUAGE
of English and other natural languages, but is not identical.) The sentences are expressed in a
language called a **knowledge representation language**.

There must be a way to add new sentences to the knowledge base, and a way to query what
is known. The standard names for these tasks are TELL and ASK, respectively. The fundamental
requirement that we will impose on TELL and ASK is that when one ASKs a question of the
knowledge base, the answer should follow from what has been told (or rather, TELLed) to the
knowledge base previously. Later in the chapter, we will be more precise about the crucial word
"follow." For now, take it to mean that the knowledge base should not just make up things as
it goes along. Determining what follows from what the KB has been TELLed is the job of the

INFERENCE
inference mechanism, the other main component of a knowledge-based agent.

Figure 6.1 shows the outline of a knowledge-based agent program. Like all our agents, it
takes a percept as input and returns an action. The agent maintains a knowledge base, *KB*, which

BACKGROUND
KNOWLEDGE
may initially contain some **background knowledge**. Each time the agent program is called, it
does two things. First, it TELLs the knowledge base what it perceives.[1]   Second, it ASKs the
knowledge base what action it should perform. In the process of answering this query, logical
reasoning is used to prove which action is better than all others, given what the agent knows and
what its goals are. The agent then performs the chosen action.

---

function KB-AGENT(*percept*) **returns** an *action*
    static: *KB*, a knowledge base
                  t, a counter, initially 0, indicating time

    TELL(*KB*, MAKE-PERCEPT-SENTENCE(*percept, t*))
    action ← ASK(*KB*, MAKE-ACTION-QUERY(*t*))
    TELL(*KB*, MAKE-ACTION-SENTENCE(*action, t*))
    t ← *t* + 1
    return *action*

Figure 6.1   A generic knowledge-based agent.

The details of the representation language are hidden inside two functions that implement
the interface between the agent program "shell" and the core representation and reasoning system.
MAKE-PERCEPT-SENTENCE takes a percept and a time and returns a sentence representing the fact
that the agent perceived the percept at the given time, and MAKE-ACTION-QUERY takes a time as
input and returns a sentence that is suitable for asking what action should be performed at that
time. The details of the inference mechanism are hidden inside TELL and ASK. Later sections
will reveal these details.

A careful examination of Figure 6.1 reveals that it is quite similar to the design of agents
with internal state described in Chapter 2. Because of the definitions of TELL and ASK, however,
the knowledge-based agent is not an arbitrary program for calculating actions based on the internal
state variable. At any point, we can describe a knowledge-based agent at three levels:

---

[1]   You might think of TELL and ASK as procedures that humans can use to communicate with knowledge bases. Don't
be confused by the fact that here it is the agent that is TELLing things to its own knowledge base.

KNOWLEDGE LEVEL
EPISTEMOLOGICAL
LEVEL

- The **knowledge level** or **epistemological level** is the most abstract; we can describe the agent by saying what it knows. For example, an automated taxi might be said to know that the Golden Gate Bridge links San Francisco and Marin County. If TELL and ASK work correctly, then most of the time we can work at the knowledge level and not worry about lower levels.

LOGICAL LEVEL

- The **logical level** is the level at which the knowledge is encoded into sentences. For example, the taxi might be described as having the logical sentence *Links*(*GGBridge*, *SF*, *Marin*) in its knowledge base.

IMPLEMENTATION
LEVEL

- The **implementation level** is the level that runs on the agent architecture. It is the level at which there are physical representations of the sentences at the logical level. A sentence such as *Links*(*GGBridge*, *SF*, *Marin*) could be represented in the KB by the string `"Links(GGBridge,SF,Marin)"` contained in a list of strings; or by a "1" entry in a three-dimensional table indexed by road links and location pairs; or by a complex set of pointers connecting machine addresses corresponding to the individual symbols. The choice of implementation is very important to the efficient performance of the agent, but it is irrelevant to the logical level and the knowledge level.

DECLARATIVE

We said that it is possible to understand the operation of a knowledge-based agent in terms of what it knows. *It is possible to construct a knowledge-based agent by* TELL*ing it what it needs to know.* The agent's initial program, before it starts to receive percepts, is built by adding one by one the sentences that represent the designer's knowledge of the environment. Provided that the representation language makes it easy to express this knowledge in the form of sentences, this simplifies the construction problem enormously. This is called the **declarative** approach to system building. Also, one can design **learning** mechanisms that output general knowledge about the environment given a series of percepts. By hooking up a learning mechanism to a knowledge-based agent, one can make the agent fully autonomous.

6.2   THE WUMPUS WORLD ENVIRONMENT

WUMPUS WORLD

Before launching into a full exposition of knowledge representation and reasoning, we will describe a simple environment class—the **wumpus world**—that provides plenty of motivation for logical reasoning. Wumpus was an early computer game, based on an agent who explores a cave consisting of rooms connected by passageways. Lurking somewhere in the cave is the wumpus, a beast that eats anyone who enters its room. To make matters worse, some rooms contain bottomless pits that will trap anyone who wanders into these rooms (except for the wumpus, who is too big to fall in). The only mitigating feature of living in this environment is the occasional heap of gold.

It turns out that the wumpus game is rather tame by modern computer game standards. However, it makes an excellent testbed environment for intelligent agents. Michael Genesereth was the first to suggest this.

Specifying the environment

Like the vacuum world, the wumpus world is a grid of squares surrounded by walls, where each square can contain agents and objects. The agent always starts in the lower left corner, a square that we will label [1,1]. The agent's task is to find the gold, return to [1,1] and climb out of the cave. An example wumpus world is shown in Figure 6.2.

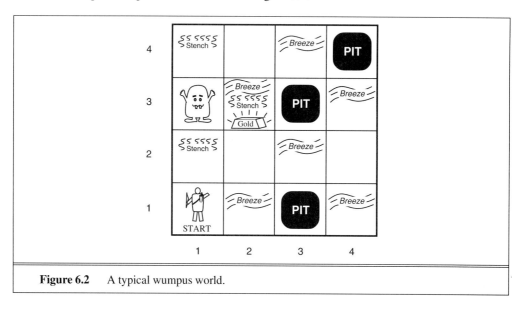

Figure 6.2   A typical wumpus world.

To specify the agent's task, we specify its percepts, actions, and goals. In the wumpus world, these are as follows:

- In the square containing the wumpus and in the directly (not diagonally) adjacent squares the agent will perceive a stench.
- In the squares directly adjacent to a pit, the agent will perceive a breeze.
- In the square where the gold is, the agent will perceive a glitter.
- When an agent walks into a wall, it will perceive a bump.
- When the wumpus is killed, it gives out a woeful scream that can be perceived anywhere in the cave.
- The percepts will be given to the agent in the form of a list of five symbols; for example, if there is a stench, a breeze, and a glitter but no bump and no scream, the agent will receive the percept [*Stench, Breeze, Glitter, None, None*]. The agent *cannot* perceive its own location.
- Just as in the vacuum world, there are actions to go forward, turn right by 90°, and turn left by 90°. In addition, the action *Grab* can be used to pick up an object that is in the same square as the agent. The action *Shoot* can be used to fire an arrow in a straight line in the direction the agent is facing. The arrow continues until it either hits and kills the wumpus or hits the wall. The agent only has one arrow, so only the first *Shoot* action has any effect.

Finally, the action *Climb* is used to leave the cave; it is effective only when the agent is in the start square.

- The agent dies a miserable death if it enters a square containing a pit or a live wumpus. It is safe (but smelly) to enter a square with a dead wumpus.

- The agent's goal is to find the gold and bring it back to the start as quickly as possible, without getting killed. To be precise, 1000 points are awarded for climbing out of the cave while carrying the gold, but there is a 1-point penalty for each action taken, and a 10,000-point penalty for getting killed.

As we emphasized in Chapter 2, an agent can do well in a single environment merely by memorizing the sequence of actions that happens to work in that environment. To provide a real test, we need to specify a complete class of environments, and insist that the agent do well, on average, over the whole class. We will assume a 4 × 4 grid surrounded by walls. The agent always starts in the square labeled (1,1), facing toward the right. The locations of the gold and the wumpus are chosen randomly, with a uniform distribution, from the squares other than the start square. In addition, each square other than the start can be a pit, with probability 0.2.

In most of the environments in this class, there is a way for the agent to safely retrieve the gold. In some environments, the agent must choose between going home empty-handed or taking a chance that could lead either to death or to the gold. And in about 21% of the environments (the ones where the gold is in a pit or surrounded by pits), there is no way the agent can get a positive score. Sometimes life is just unfair.

After gaining experience with this class of environments, we can experiment with other classes. In Chapter 22 we consider worlds where two agents explore together and can communicate with each other. We could also consider worlds where the wumpus can move, or where there are multiple troves of gold, or multiple wumpuses.[2]

Acting and reasoning in the wumpus world

We now know the rules of the wumpus world, but we do not yet have an idea of how a wumpus world agent should act. An example will clear this up and will show why a successful agent will need to have some kind of logical reasoning ability. Figure 6.3(a) shows an agent's state of knowledge at the start of an exploration of the cave in Figure 6.2, after it has received its initial percept. To emphasize that this is only a representation, we use letters such as *A* and *OK* to represent sentences, in contrast to Figure 6.2, which used (admittedly primitive) pictures of the wumpus and pits.

From the fact that there was no stench or breeze in [1,1], the agent can infer that [1,2] and [2,1] are free of dangers. They are marked with an *OK* to indicate this. From the fact that the agent is still alive, it can infer that [1,1] is also *OK*. A cautious agent will only move into a square that it knows is *OK*. Let us suppose the agent decides to move forward to [2,1], giving the scene in Figure 6.3(b).

The agent detects a breeze in [2,1], so there must be a pit in a neighboring square, either [2,2] or [3,1]. The notation *P?* indicates a possible pit. The pit cannot be in [1,1], because the

---

2 Or is it wumpi?

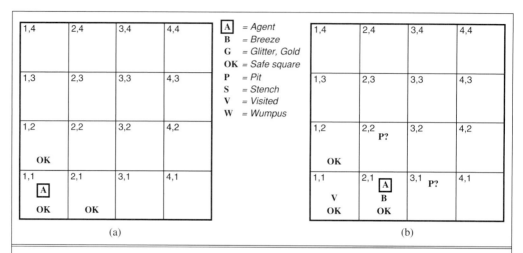

Figure 6.3   The first step taken by the agent in the wumpus world.   (a) The initial situation, after percept [*None,None,None,None,None*].   (b) After one move, with percept [*None,Breeze,None,None,None*].

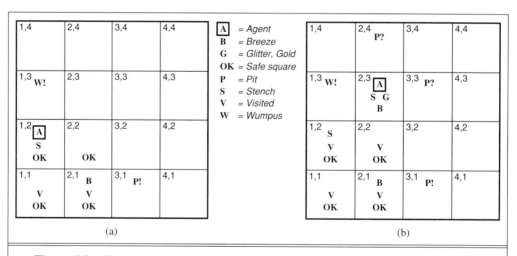

Figure 6.4   Two later stages in the progress of the agent.   (a) After the third move, with percept [*Stench,None,None,None,None*].   (b) After the fifth move, with percept [*Stench,Breeze,Glitter,None,None*].

agent was already there and did not fall in. At this point, there is only one known square that is *OK* and has not been visited yet. So the prudent agent will turn around, go back to [1,1], and then proceed to [1,2], giving the state of knowledge in Figure 6.4(a).

The agent detects a stench in [1,2], which means that there must be a wumpus nearby. But the wumpus cannot be in [1,1] (or it would have eaten the agent at the start), and it cannot be in

[2,2] (or the agent would have detected a stench when it was in [2,1]). Therefore, the agent can infer that the wumpus is in [1,3]. The notation *W!* indicates this. More interesting is that the lack of a *Breeze* percept in [1,2] means that there must be a pit in [3,1]. The reasoning is that no breeze in [1,2] means there can be no pit in [2,2]. But we already inferred that there must be a pit in either [2,2] or [3,1], so this means it must be in [3,1]. This is a fairly difficult inference, because it combines knowledge gained at different times in different places, and relies on the lack of a percept to make one crucial step. The inference is beyond the abilities of most animals, but it is typical of the kind of reasoning that a logical agent does.

After these impressive deductions, there is only one known unvisited *OK* square left, [2,2], so the agent will move there. We will not show the agent's state of knowledge at [2,2]; we just assume the agent turns and moves to [2,3], giving us Figure 6.4(b). In [2,3], the agent detects a glitter, so it should grab the gold and head for home, making sure its return trip only goes through squares that are known to be *OK*.

In the rest of this chapter, we describe how to build a logical agent that can represent beliefs such as "there is a pit in [2,2] or [3,1]" and "there is no wumpus in [2,2]," and that can make all the inferences that were described in the preceding paragraphs.

6.3   REPRESENTATION, REASONING, AND LOGIC

In this section, we will discuss the nature of representation languages, and of logical languages in particular, and explain in detail the connection between the language and the reasoning mechanism that goes with it. Together, representation and reasoning support the operation of a knowledge-based agent.

KNOWLEDGE
REPRESENTATION

The object of **knowledge representation** is to express knowledge in computer-tractable form, such that it can be used to help agents perform well. A knowledge representation language is defined by two aspects:

SYNTAX

- The **syntax** of a language describes the possible configurations that can constitute sentences. Usually, we describe syntax in terms of how sentences are represented on the printed page, but the real representation is inside the computer: each sentence is implemented by a physical configuration or physical property of some part of the agent. For now, think of this as being a physical pattern of electrons in the computer's memory.

SEMANTICS

- The **semantics** determines the facts in the world to which the sentences refer. Without semantics, a sentence is just an arrangement of electrons or a collection of marks on a page. With semantics, each sentence makes a claim about the world. And with semantics, we can say that when a particular configuration exists within an agent, the agent **believes** the corresponding sentence.

For example, the syntax of the language of arithmetic expressions says that if x and y are expressions denoting numbers, then $x \geq y$ is a sentence about numbers. The semantics of the language says that $x \geq y$ is false when y is a bigger number than x, and true otherwise.

Provided the syntax and semantics are defined precisely, we can call the language a **logic**.[3]
From the syntax and semantics, we can derive an inference mechanism for an agent that uses the
language. We now explain how this comes about.

First, recall that the semantics of the language determine the fact to which a given sentence
refers (see Figure 6.5). It is important to distinguish between facts and their representations.
Facts are part of the world,[4] whereas their representations must be encoded in some way that can
be physically stored within an agent. We cannot put the world inside a computer (nor can we put
it inside a human), so all reasoning mechanisms must operate on representations of facts, rather
than on the facts themselves. *Because sentences are physical configurations of parts of the agent,
reasoning must be a process of constructing new physical configurations from old ones. Proper
reasoning should ensure that the new configurations represent facts that actually follow from the
facts that the old configurations represent.*

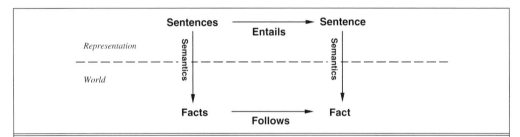

Figure 6.5   The connection between sentences and facts is provided by the semantics of the
language. The property of one fact following from some other facts is mirrored by the property of
one sentence being entailed by some other sentences. Logical inference generates new sentences
that are entailed by existing sentences.

Consider the following example. From the fact that the solar system obeys the laws of
gravitation, and the fact of the current arrangement of the sun, planets, and other bodies, it follows
(so the astronomers tell us) that Pluto will eventually spin off into the interstellar void. But if our
agent reasons improperly, it might start with representations of the first two facts and end with a
representation that means that Pluto will shortly arrive in the vicinity of Bucharest. Or we might
end up with "logical" reasoning like that in Figure 6.6.

We want to generate new sentences that are necessarily true, given that the old sentences
ENTAILMENT   are true. This relation between sentences is called **entailment**, and mirrors the relation of one
fact following from another (Figure 6.5). In mathematical notation, the relation of entailment
between a knowledge base *KB* and a sentence α is pronounced "*KB* entails α" and written as

$$KB \models \alpha.$$

An inference procedure can do one of two things: given a knowledge base *KB*, it can generate

---

[3] This is perhaps a rather broad interpretation of the term "logic," one that makes "representation language" and "logic"
synonymous. However, most of the principles of logic apply at this general level, rather than just at the level of the
particular languages most often associated with the term.

[4] As Wittgenstein (1922) put it in his famous *Tractatus Logico-Philosophicus*: "The world is everything that is the
case." We are using the word "fact" in this sense: as an "arrangement" of the world that may or may not be the case.

FIRST VILLAGER: We have found a witch. May we burn her?

ALL: A witch! Burn her!

BEDEVERE: Why do you think she is a witch?

SECOND VILLAGER: She turned *me* into a newt.

BEDEVERE: A newt?

SECOND VILLAGER *(after looking at himself for some time)*: I got better.

ALL: Burn her anyway.

BEDEVERE: Quiet! Quiet! There are ways of telling whether she is a witch.

BEDEVERE: Tell me ... what do you do with witches?

ALL: Burn them.

BEDEVERE: And what do you burn, apart from witches?

FOURTH VILLAGER: ... Wood?

BEDEVERE: So why do witches burn?

SECOND VILLAGER: *(pianissimo)* Because they're made of wood?

BEDEVERE: Good.

ALL: I see. Yes, of course.

BEDEVERE: So how can we tell if she is made of wood?

FIRST VILLAGER: Make a bridge out of her.

BEDEVERE: Ah ... but can you not also make bridges out of stone?

ALL: Yes, of course ... um ... er ...

BEDEVERE: Does wood sink in water?

ALL: No, no, it floats. Throw her in the pond.

BEDEVERE: Wait. Wait ... tell me, what also floats on water?

ALL: Bread? No, no no. Apples ... gravy ... very small rocks ...

BEDEVERE: No, no no,

KING ARTHUR: A duck!

(They all turn and look at ARTHUR. BEDEVERE looks up very impressed.)

BEDEVERE: Exactly. So ... logically ...

FIRST VILLAGER *(beginning to pick up the thread)*: If she ... weighs the same as a duck ... she's made of wood.

BEDEVERE: And therefore?

ALL: A witch!

Figure 6.6   An example of "logical" reasoning gone wrong. (Excerpted with permission from *Monty Python and the Holy Grail*, © 1977, Reed Consumer Books.)

new sentences α that purport to be entailed by *KB*. Or, given a knowledge base *KB* and another sentence α, it can report whether or not α is entailed by *KB*. An inference procedure that generates only entailed sentences is called **sound** or **truth-preserving**.

SOUND

TRUTH-PRESERVING

An inference procedure i can be described by the sentences that it can derive. If i can derive α from *KB*, a logician would write

$$KB \vdash_i \alpha,$$

PROOF

which is pronounced "Alpha is derived from *KB* by *i*" or "*i* derives alpha from *KB*." Sometimes the inference procedure is implicit and the *i* is omitted. The record of operation of a sound inference procedure is called a **proof**.

In understanding entailment and proof, it may help to think of the set of all consequences of *KB* as a haystack and α as a needle. Entailment is like the needle being in the haystack; proof is like finding it. For real haystacks, which are finite in extent, it seems obvious that a systematic examination can always decide whether the needle is in the haystack. This is the question of completeness: an inference procedure is **complete** if it can find a proof for any sentence that is entailed. But for many knowledge bases, the haystack of consequences is infinite, and completeness becomes an important issue.[5]

COMPLETE

We have said that sound inference is desirable. How is it achieved? *The key to sound inference is to have the inference steps respect the semantics of the sentences they operate upon. That is, given a knowledge base, KB, the inference steps should only derive new sentences that represent facts that follow from the facts represented by KB.* By examining the semantics of logical languages, we can extract what is called the **proof theory** of the language, which specifies the reasoning steps that are sound. Consider the following familiar example from mathematics, which illustrates syntax, semantics, and proof theory. Suppose we have the following sentence:

PROOF THEORY

$$E = mc^2$$

The syntax of the "equation language" allows two expressions to be connected by an "=" sign. An expression can be a simple symbol or number, a concatenation of two expressions, two expressions joined by a "+" sign, and so on. The semantics of the language says that the two expressions on each side of "=" refer to the same quantity; that the concatenation of two expressions refers to the quantity that is the product of the quantities referred to by each of the expressions; and so on. From the semantics, we can show that a new sentence can be generated by, for example, concatenating the same expression to both sides of the equation:

$$ET = mc^2 T$$

Most readers will have plenty of experience with inference of this sort. Logical languages are like this simple equation language, but rather than dealing with algebraic properties and numerical quantities, they must deal with more or less everything we might want to represent and about which we might want to reason.

Representation

We will now look a little more deeply into the nature of knowledge representation languages, with the aim of designing an appropriate syntax and semantics. We will begin with two familiar classes of languages, programming languages and natural languages, to see what they are good at representing and where they have problems.

Programming languages (such as C or Pascal or Lisp) are good for describing algorithms and concrete data structures. We could certainly imagine using an 4×4 array to represent the contents of the wumpus world, for example. Thus, the programming language statement *World*[2,2] $\leftarrow$ *Pit* is a fairly natural way to say that there is a pit in square [2,2]. However, most

---

[5] Compare with the case of infinite search spaces in Chapter 3, where depth-first search is not complete.

programming languages do not offer any easy way to say "there is a pit in [2,2] or [3,1]" or "there is a wumpus in *some* square." The problem is that programming languages are designed to completely describe the state of the computer and how it changes as the program executes. But we would like our knowledge representation language to support the case where we do not have complete information—where we do not know for certain how things are, but only know some possibilities for how they might or might not be. A language that does not let us do this is not *expressive* enough.

Natural languages (such as English or Spanish) are certainly expressive—we managed to write this whole book using natural language with only occasional lapses into other languages (including logic, mathematics, and the language of diagrams). But natural languages have evolved more to meet the needs of **communication** rather than representation. When a speaker points and says, "Look!" the listener comes to know that, say, Superman has finally appeared over the rooftops. But we would not want to say that the sentence "Look!" encoded that fact. Rather, the meaning of the sentence depends both on the sentence itself and on the context in which the sentence was spoken. A natural language is a good way for a speaker to get a listener to come to know something, but often this sharing of knowledge is done without explicit representation of the knowledge itself. Natural languages also suffer from ambiguity—in a phrase such as "small dogs and cats," it is not clear whether the cats are small. Contrast this to the programming language construct "$-d + c$," where the precedence rules for the language tell us that the minus sign applies to d, not to $d + c$.

A good knowledge representation language should combine the advantages of natural languages and formal languages. It should be expressive and concise so that we can say everything we need to say succinctly. It should be unambiguous and independent of context, so that what we say today will still be interpretable tomorrow. And it should be effective in the sense that there should be an inference procedure that can make new inferences from sentences in our language.

Many representation languages have been designed to try to achieve these criteria. In this book, we concentrate on first-order logic as our representation language because it forms the basis of most representation schemes in AI. Just as it would be overoptimistic to believe that one can make real progress in physics without understanding and using equations, it is important to develop a talent for working with logical notation if one is to make progress in artificial intelligence. However, it is also important *not* to get too concerned with the *specifics* of logical notation—after all, there are literally dozens of different versions, some with x's and y's and exotic mathematical symbols, and some with rather visually appealing diagrams with arrows and bubbles. The main thing to keep hold of is how a precise, formal language can represent knowledge, and how mechanical procedures can operate on expressions in the language to perform reasoning. The fundamental concepts remain the same no matter what language is being used to represent the knowledge.

Semantics

In logic, the **meaning** of a sentence is what it states about the world, that the world is *this* way and not *that* way. So how does a sentence get its meaning? How do we establish the correspondence between sentences and facts? Essentially, this is up to the person who wrote the sentence. In

INTERPRETATION   order to say what it means, the writer has to provide an **interpretation** for it; to say what fact

THE LANGUAGE OF THOUGHT

Philosophers and psychologists have long pondered how it is that humans and other animals represent knowledge. It is clear that the evolution of natural language has played an important role in developing this ability in humans. But it is also true that humans seem to represent much of their knowledge in a nonverbal form. Psychologists have done studies to confirm that humans remember the "gist" of something they have read rather than the exact words. You could look at Anderson's (1980, page 96) description of an experiment by Wanner, or you could perform your own experiment by deciding which of the following two phrases formed the opening of Section 6.3:

"In this section, we will discuss the nature of representation languages . . ."

"This section covers the topic of knowledge representation languages . . ."

In Wanner's experiment, subjects made the right choice at chance level—about 50% of the time—but remembered the overall idea of what they read with better than 90% accuracy. This indicates that the exact words are not part of the representations they formed. A similar experiment (Sachs, 1967) showed that subjects remember the words for a short time (seconds to tens of seconds), but eventually forget the words and remember only the meaning. This suggests that people process the words to form some kind of nonverbal representation which they maintain as memories.

The exact mechanism by which language enables and shapes the representation of ideas in humans remains a fascinating question. The famous **Sapir–Whorf hypothesis** claims that the language we speak profoundly influences the way in which we think and make decisions, in particular by setting up the category structure by which we divide up the world into different sorts of objects. Whorf (1956) claimed that Eskimos have many words for snow, and thus experience snow in a different way from speakers of other languages. His analysis has since been discredited (Pullum, 1991); Inuit, Yupik, and other related languages seem to have about the same number of words for snow-related concepts as English (consider blizzard, sprinkling, flurries, powder, slush, snowbank, snowdrift, etc.). Of course, different languages *do* carve up the world differently. Spanish has two words for "fish," one for the live animal and one for the food. English does not make this distinction, but it does have the cow/beef distinction. There is no evidence that this means that English and Spanish speakers think about the world in fundamentally different ways.

For our purposes, it is important to remember that the language used to represent an agent's internal knowledge is quite different from the external language used to communicate with other agents. (See Chapter 22 for the study of communication.)

it corresponds to. A sentence does not mean something *by itself*. This is a difficult concept to accept, because we are used to languages like English where the interpretation of most things was fixed a long time ago.

The idea of interpretation is easier to see in made-up languages. Imagine that one spy wants to pass a message to another, but worries that the message may be intercepted. The two spies could agree in advance on a nonstandard interpretation in which, say, the interpretation of "Pope" is a particular piece of microfilm and the interpretation of "Denver" is the pumpkin left on the porch, and so forth. Then, when the first spy sends a newspaper clipping with the headline "The Pope is in Denver," the second spy will know that the microfilm is in the pumpkin.

COMPOSITIONAL

It is possible, in principle, to define a language in which every sentence has a completely arbitrary interpretation. But in practice, all representation languages impose a *systematic* relationship between sentences and facts. The languages we will deal with are all **compositional**—the meaning of a sentence is a function of the meaning of its parts. Just as the meaning of the mathematical expression $x^2 + y^2$ is related to the meanings of x^2 and y^2, we would like the meaning of the sentence "$S_{1,4}$ and $S_{1,2}$" to be related to the meanings of "$S_{1,4}$" and "$S_{1,2}$." It would be very strange if "$S_{1,4}$" meant there is a stench in square [1,4] and "$S_{1,2}$" meant there is a stench in square [1,2], but "$S_{1,4}$ and $S_{1,2}$" meant that France and Poland drew 1–1 in last week's ice-hockey qualifying match. In Section 6.4, we describe the semantics of a simple language, the language of propositional logic, that obeys constraints like these. Such constraints make it easy to specify a proof theory that respects the semantics.

Once a sentence is given an interpretation by the semantics, the sentence says that the world is *this* way and not *that* way. Hence, it can be true or false. *A sentence is **true** under a particular interpretation if the state of affairs it represents is the case.* Note that truth depends both on the interpretation of the sentence and on the actual state of the world. For example, the sentence "$S_{1,2}$" would be true under the interpretation in which it means that there is a stench in [1,2], in the world described in Figure 6.2. But it would be false in worlds that do not have a stench in [1,2], and it would be false in Figure 6.2 under the interpretation in which it means that there is a breeze in [1,2].

Inference

The terms "reasoning" and "inference" are generally used to cover any process by which conclusions are reached. In this chapter, we are mainly concerned with sound reasoning, which we will call **logical inference** or **deduction**. Logical inference is a process that implements the entailment relation between sentences. There are a number of ways to approach the design of logical inference systems. We will begin with the idea of a **necessarily true sentence**.

LOGICAL INFERENCE
DEDUCTION

Validity and satisfiability

VALID

A sentence is **valid** or necessarily true if and only if it is true under all possible interpretations in all possible worlds, that is, regardless of what it is supposed to mean and regardless of the state of affairs in the universe being described. For example, the sentence

"There is a stench at [1,1] or there is not a stench at [1,1]."

is valid, because it is true whether or not "there is a stench in [1,1]" is true, and it is true regardless of the interpretation of "there is a stench in [1,1]." In contrast,

> "There is an open area in the square in front of me or there is a wall in the square in
> front of me."

is not valid by itself. It is only valid under the assumption that every square has either a wall or an open area in it. So the sentence

> "If every square has either a wall or an open area in it, then there is an open area in
> the square in front of me, or there is a wall in the square in front of me."

is valid.[6] There are several synonyms for valid sentences. Some authors use the terms **analytic sentences** or **tautologies** for valid sentences.

A sentence is **satisfiable** if and only if there is some interpretation in some world for which it is true. The sentence "there is a wumpus at [1,2]" is satisfiable because there might well be a wumpus in that square, even though there does not happen to be one in Figure 6.2. A

sentence that is not satisfiable is **unsatisfiable**. Self-contradictory sentences are unsatisfiable, if the contradictoriness does not depend on the meanings of the symbols. For example, the sentence

> "There is a wall in front of me and there is no wall in front of me"

is unsatisfiable.

Inference in computers

It might seem that valid and unsatisfiable sentences are useless, because they can only express things that are obviously true or false. In fact, we will see that validity and unsatisfiability are crucial to the ability of a computer to reason.

The computer suffers from two handicaps: it does not necessarily know the interpretation you are using for the sentences in the knowledge base, and it knows nothing at all about the world except what appears in the knowledge base. Suppose we ask the computer if it is OK to move to square [2,2]. The computer does not know what OK means, nor does it know what a wumpus or a pit is. So it cannot reason informally as we did on page 155. All it can do is see if its knowledge base entails the sentence "[2,2] is OK." In other words, the inference procedure has to show that the sentence "If KB is true then [2,2] is OK" is a valid sentence. If it is valid, then it does not matter that the computer does not know the interpretation you are using or that it does not know much about the world—the conclusion is guaranteed to be correct under all interpretations in all worlds in which the original KB is true. In Section 6.4, we will give an example of a formal procedure for deciding if a sentence is valid.

What makes formal inference powerful is that there is no limit to the complexity of the sentences it can handle. When we think of valid sentences, we usually think of simple examples like "The wumpus is dead or the wumpus is not dead." But the formal inference mechanism can just as well deal with valid sentences of the form "If KB then P," where KB is a conjunction of thousands of sentences describing the laws of gravity and the current state of the solar system, and P is a long description of the eventual departure of Pluto from the system.

---

6   In these examples, we are assuming that words like "if," "then," "every," "or" and "not" are part of the standard syntax of the language, and thus are not open to varying interpretation.

To reiterate, the great thing about formal inference is that it can be used to derive valid conclusions even when the computer does not know the interpretation you are using. The computer only reports valid conclusions, which must be true regardless of your interpretation. Because you know the interpretation, the conclusions will be meaningful to you, and they are guaranteed to follow from your premises. *The word "you" in this paragraph can be applied equally to human and computer agents.*

Logics

To summarize, we can say that a logic consists of the following:

1. A formal system for describing states of affairs, consisting of

   (a) the **syntax** of the language, which describes how to make sentences, and

   (b) the **semantics** of the language, which states the systematic constraints on how sentences relate to states of affairs.

2. The **proof theory**—a set of rules for deducing the entailments of a set of sentences.

We will concentrate on two kinds of logic: propositional or Boolean logic, and first-order logic (more precisely, first-order predicate calculus with equality).

PROPOSITIONAL LOGIC

In **propositional logic**, symbols represent whole propositions (facts); for example, D might have the interpretation "the wumpus is dead." which may or may not be a true proposition.

BOOLEAN CONNECTIVES

Proposition symbols can be combined using **Boolean connectives** to generate sentences with more complex meanings. Such a logic makes very little commitment to how things are represented, so it is not surprising that it does not give us much mileage as a representation language.

First-order logic commits to the representation of worlds in terms of **objects** and **predicates** on objects (i.e., properties of objects or relations between objects), as well as using **connectives** and **quantifiers**, which allow sentences to be written about everything in the universe at once. First-order logic seems to be able to capture a good deal of what we know about the world, and has been studied for about a hundred years. We will spend therefore a good deal of time looking at how to do representation and deduction using it.

ONTOLOGICAL COMMITMENTS

It is illuminating to consider logics in the light of their ontological and epistemological commitments. **Ontological commitments** have to do with the nature of *reality*. For example, propositional logic assumes that there are facts that either hold or do not in the world. Each fact can be in one of two states: true or false. First-order logic assumes more: namely, that the world consists of objects with certain relations between them that do or do not hold. Special-purpose logics make still further ontological commitments; for example, **temporal logic** assumes that the world is ordered by a set of time points or intervals, and includes built-in mechanisms for reasoning about time.

TEMPORAL LOGIC

EPISTEMOLOGICAL COMMITMENTS

Epistemological commitments have to do with the possible states of *knowledge* an agent can have using various types of logic. In both propositional and first-order logic, a sentence represents a fact and the agent either believes the sentence to be true, believes it to be false, or is unable to conclude either way. These logics therefore have three possible states of belief regarding any sentence. Systems using probability theory, on the other hand, can have any *degree* of belief, ranging from 0 (total disbelief) to 1 (total belief). For example, a probabilistic

FUZZY LOGIC

wumpus-world agent might believe that the wumpus is in [1,3] with probability 0.75. Systems based on **fuzzy logic** can have degrees of belief in a sentence, and also allow *degrees of truth*: a fact need not be true or false in the world, but can be true to a certain degree. For example, "Vienna is a large city" might be true only to degree 0.6. The ontological and epistemological commitments of various logics are summarized in Figure 6.7.

Language	Ontological Commitment (What exists in the world)	Epistemological Commitment (What an agent believes about facts)
Propositional logic	facts	true/false/unknown
First-order logic	facts, objects, relations	true/false/unknown
Temporal logic	facts, objects, relations, times	true/false/unknown
Probability theory	facts	degree of belief 0...1
Fuzzy logic	degree of truth	degree of belief 0...1

Figure 6.7   Formal languages and their ontological and epistemological commitments.

6.4   PROPOSITIONAL LOGIC: A VERY SIMPLE LOGIC

Despite its limited expressiveness, propositional logic serves to illustrate many of the concepts of logic just as well as first-order logic. We will describe its syntax, semantics, and associated inference procedures.

Syntax

The **syntax** of propositional logic is simple. The symbols of propositional logic are the logical constants *True* and *False*, proposition symbols such as P and Q, the logical connectives $\wedge$, $\vee$, $\Leftrightarrow$, $\Rightarrow$, and $\neg$, and parentheses, ( ). All sentences are made by putting these symbols together using the following rules:

- The logical constants *True* and *False* are sentences by themselves.
- A propositional symbol such as P or Q is a sentence by itself.
- Wrapping parentheses around a sentence yields a sentence, for example, $(P \wedge Q)$.
- A sentence can be formed by combining simpler sentences with one of the five logical connectives:

CONJUNCTION (LOGIC)

DISJUNCTION

  $\wedge$ (and). A sentence whose main connective is $\wedge$, such as $P \wedge (Q \vee R)$, is called a **conjunction (logic)**; its parts are the **conjuncts**. (The $\wedge$ looks like an "A" for "And.")

  $\vee$ (or). A sentence using $\vee$, such as $A \vee (P \wedge Q)$, is a **disjunction** of the **disjuncts** A and $(P \wedge Q)$. (Historically, the $\vee$ comes from the Latin "vel," which means "or." For most people, it is easier to remember as an upside-down and.)

IMPLICATION

PREMISE

CONCLUSION

⇒ (implies). A sentence such as $(P \land Q) \Rightarrow R$ is called an **implication** (or conditional). Its **premise** or **antecedent** is $P \land Q$, and its **conclusion** or **consequent** is R. Implications are also known as **rules** or **if–then** statements. The implication symbol is sometimes written in other books as ⊃ or →.

EQUIVALENCE

⇔ (equivalent). The sentence $(P \land Q) \Leftrightarrow (Q \land P)$ is an **equivalence** (also called a **biconditional**).

NEGATION

¬ (not). A sentence such as $\neg P$ is called the **negation** of P. All the other connectives combine two sentences into one; ¬ is the only connective that operates on a single sentence.

ATOMIC SENTENCES

COMPLEX
SENTENCES

LITERAL

Figure 6.8 gives a formal grammar of propositional logic; see page 854 if you are not familiar with the BNF notation. The grammar introduces **atomic sentences**, which in propositional logic consist of a single symbol (e.g., P), and **complex sentences**, which contain connectives or parentheses (e.g., $P \land Q$). The term **literal** is also used, meaning either an atomic sentence or a negated atomic sentence.

$Sentence \rightarrow AtomicSentence \mid ComplexSentence$

$AtomicSentence \rightarrow$ **True** $\mid$ **False**

$\mid P \mid Q \mid R \mid \dots$

$ComplexSentence \rightarrow (Sentence)$

$\mid Sentence\ Connective\ Sentence$

$\mid \neg Sentence$

$Connective \rightarrow \land \mid \lor \mid \Leftrightarrow \mid \Rightarrow$

Figure 6.8   A BNF (Backus–Naur Form) grammar of sentences in propositional logic.

Strictly speaking, the grammar is ambiguous—a sentence such as $P \land Q \lor R$ could be parsed as either $(P \land Q) \lor R$ or as $P \land (Q \lor R)$. This is similar to the ambiguity of arithmetic expressions such as $P + Q \times R$, and the way to resolve the ambiguity is also similar: we pick an order of precedence for the operators, but use parentheses whenever there might be confusion. The order of precedence in propositional logic is (from highest to lowest): ¬, ∧, ∨, ⇒, and ⇔. Hence, the sentence

$$\neg P \lor Q \land R \Rightarrow S$$

is equivalent to the sentence

$$((\neg P) \lor (Q \land R)) \Rightarrow S.$$

Semantics

The **semantics** of propositional logic is also quite straightforward. We define it by specifying the interpretation of the proposition symbols and constants, and specifying the meanings of the logical connectives.

A proposition symbol can mean whatever you want. That is, its interpretation can be any arbitrary fact. The interpretation of P might be the fact that Paris is the capital of France or that the wumpus is dead. A sentence containing just a proposition symbol is satisfiable but not valid: it is true just when the fact that it refers to is the case.

With logical constants, you have no choice; the sentence *True* always has as its interpretation the way the world actually is—the true fact. The sentence *False* always has as its interpretation the way the world is not.

A complex sentence has a meaning derived from the meaning of its parts. Each connective can be thought of as a function. Just as addition is a function that takes two numbers as input and returns a number, so *and* is a function that takes two truth values as input and returns a truth value. We know that one way to define a function is to make a table that gives the output value for every possible input value. For most functions (such as addition), this is impractical because of the size of the table, but there are only two possible truth values, so a logical function with two arguments needs a table with only four entries. Such a table is called a **truth table**. We give truth tables for the logical connectives in Figure 6.9. To use the table to determine, for example, the value of *True* $\lor$ *False*, first look on the left for the row where P is *true* and Q is *false* (the third row). Then look in that row under the $P \lor Q$ column to see the result: *True*.

P	Q	$\neg P$	$P \land Q$	$P \lor Q$	$P \Rightarrow Q$	$P \Leftrightarrow Q$
False	*False*	*True*	*False*	*False*	*True*	*True*
False	*True*	*True*	*False*	*True*	*True*	*False*
True	*False*	*False*	*False*	*True*	*False*	*False*
True	*True*	*False*	*True*	*True*	*True*	*True*

Figure 6.9   Truth tables for the five logical connectives.

Truth tables define the semantics of sentences such as *True* $\land$ *True*. Complex sentences such as $(P \lor Q) \land \neg S$ are defined by a process of decomposition: first, determine the meaning of $(P \land Q)$ and of $\neg S$, and then combine them using the definition of the $\land$ function. This is exactly analogous to the way a complex arithmetic expression such as $(p \times q) + -s$ is evaluated.

The truth tables for "and," "or," and "not" are in close accord with our intuitions about the English words. The main point of possible confusion is that $P \lor Q$ is true when either *or both P* and Q are true. There is a different connective called "exclusive or" ("xor" for short) that gives false when both disjuncts are true.[7] There is no consensus on the symbol for exclusive or; two choices are $\dot\lor$ and $\oplus$.

In some ways, the implication connective $\Rightarrow$ is the most important, and its truth table might seem puzzling at first, because it does not quite fit our intuitive understanding of "P implies Q"

---

[7] Latin has a separate word, *aut*, for exclusive or.

or "if *P* then *Q*." For one thing, propositional logic does not require any relation of causation or relevance between *P* and *Q*. The sentence "5 is odd implies Tokyo is the capital of Japan" is a true sentence of propositional logic (under the normal interpretation), even though it is a decidedly odd sentence of English. Another point of confusion is that any implication is true whenever its antecedent is false. For example, "5 is even implies Sam is smart" is true, regardless of whether Sam is smart. This seems bizarre, but it makes sense if you think of "$P \Rightarrow Q$" as saying, "If *P* is true, then I am claiming that *Q* is true. Otherwise I am making no claim."

Validity and inference

Truth tables can be used not only to define the connectives, but also to test for valid sentences. Given a sentence, we make a truth table with one row for each of the possible combinations of truth values for the proposition symbols in the sentence. For each row, we can calculate the truth value of the entire sentence. If the sentence is true in every row, then the sentence is valid. For example, the sentence

$$((P \vee H) \wedge \neg H) \Rightarrow P$$

is valid, as can be seen in Figure 6.10. We include some intermediate columns to make it clear how the final column is derived, but it is not important that the intermediate columns are there, as long as the entries in the final column follow the definitions of the connectives. Suppose *P* means that there is a wumpus in [1,3] and *H* means there is a wumpus in [2,2]. If at some point we learn $(P \vee H)$ and then we also learn $\neg H$, then we can use the valid sentence above to conclude that *P* is true—that the wumpus is in [1,3].

P	*H*	$P \vee H$	$(P \vee H) \wedge \neg H$	$((P \vee H) \wedge \neg H) \Rightarrow P$
False	False	False	False	True
False	True	True	False	True
True	False	True	True	True
True	True	True	False	True

Figure 6.10   Truth table showing validity of a complex sentence.

This is important. It says that if a machine has some premises and a possible conclusion, it can determine if the conclusion is true. It can do this by building a truth table for the sentence *Premises* $\Rightarrow$ *Conclusion* and checking all the rows. If every row is true, then the conclusion is entailed by the premises, which means that the fact represented by the conclusion follows from the state of affairs represented by the premises. Even though the machine has no idea what the conclusion means, the user could read the conclusions and use his or her interpretation of the proposition symbols to see what the conclusions mean—in this case, that the wumpus is in [1,3]. Thus, we have fulfilled the promise made in Section 6.3.

It will often be the case that the sentences input into the knowledge base by the user refer to a world to which the computer has no independent access, as in Figure 6.11, where it is the user who observes the world and types sentences into the computer. It is therefore essential that a reasoning system be able to draw conclusions that follow from the premises, regardless of the world to which the sentences are intended to refer. But it is a good idea for a reasoning system to follow this principle in any case. Suppose we replace the "user" in Figure 6.11 with a camera-based visual processing system that sends input sentences to the reasoning system. It makes no difference! Even though the computer now has "direct access" to the world, inference can still take place through direct operations on the syntax of sentences, without any additional information as to their intended meaning.

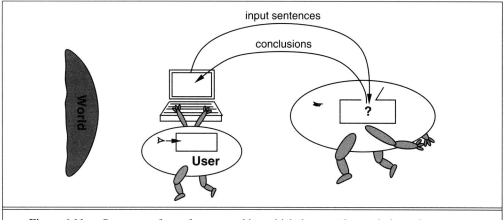

Figure 6.11   Sentences often refer to a world to which the agent has no independent access.

Models

MODEL

Any world in which a sentence is true under a particular interpretation is called a **model** of that sentence under that interpretation. Thus, the world shown in Figure 6.2 is a model of the sentence "$S_{1,2}$" under the interpretation in which it means that there is a stench in [1,2]. There are many other models of this sentence—you can make up a world that does or does not have pits and gold in various locations, and as long as the world has a stench in [1,2], it is a model of the sentence. The reason there are so many models is because "$S_{1,2}$" makes a very weak claim about the world. The more we claim (i.e., the more conjunctions we add into the knowledge base), the fewer models there will be.

Models are very important in logic, because, to restate the definition of **entailment**, *a sentence α is entailed by a knowledge base KB if the models of KB are all models of α.* If this is the case, then whenever *KB* is true, α must also be true.

In fact, we could define the meaning of a sentence by means of set operations on sets of models. For example, the set of models of $P \wedge Q$ is the intersection of the models of P and the models of Q. Figure 6.12 diagrams the set relationships for the four binary connectives.

We have said that models are worlds. One might feel that real worlds are rather messy things on which to base a formal system. Some authors prefer to think of models as *mathematical* objects. In this view, a model in propositional logic is simply a mapping from proposition symbols

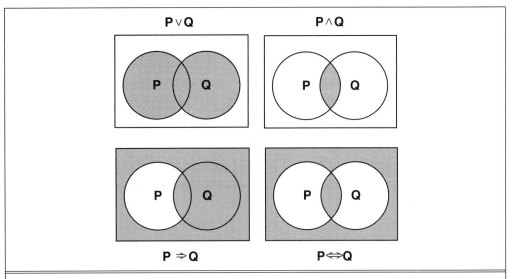

Figure 6.12   Models of complex sentences in terms of the models of their components. In each diagram, the shaded parts correspond to the models of the complex sentence.

directly to truth and falsehood, that is, the label for a row in a truth table. Then the models of a sentence are just those mappings that make the sentence true. The two views can easily be reconciled because each possible assignment of true and false to a set of proposition symbols can be viewed as an equivalence class of worlds that, under a given interpretation, have those truth values for those symbols. There may of course be many different "real worlds" that have the same truth values for those symbols. The only requirement to complete the reconciliation is that each proposition symbol be *either true or false* in each world. This is, of course, the basic ontological assumption of propositional logic, and is what allows us to expect that manipulations of symbols lead to conclusions with reliable counterparts in the actual world.

Rules of inference for propositional logic

The process by which the soundness of an inference is established through truth tables can be extended to entire *classes* of inferences. There are certain patterns of inferences that occur over and over again, and their soundness can be shown once and for all. Then the pattern can be **INFERENCE RULE**   captured in what is called an **inference rule**. Once a rule is established, it can be used to make inferences without going through the tedious process of building truth tables.

We have already seen the notation $\alpha \vdash \beta$ to say that β can be derived from α by inference. There is an alternative notation,

$$\frac{\alpha}{\beta}$$

which emphasizes that this is not a sentence, but rather an inference rule. Whenever something in the knowledge base matches the pattern above the line, the inference rule concludes the premise below the line. The letters α, β, etc., are intended to match any sentence, not just individual proposition symbols. If there are several sentences, in either the premise or the conclusion, they are separated by commas. Figure 6.13 gives a list of seven commonly used inference rules.

An inference rule is sound if the conclusion is true in all cases where the premises are true. To verify soundness, we therefore construct a truth table with one line for each possible model of the proposition symbols in the premise, and show that in all models where the premise is true, the conclusion is also true. Figure 6.14 shows the truth table for the resolution rule.

◇ **Modus Ponens** or **Implication-Elimination**: (From an implication and the premise of the implication, you can infer the conclusion.)

$$\frac{\alpha \Rightarrow \beta, \qquad \alpha}{\beta}$$

◇ **And-Elimination**: (From a conjunction, you can infer any of the conjuncts.)

$$\frac{\alpha_1 \wedge \alpha_2 \wedge \ldots \wedge \alpha_n}{\alpha_i}$$

◇ **And-Introduction**: (From a list of sentences, you can infer their conjunction.)

$$\frac{\alpha_1, \; \alpha_2, \quad \ldots, \quad \alpha_n}{\alpha_1 \wedge \alpha_2 \wedge \ldots \wedge \alpha_n}$$

◇ **Or-Introduction**: (From a sentence, you can infer its disjunction with anything else at all.)

$$\frac{\alpha_i}{\alpha_1 \vee \alpha_2 \vee \ldots \vee \alpha_n}$$

◇ **Double-Negation Elimination**: (From a doubly negated sentence, you can infer a positive sentence.)

$$\frac{\neg\neg\alpha}{\alpha}$$

◇ **Unit Resolution**: (From a disjunction, if one of the disjuncts is false, then you can infer the other one is true.)

$$\frac{\alpha \vee \beta, \qquad \neg\beta}{\alpha}$$

◇ **Resolution**: (This is the most difficult. Because β cannot be both true and false, one of the other disjuncts must be true in one of the premises. Or equivalently, implication is transitive.)

$$\frac{\alpha \vee \beta, \qquad \neg\beta \vee \gamma}{\alpha \vee \gamma} \qquad \text{or equivalently} \qquad \frac{\neg\alpha \Rightarrow \beta, \qquad \beta \Rightarrow \gamma}{\neg\alpha \Rightarrow \gamma}$$

Figure 6.13   Seven inference rules for propositional logic. The unit resolution rule is a special case of the resolution rule, which in turn is a special case of the full resolution rule for first-order logic discussed in Chapter 9.

α	β	γ	$\alpha \lor \beta$	$\neg \beta \lor \gamma$	$\alpha \lor \gamma$
False	*False*	*False*	*False*	*True*	*False*
False	*False*	*True*	*False*	*True*	*True*
False	*True*	*False*	*True*	*False*	*False*
False	*True*	*True*	*True*	*True*	*True*
True	*False*	*False*	*True*	*True*	*True*
True	*False*	*True*	*True*	*True*	*True*
True	*True*	*False*	*True*	*False*	*True*
True	*True*	*True*	*True*	*True*	*True*

Figure 6.14   A truth table demonstrating the soundness of the resolution inference rule. We have underlined the rows where both premises are true.

As we mentioned above, a logical proof consists of a sequence of applications of inference rules, starting with sentences initially in the KB, and culminating in the generation of the sentence whose proof is desired. To prove that P follows from $(P \lor H)$ and $\neg H$, for example, we simply require one application of the resolution rule, with α as P, β as H, and γ empty. The job of an inference procedure, then, is to construct proofs by finding appropriate sequences of applications of inference rules.

Complexity of propositional inference

The truth-table method of inference described on page 169 is complete, because it is always possible to enumerate the 2^n rows of the table for any proof involving n proposition symbols. On the other hand, the computation time is exponential in n, and therefore impractical. One might wonder whether there is a polynomial-time proof procedure for propositional logic based on using the inference rules from Section 6.4.

In fact, a version of this very problem was the first addressed by Cook (1971) in his theory of NP-completeness. (See also the appendix on complexity.) Cook showed that checking a set of sentences for satisfiability is NP-complete, and therefore unlikely to yield to a polynomial-time algorithm. However, this does not mean that all instances of propositional inference are going to take time proportional to 2^n. In many cases, the proof of a given sentence refers only to a small subset of the KB and can be found fairly quickly. In fact, as Exercise 6.15 shows, really hard problems are quite rare.

The use of inference rules to draw conclusions from a knowledge base relies implicitly on a general property of certain logics (including propositional and first-order logic) called MONOTONICITY **monotonicity**. Suppose that a knowledge base *KB* entails some set of sentences. A logic is monotonic if when we add some new sentences to the knowledge base, all the sentences entailed by the original *KB* are still entailed by the new larger knowledge base. Formally, we can state the property of monotonicity of a logic as follows:

if $KB_1 \models \alpha$ **then** $(KB_1 \cup KB_2) \models \alpha$

This is true regardless of the contents of KB_2—it can be irrelevant or even contradictory to KB_1.

It is fairly easy to show that propositional and first-order logic are monotonic in this sense; one can also show that probability theory is not monotonic (see Chapter 14). An inference rule such as Modus Ponens is **local** because its premise need only be compared with a small portion of the KB (two sentences, in fact). Were it not for monotonicity, we could not have any local inference rules because the rest of the KB might affect the soundness of the inference. This would potentially cripple any inference procedure.

HORN SENTENCES   There is also a useful class of sentences for which a polynomial-time inference procedure exists. This is the class called **Horn sentences**.[8] A Horn sentence has the form:

$$P_1 \wedge P_2 \wedge \ldots \wedge P_n \Rightarrow Q$$

where the P_i and Q are nonnegated atoms. There are two important special cases: First, when Q is the constant *False*, we get a sentence that is equivalent to $\neg P_1 \vee \ldots \vee \neg P_n$. Second, when $n = 1$ and $P_1 = True$, we get $True \Rightarrow Q$, which is equivalent to the atomic sentence Q. Not every knowledge base can be written as a collection of Horn sentences, but for those that can, we can use a simple inference procedure: apply Modus Ponens wherever possible until no new inferences remain to be made. We discuss Horn sentences and their associated inference procedures in more detail in the context of first-order logic (Section 9.4).

6.5   AN AGENT FOR THE WUMPUS WORLD

In this section, we show a snapshot of a propositional logic agent reasoning about the wumpus world. We assume that the agent has reached the point shown in Figure 6.4(a), repeated here as Figure 6.15, and show how the agent can conclude that the wumpus is in [1,3].

The knowledge base

On each turn, the agent's percepts are converted into sentences and entered into the knowledge base, along with some valid sentences that are entailed by the percept sentences. Let us assume that the symbol[9] $S_{1,2}$, for example, means "There is a stench in [1,2]." Similarly, $B_{2,1}$ means "There is a breeze in [2,1]." At this point, then, the knowledge base contains, among others, the percept sentences

$$\neg S_{1,1} \qquad \neg B_{1,1}$$
$$\neg S_{2,1} \qquad B_{2,1}$$
$$S_{1,2} \qquad \neg B_{1,2}$$

In addition, the agent must start out with some knowledge of the environment. For example, the agent knows that if a square has no smell, then neither the square nor any of its adjacent squares

---

8   Also known as **Horn clauses**. The name honors the logician Alfred Horn.

9   The subscripts make these symbols look like they have some kind of internal structure, but do not let that mislead you. We could have used Q or *StenchOneTwo* instead of $S_{1,2}$, but we wanted symbols that are both mnemonic and succinct.

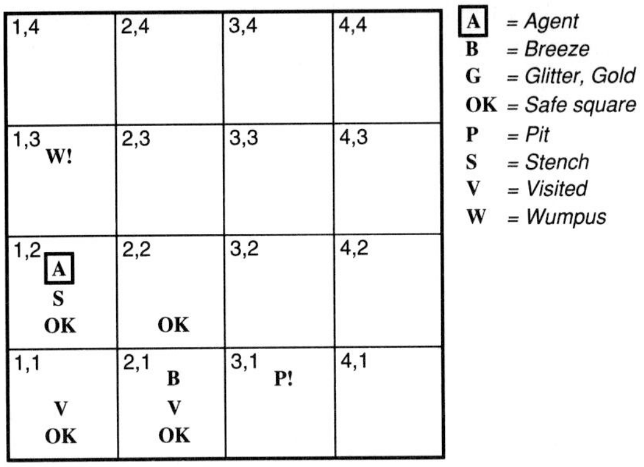

Figure 6.15   The agent's knowledge after the third move.   The current percept is [*Stench, None, None, None, None*].

can house a wumpus. The agent needs to know this for each square in the world, but here we just show sentences for three relevant squares, labeling each sentence with a rule number:

$$R_1: \quad \neg S_{1,1} \Rightarrow \neg W_{1,1} \wedge \neg W_{1,2} \wedge \neg W_{2,1}$$
$$R_2: \quad \neg S_{2,1} \Rightarrow \neg W_{1,1} \wedge \neg W_{2,1} \wedge \neg W_{2,2} \wedge \neg W_{3,1}$$
$$R_3: \quad \neg S_{1,2} \Rightarrow \neg W_{1,1} \wedge \neg W_{1,2} \wedge \neg W_{2,2} \wedge \neg W_{1,3}$$

Another useful fact is that if there is a stench in [1,2], then there must be a wumpus in [1,2] or in one or more of the neighboring squares. This fact can be represented by the sentence

$$R_4: \quad S_{1,2} \Rightarrow W_{1,3} \vee W_{1,2} \vee W_{2,2} \vee W_{1,1}$$

Finding the wumpus

Given these sentences, we will now show how an agent can mechanically conclude $W_{1,3}$. All the agent has to do is construct the truth table for $KB \Rightarrow W_{1,3}$ to show that this sentence is valid. There are 12 propositional symbols,[10] so the truth table will have $2^{12} = 4096$ rows, and every row in which the sentence KB is true also has $W_{1,3}$ true. Rather than show all 4096 rows, we use inference rules instead, but it is important to recognize that we could have done it in one (long) step just by following the truth-table algorithm.

First, we will show that the wumpus is not in one of the other squares, and then conclude by elimination that it must be in [1,3]:

1. Applying Modus Ponens with $\neg S_{1,1}$ and the sentence labelled R_1, we obtain

   $$\neg W_{1,1} \wedge \neg W_{1,2} \wedge \neg W_{2,1}$$

2. Applying And-Elimination to this, we obtain the three separate sentences

   $$\neg W_{1,1} \qquad \neg W_{1,2} \qquad \neg W_{2,1}$$

---

[10] The 12 symbols are $S_{1,1}, S_{2,1}, S_{1,2}, W_{1,1}, W_{1,2}, W_{2,1}, W_{2,2}, W_{3,1}, W_{1,3}, B_{1,1}, B_{2,1}, B_{1,2}$.

3. Applying Modus Ponens to $\neg S_{2,1}$ and the sentence labelled R_2, and then applying And-Elimination to the result, we obtain the three sentences

$$\neg W_{2,2} \qquad \neg W_{2,1} \qquad \neg W_{3,1}$$

4. Applying Modus Ponens to $S_{1,2}$ and the sentence labelled R_4, we obtain

$$W_{1,3} \vee W_{1,2} \vee W_{2,2} \vee W_{1,1}$$

5. Now we apply the unit resolution rule, where α is $W_{1,3} \vee W_{1,2} \vee W_{2,2}$ and β is $W_{1,1}$. (We derived $\neg W_{1,1}$ in step 2.) Unit resolution yields

$$W_{1,3} \vee W_{1,2} \vee W_{2,2}$$

6. Applying unit resolution again with $W_{1,3} \vee W_{1,2}$ as α and $W_{2,2}$ as β ($\neg W_{2,2}$ was derived in step 3), we obtain

$$W_{1,3} \vee W_{1,2}$$

7. Finally, one more resolution with $W_{1,3}$ as α and $W_{1,2}$ as β (we derived $\neg W_{1,2}$ in step 2) gives us the answer we want, namely, that the wumpus is in [1,3]:

$$W_{1,3}$$

Translating knowledge into action

We have shown how propositional logic can be used to infer knowledge such as the whereabouts of the wumpus. But the knowledge is only useful if it helps the agent take action. To do that, we will need additional rules that relate the current state of the world to the actions the agent should take. For example, if the wumpus is in the square straight ahead, then it is a bad idea to execute the action *Forward*. We can represent this with a series of rules, one for each location and orientation in which the agent might be. Here is the rule for the case where the agent is in [1,1] facing east:

$$A_{1,1} \wedge East_A \wedge W_{2,1} \ \Rightarrow \ \neg Forward$$

Once we have these rules, we need a way to ASK the knowledge base what action to take. Unfortunately, propositional logic is not powerful enough to represent or answer the question "what action should I take?," but it is able to answer a series of questions such as "should I go forward?" or "should I turn right?" That means that the algorithm for a knowledge-based agent using propositional logic would be as in Figure 6.16.

Problems with the propositional agent

Propositional logic allows us to get across all the important points about what a logic is and how it can be used to perform inference that eventually results in action. But propositional logic is so weak that it really cannot handle even a domain as simple as the wumpus world.

The main problem is that there are just too many propositions to handle. The simple rule "don't go forward if the wumpus is in front of you" can only be stated in propositional logic by a set of 64 rules (16 squares $\times$ 4 orientations for the agent). Naturally, it just gets worse if the

---

function PROPOSITIONAL-KB-AGENT(*percept*) **returns** an *action*
   static: *KB*, a knowledge base
         t, a counter, initially 0, indicating time

   TELL(*KB*, MAKE-PERCEPT-SENTENCE(*percept, t*))
   for each *action* **in** the list of possible actions **do**
      if ASK(*KB*, MAKE-ACTION-QUERY(*t, action*)) **then**
         $t \leftarrow t + 1$
         return *action*
  end

Figure 6.16   A knowledge-based agent using propositional logic.

---

world is larger than a 4×4 grid. Given this multiplication of rules, it will take thousands of rules to define a competent agent. The problem is not just that it is taxing to write the rules down, but also that having so many of them slows down the inference procedure. Remember that the size of a truth table is 2^n, where n is the number of propositional symbols in the knowledge base.

Another problem is dealing with change. We showed a snapshot of the agent reasoning at a particular point in time, and all the propositions in the knowledge base were true at that time. But in general the world changes over time. When the agent makes its first move, the proposition $A_{1,1}$ becomes false and $A_{2,1}$ becomes true. But it may be important for the agent to remember where it was in the past, so it cannot just forget $A_{1,1}$. To avoid confusion, we will need different propositional symbols for the agent's location at each time step. This causes difficulties in two ways. First, we do not know how long the game will go on, so we do not know how many of these time-dependent propositions we will need. Second, we will now have to go back and rewrite time-dependent versions of each rule. For example, we will need

$$A_{1,1}^0 \wedge East_A^0 \wedge W_{2,1}^0 \ \Rightarrow \ \neg Forward^0$$
$$A_{1,1}^1 \wedge East_A^1 \wedge W_{2,1}^1 \ \Rightarrow \ \neg Forward^1$$
$$A_{1,1}^2 \wedge East_A^2 \wedge W_{2,1}^2 \ \Rightarrow \ \neg Forward^2$$
$$\vdots$$
$$A_{1,1}^0 \wedge North_A^0 \wedge W_{1,2}^0 \ \Rightarrow \ \neg Forward^0$$
$$A_{1,1}^1 \wedge North_A^1 \wedge W_{1,2}^1 \ \Rightarrow \ \neg Forward^1$$
$$A_{1,1}^2 \wedge North_A^2 \wedge W_{1,2}^2 \ \Rightarrow \ \neg Forward^2$$
$$\vdots$$

where the superscripts indicate times. If we want the agent to run for 100 time steps, we will need 6400 of these rules, just to say one should not go forward when the wumpus is there.

In summary, the problem with propositional logic is that it only has one representational device: the proposition. In the next chapter, we will introduce first-order logic, which can represent *objects* and *relations* between objects in addition to propositions. In first-order logic, the 6400 propositional rules can be reduced to one.

6.6   SUMMARY

We have introduced the idea of a knowledge-based agent, and showed how we can define a logic with which the agent can reason about the world and be guaranteed to draw correct conclusions, given correct premises. We have also showed how an agent can turn this knowledge into action. The main points are as follows:

- Intelligent agents need knowledge about the world in order to reach good decisions.
- Knowledge is contained in agents in the form of **sentences** in a **knowledge representation language** that are stored in a **knowledge base**.
- A knowledge-based agent is composed of a knowledge base and an inference mechanism. It operates by storing sentences about the world in its knowledge base, using the inference mechanism to infer new sentences, and using them to decide what action to take.
- A representation language is defined by its **syntax** and **semantics**, which specify the structure of sentences and how they relate to facts in the world.
- The **interpretation** of a sentence is the fact to which it refers. If it refers to a fact that is part of the actual world, then it is **true**.
- Inference is the process of deriving new sentences from old ones. We try to design **sound** inference processes that derive true conclusions given true premises. An inference process is **complete** if it can derive *all* true conclusions from a set of premises.
- A sentence that is true in all worlds under all interpretations is called **valid**. If an implication sentence can be shown to be valid, then we can derive its consequent if we know its premise. The ability to show validity independent of meaning is essential.
- Different logics make different commitments about what the world is made of and what kinds of beliefs we can have regarding facts.
- Logics are useful for the commitments they *do not* make, because the lack of commitment gives the knowledge base writer more freedom.
- Propositional logic commits only to the existence of facts that may or may not be the case in the world being represented. It has a simple syntax and semantics, but suffices to illustrate the process of inference.
- Propositional logic can accommodate certain inferences needed by a logical agent, but quickly becomes impractical for even very small worlds.

BIBLIOGRAPHICAL AND HISTORICAL NOTES

Logic had its origins in ancient Greek philosophy and mathematics. Logical principles—principles connecting the syntactic structure of sentences with their truth and falsity, their meaning, or the validity of arguments in which they figure—can be found in scattered locations in the works of Plato (428–348 B.C.). The first known systematic study of logic was carried out by Aristotle, whose work was assembled by his students after his death in 322 B.C. as a treatise called the *Organon*, the first systematic treatise on logic. However, Aristotle's logic was very weak by modern standards; except in a few isolated instances, he did not take account of logical principles that depend essentially on embedding one entire syntactic structure within another structure of the same type, in the way that sentences are embedded within other sentences in modern propositional logic. Because of this limitation, there was a fixed limit on the amount of internal complexity within a sentence that could be analyzed using Aristotelian logic.

The closely related Megarian and Stoic schools (originating in the fifth century B.C. and continuing for several centuries thereafter) introduced the systematic study of implication and other basic constructs still used in modern propositional logic. The Stoics claimed that their logic was complete in the sense of capturing all valid inferences, but what remains is too fragmentary to tell. A good account of the history of Megarian and Stoic logic, as far as it is known, is given by Benson Mates (1953).

The ideas of creating an artificial formal language patterned on mathematical notation in order to clarify logical relationships, and of reducing logical inference to a purely formal and mechanical process, were due to Leibniz (1646–1716). Leibniz's own mathematical logic, however, was severely defective, and he is better remembered simply for introducing these ideas as goals to be attained than for his attempts at realizing them.

George Boole (1847) introduced the first reasonably comprehensive and approximately correct system of logic based on an artificial formal language with his book *The Mathematical Analysis of Logic*. Boole's logic was closely modeled on the ordinary algebra of real numbers. Boole's system subsumed the main parts of Aristotelian logic and also contained a close analogue to modern propositional logic. Although Boole's system still fell short of full propositional logic, it was close enough that other 19th-century writers following Boole could quickly fill in the gaps. The first comprehensive exposition of modern propositional logic (and first-order logic) is found in Gottlob Frege's (1879) *Begriffschrift* ("Concept Writing" or "Conceptual Notation").

Truth tables as a method of testing the validity or unsatisfiability of sentences in the language of propositional logic were independently introduced simultaneously by Ludwig Wittgenstein (1922) and by Emil Post (1921). (As a method of explaining the meanings of propositional connectives, truth tables go back to Philo of Megara.)

Quine (1982) describes "truth-value analysis," a proof method closely resembling truth tables but more efficient because, in effect, it can handle multiple lines of the truth table simultaneously. Wang (1960) takes a general proof method for first-order logic designed by Gentzen (1934) and selects a convenient and efficient subset of inference rules for use in a tree-based procedure for deciding validity in propositional logic.

John McCarthy's (1968) paper "Programs with Common Sense" promulgated the notion of agents that use logical reasoning to mediate between percepts and actions. This paper was the first to make this conception widely known, although it draws on much earlier work (McCarthy, 1958). The 1968 paper is also called the "Advice Taker" paper because it introduces a hypothetical program by that name which uses logic to enable its designers to communicate useful knowledge to it without having to write further directly executable computer code. Allen Newell's (1982) article "The Knowledge Level" focuses on the use of logic by agent designers to describe the knowledge that is, in effect, being used by the agents they are designing, whether or not the agents themselves use explicit logical formulas to represent this knowledge internally. This theme of Newell's was hinted at in 1943 by the psychologist Kenneth Craik, who writes, "My hypothesis then is that thought models, or parallels, reality—that its essential feature is not 'the mind,' 'the self,' 'sense-data,' nor propositions but symbolism, and that this symbolism is largely of the same kind as that which is familiar to us in mechanical devices which aid thought and calculation..." (Craik, 1943). Further work along these lines has been done by Rosenschein and Kaelbling (Rosenschein, 1985; Kaelbling and Rosenschein, 1990). Rosenschein and Genesereth (1987) have researched the problem of cooperative action among agents using propositional logic internally to represent the world. Gabbay (1991) has explored extensions to standard logic to enhance guidance of reasoning and retrieval from large knowledge bases.

EXERCISES

6.1   We said that truth tables can be used to establish the validity of a complex sentence. Show how they can be used to decide if a given sentence is valid, satisfiable, or unsatisfiable.

6.2   Use truth tables to show that the following sentences are valid, and thus that the equivalences hold. Some of these equivalence rules have standard names, which are given in the right column.

$$
\begin{array}{rcll}
P \wedge (Q \wedge R) & \Leftrightarrow & (P \wedge Q) \wedge R & \text{Associativity of conjunction} \\
P \vee (Q \vee R) & \Leftrightarrow & (P \vee Q) \vee R & \text{Associativity of disjunction} \\
P \wedge Q & \Leftrightarrow & Q \wedge P & \text{Commutativity of conjunction} \\
P \vee Q & \Leftrightarrow & Q \vee P & \text{Commutativity of disjunction} \\
P \wedge (Q \vee R) & \Leftrightarrow & (P \wedge Q) \vee (P \wedge R) & \text{Distributivity of } \wedge \text{ over } \vee \\
P \vee (Q \wedge R) & \Leftrightarrow & (P \vee Q) \wedge (P \vee R) & \text{Distributivity of } \vee \text{ over } \wedge \\
\neg(P \wedge Q) & \Leftrightarrow & \neg P \vee \neg Q & \text{de Morgan's Law} \\
\neg(P \vee Q) & \Leftrightarrow & \neg P \wedge \neg Q & \text{de Morgan's Law} \\
P \Rightarrow Q & \Leftrightarrow & \neg Q \Rightarrow \neg P & \text{Contraposition} \\
\neg\neg P & \Leftrightarrow & P & \text{Double Negation} \\
P \Rightarrow Q & \Leftrightarrow & \neg P \vee Q & \\
P \Leftrightarrow Q & \Leftrightarrow & (P \Rightarrow Q) \wedge (Q \Rightarrow P) & \\
P \Leftrightarrow Q & \Leftrightarrow & (P \wedge Q) \vee (\neg P \wedge \neg Q) & \\
P \wedge \neg P & \Leftrightarrow & \textit{False} & \\
P \vee \neg P & \Leftrightarrow & \textit{True} &
\end{array}
$$

6.3   Look at the following sentences and decide for each if it is valid, unsatisfiable, or neither. Verify your decisions using truth tables, or by using the equivalence rules of Exercise 6.2. Were there any that initially confused you?

a. *Smoke* $\Rightarrow$ *Smoke*

b. *Smoke* $\Rightarrow$ *Fire*

c. (*Smoke* $\Rightarrow$ *Fire*) $\Rightarrow$ ($\neg$*Smoke* $\Rightarrow$ $\neg$*Fire*)

d. *Smoke* $\vee$ *Fire* $\vee$ $\neg$*Fire*

e. $((Smoke \wedge Heat) \Rightarrow Fire) \Leftrightarrow ((Smoke \Rightarrow Fire) \vee (Heat \Rightarrow Fire))$

f. $(Smoke \Rightarrow Fire) \Rightarrow ((Smoke \wedge Heat) \Rightarrow Fire)$

g. $Big \vee Dumb \vee (Big \Rightarrow Dumb)$

h. $(Big \wedge Dumb) \vee \neg Dumb$

6.4   Is the sentence "Either $2 + 2 = 4$ and it is raining, or $2 + 2 = 4$ and it is not raining" making a claim about arithmetic, weather, or neither? Explain.

6.5   (Adapted from (Barwise and Etchemendy, 1993).) Given the following, can you prove that the unicorn is mythical? How about magical? Horned?

> If the unicorn is mythical, then it is immortal, but if it is not mythical, then it is a mortal mammal. If the unicorn is either immortal or a mammal, then it is horned. The unicorn is magical if it is horned.

6.6   What ontological and epistemological commitments are made by the language of real-number arithmetic?

6.7   Consider a world in which there are only four propositions, A, B, C, and D. How many models are there for the following sentences?

a. $A \wedge B$

b. $A \vee B$

c. $A \wedge B \wedge C$

6.8   We have defined four different binary logical connectives.

a. Are there any others that might be useful?

b. How many binary connectives can there possibly be?

c. Why are some of them not very useful?

6.9   Some agents make inferences as soon as they are told a new sentence, while others wait until they are asked before they do any inferencing. What difference does this make at the knowledge level, the logical level, and the implementation level?

6.10   We said it would take 64 propositional logic sentences to express the simple rule "don't go forward if the wumpus is in front of you." What if we represented this fact with the single rule

$$WumpusAhead \Rightarrow \neg Forward$$

Is this feasible? What effects does it have on the rest of the knowledge base?

6.11   Provide a formal syntax, semantics, and proof theory for algebraic equations including variables, numbers, $+$, $-$, $\times$, and $\div$. You should be able to provide inference steps for most standard equation manipulation techniques.

6.12   (Adapted from (Davis, 1990).) Jones, Smith, and Clark hold the jobs of programmer, knowledge engineer, and manager (not necessarily in that order). Jones owes the programmer $10. The manager's spouse prohibits borrowing money. Smith is not married. Your task is to figure out which person has which job.

Represent the facts in propositional logic. You should have nine propositional symbols to represent the possible person/job assignments. For example, you might use the symbol *SM* to indicate that Smith is the manager. You do not need to represent the relation between owing and borrowing, or being married and having a spouse; you can just use these to draw conclusions (e.g, from "Smith is not married" and "the manager's spouse" we know that Smith can't be the manager, which you can represent as $\neg SM$). The conjunction of all the relevant facts forms a sentence which you can call *KB*. The possible answers to the problem are sentences like $JP \wedge SK \wedge CM$. There are six such combinations of person/job assignments. Solve the problem by showing that only one of them is implied by *KB*, and by saying what its interpretation is.

6.13   What is the performance score that one could expect from the optimal wumpus world agent? Design an experiment wherein you look at all possible 4×4 wumpus worlds (or a random sample of them if there are too many), and for each one determine the shortest safe path to pick up the gold and return to start, and thus the best score. This gives you an idea of the expected performance score for an ideal omniscient agent. How could you determine the expected score for an optimal non-omniscient agent?

6.14   Implement a function VALIDITY that takes a sentence as input and returns either valid, satisfiable, or unsatisfiable. Use it to answer the questions in Exercise 6.12. You will need to define an implementation-level representation of sentences. The cleanest way to do this is to define an abstract data type for compound sentences. Begin by writing EVAL-TRUTH as a recursive function that takes a sentence and an assignment of truth values to proposition symbols, and returns true or false. Then call EVAL-TRUTH for all possible assignments of truth values to the proposition symbols.

6.15   SAT is the abbreviation for the satisfiability problem: given a propositional sentence, determine if it is satisfiable, and if it is, show which propositions have to be true to make the sentence true. 3SAT is the problem of finding a satisfying truth assignment for a sentence in a special format called 3-CNF, which is defined as follows:

- A **literal** is a proposition symbol or its negation (e.g., *P* or $\neg P$).
- A **clause** is a disjunction of literals; a 3-clause is a disjunction of exactly 3 literals (e.g., $P \vee Q \vee \neg R$).
- A sentence in CNF or **conjunctive normal form** is a conjunction of clauses; a 3-CNF sentence is a conjunction of 3-clauses.

For example,

$$(P \vee Q \vee \neg S) \wedge (\neg P \vee Q \vee R) \wedge (\neg P \vee \neg R \vee \neg S) \wedge (P \vee \neg S \vee T)$$

is a 3-CNF sentence with four clauses and five proposition symbols.

In this exercise, you will implement and test GSAT, an algorithm for solving SAT problems that has been used to investigate how hard 3SAT problems are. GSAT is a random-restart, hill-climbing search algorithm. The initial state is a random assignment of *true* and *false* to the proposition symbols. For example, for the preceding 3-CNF sentence, we might start with P and Q false and R, S, and T true.

The evaluation function measures the number of satisfied clauses, that is, clauses with at least one *true* disjunct. Thus, the initial state gets an evaluation of 3, because the second, third, and fourth clauses are true. If there are n proposition symbols, then there are n operators, where each operator is to change the truth assignment for one of the symbols. As a hill-climbing search, we always use the operator that yields the best evaluation (randomly choosing one if there are several equally good operators). Our example 3-CNF sentence is solved in one step, because changing S from *true* to *false* yields a solution. As with a random-restart algorithm, unless we find a solution after a certain amount of hill-climbing, we give up and start over from a new random truth assignment. After a certain number of restarts, we give up entirely. The complete algorithm is shown in Figure 6.17.

---

function GSAT(*sentence, max-restarts, max-climbs*) **returns** a truth assignment or failure

    for $i \leftarrow 1$ **to** *max-restarts* **do**
        $A \leftarrow$ A randomly generated truth assignment
        for $j \leftarrow 1$ **to** *max-climbs* **do**
            if A satisfies *sentence* **then return** A
            $A \leftarrow$ a random choice of one of the best successors of A
        end
    end
    return failure

Figure 6.17   The GSAT algorithm for satisfiability testing. The successors of an assignment A are truth assignment with one symbol flipped. A "best assignment" is one that makes the most clauses true.

Answer the following questions about the algorithm:

a. Is the GSAT algorithm sound?

b. Is it complete?

c. Implement GSAT and use it to solve the problems in Exercise 6.3.

d. Use GSAT to solve randomly generated 3SAT problems of different sizes. There are two key parameters: N, the number of propositional symbols, and C, the number of clauses. We will investigate the effects of the ratio C/N on the execution time of GSAT. With N fixed at 20, make a graph of the median execution time versus C/N for C/N from 1 to 10. (The median is a better statistic than the mean because one or two outliers can really throw off the mean.) Use N as the value of *max-restarts* and $5N$ as the value of *max-climbs*.

e. Repeat for other values of N as time permits.

f. What can you conclude about the difficulty of 3SAT problems for different values of C, N, and the ratio C/N?

See Selman *et al.* (1992) for more on GSAT. They present an implementation of GSAT that solves even the hardest 3SAT problems with $N = 70$ in under a second. GSAT can be used to solve a wide variety of problems by constructing a **reduction** from each class of problems to 3SAT. It is so efficient that it often outperforms special-purpose algorithms that are expertly designed for specific problems.

6.16   Consider the problem of designing a logical agent for the wumpus world using a Boolean circuit—that is, a collection of logic gates connecting the inputs (percept values) to outputs (action values).

a. Explain why you would need flip-flops.

b. Give an order-of-magnitude estimate of how many gates and flip-flops would you need.

7   FIRST-ORDER LOGIC

In which we introduce a logic that is sufficient for building knowledge-based agents.

In Chapter 6, we showed how a knowledge-based agent could represent the world in which it operates and use those representations to deduce what actions to take. We used propositional logic as our representation language because it is one of the simplest languages that demonstrates all the important points. Unfortunately, propositional logic has a very limited ontology, making only the commitment that the world consists of facts. This made it difficult to represent even something as simple as the wumpus world.

FIRST-ORDER LOGIC
OBJECTS
PROPERTIES
RELATIONS
FUNCTIONS

In this chapter, we examine **first-order logic**,[1] which makes a stronger set of ontological commitments. The main one is that the world consists of **objects**, that is, things with individual identities and **properties** that distinguish them from other objects.

Among these objects, various **relations** hold. Some of these relations are **functions**—relations in which there is only one "value" for a given "input." It is easy to start listing examples of objects, properties, relations, and functions:

- Objects: people, houses, numbers, theories, Ronald McDonald, colors, baseball games, wars, centuries ...
- Relations: brother of, bigger than, inside, part of, has color, occurred after, owns ...
- Properties: red, round, bogus, prime, multistoried ...
- Functions: father of, best friend, third inning of, one more than ...

Indeed, almost any fact can be thought of as referring to objects and properties or relations. Some examples follow:

- "One plus two equals three"
  Objects: one, two, three, one plus two; Relation: equals; Function: plus. (One plus two is a name for the object that is obtained by applying the function plus to the objects one and two. Three is another name for this object.)
- "Squares neighboring the wumpus are smelly."
  Objects: wumpus, square; Property: smelly; Relation: neighboring.

---

[1] Also called **first-order predicate calculus**, and sometimes abbreviated as **FOL** or **FOPC**.

- "Evil King John ruled England in 1200."
  Objects: John, England, 1200; Relation: ruled; Properties: evil, king.

First-order logic has been so important to mathematics, philosophy, and artificial intelligence precisely because those fields—and indeed, much of everyday human existence—can be usefully thought of as dealing with objects and the relations between them. We are not claiming that the world really *is* made up of objects and relations, just that dividing up the world that way helps us reason about it. First-order logic can also express facts about all of the objects in the universe. This, together with the implication connective from propositional logic, enables one to represent general laws or rules, such as the statement "Squares neighboring the wumpus are smelly."

Although first-order logic commits to the existence of objects and relations, it does not make an ontological commitment to such things as categories, time, and events, which also seem to show up in most facts about the world. Strangely enough, this reluctance to tackle categories, time, and events has not hurt the popularity of first-order logic; in fact it has contributed to its success. Important as these things are, there are just too many different ways to deal with them, and a logic that committed to a single treatment would only have limited appeal. By remaining neutral, first-order logic gives its users the freedom to describe these things in a way that is appropriate for the domain. This freedom of choice is a general characteristic of first-order logic. In the previous example we listed *King* as a property of people, but we could just as well have made *King* a relation between people and countries, or a function from countries to people (in a world in which each country has only one king).

There are many different representation schemes in use in AI, some of which we will discuss in later chapters. Some are theoretically equivalent to first-order logic and some are not. But first-order logic is universal in the sense that it can express anything that can be programmed. *We choose to study knowledge representation and reasoning using first-order logic because it is by far the most studied and best understood scheme yet devised.* Generally speaking, other proposals involving additional capabilities are still hotly debated and only partially understood. Other proposals that are a subset of first-order logic are useful only in limited domains. Despite its limitations, first-order logic will be around for a long time.

7.1   SYNTAX AND SEMANTICS

TERMS

In propositional logic every expression is a **sentence**, which represents a fact. First-order logic has sentences, but it also has **terms**, which represent objects. Constant symbols, variables, and function symbols are used to build terms, and quantifiers and predicate symbols are used to build sentences. Figure 7.1 gives a complete grammar of first-order logic, using Backus–Naur form (see page 854 if you are not familiar with this notation). A more detailed explanation of each element, describing both syntax and semantics, follows:

CONSTANT SYMBOLS

◇ **Constant symbols**: *A, B, C, John* ...

An interpretation must specify which object in the world is referred to by each constant symbol. Each constant symbol names exactly one object, but not all objects need to have names, and some can have several names. Thus, the symbol *John*, in one particular

$$
\begin{aligned}
\textit{Sentence} \;\rightarrow\; & \textit{AtomicSentence} \\
\mid\; & \textit{Sentence Connective Sentence} \\
\mid\; & \textit{Quantifier Variable,\dots\ Sentence} \\
\mid\; & \neg\ \textit{Sentence} \\
\mid\; & (\textit{Sentence}) \\[8pt]
\textit{AtomicSentence} \;\rightarrow\; & \textit{Predicate}(\textit{Term},\dots) \mid \textbf{\textit{Term = Term}} \\[8pt]
\textit{Term} \;\rightarrow\; & \textit{Function}(\textit{Term},\dots) \\
\mid\; & \textit{Constant} \\
\mid\; & \textit{Variable} \\[8pt]
\textit{Connective} \;\rightarrow\; & \Rightarrow \mid \wedge \mid \vee \mid \Leftrightarrow \\
\textit{Quantifier} \;\rightarrow\; & \forall \mid \exists \\
\textit{Constant} \;\rightarrow\; & A \mid X_1 \mid \textit{John} \mid \cdots \\
\textit{Variable} \;\rightarrow\; & a \mid x \mid s \mid \cdots \\
\textit{Predicate} \;\rightarrow\; & \textit{Before} \mid \textit{HasColor} \mid \textit{Raining} \mid \cdots \\
\textit{Function} \;\rightarrow\; & \textit{Mother} \mid \textit{LeftLegOf} \mid \cdots
\end{aligned}
$$

Figure 7.1   The syntax of first-order logic (with equality) in BNF (Backus–Naur Form).

interpretation, might refer to the evil King John, king of England from 1199 to 1216 and younger brother of Richard the Lionheart. The symbol *King* could refer to the same object/person in the same interpretation.

PREDICATE
SYMBOLS
◇ **Predicate symbols**: *Round, Brother, …*

An interpretation specifies that a predicate symbol refers to a particular relation in the model. For example, the *Brother* symbol might refer to the relation of brotherhood. *Brother* is a binary predicate symbol, and accordingly brotherhood is a relation that holds (or fails to hold) between pairs of objects. In any given model, the relation is defined by

TUPLES
the set of **tuples** of objects that satisfy it. A tuple is a collection of objects arranged in a fixed order. They are written with angle brackets surrounding the objects. In a model containing three objects, King John, Robin Hood, and Richard the Lionheart, the relation of brotherhood is defined by the set of tuples

{ ⟨King John, Richard the Lionheart⟩,
  ⟨Richard the Lionheart, King John⟩ }

Thus, formally speaking, *Brother* refers to this set of tuples under the interpretation we have chosen.

◇ **Function symbols**: *Cosine, FatherOf, LeftLegOf . . .*

Some relations are *functional*—that is, any given object is related to exactly one other object by the relation. For example, any angle has only one number that is its cosine; any person has only one person that is his or her father. In such cases, it is often more convenient to define a function symbol (e.g., *Cosine*) that refers to the appropriate relation between angles and numbers. In the model, the mapping is just a set of $n + 1$-tuples with a special property, namely, that the last element of each tuple is the value of the function for the first n elements, and each combination of the first n elements appears in exactly one tuple. A table of cosines is just such a set of tuples—for each possible angle of interest, it gives the cosine of the angle. Unlike predicate symbols, which are used to state that relations hold among certain objects, function symbols are used to refer to particular objects without using their names, as we will see in the next section.

The choice of constant, predicate, and function symbols is entirely up to the user. A mathematician might want to use + and *Cosine*, a composer *Crescendo* and *F-sharp*. The names do not matter from a formal point of view, but it enhances readability if the intended interpretation of the symbols is clear. We return to this point in Section 8.1.

Terms

A **term** is a logical expression that refers to an object. Constant symbols are therefore terms. Sometimes, it is more convenient to use an expression to refer to an object. For example, in English we might use the expression "King John's left leg" rather than giving a name to his leg. This is what function symbols are for: instead of using a constant symbol, we use *LeftLegOf*(*John*). In the general case, a complex term is formed by a function symbol followed by a parenthesized list of terms as arguments to the function symbol. It is important to remember that a complex term is just a complicated kind of name. It is not a "subroutine call" that "returns a value." There is no *LeftLegOf* subroutine that takes a person as input and returns a leg. We can reason about left legs (e.g., stating the general rule that everyone has one and then deducing that John must have one) without ever providing a definition of *LeftLegOf*. This is something that cannot be done with subroutines in programming languages.

The formal semantics of terms is straightforward. An interpretation specifies a functional relation referred to by the function symbol, and objects referred to by the terms that are its arguments. Thus, the whole term refers to the object that appears as the $(n+1)$-th entry in that tuple in the relation whose first n elements are the objects referred to by the arguments. Thus, the *LeftLegOf* function symbol might refer to the following functional relation:

{   ⟨King John, King John's left leg⟩,
    ⟨Richard the Lionheart, Richard's left leg⟩ }

and if *KingJohn* refers to King John, then *LeftLegOf*(*KingJohn*) refers, according to the relation, to King John's left leg.

Atomic sentences

Now that we have terms for referring to objects, and predicate symbols for referring to relations, we can put them together to make **atomic sentences** that state facts. An atomic sentence is formed from a predicate symbol followed by a parenthesized list of terms. For example,

> *Brother*(*Richard*, *John*)

states, under the interpretation given before, that Richard the Lionheart is the brother of King John.[2] Atomic sentences can have arguments that are complex terms:

> *Married*(*FatherOf*(*Richard*), *MotherOf*(*John*))

states that Richard the Lionheart's father is married to King John's mother (again, under a suitable interpretation). *An atomic sentence is **true** if the relation referred to by the predicate symbol holds between the objects referred to by the arguments.* The relation holds just in case the tuple of objects is in the relation. The truth of a sentence therefore depends on both the interpretation and the world.

Complex sentences

We can use **logical connectives** to construct more complex sentences, just as in propositional calculus. The semantics of sentences formed using logical connectives is identical to that in the propositional case. For example:

- *Brother*(*Richard*, *John*) ∧ *Brother*(*John*, *Richard*) is true just when John is the brother of Richard and Richard is the brother of John.
- *Older*(*John*, 30) ∨ *Younger*(*John*, 30) is true just when John is older than 30 or John is younger than 30.
- *Older*(*John*, 30) ⇒ ¬*Younger*(*John*, 30) states that if John is older than 30, then he is not younger than 30.[3]
- ¬*Brother*(*Robin*, *John*) is true just when Robin is not the brother of John.

Quantifiers

QUANTIFIERS

Once we have a logic that allows objects, it is only natural to want to express properties of entire collections of objects, rather than having to enumerate the objects by name. **Quantifiers** let us do this. First-order logic contains two standard quantifiers, called *universal* and *existential*.

Universal quantification (∀)

Recall the difficulty we had in Chapter 6 with the problem of expressing general rules in propositional logic. Rules such as "All cats are mammals" are the bread and butter of first-order logic.

---

[2] We will usually follow the argument ordering convention that $P(x, y)$ is interpreted as "x is a P of y."

[3] Although these last two sentences may seem like tautologies, they are not. There are interpretations of *Younger* and *Older* in which they are false.

To express this particular rule, we will use unary predicates *Cat* and *Mammal*; thus, "Spot is a cat" is represented by *Cat*(*Spot*), and "Spot is a mammal" by *Mammal*(*Spot*). In English, what we want to say is that for any object x, if x is a cat then x is a mammal. First-order logic lets us do this as follows:

$$\forall x \ \ Cat(x) \Rightarrow Mammal(x)$$

$\forall$ is usually pronounced "For all ...". Remember that the upside-down A stands for "all." You can think of a sentence $\forall x \ \ P$, where P is any logical expression, as being equivalent to the conjunction (i.e., the $\land$) of all the sentences obtained by substituting the name of an object for the **variable** x wherever it appears in P. The preceding sentence is therefore equivalent to

VARIABLE

$$Cat(Spot) \Rightarrow Mammal(Spot) \land$$
$$Cat(Rebecca) \Rightarrow Mammal(Rebecca) \land$$
$$Cat(Felix) \Rightarrow Mammal(Felix) \land$$
$$Cat(Richard) \Rightarrow Mammal(Richard) \land$$
$$Cat(John) \Rightarrow Mammal(John) \land$$
$$\vdots$$

Thus, it is true if and only if all these sentences are true, that is, if P is true for all objects x in the universe. Hence $\forall$ is called a **universal** quantifier.

We use the convention that all variables start with a lowercase letter, and that all constant, predicate, and function symbols are capitalized. A variable is a term all by itself, and as such can also serve as the argument of a function, for example, *ChildOf*(*x*). A term with no variables is called a **ground term**.

GROUND TERM

It is worth looking carefully at the conjunction of sentences given before. If Spot, Rebecca, and Felix are known to be cats, then the first three conjuncts allow us to conclude that they are mammals. But what about the next two conjuncts, which appear to make claims about King John and Richard the Lionheart? Is that part of the meaning of "all cats are mammals"? In fact, these conjuncts are true, but make no claim whatsoever about the mammalian qualifications of John and Richard. This is because *Cat*(*Richard*) and *Cat*(*John*) are (presumably) false. Looking at the truth table for $\Rightarrow$ (Figure 6.9), we see that the whole sentence is true whenever the left-hand side of the implication is false—*regardless* of the truth of the right-hand side. Thus, by asserting the universally quantified sentence, which is equivalent to asserting a whole list of individual implication sentences, we end up asserting the right-hand side of the rule just for those individuals for whom the left-hand side is true, and saying nothing at all about those individuals for whom the left-hand side is false. Thus, the truth-table entries for $\Rightarrow$ turn out to be perfect for writing general rules with universal quantifiers.

It is tempting to think that the presence of the condition *Cat*(*x*) on the left-hand side of the implication means that somehow the universal quantifier ranges only over cats. This is perhaps helpful but not technically correct. Again, the universal quantification makes a statement about *everything*, but it does not make any claim about whether non-cats are mammals or not. On the other hand, if we tried to express "all cats are mammals" using the sentence

$$\forall x \ \ Cat(x) \land Mammal(x)$$

this would be equivalent to

> $Cat(Spot) \land Mammal(Spot) \land$
> $Cat(Rebecca) \land Mammal(Rebecca) \land$
> $Cat(Felix) \land Mammal(Felix) \land$
> $Cat(Richard) \land Mammal(Richard) \land$
> $Cat(John) \land Mammal(John) \land$
> $\vdots$

Obviously, this does not capture what we want, because it says that Richard the Lionheart is both a cat and a mammal.

Existential quantification ($\exists$)

Universal quantification makes statements about every object. Similarly, we can make a statement about *some* object in the universe without naming it, by using an existential quantifier. To say, for example, that Spot has a sister who is a cat, we write

> $\exists x \ Sister(x, Spot) \land Cat(x)$

$\exists$ is pronounced "There exists ...". In general, $\exists x \ P$ is true if P is true for *some* object in the universe. It therefore can be thought of as equivalent to the disjunction (i.e., the $\lor$) of all the sentences obtained by substituting the name of an object for the variable x. Doing the substitution for the above sentence, we would get

> $(Sister(Spot, Spot) \land Cat(Spot)) \lor$
> $(Sister(Rebecca, Spot) \land Cat(Rebecca)) \lor$
> $(Sister(Felix, Spot) \land Cat(Felix)) \lor$
> $(Sister(Richard, Spot) \land Cat(Richard)) \lor$
> $(Sister(John, Spot) \land Cat(John)) \lor$
> $\vdots$

The existentially quantified sentence is true just in case at least one of these disjuncts is true. If Spot had two sisters who were cats, then two of the disjuncts would be true, making the whole disjunction true also. This is entirely consistent with the original sentence "Spot has a sister who is a cat."[4]

Just as $\Rightarrow$ appears to be the natural connective to use with $\forall$, $\land$ is the natural connective to use with $\exists$. Using $\land$ as the main connective with $\forall$ led to an overly strong statement in the example in the previous section; using $\Rightarrow$ with $\exists$ usually leads to a very weak statement indeed. Consider the following representation:

> $\exists x \ Sister(x, Spot) \Rightarrow Cat(x)$

---

[4] There is a variant of the existential quantifier, usually written $\exists^1$ or $\exists!$, that means "There exists exactly one ...". The same meaning can be expressed using equality statements, as we show in Section 7.1.

On the surface, this might look like a reasonable rendition of our sentence. But expanded out into a disjunction, it becomes

$$(Sister(Spot, Spot) \Rightarrow Cat(Spot)) \lor$$
$$(Sister(Rebecca, Spot) \Rightarrow Cat(Rebecca)) \lor$$
$$(Sister(Felix, Spot) \Rightarrow Cat(Felix)) \lor$$
$$(Sister(Richard, Spot) \Rightarrow Cat(Richard)) \lor$$
$$(Sister(John, Spot) \Rightarrow Cat(John)) \lor$$
$$\vdots$$

Now, this disjunction will be satisfied if any of its disjuncts are true. An implication is true if both premise and conclusion are true, *or if its premise is false.* So if Richard the Lionheart is not Spot's sister, then the implication $Sister(Spot, Richard) \Rightarrow Cat(Richard)$ is true and the entire disjunction is therefore true. So, an existentially quantified implication sentence is true in a universe containing any object for which the premise of the implication is false; hence such sentences really do not say much at all.

Nested quantifiers

We will often want to express more complex sentences using multiple quantifiers. The simplest case is where the quantifiers are of the same type. For example, "For all x and all y, if x is the parent of y then y is the child of x" becomes

$$\forall x, y \quad Parent(x, y) \Rightarrow Child(y, x)$$

$\forall x, y$ is equivalent to $\forall x \quad \forall y$. Similarly, the fact that a person's brother has that person as a sibling is expressed by

$$\forall x, y \quad Brother(x, y) \Rightarrow Sibling(y, x)$$

In other cases we will have mixtures. "Everybody loves somebody" means that for every person, there is someone that person loves:

$$\forall x \quad \exists y \quad Loves(x, y)$$

On the other hand, to say "There is someone who is loved by everyone" we write

$$\exists y \quad \forall x \quad Loves(x, y)$$

The order of quantification is therefore very important. It becomes clearer if we put in parentheses. In general, $\forall x \quad (\exists y \quad P(x, y))$, where $P(x, y)$ is some arbitrary sentence involving x and y, says that *every* object in the universe has a particular property, namely, the property that it is related to some object by the relation P. On the other hand, $\exists x \quad (\forall y \quad P(x, y))$ says that there is *some* object in the world that has a particular property, namely the property of being related by P to every object in the world.

A minor difficulty arises when two quantifiers are used with the same variable name. Consider the sentence

$$\forall x \quad [Cat(x) \lor (\exists x \quad Brother(Richard, x))]$$

Here the x in $Brother(Richard, x)$ is *existentially* quantified. The rule is that the variable belongs to the innermost quantifier that mentions it; then it will not be subject to any other quantification.

This is just like variable scoping in block-structured programming languages like Pascal and Lisp, where an occurrence of a variable name refers to the innermost block that declared the variable. Another way to think of it is this: $\exists x \; Brother(Richard, x)$ is a sentence about Richard (that he has a brother), not about x; so putting a $\forall x$ outside it has no effect. It could equally well have been written $\exists z \; Brother(Richard, z)$. Because this can be a source of confusion, we will always use different variables.

Every variable must be introduced by a quantifier before it is used. A sentence like $\forall x \; P(y)$, in which y does not have a quantifier, is incorrect.[5] The term **well-formed formula** or **wff** is sometimes used for sentences that have all their variables properly introduced.

WFF

Connections between $\forall$ and $\exists$

The two quantifiers are actually intimately connected with each other, through negation. When one says that everyone dislikes parsnips, one is also saying that there does not exist someone who likes them; and vice versa:

$\forall x \; \neg Likes(x, Parsnips)$ is equivalent to $\neg\exists x \; Likes(x, Parsnips)$

We can go one step further. "Everyone likes ice cream" means that there is no one who does not like ice cream:

$\forall x \; Likes(x, IceCream)$ is equivalent to $\neg\exists x \; \neg Likes(x, IceCream)$

Because $\forall$ is really a conjunction over the universe of objects and $\exists$ is a disjunction, it should not be surprising that they obey De Morgan's rules. The De Morgan rules for quantified and unquantified sentences are as follows:

$$\begin{array}{llll}
\forall x \; \neg P & \equiv \; \neg\exists x \; P & \neg P \wedge \neg Q & \equiv \; \neg(P \vee Q) \\
\neg\forall x \; P & \equiv \; \exists x \; \neg P & \neg(P \wedge Q) & \equiv \; \neg P \vee \neg Q \\
\forall x \; P & \equiv \; \neg\exists x \; \neg P & P \wedge Q & \equiv \; \neg(\neg P \vee \neg Q) \\
\exists x \; P & \equiv \; \neg\forall x \; \neg P & P \vee Q & \equiv \; \neg(\neg P \wedge \neg Q)
\end{array}$$

Thus, we do not really need both $\forall$ and $\exists$, just as we do not really need both $\wedge$ and $\vee$. Some formal logicians adopt a principal of parsimony, throwing out any syntactic item that is not strictly necessary. For the purposes of AI, the content, and hence the readability, of the sentences are important. Therefore, we will keep both of the quantifiers.

Equality

First-order logic includes one more way to make atomic sentences, other than using a predicate and terms as described earlier. We can use the **equality symbol** to make statements to the effect that two terms refer to the same object. For example,

EQUALITY SYMBOL

$Father(John) = Henry$

says that the object referred to by $Father(John)$ and the object referred to by $Henry$ are the same.

---

[5] Sometimes there is an assumption that all unquantified variables are introduced with an implicit $\forall$. This is the case in most logic programming languages.

IDENTITY RELATION

Equality can be viewed as a predicate symbol with a predefined meaning, namely, that it is fixed to refer to the **identity relation**. The identity relation is the set of all pairs of objects in which both elements of each pair are the same object:

$$\{ \ \langle \text{Spot}, \text{Spot} \rangle,$$
$$\langle \text{Rebecca}, \text{Rebecca} \rangle,$$
$$\langle \text{Felix}, \text{Felix} \rangle,$$
$$\langle \text{Richard the Lionheart}, \text{Richard the Lionheart} \rangle,$$
$$\langle \text{King John}, \text{King John} \rangle,$$
$$\langle \text{Henry II}, \text{Henry II} \rangle,$$
$$\dots \}$$

Thus, to see if $Father(John) = Henry$ is true in a particular interpretation, we first look in the functional relation for *Father* and find the entry

$$\{ \ \dots$$
$$\langle \text{King John}, \text{Henry II} \rangle,$$
$$\dots \}$$

Then, because *Henry* refers to Henry II, the equality statement is true because $\langle \text{Henry II}, \text{Henry II} \rangle$ is in the equality relation.

The equality symbol can be used to describe the properties of a given function, as we did above for the *Father* symbol. It can also be used with negation to insist that two terms are not the same object. To say that Spot has at least two sisters, we would write

$$\exists x, y \ \ Sister(Spot, x) \wedge Sister(Spot, y) \wedge \neg(x = y)$$

If we simply wrote

$$\exists x, y \ \ Sister(Spot, x) \wedge Sister(Spot, y)$$

that would not assert the existence of two distinct sisters, because nothing says that x and y have to be different. Consider the expansion of the existential statement into a disjunction: it will include as a disjunct

$$\dots \vee (Sister(Spot, Rebecca) \wedge Sister(Spot, Rebecca)) \vee \dots$$

which occurs when *Rebecca* is substituted for both x and y. If Rebecca is indeed Spot's sister, then the existential will be satisfied because this disjunct will be true. The addition of $\neg(x = y)$ makes the disjunct false, because $Rebecca = Rebecca$ is necessarily true. The notation $x \neq y$ is sometimes used as an abbreviation for $\neg(x = y)$.

7.2   EXTENSIONS AND NOTATIONAL VARIATIONS

In this section we look at three types of alternatives to first-order logic. First, we look at an extension called higher-order logic. Second, we consider some abbreviations that add no new power to first-order logic but do make the resulting sentences more concise. Third, we look at variations on our notation for first-order logic.

Higher-order logic

First-order logic gets its name from the fact that one can quantify over *objects* (the first-order entities that actually exist in the world) but not over relations or functions on those objects.

HIGHER-ORDER
LOGIC

Higher-order logic allows us to quantify over relations and functions as well as over objects. For example, in higher-order logic we can say that two objects are equal if and only if all properties applied to them are equivalent:

$$\forall x, y \ (x = y) \ \Leftrightarrow \ (\forall p \ p(x) \Leftrightarrow p(y))$$

Or we could say that two functions are equal if and only if they have the same value for all arguments:

$$\forall f, g \ (f = g) \ \Leftrightarrow \ (\forall x \ f(x) = g(x))$$

Higher-order logics have strictly more expressive power than first-order logic. As yet, however, logicians have little understanding of how to reason effectively with sentences in higher-order logic, and the general problem is known to be undecidable. In this book, we will stick to first-order logic, which is much better understood and still very expressive.

Functional and predicate expressions using the λ operator

It is often useful to be able to construct complex predicates and functions from simpler components, just as we can construct complex sentences from simpler components (e.g., $P \wedge Q$), or complex terms from simpler ones (e.g., $x^2 + y^3$). To turn the term $x^2 - y^2$ into a function, we need to say what its arguments are: is it the function where you square the first argument and subtract the square of the second argument, or vice versa? The operator λ (the Greek letter lambda) is traditionally used for this purpose. The function that takes the difference of the squares of its first and second argument is written as

$$\lambda x, y \ x^2 - y^2$$

λ-EXPRESSION

This λ-**expression**[6] can then be applied to arguments to yield a logical term in the same way that an ordinary, named function can:

$$(\lambda x, y \ x^2 - y^2)(25, 24) = 25^2 - 24^2 = 49$$

We will also find it useful (in Chapter 22) to generate λ-expressions for predicates. For example, the two-place predicate "are of differing gender and of the same address" can be written

$$\lambda x, y \ Gender(x) \neq Gender(y) \wedge Address(x) = Address(y)$$

As one would expect, the application of a predicate λ-expression to an appropriate number of arguments yields a logical sentence. Notice that the use of λ in this way does *not* increase the formal expressive power of first-order logic, because any sentence that includes a λ-expression can be rewritten by "plugging in" its arguments to yield a standard term or sentence.

---

[6] The same terminology is used in Lisp, where `lambda` plays exactly the same role as the λ operator.

The uniqueness quantifier $\exists$!

We have seen how to use $\exists$ to say that *some* objects exist, but there is no concise way to say that a *unique* object satisfying some predicate exists. Some authors use the notation

$$\exists! x \; King(x)$$

to mean "there exists a unique object x satisfying $King(x)$" or more informally, "there's exactly one King." You should think of this not as adding a new quantifier, $\exists!$, but rather as being a convenient abbreviation for the longer sentence

$$\exists x \; King(x) \wedge \forall y \; King(y) \; \Rightarrow \; x = y$$

Of course, if we knew from the start there was only one King, we probably would have used the constant *King* rather than the predicate *King(x)*. A more complex example is "Every country has exactly one ruler":

$$\forall c \; Country(c) \; \Rightarrow \; \exists! r \; Ruler(r, c)$$

The uniqueness operator ι

It is convenient to use $\exists!$ to state uniqueness, but sometimes it is even more convenient to have a term representing the unique object directly. The notation $\iota x P(x)$ is commonly used for this. (The symbol ι is the Greek letter iota.) To say that "the unique ruler of Freedonia is dead" or equivalently "the r that is the ruler of Freedonia is dead," we would write:

$$Dead(\iota r \, Ruler(r, Freedonia))$$

This is just an abbreviation for the following sentence:

$$\exists! r \; Ruler(r, Freedonia) \wedge \forall s \; Ruler(s, Freedonia) \; \Rightarrow \; Dead(s)$$

Notational variations

The first-order logic notation used in this book is the *de facto* standard for artificial intelligence; one can safely use the notation in a journal article without defining it, because it is recognizable to most readers. Several other notations have been developed, both within AI and especially in other fields that use logic, including mathematics, computer science, and philosophy. Here are some of the variations:

Syntax item	This book	Others
Negation (not)	$\neg P$	$\sim P \quad \overline{P}$
Conjunction (and)	$P \wedge Q$	$P \& Q \quad P \cdot Q \quad PQ \quad P, Q$
Disjunction (or)	$P \vee Q$	$P \mid Q \quad P; Q \quad P + Q$
Implication (if)	$P \Rightarrow Q$	$P \rightarrow Q \quad P \supset Q$
Equivalence (iff)	$P \Leftrightarrow Q$	$P \equiv Q \quad P \leftrightarrow Q$
Universal (all)	$\forall x \; P(x)$	$(\forall x) P(x) \quad \bigwedge x \, P(x) \quad P(x)$
Existential (exists)	$\exists x \; P(x)$	$(\exists x) P(x) \quad \bigvee x \, P(x) \quad P(Skolem_i)$
Relation	$R(x, y)$	$(R \, x \, y) \quad Rxy \quad xRy$

Two other common notations derive from implementations of logic in computer systems. The logic programming language Prolog (which we discuss further in Chapter 10) has two main differences. It uses uppercase letters for variables and lowercase for constants, whereas most other notations do the reverse. Prolog also reverses the order of implications, writing $Q :\text{-} P$ instead of $P \Rightarrow Q$. A comma is used both to separate arguments and for conjunction, and a period marks the end of a sentence:

```
cat(X)  :- furry(X), meows(X), has(X,claws).
```

In reasoning systems implemented in Lisp, a consistent prefix notation is common. Each sentence and nonconstant term is surrounded by parentheses, and the connectives come first, just like the predicate and function symbols. Because Lisp does not distinguish between uppercase and lowercase symbols, variables are usually distinguished by an initial ? or $ character, as in this example:

```
(forall ?x
   (implies (and (furry ?x) (meows ?x) (has ?x claws))
            (cat ?x)))
```

7.3   USING FIRST-ORDER LOGIC

DOMAIN

In knowledge representation, a **domain** is a section of the world about which we wish to express some knowledge. In this chapter, we start with some simple domains, using first-order logic to represent family relationships and mathematical sets. We then move on to show the knowledge that an agent in the wumpus world would need. Chapter 8 goes into more depth on the use of first-order logic for knowledge representation.

The kinship domain

The first example we consider is the domain of family relationships, or kinship. This domain includes facts such as "Elizabeth is the mother of Charles" and "Charles is the father of William," and rules such as "If x is the mother of y and y is a parent of z, then x is a grandmother of z."

Clearly, the objects in our domain are people. The properties they have include gender, and they are related by relations such as parenthood, brotherhood, marriage, and so on. Thus, we will are have two unary predicates, *Male* and *Female*. Most of the kinship relations will be binary predicates: *Parent, Sibling, Brother, Sister, Child, Daughter, Son, Spouse, Wife, Husband, Grandparent, Grandchild, Cousin, Aunt, Uncle*. We will use functions for *Mother* and *Father*, because every person has exactly one of each of these (at least according to nature's design).

We can go through each function and predicate, writing down what we know in terms of the other symbols. For example, one's mother is one's female parent:

$$\forall m, c \; Mother(c) = m \iff Female(m) \land Parent(m, c)$$

One's husband is one's male spouse:

$$\forall w, h \quad Husband(h, w) \iff Male(h) \land Spouse(h, w)$$

Male and female are disjoint categories:

$$\forall x \quad Male(x) \iff \neg Female(x)$$

Parent and child are inverse relations:

$$\forall p, c \quad Parent(p, c) \iff Child(c, p)$$

A grandparent is a parent of one's parent:

$$\forall g, c \quad Grandparent(g, c) \iff \exists p \quad Parent(g, p) \land Parent(p, c)$$

A sibling is another child of one's parents:

$$\forall x, y \quad Sibling(x, y) \iff x \neq y \land \exists p \quad Parent(p, x) \land Parent(p, y)$$

We could go on for several more pages like this, and in Exercise 7.6 we ask you to do just that.

Axioms, definitions, and theorems

AXIOMS

THEOREMS

Mathematicians write **axioms** to capture the basic facts about a domain, define other concepts in terms of those basic facts, and then use the axioms and definitions to prove **theorems**. In AI, we rarely use the term "theorem," but the sentences that are in the knowledge base initially are sometimes called "axioms," and it is common to talk of "definitions." This brings up an important question: how do we know when we have written down enough axioms to fully specify a domain? One way to approach this is to decide on a set of basic predicates in terms of which all the other predicates can be defined. In the kinship domain, for example, *Child*, *Spouse*, *Male*, and *Female* would be reasonable candidates for basic predicates. In other domains, as we will see, there is no clearly identifiable basic set.[7]

The converse problem also arises: do we have too many sentences? For example, do we need the following sentence, specifying that siblinghood is a symmetric relation?

$$\forall x, y \quad Sibling(x, y) \iff Sibling(y, x)$$

In this case, we do not. From *Sibling(John, Richard)*, we can infer that

$$\exists p \quad Parent(p, John) \land Parent(p, Richard),$$

INDEPENDENT
AXIOM

and from that we can infer *Sibling(Richard, John)*. In mathematics, an **independent axiom** is one that cannot be derived from all the other axioms. Mathematicians strive to produce a minimal set of axioms that are all independent. In AI it is common to include redundant axioms, not because they can have any effect on what can be proved, but because they can make the process of finding a proof more efficient.

DEFINITION

An axiom of the form $\forall x, y \quad P(x, y) \equiv \ldots$ is often called a **definition** of P, because it serves to define exactly for what objects P does and does not hold. It is possible to have several definitions for the same predicate; for example, a triangle could be defined both as a polygon

---

[7] In *all* cases, the set of sentences will have models other than the intended model; this follows from a theorem of Löwenheim's stating that all consistent axiom sets have a model whose domain is the integers.

with three sides and as a polygon with three angles. Many predicates will have no complete definition of this kind, because we do not know enough to fully characterize them. For example, how would you complete the sentence:

$\forall x \; Person(x) \; \Leftrightarrow \; \dots$

Fortunately, first-order logic allows us to make use of the *Person* predicate without completely defining it. Instead we can write partial specifications of properties that every person has and properties that make something a person:

$\forall x \; Person(x) \; \Rightarrow \; \dots$
$\forall x \; \dots \; \Rightarrow Person(x)$

The domain of sets

The domain of mathematical sets is somewhat more abstract than cats or kings, but nevertheless forms a coherent body of knowledge that we would like to be able to represent. We want to be able to represent individual sets, including the empty set. We need a way to build up sets by adding an element to a set or taking the union or intersection of two sets. We will want to know if an element is a member of a set, and to be able to distinguish sets from objects that are not sets.

   We will use the normal vocabulary of set theory: *EmptySet* is a constant; *Member* and *Subset* are predicates; and *Intersection*, *Union*, and *Adjoin* are functions. (*Adjoin* is the function that adds one element to a set.) *Set* is a predicate that is true only of sets. The following eight axioms provide this:

1. The only sets are the empty set and those made by adjoining something to a set.

   $\forall s \; Set(s) \; \Leftrightarrow \; (s = EmptySet) \lor (\exists x, s_2 \; Set(s_2) \land s = Adjoin(x, s_2))$

2. The empty set has no elements adjoined into it. (In other words, there is no way to decompose *EmptySet* into a smaller set and an element.)

   $\neg \exists x, s \; Adjoin(x, s) = EmptySet$

3. Adjoining an element already in the set has no effect:

   $\forall x, s \; Member(x, s) \; \Leftrightarrow \; s = Adjoin(x, s)$

4. The only members of a set are the elements that were adjoined into it. We express this recursively, saying that x is a member of s if and only if s is equal to some set s_2 adjoined with some element y, where either y is the same as x or x is a member of s_2.

   $\forall x, s \; Member(x, s) \; \Leftrightarrow$
   $\quad \exists y, s_2 \; (s = Adjoin(y, s_2) \land (x = y \lor Member(x, s_2)))$

5. A set is a subset of another if and only if all of the first set's members are members of the second set.

   $\forall s_1, s_2 \; Subset(s_1, s_2) \; \Leftrightarrow \; (\forall x \; Member(x, s_1) \; \Rightarrow \; Member(x, s_2))$

6. Two sets are equal if and only if each is a subset of the other.

   $\forall s_1, s_2 \; (s_1 = s_2) \; \Leftrightarrow \; (Subset(s_1, s_2) \land Subset(s_2, s_1))$

7. An object is a member of the intersection of two sets if and only if it is a member of each of the sets.

$$\forall\, x, s_1, s_2 \;\; Member(x, Intersection(s_1, s_2)) \;\Leftrightarrow$$
$$Member(x, s_1) \wedge Member(x, s_2)$$

8. An object is a member of the union of two sets if and only if it is a member of either set.

$$\forall\, x, s_1, s_2 \;\; Member(x, Union(s_1, s_2)) \;\Leftrightarrow$$
$$Member(x, s_1) \vee Member(x, s_2)$$

The domain of lists is very similar to the domain of sets. The difference is that lists are ordered, and the same element can appear more than once in a list. We can use the vocabulary of Lisp for lists: *Nil* is the constant list with no elements; *Cons*, *Append*, *First*, and *Rest* are functions; and *Find* is the predicate that does for lists what *Member* does for sets. *List?* is a predicate that is true only of lists. Exercise 7.8 asks you to write axioms for the list domain.

Special notations for sets, lists and arithmetic

Because sets and lists are so common, and because there is a well-defined mathematical notation for them, it is tempting to extend the syntax of first-order logic to include this mathematical notation. The important thing to remember is that when this is done, it is only a change to the syntax of the language; it does not change the semantics. The notation is just an abbreviation for the normal first-order logic notation. Such notational extensions are often called **syntactic**
SYNTACTIC SUGAR **sugar**. We will use standard mathematical notation for arithmetic and set theory from here on, and will also use the nonstandard notation $\{a|s\}$ as an abbreviation for *Adjoin(a, s)*. There is less consensus among mathematicians about the notation for lists; we have chosen the notation used by Prolog:

$$
\begin{array}{rcl rcl}
\emptyset & = & EmptySet & [] & = & Nil \\
\{x\} & = & Adjoin(x, EmptySet) & [x] & = & Cons(x, Nil) \\
\{x, y\} & = & Adjoin(x, Adjoin(y, EmptySet)) & [x, y] & = & Cons(x, Cons(y, Nil)) \\
\{x, y|s\} & = & Adjoin(x, Adjoin(y, s)) & [x, y|l] & = & Cons(x, Cons(y, l)) \\
r \cup s & = & Union(r, s) \\
r \cap s & = & Intersection(r, s) \\
x \in s & = & Member(x, s) \\
r \subseteq s & = & Subset(r, s)
\end{array}
$$

We will also use standard arithmetic notation in logical sentences, saying, for example, $x > 0$ instead of $>(x, Zero)$ and $1 + 2$ instead of $+(1, 2)$. It should be understood that each use of an infix mathematical operator is just an abbreviation for a standard prefix predicate or function. The integers are used as constant symbols, with their usual interpretation.

Asking questions and getting answers

Although we will delay discussion of the internals of TELL and ASK until chapters 9 and 10, it is important to understand how they are used in first-order logic. If we want to add the kinship sentences to a knowledge base *KB*, we would call

TELL(*KB*, ($\forall m, c \; Mother(c) = m \; \Leftrightarrow \; Female(m) \wedge Parent(m,c)$))

and so on. Now if we tell it

TELL(*KB*, (*Female(Maxi)* $\wedge$ *Parent(Maxi, Spot)* $\wedge$ *Parent(Spot, Boots)*))

then we can

ASK(*KB*, *Grandparent(Maxi, Boots)*)

ASSERTIONS
QUERIES
GOALS

and receive an affirmative answer. The sentences added using TELL are often called **assertions**, and the questions asked using ASK are called **queries** or **goals** (not to be confused with goals as used to describe an agent's desired states).

Certain people think it is funny to answer questions such as "Can you tell me the time?" with "Yes." A knowledge base should be more cooperative. When we ask a question that is existentially quantified, such as

ASK(*KB*, $\exists x \; Child(x, Spot)$)

SUBSTITUTION
BINDING LIST

we should receive an answer indicating that Boots is a child of Spot. Thus, a query with existential variables is asking "Is there an *x* such that ...," and we solve it by providing such an *x*. The standard form for an answer of this sort is a **substitution** or **binding list**, which is a set of variable/term pairs. In this particular case, the answer would be {*x/Boots*}. (If there is more than one possible answer, a list of substitutions can be returned. Different implementations of ASK do different things.)

7.4   LOGICAL AGENTS FOR THE WUMPUS WORLD

In Chapter 6 we showed the outline of a knowledge-based agent, repeated here in slightly modified form as Figure 7.2. We also hinted at how a knowledge-based agent could be constructed for the wumpus world, but the limitations of propositional logic kept us from completing the agent. With first-order logic, we have all the representational power we need, and we can turn to the more interesting question of how an agent should organize what it knows in order to take the right actions. We will consider three agent architectures: **reflex** agents[8] that merely classify their percepts and act accordingly; **model-based agents**[9] that construct an internal representation of the world and use it to act; and **goal-based agents** that form goals and try to achieve them. (Goal-based agents are usually also model-based agents.)

MODEL-BASED
AGENTS
GOAL-BASED
AGENTS

The first step in constructing an agent for the wumpus world (or for any world) is to define the interface between the environment and the agent. The percept sentence must include both the percept and the time at which it occurred; otherwise the agent will get confused about when it saw what. We will use integers for time steps. A typical percept sentence would be

Percept([*Stench, Breeze, Glitter, None, None*], 5)

---

[8]   Reflex agents are also known as **tropistic** agents. The biological term *tropism* means having a tendency to react in a definite manner to stimuli. A heliotropic plant, for example, is one that turns toward the sun.

[9]   Note that this usage of "model" is related but not identical to its meaning as a world referred to by a sentence.

---

function KB-AGENT(*percept*) **returns** an *action*
    static: *KB*, a knowledge base
          t, a counter, initially 0, indicating time

    TELL(*KB*, MAKE-PERCEPT-SENTENCE(*percept, t*))
    action ← ASK(*KB*, MAKE-ACTION-QUERY(*t*))
    TELL(*KB*, MAKE-ACTION-SENTENCE(*action, t*))
    t ← *t* + 1
    return *action*

Figure 7.2   A generic knowledge-based agent.

The agent's action must be one of the following:

$$Turn(Right), \quad Turn(Left), \quad Forward, \quad Shoot, \quad Grab, \quad Release, \quad Climb$$

To determine which one is best, the function MAKE-ACTION-QUERY creates a query such as

$$\exists a \; Action(a, 5)$$

with the intention that ASK returns a binding list such as $\{a/Grab\}$ and *Grab* is assigned as the value of the variable *action*. The agent program then calls TELL once again to record which action was taken. Because the agent does not perceive its own actions, this is the only way the *KB* could know what the agent has done.

7.5   A SIMPLE REFLEX AGENT

The simplest possible kind of agent has rules directly connecting percepts to actions. These rules resemble reflexes or instincts. For example, if the agent sees a glitter, it should do a grab in order to pick up the gold:

$$\forall s, b, u, c, t \; Percept([s, b, Glitter, u, c], t) \; \Rightarrow \; Action(Grab, t)$$

The connection between percept and action can be mediated by rules for perception, which abstract the immediate perceptual input into more useful forms:

$$\forall b, g, u, c, t \; Percept([Stench, b, g, u, c], t) \; \Rightarrow \; Stench(t)$$
$$\forall s, g, u, c, t \; Percept([s, Breeze, g, u, c], t) \; \Rightarrow \; Breeze(t)$$
$$\forall s, b, u, c, t \; Percept([s, b, Glitter, u, c], t) \; \Rightarrow \; AtGold(t)$$
$$\cdots$$

Then a connection can be made from these predicates to action choices:

$$\forall t \; AtGold(t) \; \Rightarrow \; Action(Grab, t)$$

This rule is more flexible than the direct connection, because it could be used with other means for deducing *AtGold*—for example, if one stubs one's toe on the gold.

In a more complex environment, the percept might be an entire array of gray-scale or color values (a camera image), and the perceptual rules would have to infer such things as "There's a large truck right behind me flashing its lights." Chapter 24 covers the topic of perception in more detail. Of course, computer vision is a very difficult task, whereas these rules are trivial, but the idea is the same.

Limitations of simple reflex agents

Simple reflex agents will have a hard time in the wumpus world. The easiest way to see this is to consider the *Climb* action. The optimal agent should either retrieve the gold or determine that it is too dangerous to get the gold, and then return to the start square and climb out of the cave. A pure reflex agent cannot know for sure when to *Climb*, because neither having the gold nor being in the start square is part of the percept; they are things the agent knows by forming a representation of the world.

Reflex agents are also unable to avoid infinite loops. Suppose that such an agent has picked up the gold and is headed for home. It is likely that the agent will enter one of the squares it was in before, and receive the same percept. In that case, it *must*, by definition, do exactly what it did before. Like the dung beetle of Chapter 2, it does not know whether it is carrying the gold, and thus cannot make its actions conditional on that. Randomization provides some relief, but only at the expense of risking many fruitless actions.

7.6   REPRESENTING CHANGE IN THE WORLD

In our agent design, all percepts are added into the knowledge base, and in principle the percept history is all there is to know about the world. If we allow rules that refer to past percepts as well as the current percept, then we can, in principle, extend the capabilities of an agent to the point where the agent is acting optimally.

INTERNAL MODEL   Writing such rules, however, is remarkably tedious unless we adopt certain patterns of reasoning that correspond to maintaining an **internal model** of the world, or at least of the relevant aspects thereof. Consider an example from everyday life: finding one's keys. An agent that has taken the time to build a representation of the fact "my keys are in my pocket" need only recall that fact to find the keys. In contrast, an agent that just stored the complete percept sequence would have to do a lot of reasoning to discover where the keys are. It would be theoretically *possible* for the agent to in effect rewind the video tape of its life and replay it in fast-forward, using inference rules to keep track of where the keys are, but it certainly would not be *convenient*.

    It can be shown that *any system that makes decisions on the basis of past percepts can be rewritten to use instead a set of sentences about the current world state*, provided that these sentences are updated as each new percept arrives and as each action is done.

DIACHRONIC   Rules describing the way in which the world changes (or does not change) are called **diachronic** rules, from the Greek for "across time." Representing change is one of the most important areas in knowledge representation. The real world, as well as the wumpus world, is characterized by change rather than static truth. Richard has no brother until John is born; Spot is a kitten for a while and then becomes a full-grown tomcat; the agent moves on.

The easiest way to deal with change is simply to change the knowledge base; to erase the sentence that says the agent is at [1,1], and replace it with one that says it is at [1,2]. This approach can mitigate some of the difficulties we saw with the propositional agent. If we only want the knowledge base to answer questions about the latest situation, this will work fine. But it means that all knowledge about the past is lost, and it prohibits speculation about different possible futures.

A second possibility was hinted at in Chapters 3 and 4: an agent can search through a space of past and possible future states, where each state is represented by a different knowledge base. The agent can explore hypothetical situations—what would happen if I went two squares forward? This approach allows an agent to switch its attention between several knowledge bases, but it does not allow the agent to reason about more than one situation simultaneously.

To answer questions like "was there a stench in both [1,2] and [2,3]?" or "did Richard go to Palestine before he became king?" requires representing different situations and actions in the same knowledge base. In principle, *representing situations and actions is no different from representing more concrete objects such as cats and kings, or concrete relations such as brotherhood.* We need to decide on the appropriate objects and relations, and then write axioms about them. In this chapter, we will use the simplest, and oldest, solution to the problem. In Chapter 8, we will explore more complex approaches.

Situation calculus

SITUATION
CALCULUS

Situation calculus is the name for a particular way of describing change in first-order logic. It conceives of the world as consisting of a sequence of **situations**, each of which is a "snapshot" of the state of the world. Situations are generated from previous situations by actions, as shown in Figure 7.3.

Every relation or property that can change over time is handled by giving an extra situation argument to the corresponding predicate. We use the convention that the situation argument is always the last, and situation constants are of the form S_i. Thus, instead of $At(Agent, location)$, we might have

$$At(Agent, [1, 1], S_0) \land At(Agent, [1, 2], S_1)$$

to describe the location of the agent in the first two situations in Figure 7.3. Relations or properties that are not subject to change do not need the extra situation argument. For example, we can just say $Even(8)$ instead of $Even(8, S_0)$. In the wumpus world, where walls cannot move, we can just use $Wall([0, 1])$ to say that there is a wall at [0,1].

The next step is to represent how the world changes from one situation to the next. Situation calculus uses the function $Result(action, situation)$ to denote the situation that results from performing an action in some initial situation. Hence, in the sequence shown in Figure 7.3, we have the following:

$$Result(Forward, S_0) = S_1$$
$$Result(Turn(Right), S_1) = S_2$$
$$Result(Forward, S_2) = S_3$$

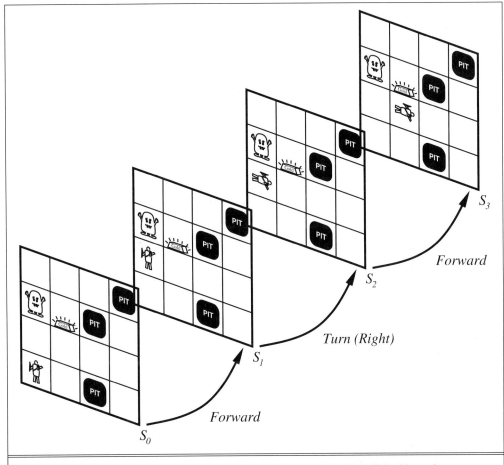

Figure 7.3   In situation calculus, the world is a sequence of situations linked by actions.

Actions are described by stating their effects. That is, we specify the properties of the situation that results from doing the action. Suppose, for example, that the agent wants to keep track of whether it is holding the gold. The description should state that, in any situation, if gold is present and the agent does a grab, then it will be holding the gold in the resulting situation. We write this in such a way as to apply to any portable object:

$Portable(Gold)$
$\forall s \; AtGold(s) \implies Present(Gold, s)$
$\forall x, s \; Present(x, s) \land Portable(x) \implies Holding(x, Result(Grab, s))$

A similar axiom says that the agent is not holding anything after a *Release* action:

$\forall x, s \; \neg Holding(x, Result(Release, s))$

EFFECT AXIOMS   These axioms are called **effect axioms**. Unfortunately, they are not sufficient to keep track of whether the agent is holding the gold. We also need to say that if the agent is holding something and does *not* release it, it will be holding it in the next state. Similarly, if the agent is not holding something and does not or cannot grab it, it will not be holding it in the next state:

$$\forall\, a,x,s\;\; Holding(x,s) \wedge (a{\neq}Release) \;\Rightarrow\; Holding(x, Result(a,s))$$
$$\forall\, a,x,s\;\; \neg Holding(x,s) \wedge (a{\neq}Grab \vee \neg(Present(x,s) \wedge Portable(x))$$
$$\Rightarrow\; \neg Holding(x, Result(a,s))$$

FRAME AXIOMS

Axioms like these that describe how the world stays the same (as opposed to how it changes) are called **frame axioms**.[10] Together, effect axioms and frame axioms provide a complete description of how the world evolves in response to the agent's actions.

We can obtain a more elegant representation by combining the effect axioms and frame axioms into a single axiom that describes how to compute the *Holding* predicate for the next time step, given its value for the current time step. The axiom has the following structure:

true afterwards $\Leftrightarrow$ [an action made it true

$\vee$ true already and no action made it false]

Notice the use of " $\Leftrightarrow$ " here. It says that the predicate will be true after the action if it is made true or if it stays true; *and* that it will be false afterwards in other cases. In the case of *Holding*, the axiom is the following:

$$\forall\, a,x,s\;\; Holding(x, Result(a,s)) \;\Leftrightarrow\; [(a{=}Grab \wedge Present(x,s) \wedge Portable(x))$$
$$\vee\;\; (Holding(x,s) \wedge a{\neq}Release)]$$

SUCCESSOR-STATE
AXIOM

This axiom is called a **successor-state axiom**. One such axiom is needed for each predicate that may change its value over time. A successor-state axiom must list all the ways in which the predicate can become true, and all the ways in which it can become false.

Keeping track of location

In the wumpus world, location is probably the most important thing to worry about; it cannot be perceived directly, but the agent needs to remember where it has been and what it saw there in order to deduce where pits and wumpuses are and to make sure it does a complete exploration for the gold. We have already seen that the initial location can be described by the sentence $At(Agent, [1,1], S_0)$. The agent also needs to know the following:

- What direction it is facing (an angle in degrees, where 0 degrees is out along the X-axis, 90 degrees is up along the Y-axis, and so on):

  $$Orientation(Agent, S_0) = 0$$

- How locations are arranged (a simple "map"). The map consists of values of the function *LocationToward*, which takes a location and a direction and gives the location that is one

---

[10] The name derives from film animation, where the background image usually remains constant as the characters move around from frame to frame.

THE FRAME PROBLEM AND ITS RELATIVES

Many AI texts refer to something called the **frame problem**. The problem was noticed soon after situation calculus was applied to reasoning about actions. Originally, it centered on the apparently unavoidable need for a large number of frame axioms that made for a very inelegant and inefficient description of actions. Many researchers considered the problem insoluble within first-order logic. There are at least three entire volumes of collected papers on the problem, and at least one author (Crockett, 1994) cites the problem as one symptom of the inevitable failure of the AI enterprise.

The proliferation of frame axioms is now called the **representational frame problem**, and as we have shown, is easily solved using successor-state axioms. The **inferential frame problem** concerns the way we make inferences about the world. When reasoning about the result of a long sequence of actions in situation calculus, one has to carry each property through all intervening situations one step at a time, *even if the property remains unchanged throughout.* This is true whether one uses frame axioms or successor-state axioms. One would like to be able to make only the changes required by the action descriptions, and have the rest available without further effort. This seems like the natural and efficient thing to do because we do not expect more than a small fraction of the world to change at any given moment. Of course, we cannot expect a *general-purpose* representation language such as first-order logic (and associated general-purpose reasoning systems) to have this bias. It is possible, however, to build *special-purpose* reasoning systems that do work efficiently for reasoning about actions that change only a small fraction of the world. These are called planning systems, and are the subject of Part IV.

Other problems besides the frame problem have surfaced in the study of reasoning about actions. The **qualification problem** arises because it is difficult, in the real world, to define the circumstances under which a given action is *guaranteed* to work. In the real world, grabbing a gold brick may not work if the brick is wet and slippery, or if it is electrified or screwed to the table, or if your back gives out when you bend over, or if the guard shoots you, and so on. If some of these conditions are left out of the successor-state axiom, then the agent is in danger of generating false beliefs.

Finally, the **ramification problem** concerns the proliferation of *implicit* consequences of actions. For example, if a gold brick is covered in dust, then when the agent picks up the brick it also picks up each particle of dust that adheres to the brick. One prefers to avoid describing the motion of the dust (if any) as part of the description of picking up things in general. It is better to state separately that the dust is stuck to the brick, and to *infer* the new location of the dust as necessary. Doing this efficiently requires a special-purpose reasoning system, just as with the frame problem.

step forward in the given direction.

$$\forall x, y \; LocationToward([x, y], 0) = [x + 1, y]$$
$$\forall x, y \; LocationToward([x, y], 90) = [x, y + 1]$$
$$\forall x, y \; LocationToward([x, y], 180) = [x - 1, y]$$
$$\forall x, y \; LocationToward([x, y], 270) = [x, y - 1]$$

From the map, it is possible to tell which square is directly ahead of the agent, or indeed of any agent p at any location l:

$$\forall p, l, s \; At(p, l, s) \Rightarrow$$
$$LocationAhead(p, s) = LocationToward(l, Orientation(p, s))$$

It is also useful to define adjacency:

$$\forall l_1, l_2 \; Adjacent(l_1, l_2) \Leftrightarrow \exists d \; l_1 = LocationToward(l_2, d)$$

- Whatever is known about the contents of the locations (geographical details on the map). In what follows we assume that the locations surrounding the 4×4 cave contain walls, and other locations do not. Sometimes the agent knows this kind of information to start, and sometimes it does not.

$$\forall x, y \; Wall([x, y]) \Leftrightarrow (x = 0 \lor x = 5 \lor y = 0 \lor y = 5)$$

- What the actions do to location. Only going forward changes location, and then only if there is no wall ahead. The successor-state axiom for location is

$$\forall a, d, p, s \; At(p, l, Result(a, s)) \Leftrightarrow$$
$$[\; (a = Forward \land l = LocationAhead(p, s) \land \neg Wall(l))$$
$$\lor (At(p, l, s) \land a \neq Forward) \;]$$

- What the actions do to orientation. Turning is the only action that changes orientation. The successor-state axiom for orientation is

$$\forall a, d, p, s \; Orientation(p, Result(a, s)) = d \Leftrightarrow$$
$$[\; (a = Turn(Right) \land d = Mod(Orientation(p, s) - 90, 360))$$
$$\lor (a = Turn(Left) \land d = Mod(Orientation(p, s) + 90, 360))$$
$$\lor (Orientation(p, s) = d \land \neg(a = Turn(Right) \lor a = Turn(Left))) \;]$$

In addition to keeping track of location and the gold, the agent should also keep track of whether the wumpus is alive or dead. We leave the problem of describing *Shoot* as an exercise.

7.7   DEDUCING HIDDEN PROPERTIES OF THE WORLD

Once the agent knows where it is, it can associate qualities with the *places* rather than just the situations, so, for example, one might say that if the agent is at a place and perceives a breeze, then that place is breezy, and if the agent perceives a stench, then that place is smelly:

$$\forall l, s \; At(Agent, l, s) \land Breeze(s) \Rightarrow Breezy(l)$$
$$\forall l, s \; At(Agent, l, s) \land Stench(s) \Rightarrow Smelly(l)$$

It is useful to know if a *place* is breezy or smelly because we know that the wumpus and the pits cannot move about. Notice that neither *Breezy* nor *Smelly* needs a situation argument.

Having discovered which places are breezy or smelly (and, very importantly, *not* smelly or *not* breezy), the agent can deduce where the pits are, and where the wumpus is. Furthermore, it can deduce which squares are safe to move to (we use the predicate *OK* to represent this), and can use this information to hunt for the gold.

SYNCHRONIC

The axioms we will write to capture the necessary information for these deductions are called **synchronic** ("same time") rules, because they relate properties of a world state to other properties of the same world state. There are two main kinds of synchronic rules:

CAUSAL RULES

◇ **Causal rules**:

Causal rules reflect the assumed direction of causality in the world: some hidden property of the world causes certain percepts to be generated. For example, we might have rules stating that squares adjacent to wumpuses are smelly and squares adjacent to pits are breezy:

$$\forall l_1, l_2, s \ \ At(Wumpus, l_1, s) \land Adjacent(l_1, l_2) \ \Rightarrow \ Smelly(l_2)$$
$$\forall l_1, l_2, s \ \ At(Pit, l_1, s) \land Adjacent(l_1, l_2) \ \Rightarrow \ Breezy(l_2)$$

MODEL-BASED REASONING

Systems that reason with causal rules are called **model-based reasoning** systems.

DIAGNOSTIC RULES

◇ **Diagnostic rules**:

Diagnostic rules infer the presence of hidden properties directly from the percept-derived information. We have already seen two diagnostic rules:

$$\forall l, s \ \ At(Agent, l, s) \land Breeze(s) \ \Rightarrow \ Breezy(l)$$
$$\forall l, s \ \ At(Agent, l, s) \land Stench(s) \ \Rightarrow \ Smelly(l)$$

For deducing the presence of wumpuses, a diagnostic rule can only draw a weak conclusion, namely, that if a location is smelly, then the wumpus must either be in that location or in an adjacent location:

$$\forall l_1, s \ \ Smelly(l_1) \ \Rightarrow$$
$$(\exists l_2 \ At(Wumpus, l_2, s) \land (l_2 = l_1 \lor Adjacent(l_1, l_2)))$$

Although diagnostic rules seem to provide the desired information more directly, it is very tricky to ensure that they derive the strongest possible conclusions from the available information. For example, the absence of stench or breeze implies that adjacent squares are OK:

$$\forall x, y, g, u, c, s \ \ Percept([None, None, g, u, c], t) \land$$
$$At(Agent, x, s) \land Adjacent(x, y) \ \Rightarrow \ OK(y)$$

But sometimes a square can be OK even when smells and breezes abound. The model-based rule

$$\forall x, t \ \ (\neg At(Wumpus, x, t) \land \neg Pit(x)) \ \Leftrightarrow \ OK(x)$$

is probably the best way to represent safety.

The distinction between model-based and diagnostic reasoning is important in many areas of AI. Medical diagnosis in particular has been an active area of research, where approaches based on direct associations between symptoms and diseases (a diagnostic approach) have gradually been replaced by approaches using an explicit model of the disease process and how it manifests itself in symptoms. The issues come up again in Chapter 14.

The important thing to remember is that *if the axioms correctly and completely describe the way the world works and the way that percepts are produced, then the inference procedure will correctly infer the strongest possible description of the world state given the available percepts.* A complete specification of the wumpus world axioms is left as an exercise.

7.8   PREFERENCES AMONG ACTIONS

So far, the only way we have to decide on actions is to write rules recommending them on the basis of certain conditions in the world. This can get very tedious. For example, generally it is a good idea to explore by moving to OK squares, but not when there is a glitter afoot. Hence our rules for exploring would also have to mention glitter. This seems arbitrary and means the rules are not **modular**: *changes in the agent's beliefs about some aspects of the world would require changes in rules dealing with other aspects also.* It is more modular to separate facts about actions from facts about goals, which means our agent can be reprogrammed simply by asking it to achieve something different. Goals describe the desirability of outcome states, regardless of how achieved. We discuss goals further in Section 7.9.

A first step is to describe the desirability of actions themselves, and leave the inference engine to choose whichever is the action that has the highest desirability. We will use a simple scale: actions can be *Great, Good, Medium, Risky,* or *Deadly.* The agent should always do a great action if it can find one; otherwise, a good one; otherwise, a medium action; and a risky one if all else fails.

$$\forall a, s \;\; Great(a, s) \;\Rightarrow\; Action(a, s)$$
$$\forall a, s \;\; Good(a, s) \wedge (\neg \exists b \;\; Great(b, s)) \;\Rightarrow\; Action(a, s)$$
$$\forall a, s \;\; Medium(a, s) \wedge (\neg \exists b \;\; Great(b, s) \vee Good(b, s)) \;\Rightarrow\; Action(a, s)$$
$$\forall a, s \;\; Risky(a, s) \wedge (\neg \exists b \;\; Great(b, s) \vee Good(b, s) \vee Medium(b, s)) \;\Rightarrow\; Action(a, s)$$

ACTION-VALUE   A system containing rules of this type is called an **action-value** system. Notice that the rules do not refer to what the actions actually *do*, just how desirable they are.

Up to the point where it finds the gold, the basic strategy for our agent will be as follows:

- Great actions include picking up the gold when found and climbing out of the cave with the gold.

- Good actions include moving to a square that's OK and has not yet been visited.

- Medium actions include moving to a square that's OK and has been visited already.

- Risky actions include moving to a square that's not known to be deadly, but is not known to be OK either.

- Deadly actions are moving into a square that is known to contain a pit or a live wumpus.

Again, we leave the specification of the action values as an exercise.

7.9   TOWARD A GOAL-BASED AGENT

The preceding set of action value statements is sufficient to prescribe a reasonably intelligent exploration policy. It can be shown (Exercise 7.15) that the agent using these axioms will always succeed in finding the gold safely whenever there is a safe sequence of actions that does so. This is about as much as we can ask from a logical agent.

Once the gold is found, the policies need to change radically. The aim now is to return to the start square as quickly as possible. What we would like to do is infer that the agent now has the **goal** of being at location [1,1]:

$$\forall s \; Holding(Gold, s) \Rightarrow GoalLocation([1, 1], s)$$

The presence of an explicit goal allows the agent to work out a sequence of actions that will achieve the goal. There are at least three ways to find such a sequence:

◇ **Inference**: It is not hard to write axioms that will allow us to ASK the *KB* for a sequence of actions that is guaranteed to achieve the goal safely. For the 4 × 4 wumpus world, this is feasible, but for larger worlds, the computational demands are too high. In any case, we have the problem of distinguishing good solutions from wasteful solutions (e.g., ones that make a long series of wandering moves before getting on the right track).

◇ **Search**: We can use a best-first search procedure (see Chapter 4) to find a path to the goal. This requires the agent to translate its knowledge into a set of operators, and accompanying state representation, so that the search algorithm can be applied.

◇ **Planning**: This involves the use of special-purpose reasoning systems designed to reason about actions. Chapter 11 describes these systems in detail, explaining their advantages over search algorithms.

7.10   SUMMARY

This chapter has shown how first-order logic can be used as the representation language for a knowledge-based agent. The important points are as follows:

• **First-order logic** is a general-purpose representation language that is based on an onto-logical commitment to the existence of objects and relations in the world.

• **Constant symbols** and **predicate symbols** name objects and relations, respectively. **Complex terms** name objects using **function symbols**. The interpretation specifies what the symbols refer to.

• An **atomic sentence** consists of a predicate applied to one or more terms; it is true just when the relation named by the predicate holds between the objects named by the terms. **Complex sentences** use connectives just like propositional logic, and **quantified sentences** allow the expression of general rules.

• It is possible to define an agent that reasons using first-order logic. Such an agent needs to

1. react to what it perceives;
2. extract abstract descriptions of the current state from percepts;
3. maintain an internal model of relevant aspects of the world that are not directly available from percepts;
4. express and use information about the desirability of actions in various circumstances;
5. use goals in conjunction with knowledge about actions to construct plans.

- Knowledge about actions and their effects can be represented using the conventions of **situation calculus**. This knowledge enables the agent to keep track of the world and to deduce the effects of plans of action.

- We have a choice of writing **diagnostic rules** that reason from percepts to propositions about the world or **causal rules** that describe how conditions in the world cause percepts to come about. Causal rules are often more flexible and entail a wider range of consequences, but can be more expensive to use in inference.

BIBLIOGRAPHICAL AND HISTORICAL NOTES

Although even Aristotle's logic deals with generalizations over objects, true first-order logic dates from the introduction of quantifiers in Gottlob Frege's (1879) *Begriffschrift* ("Concept Writing" or "Conceptual Notation"). Frege's ability to nest quantifiers was a big step forward, but he used an awkward notation. (An example appears on the front cover of this book.) The present notation for first-order logic is substantially due to Giuseppe Peano (1889), but the semantics is virtually identical to Frege's.

A major barrier to the development of first-order logic had been the concentration on one-place predicates to the exclusion of many-place relational predicates. This fixation on one-place predicates had been nearly universal in logical systems from Aristotle up to and including Boole. The first systematic treatment of the logic of relations was given by Augustus De Morgan (1864). De Morgan cited the following example to show the sorts of inferences that Aristotle's logic could not handle: "All horses are animals; therefore, the head of a horse is the head of an animal." This inference is inaccessible to Aristotle because any valid rule that can support this inference must first analyze the sentence using the two-place predicate "x is the head of y." The logic of relations was studied in depth by Charles Sanders Peirce (1870), who also developed first-order logic independently of Frege, although slightly later (Peirce, 1883).

Leopold Löwenheim (1915) gave a systematic treatment of model theory in 1915. This paper also treated the equality symbol as an integral part of logic. Löwenheim's results were further extended by Thoralf Skolem (1920). Tarski (1935) gave an explicit definition of truth and model-theoretic satisfaction in first-order logic, using set theory. (An English translation of this German article is given in (Tarski, 1956).)

McCarthy (1958) was primarily responsible for the introduction of first-order logic as a tool for building AI systems, and later (1963) proposed the use of states of the world, or situations, as objects to be reasoned about using first-order logic. The first AI system to make substantial use of general-purpose reasoning about actions in first-order logic was QA3 (Green, 1969b).

Kowalski (1979b) further advanced situation calculus by introducing propositions as objects. The frame problem was pointed out as a major problem for the use of logic in AI by McCarthy and Hayes (1969). The axiomatization we use in the chapter to avoid the representational frame problem was proposed by Charles Elkan (1992) and independently by Ray Reiter (1991). The qualification problem was also pointed out by McCarthy (1977). The inferential frame problem is discussed at length by Shoham and McDermott (1988).

There are a number of good modern introductory texts on first-order logic. Quine (1982) is one of the most readable. Enderton (1972) gives a more mathematically oriented perspective. A highly formal treatment of first-order logic, along with many more advanced topics in logic, is provided by Bell and Machover (1977). Manna and Waldinger (1985) give a readable introduction to logic from a computer science perspective. Gallier (1986) provides an extremely rigorous mathematical exposition of first-order logic, along with a great deal of material on its use in automated reasoning. *Logical Foundations of Artificial Intelligence* (Genesereth and Nilsson, 1987) provides both a solid introduction to logic and the first systematic treatment of logical agents with percepts and actions. Barwise and Etchemendy (1993) give a modern overview of logic that includes an interactive graphical logic game called *Tarski's World*.

EXERCISES

7.1   A logical knowledge base represents the world using a set of sentences with no explicit structure. An **analogical** representation, on the other hand, is one in which the representation has structure that corresponds directly to the structure of the thing represented. Consider a road map of your country as an analogical representation of facts about the country. The two-dimensional structure of the map corresponds to the two-dimensional surface of the area.

- **a**. Give five examples of *symbols* in the map language.
- **b**. An *explicit* sentence is one that the creator of the representation actually writes down. An *implicit* sentence is one that results from explicit sentences because of properties of the analogical representation. Give three examples each of *implicit* and *explicit* sentences in the map language.
- **c**. Give three examples of facts about the physical structure of your country that cannot be represented in the map language.
- **d**. Give two examples of facts that are much easier to express in the map language than in first-order logic.
- **e**. Give two other examples of useful analogical representations. What are the advantages and disadvantages of each of these languages?

7.2   Represent the following sentences in first-order logic, using a consistent vocabulary (which you must define):

- **a**. Not all students take both History and Biology.
- **b**. Only one student failed History.

   c. Only one student failed both History and Biology.

   d. The best score in History was better than the best score in Biology.

   e. Every person who dislikes all vegetarians is smart.

   f. No person likes a smart vegetarian.

   g. There is a woman who likes all men who are not vegetarians.

   h. There is a barber who shaves all men in town who do not shave themselves.

   i. No person likes a professor unless the professor is smart.

   j. Politicians can fool some of the people all of the time, and they can fool all of the people some of the time, but they can't fool all of the people all of the time.

7.3 We noted that there is often confusion because the $\Rightarrow$ connective does not correspond directly to the English "if ... then" construction. The following English sentences use "and," "or," and "if" in ways that are quite different from first-order logic. For each sentence, give both a translation into first-order logic that preserves the intended meaning in English, and a straightforward translation (as if the logical connectives had their regular first-order logic meaning). Show an unintuitive consequence of the latter translation, and say whether each translation is valid, satisfiable or invalid.

   a. One more outburst like that and you'll be in contempt of court.

   b. *Annie Hall* is on TV tonight, if you're interested.

   c. Either the Red Sox win or I'm out ten dollars.

   d. The special this morning is ham and eggs.

   e. Maybe I'll come to the party and maybe I won't.

   f. Well, I like Sandy and I don't like Sandy.

   g. I don't jump off the Empire State Building implies if I jump off the Empire State Building then I float safely to the ground.

   h. It is not the case that if you attempt this exercise you will get an F. Therefore, you will attempt this exercise.

   i. If you lived here you would be home now. If you were home now, you would not be here. Therefore, if you lived here you would not be here.

7.4 Give a predicate calculus sentence such that every world in which it is true contains exactly one object.

7.5 Represent the sentence "All Germans speak the same languages" in predicate calculus. Use *Speaks*(x, l), meaning that person x speaks language l.

7.6 Write axioms describing the predicates *GrandChild GreatGrandparent*, *Brother*, *Sister*, *Daughter*, *Son*, *Aunt*, *Uncle*, *BrotherInLaw*, *SisterInLaw*, and *FirstCousin*. Find out the proper definition of *m*th cousin *n* times removed, and write it in first-order logic.

   Write down the basic facts depicted in the family tree in Figure 7.4. Using the logical reasoning system in the code repository, TELL it all the sentences you have written down, and ASK it who are Elizabeth's grandchildren, Diana's brothers-in-law, and Zara's great-grandparents.

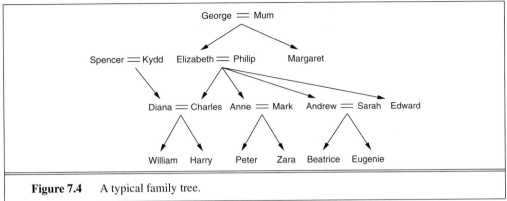

Figure 7.4   A typical family tree.

7.7 Explain what is wrong with the following proposed definition of the set membership predicate $\in$:

$$\forall x, s \ \ x \in \{x|s\}$$
$$\forall x, s \ \ x \in s \ \Rightarrow \ \forall y \ \ x \in \{y|s\}$$

7.8 Using the set axioms as examples, write axioms for the list domain, including all the constants, functions, and predicates mentioned in the chapter.

7.9 This exercise can be done without the computer, although you may find it useful to use a backward chainer to check your proof for the last part. The idea is to formalize the blocks world domain using the situation calculus. The objects in this domain are blocks, tables, and situations. The predicates are

$$On(x, y, s) \qquad ClearTop(x, s) \qquad Block(x) \qquad Table(x)$$

The only action is $PutOn(x, y)$, where x must be a block whose top is clear of any other blocks, and y can be either the table or a different block with a clear top. The initial situation S_0 has A on B on C on the table.

    a. Write an axiom or axioms describing $PutOn$.

    b. Describe the initial state, S_0, in which there is a stack of three blocks, A on B on C, where C is on the table, T.

    c. Give the appropriate query that a theorem prover can solve to generate a plan to build a stack where C is on top of B and B is on top of A. Write down the solution that the theorem prover should return. (*Hint:* The solution will be a situation described as the result of doing some actions to S_0.)

    d. Show formally that the solution fact follows from your description of the situation and the axioms for $PutOn$.

7.10 Write sentences to define the effects of the *Shoot* action in the wumpus world. As well as describing its effects on the wumpus, remember that shooting uses the agent's arrow.

7.11 In this exercise, we will consider the problem of planning a route from one city to another. The basic action taken by the robot is $Go(x, y)$, which takes it from city x to city y provided there is a direct route. *DirectRoute*(*x*, *y*) is true if and only if there is a direct route from *x* to *y*; you can assume that all such facts are already in the KB (see the map on page 62). The robot begins in Arad and must reach Bucharest.

   a. Write a suitable logical description of the initial situation of the robot.

   b. Write a suitable logical query whose solutions will provide possible paths to the goal.

   c. Write a sentence describing the *Go* action.

   d. Now suppose that following the direct route between two cities consumes an amount of fuel equal to the distance between the cities. The robot starts with fuel at full capacity. Augment your representation to include these considerations. Your action description should be such that the query you specified earlier will still result in feasible plans.

   e. Describe the initial situation, and write a new rule or rules describing the *Go* action.

   f. Now suppose some of the vertices are also gas stations, at which the robot can fill its tank using the *Fillup* action. Extend your representation to include gas stations and write all the rules needed to completely describe the *Fillup* action.

7.12 In this exercise, you will extend situation calculus to allow for actions that take place simultaneously. You will use a function called *Simultaneously*, which takes two actions as arguments and denotes the combined action. Consider a grid world containing two agents. Write axioms describing the effects of simultaneous *Forward* actions:

   a. When two agents move at once, unless they are both trying to move to the same location, the result is the same as if one had moved and then the other had moved.

   b. If the agents are trying to move to the same location, they remain in place.

7.13 Using the wumpus world simulator and the logical reasoning system in the code repository, implement a working agent for the wumpus world. You will need all of the wumpus-related axioms in the chapter, and perhaps more besides. Evaluate the performance of your agent.

7.14 How hard would it be to build a successful wumpus world agent by writing a program in your favorite programming language? Compare this to the logical reasoning agent.

7.15 Sketch an argument to the effect that a logical agent using the axioms and action preferences given in the chapter will always succeed in finding the gold safely whenever there is a safe sequence of actions that does so.

7.16 A reflex agent is one whose action is always a function of its percepts in the current time step. That is, the agent's action cannot be based on anything it learned in the past, and it cannot carry over any internal state information from one time step to the next. In the wumpus world, there are 32 different possible percepts and 6 different actions.

   a. How many different reflex agents can there be in the wumpus world?

   b. How many different 4×4 wumpus worlds are there? How many 10×10 worlds?

   c. What do you think the chances are that a reflex agent can be successful in a majority of wumpus worlds? Why?

BUILDING A
KNOWLEDGE BASE

In which we develop a methodology for building knowledge bases for particular domains, sketch a representation for the world in general, and go shopping.

The previous chapter showed that first-order logic is a powerful tool for knowledge representation and reasoning. However, a logic by itself consists of only the syntax, semantics, and proof theory. A logic does not offer any guidance as to what facts should be expressed, nor what vocabulary should be used to express them.

The process of building a knowledge base is called **knowledge engineering**. A knowledge engineer is someone who investigates a particular domain, determines what concepts are important in that domain, and creates a formal representation of the objects and relations in the domain. Often, the knowledge engineer is trained in representation but is not an expert in the domain at hand, be it circuit design, space station mission scheduling, or whatever. The knowledge engineer will usually interview the real experts to become educated about the domain and to
elicit the required knowledge, in a process called **knowledge acquisition**. This occurs prior to, or interleaved with, the process of creating formal representations. In this chapter, we will use domains that should already be fairly familiar, so that we can concentrate on the representational issues involved.

One does not become a proficient knowledge engineer just by studying the syntax and semantics of a representation language. It takes practice and exposure to lots of examples before one can develop a good style in any language, be it a language for programming, reasoning, or communicating. Sections 8.1 and 8.2 discuss the principles and pitfalls of knowledge engineering. We then show how to represent knowledge in the fairly narrow domain of electronic circuits in Section 8.3. A number of narrow domains can be tackled by similar techniques, but domains such as shopping in a supermarket seem to require much more general representations. In Section 8.4, we discuss ways to represent time, change, objects, substances, events, actions, money, measures, and so on. These are important because they show up in one form or another in every domain. Representing these very general concepts is sometimes called **ontological**
engineering. Section 8.5 describes in detail a simplified shopping environment, and uses the general ontology to develop representations capable of sustaining rational action in the domain.

8.1   PROPERTIES OF GOOD AND BAD KNOWLEDGE BASES

In Chapter 6, we said that a good knowledge representation language should be expressive, concise, unambiguous, context-insensitive, and effective. A knowledge base should, in addition, be *clear* and *correct*. The relations that matter should be defined, and the irrelevant details should be suppressed. Of course, there will be trade-offs between properties: we can make simplifications that sacrifice some correctness to gain clarity and brevity.

The question of efficiency is a little more difficult to deal with. Ideally, the separation between the knowledge base and the inference procedure should be maintained. This allows the creator of the knowledge base to worry only about the *content* of the knowledge, and not about how it will be used by the inference procedure. The same answers should be obtainable by the inference procedure, no matter how the knowledge is encoded. As far as possible, ensuring efficient inference is the task of the designer of the inference procedure and should not distort the representation.

In practice, some considerations of efficiency are unavoidable. Automatic methods exist that can eliminate the most obvious sources of inefficiency in a given encoding, in much the same way that optimizing compilers can speed up the execution of a program, but at present these methods are too weak to overcome the determined efforts of a profligate knowledge engineer who has no concern for efficiency. Even in the best case, then, the knowledge engineer should have some understanding of how inference is done, so that the representation can be designed for maximum efficiency. In the worst case, the representation language is used primarily as a way of "programming" the inference procedure.

As we will see throughout this chapter, *you cannot do, or understand, knowledge engineering by just talking about it*. To explain the general principles of good design, we need to have an example. We will start by doing the example incorrectly, and then fix it.

Every knowledge base has two potential consumers: human readers and inference procedures. A common mistake is to choose predicate names that are meaningful to the human reader, and then be lulled into assuming that the name is somehow meaningful to the inference procedure as well. The sentence *BearOfVerySmallBrain(Pooh)* might be appropriate in certain domains,[1] but from this sentence alone, the inference procedure will not be able to infer either that Pooh is a bear or that he has a very small brain; that he has a brain at all; that very small brains are smaller than small brains; or that this fact implies something about Pooh's behavior. The hard part is for the human reader to resist the temptation to make the inferences that seem to be implied by long predicate names. A knowledge engineer will often notice this kind of mistake when the inference procedure fails to conclude, for example, *Silly(Pooh)*. It is compounding the mistake to write

$$\forall b \; BearOfVerySmallBrain(b) \; \Rightarrow \; Silly(b)$$

because this expresses the relevant knowledge at too *specific* a level. Although such *VeryLong-Names* can be made to work for simple examples covering a small, sparse portion of a larger domain, they do not scale up well. Adding *AnotherVeryLongName* takes just as much work as

---

[1] Winnie the Pooh is a toy bear belonging to Christopher Robin in the well-known series of children's' books (Milne, 1926). The style of our introductory sentence in each chapter is borrowed from these works.

KNOWLEDGE ENGINEERING VS. PROGRAMMING

A useful analogy can be made between knowledge engineering and programming. Both activities can be seen as consisting of four steps:

	Knowledge Engineering	*Programming*
(1)	Choosing a logic	Choosing a programming language
(2)	Building a knowledge base	Writing a program
(3)	Implementing the proof theory	Choosing or writing a compiler
(4)	Inferring new facts	Running a program

In both activities, one writes down a description of a problem or state of affairs, and then uses the definition of the language to derive new consequences. In the case of a program, the output is derived from the input and the program; in the case of a knowledge base, answers are derived from descriptions of problems and the knowledge base.

Given these similarities, what is the point of doing "knowledge engineering" at all? Why not just admit that the final result will be a program, and set about to write that program from the start, using a traditional programming language?

The main advantage of knowledge engineering is that it requires less commitment, and thus less work. A knowledge engineer only has to decide what objects and relations are worth representing, and which relations hold among which objects. A programmer has to do all that, and in addition must decide how to compute the relations between objects, given some initial input. The knowledge engineer specifies *what* is true, and the inference procedure figures out *how* to turn the facts into a solution to the problem. Furthermore, because a fact is true regardless of what task one is trying to solve, knowledge bases can, in principle, be reused for a variety of different tasks without modification. Finally, debugging a knowledge base is made easier by the fact that any given sentence is true or false *by itself*, whereas the correctness of a program statement depends very strongly on its context.

The advantages of this **declarative approach** to system building have not been lost on other subfields of computer science. Database systems derive most of their usefulness from the fact that they provide a method to store and retrieve information in a way that is independent of the particular application. Database systems have also started to add the capability to do logical inference, thereby moving more of the functionality from the application program into the database system (Stonebraker, 1992). The field of **agent-based software engineering** (Genesereth and Ketchpel, 1994) attempts to make all sorts of systems and resources interoperable by providing a declarative interface based on first-order logic.

adding the first one. For example, to derive *Silly(Piglet)* from *ShyBabyPigOfSmallBrain(Piglet)*, we would have to write

$$\forall b \ \ ShyBabyPigOfSmallBrain(b) \ \Rightarrow \ Silly(b)$$

This is a sign that something is wrong. The first fact about silliness is of no help in a similar situation. In a properly designed knowledge base, facts that were entered for one situation should end up being used in new situations as well. As you go along, you should need fewer new facts, and fewer new predicates. This will only happen if one writes rules at the most *general* level at which the knowledge is applicable. In a good knowledge base, *BearOfVerySmallBrain(Pooh)* would be replaced by something like the following:

1. Pooh is a bear; bears are animals; animals are physical things.

    $$Bear(Pooh)$$
    $$\forall b \ \ Bear(b) \ \Rightarrow \ Animal(b)$$
    $$\forall a \ \ Animal(a) \ \Rightarrow \ PhysicalThing(a)$$

    These sentences help to tie knowledge about Pooh into a broader context. They also enable knowledge to be expressed at an appropriate level of generality, depending on whether the information is applicable to bears, animals, or all physical objects.

2. Pooh has a very small brain.

    $$RelativeSize(BrainOf(Pooh), BrainOf(TypicalBear)) = Very(Small)$$

    This provides a precise sense of "very small," which would otherwise be highly ambiguous. Is Pooh's brain very small compared to a molecule or a moon?

3. All animals (and only animals) have a brain, which is a part of the animal.

    $$\forall a \ \ Animal(a) \ \Leftrightarrow \ Brain(BrainOf(a))$$
    $$\forall a \ \ PartOf(BrainOf(a), a)$$

    This allows us to connect Pooh's brain to Pooh himself, and introduces some useful, general vocabulary.

4. If something is part of a physical thing, then it is also a physical thing:

    $$\forall x, y \ \ PartOf(x, y) \land PhysicalThing(y) \ \Rightarrow \ PhysicalThing(x)$$

    This is a very general and important fact that is seldom seen in physics textbooks!

5. Animals with brains that are small (or below) relative to the normal brain size for their species are silly.[2]

    $$\forall a \ \ RelativeSize(BrainOf(a), BrainOf(TypicalMember(SpeciesOf(a)))) \le Small$$
    $$\qquad \Rightarrow \ Silly(a)$$
    $$\forall b \ \ Bear(b) \ \Leftrightarrow \ SpeciesOf(b) = Ursidae$$
    $$TypicalBear = TypicalMember(Ursidae)$$

---

[2] It is important to remember that the goal for this knowledge base was to be consistent and useful within a world of talking stuffed animals, not to be a model of the real world. Although biologists are in agreement that brain size is not a good predictor for silliness, the rules given here are the right ones for this world.

6. Every physical thing has a size. Sizes are arranged on a scale from Tiny to Huge. A relative size is a ratio of two sizes.

$$\forall x \ \ PhysicalThing(x) \ \Rightarrow \ \exists s \ \ Size(x) = s$$
$$Tiny < Small < Medium < Large < Huge$$
$$\forall a, b \ \ RelativeSize(a, b) = Size(a)/Size(b)$$

7. The function *Very* maps a point on a scale to a more extreme value. *Medium* is the neutral value for a scale.

$$Medium = 1$$
$$\forall x \ \ x > Medium \ \Rightarrow \ Very(x) > x$$
$$\forall x \ \ x < Medium \ \Rightarrow \ Very(x) < x$$

This is more work than writing a single rule for *BearOfVerySmallBrain*, but it achieves far more. It has articulated some of the basic properties of physical things and animals, properties that will be used many times, but need be stated only once. It has begun to sketch out a hierarchy of objects (bears, animals, physical things). It has also made a representational choice for values on scales, which will come in handy later in the chapter.

Every time one writes down a sentence, one should ask oneself the following:

- Why is this true? Could I write down the facts that make it true instead?
- *How generally* is it applicable? Can I state it for a more general class of objects?
- Do I need a new predicate to denote this class of objects? How does the class relate to other classes? Is it part of a larger class? Does that class have other subclasses? What are other properties of the objects in this class?

We cannot provide a foolproof recipe for successful knowledge engineering, but we hope this example has provided some pointers.

8.2   KNOWLEDGE ENGINEERING

The knowledge engineer must understand enough about the domain in question to represent the important objects and relationships. He or she must also understand enough about the representation language to correctly encode these facts. Moreover, the knowledge engineer must also understand enough about the implementation of the inference procedure to assure that queries can be answered in a reasonable amount of time. To help focus the development of a knowledge base and to integrate the engineer's thinking at the three levels, the following five-step methodology can be used:

- *Decide what to talk about.* Understand the domain well enough to know which objects and facts need to be talked about, and which can be ignored. For the early examples in this chapter, this step is easy. In some cases, however, it can be the hardest step. Many knowledge engineering projects have failed because the knowledge engineers started to formalize the domain before understanding it. Donald Michie (1982) gives the example of a cheese factory that had a single cheese tester who decided if the Camembert was ripe by sticking his finger into a sample and deciding if it "felt right." When the cheese tester approached retirement age, the factory invested much time and money developing a complex system with steel probes that would test for just the right surface tension, but the system was next to useless. Eventually, it turned out that feel had nothing to do with it; pushing the finger in just served to break the crust and let the aroma out, and that was what the cheese tester was subconsciously relying on.

- *Decide on a vocabulary of predicates, functions, and constants.* That is, translate the important domain-level concepts into logic-level names. This involves many choices, some arbitrary and some important. Should *Size* be a function or a predicate? Would *Bigness* be a better name than *Size*? Should *Small* be a constant or a predicate? Is *Small* a measure of relative size or absolute size? Once the choices have been made, the result is a vocabulary that is known as the **ontology** of the domain. The word ontology means a particular theory of the nature of being or existence. Together, this step and the previous step are known as ontological engineering. They determine what kinds of things exist, but do not determine their specific properties and interrelationships.

ONTOLOGY

- *Encode general knowledge about the domain.* The ontology is an informal list of the concepts in a domain. By writing logical sentences or **axioms** about the terms in the ontology, we accomplish two goals: first, we make the terms more precise so that humans will agree on their interpretation. Without the axioms, we would not know, for example, whether *Bear* refers to real bears, stuffed bears, or both. Second, we make it possible to run inference procedures to automatically derive consequences from the knowledge base. Once the axioms are in place, we can say that a knowledge base has been produced.

Of course, nobody expects a knowledge base to be correct and complete on the first try. There will be a considerable debugging process. The main difference between debugging a knowledge base and debugging a program is that it is easier to look at a single logic sentence and tell if it is correct. For example, a typical error in a knowledge base looks like this:

$$\forall x \; Animal(x) \; \Rightarrow \; \exists b \; BrainOf(x) = b$$

This says that there is some object that is the value of the *BrainOf* function applied to an animal. Of course, a function has a value for *any* input, although the value may be an undefined object for inputs that are outside the expected range. So this sentence makes a vacuous claim. We can "correct" it by adding the conjunct *Brain(b)*. Then again, if we are potentially dealing with single-celled animals, we could correct it again, replacing *Animal* by, say, *Vertebrate*.

In contrast, a typical error in a program looks like this:

```
offset := position + 1
```

It is impossible to tell if this statement is correct without looking at the rest of the program to see if, for example, `offset` is used elsewhere in the program to refer to the position, or to one beyond the position; or whether the statement was accidentally included twice in different places.

Programming language statements therefore tend to depend on a lot of context, whereas logic sentences tend to be more self-contained. In that respect, a sentence in a knowledge base is more like an entire procedure in a program, not like an individual statement.

- *Encode a description of the specific problem instance.* If the ontology is well thought out, this step will be easy. It will mostly involve writing simple atomic sentences about instances of concepts that are already part of the ontology.
- *Pose queries to the inference procedure and get answers.* This is where the reward is: we can let the inference procedure operate on the axioms and problem-specific facts to derive the facts we are interested in knowing.

To understand this five-step process better, we turn to some examples of its use. We first consider the domain of Boolean electronic circuits.

8.3   THE ELECTRONIC CIRCUITS DOMAIN

Within the domain of discrete digital electronic circuits, we would like to analyze the circuit shown in Figure 8.1. The circuit purports to be a one-bit full adder, where the first two inputs are the two bits to be added, and the third input is a carry bit. The first output is the sum, and the second output is a carry bit for the next adder. The goal is to provide an analysis that determines if the circuit is in fact an adder, and that can answer questions about the value of current flow at various points in the circuit.[3] We follow the five-step process for knowledge engineering.

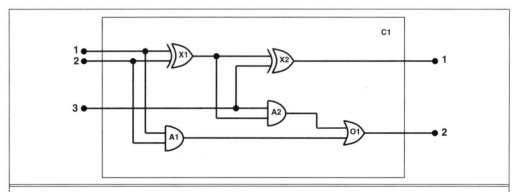

Figure 8.1   A digital circuit C1, with three inputs and two outputs, containing two XOR gates, two AND gates and one OR gate. The inputs are bit values to be added, and the outputs are the sum bit and the carry bit.

Decide what to talk about

Digital circuits are composed of wires and gates. Signals flow along wires to the input terminals of gates, and each gate produces a signal on the output terminal that flows along another wire.

---

[3]   If you are intimidated by the electronics, try to get a feel for how the knowledge base was constructed without worrying about the details.

There are four types of gates: AND, OR, and XOR gates have exactly two input terminals, and NOT gates have one. All gates have exactly one output terminal. Circuits, which are composed of gates, also have input and output terminals.

Our main purpose is to analyze the design of circuits to see if they match their specification. Thus, we need to talk about *circuits*, their *terminals*, and the *signals* at the terminals. To determine what these signals will be, we need to know about individual *gates*, and *gate types:* AND, OR, XOR, and NOT.

Not everything that is in the domain needs to show up in the ontology. We do not need to talk about the wires themselves, or the paths the wires take, or the junctions where two wires come together. All that matters is the connectivity of terminals—we can say that one output terminal is connected to another input terminal without having to mention the wire that actually connects them. There are many other factors of the domain that are irrelevant to our analysis, such as the size, shape, color, or cost of the various components.

A special-purpose ontology such as this depends not only on the domain, but also on the task to be solved. If our purpose were something other than verifying designs at the gate level, the ontology would be different. For example, if we were interested in debugging faulty circuits, then it would probably be a good idea to include the wires in the ontology, because a faulty wire can corrupt the signal flowing along it. For resolving timing faults, we would need to include gate delays. If we were interested in designing a product that would be profitable, then the cost of the circuit and its speed relative to other products on the market would be important.

Decide on a vocabulary

We now know that we want to talk about circuits, terminals, signals, gates, and gate types. The next step is to choose functions, predicates, and constants to name them. We will start from individual gates and move up to circuits.

First, we need to be able to distinguish a gate from other gates. This is handled by naming gates with constants: X_1, X_2, and so on. Next, we need to know the type of a gate.[4] A function is appropriate for this: $Type(X_1) = XOR$. This introduces the constant XOR for a particular gate type; the other constants will be called OR, AND, and NOT. The $Type$ function is not the only way to encode the ontological distinction. We could have used a type predicate: $Type(X_1, XOR)$ or several predicates, such as $XOR(X_1)$. Either of these choices would work fine, but by choosing the function $Type$, we avoid the need for an axiom that says that each individual gate can have only one type. The semantics of functions already guarantees this.

Next we consider terminals. A gate or circuit can have one or more input terminals and one or more output terminals. We could simply name each one with a constant, just as we named gates. Thus, gate X_1 could have terminals named X_1In_1, X_1In_2, and X_1Out_1. Names as long and structured as these, however, are as bad as *BearOfVerySmallBrain*. They should be replaced with a notation that makes it clear that X_1Out_1 is a terminal for gate X_1, and that it is the first output terminal. A function is appropriate for this; the function $Out(1, X_1)$ denotes the first (and only) output terminal for gate X_1. A similar function In is used for input terminals.

---

4 Note that we have used names beginning with appropriate letters—A_1, X_1, and so on—purely to make the example easier to read. The knowledge base must still contain type information for the gates.

The connectivity between gates can be represented by the predicate *Connected*, which takes two terminals as arguments, as in $Connected(Out(1, X_1), In(1, X_2))$.

Finally, we need to know if a signal is on or off. One possibility is to use a unary predicate, *On*, which is true when the signal at a terminal is on. This makes it a little difficult, however, to pose questions such as "What are all the possible values of the signals at the following terminals ... ?" We will therefore introduce as objects two "signal values" *On* or *Off*, and a function *Signal* which takes a terminal as argument and denotes a signal value.

Encode general rules

One sign that we have a good ontology is that there are very few general rules that need to be specified. A sign that we have a good vocabulary is that each rule can be stated clearly and concisely. With our example, we need only seven simple rules:

1. If two terminals are connected, then they have the same signal:
   $$\forall t_1, t_2 \quad Connected(t_1, t_2) \Rightarrow Signal(t_1) = Signal(t_2)$$

2. The signal at every terminal is either on or off (but not both):
   $$\forall t \quad Signal(t) = On \lor Signal(t) = Off$$
   $$On \neq Off$$

3. *Connected* is a commutative predicate:
   $$\forall t_1, t_2 \quad Connected(t_1, t_2) \Leftrightarrow Connected(t_2, t_1)$$

4. An OR gate's output is on if and only if any of its inputs are on:
   $$\forall g \quad Type(g) = OR \Rightarrow$$
   $$Signal(Out(1, g)) = On \Leftrightarrow \exists n \quad Signal(In(n, g)) = On$$

5. An AND gate's output is off if and only if any of its inputs are off:
   $$\forall g \quad Type(g) = AND \Rightarrow$$
   $$Signal(Out(1, g)) = Off \Leftrightarrow \exists n \quad Signal(In(n, g)) = Off$$

6. An XOR gate's output is on if and only if its inputs are different:
   $$\forall g \quad Type(g) = XOR \Rightarrow$$
   $$Signal(Out(1, g)) = On \Leftrightarrow Signal(In(1, g)) \neq Signal(In(2, g))$$

7. A NOT gate's output is different from its input:
   $$\forall g \quad (Type(g) = NOT) \Rightarrow Signal(Out(1, g)) \neq Signal(In(1, g))$$

Encode the specific instance

The circuit shown in Figure 8.1 is encoded as circuit C_1 with the following description. First, we categorize the gates:

$$Type(X_1) = XOR \quad Type(X_2) = XOR$$
$$Type(A_1) = AND \quad Type(A_2) = AND$$
$$Type(O_1) = OR$$

Then, the connections between them:

$Connected(Out(1, X_1), In(1, X_2))$ $Connected(In(1, C_1), In(1, X_1))$
$Connected(Out(1, X_1), In(2, A_2))$ $Connected(In(1, C_1), In(1, A_1))$
$Connected(Out(1, A_2), In(1, O_1))$ $Connected(In(2, C_1), In(2, X_1))$
$Connected(Out(1, A_1), In(2, O_1))$ $Connected(In(2, C_1), In(2, A_1))$
$Connected(Out(1, X_2), Out(1, C_1))$ $Connected(In(3, C_1), In(2, X_2))$
$Connected(Out(1, O_1), Out(2, C_1))$ $Connected(In(3, C_1), In(1, A_2))$

Pose queries to the inference procedure

What combinations of inputs would cause the first output of C_1 (the sum bit) to be off and the second output of C_1 (the carry bit) to be on?

$$\exists i_1, i_2, i_3 \ Signal(In(1, C_1)) = i_1 \wedge Signal(In(2, C_1)) = i_2 \wedge signal(In(3, C_1)) = i_3$$
$$\wedge \ Signal(Out(1, C_1)) = \textit{Off} \wedge Signal(Out(2, C_1)) = On$$

The answer is

$$(i_1 = On \wedge i_2 = On \wedge i_3 = \textit{Off}) \vee$$
$$(i_1 = On \wedge i_2 = \textit{Off} \wedge i_3 = On) \vee$$
$$(i_1 = \textit{Off} \wedge i_2 = On \wedge i_3 = On)$$

What are the possible sets of values of all the terminals for the adder circuit?

$$\exists i_1, i_2, i_3, o_1, o_2 \ Signal(In(1, C_1)) = i_1 \wedge Signal(In(2, C_1)) = i_2$$
$$\wedge \ Signal(In(3,_1)) = i_3 \wedge Signal(Out(1, C_1)) = o_1 \wedge Signal(Out(2, C_1)) = o_2$$

CIRCUIT
VERIFICATION

This final query will return a complete input/output table for the device, which can be used to check that it does in fact add its inputs correctly. This is a simple example of **circuit verification**. We can also use the definition of the circuit to build larger digital systems, for which the same kind of verification procedure can be carried out (see Exercises 8.1 and 8.3). Many domains are amenable to the same kind of structured knowledge-base development, in which more complex concepts are defined on top of simpler concepts.

8.4   GENERAL ONTOLOGY

This section is about a general ontology that incorporates decisions about how to represent a broad selection of objects and relations. It is encoded within first-order logic, but makes many ontological commitments that first-order logic does not make. A general ontology is rather more demanding to construct, but once done has many advantages over special-purpose ontologies.

Consider again the ontology for circuits in the previous section. It makes a large number of simplifying assumptions. For example, time is omitted completely. Signals are fixed, and there is no propagation of signals. The structure of the circuit remains constant. Now we could take a step toward generality by considering signals at particular times, and including the wire lengths and propagation delays in wires and devices. This would allow us to simulate the timing properties of the circuit, and indeed such simulations are often carried out by circuit designers. We could also introduce more interesting classes of gates, for example by describing the technology (TTL, MOS, CMOS, and so on) as well as the input/output specification. If we wanted to discuss reliability or diagnosis, we would include the possibility that the structure of the circuit, or the properties of the gates, might change spontaneously. To account for stray capacitances, we would need to move from a purely topological representation of connectivity to a more realistic description of geometric properties.

If we look at the wumpus world, similar considerations apply. Although we do include time, it has a very simple structure. Nothing happens except when the agent acts, and all changes can be considered instantaneous. A more general ontology, better suited for the real world, would allow for simultaneous changes extended over time. We also used the constant symbol *Pit* to say that there was a pit in a particular square, because all pits were identical. We could have allowed for different kinds of pits by having several individuals belonging to the class of pits but having different properties. Similarly, we might want to allow for several different kinds of animals, not just wumpuses. It might not be possible to pin down the exact species from the available percepts, so we would need to build up a wumpus-world biological taxonomy to help the agent predict behavior from scanty clues.

For any area of a special-purpose ontology, it is possible to make changes like these to move toward greater generality. An obvious question then arises: do all these ontologies converge on a general-purpose ontology? The answer is, "Possibly." In this section, we will present one version, representing a synthesis of ideas from many knowledge representation efforts in AI and philosophy. There are two major characteristics of general-purpose ontologies that distinguish them from collections of special-purpose ontologies:

- A general-purpose ontology should be applicable in more or less any special-purpose domain (with the addition of domain-specific axioms). This means that as far as possible, no representational issue can be finessed or brushed under the carpet. For example, a general ontology cannot use situation calculus, which finesses the issues of duration and simultaneity, because domains such as circuit timing analysis require those issues to be handled properly.

- In any sufficiently demanding domain, different areas of knowledge must be *unified* because reasoning and problem solving may involve several areas simultaneously. A robot circuit-repair system, for instance, needs to reason about circuits in terms of electrical connectivity and physical layout, and about time both for circuit timing analysis and estimating labor costs. The sentences describing time therefore must be capable of being combined with those describing spatial layout, and must work equally well for nanoseconds and minutes, and for angstroms and meters.

After we present the general ontology, we will apply it to write sentences describing the domain of grocery shopping. A brief reverie on the subject of shopping brings to mind a vast array of topics in need of representation: locations, movement, physical objects, shapes, sizes, grasping, releasing, colors, categories of objects, anchovies, amounts of stuff, nutrition, cooking, nonstick frying pans, taste, time, money, direct debit cards, arithmetic, economics, and so on. The domain is more than adequate to exercise our ontology, and leaves plenty of scope for the reader to do some creative knowledge representation of his or her own.

Our discussion of the general-purpose ontology is organized under the following headings, each of which is really worth a chapter by itself:

◇ **Categories**: Rather than being an entirely random collection of objects, the world exhibits a good deal of regularity. For example, there are many cases in which several objects have a number of properties in common. It is usual to define **categories**[5] that include as members all objects having certain properties. For example, we might wish to have categories for tomatoes or ten-dollar bills, for peaches or pound notes, for fruits or monetary instruments. We describe how categories can be objects in their own right, and how they are linked into a unified **taxonomic hierarchy**.

◇ **Measures**: Many useful properties such as mass, age, and price relate objects to quantities of particular types, which we call measures. We explain how measures are represented in logic, and how they relate to units of measure.

◇ **Composite objects**: It is very common for objects to belong to categories by virtue of their constituent structure. For example, cars have wheels, an engine, and so on, arranged in particular ways; typical baseball games have nine innings in which each team alternates pitching and batting. We show how such structures can be represented.

◇ **Time, Space, and Change**: In order to allow for actions and events that have different durations and can occur simultaneously, we enlarge our ontology of time. The basic picture is of a universe that is continuous in both temporal and spatial dimensions. Times, places, and objects will be parts of this universe.

◇ **Events and Processes**: Events such as the purchase of a tomato will also become individuals in our ontology. Like tomatoes, they are usually grouped into categories. Individual events take place at particular times and places. Processes are events that are continuous and homogeneous in nature, such as raining or cooking tomatoes.

◇ **Physical Objects**: We are already familiar with the representation of ordinary objects such as AND-gates and wumpuses. As things that are extended in both time and space, physical objects have much in common with events.

◇ **Substances**: Whereas objects such as tomatoes are relatively easy to pin down, substances such as tomato juice are a little slippery. Natural language usage seems to provide conflicting intuitions. Is there an object called *TomatoJuice*? Is it a category, or a real physical object? What is the connection between it and the liter of tomato juice I bought yesterday? Between it and constituent substances such as *Water*? We will see that these questions can be resolved by careful use of the ontology of space, time, and physical objects.

◇ **Mental Objects and Beliefs**: An agent will often need to reason about its own beliefs, for example, when trying to decide why it thought that anchovies were on sale. It will also need to reason about the beliefs of others, for example, in order to decide whom to ask about the right aisle to find the tomatoes. In our ontology, sentences are explicitly represented, and are believed by agents.

In this section, we will try to cover the highest levels of the ontology. The top levels of the hierarchy of categories are shown in Figure 8.2. While the scope of the effort might seem

---

[5] Categories are also called **classes**, **collections**, **kinds**, **types**, and **concepts** by other authors. They have little or nothing to do with the mathematical topic of **category theory**.

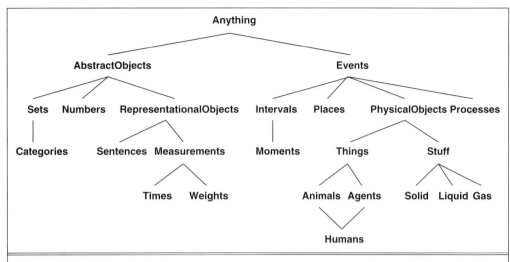

Figure 8.2   The top-level ontology of the world, showing the topics to be covered later in the chapter. Arcs indicate subset relations.

daunting at first, representing knowledge of the commonsense world can be highly illuminating. One is constantly amazed by how much one knows but never took the time to think about. With a good ontology, writing it down becomes more of a pleasure than a problem. Connections between seemingly disparate areas become obvious, and one is awed by the scope of human thought.

The following subsections fill in the details of each topic. We should first state one important caveat. We have chosen to discuss the content and organization of knowledge using first-order logic. Certain aspects of the real world are hard to capture in this language. The principal feature we must omit is the fact that almost all generalizations have exceptions, or have the status of a default in the absence of more exact information, or only hold to a degree. For example, although "tomatoes are red" is a useful rule, some tomatoes are green, yellow, or orange. Similar exceptions can be found to almost all the general statements in this section. The ability to handle exceptions and uncertain rules is extremely important, but is orthogonal to the task of understanding the general ontology. For this reason, we will delay the discussion of exceptions and defaults until Chapter 10, and the more general topic of uncertain information until Chapter 14.

Representing Categories

CATEGORIES

The organization of objects into **categories** is a vital part of knowledge representation. Although interaction with the world takes place at the level of individual objects, *much of reasoning takes place at the level of categories.* For example, a shopper might have the goal of buying *a cantaloupe*, rather than a particular cantaloupe such as *Cantaloupe*$_{37}$.[6] Categories also serve to

---

[6]   We often use subscripts as a reminder that a constant refers to an individual rather than a collection.

make predictions about objects once they are classified. One infers the presence of certain objects from perceptual input, infers category membership from the perceived properties of the objects, and then uses category information to make predictions about the objects. For example, from its green, mottled skin, large size, and ovoid shape, one can infer that an object is a watermelon; from this, one infers that it would be useful for fruit salad.

There are two main choices for representing categories in first-order logic. The first we have already seen: categories are represented by unary predicates. The predicate symbol *Tomato*, for example, represents the unary relation that is true only for objects that are tomatoes, and *Tomato*(x) means that x is a tomato.

REIFICATION

The second choice is to **reify** the category. **Reification** is the process of turning a predicate or function into an object in the language.[7] We will see several examples of reification in this chapter. In this case, we use *Tomatoes* as a constant symbol referring to the object that is the *set of all tomatoes*. We use $x \in$ *Tomatoes* to say that x is a tomato. Reified categories allow us to make assertions about the category itself, rather than about members of the category. For example, we can say *Population*(*Humans*) = 5, 000, 000, 000, even though there is no individual human with a population of five billion.

INHERITANCE

Categories perform one more important role: they serve to organize and simplify the knowledge base through **inheritance**. If we say that all instances of the category *Food* are edible, and if we assert that *Fruit* is a subclass of *Food* and *Apples* is a subclass of *Fruit*, then we know that every apple is edible. We say that the individual apples **inherit** the property of edibility, in this case from their membership in the *Food* category.

TAXONOMY

Subclass relations organize categories into a **taxonomy** or **taxonomic hierarchy**. Taxonomies have been used explicitly for centuries in technical fields. For example, systematic biology aims to provide a taxonomy of all living and extinct species; library science has developed a taxonomy of all fields of knowledge, encoded as the Dewey Decimal system; tax authorities and other government departments have developed extensive taxonomies of occupations and commercial products. Taxonomies are also an important aspect of general commonsense knowledge, as we will see in our investigations that follow.

First-order logic makes it easy to state facts about categories, either by relating objects to categories or by quantifying over their members:

- An object is a member of a category. For example:
  Tomato$_{12} \in$ *Tomatoes*

- A category is a subclass of another category. For example:
  Tomatoes $\subset$ *Fruit*

- All members of a category have some properties. For example:
  $\forall x \; x \in$ *Tomatoes* $\Rightarrow$ *Red*(x) $\land$ *Round*(x)

- Members of a category can be recognized by some properties. For example:
  $\forall x \; Red(Interior(x)) \land Green(Exterior(x)) \land x \in Melons \Rightarrow x \in Watermelons$

- A category as a whole has some properties. For example:
  Tomatoes $\in$ *DomesticatedSpecies*

---

[7] The term "reification" comes from the Latin word *res*, or thing. John McCarthy proposed the term "thingification," but it never caught on.

Notice that because *Tomatoes* is a category, and is a member of *DomesticatedSpecies*, then *DomesticatedSpecies* must be a category of categories. One can even have categories of categories of categories, but they are not much use.

Although subclass and instance relations are the most important ones for categories, we also want to be able to state relations between categories that are not subclasses of each other. For example, if we just say that *Males* and *Females* are subclasses of *Animals*, then we have not said that a male cannot be a female. We say that two or more categories are **disjoint** if they have no members in common. And even if we know that males and females are disjoint, we will not know that an animal that is not a male must be a female unless we say that males and females constitute an **exhaustive decomposition** of the animals. A disjoint exhaustive decomposition is known as a **partition**. The following examples illustrate these three concepts:

DISJOINT

EXHAUSTIVE
DECOMPOSITION
PARTITION

> *Disjoint*({*Animals*, *Vegetables*})
> *ExhaustiveDecomposition*({*Americans*, *Canadians*, *Mexicans*}, *NorthAmericans*)
> *Partition*({*Males*, *Females*}, *Animals*)

(Note that the *ExhaustiveDecomposition* of *NorthAmericans* is not a *Partition* because some people have dual citizenship.) The definitions of these three predicates are as follows:

> $\forall s \; Disjoint(s) \Leftrightarrow$
> $\qquad (\forall c_1, c_2 \; c_1 \in s \land c_2 \in s \land c_1 \neq c_2 \qquad\qquad \Rightarrow Intersection(c_1, c_2) = EmptySet)$
> $\forall s, c \; ExhaustiveDecomposition(s, c) \Leftrightarrow$
> $\qquad (\forall i \; i \in c \Leftrightarrow \exists c_2 \; c_2 \in s \land i \in c_2)$
> $\forall s, c \; Partition(s, c) \Leftrightarrow Disjoint(s) \land ExhaustiveDecomposition(s, c)$

Categories can also be *defined* by providing necessary and sufficient conditions for membership. For example, a bachelor is an unmarried, adult male:

> $\forall x \; Bachelor(x) \Leftrightarrow Male(x) \land Adult(x) \land Unmarried(x)$

As we discuss in the sidebar on natural kinds, strict logical definitions for categories are not always possible, nor always necessary.

Measures

In both scientific and commonsense theories of the world, objects have height, mass, cost, and so on. The values that we assign for these properties are called **measures**. Ordinary, quantitative measures are quite easy to represent. We imagine that the universe includes abstract "measure objects," such as the *length* that is the length of this line segment: ⊢——————————————⊣. We can call this length 1.5 inches, or 3.81 centimeters. Thus, the same length has different names in our language. Logically, this can be done by combining a **units function** with a number. If L_1 is the name of the line segment, then we can write

MEASURES

UNITS FUNCTION

> $Length(L_1) = Inches(1.5) = Centimeters(3.81)$

Conversion between units is done with sentences such as

> $\forall l \; Centimeters(2.54 \times l) = Inches(l)$
> $\forall t \; Centigrade(t) = Fahrenheit(32 + 1.8 \times t)$

NATURAL KINDS

Some categories have strict definitions: an object is a triangle if and only if it is a polygon with three sides. On the other hand, most categories in the shopping world and in the real world are **natural kind** categories with no clear-cut definition. We know, for example, that tomatoes tend to be a dull scarlet, roughly spherical, with an indentation at top where the stem was, about three to four inches in diameter, with a thin but tough skin and with flesh, seeds, and juice inside. We also know that there is variation: unripe tomatoes are green, some are smaller or larger than average, cherry tomatoes are uniformly small. Rather than having a complete definition of tomatoes, we have a set of features that serves to identify objects that are clearly typical tomatoes, but may not be able to decide for other objects. (Could there be a square tomato? a yellow one? a tomato three feet across?)

This poses a problem for a logical agent. The agent cannot be sure that an object it has perceived is a tomato, and even if it was sure, it could not be certain which of the properties of typical tomatoes this one has. This problem is an inevitable consequence of operating in inaccessible environments. The following mechanism provides a way to deal with natural kinds within a logical system.

The key idea is to separate what is true of all instances of a category from what is true only of typical instances of a category. So in addition to the category *Tomatoes*, we will also have the category *Typical(Tomatoes)*. Here *Typical* is a function that maps a category to the subclass of that category that contains only the typical instances:

$$\forall c \ \ Typical(c) \subset c$$

Most of the knowledge about natural kinds will actually be about the typical instances:

$$\forall x \ \ x \in Typical(Tomatoes) \ \Rightarrow \ Red(x) \wedge Spherical(x)$$

In this way, we can still write down useful facts about categories without providing exact definitions.

The difficulty of providing exact definitions for most natural categories was explained in depth by Wittgenstein (1953), in his book *Philosophical Investigations*. He used the example of *games* to show that members of a category shared "family resemblances" rather than necessary and sufficient characteristics. The *Investigations* also revolutionized our understanding of language, as we discuss further in Chapter 22.

The utility of the notion of strict definition was also challenged by Quine (1953). He pointed out that even the definition of "bachelor" given before is suspect; one might, for example, question a statement such as "the Pope is a bachelor." The category "bachelor" still plays a useful role in natural language and in formal knowledge representation, because it simplifies many sentences and inferences.

Similar axioms can be written for pounds and kilograms; seconds and days; dollars and cents. (Exercise 8.9 asks you to represent exchange rates between currencies, where those exchange rates can vary over time.)

Measures can be used to describe objects as follows:

$Mass(Tomato_{12}) = Kilograms(0.16)$
$Price(Tomato_{12}) = \$(0.32)$
$\forall d \ \ d \in Days \ \Rightarrow \ Duration(d) = Hours(24)$

It is very important to be able to distinguish between monetary amounts and monetary instruments:

$\forall b \ \ b \in DollarBills \ \Rightarrow \ CashValue(b) = \$(1.00)$

This will be useful when it comes to paying for things later in the chapter.

Simple, quantitative measures are easy to represent. There are other measures that present more of a problem, because they have no agreed scale of values. Exercises have difficulty, desserts have deliciousness, and poems have beauty, yet numbers cannot be assigned to these qualities. One might, in a moment of pure accountancy, dismiss such properties as useless for the purpose of logical reasoning; or, still worse, attempt to impose a numerical scale on beauty. This would be a grave mistake, because it is unnecessary. The most important aspect of measures is not the particular numerical values, but the fact that measures can be *ordered*.

Although measures are not numbers, we can still compare them using an ordering symbol such as >. For example, we might well believe that Norvig's exercises are tougher than Russell's, and that one scores less on tougher exercises:

$\forall e_1, e_2 \ \ e_1 \in Exercises \land e_2 \in Exercises \land Wrote(Norvig, e_1) \land Wrote(Russell, e_2) \ \Rightarrow$
$\qquad Difficulty(e_1) > Difficulty(e_2)$
$\forall e_1, e_2 \ \ e_1 \in Exercises \land e_2 \in Exercises \land Difficulty(e_1) > Difficulty(e_2) \ \Rightarrow$
$\qquad ExpectedScore(e_1) < ExpectedScore(e_2)$

This is enough to allow one to decide which exercises to do, even though no numerical values for difficulty were ever used. (One does, however, have to determine who wrote which exercises.) These sorts of monotonic relationships among measures form the basis for the field of **qualitative physics**, a subfield of AI that investigates how to reason about physical systems without plunging into detailed equations and numerical simulations. Qualitative physics is discussed in the historical notes section.

Composite objects

The idea that one object can be part of another is a familiar one. One's nose is part of one's head; Romania is part of Europe; this chapter is part of this book. We use the general *PartOf* relation to say that one thing is part of another. *PartOf* is transitive and reflexive. Objects can therefore be grouped into *PartOf* hierarchies, reminiscent of the *Subset* hierarchy:

$PartOf(Bucharest, Romania)$
$PartOf(Romania, EasternEurope)$
$PartOf(EasternEurope, Europe)$

From these, given the transitivity of *PartOf*, we can infer that $PartOf(Bucharest, Europe)$.

COMPOSITE OBJECT
STRUCTURE
Any object that has parts is called a **composite object**. Categories of composite objects are often characterized by the **structure** of those objects, that is, the parts and how the parts are related. For example, a biped has exactly two legs that are attached to its body:

$$\forall a \; Biped(a) \;\Rightarrow$$
$$\exists l_1, l_2, b \;\; Leg(l_1) \land Leg(l_2) \land Body(b) \land$$
$$PartOf(l_1, a) \land PartOf(l_2, a) \land PartOf(b, a) \land$$
$$Attached(l_1, b) \land Attached(l_2, b) \land$$
$$l_1 {\neq} l_2 \land \forall l_3 \;\; Leg(l_3) \land PartOf(l_3, a) \;\Rightarrow\; (l_3 = l_1 \lor l_3 = l_2)$$

This general form of sentence can be used to define the structure of any composite object, including events: for example, for all baseball games, there exist nine innings such that each is a part of the game, and so on. A generic event description of this kind is often called a
SCHEMA
SCRIPT
schema or **script**, particularly in the area of natural language understanding. Some approaches to text understanding rely mainly on the ability to recognize instances of schematic events from descriptions of their parts, so that the text can be organized into coherent events, and questions can be answered about parts not explicitly mentioned. We discuss these issues further in Chapter 22.

We can define a *PartPartition* relation analogous to the *Partition* relation for categories (see Exercise 8.4). An object is composed of the parts in its *PartPartition*, and can be viewed as deriving some properties from those parts. For example, the mass of a composite object is the sum of the masses of the parts. Notice that this is not the case with categories: categories have no mass, even though their elements might.

It is also useful to define composite objects with definite parts but no particular structure. For example, we might want to say, "The apples in this bag weigh three pounds." Rather than commit the error of assigning the weight to the *category* of apples-in-the-bag, we can make a
BUNCH
bunch out of the apples. For example, if the apples are $Apple_1$, $Apple_2$, and $Apple_3$, then

$$BunchOf(\{Apple_1, Apple_2, Apple_3\})$$

denotes the composite object with the three apples as parts. We can then use the bunch as a normal, albeit unstructured, object. Notice that $BunchOf(Apples)$ is the composite object consisting of all apples—not to be confused with *Apples*, the category.

Representing change with events

Section 7.6 showed how situation calculus could be used to represent change. Situation calculus is perfect for the vacuum world, the wumpus world, or any world in which a single agent takes discrete actions. Unfortunately, situation calculus has two problems that limit its applicability. First, situations are instantaneous points in time, which are not very useful for describing the gradual growth of a kitten into a cat, the flow of electrons along a wire, or any other process where change occurs continuously over time. Second, situation calculus works best when only one action happens at a time. When there are multiple agents in the world, or when the world can change spontaneously, situation calculus begins to break down. It is possible to prop it back up for a while by defining composite actions, as in Exercise 7.12. If there are actions that have different durations, or whose effects depend on duration, then situation calculus in its intended form cannot be used at all.

EVENT CALCULUS

EVENT

Because of these limitations, we now turn to a different approach toward representing change, which we call the **event calculus**, although the name is not standard. Event calculus is rather like a continuous version of the situation-calculus "movie" shown in Figure 7.3. We think of a particular universe as having both a "spatial" and a temporal dimension. The "spatial" dimension ranges over all of the objects in an instantaneous "snapshot" or "cross-section" of the universe.[8] The temporal dimension ranges over time. An **event** is, informally, just a "chunk" of this universe with both temporal and spatial extent. Figure 8.3 gives the general idea.

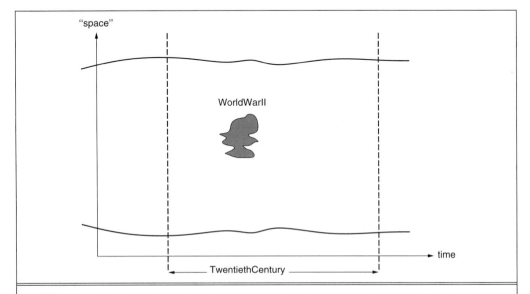

Figure 8.3   The major entities in event calculus. *Intervals* such as the *TwentiethCentury* contain as subevents all of the events occurring within a given time period. Ordinary events such as *WorldWarII* have temporal and "spatial" extent.

SUBEVENTS

Let us look at an example: World War II, referred to by the symbol *WorldWarII*. World War II has parts that we refer to as **subevents**:[9]

$SubEvent(BattleOfBritain, WorldWarII)$

Similarly, World War II is a subevent of the twentieth century:

$SubEvent(WorldWarII, TwentiethCentury)$

INTERVAL

The twentieth century is a special kind of event called an **interval**. An interval is an event that includes as subevents all events occurring in a given time period. Intervals are therefore entire temporal sections of the universe, as the figure illustrates. In situation calculus, a given fact is true in a particular situation. In event calculus, a given event occurs during a particular interval. The previous *SubEvent* sentences are examples of this kind of statement.

---

[8]   We put "spatial" in quotes because it is possible that the set of objects being considered does not include places at all; nonetheless, it is a helpful metaphor. From now on, we will leave off the quotes.

[9]   Note that *SubEvent* is a special case of the *PartOf* relation, and is also transitive and reflexive.

Like any other sort of object, events can be grouped into categories. For example, *WorldWarII* belongs to the category *Wars*. To say that a war occurred in the Middle East in 1967, we would say

$$\exists w \quad w \in Wars \wedge SubEvent(w, AD1967) \wedge PartOf(Location(w), MiddleEast)$$

To say that Shankar travelled from New York to New Delhi yesterday, we might use the category *Journeys*, as follows:

$$\exists j \quad j \in Journeys \wedge Origin(NewYork, j) \wedge Destination(NewDelhi, j)$$
$$\wedge \; Traveller(Shankar, j) \wedge SubEvent(j, Yesterday)$$

This notation can get a little tedious, particularly because we are often interested more in the event's properties than in the event itself. We can simplify the descriptions by using complex terms to name event categories. For example, *Go(Shankar, NewYork, NewDelhi)* names the category of events in which Shankar travels from New York to New Delhi. The function symbol *Go* can be defined by the following sentence:

$$\forall e, x, o, d \quad e \in Go(x, o, d) \iff$$
$$e \in Journeys \wedge Traveller(x, e) \wedge Origin(o, e) \wedge Destination(d, e)$$

Finally, we use the notation $E(c, i)$ to say that an event of *category c* is a subevent of the event (or interval) i:

$$\forall c, i \quad E(c, i) \iff \exists e \quad e \in c \wedge SubEvent(e, i)$$

Thus, we have

$$E(Go(Shankar, NewYork, NewDelhi), Yesterday)$$

which means "there was an event that was a going by Shankar from New York to New Delhi that took place sometime yesterday."

Places

PLACES

Places, like intervals, are special kinds of space-time chunks. A place can be thought of as a constant piece of space, extended through time.[10] New York and the Middle East are places, at least as far as recent history is concerned. We use the predicate *In* to denote the special kind of subevent relation that holds between places; for example:

$$In(NewYork, USA)$$

Places come in different varieties; for example, *NewYork* is an *Area*, whereas the *SolarSystem* is a *Volume*. The *Location* function, which we used earlier, maps an object to the smallest place that contains it:

$$\forall x, l \quad Location(x) = l \iff$$
$$At(x, l) \wedge \forall l_2 \quad At(x, l_2) \implies In(l, l_2)$$

MINIMIZATION

This last sentence is an example of a standard logical construction called **minimization**.

---

[10] We will not worry about local inertial coordinate frames and other things that physicists need to pin down exactly what this means. Places that *change* over time are dealt with in a later section.

Processes

The events we have seen so far have been what we call **discrete events**—they have a definite structure. Shankar's trip has a beginning, middle, and end. If interrupted halfway, the event would be different—it would not be a trip from New York to New Delhi, but instead a trip from New York to somewhere in the Eastern Mediterranean. On the other hand, the category of events denoted by *Flying(Shankar)* has a different quality. If we take a small interval of Shankar's flight, say, the third twenty-minute segment (while he waits anxiously for a second bag of honey-roasted peanuts), that event is still a member of *Flying(Shankar)*. In fact, this is true for any subinterval.

Categories of events with this property are called **process** categories or **liquid event** categories. Any subinterval of a process is also a member of the same process category. We can use the same notation used for discrete events to say that, for example, Shankar was flying at some time yesterday:

$$E(Flying(Shankar), Yesterday)$$

We often want to say that some process was going on *throughout* some interval, rather than just in some subinterval of it. To do this, we use the predicate T:

$$T(Working(Stuart), TodayLunchHour)$$

$T(c, i)$ means that some event of type c occurred over exactly the interval i—that is, the event begins and ends at the same time as the interval. Exercise 8.6 asks you to define T formally.

As well as describing processes of continuous change, liquid events can describe processes of continuous non-change. These are often called **states**. For example, "Mary being in the local supermarket" is a category of states that we might denote by $In(Mary, Supermarket_1)$. To say she was in the supermarket all this afternoon, we would write

$$T(In(Mary, Supermarket_1), ThisAfternoon)$$

An interval can also be a discontinuous sequence of times; we can represent the fact that the supermarket is closed every Sunday with

$$T(Closed(Supermarket_1), BunchOf(Sundays))$$

Special notation for combining propositions

It is tempting to write something like

$$T((At(Agent, Loc_1) \land At(Tomato_1, Loc_1)), I_3)$$

but technically this is nonsense, because a sentence appears as the first argument of the predicate T, and all arguments to predicates must be terms, not sentences. This is easily fixed by introducing a function called *And* that takes two event categories as arguments and returns a category of composite events of the appropriate kind:

$$T(And(At(Agent, Loc_1), At(Tomato_1, Loc_1)), E)$$

We can define the function *And* with the axiom

$$\forall p, q, e \ \ T(And(p, q), e) \ \Leftrightarrow \ T(p, e) \land T(q, e)$$

Thus, $And(p, q)$ is the category of composite "p-q-events," where a p-q-event is an event in which both a p and a q occur. If you think of a p-event as a piece of "videotape" of a p happening, and a q-event as a "videotape" of a q happening, then the p-q-event is like having the two pieces of tape spliced together in parallel (see Figure 8.4(a)).

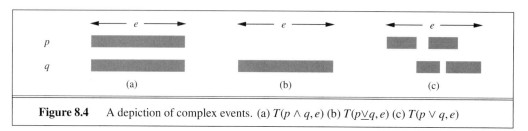

Figure 8.4   A depiction of complex events. (a) $T(p \wedge q, e)$ (b) $T(p \underline{\vee} q, e)$ (c) $T(p \vee q, e)$

Once a method for conjoining event categories is defined, it is convenient to extend the syntax to allow regular infix connective symbols to be used in place of the function name:

$$T(p \wedge q, e) \iff T(And(p, q), e) \iff T(p, e) \wedge T(q, e)$$

This is fine as long as you remember that in $T(p \wedge q, s)$, the expression $p \wedge q$ is a term denoting a category of events, not a sentence.

One might think that we can just go ahead and define similar functions for disjunctive and negated events. In fact, because the T predicate is essentially a *conjunction* (over all the subintervals of the interval in question), it can interact in two different ways with disjunction and negation. For example, consider the English sentence "One of the two shops was open all day on Sunday." This could mean, "Either the first shop was open all day on Sunday, or the second shop was open all day on Sunday" (Figure 8.4(b)), or it could mean, "At any given time on Sunday, at least one of the two shops was open" (Figure 8.4(c)). Both of these meanings are useful sorts of things to say, so we will need a concise representation for each. There are no accepted notations in this case, so we will make some up. Let $\underline{\vee}$ be used for the first kind of disjunctive event, and $\vee$ be used for the second. For the first, we have the following definition:

$$T(p \underline{\vee} q, e) \iff T(p, e) \vee T(q, e)$$

We leave the second as an exercise, along with the definitions for negated events.

Times, intervals, and actions

In this section, we flesh out the vocabulary of time intervals. Because it is a limited domain, we can be more complete in deciding on a vocabulary and encoding general rules. Time intervals are partitioned into moments and extended intervals. The distinction is that only moments have zero duration:

$$Partition(\{Moments, ExtendedIntervals\}, Intervals)$$
$$\forall i \ i \in Intervals \implies (i \in Moments \iff Duration(i) = 0)$$

Now we invent a time scale and associate points on that scale with moments, giving us absolute times. The time scale is arbitrary; we will measure it in seconds and say that the moment at midnight (GMT) on January 1, 1900, has time 0. The functions *Start* and *End* pick out the earliest and latest moments in an interval, and the function *Time* delivers the point on the time scale for a moment. The function *Duration* gives the difference between the end time and the start time.

$$\forall i \;\; Interval(i) \;\Rightarrow\; Duration(i) = (Time(End(i)) - Time(Start(i)))$$
$$Time(Start(AD1900)) = Seconds(0)$$
$$Time(Start(AD1991)) = Seconds(2871694800)$$
$$Time(End(AD1991)) = Seconds(2903230800)$$
$$Duration(AD1991) = Seconds(31536000)$$

To make these numbers easier to read, we also introduce a function *Date*, which takes six arguments (hours, minutes, seconds, month, day, and year) and returns a point on the time scale:

$$Time(Start(AD1991)) = Date(00, 00, 00, Jan, 1, 1991)$$
$$Date(12, 34, 56, Feb, 14, 1993) = Seconds(2938682096)$$

The simplest relation between intervals is *Meet*. Two intervals *Meet* if the end time of the first equals the start time of the second. It is possible to define predicates such as *Before*, *After*, *During*, and *Overlap* solely in terms of *Meet*, but it is more intuitive to define them in terms of points on the time scale. (See Figure 8.5 for a graphical representation.)

$$\forall i,j \;\; Meet(i,j) \;\Leftrightarrow\; Time(End(i)) = Time(Start(j))$$
$$\forall i,j \;\; Before(i,j) \;\Leftrightarrow\; Time(End(i)) < Time(Start(j))$$
$$\forall i,j \;\; After(j,i) \;\Leftrightarrow\; Before(i,j)$$
$$\forall i,j \;\; During(i,j) \;\Leftrightarrow\; Time(Start(j)) \le Time(Start(i)) \wedge Time(End(i)) \le Time(End(j))$$
$$\forall i,j \;\; Overlap(i,j) \;\Leftrightarrow\; \exists k \;\; During(k,i) \wedge During(k,j)$$

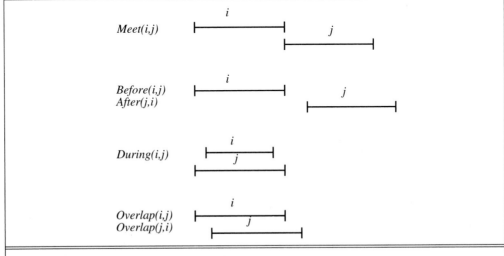

Figure 8.5   Predicates on time intervals.

For example, to say that the reign of Elizabeth II followed that of George VI, and the reign of Elvis overlapped with the 1950s, we can write the following:

$After(ReignOf(ElizabethII), ReignOf(GeorgeVI))$
$Overlap(Fifties, ReignOf(Elvis))$
$Start(Fifties) = Start(AD1950)$
$End(Fifties) = End(AD1959)$

Temporal relations among intervals are used principally in describing actions. This is done in much the same way in event calculus as it is in situation calculus. The difference is that instead of defining a resulting situation and describing it, one defines a resulting interval, in which a certain state occurs. The following examples illustrate the general idea:

1. If two people are engaged, then in some future interval, they will either marry or break the engagement.

$$\forall x, y, i_0 \ T(Engaged(x, y), i_0) \Rightarrow$$
$$\exists i_1 \ (Meet(i_0, i_1) \vee After(i_1, i_0)) \wedge$$
$$T(Marry(x, y) \vee BreakEngagement(x, y), i_1)$$

2. When two people marry, they are spouses for some interval starting at the end of the marrying event.

$$\forall x, y, i_0 \ T(Marry(x, y), i_0) \Rightarrow \exists i_1 \ T(Spouse(x, y), i_1) \wedge Meet(i_0, i_1)$$

3. The result of going from one place to another is to be at that other place.

$$\forall x, a, b, i_0 \ , \exists i_1 \ T(Go(x, a, b), i_0) \Rightarrow T(In(x, b), i_1) \wedge Meet(i_0, i_1)$$

We shall have more to say on the subject of actions and intervals in Part IV, which covers planning with these sorts of action descriptions.

Objects revisited

One purpose of situation calculus was to allow objects to have different properties at different times. Event calculus achieves the same goal. For example, we can say that Poland's area in 1426 was 233,000 square miles, whereas in 1950 it was 117,000 square miles:

$T(Area(Poland, SqMiles(233000)), AD1426)$
$T(Area(Poland, SqMiles(117000)), AD1950)$

In fact, as well as growing and shrinking, Poland has moved about somewhat on the map. We could plot its land area over time, as shown in Figure 8.6. We see that Poland has a temporal as well as spatial extent. *It turns out to be perfectly consistent to view Poland as an event.* We can then use temporal subevents such as *19thCenturyPoland*, and spatial subevents such as *CentralPoland*.

The USA has also changed various aspects over time. One aspect that changes every four or eight years, barring mishaps, is its president. In event calculus, *President(USA)* denotes an object that consists of different people at different times. *President(USA)* is the object that is George Washington from 1789 to 1796, John Adams from 1796 to 1800, and so on (Figure 8.7). To say that the president of the USA in 1994 is a Democrat, we would use

$T(Democrat(President(USA)), AD1994)$

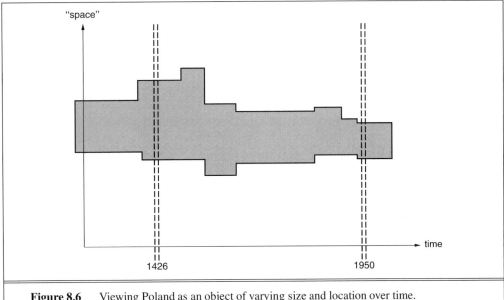

Figure 8.6   Viewing Poland as an object of varying size and location over time.

FLUENTS

Objects such as *Poland* and *President(USA)* are called **fluents**. The dictionary says that a fluent is something that is capable of flowing, like a liquid. For our purposes, a fluent is something that flows or changes across situations.

It may seem odd to reify objects that are as transient as *President(USA)*, yet fluents allow us to say some things that would otherwise be cumbersome to express. For example, "The president of the USA was male throughout the 19th century" can be expressed by

$$T(Male(President(USA)), 19thCentury)$$

even though there were 24 different presidents of the USA in the nineteenth century.

There are some things that can be easily expressed with fluents but not with situation calculus. For example, *Location(x)* denotes the place in which x is located, even if that place varies over time. We can then use sentences about the location of an object to express the fact that, for example, the location of the Empire State Building is fixed:

$$Fixed(Location(EmpireStateBuilding))$$

Without fluents, we could find a way to talk about *objects* being widespread or immobile, but we could not talk directly about the object's location over time. We leave it as an exercise to define the *Fixed* predicate (Exercise 8.7).

Substances and objects

The real world perhaps can be seen as consisting of primitive objects (particles) and composite objects built from them. By reasoning at the level of large objects such as apples and cars, we can overcome the complexity involved in dealing with vast numbers of primitive objects

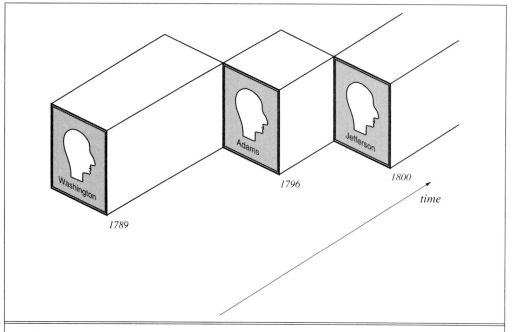

Figure 8.7   A schematic view of the object *President*(*USA*) for the first fifteen years of its existence.

INDIVIDUATION

STUFF

TEMPORAL
SUBSTANCES
SPATIAL
SUBSTANCES

COUNT NOUNS

MASS NOUNS

individually. There is, however, a significant portion of reality that seems to defy any obvious **individuation**—division into distinct objects. We give this portion the generic name **stuff**. For example, suppose I have some butter and an aardvark in front of me. I can say there is one aardvark, but there is no obvious number of "butter-objects," because any part of a butter-object is also a butter-object, at least until we get to very small parts indeed. This is the major distinction between stuff and things. If we cut an aardvark in half, we do not get two aardvarks, unfortunately. The distinction is exactly analogous to the difference between liquid and nonliquid events. In fact, some have called liquid event types **temporal substances**, whereas things like butter are **spatial substances** (Lenat and Guha, 1990).

Notice that English enforces the distinction between stuff and things. We say "an aardvark," but, except in pretentious California restaurants, one cannot say "a butter." Linguists distinguish between **count nouns**, such as aardvarks, holes, and theorems, and **mass nouns**, such as butter, water, and energy. Should we also enforce this distinction in our representation by treating butter and aardvarks differently, or can we treat them using a uniform mechanism?

To represent stuff properly, we begin with the obvious. We will need to have as objects in our ontology at least the gross "lumps" of stuff that we interact with. For example, we might recognize the butter as the same butter that was left on the table the night before; we might pick it up, weigh it, sell it, or whatever. In these senses, it is an object just like the aardvark. Let us call it *Butter₃*. We will also define the category *Butter*. Informally, its elements will be all those things of which one might say "It's butter," including *Butter₃*.

The next thing to state was mentioned earlier: with some caveats about very small parts that we will omit for now, any part of a butter-object is also a butter-object:

$$\forall x, y \;\; x \in Butter \wedge PartOf(y,x) \;\Rightarrow\; y \in Butter$$

Individual aardvarks derive properties such as approximate shape, size, weight, and diet from membership in the category of aardvarks. What sorts of properties does an object derive from being a member of the *Butter* category? Butter melts at around 30 degrees centigrade:

$$\forall x \;\; Butter(x) \;\Rightarrow\; MeltingPoint(x, Centigrade(30))$$

Butter is yellow, less dense than water, soft at room temperature, has a high fat content, and so on. On the other hand, butter has no particular size, shape, or weight. We can define more specialized categories of butter such as *UnsaltedButter*, which is also a kind of stuff because any part of an unsalted-butter-object is also an unsalted-butter-object. On the other hand, if we define a category *PoundOfButter*, which includes as members all butter-objects weighing one pound, we no longer have a substance! If we cut a pound of butter in half, we do not get two pounds of butter—another of those annoying things about the world we live in.

INTRINSIC   What is actually going on is this: there are some properties that are **intrinsic**: they belong to the very substance of the object, rather than to the object as a whole. When you cut something in half, the two pieces retain the same set of intrinsic properties—things like density, boiling point,

EXTRINSIC   flavor, color, ownership, and so on. On the other hand, **extrinsic** properties are the opposite: properties such as weight, length, shape, function, and so on are not retained under subdivision.

A class of objects that includes in its definition only *intrinsic* properties is then a substance, or mass noun; a class that includes *any* extrinsic properties in its definition is a count noun. The category *Stuff* is the most general substance category, specifying no intrinsic properties. The category *Thing* is the most general discrete object category, specifying no extrinsic properties.

It follows that an object belongs to both mass and count classes. For example, *LakeMichigan* is an element of both *Water* and *Lakes*. *Lake* specifies such extrinsic properties as (approximate) size, topological shape, and the fact that it is surrounded by land. Note that we can also handle the fact that the water in Lake Michigan changes over time, simply by viewing the lake as an event whose constituent objects change over time, in much the same way as *President(USA)*.

This approach to the representation of stuff is not the only possibility. The major competing approach considers *Butter* to be what we would call *BunchOf(Butter)*, namely, the object composed of all butter in the world. All individual butter-objects are thus *PartOf* butter, rather than instances of butter. Like any consistent knowledge representation scheme, it cannot be *proved incorrect*, but it does seem to be awkward for representing specialized kinds of substances such as *UnsaltedButter* and its relation to *Butter*.

Mental events and mental objects

The agents we have constructed so far have beliefs and can deduce new beliefs. Yet none of them has any knowledge *about* beliefs or deduction. For single-agent domains, knowledge about one's own knowledge and reasoning processes is useful for controlling inference. For example, if one knows that one does not know anything about Romanian geography, then one need not expend enormous computational effort trying to calculate the shortest path from Arad to Bucharest. In multiagent domains, it becomes important for an agent to reason about the mental processes of the other agents. Suppose a shopper in a supermarket has the goal of buying some anchovies. The agent deduces that a good plan is to go where the anchovies are, pick some up, and bring them to the checkout stand. A key step is for the shopper to realize that it cannot execute this plan until it knows where the anchovies are, and that it can come to know where they are by asking someone. The shopper should also deduce that it is better to ask a store employee than another customer, because the employee is more likely to know the answer. To do this kind of deduction, an agent needs to have a model of what other agents know, as well as some knowledge of its own knowledge, lack of knowledge, and inference procedures.

In effect, we want to have a model of the mental objects that are in someone's head (or something's knowledge base) and of the mental processes that manipulate those mental objects. The model should be faithful, but it does not have to be detailed. We do not have to be able to predict how many milliseconds it will take for a particular agent to make a deduction, nor do we have to predict what neurons will fire when an animal is faced with a particular visual stimulus. But we do want an abstract model that says that if a logical agent believes $P \vee Q$ and it learns $\neg P$, then it should come to believe Q.

The first step is to ask how mental objects are represented. That is, if we have a relation $Believes(Agent, x)$, what kind of thing is x? First of all, its clear that x cannot be a logical sentence. If $Flies(Superman)$ is a logical sentence, we can't say $Believes(Agent, Flies(Superman))$ because only terms (not sentences) can be arguments of relations. But if $Flies(Superman)$ is reified as a fluent, then it is a candidate for being a mental object, and $Believes$ can be a relation that takes an agent and a propositional fluent that the agent believes in. We could define other relations such as $Knows$ and $Wants$ to express other relationships between agents and propositions. Relations of this kind are called **propositional attitudes**.

PROPOSITIONAL
ATTITUDES

This appears to give us what we want: the ability for an agent to reason about the beliefs of agents. Unfortunately, there is a problem with this approach. If Clark and Superman are one and the same (i.e., $Clark = Superman$) then Clark flying and Superman flying are one and the same event. Thus, if the object of propositional attitudes are reified events, we must conclude that if Lois believes that Superman can fly, she also believes that Clark can fly, even if she doesn't believe that Clark is Superman. That is,

$$(Superman = Clark) \models$$
$$(Believes(Lois, Flies(Superman)) \Leftrightarrow Believes(Lois, Flies(Clark)))$$

There is a sense in which this is right: Lois does believe of a certain person, who happens to be called Clark sometimes, that that person can fly. But there is another sense in which this is wrong: if you asked Lois "Can Clark fly?" she would certainly say no. Reified objects and events work fine for the first sense of $Believes$, but for the second sense we need to reify *descriptions* of those objects and events, so that Clark and Superman can be different descriptions (even though they refer to the same object).

Technically, the property of being able to freely substitute a term for an equal term is called **referential transparency**. In first-order logic, every relation is referentially transparent. We would like to define $Believes$ (and the other propositional attitudes) as relations whose second argument is referentially **opaque**—that is, one cannot substitute an equal term for the second argument without changing the meaning.

REFERENTIAL
TRANSPARENCY

OPAQUE

SYNTACTIC THEORY

STRINGS
We will concentrate on what is called a **syntactic theory** of mental objects.[11] In this approach, we represent mental objects with **strings** written in a representation language. (We will use first-order logic itself as the representation language, but we are not required to.) A string is just a list of symbols, so the event *Flies(Clark)* can be represented by the string of characters $[F, l, i, e, s, (, C, l, a, r, k,)]$, which we will abbreviate as "*Flies(Clark)*". In this formulation, "*Clark*" $\neq$ "*Superman*" because they are two different strings consisting of different symbols. The idea is that a knowledge-based agent has a knowledge base consisting of strings that were added either via TELL or through inference. The syntactic theory models the knowledge base and the strings that are in it.

Now all we have to do is provide a syntax, semantics, and proof theory for the string representation language, just as we did in Chapter 6. The difference is that we have to define them all in first-order logic. We start by defining *Den* as the function that maps a string to the object that it denotes, and *Name* as a function that maps an object to a string that is the name of a constant that denotes the object. For example, the denotation of both "*Clark*" and "*Superman*" is the object referred to by the constant symbol *ManOfSteel*, and the name of that object could be either "*Superman*", "*Clark*", or some other constant, such as "K_{11}".

$$Den(\text{"Clark"}) = ManOfSteel \land Den(\text{"Superman"}) = ManOfSteel$$
$$Name(ManOfSteel) = \text{"}K_{11}\text{"}$$

The next step is to define inference rules for logical agents. For example, we might want to say that a logical agent can do Modus Ponens: if it believes p and believes $p \Rightarrow q$ then it will also believe q. The first attempt at writing this axiom is

$$\forall\, a, p, q \ \ LogicalAgent(a) \land Believes(a, p) \land Believes(a, \text{"}p \Rightarrow q\text{"}) \ \Rightarrow \ Believes(a, q)$$

But this is not right because the string "$p \Rightarrow q$" contains the letters 'p' and 'q' but has nothing to do with the strings that are the values of the variables p and q. In fact, "$p \Rightarrow q$" is not even a syntactically correct sentence, because only variables can be lower-case letters. The correct formulation is:

$$\forall\, a, p, q \ \ LogicalAgent(a) \land Believes(a, p) \land Believes(a, Concat(p, \text{"}\Rightarrow\text{"}, q))$$
$$\Rightarrow \ Believes(a, q)$$

where *Concat* is a function on strings that concatenates their elements together. We will abbreviate $Concat(p, \text{"}\Rightarrow\text{"}, q)$ as "$\underline{p} \Rightarrow \underline{q}$". That is, an occurrence of $\underline{x}$ within a string means to substitute in the value of the variable x. Lisp programmers will recognize this as the backquote operator.

Once we add in the other inference rules besides Modus Ponens, we will be able to answer questions of the form "given that a logical agent knows these premises, can it draw that conclusion?" Besides the normal inference rules, we need some rules that are specific to belief. For example, the following rule says that if a logical agent believes something, then it believes that it believes it.

$$\forall\, a, p \ \ LogicalAgent(a) \land Believes(a, p) \ \Rightarrow \ Believes(a, \text{"}Believes(\underline{Name(a)}, \underline{p})\text{"})$$

Note that it would not do to have just $\underline{a}$ as part of the string, because a is an agent, not a description of an agent. We use $Name(a)$ to get a string that names the agent.

---

[11] An alternative based on **modal logic** is covered in the historical notes section.

There are at least three directions we could go from here. One is to recognize that it is unrealistic to expect that there will be any real logical agents. Such an agent can, according to our axioms, deduce any valid conclusion instantaneously. This is called **logical omniscience**. It would be more realistic to define limited rational agents, which can make a limited number of deductions in a limited time. But it is very hard to axiomatize such an agent. Pretending that all agents are logically omniscient is like pretending that all problems with polynomial time bounds are tractable—it is clearly false, but if we are careful, it does not get us into too much trouble.

A second direction is to define axioms for other propositional attitudes. The relation between believing and knowing has been studied for centuries by philosophers of the mind. It is commonly said that knowledge is justified true belief. That is, if you believe something, and if it is actually true, and if you have a proof that it is true, then you know it. The proof is necessary to prevent you from saying "I know this coin flip will come up heads" and then taking credit for being right when the coin does end up heads, when actually you just made a lucky guess. If you accept this definition of knowledge, then it can be defined in terms of belief and truth:

$$\forall a, p \ Knows(a, p) \ \Leftrightarrow \ Believes(a, p) \land T(Den(p)) \land T(Den(KB(a))) \ \Rightarrow \ Den(p))$$

This version of *Knows* can be read as "knows that." It is also possible to define other kinds of knowing. For example, here is a definition of "knowing whether":

$$\forall a, p \ KnowsWhether(a, p) \ \Leftrightarrow \ Knows(a, p) \lor Knows(a, ``\neg\underline{p}")$$

Continuing our example, Lois knows whether Clark can fly if she either knows that Clark can fly or knows that he cannot.

The concept of "knowing what" is more complicated. One is tempted to say that an agent knows what Bob's phone number is if there is some x for which the agent knows $x = PhoneNumber(Bob)$. But that is not right, because the agent might know that Alice and Bob have the same number, but not know what it is (i.e., $PhoneNumber(Alice) = PhoneNumber(Bob)$), or the agent might know that there is some Skolem constant that is Bob's number without knowing anything at all about it (i.e., $K_{23} = PhoneNumber(Bob)$). A better definition of "knowing what" says that the agent has to know of some x that is a string of digits and that is Bob's number:

$$\forall a, b \ KnowsWhat(a, ``PhoneNumber(\underline{b})") \ \Leftrightarrow$$
$$\exists x \ Knows(a, ``\underline{x} = PhoneNumber(\underline{b})") \land DigitString(x)$$

Of course, for other questions we have different criteria for what is an acceptable answer. For the question "what is the capital of New York," an acceptable answer is a proper name, "Albany," not something like "the city where the state house is." To handle this, we will make *KnowsWhat* a three place relation: it takes an agent, a term, and a predicate that must be true of the answer. For example:

> $KnowsWhat(Agent, Capital(NewYork), ProperName)$
> $KnowsWhat(Agent, PhoneNumber(Bob), DigitString)$

A third direction is to recognize that propositional attitudes change over time. When we recognized that processes occur over a limited interval of time, we introduced the relation $T(process, interval)$. Similarly, we can use $Believe(agent, string, interval)$ to mean that an agent believes in a proposition over a given interval. For example, to say that Lois believed yesterday that Superman can fly, we write

> $Believes(Lois, Flies(Superman), Yesterday)$

Actually, it would be more consistent to have *Believes* be an event fluent just as *Flies* is. Then we could say that it will be true tomorrow that Lois knew that Superman could fly yesterday:

$$T(Believes(Lois, Flies(Superman), Yesterday), Tomorrow)$$

We can even say that it is true now that Jimmy knows today that Lois believes that Superman could fly yesterday:

$$T(Knows(Jimmy, Believes(Lois, Flies(Superman), Yesterday), Today), Now)$$

Knowledge and action

We have been so busy trying to represent knowledge that there is a danger of losing track of what knowledge is *for*. Recall that we are interested in building agents that perform well. That means that the only way knowledge can help is if it allows the agent to do some action it could not have done before, or if it allows the agent to choose a better action than it would otherwise have chosen. For example, if the agent has the goal of speaking to Bob, then knowing Bob's phone number can be a great help. It enables the agent to perform a dialing action and have a much better chance of reaching Bob than if the agent did not know the number and dialed randomly.

 One way of looking at this is to say that actions have **knowledge preconditions** and **knowledge effects**. For example, the action of dialing a person's number has the precondition of knowing the number, and the action of calling directory assistance sometimes has the effect of knowing the number.

Note that each action has its own requirements on the form of the knowledge, just as each question to *KnowsWhat* had its own requirements. Suppose I am in China, and the telephone there has Chinese numerals on the buttons.[12] Then knowing what Bob's number is as a digit string is not enough—I need to know it as a string of Chinese digits. Similarly, the question of whether I know where Bob lives has a different answer depending on how I want to use the information. If I'm planning to go there by taxi, all I need is an address; if I'm driving myself, I need directions; if I'm parachuting in, I need exact longitude and latitude.

8.5   THE GROCERY SHOPPING WORLD

In this section, all our hard work in defining a general ontology pays off: we will be able to define the knowledge that an agent needs to shop for a meal in a market. To demonstrate that the knowledge is sufficient, we will run a knowledge-based agent in our environment simulator. That means providing a simulated shopping world, which will by necessity be simpler than the real world. But much of the knowledge shown here is the same for simulated or real worlds. The big differences are in the complexity of vision, motion, and tactile manipulation. (These topics will be covered in Chapters 24 and 25.)

---

[12] Actually, Chinese phones have Arabic numerals, but bear with the example.

Complete description of the shopping simulation

We start by giving a PAGE (percepts, actions, goals, and environment) description of the shopping simulation. First the **percepts**:

1. The agent receives three percepts at each time step: feel, sound, and vision.

2. The feel percept is just a bump or no bump, as in the vacuum world. The agent perceives a bump only when on the previous time step it executed a *Forward* action and there is not enough room in the location it tried to move to.

3. The sound percept is a list of spoken words. The agent perceives words spoken by agents within two squares of it.

4. If the agent's camera is zoomed in, it perceives detailed visual images of each object in the square it is zoomed at.

5. If the agent's camera is not zoomed in, it perceives coarse visual images of each object in the three squares directly and diagonally ahead.

6. A visual percept consists of a relative location, approximate size, color, shape, and possibly some other features. It will be explained in detail later.

Now for the **actions**:

1. An agent can speak a string of words.

2. An agent can go one square forward.

3. An agent can turn 90° to the right or left.

4. An agent can zoom its camera in at its current square, or at any of the three squares directly or diagonally ahead.

5. An agent can also zoom its camera out.

6. An agent can grab an object that is within one square of it. To do so, it needs to specify the relative coordinates of the object, and it needs to be empty-handed.

7. An agent can release an object that it has grabbed. To do so, it needs to specify the relative coordinates of the point where it wants to release the object.

The agent's **goal** initially will be to buy all the items on a shopping list. This goal can be modified if some items are unavailable or too expensive. The agent should also try to do the shopping quickly, and avoid bumping into things. A more ambitious problem is to give the agent the goal of making dinner, and let it compose the shopping list.

The **environment** is the interior of a store, along with all the objects and people in it. As in the vacuum and wumpus worlds, the store is represented by a grid of squares, with aisles separating rows of display cases. At one end of the store are the checkout stands and their attendant clerks. Other customers and store employees may be anywhere in the store. The agent begins at the entrance, and must leave the store from the same square. There is an EXIT sign there in case the agent forgets. There are also signs marking the aisles, and smaller signs (readable only when the camera zooms in) marking some (but not necessarily all) of the items for sale.

A real agent would have to decipher the video signals from the camera (or some digitization of them). We assume that this work has already been done. Still, the vision component of a percept is a complex list of descriptions. The first component of each description is its relative position with respect to the agent's position and orientation. For example, the relative position [-2,1] is the square two squares to the agent's left and one square ahead. The second component is the size of the object, given as the average diameter of the object in meters. Next is the color of the object, given as a symbol (red, green, yellow, orange, ...), followed by the object's shape (flat, round, square, ...). Finally, we assume that an optical character recognition routine has run over the video image; if there are any letters in the visual field, they are given as a list of words. Figure 8.8 shows an overview of a supermarket, with the agent at [4,5] still dressed for the wumpus world. The agent is facing left. Figure 8.9(a) shows what the agent perceives with the camera zoomed out, and Figure 8.9(b) shows the agent's visual percept with the camera zoomed in at the square [3,6].

Organizing knowledge

The grocery shopping domain is too big to handle all at once. Instead, we will break it down into smaller clusters of knowledge, work on each cluster separately, and then see how they fit together. One good way of decomposing the domain into clusters is to consider the tasks facing the agent. This is called a functional decomposition. We divide the domain into five clusters:

◇ **Menu Planning**: The agent will need to know how to modify the shopping list when the store is out of stock of an item.

◇ **Navigating**: As in the wumpus world, the agent will need to understand the effect of movement actions and create an internal map of the world.

◇ **Gathering**: The agent must be able to find and gather the items it wants. Part of this involves inducing objects from percepts: the agent will need recognition rules to infer that a red roughly spherical object about three inches in diameter could be a tomato.

◇ **Communicating**: The agent should be able to ask questions when there is something it cannot find out on its own.

◇ **Paying**: Even a shy agent that prefers not to ask questions will need enough interagent skills to be able to pay the checkout clerk. The agent will need to know that $5.00 is too much for a single tomato, and that if the total price is $17.35, then it should receive $2.65 in change from a $20 bill.

An advantage of functional decomposition is that we can pose a problem completely within a cluster and see if the knowledge can solve it. Other kinds of decomposition often require the whole knowledge base to be fleshed out before the first question can be posed.

Menu-Planning

A good cook can walk into a market, pick out the best bargain from the various fish, fowl, or other main course ingredients that look fresh that day, select the perfect accompanying dishes, and simultaneously figure out how to make tomorrow's meal from whatever will be left over. A competent errand runner can take a shopping list and find all the items on it. Our agent will be closer to the second of these, but we will give it some ability to make intelligent choices.

Suppose the store is out of tomatoes one day. An agent with the shopping list "tomatoes, lettuce, cucumber, olive oil, vinegar" should recognize that the ingredients form a salad, and that

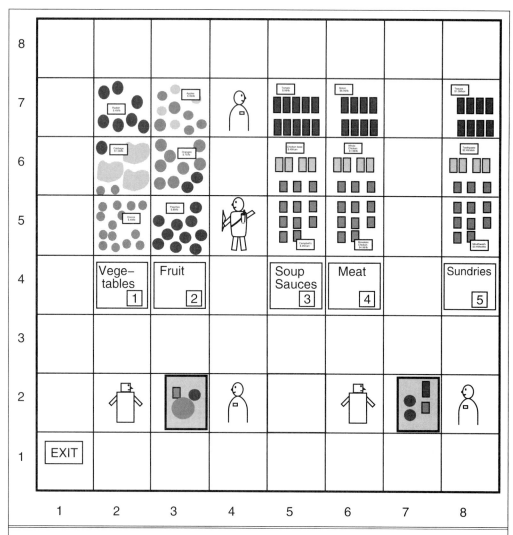

Figure 8.8   An overview of a supermarket. Note the agent at [4,5], the other shoppers at [2,2] and [6,2], the checkout clerks at [4,2] and [8,2], the signs in the fourth row, and the groceries spread throughout the world.

a red pepper would be a good substitute, as it would add color and flavor to the salad. An agent with the list "tomatoes, yellow onions, celery, a carrot, ground beef, milk, white wine, tagliatelle" should infer a Bolognese sauce (Hazan, 1973), and therefore that it is appropriate to substitute canned tomatoes.

   To make these inferences, an agent needs to understand that the items on a shopping list fit together to form one or more composite objects known as **dishes**, that the dishes go together to

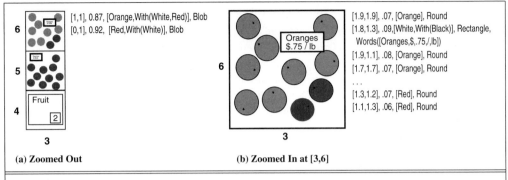

Figure 8.9   The percepts for the shopping agent at [4,5]. (a) Camera zoomed out. (b) Camera zoomed in at [3,6]. Each percept is a series of object descriptions (one per line). Each description lists a relative position, a size, a color summary, a shape, and a character string (if any).

form composite objects known as **meals**, and that an object can be recognized by its components. Our agent will be called upon to make two classes of inference. First, from a list of parts it should induce the composite object that these parts make up. This is made difficult because the parts (the items on the shopping list) may make up several composite objects, and because not all the parts will be listed (some are already at home in the cupboard). Second, the agent should be able to decide how to replace an unavailable part to complete the intended composite object. This can be done at two levels: replacing one ingredient with another to complete a dish, and if that is not possible, replacing the whole dish with another to complete the meal. Some of the necessary knowledge will involve individual dishes, and some of it will be at a general level that will also be useful for, say, replacing a faulty muffler in a car.

The first step is to convert a shopping list—a list of words—into a parts list—a list of categories. A dictionary is used to associate words with their referents:

$Referent(\text{"tomatoes"}, Tomatoes)$
$Referent(\text{"onions"}, Onions)$
$\vdots$

The next step is to describe objects in terms of their required and optional parts. If we wanted to actually prepare a dish, we would have to know more about the relations between the parts. But to do shopping, all we need is a list of the parts. We define *RequiredParts* so that *RequiredParts*($\{Lettuce, Dressing\}, GreenSalads$) means that every object that is an element of *GreenSalads* has one *RequiredPart* that is an element of *Lettuce*, and another that is an element of *Dressing*. For lettuce to be a required part of green salads means that every element of green salads has an element of lettuce as one of its parts. Similar reasoning holds for *OptionalParts*, except that only some elements of a category have to manifest the optional parts.

$$\forall r, w \ \ RequiredParts(r, w) \Rightarrow \forall p \ \ p \in r \Rightarrow RequiredPart(p, w)$$
$$\forall o, w \ \ OptionalParts(o, w) \Rightarrow \forall p \ \ p \in o \Rightarrow OptionalPart(p, w)$$
$$\forall r, w \ \ RequiredPart(r, w) \Leftrightarrow \forall c \ \ c \in w \Rightarrow \exists i \ \ i \in r \wedge PartOf(i, c)$$
$$\forall o, w \ \ OptionalPart(o, w) \Leftrightarrow \exists c \ \ c \in w \Rightarrow \exists i \ \ i \in o \wedge PartOf(o, c)$$

The next step is to describe meals and dishes in terms of their parts:

$RequiredParts(\{MainCourses\}, Meals)$
$OptionalParts(\{FirstCourses, SideDishes, Salads, Desserts, \ldots\}, Meals)$
$RequiredParts(\{Lettuce, Dressing\}, GreenSalads)$
$OptionalParts(\{Tomatoes, Cucumbers, Peppers, Carrots, \ldots\}, GreenSalads)$
$RequiredParts(\{Pasta, BologneseSauce\}, PastaBolognese,)$
$OptionalParts(\{GratedCheese\}, PastaBolognese)$
$RequiredParts(\{Onions, OliveOil, Butter, Celery, Carrots, GroundBeef, Salt,$
$\quad WhiteWines, Milk, TomatoStuff\}, BologneseSauce)$

Then we need taxonomic information for dishes and foods:

$GreenSalads \subset Salads$
$Salads \subset Dishes$
$PastaBolognese \subset FirstCourses$
$FirstCourses \subset Dishes$
$Tomatoes \subset TomatoStuff$
$CannedTomatoes \subset TomatoStuff$
$Tagliatelle \subset Pasta$

Now we want to be able to determine what dishes can be made from the shopping list "tomatoes, yellow onions, celery, a carrot, ground beef, milk, white wine, tagliatelle." As mentioned earlier, this is complicated by the fact that the salt, butter, and olive oil that are required for the Bolognese dish are not on the shopping list. We define the predicate *CanMake* to hold between a shopping list and a dish if the categories on the list, when combined with typical staples, cover all the required parts of the dish.

$\forall l, d \ CanMake(l, d) \ \Leftrightarrow \ d \in Dishes \wedge RequiredParts(p, d) \wedge p \subset Union(l, Staples)$
$\{Salt, Butter, OliveOil\} \subset Staples$

With what we have so far, this would allow us to infer that Pasta Bolognese is the only dish that can be made from the shopping list. The next question is what to do if fresh tomatoes are not available. It turns out that all we have to do is replace the shopping list (or the part of the shopping list that makes up this dish) with the list of part categories for this dish. In this case, that means that *Tomatoes* would be replaced by *TomatoStuff*, which could be satisfied by gathering an instance of *CannedTomatoes*.

Navigating

An agent that wants to find a book in a library could traverse the entire library, looking at each book until the desired one is found. But it would be more efficient to find the call number for the book, find a map describing where that number can be found, and go directly there. It is the same way with a supermarket, although the catalog system is not as good. A shopping agent should know that supermarkets are arranged into aisles, that aisles have signs describing their contents (in rough terms), and that objects that are near each other in the taxonomic hierarchy are likely to be near each other in physical space. For example, British immigrants to the United States learn that to find a package of tea, they should look for the aisle marked "Coffee."

Most of the navigation problem is the same as in the vacuum or wumpus world. The agent needs to remember where it started, and can compute its current location from the movements it has made where it is now. The supermarket is not as hostile as the wumpus world so it is safer to explore, but an agent can find better routes if it knows that supermarkets are generally laid out in aisles. Supermarkets also provide aisle numbers, unlike the wumpus world, so that the agent does not need to rely on dead reckoning. On the second trip to a store, it can save a lot of wandering by remembering where things are. It is not helpful, however, to remember the exact location of each individual item, because the tomato that is at location $[x, y]$ today will probably be gone tomorrow. Because much of the logic is the same as for the wumpus world, it will not be repeated here.

A typical navigation problem is to locate the tomatoes. The following strategy is usually believed to work:

1. If the agent knows the location of the tomatoes from a previous visit, calculate a path to that spot from the current location.

2. Otherwise, if the location of the vegetable aisle is known, plan a path there.

3. Otherwise, move along the front of the store until a sign for the vegetable aisle is spotted.

4. If none of these work, wander about and find someone to ask where the tomatoes are. (This is covered in the "Communicating" section.)

5. Once the vegetable aisle is found, move down the aisle with the camera zoomed out, looking for something red. When spotted, zoom in to see if they are in fact tomatoes. (This is covered in the "Gathering" section.)

Gathering

Once in the right aisle, the agent still needs to find the items on its list. This is done by matching the visual percepts against the expected percepts from each category of objects. In the wumpus world, this kind of perception is trivial—a breeze signals a pit and a stench signals a wumpus. But in the grocery shopping world, there are thousands of different kinds of objects and many of them (such as tomatoes and apples) present similar percepts. The agent never can be sure that it has classified an object correctly based on its percepts, but it can know when it has made a good guess. The shopping agent can use the following classification rules:

1. If only one known category matches a percept, assume the object is a member of that category. (This may lead to an error when an unknown object is sighted.)

2. If a percept matches several categories, but there is a sign nearby that identifies one of them, assume the object is a member of that category.

3. If there is an aisle sign that identifies one category (or one supercategory), assume the object is of that category. For example, we could categorize a round, red percept as a tomato rather than an apple if we were in an aisle marked "Vegetables" and not "Fruit." At a cricket match, it would be something else altogether.

To implement this, we start with a set of *causal* rules for percepts:

$$\forall x \ \ x \in Tomatoes \ \Rightarrow \ SurfaceColor(x, Red)$$
$$\forall x \ \ x \in Oranges \ \Rightarrow \ SurfaceColor(x, Orange)$$
$$\forall x \ \ x \in Apples \ \Rightarrow \ SurfaceColor(x, Red) \lor SurfaceColor(x, Green)$$
$$\forall x \ \ x \in Tomatoes \ \Rightarrow \ Shape(x, Round)$$
$$\forall x \ \ x \in Oranges \ \Rightarrow \ Shape(x, Round)$$
$$\vdots$$
$$\forall x \ \ SurfaceColor(x, c) \land Visible(x) \ \Rightarrow \ CausesColorPercept(x, c)$$
$$\forall x \ \ Shape(x, s) \land Visible(x) \ \Rightarrow \ CausesShapePercept(x, s)$$

These rules, and many more like them, give a flavor of a causal theory of how percepts are formed by objects in the world. Notice how simplistic it is. For example, it does not mention lighting at all. (Fortunately, the lights are always on in our supermarket.) From these rules, the agent will be able to deduce a set of possible objects that might explain its percepts. Knowledge about what sorts of objects appear where will usually eliminate all but one category. Of course, the fact that the agent only *knows about* one sort of object that might produce a given percept does not mean that the percept must be produced by that sort of object. Logically, there might be other sorts of objects (e.g., plastic tomatoes) that produce the same percept as the known category. This can be handled either by a **domain closure** axiom, stating that the known categories are all the ones there are, or by a default assumption, as described in Chapter 15.

DOMAIN CLOSURE

The other part of the gathering problem is manipulation: being able to pick up objects and carry them. In our simulation, we just assume a primitive action to grasp an object, and that the agent can carry all the items it will need. In the real world, the actions required to pick up a bunch of bananas without bruising them and a gallon jug of milk without dropping it pose serious problems. Chapter 25 considers them in more detail.

Communicating

The successful shopper knows when to ask questions (Where are the anchovies? Are these tomatillas?). Unfortunately, being able to carry on a conversation is a difficult task, so we will delay covering it until Chapter 22. Instead, we will cover a simpler form of one-way communication: reading signs. If a word appears on an aisle's sign, then members of the category that the word refers to will be located in that aisle.

$$\forall a \ \ (a \in Aisles \land \exists s, w \ \ SignOf(s, a) \land w \in Words(s)) \ \Rightarrow$$
$$\exists x, c \ \ Referent(w, c) \land x \in c \land At(x, a)$$

If a word appears on a small sign, then items of that category will be located nearby.

$$\forall s, w, l \ \ (s \in Signs \land Size(s) < Meters(.3) \land w \in Words(s) \land At(s, l)) \ \Rightarrow$$
$$\exists x, c \ \ Referent(w, c) \land x \in c \land At(x, AreaAround(l))$$

Paying

The shopping agent also has to know enough so that it will not overpay for an item. First, it needs to know typical fair prices for items, for example:

$$\forall g \quad g \in Typical(GroundBeef) \land Weight(g) = Pounds(1) \;\Rightarrow\; \$(1) \leq FairPrice(g) \leq \$(2)$$

The agent should know that total price is roughly proportional to quantity, but that often discounts are given for buying larger sizes. The following rule says that this discount can be up to 50%:

$$\forall q, c, w, p \quad q \in c \land Weight(q) = w \land Price(q) = p \;\Rightarrow\;$$
$$\forall m, q_2 \quad m > 1 \land q_2 \in c \land Weight(q_2) = m \times w \;\Rightarrow\;$$
$$(1 + \tfrac{m-1}{2}) \times p \leq FairPrice(q_2) \leq m \times p$$

Most importantly, the agent should know that it is a bad deal to pay more than the fair price for an item, and that buying anything that is a bad deal is a bad action:

$$\forall i \quad Price(i) > FairPrice(i) \;\Rightarrow\; BadDeal(i)$$
$$\forall i \quad BadDeal(i) \;\Rightarrow\; \forall a \;\; Bad(Buy(a, i))$$

Buying events belong to the category $Buy(b, x, s, p)$—buyer b buying object x from seller s for price p. The complete description of buying is quite complex, but follows the general pattern laid down earlier in the chapter for marriage. The preconditions include the fact that p is the price of the object x; that b has at least that much money in the form of one or more monetary instruments; and that s owns x. The event includes a monetary exchange that results in a net gain of p for s, and finally b owns x. Exercise 8.10 asks you to complete this description.

One final thing an agent needs to know about shopping: it is bad form to exit a shop while carrying something that the shop owns.

$$\forall a, x, s, i \quad s \in Shops \land T(Carrying(a, x) \land At(x, s) \land Owns(s, x)) \;\Rightarrow\;$$
$$T(Bad(Exit(a)), i)$$

An agent with the goal of exiting will use this goal to set up the subgoal of owning all the objects it is carrying. So all we need now is a description of the parts of a buying event, so that the agent can execute the buying. In a supermarket, a buying event consists of going to a checkout stand, placing all the items on the stand, waiting for the cashier to ring them up, placing a sum of money equal to the total price on the stand, and picking up the items again. Note that if the total is $4, it will not do to place the same dollar bill onto the checkout stand four times.

$$\forall b, m, s, p, e \quad e \in SupermarketBuy(b, m, s, p) \;\Rightarrow\;$$
$$\exists e_1, e_2, e_3, e_4, e_5 \quad e_1 = Go(b, c) \land CheckoutStand(c) \land$$
$$e_2 = Put(b, m, c) \land e_3 = TotalUpPrice(s, m) \land$$
$$e_4 = Put(b, p, c) \land e_5 = Grab(b, m) \land$$
$$Before(e_1, e_2) \land Before(e_2, e_3) \land Before(e_3, e_4) \land Before(e_4, e_5) \land$$
$$PartOf(e_1, e) \land PartOf(e_2, e) \land PartOf(e_3, e) \land PartOf(e_4, e) \land PartOf(e_5, e)$$

Now we have touched on all the major areas of knowledge necessary for an agent to cope with the grocery shopping world. A complete specification would make this chapter too long, but we have outlined the approach one would take to complete this specification. Although it is hard work, building actual knowledge bases of this kind is an invaluable experience.

8.6   SUMMARY

This has been the most detailed chapter of the book so far. As we said earlier in the chapter, one *cannot* understand knowledge representation without doing it, or at least seeing it. The following are some of the major points of the chapter:

- The process of representing knowledge of a domain goes through several stages. The first, informal stage involves deciding what kinds of objects and relations need to be represented (the ontology). Then a vocabulary is selected, and used to encode general knowledge of the domain. After encoding specific problem instances, automated inference procedures can be used to solve them.

- Good representations eliminate irrelevant detail, capture relevant distinctions, and express knowledge at the most general level possible.

- Constructing knowledge-based systems has advantages over programming: the knowledge engineer has to concentrate only on what's true about the domain, rather than on solving the problems and encoding the solution process; the same knowledge can often be used in several ways; debugging knowledge is often simpler than debugging programs.

- Special-purpose ontologies, such as the one constructed for the circuits domain, can be effective within the domain but often need to be generalized to broaden their coverage.

- A general-purpose ontology needs to cover a wide variety of knowledge, and should be capable in principle of handling any domain.

- We presented a general ontology based around categories and the event calculus. We covered structured objects, time and space, change, processes, substances, and beliefs.

- We presented a detailed analysis of the shopping domain, exercising the general ontology and showing how the domain knowledge can be used by a shopping agent.

Finally, it is worth recalling that the nature of an appropriate representation depends on the world being represented and the intended range of uses of the representation. The representation choices in this chapter are specific to the world of human experience, but this is unavoidable.

BIBLIOGRAPHICAL AND HISTORICAL NOTES

There are plausible claims (Briggs, 1985) that formal knowledge representation research began with classical Indian theorizing about the grammar of Shastric Sanskrit, which dates back to the first millennium B.C. Shastric Sanskrit grammatical theory proposed not only a formal syntax and vocabulary for a general-purpose language, but also provided an analysis of its semantics. Shastric Sanskrit grammatical theory therefore can be regarded as the earliest instance of systematic representation of knowledge in a specific area in order to facilitate inference. In the West, the use of definitions of terms in ancient Greek mathematics can be regarded as the earliest instance. Indeed, the development of technical terminology or artificial languages in any field can be regarded as a form of knowledge representation research. The connection between knowledge representation in this sense, and knowledge representation in AI, is closer than it may seem; twentieth century AI research draws widely upon the formalisms of other fields, especially logic and philosophy. Aristotle (384–322 B.C.) developed a comprehensive system of what we would now call ontology and knowledge representation in connection with his work in logic, natural science, and philosophical metaphysics.

Besides the logicist tradition started by McCarthy, which we discussed in Chapter 6, there have been many other threads in the history of representation in AI. Early discussions in the field tended to focus on "*problem* representation" rather than "*knowledge* representation." The emphasis was on formulating the problem to be solved, rather than formulating the resources available to the program. A conscious focus on knowledge representation had to await the discovery that high performance in AI problem solving required the accumulation and use of large amounts of problem-specific knowledge. The realization that AI systems needed such knowledge was largely driven by two types of research. The first was the attempt to match human performance in the everyday world, particularly in understanding natural human languages and in rapid, content-based retrieval from a general-purpose memory. The second was the design of "expert systems"—also, significantly, called "knowledge-based systems"—that could match (or, in some cases, exceed) the performance of human experts on narrowly defined tasks. The need for problem-specific knowledge was stressed forcefully by the designers of DENDRAL, the first expert system, which interpreted the output of a mass spectrometer, a type of instrument used for analysis of the structure of organic chemical compounds. An early statement of the DENDRAL philosophical perspective can be found in Feigenbaum, Buchanan, and Lederberg(1971); Lindsay *et al.* (1980) provide a book-length description of the DENDRAL project, along with a complete bibliography from 1964 to 1979. Although the success of DENDRAL was instrumental in bringing the AI research community as a whole to realize the importance of knowledge representation, the representational formalisms used in DENDRAL are highly specific to the domain of chemistry. As expert systems continued to succeed and proliferate, expert system researchers became interested in standardized knowledge representation formalisms and ontologies that could reduce the difficulty of creating a new expert system in yet another previously unexplored field. In so doing, they ventured into territory previously explored by philosophers of science and of language. The discipline imposed in AI by the need for one's theories to "work" has led to more rapid and deeper progress than was the case when these problems were the exclusive domain of philosophy (although it has at times also led to the repeated reinvention of the wheel).

Research in memory and natural language processing (NLP) also had to deal with the need for general-purpose knowledge representation languages from the very start. Indeed, Ross Quillian's (1961) work on "semantic networks" predates DENDRAL. Because of the need to get heterogeneous bodies of knowledge to interact fruitfully, memory and NLP research was the original spark for semantic networks, frames, and other very general formalisms. Such "knowledge representation languages" are covered in greater detail in Chapter 10. The present chapter focuses instead on the content of the knowledge itself and on the representational concepts that are common to a number of distinct formalisms.

The creation of comprehensive taxonomies or classifications dates back to ancient times. Aristotle strongly emphasized classification and categorization schemes. His *Organon*, a collection of works on logic assembled by his students after his death, included a treatise called *Categories* in which he attempted a comprehensive high-level classification and also introduced the use of genus and species for lower-level classification, although these terms did not have the precise and specifically biological sense which is now attached to them. Our present system of biological classification, including the use of "binomial nomenclature" (classification via genus and species in the technical sense), was invented by the Swedish biologist Carolus Linnaeus, or Carl von Linne (1707–1778). Lakoff (1987) presents a model of classification based on prototypes rather than strict categorical boundaries.

Within modern AI specifically, comprehensive taxonomies have usually been developed as part of large projects that also included research in other areas of knowledge representation. These include the "commonsense summer" project led by Jerry Hobbs (1985) and the knowledge representation portion of the ensuing TACITUS natural language interpretation project (Hobbs, 1986; Hobbs *et al.*, 1990), as well as the massive CYC project (Lenat and Guha, 1990). The taxonomy used in this chapter was developed by the authors, based in part on their experience in the CYC project and in part on work by Hwang and Schubert (1993) and Davis (1990). An inspirational discussion of the general project of commonsense knowledge representation appears in Hayes's (1978; 1985b) "The Naive Physics Manifesto."

The philosophical study of the part-whole relation was initiated by the Polish logician Leśniewski (1916), who was a hardcore "nominalist" or skeptic about abstract entities such as sets and numbers. He intended his "mereology" (the name is derived from the Greek word for "part") as a substitute for mathematical set theory. Although mereology showed promise as a way of analyzing the distinction between mass nouns and count nouns, Leśniewski's publications are extremely difficult to follow, because they are written in a very idiosyncratic formal notation with (in some cases) almost no natural-language commentary. A more readable exposition and axiomatization of mereology was provided in 1940 by the philosophers Nelson Goodman (another hardcore nominalist) and Henry Leonard under the name of "the calculus of individuals" (Leonard and Goodman, 1940). Goodman's *The Structure of Appearance* (1977) applies the calculus of individuals to what in AI would be called knowledge representation. Quine (1960) also supports the nominalist view of substances. Harry Bunt (1985) has provided an extensive analysis of its use in knowledge representation.

Few if any AI researchers have any problems with abstract entities; the pragmatic "Ontological Promiscuity" endorsed by Hobbs (1985) in the article of that title is more typical. The position adopted in this chapter, in which substances are categories of objects, was championed by Richard Montague (1973). It has also been adopted in the CYC project. Copeland (1993) mounts a serious but not invincible attack.

Several different approaches have been taken in the study of time and events. The oldest approach is **temporal logic**, which is a form of modal logic in which modal operators are used specifically to refer to the times at which facts are true. Typically, in temporal logic, "$\Box p$" means "p will be true at all times in the future," and "$\Diamond p$" means "p will be true at some time in the future." The study of temporal logic was initiated by Aristotle and the Megarian and Stoic schools in ancient Greece.

TEMPORAL LOGIC

In modern times, Findlay (1941) was the first to conceive the idea of a "formal calculus" for reasoning about time; Findlay also sketched a few proposed laws of temporal logic. The further development of modern temporal logic was carried out by a number of researchers, including Arthur Prior (1967). The modern development was actually strongly influenced by historical studies of Megarian and Stoic temporal logic. Burstall (1974) introduced the idea of using modal logic to reason about computer programs. Soon thereafter, Vaughan Pratt (1976) designed **dynamic logic**, in which modal operators indicate the effects of programs or other actions. For instance, in dynamic logic, if α is the name of a program, then "$[\alpha]p$" might mean "p would be true in all world states resulting from executing program α in the current world state", and "$\langle\alpha\rangle p$" might mean "p would be true in at least one world state resulting from executing program α in the current world state." Dynamic logic was applied to the actual analysis of programs by Fischer and Ladner (1977). Pnueli (1977) introduced the idea of using classical temporal logic to reason about programs. Shoham (1988) discusses the use of temporal logic in AI.

Despite the long history of temporal logic, the considerable mathematical theory built up around it, and its extensive use in other branches of computer science, AI research on temporal reasoning has more often taken a different approach. A temporal logic is usually conceptualized around an underlying model involving events, world states, or temporal intervals. The tendency in AI has been to refer to these events, states, and intervals directly, using terms that denote them, rather than indirectly through the interpretation of the sentence operators of temporal logic. The language used is typically either first-order logic or, in some cases, a restricted algebraic formalism geared toward efficient computation (but still capable of being embedded within first-order logic). This approach may allow for greater clarity and flexibility in some cases. Also, temporal knowledge expressed in first-order logic can be more easily integrated with other knowledge that has been accumulated in that notation.

One of the earliest formalisms of this kind was McCarthy's situation calculus, mentioned in Chapter 7. McCarthy (1963) introduced situational fluents and made extensive use of them in later papers. Recent work by Raymond Reiter (1991) and others in the "cognitive robotics" project at the University of Toronto (Scherl and Levesque, 1993) has re-emphasized the use of situation calculus for knowledge representation. The relationship between temporal logic and situation calculus was analyzed by McCarthy and Hayes (1969). They also brought to the attention of AI researchers the work of philosophers such as Donald Davidson on events. Davidson's research, collected in (Davidson, 1980), had a heavy emphasis on the analysis of natural language, particularly of the adverb. It has strongly influenced later AI research, particularly in natural language understanding. Other philosophical and linguistic approaches to events that are of significance for AI research are those of Zeno Vendler (1967; 1968), Alexander Mourelatos (1978), and Emmon Bach (1986).

James Allen's introduction of time intervals, and a small, fixed set of relationships between them, as the primitives for reasoning about time (Allen, 1983; Allen, 1984) marked a major advance over situation calculus and other systems based on time points or instantaneous events. Preliminary versions of Allen's work were available as technical reports as early as 1981. Peter Ladkin (1986a; 1986b) introduced "concave" time intervals (intervals with gaps; essentially, unions of ordinary "convex" time intervals) and applied the techniques of mathematical abstract algebra to time representation. Allen (1991) systematically investigates the wide variety of techniques currently available for time representation. Shoham (1987) describes the reification of events and sets forth a novel scheme of his own for the purpose. The term "event calculus" is also used by Kowalski and Sergot (1986), who show how to reason about events in a logic programming system.

The syntactic theory of mental objects was first studied in depth by Kaplan and Montague (1960), who showed that it led to paradoxes if not handled carefully. Because it has a natural model in terms of beliefs as physical configurations of a computer or a brain, it has been popular in AI in recent years. Konolige (1982) and Haas (1986) used it to describe inference engines of limited power, and Morgenstern (1987) showed how it could be used to describe knowledge preconditions in planning. The methods for planning observation actions in Chapter 13 are based on the syntactic theory.

MODAL LOGIC

Modal logic is the classical method for reasoning about knowledge in philosophy. Modal logic augments first-order logic with modal operators, such as B (believes) and K (knows), that take *sentences* as arguments rather than terms. The proof theory for modal logic restricts substitution within modal contexts, thereby achieving referential opacity. The modal logic of knowledge was invented by Jaakko Hintikka (1962). Saul Kripke (1963) defined the semantics

POSSIBLE WORLDS

of the modal logic of knowledge in terms of **possible worlds**. Roughly speaking, a world is possible for an agent if it is consistent with everything the agent knows. From this, one can derive rules of inference involving the K operator. Robert C. Moore relates the modal logic of knowledge to a style of reasoning about knowledge which refers directly to possible worlds in first-order logic (Moore, 1980; Moore, 1985a). Modal logic can be an intimidatingly arcane field, but has also found significant applications in reasoning about information in distributed computer systems (Halpern, 1987). For an excellent comparison of the syntactic and modal theories of knowledge, see (Davis, 1990).

For obvious reasons, this chapter does not cover *every* area of knowledge representation in depth. The three principal topics omitted are the following:

QUALITATIVE
PHYSICS

◇ **Qualitative physics**: A subfield of knowledge representation concerned specifically with constructing a logical, nonnumeric theory of physical objects and processes. The term was coined by Johan de Kleer (1975), although the enterprise could be said to have started in Fahlman's (1974) BUILD. BUILD was a sophisticated planner for constructing complex towers of blocks. Fahlman discovered in the process of designing it that most of the effort (80%, by his estimate) went into modelling the physics of the blocks world to determine the stability of various subassemblies of blocks, rather than into planning per se. He sketches a hypothetical naive-physics like process to explain why young children can solve BUILD-like problems without access to the high-speed floating-point arithmetic used in BUILD's physical modelling. Hayes (1985a) uses "histories," four-dimensional slices of space-time similar to Davidson's events, to construct a fairly complex naive physics of liquids. Hayes was the first to prove that a bath with the plug in will eventually overflow if the tap keeps running; and that a person who falls into a lake will get wet all over. De Kleer and Brown (1985) and Ken Forbus (1985) attempted to construct something like a general-purpose theory of the physical world, based on qualitative abstractions of physical equations. In recent years, qualitative physics has developed to the point where it is possible to analyze an impressive variety of complex physical systems (Sacks and Joskowicz, 1993; Yip, 1991). Qualitative techniques have been also used to construct novel designs for clocks, windscreen wipers, and six-legged walkers (Subramanian, 1993; Subramanian and Wang, 1994). The collection *Readings in Qualitative Reasoning about Physical Systems* (Weld and de Kleer, 1990) provides a good introduction to the field.

SPATIAL REASONING

◇ **Spatial reasoning**: The reasoning necessary to navigate in the wumpus world and supermarket world is trivial in comparison to the rich spatial structure of the real world. The most complete attempt to capture commonsense reasoning about space appears in the work of Ernest Davis (1986; 1990). As with qualitative physics, it appears that an agent can go a long way, so to speak, without resorting to a full metric representation. When such a representation is necessary, techniques developed in robotics (Chapter 25) can be used.

PSYCHOLOGICAL
REASONING

◇ **Psychological reasoning**: The development of a working *psychology* for artificial agents to use in reasoning about themselves and other agents. This is often based on so-called "folk psychology," the theory that humans in general are believed to use in reasoning about themselves and other humans. When AI researchers provide their artificial agents with psychological theories for reasoning about other agents, the theories are frequently based on the researchers' description of the logical agents' own design. Also, this type of psychological theorizing frequently takes place within the context of natural language understanding, where divining the speaker's intentions is of paramount importance. For this reason, the historical and bibliographical background for this topic has been relegated to other chapters, especially Chapter 22.

The proceedings of the international conferences on *Principles of Knowledge Representation and Reasoning* provide the most up-to-date sources for work in this area. *Readings in Knowledge Representation* (Brachman and Levesque, 1985) and *Formal Theories of the Commonsense World* (Hobbs and Moore, 1985) are excellent anthologies on knowledge representation; the former focuses more on historically important papers in representation languages and formalisms, the latter on the accumulation of the knowledge itself. *Representations of Commonsense Knowledge* (Davis, 1990) is a good recent textbook devoted specifically to knowledge representation rather than AI in general. Hughes and Cresswell (1968; 1984) and Chellas (1980) are introductory texts on modal logic; *A Manual of Intensional Logic* (van Benthem, 1985) provides a useful survey of the field. The proceedings of the annual conference *Theoretical Aspects of Reasoning About Knowledge* (TARK) contain many interesting papers from AI, distributed systems, and game theory. Rescher and Urquhart (1971) and van Benthem (1983) cover temporal logic specifically. David Harel (1984) provides an introduction to dynamic logic.

EXERCISES

8.1   Extend the vocabulary from Section 8.3 to define addition and an adder circuit.

8.2   Represent the following six sentences using the representations developed in the chapter.

   a. Water is a liquid between 0 and 100 degrees.

   b. Water boils at 100 degrees.

   c. The water in John's water bottle is frozen.

   d. Perrier is a kind of water.

   e. John has Perrier in his water bottle.

   f. All liquids have a freezing point. (Don't use HasFreezingPoint!)

Now repeat the exercise using a representation based on the mereological approach, in which, for example, *Water* is an object containing as parts all the water in the world.

8.3 Encode the description of the 4-bit adder in Figure 8.10 and pose queries to verify that it is in fact correct.

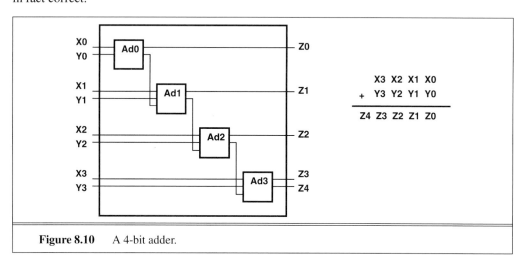

Figure 8.10   A 4-bit adder.

8.4 Write definitions for the following:

a. *ExhaustivePartDecomposition*
b. *PartPartition*
c. *PartwiseDisjoint*

These should be analogous to those for *ExhaustiveDecomposition*, *Partition*, and *Disjoint*.

8.5 Write a set of sentences that allows one to calculate the price of an individual tomato (or other object), given the price per pound. Extend the theory to allow the price of a bag of tomatoes to be calculated.

8.6 This exercise concerns the relationships between event categories and the time intervals in which they occur.

a. Define the predicate $T(c, i)$ in terms of *SubEvent* and $\in$.
b. Explain precisely why we do not need two different notations ($\wedge$ and $\underline{\wedge}$) to describe conjunctive event categories.
c. Give a formal definition for $T(p \vee q, i)$.
d. Give formal definitions for $T(\neg p, i)$ and $T(\neg p, i)$, analogous to those using $\underline{\vee}$ and $\vee$.

8.7 Define the predicate *Fixed*, where *Fixed*(*Location*(x)) means that the location of object x is fixed over time.

8.8 Define the predicates *Before*, *After*, *During*, and *Overlap* using the predicate *Meet* and the functions *Start* and *End*, but not the function *Time* or the predicate <.

8.9   Construct a representation for exchange rates between currencies that allows fluctuations on a daily basis.

8.10   In this chapter, we sketched some of the properties of buying events. Provide a formal logical description of buying using event calculus.

8.11   Describe the event of trading something for something else. Describe buying as a kind of trading where one of the objects is a sum of money.

8.12   The exercises on buying and trading used a fairly primitive notion of ownership. For example, the buyer starts by *owning* the dollar bills. This picture begins to break down when, for example, one's money is in the bank, because there is no longer any specific collection of dollar bills that one owns. The picture is complicated still further by borrowing, leasing, renting, and bailment. Investigate the various commonsense and legal concepts of ownership, and propose a scheme by which they can be represented formally.

8.13   You are to create a system for advising computer science undergraduates on what courses to take over an extended period in order to satisfy the program requirements. (Use whatever requirements are appropriate for your institution.) First, decide on a vocabulary for representing all the information, then represent it; then use an appropriate query to the system, that will return a legal program of study as a solution. You should allow for some tailoring to individual students, in that your system should ask the student what courses or equivalents he has already taken, and not generate programs that repeat those courses.

Suggest ways in which your system could be improved, for example to take into account knowledge about student preferences, workload, good and bad instructors, and so on. For each kind of knowledge, explain how it could be expressed logically. Could your system easily incorporate this information to find the *best* program of study for a student?

8.14   Figure 8.2 shows the top levels of a hierarchy for everything. Extend it to include as many real categories as possible. A good way to do this is to cover all the things in your everyday life. This includes objects and events. Start with waking up, proceed in an orderly fashion noting everything that you see, touch, do, and think about. For example, a random sampling produces music, news, milk, walking, driving, gas, Soda Hall, carpet, talking, Professor Fateman, chicken curry, tongue, $4, sun, the daily newspaper, and so on.

You should produce both a single hierarchy chart (large sheet of paper) and a listing of objects and categories with one or more relations satisfied by members of each category. Every object should be in a category, and every category should be incorporated in the hierarchy.

8.15   (Adapted from an example by Doug Lenat.) Your mission is to capture, in logical form, enough knowledge to answer a series of questions about the following simple sentence:

> Yesterday John went to the North Berkeley Safeway and bought two pounds of tomatoes and a pound of ground beef.

Start by trying to represent its content as a series of assertions. You should write sentences that have straightforward logical structure (e.g., statements that objects have certain properties; that objects are related in certain ways; that all objects satisfying one property satisfy another). The following may help you get started:

- Which classes, individuals, relations, and so on, would you need? What are their parents, siblings and so on? (You will need events and temporal ordering, among other things.)
- Where would they fit in a more general hierarchy?
- What are the constraints and interrelationships among them?
- How detailed must you be about each of the various concepts?

The knowledge base you construct must be capable of answering a list of questions that we will give shortly. Some of the questions deal with the material stated explicitly in the story, but most of them require one to know other background knowledge—to read between the lines. You'll have to deal with what kind of things are at a supermarket, what is involved with purchasing the things one selects, what will purchases be used for, and so on. Try to make your representation as general as possible. To give a trivial example: don't say "People buy food from Safeway," because that won't help you with those who shop at another supermarket. Don't say "Joe made spaghetti with the tomatoes and ground beef," because that won't help you with anything else at all. Also, don't turn the questions into answers; for example, question (c) asks "Did John buy any meat?"—not "Did John buy a pound of ground beef?"

Sketch the chains of reasoning that would answer the questions. In the process of doing so, you will no doubt need to create additional concepts, make additional assertions, and so on. If possible, use a logical reasoning system to demonstrate the sufficiency of your knowledge base. Many of the things you write may only be approximately correct in reality, but don't worry too much; the idea is to extract the common sense that lets you answer these questions at all.

   a. Is John a child or an adult? [Adult]

   b. Does John now have at least 2 tomatoes? [Yes]

   c. Did John buy any meat? [Yes]

   d. If Mary was buying tomatoes at the same time as John, did he see her? [Yes]

   e. Are the tomatoes made in the supermarket? [No]

   f. What is John going to do with the tomatoes? [Eat them]

   g. Does Safeway sell deodorant? [Yes]

   h. Did John bring any money to the supermarket? [Yes]

   i. Does John have less money after going to the supermarket? [Yes]

8.16   Make the necessary additions/changes to your knowledge base from the previous exercise so that the following questions can be answered. Show that they can indeed be answered by the KB, and include in your report a discussion of the fixes, explaining why they were needed, whether they were minor or major, and so on.

   a. Are there other people in Safeway while John is there? [Yes—staff!]

   b. Did Mary see John? [Yes]

   c. Is John a vegetarian? [No]

   d. Who owns the deodorant in Safeway? [Safeway Corporation]

   e. Did John have an ounce of ground beef? [Yes]

   f. Does the Shell station next door have any gas? [Yes]

   g. Do the tomatoes fit in John's car trunk? [Yes]

9 INFERENCE IN FIRST-ORDER LOGIC

In which we define inference mechanisms that can efficiently answer questions posed in first-order logic.

Chapter 6 defined the notion of **inference**, and showed how sound and complete inference can be achieved for propositional logic. In this chapter, we extend these results to first-order logic. In Section 9.1 we provide some additional basic inference rules to deal with quantifiers. In Section 9.2, we show how these inference rules, along with those for propositional logic, can be chained together to make proofs. By examining these proofs, we can come up with more powerful inference rules that make proofs much shorter and more intuitive. This makes it possible to design inference procedures that are sufficiently powerful to be of use to a knowledge-based agent. These rules and procedures are discussed in Sections 9.3 and 9.4. Section 9.5 describes the problem of completeness for first-order inference, and discusses the remarkable result, obtained by Kurt Gödel, that if we extend first-order logic with additional constructs to handle mathematical induction, then there is no complete inference procedure; even though the needle is in the metaphorical haystack, no procedure can guarantee to find it. Section 9.6 describes an inference procedure called **resolution** that is complete for any set of sentences in first-order logic, and Section 9.7 proves that it is complete.

9.1 INFERENCE RULES INVOLVING QUANTIFIERS

In Section 6.4, we saw the inference rules for propositional logic: Modus Ponens, And-Elimination, And-Introduction, Or-Introduction, and Resolution. These rules hold for first-order logic as well. But we will need additional inference rules to handle first-order logic sentences with quantifiers. The three additional rules we introduce here are more complex than previous ones, because we have to talk about substituting particular individuals for the variables. We will use the notation $\text{SUBST}(\theta, \alpha)$ to denote the result of applying the substitution (or binding list) θ to the sentence α. For example:

$$\text{SUBST}(\{x/Sam, y/Pam\}, Likes(x, y)) = Likes(Sam, Pam)$$

The three new inference rules are as follows:

UNIVERSAL
ELIMINATION
◇ **Universal Elimination**: For any sentence α, variable v, and ground term[1] g:

$$\frac{\forall v \; \alpha}{\text{SUBST}(\{v/g\}, \alpha)}$$

For example, from $\forall x \; Likes(x, IceCream)$, we can use the substitution $\{x/Ben\}$ and infer $Likes(Ben, IceCream)$.

EXISTENTIAL
ELIMINATION
◇ **Existential Elimination**: For any sentence α, variable v, and constant symbol k that does not appear elsewhere in the knowledge base:

$$\frac{\exists v \; \alpha}{\text{SUBST}(\{v/k\}, \alpha)}$$

For example, from $\exists x \; Kill(x, Victim)$, we can infer $Kill(Murderer, Victim)$, as long as $Murderer$ does not appear elsewhere in the knowledge base.

EXISTENTIAL
INTRODUCTION
◇ **Existential Introduction**: For any sentence α, variable v that does not occur in α, and ground term g that does occur in α:

$$\frac{\alpha}{\exists v \; \text{SUBST}(\{g/v\}, \alpha)}$$

For example, from $Likes(Jerry, IceCream)$ we can infer $\exists x \; Likes(x, IceCream)$.

You can check these rules using the definition of a universal sentence as the conjunction of all its possible instantiations (so Universal Elimination is like And-Elimination) and the definition of an existential sentence as the disjunction of all its possible instantiations.

It is very important that the constant used to replace the variable in the Existential Elimination rule is new. If we disregard this requirement, it is easy to produce consequences that do not follow logically. For example, suppose we have the sentence $\exists x \; Father(x, John)$ ("John has a father"). If we replace the variable x by the constant $John$, we get $Father(John, John)$, which is certainly not a logical consequence of the original sentence. Basically, the existential sentence says there is some object satisfying a condition, and the elimination process is just giving a name to that object. Naturally, that name must not already belong to another object. Mathematics provides a nice example: suppose we discover that there is a number that is a little bigger than 2.71828 and that satisfies the equation $d(x^y)/dy = x^y$ for x. We can give this number a name, such as e, but it would be a mistake to give it the name of an existing object, like π.

9.2   AN EXAMPLE PROOF

Having defined some inference rules, we now illustrate how to use them to do a proof. From here, it is only a short step to an actual proof procedure, because the application of inference rules is simply a question of matching their premise patterns to the sentences in the KB and then adding

---

[1]   Recall from Chapter 7 that a ground term is a term that contains no variables—that is, either a constant symbol or a function symbol applied to some ground terms.

their (suitably instantiated) conclusion patterns. We will begin with the situation as it might be described in English:

> The law says that it is a crime for an American to sell weapons to hostile nations. The country Nono, an enemy of America, has some missiles, and all of its missiles were sold to it by Colonel West, who is American.

What we wish to prove is that West is a criminal. We first represent these facts in first-order logic, and then show the proof as a sequence of applications of the inference rules.[2]

"... it is a crime for an American to sell weapons to hostile nations":

$$\forall x, y, z \; American(x) \land Weapon(y) \land Nation(z) \land Hostile(z) \\ \land \, Sells(x, z, y) \Rightarrow Criminal(x) \tag{9.1}$$

"Nono ... has some missiles":

$$\exists x \; Owns(Nono, x) \land Missile(x) \tag{9.2}$$

"All of its missiles were sold to it by Colonel West":

$$\forall x \; Owns(Nono, x) \land Missile(x) \Rightarrow Sells(West, Nono, x) \tag{9.3}$$

We will also need to know that missiles are weapons:

$$\forall x \; Missile(x) \Rightarrow Weapon(x) \tag{9.4}$$

and that an enemy of America counts as "hostile":

$$\forall x \; Enemy(x, America) \Rightarrow Hostile(x) \tag{9.5}$$

"West, who is American ...":

$$American(West) \tag{9.6}$$

"The country Nono ...":

$$Nation(Nono) \tag{9.7}$$

"Nono, an enemy of America ...":

$$Enemy(Nono, America) \tag{9.8}$$

$$Nation(America) \tag{9.9}$$

The proof consists of a series of applications of the inference rules:

From (9.2) and Existential Elimination:

$$Owns(Nono, M1) \land Missile(M1) \tag{9.10}$$

From (9.10) and And-Elimination:

$$Owns(Nono, M1) \tag{9.11}$$

$$Missile(M1) \tag{9.12}$$

From (9.4) and Universal Elimination:

$$Missile(M1) \Rightarrow Weapon(M1) \tag{9.13}$$

---

[2] Our representation of the facts will not be ideal according to the standards of Chapter 8, because this is mainly an exercise in proof rather than knowledge representation.

From (9.12), (9.13), and Modus Ponens:

$$Weapon(M1) \tag{9.14}$$

From (9.3) and Universal Elimination:

$$Owns(Nono, M1) \land Missile(M1) \Rightarrow Sells(West, Nono, M1) \tag{9.15}$$

From (9.15), (9.10), and Modus Ponens:

$$Sells(West, Nono, M1) \tag{9.16}$$

From (9.1) and Universal Elimination (three times):

$$American(West) \land Weapon(M1) \land Nation(Nono) \land Hostile(Nono)$$
$$\land \; Sells(West, Nono, M1) \Rightarrow Criminal(West) \tag{9.17}$$

From (9.5) and Universal Elimination:

$$Enemy(Nono, America) \Rightarrow Hostile(Nono) \tag{9.18}$$

From (9.8), (9.18), and Modus Ponens:

$$Hostile(Nono) \tag{9.19}$$

From (9.6), (9.7), (9.14), (9.16), (9.19), and And-Introduction:

$$American(West) \land Weapon(M1) \land Nation(Nono)$$
$$\land \; Hostile(Nono) \land Sells(West, Nono, M1) \tag{9.20}$$

From (9.17), (9.20), and Modus Ponens:

$$Criminal(West) \tag{9.21}$$

If we formulate the process of finding a proof as a search process, then obviously this proof is the solution to the search problem, and equally obviously it would have to be a pretty smart program to find the proof without following any wrong paths. As a search problem, we would have

Initial state = KB (sentences 9.1–9.9)

Operators = applicable inference rules

Goal test = KB containing *Criminal(West)*

This example illustrates some important characteristics:

- The proof is 14 steps long.
- The branching factor increases as the knowledge base grows; this is because some of the inference rules combine existing facts.
- Universal Elimination can have an enormous branching factor on its own, because we can replace the variable by any ground term.
- We spent a lot of time combining atomic sentences into conjunctions, instantiating universal rules to match, and then applying Modus Ponens.

Thus, we have a serious difficulty, in the form of a collection of operators that give long proofs and a large branching factor, and hence a potentially explosive search problem. We also have an opportunity, in the form of an identifiable pattern of application of the operators (combining atomic sentences, instantiating universal rules, and then applying Modus Ponens). If we can define a better search space in which a single operator takes these three steps, then we can find proofs more efficiently.

9.3   GENERALIZED MODUS PONENS

In this section, we introduce a generalization of the Modus Ponens inference rule that does in a single blow what required an And-Introduction, Universal Elimination, and Modus Ponens in the earlier proof. The idea is to be able to take a knowledge base containing, for example:

> $Missile(M1)$
> $Owns(Nono, M1)$
> $\forall x \; Missile(x) \land Owns(Nono, x) \Rightarrow Sells(West, Nono, x)$

and infer in one step the new sentence

> $Sells(West, Nono, M1)$

Intuitively, this inference seems quite obvious. The key is to find some x in the knowledge base such that x is a missile and Nono owns x, and then infer that West sells this missile to Nono. More generally, if there is some substitution involving x that makes the premise of the implication identical to sentences already in the knowledge base, then we can assert the conclusion of the implication, after applying the substitution. In the preceding case, the substitution $\{x/M1\}$ achieves this.

We can actually make Modus Ponens do even more work. Suppose that instead of knowing $Owns(Nono, M1)$, we knew that everyone owns $M1$ (a communal missile, as it were):

> $\forall y \; Owns(y, M1)$

Then we would still like to be able to conclude that $Sells(West, Nono, M1)$. This inference could be carried out if we first applied Universal Elimination with the substitution $\{y/Nono\}$ to get $Owns(Nono, M1)$. The generalized version of Modus Ponens can do it in one step by finding a substitution for both the variables in the implication sentence and the variables in the sentences to be matched. In this case, applying the substitution $\{x/M1, y/Nono\}$ to the premise $Owns(Nono, x)$ and the sentence $Owns(y, M1)$ will make them identical. If this can be done for all the premises of the implication, then we can infer the conclusion of the implication. The rule is as follows:

GENERALIZED
MODUS PONENS

◇ **Generalized Modus Ponens**: For atomic sentences p_i, p_i', and q, where there is a substitution θ such that $\text{SUBST}(\theta, p_i') = \text{SUBST}(\theta, p_i)$, for all i:

$$\frac{p_1', \; p_2', \; \ldots, \; p_n', \; (p_1 \land p_2 \land \ldots \land p_n \Rightarrow q)}{\text{SUBST}(\theta, q)}$$

There are $n + 1$ premises to this rule: the n atomic sentences p_i' and the one implication. There is one conclusion: the result of applying the substitution to the consequent q. For the example with West and the missile:

p_1' is $Missile(M1)$	p_1 is $Missile(x)$
p_2' is $Owns(y, M1)$	p_2 is $Owns(Nono, x)$
θ is $\{x/M1, y/Nono\}$	q is $Sells(West, Nono, x)$
$\text{SUBST}(\theta, q)$ is $Sells(West, Nono, M1)$	

Generalized Modus Ponens is an efficient inference rule for three reasons:

  1. It takes bigger steps, combining several small inferences into one.

2. It takes sensible steps—it uses substitutions that are guaranteed to help rather than randomly trying Universal Eliminations. The **unification** algorithm takes two sentences and returns a substitution that makes them look the same if such a substitution exists.

3. It makes use of a precompilation step that converts all the sentences in the knowledge base into a **canonical form**. Doing this once and for all at the start means we need not waste time trying conversions during the course of the proof.

We will deal with canonical form and unification in turn.

Canonical Form

We are attempting to build an inferencing mechanism with one inference rule—the generalized version of Modus Ponens. That means that all sentences in the knowledge base should be in a form that matches one of the premises of the Modus Ponens rule—otherwise, they could never be used. In other words, the canonical form for Modus Ponens mandates that each sentence in the knowledge base be either an atomic sentence or an implication with a conjunction of atomic sentences on the left hand side and a single atom on the right. As we saw on page 174, sentences

of this form are called **Horn sentences**, and a knowledge base consisting of only Horn sentences is said to be in Horn Normal Form.

We convert sentences into Horn sentences when they are first entered into the knowledge base, using Existential Elimination and And-Elimination.[3] For example, $\exists x \; Owns(Nono, x) \land Missile(x)$ is converted into the two atomic Horn sentences $Owns(Nono, M1)$ and $Missle(M1)$. Once the existential quantifiers are all eliminated, it is traditional to drop the universal quantifiers, so that $\forall y \; Owns(y, M1)$ would be written as $Owns(y, M1)$. This is just an abbreviation—the meaning of y is still a universally quantified variable, but it is simpler to write and read sentences without the quantifiers. We return to the issue of canonical form on page 278.

Unification

The job of the unification routine, UNIFY, is to take two atomic sentences p and q and return a substitution that would make p and q look the same. (If there is no such substitution, then UNIFY should return *fail*.) Formally,

$$\text{UNIFY}(p, q) = \theta \text{ where } \text{SUBST}(\theta, p) = \text{SUBST}(\theta, q)$$

θ is called the **unifier** of the two sentences. We will illustrate unification in the context of an example, delaying discussion of detailed algorithms until Chapter 10. Suppose we have a rule

$$Knows(John, x) \Rightarrow Hates(John, x)$$

("John hates everyone he knows") and we want to use this with the Modus Ponens inference rule to find out whom he hates. In other words, we need to find those sentences in the knowledge base

---

[3] We will see in Section 9.5 that not all sentences can be converted into Horn form. Fortunately, the sentences in our example (and in many other problems) can be.

that unify with *Knows(John, x)*, and then apply the unifier to *Hates(John, x)*. Let our knowledge base contain the following sentences:

$$Knows(John, Jane)$$
$$Knows(y, Leonid)$$
$$Knows(y, Mother(y))$$
$$Knows(x, Elizabeth)$$

(Remember that x and y are implicitly universally quantified.) Unifying the antecedent of the rule against each of the sentences in the knowledge base in turn gives us:

$$\text{UNIFY}(Knows(John, x), \ Knows(John, Jane)) = \{x/Jane\}$$
$$\text{UNIFY}(Knows(John, x), \ Knows(y, Leonid)) = \{x/Leonid, y/John\}$$
$$\text{UNIFY}(Knows(John, x), \ Knows(y, Mother(y))) = \{y/John, x/Mother(John)\}$$
$$\text{UNIFY}(Knows(John, x), \ Knows(x, Elizabeth)) = fail$$

The last unification fails because x cannot take on the value *John* and the value *Elizabeth* at the same time. But intuitively, from the facts that John hates everyone he knows and that everyone knows Elizabeth, we should be able to infer that John hates Elizabeth. It should not matter if the sentence in the knowledge base is *Knows(x, Elizabeth)* or *Knows(y, Elizabeth)*.

STANDARDIZE APART   One way to handle this problem is to **standardize apart** the two sentences being unified, which means renaming the variables of one (or both) to avoid name clashes. After standardizing apart, we would have

$$\text{UNIFY}(Knows(John, x_1), \ Knows(x_2, Elizabeth)) = \{x_1/Elizabeth, x_2/John\}$$

The renaming is valid because $\forall x \ Knows(x, Elizabeth)$ and $\forall x_2 \ Knows(x_2, Elizabeth)$ have the same meaning. (See also Exercise 9.2.)

There is one more complication: we said that UNIFY should return a substitution that makes the two arguments look the same. But if there is one such substitution, then there are an infinite number:

$$\begin{aligned} \text{UNIFY}(Knows(John, x), Knows(y, z)) \ = \ & \{y/John, x/z\} \\ \text{or} \ & \{y/John, x/z, w/Freda\} \\ \text{or} \ & \{y/John, x/John, z/John\} \\ \text{or} \ & \cdots \end{aligned}$$

MOST GENERAL UNIFIER   Thus, we insist that UNIFY returns the **most general unifier** (or MGU), which is the substitution that makes the least commitment about the bindings of the variables. In this case it is $\{y/John, x/z\}$.

Sample proof revisited

Let us solve our crime problem using Generalized Modus Ponens. To do this, we first need to put the original knowledge base into Horn form. Sentences (9.1) through (9.9) become

$$American(x) \land Weapon(y) \land Nation(z) \land Hostile(z)$$
$$\land \ Sells(x, z, y) \Rightarrow Criminal(x) \tag{9.22}$$
$$Owns(Nono, M1) \tag{9.23}$$

$$Missile(M1) \tag{9.24}$$

$$Owns(Nono, x) \land Missile(x) \Rightarrow Sells(West, Nono, x) \tag{9.25}$$

$$Missile(x) \Rightarrow Weapon(x) \tag{9.26}$$

$$Enemy(x, America) \Rightarrow Hostile(x) \tag{9.27}$$

$$American(West) \tag{9.28}$$

$$Nation(Nono) \tag{9.29}$$

$$Enemy(Nono, America) \tag{9.30}$$

$$Nation(America) \tag{9.31}$$

The proof involves just four steps. From (9.24) and (9.26) using Modus Ponens:

$$Weapon(M1) \tag{9.32}$$

From (9.30) and (9.27) using Modus Ponens:

$$Hostile(Nono) \tag{9.33}$$

From (9.23), (9.24), and (9.25) using Modus Ponens:

$$Sells(West, Nono, M1) \tag{9.34}$$

From (9.28), (9.32), (9.29), (9.33), (9.34) and (9.22), using Modus Ponens:

$$Criminal(West) \tag{9.35}$$

This proof shows how natural reasoning with Generalized Modus Ponens can be. (In fact, one might venture to say that it is not unlike the way in which a human might reason about the problem.) In the next section, we describe systematic reasoning algorithms using Modus Ponens. These algorithms form the basis for many large-scale applications of AI, which we describe in Chapter 10.

9.4   FORWARD AND BACKWARD CHAINING

Now that we have a reasonable language for representing knowledge, and a reasonable inference rule (Generalized Modus Ponens) for using that knowledge, we will study how a reasoning program is constructed.

The Generalized Modus Ponens rule can be used in two ways. We can start with the sentences in the knowledge base and generate new conclusions that in turn can allow more inferences to be made. This is called **forward chaining**. Forward chaining is usually used when a new fact is added to the database and we want to generate its consequences. Alternatively, we can start with something we want to prove, find implication sentences that would allow us to conclude it, and then attempt to establish their premises in turn. This is called **backward chaining**, because it uses Modus Ponens backwards. Backward chaining is normally used when there is a goal to be proved.

FORWARD CHAINING

BACKWARD
CHAINING

Forward-chaining algorithm

Forward chaining is normally triggered by the addition of a new fact p to the knowledge base. It can be incorporated as part of the TELL process, for example. The idea is to find all implications that have p as a premise; then if the other premises are already known to hold, we can add the consequent of the implication to the knowledge base, triggering further inference (see Figure 9.1).

RENAMING

The FORWARD-CHAIN procedure makes use of the idea of a **renaming**. One sentence is a renaming of another if they are identical except for the names of the variables. For example, $Likes(x, IceCream)$ and $Likes(y, IceCream)$ are renamings of each other because they only differ in the choice of x or y, but $Likes(x, x)$ and $Likes(x, y)$ are not renamings of each other.

COMPOSITION

We also need the idea of a **composition** of substitutions. COMPOSE(θ_1, θ_2) is the substitution whose effect is identical to the effect of applying each substitution in turn. That is,

$$\text{SUBST}(\text{COMPOSE}(\theta_1, \theta_2), p) = \text{SUBST}(\theta_2, \text{SUBST}(\theta_1, p))$$

We will use our crime problem again to illustrate how FORWARD-CHAIN works. We will begin with the knowledge base containing only the implications in Horn form:

$$American(x) \wedge Weapon(y) \wedge Nation(z) \wedge Hostile(z)$$
$$\wedge Sells(x, z, y) \Rightarrow Criminal(x) \tag{9.36}$$

$$Owns(Nono, x) \wedge Missile(x) \Rightarrow Sells(West, Nono, x) \tag{9.37}$$

$$Missile(x) \Rightarrow Weapon(x) \tag{9.38}$$

$$Enemy(x, America) \Rightarrow Hostile(x) \tag{9.39}$$

---

procedure FORWARD-CHAIN(KB, p)

  if there is a sentence in KB that is a renaming of p **then return**
  Add p to KB
  for each ($p_1 \wedge \ldots \wedge p_n \Rightarrow q$) **in** KB such that for some i, UNIFY$(p_i, p) = \theta$ succeeds **do**
    FIND-AND-INFER($KB, [p_1, \ldots, p_{i-1}, p_{i+1}, \ldots, p_n], q, \theta$)
  end

---

procedure FIND-AND-INFER($KB, premises, conclusion, \theta$)

  if $premises = [\,]$ **then**
    FORWARD-CHAIN(KB, SUBST$(\theta, conclusion)$)
  else for each p' **in** KB such that UNIFY$(p', \text{SUBST}(\theta, \text{FIRST}(premises))) = \theta_2$ **do**
    FIND-AND-INFER(KB, REST$(premises), conclusion,$ COMPOSE(θ, θ_2))
  end

Figure 9.1   The forward-chaining inference algorithm. It adds to KB all the sentences that can be inferred from the sentence p. If p is already in KB, it does nothing. If p is new, consider each implication that has a premise that matches p. For each such implication, if all the remaining premises are in KB, then infer the conclusion. If the premises can be matched several ways, then infer each corresponding conclusion. The substitution θ keeps track of the way things match.

Now we add the atomic sentences to the knowledge base one by one, forward chaining each time and showing any additional facts that are added:

FORWARD-CHAIN(*KB*, *American*(*West*))

Add to the KB. It unifies with a premise of (9.36), but the other premises of (9.36) are not known, so FORWARD-CHAIN returns without making any new inferences.

FORWARD-CHAIN(*KB*, *Nation*(*Nono*))

Add to the KB. It unifies with a premise of (9.36), but there are still missing premises, so FORWARD-CHAIN returns.

FORWARD-CHAIN(*KB*, *Enemy*(*Nono*, *America*))

Add to the KB. It unifies with the premise of (9.39), with unifier $\{x/Nono\}$. Call

FORWARD-CHAIN(*KB*, *Hostile*(*Nono*))

Add to the KB. It unifies with a premise of (9.36). Only two other premises are known, so processing terminates.

FORWARD-CHAIN(*KB*, *Owns*(*Nono*, *M*1))

Add to the KB. It unifies with a premise of (9.37), with unifier $\{x/M1\}$. The other premise, now *Missile*(*M*1), is not known, so processing terminates.

FORWARD-CHAIN(*KB*, *Missile*(*M*1))

Add to the KB. It unifies with a premise of (9.37) and (9.38). We will handle them in that order.

- *Missile*(*M*1) unifies with a premise of (9.37) with unifier $\{x/M1\}$. The other premise, now *Owns*(*Nono*, *M*1), is known, so call

  FORWARD-CHAIN(*KB*, *Sells*(*West*, *Nono*, *M*1))

  Add to the KB. It unifies with a premise of (9.36), with unifier $\{x/West, y/M1, z/Nono\}$. The premise *Weapon*(*M*1) is unknown, so processing terminates.
- *Missile*(*M*1) unifies with a premise of (9.38) with unifier $\{x/M1\}$. Call

  FORWARD-CHAIN(*KB*, *Weapon*(*M*1))

  Add to the KB. It unifies with a premise of (9.36), with unifier $\{y/M1\}$. The other premises are all known, with accumulated unifier $\{x/West, y/M1, z/Nono\}$. Call

  FORWARD-CHAIN(*KB*, *Criminal*(*West*))

  Add to the KB. Processing terminates.

As can be seen from this example, forward chaining builds up a picture of the situation gradually as new data comes in. Its inference processes are not directed toward solving any particular problem; for this reason it is called a **data-driven** or **data-directed** procedure. In this example, there were no rules capable of drawing irrelevant conclusions, so the lack of directedness was not a problem. In other cases (for example, if we have several rules describing the eating habits of Americans and the price of missiles), FORWARD-CHAIN will generate many irrelevant conclusions. In such cases, it is often better to use backward chaining, which directs all its effort toward the question at hand.

Backward-chaining algorithm

Backward chaining is designed to find all answers to a question posed to the knowledge base. Backward chaining therefore exhibits the functionality required for the ASK procedure. The backward-chaining algorithm BACK-CHAIN works by first checking to see if answers can be provided directly from sentences in the knowledge base. It then finds all implications whose conclusion unifies with the query, and tries to establish the premises of those implications, also by backward chaining. If the premise is a conjunction, then BACK-CHAIN processes the conjunction conjunct by conjunct, building up the unifier for the whole premise as it goes. The algorithm is shown in Figure 9.2. (Here UNIFY is assumed to standardize apart its second argument.)

Figure 9.3 is the proof tree for deriving $Criminal(West)$ from sentences (9.22) through (9.30). As a diagram of the backward chaining algorithm, the tree should be read depth-first, left to right. To prove $Criminal(x)$ we have to prove the five conjuncts below it. Some of these are in the knowledge base, and others require further backward chaining. Each leaf node has the substitution used to obtain it written below. Note that once one branch of a conjunction succeeds, its substitution is applied to subsequent branches. Thus, by the time BACK-CHAIN gets to $Sells(x, z, y)$, all the variables are instantiated. Figure 9.3 can also be seen as a diagram of forward chaining. In this interpretation, the premises are added at the bottom, and conclusions are added once all their premises are in the KB. Figure 9.4 shows what can happen if an incorrect choice is made in the search—in this case, choosing America as the nation in question. There is no way to prove that America is a hostile nation, so the proof fails to go through, and we have to back up and consider another branch in the search space.

---

function BACK-CHAIN(*KB, q*) **returns** a set of substitutions

   BACK-CHAIN-LIST(*KB*, [*q*], {})

---

function BACK-CHAIN-LIST(*KB, qlist, θ*) **returns** a set of substitutions
   inputs: *KB*, a knowledge base
         qlist, a list of conjuncts forming a query (*θ* already applied)
         θ, the current substitution
   local variables: *answers*, a set of substitutions, initially empty

   if *qlist* is empty **then return** {*θ*}
   q ← FIRST(*qlist*)
         for each q_i' in *KB* such that $\theta_i \leftarrow$ UNIFY(q, q_i') succeeds **do**
            Add COMPOSE(θ, θ_i) to *answers*
         end
         for each sentence ($p_1 \wedge \ldots \wedge p_n \Rightarrow q_i'$) **in** *KB* such that $\theta_i \leftarrow$ UNIFY(q, q_i') succeeds **do**
            answers ← BACK-CHAIN-LIST(*KB*, SUBST$(\theta_i, [p_1 \ldots p_n])$, COMPOSE$(\theta, \theta_i)$) ∪ *answers*
         end
   return the union of BACK-CHAIN-LIST(*KB*, REST(*qlist*), *θ*) for each *θ* ∈ *answers*

Figure 9.2   The backward-chaining algorithm.

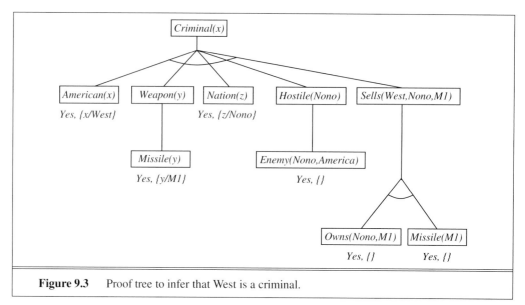

Figure 9.3   Proof tree to infer that West is a criminal.

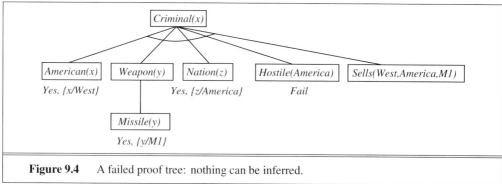

Figure 9.4   A failed proof tree: nothing can be inferred.

9.5 COMPLETENESS

Suppose we have the following knowledge base:

$$\forall x \ P(x) \Rightarrow Q(x)$$
$$\forall x \ \neg P(x) \Rightarrow R(x)$$
$$\forall x \ Q(x) \Rightarrow S(x) \tag{9.40}$$
$$\forall x \ R(x) \Rightarrow S(x)$$

Then we certainly want to be able to conclude $S(A)$; $S(A)$ is true if $Q(A)$ or $R(A)$ is true, and one of those must be true because either $P(A)$ is true or $\neg P(A)$ is true.

Unfortunately, chaining with Modus Ponens cannot derive $S(A)$ for us. The problem is that $\forall x \; \neg P(x) \Rightarrow R(x)$ cannot be converted to Horn form, and thus cannot be used by Modus Ponens. That means that a proof procedure using Modus Ponens is **incomplete**: there are sentences entailed by the knowledge base that the procedure cannot infer.

INCOMPLETE

The question of the existence of complete proof procedures is of direct concern to mathematicians. If a complete proof procedure can be found for mathematical statements, two things follow: first, all conjectures can be established mechanically; second, all of mathematics can be established as the logical consequence of a set of fundamental axioms. A complete proof procedure for first-order logic would also be of great value in AI: barring practical issues of computational complexity, it would enable a machine to solve any problem that can be stated in the language.

The question of completeness has therefore generated some of the most important mathematical work of the twentieth century. This work culminated in the results proved by the German mathematician Kurt Gödel in 1930 and 1931. Gödel has some good news for us; his **completeness theorem** showed that, for first-order logic, any sentence that is entailed by another set of sentences can be proved from that set. That is, we can find inference rules that allow a **complete** proof procedure R:

COMPLETENESS
THEOREM

$$\text{if } KB \models \alpha \text{ then } KB \vdash_R \alpha$$

The completeness theorem is like saying that a procedure for finding a needle in a haystack does exist. This is not a trivial claim, because universally quantified sentences and arbitrarily nested function symbols add up to haystacks of infinite size. Gödel showed that a proof procedure exists, but he did not demonstrate one; it was not until 1965 that Robinson published his **resolution algorithm**, which we discuss in the next section.

RESOLUTION
ALGORITHM

There is one problem with the completeness theorem that is a real nuisance. Note that we said that *if* a sentence follows, then it can be proved. Normally, we do not know until the proof is done that the sentence *does* follow; what happens when the sentence doesn't follow? Can we tell? Well, for first-order logic, it turns out that we cannot; our proof procedure can go on and on, but we will not know if it is stuck in a hopeless loop or if the proof is just about to pop out. (This is like the halting problem for Turing machines.) Entailment in first-order logic is thus **semidecidable**, that is, we can show that sentences follow from premises, if they do, but we cannot always show it if they do not. As a corollary, **consistency** of sets of sentences (the question of whether there is a way to make all the sentences true) is also semidecidable.

SEMIDECIDABLE

9.6   RESOLUTION: A COMPLETE INFERENCE PROCEDURE

Recall from Chapter 6 that the simple version of the resolution inference rule for propositional logic has the following form:

$$\frac{\alpha \vee \beta, \; \neg\beta \vee \gamma}{\alpha \vee \gamma} \qquad \text{or equivalently} \qquad \frac{\neg\alpha \Rightarrow \beta, \; \beta \Rightarrow \gamma}{\neg\alpha \Rightarrow \gamma}$$

The rule can be understood in two ways. First, we can see it as reasoning by cases. If β is false, then from the first disjunction, α must be true; but if β is true, then from the second disjunction γ must be true. Hence, either α or γ must be true. The second way to understand it is as transitivity of implication: from two implications, we derive a third that links the premise of the first to the conclusion of the second. Notice that Modus Ponens does not allow us to derive new implications; it only derives atomic conclusions. Thus, the resolution rule is more powerful than Modus Ponens. In this section, we will see that a generalization of the simple resolution rule can serve as the sole inference rule in a complete inference procedure for first-order logic.

The resolution inference rule

In the simple form of the resolution rule, the premises have exactly two disjuncts. We can extend that to get a more general rule that says that for two disjunctions of any length, if one of the disjuncts in one clause (p_j) unifies with the negation of a disjunct in the other (q_k), then infer the disjunction of all the disjuncts except for those two:

GENERALIZED
RESOLUTION
(DISJUNCTIONS)

$\diamond$ **Generalized Resolution (disjunctions)**: For literals p_i and q_i,
where $\text{UNIFY}(p_j, \neg q_k) = \theta$:

$$\frac{\begin{array}{c} p_1 \vee \ldots p_j \ldots \vee p_m, \\ q_1 \vee \ldots q_k \ldots \vee q_n \end{array}}{\text{SUBST}(\theta, (p_1 \vee \ldots p_{j-1} \vee p_{j+1} \ldots p_m \vee q_1 \ldots q_{k-1} \vee q_{k+1} \ldots \vee q_n))}$$

Equivalently, we can rewrite this in terms of implications:

GENERALIZED
RESOLUTION
(IMPLICATIONS)

$\diamond$ **Generalized Resolution (implications)**: For atoms p_i, q_i, r_i, s_i
where $\text{UNIFY}(p_j, q_k) = \theta$:

$$\frac{\begin{array}{c} p_1 \wedge \ldots p_j \ldots \wedge p_{n_1} \Rightarrow r_1 \vee \ldots r_{n_2} \\ s_1 \wedge \ldots \wedge s_{n_3} \Rightarrow q_1 \vee \ldots q_k \ldots \vee q_{n_4} \end{array}}{\text{SUBST}(\theta, (p_1 \wedge \ldots p_{j-1} \wedge p_{j+1} \wedge p_{n_1} \wedge s_1 \wedge \ldots s_{n_3} \Rightarrow r_1 \vee \ldots r_{n_2} \vee q_1 \vee \ldots q_{k-1} \vee q_{k+1} \vee \ldots \vee q_{n_4}))}$$

Canonical forms for resolution

In the first version of the resolution rule, every sentence is a disjunction of literals. All the disjunctions in the KB are assumed to be joined in one big, implicit conjunction (as in a normal

CONJUNCTIVE
NORMAL FORM

KB), so this form is called **conjunctive normal form** (or CNF), even though each individual sentence is a disjunction (confusing, isn't it?).

In the second version of the resolution rule, each sentence is an implication with a conjunction of atoms on the left and a disjunction of atoms on the right. We call this **implicative normal**

IMPLICATIVE
NORMAL FORM

form (or INF), although the name is not standard. We can transform the sentences in (9.40) into either of the two forms, as we now show. (Notice that we have standardized apart the variable names in these sentences.)

Conjunctive Normal Form	Implicative Normal Form	
$\neg P(w) \lor Q(w)$	$P(w) \Rightarrow Q(w)$	
$P(x) \lor R(x)$	$True \Rightarrow P(x) \lor R(x)$	
$\neg Q(y) \lor S(y)$	$Q(y) \Rightarrow S(y)$	(9.41)
$\neg R(z) \lor S(z)$	$R(z) \Rightarrow S(z)$	

The two forms are notational variants of each other, and as we will see on page 281, any set of sentences can be translated to either form. Historically, conjunctive normal form is more common, but we will use implicative normal form, because we find it more natural.

It is important to recognize that *resolution is a generalization of modus ponens.* Clearly, the implicative normal form is more general than Horn form, because the right-hand side can be a disjunction, not just a single atom. But at first glance it seems that Modus Ponens has the ability to combine atoms with an implication to infer a conclusion in a way that resolution cannot do. This is just an illusion—once we realize that an atomic sentence α in implicative normal form is written as $True \Rightarrow \alpha$, we can see that modus ponens is just a special case of resolution:

$$\frac{\alpha, \ \alpha \Rightarrow \beta}{\beta} \quad \text{is equivalent to} \quad \frac{True \Rightarrow \alpha, \ \alpha \Rightarrow \beta}{True \Rightarrow \beta}$$

Even though $True \Rightarrow \alpha$ is the "correct" way to write an atomic sentence in implicative normal form, we will sometimes write α as an abbreviation.

Resolution proofs

One could use resolution in a forward- or backward-chaining algorithm, just as Modus Ponens is used. Figure 9.5 shows a three-step resolution proof of $S(A)$ from the KB in (9.41).

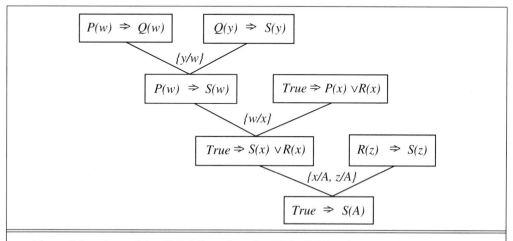

Figure 9.5   A proof that $S(A)$ follows from the KB in (9.41), using resolution. Each "vee" in the proof tree represents a resolution step: the two sentences at the top are the premises, and the one at the bottom is the conclusion or **resolvent**. The substitution is shown for each resolution.

Technically, the final resolvent should be *True* $\Rightarrow$ $S(A) \lor S(A)$, but we have taken the liberty of removing the redundant disjunct. In some systems, there is a separate inference rule called **factoring** to do this, but it is simpler to just make it be part of the resolution rule.

Chaining with resolution is more powerful than chaining with Modus Ponens, but it is still not complete. To see that, consider trying to prove $P \lor \neg P$ from the empty KB. The sentence is valid, but with nothing in the KB, there is nothing for resolution to apply to, and we are unable to prove anything.

One complete inference procedure using resolution is **refutation**, also known as **proof by contradiction** and **reductio ad absurdum**. The idea is that to prove P, we assume P is false (i.e., add $\neg P$ to the knowledge base) and prove a contradiction. If we can do this, then it must be that the knowledge base implies P. In other words:

$$(KB \land \neg P \Rightarrow \text{False}) \Leftrightarrow (KB \Rightarrow P)$$

Proof by contradiction is a powerful tool throughout mathematics, and resolution gives us a simple, sound, complete way to apply it. Figure 9.6 gives an example of the method. We start with the knowledge base of (9.41) and are attempting to prove $S(A)$. We negate this to get $\neg S(A)$, which in implicative normal form is $S(A) \Rightarrow \text{False}$, and add it to the knowledge base. Then we apply resolution until we arrive at a contradiction, which in implicative normal form is $\text{True} \Rightarrow \text{False}$. It takes one more step than in Figure 9.5, but that is a small price to pay for the security of a complete proof method.

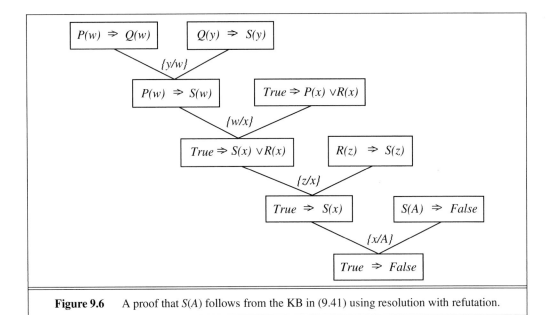

Figure 9.6   A proof that $S(A)$ follows from the KB in (9.41) using resolution with refutation.

Conversion to Normal Form

So far, we have claimed that resolution is complete, but we have not shown it. In this section we show that *any* first-order logic sentence can be put into implicative (or conjunctive) normal form, and in the following section we will show that from a set of sentences in normal form we can prove that a given sentence follows from the set.

We present the procedure for converting to normal form, step by step, showing that each step does not change the meaning; it should be fairly clear that all possible sentences are dealt with properly. You should understand why each of the steps in this procedure is valid, but few people actually manage to remember them all.

◇ **Eliminate implications**: Recall that $p \Rightarrow q$ is the same as $\neg p \vee q$. So replace all implications by the corresponding disjunctions.

◇ **Move ¬ inwards**: Negations are allowed only on atoms in conjunctive normal form, and not at all in implicative normal form. We eliminate negations with wide scope using de Morgan's laws (see Exercise 6.2), the quantifier equivalences and double negation:

$$\neg(p \vee q) \quad \text{becomes} \quad \neg p \wedge \neg q$$
$$\neg(p \wedge q) \quad \text{becomes} \quad \neg p \vee \neg q$$
$$\neg \forall x, p \quad \text{becomes} \quad \exists x \; \neg p$$
$$\neg \exists x, p \quad \text{becomes} \quad \forall x \; \neg p$$
$$\neg\neg p \quad \text{becomes} \quad p$$

◇ **Standardize variables**: For sentences like $(\forall x \; P(x)) \vee (\exists x \; Q(x))$ that use the same variable name twice, change the name of one of the variables. This avoids confusion later when we drop the quantifiers.

◇ **Move quantifiers left**: The sentence is now in a form in which all the quantifiers can be moved to the left, in the order in which they appear, without changing the meaning of the sentence. It is tedious to prove this properly; it involves equivalences such as

$$p \vee \forall x \; q \quad \text{becomes} \quad \forall x \; p \vee q$$

which is true because p here is guaranteed not to contain an x.

SKOLEMIZATION

◇ **Skolemize**: **Skolemization** is the process of removing existential quantifiers by elimination. In the simple case, it is just like the Existential Elimination rule of Section 9.1—translate $\exists x \; P(x)$ into $P(A)$, where A is a constant that does not appear elsewhere in the KB. But there is the added complication that some of the existential quantifiers, even though moved left, may still be nested inside a universal quantifier. Consider "Everyone has a heart":

$$\forall x \; Person(x) \Rightarrow \exists y \; Heart(y) \wedge Has(x, y)$$

If we just replaced y with a constant, H, we would get

$$\forall x \; Person(x) \Rightarrow Heart(H) \wedge Has(x, H)$$

which says that everyone has the same heart H. We need to say that the heart they have is not necessarily shared, that is, it can be found by applying to each person a function that maps from person to heart:

$$\forall x \; Person(x) \Rightarrow Heart(F(x)) \wedge Has(x, F(x))$$

where F is a function name that does not appear elsewhere in the KB. F is called a **Skolem function**. In general, the existentially quantified variable is replaced by a term that consists of a Skolem function applied to all the variables universally quantified *outside* the existential quantifier in question. Skolemization eliminates all existentially quantified variables, so we are now free to drop the universal quantifiers, because any variable must be universally quantified.

◊ **Distribute** $\wedge$ **over** $\vee$: $(a \wedge b) \vee c$ becomes $(a \vee c) \wedge (b \vee c)$.

◊ **Flatten nested conjunctions and disjunctions**: $(a \vee b) \vee c$ becomes $(a \vee b \vee c)$, and $(a \wedge b) \wedge c$ becomes $(a \wedge b \wedge c)$.

At this point, the sentence is in conjunctive normal form (CNF): it is a conjunction where every conjunct is a disjunction of literals. This form is sufficient for resolution, but it may be difficult for us humans to understand.

◊ **Convert disjunctions to implications**: Optionally, you can take one more step to convert to implicative normal form. For each conjunct, gather up the negative literals into one list, the positive literals into another, and build an implication from them:
$(\neg a \vee \neg b \vee c \vee d)$ becomes $(a \wedge b \Rightarrow c \vee d)$

Example proof

We will now show how to apply the conversion procedure and the resolution refutation procedure on a more complicated example, which is stated in English as:

> Jack owns a dog.
> Every dog owner is an animal lover.
> No animal lover kills an animal.
> Either Jack or Curiosity killed the cat, who is named Tuna.
> Did Curiosity kill the cat?

First, we express the original sentences (and some background knowledge) in first-order logic:

A. $\exists x\ Dog(x) \wedge Owns(Jack, x)$
B. $\forall x\ (\exists y\ Dog(y) \wedge Owns(x, y)) \Rightarrow AnimalLover(x)$
C. $\forall x\ AnimalLover(x) \Rightarrow \forall y\ Animal(y) \Rightarrow \neg Kills(x, y)$
D. $Kills(Jack, Tuna) \vee Kills(Curiosity, Tuna)$
E. $Cat(Tuna)$
F. $\forall x\ Cat(x) \Rightarrow Animal(x)$

Now we have to apply the conversion procedure to convert each sentence to implicative normal form. We will use the shortcut of writing P instead of *True* $\Rightarrow$ P:

A1. $Dog(D)$
A2. $Owns(Jack, D)$
B. $Dog(y) \wedge Owns(x, y) \Rightarrow AnimalLover(x)$
C. $AnimalLover(x) \wedge Animal(y) \wedge Kills(x, y) \Rightarrow$ *False*
D. $Kills(Jack, Tuna) \vee Kills(Curiosity, Tuna)$
E. $Cat(Tuna)$
F. $Cat(x) \Rightarrow Animal(x)$

The problem is now to show that *Kills(Curiosity, Tuna)* is true. We do that by assuming the negation, *Kills(Curiosity, Tuna)* $\Rightarrow$ *False*, and applying the resolution inference rule seven times, as shown in Figure 9.7. We eventually derive a contradiction, *False*, which means that the assumption must be false, and *Kills(Curiosity, Tuna)* is true after all. In English, the proof could be paraphrased as follows:

> Suppose Curiosity did *not* kill Tuna. We know that either Jack or Curiosity did, thus Jack must have. But Jack owns D, and D is a dog, so Jack is an animal lover. Furthermore, Tuna is a cat, and cats are animals, so Tuna is an animal. Animal lovers don't kill animals, so Jack couldn't have killed Tuna. But this is a contradiction, because we already concluded that Jack must have killed Tuna. Hence, the original supposition (that Curiosity did not kill Tuna) must be wrong, and we have proved that Curiosity *did* kill Tuna.

The proof answers the question "Did Curiosity kill the cat?" but often we want to pose more general questions, like "Who killed the cat?" Resolution can do this, but it takes a little more work to obtain the answer. The query can be expressed as $\exists w$ *Kills(w, Tuna)*. If you repeat the proof tree in Figure 9.7, substituting the negation of this query, *Kills(w, Tuna)* $\Rightarrow$ *False* for the old query, you end up with a similar proof tree, but with the substitution {*w/Curiosity*} in one of the steps. So finding an answer to "Who killed the cat" is just a matter of looking in the proof tree to find the binding of *w*. It is straightforward to maintain a composed unifier so that a solution is available as soon as a contradiction is found.

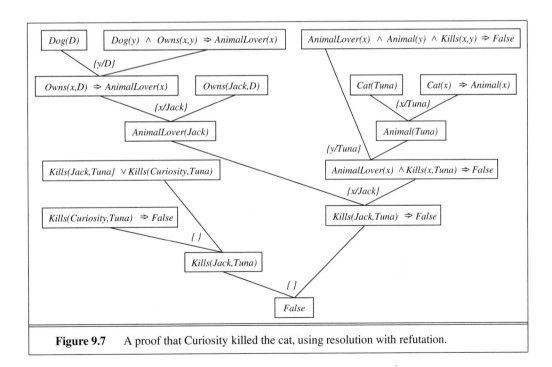

Figure 9.7   A proof that Curiosity killed the cat, using resolution with refutation.

Dealing with equality

There is one problem that we have not dealt with so far, namely, finding appropriate inference rules for sentences containing the equality symbol. Unification does a good job of matching variables with other terms: $P(x)$ unifies with $P(A)$. But $P(A)$ and $P(B)$ fail to unify, even if the sentence $A = B$ is in the knowledge base. The problem is that unification only does a syntactic test based on the appearance of the argument terms, not a true semantic test based on the objects they represent. Of course, no semantic test is available because the inference system has no access to the objects themselves, but it should still be able to take advantage of what knowledge it has concerning the identities and differences among objects.

One way to deal with this is to axiomatize equality, by writing down its properties. We need to say that equality is reflexive, symmetric, and transitive, and we also have to say that we can substitute equals for equals in any predicate or function. So we need three basic axioms, and then one for each predicate and function:

$$\forall x \; x = x$$
$$\forall x, y \; x = y \; \Rightarrow \; y = x$$
$$\forall x, y, z \; x = y \wedge y = z \; \Rightarrow \; x = z$$
$$\forall x, y \; x = y \; \Rightarrow \; (P_1(x) \Leftrightarrow P_1(y))$$
$$\forall x, y \; x = y \; \Rightarrow \; (P_2(x) \Leftrightarrow P_2(y))$$
$$\vdots$$
$$\forall w, x, y, z \; w = y \wedge x = z \; \Rightarrow \; (F_1(w, x) = F_1(y, z))$$
$$\forall w, x, y, z \; w = y \wedge x = z \; \Rightarrow \; (F_2(w, x) = F_2(y, z))$$
$$\vdots$$

The other way to deal with equality is with a special inference rule. The **demodulation** rule takes an equality statement $x = y$ and any sentence with a nested term that unifies with x and derives the same sentence with y substituted for the nested term. More formally, we can define the inference rule as follows:

DEMODULATION

$\diamond$ **Demodulation**: For any terms x, y, and z, where $\text{UNIFY}(x, z) = \theta$:

$$\frac{x = y, \quad (\ldots z \ldots)}{(\ldots \text{SUBST}(\theta, y) \ldots)}$$

If we write all our equalities so that the simpler term is on the right (e.g., $(x + 0) = 0$), then demodulation will do simplification, because it always replaces an expression on the left with one on the right. A more powerful rule called **paramodulation** deals with the case where we do not know $x = y$, but we do know, say, $x = y \vee P(x)$.

PARAMODULATION

Resolution strategies

We know that repeated applications of the resolution inference rule will find a proof if one exists, but we have no guarantee of the efficiency of this process. In this section we look at four of the strategies that have been used to guide the search toward a proof.

Unit preference

UNIT CLAUSE

This strategy prefers to do resolutions where one of the sentences is a single literal (also known as a **unit clause**). The idea behind the strategy is that we are trying to produce a very short sentence, $True \Rightarrow False$, and therefore it might be a good idea to prefer inferences that produce shorter sentences. Resolving a unit sentence (such as P) with any other sentence (such as $P \wedge Q \Rightarrow R$) always yields a sentence (in this case, $Q \Rightarrow R$) that is shorter than the other sentence. When the unit preference strategy was first tried for propositional inference in 1964, it led to a dramatic speedup, making it feasible to prove theorems that could not be handled without the preference. Unit preference by itself does not, however, reduce the branching factor in medium-sized problems enough to make them solvable by resolution. It is, nonetheless, a useful heuristic that can be combined with other strategies.

Set of support

SET OF SUPPORT

Preferences that try certain resolutions first are helpful, but in general it is more effective to try to eliminate some potential resolutions altogether. The set of support strategy does just that. It starts by identifying a subset of the sentences called the **set of support**. Every resolution combines a sentence from the set of support with another sentence, and adds the resolvent into the set of support. If the set of support is small relative to the whole knowledge base, this will cut the search space dramatically.

We have to be careful with this approach, because a bad choice for the set of support will make the algorithm incomplete. However, if we choose the set of support S so that the remainder of the sentences are jointly satisfiable, then set-of-support resolution will be complete. A common approach is to use the negated query as the set of support, on the assumption that the original knowledge base is consistent. (After all, if it is not consistent, then the fact that the query follows from it is vacuous.) The set-of-support strategy has the additional advantage of generating proof trees that are often easy for humans to understand, because they are goal-directed.

Input resolution

INPUT RESOLUTION

In the **input resolution** strategy, every resolution combines one of the input sentences (from the KB or the query) with some other sentence. The proofs in Figure 9.5 and Figure 9.6 use only input resolutions; they have the characteristic shape of a diagonal "spine" with single sentences combining onto the spine. Clearly, the space of proof trees of this shape is smaller than the space of all proof graphs. In Horn knowledge bases, Modus Ponens is a kind of input resolution strategy, because it combines an implication from the original KB with some other sentences. Thus, it should not be surprising that input resolution is complete for knowledge bases that are in Horn form, but incomplete in the general case.

LINEAR RESOLUTION

The **linear resolution** strategy is a slight generalization that allows P and Q to be resolved together if either P is in the original KB or if P is an ancestor of Q in the proof tree. Linear resolution is complete.

Subsumption

SUBSUMPTION   The **subsumption** method eliminates all sentences that are subsumed by (i.e., more specific than) an existing sentence in the KB. For example, if $P(x)$ is in the KB, then there is no sense in adding $P(A)$, and even less sense in adding $P(A) \lor Q(B)$. Subsumption helps keep the KB small, which helps keep the search space small.

9.7   COMPLETENESS OF RESOLUTION

This section proves that resolution is complete. It can be safely skipped by those who are willing to take it on faith.

REFUTATION-
COMPLETE

       Before we show that resolution is complete, we need to be more precise about the particular flavor of completeness that we will establish. Resolution is **refutation-complete**, which means that *if* a set of sentences is unsatisfiable, then resolution will derive a contradiction. Resolution cannot be used to generate all logical consequences of a set of sentences, but it can be used to establish that a given sentence is entailed by the set. Hence, it can be used to find all answers to a given question, using the negated-goal method described before.

       We will take it as given that any sentence in first-order logic (without equality) can be rewritten in normal form. This can be proved by induction on the form of the sentence, using atomic sentences as the base case (Davis and Putnam, 1960). Our goal therefore is to prove the following: *if S is an unsatisfiable set of sentences in clausal form, then the application of a finite number of resolution steps to S will yield a contradiction.*

       Our proof sketch follows the original proof due to Robinson, with some simplifications from Genesereth and Nilsson (1987). The basic structure of the proof is shown in Figure 9.8, and is as follows:

1. We begin by observing that if S is unsatisfiable, then there exists a particular set of *ground instances* of the sentences of S, such that this set is also unsatisfiable (Herbrand's theorem).
2. We then show that resolution is complete for ground sentences (i.e., propositional logic). This is easy because the set of consequences of a propositional theory is always finite.
3. We then use a **lifting lemma** to show that, for any resolution proof using the set of ground sentences, there is a corresponding proof using the first-order sentences from which the ground sentences were obtained.

To carry out the first step, we will need three new concepts:

HERBRAND
UNIVERSE

    ◇ **Herbrand universe**: If S is a set of clauses, then H_S, the Herbrand universe of S, is the set of all ground terms constructible from the following:

        a. The function symbols in S, if any.
        b. The constant symbols in S, if any; if none, then the constant symbol A.

    For example, if S contains just the clause $P(x, F(x, A)) \land Q(x, A) \Rightarrow R(x, B)$, then H_S is the following infinite set of ground sentences:

$$\{A, B, F(A, A), F(A, B), F(B, A), F(B, B), F(A, F(A, A)), F(A, F(A, B)), \ldots\}$$

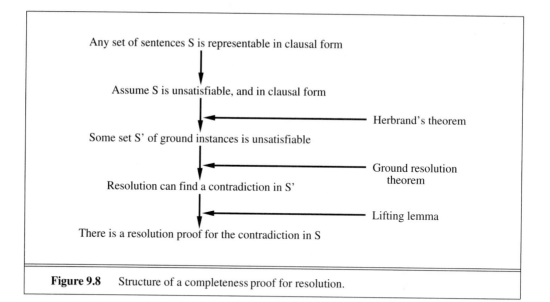

Figure 9.8   Structure of a completeness proof for resolution.

SATURATION

◇ **Saturation**: If S is a set of clauses, and P is a set of ground terms, then $P(S)$, the saturation of S with respect to P, is the set of all ground clauses obtained by applying all possible consistent substitutions for variables in S with ground terms in P.

HERBRAND BASE

◇ **Herbrand base**: The saturation of a set of clauses S with respect to its Herbrand universe is called the Herbrand base of S, written as $H_S(S)$. For example, if S contains just the clause given above, then

$$H_S(S) \;=\; \{P(A, F(A,A)) \land Q(A,A) \;\Rightarrow\; R(A,B),$$
$$P(B, F(B,A)) \land Q(B,A) \;\Rightarrow\; R(B,B),$$
$$P(F(A,A), F(F(A,A),A)) \land Q(F(A,A),A) \;\Rightarrow\; R(F(A,A),B),$$
$$P(F(A,B), F(F(A,B),A)) \land Q(F(A,B),A) \;\Rightarrow\; R(F(A,B),B),$$
$$\ldots\}$$

Notice that both the Herbrand universe and the Herbrand base can be infinite even if the original set of sentences S is finite.

HERBRAND'S
THEOREM

These definitions allow us to state a form of **Herbrand's theorem** (Herbrand, 1930):

If a set of clauses S is unsatisfiable, then there exists a finite subset of $H_S(S)$ that is also unsatisfiable.

RESOLUTION
CLOSURE

Let S' be this finite subset. Now it will be useful to introduce the **resolution closure** of S', which is the set of all clauses derivable by repeated application of the resolution inference step to clauses in S' or their derivatives. (To construct this closure, we could run a breadth-first search to completion using the resolution inference rule as the successor generator.) Let T be the resolution closure of S', and let $A_{S'} = \{A_1, A_2, \ldots, A_k\}$ be the set of atomic sentences occurring in S'. Notice that because S' is finite, $A_{S'}$ must also be finite. And because the clauses in T are constructed

GÖDEL'S INCOMPLETENESS THEOREM

By slightly extending the language of first-order logic to allow for the **mathematical induction schema** in arithmetic, Gödel was able to show, in his **incompleteness theorem**, that there are true arithmetic sentences that cannot be proved.

The proof of the incompleteness theorem is somewhat beyond the scope of this book, occupying, as it does, at least 30 pages, but we can give a hint here. We begin with the logical theory of numbers. In this theory, there is a single constant, 0, and a single function, S (the successor function). In the intended model, $S(0)$ denotes 1, $S(S(0))$ denotes 2, and so on; the language therefore has names for all the natural numbers. The vocabulary also includes the function symbols +, ×, and *Expt* (exponentiation), and the usual set of logical connectives and quantifiers. The first step is to notice that the set of sentences that we can write in this language can be enumerated. (Imagine defining an alphabetical order on the symbols and then arranging in alphabetical order each of the sets of sentences of length 1, 2, and so on.) We can then number each sentence α with a unique natural number #α (the **Gödel number**). This is crucial: number theory contains a name for each of its own sentences. Similarly, we can number each possible proof P with a Gödel number $G(P)$, because a proof is simply a finite sequence of sentences.

Now suppose we have a set A of sentences that are true statements about the natural numbers. Recalling that A can be named by a given set of integers, we can imagine writing in our language a sentence $\alpha(j, A)$ of the following sort:

> $\forall i$ i is not the Gödel number of a proof of the sentence whose Gödel number is j, where the proof uses only premises in A.

Then let σ be the sentence $\alpha(\#\sigma, A)$, that is, a sentence that states its own unprovability from A. (That this sentence always exists is true but not entirely obvious.)

Now we make the following ingenious argument. Suppose that σ *is* provable from A; then σ is false (because σ says it cannot be proved). But then we have a false sentence that is provable from A, so A cannot consist of only true sentences—a violation of our premise. Therefore σ is *not* provable from A. But this is exactly what σ itself claims; hence σ is a true sentence.

So, we have shown (barring 29 and a half pages) that for any set of true sentences of number theory, and in particular any set of basic axioms, there are other true sentences that *cannot* be proved from those axioms. This establishes, among other things, that we can never prove all the theorems of mathematics *within any given system of axioms*. Clearly, this was an important discovery for mathematics. Its significance for AI has been widely debated, beginning with speculations by Gödel himself. We take up the debate in Chapter 26.

entirely from members of $A_{S'}$, T must be finite because only a finite number of distinct clauses can be constructed from a finite vocabulary of atomic sentences. To illustrate these definitions, we will use a slimmed-down example:

$$S' = \{\, P(A), \; P(A) \Rightarrow Q(A), \; Q(A) \Rightarrow \textit{False} \,\}$$
$$A_{S'} = \{P(A), \; Q(A), \; \textit{False}\}$$
$$T = \{\, P(A), \; P(A) \Rightarrow Q(A), \; Q(A) \Rightarrow \textit{False}, \; Q(A), \; P(A) \Rightarrow \textit{False}, \textit{False} \,\}$$

Now we can state a completeness theorem for resolution on ground clauses. This is called the **ground resolution theorem**:

> If a set of ground clauses is unsatisfiable, then the resolution closure of those clauses contains the clause *False*.

We prove this theorem by showing its contrapositive: if the closure T does *not* contain *False*, then S' is satisfiable; in fact, we can construct a satisfying assignment for the atomic sentences in S'. The construction procedure is as follows:

> Pick an assignment (*True* or *False*) for each atomic sentence in $A_{S'}$ in some fixed order $A_1, \ldots, A_k$:
>
> – If there is a clause in T containing the literal $\neg A_i$, such that all its other literals are false under the assignment chosen for $A_1, \ldots, A_{i-1}$, then assign A_i to be *False*.
> – Otherwise, assign A_i to be *True*.

It is easy to show that the assignment so constructed will satisfy S', provided T is closed under resolution and does not contain the clause *False* (Exercise 9.10).

Now we have established that there is always a resolution proof involving some finite subset of the Herbrand base of S. The next step is to show that there is a resolution proof using the clauses of S itself, which are not necessarily ground clauses. We start by considering a single application of the resolution rule. Robinson's basic lemma implies the following fact:

> Let C_1 and C_2 be two clauses with no shared variables, and let C_1' and C_2' be ground instances of C_1 and C_2. If C' is a resolvent of C_1' and C_2', then there exists a clause C such that (1) C is a resolvent of C_1 and C_2, and (2) C' is a ground instance of C.

LIFTING LEMMA   This is called a **lifting lemma**, because it lifts a proof step from ground clauses up to general first-order clauses. In order to prove his basic lifting lemma, Robinson had to invent unification and derive all of the properties of most general unifiers. Rather than repeat the proof here, we simply illustrate the lemma:

$$C_1 = P(x, F(x, A)) \wedge Q(x, A) \Rightarrow R(x, B)$$
$$C_2 = N(G(y), z) \Rightarrow P(H(y), z)$$
$$C_1' = P(H(B), F(H(B), A)) \wedge Q(H(B), A) \Rightarrow R(H(B), B)$$
$$C_2' = N(G(B), F(H(B), A)) \Rightarrow P(H(B), F(H(B), A))$$
$$C' = N(G(B), F(H(B), A)) \wedge Q(H(B), A) \Rightarrow R(H(B), B)$$
$$C = N(G(y), F(H(y), A)) \wedge Q(H(y), A) \Rightarrow R(H(y), B)$$

We see that indeed C' is a ground instance of C. In general, for C_1' and C_2' to have any resolvents, they must be constructed by first applying to C_1 and C_2 the most general unifier of a pair of complementary literals in C_1 and C_2. From the lifting lemma, it is easy to derive a similar statement about any sequence of applications of the resolution rule:

> For any clause C' in the resolution closure of S', there is a clause C in the resolution closure of S, such that C' is a ground instance of C and the derivation of C is the same length as the derivation of C'.

From this fact, it follows that if the clause *False* appears in the resolution closure of S', it must also appear in the resolution closure of S. This is because *False* cannot be a ground instance of any other clause. To recap: we have shown that if S is unsatisfiable, then there is a finite derivation of the clause *False* using the resolution rule.

The lifting of theorem proving from ground clauses to first-order clauses provided a vast increase in power. This derives from the fact that the first-order proof need instantiate variables only as far as necessary for the proof, whereas the ground-clause methods were required to examine a huge number of arbitrary instantiations.

9.8   SUMMARY

We have presented an analysis of logical inference in first-order logic, and a number of algorithms for doing it.

- A simple extension of the propositional inference rules allows the construction of proofs for first-order logic. Unfortunately, the branching factor for the quantifier is huge.

- The use of **unification** to identify appropriate substitutions for variables eliminates the instantiation step in first-order proofs, making the process much more efficient.

- A generalized version of **Modus Ponens** uses unification to provide a natural and powerful inference rule, which can be used in a backward-chaining or forward-chaining algorithm.

- The canonical form for Modus Ponens is **Horn form**:

$$p_1 \wedge \ldots \wedge p_n \Rightarrow q, \text{ where } p_i \text{ and } q \text{ are atoms.}$$

This form cannot represent all sentences, and Modus Ponens is not a complete proof system.

- The generalized **resolution** inference rule provides a complete system for proof by refutation. It requires a normal form, but *any* sentence can be put into the form.

- Resolution can work with either **conjunctive normal form**—each sentence is a disjunction of literals—or **implicative normal form**—each sentence is of the form

$$p_1 \wedge \ldots \wedge p_n \Rightarrow q_1 \vee \ldots \vee q_m, \text{ where } p_i \text{ and } q_i \text{ are atoms.}$$

- Several strategies exist for reducing the search space of a resolution system without compromising completeness.

BIBLIOGRAPHICAL AND HISTORICAL NOTES

SYLLOGISM

Logical inference was studied extensively in Greek mathematics. The type of inference most carefully studied by Aristotle was the **syllogism**. The syllogism is divided into "figures" and "moods," depending on the order of the terms (which we would call predicates) in the sentences, the degree of generality (which we would today interpret through quantifiers) applied to each term, and whether each term is negated. The most fundamental syllogism is that of the first mood of the first figure:

> All S are M.
> All M are P.
> Therefore, all S are P.

Aristotle tried to prove the validity of other syllogisms by "reducing" them to those of the first figure. He was much less precise in describing what this "reduction" should involve than he was in characterizing the syllogistic figures and moods themselves.

Rigorous and explicit analysis of inference rules was one of the strong points of Megarian and Stoic propositional logic. The Stoics took five basic inference rules as valid without proof and then rigorously derived all others from these five. The first and most important of the five rules was the one known today as Modus Ponens. The Stoics were much more precise about what was meant by derivation than Aristotle had been about what was meant by reduction of one syllogism to another. They also used the "Principle of Conditionalization," which states that if q can be inferred validly from p, then the conditional "$p \Rightarrow q$" is logically true. Both these principles figure prominently in contemporary logic.

Inference rules, other than logically valid schemas, were not a major focus either for Boole or for Frege. Boole's logic was closely modeled on the algebra of numbers. It relied mainly on the **equality substitution** inference rule, which allows one to conclude $P(t)$ given $P(s)$ and $s = t$. Logically valid schemas were used to obtain equations to which equality substitution could be applied. Whereas Frege's logic was much more general than Boole's, it too relied on an abundance of logically valid schemas plus a single inference rule that had premises—in Frege's case, this rule was Modus Ponens. Frege took advantage of the fact that the effect of an inference rule of the form "From p infer q" can be simulated by applying Modus Ponens to p along with a logically valid schema $p \Rightarrow q$. This "axiomatic" style of exposition, using Modus Ponens plus a number of logically valid schemas, was employed by a number of logicians after Frege; most notably, it was used in *Principia Mathematica* (Whitehead and Russell, 1910).

One of the earliest types of systems (after Frege) to focus prominently on inference rules was **natural deduction**, introduced by Gerhard Gentzen (1934) and by Stanisław Jáskowski (1934). Natural deduction is called "natural" because it does not require sentences to be subjected to extensive preprocessing before it can be applied to them (as many other proof procedures do) and because its inference rules are thought to be more intuitive than, say, the resolution rule. Natural deduction makes frequent use of the Principle of Conditionalization. The objects manipulated by Gentzen's inference rules are called *sequents*. A sequent can be regarded either as a logical argument (a pair of a set of premises and a set of alternative conclusions, intended to be an instance of some valid rule of inference) or as a sentence in implicative normal form. Prawitz (1965) offers a book-length treatment of natural deduction. Gallier (1986) uses Gentzen sequents to expound the theoretical underpinnings of automated deduction.

Conjunctive normal form and disjunctive normal form for propositional formulas were known to Schröder (1877), although the principles underlying the construction of these forms go back at least to Boole. The use of clausal form (conjunctive normal form for first-order logic) depends upon certain techniques for manipulating quantifiers, in particular skolemization. Whitehead and Russell (1910) expounded the so-called *rules of passage* (the actual term is from Herbrand (1930)) that are used to move quantifiers to the front of formulas. (Moving all the quantifiers to the front of a formula is called *prenexing* the formula, and a formula with all the quantifiers in front is said to be in **prenex form**.) Horn form was introduced by Alfred Horn (1951). What we have called "implicative normal form" was used (with a right-to-left implication symbol) in Robert Kowalski's (1979b) *Logic for Problem Solving*, and this way of writing clauses is sometimes called "Kowalski form."

Skolem constants and Skolem functions were introduced, appropriately enough, by Thoralf Skolem (1920). The general procedure for skolemization is given in (Skolem, 1928), along with the important notion of the Herbrand universe.

Herbrand's theorem, named after the French logician Jacques Herbrand (1930), has played a vital role in the development of automated reasoning methods, both before and after Robinson's introduction of resolution. This is reflected in our reference to the "Herbrand universe" rather than the "Skolem universe," even though Skolem really invented this concept (and indeed Herbrand does not explicitly use Skolem functions and constants, but a less elegant although roughly equivalent device). Herbrand can also be regarded as the inventor of unification, because a variant of the unification algorithm occurs in (Herbrand, 1930).

First-order logic was shown to have complete proof procedures by Gödel (1930), using methods similar to those of Skolem and Herbrand. Alan Turing (1936) and Alonzo Church (1936) simultaneously showed, using very different proofs, that validity in first-order logic was not decidable. The excellent text by Enderton (1972) explains all of these results in a rigorous yet moderately understandable fashion.

The first mechanical device to carry out logical inferences was constructed by the third Earl of Stanhope (1753–1816). The Stanhope Demonstrator could handle syllogisms and certain inferences in the theory of probability. The first mechanical device to carry out inferences in *mathematical* logic was William Stanley Jevons's "logical piano," constructed in 1869. Jevons was one of the nineteenth-century logicians who expanded and improved Boole's work; the logical piano carried out reasoning in Boolean logic. An entertaining and instructive history of these and other early mechanical devices for reasoning is given by Martin Gardner (1968).

The first published results from research on automated deduction using electronic computers were those of Newell, Shaw, and Simon (1957) on the Logic Theorist. This program was based on an attempt to model human thought processes. Martin Davis (1957) had actually designed a program that came up with a proof in 1954, but the Logic Theorist's results were published slightly earlier. Both Davis's 1954 program and the Logic Theorist were based on somewhat ad hoc methods that did not strongly influence later automated deduction.

It was Abraham Robinson who suggested attempting to use Herbrand's Theorem to generate proofs mechanically. Gilmore (1960) wrote a program that uses Robinson's suggestion in a way influenced by the "Beth tableaux" method of proof (Beth, 1955). Davis and Putnam (1960) introduced clausal form, and produced a program that attempted to find refutations by substituting members of the Herbrand universe for variables to produce ground clauses and then looking for propositional inconsistencies among the ground clauses. Prawitz (1960) developed the key idea of letting the quest for propositional inconsistency drive the search process, and generating terms from the Herbrand universe only when it was necessary to do so in order to establish propositional inconsistency. After further development by other researchers, this idea led J. A. Robinson (no relation) to develop the resolution method (Robinson, 1965), which used unification in its modern form to allow the demonstration of propositional inconsistency without necessarily making explicit use of terms from the Herbrand universe. The so-called "inverse method" developed at about the same time by the Soviet researcher S. Maslov (1964; 1967) is based on principles somewhat different from Robinson's resolution method but offers similar computational advantages in avoiding the unnecessary generation of terms in the Herbrand universe. The relations between resolution and the inverse method are explored by Maslov (1971) and by Kuehner (1971).

The demodulation rule described in the chapter was intended to eliminate equality axioms by combining equality substitution with resolution, and was introduced by Wos (1967). Term rewriting systems such as the Knuth–Bendix algorithm (Knuth and Bendix, 1970) are based on demodulation, and have found wide application in programming languages. The paramodulation inference rule (Wos and Robinson, 1968) is a more general version of demodulation that provides a complete proof procedure for first-order logic with equality.

In addition to demodulation and paramodulation for equality reasoning, other special-purpose inference rules have been introduced to aid reasoning of other kinds. Boyer and Moore (1979) provide powerful methods for the use of mathematical induction in automated reasoning, although their logic unfortunately lacks quantifiers and does not quite have the full power of first-order logic. Stickel's (1985) "theory resolution" and Manna and Waldinger's (1986) method of "special relations" provide general ways of incorporating special-purpose inference rules into a resolution-style framework.

A number of control strategies have been proposed for resolution, beginning with the unit preference strategy (Wos *et al.*, 1964). The set of support strategy was proposed by Wos *et al.* (1965), to provide a degree of goal-directedness in resolution. *Linear resolution* first appeared in (Loveland, 1968). Wolfgang Bibel (1981) developed the **connection method** which allows complex deductions to be recognized efficiently. Developments in resolution control strategies, and the accompanying growth in the understanding of the relationship between completeness and syntactic restrictions on clauses, contributed significantly to the development of **logic programming** (see Chapter 10). Genesereth and Nilsson (1987, Chapter 5) provide a short but thorough analysis of a wide variety of control strategies.

There are a number of good general-purpose introductions to automated deduction and to the theory of proof and inference; some were mentioned in Chapter 7. Additional textbooks on matters related to completeness and undecidability include *Computability and Logic* (Boolos and Jeffrey, 1989), *Metalogic* (Hunter, 1971), and (for an entertaining and unconventional, yet highly rigorous approach) *A Course in Mathematical Logic* (Manin, 1977). Many of the most important papers from the turn-of-the-century development of mathematical logic are to be found in *From Frege to Gödel: A Source Book in Mathematical Logic* (van Heijenoort, 1967). The journal of record for the field of pure mathematical logic (as opposed to automated deduction) is *The Journal of Symbolic Logic*.

Textbooks geared toward automated deduction include (in addition to those mentioned in Chapter 7) the classic *Symbolic Logic and Mechanical Theorem Proving* (Chang and Lee, 1973) and, more recently, *Automated Reasoning: Introduction and Applications* (Wos *et al.*, 1992). The two-volume anthology *Automation of Reasoning* (Siekmann and Wrightson, 1983) includes many important papers on automated deduction from 1957 to 1970. The historical summaries prefacing each volume provide a concise yet thorough overview of the history of the field. Further important historical information is available from Loveland's "Automated Theorem Proving: A Quarter-Century Review" (1984) and from the bibliography of (Wos *et al.*, 1992).

The principal journal for the field of theorem proving is the *Journal of Automated Reasoning*; important results are also frequently reported in the proceedings of the annual Conferences on Automated Deduction (CADE). Research in theorem proving is also strongly related to the use of logic in analyzing programs and programming languages, for which the principal conference is Logic in Computer Science.

EXERCISES

9.1   For each of the following pairs of atomic sentences, give the most general unifier, if it exists.

  a. $P(A, B, B)$, $P(x, y, z)$.
  b. $Q(y, G(A, B))$, $Q(G(x, x), y)$.
  c. $Older(Father(y), y)$, $Older(Father(x), John)$.
  d. $Knows(Father(y), y)$, $Knows(x, x)$.

9.2   One might suppose that we can avoid the problem of variable conflict in unification by standardizing apart all of the sentences in the knowledge base once and for all. Show that for some sentences, this approach cannot work. (*Hint*: Consider a sentence, one part of which unifies with another.)

9.3   Show that the final state of the knowledge base after a series of calls to FORWARD-CHAIN is independent of the order of the calls. Does the number of inference steps required depend on the order in which sentences are added? Suggest a useful heuristic for choosing an order.

9.4   Write down logical representations for the following sentences, suitable for use with Generalized Modus Ponens:

  a. Horses, cows, and pigs are mammals.
  b. An offspring of a horse is a horse.
  c. Bluebeard is a horse.
  d. Bluebeard is Charlie's parent.
  e. Offspring and parent are inverse relations.
  f. Every mammal has a parent.

9.5   In this question we will use the sentences you wrote in Exercise 9.4 to answer a question using a backward-chaining algorithm.

   a. Draw the proof tree generated by an exhaustive backward-chaining algorithm for the query $\exists h \; Horse(h)$.

   b. What do you notice about this domain?

   c. How many solutions for h actually follow from your sentences?

   d. Can you think of a way to find all of them? (*Hint*: You might want to consult (Smith *et al.*, 1986).)

9.6   A popular children's riddle is "Brothers and sisters have I none, but that man's father is my father's son." Use the rules of the family domain (Chapter 7) to show who that man is. You may use any of the inference methods described in this chapter.

9.7   How can resolution be used to show that a sentence is

   a. Valid?

   b. Unsatisfiable?

9.8   From "Horses are animals," it follows that "The head of a horse is the head of an animal." Demonstrate that this inference is valid by carrying out the following steps:

   a. Translate the premise and the conclusion into the language of first-order logic. Use three predicates: $HeadOf(h, x)$, $Horse(x)$, and $Animal(x)$.

   b. Negate the conclusion, and convert the premise and the negated conclusion into conjunctive normal form.

   c. Use resolution to show that the conclusion follows from the premise.

9.9   Here are two sentences in the language of first-order logic:

   (A): $\forall x \; \exists y \; (x \geq y)$
   (B): $\exists y \; \forall x \; (x \geq y)$

   a. Assume that the variables range over all the natural numbers $0, 1, 2, \ldots, \infty$, and that the "$\geq$" predicate means "greater than or equal to." Under this interpretation, translate these sentences into English.

   b. Is (A) true under this interpretation?

   c. Is (B) true under this interpretation?

   d. Does (A) logically entail (B)?

   e. Does (B) logically entail (A)?

   f. Try to prove that (A) follows from (B) using resolution. Do this even if you think that (B) does not logically entail (A); continue until the proof breaks down and you cannot proceed (if it does break down). Show the unifying substitution for each resolution step. If the proof fails, explain exactly where, how, and why it breaks down.

   g. Now try to prove that (B) follows from (A).

9.10 In this exercise, you will complete the proof of the ground resolution theorem given in the chapter. The proof rests on the claim that if T is the resolution closure of a set of ground clauses S', and T does not contain the clause *False*, then a satisfying assignment can be constructed for S' using the construction given in the chapter. Show that the assignment does indeed satisfy S', as claimed.

10 LOGICAL REASONING SYSTEMS

In which we show how to build efficient programs that reason with logic.

10.1 INTRODUCTION

We have explained that it is a good idea to build agents as reasoning systems—systems that explicitly represent and reason with knowledge. The main advantage of such systems is a high degree of modularity. The control structure can be isolated from the knowledge, and each piece of knowledge can be largely independent of the others. This makes it easier to experiment with the system and modify it, makes it easier for the system to explain its workings to another agent, and, as we will see in Part VI, makes it easier for the system to learn on its own.

In this chapter the rubber hits the road, so to speak, and we discuss ways in which these advantages can be realized in an actual, efficient system. Automated reasoning systems come in several flavors, each designed to address different kinds of problems. We group them into four main categories:

THEOREM PROVERS
LOGIC
PROGRAMMING
LANGUAGES

◇ **Theorem provers** and **logic programming languages**: Theorem provers use resolution (or some other complete inference procedure) to prove sentences in full first-order logic, often for mathematical and scientific reasoning tasks. They can also be used to answer questions: the proof of a sentence containing variables serves as an answer to a question because it instantiates the variables. Logic programming languages typically restrict the logic, disallowing full treatment of negation, disjunction, and/or equality. They usually use backward chaining, and may include some nonlogical features of programming languages (such as input and output). Examples of theorem provers: SAM, AURA, OTTER. Examples of logic programming languages: Prolog, MRS, LIFE.

PRODUCTION
SYSTEMS

◇ **Production systems**: Like logic programming languages, these use implications as their primary representation. The consequent of each implication is interpreted as an action recommendation, rather than simply a logical conclusion. Actions include insertions and

297

deletions from the knowledge base as well as input and output. Production systems operate with a forward-chaining control structure. Some have a conflict resolution mechanism to decide which action to take when more than one is recommended. Examples: OPS-5, CLIPS, SOAR.

FRAME SYSTEMS
SEMANTIC
NETWORKS

◇ **Frame systems** and **semantic networks**: These systems use the metaphor that objects are nodes in a graph, that these nodes are organized in a taxonomic structure, and that links between nodes represent binary relations. In frame systems the binary relations are thought of as slots in one frame that are filled by another, whereas in semantic networks, they are thought of as arrows between nodes. The choice between the frame metaphor and the semantic network metaphor determines whether you draw the resulting networks as nested boxes or as graphs, but the meaning and implementation of the two types of systems can be identical. In this chapter we will say "semantic network" to mean "semantic network or frame system." Examples of frame systems: OWL, FRAIL, KODIAK. Examples of semantic networks: SNEPS, NETL, Conceptual Graphs.

DESCRIPTION LOGIC
SYSTEMS

◇ **Description logic systems**: These systems evolved from semantic networks due to pressure to formalize what the networks mean while retaining the emphasis on taxonomic structure as an organizing principle. The idea is to express and reason with complex definitions of, and relations among, objects and classes. Description logics are sometimes called **terminological logics**, because they concentrate on defining terms. Recent work has concentrated on the trade-off between expressivity in the language and the computational complexity of certain operations. Examples: KL-ONE, CLASSIC, LOOM.

TERMINOLOGICAL
LOGICS

In this chapter, we will see how each of the four types of systems can be implemented, and how each of the following five tasks is addressed:

1. Add a new fact to the knowledge base. This could be a percept, or a fact derived via inference. We call this function TELL.

2. Given a knowledge base and a new fact, derive some of the facts implied by the conjunction of the knowledge base and the new fact. In a forward-chaining system, this is part of TELL.

3. Decide if a query is entailed by the knowledge base. We call this function ASK. Different versions of ASK do different things, ranging from just confirming that the query is entailed to returning a set of all the possible substitutions that make the query true.

4. Decide if a query is explicitly stored in the knowledge base—a restricted version of ASK.

5. Remove a sentence from the knowledge base. It is important to distinguish between correcting a sentence that proves to be false, forgetting a sentence that is no longer useful (perhaps because it was only relevant in the past), and updating the knowledge base to reflect a change in the world, while still remembering how the world was in the past. (Some systems can make this distinction; others rely on the knowledge engineer to keep things straight.)

All knowledge-based systems rely on the fundamental operation of retrieving sentences satisfying certain conditions—for example, finding an atomic sentence that unifies with a query, or finding an implication that has a given atomic sentence as one of its premises. We will therefore begin with techniques for maintaining a knowledge base in a form that supports efficient retrieval.

10.2   INDEXING, RETRIEVAL, AND UNIFICATION

The functions TELL and ASK can in general do complicated reasoning using forward and backward chaining or resolution. In this section, we consider two simpler functions that implement the part of TELL and ASK that deals directly with the physical implementation of the knowledge base. We call these functions STORE and FETCH. We also describe the implementation of a unification algorithm, another basic component of knowledge-based systems.

Implementing sentences and terms

The first step in building a reasoning system is to define the data types for sentences and terms. This involves defining both the syntax of sentences—the format for interacting with the user at the logic level—and the internal representation in which the system will store and manipulate sentences at the implementation level. There may be several internal representations for different aspects of sentences. For example, there may be one form that allows the system to print sentences and another to represent sentences that have been converted to clausal form.

Our basic data type will represent the application of an operator (which could be a predicate, a function symbol or a logical connective) to a list of arguments (which could be terms or sentences). We will call this general data type a COMPOUND. It has fields for the operator (OP) and arguments (ARGS). For example, let c be the compound $P(x) \land Q(x)$; then $\text{OP}[c] = \land$ and $\text{ARGS}[c] = [\, P(x),\ Q(x)\,]$.

Store and fetch

Now that we have a data type for sentences and terms, we need to be able to maintain a set of sentences in a knowledge base, which means storing them in such a way that they can be fetched efficiently. Typically, FETCH is responsible for finding sentences in the knowledge base that unify with the query, or at least have the same syntactic structure. ASK is responsible for the inference strategy, which results in a series of calls to FETCH. *The computational cost of inference is dominated by two aspects: the search strategy used by ASK and the data structures used to implement FETCH.*

The call STORE(KB,S) adds each conjunct of the sentence S to the knowledge base KB. The simplest approach is to implement the knowledge base as an array or linked list of conjuncts. For example, after

TELL(KB, $A \land \neg B$)
TELL(KB, $\neg C \land D$)

the KB will contain a list with the elements

$[A, \neg B, \neg C, D]$

The call FETCH(KB,Q) must then go through the elements of the knowledge base one at a time until it either finds a conjunct that matches Q or reaches the end. With this approach FETCH takes

$O(n)$ time on an n-element *KB*. STORE takes $O(1)$ time to add a conjunct to the *KB*, but if we want to ensure that no duplicates are added, then STORE is also $O(n)$. This is impractical if one wants to do serious inference.

Table-based indexing

A better approach is to implement the knowledge base as a hash table.[1] If we only had to deal with ground literal sentences[2] we could implement STORE so that when given P it stores the value *true* in the hash table under the key P, and when given $\neg P$, it stores *false* under the key P. Then FETCH could do a simple lookup in the hash table, and both FETCH and STORE would be $O(1)$.

There are two problems with this approach: it does not deal with complex sentences other than negated sentences, and it does not deal with variables within sentences. So FETCH would not be able to find "an implication with P as consequent," such as might be required by a backward-chaining algorithm; nor could it find *Brother(Richard, John)* when given a query $\exists x \ Brother(Richard, x)$.

The solution is to make STORE maintain a more complex table. We assume the sentences are all converted to a normal form. (We use implicative normal form.) The keys to the table will be predicate symbols, and the value stored under each key will have four components:

- A list of positive literals for that predicate symbol.
- A list of negative literals.
- A list of sentences in which the predicate is in the conclusion.
- A list of sentences in which the predicate is in the premise.

So, given the knowledge base:

$$Brother(Richard, John)$$
$$Brother(Ted, Jack) \land Brother(Jack, Bobbie)$$
$$\neg Brother(Ann, Sam)$$
$$Brother(x, y) \ \Rightarrow \ Male(x)$$
$$Brother(x, y) \land Male(y) \ \Rightarrow \ Brother(y, x)$$
$$Male(Jack) \land Male(Ted) \land \ldots \land \neg Male(Ann) \land \ldots$$

the table for the knowledge base would be as shown in Figure 10.1.

Now suppose that we ask the query

$$\text{ASK}(KB, Brother(Jack, Ted))$$

and that ASK uses backward chaining (see Section 9.4). It would first call FETCH to find a positive literal matching the query. Because that fails, FETCH is called to find an implication with *Brother* as the consequent. The query matches the consequent, the antecedent becomes the new goal after the appropriate substitution is applied, and the procedure begins again.

---

[1] A hash table is a data structure for storing and retrieving information indexed by fixed *keys*. For practical purposes, a hash table can be considered to have constant storage and retrieval times, even when the table contains a vary large number of items.

[2] Remember that a **ground literal** contains no variables. It is either an atomic sentence such as *Brother(Richard, John)* or a negated atomic sentence such as $\neg Brother(Ann, Victoria)$.

Key	Positive	Negative	Conclusion	Premise
Brother	*Brother(Richard,John)* *Brother(Ted,Jack)* *Brother(Jack,Bobbie)*	*¬Brother(Ann,Sam)*	$Brother(x,y) \land Male(y)$ $\Rightarrow Brother(y,x)$	$Brother(x,y) \land Male(y)$ $\Rightarrow Brother(y,x)$ $Brother(x,y) \Rightarrow Male(x)$
Male	*Male(Jack)* *Male(Ted)* . . .	*¬Male(Ann)* . . .	$Brother(x,y) \Rightarrow Male(x)$	$Brother(x,y) \land Male(y)$ $\Rightarrow Brother(y,x)$

Figure 10.1   Table-based indexing for a collection of logical sentences.

Because in first-order logic the predicate is always fixed in a query, the simple device of dividing up the knowledge base by predicate reduces the cost of fetching considerably. But why stop with just the predicate?

Tree-based indexing

Table-based indexing is ideal when there are many predicate symbols and a few clauses for each symbol. But in some applications, there are many clauses for a given predicate symbol. For example, in a knowledge base for the U.S. Census Bureau that uses social security numbers to represent people, the query *Brother*(012-34-5678, x) would require a search through millions of *Brother* literals.

To make this search efficient, we need to index on the arguments as well as on the predicate symbols themselves. One way to do this is to change the table entry for *Brother* so that each entry is itself a table, indexed by the first argument, rather than just a list. So to answer the query *Brother*(012-34-5678, x), we first look in the predicate table under *Brother*, and then look in that entry under 012-34-5678. Both table lookups take a small constant amount of time, so the complete FETCH is efficient. We can view the process of searching for a matching literal as a walk down a tree, where the branch at each point is dictated by the symbol at the appropriate point in the query sentence (Figure 10.2).

TREE-BASED INDEXING

COMBINED INDEXING

Tree-based indexing is one form of **combined indexing**, in that it essentially makes a combined key out of the sequence of predicate and argument symbols in the query. Unfortunately, it provides little help when one of the symbols in the sequence is a variable, because every branch has to be followed in that case. Suppose our census knowledge base has a predicate *Taxpayer* with four arguments: a person, a zip code, a net income to the nearest thousand, and the number of dependents, for example:

Taxpayer(012-34-5678, 02138, 32000, 10)

Suppose we were interested in finding all the people in zip code 02138 with exactly 10 dependents:

FETCH(*Taxpayer*(p, 02138, i, 10))

There are tens of thousands of people with that zip code, and hundreds of thousands of people in the country with 10 dependents, but there are probably only a few people that match both criteria. To find those people without undue effort, we need a combined index based on both the second and fourth argument. If we are to deal with every possible set of variable positions, we will need

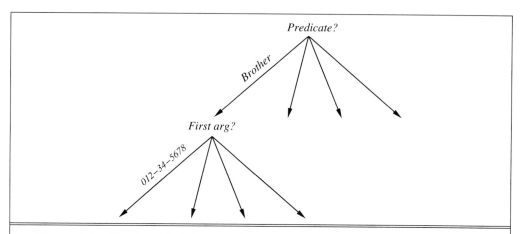

Figure 10.2   Tree-based indexing organizes a knowledge base into a nested series of hash tables. Each node in the tree is a hash table indexed by the value at a particular sentence position.

2^n combined indices, where n is the number of symbol positions in the sentences being stored. When sentences include complex terms, n can easily grow quite large. At some point, the extra storage needed for the indices and the extra work that STORE must do to maintain them outweigh the benefits. We can respond by adopting a fixed policy, such as maintaining indices only on keys composed of predicate plus each argument; or by using an adaptive policy that creates indices to meet the demands of the kinds of queries being asked.

CROSS-INDEXING   The **cross-indexing** strategy indexes entries in several places, and when faced with a query chooses the most promising place for retrieval. Suppose we have the query

FETCH(*Taxpayer*(*p*, 02138, 20000, 3))

and the four available indices key on *Taxpayer* plus each of the four argument positions separately. A sentence matching the query will be indexed under *Taxpayer*(_, 02138, _, _), *Taxpayer*(_, _, 20000, _), and *Taxpayer*(_, _, _, 3). The best strategy is usually to search through whichever of these collections of sentences is smallest.

The unification algorithm

In Section 9.3 we showed how two statements such as

$Knows(John, x) \Rightarrow Hates(John, x)$
$Knows(John, Jane)$

can be combined to infer *Hates*(*John*, *Jane*). The key to this Modus Ponens inference is to unify *Knows*(*John*, *x*) and *Knows*(*John*, *Jane*). This unification yields as a result the substitution {*x*/*Jane*}, which can then be applied to *Hates*(*John*, *x*) to give the solution *Hates*(*John*, *Jane*).

We have seen that by clever indexing, we can reduce the number of calls to the unification algorithm, but this number still can be quite large. Thus, the unification algorithm should be efficient. The algorithm shown in Figure 10.3 is reasonably simple. It recursively explores the two expressions simultaneously, building up a unifier as it goes along but failing if it ever finds two corresponding points in the structures that do not match. Unfortunately, it has one expensive step. The **occur-check** takes time linear in the size of the expression being checked, and is done for each variable found. It makes the time complexity of the algorithm $O(n^2)$ in the size of the expressions being unified. Later we will see how to make this algorithm more efficient by eliminating the need for explicit representations of substitutions. On page 308, we see how unification can be extended to handle more information besides equality.

---

function UNIFY(x, y) **returns** a substitution to make x and y identical, if possible

  UNIFY-INTERNAL(x, y, { })

---

function UNIFY-INTERNAL(x, y, θ) **returns** a substitution to make x and y identical (given θ)
  inputs: x, a variable, constant, list, or compound
       y, a variable, constant, list, or compound
       θ, the substitution built up so far

  if θ = failure **then return** failure
  else if x = y **then return** θ
  else if VARIABLE?(x) **then return** UNIFY-VAR(x, y, θ)
  else if VARIABLE?(y) **then return** UNIFY-VAR(y, x, θ)
  else if COMPOUND?(x) **and** COMPOUND?(y) **then**
    return UNIFY-INTERNAL(ARGS[x], ARGS[y], UNIFY-INTERNAL(OP[x], OP[y], θ))
  else if LIST?(x) **and** LIST?(y) **then**
    return UNIFY-INTERNAL(REST[x], REST[y], UNIFY-INTERNAL(FIRST[x], FIRST[y], θ))
  else return failure

---

function UNIFY-VAR(var, x, θ) **returns** a substitution
  inputs: var, a variable
      x, any expression
      θ, the substitution built up so far

  if {var/val} ∈ θ
    then return UNIFY-INTERNAL(val, x, θ)
  else if {x/val} ∈ θ
    then return UNIFY-INTERNAL(var, val, θ)
  else if var occurs anywhere in x /* occur-check */
    then return failure
  else return add {x/var} to θ

Figure 10.3   The unification algorithm. The algorithm works by comparing the structures of the inputs, element by element. The substitution θ that is the argument to UNIFY-INTERNAL is built up along the way, and used to make sure that later comparisons are consistent with bindings that were established earlier.

10.3   LOGIC PROGRAMMING SYSTEMS

We now turn from the details of implementing a knowledge base to a comparison of ways in which a knowledge base can be constructed and used. We start with logic programming.

We have seen that the declarative approach has many advantages for building intelligent systems. Logic programming tries to extend these advantages to all programming tasks. *Any computation can be viewed as a process of making explicit the consequences of choosing a particular program for a particular machine and providing particular inputs.* Logic programming views the program and inputs as logical statements about the world, and the process of making consequences explicit as a process of inference. The relation between logic and algorithms is summed up in Robert Kowalski's equation

$$Algorithm = Logic + Control$$

PROLOG
A logic programming language makes it possible to write algorithms by augmenting logical sentences with information to control the inference process. **Prolog** is by far the most widely used logic programming language. Its users number in the hundreds of thousands. It is used primarily as a rapid-prototyping language and for symbol-manipulation tasks such as writing compilers (Van Roy, 1990) and parsing natural language (Pereira and Warren, 1980). It has also been used to develop expert system applications in legal, medical, financial, and other domains.

The Prolog language

We have already explained the notational conventions of Prolog in Chapter 7. Viewed as a logical knowledge base, a Prolog program has the following characteristics:

- A program consists of a sequence of sentences, implicitly conjoined. All variables have implicit universal quantification, and variables in different sentences are considered distinct.
- Only Horn clause sentences are acceptable. This means that each sentence is either an atomic sentence or an implication with no negated antecedents and an atomic consequent.
- Terms can be constant symbols, variables, or functional terms.
- Queries can include conjunctions, disjunctions, variables, and functional terms.

NEGATION AS FAILURE
- Instead of negated antecedents in implications, Prolog uses a **negation as failure** operator: a goal not P is considered proved if the system fails to prove P.
- All syntactically distinct terms are assumed to refer to distinct objects. That is, you cannot assert $A = B$ or $A = F(x)$, where A is a constant. You can assert $x = B$ or $x = F(y)$, where x is a variable.
- There is a large set of built-in predicates for arithmetic, input/output, and various system and knowledge base functions. Literals using these predicates are "proved" by executing code rather than doing further inference. In Prolog notation (where capitalized names are variables), the goal X is 4+3 succeeds with X bound to 7. However, the goal 5 is X+Y cannot be proved, because the built-in functions do not do arbitrary equation solving.[3]

---

[3] Note that if proper axioms are provided for addition, such goals can be solved by inference within a Prolog program.

As an example, here is a Prolog program for the *Member* relation, given both in normal first-order logic notation and in the format actually used by Prolog:

$$\forall x, l \; Member(x, [x|l])$$
```
member(X,[X|L]).
```

$$\forall x, y, l \; Member(x, l) \Rightarrow$$
$$Member(x, [y|l])$$
```
member(X,[Y|L]) :-
  member(X,L).
```

HEAD

BODY

As we mentioned in Chapter 7, the Prolog representation has the consequent, or **head**, on the left-hand side, and the antecedents, or **body**, on the right. A Prolog clause is often read as "To prove ⟨the head⟩, prove ⟨the body⟩." To preserve this intuitive reading along with our logical notation, we will compromise and write Prolog clauses using a leftward implication. For example, the second clause of the *Member* definition becomes

$$Member(x, [y|l]) \Leftarrow Member(x, l)$$

The definition of *Member* can be used to answer several kinds of queries. It can be used to confirm that *Member*(2, [1, 2, 3]) is true. It can also enumerate the three values of x that make *Member*(x, [1, 2, 3]) true. It can be used to find the value of x such that *Member*(2, [1, x, 3]) is true. It even can be used to enumerate the lists for which *Member*(1, *list*) is true.

Implementation

The designers of Prolog made a number of implementation decisions designed to provide a simple, fast execution model:

- All inferences are done by backward chaining, with depth-first search. That means that whenever there is a dead end in the attempt to prove a sentence, Prolog backs up to the most recent step that has alternatives.
- The order of search through the conjuncts of an antecedent is strictly left to right, and clauses in the knowledge base are applied in first-to-last order.
- The occur-check is omitted from the unification routine.

The omission of the occur-check makes Prolog inference unsound, but actual errors happen very seldom in practice. The use of depth-first search makes Prolog incomplete, because of infinite paths created by circular sentences (but see page 311 for another approach). Programmers must therefore keep termination in mind when writing recursive sentences. Despite these caveats, one good point of Prolog is that *the execution model is simple enough that a trained programmer can add control information to yield an efficient program.*

Like our BACK-CHAIN algorithm (page 275), Prolog enumerates all the solutions to a query, but it does not gather them into a set. Instead, it is up to the user's program to do what it will with each solution as it is enumerated. The most common thing to do is to print the answers. In fact, Prolog's top level does this automatically. A query such as

```
member(loc(X,X),[loc(1,1),loc(2,1),loc(2,2)])?
```

results in the user seeing two pieces of output, "X = 1" and "X = 2".

The execution of a Prolog program can happen in two modes: interpreted and compiled. Compilation is discussed in the next subsection. Interpretation essentially amounts to running the BACK-CHAIN algorithm from Section 9.4, with the program as the knowledge base. We say "essentially," because Prolog interpreters contain a variety of improvements designed to maximize speed. Here we consider only two.

First, instead of constructing the list of all possible answers for each subgoal before continuing to the next, Prolog interpreters generate one answer and a "promise" to generate the CHOICE POINT rest when the current answer has been fully explored. This promise is called a **choice point**. When the depth-first search completes its exploration of the possible solutions arising from the current answer and backs up to the choice point, the choice point is expanded to yield a new answer for the subgoal and a new choice point. This approach saves both time and space. It also provides a very simple interface for debugging because at all times there is only a single solution path under consideration.

Second, our simple implementation of BACK-CHAIN spends a good deal of time generating substitutions and applying them to query lists. Prolog eliminates the need for a *substitution* data type by implementing logic variables that can remember their current binding. At any point in time every variable in the program is either unbound or is bound to some value. Together, these variables and values implicitly define a substitution. Of course, there is only one such substitution at a time, but that is all we need. The substitution is the right one for the current path in the search tree. Extending the path can only add new variable bindings, because an attempt to add a different binding for an already-bound variable results in a failure of unification. When a path in the search fails, Prolog will back up to a previous choice point, and then it may have to unbind some variables. This is done by keeping track of all the variables that have been bound in a stack TRAIL called the **trail**. As each new variable is bound by UNIFY-VAR, the variable is pushed onto the trail stack. When a goal fails and it is time to back up to a previous choice point, each of the variables is unbound as it is removed from the trail.

Compilation of logic programs

It is possible to make a reasonably efficient Prolog interpreter by following the guidelines in the previous subsection. But interpreting programs in any language, including Prolog, is necessarily slower than running compiled code. This is because the interpreter always behaves as if it has never seen the program before. A Prolog interpreter must do database retrieval to find sentences that match the goal, and analysis of sentence structure to decide what subgoals to generate. All serious heavy-duty Prolog programming is done with compiled code. The great advantage of compilation is that when it is time to execute the inference process, we can use inference routines specifically designed for the sentences in the knowledge base. Prolog basically generates a miniature theorem prover for each different predicate, thereby eliminating much of the overhead OPEN-CODE of interpretation. It is also possible to **open-code** the unification routine for each different call, thereby avoiding explicit analysis of term structure. (For details of open-coded unification, see Warren *et al.* (1977).)

The instruction sets of today's computers give a poor match with Prolog's semantics, so most Prolog compilers compile into an intermediate language rather than directly into machine language. The most popular intermediate language is the Warren Abstract Machine, or WAM, named after David H. D. Warren, one of the implementors of the first Prolog compiler. The WAM is an abstract instruction set that is suitable for Prolog and can be either interpreted or translated into machine language. Other compilers translate Prolog into a high-level language such as Lisp or C, and then use that language's compiler to translate to machine language. For example, the definition of the *Member* predicate can be compiled into the code shown in Figure 10.4.

---

procedure MEMBER(*item, list, continuation*)

    trail ← GLOBAL-TRAIL-POINTER()
    if UNIFY([*item* | NEW-VARIABLE()], *list*) **then** CALL(*continuation*)
    RESET-TRAIL(*trail*)
    rest ← NEW-VARIABLE()
    if UNIFY(*list*, [NEW-VARIABLE() | *rest*]) **then** MEMBER(*item, rest, continuation*)

Figure 10.4   Pseudocode representing the result of compiling the *Member* predicate. The function NEW-VARIABLE returns a new variable, distinct from all other variables so far used. The procedure CALL(*continuation*) continues execution with the specified continuation.

There are several points worth mentioning:

- Rather than having to search the knowledge base for *Member* clauses, the clauses are built into the procedure and the inferences are carried out simply by calling the procedure.

- As described earlier, the current variable bindings are kept on a trail. The first step of the procedure saves the current state of the trail, so that it can be restored by RESET-TRAIL if the first clause fails. This will undo any bindings generated by the first call to UNIFY.

CONTINUATIONS

- The trickiest part is the use of **continuations** to implement choice points. You can think of a continuation as packaging up a procedure and a list of arguments that together define what should be done next whenever the current goal succeeds. It would not do just to return from a procedure like MEMBER when the goal succeeds, because it may succeed in several ways, and each of them has to be explored. The continuation argument solves this problem because it can be called each time the goal succeeds. In the MEMBER code, if *item* unifies with the first element of the *list*, then the MEMBER predicate has succeeded. We then CALL the continuation, with the appropriate bindings on the trail, to do whatever should be done next. For example, if the call to MEMBER were at the top level, the continuation would print the bindings of the variables.

Before Warren's work on compilation of inference in Prolog, logic programming was too slow for general use. Compilers by Warren and others allowed Prolog to achieve speeds of up to 50,000 LIPS (logical inferences per second) on standard 1990-model workstations. More recently, application of modern compiler technology, including type inference, open-coding, and interprocedural data-flow analysis has allowed Prolog to reach speeds of several million LIPS, making it competitive with C on a variety of standard benchmarks (Van Roy, 1990). Of course, the fact that one can write a planner or natural language parser in a few dozen lines of Prolog makes it somewhat more desirable than C for prototyping most small-scale AI research projects.

Other logic programming languages

Although Prolog is the only accepted standard for logic programming, there are many other useful systems, each extending the basic Prolog model in different ways.

The parallelization of Prolog is an obvious direction to explore. If we examine the work done by a Prolog program, there are two principal sources of parallelism. The first, called OR-PARALLELISM **OR-parallelism**, comes from the possibility of a goal unifying with many different literals and implications in the knowledge base. Each gives rise to an independent branch in the search space that can lead to a potential solution, and all such branches can be solved in parallel. The second, AND-PARALLELISM called **AND-parallelism**, comes from the possibility of solving each conjunct in the body of an implication in parallel. And-parallelism is more difficult to achieve, because solutions for the whole conjunction require consistent bindings for all the variables. Each conjunctive branch must communicate with the other branches to ensure a global solution. A number of projects have been successful in achieving a degree of parallel inference, but the most advanced is probably the PIM (Parallel Inference Machine) project, part of the Fifth Generation Computing Systems project in Japan. PIM has achieved speeds of 64 million LIPS.

Prolog can be enriched, rather than just accelerated, by generalizing the notion of the binding of a variable. Prolog's logic variables are very useful because they allow a programmer to generate a partial solution to a problem, leaving some of the variables unbound, and then later fill in the values for those variables. Unfortunately, there is no way in Prolog to specify *constraints* on values: for example, to say that $X < 3$, and then later in the computation determine CONSTRAINT LOGIC PROGRAMMING the exact value of X. The **constraint logic programming** (CLP) formalism extends the notions of variables and unification to allow such constraints. Consider this definition of a triangle based on the lengths of the three sides:

$$Triangle(x, y, z) \Leftarrow (x > 0) \land (y > 0) \land (z > 0) \land (x + y > z) \land (y + z > x) \land (x + z > y)$$

In either Prolog or CLP, this definition can be used to confirm $Triangle(3, 4, 5)$. But only in CLP would the query $Triangle(x, 4, 5)$ give the binding specified by the constraint $\{x > 1 \land x < 9\}$; in standard Prolog, this query would fail.

As well as using arithmetical constraints on variables, it is possible to use logical constraints. For example, we can insist that a particular variable refer to a *Person*. In standard Prolog, this can only be done by inserting the conjunct *Person*(p) into the body of a clause. Then, when the clause is used, the system will attempt to solve the remainder of the clause with p bound to each different person in the knowledge base. In languages such as Login and Life, literals containing TYPE PREDICATES **type predicates** such as *Person* are implemented as constraints. Inference is delayed until the constraints need to be resolved. Thus, *Person*(p) just means that the variable p is constrained to be a person; it does not generate alternative bindings for p. The use of types can simplify programs, and the use of constraints can speed up their execution.

Advanced control facilities

Going back to our census knowledge base, consider the query "What is the income of the spouse of the president?" This might be stated in Prolog as

$$Income(s, i) \land Married(s, p) \land Occupation(p, President)$$

This query will be expensive to compute, because it must enumerate all person/income pairs, then fetch the spouse for each person (failing on those that are not married, and looping on anyone who is married multiple times), and finally check for the one person whose occupation is president. Conjunctive queries like this often can be answered more efficiently if we first spend some time to reorder the conjuncts to reduce the expected amount of computation. For this query, a better ordering is

$$Occupation(p, President) \land Married(s, p) \land Income(s, i)$$

This yields the same answer, but with no backtracking at all, assuming that the *Occupation* and *Married* predicates are indexed by their second arguments.

METAREASONING
                This reordering process is an example of **metareasoning**, or reasoning about reasoning. As with constraint satisfaction search (Section 3.7), the heuristic we are using for conjunct ordering is to put the most constraining conjuncts first. In this case it is clear that only one p satisfies $Occupation(p, President)$, but it is not always easy to predict in advance how many solutions there will be to a predicate. Even if it were, it would not be a good idea to try all $n!$ permutations of an n-place conjunction for large n. Languages such as MRS (Genesereth and Smith, 1981; Russell, 1985) allow the programmer to write metarules to decide which conjuncts are tried first. For example, the user could write a rule saying that the goal with the fewest variables should be tried first.

                Some systems change the way backtracking is done rather than attempting to reorder conjuncts. Consider the problem of finding all people x who come from the same town as the president. One inefficient ordering of this query is:

$$Resident(p, town) \land Resident(x, town) \land Occupation(p, President)$$

Prolog would try to solve this by enumerating all residents p of any town, then enumerating all residents x of that town, and then checking if p is the president. When the $Occupation(p, President)$ goal fails, Prolog backtracks to the *most recent* choice point, which is the $Resident(x, town)$ goal.

CHRONOLOGICAL BACKTRACKING
This is called **chronological backtracking**; although simple, it is sometimes inefficient. Clearly, generating a new x cannot possibly help p become president!

BACKJUMPING
                The technique of **backjumping** avoids such pointless repetition. In this particular problem, a backjumping search would backtrack two steps to $Resident(p, town)$ and generate a new binding for p. Discovering where to backjump to at compilation time is easy for a compiler that keeps global dataflow information. Sometimes, in addition to backjumping to a reasonable spot, the system will cache the combination of variables that lead to the dead end, so that they will not be repeated again in another branch of the search. This is called **dependency-directed**

DEPENDENCY-DIRECTED BACKTRACKING
backtracking. In practice, the overhead of storing all the dead ends is usually too great—as with heuristic search, memory is often a stronger constraint than time. In practice, there are many more backjumping systems than full dependency-directed backtracking systems.

                The final kind of metareasoning is the most complicated: being able to remember a previously computed inference rather than having to derive it all over again. This is important because most logical reasoning systems are given a series of related queries. For example, a logic-based agent repeatedly ASKs its knowledge base the question "what should I do now?" Answering this question will involve subgoals that are similar or identical to ones answered the previous time around. The agent could just store every conclusion that it is able to prove, but this would soon exhaust memory. There must be some guidance to decide which conclusions are worth storing and which should be ignored, either because they are easy to recompute or because they are unlikely to be asked again. Chapter 21 discusses these issues in the general context of an agent trying to take advantage of its previous reasoning experiences.

10.4   THEOREM PROVERS

Theorem provers (also known as automated reasoners) differ from logic programming languages in two ways. First, most logic programming languages only handle Horn clauses, whereas theorem provers accept full first-order logic. Second, Prolog programs intertwine logic and control. The programmer's choice in writing $A \Leftarrow B \land C$ instead of $A \Leftarrow C \land B$ affects the execution of the program. In theorem provers, the user can write either of these, or another form such as $\neg B \Leftarrow C \land \neg A$, and the results will be exactly the same. Theorem provers still need control information to operate efficiently, but this information is kept distinct from the knowledge base, rather than being part of the knowledge representation itself. Most of the research in theorem provers is in finding control strategies that are generally useful. In Section 9.6 we covered three generic strategies: unit preference, linear input resolution, and set of support.

Design of a theorem prover

In this section, we describe the theorem prover OTTER (Organized Techniques for Theorem-proving and Effective Research) (McCune, 1992), with particular attention to its control strategy. In preparing a problem for OTTER, the user must divide the knowledge into four parts:

- A set of clauses known as the **set of support** (or *sos*), which defines the important facts about the problem. Every resolution step resolves a member of the set of support against another axiom, so the search is focused on the set of support.
- A set of **usable axioms** that are outside the set of support. These provide background knowledge about the problem area. The boundary between what is part of the problem (and thus in *sos*) and what is background (and thus in the usable axioms) is up to the user's judgment.
- A set of equations known as **rewrites** or **demodulators**. Although demodulators are equations, they are always applied in the left to right direction. Thus, they define a canonical form into which all terms will be simplified. For example, the demodulator $x + 0 = x$ says that every term of the form $x + 0$ should be replaced by the term x.
- A set of parameters and clauses that defines the control strategy. In particular, the user specifies a heuristic function to control the search and a filtering function that eliminates some subgoals as uninteresting.

OTTER works by continually resolving an element of the set of support against one of the usable axioms. Unlike Prolog, it uses a form of best-first search. Its heuristic function measures the "weight" of each clause, where lighter clauses are preferred. The exact choice of heuristic is up to the user, but generally, the weight of a clause should be correlated with its size and/or difficulty.

Unit clauses are usually treated as very light, so that the search can be seen as a generalization of the unit preference strategy. At each step, OTTER moves the "lightest" clause in the set of support to the usable list, and adds to the usable list some immediate consequences of resolving the lightest clause with elements of the usable list. OTTER halts when it has found a refutation or when there are no more clauses in the set of support. The algorithm is shown in more detail in Figure 10.5.

---

procedure OTTER(*sos, usable*)
    inputs: *sos*, a set of support—clauses defining the problem (a global variable)
               usable, background knowledge potentially relevant to the problem

    repeat
        clause ← the lightest member of *sos*
        move *clause* from *sos* to *usable*
        PROCESS(INFER(*clause, usable*), *sos*)
    until *sos* = [ ] **or** a refutation has been found

---

function INFER(*clause, usable*) **returns** clauses

    resolve *clause* with each member of *usable*
    return the resulting clauses after applying FILTER

---

procedure PROCESS(*clauses, sos*)

    for each *clause* **in** *clauses* **do**
        clause ← SIMPLIFY(*clause*)
        merge identical literals
        discard clause if it is a tautology
        sos ← [*clause* | *sos*]
        if *clause* has no literals **then** a refutation has been found
        if *clause* has one literal **then** look for unit refutation
    end

Figure 10.5   Sketch of the OTTER theorem prover. Heuristic control is applied in the selection of the "lightest" clause, and in the FILTER function that eliminates uninteresting clauses from consideration.

Extending Prolog

An alternative way to build a theorem prover is to start with a Prolog compiler and extend it to get a sound and complete reasoner for full first-order logic. This was the approach taken in the Prolog Technology Theorem Prover, or PTTP (Stickel, 1988). PTTP includes five significant changes to Prolog to restore completeness and expressiveness:

- The occurs check is put back into the unification routine to make it sound.

- The depth-first search is replaced by an iterative deepening search. This makes the search strategy complete and takes only a constant factor more time.
- Negated literals (such as $\neg P(x)$) are allowed. In the implementation, there are two separate routines, one trying to prove P and one trying to prove $\neg P$.

LOCKING
- A clause with n atoms is stored as n different rules. For example, $A \Leftarrow B \wedge C$ would also be stored as $\neg B \Leftarrow C \wedge \neg A$ and as $\neg C \Leftarrow B \wedge \neg A$. This technique, known as **locking**, means that the current goal need only be unified with the head of each clause but still allows for proper handling of negation.
- Inference is made complete (even for non-Horn clauses) by the addition of the linear input resolution rule: If the current goal unifies with the negation of one of the goals on the stack, then the goal can be considered solved. This is a way of reasoning by contradiction. Suppose we are trying to prove P and that the current goal is $\neg P$. This is equivalent to saying that $\neg P \Rightarrow P$, which entails P.

Despite these changes, PTTP retains the features that make Prolog fast. Unifications are still done by modifying variables directly, with unbinding done by unwinding the trail during backtracking. The search strategy is still based on input resolution, meaning that every resolution is against one of the clauses given in the original statement of the problem (rather than a derived clause). This makes it feasible to compile all the clauses in the original statement of the problem.

The main drawback of PTTP is that the user has to relinquish all control over the search for solutions. Each inference rule is used by the system both in its original form and in the contrapositive form. This can lead to unintuitive searches. For example, suppose we had the rule

$$(f(x, y) = f(a, b)) \Leftarrow (x = a) \wedge (y = b)$$

As a Prolog rule, this is a reasonable way to prove that two f terms are equal. But PTTP would also generate the contrapositive:

$$(x \neq a) \Leftarrow (f(x, y) \neq f(a, b)) \wedge (y = b)$$

It seems that this is a wasteful way to prove that any two terms x and a are different.

Theorem provers as assistants

So far, we have thought of a reasoning system as an independent agent that has to make decisions and act on its own. Another use of theorem provers is as an assistant, providing advice to, say, a mathematician. In this mode the mathematician acts as a supervisor, mapping out the strategy for determining what to do next and asking the theorem prover to fill in the details. This alleviates the problem of semi-decidability to some extent, because the supervisor can cancel a query and try another approach if the query is taking too much time. A theorem prover can also act as a

PROOF-CHECKER
proof-checker, where the proof is given by a human as a series of fairly large steps; the individual inferences required to show that each step is sound are filled in by the system.

SOCRATIC
REASONER
A **Socratic reasoner** is a theorem prover whose ASK function is incomplete, but which can always arrive at a solution if asked the right series of questions. Thus, Socratic reasoners make good assistants, provided there is a supervisor to make the right series of calls to ASK. ONTIC (McAllester, 1989) is an example of a Socratic reasoning system for mathematics.

Practical uses of theorem provers

Theorem provers have come up with novel mathematical results. The SAM (Semi-Automated Mathematics) program was the first, proving a lemma in lattice theory (Guard *et al.*, 1969). The AURA program has also answered open questions in several areas of mathematics (Wos and Winker, 1983). The Boyer–Moore theorem prover (Boyer and Moore, 1979) has been used and extended over many years, and was used by Natarajan Shankar to give the first fully rigorous, formal proof of Gödel's Incompleteness Theorem (Shankar, 1986). The OTTER program is one of the strongest theorem provers; it has been used to solve several open questions in combinatorial logic, and achieves approximately 2,000 LIPS on a 1990-model workstation.

VERIFICATION

SYNTHESIS

Theorem provers can be applied to the problems involved in the **verification** and **synthesis** of both hardware and software, because both domains can be given correct axiomatizations. In the case of software, the axioms state the properties of each syntactic element of the programming language. (Reasoning about programs is quite similar to reasoning about actions in the situation calculus.) An algorithm is verified by showing that its outputs meet the specifications for all inputs. The RSA public key encryption algorithm and the Boyer-Moore string matching algorithm have been verified this way (Boyer and Moore, 1984). In the case of hardware, the axioms describe the interactions between signals and circuit elements (see Chapter 8 for an example). The design of a 16-bit adder has been verified by AURA (Wojcik, 1983). Logical reasoners designed specially for verification have been able to verify entire CPUs, including timing properties (Srivas and Bickford, 1990). The MRS theorem prover has been applied to the problem of diagnosing computer systems using structural and behavioral specifications (Genesereth, 1984).

DEDUCTIVE
SYNTHESIS

The formal synthesis of algorithms was one of the first uses of theorem provers, as outlined by Cordell Green (1969a) who built on earlier ideas by Simon (1963). The idea is to prove a theorem to the effect that "there exists a program p satisfying a certain specification." If the proof is constrained to be constructive, the program can be extracted. Although fully automated **deductive synthesis**, as it is called, has not yet become feasible for general-purpose programming, hand-guided deductive synthesis has been successful in designing several novel and sophisticated algorithms. Synthesis of special-purpose programs is also an active area of research. In the area of hardware synthesis, the AURA theorem prover has been applied to design circuits that are more compact than any previous design (Wojciechowski and Wojcik, 1983). For many circuit designs, propositional logic is sufficient because the set of interesting propositions is fixed by the set of circuit elements. Application of propositional inference in hardware synthesis is now a standard technique with many large-scale applications (see, e.g., Nowick *et al.* (1993)).

10.5   FORWARD-CHAINING PRODUCTION SYSTEMS

Prolog and most other logic programming languages are backward chaining. Given a query, they search for a constructive proof that establishes some substitution that satisfies the query. An alternative is a **forward-chaining** approach in which there are no queries. Instead, inference rules are applied to the knowledge base, yielding new assertions. This process repeats forever, or until some stopping criterion is met. The forward-chaining approach is appropriate for the design of an agent—on each cycle, we add the percepts to the knowledge base and run the forward chainer, which chooses an action to perform according to a set of condition-action rules.

Theoretically, we could implement a production system with a theorem prover, using resolution to do forward chaining over a full first-order knowledge base. A more restricted language, on the other hand, can provide greater efficiency because the branching factor is reduced. The typical production system has these features:

- The system maintains a knowledge base called the **working memory**. This contains a set of positive literals with no variables.

- The system also maintains a separate **rule memory**. This contains a set of inference rules, each of the form $p_1 \wedge p_2 \cdots \Rightarrow act_1 \wedge act_2 \cdots$, where the p_i are literals, and the act_i are actions to take when the p_i are all satisfied. Allowable actions are adding and deleting elements from the working memory, and possibly other actions (such as printing a value).

- In each cycle, the system computes the subset of rules whose left-hand side is satisfied by the current contents of the working memory. This is called the **match phase**.

- The system then decides which of the rules should be executed. This is called the **conflict resolution phase**.

- The final step in each cycle is to execute the action(s) in the chosen rule(s). This is called the **act phase**.

Match phase

Unification addresses the problem of matching a pair of literals, where either literal can contain variables. We can use unification in a straightforward way to implement a forward-chaining production system, but this is very inefficient. If there are w elements in working memory and r rules each with n elements in the left-hand side, and solving a problem requires c cycles, then the naive match algorithm must perform $wrnc$ unifications. A simple expert system might have

RETE
$w = 100, r = 200, n = 5, c = 1000$, so this is a hundred million unifications. The **rete** algorithm[4] used in the OPS-5 production system was the first to seriously address this problem. The rete algorithm is best explained by example. Suppose we have the following rule memory:

$$A(x) \wedge B(x) \wedge C(y) \Rightarrow \text{add } D(x)$$
$$A(x) \wedge B(y) \wedge D(x) \Rightarrow \text{add } E(x)$$
$$A(x) \wedge B(x) \wedge E(x) \Rightarrow \text{delete } A(x)$$

and the following working memory:

$$\{A(1), A(2), B(2), B(3), B(4), C(5)\}$$

The rete algorithm first compiles the rule memory into the network shown in Figure 10.6. In this diagram, the circular nodes represent fetches (not unifications) to working memory. Under node A, the working memory elements $A(1)$ and $A(2)$ are fetched and stored. The square nodes indicate unifications. Of the six possible $A \times B$ combinations at the $A = B$ node, only $A(2)$ and $B(2)$ satisfy the unification. Finally, rectangular boxes indicate actions. With the initial working

---

[4] Rete is Latin for net. It rhymes with treaty.

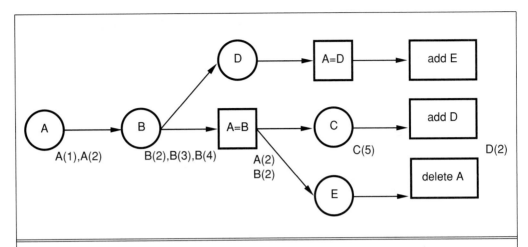

Figure 10.6   A rete network.   Circles represent predicate tests.   A square containing, for example, $A = B$ represents a constraint that the solutions to the A and B tests must be equal. Rectangles are actions.

memory the "*add D*" rule is the only one that fires, resulting in the addition of the sentence $D(2)$ to working memory.

One obvious advantage of the rete network is that it eliminates duplication between rules. All three of the rules start with a conjunction of A and B, and the network allows that part to be shared. The second advantage of rete networks is in eliminating duplication over time. Most production systems make only a few changes to the knowledge base on each cycle. This means that most of the tests at cycle $t + 1$ will give the same result as at cycle t. The rete network modifies itself after each addition or deletion, but if there are few changes, then the cost of each update will be small relative to the whole job of maintaining the indexing information. The network thus represents the saved intermediate state in the process of testing for satisfaction of a set of conjuncts. In this case, adding $D(2)$ will result in the activation of the "add E" rule, but will not have any effect on the rest of the network. Adding or deleting an A, however, will have a bigger effect that needs to be propagated through much of the network.

Conflict resolution phase

Some production systems execute the actions of all rules that pass the match phase. Other production systems treat these rules only as suggestions, and use the conflict resolution phase to decide which of the suggestions to accept. This phase can be thought of as the control strategy. Some of the strategies that have been used are as follows:

- *No duplication.* Do not execute the same rule on the same arguments twice.

- *Recency.* Prefer rules that refer to recently created working memory elements.

- *Specificity.* Prefer rules that are more specific.[5] For example, the second of these two rules would be preferred:

$$Mammal(x) \ \Rightarrow \ \text{add } Legs(x, 4)$$
$$Mammal(x) \wedge Human(x) \ \Rightarrow \ \text{add } Legs(x, 2)$$

- *Operation priority.* Prefer actions with higher priority, as specified by some ranking. For example, the second of the following two rules should probably have a higher priority:

$$ControlPanel(p) \wedge Dusty(p) \ \Rightarrow \ Action(Dust(p))$$
$$ControlPanel(p) \wedge MeltdownLightOn(p) \ \Rightarrow \ Action(Evacuate)$$

Practical uses of production systems

Forward-chaining production systems formed the foundation of much early work in AI. In particular, the XCON system (originally called R1 (McDermott, 1982)) was built using a production system (rule-based) architecture. XCON contains several thousand rules for designing configurations of computer components for customers of the Digital Equipment Corporation. It was one of the first clear commercial successes in the emerging field of expert systems. Many other similar systems have been built using the same underlying technology, which has been implemented in the general-purpose language OPS-5. A good deal of work has gone into designing matching algorithms for production system languages, as we have seen; implementations on parallel hardware have also been attempted (Acharya *et al.*, 1992).

COGNITIVE
ARCHITECTURES
        Production systems are also popular in **cognitive architectures**—that is, models of human reasoning—such as ACT (Anderson, 1983) and SOAR (Laird *et al.*, 1987). In such systems, the "working memory" of the system models human short-term memory, and the productions are part of long-term memory. Both ACT and SOAR have sophisticated mechanisms for conflict resolution, and for saving the results of expensive reasoning in the form of new productions. These can be used to avoid reasoning in future situations (see also Section 21.2).

10.6   FRAME SYSTEMS AND SEMANTIC NETWORKS

EXISTENTIAL
GRAPHS
        In 1896, seven years after Peano developed what is now the standard notation for first-order logic, Charles Peirce proposed a graphical notation called **existential graphs** that he called "the logic of the future." Thus began a long-running debate between advocates of "logic" and advocates of "semantic networks." What is unfortunate about this debate is that it obscured the underlying unity of the field. It is now accepted that every semantic network or frame system could just as well have been defined as sentences in a logic, and most accept that it could be first-order logic.[6] (We will show how to execute this translation in detail.) The important thing with any representation language is to understand the semantics, and the proof theory; the details of the syntax are less important. *Whether the language uses strings or nodes and links, and whether it*

---

[5]   For more on the use of specificity to implement default reasoning, see Chapter 14.

[6]   There are a few problems having to do with handling exceptions, but they too can be handled with a little care.

is called a semantic network or a logic, has no effect on its meaning or on its implementation.

Having said this, we should also say that the format of a language can have a *significant* effect on its clarity for a human reader. Some things are easier to understand in a graphical notation; some are better shown as strings of characters. Fortunately, there is no need to choose one or the other; the skilled AI practitioner can translate back and forth between notations, choosing the one that is best for the task at hand, but drawing intuitions from other notations. Some systems, such as the CYC system mentioned in Chapter 8, provide both kinds of interfaces.

Besides the appeal of pretty node-and-link diagrams, semantic networks have been successful for the same reason that Prolog is more successful than full first-order logic theorem provers: because most semantic network formalisms have a very simple execution model. Programmers can build a large network and still have a good idea about what queries will be efficient, because (a) it is easy to visualize the steps that the inference procedure will go through, and (b) the query language is so simple that difficult queries cannot be posed. This may be the reason why many of the pioneering researchers in commonsense ontology felt more comfortable developing their theories with the semantic network approach.

Syntax and semantics of semantic networks

Semantic networks concentrate on categories of objects and the relations between them. It is very natural to draw the link

$$Cats \xrightarrow{Subset} Mammals$$

to say that cats are mammals. Of course, it is just as easy to write the logical sentence *Cats* ⊂ *Mammals*, but when semantic networks were first used in AI (around 1961), this was not widely appreciated; people thought that in order to use logic they would have to write

$$\forall x \; Cat(x) \; \Rightarrow \; Mammal(x)$$

which seemed a lot more intimidating. It was also felt that $\forall x$ did not allow exceptions, but that $\xrightarrow{Subset}$ was somehow more forgiving.[7]

We now recognize that semantics is more important than notation. Figure 10.7 gives an example of a typical frame-based network, and a translation of the network into first-order logic. This network can be used to answer the query "How many legs does Opus have?" by following the chain of $\xrightarrow{Member}$ and $\xrightarrow{Subset}$ links from Opus to Penguins to Birds, and seeing that birds have two legs. This is an example of **inheritance**, as described in Section 8.4. That is clear enough, but what happens, when, say, there are two different chains to two different numbers of legs? Ironically, semantic networks sometimes lack a clear semantics. Often the user is left to induce the semantics of the language from the behavior of the program that implements it. Consequently, users often think of semantic networks at the implementation level rather than the logical level or the knowledge level.

---

[7] In many systems, the name *IsA* was given to both subset and set-membership links, in correspondence with English usage: "a cat is a mammal" and "Fifi is a cat." This can lead directly to inconsistencies, as pointed out by Drew McDermott (1976) in his article "Artificial Intelligence Meets Natural Stupidity." Some systems also failed to distinguish between properties of members of a category and properties of the category as a whole.

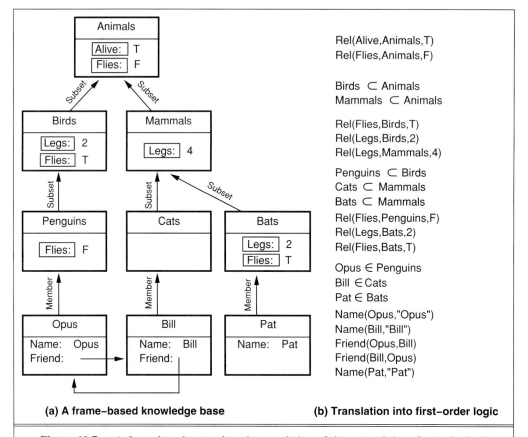

Rel(Alive,Animals,T)
Rel(Flies,Animals,F)

Birds ⊂ Animals
Mammals ⊂ Animals

Rel(Flies,Birds,T)
Rel(Legs,Birds,2)
Rel(Legs,Mammals,4)

Penguins ⊂ Birds
Cats ⊂ Mammals
Bats ⊂ Mammals
Rel(Flies,Penguins,F)
Rel(Legs,Bats,2)
Rel(Flies,Bats,T)

Opus ∈ Penguins
Bill ∈ Cats
Pat ∈ Bats
Name(Opus,"Opus")
Name(Bill,"Bill")
Friend(Opus,Bill)
Friend(Bill,Opus)
Name(Pat,"Pat")

(a) A frame–based knowledge base   **(b) Translation into first–order logic**

Figure 10.7   A frame-based network and a translation of the network into first-order logic.
Boxed relation names in the network correspond to relations holding for all members of the set
of objects.

The semantics of a simple semantic network language can be stated by providing first-order
logical equivalents for assertions in the network language. We first define a version in which
exceptions are not allowed. In addition to $\xrightarrow{Subset}$ and $\xrightarrow{Member}$ links, we find that there is a need for
at least three other kinds of links: one that says a relation R holds between two objects, A and B;
one that says R holds between every element of the class A and the object B; and one that says
that R holds between every element of A and some element of B. The five standard link types
are summarized in Figure 10.8.[8] Notice that a theorem prover or logic programming language
could take the logical translations of the links and do inheritance by ordinary logical inference. A
semantic network system uses uses special-purpose algorithms for following links, and therefore
can be faster than general logical inference.

---

[8]   Because assertions of the form $A \xrightarrow{\boxed{R}} B$ are so common, we use the abbreviation $Rel(R, A, B)$ as syntactic sugar in the
logical translation (Figure 10.7).

Link Type	Semantics	Example
$A \xrightarrow{Subset} B$	$A \subset B$	$Cats \subset Mammals$
$A \xrightarrow{Member} B$	$A \in B$	$Bill \in Cats$
$A \xrightarrow{R} B$	$R(A,B)$	$Bill \xrightarrow{Age} 12$
$A \xrightarrow{\boxed{R}} B$	$\forall x \ x \in A \ \Rightarrow \ R(x,B)$	$Birds \xrightarrow{\boxed{Legs}} 2$
$A \xrightarrow{\boxed{\boxed{R}}} B$	$\forall x \ \exists y \ x \in A \ \Rightarrow \ y \in B \wedge R(x,y)$	$Birds \xrightarrow{\boxed{Parent}} Birds$

Figure 10.8   Link types in semantic networks, and their meanings.

Inheritance with exceptions

As we saw in Chapter 8, natural kinds are full of exceptions. The diagram in Figure 10.7 says that mammals have 4 legs, but it also says that bats, which are mammals, have 2 legs. According to the straightforward logical semantics, this is a contradiction. To fix the problem, we will change the semantic translation of a boxed-R link from A to B to mean that every member of A must have an R relation to B *unless there is some intervening A' for which $Rel(R, A', B')$*. Then Figure 10.7 will unambiguously mean that bats have 2 legs, not 4. Notice that $Rel(R, A, B)$ no longer means that every A is related by R to B; instead it means that B is a **default value** for the R relation for members of A, but the default can be overridden by other information.

DEFAULT VALUE

It may be intuitive to think of inheritance with exceptions by following links in a diagram, but it is also possible—and instructive—to define the semantics in first-order logic. The first step in the logical translation is to **reify** relations: a relation R becomes an object, not a predicate. That means that $Rel(R, A, B)$ is just an ordinary atomic sentence, not an abbreviation for a complex sentence. It also means that we can no longer write $R(x, B)$, because R is an object, not a predicate. We will use $Val(R, x, B)$ to mean that the equivalent of an $R(x, B)$ relation is explicitly asserted in the semantic network, and $Holds(R, x, B)$ to mean that $R(x, B)$ can be inferred. We then can define $Holds$ by saying that a relation R holds between x and b if either there is an explicit Val predication or there is a Rel on some parent class p of which x is an element, and there is no Rel on any intervening class i. (A class i is intervening if x is an element of i and i is a subset of p.) In other words:

$$\forall r, x, b \ \ Holds(r, x, b) \ \Leftrightarrow$$
$$Val(r, x, b) \vee (\exists p \ x \in p \wedge Rel(r, p, b) \wedge \neg InterveningRel(x, p, r))$$
$$\forall x, p, r \ \ InterveningRel(x, p, r) \ \Leftrightarrow$$
$$\exists i \ Intervening(x, i, p) \wedge \exists b' \ Rel(r, i, b')$$
$$\forall a, i, p \ \ Intervening(x, i, p) \ \Leftrightarrow \ (x \in i) \wedge (i \subset p)$$

Note that the $\subset$ symbol means proper subset (e.g., $i \subset p$ means that i is a subset of p and is not equal to p). The next step is to recognize that it is important not only to know what Rel and Val relations hold, but also what ones *do not* hold. Suppose we are trying to find the n that satisfies $Holds(Legs, Opus, n)$. We know $Rel(Legs, Birds, 2)$ and we know Opus is a bird, but the definition of $Holds$ does not allow us to infer anything unless we can prove there is no $Rel(Legs, i, b)$ for $i = Penguins$ or any other intervening category. If the knowledge base only contains positive *Rel* atoms (i.e., *Rel*(*Legs*, *Birds*, 2) ∧ *Rel*(*Flies*, *Birds*, *T*)), then we are stuck. Therefore, the translation of a semantic network like Figure 10.7 should include sentences that say that the *Rel* and *Val* relations that are shown are the only ones that are true:

$$\forall r, a, b \ Rel(r, a, b) \ \Leftrightarrow \ [r, a, b] \in \{[Alive, Animal, T], [Flies, Animal, F], \ldots\}$$
$$\forall r, a, b \ Val(r, a, b) \ \Leftrightarrow \ [r, a, b] \in \{[Friend, Opus, Bill], [Friend, Bill, Opus], \ldots\}$$

Multiple inheritance

MULTIPLE
INHERITANCE

Some semantic network systems allow **multiple inheritance**—that is, an object can belong to more than one category and can therefore inherit properties along several different paths. In some cases, this will work fine. For example, some people might belong to both the categories *Billionaire* and *PoloPlayer*, in which case we can infer that they are rich and can ride a horse.

It is possible, however, for two inheritance paths to produce conflicting answers. An example of this difficulty is shown in Figure 10.9. Opus is a penguin, and therefore speaks only in squawks. Opus is a cartoon character, and therefore speaks English.[9] In the simple logical translation given earlier, we would be able to infer both conclusions, which, with appropriate background knowledge, would lead to a contradiction. Without additional information indicating some preference for one path, there is no way to resolve the conflict.

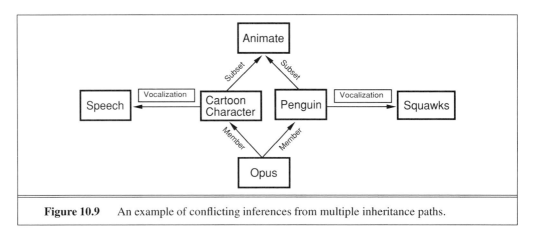

Figure 10.9   An example of conflicting inferences from multiple inheritance paths.

Inheritance and change

A knowledge base is not of much use to an agent unless it can be expanded. In systems based on first-order logic, we use TELL to add a new sentence to the knowledge base, and we enjoy the

---

[9]   The classical example of multiple inheritance conflict is called the "Nixon diamond." It arises from the observation that Richard Nixon was both a Quaker (and hence a pacifist) and a Republican (and hence not a pacifist). Because of its potential for controversy, we will avoid this particular example. The other canonical example involves a bird called Tweety, about whom the less said the better.

property of **monotonicity**: if P follows from KB, then it still follows when KB is augmented by TELL(KB,S). In other words,

$$\text{if } KB \vdash P \text{ then } (KB \wedge S) \vdash P$$

NONMONOTONIC

Inheritance with exceptions is **nonmonotonic**: from the semantic network in Figure 10.7 it follows that Bill has 4 legs, but if we were to add the new statement $Rel(Legs, Cats, 3)$, then it no longer follows that Bill has 4 legs. There are two ways to deal with this.

First, we could switch from first-order logic to a **nonmonotonic logic** that explicitly deals with default values. Nonmonotonic logics allow you to say that a proposition P should be treated as true until additional evidence allows you to prove that P is false. There has been quite a lot of interesting theoretical work in this area, but so far its impact on practical systems has been smaller than other approaches, so we will not address it in this chapter.

Second, we could treat the addition of the new statement as a RETRACT followed by a TELL. Given the way we have defined Rel, this makes perfect sense. We do not make statements of the form TELL($KB, Rel(R,A,B)$). Instead, we make one big equivalence statement of the form

$$\text{TELL}(KB, \ \forall r, a, b \ \ Rel(r, a, b) \ \Leftrightarrow \ \ldots)$$

where the ... indicate all the possible Rel's. So to add $Rel(Legs, Cats, 3)$, we would have to remove the old equivalence statement and replace it by a new one. Once we have altered the knowledge base by removing a sentence from it (and not just adding a new one) we should not be surprised at the nonmonotonicity. Section 10.8 discusses implementations of RETRACT.

Implementation of semantic networks

Once we have decided on a meaning for our networks, we can start to implement the network. Of course, we could choose to implement the network with a theorem prover or logic programming language, and in some cases this would be the best choice. But for networks with simple semantics, a more straightforward implementation is possible. A node in a network is represented by a data structure with fields for the basic taxonomic connections: which categories it is a member of; what elements it has; what immediate subsets and supersets. It also has fields for other relations in which it participates. The RELS-IN and RELS-OUT fields handle ordinary (unboxed) links, and the ALL-RELS-IN and ALL-RELS-OUT fields handle boxed links. Here is the data type definition for nodes:

---

datatype SEM-NET-NODE
    components: NAME, MEMBERSHIPS, ELEMENTS, SUPERS, SUBS,
        RELS-IN, RELS-OUT, ALL-RELS-IN, ALL-RELS-OUT

Each of the four REL-fields is organized as a table indexed by the relation. We use the function LOOKUP(key, $table$) to find the value associated with a key in a table. So, if we have the two links $Opus \xrightarrow{Friend} Bill$ and $Opus \xrightarrow{Friend} Steve$, then LOOKUP($Friend$,RELS-OUT($Opus$)) gives us the set $\{Bill, Steve\}$.

The code in Figure 10.10 implements everything you need in order to ASK the network whether subset, membership, or other relations hold between two objects. Each of the functions simply follows the appropriate links until it finds what it is looking for, or runs out of links. The code does not handle double-boxed links, nor does it handle exceptions. Also, the code that TELLs the network about new relations is not shown, because it is straightforward.

The code can be extended with other functions to answer other questions. One problem with this approach is that it is easy to become carried away with the data structures and forget their underlying semantics. For example, we could easily define a NUMBER-OF-SUBKINDS function that returns the length of the list in the SUBS slot. For Figure 10.7, NUMBER-OF-SUBKINDS(*Animal*) = 2. This may well be the answer the user wanted, but its logical status is dubious. First of all, it

---

function MEMBER?(*element, category*) **returns** *True* or *False*

   for each *c* **in** MEMBERSHIPS[*element*] **do**
      if SUBSET?(*c, category*) **then return** *True*
   return *False*

---

function SUBSET?(*sub, super*) **returns** *True* or *False*

   if *sub* = *super* **then return** *True*
   for each *c* **in** SUPERS[*sub*] **do**
      if SUBSET?(*c, super*) **then return** *True*
   return *False*

---

function RELATED-TO?(*source, relation, destination*) **returns** *True* or *False*

   if *relation* appears in RELS-OUT(*source*) **then**
      return MEMBER([*relation, destination*], RELS-OUT(*node*))
   else for each *c* **in** MEMBERSHIPS(*source*) **do**
      if ALL-RELATED-TO?(*c, relation, destination*) **then return** *True*
   end
   return *False*

---

function ALL-RELATED-TO?(*source, relation, destination*) **returns** *True* or *False*

   if *relation* appears in ALL-RELS-OUT(*source*) **then**
      return MEMBER([*relation, destination*], ALL-RELS-OUT(*node*))
   else for each *c* **in** SUPERS(category) **do**
      if ALL-RELATED-TO?(*c, relation, destination*) **then return** *True*
   end
   return *False*

Figure 10.10   Basic routines for inheritance and relation testing in a simple exception-free semantic network. Note that the function MEMBER? is defined here to operate on semantic network nodes, while the function MEMBER is a utility that operates on sets.

is likely that there are species of animals that are not represented in the knowledge base. Second, it may be that some nodes denote the same object. Perhaps *Dog* and *Chien* are two nodes with an equality link between them. Do these count as one or two? Finally, is *Dog-With-Black-Ears* a kind of animal? How about *Dog-On-My-Block-Last-Thursday*? It is easy to answer these questions based on what is stored in the knowledge base, but it is better to have a clear semantics so that the questions can be answered about the world, rather than about the current state of the internal representation.

Expressiveness of semantic networks

The networks we have discussed so far are extremely limited in their expressiveness. For example, it is not possible to represent negation (Opus does not ride a bicycle), disjunction (Opus appears in either the *Times* or the *Dispatch*), or quantification (all of Opus' friends are cartoon characters). These constructs are essential in many domains.

PARTITIONED
SEMANTIC
NETWORKS

PROCEDURAL
ATTACHMENT

Some semantic networks extend the notation to allow all of first-order logic. Peirce's original existential graphs, **partitioned semantic networks** (Hendrix, 1975), and SNEPS (Shapiro, 1979) all take this approach. A more common approach retains the limitations on expressiveness and uses **procedural attachment** to fill in the gaps. Procedural attachment is a technique where a function written in a programming language can be stored as the value of some relation, and used to answer ASK calls about that relation (and sometimes TELL calls as well).

What do semantic networks provide in return for giving up expressiveness? We have already seen two advantages: they are able to capture inheritance information in a modular way, and their simplicity makes them easy to understand. Efficiency is often claimed as a third advantage: because inference is done by following links, rather than retrieving sentences from a knowledge base and performing unifications, it can operate with only a few machine cycles per inference step. But if we look at the kinds of computations done by compiled Prolog programs, we see there is not much difference. A compiled Prolog program for a set of subset and set-membership sentences, combined with general properties of categories, does almost the same computations as a semantic network.

10.7   DESCRIPTION LOGICS

SUBSUMPTION

CLASSIFICATION

The syntax of first-order logic is designed to make it easy to say things about objects. *Description logics are designed to focus on categories and their definitions.* They provide a reasonably sophisticated facility for defining categories in terms of existing relations, with much greater expressiveness than typical semantic network languages. The principal inference tasks are **subsumption**—checking if one category is a subset of another based on their definitions—and **classification**—checking if an object belongs to a category. In some description logics, objects are also viewed as categories defined by the object's description and (presumably) containing only one member. This way of looking at representation is a significant departure from the object-centered view that is most compatible with first-order logical syntax.

The CLASSIC language (Borgida *et al.*, 1989) is a typical description logic. The syntax of CLASSIC descriptions is shown in Figure 10.11.[10] For example, to say that bachelors are unmarried, adult males we would write

Bachelor = And(Unmarried, Adult, Male)

The equivalent in first-order logic would be

$\forall x \; Bachelor(x) \; \Leftrightarrow \; Unmarried(x) \land Adult(x) \land Male(x)$

Notice that the description logic effectively allows direct logical operations on predicates, rather than having to first create sentences to be joined by connectives. Any description in CLASSIC can be written in first-order logic, but some descriptions are more straightforward in CLASSIC. For example, to describe the set of men with at least three sons who are all unemployed and married to doctors, and at most two daughters who are all professors in physics or chemistry departments, we would use

And(Man, AtLeast(3, Son), AtMost(2, Daughter),
         All(Son, And(Unemployed, Married, All(Spouse, Doctor))),
         All(Daughter, And(Professor, Fills(Department, Physics, Chemistry)))))

We leave it as an exercise to translate this into first-order logic.

Concept → **Thing** | *ConceptName*
         | **And**(*Concept*, ...)
         | **All**(*RoleName, Concept*)
         | **AtLeast**(*Integer, RoleName*)
         | **AtMost**(*Integer, RoleName*)
         | **Fills**(*RoleName, IndividualName*, ...)
         | **SameAs**(*Path, Path*)
         | **OneOf**(*IndividualName*, ...)
Path → [*RoleName*, ...]

Figure 10.11   The syntax of descriptions in a subset of the CLASSIC language.

Perhaps the most important aspect of description logics is the emphasis on tractability of inference. A problem instance is solved by describing it and asking if it is subsumed by one of several possible solution categories. In standard first-order logic systems, predicting the solution time is often impossible. It is often left to the user to engineer the representation to detour around sets of sentences that seem to be causing the system to take several weeks to solve a problem. The thrust in description logics, on the other hand, is to ensure that subsumption-testing can be solved in time polynomial in the size of the problem description. The CLASSIC language satisfies this condition, and is currently the most comprehensive language to do so.

---

[10] Notice that the language does *not* allow one to simply state that one concept, or category, is a subset of another. This is a deliberate policy: subsumption between categories must be derivable from some aspects of the descriptions of the categories. If not, then something is missing from the descriptions.

This sounds wonderful in principle, until one realizes that it can only have one of two consequences: hard problems either cannot be stated at all, or require exponentially large descriptions! However, the tractability results do shed light on what sorts of constructs cause problems, and thus help the user to understand how different representations behave. For example, description logics usually lack *negation* and *disjunction*. These both force first-order logical systems to essentially go through an exponential case analysis in order to ensure completeness. For the same reason, they are excluded from Prolog. CLASSIC only allows a limited form of disjunction in the *Fills* and *OneOf* constructs, which allow disjunction over explicitly enumerated individuals but not over descriptions. With disjunctive descriptions, nested definitions can lead easily to an exponential number of alternative routes by which one category can subsume another.

Practical uses of description logics

Because they combine clear semantics and simple logical operations, description logics have become popular with both the theoretical and practical AI communities. Applications have included financial management (Mays *et al.*, 1987), database interfaces (Beck *et al.*, 1989), and software information systems (Devanbu *et al.*, 1991). Because of the gradual extension of the class of tractable languages, and a better understanding of what kinds of constructs cause intractability, the efficiency of description logic systems has improved by several orders of magnitude over the last decade.

10.8   MANAGING RETRACTIONS, ASSUMPTIONS, AND EXPLANATIONS

We have said a great deal about TELL and ASK, but so far very little about RETRACT. Most logical reasoning systems, regardless of their implementation, have to deal with RETRACT. As we have seen, there are three reasons for retracting a sentence. It may be that a fact is no longer important, and we want to forget about it to free up space for other purposes. It may be that the system is tracking the current state of the world (without worrying about past situations) and that the world changes. Or it may be that the system assumed (or determined) that a fact was true, but now wants to assume (or comes to determine) that it is actually false. In any case, we want to be able to retract a sentence from the knowledge base without introducing any inconsistencies, and we would like the interaction with the knowledge base as a whole (the cycle of TELL, ASK and RETRACT requests) to be efficient.

It takes a little experience to appreciate the problem. First, it is important to understand the distinction between RETRACT(KB, P) and TELL(KB, $\neg P$). Assuming that the knowledge base already contains P, adding $\neg P$ with TELL will allow us to conclude both P and $\neg P$, whereas removing P with RETRACT will allow us to conclude neither P nor $\neg P$. Second, if the system does any forward chaining, then RETRACT has some extra work to do. Suppose the knowledge base was told P and $P \Rightarrow Q$, and used that to infer Q and add it to the knowledge base. Then RETRACT(KB, P) must remove both P and Q to keep the knowledge base consistent. However, if there is some other independent reason for believing Q (perhaps both R and $R \Rightarrow Q$ have been

TRUTH
MAINTENANCE

asserted), then Q does not have to be removed after all. The process of keeping track of which additional propositions need to be retracted when we retract P is called **truth maintenance**.

The simplest approach to truth maintenance is to use chronological backtracking (see page 309). In this approach, we keep track of the order in which sentences are added to the knowledge base by numbering them from P_1 to P_n. When the call RETRACT(P_i) is made, the system reverts to the state just before P_i was added. If desired, the sentences P_{i+1} through P_n can then be added again. This is simple, and it guarantees that the knowledge base will be consistent, but it means that retraction is $O(n)$, where n is the size of the knowledge base. We would prefer a more efficient approach that does not require us to duplicate all the work for P_{i+1} to P_n.

TRUTH
MAINTENANCE
SYSTEM

A **truth maintenance system** or **TMS** is a program that keeps track of dependencies between sentences so that retraction (and some other operations) will be more efficient. A TMS actually performs four important jobs. First, a TMS enables dependency-directed backtracking, to avoid the inefficiency of chronological backtracking.

EXPLANATIONS

A second and equally important job is to provide **explanations** of propositions. A proof is one kind of explanation—if we ask, "Explain why you believe P is true?" then a proof of P is a good explanation. If a proof is not possible, then a good explanation is one that involves

ASSUMPTIONS

assumptions. For example, if we ask, "Explain why the car won't start," there may not be enough evidence to prove anything, but a good explanation is, "If we assume that there is gas in the car and that it is reaching the cylinders, then the observed absence of activity proves that the electrical system must be at fault." Technically, an explanation E of a sentence P is defined as a set of sentences such that E entails P. The sentences in E must either be known to be true (i.e., they are in the knowledge base), or they must be known to be assumptions that the problem-solver has made. To avoid having the whole knowledge base as an explanation, we will insist that E is minimal, that is, that there is no proper subset of E that is also an explanation.

The ability to deal with assumptions and explanations is critical for the third job of a TMS: doing default reasoning. In a taxonomic system that allows exceptions, stating that Opus is a penguin does not sanction an irrefutable inference that Opus has two legs, because additional information about Opus might override the derived belief. A TMS can deliver the explanation that Opus, being a penguin, has two legs *provided he is not an abnormal penguin*. Here, the lack of abnormality is made into an explicit assumption. Finally, TMSs help in dealing with inconsistencies. If adding P to the knowledge base results in a logical contradiction, a TMS can help pinpoint an explanation of what the contradiction is.

JTMS

There are several types of TMSs. The simplest is the justification-based truth maintenance system or **JTMS**. In a JTMS, each sentence in the knowledge base is annotated with a justification that identifies the sentences from which it was inferred, if any. For example, if Q is inferred by Modus Ponens from P, then the set of sentences $\{P, \ P \ \Rightarrow \ Q\}$ could serve as a justification of the sentence Q. Some sentences will have more than one justification. Justifications are used to do selective retractions. If after adding P_1 through P_n we get a call to RETRACT(P_i), then the JTMS will remove from the knowledge base exactly those sentences for which P_i is a required part of every justification. So, if a sentence Q had $\{P_i, \ P_i \ \Rightarrow \ Q\}$ as its only justification, it would be removed; if it had the additional justification $\{P_i, \ P_i \vee R \ \Rightarrow \ Q\}$, then it would still be removed; but if it also had the justification $\{R, \ P_i \vee R \ \Rightarrow \ Q\}$, then it would be spared.

In most JTMS implementations, it is assumed that sentences that are considered once will probably be considered again, so rather than removing a sentence from the knowledge base when it loses all justification, we merely mark the sentence as being *out* of the knowledge base. If a subsequent assertion restores one of the justifications, then we mark the sentence as being back *in*. In this way, the JTMS retains all of the inference chains that it uses, and need not rederive sentences when a justification becomes valid again.

To solve the car diagnosis problem with a JTMS, we would first assume (that is, assert) that there is gas in the car and that it is reaching the cylinders. These sentences would be labelled as *in*. Given the right background knowledge, the sentence representing the fact that the car will not start would also become labelled *in*. We could then ask the JTMS for an explanation. On the other hand, if it turned out that the assumptions were not sufficient (i.e., they did not lead to "car won't start" being *in*), then we would retract the original assumptions and make some new ones. We still have a search problem—the TMS does only part of the job.

ATMS   The JTMS was the first type of TMS, but the most popular type is the **ATMS** or assumption-based truth maintenance system. The difference is that a JTMS represents one consistent state of the world at a time. The maintenance of justifications allows you to quickly move from one state to another by making a few retractions and assertions, but at any time only one state is represented. An ATMS represents *all* the states that have ever been considered at the same time. Whereas a JTMS simply labels each sentence as being *in* or *out*, an ATMS keeps track, for each sentence, of which assumptions would cause the sentence to be true. In other words, each sentence has a label that consists of a set of assumption sets. The sentence holds just in those cases where all the assumptions in one of the assumption sets hold.

To solve problems with an ATMS, we can make assumptions (such as P_i or "gas in car") in any order we like. Instead of retracting assumptions when one line of reasoning fails, we just assert all the assumptions we are interested in, even if they contradict each other. We then can check a particular sentence to determine the conditions under which it holds. For example, the label on the sentence Q would be $\{\{P_i\}, \{R\}\}$, meaning that Q is true under the assumption that P_i is true or under the assumption that R is true. A sentence that has the empty set as one of its assumption sets is necessarily true—it is true with no assumptions at all. On the other hand, a sentence with no assumption sets is just false.

The algorithms used to implement truth maintenance systems are a little complicated, and we do not cover them here. The computational complexity of the truth maintenance problem is at least as great as that of propositional inference—that is, NP-hard. Therefore, you should not expect truth maintenance to be a panacea (except for trivially small problems). But when used carefully (for example, with an informed choice about what is an assumption and what is a fact that can not be retracted), a TMS can be an important part of a logical system.

10.9   SUMMARY

This chapter has provided a connection between the conceptual foundations of knowledge representation and reasoning, explained in Chapters 6 through 9, and the practical world of actual reasoning systems. We emphasize that real understanding of these systems can only be obtained by trying them out.

We have described implementation techniques and characteristics of four major classes of logical reasoning systems:

- Logic programming systems and theorem provers.
- Production systems.
- Semantic networks.
- Description logics.

We have seen that there is a trade-off between the expressiveness of the system and its efficiency. Compilation can provide significant improvements in efficiency by taking advantage of the fact that the set of sentences is fixed in advance. Usability is enhanced by providing a clear semantics for the representation language, and by simplifying the execution model so that the user has a good idea of the computations required for inference.

BIBLIOGRAPHICAL AND HISTORICAL NOTES

Work on indexing and retrieval in knowledge bases appears in the literatures of both AI and databases. The two major texts on AI programming (Charniak *et al.*, 1987; Norvig, 1992) discuss the topic in depth. The text by Forbus and de Kleer (1993) also covers much of this ground. The standard reference on management of databases and knowledge bases is (Ullman, 1989). Jack Minker was a major pioneer in the development of the theory of deductive databases (Gallaire and Minker, 1978; Minker, 1988). Colomb (1991) presents some interesting ideas about using hardware to aid indexing of Prolog programs.

As mentioned in Chapter 9, unification was foreshadowed by Herbrand (1930), and formally introduced by Robinson (1965) in the same article that unveiled the resolution inference rule. Extending work by Boyer and Moore (1972), Martelli and Montanari (1976) and Paterson and Wegman (1978) developed unification algorithms that run in linear time and space via sharing of structure among representations of terms. Unification is surveyed by Knight (1989) and by Lassez et al. (1988). Shieber (1986) covers the use of unification in natural language processing.

Prolog was developed, and the first interpreter written, by the French researcher Alain Colmerauer in 1972 (Roussel, 1975; Colmerauer *et al.*, 1973); Colmerauer (1985) also gives an English-language survey of Prolog. Much of the theoretical background was developed by Robert Kowalski (1974; 1979b; 1979a) in collaboration with Colmerauer. Kowalski (1988) and Cohen (1988) provide good historical overviews of the origins of Prolog. *Foundations of Logic Programming* (Lloyd, 1987) is a theoretical analysis of the underpinnings of Prolog and other logic programming languages. Ait-Kaci (1991) gives a clear exposition of the Warren Abstract Machine (WAM) model of computation (Warren, 1983).

Recently, much of the effort in logic programming has been aimed toward increasing efficiency by building information about specific domains or specific inference patterns into the logic programming language. The language LOGIN (Ait-Kaci and Nasr, 1986) incorporates efficient handling of inheritance reasoning. Constraint logic programming (CLP) is based on the use of constraint satisfaction, together with a background theory, to solve constraints on variables (Roach *et al.*, 1990), rather than the simple equality propagation used in normal unification. (Herbrand's original formulation had also used constraining equations rather than syntactic matching.) CLP is analyzed theoretically in (Jaffar and Lassez, 1987). Jaffar *et al.* (1992a) work specifically in the domain of the real numbers, using a logic programming language called CLP(R). Concurrent CLP is addressed by Saraswat (1993). Jaffar *et al.* (1992b) present the Constraint Logic Abstract Machine (CLAM), a WAM-like abstraction designed to aid in the analysis of CLP(R). Ait-Kaci and Podelski (1993) describe a sophisticated constraint logic programming language called LIFE, which combines constraint logic programming with functional programming and with inheritance reasoning (as in LOGIN). Prolog III (Colmerauer, 1990) builds in several assorted types of reasoning into a Prolog-like language. Volume 58 (1992) of the journal *Artificial Intelligence* is devoted primarily to constraint-based systems. Kohn (1991) describes an ambitious project to use constraint logic programming as the foundation for a real-time control architecture, with applications to fully automatic pilots.

Aside from the development of constraint logic and other advanced logic programming languages, there has been considerable effort to speed up the execution of Prolog by highly optimized compilation and the use of parallel hardware, especially in the Japanese Fifth Generation computing project. Van Roy (1990) examines some of the issues involved in fast execution on serial hardware. Feigenbaum and Shrobe (1993) provide a general account and evaluation of the Fifth Generation project. The Fifth Generation's parallel hardware prototype was the PIM, or Parallel Inference Machine (Taki, 1992). Logic programming of the PIM was based on the formalism of guarded Horn clauses (Ueda, 1985) and the GHC and KL1 languages that grew out of it (Furukawa, 1992). A number of applications of parallel logic programming are covered by Nitta *et al.* (1992). Other languages for parallel logic programming include Concurrent Prolog (Shapiro, 1983) and PARLOG (Clark and Gregory, 1986).

FUNCTIONAL
PROGRAMMING

Logic programming is not the only paradigm of programming that has been prominent in AI. **Functional programming** models programs not as collections of logical clauses but as descriptions of mathematical functions. Functional programming is based on the **lambda calculus** (Church, 1941) and **combinatory logic** (Schönfinkel, 1924; Curry and Feys, 1958), two sophisticated mathematical notations for describing and reasoning about functions. The earliest functional programming language, dating from 1958, was **Lisp**, which is due to John McCarthy. Its history and prehistory is described in detail in (McCarthy, 1978). Incidentally, McCarthy denies (p. 190) that Lisp was intended as an actual implementation of the lambda-calculus (as has often been asserted), although it does borrow certain features. Lisp stands for LISt Processing, the use of **linked lists** whose elements are connected by pointers (rather than by proximity in the machine's address space, as arrays are) to create data structures of great flexibility. The list processing technique predated Lisp and functional programming (Newell and Shaw, 1957; Gelernter *et al.*, 1960). After its invention, Lisp proliferated into a wide variety of dialects, partly because the language had been designed to be easy to modify and extend. In the past two decades, there has been an effort to reunify the language as **Common Lisp**, described in great detail by Steele (1990). Both of the two major AI programming texts mentioned above assume the use of Lisp. A number of other functional programming languages have been developed around a small, clean core of definitions. These include SCHEME, DYLAN, and ML.

The so-called **problem-solving languages** were precursors of logic programming in that they attempted to incorporate inference-like mechanisms, although they were not logic programming languages as such and had control structures other than backtracking. PLANNER (Hewitt, 1969), although never actually implemented, was a very complex language that used automatic backtracking mechanisms analogous to the Prolog control structure. A subset known as MICRO-PLANNER (Sussman and Winograd, 1970) was implemented and used in the SHRDLU natural language understanding system (Winograd, 1972). The CONNIVER language (Sussman and McDermott, 1972) allowed finer programmer control over backtracking than MICRO-PLANNER. CONNIVER was used in the HACKER (Sussman, 1975) and BUILD (Fahlman, 1974) planning systems. QLISP (Sacerdoti *et al.*, 1976) used pattern matching to initiate function calls, as Prolog does; it was used in the NOAH planning system (Sacerdoti, 1975; Sacerdoti, 1977). More recently, POPLOG (Sloman, 1985) has attempted to incorporate several programming languages, including Lisp, Prolog, and POP-11 (Barrett *et al.*, 1985), into an integrated system.

Reasoning systems with metalevel capabilities were first proposed by Hayes (1973), but his GOLUX system was never built (a fate that also befell Doyle's (1980) ambitious SEAN system). AMORD (de Kleer *et al.*, 1977) put some of these ideas into practice, as did TEIRESIAS (Davis, 1980) in the field of rule-based expert systems. In the area of logic programming systems, MRS (Genesereth and Smith, 1981; Russell, 1985) provided extensive metalevel facilities. Dincbas and Le Pape (1984) describe a similar system called METALOG. The work of David E. Smith (1989) on controlling logical inference builds on MRS. Alan Bundy's (1983) PRESS system used logical reasoning at the metalevel to guide the use of equality reasoning in solving algebra and trigonometry problems. It was able to attain humanlike performance on the British A-level exams for advanced precollege students, although equality reasoning had previously been thought to be a very difficult problem for automated reasoning systems. Guard *et al.* (1969) describe the early SAM theorem prover, which helped to solve an open problem in lattice theory. Wos and Winker (1983) give an overview of the contributions of AURA theorem prover toward solving open problems in various areas of mathematics and logic. McCune (1992) follows up on this, recounting the accomplishments of AURA's successor OTTER in solving open problems. McAllester (1989) describes the ONTIC expert assistant system for mathematics research.

A Computational Logic (Boyer and Moore, 1979) is the basic reference on the Boyer-Moore theorem prover. Stickel (1988) covers the Prolog Technology Theorem Prover (PTTP), which incorporates the technique of locking introduced by Boyer (1971).

Early work in automated program synthesis was done by Simon (1963), Green (1969a), and Manna and Waldinger (1971). The transformational system of Burstall and Darlington (1977) used equational reasoning with recursion equations for program synthesis. Barstow (1979) provides an early book-length treatment. RAPTS (Paige and Henglein, 1987) takes an approach that views automated synthesis as an extension of the process of compilation. KIDS (Smith, 1990) is one of the strongest modern systems; it operates as an expert assistant. Manna and Waldinger (1992) give a tutorial introduction to the current state of the art, with emphasis on their own deductive approach. *Automating Software Design* (Lowry and McCartney, 1991) is an anthology; the articles describe a number of current approaches.

There are a number of textbooks on logic programming and Prolog. *Logic for Problem Solving* (Kowalski, 1979b) is an early text on logic programming in general, with a number of exercises. Several textbooks on Prolog are available (Clocksin and Mellish, 1987; Sterling and Shapiro, 1986; O'Keefe, 1990; Bratko, 1990). Despite focusing on Common Lisp, Norvig (1992) gives a good deal of basic information about Prolog, as well as suggestions for implementing

Prolog interpreters and compilers in Common Lisp. Several textbooks on automated reasoning were mentioned in Chapter 9. Aside from these, a unique text by Bundy (1983) provides reasonably broad coverage of the basics while also providing treatments of more advanced topics such as meta-level inference (using PRESS as one case study) and the use of higher-order logic. The *Journal of Logic Programming* and the *Journal of Automated Reasoning* are the principal journals for logic programming and theorem proving respectively. The major conferences in these fields are the annual International Conference on Automated Deduction (CADE) and International Conference on Logic Programming.

Aside from classical examples like the semantic networks used in Shastric Sanskrit grammar described in Chapter 8, or Peirce's existential graphs as described by Roberts (1973), modern work on semantic networks in AI began in the 1960s with the work of Quillian (1961; 1968). Charniak's (1972) thesis served to underscore the full extent to which heterogeneous knowledge on a wide variety of topics is essential for the interpretation of natural language discourse.

Minsky's (1975) so-called "frames paper" served to place knowledge representation on the map as a central problem for AI. The specific formalism suggested by Minsky, however, that of so-called "frames," was widely criticized as, at best, a trivial extension of the techniques of object-oriented programming, such as inheritance and the use of default values (Dahl *et al.*, 1970; Birtwistle *et al.*, 1973), which predated Minsky's frames paper. It is not clear to what extent the latter papers on object-oriented programming were influenced in turn by early AI work on semantic networks.

The question of semantics arose quite acutely with respect to Quillian's semantic networks (and those of others who followed his approach), with their ubiquitous and very vague "ISA links," as well as other early knowledge representation formalisms such as that of MERLIN (Moore and Newell, 1973) with its mysterious "flat" and "cover" operations. Woods' (1975) famous article "What's In a Link?" drew the attention of AI researchers to the need for precise semantics in knowledge representation formalisms. Brachman (1979) elaborated on this point and proposed solutions. Patrick Hayes's (1979) "The Logic of Frames" cut even deeper by claiming that most of whatever content such knowledge representations *did* have was merely sugar-coated logic: "Most of 'frames' is just a new syntax for parts of first-order logic." Drew McDermott's (1978b) "Tarskian Semantics, or, No Notation Without Denotation!" argued that the kind of semantical analysis used in the formal study of first-order logic, based on Tarski's definition of truth, should be the standard for *all* knowledge representation formalisms. Measuring all formalisms by the "logic standard" has many advocates but remains a controversial idea; notably, McDermott himself has reversed his position in "A Critique of Pure Reason" (McDermott, 1987). NETL (Fahlman, 1979) was a sophisticated semantic network system whose ISA links (called "virtual copy" or VC links) were based more on the notion of "inheritance" characteristic of frame systems or of object-oriented programming languages than on the subset relation, and were much more precisely defined than Quillian's links from the pre-Woods era. NETL is particularly intriguing because it was intended to be implemented in parallel hardware to overcome the difficulty of retrieving information from large semantic networks. David Touretzky (1986) subjects inheritance to rigorous mathematical analysis. Selman and Levesque (1993) discuss the complexity of inheritance with exceptions, showing that in most formulations it is NP-complete.

The development of description logics is merely the most recent stage in a long line of research aimed at finding useful subsets of first-order logic for which inference is computationally tractable. Hector Levesque and Ron Brachman (1987) showed that certain logical constructs, notably certain uses of disjunction and negation, were primarily responsible for the intractability of logical inference. Building on the KL-ONE system (Schmolze and Lipkis, 1983), a number of systems have been developed whose designs incorporate the results of theoretical complexity analysis, most notably KRYPTON (Brachman *et al.*, 1983) and Classic (Borgida *et al.*, 1989). The result has been a marked increase in the speed of inference, and a much better understanding of the interaction between complexity and expressiveness in reasoning systems. On the other hand, as Doyle and Patil (1991) argue, restricting the expressiveness of a language either makes it impossible to solve certain problems, or encourages the user to circumvent the language restrictions using nonlogical means.

The study of truth maintenance systems began with the TMS (Doyle, 1979) and RUP (McAllester, 1980) systems, both of which were essentially JTMSs. The ATMS approach was described in a series of papers by Johan de Kleer (1986c; 1986a; 1986b). *Building Problem Solvers* (Forbus and de Kleer, 1993) explains in depth how TMSs can be used in AI applications.

EXERCISES

10.1   Recall that inheritance information in semantic networks can be captured logically by suitable implication sentences. In this exercise, we will consider the efficiency of using such sentences for inheritance.

    a. Consider the information content in a used-car catalogue such as Kelly's "Blue Book": that, for example, 1973 Dodge Vans are worth $575. Suppose all this information (for 11,000 models) is encoded as logical rules, as suggested in the chapter. Write down three such rules, including that for 1973 Dodge Vans. How would you use the rules to find the value of a *particular* car (e.g., JB, which is a 1973 Dodge Van) given a backward-chaining theorem prover such as Prolog?

    b. Compare the time efficiency of the backward-chaining method for solving this problem with the inheritance method used in semantic nets.

    c. Explain how forward chaining allows a logic-based system to solve the same problem efficiently, assuming that the KB contains only the 11,000 rules about price.

    d. Describe a situation in which neither forward nor backward chaining on the rules will allow the price query for an individual car to be handled efficiently.

    e. Can you suggest a solution enabling this type of query to be solved efficiently in all cases in logic systems? (*Hint:* Remember that two cars of the same category have the same price.)

10.2   The following Prolog code defines a relation R.

```
R([],X,X).
R([A|X],Y,[A|Z]) :- R(X,Y,Z)
```

    a. Show the proof tree and solution obtained for the queries

$$R([1,2],L,[1,2,3,4]) \quad \text{and} \quad R(L,M,[1,2,3,4])$$

b. What standard list operation does R represent?

c. Define the Prolog predicate last(L,X) (X is the last element of list L) using R and no other predicates.

10.3   In this exercise, we will look at sorting in Prolog.

a. Write Prolog clauses that define the predicate sorted(L), which is true if and only if list L is sorted in ascending order.

b. Write a Prolog definition for the predicate perm(L,M), which is true if and only if L is a permutation of M.

c. Define sort(L,M) (M is a sorted version of L) using perm and sorted.

d. Run sort on longer and longer lists until you lose patience. What is the time complexity of your program?

e. Write a faster sorting algorithm, such as insertion sort or quicksort, in Prolog.

10.4   In this exercise, we will look at the recursive application of rewrite rules using logic programming. A rewrite rule (or demodulator in OTTER terminology) is an equation with a specified direction. For example, the rewrite rule $x + 0 \rightarrow x$ suggests replacing any expression that matches $x + 0$ with the expression x. The application of rewrite rules is a central part of mathematical reasoning systems, for example, in expression simplification and symbolic differentiation. We will use the predicate $Rewrite(x, y)$ to represent rewrite rules. For example, the earlier rewrite rule is written as $Rewrite(x + 0, x)$. We will also need some way to define primitive terms that cannot be further simplified. For example, we can use $Primitive(0)$ to say that 0 is a primitive term.

a. Write a definition of a predicate $Simplify(x, y)$, that is true when y is a simplified version of x; that is, no further rewrite rules are applicable to any subexpression of y.

b. Write a collection of rules for simplification of expressions involving arithmetic operators, and apply your simplification algorithm to some sample expressions.

c. Write a collection of rewrite rules for symbolic differentiation, and use them along with your simplification rules to differentiate and simplify expressions involving arithmetic expressions, including exponentiation.

10.5   In this exercise, we will consider the implementation of search algorithms in Prolog. Suppose that successor(X,Y) is true when state Y is a successor of state X; and that goal(X) is true when X is a goal state. Write a definition for solve(X,P), which means that P is a path (list of states) beginning with X, ending in a goal state, and consisting of a sequence of legal steps as defined by successor. You will find that depth-first search is the easiest way to do this. How easy would it be to add heuristic search control?

10.6   Why do you think that Prolog includes no heuristics for guiding the search for a solution to the query?

10.7   Assume we put into a logical database a segment of the U.S. census data listing the age, city of residence, date of birth, and mother of every person, and where the constant symbol for each person is just their social security number. Thus, Ron's age is given by $Age(443\text{-}65\text{-}1282, 76)$.

Which of the indexing schemes S1–S5 following enable an efficient solution for which of the queries Q1–Q4 (assuming normal backward chaining).

◇ **S1**: an index for each atom in each position.

◇ **S2**: an index for each first argument.

◇ **S3**: an index for each predicate atom.

◇ **S4**: an index for each *combination* of predicate and first argument.

◇ **S5**: an index for each *combination* of predicate and second argument, and an index for each first argument (nonstandard).

◇ **Q1**: $Age(443\text{-}44\text{-}4321, x)$

◇ **Q2**: $ResidesIn(x, Houston)$

◇ **Q3**: $Mother(x, y)$

◇ **Q4**: $Age(x, 34) \wedge ResidesIn(x, TinyTownUSA)$

10.8   We wouldn't want a semantic network to contain both $Age(Bill, 12)$ and $Age(Bill, 10)$, but its fine if it contains both $Friend(Bill, Opus)$ and $Friend(Bill, Steve)$. Modify the functions in Figure 10.10 so that they make the distinction between logical functions and logical relations, and treat each properly.

10.9   The code repository contains a logical reasoning system whose components can be replaced by other versions. Re-implement some or all of the following components, and make sure that the resulting system works using the circuit example from Chapter 8.

    a. Basic data types and access functions for sentences and their components.

    b. STORE and FETCH for atomic sentences (disregarding efficiency).

    c. Efficient indexing mechanisms for STORE and FETCH.

    d. A unification algorithm.

    e. A forward-chaining algorithm.

    f. A backward-chaining algorithm using iterative deepening.

Part IV

ACTING LOGICALLY

In Part II, we saw that an agent cannot always select actions based solely on the percepts that are available at the moment, or even the internal model of the current state. We saw that **problem-solving agents** are able to plan ahead—to consider the consequences of *sequences* of actions—before acting. In Part III, we saw that a **knowledge-based agent** can select actions based on explicit, logical representations of the current state and the effects of actions. This allows the agent to succeed in complex, inaccessible environments that are too difficult for a problem-solving agent.

In Part IV, we put these two ideas together to build **planning agents**. At the most abstract level, the task of planning is the same as problem solving. Planning can be viewed as a type of problem solving in which the agent uses beliefs about actions and their consequences to search for a solution over the more abstract space of plans, rather than over the space of situations. Planning algorithms can also be viewed as special-purpose theorem provers that reason efficiently with axioms describing actions.

Chapter 11 introduces the basic ideas of planning, including the need to divide complex problems into **subgoals** whose solutions can be combined to provide a solution for the complete problem. Chapter 12 extends these ideas to more expressive representations of states and actions, and discusses real-world planning systems. Chapter 13 considers the execution of plans, particularly for cases in which unknown contingencies must be handled.

11 PLANNING

In which we see how an agent can take advantage of problem structure to construct complex plans of action.

PLANNING AGENT

In this chapter, we introduce the basic ideas involved in planning systems. We begin by specifying a simple **planning agent** that is very similar to a problem-solving agent (Chapter 3) in that it constructs plans that achieve its goals, and then executes them. Section 11.2 explains the limitations of the problem-solving approach, and motivates the design of planning systems. The planning agent differs from a problem-solving agent in its representations of goals, states, and actions, as described in Section 11.4. The use of explicit, logical representations enables the planner to direct its deliberations much more sensibly. The planning agent also differs in the way it represents and searches for solutions. The remainder of the chapter describes in detail the basic **partial-order planning** algorithm, which searches through the space of plans to find one that is guaranteed to succeed. The additional flexibility gained from the partially ordered plan representation allows a planning agent to handle quite complicated domains.

11.1 A SIMPLE PLANNING AGENT

When the world state is accessible, an agent can use the percepts provided by the environment to build a complete and correct model of the current world state. Then, given a goal, it can call a suitable planning algorithm (which we will call IDEAL-PLANNER) to generate a plan of action. The agent can then execute the steps of the plan, one action at a time.

The algorithm for the simple planning agent is shown in Figure 11.1. This should be compared with the problem-solving agent shown in Figure 3.1. The planning algorithm IDEAL-PLANNER can be any of the planners described in this chapter or Chapter 12. We assume the existence of a function STATE-DESCRIPTION, which takes a percept as input and returns an initial state description in the format required by the planner, and a function MAKE-GOAL-QUERY, which is used to ask the knowledge base what the next goal should be. Note that the agent must deal with the case where the goal is infeasible (it just ignores it and tries another), and the case

```
function SIMPLE-PLANNING-AGENT(percept) returns an action
    static: KB, a knowledge base (includes action descriptions)
            p, a plan, initially NoPlan
            t, a counter, initially 0, indicating time
    local variables: G, a goal
                     current, a current state description

    TELL(KB, MAKE-PERCEPT-SENTENCE(percept, t))
    current ← STATE-DESCRIPTION(KB, t)
    if p = NoPlan then
        G ← ASK(KB, MAKE-GOAL-QUERY(t))
        p ← IDEAL-PLANNER(current, G, KB)
    if p = NoPlan or p is empty then action ← NoOp
    else
        action ← FIRST(p)
        p ← REST(p)
    TELL(KB, MAKE-ACTION-SENTENCE(action, t))
    t ← t + 1
    return action
```

Figure 11.1   A simple planning agent. The agent first generates a goal to achieve, and then constructs a plan to achieve it from the current state. Once it has a plan, it keeps executing it until the plan is finished, then begins again with a new goal.

where the complete plan is in fact empty, because the goal is already true in the initial state. The agent interacts with the environment in a minimal way—it uses its percepts to define the initial state and thus the initial goal, but thereafter it simply follows the steps in the plan it has constructed. In Chapter 13, we discuss more sophisticated agent designs that allow more interaction between the world and the planner during plan execution.

11.2   FROM PROBLEM SOLVING TO PLANNING

Planning and problem solving are considered different subjects because of the differences in the representations of goals, states, and actions, and the differences in the representation and construction of action sequences. In this section, we first describe some of the difficulties encountered by a search-based problem-solving approach, and then introduce the methods used by planning systems to overcome these difficulties.

Recall the basic elements of a search-based problem-solver:

- **Representation of actions.** Actions are described by programs that generate successor state descriptions.
- **Representation of states.** In problem solving, a complete description of the initial state is

given, and actions are represented by a program that generates complete state descriptions. Therefore, all state representations are complete. In most problems, a state is a simple data structure: a permutation of the pieces in the eight puzzle, the position of the agent in a route-finding problem, or the position of the six people and the boat in the missionaries and cannibals problem. State representations are used only for successor generation, heuristic function evaluation, and goal testing.

- **Representation of goals.** The only information that a problem-solving agent has about its goal is in the form of the goal test and the heuristic function. Both of these can be applied to states to decide on their desirability, but they are used as "black boxes." That is, the problem-solving agent cannot "look inside" to select actions that might be useful in achieving the goal.

- **Representation of plans.** In problem solving, a solution is a sequence of actions, such as "Go from Arad to Sibiu to Fagaras to Bucharest." During the construction of solutions, search algorithms consider only unbroken sequences of actions beginning from the initial state (or, in the case of bidirectional search, ending at a goal state).

Let us see how these design decisions affect an agent's ability to solve the following simple problem: "Get a quart of milk and a bunch of bananas and a variable-speed cordless drill." Treating this as a problem-solving exercise, we need to specify the initial state: the agent is at home but without any of the desired objects, and the operator set: all the things that the agent can do. We can optionally supply a heuristic function: perhaps the number of things that have not yet been acquired.

Figure 11.2 shows a very small part of the first two levels of the search space for this problem, and an indication of the path toward the goal. The actual branching factor would be in the thousands or millions, depending on how actions are specified, and the length of the solution could be dozens of steps. Obviously, there are too many actions and too many states to consider. The real difficulty is that the heuristic evaluation function can only choose among states to decide which is closer to the goal; it cannot eliminate actions from consideration. Even if the evaluation function could get the agent into the supermarket, the agent would then resort to a guessing game. The agent makes guesses by considering actions—buying an orange, buying tuna fish, buying corn flakes, buying milk—and the evaluation function ranks these guesses—bad, bad, bad, good. The agent then knows that buying milk is a good thing, but has no idea what to try next and must start the guessing process all over again.

The fact that the problem-solving agent considers sequences of actions starting from the initial state also contributes to its difficulties. It forces the agent to decide first what to do in the initial state, where the relevant choices are essentially to go to any of a number of other places. Until the agent has figured out *how* to obtain the various items—by buying, borrowing, leasing, growing, manufacturing, stealing—it cannot really decide where to go. The agent therefore needs a more flexible way of structuring its deliberations, so that it can work on whichever part of the problem is most likely to be solvable given the current information.

 The first key idea behind planning is to *"open up" the representation of states, goals, and actions.* Planning algorithms use descriptions in some formal language, usually first-order logic or a subset thereof. States and goals are represented by sets of sentences, and actions are represented by logical descriptions of preconditions and effects. This enables the planner to make

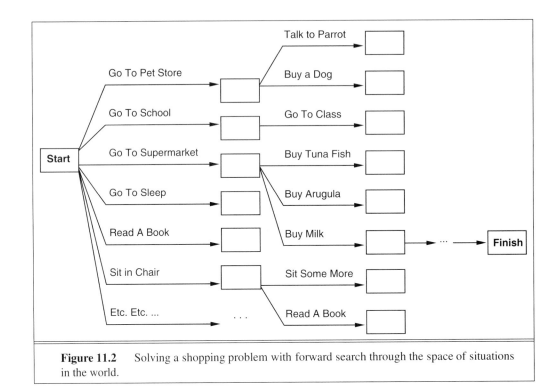

Figure 11.2   Solving a shopping problem with forward search through the space of situations in the world.

direct connections between states and actions. For example, if the agent knows that the goal is a conjunction that includes the conjunct *Have*(*Milk*), and that *Buy*(*x*) achieves *Have*(*x*), then the agent knows that it is worthwhile to consider a plan that includes *Buy*(*Milk*). It need not consider irrelevant actions such as *Buy*(*WhippingCream*) or *GoToSleep*.

The second key idea behind planning is that *the planner is free to add actions to the plan wherever they are needed, rather than in an incremental sequence starting at the initial state.* For example, the agent may decide that it is going to have to *Buy*(*Milk*), even before it has decided where to buy it, how to get there, or what to do afterwards. There is no necessary connection between the order of planning and the order of execution. By making "obvious" or "important" decisions first, the planner can reduce the branching factor for future choices and reduce the need to backtrack over arbitrary decisions. Notice that the representation of states as sets of logical sentences plays a crucial role in making this freedom possible. For example, when adding the action *Buy*(*Milk*) to the plan, the agent can represent the state in which the action is executed as, say, *At*(*Supermarket*). This actually represents an entire class of states—states with and without bananas, with and without a drill, and so on. Search algorithms that require complete state descriptions do not have this option.

The third and final key idea behind planning is that *most parts of the world are independent of most other parts.* This makes it feasible to take a conjunctive goal like "get a quart of milk *and* a bunch of bananas *and* a variable-speed cordless drill" and solve it with a divide-and-conquer strategy. A subplan involving going to the supermarket can be used to achieve the first two conjuncts, and another subplan (e.g., either going to the hardware store or borrowing from a neighbor) can be used to achieve the third. The supermarket subplan can be further divided into a milk subplan and a bananas subplan. We can then put all the subplans together to solve the whole problem. This works because there is little interaction between the two subplans: going to the supermarket does not interfere with borrowing from a neighbor, and buying milk does not interfere with buying bananas (unless the agent runs out of some resource, like time or money).

Divide-and-conquer algorithms are efficient because it is almost always easier to solve several small sub-problems rather than one big problem. However, divide-and-conquer fails in cases where the cost of combining the solutions to the sub-problems is too high. Many puzzles have this property. For example, the goal state in the eight puzzle is a conjunctive goal: to get tile 1 in position *A and* tile 2 in position *B and* ... up to tile 8. We could treat this as a planning problem and plan for each subgoal independently, but the reason that puzzles are "tricky" is that it is difficult to put the subplans together. It is easy to get tile 1 in position *A*, but getting tile 2 in position *B* is likely to move tile 1 out of position. For tricky puzzles, the planning techniques in this chapter will not do any better than problem-solving techniques of Chapter 4. Fortunately, the real world is a largely benign place where subgoals tend to be nearly independent. If this were not the case, then the sheer size of the real world would make successful problem solving impossible.

11.3   PLANNING IN SITUATION CALCULUS

Before getting into planning techniques in detail, we present a formulation of planning as a logical inference problem, using situation calculus (see Chapter 7). A planning problem is represented in situation calculus by logical sentences that describe the three main parts of a problem:

- **Initial state:** An arbitrary logical sentence about a situation S_0. For the shopping problem, this might be[1]

  $At(Home, S_0) \land \neg Have(Milk, S_0) \land \neg Have(Bananas, S_0) \land \neg Have(Drill, S_0)$

- **Goal state:** A logical query asking for suitable situations. For the shopping problem, the query would be

  $\exists s \ At(Home, s) \land Have(Milk, s) \land Have(Bananas, s) \land Have(Drill, s)$

- **Operators:** A set of descriptions of actions, using the action representation described in Chapter 7. For example, here is a successor-state axiom involving the *Buy(Milk)* action:

  $$\forall a, s \ Have(Milk, Result(a, s)) \iff [(a = Buy(Milk) \land At(Supermarket, s)$$
  $$\lor \ (Have(Milk, s) \land a \neq Drop(Milk))]$$

Recall that situation calculus is based on the idea that actions transform states: *Result(a, s)* names the situation resulting from executing action *a* in situation *s*. For the purposes of planning, it

---

[1] A better representation might be along the lines of $\neg \exists m \ Milk(m) \land Have(m, S_0)$, but we have chosen the simpler notation to facilitate the explanation of planning methods. Notice that partial state information is handled automatically by a logical representation, whereas problem-solving algorithms required a special multiple-state representation.

will be useful to handle action sequences as well as single actions. We will use $Result'(l, s)$ to mean the situation resulting from executing the sequence of actions l starting in s. $Result'$ is defined by saying that an empty sequence of actions has no effect on a situation, and the result of a nonempty sequence of actions is the same as applying the first action, and then applying the rest of the actions from the resulting situation:

$$\forall s \; Result'([\,], s) = s$$
$$\forall a, p, s \; Result'([a|p], s) = Result'(p, Result(a, s))$$

A solution to the shopping problem is a plan p that when applied to the start state S_0 yields a situation satisfying the goal query. In other words, a p such that

$$At(Home, Result'(p, S_0)) \wedge Have(Milk, Result'(p, S_0)) \wedge Have(Bananas, Result'(p, S_0))$$
$$\wedge \; Have(Drill, Result'(p, S_0))$$

If we hand this query to ASK, we end up with a solution such as

$$p = [Go(SuperMarket), Buy(Milk), Buy(Banana),$$
$$Go(HardwareStore), Buy(Drill), Go(Home)]$$

From the theoretical point of view, there is little more to say. We have a formalism for expressing goals and plans, and we can use the well-defined inference procedure of first-order logic to find plans. It is true that there are some limitations in the expressiveness of situation calculus, as discussed in Section 8.4, but situation calculus is sufficient for most planning domains.

Unfortunately, a good theoretical solution does not guarantee a good practical solution. We saw in Chapter 3 that problem solving takes time that is exponential in the length of the solution in the worst case, and in Chapter 9, we saw that logical inference is only semidecidable. If you suspect that planning by unguided logical inference would be inefficient, you're right. Furthermore, the inference procedure gives us no guarantees about the resulting plan p other than that it achieves the goal. In particular, note that if p achieves the goal, then so do $[Nothing|p]$ and $[A, A^{-1}|p]$, where $Nothing$ is an action that makes no changes (or at least no relevant changes) to the situation, and A^{-1} is the inverse of A (in the sense that $s = Result(A^{-1}, Result(A, s))$). So we may end up with a plan that contains irrelevant steps if we use unguided logical inference.

To make planning practical we need to do two things: (1) Restrict the language with which we define problems. With a restrictive language, there are fewer possible solutions to search

PLANNER

through. (2) Use a special-purpose algorithm called a **planner** rather than a general-purpose theorem prover to search for a solution. The two go hand in hand: every time we define a new problem-description language, we need a new planning algorithm to process the language. The remainder of this chapter and Chapter 12 describe a series of planning languages of increasing complexity, along with planning algorithms for these languages. Although we emphasize the algorithms, it is important to remember that *we are always dealing with a logic: a formal language with a well-defined syntax, semantics, and proof theory.* The proof theory says what can be inferred about the results of action sequences, and therefore what the legal plans are. The algorithm enables us to find those plans. The idea is that the algorithm can be designed to process the restricted language more efficiently than a resolution theorem prover.

11.4   BASIC REPRESENTATIONS FOR PLANNING

The "classical" approach that most planners use today describes states and operators in a restricted language known as the STRIPS language,[2] or in extensions thereof. The STRIPS language lends itself to efficient planning algorithms, while retaining much of the expressiveness of situation calculus representations.

Representations for states and goals

In the STRIPS language, states are represented by conjunctions of function-free ground literals, that is, predicates applied to constant symbols, possibly negated. For example, the initial state for the milk-and-bananas problem might be described as

$$At(Home) \land \neg Have(Milk) \land \neg Have(Bananas) \land \neg Have(Drill) \land \cdots$$

As we mentioned earlier, a state description does not need to be complete. An incomplete state description, such as might be obtained by an agent in an inaccessible environment, corresponds to a set of possible complete states for which the agent would like to obtain a successful plan. Many planning systems instead adopt the convention—analogous to the "negation as failure" convention used in logic programming—that if the state description does not mention a given positive literal then the literal can be assumed to be false.

Goals are also described by conjunctions of literals. For example, the shopping goal might be represented as

$$At(Home) \land Have(Milk) \land Have(Bananas) \land Have(Drill)$$

Goals can also contain variables. For example, the goal of being at a store that sells milk would be represented as

$$At(x) \land Sells(x, Milk)$$

As with goals given to theorem provers, the variables are assumed to be existentially quantified. However, one must distinguish clearly between a goal given to a planner and a query given to a theorem prover. The former asks for a sequence of actions that *makes the goal true if executed*, and the latter asks whether the query sentence *is true* given the truth of the sentences in the knowledge base.

Although representations of initial states and goals are used as inputs to planning systems, it is quite common for the planning process itself to maintain only implicit representations of states. Because most actions change only a small part of the state representation, it is more efficient to keep track of the changes. We will see how this is done shortly.

---

[2] Named after a pioneering planning program known as the STanford Research Institute Problem Solver. There are two unfortunate things about the name STRIPS. First, the organization no longer uses the name "Stanford" and is now known as SRI International. Second, the program is what we now call a planner, not a problem solver, but when it was developed in 1970, the distinction had not been articulated. Although the STRIPS planner has long since been superseded, the STRIPS language for describing actions has been invaluable, and many "STRIPS-like" variants have been developed.

Representations for actions

Our STRIPS operators consist of three components:

- The **action description** is what an agent actually returns to the environment in order to do something. Within the planner it serves only as a name for a possible action.

- The **precondition** is a conjunction of atoms (positive literals) that says what must be true before the operator can be applied.

- The **effect** of an operator is a conjunction of literals (positive or negative) that describes how the situation changes when the operator is applied.[3]

Here is an example of the syntax we will use for forming a STRIPS operator for going from one place to another:

$$Op(\text{ACTION}:Go(there), \text{PRECOND}:At(here) \land Path(here, there),$$
$$\text{EFFECT}:At(there) \land \neg At(here))$$

(We will also use a graphical notation to describe operators, as shown in Figure 11.3.) Notice that there are no explicit situation variables. Everything in the precondition implicitly refers to the situation immediately before the action, and everything in the effect implicitly refers to the situation that is the result of the action.

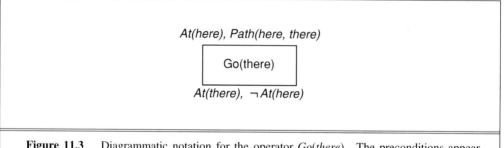

Figure 11.3   Diagrammatic notation for the operator *Go(there)*. The preconditions appear above the action, and the effects below.

An operator with variables is known as an **operator schema**, because it does not correspond to a single executable action but rather to a family of actions, one for each different instantiation of the variables. Usually, only fully instantiated operators can be executed; our planning algorithms will ensure that each variable has a value by the time the planner is done. As with state descriptions, the language of preconditions and effects is quite restricted. The precondition must be a conjunction of positive literals, and the effect must be a conjunction of positive and/or negative literals. All variables are assumed universally quantified, and there can be no additional quantifiers. In Chapter 12, we will relax these restrictions.

We say that an operator o is **applicable** in a state s if there is some way to instantiate the variables in o so that every one of the preconditions of o is true in s, that is, if $Precond(o) \subset s$. In the resulting state, all the positive literals in $Effect(o)$ hold, as do all the literals that held in s,

---

[3] The original version of STRIPS divided the effects into an **add list** and a **delete list**.

except for those that are negative literals in *Effect(o)*. For example, if the initial situation includes the literals

$$At(Home),\ Path(Home, Supermarket), \ldots$$

then the action *Go(Supermarket)* is applicable, and the resulting situation contains the literals

$$\neg At(Home),\ At(Supermarket),\ Path(Home, Supermarket), \ldots$$

Situation Space and Plan Space

In Figure 11.2, we showed a search space of *situations* in the world (in this case the shopping world). A path through this space from the initial state to the goal state constitutes a plan for the shopping problem. If we wanted, we could take a problem described in the STRIPS language and solve it by starting at the initial state and applying operators one at a time until we reached a state that includes all the literals in the goal. We could use any of the search methods of Part II. An algorithm that did this would clearly be considered a problem solver, but we could also consider it a planner. We would call it a **situation space** planner because it searches through the space of possible situations, and a **progression** planner because it searches forward from the initial situation to the goal situation. The main problem with this approach is the high branching factor and thus the huge size of the search space.

One way to try to cut the branching factor is to search backwards, from the goal state to the initial state; such a search is called **regression** planning. This approach is *possible* because the operators contain enough information to regress from a partial description of a result state to a partial description of the state before an operator is applied. We cannot get complete descriptions of states this way, but we don't need to. The approach is *desirable* because in typical problems the goal state has only a few conjuncts, each of which has only a few appropriate operators, whereas the initial state usually has many applicable operators. (An operator is appropriate to a goal if the goal is an effect of the operator.) Unfortunately, searching backwards is complicated somewhat by the fact that we often have to achieve a conjunction of goals, not just one. The original STRIPS algorithm was a situation-space regression planner that was incomplete (it could not always find a plan when one existed) because it had an inadequate way of handling the complication of conjunctive goals. Fixing this incompleteness makes the planner very inefficient.

In summary, the nodes in the search tree of a situation-space planner correspond to situations, and the path through the search tree is the plan that will be ultimately returned by the planner. Each branch point adds another step to either the beginning (regression) or end (progression) of the plan.

An alternative is to search through the space of *plans* rather than the space of *situations*. That is, we start with a simple, incomplete plan, which we call a **partial plan**. Then we consider ways of expanding the partial plan until we come up with a complete plan that solves the problem. The operators in this search are operators on plans: adding a step, imposing an ordering that puts one step before another, instantiating a previously unbound variable, and so on. The solution is the final plan, and the path taken to reach it is irrelevant.

Operations on plans come in two categories. **Refinement operators** take a partial plan and add constraints to it. One way of looking at a partial plan is as a representation for a set

SITUATION SPACE

PROGRESSION

REGRESSION

PARTIAL PLAN

REFINEMENT
OPERATORS

MODIFICATION
OPERATOR

of complete, fully constrained plans. Refinement operators eliminate some plans from this set, but they never add new plans to it. Anything that is not a refinement operator is a **modification operator**. Some planners work by constructing potentially incorrect plans, and then "debugging" them using modification operators. In this chapter, we use only refinement operators.

Representations for plans

If we are going to search through a space of plans, we need to be able to represent them. We can settle on a good representation for plans by considering partial plans for a simple problem: putting on a pair of shoes. The goal is the conjunction of *RightShoeOn* ∧ *LeftShoeOn*, the initial state has no literals at all, and the four operators are

> *Op*(ACTION:*RightShoe*, PRECOND:*RightSockOn*, EFFECT:*RightShoeOn*)
> *Op*(ACTION:*RightSock*, EFFECT:*RightSockOn*)
> *Op*(ACTION:*LeftShoe*, PRECOND:*LeftSockOn*, EFFECT:*LeftShoeOn*)
> *Op*(ACTION:*LeftSock*, EFFECT:*LeftSockOn*)

LEAST COMMITMENT

A partial plan for this problem consists of the two steps *RightShoe* and *LeftShoe*. But which step should come first? Many planners use the principle of **least commitment**, which says that one should only make choices about things that you currently care about, leaving the other choices to be worked out later. This is a good idea for programs that search, because if you make a choice about something you don't care about now, you are likely to make the wrong choice and have to backtrack later. A least commitment planner could leave the ordering of the two steps unspecified. When a third step, *RightSock*, is added to the plan, we want to make sure that putting on the right sock comes before putting on the right shoe, but we do not care where they come with respect to the left shoe. A planner that can represent plans in which some steps are ordered (before or after) with respect to each other and other steps are unordered is called a **partial order**

PARTIAL ORDER

TOTAL ORDER

planner. The alternative is a **total order** planner, in which plans consist of a simple list of steps. A totally ordered plan that is derived from a plan *P* by adding ordering constraints is called a

LINEARIZATION

linearization of *P*.

The socks-and-shoes example does not show it, but planners also have to commit to bindings for variables in operators. For example, suppose one of your goals is *Have(Milk)*, and you have the action *Buy(item, store)*. A sensible commitment is to choose this action with the variable *item* bound to *Milk*. However, there is no good reason to pick a binding for *store*, so the principle of least commitment says to leave it unbound and make the choice later. Perhaps another goal will be to buy an item that is only available in one specialty store. If that store also carries milk, then we can bind the variable *store* to the specialty store at that time. By delaying the commitment to a particular store, we allow the planner to make a good choice later. This strategy can also help prune out bad plans. Suppose that for some reason the branch of the search space that includes the partially instantiated action *Buy(Milk, store)* leads to a failure for some reason unrelated to the choice of store (perhaps the agent has no money). If we had committed to a particular store, then the search algorithm would force us to backtrack and consider another store. But if we have not committed, then there is no choice to backtrack over and we can discard this whole branch of the search tree without having to enumerate any of the stores. Plans in which every variable is

FULLY INSTANTIATED
PLANS

bound to a constant are called **fully instantiated plans**.

PLAN

In this chapter, we will use a representation for plans that allows for deferred commitments about ordering and variable binding. A **plan** is formally defined as a data structure consisting of the following four components:

- A set of plan steps. Each step is one of the operators for the problem.

- A set of step ordering constraints. Each ordering constraint is of the form $S_i \prec S_j$, which is read as "S_i before S_j" and means that step S_i must occur sometime before step S_j (but not necessarily immediately before).[4]

- A set of variable binding constraints. Each variable constraint is of the form $v = x$, where v is a variable in some step, and x is either a constant or another variable.

CAUSAL LINKS

- A set of **causal links**.[5] A causal link is written as $S_i \xrightarrow{c} S_j$ and read as "S_i achieves c for S_j." Causal links serve to record the purpose(s) of steps in the plan: here a purpose of S_i is to achieve the precondition c of S_j.

The initial plan, before any refinements have taken place, simply describes the unsolved problem. It consists of two steps, called *Start* and *Finish*, with the ordering constraint *Start* $\prec$ *Finish*. Both *Start* and *Finish* have null actions associated with them, so when it is time to execute the plan, they are ignored. The *Start* step has no preconditions, and its effect is to add all the propositions that are true in the initial state. The *Finish* step has the goal state as its precondition, and no effects. By defining a problem this way, our planners can start with the initial plan and manipulate it until they come up with a plan that is a solution. The shoes-and-socks problem is defined by the four operators given earlier and an initial plan that we write as follows:

Plan(STEPS:{ S_1: *Op*(ACTION:*Start*),
$\qquad\qquad$ S_2: *Op*(ACTION:*Finish*,
$\qquad\qquad\qquad\qquad$ PRECOND:*RightShoeOn* $\wedge$ *LeftShoeOn*)},
$\qquad$ ORDERINGS: $\{S_1 \prec S_2\}$,
$\qquad$ BINDINGS: {},
$\qquad$ LINKS: {})

As with individual operators, we will use a graphical notation to describe plans (Figure 11.4(a)). The initial plan for the shoes-and-socks problem is shown in Figure 11.4(b). Later in the chapter we will see how this notation is extended to deal with more complex plans.

Figure 11.5 shows a partial-order plan that is a solution to the shoes-and-socks problem, and six linearizations of the plan. This example shows that the partial-order plan representation is powerful because it allows a planner to ignore ordering choices that have no effect on the correctness of the plan. As the number of steps grows, the number of possible ordering choices grows exponentially. For example, if we added a hat and a coat to the problem, which interact neither with each other nor with the shoes and socks, then there would still be one partial plan that represents all the solutions, but there would be 180 linearizations of that partial plan. (Exercise 11.1 asks you to derive this number).

---

[4] We use the notation $A \prec B \prec C$ to mean $(A \prec B) \wedge (B \prec C)$.

[5] Some authors call causal links **protection intervals**.

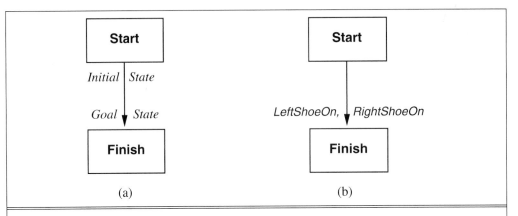

Figure 11.4   (a) Problems are defined by partial plans containing only *Start* and *Finish* steps. The initial state is entered as the effects of the *Start* step, and the goal state is the precondition of the *Finish* step. Ordering constraints are shown as arrows between boxes. (b) The initial plan for the shoes-and-socks problem.

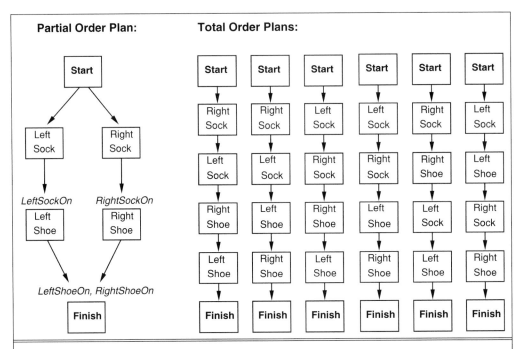

Figure 11.5   A partial-order plan for putting on shoes and socks (including preconditions on steps), and the six possible linearizations of the plan.

Solutions

A **solution** is a plan that an agent can execute, and that guarantees achievement of the goal. If we wanted to make it really easy to check that a plan is a solution, we could insist that only fully instantiated, totally ordered plans can be solutions. But this is unsatisfactory for three reasons. First, for problems like the one in Figure 11.5, it is more natural for the planner to return a partial-order plan than to arbitrarily choose one of the many linearizations of it. Second, some agents are capable of performing actions in parallel, so it makes sense to allow solutions with parallel actions. Lastly, when creating plans that may later be combined with other plans to solve larger problems, it pays to retain the flexibility afforded by the partial ordering of actions. SOLUTION   Therefore, we allow partially ordered plans as solutions using a simple definition: a **solution** is a **complete**, **consistent** plan. We need to define these terms.

COMPLETE PLAN   A **complete plan** is one in which every precondition of every step is **achieved** by some ACHIEVED   other step. A step achieves a condition if the condition is one of the effects of the step, and if no other step can possibly cancel out the condition. More formally, a step S_i achieves a precondition c of the step S_j if (1) $S_i \prec S_j$ and $c \in \text{EFFECTS}(S_i)$; and (2) there is no step S_k such that $(\neg c) \in \text{EFFECTS}(S_k)$, where $S_i \prec S_k \prec S_j$ in some linearization of the plan.

CONSISTENT PLAN   A **consistent plan** is one in which there are no contradictions in the ordering or binding constraints. A contradiction occurs when both $S_i \prec S_j$ and $S_j \prec S_i$ hold or both $v = A$ and $v = B$ hold (for two different constants A and B). Both $\prec$ and $=$ are transitive, so, for example, a plan with $S_1 \prec S_2, S_2 \prec S_3$, and $S_3 \prec S_1$ is inconsistent.

The partial plan in Figure 11.5 is a solution because all the preconditions are achieved. From the preceding definitions, it is easy to see that any linearization of a solution is also a solution. Hence the agent can execute the steps in any order consistent with the constraints, and still be assured of achieving the goal.

11.5   A PARTIAL-ORDER PLANNING EXAMPLE

In this section, we sketch the outline of a partial-order regression planner that searches through plan space. The planner starts with an initial plan representing the start and finish steps, and on each iteration adds one more step. If this leads to an inconsistent plan, it backtracks and tries another branch of the search space. *To keep the search focused, the planner only considers adding steps that serve to achieve a precondition that has not yet been achieved.* The causal links are used to keep track of this.

We illustrate the planner by returning to the problem of getting some milk, a banana, and a drill, and bringing them back home. We will make some simplifying assumptions. First, the *Go* action can be used to travel between any two locations. Second, the description of the *Buy* action ignores the question of money (see Exercise 11.2). The initial state is defined by the following operator, where *HWS* means hardware store and *SM* means supermarket:

$Op(\text{ACTION}:Start, \text{EFFECT}:At(Home) \wedge Sells(HWS, Drill)$
$\wedge Sells(SM, Milk), Sells(SM, Banana))$

The goal state is defined by a *Finish* step describing the objects to be acquired and the final destination to be reached:

> *Op*(ACTION:*Finish*,
>   PRECOND:*Have(Drill)* ∧ *Have(Milk)* ∧ *Have(Banana)* ∧ *At(Home)*)

The actions themselves are defined as follows:

> *Op*(ACTION:*Go(there)*, PRECOND:*At(here)*,
>   EFFECT:*At(there)* ∧ ¬*At(here)*)
> *Op*(ACTION:*Buy(x)*, PRECOND:*At(store)* ∧ *Sells(store, x)*,
>   EFFECT:*Have(x)*)

Figure 11.6 shows a diagram of the initial plan for this problem. We will develop a solution to the problem step by step, showing at each point a figure illustrating the partial plan at that point in the development. As we go along, we will note some of the properties we require for the planning algorithm. After we finish the example, we will present the algorithm in detail.

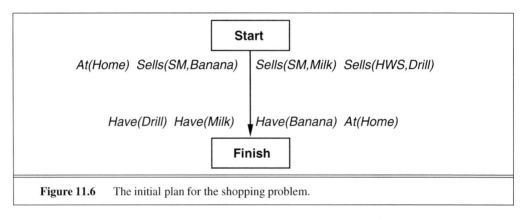

Figure 11.6   The initial plan for the shopping problem.

The first thing to notice about Figure 11.6 is that there are many possible ways in which the initial plan can be elaborated. Some choices will work, and some will not. As we work out the solution to the problem, we will show some correct choices and some incorrect choices. For simplicity, we will start with some correct choices. In Figure 11.7 (top), we have selected three *Buy* actions to achieve three of the preconditions of the *Finish* action. In each case there is only one possible choice because the operator library offers no other way to achieve these conditions.

The bold arrows in the figure are causal links. For example, the leftmost causal link in the figure means that the step *Buy(Drill)* was added in order to achieve the *Finish* step's *Have(Drill)* precondition. The planner will make sure that this condition is maintained by **protecting** it: if a step might delete the *Have(Drill)* condition, then it will not be inserted between the *Buy(Drill)* step and the *Finish* step. Light arrows in the figure show ordering constraints. By definition, all actions are constrained to come after the *Start* action. Also, all causes are constrained to come before their effects, so you can think of each bold arrow as having a light arrow underneath it.

The second stage in Figure 11.7 shows the situation after the planner has chosen to achieve the *Sells* preconditions by linking them to the initial state. Again, the planner has no choice here because there is no other operator that achieves *Sells*.

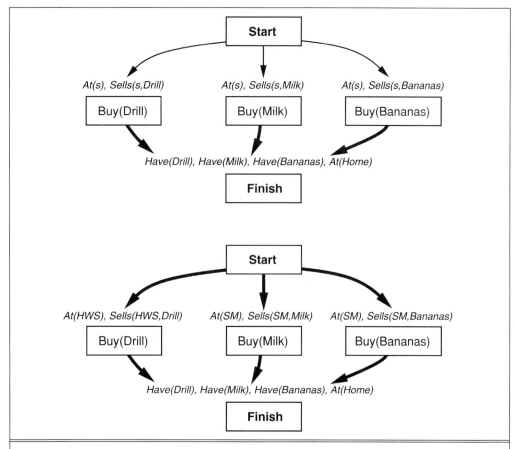

Figure 11.7   Top: A partial plan that achieves three of the four preconditions of *Finish*. The heavy arrows show causal links. Bottom: Refining the partial plan by adding causal links to achieve the *Sells* preconditions of the *Buy* steps.

Although it may not seem like we have done much yet, this is actually quite an improvement over what we could have done with the problem-solving approach. First, out of all the things that one can buy, and all the places that one can go, we were able to choose just the right *Buy* actions and just the right places, without having to waste time considering the others. Then, once we have chosen the actions, we need not decide how to order them; a partial-order planner can make that decision later.

In Figure 11.8, we extend the plan by choosing two *Go* actions to get us to the hardware store and supermarket, thus achieving the *At* preconditions of the *Buy* actions.

So far, everything has been easy. A planner could get this far without having to do any search. Now it gets harder. The two *Go* actions have unachieved preconditions that interact with each other, because the agent cannot be *At* two places at the same time. Each *Go* action has a precondition $At(x)$, where x is the location that the agent was at before the *Go* action. Suppose

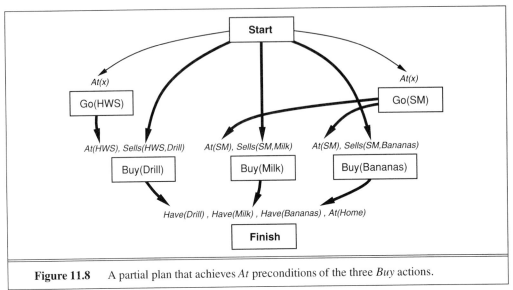

Figure 11.8   A partial plan that achieves *At* preconditions of the three *Buy* actions.

the planner tries to achieve the preconditions of *Go(HWS)* and *Go(SM)* by linking them to the *At(Home)* condition in the initial state. This results in the plan shown in Figure 11.9.

Unfortunately, this will lead to a problem. The step *Go(HWS)* adds the condition *At(HWS)*, but it also deletes the condition *At(Home)*. So if the agent goes to the hardware store, it can no longer go from home to the supermarket. (That is, unless it introduces another step to go back home from the hardware store—but the causal link means that the start step, not some other step,

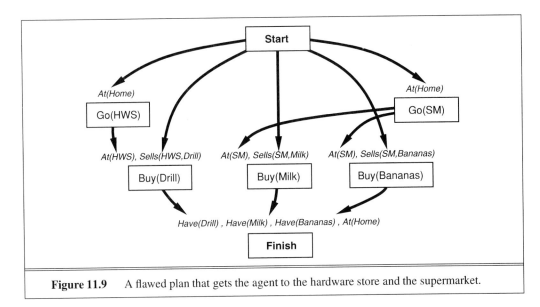

Figure 11.9   A flawed plan that gets the agent to the hardware store and the supermarket.

achieves the *At(Home)* precondition.) On the other hand, if the agent goes to the supermarket first, then it cannot go from home to the hardware store.

At this point, we have reached a dead end in the search for a solution, and must back up and try another choice. The interesting part is seeing how *a planner could notice that this partial plan is a dead end without wasting a lot of time on it.* The key is that the the causal links in a partial plan are **protected links**. A causal link is protected by ensuring that **threats**—that is, steps that might delete (or **clobber**) the protected condition—are ordered to come before or after the protected link. Figure 11.10(a) shows a threat: The causal link $S_1 \xrightarrow{c} S_2$ is threatened by the new step S_3 because one effect of S_3 is to delete c. The way to resolve the threat is to add ordering constraints to make sure that S_3 does not intervene between S_1 and S_2. If S_3 is placed before S_1 this is called **demotion** (see Figure 11.10(b)), and if it is placed after S_2, it is called **promotion** (see Figure 11.10(c)).

PROTECTED LINKS

THREATS

DEMOTION

PROMOTION

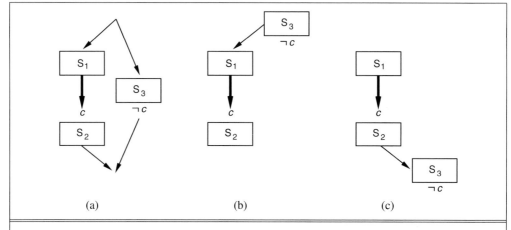

(a)   (b)   (c)

Figure 11.10   Protecting causal links. In (a), the step S_3 threatens a condition c that is established by S_1 and protected by the causal link from S_1 to S_2. In (b), S_3 has been demoted to come before S_1, and in (c) it has been promoted to come after S_2.

In Figure 11.9, there is no way to resolve the threat that each *Go* step poses to the other. Whichever *Go* step comes first will delete the *At(Home)* condition on the other step. Whenever the planner is unable to resolve a threat by promotion or demotion, it gives up on the partial plan and backs up to try a different choice at some earlier point in the planning process.

Suppose the next choice is to try a different way to achieve the *At(x)* precondition of the *Go(SM)* step, this time by adding a causal link from *Go(HWS)* to *Go(SM)*. In other words, the plan is to go from home to the hardware store and then to the supermarket. This introduces another threat. Unless the plan is further refined, it will allow the agent to go from the hardware store to the supermarket without first buying the drill (which was why it went to the hardware store in the first place). However much this might resemble human behavior, we would prefer our planning agent to avoid such forgetfulness. Technically, the *Go(SM)* step threatens the *At(HWS)* precondition of the *Buy(Drill)* step, which is protected by a causal link. The threat is resolved by constraining *Go(SM)* to come after *Buy(Drill)*. Figure 11.11 shows this.

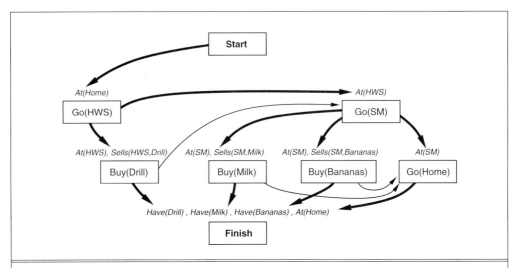

Figure 11.11   Causal link protection in the shopping plan. The $Go(HWS) \xrightarrow{At(HWS)} Buy(Drill)$ causal link is protected ordering the $Go(SM)$ step after $Buy(Drill)$, and the $Go(SM) \xrightarrow{At(SM)}$ $Buy(Milk/Bananas)$ link is protected by ordering $Go(Home)$ after $Buy(Milk)$ and $Buy(Bananas)$.

Only the $At(Home)$ precondition of the *Finish* step remains unachieved.   Adding a $Go(Home)$ step achieves it, but introduces an $At(x)$ precondition that needs to be achieved.[6] Again, the protection of causal links will help the planner decide how to do this:

- If it tries to achieve $At(x)$ by linking to $At(Home)$ in the initial state, there will be no way to resolve the threats caused by $Go(HWS)$ and $Go(SM)$.
- If it tries to link $At(x)$ to the $Go(HWS)$ step, there will be no way to resolve the threat posed by the $Go(SM)$ step, which is already constrained to come after $Go(HWS)$.
- A link from $Go(SM)$ to $At(x)$ means that x is bound to SM, so that now the $Go(Home)$ step deletes the $At(SM)$ condition. This results in threats to the $At(SM)$ preconditions of $Buy(Milk)$ and $Buy(Bananas)$, but these can be resolved by ordering $Go(Home)$ to come after these steps (Figure 11.11).

Figure 11.12 shows the complete solution plan, with the steps redrawn to reflect the ordering constraints on them. The result is an almost totally ordered plan; the only ambiguity is that $Buy(Milk)$ and $Buy(Bananas)$ can come in either order.

Let us take stock of what our partial-order planner has accomplished. It can take a problem that would require many thousands of search states for a problem-solving approach, and solve it with only a few search states. Moreover, the least commitment nature of the planner means it only needs to search at all in places where subplans interact with each other. Finally, the causal links allow the planner to recognize when to abandon a doomed plan without wasting a lot of time expanding irrelevant parts of the plan.

---

[6] Notice that the $Go(Home)$ step also has the effect $\neg At(x)$, meaning that the step will delete an At condition for some location yet to be decided. This is a **possible threat** to protected conditions in the plan such as $At(SM)$, but we will not worry about it for now. Possible threats are dealt with in Section 11.7.

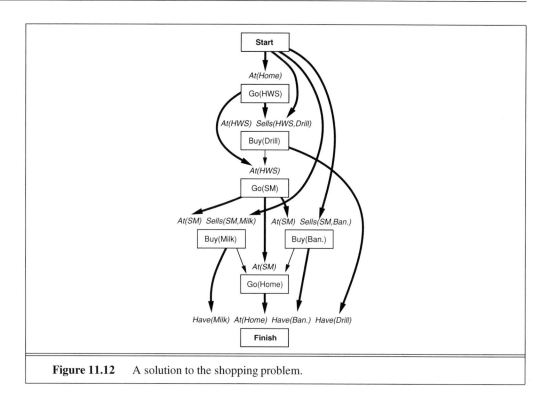

Figure 11.12   A solution to the shopping problem.

11.6   A PARTIAL-ORDER PLANNING ALGORITHM

In this section, we develop a more formal algorithm for the planner sketched in the previous section. We call the algorithm POP, for Partial-Order Planner. The algorithm appears in Figure 11.13. (Notice that POP is written as a *nondeterministic* algorithm, using **choose** and **fail** rather than explicit loops. Nondeterministic algorithms are explained in Appendix B.)

POP starts with a minimal partial plan, and on each step extends the plan by achieving a precondition c of a step S_{need}. It does this by choosing some operator—either from the existing steps of the plan or from the pool of operators—that achieves the precondition. It records the causal link for the newly achieved precondition, and then resolves any threats to causal links. The new step may threaten an existing causal link or an existing step may threaten the new causal link. If at any point the algorithm fails to find a relevant operator or resolve a threat, it backtracks to a previous choice point. An important subtlety is that the selection of a step and precondition in SELECT-SUBGOAL is *not* a candidate for backtracking. The reason is that every precondition needs to be considered eventually, and the handling of preconditions is commutative: handling c_1 and then c_2 leads to exactly the same set of possible plans as handling c_2 and then c_1. So we

---

function POP(*initial, goal, operators*) **returns** *plan*

   plan ← MAKE-MINIMAL-PLAN(*initial, goal*)
   loop do
      if SOLUTION?(*plan*) **then return** *plan*
      S_{need}, c ← SELECT-SUBGOAL(*plan*)
      CHOOSE-OPERATOR(*plan, operators*, S_{need}, c)
      RESOLVE-THREATS(*plan*)
   end

---

function SELECT-SUBGOAL(*plan*) **returns** S_{need}, c

   pick a plan step S_{need} from STEPS(*plan*)
      with a precondition c that has not been achieved
   return S_{need}, c

---

procedure CHOOSE-OPERATOR(*plan, operators*, S_{need}, c)

   choose a step S_{add} from *operators* or STEPS(*plan*) that has c as an effect
   if there is no such step **then fail**
   add the causal link $S_{add} \xrightarrow{c} S_{need}$ to LINKS(*plan*)
   add the ordering constraint $S_{add} \prec S_{need}$ to ORDERINGS(*plan*)
   if S_{add} is a newly added step from *operators* **then**
      add S_{add} to STEPS(*plan*)
      add *Start* $\prec S_{add} \prec$ *Finish* to ORDERINGS(*plan*)

---

procedure RESOLVE-THREATS(*plan*)

   for each S_{threat} that threatens a link $S_i \xrightarrow{c} S_j$ in LINKS(*plan*) **do**
      choose either
         Promotion: Add $S_{threat} \prec S_i$ to ORDERINGS(*plan*)
         Demotion: Add $S_j \prec S_{threat}$ to ORDERINGS(*plan*)
      if not CONSISTENT(*plan*) **then fail**
   end

Figure 11.13   The partial-order planning algorithm, POP.

can just pick a precondition and move ahead without worrying about backtracking. The pick we make affects only the speed, and not the possibility, of finding a solution.

Notice that POP is a regression planner, because it starts with goals that need to be achieved and works backwards to find operators that will achieve them. Once it has achieved all the preconditions of all the steps, it is done; it has a solution. POP *is sound and complete.* Every plan it returns is in fact a solution, and if there is a solution, then it will be found (assuming a breadth-first or iterative deepening search strategy). At this point, we suggest that the reader return to the example of the previous section, and trace through the operation of POP in detail.

11.7   PLANNING WITH PARTIALLY INSTANTIATED OPERATORS

The version of POP in Figure 11.13 outlines the algorithm, but leaves some details unspecified. In particular, it does not deal with variable binding constraints. For the most part, all this entails is being diligent about keeping track of binding lists and unifying the right expressions at the right time. The implementation techniques of Chapter 10 are applicable here.

POSSIBLE THREAT

There is one substantive decision to make: in RESOLVE-THREATS, should an operator that has the effect, say, $\neg At(x)$ be considered a threat to the condition $At(Home)$? Currently we can distinguish between threats and non-threats, but this is a **possible threat**. There are three main approaches to dealing with possible threats:

- **Resolve now with an equality constraint:** Modify RESOLVE-THREATS so that it resolves all possible threats as soon as they are recognized. For example, when the planner chooses the operator that has the effect $\neg At(x)$, it would add a binding such as $x = HWS$ to make sure it does not threaten $At(Home)$.

- **Resolve now with an inequality constraint:** Extend the language of variable binding constraints to allow the constraint $x \neq Home$. This has the advantage of being a lower commitment—it does not require an arbitrary choice for the value of x—but it is a little more complicated to implement, because the unification routines we have used so far all deal with equalities, not inequalities.

- **Resolve later:** The third possibility is to ignore possible threats, and only deal with them when they become *necessary* threats. That is, RESOLVE-THREATS would not consider $\neg At(x)$, to be a threat to $At(Home)$. But if the constraint $x = Home$ were ever added to the plan, then the threat would be resolved (by promotion or demotion). This approach has the advantage of being low commitment, but has the disadvantage of making it harder to decide if a plan is a solution.

Figure 11.14 shows an implementation of the changes to CHOOSE-OPERATOR, along with the changes to RESOLVE-THREATS that are necessary for the third approach. It is certainly possible (and advisable) to do some bookkeeping so that RESOLVE-THREATS will not need to go through a triply nested loop on each call.

When partially instantiated operators appear in plans, the criterion for solutions needs to be refined somewhat. In our earlier definition (page 349), we were concerned mainly with the question of partial ordering; a solution was defined as a partial plan such that all linearizations are guaranteed to achieve the goal. With partially instantiated operators, we also need to ensure that all instantiations will achieve the goal. We therefore extend the definition of achievement for a step in a plan as follows:

A step S_i **achieves** a precondition c of the step S_j if (1) $S_i \prec S_j$ and S_i has an effect that necessarily unifies with c; and (2) there is no step S_k such that $S_i \prec S_k \prec S_j$ in some linearization of the plan, and S_k has an effect that possibly unifies with $\neg c$.

The POP algorithm can be seen as constructing a proof that each precondition of the goal step is achieved. CHOOSE-OPERATOR comes up with the S_i that achieves (1), and RESOLVE-THREATS makes sure that (2) is satisfied by promoting or demoting possible threats. The tricky part is that

---

procedure CHOOSE-OPERATOR($plan$, $operators$, S_{need}, c)

    choose a step S_{add} from $operators$ or STEPS($plan$) that has c_{add} as an effect
           such that u = UNIFY(c, c_{add}, BINDINGS($plan$))
    if there is no such step
        then fail
    add u to BINDINGS($plan$)
    add $S_{add} \xrightarrow{c} S_{need}$ to LINKS($plan$)
    add $S_{add} \prec S_{need}$ to ORDERINGS($plan$)
    if S_{add} is a newly added step from $operators$ **then**
        add S_{add} to STEPS($plan$)
        add $Start \prec S_{add} \prec Finish$ to ORDERINGS($plan$)

---

procedure RESOLVE-THREATS($plan$)

    for each $S_i \xrightarrow{c} S_j$ in LINKS($plan$) **do**
        for each S_{threat} in STEPS($plan$) **do**
            for each c' in EFFECT(S_{threat}) **do**
                if SUBST(BINDINGS($plan$), c) = SUBST(BINDINGS($plan$), $\neg c'$) **then**
                    choose either
                        Promotion: Add $S_{threat} \prec S_i$ to ORDERINGS($plan$)
                        Demotion: Add $S_j \prec S_{threat}$ to ORDERINGS($plan$)
                if not CONSISTENT($plan$)
                    then fail
            end
        end
    end

Figure 11.14   Support for partially instantiated operators in POP.

if we adopt the "resolve-later" approach, then there will be possible threats that are not resolved away. We therefore need some way of checking that these threats are all gone before we return the plan. It turns out that if the initial state contains no variables and if every operator mentions all its variables in its precondition, then any complete plan generated by POP is guaranteed to be fully instantiated. Otherwise we will need to change the function SOLUTION? to check that there are no uninstantiated variables and choose bindings for them if there are. If this is done, then POP is guaranteed to be a sound planner in all cases.

It is harder to see that POP is complete—that is, finds a solution whenever one exists—but again it comes down to understanding how the algorithm mirrors the definition of achievement. The algorithm generates every possible plan that satisfies part (1), and then filters out those plans that do not satisfy part (2) or that are inconsistent. Thus, if there is a plan that is a solution, POP will find it. So if you accept the definition of **solution** (page 349), you should accept that POP is a sound and complete planner.

11.8   KNOWLEDGE ENGINEERING FOR PLANNING

The methodology for solving problems with the planning approach is very much like the general knowledge engineering guidelines of Section 8.2:

- Decide what to talk about.
- Decide on a vocabulary of conditions (literals), operators, and objects.
- Encode operators for the domain.
- Encode a description of the specific problem instance.
- Pose problems to the planner and get back plans.

We will cover each of these five steps, demonstrating them in two domains.

The blocks world

What to talk about: The main consideration is that operators are so restricted in what they can express (although Chapter 12 relaxes some of the restrictions). In this section we show how to define knowledge for a classic planning domain: the blocks world. This domain consists of a set of cubic blocks sitting on a table. The blocks can be stacked, but only one block can fit directly on top of another. A robot arm can pick up a block and move it to another position, either on the table or on top of another block. The arm can only pick up one block at a time, so it cannot pick up a block that has another one on it. The goal will always be to build one or more stacks of blocks, specified in terms of what blocks are on top of what other blocks. For example, a goal might be to make two stacks, one with block A on B, and the other with C on D.

Vocabulary: The objects in this domain are the blocks and the table. They are represented by constants. We will use $On(b, x)$ to indicate that block b is on x, where x is either another block or the table. The operator for moving block b from a position on top of x to a position on top y will be $Move(b, x, y)$. Now one of the preconditions on moving b is that no other block is on it. In first-order logic this would be $\neg \exists x \; On(x, b)$ or alternatively $\forall x \; \neg On(x, b)$. But our language does not allow either of these forms, so we have to think of something else. The trick is to invent a predicate to represent the fact that no block is on b, and then make sure the operators properly maintain this predicate. We will use $Clear(x)$ to mean that nothing is on x.

Operators: The operator $Move$ moves a block b from x to y if both b and y are clear, and once the move is made, x becomes clear but y is clear no longer. The formal description of $Move$ is as follows:

$Op(\text{ACTION:}Move(b, x, y),$
  $\quad \text{PRECOND:}On(b, x) \wedge Clear(b) \wedge Clear(y),$
  $\quad \text{EFFECT:}On(b, y) \wedge Clear(x) \wedge \neg On(b, x) \wedge \neg Clear(y))$

Unfortunately, this operator does not maintain $Clear$ properly when x or y is the table. When $x = Table$, this operator has the effect $Clear(Table)$, but the table should not become clear, and when $y = Table$, it has the precondition $Clear(Table)$, but the table does not have to be clear to move a block onto it. To fix this, we do two things. First, we introduce another operator to move a block b from x to the table:

> Op(ACTION:*MoveToTable*(b, x),
>   PRECOND:*On*$(b, x) \wedge$ *Clear*(b),
>   EFFECT:*On*$(b, Table) \wedge$ *Clear*$(x) \wedge \neg On(b, x)$)

Second, we take the interpretation of *Clear*(x) to be "there is a clear space on x to hold a block." Under this interpretation, *Clear*$(Table)$ will always be part of the initial situation, and it is proper that *Move*$(b, Table, y)$ has the effect *Clear*$(Table)$. The only problem is that nothing prevents the planner from using *Move*$(b, x, Table)$ instead of *MoveToTable*(b, x). We could either live with this problem—it will lead to a larger-than-necessary search space, but will not lead to incorrect answers—or we could introduce the predicate *Block* and add *Block*$(b) \wedge$ *Block*(y) to the precondition of *Move*.

Finally, there is the problem of spurious operations like *Move*(B, C, C), which should be a no-op, but which instead has contradictory effects. It is common to ignore problems like this, because they tend not to have any effect on the plans that are produced. To really fix the problem, we need to be able to put inequalities in the precondition: $b \neq x \neq y$.

Shakey's world

The original STRIPS program was designed to control Shakey,[7] a robot that roamed the halls of SRI in the early 1970s. It turns out that most of the work on STRIPS involved simulations where the actions performed were just printing to a terminal, but occasionally Shakey would actually move around, grab, and push things, based on the plans created by STRIPS. Figure 11.15 shows a version of Shakey's world consisting of four rooms lined up along a corridor, where each room has a door and a light switch.

Shakey can move from place to place, push movable objects (such as boxes), climb on and off of rigid objects (such as boxes), and turn light switches on and off. We will develop the vocabulary of literals along with the operators:

1. Go from current location to location y: *Go*(y)
   This is similar to the *Go* operator used in the shopping problem, but somewhat restricted. The precondition *At*$(Shakey, x)$ establishes the current location, and we will insist that x and y be *In* the same room: *In*$(x, r) \wedge In(y, r)$. To allow Shakey to plan a route from room to room, we will say that the door between two rooms is *In* both of them.

2. Push an object b from location x to location y: *Push*(b, x, y)
   Again we will insist that the locations be in the same room. We introduce the predicate *Pushable*(b), but otherwise this is similar to *Go*.

3. Climb up onto a box: *Climb*(b).
   We introduce the predicate *On* and the constant *Floor*, and make sure that a precondition of *Go* is *On*$(Shakey, Floor)$. For *Climb*(b), the preconditions are that Shakey is *At* the same place as b, and b must be *Climbable*.

---

7 Shakey's name comes from the fact that its motors made it a little unstable when it moved.

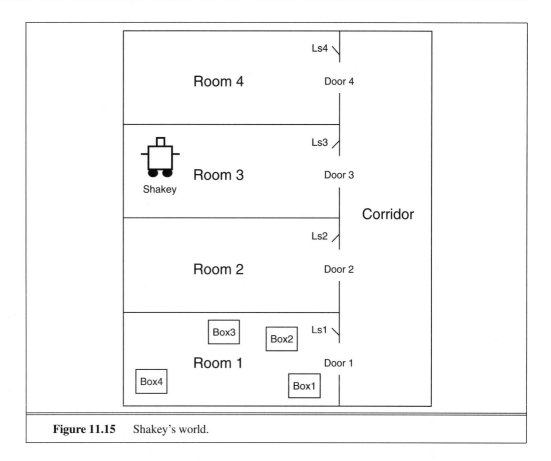

Figure 11.15   Shakey's world.

4. Climb down from a box: *Down(b)*.
   This just undoes the effects of a *Climb*.

5. Turn a light switch on: *TurnOn(ls)*.
   Because Shakey is short, this can only be done when Shakey is on top of a box that is at the light switch's location.[8]

6. Turn a light switch off: *TurnOff(ls)*.
   This is similar to *TurnOn*. Note that it would not be possible to represent toggling a light switch as a STRIPS action, because there are no conditionals in the language to say that the light becomes on if it was off and off if it was on. (Section 12.4 will add conditionals to the language.)

In situation calculus, we could write an axiom to say that every box is pushable and climbable. But in STRIPS, we have to include individual literals for each box in the initial state. We also have to include the complete map of the world in the initial state, in terms of what objects are *In* which

---

[8] Shakey was never dextrous enough to climb on a box or toggle a switch, but STRIPS was capable of finding plans using these actions.

rooms, and which locations they are *At*. We leave this, and the specification of the operators, as an exercise.

In conclusion, it is possible to represent simple domains with STRIPS operators, but it requires ingenuity in coming up with the right set of operators and predicates in order to stay within the syntactic restrictions that the language imposes.

11.9   SUMMARY

In this chapter, we have defined the planning problem and shown that situation calculus is expressive enough to deal with it. Unfortunately, situation calculus planning using a general-purpose theorem prover is very inefficient. Using a restricted language and special-purpose algorithms, planning systems can solve quite complex problems. Thus, planning comes down to an exercise in finding a language that is just expressive enough for the problems you want to solve, but still admits a reasonably efficient algorithm. The points to remember are as follows:

- Planning agents use lookahead to come up with actions that will contribute to goal achievement. They differ from problem-solving agents in their use of more flexible representations of states, actions, goals, and plans.

- The STRIPS language describes actions in terms of their preconditions and effects. It captures much of the expressive power of situation calculus, but not all domains and problems can be described in the STRIPS language.

- It is not feasible to search through the space of situations in complex domains. Instead we search through the space of plans, starting with a minimal plan and extending it until we find a solution. For problems in which most subplans do not interfere with each other, this will be efficient.

- The principle of least commitment says that a planner (or any search algorithm) should avoid making decisions until there is a good reason to make a choice. Partial-ordering constraints and uninstantiated variables allow us to follow a least-commitment approach.

- The causal link is a useful data structure for recording the purposes for steps. Each causal link establishes a protection interval over which a condition should not be deleted by another step. Causal links allow early detection of unresolvable conflicts in a partial plan, thereby eliminating fruitless search.

- The POP algorithm is a sound and complete algorithm for planning using the STRIPS representation.

- The ability to handle partially instantiated operators in POP reduces the need to commit to concrete actions with fixed arguments, thereby improving efficiency.

BIBLIOGRAPHICAL AND HISTORICAL NOTES

The roots of AI planning lie partly in problem solving through state-space search and associated techniques such as problem reduction and means–ends analysis, especially as embodied in Newell and Simon's GPS, and partly in theorem proving and situation calculus, especially as embodied in the QA3 theorem proving system (Green, 1969b). Planning has also been historically motivated by the needs of robotics. STRIPS (Fikes and Nilsson, 1971), the first major planning system, illustrates the interaction of these three influences. STRIPS was designed as the planning component of the software for the Shakey robot project at SRI International. Its overall control structure was modeled on that of GPS, and it used a version of QA3 as a subroutine for establishing preconditions for actions. Lifschitz (1986) offers careful criticism and formal analysis of the STRIPS system. Bylander (1992) shows simple planning in the fashion of STRIPS to be PSPACE-complete. Fikes and Nilsson (1993) give a historical retrospective on the STRIPS project and a survey of its relationship to more recent planning efforts.

For several years, terminological confusion has reigned in the field of planning. Some authors (Genesereth and Nilsson, 1987) use the term **linear** to mean what we call totally ordered, and **nonlinear** for partially ordered. Sacerdoti (1975), who originated the term, used "linear" to refer to a property that we will call **noninterleaved**. Given a set of subgoals, a noninterleaved planner can find plans to solve each subgoal, but then it can only combine them by placing all the steps for one subplan before or after all the steps of the others. Many early planners of the 1970s were noninterleaved, and thus were incomplete—they could not always find a solution when one exists. This was forcefully driven home by the Sussman Anomaly (see Exercise 11.4), found during experimentation with the HACKER system (Sussman, 1975). (The anomaly was actually found by Allen Brown, not by Sussman himself, who thought at the time that assuming linearity to begin with was often a workable approach.) HACKER introduced the idea of protecting subgoals, and was also an early example of plan learning.

Goal regression planning, in which steps in a totally ordered plan are reordered so as to avoid conflict between subgoals, was introduced by Waldinger (1975) and also used by Warren's (1974) WARPLAN. WARPLAN is also notable in that it was the first planner to be written using a logic programming language (Prolog), and is one of the best examples of the remarkable economy that can sometimes be gained by using logic programming: WARPLAN is only 100 lines of code, a small fraction of the size of comparable planners of the time. INTERPLAN (Tate, 1975b; Tate, 1975a) also allowed arbitrary interleaving of plan steps to overcome the Sussman anomaly and related problems.

The construction of partially ordered plans (then called **task networks**) was pioneered by the NOAH planner (Sacerdoti, 1975; Sacerdoti, 1977), and thoroughly investigated in Tate's (1977) NONLIN system, which also retained the clear conceptual structure of its predecessor INTERPLAN. INTERPLAN and NONLIN provide much of the grounding for the work described in this chapter and the next, particularly in the use of causal links to detect potential protection violations. NONLIN was also the first planner to use an explicit algorithm for determining the truth or falsity of conditions at various points in a partially specified plan.

TWEAK (Chapman, 1987) formalizes a generic, partial-order planning system. Chapman provides detailed analysis, including proofs of completeness and intractability (NP-hardness and undecidability) of various formulations of the planning problem and its subcomponents. The POP algorithm described in the chapter is based on the SNLP algorithm (Soderland and Weld, 1991), which is an implementation of the planner described by McAllester and Rosenblitt (1991). Weld contributed several useful suggestions to the presentation in this chapter.

A number of important papers on planning were presented at the Timberline workshop in 1986, and its proceedings (Georgeff and Lansky, 1986) are an important source. *Readings in Planning* (Allen *et al.*, 1990) is a comprehensive anthology of many of the best articles in the field, including several good survey articles. *Planning and Control* (Dean and Wellman, 1991) is a good general introductory textbook on planning, and is particularly remarkable because it makes a particular effort to integrate classical AI planning techniques with classical and modern control theory, metareasoning, and reactive planning and execution monitoring. Weld (1994) provides an excellent survey of modern planning algorithms.

Planning research has been central to AI since its inception, and papers on planning are a staple of mainstream AI journals and conferences, but there are also specialized conferences devoted exclusively to planning, like the Timberline workshop, the 1990 DARPA Workshop on Innovative Approaches to Planning, Scheduling, and Control, or the International Conferences on AI Planning Systems.

EXERCISES

11.1   Define the operator schemata for the problem of putting on shoes and socks and a hat and coat, assuming that there are no preconditions for putting on the hat and coat. Give a partial-order plan that is a solution, and show that there are 180 different linearizations of this solution.

11.2   Let us consider a version of the milk/banana/drill shopping problem in which money is included, at least in a simple way.

    a. Let *CC* denote a credit card that the agent can use to buy any object. Modify the description of *Buy* so that the agent has to have its credit card in order to buy anything.

    b. Write a *PickUp* operator that enables the agent to *Have* an object if it is portable and at the same location as the agent.

    c. Assume that the credit card is at home, but *Have(CC)* is initially false. Construct a partially ordered plan that achieves the goal, showing both ordering constraints and causal links.

    d. Explain in detail what happens during the planning process when the agent explores a partial plan in which it leaves home without the card.

11.3   There are many ways to characterize planners. For each of the following dichotomies, explain what they mean, and how the choice between them affects the efficiency and completeness of a planner.

    a. Situation space vs. plan space.

    b. Progressive vs. regressive.

   c. Refinement vs. debugging.

   d. Least commitment vs. more commitment.

   e. Bound variables vs. unbound variables.

   f. Total order vs. partial order.

   g. Interleaved vs. noninterleaved.

   h. Unambiguous preconditions vs. ambiguous preconditions.

   i. Systematic vs. unsystematic.

SUSSMAN ANOMALY   **11.4**   Figure 11.16 shows a blocks-world planning problem known as the **Sussman anomaly**. The problem was considered anomalous because the noninterleaved planners of the early 1970s could not solve it. Encode the problem using STRIPS operators, and use POP to solve it.

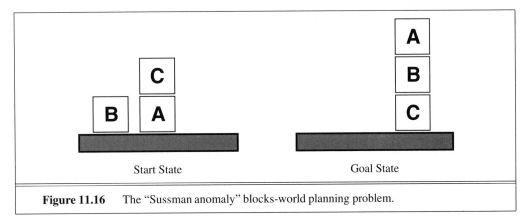

Figure 11.16   The "Sussman anomaly" blocks-world planning problem.

11.5   Suppose that you are the proud owner of a brand new time machine. That means that you can perform actions that affect situations in the past. What changes would you have to make to the planners in this chapter to accommodate such actions?

11.6   The POP algorithm shown in the text is a regression planner, because it adds steps whose effects satisfy unsatisfied conditions in the plan. Progression planners add steps whose preconditions are satisfied by conditions known to be true in the plan. Modify POP so that it works as a progression planner, and compare its performance to the original on several problems of your choosing.

11.7   In this exercise, we will look at planning in Shakey's world.

   a. Describe Shakey's six actions in situation calculus notation.

   b. Translate them into the STRIPS language.

   c. Either manually or using a partial-order planner, construct a plan for Shakey to get *Box*2 into *Room*2 from the starting configuration in Figure 11.15.

   d. Suppose Shakey has n boxes in a room and needs to move them all into another room. What is the complexity of the planning process in terms of n?

11.8   POP is a nondeterministic algorithm, and has a choice about which operator to add to the plan at each step and how to resolve each threat. Can you think of any domain-independent heuristics for ordering these choices that are likely to improve POP's efficiency? Will they help in Shakey's world? Are there any additional, domain-dependent heuristics that will improve the efficiency still further?

11.9   In this exercise we will consider the monkey-and-bananas problem, in which there is a monkey in a room with some bananas hanging out of reach from the ceiling, but a box is available that will enable the monkey to reach the bananas if he climbs on it. Initially, the monkey is at A, the bananas at B, and the box at C. The monkey and box have height *Low*, but if the monkey climbs onto the box he will have height *High*, the same as the bananas. The actions available to the monkey include *Go* from one place to another, *Push* an object from one place to another, *Climb* onto an object, and *Grasp* an object. Grasping results in holding the object if the monkey and object are in the same place at the same height.

   a. Write down the initial state description in predicate calculus.

   b. Write down STRIPS-style definitions of the four actions, providing at least the obvious preconditions.

   c. Suppose the monkey wants to fool the scientists, who are off to tea, by grabbing the bananas but leaving the box in its original place. Write this as a general goal (i.e., not assuming the box is necessarily at C) in the language of situation calculus. Can this goal be solved by a STRIPS-style system?

   d. Your axiom for pushing is probably incorrect, because if the object is too heavy, its position will remain the same when the *Push* operator is applied. Is this an example of the frame problem or the qualification problem?

12 PRACTICAL PLANNING

In which planning algorithms meet the real world and survive, albeit with some significant modifications.

12.1 PRACTICAL PLANNERS

Chapter 11 showed how a partial-order planner's search through the space of plans can be more efficient than a problem-solver's search through the space of situations. On the other hand, the POP planner can only handle problems that are stated in the STRIPS language, and its search process is so unguided that it can still only be used for small problems. In this chapter we begin by surveying existing planners that operate in complex, realistic domains. This will help to pinpoint the weaknesses of POP and suggest the necessary extensions. We then show how the planning language and algorithms of Chapter 11 can be extended and the search focused to handle domains like these.

Spacecraft assembly, integration, and verification

OPTIMUM-AIV is a planner that is used by the European Space Agency to help in the assembly, integration, and verification (AIV) of spacecraft. The system is used both to generate plans and to monitor their execution. During monitoring, the system reminds the user of upcoming activities, and can suggest repairs to the plan when an activity is performed late, cancelled, or reveals something unexpected. In fact, the ability to quickly replan is the principal objective of OPTIMUM-AIV. The system does not execute the plans; that is done by humans with standard construction and test equipment.

In complex projects like this, it is common to use scheduling tools from operations research (OR) such as PERT charts or the critical path method. These tools essentially take a *hand-constructed* complete partial-order plan and generate an optimal schedule for it. Actions are treated as objects that take up time and have ordering constraints; their effects are ignored. This avoids the need for knowledge engineering, and for one-shot problems it may be the most appropriate solution. For most practical applications, however, there will be many related problems to solve, so it is worth the effort to describe the domain and then have the plans automatically generated. This is especially important during the *execution* of plans. If a step of a plan fails, it is often necessary to replan quickly to get the project back on track. PERT charts do not contain the causal links and other information needed to see how to fix a plan, and human replanning is often too slow.

The success of real-world AI systems requires integration into the environment in which they operate. It is vital that a planner be able to access existing databases of project information in whatever format they might have, and that the planner's input and output representations be in a form that is both expressive and easily understood by users. The STRIPS language is insufficient for the AIV domain because it cannot express four key concepts:

1. **Hierarchical plans:** Obviously, launching a spacecraft is more complicated than shopping for groceries. One way to handle the increased complexity is to specify plans at varying levels of detail. The top-level plan might be: prepare booster rocket, prepare capsule, load cargo, and launch. There might be a dozen intermediate levels before we finally get down to the level of executable actions: insert nut *A* into hole *B* and fasten with bolt *C*. Adding the ability to represent hierarchical plans can make the difference between feasible and infeasible computation, and it can make the resulting plan easier to understand. It also allows the user to provide guidance to the planner in the form of a partially specified, abstract plan for which the planner can fill in the details.

2. **Complex conditions:** STRIPS operators are essentially propositional. True, they do allow variables, but the variables are used in a very limited way. For example, there is no universal quantification, and without it we cannot describe the fact that the *Launch* operator causes *all* the objects that are in the spacecraft to go into orbit. Similarly, STRIPS operators are unconditional: we cannot express the fact that if all systems are go, then the *Launch* will put the spacecraft into orbit, otherwise it will put it into the ocean.

3. **Time:** Because the STRIPS language is based on situation calculus it assumes that all actions occur instantaneously, and that one action follows another with no break in between. Real-world projects need a better model of time. They must represent the fact that projects have deadlines (the spacecraft must be launched on June 17), actions have durations (it takes 6 hours to test the *XYZ* assembly), and steps of plans may have time windows (the machine that tests the *XYZ* assembly is available from May 1 to June 1 (except weekends), but it must be reserved one week ahead of time). Indeed, the major contribution of traditional OR techniques is to satisfy time constraints for a complete partial-order plan.

4. **Resources:** A project normally has a budget that cannot be exceeded, so the plan must be constrained to spend no more money than is available. Similarly, there are limits on the number of workers that are available, and on the number of assembly and test stations. Resource limitations may be placed on the number of things that may be used at at one time (e.g., people) or on the total amount that may be used (e.g., money). Action descriptions must incorporate resource consumption and generation, and planning algorithms must be able to handle constraints on resources efficiently.

OPTIMUM-AIV is based on the open planning architecture O-PLAN (Currie and Tate, 1991). O-PLAN is similar to the POP planner of Chapter 11, except that it is augmented to accept a more expressive language that can represent time, resources, and hierarchical plans. It also accepts heuristics for guiding the search and records its reasons for each choice, which makes it easier to replan when necessary. O-PLAN has been applied to a variety of problems, including software procurement planning at Price Waterhouse, back axle assembly process planning at Jaguar Cars, and complete factory production planning at Hitachi.

Job shop scheduling

The problem that a factory solves is to take in raw materials and components, and assemble them into finished products. The problem can be divided into a planning task (deciding what assembly steps are going to be performed) and a scheduling task (deciding when and where each step will be performed). In many modern factories, the planning is done by hand and the scheduling is done with an automated tool.

O-PLAN is being used by Hitachi for job shop planning and scheduling in a system called TOSCA. A typical problem involves a product line of 350 different products, 35 assembly machines, and over 2000 different operations. The planner comes up with a 30-day schedule for three 8-hour shifts a day. In general, TOSCA follows the partial-order, least-commitment planning approach. It also allows for "low-commitment" decisions: choices that impose constraints on the plan or on a particular step. For example, the system might choose to schedule an action to be carried out on a class of machine without specifying any particular one.

Factories with less diversity of products often follow a fixed plan, but still have a need for automated scheduling. The ISIS system (Fox and Smith, 1984) was developed specifically for scheduling. It was first tested at the Westinghouse turbine component plant in Winston-Salem, NC. The plant makes thousands of different turbine blades, and for each one, there are one or more plans, called process routings. When an order comes in, one of the plans is chosen and a time for it is scheduled. The time depends on the criticality of the order: whether it is an urgent replacement for a failed blade in service, a scheduled maintenance part that has plenty of lead time but must arrive on time, or just a stock order to build up the reserves.

Traditional scheduling methods such as PERT are capable of finding a feasible ordering of steps subject to time constraints, but it turns out that human schedulers using PERT spend 80% to 90% of their time communicating with other workers to discover what the real constraints are. A successful automated scheduler needs to be able to represent and reason with these additional constraints. Factors that are important include the cost of raw materials on hand, the value of finished but unshipped goods, accurate forecasts of future needs, and minimal disruption of existing procedures. ISIS uses a hierarchical, least-commitment search to find high-quality plans that satisfy all of these requirements.

Scheduling for space missions

Planning and scheduling systems have been used extensively in planning space missions as well as in constructing spacecraft. There are two main reasons for this. First, spacecraft are very expensive and sometimes contain humans, and any mistake can be costly and irrevocable. Second, space missions take place in space, which does not contain many other agents to mess up the expected effects of actions. Planners have been used by the ground teams for the Hubble space telescope and at least three spacecraft: Voyager, UOSAT-II, and ERS-1. In each case, the goal is to orchestrate the observational equipment, signal transmitters, and attitude- and velocity-control mechanisms, in order to maximize the value of the information gained from observations while obeying resource constraints on time and energy.

Mission scheduling often involves very complex temporal constraints, particularly those involving periodic events. For example, ERS-1, the European Earth Resource Observation satellite, completes an orbit every 100 minutes, and returns to the same point every 72 hours. An observation of a particular point on the earth's surface thus can be made at any one of a number of times, each separated by 72 hours, but at no other time. Satellites also have resource constraints on their power output: they cannot exceed a fixed maximum output, and they must be sure not to discharge too much power over a period of time. Other than that, a satellite can be considered as a job-shop scheduling problem, where the telescopes and other instruments are the machines, and the observations are the products. PlanERS-1 is a planner based on O-PLAN that produces observation plans for the ERS-1.

The Hubble space telescope (HST) is a good example of the need for automated planning tools. After it was launched in April 1990, the primary mirror was found to be out of focus. Using Bayesian techniques for image reconstruction (see Chapter 24), the ground team was able to compensate for the defect to a degree, enabling the HST to deliver novel and important data on Pluto, a gravitational lens, a supernova, and other objects. In 1993, shuttle astronauts repaired most of the problems with the primary mirror, opening up the possibility of a new set of observations. The ground team is constantly learning more about what the HST can and cannot do, and it would be impossible to update the observation plans to reflect this ever-increasing knowledge without automated planning and scheduling tools.

Any astronomer can submit a proposal to the HST observing committee. Proposals are classified as high priority (which are almost always executed and take up about 70% of the available observing time), low priority (which are scheduled as time allows), or rejected. Proposals are received at the rate of about one per day, which means there are more proposals than can be executed. Each proposal includes a machine-readable specification of which instrument should be pointed at which celestial object, and what kind of exposure should be made. Some observations can be done at any time, whereas others are dependent on factors such as the alignment of planets and whether the HST is in the earth's shadow. There are some constraints that are unique to this domain. For example, an astronomer may request periodic observations of a quasar over a period of months or years subject to the constraint that each observation be taken under the same shadow conditions.

The HST planning system is split into two parts. A long-term scheduler, called SPIKE, first schedules observations into one-week segments. The heuristic is to assign high-priority proposals so that they can all be executed within the scheduled segment, and then to pack each segment with extra low-priority proposals until they are about 20% above capacity. This is done a year or more ahead of time. A multiyear schedule with 5000 observations or so can be created in less than an hour, so replanning is easy. After each segment is scheduled, a short-term planner, SPSS, does the detailed planning of each segment, filling in the time between high-priority tasks with as many low-priority ones as possible. The system also calculates the commands for the platform attitude controls so that the observation plan can be executed. It can check the feasibility of proposals and detailed schedules much faster than human experts.

Buildings, aircraft carriers, and beer factories

SIPE (System for Interactive Planning and Execution monitoring) was the first planner to deal with the problem of replanning, and the first to take some important steps toward expressive operators. It is similar to O-PLAN in the range of its features and in its applicability. It is not in everyday practical use, but it has been used in demonstration projects in several domains, including planning operations on the flight deck of an aircraft carrier and job-shop scheduling for an Australian beer factory. Another study used SIPE to plan the construction of multistory buildings, one of the most complex domains ever tackled by a planner.

SIPE allows deductive rules to operate over states, so that the user does not have to specify all relevant literals as effects of each operator. It allows for an inheritance hierarchy among object classes and for an expressive set of constraints. This means it is applicable to a wide variety of domains, but its generality comes at a cost. For example, in the building construction domain, it was found that SIPE needed time $O(n^{2.5})$ for an n-story building. This suggests a high degree of interaction between stories, when in fact the degree of interaction should be much lower: if you remember to build from the ground up and make sure that the elevator shafts line up, it should be possible to get performance much closer to $O(n)$.

The examples in this and the preceding sections give an idea of the state of the art of planning systems. They are good enough to model complex domains, but have not yet gained practical acceptance beyond a few pilot projects. Clearly, to achieve the degree of flexibility and efficiency needed to exceed the capabilities of human planners armed with traditional scheduling tools, we need to go far beyond the limited STRIPS language.

12.2   HIERARCHICAL DECOMPOSITION

The grocery shopping example of Chapter 11 produced solutions at a rather high level of abstraction. A plan such as

   [*Go*(*Supermarket*), *Buy*(*Milk*), *Buy*(*Bananas*), *Go*(*Home*)]

is a good high-level description of what to do, but it is a long way from the type of instructions that can be fed directly to the agent's effectors. Thus, it is insufficient for an agent that wants to actually *do* anything. On the other hand, a low-level plan such as

   [*Forward*(1 *cm*), *Turn*(1 deg), *Forward*(1 *cm*), . . .]

would have to be many thousands of steps long to solve the shopping problem. The space of plans of that length is so huge that the techniques of Chapter 11 would probably not find a solution in a reasonable amount of time.

HIERARCHICAL
DECOMPOSITION
ABSTRACT
OPERATOR

PRIMITIVE
OPERATOR

To resolve this dilemma, all the practical planners we surveyed have adopted the idea of **hierarchical decomposition**:[1] that an **abstract operator** can be decomposed into a group of steps that forms a plan that implements the operator. These decompositions can be stored in a library of plans and retrieved as needed.

Consider the problem of building a frame house. The abstract operator *Build(House)* can be decomposed into a plan that consists of the four steps *Obtain Permit, Hire Builder, Construction,* and *Pay Builder*, as depicted in Figure 12.1. The steps of this plan may in turn be further decomposed into even more specific plans. We show a decomposition of the *Construction* step. We could continue decomposing until we finally get down to the level of *Hammer(Nail)*. The plan is complete when every step is a **primitive operator**—one that can be directly executed by the agent. Hierarchical decomposition is most useful when operators can be decomposed in more than one way. For example, the *Build Walls* operator can be decomposed into a plan involving wood, bricks, concrete, or vinyl.

To make the idea of hierarchical planning work, we have to do two things. (1) Provide an extension to the STRIPS language to allow for nonprimitive operators. (2) Modify the planning algorithm to allow the replacement of a nonprimitive operator with its decomposition.

Extending the language

To incorporate hierarchical decomposition, we have to make two additions to the description of each problem domain.

First, we partition the set of operators into primitive and nonprimitive operators. In our domain, we might define *Hammer(Nail)* to be primitive and *Build(House)* to be nonprimitive. In general, the distinction between primitive and nonprimitive is relative to the agent that will execute the plan. For the general contractor, an operator such as *Install(FloorBoards)* would be primitive, because all the contractor has to do is order a worker to do the installation. For the worker, *Install(FloorBoards)* would be nonprimitive, and *Hammer(Nail)* would be primitive.

Second, we add a set of decomposition methods. Each method is an expression of the form $Decompose(o, p)$, which means that a nonprimitive operator that unifies with o can be decomposed into a plan p. Here is decomposition of *Construction* from Figure 12.1:

$$Decompose(Construction,$$
$$Plan(\text{STEPS}:\{S_1 : Build(Foundation), S_2 : Build(Frame),$$
$$S_3 : Build(Roof), S_4 : Build(Walls),$$
$$S_5 : Build(Interior)\}$$
$$\text{ORDERINGS}:\{S_1 \prec S_2 \prec S_3 \prec S_5, \quad S_2 \prec S_4 \prec S_5\},$$
$$\text{BINDINGS}:\{\},$$
$$\text{LINKS}:\{S_1 \xrightarrow{Foundation} S_2, S_2 \xrightarrow{Frame} S_3, S_2 \xrightarrow{Frame} S_4, S_3 \xrightarrow{Roof} S_5, S_4 \xrightarrow{Walls} S_5\}))$$

A decomposition method is like a subroutine or macro definition for an operator. As such, it is important to make sure that the decomposition is a correct implementation of the operator. We

---

[1] For hierarchical decomposition, some authors use the term **operator reduction** (reducing a high-level operator to a set of lower-level ones), and some use **operator expansion** (expanding a macro-like operator into the structure that implements it). This kind of planning is also called **hierarchical task network** planning.

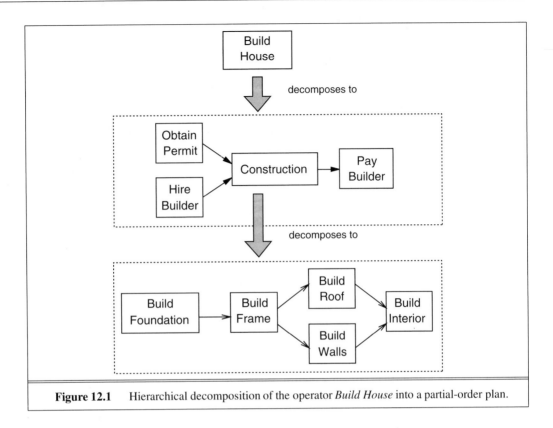

Figure 12.1   Hierarchical decomposition of the operator *Build House* into a partial-order plan.

say that a plan *p* correctly implements an operator *o* if it is a complete and consistent plan for the problem of achieving the effects of *o* given the preconditions of *o*:

1. *p* must be consistent. (There is no contradiction in the ordering or variable binding constraints of *p*.)

2. Every effect of *o* must be asserted by at least one step of *p* (and is not denied by some other, later step of *p*).

3. Every precondition of the steps in *p* must be achieved by a step in *p* or be one of the preconditions of *o*.

This guarantees that it is possible to replace a nonprimitive operator with its decomposition and have everything hook up properly. Although one will need to check for possible threats arising from interactions between the newly introduced steps and conditions and the existing steps and conditions, there is no need to worry about interactions among the steps of the decomposition itself. Provided there is not too much interaction *between* the different parts of the plan, hierarchical planning allows very complex plans to be built up cumulatively from simpler subplans. It also allows plans to be generated, saved away, and then re-used in later planning problems.

Modifying the planner

We can derive a hierarchical decomposition planner, which we call HD-POP, from the POP planner of Figure 11.13. The new algorithm in shown in Figure 12.2. There are two principal changes. First, as well as finding ways to achieve unachieved conditions in the plan, the algorithm must find a way to decompose nonprimitive operators. Because both kinds of refinements must be carried out to generate a complete, primitive plan, there is no need to introduce a backtracking choice of one or the other. HD-POP simply does one of each on each iteration; more sophisticated strategies can be used to reduce the branching factor. Second, the algorithm takes a *plan* as input, rather than just a goal. We have already seen that a goal can be represented as a *Start–Finish* plan, so this is compatible with the POP approach. However, it will often be the case that the user has some idea of what general kinds of activities are needed, and allowing more extensive plans as inputs means that this kind of guidance can be provided.

---

function HD-POP(*plan, operators, methods*) **returns** *plan*
   inputs: *plan*, an abstract plan with start and goal steps (and possibly other steps)

   loop do
      if SOLUTION?(*plan*) **then return** *plan*
      S_{need}, $c \leftarrow$ SELECT-SUB-GOAL(*plan*)
      CHOOSE-OPERATOR(*plan, operators, S_{need}, c*)
      $S_{nonprim} \leftarrow$ SELECT-NONPRIMITIVE(*plan*)
      CHOOSE-DECOMPOSITION(*plan, methods, $S_{nonprim}$*)
      RESOLVE-THREATS(*plan*)
   end

Figure 12.2   A hierarchical decomposition partial-order planning algorithm, HD-POP. On each iteration of the loop we first achieve an unachieved condition (CHOOSE-OPERATOR), then decompose a nonprimitive operator (CHOOSE-DECOMPOSITION), then resolve threats.

To make HD-POP work, we have to change SOLUTION? to check that every step of the plan is primitive. The other functions from Figure 11.13 remain unchanged. There are two new procedures: SELECT-NONPRIMITIVE arbitrarily selects a nonprimitive step from the plan. The function CHOOSE-DECOMPOSITION picks a decomposition method for the plan and applies it. If *method* is chosen as the decomposition for the step $S_{nonprim}$, then the fields of the *plan* are altered as follows:

- STEPS: Add all the steps of *method* to the plan, but remove $S_{nonprim}$.
- BINDINGS: Add all the variable binding constraints of *method* to the plan. Fail if this introduces a contradiction.
- ORDERINGS: Following the principle of least commitment, we replace each ordering constraint of the form $S_a \prec S_{nonprim}$ with constraint(s) that order S_a before the *latest* step(s) of *method*. That is, if S_m is a step of *method*, and there is no other S_j in *method* such that $S_m \prec S_j$, then add the constraint $S_a \prec S_m$. Similarly, replace each constraint of the form

$S_{nonprim} \prec S_z$ with constraint(s) that order S_z after the *earliest* step(s) of *method*. We then call RESOLVE-THREATS to add any additional ordering constraints that may be needed.

- LINKS: It is easier to match up causal links with the right substeps of *method* than it is to match up ordering constraints. If $S_i \xrightarrow{c} S_{nonprim}$ was a causal link in *plan*, replace it by a set of links $S_i \xrightarrow{c} S_m$, where each S_m is a step of *method* that has c as a precondition, and there is no earlier step of *method* that has c as a precondition. (If there are several such steps with c as a precondition, then put in a causal link for each one. If there are none, then the causal link from S_i can be dropped, because c was an unnecessary precondition of $S_{nonprim}$.) Similarly, for each link $S_{nonprim} \xrightarrow{c} S_j$ in *plan*, replace it with a set of links $S_m \xrightarrow{c} S_j$, where S_m is a step of *method* that has c as an effect and there is no later step of *method* with c as an effect.

In Figure 12.3, we show a more detailed diagram of the decomposition of a plan step, in the context of a larger plan. Notice that one of the causal links that leads into the nonprimitive step *Build House* ends up being attached to the first step of the decomposition, but the other causal link is attached to a later step.

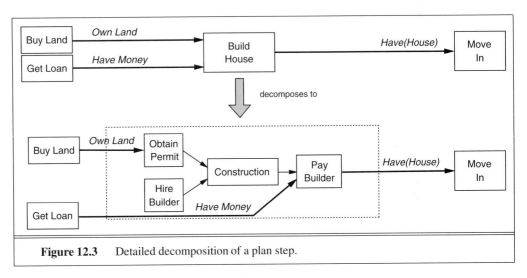

Figure 12.3   Detailed decomposition of a plan step.

12.3   ANALYSIS OF HIERARCHICAL DECOMPOSITION

Hierarchical decomposition *seems* like a good idea, on the same grounds that subroutines or macros are a good idea in programming: they allow the programmer (or knowledge engineer) to specify the problem in pieces of a reasonable size. The pieces can be combined hierarchically to create large plans, without incurring the enormous combinatorial cost of constructing large plans from primitive operators. In this section, we will make this intuitive idea more precise.

ABSTRACT
SOLUTION
Suppose that there is a way to string four abstract operators together to build a house—for example, the four operators shown in Figure 12.1. We will call this an **abstract solution**—a plan that contains abstract operators, but is consistent and complete. Finding a small abstract solution, if one exists, should not be too expensive. Continuing this process, we should be able to obtain a primitive plan without too much backtracking.

This assumes, however, that in finding an abstract solution, and in rejecting other abstract plans as inconsistent, one is doing useful work. One would *like* the following properties to hold:

DOWNWARD
SOLUTION
- If p is an abstract solution, then there is a primitive solution of which p is an abstraction. If this property holds, then once an abstract solution is found we can prune away all other abstract plans from the search tree. This property is the **downward solution** property.

UPWARD SOLUTION
- If an abstract plan is inconsistent, then there is no primitive solution of which it is an abstraction. If this property holds, then we can prune away all the descendants of any inconsistent abstract plan. This is called the **upward solution** property because it also means that all complete abstractions of primitive solutions are abstract solutions.

Figure 12.4 illustrates these two notions graphically. Each box represents an entire plan (not just a step), and each arc represents a decomposition step in which an abstract operator is expanded. At the top is a very abstract plan, and at the bottom are plans with only primitive steps. The boxes with bold outlines are (possibly abstract) solutions, and the ones with dotted outlines are inconsistent. Plans marked with an "X" need not be examined by the planning algorithm. (The figure shows only complete or inconsistent plans, leaving out consistent but incomplete plans and the achievement steps that are applied to them.)

To get a more quantitative feel for how these properties affect the search, we need a simplified model of the search space. Assume that there is at least one solution with n primitive steps, and that the time to resolve threats and handle constraints is negligible: all we will be concerned with is the time it takes to choose the right set of steps. Figure 12.5 defines the search space in terms of the parameters b, s, and d.

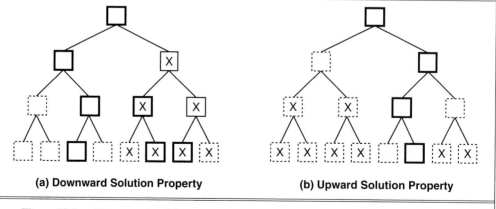

(a) Downward Solution Property   **(b) Upward Solution Property**

Figure 12.4   The upward and downward solution properties in plan space (abstract plans on top, primitive plans on the bottom). Bold outlined boxes are solutions, dotted outlines are inconsistent, and boxes marked with an "X" can be pruned away in a left-to-right search.

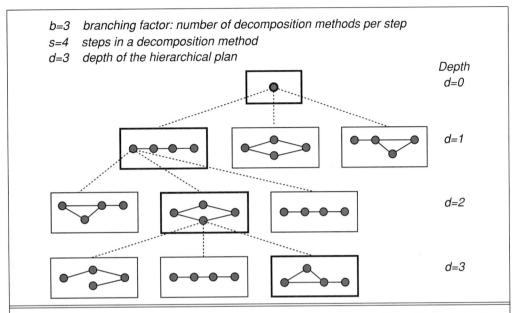

b=3   *branching factor: number of decomposition methods per step*
s=4   *steps in a decomposition method*
d=3   *depth of the hierarchical plan*

Figure 12.5   A portion of the search space for hierarchical decomposition with depth $d = 3$; branching factor $b = 3$ decompositions per step; $s = 4$ steps per decomposition method. A solution will have $n = s^d$ steps ($n = 64$ in this case). We also assume that $1/b$ decompositions will lead to a solution.

A nonhierarchical planner would have to generate an n-step plan, choosing among b possibilities for each one. (We are also assuming that the number of decompositions per nonprimitive step, b, is the same as the number of applicable new operators for an open precondition of a primitive step.) Thus, it takes time $O(b^n)$ in the worst case. *With a hierarchical planner, we can adopt the strategy of only searching decompositions that lead to abstract solutions.* (In our simplified model, exactly 1 of every b decompositions is a solution. In more realistic models, we need to consider what to do when there are zero or more than one solution.) The planner has to look at sb steps at depth $d = 1$. At depth $d = 2$, it looks at another sb steps for each step it decomposes, but it only has to decompose $1/b$ of them, for a total of bs^2. Thus, the total number of plans considered is

$$\sum_{i=1}^{d} bs^i = O(bs^d)$$

To give you an idea of the difference, for the parameter values in Figure 12.5, a nonhierarchical planner has to inspect 3×10^{30} plans, whereas a hierarchical planner looks at only 576.

The upward and downward solution properties seem to be enormously powerful. At first glance, it may seem that they are necessary consequences of the correctness conditions for decompositions (page 373). In fact, neither property is guaranteed to hold. Without these properties, or some reasonable substitute, a hierarchical planner does no better than a nonhierarchical planner in the worst case (although it may do better in the average case).

Figure 12.6 shows an example where the upward solution property does not hold. That is, the abstract solution is inconsistent, but there is a decomposition that solves the problem. The problem is taken from the O. Henry story *The Gift of the Magi*. A poor couple has only two prized possessions; he a gold watch and she her beautiful long hair. They each plan to buy presents to make the other happy. He decides to trade his watch to buy a fancy comb for her hair, and she decides to sell her hair to get a gold chain for his watch. As Figure 12.6(b) shows, the resulting abstract plan is inconsistent. However, it is still possible to decompose this inconsistent plan into a consistent solution, if the right decomposition methods are available. In Figure 12.6(c) we decompose the "Give Comb" step with an "installment plan" method. In the first step of the decomposition, the husband takes possession of the comb, and gives it to his wife, while agreeing to deliver the watch in payment at a later date. In the second step, the watch is handed over and the obligation is fulfilled. A similar method decomposes the "Give Chain" step. As long as both giving steps are ordered before the delivery steps, this decomposition solves the problem.

UNIQUE MAIN
SUBACTION
        One way to guarantee the upward solution property is to make sure that each decomposition method satisfies the **unique main subaction** condition: that there is one step of the decomposed plan to which all preconditions and effects of the abstract operator are attached. In the Magi example, the unique main subaction condition does not hold. It does not hold in Figure 12.3 either, although it would be if *Own Land* were a precondition of the Pay Builder step. Sometimes

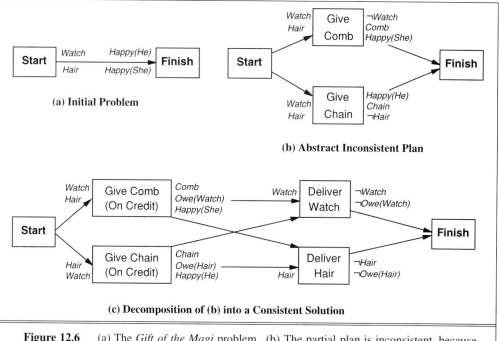

(a) Initial Problem

(b) Abstract Inconsistent Plan

(c) Decomposition of (b) into a Consistent Solution

Figure 12.6   (a) The *Gift of the Magi* problem. (b) The partial plan is inconsistent, because there is no way to order the two abstract steps without a conflict. (c) A decomposition that solves the problem. This violates the upward solution property, because the inconsistent plan in (b) now has a solution.

it is worthwhile to do some preprocessing of the decomposition methods to put them in a form that satisfies the unique main subaction condition so that we can freely cut off search when we hit an inconsistent abstract plan without fear of missing any solutions.

It is important to remember that even when the upward solution property fails to hold, it is still a reasonable heuristic to prefer applications of decomposition to consistent plans rather than inconsistent ones. Similarly, even when the downward solution property is violated, it makes more sense to pursue the refinement of abstract solutions than that of inconsistent plans, even though the abstract solution may not lead to a real solution. (Exercise 12.4 asks you to find an example of the violation of the downward solution property.)

Decomposition and sharing

In CHOOSE-DECOMPOSITION, we just merge each step of the decomposition into the existing plan. This is appropriate for a divide-and-conquer approach—we solve each subproblem separately, and then combine it into the rest of the solution. But often the only solution to a problem involves combining the two solutions by *sharing* steps rather than by joining distinct sets of steps. For example, consider the problem "enjoy a honeymoon and raise a baby." A planner might choose the decomposition "get married and go on honeymoon" for the first subproblem and "get married and have a baby" for the second, but the planner could get into a lot of trouble if the two "get married" steps are different. Indeed, if a precondition to "get married" is "not married," and divorce is not an option, then there is no way that a planner can merge the two subplans without sharing steps. Hence a sharing mechanism is required for a hierarchical planner to be complete.

Sharing can be implemented by adding a choice point in CHOOSE-DECOMPOSITION for every operator in a decomposition: either a new step is created to instantiate the operator or an existing step is used. This is exactly analogous to the existing choice point in CHOOSE-OPERATOR. Although this introduces a lot of additional choice points, many of them will have only a single alternative if no operators are available for sharing. Furthermore, it is a reasonable heuristic to prefer sharing to non-sharing.

CRITICS

Many hierarchical planners use a different mechanism to handle this problem: they merge decompositions without sharing but allow **critics** to modify the resulting plan. A critic is a function that takes a plan as input and returns a modified plan with some conflict or other anomaly corrected. Theoretically, using critics is no more or less powerful than putting in all the choice points, but it can be easier to manage the search space with a well-chosen set of critics.

Note that the choice of sharing versus merging steps has an effect on the efficiency of planning, as well as on completeness. An interesting example of the costs and benefits of sharing occurs in optimizing compilers. Consider the problem of compiling $\sin(x)+\cos(x)$ for a sequential computer. Most compilers accomplish this by merging two separate subroutine calls in a trivial way: all the steps of sin come before any of the steps of cos (or vice versa). If we allowed sharing instead of merging, we could actually get a more efficient solution, because the two computations have many steps in common. Most compilers do not do this because it would take too much time to consider all the possible shared plans. Instead, most compilers take the critic approach: a peephole optimizer is just a kind of critic.

Decomposition versus approximation

The literature on planning is confusing because authors have not agreed on their terminology. There are two completely separate ideas that have gone under the name **hierarchical planning**. **Hierarchical decomposition**, as we have seen, is the idea that an abstract, nonprimitive operator can be decomposed into a more complex network of steps. The abstraction here is on the granularity with which operators interact with the world. Second, **abstraction hierarchies** capture the idea that a single operator can be planned with at different levels of abstraction. At the primitive level, the operator has a full set of preconditions and effects; at higher levels, the planner ignores some of these details.

APPROXIMATION
HIERARCHY

CRITICALITY LEVEL

To avoid confusion, we will use the term **approximation hierarchy** for this kind of abstraction, because the "abstract" version of an operator is slightly incorrect, rather than merely abstract. An approximation hierarchy planner takes an operator and partitions its preconditions according to their **criticality level**, for example:

Op(ACTION:$Buy(x)$,
        EFFECT:$Have(x) \land \neg Have(Money)$,
        PRECOND:1: $Sells(store, x) \land$
                2: $At(store) \land$
                3: $Have(Money))$

Conditions labelled with lower numbers are considered more critical. In the case of buying something, there is not much one can do if the store does not sell it, so it is vital to choose the right store. An approximation hierarchy planner first solves the problem using only the preconditions of criticality 1. The solution would be a plan that buys the right things at the right stores, but does not worry about how to travel between stores or how to pay for the goods. The idea is that it will be easy to find an abstract solution like this, because most of the pesky details are ignored. Once a solution is found, it can be expanded by considering the preconditions at criticality level 2. Then we get a plan that takes travel into consideration, but still does not worry about paying. We keep expanding the solution in this way until all the preconditions are satisfied.

In the framework we have presented, we do not really need to change the language or the planner to support approximation hierarchy planning. All we have to do is provide the right decomposition methods and abstract operators. First, we define Buy_1, which has just the precondition at criticality level 1, and has a single decomposition method to Buy_2, which has preconditions at criticality 1 and 2, and so on. Clearly, any domain generated this way has the unique main subaction property—the decomposition has only one step, and it has all the preconditions and effects of the abstract operator. Therefore, the upward solution property holds.

If we add a heuristic that causes the planning algorithm to backtrack to choice points involving low-number preconditions first, then we get an approximation hierarchy planner using our standard hierarchical decomposition planner. Thus, the criticality levels used in approximation hierarchy planning can be seen as providing control information to guide the planning search. In this sense, criticality levels are a rather crude tool because they do not allow the criticality to depend on context. (For example, money might be a critical precondition if one is buying a house.) One promising approach is to replace criticality levels with descriptions of how likely the operator is to succeed in various combinations of circumstances.

12.4   MORE EXPRESSIVE OPERATOR DESCRIPTIONS

Hierarchical planning addresses the problem of efficiency, but we still need to make our representation language more expressive in order to broaden its applicability. The extensions include allowing for the effects of an action to depend on the circumstances in which it is executed; allowing disjunctive and negated preconditions; and allowing universally quantified preconditions and effects. We conclude the section with a planning algorithm, POP-DUNC (Partial-Order Planner with Disjunction, Universal quantification, Negation and Conditional effects).

Conditional effects

CONDITIONAL
EFFECTS

Operators with **conditional effects** have different effects depending on what the world is like when they are executed. We will return to the blocks world of Section 11.8 for some of our examples. Conceptually, the simple blocks world has only one real action—moving a block from one place to another—but we were forced to introduce two operators in order to maintain the *Clear* predicate properly:

Op(ACTION:$Move(b, x, y)$,
　　PRECOND:$On(b, x) \land Clear(b) \land Clear(y)$,
　　EFFECT:$On(b, y) \land Clear(x) \land \neg On(b, x) \land \neg Clear(y)$)

Op(ACTION:$MoveToTable(b, x)$,
　　PRECOND:$On(b, x) \land Clear(b)$,
　　EFFECT:$On(b, Table) \land Clear(x) \land \neg On(b, x)$)

Suppose that the initial situation includes $On(A, B)$ and we have the goal $Clear(B)$. We can achieve the goal by moving A off B, but unfortunately we are forced to choose whether we want to move A to the table or to somewhere else. This introduces a premature commitment and can lead to inefficiency.

We can eliminate the premature commitment by extending the operator language to include conditional effects. In this case, we can define a single operator $Move(b, x, y)$ with a conditional effect that says, "if y is not the table then an effect is $\neg Clear(y)$." We will use the syntax "*effect* **when** *condition*" to denote this, where *effect* and *condition* are both literals or conjunctions of literals. We place this syntax in the EFFECT slot of an operator, but it is really a combination of a precondition and an effect: the *effect* part refers to the situation that is the result of the operator, and the *condition* part refers to the situation before the operator is applied. Thus, "Q **when** P" is not the same as the logical statement $P \Rightarrow Q$; rather it is equivalent to the situation calculus statement $P(s) \Rightarrow Q(Result(act, s))$. The conditional *Move* operator is written as follows:

Op(ACTION:$Move(b, x, y)$,
　　PRECOND:$On(b, x) \land Clear(b) \land Clear(y)$,
　　EFFECT:$On(b, y) \land Clear(x) \land \neg On(b, x)$
　　　　$\land \neg Clear(y)$ **when** $y \neq Table$)

Now we have to incorporate this new syntax into the planner. Two changes are required. First, in SELECT-SUB-GOAL, we have to decide if a precondition c in a conditional effect of the form e **when** c should be considered as a candidate for selection. The answer is that if the effect e supplies a condition that is protected by a causal link, then we should consider selecting c, but not until the causal link is there. This is because the causal link means that the plan will not work unless c is also true. Considering the operator just shown, the planner would usually have no need to establish $y{\neq}Table$ because $\neg Clear(y)$ is not usually needed as a precondition of some other step in the plan. Thus, the planner can usually use the table if it needs somewhere to put a block that does not need to be anywhere special.

Second, we have another possibility for RESOLVE-THREAT. Any step that has the effect ($\neg c'$ **when** p) is a possible threat to the causal link $S_i \xrightarrow{c} S_j$ whenever c and c' unify. We can

resolve the threat by making sure that p does not hold. We call this technique **confrontation**. In the blocks world, if we need a given block to be clear in order to carry out some step, then it is possible for the $Move(b, x, y)$ operator to threaten this condition if y is uninstantiated. However, the threat only occurs if $y{\neq}Table$; confrontation removes the threat by setting $y = Table$. A version of RESOLVE-THREATS that incorporates confrontation appears in Figure 12.7.

---

procedure RESOLVE-THREATS(*plan*)

    for each $S_i \xrightarrow{c} S_j$ **in** LINKS(*plan*) **do**
        for each S_{threat} **in** STEPS(*plan*) **do**
            for each c' **in** EFFECT(S_{threat}) **do**
                if SUBST(BINDINGS(*plan*), c) = SUBST(BINDINGS(*plan*), $\neg c'$) **then**
                    choose either
                        Promotion: Add $S_{threat} \prec S_i$ to ORDERINGS(*plan*)
                        Demotion: Add $S_j \prec S_{threat}$ to ORDERINGS(*plan*)
                        Confrontation: **if** c' is really of the form (c' **when** p) **then**
                              CHOOSE-OPERATOR(*plan, operators*, S_{threat}, $\neg p$)
                              RESOLVE-THREATS(*plan*)
                  if not CONSISTENT(*plan*) **then fail**
        end
        end
    end

Figure 12.7   A version of RESOLVE-THREATS with the confrontation technique for resolving conditional effects.

Negated and disjunctive goals

The confrontation technique calls CHOOSE-OPERATOR with the goal $\neg p$. This is something new: so far we have insisted that all goals (preconditions) be positive literals. Dealing with negated literals as goals does not add much complexity: we still just have to check for effects that match the goal. We do have to make sure that our unification function allows p to match $\neg\neg p$. We also have to treat the initial state specially: we do not want to specify all the conditions that are false in the initial state, so we say that a goal of the form $\neg p$ can be matched either by an explicit effect that unifies with $\neg p$ or by the initial state, if it does not contain p.

DISJUNCTIVE
PRECONDITIONS

While we are at it, it is easy to add **disjunctive preconditions**. In SELECT-SUB-GOAL, if we choose a step with a precondition of the form $p \lor q$, then we nondeterministically choose to return either p or q and reserve the other one as a backtrack point. Of course, any operator with the precondition $p \lor q$ could be replaced with two operators, one with p as a precondition and one with q, but then the planner would have to commit to one or the other. Keeping the conditions in a single operator allows us to delay making the commitment.

DISJUNCTIVE
EFFECTS

Whereas disjunctive preconditions are easy to handle, **disjunctive effects** are very difficult to incorporate. They change the environment from deterministic to nondeterministic. A disjunctive effect is used to model random effects, or effects that are not determined by the preconditions of the operator. For example, the operator *Flip(coin)* would have the disjunctive effect *Heads(coin)* $\lor$ *Tails(coin)*. In some cases, a single plan can guarantee goal achievement even in the face of disjunctive effects. For example, an operator such as *TurnHeadsSideUp(coin)* will coerce the world into a known state even after a flip. In most cases, however, the agent needs to develop a different plan to handle each possible outcome. We develop algorithms for this kind of planning in Chapter 13.

Universal quantification

In defining the blocks world, we had to introduce the condition *Clear(b)*. In this section, we extend the language to allow **universally quantified preconditions**. Instead of writing *Clear(b)* as a precondition, we can use $\forall x \; Block(x) \; \Rightarrow \; \neg On(x, b)$ instead. Not only does this relieve us of the burden of making each operator maintain the *Clear* predicate, but it also allows us to handle more complex domains, such as a blocks world with different size blocks.

UNIVERSALLY
QUANTIFIED
PRECONDITIONS

UNIVERSALLY
QUANTIFIED
EFFECTS

We also allow for **universally quantified effects**. For example, in the shopping domain we could define the operator *Carry(bag, x, y)* so that it has the effect that all objects that are in the bag are at y and are no longer at x. There is no way to define this operator without universal quantification. Here is the syntax we will use:

$Op(\text{ACTION:}Carry(bag, x, y),$
$\quad\text{PRECOND:}Bag(bag) \land At(bag, x),$
$\quad\text{EFFECT:}At(bag, y), \neg At(bag, x) \land$
$\qquad \forall i \; Item(i) \; \Rightarrow \; (At(i, y) \land \neg At(i, x)) \textbf{ when } In(i, bag))$

Although this *looks* like full first-order logic with quantifiers and implications, it is not. The syntax—and the corresponding semantics—is strictly limited. We will only allow worlds with a finite, static, typed universe of objects, so that the universally quantified condition can be satisfied by enumeration. The description of the initial state must mention all the objects and give each one a **type**, specified as a unary predicate. For example, $Bag(B) \land Item(I_1) \land Item(I_2) \land Item(B)$. Notice that is possible for an object to have more than one type: B is both a bag and an item. The **static universe** requirement means that the objects mentioned in the initial state cannot change type or be destroyed, and no new objects can be created. That is, no operator except *Start* can have $Bag(x)$ or $\neg Bag(x)$ as an effect. With this semantics of objects in mind, we can extend the syntax of preconditions and effects by allowing the form

$$\forall x\ T(x)\ \Rightarrow\ C(x)$$

where T is a unary type predicate on x, and C is a condition involving x. The finite, static, typed universe means that we can always expand this form into an equivalent conjunctive expression with no quantifiers:

$$\forall x\ T(x)\ \Rightarrow\ C(x)\ \equiv\ C(x_1) \wedge \ldots \wedge C(x_n)$$

where $x_1, \ldots, x_n$ are the objects in the initial state that satisfy $T(x)$. Here is an example:

Initial State: $Bag(B) \wedge Milk(M_1) \wedge Milk(M_2) \wedge Milk(M_3)$
Expression: $\forall x\ Milk(x)\ \Rightarrow\ In(x, B)$
Expansion: $In(M_1, B) \wedge In(M_2, B) \wedge In(M_3, B)$

In our planner, we will expand universally quantified goals to eliminate the quantifier. This can be inefficient because it can lead to large conjunctions that need to be satisfied, but there is no general solution that does any better.

For universally quantified effects, we are better off. We do not need to expand out the effect because we may not care about many of the resulting conjuncts. Instead we leave the universally quantified effect as it is, but make sure that RESOLVE-THREATS can notice that a universally quantified effect is a threat and that CHOOSE-OPERATOR can notice when a universally quantified effect can be used as a causal link.

Some domains are dynamic in that objects are created or destroyed, or change their type over time. Plans in which objects are first made, then used, seem quite natural. Our insistence on a static set of objects might seem to make it impossible to handle such domains. In fact, we can often finesse the problem by specifying broad static types in the universally quantified expressions and using additional dynamic unary predicates to make finer discriminations. In particular, we can use the dynamic predicate to distinguish between potential and actual objects. We begin with a supply of non-*Actual* objects, and object creation is handled by operators that make objects *Actual*. Suppose that in the house-building domain there are two possible sites for the house. In the initial state we could include $House(H_1) \wedge House(H_2)$, where we take *House* to mean that its argument is a possible house: something that might exist in some points of some plans, but not in others. In the initial state neither $Actual(H_1)$ nor $Actual(H_2)$ holds, but that can change: the $Build(x)$ operator has $Actual(x)$ as an effect, and the $Demolish(x)$ operator has $\neg Actual(x)$ as an effect.

If there were an infinite number of possible houses (or just a million), then this approach would not work. But objects that can potentially exist in large, undifferentiated quantities can often be treated as resources, which are covered in the next section.

A planner for expressive operator descriptions

We now combine all the extensions to create our POP-DUNC algorithm. Because the top level of POP-DUNC is identical to that of POP (Figure 11.13), we will not repeat it here. Figure 12.8 shows the parts of POP-DUNC that differ from the original. SELECT-SUB-GOAL is modified to expand out universally quantified preconditions and to choose one of two possible ways to satisfy

---

function SELECT-SUB-GOAL(*plan*) **returns** *plan, precondition conjunct*

    pick a plan step S_{need} from STEPS(*plan*) with a precondition conjunct c that has not been achieved
    if c is a universally quantified expression **then**
        return S_{need}, EXPANSION(c)
    else if c is a disjunction $c_1 \lor c_2$ **then**
        return S_{need}, **choose**(c_1, c_2)
    else return S_{need}, c

---

procedure CHOOSE-OPERATOR(*plan, operators, S_{need}, c*)

    choose a step S_{add} from *operators* or STEPS(*plan*) that has c_{add} as an effect
        such that $u =$ UNIFY(c, c_{add}, BINDINGS(*plan*))
    if there is no such step **then fail**
    $u' \leftarrow u$ without the universally quantified variables of c_{add}
    add u' to BINDINGS(*plan*)
    add $S_{add} \xrightarrow{c} S_{need}$ to LINKS(*plan*)
    add $S_{add} \prec S_{need}$ to ORDERINGS(*plan*)
    if S_{add} is a newly added step from *operators* **then**
        add S_{add} to STEPS(*plan*)
        add *Start* $\prec S_{add} \prec$ *Finish* to ORDERINGS(*plan*)

---

procedure RESOLVE-THREATS(*plan*)

    for each $S_i \xrightarrow{c} S_j$ **in** LINKS(*plan*) **do**
        for each S_{threat} **in** STEPS(*plan*) **do**
            for each c' **in** EFFECT(S_{threat}) **do**
                if SUBST(BINDINGS(*plan*), c) $=$ SUBST(BINDINGS(*plan*), $\neg c'$) **then**
                    choose either
                        Promotion: Add $S_{threat} \prec S_i$ to ORDERINGS(*plan*)
                        Demotion: Add $S_j \prec S_{threat}$ to ORDERINGS(*plan*)
                        Confrontation: **if** c' is really of the form (c' *when p*) **then**
                              CHOOSE-OPERATOR(*plan, operators, S_{threat},* $\neg p$)
                              RESOLVE-THREATS(*plan*)
                  if not CONSISTENT(*plan*) **then fail**
        end
        end
    end

Figure 12.8   The relevant components of POP-DUNC.

---

a disjunctive precondition. CHOOSE-OPERATOR is modified only slightly, to handle universally quantified variables properly. RESOLVE-THREATS is modified to include confrontation as one method of resolving a threat from a conditional effect.

12.5   RESOURCE CONSTRAINTS

In Chapter 11, we tackled the problem of shopping, but ignored money. In this section, we consider how to handle money and other resources properly. To do this, we need a language in which we can express a precondition such as *Have*($1.89), and we need a planning algorithm that will handle this efficiently. The former is theoretically possible with what we already have. We can represent each coin and bill in the world in the initial state: *Dollar*(d_1) ∧ *Dollar*(d_2) ∧ *Quarter*(q_1) ∧ .... We can then add decomposition methods to enumerate the ways it is possible to have a dollar. We have to be careful about inequality constraints, because we would not want the goal *Have*($2.00) to be satisfied by *Have*(d_1) ∧ *Have*(d_1). The final representation would be a little unintuitive and extremely verbose, but we could do it.

The problem is that the representation is totally unsuited for planning. Let us say we pose the problem *Have*($1,000,000$), and the best the planner can come up with is a plan that generates $1000. The planner would then backtrack looking for another plan. For every step that achieved, say, *Have*(d_1), the planner would have to consider *Have*(d_2) instead. The planner would end up generating all combinations of all the coins and bills in the world that total $1000. Clearly, this is a waste of search time, and it fails to capture the idea that it is the quantity of money you have that is important, not the identity of the coins and bills.

Using measures in planning

The solution is to introduce numeric-valued **measures** (see Chapter 8). Recall that a measure is an *amount* of something, such as money or volume. Measures can be referred to by logical terms such as $(1.50) or *Gallons*(6) or *GasLevel*. Measure functions such as *Volume* apply to objects such as *GasInCar* to yield measures: *GasLevel* = *Volume*(*GasInCar*) = *Gallons*(6). In planning problems, we are usually interested in amounts that change over time. A situation calculus representation would therefore include a situation argument (e.g., *GasLevel*(*s*)), but as usual in planning we will leave the situation implicit. We will call expressions such as *GasLevel*

MEASURE FLUENTS   **measure fluents**.

Planners that use measures typically require them to be "declared" up front with associated range information. For example, in a shopping problem, we might want to state that the amount of money the agent has, *Cash*, must be nonnegative; that the amount of gas in the tank, *GasLevel*, can range up to 15 gallons; that the price of gas ranges from $1.00 to $1.50 per gallon; and that the price of milk ranges from $1.00 to $1.50 per quart:

$$\$(0) \leq Cash$$
$$Gallons(0) \leq GasLevel \leq Gallons(15)$$
$$\$(1.00) \leq UnitPrice(Gas) \times Gallons(1) \leq \$(1.50)$$
$$\$(1.00) \leq UnitPrice(Milk) \times Quarts(1) \leq \$(1.50)$$

RESOURCES   Measures such as the price of gas are realities with which the planner must deal, but over which it has little control. Other measures, such as *Cash* and *GasLevel*, are treated as **resources** that can be produced and consumed. That is, there are operators such as *Drive* that require and consume the *GasLevel* resource, and there are operators such as *FillUp* that produce more of the *GasLevel* resource (while consuming some of the *Cash* resource).

To represent this, we allow inequality tests involving measures in the precondition of an operator. In the effect of an operator, we allow numeric assignment statements, where the left-hand side is a measure fluent and the right-hand side is an arithmetic expression involving measures. This is like an assignment and not like an equality in that the right-hand side refers to values *before* the action and the left-hand side refers to the value of the measure fluent *after* the action. As usual, the initial state is described by the effects of the start action:

Op(ACTION:*Start*,
        EFFECT: $Cash \leftarrow \$(12.50) \land$
                $GasLevel \leftarrow Gallons(5) \land$
                $\vdots$

The *Buy* action reduces the amount of Cash one has:

Op(ACTION:*Buy*(x, *store*),
        EFFECT:$Have(x) \land Cash \leftarrow Cash - Price(x, store))$

Getting gas can be described by an abstract *Fillup* operator:

Op(ACTION:*Fillup*(*GasLevel*),
        EFFECT: $GasLevel \leftarrow Gallons(15) \land$
                $Cash \leftarrow Cash - (UnitPrice(Gas) \times (Gallons(15) - GasLevel)))$

The declared upper and lower bounds serve as implicit preconditions for each operator. For example, *Buy*(x) has the implicit precondition $Cash \geq Price(x)$ to ensure that the quantity will be within range after the action. It takes some reasonably sophisticated algebraic manipulation code to automatically generate these preconditions, but it is less error-prone to do that than to require the user to explicitly write down the preconditions.

These examples should give you an idea of the versatility and power of using measures to reason about consumable resources. Although practical planners such as SIPE, O-PLAN, and DEVISER all have mechanisms for resource allocation, the theory behind them has not been formulated in a clean way, and there is disagreement about just what should be represented and how it should be reasoned with. We will sketch an outline of one approach.

It is a good idea to plan for scarce resources first. This can be done using an abstraction hierarchy of preconditions, as in Section 12.3, or by a special resource mechanism. Either way, it is desirable to delay the choice of a causal link for the resource measures. That is, when planning to buy a quart of milk, it is a good idea to check if $Cash \geq (Quarts(1) \times UnitPrice(Milk, store))$, but it would be premature to establish a causal link to that precondition from either the start state or some other step. The idea is to first pick the steps of the plan and do a rough check to see if the resource requirements are satisfiable. If they are, then the planner can continue with the normal mechanism of resolving threats for all the preconditions.

An easy way of doing the rough check on resources is to keep track of the minimum and maximum possible values of each quantity at each step in the plan. For example, if in the initial state we have $Cash \leftarrow \$(12.50)$ and in the description of measures we have $\$(0.50) \leq UnitPrice(Bananas, store) \times Pounds(1) \leq \$(1.00)$ and $\$(1.00) \leq UnitPrice(Milk, store) \times Quarts(1) \leq \$(1.50)$, then a plan with the steps *Buy*(*Milk*) and *Buy*(*Bananas*) will have the range $\$(10.00) \leq Cash \leq \$(11.00)$ at the finish. If we started out with less than $\$(1.50)$, then this approach would lead to failure quickly, without having to try all permutations of *Buy* steps at all combinations of stores.

There is a trade-off in deciding how much of the resource quantity information we want to deal with in the rough check. We could implement a full constraint satisfaction problem solver for arbitrary arithmetic inequalities (making sure we tie this process in with the normal unification of variables). However, with complicated domains, we can end up spending just as long solving the constraint satisfaction problem as we would have spent resolving all the conflicts.

Temporal constraints

In most ways, time can be treated like any other resource. The initial state specifies a start time for the plan, for example, $Time \leftarrow 8{:}30$. (Here 8:30 is a shorthand for $Minutes(8 \times 60 + 30)$.) We then can say how much time each operation consumes. (In the case of time, of course, consumption means *adding* to the amount.) Suppose it takes 10 seconds to pump each gallon of gas, and 3 minutes to do the rest of the *Fillup* action. Then an effect of *Fillup* is

$$Time \leftarrow Time + Minutes(3) + (Seconds(10)/Gallons(1)) \times (Gallons(15) - GasLevel))$$

It is handy to provide the operator $Wait(x)$, which has the effect $Time \leftarrow Time + x$ and no other preconditions or effects (at least in static domains).

There are two ways in which time differs from other resources. First, actions that are executed in parallel consume the maximum of their respective times rather than the sum. Second, constraints on the time resource have to be consistent with ordering constraints. That is, if $S_i \prec S_j$ is one of the ordering constraints, then *Time* at S_i must be less than *Time* at S_j.

Another important constraint is that time never goes backward. This implies that no operators generate time instead of consuming it. Thus, if the goal state specifies a deadline (a maximum time), and you have a partial plan whose steps require more time than is allowed, you can backtrack immediately, without considering any completions of the plan. (See Exercise 12.9 for more on this.)

12.6   SUMMARY

In this chapter we have seen several ways to extend the planning language—the representation of states and operators—to allow the planner to handle more complex, realistic domains. Each extension requires a corresponding change to the planning algorithm, and there is often a difficult trade-off between expressiveness and worst-case efficiency. However, when the more expressive representations are used wisely, they can lead to an increase in efficiency.

We have tried to present the field of planning in a way that emphasizes the best aspects of progress in AI. The field started with a vague set of requirements (to control a robot) and after some experimenting with an initially promising but ultimately intractable approach (situation calculus and theorem proving) settled down to a well-understood paradigm (STRIPS-style planning). From there, progress was made by a series of implementations, and formalizations of ever more ambitious variations on the basic planning language.

- The STRIPS language is too restricted for complex, realistic domains, but can be extended in several ways.

- Planners based on extended STRIPS-like languages and partial-order least-commitment algorithms have proven capable of handling complex domains such as spacecraft missions and manufacturing.

- **Hierarchical decomposition** allows nonprimitive operators to be included in plans, with a known decomposition into more primitive steps.

- Hierarchical decomposition is most effective when it serves to prune the search space. Pruning is guaranteed when either the **downward solution** property (every abstract solution can be decomposed into a primitive solution) or **upward solution** property (inconsistent abstract plans have no primitive solutions) holds.

- We can make the planning language closer to situation calculus by allowing **conditional effects** (the effect of an operator depends on what is true when it is executed) and **universal quantification** (the precondition and effect can refer to all objects of a certain class).

- Many actions consume **resources**, such as money, gas, or raw materials. It is convenient to treat these as numeric measures in a pool rather than try to reason about, say, each individual coin and bill in the world. Actions can generate and consume resources, and it is usually cheap and effective to check partial plans for satisfaction of resource constraints before attempting further refinements.

- Time is one of the most important resources. With a few exceptions, time can be handled with the general mechanisms for manipulating resource measures.

BIBLIOGRAPHICAL AND HISTORICAL NOTES

MACROPS

Abstract and hierarchical planning was introduced in the ABSTRIPS system (Sacerdoti, 1974), a variant of STRIPS. (Actually, the facility in STRIPS itself for learning **macrops**—"macro-operators" consisting of a sequence of bottom-level steps—could be considered the first mechanism for hierarchical planning.) Hierarchy was also used in the LAWALY system (Siklossy and Dreussi, 1973). Wilkins (1986) discusses some ambiguities in the meaning of the term "hierarchical planning." Yang (1990) explains the "unique main subaction" property in the context of abstraction planning. Erol, Hendler, and Nau (1994) present a complete hierarchical decomposition planner to which our HD-POP owes a great deal.

Work on deciding what hierarchical plans are worth knowing about and how to adapt previously constructed plans to novel situations goes under the name adaptive planning (Alterman, 1988) or case-based planning (Hammond, 1989).

Continuous time was first dealt with by DEVISER (Vere, 1983). A more recent planner focusing on the treatment of continuous time constraints is FORBIN (Dean *et al.*, 1990). NONLIN+ (Tate and Whiter, 1984) and SIPE (Wilkins, 1988; Wilkins, 1990) could reason about the allocation of limited resources to various plan steps. MOLGEN (Stefik, 1981b; Stefik, 1981a) allowed reasoning about objects that are only partially specified (via constraints). GARI (Descotte and Latombe, 1985) allowed hierarchical reasoning with constraints, in that some lower-level constraints are given lower priorities and may be violated at some stages during plan construction. O-PLAN (Bell and Tate, 1985) had a uniform, general representation for constraints on time and resources.

Classical situation calculus had allowed the full predicate calculus for describing the preconditions and effects of plan steps. Later formalisms have tried to get much of this expressiveness back, without sacrificing the efficiency gained by the use of STRIPS operators. The ADL planning formalism (Pednault, 1986) allows for multiagent planning and avoids the problems with the STRIPS formalism that were pointed out by Lifschitz (1986). PEDESTAL (McDermott, 1991) was the first (partial) implementation of ADL. UCPOP (Penberthy and Weld, 1992; Barrett *et al.*, 1993) is a more complete implementation of ADL that also allows for partial-order planning. POP-DUNC is based largely on this work. Weld (1994) describes UCPOP and gives a general introduction to partial-order planning with actions having conditional effects. Kambhampati and Nau (1993) analyze the applicability of Chapman's (1987) NP-hardness results to actions with conditional effects. Wolfgang Bibel (1986) has attempted to revive the use of full predicate calculus for planning, counting on advances in theorem proving to avoid the intractability that this led to in the early days of planning.

The improvements in the richness of the representations used in modern planners have helped make them more nearly equal to the challenges of real-world planning tasks than was STRIPS. Several systems have been used to plan for scientific experimentation and observation. MOLGEN was used in the design of scientific experiments in molecular genetics. T-SCHED (Drabble, 1990) was used to schedule mission command sequences for the UOSAT-II satellite. PLAN-ERS1 (Fuchs *et al.*, 1990), based on O-PLAN, was used for observation planning at the European Space Agency; SPIKE (Johnston and Adorf, 1992) was used for observation planning at NASA for the Hubble space telescope. Manufacturing has been another fertile application area for advanced planning systems. OPTIMUM-AIV (Aarup *et al.*, 1994), based on O-PLAN, has been used in spacecraft assembly at the European Space Agency. ISIS (Fox *et al.*, 1981; Fox, 1990) has been used for job shop scheduling at Westinghouse. GARI planned the machining and construction of mechanical parts. FORBIN was used for factory control. NONLIN+ was used for naval logistics planning. SIPE has had a number of applications, including planning for aircraft carrier flight deck operations.

EXERCISES

12.1   Give decompositions for the *Hire Builder* and *Obtain Permit* steps in Figure 12.1, and show how the decomposed subplans connect into the overall plan.

12.2   Rework the previous exercise using an approximation hierarchy. That is, assign criticality levels to each precondition of each step. How did you decide which preconditions get higher criticality levels?

12.3   Give an example in the house-building domain of two abstract subplans that cannot be merged into a consistent plan without sharing steps. (*Hint:* Places where two physical parts of the house come together are also places where two subplans tend to interact.)

12.4   Construct an example of the violation of the downward solution property. That is, find an abstract solution such that, when one of the steps is decomposed, the plan becomes inconsistent in that one of its threats cannot be resolved.

12.5   Prove that the upward solution property always holds for approximation hierarchy planning (see page 380). You may use Tenenberg (1988) for hints.

12.6   Add existential quantifiers (∃) to the plan language, using whatever syntax restrictions you find reasonable, and extend the planner to accommodate them.

12.7   Write operators for the shopping domain that will enable the planner to achieve the goal of having three oranges by grabbing a bag, going to the store, grabbing the oranges, paying for them, and returning home. Model money as a resource. Use universal quantification in the operators, and show that the original contents of the bag will still be there at the end of the plan.

12.8   We said in Section 11.6 that the SELECT-SUB-GOAL part of the POP algorithm was *not* a backtrack point—that we can work on subgoals in any order without affecting completeness (although the choice certainly has an effect on efficiency). When we change the SELECT-SUB-GOAL part to handle hierarchical decomposition, do we need to make it a backtrack point?

12.9   Some domains have resources that are monotonically decreasing or increasing. For example, time is monotonically increasing, and if there is a *Buy* operator, but no *Earn*, *Beg*, *Borrow*, or *Steal*, then money is monotonically decreasing. Knowing this can cut the search space: if you have a partial plan whose steps require more money than is available, then you can avoid considering any of the possible completions of the plan.

    a. Explain how to determine if a measure is monotonic, given a set of operator descriptions.

    b. Design an experiment to analyze the efficiency gains resulting from the use of monotonic resources in planning.

12.10   Some of the operations in standard programming languages can be modelled as actions that change the state of the world. For example, the assignment operation changes the contents of a memory location; the print operation changes the state of the output stream. A program consisting of these operations can also be considered as a plan, whose goal is given by the specification of the program. Therefore, planning algorithms can be used to construct programs that achieve a given specification.

    a. Write an operator schema for the assignment operator (assigning the value of one variable to another).

    b. Show how object creation can be used by a planner to produce a plan for exchanging the values of two variables using a temporary variable.

13 PLANNING AND ACTING

In which planning systems must face up to the awful prospect of actually having to take their own advice.

The assumptions required for flawless planning and execution, given the algorithms in the previous chapters, are that the world be accessible, static, and deterministic—just as for our simple search methods. Furthermore, the action descriptions must be correct and complete, describing all the consequences exactly. We described a planning agent in this ideal case in Chapter 11; the resemblance to the simple problem-solving agent of Chapter 3 was no coincidence.

In real-world domains, agents have to deal with both incomplete and incorrect information. Incompleteness arises because the world is inaccessible; for example, in the shopping world, the agent may not know where the milk is kept unless it asks. Incorrectness arises because the world does not necessarily match the agent's model of it; for example, the price of milk may have doubled overnight, and the agent's wallet may have been pickpocketed.

There are two different ways to deal with the problems arising from incomplete and incorrect information:

◇ **Conditional planning**: Also known as **contingency planning**, conditional planning deals with incomplete information by constructing a conditional plan that accounts for each possible situation or **contingency** that could arise. The agent finds out which part of the plan to execute by including **sensing actions** in the plan to test for the appropriate conditions. For example, the shopping agent might want to include a sensing action in its shopping plan to check the price of some object in case it is too expensive. Conditional planning is discussed in Section 13.1.

◇ **Execution monitoring**: The simple planning agent described in Chapter 11 executes its plan "with its eyes closed"—once it has a plan to execute, it does not use its percepts to select actions. Obviously this is a very fragile strategy when there is a possibility that the agent is using incorrect information about the world. By monitoring what is happening while it executes the plan, the agent can tell when things go wrong. It can then do **replanning** to find a way to achieve its goals from the new situation. For example, if the agent discovers that it does not have enough money to pay for all the items it has picked up, it can return some and replace them with cheaper versions. In Section 13.2 we look at a simple replanning agent that implements this strategy. Section 13.3 elaborates on this design to provide a full integration of planning and execution.

Execution monitoring is related to conditional planning in the following way. An agent that builds a plan and then executes it while watching for errors is, in a sense, taking into account the possible conditions that constitute execution errors. Unlike a conditional planner, however, the execution monitoring agent is actually **deferring** the job of dealing with those conditions until they actually arise. The two approaches of course can be combined by planning for some contingencies and leaving others to be dealt with later if they occur. In Section 13.4, we will discuss when one might prefer to use one or the other approach.

DEFERRING

13.1   CONDITIONAL PLANNING

We begin by looking at the nature of conditional plans and how an agent executes them. This will help to clarify the relationship between sensing actions in the plan and their effects on the agent's knowledge base. We then explain how to construct conditional plans.

The nature of conditional plans

Let us consider the problem of fixing a flat tire. Suppose we have the following three action schemata:

Op(ACTION:$Remove(x)$,
   PRECOND:$On(x)$,
   EFFECT:$Off(x) \wedge ClearHub(x) \wedge \neg On(x)$)
Op(ACTION:$PutOn(x)$,
   PRECOND:$Off(x) \wedge ClearHub(x)$,
   EFFECT:$On(x) \wedge \neg ClearHub(x) \wedge \neg Off(x)$)
Op(ACTION:$Inflate(x)$,
   PRECOND:$Intact(x) \wedge Flat(x)$,
   EFFECT:$Inflated(x) \wedge \neg Flat(x)$)

If our goal is to have an inflated tire on the wheel:

$On(x) \wedge Inflated(x)$

and the initial conditions are

$Inflated(Spare) \wedge Intact(Spare) \wedge Off(Spare) \wedge On(Tire_1) \wedge Flat(Tire_1)$

then any of the standard planners described in the previous chapters would be able to come up with the following plan:

$[Remove(Tire_1), PutOn(Spare)]$

If the absence of $Intact(Tire_1)$ in the initial state really means that the tire is not intact (as the standard planners assume), then this is all well and good. But suppose we have incomplete knowledge of the world—the tire may be flat because it is punctured, or just because it has not been pumped up lately. Because changing a tire is a dirty and time-consuming business, it would be better if the agent could execute a conditional plan: if $Tire_1$ is intact, then inflate it. If not, remove it and put on the spare. To express this formally, we can extend our original notation for plan steps with a conditional step $If(<Condition>,<ThenPart>,<ElsePart>,)$. Thus, the tire-fixing plan now includes the step

$$If(Intact(Tire_1),[Inflate(Tire_1)],[Remove(Tire_1),PutOn(Spare)])$$

Thus, the conditional planning agent can sometimes do better than the standard planning agents described earlier. Furthermore, there are cases where a conditional plan is the only possible plan. If the agent does not know if its spare tire is flat or inflated, then the standard planner will fail, whereas the conditional planner can insert a second conditional step that inflates the spare if necessary. Lastly, if there is a possibility that both tires have holes, then neither planner can come up with a guaranteed plan. In this case, a conditional planner can plan for all the cases where success is possible, and insert a *Fail* action on those branches where no completion is possible.

Plans that include conditional steps are executed as follows. When the conditional step is executed, the agent first tests the condition against its knowledge base. It then continues executing either the then-part or the else-part, depending on whether the condition is true or false. The then-part and the else-part can themselves be plans, allowing arbitrary nesting of conditionals. The conditional planning agent design is shown in Figure 13.1. Notice that it deals with nested conditional steps by following the appropriate conditional branches until it finds a real action to do. (The conditional planning algorithm itself, CPOP, will be discussed later.)

The crucial part of executing conditional plans is that the agent must, at the time of execution of a conditional step, be able to decide the truth or falsehood of the condition—that is, *the condition must be known to the agent* at that point in the plan. If the agent does not know if $Tire_1$ is intact or not, it cannot execute the previously shown plan. What the agent knows at any point is of course determined by the sequence of percepts up to that point, the sequence of actions carried out, and the agent's initial knowledge. In this case, the initial conditions in the knowledge base do not say anything about $Intact(Tire_1)$. Furthermore, the agent may have no actions that cause $Intact(Tire_1)$ to become true.[1] *To ensure that a conditional plan is executable, the agent must insert actions that cause the relevant conditions to become known by the agent.*

Facts become known to the agent through its percepts, so what we mean by the previous remark is that the agent must act in such a way as to make sure it receives the appropriate percepts. For example, one way to come to know that a tire is intact is to put some air into it and place one's listening device in close proximity. A hissing percept then enables the agent to infer that the tire is not intact.[2] Suppose we use the name $CheckTire(x)$ to refer to an action that establishes the state of the tire x. This is an example of a **sensing action**.

Using the situation calculus description of sensing actions described in Chapter 8, we would write

$$\forall x,s \ \ Tire(x) \ \Rightarrow \ KnowsWhether("Intact(\underline{x})",Result(CheckTire(x),s))$$

---

[1] Note that if, for example, a $Patch(Tire_1)$ action were available, then a standard plan could be constructed.

[2] Agents without sound percepts can wet the tire. A bubbling visual percept then suggests the tire is compromised.

---

function CONDITIONAL-PLANNING-AGENT(*percept*) **returns** an *action*
    static: *KB*, a knowledge base (includes action descriptions)
            p, a plan, initially *NoPlan*
            t, a counter, initially 0, indicating time
            G, a goal

    TELL(*KB*, MAKE-PERCEPT-SENTENCE(*percept*, *t*))
    current ← STATE-DESCRIPTION(*KB*, *t*)
    if *p* = *NoPlan* **then** *p* ← CPOP(*current*, *G*, *KB*)
    if *p* = *NoPlan* **or** *p* is empty **then** *action* ← *NoOp*
    else
        action ← FIRST(*p*)
        while CONDITIONAL?(*action*) **do**
            if ASK(*KB*, CONDITION-PART[*action*]) **then** *p* ← APPEND(THEN-PART[*action*], REST(*p*))
            else *p* ← APPEND(ELSE-PART[*action*], REST(*p*))
            action ← FIRST(*p*)
        end
        p ← REST(*p*)
    TELL(*KB*, MAKE-ACTION-SENTENCE(*action*, *t*))
    t ← *t* + 1
    return *action*

Figure 13.1   A conditional planning agent.

In our action schema format, we would write

    Op(ACTION:*CheckTire*(*x*),
        PRECOND:*Tire*(*x*),
        EFFECT:*KnowsWhether*("*Intact*(*x*)"))

Notice that as well as having knowledge effects, a sensing action can have ordinary effects. For example, if the *CheckTire* action uses the water method, then the tire will become wet. Sensing actions can also have preconditions that need to be established. For example, we might need to fetch the pump in order to put some air in the tire in order to check it. *A conditional planner therefore will sometimes create plans that involve carrying out ordinary actions for the purpose of obtaining some needed information.*

An algorithm for generating conditional plans

CONTEXT

The process of generating conditional plans is much like the planning process described in Chapter 11. The main additional construct is the **context** of a step in the plan. A step's context is simply the union of the conditions that must hold in order for the step to be executed—essentially, it describes the "branch" on which the step lies. For example, the action *Inflate*(*Tire*$_1$) in the earlier plan has a context *Intact*(*Tire*$_1$). Once it is established that a step has a certain context, then subsequent steps in the plan inherit that context. Because it cannot be the case that two steps with distinct contexts can both be executed, such steps cannot interfere with each other. Contexts are therefore essential for keeping track of which steps can establish or violate the preconditions of which other steps. An example will make this clear.

The flat-tire plan begins with the usual start and finish steps (Figure 13.2). Notice that the finish step has the context *True*, indicating that no assumptions have been made so far.

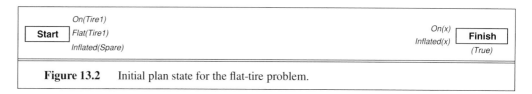

Figure 13.2   Initial plan state for the flat-tire problem.

There are two open conditions to be resolved: $On(x)$ and $Inflated(x)$. The first is satisfied by adding a link from the start step, with the unifier $\{x/Tire_1\}$. The second is satisfied by adding the step $Inflate(Tire_1)$, which has preconditions $Flat(Tire_1)$ and $Intact(Tire_1)$ (see Figure 13.3).

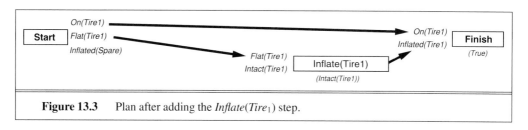

Figure 13.3   Plan after adding the $Inflate(Tire_1)$ step.

The open condition $Flat(Tire_1)$ is satisfied by adding a link from the start step. The interesting part is what to do with the $Intact(Tire_1)$ condition. In the statement of the problem there are no actions that can make the tire intact—that is, no action schema with the effect $Intact(x)$. At this point a standard causal-link planner would abandon this plan and try another way to achieve the goal. There is, however, an action $CheckTire(x)$ that allows one to *know* the truth value of a proposition that unifies with $Intact(Tire_1)$. If (and this is sometimes a big if) the outcome of checking the tire is that the tire is known to be intact, then the $Inflate(Tire_1)$ step can be achieved. We therefore add the $CheckTire$ step to the plan with a **conditional link** (shown as a dotted arrow in Figure 13.4) to the $Inflate(Tire_1)$ step. The $CheckTire$ step is called a **conditional step** because it will become a branch point in the final plan. The inflate step and the finish step now acquire a context label stating that they are assuming the outcome $Intact(Tire_1)$ rather than $\neg Intact(Tire_1)$. Because $CheckTire$ has no preconditions in our simple formulation, the plan is complete *given the context of the finish step*.

Obviously, we cannot stop here. We need a plan that works in both cases. The conditional planner ensures this by adding a second copy of the original finish step, labelled with a context that is the negation of the existing context (see Figure 13.5).[3] In this way, the planner covers an

CONDITIONAL LINK

CONDITIONAL STEP

_____

[3] If the solution of this new branch requires further context assumptions, then a third copy of the finish step will be added whose context is the negation of the disjunction of the existing finish steps. This continues until no more assumptions are needed.

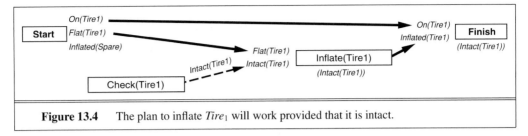

Figure 13.4   The plan to inflate *Tire₁* will work provided that it is intact.

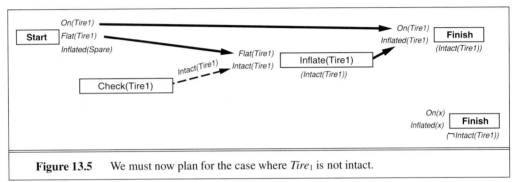

Figure 13.5   We must now plan for the case where *Tire₁* is not intact.

exhaustive set of possibilities—for every possible outcome, there is a corresponding finish step, and a path to get to the finish step.

Now we need to solve the goal when *Tire₁* has a hole in it. Here the context is very useful. If we were to try to add the step *Inflate(Tire₁)* to the plan, we would immediately see that the precondition *Intact(Tire₁)* is inconsistent with the context ¬*Intact(Tire₁)*. Thus, the only ways to satisfy the *Inflated(x)* condition are to link it to the start step with the unifier {*x/spare*} or to add an *Inflate* step for the spare. Because the latter leads to a dead end (because the spare is not flat), we choose the former. This leads to the plan state in Figure 13.6.

The steps *Remove(Tire₁)* and *PutOn(Spare)* are now added to the plan to satisfy the condition *On(Spare)*, using standard causal-link addition. Initially, the steps would have a *True*

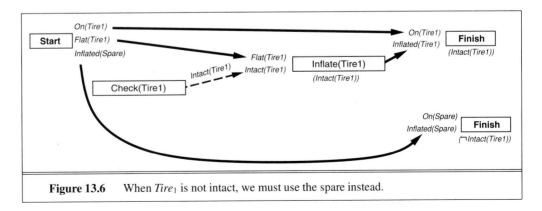

Figure 13.6   When *Tire₁* is not intact, we must use the spare instead.

context, because it has not yet been established that they can only be executed under certain circumstances. This means that we have to check how the steps interact with other steps in the plan. In particular, the *Remove(Tire₁)* step threatens the causal link protecting *On(Tire₁)* in the first finish step (the one with the context (*Intact(Tire₁)*)). In a standard causal-link planner, the only solution would be to promote or demote the *Remove(Tire₁)* step so that it cannot interfere.

CONDITIONING

In the conditional planner, we can also resolve the threat by **conditioning** the step so that its context becomes incompatible with the context of the step whose precondition it is threatening (in this case, the first finish step). Conditioning is achieved by finding a conditional step that has a possible outcome that would make the threatening step's context incompatible with the causal link's context. In this case, the *CheckTire* step has a possible outcome ¬*Intact(Tire₁)*. If we make a conditional link from the *CheckTire* step to the *Remove(Tire₁)* step, then the remove step is no longer a threat. The new context is inherited by the *PutOn(Spare)* step, and the plan is now complete (Figure 13.7).

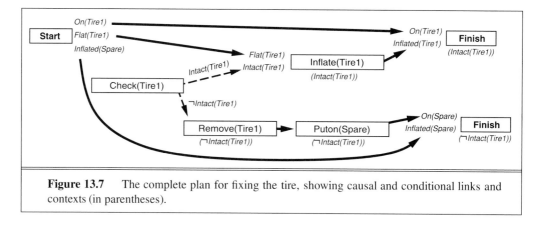

Figure 13.7   The complete plan for fixing the tire, showing causal and conditional links and contexts (in parentheses).

The algorithm is called CPOP (for Conditional Partial-Order Planner). It builds on the POP algorithm, and extends it by incorporating contexts, multiple finish steps and the conditioning process for resolving potential threats. It is shown in Figure 13.8.

Extending the plan language

The conditional steps we used in the previous section had only two possible outcomes. In some cases, however, a sensing action can have any number of outcomes. For example, checking the color of some object might result in a sentence of the form *Color(x, c)* being known for some value of *c*. Sensing actions of this type can be used in **parameterized plans**, where the exact actions to be carried out will not be known until the plan is executed. For example, suppose we have a goal such as

PARAMETERIZED
PLANS

$$Color(Chair, c) \wedge Color(Table, c)$$

---

function CPOP(*initial, goals, operators*) **returns** *plan*

plan ← MAKE-PLAN(*initial, goals*)
loop do

    Termination:
        if there are no unsatisfied preconditions
            and the contexts of the finish steps are exhaustive
            then return *plan*

    Alternative context generation:
        if the plans for existing finish steps are complete and have contexts $C_1 \ldots C_n$ **then**
            add a new finish step with a context $\neg (C_1 \vee \ldots \vee C_n)$
            this becomes the *current context*

    Subgoal selection and addition:
        find a plan step S_{need} with an open precondition c

    Action selection:
        choose a step S_{add} from *operators* or STEPS(*plan*) that adds c or
            knowledge of c and has a context compatible with the current context
        if there is no such step
            then fail
        add $S_{add} \xrightarrow{c} S_{need}$ to LINKS(*plan*)
        add $S_{add} < S_{need}$ to ORDERINGS(*plan*)
        if S_{add} is a newly added step **then**
            add S_{add} to STEPS(*plan*)
            add *Start* < S_{add} < *Finish* to ORDERINGS(*plan*)

    Threat resolution:
        for each step S_{threat} that potentially threatens any causal link $S_i \xrightarrow{c} S_j$
            with a compatible context **do**
        choose one of
            Promotion: Add $S_{threat} < S_i$ to ORDERINGS(*plan*)
            Demotion: Add $S_j < S_{threat}$ to ORDERINGS(*plan*)
            Conditioning:
                 find a conditional step S_{cond} possibly before both S_{threat} and S_j, where
                     1. the context of S_{cond} is compatible with the contexts of S_{threat} and S_j;
                     2. the step has outcomes consistent with S_{threat} and S_j, respectively
                 add conditioning links for the outcomes from S_{cond} to S_{threat} and S_j
                 augment and propagate the contexts of S_{threat} and S_j
        if no choice is consistent
            then fail
        end
end

Figure 13.8   The CPOP algorithm for constructing conditional plans.

("the chair and table are the same color"). The chair is initially unpainted, and we have some paints and a paintbrush. Then we might use the plan

$$[SenseColor(Table), KnowsWhat("Color(Table, \underline{c})"), GetPaint(c), Paint(Chair, c)]$$

RUNTIME VARIABLE

The last two steps are parameterized, because until execution the agent will not know the value of c. We call c a **runtime variable**, as distinguished from normal planning variables whose values are known as soon as the plan is made. The step $SenseColor(Table)$ will have the effect of providing percepts sufficient to allow the agent to deduce the color of the table. Then the action $KnowsWhat("Color(Table, \underline{c})")$ is executed simply by querying the knowledge base to establish a value for the variable c. This value can be used in subsequent steps such as $GetPaint(c)$, or in conditional steps such as $If(c = Green, [\ldots], [\ldots])$. Sensing actions are defined just as in the binary-condition case:

$$Op(\text{ACTION:}SenseColor(x),$$
$$\text{EFFECT:}KnowsWhat("Color(\underline{x}, \underline{c})"))$$

In situation calculus, the action would be described by

$$\forall x, s \; \exists c \; KnowsWhat("Color(\underline{x}, \underline{c})", Result(SenseColor(x), s))$$

The variables x and c are treated differently by the planner. Logically, c is existentially quantified in the situation calculus representation, and thus must be treated as a Skolem function of the object being sensed and the situation in which it is sensed. In the planner, runtime variables like c unify only with ordinary variables, and not with constants or with each other. This corresponds exactly to what would happen with Skolem functions.

When we have the ability to discover that certain facts *are* true, as well as the ability to cause them to *become* true, then we may wish to have some control over which facts are changed and which are preserved. For example, the goal of having the table and chair the same color can be achieved by painting them both black, regardless of what color the table is at the start. This can be prevented by protecting the table's color so that the agent has to sense it, rather than painting over it. A **maintenance goal** can be used to specify this:

MAINTENANCE GOAL

$$Color(Chair, c) \land Color(Table, c) \land Maintain(Color(Table, x))$$

The *Maintain* goal will ensure that no action is inserted in the plan that has an ordinary causal effect that changes the color of the table. This is done in a causal-link planner by adding a causal link from the start step to the finish step protecting the table's initial color.

Plans with conditionals start to look suspiciously like programs. Moreover, executing such plans starts to look rather like interpreting a program. The similarity becomes even stronger when we include loops in plans. A loop is like a conditional, except that when the condition holds, a portion of the plan is repeated. For example, we might include a looping step to make sure the chair is painted properly:

$$While(Knows("UnevenColor(Chair)"), [Paint(Chair, c), CheckColor(Chair)])$$

AUTOMATIC
PROGRAMMING

Techniques for generating plans with conditionals and loops are almost identical to those for generating programs from logical specifications (so-called **automatic programming**). Even a standard planner can do automatic programming of a simple kind if we encode as STRIPS operators the actions corresponding to assignment statements, procedure calls, printing, and so on.

13.2   A SIMPLE REPLANNING AGENT

As long as the world behaves exactly as the action descriptions describe it, then executing a plan in the ideal or incomplete-information cases will always result in goal achievement. As each step is executed, the world state will be as predicted—as long as nothing goes wrong.

"Something going wrong" means that the world state after an action is not as predicted. More specifically, the remaining plan segment will fail if any of its preconditions is not met. The preconditions of a plan segment (as opposed to an individual step) are all those preconditions of the steps in the segment that are not established by other steps in the segment. It is straightforward to annotate a plan at each step with the preconditions required for successful completion of the remaining steps. In terms of the plan description adopted in Chapter 11, the required conditions are just the propositions protected by all the causal links beginning at or before the current step and ending at or after it. Then we can detect a potential failure by comparing the current preconditions with the state description generated from the percept sequence. This is the standard model of execution monitoring, first used by the original STRIPS planner. STRIPS also introduced the **triangle table**, an efficient representation for fully annotated plans.

TRIANGLE TABLE

ACTION MONITORING

A second approach is to check the preconditions of each action as it is executed, rather than checking the preconditions of the entire remaining plan. This is called **action monitoring**. As well as being simpler and avoiding the need for annotations, this method fits in well with realistic systems where an individual action failure can be recognized. For example, if a robot agent issues a command to the motor subsystem to move two meters forward, the subsystem can report a failure if the robot bumps into an obstacle that materialized unexpectedly. On the other hand, action monitoring is less effective than execution monitoring, because it does not look ahead to see that an unexpected current state will cause an action failure some time in the future. For example, the obstacle that the robot bumped into might have been knocked off the table by accident much earlier in the plan. An agent using execution monitoring could have realized the problem and picked it up again.

Action monitoring is also useful when a goal is serendipitously achieved. That is, if someone or something else has already changed the world so that the goal is achieved, action monitoring notices this and avoids wasting time by going through the rest of the plan.

These forms of monitoring require that the percepts provide enough information to tell if a plan or action is about to fail. In an inaccessible world where the relevant conditions are not perceivable, more complicated strategies are needed to cope with undetected but potentially serious deviations from expectations. This issue is beyond the scope of the current chapter.

We can divide the causes of plan failure into two kinds, depending on whether it is possible to anticipate the possible contingencies:

BOUNDED
INDETERMINACY

◇ **Bounded indeterminacy**: In this case, actions can have unexpected effects, but the possible effects can be enumerated and described as part of the action description axiom. For example, the result of opening a can of paint can be described as the disjunction of having paint available, having an empty can, or spilling the paint. Using a combination of CPOP and the "D" (disjunctive) part of POP-DUNC we can generate conditional plans to deal with this kind of indeterminacy.

UNBOUNDED
INDETERMINACY
◇ **Unbounded indeterminacy**: In this case, the set of possible unexpected outcomes is too large to be completely enumerated. This would be the case in very complex and/or dynamic domains such as driving, economic planning, and military strategy. In such cases, we can plan for at most a limited number of contingencies, and must be able to *replan* when reality does not behave as expected.

The next subsection describes a simple method for replanning based on trying to get the plan "back on track" as quickly as possible. Section 13.3 describes a more comprehensive approach that deals with unexpected conditions as an integral part of the decision-making process.

Simple replanning with execution monitoring

One approach to replanning based on execution monitoring is shown in Figure 13.9. The simple planning agent is modified so that it keeps track of both the remaining plan segment p and the complete plan q. Before carrying out the first action of p, it checks to see whether the preconditions of the p are met. If not, it calls CHOOSE-BEST-CONTINUATION to choose some point in the complete plan q such that the plan p' from that point to the end of q is easiest to achieve from the current state. The new plan is to first achieve the preconditions of p' and then execute it.

Consider how REPLANNING-AGENT will perform the task of painting the chair to match the table. Suppose that the motor subsystem responsible for the painting action is imperfect and sometimes leaves small areas unpainted. Then after the $Paint(Chair, c)$ action is done, the execution-monitoring part will check the preconditions for the rest of the plan; the preconditions

---

function REPLANNING-AGENT(*percept*) **returns** an *action*
   static: *KB*, a knowledge base (includes action descriptions)
           p, an annotated plan, initially *NoPlan*
           q, an annotated plan, initially *NoPlan*
           G, a goal

   TELL(*KB*, MAKE-PERCEPT-SENTENCE(*percept*, *t*))
   current ← STATE-DESCRIPTION(*KB*, *t*)
   if *p* = *NoPlan* **then**
      p ← PLANNER(*current*, *G*, *KB*)
      q ← *p*
      if *p* = *NoPlan* **or** *p* is empty **then return** *NoOp*
   if PRECONDITIONS(*p*) not currently true in *KB* **then**
      p' ← CHOOSE-BEST-CONTINUATION(*current*, *q*)
      p ← APPEND(PLANNER(*current*, PRECONDITIONS(*p'*), *KB*), *p'*)
      q ← *p*
   action ← FIRST(*p*)
   p ← REST(*p*)
   return *action*

Figure 13.9   An agent that does execution monitoring and replanning.

are just the goal conditions because the remaining plan p is now empty, and the agent will detect that the chair is not all the same color as the table. Looking at the original plan q, the current state is identical to the precondition before the chair-painting step, so the agent will now try to paint over the bare spots. This behavior will cycle until the chair is completely painted.

Suppose instead that the agent runs out of paint during the painting process. This is not envisaged by the action description for *Paint*, but it will be detected because the chair will again not be completely painted. At this point, the current state matches the precondition of the plan beginning with *GetPaint*, so the agent will go off and get a new can of paint before continuing.

Consider again the agent's behavior in the first case, as it paints and repaints the chair. Notice that the *behavior* is identical to that of a conditional planning agent running the looping plan shown earlier. *The difference lies in the time at which the computation is done and the information is available to the computation process.* The conditional planning agent reasons explicitly about the possibility of uneven paint, and prepares for it even though it may not occur. The looping behavior results from a looping plan. The replanning agent assumes at planning time that painting succeeds, but during execution checks on the results and plans just for those contingencies that actually arise. The looping behavior results not from a looping plan but from the interaction between action failures and a persistent replanner.

We should mention the question of **learning** in response to failed expectations about the results of actions. Consider a plan for the painting agent that includes an action to open a door (perhaps to the paint store). If the door sticks a little, the replanning agent will try again until the door opens. But if the door is locked, the agent has a problem. Of course, if the agent already knows about locked doors, then *Unlocked* will be a precondition of opening the door, and the agent will have inserted a *CheckIfLocked* action that observes the state of the door, and perhaps a conditional branch to fetch the key. But if the agent does not know about locked doors, it will continue pulling on the door indefinitely. What we would like to happen is for the agent to learn that its action description is wrong; in this case, there is a missing precondition. We will see how this kind of learning can take place in Chapter 21.

13.3   FULLY INTEGRATED PLANNING AND EXECUTION

In this section, we describe a more comprehensive approach to plan execution, in which the planning and execution processes are fully integrated. Rather than thinking of the planner and execution monitor as separate processes, one of which passes its results to the other, we can

SITUATED PLANNING
AGENT
think of them as a single process in a **situated planning agent**.[4] The agent is thought of as always being *part of the way through* executing a plan—the grand plan of living its life. Its activities include executing some steps of the plan that are ready to be executed; refining the plan to resolve any of the standard deficiencies (open conditions, potential clobbering, and so on); refining the plan in the light of additional information obtained during execution; and fixing the

---

[4] The word "situated," which became popular in AI in the late 1980s, is intended to emphasize that the process of deliberation takes place in an agent that is directly connected to an environment. In this book all the agents are "situated," but the situated planning agent integrates deliberation and action to a greater extent than some of the other designs.

plan in the light of unexpected changes in the environment, which might include recovering from execution errors or removing steps that have been made redundant by serendipitous occurrences. Obviously, when it first gets a new goal the agent will have no actions ready to execute, so it will spend a while generating a partial plan. It is quite possible, however, for the agent to begin execution before the plan is complete, especially when it has independent subgoals to achieve. The situated agent continuously monitors the world, updating its world model from new percepts even if its deliberations are still continuing.

As in the discussion of the conditional planner, we will first go through an example and then give the planning algorithm. We will keep to the formulation of steps and plans used by the partial-order planner POP, rather than the more expressive languages used in Chapter 12. It is, of course, possible to incorporate more expressive languages, as well as conditional planning techniques, into a situated planner.

The example we will use is a version of the blocks world. The start state is shown in Figure 13.10(a), and the goal is $On(C, D) \land On(D, B)$. The action we will need is $Move(x, y)$, which moves block x onto block y, provided both are clear. Its action schema is

$Op(\text{ACTION:}Move(x, y),$
$\quad \text{PRECOND:}Clear(x) \land Clear(y) \land On(x, z),$
$\quad \text{EFFECT:}On(x, y) \land Clear(z) \land \neg On(x, z) \land \neg Clear(y))$

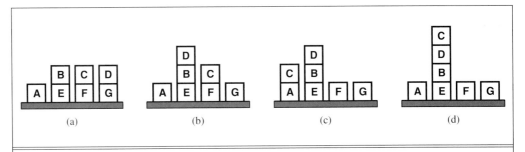

Figure 13.10   The sequence of states as the situated planning agent tries to reach the goal state $On(C, D) \land On(D, B)$ as shown in (d). The start state is (a). At (b), another agent has interfered, putting D on B. At (c), the agent has executed $Move(C, D)$ but has failed, dropping C on A instead. It retries $Move(C, D)$, reaching the goal state (d).

The agent first constructs the plan shown in Figure 13.11. Notice that although the preconditions of both actions are satisfied by the initial state, there is an ordering constraint putting $Move(D, B)$ before $Move(C, D)$. This is needed to protect the condition $Clear(D)$ until $Move(D, B)$ is completed.

At this point, the plan is ready to be executed, but nature intervenes. An external agent moves D onto B (perhaps the agent's teacher getting impatient), and the world is now in the state shown in Figure 13.10(b). Now $Clear(B)$ and $On(D, G)$ are no longer true in the initial state, which is updated from the new percept. The causal links that were supplying the preconditions $Clear(B)$ and $On(D, G)$ for the $Move(D, B)$ action become invalid, and must be removed from the plan. The new plan is shown in Figure 13.12. Notice that two of the preconditions for $Move(D, B)$

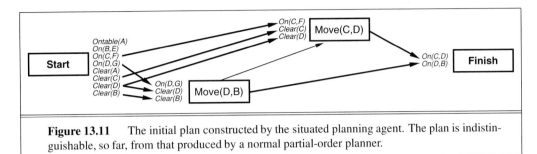

Figure 13.11   The initial plan constructed by the situated planning agent. The plan is indistinguishable, so far, from that produced by a normal partial-order planner.

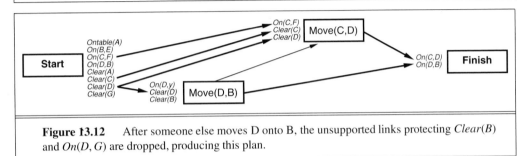

Figure 13.12   After someone else moves D onto B, the unsupported links protecting *Clear*(B) and *On*(D, G) are dropped, producing this plan.

are now open, and the precondition *On*(D, y) is now uninstantiated because there is no reason to assume the move will be from G any more.

Now the agent can take advantage of the "helpful" interference by noticing that the causal link protecting *On*(D, B) and supplied by *Move*(D, B) can be replaced by a direct link from START. This process is called **extending** a causal link, and is done whenever a condition can be supplied by an earlier step instead of a later one without causing a new threat.

EXTENDING

Once the old link from *Move*(D, B) is removed, the step no longer supplies any causal links at all. It is now a **redundant step**. All redundant steps are dropped from the plan, along with any links supplying them. This gives us the plan shown in Figure 13.13.

REDUNDANT STEP

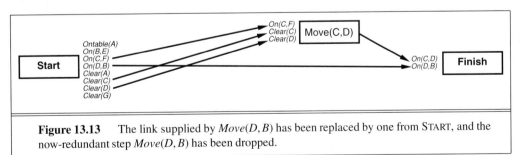

Figure 13.13   The link supplied by *Move*(D, B) has been replaced by one from START, and the now-redundant step *Move*(D, B) has been dropped.

Now the step *Move*(C, D) is ready to be executed, because all of its preconditions are satisfied by the START step, no other steps are necessarily before it, and it does not threaten any other link in the plan. The step is removed from the plan and executed. Unfortunately, the agent is clumsy and drops C onto A instead of D, giving the state shown in Figure 13.10(c). The new plan state is shown in Figure 13.14. Notice that although there are now no actions in the plan, there is still an open condition for the FINISH step.

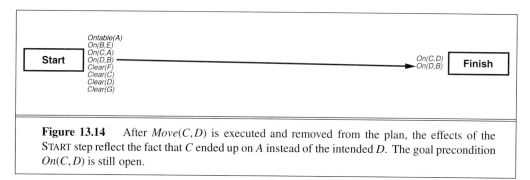

Figure 13.14   After *Move*(*C*, *D*) is executed and removed from the plan, the effects of the START step reflect the fact that *C* ended up on *A* instead of the intended *D*. The goal precondition *On*(*C*, *D*) is still open.

The agent now does the same planning operations as a normal planner, adding a new step to satisfy the open condition. Once again, *Move*(*C*, *D*) will satisfy the goal condition. Its preconditions are satisfied in turn by new causal links from the START step. The new plan appears in Figure 13.15.

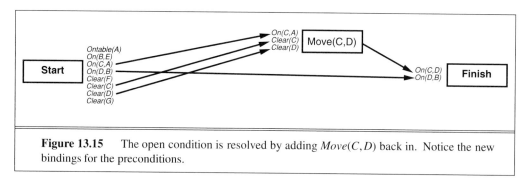

Figure 13.15   The open condition is resolved by adding *Move*(*C*, *D*) back in. Notice the new bindings for the preconditions.

Once again, *Move*(*C*, *D*) is ready for execution. This time it works, resulting in the goal state shown in Figure 13.10(d). Once the step is dropped from the plan, the goal condition *On*(*C*, *D*) becomes open again. Because the START step is updated to reflect the new world state, however, the goal condition can be satisfied immediately by a link from the START step. This is the normal course of events when an action is successful. The final plan state is shown in Figure 13.16. Because all the goal conditions are satisfied by the START step and there are no remaining actions, the agent resets the plan and looks for something else to do.

The complete agent design is shown in Figure 13.17 in much the same form as used for POP and CPOP, although we abbreviate the part in common (resolving standard flaws). One significant structural difference is that planning and acting are the same "loop" as implemented by the coupling between agent and environment. After each plan modification, an action is returned (even if it is a *NoOp*) and the world model is updated from the new percept. We assume that each action finishes executing before the next percept arrives. To allow for extended execution with a completion signal, an executed action must remain in the plan until it is completed.

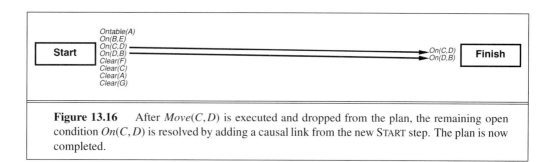

Figure 13.16   After *Move*(*C*, *D*) is executed and dropped from the plan, the remaining open condition *On*(*C*, *D*) is resolved by adding a causal link from the new START step. The plan is now completed.

13.4   DISCUSSION AND EXTENSIONS

We have arrived at an agent design that addresses many of the issues arising in real domains:

- The agent can use explicit domain descriptions and goals to control its behavior.
- By using partial-order planning, it can take advantage of problem decomposition to deal with complex domains without necessarily suffering exponential complexity.
- By using the techniques described in Chapter 12, it can handle domains involving conditional effects, universally quantified effects, object creation and deletion, and ramifications. It can also use "canned plans" to achieve subgoals.
- It can deal with errors in its domain description, and, by incorporating conditional planning, it can plan to obtain information when more is needed.
- It can deal with a dynamically changing world by incrementally fixing its plan as it detects errors and unfulfilled preconditions.

Clearly, this is progress. It is, however, a good idea to examine each advance in capabilities and try to see where it breaks down.

Comparing conditional planning and replanning

Looking at conditional planning, we see that almost all actions in the real world have a variety of possible outcomes besides the expected outcome. The number of possible conditions that must be planned for grows exponentially with the number of steps in the plan. Given that only one set of conditions will actually occur, this seems rather wasteful as well as impractical. Many of the events being planned for have only an infinitesimal chance of occurring.

Looking at replanning, we see that the planner is basically assuming no action failures, and then fixing problems as they arise during execution. This too has its drawbacks. The planner may produce very "fragile" plans, which are very hard to fix if anything goes wrong. For example, the entire existence of "spare tires" is a result of conditional planning rather than replanning. If the agent does not plan for a puncture, then it will not see the need for a spare tire. Unfortunately, without a spare tire, even the most determined replanning agent might be faced with a long walk.

---

function SITUATED-PLANNING-AGENT(*percept*) **returns** an *action*
   static: *KB*, a knowledge base (includes action descriptions)
         p, a plan, initially *NoPlan*
         t, a counter, initially 0, indicating time
         G, a goal

   TELL(*KB*, MAKE-PERCEPT-SENTENCE(*percept, t*))
   current ← STATE-DESCRIPTION(*KB, t*)
   EFFECTS(START(*p*)) ← *current*
   if *p* = *NoPlan* **then**
      G ← ASK(*KB*, MAKE-GOAL-QUERY(*t*))
      p ← MAKE-PLAN(*current, G, KB*)
   action ← *NoOp* (the default)

   Termination:
      if there are no open preconditions and *p* has no steps other than START and FINISH **then**
         p ← *NoPlan* and skip remaining steps

   Resolving standard flaws:
      resolve any open condition by adding a causal link from any existing
         possibly prior step or a new step
      resolve potential threats by promotion or demotion

   Remove unsupported causal links:
      if there is a causal link START $\xrightarrow{c}$ *S* protecting a proposition *c*
      that no longer holds in START **then**
         remove the link and any associated bindings

   Extend causal links back to earliest possible step:
      if there is a causal link $S_j \xrightarrow{c} S_k$ such that
      another step S_i exists with $S_i < S_j$ and the link $S_i \xrightarrow{c} S_k$ is safe **then**
         replace $S_j \xrightarrow{c} S_k$ with $S_i \xrightarrow{c} S_k$

   Remove redundant actions:
      remove any step *S* that supplies no causal links

   Execute actions when ready for execution:
      if a step *S* in the plan other than FINISH satisfies the following:
         (a) all preconditions satisfied by START;
         (b) no other steps necessarily between START and *S*; and
         (c) *S* does not threaten any causal link in *p* **then**
            add ordering constraints to force all other steps after *S*
            remove *S* from *p*, and all causal links to and from *S*
            action ← the action in *S*

   TELL(*KB*, MAKE-ACTION-SENTENCE(*action, t*))
   t ← *t* + 1
   return *action*

Figure 13.17   A situated planning agent.

Conditional planning and replanning are really two extremes of a continuous spectrum. One way to construct intermediate systems is to specify disjunctive outcomes for actions where more than one outcome is reasonably likely. Then the agent can insert a sensing action to see which outcome occurred and construct a conditional plan accordingly. Other contingencies are dealt with by replanning. Although this approach has its merits, it requires the agent designer to decide which outcomes need to be considered. This also means that the decision must be made once for each action schema, rather than depending on the particular context of the action. In the case of the provision of spare tires, for example, it is clear that the decision as to which contingencies to plan for depends not just on the likelihood of occurrence—after all, punctures are quite rare—but also on the cost of an action failure. An unlikely condition needs to be taken into account if it would result in catastrophe (e.g., a puncture when driving across a remote desert). Even if a conditional plan can be constructed, it might be better to plan around the suspect action altogether (e.g., by bringing two spare tires or crossing the desert by camel).

What all this suggests is that when faced with a complex domain and incomplete and incorrect information, the agent needs a way to assess the likelihoods and costs of various outcomes. Given this information, it should construct a plan that maximizes the probability of success and minimizes costs, while ignoring contingencies that are unlikely or are easy to deal with. Part V of this book deals with these issues in depth.

Coercion and abstraction

Although incomplete and incorrect information is the normal situation in real domains, there are techniques that still allow an agent to make quite complex, long-range plans without requiring the full apparatus of reasoning about likelihoods.

COERCION

The first method an agent can apply is **coercion**, which reduces uncertainty about the world by forcing it into a known state regardless of the initial state. A simple example is provided by the table-painting problem. Suppose that some aspects of the world are permanently inaccessible to the agent's senses—for example, it may have only a black and white camera. In this case, the agent can pick up a can of paint and paint both the chair and the table from the same can. This achieves the goal and reduces uncertainty. Furthermore, if the agent can read the label on the can, it will even know the color of the chair and table.

A second technique is **abstraction**. Although we have discussed abstraction as a tool for handling complexity (see Chapter 12), it also allows the agent to ignore details of a problem about which it may not have exact and complete knowledge. For example, if the agent is currently in London and plans to spend a week in Paris, it has a choice as to whether to plan the trip at an abstract level (fly out on Sunday, return the following Saturday) or a detailed level (take flight BA 216 and then taxi number 13471 via the Boulevard Peripherique). At the abstract level, the agent has actions such as $Fly(London, Paris)$ that are reasonably certain to work. Even with delays, oversold flights, and so on, the agent will still get to Paris. At the detailed level, there is missing information (flight schedules, which taxi will turn up, Paris traffic conditions) and the possibility of unexpected situations developing that would lead to a particular flight being missed.

AGGREGATION

Aggregation is another useful form of abstraction for dealing with large numbers of objects. For example, in planning its cash flows, the U.S. Government assumes a certain number of taxpayers will send in their tax returns by any given date. At the level of individual taxpayers, there is almost complete uncertainty, but at the aggregate level, the system is reliable. Similarly, in trying to pour water from one bottle into another using a funnel, it would be hopeless to plan the path of each water molecule because of uncertainty as well as complexity, yet the pouring as an aggregated action is very reliable.

The discussion of abstraction leads naturally to the issue of the connection between plans and physical actions. Our agent designs have assumed that the actions returned by the planner (which are concrete instances of the actions described in the knowledge base) are directly executable in the environment. A more sophisticated design might allow planning at a higher level of abstraction and incorporate a "motor subsystem" that can take an action from the plan and generate a sequence of primitive actions to be carried out. The subsystem might, for example, generate a speech signal from an utterance description returned by the planner; or it might generate stepper-motor commands to turn the wheels of a robot to carry out a "move" action in a motion plan. We discuss the connection between planning and motor programs in more detail in Chapter 25. Note that the subsystem might itself be a planner of some sort; its goal is to find a sequence of lower-level actions that achieve the effects of the higher-level action specified in the plan. In any case, the actions generated by the higher-level planner must be capable of execution independently of each other, because the lower-level motor system cannot allow for interactions or interleavings among the subplans that implement different actions.

13.5 SUMMARY

The world is not a tidy place. When the unexpected or unknown occurs, an agent needs to do something to get back on track. This chapter shows how conditional planning and replanning can help an agent recover.

- Standard planning algorithms assume complete and correct information. Many domains violate this assumption.

- Incomplete information can be dealt with using sensing actions to obtain the information needed. **Conditional plans** include different subplans in different contexts, depending on the information obtained.

- Incorrect information results in unsatisfied preconditions for actions and plans. **Execution monitoring** detects violations of the preconditions for successful completion of the plan. **Action monitoring** detects actions that fail.

- A simple **replanning agent** uses execution monitoring and splices in subplans as needed.

- A more comprehensive approach to plan execution involves incremental modifications to the plan, including execution of steps, as conditions in the environment evolve.

- **Abstraction** and **coercion** can overcome the uncertainty inherent in most real domains.

BIBLIOGRAPHICAL AND HISTORICAL NOTES

Early planners, which lacked conditionals and loops, sometimes resorted to a coercive style in response to environmental uncertainty. Sacerdoti's NOAH used coercion in its solution to the "keys and boxes" problem, a planning challenge problem in which the planner knows little about the initial state. Mason (1993) argued that sensing often can and should be dispensed with in robotic planning, and describes a sensorless plan that can move a tool into a specific position on a table by a sequence of tilting actions *regardless* of the initial position.

WARPLAN-C (Warren, 1976), a variant of WARPLAN, was one of the earliest planners to use conditional actions. Olawski and Gini (1990) lay out the major issues involved in conditional planning. Recent systems for partial-order conditional planning include UWL (Etzioni *et al.*, 1992) and CNLP (Peot and Smith, 1992), on which CPOP is based). C-BURIDAN (Draper *et al.*, 1994) handles conditional planning for actions with probabilistic outcomes, thereby connecting to the work on Markov decision problems described in Chapter 17.

There is a close relation between conditional planning and automated program synthesis, for which there are a number of references in Chapter 10. The two fields have usually been pursued separately because of the enormous difference in typical cost between execution of machine instructions and execution of actions by robot vehicles or manipulators. Linden (1991) attempts explicit cross-fertilization between the two fields.

The earliest major treatment of execution monitoring was PLANEX (Fikes *et al.*, 1972), which worked with the STRIPS planner to control the robot Shakey. PLANEX used triangle tables to allow recovery from partial execution failure without complete replanning. Shakey's model of execution is discussed further in Chapter 25. The NASL planner (McDermott, 1978a) treated a planning problem simply as a specification for carrying out a complex action, so that execution and planning were completely unified. It used theorem proving to reason about these complex actions. IPEM (Integrated Planning, Execution, and Monitoring) (Ambros-Ingerson and Steel, 1988), which was the first system to smoothly integrate partial-order planning and planning execution, forms the basis for the discussion in this chapter.

A system that contains an explicitly represented agent function, whether implemented as a table or a set of condition–action rules, need not worry about unexpected developments in the environment. All it has to do is to execute whatever action its function recommends for the state in which it finds itself (or in the case of inaccessible environments, the percept sequence to REACTIVE PLANNING date). The field of **reactive planning** aims to take advantage of this fact, thereby avoiding the complexities of planning in dynamic, inaccessible environments. "Universal plans" (Schoppers, 1987) were developed as a scheme for reactive planning, but turned out to be a rediscovery of the idea of **policies** in Markov decision processes. Brooks's (1986) subsumption architecture (also discussed in Chapter 25) uses a layered finite state machine to represent the agent function, and stresses the use of minimal internal state. Another important manifestation of the reactive planning paradigm is Pengi (Agre and Chapman, 1987), designed as a response to the criticism of classical AI planning in Chapman (1987). Ginsberg (1989) made a spirited attack on reactive planning, including intractability results for some formulations of the reactive planning problem. For an equally spirited response, see Schoppers (1989).

EXERCISES

13.1   Consider how one might use a planning system to play chess.

    a. Write action schemata for legal moves. Make sure to include in the state description some way to indicate whose move it is. Will basic STRIPS actions suffice?

    b. Explain how the opponent's moves can be handled by conditional steps.

    c. Explain how the planner would represent and achieve the goal of winning the game.

    d. How might we use the planner to do a finite-horizon lookahead and pick the best move, rather than planning for outright victory?

    e. How would a replanning approach to chess work? What might be an appropriate way to combine conditional planning and replanning for chess?

13.2   Discuss the application of conditional planning and replanning techniques to the vacuum world and wumpus world.

 13.3   Represent the actions for the flat-tire domain in the appropriate format, formulate the initial and goal state descriptions, and use the POP algorithm to solve the problem.

 13.4   This exercise involves the use of POP to *actually* fix a flat tire (in simulation).

    a. Build an environment simulator for the flat-tire world. Your simulator should be able to update the state of the environment according to the actions taken by the agent. The easiest way to do this is to take the postconditions directly from the operator descriptions and use TELL and RETRACT to update a logical knowledge base representing the world state.

    b. Implement a planning agent for your environment, and show that it fixes the tire.

 13.5   In this exercise, we will add nondeterminism to the environment from Exercise 13.4.

    a. Modify your environment so that with probability 0.1, an action fails—that is, one of the effects does not occur. Show an example of a plan not working because of an action failure.

    b. Modify your planning agent to include a simple replanning capability. It should call POP to construct a repair plan to get back to the desired state along the solution path, execute the repair plan (calling itself recursively, of course, if the repair plan fails), and then continue executing the original plan from there. (You may wish to start by having failed actions do nothing at all, so that this recursive repair method automatically results in a "loop-until-success" behavior; this will probably be easier to debug!)

    c. Show that your agent can fix the tire in this new environment.

13.6   **Softbots** construct and execute plans in software environments. One typical task for softbots is to find copies of technical reports that have been published at some other institution. Suppose that the softbot is given the task "Get me the most recent report by X on topic Y." Relevant actions include logging on to a library information system and issuing queries, using an Internet directory to find X's institution, sending email to X; connecting to X's institution by `ftp`, and so on. Write down formal representations for a representative set of actions, and discuss what sort of planning and execution algorithms would be needed.

Part V

UNCERTAIN KNOWLEDGE AND REASONING

Parts III and IV covered the **logical agent** approach to AI. We used first-order logic as the language to represent facts, and we showed how standard inference procedures and planning algorithms can derive new beliefs and hence identify desirable actions. In Part V, we reexamine the very foundation of the logical approach, describing how it must be changed to deal with the often unavoidable problem of uncertain information. **Probability theory** provides the basis for our treatment of systems that reason under uncertainty. Also, because actions are no longer certain to achieve goals, agents will need ways of weighing up the desirability of goals and the likelihood of achieving them. For this, we use **utility theory**. Probability theory and utility theory together constitute **decision theory**, which allows us to build rational agents for uncertain worlds.

Chapter 14 covers the basics of probability theory, including the representation language for uncertain beliefs. **Belief networks**, a powerful tool for representing and reasoning with uncertain knowledge, are described in detail in Chapter 15, along with several other formalisms for handling uncertainty. Chapter 16 develops utility theory and decision theory in some depth. Finally, Chapter 17 describes the full decision-theoretic agent design for uncertain environments, thereby generalizing the planning methods of Part IV.

14 UNCERTAINTY

In which we see what an agent should do when not all is crystal clear.

14.1 ACTING UNDER UNCERTAINTY

One problem with first-order logic, and thus with the logical-agent approach, is that *agents almost never have access to the whole truth about their environment.* Some sentences can be ascertained directly from the agent's percepts, and others can be inferred from current and previous percepts together with knowledge about the properties of the environment. In almost every case, however, even in worlds as simple as the wumpus world in Chapter 6, there will be important questions to which the agent cannot find a categorical answer. The agent must therefore act under **uncertainty**. For example, a wumpus agent often will find itself unable to discover which of two squares contains a pit. If those squares are en route to the gold, then the agent might have to take a chance and enter one of the two squares.

UNCERTAINTY

Uncertainty can also arise because of incompleteness and incorrectness in the agent's understanding of the properties of the environment. The **qualification problem**, mentioned in Chapter 7, says that many rules about the domain will be incomplete, because there are too many conditions to be explicitly enumerated, or because some of the conditions are unknown. Suppose, for example, that the agent wants to drive someone to the airport to catch a flight, and is considering a plan A_{90} that involves leaving home 90 minutes before the flight departs and driving at a reasonable speed. Even though the airport is only about 15 miles away, the agent will not be able to reach a definite conclusion such as "Plan A_{90} will get us to the airport in time," but rather only the weaker conclusion "Plan A_{90} will get us to the airport in time, as long as my car doesn't break down or run out of gas, and I don't get into an accident, and there are no accidents on the bridge, and the plane doesn't leave early, and there's no earthquake, ..."[1] A logical

---

[1] Conditional planning can overcome uncertainty to some extent, but only if the agent's sensing actions can obtain the required information, and if there are not too many different contingencies.

agent therefore will not believe that plan A_{90} will necessarily achieve the goal, and that makes it difficult for the logical agent to conclude that plan A_{90} is the right thing to do.

Nonetheless, let us suppose that A_{90} is in fact the right thing to do. What do we mean by saying this? As we discussed in Chapter 2, we mean that out of all the possible plans that could be executed, A_{90} is expected to maximize the agent's performance measure, given the information it has about the environment. The performance measure includes getting to the airport in time for the flight, avoiding a long, unproductive wait at the airport, and avoiding speeding tickets along the way. The information the agent has cannot guarantee any of these outcomes for A_{90}, but it can provide some degree of belief that they will be achieved. Other plans, such as A_{120}, might increase the agent's belief that it will get to the airport on time, but also increase the likelihood of a long wait. *The right thing to do, the **rational decision**, therefore, depends on both the relative importance of various goals and the likelihood that, and degree to which, they will be achieved.* The remainder of this section sharpens up these ideas, in preparation for the development of the general theories of uncertain reasoning and rational decisions that we present in this and subsequent chapters.

Handling uncertain knowledge

In this section, we look more closely at the nature of uncertain knowledge. We will use a simple diagnosis example to illustrate the concepts involved. Diagnosis—whether for medicine, automobile repair, or whatever—is a task that almost always involves uncertainty. If we tried to build a dental diagnosis system using first-order logic, we might propose rules such as

$\forall p \; Symptom(p, Toothache) \;\Rightarrow\; Disease(p, Cavity)$

The problem is that this rule is wrong. Not all patients with toothaches have cavities; some of them may have gum disease, or impacted wisdom teeth, or one of several other problems:

$\forall p \; Symptom(p, Toothache) \;\Rightarrow$
$\quad Disease(p, Cavity) \lor Disease(p, GumDisease) \lor Disease(p, ImpactedWisdom) \ldots$

Unfortunately, in order to make the rule true, we have to add an almost unlimited list of possible causes. We could try turning the rule into a causal rule:

$\forall p \; Disease(p, Cavity) \;\Rightarrow\; Symptom(p, Toothache)$

But this rule is not right either; not all cavities cause pain. The only way to fix the rule is to make it logically exhaustive: to extend the left-hand side to cover all possible reasons why a cavity might or might not cause a toothache. Even then, for the purposes of diagnosis, one must also take into account the possibility that the patient may have a toothache and a cavity that are unconnected.

Trying to use first-order logic to cope with a domain like medical diagnosis thus fails for three main reasons:

LAZINESS
$\Diamond$ **Laziness**: It is too much work to list the complete set of antecedents or consequents needed to ensure an exceptionless rule, and too hard to use the enormous rules that result.

THEORETICAL
IGNORANCE
$\Diamond$ **Theoretical ignorance**: Medical science has no complete theory for the domain.

PRACTICAL
IGNORANCE

◇ **Practical ignorance**: Even if we know all the rules, we may be uncertain about a particular patient because all the necessary tests have not or cannot be run.

The connection between toothaches and cavities is just not a logical consequence in either direction. This is typical of the medical domain, as well as most other judgmental domains: law, business, design, automobile repair, gardening, dating, and so on. The agent's knowledge can at best provide only a **degree of belief** in the relevant sentences. Our main tool for dealing with degrees of belief will be **probability theory**, which assigns a numerical degree of belief between 0 and 1 to sentences.[2]

DEGREE OF BELIEF

PROBABILITY
THEORY

*Probability provides a way of **summarizing** the uncertainty that comes from our laziness and ignorance.* We may not know for sure what afflicts a particular patient, but we believe that there is, say, an 80% chance—that is, a probability of 0.8—that the patient has a cavity if he or she has a toothache. This probability could be derived from statistical data—80% of the toothache patients seen so far have had cavities—or from some general rules, or from a combination of evidence sources. The 80% summarizes those cases in which all the factors needed for a cavity to cause a toothache are present, as well as other cases in which the patient has both toothache and cavity but the two are unconnected. The missing 20% summarizes all the other possible causes of toothache that we are too lazy or ignorant to confirm or deny.

A probability of 0 for a given sentence corresponds to an unequivocal belief that the sentence is false, while a probability of 1 corresponds to an unequivocal belief that the sentence is true. Probabilities between 0 and 1 correspond to intermediate degrees of belief in the truth of the sentence. The sentence itself is *in fact* either true or false. It is important to note that a degree of belief is different from a degree of truth. A probability of 0.8 does not mean "80% true" but rather an 80% degree of belief—that is, a fairly strong expectation. If an agent assigns a probability of 0.8 to a sentence, then the agent expects that in 80% of cases that are indistinguishable from the current situation as far as the agent's knowledge goes, the sentence will turn out to be actually true. Thus, probability theory makes the same ontological commitment as logic, namely, that facts either do or do not hold in the world. Degree of truth, as opposed to degree of belief, is the subject of **fuzzy logic**, which is covered in Section 15.6.

Before we plunge into the details of probability, let us pause to consider the status of probability statements such as "The probability that the patient has a cavity is 0.8." In propositional and first-order logic, a sentence is true or false depending on the interpretation and the world; it is true just when the fact it refers to is the case. Probability statements do not have quite the same kind of semantics.[3] This is because the probability that an agent assigns to a proposition depends on the percepts that it has received to date. In discussing uncertain reasoning, we call this the **evidence**. For example, suppose that the agent has drawn a card from a shuffled pack. Before looking at the card, the agent might assign a probability of 1/52 to its being the ace of spades. After looking at the card, an appropriate probability for the same proposition would be 0 or 1. Thus, an assignment of probability to a proposition is analogous to saying whether or not a given logical sentence (or its negation) is entailed by the knowledge base, rather than whether or not it

EVIDENCE

---

[2] Until recently, it was thought that probability theory was too unwieldy for general use in AI, and many approximations and alternatives to probability theory were proposed. Some of these will be covered in Section 15.6.

[3] The *objectivist* view of probability, however, claims that probability statements *are* true or false in the same way as logical sentences. In Section 14.5, we discuss this claim further.

is true. Just as entailment status can change when more sentences are added to the knowledge base, probabilities can change when more evidence is acquired.[4]

All probability statements must therefore indicate the evidence with respect to which the probability is being assessed. As the agent receives new percepts, its probability assessments are updated to reflect the new evidence. Before the evidence is obtained, we talk about **prior** or **unconditional** probability; after the evidence is obtained, we talk about **posterior** or **conditional** probability. In most cases, an agent will have some evidence from its percepts, and will be interested in computing the conditional probabilities of the outcomes it cares about given the evidence it has. In some cases, it will also need to compute conditional probabilities with respect to the evidence it has plus the evidence it expects to obtain during the course of executing some sequence of actions.

Uncertainty and rational decisions

The presence of uncertainty changes radically the way in which an agent makes decisions. A logical agent typically has a single (possibly conjunctive) goal, and executes any plan that is guaranteed to achieve it. An action can be selected or rejected on the basis of whether or not it achieves the goal, regardless of what other actions achieve. When uncertainty enters the picture, this is no longer the case. Consider again the A_{90} plan for getting to the airport. Suppose it has a 95% chance of succeeding. Does this mean it is a rational choice? Obviously, the answer is "Not necessarily." There might be other plans, such as A_{120}, with higher probabilities of success. If it is vital not to miss the flight, then it might be worth risking the longer wait at the airport. What about A_{1440}, a plan that involves leaving home 24 hours in advance? In most circumstances, this is not a good choice, because although it almost guarantees getting there on time, it involves an intolerable wait.

PREFERENCES   To make such choices, an agent must first have **preferences** between the different possible outcomes of the various plans. A particular outcome is a completely specified state, including such factors as whether or not the agent arrives in time, and the length of the wait at the airport. UTILITY THEORY   We will be using **utility theory** to represent and reason with preferences. The term **utility** is used here in the sense of "the quality of being useful," not in the sense of the electric company or water works. Utility theory says that every state has a degree of usefulness, or utility, to an agent, and that the agent will prefer states with higher utility.

The utility of a state is relative to the agent whose preferences the utility function is supposed to represent. For example, the payoff functions for games in Chapter 5 are utility functions. The utility of a state in which White has won a game of chess is obviously high for the agent playing White, but low for the agent playing Black. Or again, some players (including the authors) might be happy with a draw against the world champion, whereas other players (including the former world champion) might not. There is no accounting for taste or preferences: you might think that an agent who prefers jalapeño-bubble-gum ice cream to chocolate-chocolate-chip is odd or even misguided, but you could not say the agent is irrational.

---

[4] This is quite different from a sentence becoming true or false as the world changes. Handling a changing world using probabilities requires the same kinds of mechanisms—situations, intervals and events—as we used in Chapter 8 for logical representations.

It is also interesting that utility theory allows for altruism. It is perfectly consistent for an agent to assign high utility to a state where the agent itself suffers a concrete loss but others profit. Here, "concrete loss" must denote a reduction in "personal welfare" of the kind normally associated with altruism or selfishness—wealth, prestige, comfort, and so on—rather than a loss of utility *per se*. Therefore, utility theory is necessarily "selfish" only if one equates a preference for the welfare of others with selfishness; conversely, altruism is only inconsistent with the principle of utility maximization if one's goals do *not* include the welfare of others.

DECISION THEORY   Preferences, as expressed by utilities, are combined with probabilities in the general theory of rational decisions called **decision theory**:

Decision theory = probability theory + utility theory

 The fundamental idea of decision theory is that *an agent is rational if and only if it chooses the action that yields the highest expected utility, averaged over all the possible outcomes of the action.* This is called the principle of Maximum Expected Utility (MEU). Probabilities and utilities are therefore combined in the evaluation of an action by weighting the utility of a particular outcome by the probability that it occurs. We saw this principle in action in Chapter 5, where we examined optimal decisions in backgammon. We will see that it is in fact a completely general principle.

Design for a decision-theoretic agent

The structure of an agent that uses decision theory to select actions is identical, at an abstract level, to that of the logical agent described in Chapter 6. Figure 14.1 shows what needs to be done. In this chapter and the next, we will concentrate on the task of computing probabilities for current states and for the various possible outcomes of actions. Chapter 16 covers utility theory in more depth, and Chapter 17 fleshes out the complete agent architecture.

```
function DT-AGENT( percept) returns an action
    static: a set probabilistic beliefs about the state of the world

    calculate updated probabilities for current state based on
        available evidence including current percept and previous action
    calculate outcome probabilities for actions,
        given action descriptions and probabilities of current states
    select action with highest expected utility
        given probabilities of outcomes and utility information
    return action
```

Figure 14.1   A decision-theoretic agent that selects rational actions. The steps will be fleshed out in the next four chapters.

14.2   BASIC PROBABILITY NOTATION

Now that we have set up the general framework for a rational agent, we will need a formal language for representing and reasoning with uncertain knowledge. Any notation for describing degrees of belief must be able to deal with two main issues: the nature of the sentences to which degrees of belief are assigned, and the dependence of the degree of belief on the agent's state of knowledge. The version of probability theory we present uses an extension of propositional logic for its sentences. The dependence on experience is reflected in the syntactic distinction between prior probability statements, which apply before any evidence is obtained, and conditional probability statements, which include the evidence explicitly.

Prior probability

UNCONDITIONAL
PRIOR PROBABILITY

We will use the notation $P(A)$ for the **unconditional** or **prior probability** that the proposition A is true. For example, if *Cavity* denotes the proposition that a particular patient has a cavity,

$$P(Cavity) = 0.1$$

means that *in the absence of any other information*, the agent will assign a probability of 0.1 (a 10% chance) to the event of the patient's having a cavity. It is important to remember that $P(A)$ can only be used when there is no other information. As soon as some new information B is known, we have to reason with the conditional probability of A given B instead of $P(A)$. Conditional probabilities are covered in the next section.

The proposition that is the subject of a probability statement can be represented by a proposition symbol, as in the $P(A)$ example. Propositions can also include equalities involving so-called **random variables**. For example, if we are concerned about the random variable *Weather*, we might have

RANDOM VARIABLES

$$P(Weather = Sunny) = 0.7$$
$$P(Weather = Rain) = 0.2$$
$$P(Weather = Cloudy) = 0.08$$
$$P(Weather = Snow) = 0.02$$

DOMAIN

Each random variable X has a **domain** of possible values $\langle x_1, \ldots, x_n \rangle$ that it can take on.[5] We will usually deal with discrete sets of values, although continuous random variables will be discussed briefly in Chapter 15. We can view proposition symbols as random variables as well, if we assume that they have a domain $\langle true, false \rangle$. Thus, the expression $P(Cavity)$ can be viewed as shorthand for $P(Cavity = true)$. Similarly, $P(\neg Cavity)$ is shorthand for $P(Cavity = false)$. Usually, we will use the letters A, B, and so on for Boolean random variables, and the letters X, Y, and so on for multivalued variables.

Sometimes, we will want to talk about the probabilities of all the possible values of a random variable. In this case, we will use an expression such as $\mathbf{P}(Weather)$, which denotes a

---

[5] In probability, the variables are capitalized, while the values are lowercase. This is unfortunately the reverse of logical notation, but it is the tradition.

vector of values for the probabilities of each individual state of the weather. Given the preceding values, for example, we would write

$$\mathbf{P}(\textit{Weather}) = \langle 0.7, 0.2, 0.08, 0.02 \rangle$$

PROBABILITY
DISTRIBUTION

This statement defines a **probability distribution** for the random variable *Weather*.

We will also use expressions such as $\mathbf{P}(\textit{Weather}, \textit{Cavity})$ to denote the probabilities of all combinations of the values of a set of random variables. In this case, $\mathbf{P}(\textit{Weather}, \textit{Cavity})$ denotes a 4×2 table of probabilities. We will see that this notation simplifies many equations.

We can also use logical connectives to make more complex sentences and assign probabilities to them. For example,

$$P(\textit{Cavity} \wedge \neg \textit{Insured}) = 0.06$$

says there is an 6% chance that a patient has a cavity and has no insurance.

Conditional probability

CONDITIONAL

POSTERIOR

Once the agent has obtained some evidence concerning the previously unknown propositions making up the domain, prior probabilities are no longer applicable. Instead, we use **conditional** or **posterior** probabilities, with the notation $P(A|B)$. This is read as "the probability of A given that *all we know* is B." For example,

$$P(\textit{Cavity}|\textit{Toothache}) = 0.8$$

indicates that if a patient is observed to have a toothache, and no other information is yet available, then the probability of the patient having a cavity will be 0.8. It is important to remember that $P(A|B)$ can only be used when all we know is B. As soon as we know C, then we must compute $P(A|B \wedge C)$ instead of $P(A|B)$. A prior probability $P(A)$ can be thought of as a special case of conditional probability $P(A|\ )$, where the probability is conditioned on no evidence.

We can also use the $\mathbf{P}$ notation with conditional probabilities. $\mathbf{P}(X|Y)$ is a two-dimensional table giving the values of $P(X = x_i | Y = y_j)$ for each possible i, j. Conditional probabilities can be defined in terms of unconditional probabilities. The equation

$$P(A|B) = \frac{P(A \wedge B)}{P(B)} \qquad (14.1)$$

holds whenever $P(B) > 0$. This equation can also be written as

$$P(A \wedge B) = P(A|B)P(B)$$

PRODUCT RULE

which is called the **product rule**. The product rule is perhaps easier to remember: it comes from the fact that for A and B to be true, we need B to be true, and then A to be true given B. We can also have it the other way around:

$$P(A \wedge B) = P(B|A)P(A)$$

In some cases, it is easier to reason in terms of prior probabilities of conjunctions, but for the most part, we will use conditional probabilities as our vehicle for probabilistic inference.

We can also extend our $\mathbf{P}$ notation to handle equations like these, providing a welcome degree of conciseness. For example, we might write

$$\mathbf{P}(X, Y) = \mathbf{P}(X|Y)\mathbf{P}(Y)$$

which denotes a set of equations relating the corresponding individual entries in the tables (*not a matrix multiplication of the tables*). Thus, one of the equations might be

$$P(X = x_1 \land Y = y_2) = P(X = x_1 | Y = y_2)P(Y = y_2)$$

In general, if we are interested in the probability of a proposition A, and we have accumulated evidence B, then the quantity we must calculate is $P(A|B)$. Sometimes we will not have this conditional probability available directly in the knowledge base, and we must resort to probabilistic inference, which we describe in later sections.

As we have already said, probabilistic inference does not work like logical inference. It is tempting to interpret the statement $P(A|B) = 0.8$ to mean "whenever B is true, conclude that $P(A)$ is 0.8." This is wrong on two counts: first, $P(A)$ always denotes the prior probability of A, not the posterior given some evidence; second, the statement $P(A|B) = 0.8$ is only applicable when B is the only available evidence. When additional information C is available, we must calculate $P(A|B \land C)$, which may bear little relation to $P(A|B)$. In the extreme case, C might tell us directly whether A is true or false. If we examine a patient who complains of toothache, and discover a cavity, then we have additional evidence *Cavity*, and we conclude (trivially) that $P(Cavity|Toothache \land Cavity) = 1.0$.

14.3   THE AXIOMS OF PROBABILITY

In order to define properly the semantics of statements in probability theory, we will need to describe how probabilities and logical connectives interact. We take as given the properties of the connectives themselves, as defined in Chapter 6. As for probabilities, it is normal to use a small set of axioms that constrain the probability assignments that an agent can make to a set of propositions. The following axioms are in fact sufficient:

1. All probabilities are between 0 and 1.
   $$0 \leq P(A) \leq 1$$

2. Necessarily true (i.e., valid) propositions have probability 1, and necessarily false (i.e., unsatisfiable) propositions have probability 0.
   $$P(True) = 1 \qquad P(False) = 0$$

3. The probability of a disjunction is given by
   $$P(A \lor B) = P(A) + P(B) - P(A \land B)$$

The first two axioms serve to define the probability scale. The third is best remembered by reference to the Venn diagram shown in Figure 14.2. The figure depicts each proposition as a set, which can be thought of as the set of all possible worlds in which the proposition is true. The total probability of $A \lor B$ is seen to be the sum of the probabilities assigned to A and B, but with $P(A \land B)$ subtracted out so that those cases are not counted twice.

From these three axioms, we can derive all other properties of probabilities. For example, if we let B be $\neg A$ in the last axiom, we obtain an expression for the probability of the negation of

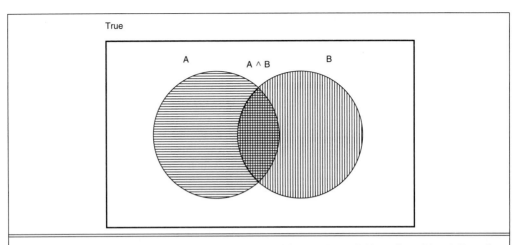

Figure 14.2   A Venn diagram showing the propositions A, B, $A \vee B$ (the union of A and B), and $A \wedge B$ (the intersection of A and B) as sets of possible worlds.

a proposition in terms of the probability of the proposition itself:

$$
\begin{aligned}
P(A \vee \neg A) &= P(A) + P(\neg A) - P(A \wedge \neg A) && \text{(by 3 with } B = \neg A) \\
P(\textit{True}) &= P(A) + P(\neg A) - P(\textit{False}) && \text{(by logical equivalence)} \\
1 &= P(A) + P(\neg A) && \text{(by 2)} \\
P(\neg A) &= 1 - P(A) && \text{(by algebra)}
\end{aligned}
$$

Why the axioms of probability are reasonable

The axioms of probability can be seen as restricting the set of probabilistic beliefs that an agent can hold. This is somewhat analogous to the logical case, where a logical agent cannot simultaneously believe A, B, and $\neg(A \wedge B)$, for example. There is, however, an additional complication. In the logical case, the semantic definition of conjunction means that at least one of the three beliefs just mentioned *must be false in the world*, so it is unreasonable for an agent to believe all three. With probabilities, on the other hand, statements refer not to the world directly, but to the agent's own state of knowledge. Why, then, can an agent not hold the following set of beliefs, given that these probability assignments clearly violate the third axiom?

$$
\begin{aligned}
P(A) &= 0.4 \\
P(B) &= 0.3 \\
P(A \wedge B) &= 0.0 \\
P(A \vee B) &= 0.8
\end{aligned}
\tag{14.2}
$$

This kind of question has been the subject of decades of intense debate between those who advocate the use of probabilities as the only legitimate form for degrees of belief, and those who advocate alternative approaches. Here, we give one argument for the axioms of probability, first stated in 1931 by Bruno de Finetti.

The key to de Finetti's argument is the connection between degree of belief and actions. The idea is that if an agent has some degree of belief in a proposition, A, then the agent should be able to state odds at which it is indifferent to a bet for or against A. Think of it as a game between two agents: Agent 1 states "my degree of belief in event A is 0.4." Agent 2 is then free to choose whether to bet for or against A, at stakes that are consistent with the stated degree of belief. That is, Agent 2 could choose to bet that A will occur, betting \$4 against Agent 1's \$6. Or Agent 2 could bet \$6 against \$4 that A will not occur.[6] If an agent's degrees of belief do not accurately reflect the world, then you would expect it would tend to lose money over the long run, depending on the skill of the opposing agent.

But de Finetti proved something much stronger: *if Agent 1 expresses a set of degrees of belief that violate the axioms of probability theory then there is a betting strategy for Agent 2 that* guarantees *that Agent 1 will lose money.* So if you accept the idea that an agent should be willing to "put its money where its probabilities are," then you should accept that it is irrational to have beliefs that violate the axioms of probability.

One might think that this betting game is rather contrived. For example, what if one refuses to bet? Does that scupper the whole argument? The answer is that the betting game is an abstract model for the decision-making situation in which every agent is *unavoidably* involved at every moment. Every action (including inaction) is a kind of bet, and every outcome can be seen as a payoff of the bet. One can no more refuse to bet than one can refuse to allow time to pass.

We will not provide the proof of de Finetti's theorem (see Exercise 14.15), but we will show an example. Suppose that Agent 1 has the set of degrees of belief from Equation (14.2). If Agent 2 chooses to bet \$4 on A, \$3 on B, and \$2 on $\neg(A \lor B)$, then Figure 14.3 shows that Agent 1 always loses money, regardless of the outcomes for A and B.

Agent 1		Agent 2		Outcome for Agent 1			
Proposition	Belief	Bet	Stakes	$A \land B$	$A \land \neg B$	$\neg A \land B$	$\neg A \land \neg B$
A	0.4	A	4 to 6	-6	-6	4	4
B	0.3	B	3 to 7	-7	3	-7	3
$A \lor B$	0.8	$\neg(A \lor B)$	2 to 8	2	2	2	-8
				-11	-1	-1	-1

Figure 14.3   Because Agent 1 has inconsistent beliefs, Agent 2 is able to devise a set of bets that guarantees a loss for Agent 1, no matter what the outcome of A and B.

Other strong philosophical arguments have been put forward for the use of probabilities, most notably those of Cox (1946) and Carnap (1950). The world being the way it is, however, practical demonstrations sometimes speak louder than proofs. The success of reasoning systems based on probability theory has been much more effective in making converts. We now look at how the axioms can be deployed to make inferences.

---

[6]   One might argue that the agent's preferences for different bank balances are such that the possibility of losing \$1 is not counterbalanced by an equal possibility of winning \$1. We can make the bet amounts small enough to avoid this problem, or we can use the more sophisticated treatment due to Savage (1954) to circumvent this issue altogether.

The joint probability distribution

JOINT PROBABILITY
DISTRIBUTION

In this section, we define the **joint probability distribution** (or "joint" for short), which completely specifies an agent's probability assignments to all propositions in the domain (both simple and complex).

ATOMIC EVENT

A probabilistic model of a domain consists of a set of random variables that can take on particular values with certain probabilities. Let the variables be $X_1 \ldots X_n$. An **atomic event** is an assignment of particular values to all the variables—in other words, a complete specification of the state of the domain.

The joint probability distribution $\mathbf{P}(X_1, \ldots, X_n)$ assigns probabilities to all possible atomic events. Recall that $\mathbf{P}(X_i)$ is a one-dimensional vector of probabilities for the possible values of the variable X_i. Then the joint is an n-dimensional table with a value in every cell giving the probability of that specific state occurring. Here is a joint probability distribution for the trivial medical domain consisting of the two Boolean variables *Toothache* and *Cavity*:

	Toothache	¬*Toothache*
Cavity	0.04	0.06
¬*Cavity*	0.01	0.89

Because the atomic events are mutually exclusive, any conjunction of atomic events is necessarily false. Because they are collectively exhaustive, their disjunction is necessarily true. Hence, from the second and third axioms of probability, the entries in the table sum to 1. In the same way, the joint probability distribution can be used to compute any probabilistic statement we care to know about the domain, by expressing the statement as a disjunction of atomic events and adding up their probabilities. Adding across a row or column gives the unconditional probability of a variable, for example, $P(Cavity) = 0.06 + 0.04 = 0.10$. As another example:

$$P(Cavity \vee Toothache) = 0.04 + 0.01 + 0.06 = 0.11$$

Recall that we can make inferences about the probabilities of an unknown proposition A, given evidence B, by calculating $P(A|B)$. A query to a probabilistic reasoning system will therefore ask for the value of a particular conditional probability. Conditional probabilities can be found from the joint using Equation (14.1):

$$P(Cavity|Toothache) = \frac{P(Cavity \wedge Toothache)}{P(Toothache)} = \frac{0.04}{0.04 + 0.01} = 0.80$$

Of course, in a realistic problem, there might be hundreds or thousands of random variables to consider, not just two. In general it is not practical to define all the 2^n entries for the joint probability distribution over n Boolean variables, but it is important to remember that if we could define all the numbers, then we could read off any probability we were interested in.

Modern probabilistic reasoning systems sidestep the joint and work directly with conditional probabilities, which are after all the values that we are interested in. In the next section, we introduce a basic tool for this task.

14.4   BAYES' RULE AND ITS USE

Recall the two forms of the product rule:

$$P(A \wedge B) = P(A|B)P(B)$$
$$P(A \wedge B) = P(B|A)P(A)$$

Equating the two right-hand sides and dividing by $P(A)$, we get

$$P(B|A) = \frac{P(A|B)P(B)}{P(A)} \qquad (14.3)$$

BAYES' RULE   This equation is known as **Bayes' rule** (also Bayes' law or Bayes' theorem).[7]   This simple equation underlies all modern AI systems for probabilistic inference. The more general case of multivalued variables can be written using the **P** notation as follows:

$$\mathbf{P}(Y|X) = \frac{\mathbf{P}(X|Y)\mathbf{P}(Y)}{\mathbf{P}(X)}$$

where again this is to be taken as representing a set of equations relating corresponding elements of the tables. We will also have occasion to use a more general version conditionalized on some background evidence E:

$$\mathbf{P}(Y|X, E) = \frac{\mathbf{P}(X|Y, E)\mathbf{P}(Y|E)}{\mathbf{P}(X|E)} \qquad (14.4)$$

The proof of this form is left as an exercise.

Applying Bayes' rule: The simple case

On the surface, Bayes' rule does not seem very useful. It requires three terms—a conditional probability and two unconditional probabilities—just to compute one conditional probability.

Bayes' rule is useful in practice because there are many cases where we do have good probability estimates for these three numbers and need to compute the fourth. In a task such as medical diagnosis, we often have conditional probabilities on causal relationships and want to derive a diagnosis. A doctor knows that the disease meningitis causes the patient to have a stiff neck, say, 50% of the time. The doctor also knows some unconditional facts: the prior probability of a patient having meningitis is 1/50,000, and the prior probability of any patient having a stiff neck is 1/20. Letting S be the proposition that the patient has a stiff neck and M be the proposition that the patient has meningitis, we have

$$P(S|M) \;=\; 0.5$$
$$P(M) \;=\; 1/50000$$
$$P(S) \;=\; 1/20$$
$$P(M|S) \;=\; \frac{P(S|M)P(M)}{P(S)} = \frac{0.5 \times 1/50000}{1/20} = 0.0002$$

---

[7] According to rule 1 on page 1 of Strunk and White's *The Elements of Style*, it should be Bayes's rather than Bayes'. The latter is, however, more commonly used.

That is, we expect only one in 5000 patients with a stiff neck to have meningitis. Notice that even though a stiff neck is strongly indicated by meningitis (probability 0.5), the probability of meningitis in the patient remains small. This is because the prior on stiff necks is much higher than that for meningitis.

One obvious question to ask is why one might have available the conditional probability in one direction but not the other. In the meningitis case, perhaps the doctor knows that 1 out of 5000 patients with stiff necks has meningitis, and therefore has no need to use Bayes' rule. Unfortunately, *diagnostic knowledge is often more tenuous than causal knowledge*. If there is a sudden epidemic of meningitis, the unconditional probability of meningitis, $P(M)$, will go up. The doctor who derived $P(M|S)$ from statistical observation of patients before the epidemic will have no idea how to update the value, but the doctor who computes $P(M|S)$ from the other three values will see that $P(M|S)$ should go up proportionately to $P(M)$. Most importantly, the causal information $P(S|M)$ is *unaffected* by the epidemic, because it simply reflects the way meningitis works. The use of this kind of direct causal or model-based knowledge provides the crucial robustness needed to make probabilistic systems feasible in the real world.

Normalization

Consider again the equation for calculating the probability of meningitis given a stiff neck:

$$P(M|S) = \frac{P(S|M)P(M)}{P(S)}$$

Suppose we are also concerned with the possibility that the patient is suffering from whiplash W given a stiff neck:

$$P(W|S) = \frac{P(S|W)P(W)}{P(S)}$$

RELATIVE
LIKELIHOOD Comparing these two equations, we see that in order to compute the **relative likelihood** of meningitis and whiplash, given a stiff neck, we need not assess the prior probability $P(S)$ of a stiff neck. To put numbers on the equations, suppose that $P(S|W) = 0.8$ and $P(W) = 1/1000$. Then

$$\frac{P(M|S)}{P(W|S)} = \frac{P(S|M)P(M)}{P(S|W)P(W)} = \frac{0.5 \times 1/50000}{0.8 \times 1/1000} = \frac{1}{80}$$

That is, whiplash is 80 times more likely than meningitis, given a stiff neck.

In some cases, relative likelihood is sufficient for decision making, but when, as in this case, the two possibilities yield radically different utilities for various treatment actions, one needs exact values in order to make rational decisions. It is still possible to avoid direct assessment of the prior probability of the "symptoms," by considering an exhaustive set of cases. For example, we can write equations for M and for $\neg M$:

$$P(M|S) = \frac{P(S|M)P(M)}{P(S)}$$

$$P(\neg M|S) = \frac{P(S|\neg M)P(\neg M)}{P(S)}$$

Adding these two equations, and using the fact that $P(M|S) + P(\neg M|S) = 1$, we obtain

$$P(S) = P(S|M)P(M) + P(S|\neg M)P(\neg M)$$

Substituting into the equation for $P(M|S)$, we have

$$P(M|S) = \frac{P(S|M)P(M)}{P(S|M)P(M) + P(S|\neg M)P(\neg M)}$$

This process is called **normalization**, because it treats $1/P(S)$ as a normalizing constant that allows the conditional terms to sum to 1. Thus, in return for assessing the conditional probability $P(S|\neg M)$, we can avoid assessing $P(S)$ and still obtain exact probabilities from Bayes' rule. In the general, multivalued case, we obtain the following form for Bayes' rule:

$$\mathbf{P}(Y|X) = \alpha \mathbf{P}(X|Y)\mathbf{P}(Y)$$

where α is the normalization constant needed to make the entries in the table $\mathbf{P}(Y|X)$ sum to 1. The normal way to use normalization is to calculate the unnormalized values, and then scale them all so that they add to 1 (Exercise 14.7).

Using Bayes' rule: Combining evidence

Suppose we have two conditional probabilities relating to cavities:

$P(Cavity|Toothache) = 0.8$
$P(Cavity|Catch) = 0.95$

which might perhaps have been computed using Bayes' rule. What can a dentist conclude if her nasty steel probe catches in the aching tooth of a patient? If we knew the whole joint distribution, it would be easy to read off $P(Cavity|Toothache \land Catch)$. Alternatively, we could use Bayes' rule to reformulate the problem:

$$P(Cavity|Toothache \land Catch) = \frac{P(Toothache \land Catch|Cavity)P(Cavity)}{P(Toothache \land Catch)}$$

For this to work, we need to know the conditional probabilities of the pair $Toothache \land Catch$ given *Cavity*. Although it seems feasible to estimate conditional probabilities (given *Cavity*) for n different individual variables, it is a daunting task to come up with numbers for n^2 pairs of variables. To make matters worse, a diagnosis may depend on dozens of variables, not just two. That means we need an exponential number of probability values to complete the diagnosis— we might as well go back to using the joint. This is what first led researchers away from probability theory toward approximate methods for evidence combination that, while giving incorrect answers, require fewer numbers to give any answer at all.

In many domains, however, the application of Bayes' rule can be simplified to a form that requires fewer probabilities in order to produce a result. The first step is to take a slightly different view of the process of incorporating multiple pieces of evidence. The process of
Bayesian updating incorporates evidence one piece at a time, modifying the previously held belief in the unknown variable. Beginning with *Toothache*, we have (writing Bayes' rule in such a way as to reveal the updating process):

$$P(Cavity|Toothache) = P(Cavity)\frac{P(Toothache|Cavity)}{P(Toothache)}$$

When *Catch* is observed, we can apply Bayes' rule with *Toothache* as the constant conditioning context (see Exercise 14.5):

$$P(Cavity|Toothache \wedge Catch) = P(Cavity|Toothache) \frac{P(Catch|Toothache \wedge Cavity)}{P(Catch|Toothache)}$$

$$= P(Cavity) \frac{P(Toothache|Cavity)}{P(Toothache)} \frac{P(Catch|Toothache \wedge Cavity)}{P(Catch|Toothache)}$$

Thus, in Bayesian updating, as each new piece of evidence is observed, the belief in the unknown variable is multiplied by a factor that depends on the new evidence. Exercise 14.8 asks you to prove that this process is order-independent, as we would hope.

So far we are not out of the woods, because the multiplication factor depends not just on the new evidence, but also on the evidence already obtained. Finding a value for the numerator, $P(Catch|Toothache \wedge Cavity)$, is not necessarily any easier than finding a value for $P(Toothache \wedge Catch|Cavity)$. We will need to make a substantive assumption in order to simplify our expressions. The key observation, in the cavity case, is that the cavity is the *direct cause* of both the toothache and the probe catching in the tooth. Once we know the patient has a cavity, we do not expect the probability of the probe catching to depend on the presence of a toothache; similarly, the probe catching is not going to change the probability that the cavity is causing a toothache. Mathematically, these properties are written as

$$P(Catch|Cavity \wedge Toothache) = P(Catch|Cavity)$$
$$P(Toothache|Cavity \wedge Catch) = P(Toothache|Cavity)$$

CONDITIONAL INDEPENDENCE These equations express the **conditional independence** of *Toothache* and *Catch* given *Cavity*. Given conditional independence, we can simplify the equation for updating:

$$P(Cavity|Toothache \wedge Catch) = P(Cavity) \frac{P(Toothache|Cavity)}{P(Toothache)} \frac{P(Catch|Cavity)}{P(Catch|Toothache)}$$

There is still the term $P(Catch|Toothache)$, which might seem to involve considering all pairs (triples, etc.) of symptoms, but in fact this term goes away. Notice that the product of the denominators is $P(Catch|Toothache)P(Toothache)$, or $P(Toothache \wedge Catch)$. We can eliminate this term by normalization, as before, provided we also assess $P(Toothache|\neg Cavity)$ and $P(Catch|\neg Cavity)$. Thus, we are back where we were with a single piece of evidence: we just need to evaluate the prior for the cause, and the conditional probabilities of each of its effects.

We can also use conditional independence in the multivalued case. To say that X and Y are independent given Z, we write

$$\mathbf{P}(X|Y, Z) = \mathbf{P}(X|Z)$$

which represents a set of individual conditional independence statements. The corresponding simplification of Bayes' rule for multiple evidence is

$$\mathbf{P}(Z|X, Y) = \alpha \mathbf{P}(Z)\mathbf{P}(X|Z)\mathbf{P}(Y|Z)$$

where α is a normalization constant such that the entries in $\mathbf{P}(Z|X, Y)$ sum to 1.

It is important to remember that this simplified form of Bayesian updating only works when the conditional independence relationships hold. Conditional independence information therefore is crucial to making probabilistic systems work effectively. In Chapter 15, we show how it can be represented and manipulated in a systematic fashion.

14.5   WHERE DO PROBABILITIES COME FROM?

FREQUENTIST

OBJECTIVIST

SUBJECTIVIST

There has been endless debate over the source and status of probability numbers. The **frequentist** position is that the numbers can come only from *experiments*: if we test 100 people and find that 10 of them have a cavity, then we can say the probability of a cavity is approximately 0.1. A great deal of work has gone into making such statistical assessments reliable. The **objectivist** view is that probabilities are real aspects of the universe—propensities of objects to behave in certain ways—rather than being just descriptions of an observer's degree of belief. In this view, frequentist measurements are attempts to observe the real probability value. The **subjectivist** view describes probabilities as a way of characterizing an agent's beliefs, rather than having any external physical significance. This allows the doctor or analyst to make these numbers up, to say, "In my opinion, I expect the probability of a cavity to be about 0.1." Several more reliable techniques, such as the betting systems described earlier, have also been developed for eliciting probability assessments from humans.

In the end, even a strict frequentist position involves subjective analysis, so the difference probably has little practical importance. Consider the probability that the sun will still exist tomorrow (a question first raised by Hume's *Inquiry*). There are several ways to compute this:

- The probability is undefined, because there has never been an experiment that tested the existence of the sun *tomorrow*.
- The probability is 1, because in all the experiments that have been done (on past days) the sun has existed.
- The probability is $1 - \epsilon$, where ϵ is the proportion of stars in the universe that go supernova and explode per day.
- The probability is $(d + 1)/(d + 2)$, where d is the number of days that the sun has existed so far. (This formula is due to Laplace.)
- The probability can be derived from the type, age, size, and temperature of the sun, even though we have never observed another star with those exact properties.

REFERENCE CLASS

The first three of these methods are frequentist, whereas the last two are subjective. But even if you prefer not to allow subjective methods, the choice of which of the first three experiments to use is a subjective choice known as the **reference class** problem. It is the same problem faced by the doctor who wants to know the chances that a patient has a particular disease. The doctor wants to consider other patients who are similar in important ways—age, symptoms, perhaps sex—and see what proportion of them had the disease. But if the doctor considered everything that is known about the patient—weight to the nearest gram, hair color, maternal grandmother's maiden name—the result would be that there are no other patients who are exactly the same, and thus no reference class from which to collect experimental data. This has been a vexing problem in the philosophy of science. Carnap (along with other philosophers) tried in vain to find a way of reducing theories to objective truth—to show how a series of experiments necessarily leads to one theory and not another. The approach we will take in the next chapter is to minimize the number of probabilities that need to be assessed, and to maximize the number of cases available for each assessment, by taking advantage of independence relationships in the domain.

14.6 SUMMARY

This chapter shows that probability is the right way to reason about uncertainty.

- Uncertainty arises because of both laziness and ignorance. It is inescapable in complex, dynamic, or inaccessible worlds.

- Uncertainty means that many of the simplifications that are possible with deductive inference are no longer valid.

- Probabilities express the agent's inability to reach a definite decision regarding the truth of a sentence, and summarize the agent's beliefs.

- Basic probability statements include **prior probabilities** and **conditional probabilities** over simple and complex propositions.

- The axioms of probability specify constraints on reasonable assignments of probabilities to propositions. An agent that violates the axioms will behave irrationally in some circumstances.

- The **joint probability distribution** specifies the probability of each complete assignment of values to random variables. It is usually far too large to create or use.

- **Bayes' rule** allows unknown probabilities to be computed from known, stable ones.

- In the general case, combining many pieces of evidence may require assessing a large number of conditional probabilities.

- **Conditional independence** brought about by direct causal relationships in the domain allows **Bayesian updating** to work effectively even with multiple pieces of evidence.

BIBLIOGRAPHICAL AND HISTORICAL NOTES

Although games of chance date back at least to around 300 B.C., the mathematical analysis of odds and probability appears to be much later. Some work done by Mahaviracarya in India is dated to roughly the ninth century A.D. In Europe, the first attempts date only to the Italian Renaissance, beginning around 1500 A.D. The first significant systematic analyses were produced by Girolamo Cardano around 1565, but they remained unpublished until 1663. By that time, the discovery by Blaise Pascal (in correspondence with Pierre Fermat in 1654) of a systematic way of calculating probabilities had for the first time established probability as a widely and fruitfully studied mathematical discipline. The first published textbook on probability was *De Ratiociniis in Ludo Aleae* (Huygens, 1657). Pascal also introduced conditional probability, which is covered in Huygens's textbook. The Rev. Thomas Bayes (1702–1761) introduced the rule for reasoning about conditional probabilities that was named after him. It was published posthumously (Bayes, 1763). Kolmogorov (1950, first published in German in 1933) presented probability theory in a rigorously axiomatic framework for the first time. Rényi (1970) later gave an axiomatic presentation that took conditional probability, rather than absolute probability, as primitive.

Pascal used probability in ways that required both the objective interpretation, as a property of the world based on symmetry or relative frequency, and the subjective interpretation as degree of belief: the former in his analyses of probabilities in games of chance, the latter in the famous "Pascal's wager" argument about the possible existence of God. However, Pascal did not clearly realize the distinction between these two interpretations. The distinction was first drawn clearly by James Bernoulli (1654–1705).

Leibniz introduced the "classical" notion of probability as a proportion of enumerated, equally probable cases, which was also used by Bernoulli, although it was brought to prominence by Laplace (1749–1827). This notion is ambiguous between the frequency interpretation and the subjective interpretation. The cases can be thought to be equally probable either because of a natural, physical symmetry between them, or simply because we do not have any knowledge that would lead us to consider one more probable than another. The use of this latter, subjective consideration to justify assigning equal probabilities is known as the *principle of indifference* (Keynes, 1921).

The debate between objective and subjective interpretations of probability became sharper in the twentieth century. Kolmogorov (1963), R. A. Fisher (1922), and Richard von Mises(1928) were advocates of the relative frequency interpretation. Karl Popper's (1959, first published in German in 1934) "propensity" interpretation traces relative frequencies to an underlying physical symmetry. Frank Ramsey (1931), Bruno de Finetti (1937), R. T. Cox (1946), Leonard Savage (1954), and Richard Jeffrey (1983) interpreted probabilities as the degrees of belief of specific individuals. Their analyses of degree of belief were closely tied to utilities and to behavior, specifically to the willingness to place bets. Rudolf Carnap, following Leibniz and Laplace, offered a different kind of subjective interpretation of probability: not as any actual individual's degree of belief, but as the degree of belief that an idealized individual *should* have in a particular proposition *p* given a particular body of evidence *E*. Carnap attempted to go further than Leibniz

CONFIRMATION

or Laplace by making this notion of degree of **confirmation** mathematically precise, as a logical relation between *p* and *E*. The study of this relation was intended to constitute a mathematical

INDUCTIVE LOGIC

discipline called **inductive logic**, analogous to ordinary deductive logic (Carnap, 1948; Carnap, 1950). Carnap was not able to extend his inductive logic much beyond the propositional case, and Putnam (1963) showed that some fundamental difficulties would prevent a strict extension to languages capable of expressing arithmetic.

The question of reference classes is closely tied to the attempt to find an inductive logic. The approach of choosing the "most specific" reference class of sufficient size was formally proposed by Reichenbach (1949). Various attempts have been made to formulate more sophisticated policies in order to avoid some obvious fallacies that arise with Reichenbach's rule, notably by Henry Kyburg (1977; 1983), but such approaches remain somewhat *ad hoc*. More recent work by Bacchus, Grove, Halpern, and Koller (1992) extends Carnap's methods to first-order theories on finite domains, thereby avoiding many of the difficulties associated with reference classes.

Bayesian probabilistic reasoning has been used in AI since the 1960s, especially in medical diagnosis. It was used not only to make a diagnosis from available evidence, but also to select further questions and tests when available evidence was inconclusive (Gorry, 1968; Gorry *et al.*, 1973), using the theory of information value (Section 16.6). One system outperformed human experts in the diagnosis of acute abdominal illnesses (de Dombal *et al.*, 1974). These early Bayesian systems suffered from a number of problems, however. Because they lacked any theoretical model of the conditions they were diagnosing, they were vulnerable to unrepresentative data occurring in situations for which only a small sample was available (de Dombal *et al.*, 1981). Even more fundamentally, because they lacked a concise formalism (such as the one to be described in Chapter 15) for representing and using conditional independence information, they depended on the acquisition, storage, and processing of enormous amounts of probabilistic data. De Dombal's system, for example, was built by gathering and analyzing enough clinical cases to provide meaningful data for every entry in a large joint probability table. Because of these difficulties, probabilistic methods for coping with uncertainty fell out of favor in AI from the 1970s to the mid-1980s. In Chapter 15, we will examine the alternative approaches that were taken and the reason for the resurgence of probabilistic methods in the late 1980s.

There are many good introductory textbooks on probability theory, including those by Chung (1979) and Ross (1988). Morris DeGroot (1989) offers a combined introduction to probability and statistics from a Bayesian standpoint, as well as a more advanced text (1970). Richard Hamming's (1991) textbook gives a mathematically sophisticated introduction to probability theory from the standpoint of a propensity interpretation based on physical symmetry. Hacking (1975) and Hald (1990) cover the early history of the concept of probability.

EXERCISES

14.1 Show from first principles that

$$P(A|B \wedge A) = 1$$

14.2 Consider the domain of dealing five-card poker hands from a standard deck of 52 cards, under the assumption that the dealer is fair.

   a. How many atomic events are there in the joint probability distribution (i.e., how many five-card hands are there)?
   b. What is the probability of each atomic event?
   c. What is the probability of being dealt a royal straight flush (the ace, king, queen, jack and ten of the same suit)?
   d. What is the probability of four of a kind?

14.3 After your yearly checkup, the doctor has bad news and good news. The bad news is that you tested positive for a serious disease, and that the test is 99% accurate (i.e., the probability of testing positive given that you have the disease is 0.99, as is the probability of testing negative given that you don't have the disease). The good news is that this is a rare disease, striking only one in 10,000 people. Why is it good news that the disease is rare? What are the chances that you actually have the disease?

14.4 Would it be rational for an agent to hold the three beliefs $P(A) = 0.4$, $P(B) = 0.3$, and $P(A \vee B) = 0.5$? If so, what range of probabilities would be rational for the agent to hold for $A \wedge B$? Make up a table like the one in Figure 14.3 and show how it supports your argument about rationality. Then draw another version of the table where $P(A \lor B) = 0.7$. Explain why it is rational to have this probability, even though the table shows one case that is a loss and three that just break even. (*Hint:* what is Agent 1 committed to about the probability of each of the four cases, especially the case that is a loss?)

14.5   It is quite often useful to consider the effect of some specific propositions in the context of some general background evidence that remains fixed, rather than in the complete absence of information. The following questions ask you to prove more general versions of the product rule and Bayes' rule, with respect to some background evidence E:

    a. Prove the conditionalized version of the general product rule:

$$\mathbf{P}(A, B|E) = \mathbf{P}(A|B, E)\mathbf{P}(B|E)$$

    b. Prove the conditionalized version of Bayes' rule:

$$\mathbf{P}(A|B, C) = \frac{\mathbf{P}(B|A, C)\mathbf{P}(A|C)}{\mathbf{P}(B|C)}$$

14.6   Show that the statement

$$\mathbf{P}(A, B|C) = \mathbf{P}(A|C)\mathbf{P}(B|C)$$

is equivalent to the statement

$$\mathbf{P}(A|B, C) = \mathbf{P}(A|C)$$

and also to

$$\mathbf{P}(B|A, C) = \mathbf{P}(B|C)$$

14.7   In this exercise, you will complete the normalization calculation for the meningitis example. First, make up a suitable value for $P(S|\neg M)$, and use it to calculate unnormalized values for $P(M|S)$ and $P(\neg M|S)$ (i.e., ignoring the $P(S)$ term in the Bayes' rule expression). Now normalize these values so that they add to 1.

14.8   Show that the degree of belief after applying the Bayesian updating process is independent of the order in which the pieces of evidence arrive. That is, show that $P(A|B, C) = P(A|C, B)$ using the Bayesian updating rule.

14.9   This exercise investigates the way in which conditional independence relationships affect the amount of information needed for probabilistic calculations.

    a. Suppose we wish to calculate $P(H|E_1, E_2)$, and we have no conditional independence information. Which of the following sets of numbers are sufficient for the calculation?

        (i) $\mathbf{P}(E_1, E_2)$, $\mathbf{P}(H)$, $\mathbf{P}(E_1|H)$, $\mathbf{P}(E_2|H)$
        (ii) $\mathbf{P}(E_1, E_2)$, $\mathbf{P}(H)$, $\mathbf{P}(E_1, E_2|H)$
        (iii) $\mathbf{P}(H)$, $\mathbf{P}(E_1|H)$, $\mathbf{P}(E_2|H)$

    b. Suppose we know that $\mathbf{P}(E_1|H, E_2) = \mathbf{P}(E_1|H)$ for all values of H, E_1, E_2. Now which of the above three sets are sufficient?

14.10   Express the statement that X and Y are conditionally independent given Z as a constraint on the joint distribution entries for $\mathbf{P}(X, Y, Z)$.

14.11   (Adapted from Pearl (1988).) You are a witness of a night-time hit-and-run accident involving a taxi in Athens. All taxis in Athens are blue or green. You swear, under oath, that the taxi was blue. Extensive testing shows that under the dim lighting conditions, discrimination between blue and green is 75% reliable. Is it possible to calculate the most likely color for the taxi? (Hint: distinguish carefully between the proposition that the taxi *is* blue and the proposition that it *appears* blue.)

What now, given that 9 out of 10 Athenian taxis are green?

14.12   (Adapted from Pearl (1988).) Three prisoners, A, B, and C, are locked in their cells. It is common knowledge that one of them will be executed the next day and the others pardoned. Only the governor knows which one will be executed. Prisoner A asks the guard a favor: "Please ask the governor who will be executed, and then take a message to one of my friends B and C to let him know that he will be pardoned in the morning." The guard agrees, and comes back later and tells A that he gave the pardon message to B.

What are A's chances of being executed, given this information? (Answer this *mathematically*, not by energetic waving of hands.)

14.13   This exercise concerns Bayesian updating in the meningitis example. Starting with a patient about whom we know nothing, show how the probability of having meningitis, $P(M)$, is updated after we find the patient has a stiff neck. Next, show how $P(M)$ is updated again when we find the patient has a fever. (Say what probabilities you need to compute this, and make up values for them.)

14.14   In previous chapters, we found the technique of **reification** useful in creating representations in first-order logic. For example, we handled change by reifying situations, and belief by reifying sentences. Suppose we try to do this for uncertain reasoning by reifying probabilities, thus embedding probability entirely *within* first-order logic. Which of the following are true?

   a. This would not work.

   b. This would work fine; in fact, it is just another way of describing probability theory.

   c. This would work fine; it would be an alternative to probability theory.

14.15   Prove that the three axioms of probability are necessary for rational behavior in betting situations, as shown by de Finetti.

15 PROBABILISTIC REASONING SYSTEMS

In which we explain how to build reasoning systems that use network models to reason with uncertainty according to the laws of probability theory.

Chapter 14 gave the syntax and semantics of probability theory. This chapter introduces an inference mechanism, thus giving us everything we need to build an uncertain-reasoning system.

The main advantage of probabilistic reasoning over logical reasoning is in allowing the agent to reach rational decisions even when there is not enough information to prove that any given action will work. We begin by showing how to capture uncertain knowledge in a natural and efficient way. We then show how probabilistic inference, although exponentially hard in the worst case, can be done efficiently in many practical situations. We conclude the chapter with a discussion of knowledge engineering techniques for building probabilistic reasoning systems, a case study of one successful system, and a survey of alternate approaches.

15.1 REPRESENTING KNOWLEDGE IN AN UNCERTAIN DOMAIN

In Chapter 14, we saw that the joint probability distribution can answer any question about the domain, but can become intractably large as the number of variables grows. Furthermore, specifying probabilities for atomic events is rather unnatural and may be very difficult unless a large amount of data is available from which to gather statistical estimates.

We also saw that, in the context of using Bayes' rule, conditional independence relationships among variables can simplify the computation of query results and greatly reduce the number of conditional probabilities that need to be specified. We use a data structure called a **belief network**[1] to represent the dependence between variables and to give a concise specification of the joint probability distribution. A belief network is a graph in which the following holds:

BELIEF NETWORK

---

[1] This is the most common name, but there are many others, including **Bayesian network**, **probabilistic network**, **causal network**, and **knowledge map**. An extension of belief networks called a **decision network** or **influence diagram** will be covered in Chapter 16.

1. A set of random variables makes up the nodes of the network.
2. A set of directed links or arrows connects pairs of nodes. The intuitive meaning of an arrow from node X to node Y is that X has a *direct influence* on Y.
3. Each node has a conditional probability table that quantifies the effects that the parents have on the node. The parents of a node are all those nodes that have arrows pointing to it.
4. The graph has no directed cycles (hence is a directed, acyclic graph, or DAG).

It is usually easy for a domain expert to decide what direct conditional dependence relationships hold in the domain—much easier, in fact, than actually specifying the probabilities themselves. Once the topology of the belief network is specified, we need only specify conditional probabilities for the nodes that participate in direct dependencies, and use those to compute any other probability values.

Consider the following situation. You have a new burglar alarm installed at home. It is fairly reliable at detecting a burglary, but also responds on occasion to minor earthquakes. (This example is due to Judea Pearl, a resident of Los Angeles; hence the acute interest in earthquakes.) You also have two neighbors, John and Mary, who have promised to call you at work when they hear the alarm. John always calls when he hears the alarm, but sometimes confuses the telephone ringing with the alarm and calls then, too. Mary, on the other hand, likes rather loud music and sometimes misses the alarm altogether. Given the evidence of who has or has not called, we would like to estimate the probability of a burglary. This simple domain is described by the belief network in Figure 15.1.

The topology of the network can be thought of as an abstract knowledge base that holds in a wide variety of different settings, because it represents the general structure of the causal processes in the domain rather than any details of the population of individuals. In the case of the burglary network, the topology shows that burglary and earthquakes directly affect the probability of the alarm going off, but whether or not John and Mary call depends only on the alarm—the network thus represents our assumption that they do not perceive any burglaries directly, and they do not feel the minor earthquakes.

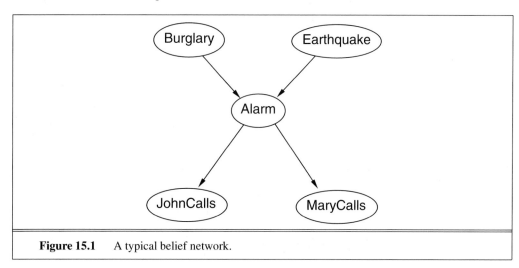

Figure 15.1   A typical belief network.

Notice that the network does not have nodes corresponding to Mary currently listening to loud music, or to the telephone ringing and confusing John. These factors are summarized in the uncertainty associated with the links from *Alarm* to *JohnCalls* and *MaryCalls*. This shows both laziness and ignorance in operation: it would be a lot of work to determine any reason why those factors would be more or less likely in any particular case, and we have no reasonable way to obtain the relevant information anyway. The probabilities actually summarize a *potentially infinite* set of possible circumstances in which the alarm might fail to go off (high humidity, power failure, dead battery, cut wires, dead mouse stuck inside bell, . . .) or John or Mary might fail to call and report it (out to lunch, on vacation, temporarily deaf, passing helicopter, . . .). In this way, a small agent can cope with a very large world, at least approximately. The degree of approximation can be improved if we introduce additional relevant information.

CONDITIONAL
PROBABILITY TABLE

CONDITIONING CASE

Once we have specified the topology, we need to specify the **conditional probability table** or CPT for each node. Each row in the table contains the conditional probability of each node value for a **conditioning case**. A conditioning case is just a possible combination of values for the parent nodes (a miniature atomic event, if you like). For example, the conditional probability table for the random variable *Alarm* might look like this:

Burglary	Earthquake	$\mathbf{P}(Alarm|Burglary, Earthquake)$	
		True	False
True	*True*	0.950	0.050
True	*False*	0.950	0.050
False	*True*	0.290	0.710
False	*False*	0.001	0.999

Each row in a conditional probability table must sum to 1, because the entries represent an exhaustive set of cases for the variable. Hence only one of the two numbers in each row shown above is independently specifiable. In general, a table for a Boolean variable with n Boolean parents contains 2^n independently specifiable probabilities. A node with no parents has only one row, representing the prior probabilities of each possible value of the variable.

The complete network for the burglary example is shown in Figure 15.2, where we show just the conditional probability for the *True* case of each variable.

15.2   THE SEMANTICS OF BELIEF NETWORKS

The previous section described what a network is, but not what it means. There are two ways in which one can understand the semantics of belief networks. The first is to see the network as a representation of the joint probability distribution. The second is to view it as an encoding of a collection of conditional independence statements. The two views are equivalent, but the first turns out to be helpful in understanding how to *construct* networks, whereas the second is helpful in designing inference procedures.

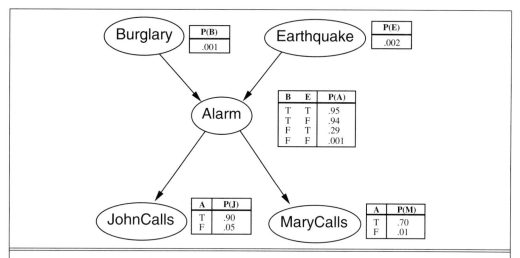

Figure 15.2   A typical belief network with conditional probabilities. The letters B, E, A, J, and M stand for *Burglary*, *Earthquake*, *Alarm*, *JohnCalls*, and *MaryCalls*, respectively. All variables (nodes) are Boolean, so the probability of, say, $\neg P(A)$ in any row of its table is $1 - P(A)$.

Representing the joint probability distribution

A belief network provides a complete description of the domain. Every entry in the joint probability distribution can be calculated from the information in the network. A generic entry in the joint is the probability of a conjunction of particular assignments to each variable, such as $P(X_1 = x_1 \wedge \ldots \wedge X_n = x_n)$. We use the notation $P(x_1, \ldots, x_n)$ as an abbreviation for this. The value of this entry is given by the following formula:

$$P(x_1, \ldots, x_n) = \prod_{i=1}^{n} P(x_i | Parents(X_i)) \tag{15.1}$$

Thus, each entry in the joint is represented by the product of the appropriate elements of the conditional probability tables (CPTs) in the belief network. The CPTs therefore provide a decomposed representation of the joint.

To illustrate this, we can calculate the probability of the event that the alarm has sounded but neither a burglary nor an earthquake has occurred, and both John and Mary call. We use single-letter names for the variables:

$$P(J \wedge M \wedge A \wedge \neg B \wedge \neg E)$$
$$= P(J|A)P(M|A)P(A|\neg B \wedge \neg E)P(\neg B)P(\neg E)$$
$$= 0.90 \times 0.70 \times 0.001 \times 0.999 \times 0.998 = 0.00062$$

Section 14.3 explained that the joint distribution can be used to answer any query about the domain. If a belief network is a representation of the joint, then it too can be used to answer any query. Trivially, this can be done by first computing all the joint entries. We will see below that there are much better methods.

A method for constructing belief networks

Equation (15.1) defines what a given belief network means. It does not, however, explain how to *construct* a belief network such that the resulting joint distribution is a good representation of a given domain. We will now show that Equation (15.1) implies certain conditional independence relationships that can be used to guide the knowledge engineer in constructing the topology of the network. First, we rewrite the joint in terms of a conditional probability using the definition of conditional probability:

$$P(x_1, \ldots, x_n) = P(x_n|x_{n-1}, \ldots, x_1)P(x_{n-1}, \ldots, x_1)$$

Then we repeat this process, reducing each conjunctive probability to a conditional probability and a smaller conjunction. We end up with one big product:

$$P(x_1, \ldots, x_n) = P(x_n|x_{n-1}, \ldots, x_1)P(x_{n-1}|x_{n-2}, \ldots, x_1) \cdots P(x_2|x_1)P(x_1)$$

$$= \prod_{i=1}^{n} P(x_i|x_{i-1}, \ldots, x_1)$$

Comparing this with Equation (15.1), we see that the specification of the joint is equivalent to the general assertion that

$$\mathbf{P}(X_i|X_{i-1}, \ldots, X_1) = P(X_i|Parents(X_i)) \tag{15.2}$$

provided that $Parents(X_i) \subseteq \{x_{i-1}, \ldots, x_1\}$. This last condition is easily satisfied by labelling the nodes in any order that is consistent with the partial order implicit in the graph structure.

What the preceding equation says is that the belief network is a correct representation of the domain only if each node is conditionally independent of its predecessors in the node ordering, given its parents. Hence, in order to construct a belief network with the correct structure for the domain, we need to choose parents for each node such that this property holds. Intuitively, the parents of node X_i should contain all those nodes in $X_1, \ldots, X_{i-1}$ that directly influence X_i. For example, suppose we have completed the network in Figure 15.1 except for the choice of parents for *MaryCalls*. *MaryCalls* is certainly influenced by whether or not there is a *Burglary* or an *Earthquake*, but it is not *directly* influenced. Intuitively, our knowledge of the domain tells us that these events only influence Mary's calling behavior through their effect on the alarm. Also, given the state of the alarm, whether or not John calls has no influence on Mary's calling. Formally speaking, we believe that the following conditional independence statement holds:

$$\mathbf{P}(MaryCalls|JohnCalls, Alarm, Earthquake, Burglary) = \mathbf{P}(MaryCalls|Alarm)$$

The general procedure for incremental network construction is as follows:

1. Choose the set of relevant variables X_i that describe the domain.
2. Choose an ordering for the variables.
3. While there are variables left:
    (a) Pick a variable X_i and add a node to the network for it.
    (b) Set *Parents(X_i)* to some minimal set of nodes already in the net such that the conditional independence property (15.2) is satisfied.
    (c) Define the conditional probability table for X_i.

Because each node is only connected to earlier nodes, this construction method guarantees that the network is acyclic. Another important property of belief networks is that they contain no redundant probability values, except perhaps for one entry in each row of each conditional probability table. This means that *it is impossible for the knowledge engineer or domain expert to create a belief network that violates the axioms of probability.* We will see examples of the application of the construction method in the next section.

Compactness and node ordering

As well as being a complete and nonredundant representation of the domain, a belief network can often be far more *compact* than the full joint. This property is what makes it feasible to handle a large number of pieces of evidence without the exponential growth in conditional probability values that we saw in the discussion of Bayesian updating in Section 14.4.

The compactness of belief networks is an example of a very general property of **locally structured** (also called **sparse**) systems. In a locally structured system, each subcomponent interacts directly with only a bounded number of other components, regardless of the total number of components. Local structure is usually associated with linear rather than exponential growth in complexity. In the case of belief networks, it is reasonable to suppose that in most domains each random variable is directly influenced by at most k others, for some constant k. If we assume Boolean variables for simplicity, then the amount of information needed to specify the conditional probability table for a node will be at most 2^k numbers, so the complete network can be specified by $n2^k$ numbers. In contrast, the joint contains 2^n numbers. To make this concrete, suppose we have 20 nodes ($n = 20$) and each has at most 5 parents ($k = 5$). Then the belief network requires 640 numbers, but the full joint requires over a million.

There are domains in which each variable can be influenced directly by all the others, so that the network is fully connected. Then specifying the conditional probability tables requires the same amount of information as specifying the joint. The reduction in information that occurs in practice comes about because real domains have a lot of structure, which networks are very good at capturing. In some domains, there will be slight dependencies that should strictly be included by adding a new link. But if these dependencies are very tenuous, then it may not be worth the additional complexity in the network for the small gain in accuracy. For example, one might object to our burglary network on the grounds that if there is an earthquake, then John and Mary would not call even if they heard the alarm, because they assume the earthquake is the cause. Whether to add the link from *Earthquake* to *JohnCalls* and *MaryCalls* (and thus enlarge the tables) depends on the importance of getting more accurate probabilities compared to the cost of specifying the extra information.

Even in a locally structured domain, constructing a locally structured belief network is not a trivial problem. We require not only that each variable is directly influenced by only a few others, but also that the network topology actually reflects those direct influences with the appropriate set of parents. Because of the way that the construction procedure works, the "direct influencers" will have to be added to the network first if they are to become parents of the node they influence. Therefore, *the correct order to add nodes is to add the "root causes" first, then the variables they influence,* and so on until we reach the "leaves," which have no direct causal influence on the other variables.

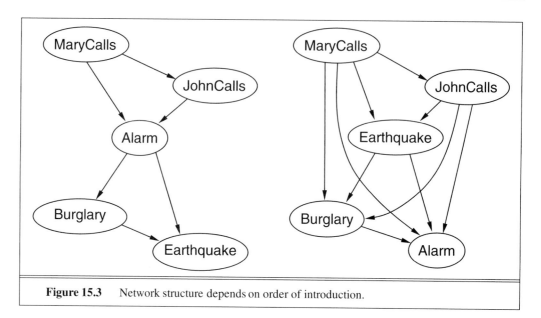

Figure 15.3   Network structure depends on order of introduction.

What happens if we happen to choose the wrong order? Let us consider the burglary example again. Suppose we decide to add the nodes in the order *MaryCalls, JohnCalls, Alarm, Burglary, Earthquake*. We get a somewhat more complicated network (Figure 15.3, left). The process goes as follows:

- Adding *MaryCalls*: no parents.
- Adding *JohnCalls*: if Mary calls, that probably means the alarm has gone off, which of course would make it more likely that John calls. Therefore, there is a dependence:

  $$P(JohnCalls|MaryCalls) \neq P(JohnCalls)$$

  Hence, *JohnCalls* needs *MaryCalls* as a parent.

- Adding *Alarm*: clearly, if both call, it is more likely that the alarm has gone off than if just one or neither call, so we need both *MaryCalls* and *JohnCalls* as parents.
- Adding *Burglary*: if we know the alarm state, then the call (or lack of it) from John or Mary might tell us about whether our telephone is ringing or whether Mary's music is on loud, but it does not give us further information about a burglary. That is,

  $$P(Burglary|Alarm, JohnCalls, MaryCalls) = P(Burglary|Alarm)$$

  Hence we need just *Alarm* as parent.

- Adding *Earthquake*: if the alarm is on, it is more likely that there has been an earthquake (because the alarm is an earthquake detector of sorts). But if we know there has been a burglary, then that accounts for the alarm and the probability of an earthquake would be only slightly above normal. Hence we need both *Alarm* and *Burglary* as parents:

  $$P(Earthquake|Burglary, Alarm, JohnCalls, MaryCalls) = P(Earthquake|Burglary, Alarm)$$

The resulting network has two more links than the original network in Figure 15.1, and requires three more probabilities to be specified. But the worst part is that some of the links represent tenuous relationships that require difficult and unnatural probability judgments, such as assessing the probability of *Earthquake* given *Burglary* and *Alarm*. This phenomenon is quite general. If we try to build a diagnostic model with links from symptoms to causes (as from *MaryCalls* to *Alarm*, or *Alarm* to *Burglary*), we end up having to specify additional dependencies between otherwise independent causes, and often between separately occurring symptoms as well. *If we stick to a causal model, we end up having to specify fewer numbers, and the numbers will often be easier to come up with.* In the domain of medicine, for example, it has been shown by Tversky and Kahneman (1982) that expert physicians prefer to give probability judgments for causal rules rather than for diagnostic ones.

The right-hand side of Figure 15.3 shows a really bad ordering of nodes: *MaryCalls*, *JohnCalls*, *Earthquake*, *Burglary*, *Alarm*. This network requires 31 distinct probabilities to be specified—exactly the same as the full joint distribution. It is important to realize, however, that any of the three networks can represent *exactly the same joint distribution*. The last two versions simply fail to represent all the conditional independence relationships, and end up specifying a lot of unnecessary numbers instead.

Representation of conditional probability tables

Even with a fairly small number of parents, a node's conditional probability table still requires a lot of numbers. Filling in the table would appear to require a good deal of time and also a lot of experience with all the possible conditioning cases. In fact, this is a worst-case scenario, where the relationship between the parents and the child is completely arbitrary. Usually, such relationships fall into one of several categories that have **canonical distributions**—that is, they fit some standard pattern. In such cases, the complete table can be specified by naming the pattern and perhaps supplying a few parameters.

CANONICAL
DISTRIBUTIONS

The simplest example is provided by **deterministic nodes**. A deterministic node has its value specified exactly by the values of its parents, with no uncertainty. The relationship can be a logical one—for example, the relationship between parent nodes *Canadian*, *US*, *Mexican* and the child node *NorthAmerican* is simply that the child is the disjunction of the parents. The relationship can also be numerical—for example, if the parent nodes are the prices of a particular model of car at several dealers, and the child node is the price that a bargain hunter ends up paying, then the child node is the minimum of the parent values; or if the parent nodes are the inflows (rivers, runoff, precipitation) into a lake and the outflows (rivers, evaporation, seepage) from the lake and the child is the change in lake level, then the child is the difference between the inflow parents and the outflow parents.

DETERMINISTIC
NODES

Uncertain relationships can often be characterized by so-called "noisy" logical relationships. The standard example is the so-called **noisy-OR** relation, which is a generalization of the logical OR. In propositional logic, we might say *Fever* is true if and only if *Cold*, *Flu*, or *Malaria* is true. The noisy-OR model adds some uncertainty to this strict logical approach. The model makes three assumptions. First, it assumes that each cause has an independent chance of causing the effect. Second, it assumes that all the possible causes are listed. (This is not as strict as it seems, because we can always add a so-called **leak node** that covers "miscellaneous causes.") Third, it assumes that whatever inhibits, say, *Cold* from causing a fever is independent of whatever inhibits *Flu* from causing a fever. These inhibitors are not represented as nodes but

NOISY-OR

LEAK NODE

rather are summarized as "noise parameters." If $P(Fever|Cold) = 0.4$, $P(Fever|Flu) = 0.8$, and $P(Fever|Malaria) = 0.9$, then the noise parameters are 0.6, 0.2, and 0.1, respectively. If no parent node is true, then the output node is false with 100% certainty. If exactly one parent is true, then the output is false with probability equal to the noise parameter for that node. In general, the probability that the output node is *False* is just the product of the noise parameters for all the input nodes that are true. For this example, we have the following:

Cold	Flu	Malaria	P(Fever)	P(¬Fever)
F	F	F	0.0	1.0
F	F	T	0.9	0.1
F	T	F	0.8	0.2
F	T	T	0.98	$0.02 = 0.2 \times 0.1$
T	F	F	0.4	0.6
T	F	T	0.94	$0.06 = 0.6 \times 0.1$
T	T	F	0.88	$0.12 = 0.6 \times 0.2$
T	T	T	0.988	$0.012 = 0.6 \times 0.2 \times 0.1$

In general, noisy logical relationships in which a variable depends on k parents can be described using $O(k)$ parameters instead of $O(2^k)$ for the full conditional probability table. This makes assessment and learning much easier. For example, the CPSC network (Pradhan *et al.*, 1994) uses noisy-OR and noisy-MAX, and requires "only" 8,254 values instead of 133,931,430 for a network with full CPTs.

Conditional independence relations in belief networks

The preceding analysis shows that a belief network expresses the conditional independence of a node and its predecessors, given its parents, and uses this independence to design a construction method for networks. If we want to design inference algorithms, however, we will need to know whether more general conditional independences hold. If we are given a network, is it possible to "read off" whether a set of nodes X is independent of another set Y, given a set of evidence nodes E? The answer is yes, and the method is provided by the notion of **direction-dependent**

D-SEPARATION   **separation** or **d-separation**.

First, we will say what d-separation is good for. *If every undirected path[2] from a node in X to a node in Y is d-separated by E, then X and Y are conditionally independent given E.* The definition of d-separation is somewhat complicated. We will need to appeal to it several times in constructing our inference algorithms. Once this is done, however, the process of constructing and using belief networks does not involve any uses of d-separation.

A set of nodes E d-separates two sets of nodes X and Y if every undirected path from a
BLOCKED   node in X to a node in Y is **blocked** given E. A path is blocked given a set of nodes E if there is a node Z on the path for which one of three conditions holds:

1. Z is in E and Z has one arrow on the path leading in and one arrow out.

---

[2] An undirected path is a path through the network that ignores the direction of the arrows.

2. Z is in E and Z has both path arrows leading out.

3. Neither Z nor any descendant of Z is in E, and both path arrows lead in to Z.

Figure 15.4 shows these three cases. The proof that d-separated nodes are conditionally independent is also complicated. We will use Figure 15.5 to give examples of the three cases:

1. Whether there is *Gas* in the car and whether the car *Radio* plays are independent given evidence about whether the *SparkPlugs* fire.

2. *Gas* and *Radio* are independent if it is known if the *Battery* works.

3. *Gas* and *Radio* are independent given no evidence at all. But they are dependent given evidence about whether the car *Starts*. For example, if the car does not start, then the radio playing is increased evidence that we are out of gas. *Gas* and *Radio* are also dependent given evidence about whether the car *Moves*, because that is enabled by the car starting.

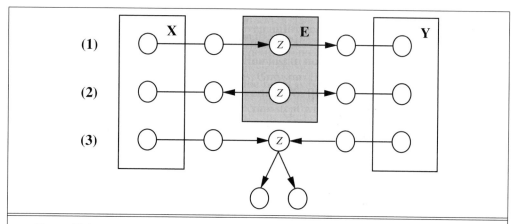

Figure 15.4   Three ways in which a path from X to Y can be blocked, given the evidence E. If every path from X to Y is blocked, then we say that E d-separates X and Y.

15.3   INFERENCE IN BELIEF NETWORKS

The basic task for any probabilistic inference system is to compute the posterior probability distribution for a set of **query variables**, given exact values for some **evidence variables**. That is, the system computes **P**(*Query*|*Evidence*). In the alarm example, *Burglary* is an obvious query variable, and *JohnCalls* and *MaryCalls* could serve as evidence variables. Of course, belief networks are flexible enough so that any node can serve as either a query or an evidence variable. There is nothing to stop us from asking **P**(*Alarm*|*JohnCalls*, *Earthquake*), although it would be somewhat unusual. In general, *an agent gets values for evidence variables from its percepts (or from other reasoning), and asks about the possible values of other variables so that it can decide*

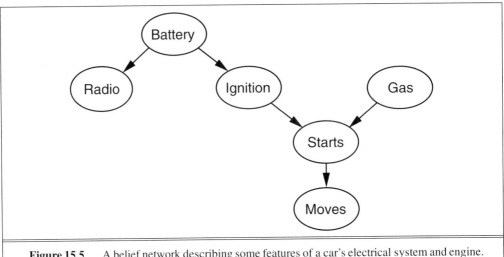

Figure 15.5   A belief network describing some features of a car's electrical system and engine.

what action to take. The two functions we need are BELIEF-NET-TELL, for adding evidence to the network, and BELIEF-NET-ASK, for computing the posterior probability distribution for a given query variable.

The nature of probabilistic inferences

Before plunging into the details of the inference algorithms, it is worthwhile to examine the kinds of things such algorithms can achieve. We will see that a single mechanism can account for a very wide variety of plausible inferences under uncertainty.

Consider the problem of computing $P(Burglary|JohnCalls)$, the probability that there is a burglary given that John calls. This task is quite tricky for humans, and therefore for many reasoning systems that attempt to encode human judgment. The difficulty is not the complexity of the problem, but keeping the reasoning straight. An incorrect but all-too-common line of reasoning starts by observing that when the alarm goes off, *JohnCalls* will be true 90% of the time. The alarm is fairly accurate at reflecting burglaries, so $P(Burglary|JohnCalls)$ should also be about 0.9, or maybe 0.8 at worst. The problem is that this line of reasoning ignores the prior probability of John calling. Over the course of 1000 days, we expect one burglary, for which John is very likely to call. However, John also calls with probability 0.05 when there actually is no alarm—about 50 times over 1000 days. Thus, we expect to receive about 50 false alarms from John for every 1 burglary, so $P(Burglary|JohnCalls)$ is about 0.02. In fact, if we carry out the exact computation, we find that the true value is 0.016. It is less than our 0.02 estimate because the alarm is not perfect.

Now suppose that as soon as we get off the phone with John, Mary calls. We are now interested in incrementally updating our network to give $P(Burglary|JohnCalls \wedge MaryCalls)$. Again, humans often overestimate this value; the correct answer is only 0.29. We can also determine that $P(Alarm|JohnCalls \wedge MaryCalls)$ is 0.76 and $P(Earthquake|JohnCalls \wedge MaryCalls)$ is 0.18.

In both of these problems, the reasoning is diagnostic. But belief networks are not limited to diagnostic reasoning and in fact can make four distinct kinds of inference:

$\diamond$ **Diagnostic inferences** (from effects to causes).
Given that *JohnCalls*, infer that $P(Burglary|JohnCalls) = 0.016$.

$\diamond$ **Causal inferences** (from causes to effects).
Given *Burglary*, $P(JohnCalls|Burglary) = 0.86$ and $P(MaryCalls|Burglary) = 0.67$.

$\diamond$ **Intercausal inferences** (between causes of a common effect).
Given *Alarm*, we have $P(Burglary|Alarm) = 0.376$. But if we add the evidence that *Earthquake* is true, then $P(Burglary|Alarm \wedge Earthquake)$ goes down to 0.003. Even though burglaries and earthquakes are independent, the presence of one makes the other

less likely. This pattern of reasoning is also known as **explaining away**.[3]

$\diamond$ **Mixed inferences** (combining two or more of the above).
Setting the effect *JohnCalls* to true and the cause *Earthquake* to false gives

$$P(Alarm|JohnCalls \wedge \neg Earthquake) = 0.03$$

This is a simultaneous use of diagnostic and causal inference. Also,

$$P(Burglary|JohnCalls \wedge \neg Earthquake) = 0.017$$

This is a combination of intercausal and diagnostic inference.

These four patterns are depicted in Figure 15.6. Besides calculating the belief in query variables given definite values for evidence variables, belief networks can also be used for the following:

- Making decisions based on probabilities in the network and on the agent's utilities.
- Deciding which additional evidence variables should be observed in order to gain useful information.

- Performing **sensitivity analysis** to understand which aspects of the model have the greatest impact on the probabilities of the query variables (and therefore must be accurate).
- Explaining the results of probabilistic inference to the user.

These tasks are discussed further in Chapter 16. In this chapter, we focus on computing posterior probabilities of query variables. In Chapter 18, we show how belief networks can be learned from example cases.

An algorithm for answering queries

In this section, we will derive an algorithm for BELIEF-NET-ASK. This is a rather technical section, and some of the mathematics and notation are unavoidably intricate. The algorithm itself, however, is very simple. Our version will work rather like the backward-chaining algorithm in Chapter 9, in that it begins at the query variable and chains along the paths from that node until it reaches evidence nodes. Because of the complications that may arise when two different paths

converge on the same node, we will derive an algorithm that works only on **singly connected**

---

[3] To get this effect, we do not have to *know* that *Earthquake* is true, we just need some evidence for it. When one of the authors first moved to California, he lived in a rickety house that shook when large trucks went by. After one particularly large shake, he turned on the radio, heard the Carole King song *I Feel the Earth Move*, and considered this strong evidence that a large truck had not gone by.

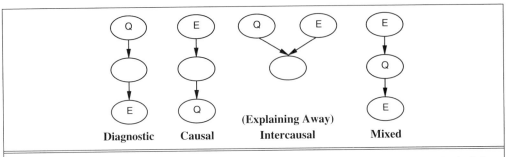

Figure 15.6   Simple examples of four patterns of reasoning that can be handled by belief networks. E represents an evidence variable and Q is a query variable.

POLYTREES

networks, also known as **polytrees**. In such networks, there is at most one undirected path between any two nodes in the network. Algorithms for general networks (Section 15.4) will use the polytree algorithms as their main subroutine.

Figure 15.7 shows a generic singly connected network. Node X has parents $\mathbf{U} = U_1 \ldots U_m$, and children $\mathbf{Y} = Y_1 \ldots Y_n$. For each child and parent we have drawn a box that contains all the node's descendants and ancestors (except for X). The singly connected property means that all the boxes are disjoint and have no links connecting them. We are assuming that X is the query variable, and that there is some set of evidence variables E. The aim is to compute $\mathbf{P}(X|E)$. (Obviously, if X is itself an evidence variable in E, then calculating $\mathbf{P}(X|E)$ is trivial. We will assume that X is not in E.)

In order to derive the algorithm, it will be helpful to be able to refer to different portions of the total evidence. The first distinction we will need is the following:

CAUSAL SUPPORT

E_X^+ is the the **causal support** for X—the evidence variables "above" X that are connected to X through its parents.

EVIDENTIAL
SUPPORT

E_X^- is the **evidential support** for X—the evidence variables "below" X that are connected to X through its children.

Sometimes we will need to exclude certain paths when considering evidence connected to a certain variable. For example, we will use $E_{U_i \setminus X}$ to refer to all the evidence connected to node U_i *except* via the path from X. Similarly, $E_{Y_i \setminus X}^+$ means all the evidence connected to Y_i through its parents *except* for X. Notice that the total evidence E can be written as E_X (all the evidence connected to X) and as $E_{X \setminus}$ (all the evidence connected to X with no exceptions).

Now we are ready to compute $\mathbf{P}(X|E)$. The general strategy is roughly the following:

- Express $\mathbf{P}(X|E)$ in terms of the contributions of E_X^+ and E_X^-.
- Compute the contribution of E_X^+ by computing its effect on the parents of X, and then passing that effect on to X. Notice that computing the effect on each parent of X is a recursive instance of the problem of computing the effect on X.
- Compute the contribution of E_X^- by computing its effect on the children of X, and then passing that effect on to X. Notice that computing the effect on each child of X is a recursive instance of the problem of computing the effect on X.

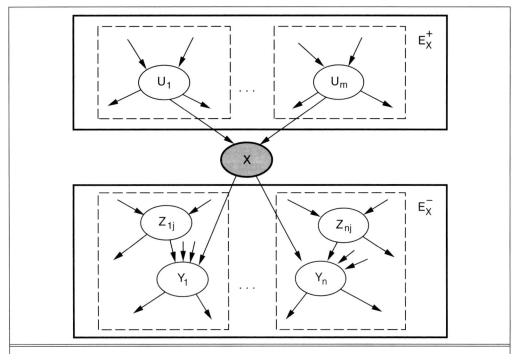

Figure 15.7   A generic singly connected network. The network is shown partitioned according to the parents and children of the query variable X.

Our derivation will work by applying Bayes' rule and other standard methods for manipulating probability expressions, until we have massaged the formulas into something that looks like a recursive instance of the original problems. Along the way, we will use simplifications sanctioned by the conditional independence relationships inherent in the network structure.

The total evidence E consists of the evidence above X and the evidence below X, since we are assuming that X itself is not in E. Hence, we have

$$\mathbf{P}(X|E) = \mathbf{P}(X|E_X^-, E_X^+)$$

To separate the contributions of E_X^+ and E_X^-, we apply the conditionalized version of Bayes' rule (Equation (14.4)) keeping E_X^- as fixed background evidence:

$$\mathbf{P}(X|E_X^-, E_X^+) = \frac{\mathbf{P}(E_X^-|X, E_X^+)\mathbf{P}(X|E_X^+)}{\mathbf{P}(E_X^-|E_X^+)}$$

Because X d-separates E_X^+ from E_X^- in the network, we can use conditional independence to simplify the first term in the numerator. Also, we can treat $1/\mathbf{P}(E_X^-|E_X^+)$ as a normalizing constant, giving us

$$\mathbf{P}(X|E) = \alpha\mathbf{P}(E_X^-|X)\mathbf{P}(X|E_X^+)$$

So now we just need to compute the two terms $\mathbf{P}(E_X^-|X)$ and $\mathbf{P}(X|E_X^+)$. The latter is easier, so we shall look at it first.

We compute $\mathbf{P}(X|E_X^+)$ by considering all the possible configurations of the *parents* of X, and how likely they are given E_X^+. Given each configuration, we know the probability of X directly from the CPT; we then average those probabilities, weighted by the likelihood of each configuration. To say this formally, let $\mathbf{U}$ be the vector of parents $U_1, \ldots, U_m$, and let $\mathbf{u}$ be an assignment of values to them.[4] Then we have

$$\mathbf{P}(X|E_X^+) = \sum_{\mathbf{u}} \mathbf{P}(X|\mathbf{u}, E_X^+)P(\mathbf{u}|E_X^+)$$

Now $\mathbf{U}$ d-separates X from E_X^+, so we can simplify the first term to $\mathbf{P}(X|\mathbf{u})$. We can simplify the second term by noting that E_X^+ d-separates each U_i from the others, and by remembering that the probability of a conjunction of independent variables is equal to the product of their individual probabilities. This gives us

$$\mathbf{P}(X|E_X^+) = \sum_{\mathbf{u}} \mathbf{P}(X|\mathbf{u}) \prod_i \mathbf{P}(u_i|E_X^+)$$

The final step is to simplify the last term of this equation by partitioning E_X^+ into $E_{U_1 \setminus X}, \ldots, E_{U_m \setminus X}$ (the separate boxes in Figure 15.7) and using the fact that $E_{U_i \setminus X}$ d-separates U_i from all the other evidence in E_X^+. So that gives us

$$\mathbf{P}(X|E_X^+) = \sum_{\mathbf{u}} \mathbf{P}(X|\mathbf{u}) \prod_i \mathbf{P}(u_i|E_{U_i \setminus X})$$

which we can plug into our earlier equation to yield

$$\mathbf{P}(X|E) = \alpha \mathbf{P}(E_X^-|X) \sum_{\mathbf{u}} \mathbf{P}(X|\mathbf{u}) \prod_i \mathbf{P}(U_i|E_{u_i \setminus X}) \tag{15.3}$$

Finally, this is starting to look like an algorithm: $\mathbf{P}(X|\mathbf{u})$ is a lookup in the conditional probability table of X, and $\mathbf{P}(U_i|E_{U_i \setminus X})$ is a recursive instance of the original problem, which was to compute $\mathbf{P}(X|E)$—that is, $\mathbf{P}(X|E_{X \setminus})$. Note that the set of evidence variables in the recursive call is a proper subset of those in the original call—a good sign that the algorithm will terminate.

Now we return to $\mathbf{P}(E_X^-|X)$, with an eye toward coming up with another recursive solution. In this case we average over the values of Y_i, the children of X, but we will also need to include Y_i's parents. We let $\mathbf{Z}_i$ be the parents of Y_i other than X, and let $\mathbf{z}_i$ be an assignment of values to the parents. The derivation is similar to the previous one. First, because the evidence in each Y_i box is conditionally independent of the others given X, we get

$$\mathbf{P}(E_X^-|X) = \prod_i \mathbf{P}(E_{Y_i \setminus X}|X)$$

Averaging over Y_i and $\mathbf{z}_i$ yields

$$\mathbf{P}(E_X^-|X) = \prod_i \sum_{y_i} \sum_{\mathbf{z}_i} \mathbf{P}(E_{Y_i \setminus X}|X, y_i, \mathbf{z}_i)\mathbf{P}(y_i, \mathbf{z}_i|X)$$

Breaking $E_{Y_i \setminus X}$ into the two independent components $E_{Y_i}^-$ and $E_{Y_i \setminus X}^+$:

$$\mathbf{P}(E_X^-|X) = \prod_i \sum_{y_i} \sum_{\mathbf{z}_i} \mathbf{P}(E_{Y_i}^-|X, y_i, \mathbf{z}_i)\mathbf{P}(E_{Y_i \setminus X}^+|X, y_i, \mathbf{z}_i)\mathbf{P}(y_i, \mathbf{z}_i|X)$$

---

4   For example, if there are two Boolean parents, U_1 and U_2, then $\mathbf{u}$ ranges over four possible assignments, of which [*true, false*] is one.

$E_{Y_i}^-$ is independent of X and $\mathbf{z}_i$ given y_i, and $E_{Y_i\setminus X}^+$ is independent of X and y_i. We can also pull a term with no $\mathbf{z}_i$ out of the $\mathbf{z}_i$ summation:

$$\mathbf{P}(E_X^-|X) = \prod_i \sum_{y_i} P(E_{Y_i}^-|y_i) \sum_{\mathbf{z}_i} \mathbf{P}(E_{Y_i\setminus X}^+|\mathbf{z}_i)\mathbf{P}(y_i, \mathbf{z}_i|X)$$

Apply Bayes' rule to $\mathbf{P}(E_{Y_i\setminus X}^+|\mathbf{z}_i)$:

$$\mathbf{P}(E_X^-|X) = \prod_i \sum_{y_i} P(E_{Y_i}^-|y_i) \sum_{\mathbf{z}_i} \frac{P(\mathbf{z}_i|E_{Y_i\setminus X}^+)P(E_{Y_i\setminus X}^+)}{P(\mathbf{z}_i)}\mathbf{P}(y_i, \mathbf{z}_i|X)$$

Rewriting the conjunction $Y_i, \mathbf{z}_i$:

$$\mathbf{P}(E_X^-|X) = \prod_i \sum_{y_i} P(E_{Y_i}^-|y_i) \sum_{\mathbf{z}_i} \frac{P(\mathbf{z}_i|E_{Y_i\setminus X}^+)P(E_{Y_i\setminus X}^+)}{P(\mathbf{z}_i)}\mathbf{P}(y_i|X, \mathbf{z}_i)\mathbf{P}(\mathbf{z}_i|X)$$

Now $\mathbf{P}(\mathbf{z}_i|X) = P(\mathbf{z}_i)$, because $\mathbf{Z}$ and X are d-separated, so we can cancel them out. We can also replace $P(E_{Y_i\setminus X}^+)$ by a normalizing constant β_i:

$$\mathbf{P}(E_X^-|X) = \prod_i \sum_{y_i} P(E_{Y_i}^-|y_i) \sum_{\mathbf{z}_i} \beta_i P(\mathbf{z}_i|E_{Y_i\setminus X}^+)\mathbf{P}(y_i|X, \mathbf{z}_i)$$

Finally, the parents of Y_i (the Z_{ij}) are independent of each other, so we can multiply them together, just as we did with the U_i parents previously. We also combine the β_i into one big normalizing constant β:

$$\mathbf{P}(E_X^-|X) = \beta \prod_i \sum_{y_i} P(E_{Y_i}^-|y_i) \sum_{\mathbf{z}_i} \mathbf{P}(y_i|X, \mathbf{z}_i) \prod_j P(z_{ij}|E_{Z_{ij}\setminus Y_i}) \tag{15.4}$$

Notice that each of the terms in the final expression is easily evaluated:

- $P(E_{Y_i}^-|y_i)$ is a recursive instance of $\mathbf{P}(E_X^-|X)$.
- $P(y_i|x\mathbf{z}_i)$ is a conditional probability table entry for Y_i.
- $P(z_{ij}|E_{Z_{ij}\setminus Y_i})$ is a recursive instance of the $\mathbf{P}(X|E)$ calculation—that is, $\mathbf{P}(X|E_{X\setminus})$

It is now a simple matter to turn all this into an algorithm. We will need two basic routines. SUPPORT-EXCEPT(X,V) computes $\mathbf{P}(X|E_{X\setminus V})$, using a slight generalization of Equation (15.3) to handle the "except" variable V. EVIDENCE-EXCEPT(X,V) computes $P(E_{X\setminus V}^-|X)$, using a generalization of Equation (15.4). The algorithms are shown in Figure 15.8.

The computation involves recursive calls that spread out from X along all paths in the network. The recursion terminates on evidence nodes, root nodes (which have no parents), and leaf nodes (which have no children). Each recursive call excludes the node from which it was called, so each node in the tree is covered only once. Hence the algorithm is linear in the number of nodes in the network. Remember that this only works because the network is a *polytree*. If there were more than one path between a pair of nodes, then either our recursions would count the same evidence more than once or they would fail to terminate.

We have chosen to present a "backward-chaining" algorithm because it is the simplest algorithm for polytrees. One drawback is that it computes the probability distribution for just one variable. If we wanted the posterior distributions for all the non-evidence variables, we would have to run the algorithm once for each. This would give a quadratic runtime, and

---

function BELIEF-NET-ASK(X) **returns** a probability distribution over the values of X
  inputs: X, a random variable

  SUPPORT-EXCEPT(X, *null*)

---

function SUPPORT-EXCEPT(X, V) **returns** $\mathbf{P}(X|E_{X\setminus V})$

  if EVIDENCE?(X) **then return** observed point distribution for X
  else
      calculate $\mathbf{P}(E^-_{X\setminus V}|X) =$ EVIDENCE-EXCEPT(X, V)
      $U \leftarrow$ PARENTS[X]
      if U is empty
          then return $\alpha\ \mathbf{P}(E^-_{X\setminus V}|X)\ \mathbf{P}(X)$
      else
          for each U_i **in** U
              calculate and store $\mathbf{P}(U_i|E_{U_i\setminus X}) =$ SUPPORT-EXCEPT(U_i, X)
          return $\alpha\ \mathbf{P}(E^-_{X\setminus V}|X)\ \sum_{\mathbf{u}}\mathbf{P}(X|\mathbf{u})\ \prod_i \mathbf{P}(U_i|E_{u_i\setminus X})$

---

function EVIDENCE-EXCEPT(X, V) **returns** $\mathbf{P}(E^-_{X\setminus V}|X)$

  $\mathbf{Y} \leftarrow$ CHILDREN[X] $- V$
  if Y is empty
      then return a uniform distribution
  else
      for each Y_i **in Y do**
          calculate $\mathbf{P}(E^-_{Y_i}|y_i) =$ EVIDENCE-EXCEPT(Y_i, null)
          $\mathbf{Z}_i \leftarrow$ PARENTS[Y_i] $- X$
          for each Z_{ij} **in** $\mathbf{Z}_i$
              calculate $\mathbf{P}(Z_{ij}|E_{Z_{ij}\setminus Y_i}) =$ SUPPORT-EXCEPT(Z_{ij}, Y_i)
      return $\beta\ \prod_i\ \sum_{y_i} P(E^-_{Y_i}|y_i)\ \sum_{\mathbf{z}_i}\mathbf{P}(y_i|X,\mathbf{z}_i)\ \prod_j P(z_{ij}|E_{Z_{ij}\setminus Y_i})$

Figure 15.8 A backward-chaining algorithm for solving probabilistic queries on a polytree. To simplify the presentation, we have assumed that the network is fixed and already primed with evidence, and that evidence variables satisfy the predicate EVIDENCE?. The probabilities $\mathbf{P}(X|\mathbf{U})$, where $\mathbf{U}$ denotes the parents of X, are available from the CPT for X. Calculating the expressions $\alpha \ldots$ and $\beta \ldots$ is done by normalization.

would involve many repeated calculations. A better way to arrange things is to "memoize" the computations by forward-chaining from the evidence variables. Given careful bookkeeping, the entire computation can be done in linear time. It is interesting to note that the forward-chaining version can be viewed as consisting of "messages" being "propagated" through the network. This leads to a simple implementation on parallel computers, and an intriguing analogy to message propagation among neurons in the brain (see Chapter 19).

15.4   INFERENCE IN MULTIPLY CONNECTED BELIEF NETWORKS

MULTIPLY
CONNECTED

A **multiply connected** graph is one in which two nodes are connected by more than one path. One way this happens is when there are two or more possible causes for some variable, and the causes share a common ancestor. Alternatively, one can think of multiply connected networks as representing situations in which one variable can influence another through more than one causal mechanism. For example, Figure 15.9 shows a situation in which whether it is cloudy has a causal link to whether it rains, and also a causal link to whether the lawn sprinklers are turned on (because a gardener who observes clouds is less likely to turn the sprinklers on). Both rain and sprinklers have an effect on whether the grass gets wet.

There are three basic classes of algorithms for evaluating multiply connected networks, each with its own areas of applicability:

CLUSTERING

◇ **Clustering** methods transform the network into a probabilistically equivalent (but topologically different) polytree by merging offending nodes.

CONDITIONING

◇ **Conditioning** methods do the transformation by instantiating variables to definite values, and then evaluating a polytree for each possible instantiation.

STOCHASTIC
SIMULATION

◇ **Stochastic simulation** methods use the network to generate a large number of concrete models of the domain that are consistent with the network distribution. They give an approximation of the exact evaluation.

In the general case, exact inference in belief networks is known to be NP-hard. It is fairly straightforward to prove this, because a general belief network can represent any propositional logic problem (if all the probabilities are 1 or 0) and propositional logic problems are known to be NP-complete. For very large networks, approximation using stochastic simulation is currently the method of choice. The problem of approximating the posterior probabilities to within an arbitrary tolerance is itself NP-hard, but for events that are not too unlikely the calculations are usually feasible.

Clustering methods

MEGANODE

One way of evaluating the network in Figure 15.9 is to transform it into a polytree by combining the *Sprinkler* and *Rain* node into a **meganode** called *Sprinkler+Rain*, as shown in Figure 15.10. The two Boolean nodes are replaced by a meganode that takes on four possible values: *TT*, *TF*, *FT*, and *FF*. The meganode has only one parent, the Boolean variable *Cloudy*, so there are two conditioning cases. Once the network has been converted to a polytree, a linear-time algorithm can be applied to answer queries. Queries on variables that have been clustered can be answered by averaging over the values of the other variables in the cluster.

Although clustering makes it possible to use a linear-time algorithm, the NP-hardness of the problem does not go away. In the worst case, the *size* of the network increases exponentially, because the conditional probability tables for the clusters involve the cross-product of the domains of the variables. In Figure 15.10, there are six independently specifiable numbers in *Sprinkler+Rain*, as opposed to four total in *Sprinkler* and *Rain*. (One of the numbers in each row is not independent, because the row must sum to 1. In Figure 15.9, we dropped one of the two columns, but here we show all four.)

The tricky part about clustering is choosing the right meganodes. There are several ways to make this choice, but all of them ultimately produce meganodes with large probability tables. Despite this problem, clustering methods are currently the most effective approach for exact evaluation of multiply connected networks.

Cutset conditioning methods

The **cutset conditioning** method takes the opposite approach. Instead of transforming the network into one complex polytree, this method transforms the network into several simpler

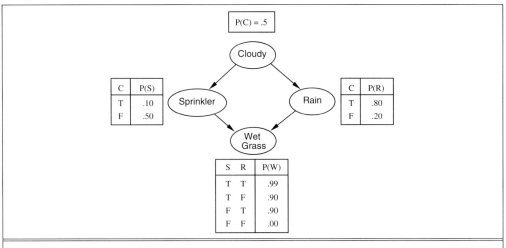

Figure 15.9   A multiply connected network with conditional probability tables.

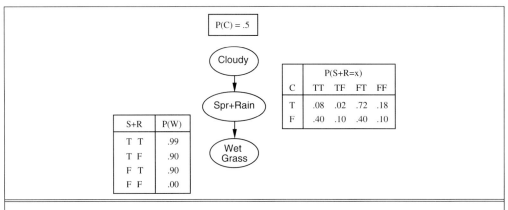

Figure 15.10   A clustered equivalent of the multiply connected network.

polytrees. Each simple network has one or more variables *instantiated* to a definite value. $P(X|E)$ is computed as a weighted average over the values computed by each polytree.

CUTSET

A set of variables that can be instantiated to yield polytrees is called a **cutset**. In Figure 15.11, the cutset is just {*Cloudy*}, and because it is a Boolean variable, there are just two resulting polytrees. In general, the number of resulting polytrees is exponential in the size of the cutset, so we want to find a small cutset if possible.

Cutset conditioning can be approximated by evaluating only some of the resulting polytrees. The error in the approximation is bounded by the total probability weight of the polytrees not yet evaluated. The obvious approach is to evaluate the most likely polytrees first. For example, if we need an answer accurate to within 0.1, we evaluate trees in decreasing order of likelihood until BOUNDED CUTSET CONDITIONING the total probability exceeds 0.9. This technique is called **bounded cutset conditioning**, and is useful in systems that need to make approximately correct decisions quickly.

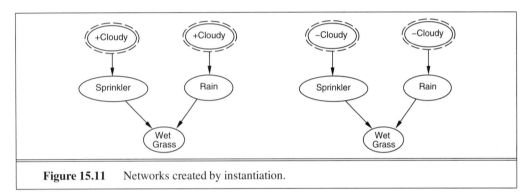

Figure 15.11   Networks created by instantiation.

Stochastic simulation methods

LOGIC SAMPLING

In the stochastic simulation method known as **logic sampling**, we run repeated simulations of the world described by the belief network, and estimate the probability we are interested in by counting the frequencies with which relevant events occur. Each round of the simulation starts by randomly choosing a value for each root node of the network, weighting the choice by the prior probabilities. If the prior $P(Cloudy) = 0.5$, then we would pick *Cloudy = True* half the time, and *Cloudy = False* half the time. Whatever value is chosen, we can then choose values randomly for *Sprinkler* and *Rain*, using the conditional probabilities of those nodes given the known value of *Cloudy*. Finally, we do the same for *WetGrass*, and the first round is done.

To estimate $P(WetGrass|Cloudy)$ (or in general $\mathbf{P}(X|E)$), we repeat the process many times, and then compute the ratio of the number of runs where *WetGrass* and *Cloudy* are true to the number of runs where just *Cloudy* is true. This will always converge to the right value, although it may take many runs.

The main problem is when we are interested in some assignment of values to E that rarely occurs. For example, suppose we wanted to know

$P(WetGrass|Sprinkler \wedge Rain)$

Because *Sprinkler* ∧ *Rain* is rare in the world, most of the simulation rounds would end up with different values for these evidence variables, and we would have to discard those runs. The fraction of useful runs decreases exponentially with the number of evidence variables.

We can get around this problem with an approach called **likelihood weighting**. The idea is that every time we reach an evidence variable, instead of randomly choosing a value (according to the conditional probabilities), we take the given value for the evidence variable, but use the conditional probabilities to see how likely that is. For example, to compute $P(WetGrass|Rain)$ we would do the following:

1. Choose a value for *Cloudy* with prior $P(Cloudy) = 0.5$. Assume we choose *Cloudy = False*.
2. Choose a value for *Sprinkler*. We see that $P(Sprinkler|\neg Cloudy) = 0.5$, so we randomly choose a value given that distribution. Assume we choose *Sprinkler = True*.
3. Look at *Rain*. This is an evidence variable that has been set to *True*, so we look at the table to see that $P(Rain|\neg Cloudy) = 0.2$. This run therefore counts as 0.2 of a complete run.
4. Look at *WetGrass*. Choose randomly with $P(WetGrass|Sprinkler \wedge Rain) = 0.99$; assume we choose *WetGrass = True*.
5. We now have completed a run with likelihood 0.2 that says *Wetgrass = True* given *Rain*. The next run will result in a different likelihood, and (possibly) a different value for *WetGrass*. We continue until we have accumulated enough runs, and then add up the evidence for each value, weighted by the likelihood score.

Likelihood weighting usually converges considerably faster than logic sampling, and can handle very large networks. In the CPSC project (Pradhan *et al.*, 1994), for example, a belief network has been constructed for internal medicine that contains 448 nodes, 906 links and 8,254 conditional probability values. (The front cover shows a small portion of the network.) Likelihood weighting typically obtains accurate values in around 35 minutes on this network.

The main difficulty with likelihood weighting, and indeed with any stochastic sampling method, is that it takes a long time to reach accurate probabilities for unlikely events. In general, the runtime necessary to reach a given level of accuracy is inversely proportional to the probability of the event. Events such as the meltdown of a nuclear reactor on a particular day are *extremely* unlikely, but there is a very big difference between 10^{-5} and 10^{-10}, so we still need to get accurate values. Researchers are currently working to find ways around this problem.

15.5   KNOWLEDGE ENGINEERING FOR UNCERTAIN REASONING

The approach to knowledge engineering for probabilistic reasoning systems is very much like the approach for logical reasoning systems outlined in Section 8.2:

- *Decide what to talk about.* This remains a difficult step. It is important to decide which factors will be modelled, and which will just be summarized by probability statements. In an expert system of all dental knowledge, we will certainly want to talk about toothaches, gum disease, and cavities. We may want to know if a patient's parents have a history of gum disease, but we probably do not need to talk about the patient's third cousins. Once we have an initial set of factors, we can extend the model by asking, "What directly influences this factor?" and "What does this factor directly influence?"

- *Decide on a vocabulary of random variables.* Determine the variables you want to use, and what values they can take on. Sometimes it is useful to quantize a continuous-valued variable into discrete ranges.

- *Encode general knowledge about the dependence between variables.* Here there is a qualitative part, where we say what variables are dependent on what others, and a quantitative part, where we specify probability values. The values can come either from the knowledge engineer's (or expert's) subjective experience, or from measurements of frequencies in a database of past experiences, or from some combination of the two.

- *Encode a description of the specific problem instance.* For example, we say that the particular patient we are interested in is a 34-year-old female with moderate to severe pain in the lower jaw.

- *Pose queries to the inference procedure and get answers.* The most common query is to ask for the value of some hypothesis variable. For example, given the patient's symptoms, what is the probability of gum disease, or of any other disorder. It is also common to use sensitivity analysis to determine how robust the answers are with respect to perturbations in the conditional probability table values.

Case study: The Pathfinder system

PATHFINDER is a diagnostic expert system for lymph-node diseases, built by members of the Stanford Medical Computer Science program during the 1980s (see Heckerman (1991) for a discussion). The system deals with over 60 diseases and over 100 disease findings (symptoms and test results). Four versions of the system have been built, and the history is instructive because it shows a trend toward increasing sophistication in reasoning with uncertainty.

PATHFINDER I was a rule-based system written with the logical metareasoning system MRS. It did not do any uncertain reasoning.

PATHFINDER II experimented with several methods for uncertain reasoning, including certainty factors and the Dempster–Shafer theory (see Section 15.6). The results showed that a simplified Bayesian model (in which all disease findings were assumed to be independent) outperformed the other methods. One interesting result of the experiment was that 10% of cases were diagnosed incorrectly because the expert had given a probability of zero to an unlikely but possible event.

PATHFINDER III used the same simplified Bayesian model, but with a reassessment of the probabilities using a different protocol and paying attention to low-probability events.

PATHFINDER IV used a belief network to represent the dependencies that could not be handled in the simplified Bayesian model. The author of the system sat down with an expert physician and followed the knowledge engineering approach described earlier. Deciding on a vocabulary took 8 hours, devising the topology of the network took 35 hours, and making the 14,000 probability assessments took another 40 hours. The physician reportedly found it easy to think in terms of probabilities on causal links, and a concept called **similarity networks** made it easier for the expert to assess a large number of probabilities. The network constructed in this process covers one of the 32 major areas of pathology. The plan is to cover all of pathology through consultations with leading experts in each area.

An evaluation of PATHFINDER III and IV used 53 actual cases of patients who were referred to a lymph-node specialist. As referrals, these cases were probably of above-average difficulty. In a blind evaluation, expert analysis of the diagnoses showed that PATHFINDER III scored an average 7.9 out of 10, and PATHFINDER IV scored 8.9, significantly better. The difference amounts to saving one life every thousand cases or so. A recent comparison showed that Pathfinder is now outperforming the experts who were consulted during its creation—those experts being some of the world's leading pathologists.

15.6   OTHER APPROACHES TO UNCERTAIN REASONING

Other sciences (e.g., physics, genetics, economics) have long favored probability as a model for uncertainty. Pierre Laplace said in 1819 that "Probability theory is nothing but common sense reduced to calculation." James Maxwell said in 1850 that "the true logic for this world is the calculus of Probabilities, which takes account of the magnitude of the probability which is, or ought to be, in a reasonable man's mind." Stephen Jay Gould (1994) claimed that "misunderstanding of probability may be the greatest of all general impediments to scientific literacy."

Given this long tradition, it is perhaps surprising that AI has considered many alternatives to probability. The earliest expert systems of the 1970s ignored uncertainty and used strict logical reasoning, but soon it became clear that this was impractical for most real-world domains. The next generation of expert systems (especially in medical domains) used probabilistic techniques. Initial results were promising, but they did not scale up because of the exponential number of probabilities required in the full joint distribution. (Belief net algorithms were not known then.) As a result, probabilistic approaches fell out of favor from roughly 1975 to 1988, and a variety of alternatives were tried for a variety of reasons:

- One common view is that probability theory is essentially numerical, whereas human judgmental reasoning is more "qualitative." Certainly, we are not consciously aware of doing numerical calculations of degrees of belief. (On the other hand, it might be that we have some kind of numerical degrees of belief encoded directly in strengths of connections and activations in our neurons. In that case, the difficulty of conscious access to those strengths is only to be expected.) One should also note that qualitative reasoning mechanisms can be built directly on top of probability theory, so that the "no numbers" argument against probability has little force. Nonetheless, some qualitative schemes have a good deal of appeal in their own right. One of the most well-studied is **default reasoning**, which treats conclusions not as "believed to a certain degree," but as "believed until a better reason is found to believe something else."

- **Rule-based** approaches to uncertainty also have been tried. Such approaches hope to build on the success of logical rule-based systems, but add a sort of "fudge factor" to each rule to accommodate uncertainty. These methods were developed in the mid-1970s, and formed the basis for a large number of expert systems in medicine and other areas.

- One area that we have not addressed so far is the question of **ignorance**, as opposed to uncertainty. Consider flipping a coin. If we know the coin to be fair, then a probability of 0.5 for heads is reasonable. If we know the coin is biased, but we do not know which way, then 0.5 is the only reasonable probability. Obviously, the two cases are different, yet probability seems not to distinguish them. The **Dempster–Shafer theory** uses **interval-valued** degrees of belief to represent an agent's knowledge of the probability of a proposition. Other methods using second-order probabilities are also discussed.

- Probability makes the same ontological commitment as logic: that events are true or false in the world, even if the agent is uncertain as to which is the case. Researchers in **fuzzy logic** have proposed an ontology that allows **vagueness**: that an event can be "sort of" true. Vagueness and uncertainty are in fact orthogonal issues, as we will see.

The following sections treat each of these approaches in slightly more depth. We will not provide detailed technical material, but we provide references for further study.

Default reasoning

Commonsense reasoning is often said to involve "jumping to conclusions." For example, when one sees a car parked on the street, one would normally be willing to accept that it has four wheels even though only three are visible. (If you feel that the existence of the fourth wheel is dubious, consider also the question as to whether the three visible wheels are real or merely cardboard facsimiles.) Probability theory can certainly provide a conclusion that the fourth wheel exists with high probability. On the other hand, introspection suggests that the possibility of the car not having four wheels does not even arise *unless some new evidence presents itself*. Thus, it seems that the four-wheel conclusion is reached *by default*, in the absence of any reason to doubt it. If new evidence arrives—for example, if one sees the owner carrying a wheel and notices that the car is jacked up—then the conclusion can be retracted. This kind of reasoning is said to exhibit **nonmonotonicity**, because the set of beliefs does not grow monotonically over time as new evidence arrives. First-order logic, on the other hand, exhibits strict **monotonicity**.

NONMONOTONICITY

MONOTONICITY

DEFAULT LOGIC

NONMONOTONIC LOGIC

CIRCUMSCRIPTION

Reasoning schemes such as **default logic** (Reiter, 1980), **nonmonotonic logic** (McDermott and Doyle, 1980) and **circumscription** (McCarthy, 1980) are designed to handle reasoning with default rules and retraction of beliefs. Although the technical details of these systems are quite different, they share a number of problematic issues that arise with default reasoning:

- What is the *semantic* status of default rules? If "Cars have four wheels" is false, what does it mean to have it in one's knowledge base? What is a good set of default rules to have? Without a good answer to these questions, default reasoning systems will be nonmodular, and it will be hard to develop a good knowledge engineering methodology.

SPECIFICITY PREFERENCE

- What happens when the evidence matches the premises of two default rules with conflicting conclusions? We saw examples of this in the discussion of multiple inheritance in Section 10.6. In some schemes, one can express priorities between rules so that one rule takes precedence. **Specificity preference** is a commonly used form of priority in which a special-case rule takes precedence over the general case. For example, "Three-wheeled cars have three wheels" takes precedence over "Cars have four wheels."

- Sometimes a system may draw a number of conclusions on the basis of a belief that is later retracted. How can a system keep track of which conclusions need to be retracted as a result? Conclusions that have multiple justifications, only some of which have been abandoned, should be retained; whereas those with no remaining justifications should be dropped. These problems have been addressed by **truth maintenance systems**, which are discussed in Section 10.8.

- How can beliefs that have default status be used to make decisions? This is probably the hardest issue for default reasoning. Decisions often involve trade-offs, and one therefore needs to compare the *strength* of belief in the outcomes of different actions. In cases where the same kinds of decisions are being made repeatedly, it is possible to interpret default rules as "threshold probability" statements. For example, the default rule "My brakes are always OK" really means "The probability that my brakes are OK, given no other information, is sufficiently high that the optimal decision is for me to drive without checking them." When the decision context changes—for example, when one is driving a heavily laden truck down a steep mountain road—the default rule suddenly becomes inappropriate, even though there is no new evidence to suggest that the brakes are faulty.

To date, no default reasoning system has successfully addressed all of these issues. Furthermore, most systems are formally undecidable, and very slow in practice. There have been several attempts to subsume default reasoning in a probabilistic system, using the idea that a default rule is basically a conditional probability of $1 - \epsilon$. For reasons already mentioned, such an approach is likely to require a full integration of decision making before it fully captures the desirable features of default reasoning.

Rule-based methods for uncertain reasoning

In addition to monotonicity, logical reasoning systems have three other important properties that probabilistic reasoners lack:

LOCALITY

◇ **Locality**: In logical systems, whenever we have a rule of the form $A \Rightarrow B$, we can conclude B given evidence A, *without worrying about any other rules*. In probabilistic systems, we need to consider *all* of the available evidence.

DETACHMENT

◇ **Detachment**: Once a logical proof is found for a proposition B, the proposition can be used regardless of how it was derived. That is, it can be **detached** from its justification. In dealing with probabilities, on the other hand, the source of the evidence for a belief is important for subsequent reasoning.

TRUTH-
FUNCTIONALITY

◇ **Truth-functionality**: In logic, the truth of complex sentences can be computed from the truth of the components. Probability combination does not work this way, except under strong independence assumptions.

These properties confer obvious computational advantages. There have been several attempts to devise uncertain reasoning schemes by attaching degrees of belief to propositions and rules in what is essentially a logical system. This means treating degree of belief as a generalized truth value, in order to retain truth-functionality. That is, each proposition is assigned a degree of belief, and the degree of belief in, say, $A \lor B$ is a function of the belief in A and the belief in B.

The bad news for truth-functional systems is that the properties of *locality, detachment, and truth-functionality are simply not appropriate for uncertain reasoning.* Let us look at truth-functionality first. Let H_1 be the event of a coin coming up heads on a fair flip, let T_1 be the event of the coin coming up tails on that same flip, and let H_2 be the event of the coin coming up heads on a second flip. Clearly, all three events have the same probability, 0.5, and so a truth-functional system must assign the same belief to the conjunction of any two of them. But we can see that the probability of the conjunction depends on the events themselves, and not just on their probabilities:

$P(A)$	$P(B)$	$P(A \lor B)$
	$P(H_1) = 0.5$	$P(H_1 \lor H_1) = 0.50$
$P(H_1) = 0.5$	$P(T_1) = 0.5$	$P(H_1 \lor T_1) = 1.00$
	$P(H_2) = 0.5$	$P(H_1 \lor H_2) = 0.75$

It gets worse when we chain evidence together. Truth-functional systems have **rules** of the form $A \mapsto B$, which allow us to compute the belief in B as a function of the belief in the rule and the belief in A. Both forward- and backward-chaining systems can be devised. The belief in the rule is assumed to be constant, and is usually specified by the knowledge engineer, for example, $A \mapsto_{0.9} B$.

Consider the wet-grass situation from Section 15.4. If we wanted to be able to do both causal and diagnostic reasoning, we would need the two rules:

$$Rain \mapsto WetGrass \qquad \text{and} \qquad WetGrass \mapsto Rain$$

If we are not careful, these two rules will act in a feedback loop so that evidence for *Rain* increases the belief in *WetGrass*, which in turn increases the belief in *Rain* even more. Clearly, uncertain reasoning systems need to keep track of the paths along which evidence is propagated.

Intercausal reasoning (or explaining away) is also tricky. Consider what happens when we have the two rules:

$$Sprinkler \mapsto WetGrass \qquad \text{and} \qquad WetGrass \mapsto Rain$$

Suppose we see that the sprinkler is on. Chaining forward through our rules, this increases the belief that the grass will be wet, which in turn increases the belief that it is raining. But this is ridiculous: the fact that the sprinkler is on explains away the wet grass, and should *reduce* the belief in rain. In a truth-functional system, the transitively derived rule *Sprinkler* $\mapsto$ *Rain* is unavoidable.

Given these difficulties, how is it possible that truth-functional systems were ever considered useful? The answer lies in restricting the tasks required of them, and in carefully engineering the rule base so that undesirable interactions do not occur. The most famous example of a truth-CERTAINTY FACTORS functional system for uncertain reasoning is the **certainty factors** model, which was developed for the MYCIN medical diagnosis program and widely used in expert systems of the late 1970s and 1980s. Almost all uses of certainty factors involved rule sets that were either purely diagnostic (as in MYCIN) or purely causal. Furthermore, evidence was only entered at the "roots" of the rule set, and most rule sets were singly connected. Heckerman (1986) has shown that under these circumstances, a minor variation on certainty-factor inference was exactly equivalent to Bayesian inference on polytrees. In other circumstances, certainty factors could yield disastrously incorrect degrees of belief through overcounting of evidence. Details of the method can be found under the "Certainty Factors" entry in *Encyclopedia of AI*, but the use of certainty factors is no longer recommended (even by one of its inventors—see the foreword to Heckerman (1991)).

Representing ignorance: Dempster–Shafer theory

DEMPSTER–SHAFER

BELIEF FUNCTION

The **Dempster–Shafer** theory is designed to deal with the distinction between **uncertainty** and **ignorance**. Rather than computing the probability of a proposition, it computes the probability that the evidence supports the proposition. This measure of belief is called a **belief function**, written $Bel(X)$.

We return to coin flipping for an example of belief functions. Suppose a shady character comes up to you and offers to bet you $10 that his coin will come up heads on the next flip. Given that the coin may or may not be fair, what belief should you ascribe to the event of it coming up heads? Dempster–Shafer theory says that because you have no evidence either way, you have to say that the belief $Bel(Heads) = 0$, and also that $Bel(\neg Heads) = 0$. This makes Dempster–Shafer reasoning systems skeptical in a way that has some intuitive appeal. Now suppose you have an expert at your disposal who testifies with 90% certainty that the coin is fair (i.e., he is 90% sure that $P(Heads) = 0.5$). Then Dempster–Shafer theory gives $Bel(Heads) = 0.9 \times 0.5 = 0.45$ and likewise $Bel(\neg Heads) = 0.45$. There is still a 0.1 "gap" that is not accounted for by the evidence. "Dempster's rule" (Dempster, 1968) shows how to combine evidence to give new values for Bel, and Shafer's work extends this into a complete computational model.

As with default reasoning, there is a problem in connecting beliefs to actions. With probabilities, decision theory says that if $P(Heads) = P(\neg Heads) = 0.5$ then (assuming that winning $10 and losing $10 are considered equal opposites) the reasoner will be indifferent between the action of accepting and declining the bet. A Dempster–Shafer reasoner has $Bel(\neg Heads) = 0$, and thus no reason to accept the bet, but then it also has $Bel(Heads) = 0$, and thus no reason to decline it. Thus, it seems that the Dempster–Shafer reasoner comes to the same conclusion about how to act in this case. Unfortunately, Dempster–Shafer theory allows no definite decision in many other cases where probabilistic inference does yield a specific choice. In fact, the notion of utility in the Dempster–Shafer model is not yet well-understood, partly because the semantics of Bel is not defined precisely with respect to decision making.

One interpretation of Dempster–Shafer theory is that it defines a probability interval—the interval for *Heads* is [0, 1] before our expert testimony, and [0.45, 0.55] after. The width of the interval can be a good aid in deciding when we need to acquire more evidence: it can tell you that the expert's testimony will help you if you do not know whether the coin is fair, but will not help you if you have already determined that the coin is fair. In the Bayesian approach, this kind of reasoning can be done easily by examining how much one's belief would change if one were to acquire more evidence. For example, knowing whether the coin is fair would have a significant impact on the belief that it will come up heads. A Bayesian probability therefore has an "implicit" uncertainty associated with the various possible changes that it might undergo as a result of future observations.

Representing vagueness: Fuzzy sets and fuzzy logic

FUZZY SET THEORY

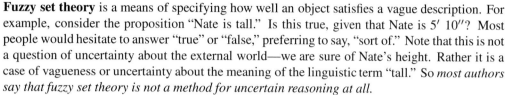

Fuzzy set theory is a means of specifying how well an object satisfies a vague description. For example, consider the proposition "Nate is tall." Is this true, given that Nate is 5′ 10″? Most people would hesitate to answer "true" or "false," preferring to say, "sort of." Note that this is not a question of uncertainty about the external world—we are sure of Nate's height. Rather it is a case of vagueness or uncertainty about the meaning of the linguistic term "tall." So *most authors say that fuzzy set theory is not a method for uncertain reasoning at all.*

Another way to think of this is as similarity to a prototype—how close is Nate to our prototype for tall person? We could express this in logical notation by making *TallPerson* a constant and having a function *Similarity* that compares things to it:

$$Similarity(Nate, TallPerson) = SortOf$$

Fuzzy set theory takes a slightly different approach: it treats *TallPerson* as a fuzzy predicate and says that the truth value of *TallPerson(Nate)* is a number between 0 and 1, rather than being just *True* or *False*. The name "fuzzy set" derives from the interpretation of the predicate as implicitly defining a set of its members, a set that does not have sharp boundaries. Consider a kennel with 60 rottweilers and 40 retrievers. If we pick a dog at random, the probability of it being a rottweiler is 0.6; this is uncertainty. The uncertainty can be resolved by looking at the dog. But if a rottweiler and a retriever were to mate, then the puppies would be half rottweiler, half retriever. There is no uncertainty here, no additional evidence we can gather to determine the breed of the puppies. Rather, this is a case of fuzziness at the boundary between two breeds.

FUZZY LOGIC

Fuzzy logic takes a complex sentence such as *TallPerson(Nate)* ∨ *Smart(Nate)* and determines its truth value as a function of the truth values of its components. The rules for evaluating the fuzzy truth, T, of a complex sentence are

$$T(A \wedge B) = \min(T(A), T(B))$$
$$T(A \vee B) = \max(T(A), T(B))$$
$$T(\neg A) = 1 - T(A)$$

Fuzzy logic is therefore a truth-functional system, and is thus subject to all the usual problems. It has the additional problem that it is inconsistent with normal propositional or first-order logic. We would like any logic to ensure that standard equivalences such as $A \vee \neg A \Leftrightarrow True$ hold, but in fuzzy logic, $T(A \vee \neg A) \neq T(True)$.

Despite these serious semantic difficulties, fuzzy logic has been very successful in commercial applications, particularly in control systems for products such as automatic transmissions, trains, video cameras, and electric shavers. Elkan (1993) argues that these applications are successful because they have small rule bases, have no chaining of inferences, and have tunable parameters that can be adjusted to improve the system's performance (often by learning techniques). The fact that they are implemented with fuzzy operators is incidental to their success. Elkan predicts that when more complex applications are tackled with fuzzy logic, they will run into the same kinds of problems that plagued knowledge-based systems using certainty factors and other approaches. As one might expect, the debate continues.

15.7   SUMMARY

Both Chapter 9 and this chapter are concerned with reasoning properly, but there is a difference in just what that means. In first-order logic, proper reasoning means that conclusions follow from premises—that if the initial knowledge base faithfully represents the world, then the inferences also faithfully represent the world. In probability, we are dealing with beliefs, not with the state of the world, so "proper reasoning" means having beliefs that allow an agent to act rationally.

In Chapter 10, we saw a variety of approaches to the problem of implementing logical reasoning systems. In this chapter, we see much more of a consensus: efficient reasoning with probability is so new that there is one main approach—belief networks—with a few minor variations. The main points are as follows:

- **Conditional independence** information is a vital and robust way to structure information about an uncertain domain.

- **Belief networks** are a natural way to represent conditional independence information. The links between nodes represent the qualitative aspects of the domain, and the conditional probability tables represent the quantitative aspects.

- A belief network is a complete representation for the joint probability distribution for the domain, but is often exponentially smaller in size.

- Inference in belief networks means computing the probability distribution of a set of query variables, given a set of evidence variables.

- Belief networks can reason causally, diagnostically, in mixed mode, or intercausally. No other uncertain reasoning mechanism can handle all these modes.

- The complexity of belief network inference depends on the network structure. In **polytrees** (singly connected networks), the computation time is linear in the size of the network.

- There are various inference techniques for general belief networks, all of which have exponential complexity in the worst case. In real domains, the local structure tends to make things more feasible, but care is needed to construct a tractable network with more than a hundred nodes.

- It is also possible to use approximation techniques, including **stochastic simulation**, to get an estimate of the true probabilities with less computation.

- Various alternative systems for reasoning with uncertainty have been suggested. All the **truth-functional** systems have serious problems with mixed or intercausal reasoning.

BIBLIOGRAPHICAL AND HISTORICAL NOTES

The use of networks to represent probabilistic information began early in the twentieth century, with the work of Sewall Wright on the probabilistic analysis of genetic inheritance and animal growth factors (Wright, 1921; Wright, 1934). One of his networks appears on the cover of this book. I. J. Good (1961) investigated the use of Bayesian inference in belief networks.[5] The **influence diagram** or **decision network** representation for decision problems, which incorporated a DAG representation for random variables, was used in decision analysis in the late 1970s (see Chapter 16), but no interesting evaluation algorithms were developed for decision networks until 1986 (Shachter, 1986). Judea Pearl (1982a) developed the message-passing method for carrying out inference in networks that had the form of trees. Jin Kim (Kim and Pearl, 1983) extended the method to all singly connected networks. The backward-chaining algorithm given in the text was derived by the authors, but has much in common with the methods of Pearl (1988) and of Shachter et al. (1990). Gregory Cooper (1990) showed that the general problem of inference in unconstrained belief networks is NP-hard, and Paul Dagum and Mike Luby (1993) showed the corresponding approximation problem to be NP-hard.

David Spiegelhalter and Steffen Lauritzen pioneered the use of clustering for inference in multiply connected networks (Spiegelhalter, 1986; Lauritzen and Spiegelhalter, 1988). Finn Jensen and colleagues (1990) developed an object-oriented computational scheme for clustering. The scheme is implemented in the HUGIN system, an efficient and widely used tool for uncertain reasoning (Andersen et al., 1989). Eric Horvitz, H. Jacques Suermondt, and Gregory Cooper (1989) developed bounded cutset conditioning, building on earlier work on cutsets (Pearl, 1986). The logic sampling method is due to Max Henrion (1988), and likelihood weighting was developed by Fung and Chang (1989) and Shachter and Peot (1989). A large-scale application of likelihood weighting to medical diagnosis appears in Shwe and Cooper (1991). The latter paper also incorporates elements of the "Markov blanket" simulation scheme developed by Pearl (1987). The first expert system using belief networks was CONVINCE (Kim, 1983; Kim and Pearl, 1987). More recent systems include the MUNIN system for diagnosing neuromuscular disorders (Andersen et al., 1989) and the PATHFINDER system for pathology (Heckerman, 1991).

The extension of belief networks to handle continuous random variables is an important topic of current research. The basic technical problem is that the distributions must be representable by a finite number of parameters, and must come from a family of distributions that is closed under belief net updating. To date, only Gaussian distributions have been used. Networks with continuous variables but no discrete variables have been considered (Pearl, 1988; Shachter and Kenley, 1989). Such networks can be evaluated in polynomial time, regardless of topology. The inclusion of discrete variables has been investigated by Lauritzen and Wermuth (1989), and implemented in the cHUGIN system (Olesen, 1993). Currently, exact algorithms are known only for the case in which discrete variables are ancestors, not descendants, of continuous variables. Stochastic simulation algorithms, on the other hand, can handle arbitrary distributions and topologies.

QUALITATIVE
PROBABILISTIC
NETWORKS

Qualitative probabilistic networks (Wellman, 1990) provide a purely qualitative abstraction of belief networks, using the notion of positive and negative influences between variables. Wellman shows that in many cases such information is sufficient for optimal decision making without the need for precise specification of probability values. Work by Adnan Darwiche and Matt Ginsberg (1992) extracts the basic properties of conditioning and evidence combination from probability theory and shows that they can also be applied in logical and default reasoning.

---

5   I. J. Good was chief statistician for Turing's codebreaking team in World II. In *2001: A Space Odyssey*, Arthur C. Clarke credited Good and Minsky with making the breakthrough that led to the development of the HAL computer.

The literature on default and nonmonotonic reasoning is very large. Early work is collected in *Readings in Nonmonotonic Reasoning* (Ginsberg, 1987). Shoham (1988) discusses the nonmonotonic nature of reasoning about time and change, and proposes a semantics based on general preferences between possible models of a default knowledge base. Geffner (1992) provides an excellent introduction to default reasoning, including early philosophical work on default conditionals. Some informative computational complexity results on default reasoning have been derived by Kautz and Selman (1991). Bain and Muggleton (1991) provide methods for learning default rules, suggesting a role for them as compact representations of data containing regularities with exceptions. **Autoepistemic logic** (Moore, 1985b) attempts to explain nonmonotonicity as arising from the agent's reflection on its own states of knowledge. A comprehensive retrospective and summary of work in this area is given by Moore (1993).

Applications of nonmonotonic reasoning have been largely limited to improving the theoretical underpinnings of logic programming. The use of negation as failure in Prolog can be viewed as source of nonmonotonicity because adding new facts will rule out some potential derivations (Clark, 1978). An important subclass of the so-called default theories in the default logic of (Reiter, 1980) can be shown to be equivalent to logic programs in a language in which both negation as failure and classical logical negation are available (Gelfond and Lifschitz, 1991). The same is true of circumscriptive theories (Gelfond and Lifschitz, 1988). Autoepistemic logic can, in turn, be closely imitated by circumscription (Lifschitz, 1989).

Certainty factors were invented for use in the medical expert system MYCIN (Shortliffe, 1976), which was intended both as an engineering solution and as a model of human judgment under uncertainty. The collection *Rule-Based Expert Systems* (Buchanan and Shortliffe, 1984) provides a complete overview of MYCIN and its descendants. David Heckerman (1986) showed that a slightly modified version of certainty factors can be analyzed as a disguised form of reasoning with standard probability theory. The PROSPECTOR expert system (Duda *et al.*, 1979) used a rule-based approach in which the rules were justified by a global independence assumption. More recently, Bryan Todd has shown that a rule-based system can perform correct Bayesian inference, provided that the structure of the rule set exactly reflects a set of conditional independence statements that is equivalent to the topology of a belief network (Todd *et al.*, 1993).

Dempster–Shafer theory originates with a paper by Arthur Dempster (1968) proposing a generalization of probability to interval values, and a combination rule for using them. Later work by Glenn Shafer (1976) led to the Dempster-Shafer theory being viewed as a competing approach to probability. Ruspini *et al.* (1992) analyze the relationship between the Dempster-Shafer theory and standard probability theory from an AI standpoint. Shenoy (1989) has proposed a method for decision making with Dempster–Shafer belief functions.

Fuzzy sets were developed by Lotfi Zadeh (1965) in response to the perceived difficulty of providing exact inputs for intelligent systems. The text by Zimmermann (1991) provides a thorough introduction to fuzzy set theory. As we mentioned in the text, fuzzy logic has often been perceived incorrectly as a direct competitor to probability theory whereas in fact it addresses POSSIBILITY THEORY a different set of issues. **Possibility theory** (Zadeh, 1978) was introduced to handle uncertainty in fuzzy systems, and has much in common with probability. Dubois and Prade (1994) provide a thorough survey of the connections between possibility theory and probability theory. An interesting interview/debate with Lotfi Zadeh (the founder of fuzzy logic) and William Kahan (the Turing award winner) appears in Woehr (1994).

The three approaches to quantitative reasoning about uncertainty just surveyed—fuzzy logic, certainty factors, and Dempster–Shafer theory—were the three main alternatives to which AI researchers resorted after early probabilistic systems fell out of favor in the early 1970s, as described in Chapter 14. The later development of nonmonotonic logics in the early 1980s was also, in part, a response to the need for an effective method for handling uncertainty. The resurgence of probability depended mainly on the discovery of belief networks as a method for representing and using conditional independence information. This resurgence did not come without a fight—probabilistic methods were attacked both by logicists, who believed that numerical approaches to AI were both unnecessary and introspectively implausible, and by supporters of the other quantitative approaches to uncertainty. Peter Cheeseman's (1985) pugnacious "In Defense of Probability," and his later article "An Inquiry into Computer Understanding" (Cheeseman, 1988, with commentaries) give something of the flavor of the debate.

It is fair to say that certainty factors are now of historical interest only (for reasons noted above), and although fuzzy logic is a healthy, ongoing enterprise, it is increasingly perceived as a way of handling continuous-valued variables rather than uncertainty. Nonmonotonic logics continue to be of interest as a purely qualitative mechanism, although there is a good deal of work aimed at showing how nonmonotonic inference is best viewed as a special case of probabilistic reasoning with probabilities close to 0 or 1 (Goldszmidt *et al.*, 1990). Dempster–Shafer theory is still perceived by its supporters as a viable alternative to Bayesian systems. Nonprobabilists continue to be irritated by the dogmatic "Bayesianity" of the probabilists.

Probabilistic Reasoning in Intelligent Systems: Networks of Plausible Inference (Pearl, 1988) is a comprehensive textbook and reference on belief networks, by one of the major contributors to the field. *Probabilistic Reasoning in Expert Systems: Theory and Algorithms* (Neapolitan, 1990) gives a relatively readable introduction to belief networks from the standpoint of their use in expert systems. *Readings in Uncertain Reasoning* (Shafer and Pearl, 1990) is a voluminous collection of important papers about probability, belief networks, and other formalisms for reasoning about uncertainty, and their applications in AI. *Uncertainty in Artificial Intelligence* (Kanal and Lemmer, 1986) is an anthology containing a number of important early papers about belief networks and other matters having to do with reasoning under uncertainty. Although this volume is not numbered, a series of numbered anthologies with the same title have also been published. New research on probabilistic reasoning appears both in mainstream AI journals such as *Artificial Intelligence* and in more specialized journals such as the *International Journal of Approximate Reasoning*. The proceedings of the Conferences on Uncertainty in Artificial Intelligence (known as UAI) are an excellent source for current research.

EXERCISES

15.1   Consider the problem of dealing with a car that will not start, as diagrammed in Figure 15.5.

  a. Extend the network with the Boolean variables *IcyWeather* and *StarterMotorWorking*.

  b. Give reasonable conditional probability tables for all the nodes.

   c. How many independent values are contained in the joint probability distribution for eight
      Boolean nodes, assuming no conditional independence relations hold among them?

   d. How many independent probability values do your network tables contain?

   e. The conditional probability table for *Starts* is a canonical one. Describe, in English, what
      its structure will be in general, as more possible causes for not starting are added.

15.2   In your local nuclear power station, there is an alarm that senses when a temperature
gauge exceeds a given threshold. The gauge measures the core temperature. Consider the
Boolean variables A (alarm sounds), F_A (alarm is faulty), and F_G (gauge is faulty), and the
multivalued nodes G (gauge reading) and T (actual core temperature).

   a. Draw a belief net for this domain, given that the gauge is more likely to fail when the core
      temperature gets too high.

   b. Is your network a polytree?

   c. Suppose there are just two possible actual and measured temperatures, Normal and High;
      and that the gauge gives the incorrect temperature $x\%$ of the time when it is working, but
      $y\%$ of the time when it is faulty. Give the conditional probability table associated with G.

   d. Suppose the alarm works unless it is faulty, in which case it never goes off. Give the
      conditional probability table associated with A.

   e. Suppose the alarm and gauge are working, and the alarm sounds. Calculate the probability
      that the core temperature is too high.

   f. In a given time period, the probability that the temperature exceeds threshold is p. The cost
      of shutting down the reactor is c_s; the cost of not shutting it down when the temperature is
      in fact too high is c_m (m is for meltdown). Assuming the gauge and alarm to be working
      normally, calculate the maximum value for x for which the gauge is of any use (i.e., if x is
      any higher than this, we have to shut down the reactor all the time).

   g. Suppose we add a second temperature gauge H, connected so that the alarm goes off when
      either gauge reads High. Where do H and F_H (the event of H failing) go in the network?

   h. Are there circumstances under which adding a second gauge would mean that we would
      need *more* accurate (i.e., more likely to give the correct temperature) gauges? Why (not)?

15.3   Two astronomers, in different parts of the world, make measurements M_1 and M_2 of the
number of stars N in some small region of the sky, using their telescopes. Normally, there is
a small possibility of error by up to one star. Each telescope can also (with a slightly smaller
probability) be badly out of focus (events F_1 and F_2), in which case the scientist will undercount
by three or more stars. Consider the three networks shown in Figure 15.12.

   a. Which of these belief networks correctly (but not necessarily efficiently) represent the
      above information?

   b. Which is the best network?

   c. Give a reasonable conditional probability table for the values of $\mathbf{P}(M_1|N)$. (For simplicity,
      consider only the possible values 1, 2, and 3 in this part.)

   d. Suppose $M_1 = 1$ and $M_3 = 3$. What are the possible numbers of stars?

   e. Of these, which is the most likely number?

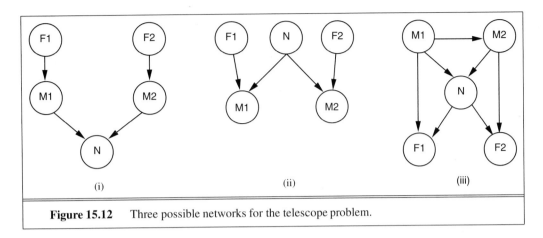

Figure 15.12   Three possible networks for the telescope problem.

15.4   You are an AI consultant for a credit card company, and your task is to construct a belief net that will allow the company to determine whether or not to grant a person a card.

a. What are the evidence variables?   These are the variables for which you can obtain information, on the basis of which it is legal to make decisions, and that are relevant to the decision. Thus, *Age* might be one of your variables, but *VotingRecord* and *HairColor* would not.

b. What is the output variable (i.e., what proposition is the company going to examine the probabilities of in order to determine whether to grant a card)? This should not be *Decision* with values *yes* and *no* because the company has control over the value of this variable.

c. Construct your network by incrementally adding variables in causal order, as described in the chapter. You may wish to add intermediate nodes such as *Reliability* and *FutureIncome*. (Remember that the company cares about what will happen in the future, not about the past *per se*.) Set the conditional probabilities for each node. Write commentary to describe your reasoning in choosing your variables and links. If you find that a node has too many predecessors (so that the conditional probability table becomes too big), that is a good hint that you need some intermediate variables.

d. Build a file of test data corresponding to your evidence variables. As far as possible these should be real people! Do some interviewing to get real data if you can; try to get a wide variety of cases, from deadbeats to trust-fund babies. Run the data through your network to see if the net's results correspond to your own judgements. Examine not only the output variable, but the value of other intermediate variables. You may need to go through several iterations of steps (c) and (d).

e. Write a report showing various test cases and explaining the advantages of your approach. Your report should be enough to convince the company to adopt your product.

15.5   You are an AI consultant for an auto insurance company. Your task is construct a belief network that will allow the company to decide how much financial risk they run from various policy holders, given certain data about the policy holders. (In case you think all class projects are just toys to amuse sadistic instructors, bear in mind that a 1% improvement in risk assessment is worth well over a billion dollars a year.)

In order to design a belief network, you need *output variables* and *evidence variables*. The output variables are those for which the insurance company is trying to get a probability distribution for their possible values. The evidence variables are those variables for which you can obtain information, on the basis of which it is legal to make decisions, and that are relevant to the decision.

Output variables represent the costs of various catastrophic events that the insurance company might have to reimburse. (We do not consider the ways in which the company tries to avoid payment.) In the automobile insurance domain, the major output variables are medical cost (*MedCost*), property cost (*PropCost*), and intangible liability cost (*ILiCost*). Medical and property costs are those incurred by *all* individuals involved in an accident; auto theft or vandalism might also incur property costs. Intangible liability costs are legal penalties for things like "pain and suffering," punitive damages, and so forth, that a driver might incur in an accident in which he or she is at fault.

Evidence variables for this domain include the driver's age and record; whether or not he or she owns another car; how far he or she drives per year; the vehicle's make, model and year; whether it has safety equipment such as an airbag and antilock brakes; where it is garaged and whether it has an antitheft device.

Build a network for this problem. You will need to decide on suitable domains for the variables, bearing in mind the need to discretize (unless you plan to use a stochastic simulation algorithm). You will also need to add intermediate nodes such as *DrivingSkill* and *AutoRuggedness*. Write commentary to describe your reasoning in choosing your domains, variables, links, and inference algorithm. If you find that a node has too many predecessors (so that the conditional probability table becomes too big), that is a good hint that you need some intermediate variables. Generate a few reasonable-looking test cases to get a feeling for what your network does with them. How would you convince the insurance company to adopt your product?

 15.6 Is probabilistic reasoning monotonic or nonmonotonic? Do these concepts even apply to probabilities?

16 MAKING SIMPLE DECISIONS

In which we see how an agent should make decisions so that it gets what it wants—on average, at least.

In this chapter, we return to the idea of utility theory that was introduced in Chapter 14 and show how it is combined with probability theory to yield a decision-theoretic agent—one that can make rational decisions based on what it believes and what it wants. Such an agent can make decisions in contexts where uncertainty and conflicting goals leave a logical agent with no way to decide.

Section 16.1 introduces the basic principle of decision theory: the maximization of expected utility. Section 16.2 shows that the behavior of any rational agent can be captured by supposing a utility function that is being maximized. Section 16.3 discusses the nature of utility functions in more detail, and in particular their relation to individual quantities such as money. Section 16.4 shows how to handle utility functions that depend on several quantities. In Section 16.5, we describe the implementation of decision-making systems. In particular, we introduce a formalism called **decision networks** (also known as **influence diagrams**) that extends belief networks by incorporating actions and utilities. The remainder of the chapter discusses issues that arise in applications of decision theory to expert systems.

16.1 COMBINING BELIEFS AND DESIRES UNDER UNCERTAINTY

In the *Port-Royal Logic*, written in 1662, the French philosopher Arnauld stated that

> To judge what one must do to obtain a good or avoid an evil, it is necessary to consider not only the good and the evil in itself, but also the probability that it happens or does not happen; and to view geometrically the proportion that all these things have together.

These days, it is more common in scientific texts to talk of utility rather than good and evil, but the principle is exactly the same. An agent's preferences between world states are captured by a **utility function**, which assigns a single number to express the desirability of a state. Utilities are combined with the outcome probabilities for actions to give an expected utility for each action.

We will use the notation $U(S)$ to denote the utility of state S according to the agent that is making the decisions. For now, we will consider states as complete snapshots of the world, similar to the **situations** of Chapter 7. This will simplify our initial discussions, but it can become rather cumbersome to specify the utility of each possible state separately. In Section 16.4, we will see how states can be decomposed under some circumstances for the purpose of utility assignment.

A nondeterministic action A will have possible outcome states $Result_i(A)$, where the index i ranges over the different outcomes. Prior to the execution of A, the agent assigns probability $P(Result_i(A)|Do(A), E)$ to each outcome, where E summarizes the agent's available evidence about the world, and $Do(A)$ is the proposition that action A is executed in the current state. Then we can calculate the **expected utility** of the action given the evidence, $EU(A|E)$, using the following formula:

EXPECTED UTILITY

$$EU(A|E) = \sum_i P(Result_i(A)|E, Do(A))\, U(Result_i(A)) \qquad (16.1)$$

MAXIMUM EXPECTED UTILITY

The principle of **maximum expected utility** (MEU) says that a rational agent should choose an action that maximizes the agent's expected utility.

In a sense, the MEU principle could be seen as defining all of AI.[1] All an intelligent agent has to do is calculate the various quantities, maximize over its actions, and away it goes. But this does not mean that the AI problem is *solved* by the definition!

Although the MEU principle defines the right action to take in any decision problem, the computations involved can be prohibitive, and sometimes it is difficult even to formulate the problem completely. Knowing the initial state of the world requires perception, learning, knowledge representation, and inference. Computing $P(Result_i(A)|Do(A), E)$ requires a complete causal model of the world and, as we saw in Chapter 15, NP-complete updating of belief nets. Computing the utility of each state, $U(Result_i(A))$, often requires search or planning, because an agent does not know how good a state is until it knows where it can get to from that state. So, decision theory is not a panacea that solves the AI problem. But it does provide a framework in which we can see where all the components of an AI system fit in.

The MEU principle has a clear relation to the idea of performance measures introduced in Chapter 2. The basic idea is very simple. Consider the possible environments that could lead to an agent having a given percept history, and consider the different possible agents that we could design. *If an agent maximizes a utility function that correctly reflects the performance measure by which its behavior is being judged, then it will achieve the highest possible performance score, if we average over the possible environments in which the agent could be placed.* This is the central justification for the MEU principle itself.

ONE-SHOT DECISIONS

In this chapter, we will only be concerned with single or **one-shot decisions**, whereas Chapter 2 defined performance measures over environment histories, which usually involve many decisions. In the next chapter, which covers the case of **sequential decisions**, we will show how these two views can be reconciled.

---

[1]   Actually, it is not quite true that AI is, even in principle, a field that attempts to build agents that maximize their expected utility. We believe, however, that understanding such agents is a good place to start. This is a difficult methodological question, to which we return in Chapter 27.

16.2   THE BASIS OF UTILITY THEORY

Intuitively, the principle of Maximum Expected Utility (MEU) seems like a reasonable way to make decisions, but it is by no means obvious that it is the *only* rational way. After all, why should maximizing the *average* utility be so special—why not try to maximize the sum of the cubes of the possible utilities, or try to minimize the worst possible loss? Also, couldn't an agent act rationally just by expressing preferences between states without giving them numeric values? Finally, why should a utility function with the required properties exist at all? Perhaps a rational agent can have a preference structure that is too complex to be captured by something as simple as a single real number for each state.

Constraints on rational preferences

These questions can be answered by writing down some constraints on the preferences that a rational agent should have, and then showing that the MEU principle can be derived from the constraints. Writing down these constraints is a way of defining the semantics of preferences. The idea is that, given some preferences on individual atomic states, the theory should allow one to derive results about preferences for complex decision-making scenarios. This is analogous to the way that the truth value of a complex logical sentence is derived from the truth value of its component propositions, and the way the probability of a complex event is derived from the probability of atomic events.

LOTTERIES   In the language of utility theory, the complex scenarios are called **lotteries** to emphasize the idea that the different attainable outcomes are like different prizes, and that the outcome is determined by chance. The lottery L, in which there are two possible outcomes—state A with probability p and state B with the remaining probability—is written

$$L = [p, A; \ 1 - p, B]$$

In general, a lottery can have any number of outcomes. Each outcome can be either an atomic state or another lottery. A lottery with only one outcome can be written either as A or $[1, A]$. It is the decision-maker's job to choose among lotteries. Preferences between prizes are used to determine preferences between lotteries. The following notation is used to express preferences or the lack of a preference between lotteries or states:

$A \succ B$ A is preferred to B

$A \sim B$ the agent is indifferent between A and B

$A \succsim B$ the agent prefers A to B or is indifferent between them

Now we impose reasonable constraints on the preference relation, much as we imposed rationality constraints on degrees of belief in order to obtain the axioms of probability in Chapter 14. One reasonable constraint is that preference should be **transitive**, that is, if $A \succ B$ and $B \succ C$, then we would expect $A \succ C$. We argue for transitivity by showing that an agent whose preferences do not respect transitivity would behave irrationally. Suppose, for example, that an agent has the nontransitive preferences $A \succ B \succ C \succ A$, where A, B, and C are goods that can be freely exchanged. If the agent currently has A, then we could offer to trade C for A and some cash. The agent prefers C, and so would be willing to give up some amount of cash to make this trade. We could then offer to trade B for C, extracting more cash, and finally trade A for B. This brings us back where we started from, except that the agent has less money. It seems reasonable to claim that in this case the agent has not acted rationally.

The following six constraints are known as the axioms of utility theory. They specify the most obvious semantic constraints on preferences and lotteries.

ORDERABILITY

◇ **Orderability**: Given any two states, a rational agent must either prefer one to the other or else rate the two as equally preferable. That is, an agent should know what it wants.

$$(A \succ B) \vee (B \succ A) \vee (A \sim B)$$

TRANSITIVITY

◇ **Transitivity**: Given any three states, if an agent prefers A to B and prefers B to C, then the agent must prefer A to C.

$$(A \succ B) \wedge (B \succ C) \Rightarrow (A \succ C)$$

CONTINUITY

◇ **Continuity**: If some state B is between A and C in preference, then there is some probability p for which the rational agent will be indifferent between getting B for sure and the lottery that yields A with probability p and C with probability $1 - p$.

$$A \succ B \succ C \Rightarrow \exists p \ [p, A; \ 1 - p, C] \sim B$$

SUBSTITUTABILITY

◇ **Substitutability**: If an agent is indifferent between two lotteries, A and B, then the agent is indifferent between two more complex lotteries that are the same except that B is substituted for A in one of them. This holds regardless of the probabilities and the other outcome(s) in the lotteries.

$$A \sim B \ \Rightarrow \ [p, A; \ 1 - p, C] \sim [p, B; 1 - p, C]$$

MONOTONICITY

◇ **Monotonicity**: Suppose there are two lotteries that have the same two outcomes, A and B. If an agent prefers A to B, then the agent must prefer the lottery that has a higher probability for A (and vice versa).

$$A \succ B \ \Rightarrow \ (p \geq q \ \Leftrightarrow \ [p, A; \ 1 - p, B] \succsim [q, A; \ 1 - q, B])$$

DECOMPOSABILITY

◇ **Decomposability**: Compound lotteries can be reduced to simpler ones using the laws of probability. This has been called the "no fun in gambling" rule because it says that an agent should not prefer (or disprefer) one lottery just because it has more choice points than another.[2]

$$[p, A; \ 1 - p, [q, B; \ 1 - q, C]] \sim [p, A; \ (1 - p)q, B; \ (1 - p)(1 - q), C]$$

... and then there was Utility

Notice that the axioms of utility theory do not say anything about utility. They only talk about preferences. Preference is assumed to be a basic property of rational agents. The existence of a utility function *follows* from the axioms of utility:

---

[2] It is still possible to account for an agent who enjoys gambling by reifying the act of gambling itself: just include in the appropriate outcome states the proposition "participated in a gamble," and base utilities in part on that proposition.

1. **Utility principle**

   If an agent's preferences obey the axioms of utility, then there exists a real-valued function U that operates on states such that $U(A) > U(B)$ if and only if A is preferred to B, and $U(A) = U(B)$ if and only if the agent is indifferent between A and B.

   $$U(A) > U(B) \iff A \succ B$$
   $$U(A) = U(B) \iff A \sim B$$

2. **Maximum Expected Utility principle**

   The utility of a lottery is the sum of the probabilities of each outcome times the utility of that outcome.

   $$U([p_1, S_1; \ldots; p_n, S_n]) = \sum_i p_i U(S_i)$$

In other words, once the probabilities and utilities of the possible outcome states are specified, the utility of a compound lottery involving these states can be computed. $U([p_1, S_1; p_2, S_2; \ldots])$ is completely determined by $U(S_i)$ and the probability values.

It is important to remember that the existence of a utility function that describes an agent's preference behavior does not necessarily mean that the agent is *explicitly* maximizing that utility function in its own deliberations. As we showed in Chapter 2, rational behavior can be generated in any number of ways, some of which are more efficient than explicit utility maximization. By observing an agent's preferences, however, it is possible to construct the utility function that represents what it is that the agent's actions are trying to achieve.

16.3   UTILITY FUNCTIONS

Utility is a function that maps from states to real numbers. Is that all we can say about utility functions? Strictly speaking, that is it. Beyond the constraints listed earlier, an agent can have any preferences it likes. For example, an agent might prefer to have a prime number of dollars in its bank account; in which case, if it had $16 it would give away $3. It might prefer a dented 1973 Ford Pinto to a shiny new Mercedes. Preferences can also interact: for example, it might only prefer prime numbers of dollars when it owns the Pinto, but when it owns the Mercedes, it might prefer more dollars to less.

If all utility functions were as arbitrary as this, however, then utility theory would not be of much help because we would have to observe the agent's preferences in every possible combination of circumstances before being able to make any predictions about its behavior. Fortunately, the preferences of real agents are usually more systematic. Conversely, there are systematic ways of designing utility functions that, when installed in an artificial agent, cause it to generate the kinds of behavior we want.

The utility of money

Utility theory has its roots in economics, and economics provides one obvious candidate for a utility measure: money (or more specifically, an agent's total net assets). The almost universal exchangeability of money for all kinds of goods and services suggests that money plays a significant role in human utility functions.[3]

MONOTONIC
PREFERENCE

VALUE FUNCTION

ORDINAL UTILITY

If we restrict our attention to actions that only affect the amount of money that an agent has, then it will usually be the case that the agent prefers more money to less, all other things being equal. We say that the agent exhibits a **monotonic preference** for money. This is not, however, sufficient to guarantee that money behaves as a utility function. Technically speaking, money behaves as a **value function** or **ordinal utility** measure, meaning just that the agent prefers to have more rather than less when considering *definite amounts*. To understand monetary decision making under uncertainty, we also need to examine the agent's preferences between lotteries involving money.

Suppose you have triumphed over the other competitors in a television game show. The host now offers you a choice: you can either take the $1,000,000 prize or you can gamble it on the flip of a coin. If the coin comes up heads, you end up with nothing, but if it comes up tails, you get $3,000,000. If you're like most people, you would decline the gamble and pocket the million. Are you being irrational?

EXPECTED
MONETARY VALUE

Assuming you believe that the coin is fair, the **expected monetary value** (EMV) of the gamble is $\frac{1}{2}(\$0) + \frac{1}{2}(\$3{,}000{,}000) = \$1{,}500{,}000$, and the EMV of taking the original prize is of course $1,000,000, which is less. But that does not necessarily mean that accepting the gamble is a better decision. Suppose we use S_n to denote the state of possessing total wealth $n, and that your current wealth is $k. Then the expected utilities of the two actions of accepting and declining the gamble are

$$EU(Accept) \;=\; \tfrac{1}{2}U(S_k) + \tfrac{1}{2}U(S_{k+3{,}000{,}000})$$
$$EU(Decline) \;=\; U(S_{k+1{,}000{,}000})$$

To determine what to do, we need to assign utilities to the outcome states. Utility is not directly proportional to monetary value because the utility—the positive change in lifestyle—for your first million is very high (or so we are told), whereas the utility for additional millions is much smaller. Suppose you assign a utility of 5 to your current financial status (S_k), a 10 to the state $S_{k+3{,}000{,}000}$, and an 8 to the state $S_{k+1{,}000{,}000}$. Then the rational action would be to decline, because the expected utility of accepting is only 7.5 (less than the 8 for declining). On the other hand, suppose that you happen to have $500,000,000 in the bank already (and appear on game shows just for fun, one assumes). In this case, the gamble is probably acceptable, provided that you prefer more money to less, because the additional benefit of the 503rd million is probably about the same as that of the 501st million.

In 1738, long before television game shows, Bernoulli came up with an even more compelling example, known as the St. Petersburg paradox. Suppose you are offered a chance to play a game in which a fair coin is tossed repeatedly until it comes up heads. If the first heads appears on the nth toss, you win 2^n dollars. How much would you pay for a chance to play this game?

---

[3]   This despite the assurances of a well-known song to the effect that the best things in life are free.

The probability of the first head showing up on the nth toss is $1/2^n$, so the expected monetary value (EMV) of this game is

$$EMV(St.P.) = \sum_i P(Heads_i)MV(Heads_i) = \sum_i \frac{1}{2^i}2^i = \frac{2}{2} + \frac{4}{4} + \frac{8}{8} + \cdots = \infty$$

Thus, an agent who is trying to maximize its expected monetary gain should be willing to pay *any* finite sum for a chance to play this game. Somehow this does not seem rational to most people. Bernoulli resolved the alleged paradox by positing that the utility of money is measured on a logarithmic scale (at least for positive amounts):

$$U(S_{k+n}) = \log_2 n \qquad \text{(for } n > 0)$$

With this utility function, the expected utility of the game is 2:

$$EU(St.P.) = \sum_i P(Heads_i)U(Heads_i) = \sum_i \frac{1}{2^i}\log_2 2^i = \frac{1}{2} + \frac{2}{4} + \frac{3}{8} + \cdots = 2$$

which means that a rational agent with the given utility scale should be willing to pay up to \$4 for a chance to play the game, because $U(S_{k+4}) = \log_2 4 = 2$.

Bernoulli chose $\log_2$ as the utility function just to make this problem work out. However, in a pioneering study of actual utility functions, Grayson (1960) found an almost perfect fit to the logarithmic form. One particular curve, for a certain Mr. Beard, is shown in Figure 16.1(a). The data obtained for Mr. Beard's preferences are consistent with a utility function

$$U(S_{k+n}) = -263.31 + 22.09\log(n + 150,000)$$

for the range between $n = -\$150,000$ and $n = \$800,000$.

We should not assume that this is the definitive utility function for monetary value, but it is likely that most people have a utility function that is concave for positive wealth. Going into debt is usually considered disastrous, but preferences between different levels of debt can display a reversal of the concavity associated with positive wealth. For example, someone already

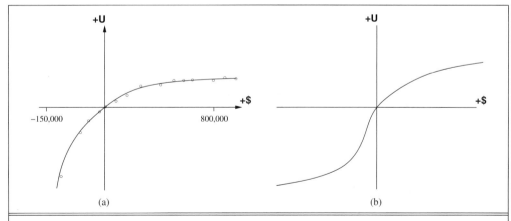

Figure 16.1   The utility of money. (a) Empirical data for Mr. Beard over a limited range. (b) A typical curve for the full range.

$10,000,000 in debt might well accept a gamble on a fair coin with a gain of $10,000,000 for heads and a loss of $20,000,000 for tails.[4] This yields the S-shaped curve shown in Figure 16.1(b).

If we restrict our attention to the positive part of the curves, where the slope is decreasing, then for any lottery L, the utility of being faced with that lottery is less than the utility of being handed the expected monetary value of the lottery as a sure thing:

$$U(S_L) < U(S_{EMV(L)})$$

RISK-AVERSE

RISK-SEEKING
CERTAINTY
EQUIVALENT

INSURANCE
PREMIUM

That is, agents with curves of this shape are **risk-averse**: they prefer a sure thing with a payoff that is less than the expected monetary value of a gamble. On the other hand, in the "desperate" region at large negative wealth in Figure 16.1(b), the behavior is **risk-seeking**. The value an agent will accept in lieu of a lottery is called the **certainty equivalent** of the lottery. Studies have shown that most people will accept about $400 in lieu of a gamble that gives $1000 half the time and $0 the other half—that is, the certainty equivalent of the lottery is $400. The difference between the expected monetary value of a lottery and its certainty equivalent is called the **insurance premium**. Risk aversion is the basis for the insurance industry, because it means that insurance premiums are positive. People would rather pay a small insurance premium than gamble with the price of their house against the possibility of a fire. From the insurance company's point of view, the risk is very low because the law of large numbers makes it almost certain that the claims it pays will be substantially less than the premiums it receives.

RISK-NEUTRAL

Notice that for *small* changes in wealth relative to the current wealth, almost any curve will be approximately linear. An agent that has a linear curve is said to be **risk-neutral**. For gambles with small sums, therefore, we expect risk neutrality. In a sense, this justifies the simplified procedure that proposed small gambles to assess probabilities and to justify the axioms of probability in Chapter 14.

Utility scales and utility assessment

The axioms of utility do not specify a unique utility function for an agent, given its preference behavior. It is simple to see that an agent using a utility function

$$U'(S) = k_1 + k_2 U(S),$$

where k_1 is a constant and k_2 is any *positive* constant, will behave identically to an agent using $U(S)$, provided they have the same beliefs.[5] The scale of utilities is therefore somewhat arbitrary.

NORMALIZED
UTILITIES

STANDARD LOTTERY

One common procedure for assessing utilities is to establish a scale with a "best possible prize" at $U(S) = u_\top$ and a "worst possible catastrophe" at $U(S) = u_\perp$. **Normalized utilities** use a scale with $u_\perp = 0$ and $u_\top = 1$. Utilities of intermediate outcomes are assessed by asking the agent to indicate a preference between the given outcome state S and a **standard lottery** $[p, u_\top; (1 - p), u_\perp]$. The probability p is adjusted until the agent is indifferent between S and the standard lottery. Assuming normalized utilities, the utility of S is given by p.

In medical, transportation, and environmental decision problems, among others, people's lives are at stake. In such cases, $u_\perp$ is the value assigned to immediate death (or perhaps many

---

[4]   Such behavior might be called desperate, but it is nonetheless perfectly rational if one is already in a desperate situation.

[5]   In Chapter 5, we saw that move choice in *deterministic* games is unchanged by any monotonic transformation of the evaluation function, but in backgammon, where positions are lotteries, only linear transformations preserve move choice.

HUMAN JUDGMENT AND FALLIBILITY

Decision theory is a **normative** theory: it describes how a rational agent *should* act. The application of economic theory would be greatly enhanced if it were also a **descriptive** theory of actual human decision making. However, there is experimental evidence indicating that people systematically violate the axioms of utility theory. An example is given by the psychologists Tversky and Kahneman (1982), based on an example by the economist Allais (1953). Subjects in this experiment are given a choice between lotteries A and B, and then between C and D:

A :   80% chance of $4000 C : 20% chance of $4000
B : 100% chance of $3000 D : 25% chance of $3000

The majority of subjects choose B over A and C over D. But if we assign $U(\$0) = 0$, then the first of these choices implies that $0.8U(\$4000) < U(\$3000)$, whereas the second choice implies exactly the reverse. In other words, there seems to be no utility function that is consistent with these choices. One possible conclusion is that humans are simply irrational by the standards of our utility axioms. An alternative view is that the analysis does not take into account **regret**—the feeling that humans know they would experience if they gave up a certain reward (B) for an 80% chance at a higher reward, and then lost. In other words, if A is chosen, there is a 20% chance of getting no money and feeling like a complete idiot.

Kahneman and Tversky go on to develop a descriptive theory that explains how people are risk-averse with high-probability events, but are willing to take more risks with unlikely payoffs. The connection between this finding and AI is that the choices our agents can make are only as good as the preferences they are based on. If our human informants insist on contradictory preference judgments, there is nothing our agent can do to be consistent with them.

Fortunately, preference judgments made by humans are often open to revision in the light of further consideration. In early work at Harvard Business School on assessing the utility of money, Keeney and Raiffa (1976, p. 210) found the following:

> A great deal of empirical investigation has shown that there is a serious deficiency in the assessment protocol. Subjects tend to be too risk-averse in the small and therefore ... the fitted utility functions exhibit unacceptably large risk premiums for lotteries with a large spread. ... Most of the subjects, however, can reconcile their inconsistencies and feel that they have learned an important lesson about how they want to behave. As a consequence, some subjects cancel their automobile collision insurance and take out more term insurance on their lives.

Even today, human (ir)rationality is the subject of intensive investigation.

deaths). *Although nobody feels comfortable with putting a value on human life, it is a fact that trade-offs are made all the time.* Aircraft are given a complete overhaul at intervals determined by trips and miles flown, rather than after every trip. Car bodies are made with relatively thin sheet metal to reduce costs, despite the decrease in accident survival rates. Leaded fuel is still widely used even though it has known health hazards. Paradoxically, a refusal to "put a monetary value on life" means that life is often *undervalued*. Ross Shachter relates an experience with a government agency that commissioned a study on removing asbestos from schools. The study assumed a particular dollar value for the life of a school-age child, and argued that the rational choice under that assumption was to remove the asbestos. The government agency, morally outraged, rejected the report out of hand. It then decided against asbestos removal.

MICROMORT

QALY

Some attempts have been made to find out the value that people place on their own lives. Two common "currencies"[6] used in medical and safety analysis are the **micromort** (a one in a million chance of death) and the **QALY**, or quality-adjusted life year (equivalent to a year in good health with no infirmities). A number of studies across a wide range of individuals have shown that a micromort is worth about $20 (1980 dollars). We have already seen that utility functions need not be linear, so this does not imply that a decision maker would kill himself for $20 million. Again, the local linearity of any utility curve means that micromort and QALY values are useful for small incremental risks and rewards, but not necessarily for large risks.

16.4 MULTIATTRIBUTE UTILITY FUNCTIONS

Decision making in the field of public policy involves both millions of dollars and life and death. For example, in deciding what levels of a carcinogenic substance to allow into the environment, policy makers must weigh the prevention of deaths against the economic hardship that might result from the elimination of certain products and processes. Siting a new airport requires consideration of the disruption caused by construction; the cost of land; the distance from centers of population; the noise of flight operations; safety issues arising from local topography and weather conditions; and so on. Problems like these, in which outcomes are characterized by two

MULTIATTRIBUTE
UTILITY THEORY

or more attributes, are handled by **multiattribute utility theory**, or MAUT.

We will call the attributes X_1, X_2, and so on; their values will be x_1, x_2, and so on; and a complete vector of attribute values will be $\mathbf{x} = \langle x_1, x_2, \ldots \rangle$. Each attribute is generally assumed to have discrete or continuous scalar values. For simplicity, we will assume that each attribute is defined in such a way that, all other things being equal, higher values of the attribute correspond to higher utilities. For example, if we choose as an attribute in the airport problem *AbsenceOfNoise*, then the greater its value, the better the solution. In some cases, it may be necessary to subdivide the range of values so that utility varies monotonically within each range.

REPRESENTATION
THEOREMS

The basic approach adopted in multiattribute utility theory is to identify regularities in the preference behavior we would expect to see, and to use what are called **representation theorems**

---

6 We use quotation marks because these measures are definitely not currencies in the standard sense of being exchangeable for goods at constant rates regardless of the current "wealth" of the agent making the exchange.

to show that an agent with a certain kind of preference structure has a utility function

$$U(x_1, \ldots, x_n) = f[f_1(x_1), \ldots, f_n(x_n)]$$

where f is, we hope, a simple function such as addition. Notice the similarity to the use of belief networks to decompose the joint probability of several random variables.

Dominance

STRICT DOMINANCE

Suppose that airport site S_1 costs less, generates less noise pollution, and is safer than site S_2. One would not hesitate to reject S_2. We say that there is **strict dominance** of S_1 over S_2. In general, if an option is of lower value on all attributes than some other option, it need not be considered further. Strict dominance is often very useful in narrowing down the field of choices to the real contenders, although it seldom yields a unique choice. Figure 16.2(a) shows a schematic diagram for the two-attribute case.

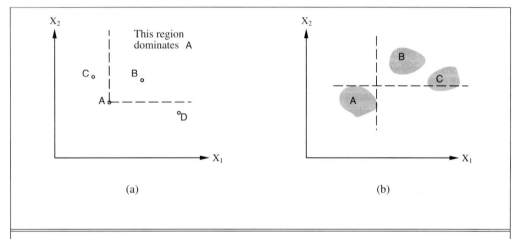

Figure 16.2   Strict dominance. (a) Deterministic: Option A is strictly dominated by B but not by C or D. (b) Uncertain: A is strictly dominated by B but not by C.

That is fine for the deterministic case, in which the attribute values are known for sure. What about the general case, where the action outcomes are uncertain? A direct analogue of strict dominance can be constructed, where, despite the uncertainty, all possible concrete outcomes for S_1 strictly dominate all possible outcomes for S_2. (See Figure 16.2(b) for a schematic depiction.) Of course, this will probably occur even less often than in the deterministic case.

STOCHASTIC DOMINANCE

Fortunately, there is a more useful generalization called **stochastic dominance**, which occurs very frequently in real problems. Stochastic dominance is easiest to understand in the context of a single attribute. Suppose that we believe the cost of siting the airport at S_1 to be normally distributed around $3.7 billion, with standard deviation $0.4 billion; and the cost at S_2 to be normally distributed around $4.0 billion, with standard deviation $0.35 billion. Figure 16.3(a) shows these distributions, with cost plotted as a negative value. Then, given only the information

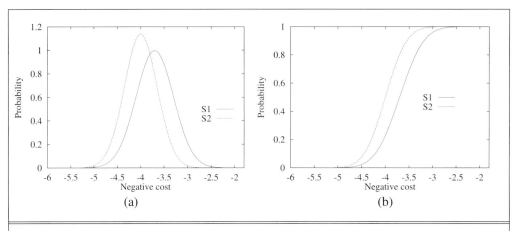

Figure 16.3   Stochastic dominance. (a) S_1 stochastically dominates S_2 on cost. (b) Cumulative distributions for the negative cost of S_1 and S_2.

that utility decreases with cost, we can say that S_1 stochastically dominates S_2—that is, S_2 can be discarded. It is important to note that this does *not* follow from comparing the expected costs. For example, if we knew the cost of S_1 to be *exactly* \$3.7 billion, then we would be *unable* to make a decision without additional information on the utility of money.[7]

The exact relationship between the attribute distributions needed to establish stochastic dominance is best seen by examining the *cumulative* distributions, shown in Figure 16.3(b). The cumulative distribution measures the probability that the cost is less than or equal to any given amount—that is, it integrates the original distribution. If the cumulative distribution for S_1 is always to the right of the cumulative distribution for S_2, then stochastically speaking S_1 is cheaper than S_2. Formally, if two actions A_1 and A_2 lead to probability distributions $p_1(x)$ and $p_2(x)$ on attribute X, then A_1 stochastically dominates A_2 on X if

$$\forall x \quad \int_{-\infty}^{x} p_1(x')\, dx' \geq \int_{-\infty}^{x} p_2(x')\, dx'$$

If an action is stochastically dominated by another action on all attributes, then it can be discarded.

The stochastic dominance condition might seem rather technical, and perhaps not so easy to determine without extensive probability calculations. In fact, it can be decided very easily in many cases. Suppose, for example, that the construction cost depends on the distance to centers of population. The cost itself is uncertain, but the greater the distance, the greater the cost. If S_1 is less remote than S_2, then S_1 will dominate S_2 on cost. Although we will not present them here, there exist algorithms for propagating this kind of qualitative information among uncertain variables in **qualitative probabilistic networks**, enabling a system to make rational decisions based on stochastic dominance without ever needing to use numerical probabilities or utilities.

---

[7] It might seem odd that *more* information on the cost of S_1 could make the agent *less* able to decide. The paradox is resolved by noting that the decision reached in the absence of exact cost information is less likely to be correct.

Preference structure and multiattribute utility

Suppose we have n attributes, each of which has m distinct possible values. This gives a set of possible outcomes of size m^n. In the worst case, the agent's utility function yields an arbitrary set of preferences over these m^n states with no regularities beyond those implied by the basic axioms of utility. Multiattribute utility theory is based on the supposition that most utility functions have much more structure than that, allowing us to use simplified decision procedures.

Preferences without uncertainty

PREFERENCE
INDEPENDENCE

Let us begin by considering the case in which there is no uncertainty in the outcomes of actions, and we are just considering preferences between concrete outcomes. In this case, the basic regularity in preference structure is called **preference independence**. Two attributes X_1 and X_2 are preferentially independent of a third attribute X_3 if the preference between outcomes $\langle x_1, x_2, x_3 \rangle$ and $\langle x_1', x_2', x_3 \rangle$ does not depend on the particular value x_3 for attribute X_3.

Going back to the airport example, where we have (among other attributes) *Noise*, *Cost*, and *Deaths* to consider, one may propose that *Noise* and *Cost* are preferentially independent of *Deaths*. For example, if we prefer a state with 20,000 people residing in the flight path and a construction cost of \$4 billion to a state with 70,000 people residing in the flight path and a cost of \$3.7 billion when the safety level is 0.06 deaths per million passenger miles in both cases, then we would have the same preference when the safety level is 0.13 or 0.01; and the same independence would hold for preferences between any other pair of values for *Noise* and *Cost*. It is also apparent that *Cost* and *Deaths* are preferentially independent of *Noise*, and that *Noise* and *Deaths* are preferentially independent of *Cost*. We say that the set of attributes $\{Noise, Cost, Deaths\}$

MUTUAL
PREFERENTIAL
INDEPENDENCE

exhibits **mutual preferential independence** (MPI). MPI says that whereas each attribute may be important, it does not affect the way in which one trades off the other attributes against each other.

Mutual preferential independence is something of a mouthful, but thanks to a remarkable theorem due to the economist Debreu (1960), we can derive from it a very simple form for the agent's value function: *If attributes $X_1, \ldots, X_n$ are mutually preferentially independent, then the agent's preference behavior can be described as maximizing the function*

$$V(S) = \sum_i V_i(X_i(S))$$

where each V_i is a value function referring only to the attribute X_i. For example, it might well be the case that the airport decision can be made using a value function

$$V(S) = -Noise \times 10^4 - Cost - Deaths \times 10^{12}$$

ADDITIVE VALUE
FUNCTION

A value function of this type is called an **additive value function**. Additive functions are an extremely natural way to describe an agent's value function, and are valid in many real-world situations. Even when MPI does not strictly hold, as might be the case at extreme values of the attributes, an additive value function can still provide a good approximation to the agent's preferences. This is especially true when the violations of MPI occur in portions of the attribute ranges that are unlikely to occur in practice.

Preferences with uncertainty

When uncertainty is present in the domain, we will also need to consider the structure of preferences between lotteries and to understand the resulting properties of utility functions, rather than just value functions. The mathematics of this problem can become quite complicated, so we will give just one of the main results to give a flavor of what can be done. The reader is referred to Keeney and Raiffa (1976) for a thorough survey of the field.

The basic notion of **utility independence** extends preference independence to cover lotteries: a set of attributes **X** is utility-independent of a set of attributes **Y** if preferences between lotteries on the attributes in **X** are independent of the particular values of the attributes in **Y**. A set

of attributes is **mutually utility-independent** (MUI) if each subset is utility-independent of the remaining attributes. Again, it seems reasonable to propose that the airport attributes are MUI.

MUI implies that the agent's behavior can be described using a **multiplicative utility**

function (Keeney, 1974). The general form of a multiplicative utility function is best seen by looking at the case for three attributes. For simplicity, we will use U_i to mean $U_i(X_i(s))$:

$$U = k_1 U_1 + k_2 U_2 + k_3 U_3 + k_1 k_2 U_1 U_2 + k_2 k_3 U_2 U_3 + k_3 k_1 U_3 U_1 + k_1 k_2 k_3 U_1 U_2 U_3$$

Although this does not look very simple, it contains three single-attribute utility functions and just three constants. In general, an n-attribute problem exhibiting MUI can be modelled using n single-attribute utilities and n constants. Each of the single-attribute utility functions can be developed independently of the other attributes, and this combination will be guaranteed to generate the correct overall preferences. Additional assumptions are required to obtain a purely additive utility function.

16.5   DECISION NETWORKS

In this section, we will look at a general mechanism for making rational decisions. The notation

is often called an **influence diagram** (Howard and Matheson, 1984), but we will use the more

descriptive term **decision network**. Decision networks combine belief networks with additional node types for actions and utilities. We will use the airport siting problem as an example.

Representing a decision problem using decision networks

In its most general form, a decision network represents information about the agent's current state, its possible actions, the state that will result from the agent's action, and the utility of that state. It therefore provides a substrate for implementing utility-based agents of the type first introduced in Section 2.3. Figure 16.4 shows a decision network for the airport siting problem. It illustrates the three types of nodes used:

◇ **Chance nodes** (ovals) represent random variables, just as they do in belief nets. The agent may be uncertain about the construction cost, the level of air traffic and the potential for litigation, as well as the *Deaths*, *Noise*, and total *Cost* variables, each of which also depends

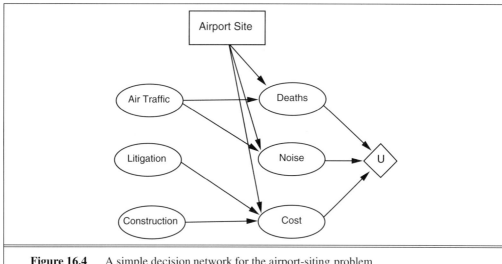

Figure 16.4   A simple decision network for the airport-siting problem.

on the site chosen. Each chance node has associated with it a conditional probability table (CPT) that is indexed by the state of the parent nodes. In decision networks, the parent nodes can include decision nodes as well as chance nodes. Note that each of the current-state chance nodes could be part of a large belief network for assessing construction costs, air traffic levels, or litigation potential. For simplicity, these are omitted.

DECISION NODES   ◇ **Decision nodes** (rectangles) represent points where the decision-maker has a choice of actions. In this case, the *AirportSite* action can take on a different value for each site under consideration. The choice influences the cost, safety, and noise that will result. In this chapter, we will assume that we are dealing with a single decision node. Chapter 17 deals with cases where more than one decision must be made.

UTILITY NODES   ◇ **Utility nodes** (diamonds) represent the agent's utility function.[8] The utility node has as parents all those variables describing the outcome state that directly affect utility. The table associated with a utility node is thus a straightforward tabulation of the agent's utility as a function of the attributes that determine it. As with canonical CPTs, multiattribute utility functions can be represented by a structured description rather than a simple tabulation.

A simplified form is also used in many cases. The notation remains identical, but the chance nodes describing the outcome state are omitted. Instead, the utility node is connected directly to the current-state nodes and the decision node. In this case, rather than representing a utility function on states, the table associated with the utility node represents the *expected* utility associated with each action, as defined in Equation (16.1). We therefore call such tables ACTION-UTILITY **action-utility tables**. Figure 16.5 shows the action-utility representation of the airport problem.
TABLES   Notice that because the *Noise*, *Deaths*, and *Cost* chance nodes in Figure 16.4 refer to future states, they can never have their values set as evidence variables. Thus, the simplified version

---

[8]   These nodes are often called **value nodes** in the literature. We prefer to maintain the distinction between utility and value functions, as discussed earlier, because the outcome state may represent a lottery.

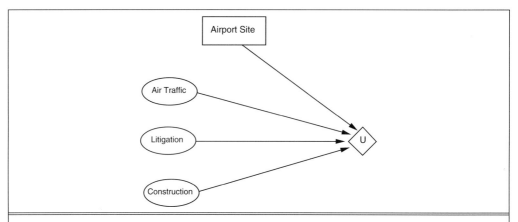

Figure 16.5   A simplified representation of the airport-siting problem. Chance nodes corresponding to outcome states have been factored out.

that omits these nodes can be used whenever the more general form can be used. Although the simplified form contains fewer nodes, the omission of an explicit description of the outcome of the siting decision means that it is less flexible with respect to changes in circumstances. For example, in Figure 16.4, a change in aircraft noise levels can be reflected by a change in the conditional probability table associated with the *Noise* node, whereas a change in the weight accorded to noise pollution in the utility function can be reflected by a change in the utility table. In the action-utility diagram, Figure 16.5, on the other hand, all such changes have to be reflected by changes to the action-utility table. Essentially, the action-utility formulation is a *compiled* version of the original formulation.

Evaluating decision networks

Actions are selected by evaluating the decision network for each possible setting of the decision node. Once the decision node is set, it behaves exactly like a chance node that has been set as an evidence variable. The algorithm for evaluating decision networks is the following:

1. Set the evidence variables for the current state.
2. For each possible value of the decision node:
   (a) Set the decision node to that value.
   (b) Calculate the posterior probabilities for the parent nodes of the utility node, using a standard probabilistic inference algorithm.
   (c) Calculate the resulting utility for the action.
3. Return the action with the highest utility.

This is a straightforward extension of the belief network algorithm, and can be incorporated directly into the agent design given in Figure 14.1. We will see in Chapter 17 that the possibility of executing several actions in sequence makes the problem much more interesting.

16.6   THE VALUE OF INFORMATION

In the preceding analysis, we have assumed that all relevant information, or at least all available information, is provided to the agent before it makes its decision. In practice, this is hardly ever the case. *One of the most important parts of decision making is knowing what questions to ask.* For example, a doctor cannot expect to be provided with the results of *all possible* diagnostic tests and questions at the time a patient first enters the consulting room.[9] Tests are often expensive and sometimes hazardous (both directly and because of associated delays). Their importance depends on two factors: whether the different possible outcomes would make a significant difference to the optimal course of action, and the likelihood of the various outcomes.

INFORMATION VALUE
THEORY

This section describes **information value theory**, which enables an agent to choose what information to acquire.   The acquisition of information is achieved by **sensing actions**, as described in Chapter 13. Because the agent's utility function seldom refers to the contents of the agent's internal state, whereas the whole purpose of sensing actions is to affect the internal state, we must evaluate sensing actions by their effect on the agent's subsequent actions. Information value theory is therefore a special kind of sequential decision making.

A simple example

Suppose an oil company is hoping to buy one of n indistinguishable blocks of ocean drilling rights. Let us assume further that exactly one of the blocks contains oil worth C dollars, and that the price of each block is C/n dollars. If the company is risk-neutral, then it will be indifferent between buying a block or not.

Now suppose that a seismologist offers the company the results of a survey of block number 3, which indicates definitively whether the block contains oil. How much should the company be willing to pay for the information? The way to answer this question is to examine what the company would do if it had the information:

- With probability $1/n$, the survey will show that block 3 contains the oil. In this case, the company will buy block 3 for C/n dollars, and make a profit of $C - C/n = (n-1)C/n$ dollars.

- With probability $(n-1)/n$, the survey will show that the block contains no oil, in which case the company will buy a different block. Now the probability of finding oil in one of the other blocks changes from $1/n$ to $1/(n-1)$, so the company makes an expected profit of $C/(n-1) - C/n = C/n(n-1)$ dollars.

Now we can calculate the expected profit given the survey information:

$$\frac{1}{n} \times \frac{(n-1)C}{n} + \frac{n-1}{n} \times \frac{C}{n(n-1)} = C/n$$

Therefore, the company should be willing to pay the seismologist up to C/n dollars for the information: the information is worth as much as the block itself.

---

[9]   In the United States, the only question that is always asked beforehand is whether the patient has insurance.

The value of information derives from the fact that *with* the information, one's course of action may change to become more appropriate to the actual situation. One can discriminate according to the situation, whereas without the information one has to do what's best on average over the possible situations. In general, the value of a given piece of information is defined to be the difference in expected value between best actions before and after information is obtained.

A general formula

VALUE OF PERFECT
INFORMATION

It is simple to derive a general mathematical formula for the value of information. Usually, we assume that exact evidence is obtained about the value of some random variable E_j, so the phrase **value of perfect information** (VPI) is used. Let the agent's current knowledge be E. Then the value of the current best action α is defined by

$$EU(\alpha|E) = \max_A \sum_i U(Result_i(A)) \, P(Result_i(A)|E, Do(A))$$

and the value of the new best action (after the new evidence E_j is obtained) will be

$$EU(\alpha_{E_j}|E, E_j) = \max_A \sum_i U(Result_i(A)) \, P(Result_i(A)|E, Do(A), E_j)$$

But E_j is a random variable whose value is *currently* unknown, so we must average over all possible values e_{jk} that we might discover for E_j, using our *current* beliefs about its value. The value of discovering E_j is then defined as

$$VPI_E(E_j) = \left(\sum_k P(E_j = e_{jk}|E) EU(\alpha_{e_{jk}}|E, E_j = e_{jk}) \right) - EU(\alpha|E)$$

In order to get some intuition for this formula, consider the simple case where there are only two actions A_1 and A_2 from which to choose. Their current expected utilities are U_1 and U_2. The information E_j will yield some new expected utility U_1' and U_2' for the actions, but before we obtain E_j, we will have some probability distributions over the possible values of U_1' and U_2' (which we will assume are independent).

Suppose that A_1 and A_2 represent two different routes through a mountain range in winter. A_1 is a nice, straight highway through a low pass, and A_2 is a winding dirt road over the top. Just given this information, A_1 is clearly preferable, because it is quite likely that the second route is blocked by avalanches, whereas it is quite unlikely that the first route is blocked by traffic. U_1 is therefore clearly higher than U_2. It is possible to obtain satellite reports E_j on the actual state of each road, which would give new expectations U_1' and U_2' for the two crossings. The distributions for these expectations are shown in Figure 16.6(a). Obviously, in this case, it is not worth the expense of obtaining satellite reports, because it is so unlikely that they will cause a change of plan. With no change of plan, information has no value.

Now suppose that we are choosing between two different winding dirt roads of slightly different lengths, and we are carrying a seriously injured passenger. Then, although U_1 and U_2 may be quite close, the distributions of U_1' and U_2' are very broad. There is a significant possibility that the second route will turn out to be clear whereas the first is blocked, and in this case the difference in utilities will be very high. The VPI formula indicates that it might be worth getting the satellite reports. This situation is shown in Figure 16.6(b).

Now suppose that we are choosing between the two dirt roads in summertime, when blockage by avalanches is unlikely. In this case, satellite reports might show one route to be more scenic than the other because of flowering alpine meadows, or perhaps wetter because of errant streams. It is therefore quite likely that we would change our plan if we had the information. But in this case, the difference in value between the two routes is still likely to be very small, so we will not bother to obtain the reports. This situation is shown in Figure 16.6(c).

In summary, we can say that *information has value to the extent that it is likely to cause a change of plan, and to the extent that the new plan will be significantly better than the old plan.*

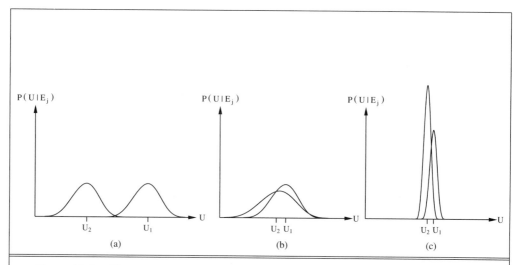

Figure 16.6   Three generic cases for the value of information. In (a), A_1 will almost certainly remain superior to A_2, so the information is not needed. In (b), the choice is unclear and the information is crucial. In (c), the choice is unclear but because it makes little difference, the information is less valuable.

Properties of the value of information

One might ask if it is possible for information to be deleterious—can it actually have negative expected value? Intuitively, one should expect this to be impossible. After all, one could in the worst case just ignore the information and pretend one has never received it. This is confirmed by the following theorem, which applies to any decision-theoretic agent: *The value of information is nonnegative:*

$$\forall j, E \ VPI_E(E_j) \geq 0$$

proof as an exercise (Exercise 16.11). It is important to remember that VPI depends on the current state of information, which is why it is subscripted. It can change as more information is acquired. In the extreme case, it will become zero if the variable in question already has a known value. Thus, VPI is not additive. That is,

$$VPI_E(E_j, E_k) \neq VPI_E(E_j) + VPI_E(E_k) \qquad \text{(in general)}$$

It is, however, order-independent, which should be intuitively obvious. That is,

$$VPI_E(E_j, E_k) = VPI_E(E_j) + VPI_{E,E_j}(E_k) = VPI_E(E_k) + VPI_{E,E_k}(E_j)$$

Order independence distinguishes sensing actions from ordinary actions, and simplifies the problem of calculating the value of a sequence of sensing actions.

Implementing an information-gathering agent

As we mentioned earlier, a sensible agent should ask questions of the user in a reasonable order, should avoid asking questions that are irrelevant, should take into account the importance of each piece of information in relation to its cost, and should stop asking questions when appropriate. All of these capabilities can be achieved by using the value of information as a guide.

Figure 16.7 shows the overall design of an agent that can gather information intelligently before acting. For now, we will assume that with each observable evidence variable E_j, there is an associated cost, $Cost(E_j)$, which reflects the cost of obtaining the evidence through tests, consultants, questions, or whatever. The agent requests what appears to be the most valuable piece of information, compared to its cost. We assume that the result of the action $Request(E_j)$ is that the next percept provides the value of E_j. If no observation is worth its cost, the agent selects a non-information-gathering action.

---

function INFORMATION-GATHERING-AGENT(*percept*) **returns** an *action*
    static: D, a decision network

    integrate *percept* into D
    $j \leftarrow$ the value that maximizes $VPI(E_j) \; - \; Cost(E_j)$
    if $VPI(E_j) > Cost(E_j)$
        then return REQUEST(E_j)
    else return the best action from D

Figure 16.7   Design of a simple information-gathering agent. The agent works by repeatedly selecting the observation with the highest information value, until the costs of observing are greater than the benefits.

MYOPIC

    The agent algorithm we have described implements a form of information gathering that is called **myopic**. This is because it uses the VPI formula short-sightedly, calculating the value of information assuming that only a single evidence variable will be acquired. If there is no single evidence variable that will help a lot, a myopic agent may hastily take an action when it would have been better to request two or more variables first, and then take action. Myopic control is based on the same heuristic idea as greedy search, and often works well in practice. (For example, it has been shown to outperform expert physicians in selecting diagnostic tests.)

However, a perfectly rational information-gathering agent should consider all possible sequences of information requests terminating in an external action. Because VPI is order-independent, this is somewhat simplified by the fact that any permutations of a given sequence of information requests has the same value. Thus, one need consider only subsets of the possible information requests, without worrying about ordering.

16.7   DECISION-THEORETIC EXPERT SYSTEMS

DECISION ANALYSIS   The field of **decision analysis**, which evolved in the 1950s and 1960s, studies the application of decision theory to actual decision problems. It is used to help make rational decisions in important domains where the stakes are high, such as business, government, law, military strategy, medical diagnosis and public health, engineering design, and resource management. The process involves a careful study of the possible actions and outcomes as well as the preferences placed on each
DECISION MAKER   outcome. It is traditional in decision analysis to talk about two roles: the **decision maker** states
DECISION ANALYST   preferences between outcomes, and the **decision analyst** enumerates the possible actions and outcomes and elicits preferences from the decision maker to determine the best course of action. Until the early 1980s, the use of computers in decision analysis was quite limited, and the main purpose of analysis was seen as helping humans to make decisions that actually reflect their own preferences.

As we discussed in Chapter 15, early expert system research concentrated on answering questions, rather than making decisions. Those systems that did recommend actions rather than providing opinions on matters of fact generally did so using condition-action rules, rather than with explicit representations of outcomes and preferences. The eventual emergence of belief networks made it possible to build large-scale systems that generated sound probabilistic inferences from evidence. The addition of decision networks means that expert systems can be developed that recommend optimal decisions, reflecting the preferences of the user as well as the available evidence.

There are many advantages that accrue from the inclusion of explicit utility models and calculations in the expert system framework. The expert benefits from the process of making his or her (or the client's) preferences explicit, and the system can automate the action selection process as well as the process of drawing conclusions from evidence. A system that incorporates utilities can avoid one of the most common pitfalls associated with the consultation process: confusing likelihood and importance. A common strategy in early medical expert systems, for example, was to rank possible diagnoses in order of likelihood, and report the most likely. Unfortunately, this can be disastrous, because it will miss cases of relatively rare, but treatable, conditions that are easily confused with more common diseases. The confusion of Hodgkin's disease (a form of cancer) with mononucleosis (a mild and very common viral infection) is a classic case in point. (For the majority of patients in general practice, moreover, the most *likely* diagnosis is "There's nothing wrong with you.") Obviously, a testing or treatment plan should depend both on probabilities and utilities. Finally, the availability of utility information helps in the knowledge engineering and consultation process, as we now explain.

The knowledge engineering process required for building and using decision-theoretic expert system is as follows:

- **Determine the scope of the problem**. Determine what are the possible actions, outcomes, and evidence to consider. Normally, the analyst will have to interview one or more experts in the domain to discover the important factors. Note that we recommended the same sort of determination as the first step of knowledge engineering in Section 8.2.

- **Lay out the topology**. Once all the relevant factors are determined, we need to know which ones are influenced by which others. It is particularly important to understand which aspects of the outcome state determine its utility.

- **Assign probabilities**. In decision networks, the conditional probabilities reflect not only causal influences between random variables, but also the effects of actions.

- **Assign utilities**. A utility function is often assessed using the techniques described earlier. Computer programs exist that automate the task of extracting preferences for various lotteries and constructing a utility function. Identifying the preference structure of multiattribute utility functions is also vital in reducing the dimensionality of the assessment problem. It can reduce the number of questions exponentially.

- **Enter available evidence**. For each specific case in which the system is used, there may be some initial evidence available.

- **Evaluate the diagram**. Calculate the optimal action according to the existing evidence.

- **Obtain new evidence**. Calculate the value of information, comparing it with the costs of acquisition, and perform the appropriate observations, if any. Notice that purely inferential expert systems, without utilities, cannot decide what new evidence to acquire.

- **Perform sensitivity analysis**. This important step checks to see if the best decision is sensitive to small changes in the assigned probabilities and utilities by systematically varying these parameters and running the evaluation again. If small changes lead to significantly different decisions, then it may be worthwhile to spend more resources to collect better data. If all variations lead to the same decision, then the user will have more confidence that it is the right decision.

Sensitivity analysis is particularly important, because one of the main criticisms of probabilistic approaches to expert systems is that it is too difficult to assess the numerical probabilities required. Sensitivity analysis often reveals that many of the numbers need only be specified very approximately—within, say, 0.2 of the value that might be obtained from an exhaustive analysis. Some systems allow probabilities to be specified as ranges. This leads to ranges for the utilities of actions. If the range of one action dominates the ranges of all others, then no further probability assessment need occur. For example, it might be the case that the optimal siting of an airport is insensitive to the predicted air traffic over a large range of values, given the system's beliefs about the other relevant factors, so that the user can remain unruffled by his or her lack of expertise on air traffic prediction.

16.8   SUMMARY

This chapter shows how to combine utility theory with probability to enable an agent to select actions that will maximize its expected performance.

- **Probability theory** describes what an agent should believe on the basis of evidence, **utility theory** describes what an agent wants, and **decision theory** puts the two together to describe what an agent should do.

- We can use decision theory to build a system that makes decisions by considering all possible actions and choosing the one that leads to the best expected outcome. Such a system is known as a **rational agent**.

- Utility theory shows that an agent whose preferences between lotteries are consistent with a set of simple axioms can be described as possessing a utility function; furthermore, the agent selects actions as if maximizing its expected utility.

- **Multiattribute utility theory** deals with utilities that depend on several distinct attributes of states. **Stochastic dominance** is a particularly useful technique for making unambiguous decisions even without precise utility values for attributes.

- **Decision networks** provide a simple formalism for expressing and solving decision problems. They are a natural extension of belief networks, containing decision and utility nodes in addition to chance nodes.

- Sometimes solving a problem involves finding more information before making a decision. The **value of information** is defined as the expected improvement in utility compared to making a decision without the information.

- **Expert systems** that incorporate utility information have additional capabilities compared to pure inference systems. In addition to being able to make decisions, they can decide to acquire information based on its value, and they can calculate the sensitivity of their decisions to small changes in probability and utility assessments.

BIBLIOGRAPHICAL AND HISTORICAL NOTES

One of the earliest applications of the principle of maximum expected utility (although a deviant one involving infinite utilities) was Pascal's Wager, first published as part of the *Port-Royal Logic* (Arnauld, 1662). The derivation of numerical utilities from preference (utility ordering) was first carried out by Ramsey (1931); the axioms for preference in the present text are closer in form to those rediscovered in *Theory of Games and Economic Behavior* (Von Neumann and Morgenstern, 1944). A good presentation of these axioms, in the course of a discussion on risk preference, is given by Howard (1977). Ramsey had derived subjective probabilities (not just utilities) from an agent's preferences; Savage (1954) and Jeffrey (1983) carry out more recent constructions of this kind. Von Winterfeldt and Edwards (1986) provide a modern perspective on decision analysis and its relationship to human preference structures.

The St. Petersburg paradox was first presented by Bernoulli (1738). Jeffrey (1983) presents a resolution of the paradox based not on logarithmic utility functions, but on denying that playing the game is a real possibility (because no one could have a bank from which rewards of arbitrarily high utility could be paid out).

The micromort utility measure is discussed by Howard (1989). QALYs are much more widely used in medical and social policy decision-making than are micromorts; see (Russell, 1990) for a typical example of an argument for a major change in public health policy on grounds of increased expected utility measured in QALYs.

The book *Decisions with Multiple Objectives: Preferences and Value Trade-Offs* (Keeney and Raiffa, 1976) gives a thorough introduction to multiattribute utility theory. It describes early computer implementations of methods for eliciting the necessary parameters for a multiattribute utility function, and includes extensive accounts of real applications of the theory. In AI, the principal reference for MAUT is Wellman's (1985) paper, which includes a system called URP (Utility Reasoning Package) that can use a collection of statements about preference independence and conditional independence to analyze the structure of decision problems. The use of stochastic dominance together with qualitative probability models was investigated extensively by Wellman (1988; 1990). Wellman and Doyle (1992) provide a preliminary sketch of how a complex set of utility-independence relationships might be used to provide a structured model of a utility function, in much the same way that belief networks provide a structured model of joint probability distributions.

Decision theory has been a standard tool in economics, finance, and management science since the 1950s. Until the 1980s, decision trees were the main tool used for representing simple decision problems. Decision networks or influence diagrams were introduced by Howard and Matheson (1984), although the underlying concepts were developed much earlier by a group (including Howard and Matheson) at SRI (Miller *et al.*, 1976). Howard and Matheson's method involved the derivation of a decision tree from a decision network, but in general the tree is of exponential size. Shachter (1986) developed a method for making decisions based directly on a decision network, without the creation of an intermediate decision tree. The collection by Oliver and Smith (1990) has a number of useful articles on decision networks, as does the 1990 special issue of the journal *Networks*. Papers on decision networks and utility modelling also appear regularly in the journal *Management Science*.

Information value theory was first analyzed by Ron Howard (1966). His paper ends with the following remark:

> If information value theory and associated decision theoretic structures do not in the future occupy a large part of the education of engineers, then the engineering profession will find that its traditional role of managing scientific and economic resources for the benefit of man has been forfeited to another profession.

To date, the implied revolution in managerial methods has not occurred, although as the use of information value theory in systems such as Pathfinder becomes more widespread, it may yet become part of every decision-maker's armory.

Surprisingly few AI researchers adopted decision-theoretic tools after the early applications in medical decision making described in Chapter 14. One of the few exceptions was Jerry Feldman, who applied decision theory to problems in vision (Feldman and Yakimovsky, 1974) and planning (Feldman and Sproull, 1977). After the resurgence of interest in probabilistic methods in AI in the 1980s, decision-theoretic expert systems gained widespread acceptance (Horvitz *et al.*, 1988)—in fact, from 1991 onward, the cover design of the journal *Artificial Intelligence* has depicted a decision network, although some artistic license appears to have been taken with the direction of the arrows.

EXERCISES

16.1   (Adapted from David Heckerman.) This exercise concerns the **Almanac Game**, which is used by decision analysts to calibrate numeric estimations. For each of the questions below, give your best guess of the answer, that is, a number that you think is as likely to be too high as it is to be too low. Also give your guess at a 25th percentile estimate, that is, a number that you think has a 25% chance of being too high, and a 75% chance of being too low. Do the same for the 75th percentile. (Thus, you should give three estimates in all—low, median, and high—for each question.)

   a. Number of passengers who flew between New York and Los Angeles in 1989.
   b. Population of Warsaw in 1992.
   c. Year in which Coronado discovered the Mississippi River.
   d. Number of votes received by Jimmy Carter in the 1976 presidential election.
   e. Number of newspapers in the U.S. in 1990.
   f. Height of Hoover Dam in feet.
   g. Number of eggs produced in Oregon in 1985.
   h. Number of Buddhists in the world in 1992.
   i. Number of deaths due to AIDS in the U.S. in 1981.
   j. Number of U.S. patents granted in 1901.

The correct answers appear after the last exercise for this chapter. From the point of view of decision analysis, the interesting thing is not how close your median guesses came to the real answers, but rather how often the real answer came within your 25% and 75% bounds. If it was about half the time, then your bounds are accurate. But if you're like most people, you will be more sure of yourself than you should be, and fewer than half the answers will fall within the bounds. With practice, you can calibrate yourself to give realistic bounds, and thus be more useful in supplying information for decision making. Try this second set of questions and see if there is any improvement:

   a. Year of birth of Zsa Zsa Gabor.
   b. Maximum distance from Mars to the sun in miles.
   c. Value in dollars of exports of wheat from the U.S. in 1992.
   d. Tons handled by the port of Honolulu in 1991.
   e. Annual salary in dollars of the governor of California in 1993.

      f. Population of San Diego in 1990.

      g. Year in which Roger Williams founded Providence, R.I.

      h. Height of Mt. Kilimanjaro in feet.

      i. Length of the Brooklyn Bridge in feet.

      j. Number of deaths due to automobile accidents in the U.S. in 1992.

16.2   Tickets to the state lottery cost $1. There are two possible prizes: a $10 payoff with probability 1/50, and a $1,000,000 payoff with probability 1/2,000,000. What is the expected monetary value of a lottery ticket? When (if ever) is it rational to buy a ticket? Be precise—show an equation involving utilities. You may assume that $U(\$10) = 10 \times U(\$1)$, but you may not make any assumptions about $U(\$1,000,000)$. Sociological studies show that people with lower income buy a disproportionate number of lottery tickets. Do you think this is because they are worse decision makers or because they have a different utility function?

16.3   Assess your own utility for different incremental amounts of money. Do this by running a series of preference tests between some definite amount M_1 and a lottery $[p, M_2; (1 - p), 0]$. Choose different values of $M_1 1$ and M_2, and vary p until you are indifferent between the two choices. Plot the resulting utility function.

16.4   Write a computer program to automate the process in Exercise 16.3. Try your program out on several people of different net worth and political outlook. Comment on the consistency of your results, both across individuals and within the set of choices made by a single individual.

LEXICOGRAPHIC
PREFERENCE

16.5   It has sometimes been suggested that **lexicographic preference** is a form of rational behavior that is not captured by utility theory. Lexicographic preferences rank attributes in some order $X_1, \ldots, X_n$, and treat each attribute as infinitely more important than attributes later in the order. In choosing between two prizes, the value of attribute X_i only matters if the prizes have the same values for $X_1, \ldots, X_{i-1}$. In a lottery, an infinitesimal probability of a tiny improvement in a more important attribute is considered better than a dead certainty of a huge improvement in a less important attribute. For example, in the airport-siting problem, it might be proposed that preserving human life is of paramount importance, and therefore if one site is more dangerous than another, it should be ruled out immediately, without considering the other attributes. Only if two sites are equally safe should they be compared on other attributes such as cost.

      a. Give a precise definition of lexicographic preference between deterministic outcomes.

      b. Give a precise definition of lexicographic preference between lotteries.

      c. Does lexicographic preference violate any of the axioms of utility theory? If so, give an example. (*Hint:* consider pair-wise preference comparisons of three different possibilities.)

      d. Suggest a set of attributes for which you might exhibit lexicographic preferences.

16.6   Show that if X_1 and X_2 are preferentially independent of X_3, and X_2 and X_3 are preferentially independent of X_1, then it follows that X_3 and X_1 are preferentially independent of X_2.

16.7   Encode the airport-siting problem as shown in Figure 16.4, provide reasonable probabilities and utilities, and solve the problem for the case of choosing among three sites. What happens if changes in technology mean that each aircraft generates half as much noise? What if noise avoidance becomes three times more important?

16.8 Repeat Exercise 16.7, using the action-utility representation shown in Figure 16.5.

16.9 For either of the airport-siting diagrams constructed in Exercises 16.7 and 16.8, to which conditional probability table entry is the utility most sensitive, given the available evidence?

16.10 (Adapted from Pearl (1988).) A used-car buyer can decide to carry out various tests with various costs (e.g., kick the tires, take the car to a qualified mechanic), and then, depending on the outcome of the tests, decide which car to buy. We will assume that the buyer is deciding whether to buy car c_1, that there is time to carry out at most one test, and that t_1 is the test of c_1 and costs \$50.

A car can be in good shape (quality q^+) or bad shape (quality q^-), and the tests may help to indicate what shape the car is in. Car c_1 costs \$1,500, and its market value is \$2,000 if it is in good shape; if not, \$700 in repairs will be needed to make it in good shape. The buyer's estimate is that c_1 has a 70% chance of being in good shape.

  a. Calculate the expected net gain from buying c_1, given no test.

  b. Tests can be described by the probability that the car will pass or fail given that the car is in good or bad shape. We have the following information:
  $P(pass(c_1, t_1)|q^+(c_1)) = 0.8$
  $P(pass(c_1, t_1)|q^-(c_1)) = 0.35$
  Use Bayes' theorem to calculate the probability that the car will pass (or fail) its test, and hence the probability that it is in good (or bad) shape given each possible test outcome.

  c. Calculate the optimal decisions given either a pass or a fail, and their expected utilities.

  d. Calculate the value of information of the test, and derive an optimal conditional plan for the buyer.

16.11 Prove that the value of information is nonnegative, as stated in Section 16.6.

16.12 How much is a micromort worth to you? Devise a protocol to determine this.

The answers for Exercise 16.1 (where M stands for million): First set: 3M, 1.6M, 1541, 41M, 1611, 221, 649M, 295M, 132, 25546. Second set: 1917, 155M, 4500M, 11M, 120000, 1.1M, 1636, 19340, 1595, 41710.

17 MAKING COMPLEX DECISIONS

In which we examine methods for deciding what to do today, given that we will have a chance to act again tomorrow.

In this chapter, we address the computational issues involved in making decisions. Whereas Chapter 16 was concerned with single decision problems, in which the utility of each action's outcome was well-known, in this chapter we will be concerned with **sequential decision problems**, where the agent's utility depends on a sequence of decisions. Sequential decision problems, which include utilities, uncertainty, and sensing, generalize the search and planning problems described in Parts II and IV.

The chapter divides roughly into two parts. Sections 17.1 through 17.3 deal with classical techniques from control theory, operations research, and decision analysis that were developed to solve sequential decision problems under uncertainty. They operate in much the same way that the search algorithms of Part II solved sequential decision problems in deterministic domains: by looking for a sequence of actions that leads to a good state. The difference is that what they return is not the fixed sequence of actions, but rather a **policy**—that is, a set of situation–action rules for each state—arrived at by calculating utilities for each state.

The second part, Sections 17.4 through 17.6, develops a complete sketch of a decision-theoretic agent using a richer representation of states in terms of random variables in a belief network. We also show how to efficiently update the network over time, and how to be able to safely forget things about the past.

17.1 SEQUENTIAL DECISION PROBLEMS

Suppose that an agent is situated in the environment shown in Figure 17.1. Beginning in the start state, it must execute a sequence of actions. The environment terminates when the agent reaches one of the states marked +1 or −1. In each location, the available actions are called *North*, *South*, *East*, and *West*. We will assume for now that the agent knows which state it is in initially, and that it knows the effects of all of its actions on the state of the world.

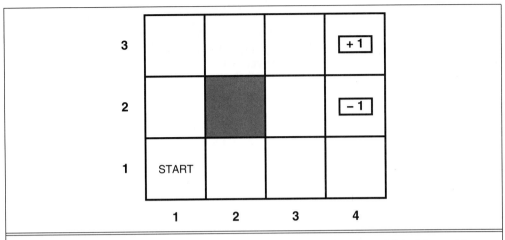

Figure 17.1   A simple environment that presents the agent with a sequential decision problem.

In the deterministic version of the problem, each action reliably moves one square in the intended direction, except that moving into a wall results in no change in position. In the stochastic version, the actions are unreliable. Each action achieves the intended effect with probability 0.8, but the rest of the time, the action moves the agent at right angles to the intended direction. For example, from the start square (1,1), the action *North* moves the agent to (1,2) with probability 0.8, but with probability 0.1, it moves *East* to (2,1), and with probability 0.1, it moves *West*, bumps into the wall, and stays in (1,1). We will use the term **transition model** (or just "model," where no confusion can arise) to refer to the set of probabilities associated with the possible transitions between states after any given action. The notation M_{ij}^a means the probability of reaching state j if action a is done in state i.

The tricky part is the utility function. Other than the terminal states (the ones marked +1 and −1), there is no indication of a state's utility. So we have to base the utility function on a sequence of states—an **environment history**—rather than on a single state. Let us suppose that the utility for a sequence will be the terminal state's value minus 1/25th the length of the sequence, so a sequence of length 6 that leads to the +1 box has utility 0.76.

In the deterministic case, with knowledge of the initial state and the effects of actions, the problem can be solved directly by the search algorithms described in Chapter 3. This is true *regardless* of whether the environment is accessible or inaccessible. The agent knows exactly which state it will be in after any given action, so there is no need for sensing.

In the more general, stochastic case, the agent will not know exactly which state it will reach after any given sequence of actions. For example, if the agent is in location (3,2), then the action sequence [*North, East*] might end up in any of five states (see Exercise 17.1), and reaches the +1 state at (4,3) with probability only 0.64.

One tempting way to deal with action sequences would be to consider sequences as long actions. Then one could simply apply the basic Maximum Expected Utility principle to sequences. The rational action would then be the first action of the optimal sequence. Now, although this approach is closely related to the way that search algorithms work, it has a fundamental flaw. It assumes that the agent is required to *commit* to an entire sequence of actions before executing it. If the agent has no sensors, then this is the best it can do. But if the agent can acquire new sensory information after each action, then committing to an entire sequence is irrational. For example, consider the sequence [*North, East*], starting at (3,2). With probability 0.1, *North* bumps the agent into the wall, leaving it still in (3,2). In this case, carrying on with the sequence and executing *East* would be a bad choice.

In reality, the agent will have the opportunity to choose a new action after each step, *given whatever additional information its sensors provide*. We therefore need an approach much more like the conditional planning algorithms of Chapter 13, rather than the search algorithms of Chapter 3. Of course, these will have to be extended to handle probabilities and utilities. We will also have to deal with the fact that the "conditional plan" for a stochastic environment may have to be of infinite size, because it is possible, although unlikely, for the agent to get stuck in one place (or in a loop) no matter how hard it tries not to.

We begin our analysis with the case of **accessible** environments. In an accessible environment, the agent's percept at each step will identify the state it is in. If it can calculate the optimal action for each state, then that will completely determine its behavior. No matter what the outcome of any action, the agent will always know what to do next.

POLICY   A complete mapping from states to actions is called a **policy**. Given a policy, it is possible to calculate the expected utility of the possible environment histories generated by that policy. The problem, then, is not to calculate the optimal action sequence, but to calculate the optimal policy—that is, the policy that results in the highest expected utility. An optimal policy for the world in Figure 17.1 is shown in Figure 17.2(a). Notice that because the cost of taking a step is fairly small compared to the penalty for ending up in (4,2) by accident, the optimal policy for the state (3,1) is conservative. The policy recommends taking the long way round, rather than taking the short cut and thereby risking entering (4,2). As the cost of taking a step is increased, the optimal policy will, at some point, switch over to the more direct route (see Exercise 17.4). As the cost of a step is decreased, the policy will become *extremely* conservative. For example, if the cost is 0.01, the policy for the state (3,2) is to head *West* directly into the wall, thereby avoiding any chance of falling into (4,2).

Once a policy has been calculated from the transition model and the utility function, it is a trivial matter to decide what to do. A policy represents the agent function explicitly, and is therefore a description of a simple reflex agent, computed from the information used for a utility-based agent. Figure 17.3 shows the corresponding agent design.

MARKOV DECISION PROBLEM
MDP

The problem of calculating an optimal policy in an accessible, stochastic environment with a known transition model is called a **Markov decision problem** (**MDP**), after the Russian statistician Andrei A. Markov. Markov's work is so closely associated with the assumption of accessibility, that decision problems are often divided into "Markov" and "non-Markov." More strictly, we say the **Markov property** holds if the transition probabilities from any given state depend only on the state and not on previous history. The next two sections give algorithms for calculating optimal policies in Markov decision problems.

MARKOV PROPERTY

POMDP

In an **inaccessible** environment, the percept does not provide enough information to determine the state or the associated transition probabilities. In the operations research literature, such problems are called **partially observable Markov decision problems**, or **POMDP**. Methods used for MDPs are not directly applicable to POMDPs. For example, suppose our agent

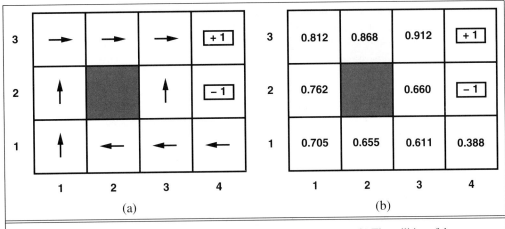

Figure 17.2   (a) An optimal policy for the stochastic environment. (b) The utilities of the states.

---

function SIMPLE-POLICY-AGENT(*percept*) **returns** an *action*
    static: *M*, a transition model
            U, a utility function on environment histories
            P, a policy, initially unknown

    if *P* is unknown **then** *P* ← the optimal policy given *U*, *M*
    return *P*[*percept*]

Figure 17.3   An agent that calculates and uses an optimal policy.

---

is equipped with a sonar ring that gives it the distance to the nearest wall in each of the four directions. For such an agent, the locations (2,1) and (2,3) are indistinguishable, yet different actions are needed in each. Furthermore, the Markov property does not hold for percepts (as opposed to states), because the next percept does not depend just on the current *percept* and the action taken.

The correct approach for POMDPs is to calculate a probability distribution over the possible states given all previous percepts, and to base decisions on this distribution. Although the optimal decision is not uniquely determined by the current percept, it *is* determined uniquely (up to ties) by the agent's probability distribution over the possible states that it could be in. For example, the sonar-equipped agent might believe that it is in state (2,1) with probability 0.8 and in state (2,3) with probability 0.2. The utility of action *A* is then

    0.8 × utility of doing *A* in (2,1) given current beliefs +
    0.2 × utility of doing *A* in (2,3) given current beliefs

This seems simple enough. Unfortunately, in POMDPs, calculating the utility of an action in a state is made more difficult by the fact that actions will cause the agent to obtain new percepts, which will cause the agent's beliefs to change in complex ways that depend on its current beliefs.

Essentially, the agent must take into account the *information* that it might obtain, as well as the state it will reach. POMDPs therefore include the value of information (Section 16.6) as one component of the decision problem.

The standard method for solving a POMDP is to construct a new MDP in which the current probability distribution over states plays the role of the state variable. Unfortunately, the new MDP is not easy to solve. The new state space is characterized by real-valued probabilities, and is therefore infinite. Exact solution methods for POMDPs require some fairly advanced tools, and are beyond the scope of this book. The bibliographical notes at the end of this chapter provide pointers to suitable additional reading.

Instead of trying to find exact solutions, one can often obtain a good approximation using a limited lookahead. (See, for example, the algorithms in Chapter 5.) Section 17.4 shows how this approach can be realized for POMDPs using the technology of decision networks. Before tackling POMDPs, however, we first present the most common solution methods for making decisions in accessible worlds.

17.2   VALUE ITERATION

VALUE ITERATION

In this section, we present an algorithm for calculating an optimal policy called **value iteration**. The basic idea is to calculate the utility of each state, $U(state)$, and then use the state utilities to select an optimal action in each state.

The difficult part about calculating $U(state)$ is that we do not know where an action will lead. We can think of a sequence of actions as generating a tree of possible histories, with the current state as the root of the tree, and each path from the root to a leaf representing a possible history of states. We use the notation $H(state, policy)$ to denote the history tree starting from *state* and taking action according to *policy*. This can be thought of as a random variable that is dependent on the transition model M. Then the utility of a state i is given by the expected utility of the history beginning at that state and following an optimal policy:

$$U(i) \equiv EU(H(i, policy^*)|M) \equiv \sum P(H(i, policy^*)|M)U_h(H(i, policy^*)) \qquad (17.1)$$

where *policy** is an optimal policy defined by the transition model M and the utility function on histories U_h. We will explain shortly how to derive an optimal policy.

Having a utility function on states is only useful to the extent that it can be used to make rational decisions, using the Maximum Expected Utility principle (Equation (16.1), page 472). In the case of sequential decisions, we have to be quite careful about this. For a utility function on states (U) to make sense, we require that the utility function on histories (U_h) have the property SEPARABILITY of **separability**. A utility function U_h is separable if and only if we can find a function f such that

$$U_h([s_0, s_1, \ldots, s_n]) = f(s_0, U_h([s_1, \ldots, s_n]))$$

(Exercise 17.2 asks you to construct a utility function violating this property.) The simplest form ADDITIVE of separable utility function is **additive**:

$$U_h([s_0, s_1, \ldots, s_n]) = R(s_0) + U_h([s_1, \ldots, s_n]))$$

REWARD FUNCTION
where R is called a **reward function**.[1] Consider again the utility function defined for Figure 17.1: an environment history of length n terminating in a state of value v has a utility of $v - (1/25)n$. This utility function is separable and additive, and the reward function R is -1/25 for nonterminal states, +1 for state (4,3) and −1 for state (4,2). As we discuss in what follows, utility functions over histories are almost always additive in practice. Notice that additivity was implicit in our use of path cost functions in heuristic search algorithms (Chapter 4).

Given an additive utility function U_h, we can recover the standard Maximum Expected Utility principle that an optimal action is one with maximal expected utility of outcome states:

$$policy^*(i) = \arg\max_a \sum_j M_{ij}^a U(j) \tag{17.2}$$

where M_{ij}^a is the probability of reaching state j if action a is taken in state i, and $\arg\max_a f(a)$ returns the value of a with the highest value for $f(a)$. Similarly, the utility of a state can be expressed in terms of the utility of its successors:

$$U(i) = R(i) + \max_a \sum_j M_{ij}^a U(j) \tag{17.3}$$

DYNAMIC
PROGRAMMING
Equation (17.3) is the basis for **dynamic programming**, an approach to solving sequential decision problems developed in the late 1950s by Richard Bellman (1957).

The simplest dynamic programming context involves an n-step decision problem, where the states reached after n steps are considered terminal states and have known utilities. If there are $|A|$ possible actions at each step, then the total complexity of a naive approach—exhaustive enumeration—would be $O(|A|^n)$. The dynamic programming approach starts by calculating the utilities of all states at step $n - 1$ in terms of the utilities of the terminal states. One then calculate the utilities of states at step $n - 2$, and so on. Because calculating the utility of one state, using Equation (17.3), costs $O(|A|)$, the total cost of solving the decision problem is no more than $O(n|A||S|)$, where $|S|$ is the number of possible states. In small state spaces, this can be a huge saving.[2] Dynamic programming has since become a field of its own, with a huge array of applications and a large library of techniques for different types of separable utility functions.

In most of the decision problems that AI is interested in (including the world of Figure 17.1), the environment histories are potentially of unbounded length because of loops. This means that there is no n for which to start the n-step dynamic programming algorithm. Fortunately, there is a simple algorithm for approximating the utilities of states to any degree of accuracy using an iterative procedure. We apply Equation (17.3) repeatedly, on each step updating the utility of each state based on the old utility estimates of the neighboring states:

$$U_{t+1}(i) \leftarrow R(i) + \max_a \sum_j M_{ij}^a U_t(j) \tag{17.4}$$

where $U_t(i)$ is the utility estimate for state i after t iterations. As $t \to \infty$, the utility values will converge to stable values given certain conditions on the environment. The algorithm, called VALUE-ITERATION, is shown in Figure 17.4.

---

[1] Thus, the utility function is additive, in the sense defined in Chapter 16, given attributes corresponding to the rewards received in each state in the sequence. There are some problems in applying this equation to infinite histories, which will be discussed later.

[2] The saving is of the same sort as that achieved by checking repeated states during search (Section 3.6).

function VALUE-ITERATION(M, R) **returns** a utility function
   inputs: M, a transition model
         R, a reward function on states
   local variables: U, utility function, initially identical to R
                 U', utility function, initially identical to R

   repeat
      $U \leftarrow U'$
      for each state i **do**
         $U'[i] \leftarrow R[i] + \max_a \sum_j M_{ij}^a\ U[j]$
      end
   until CLOSE-ENOUGH(U, U')
   return U

Figure 17.4   The value iteration algorithm for calculating utilities of states.

Given a utility function on states, it is trivial to calculate a corresponding policy using Equation (17.2). Furthermore, the policy will actually be optimal, as proved by Bellman and Dreyfus (1962). We can apply value iteration to the environment shown in Figure 17.1, which yields the utility values shown in Figure 17.2(b). In Figure 17.5, we show the utility values of some of the states at each iteration step of the algorithm. Notice how the states at different distances from (4,3) accumulate negative reward until, at some point, a path is found to (4,3) whereupon the utilities start to increase.

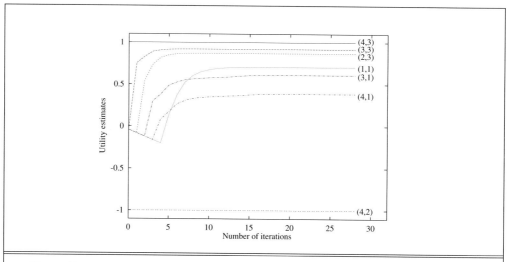

Figure 17.5   The utility values for selected states at each iteration step in the application of VALUE-ITERATION to the 4×3 world in Figure 17.1.

RMS ERROR

How long should value iteration be allowed to run? Do we require the values to converge? These are nontrivial questions. There are two obvious ways to measure the progress of value iteration. The first uses the **RMS error** (RMS stands for "root mean square") of the utility values compared to the correct values. The second assumes that the estimated utility values are not in themselves important—what counts is the policy that they imply. The policy corresponding to an estimated utility function U_t is derived using Equation (17.2). We can measure the quality of

POLICY LOSS

a policy using the expected **policy loss**—the difference between the expected utility obtained by an agent using the policy, compared with an agent using the optimal policy. Figure 17.6 shows how both measures approach zero as the value iteration process proceeds. Notice that the policy (which is chosen from a discrete, finite set of possible policies) becomes exactly optimal long before the utility estimates have converged to their correct values.

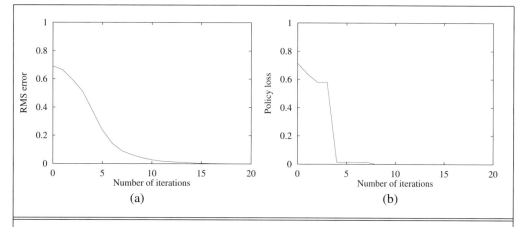

Figure 17.6   (a) The RMS (root mean square) error of the utility estimates compared to the correct values, as a function of iteration number during value iteration. (b) The expected policy loss compared to the optimal policy.

17.3   POLICY ITERATION

POLICY ITERATION

In the previous section, we observed that the optimal policy is often not very sensitive to the exact utility values. This insight suggests an alternative way to find optimal policies. The **policy iteration** algorithm works by picking a policy, then calculating the utility of each state *given that policy*. It then updates the policy at each state using the utilities of the successor states

VALUE DETERMINATION

(Equation (17.2)), and repeats until the policy stabilizes. The step in which utility values are determined from a given policy is called **value determination**. The basic idea behind policy iteration, as compared to value iteration, is that value determination should be simpler than value iteration because the action in each state is fixed by the policy. The policy iteration algorithm is shown in Figure 17.7.

function POLICY-ITERATION(M, R) **returns** a policy
  inputs: M, a transition model
          R, a reward function on states
  local variables: U, a utility function, initially identical to R
                P, a policy, initially optimal with respect to U

  repeat
     U ← VALUE-DETERMINATION(P, U, M, R)
     unchanged? ← true
     for each state i **do**
       if $\max_a \sum_j M_{ij}^a U[j] > \sum_j M_{ij}^{P[i]} U[j]$ **then**
          $P[i] \leftarrow \arg\max_a \sum_j M_{ij}^a U[j]$
          unchanged? ← false
    end
  until *unchanged?*
  return P

Figure 17.7   The policy iteration algorithm for calculating an optimal policy.

The VALUE-DETERMINATION algorithm can be implemented in one of two ways. The first is a simplification of the VALUE-ITERATION algorithm, replacing Equation (17.4) with

$$U_{t+1}(i) \leftarrow R(i) + \sum_j M_{ij}^{Policy(i)} U_t(j)$$

and using the current utility estimates from policy iteration as the initial values. (Here *Policy(i)* is the action suggested by the policy in state i.) While this can work well in some environments, it will often take a very long time to converge in the early stages of policy iteration. This is because the policy will be more or less random, so that many steps can be required to reach terminal states.

The second approach is to solve for the utilities directly. Given a fixed policy P, the utilities of states obey a set of equations of the form

$$U(i) = R(i) + \sum_j M_{ij}^{P(i)} U_t(j)$$

For example, suppose P is the policy shown in Figure 17.2(a). Then using the transition model M, we can construct the following set of equations:

$$u_{(1,1)} = 0.8u_{(1,2)} + 0.1u_{(1,1)} + 0.1u_{(2,1)}$$
$$u_{(1,2)} = 0.8u_{(1,3)} + 0.2u_{(1,2)}$$

and so on. This gives a set of 11 linear equations in 11 unknowns, which can be solved by linear algebra methods such as Gaussian elimination. For small state spaces, value determination using exact solution methods is often the most efficient approach.

HOW IMMORTAL AGENTS DECIDE WHAT TO DO

Making decisions is not easy when one lives forever. The total reward obtained by a policy can easily be unbounded. Because one cannot easily compare infinities, it is difficult to say which policy is rational; moreover, both value iteration and policy iteration will fail to terminate. If the agent's lifetime is finite but contains millions of steps, then these algorithms are intractable. These difficulties arise from fundamental problems associated with specifying utilities over histories so that the resulting "optimal" behavior makes intuitive sense. The same issues arise for humans. Should one live fast and die young, or live an unexciting life to a ripe old age?

One of the most common approaches is to use **discounting**. A discounting function considers rewards received in future time steps to be less valuable than rewards received in the current time step. Suppose that an environment history H contains a stream of rewards, such that the agent receives reward R_i at the ith future time step. The standard method of discounting uses the utility function $U(H) = \sum_i \gamma^i R_i$, where γ is the **discount factor**. Provided $0 \leq \gamma < 1$, this sum will converge to a finite amount. Discounting can be interpreted in at least three different ways:

- As a trick to get rid of the infinities. Essentially, it is a smoothed-out version of the limited-horizon algorithms used in game-playing—the smaller the value of γ, the shorter the effective horizon.

- As an accurate model of both animal and human preference behavior. In economics, it is widely used in assessing the value of investments.

- As a natural preference-independence assumption associated with rewards over time. Discounting *follows* from an assumption of **stationarity**. Stationarity means the following: if two reward sequences $R_1, R_2, R_3, \ldots$ and $S_1, S_2, S_3, \ldots$ begin with the same reward (i.e., $R_1 = S_1$) then the two sequences should be preference-ordered the same way as the sequences $R_2, R_3, \ldots$ and $S_2, S_3, \ldots$. If stationarity seems like a reasonable assumption, then discounting is a reasonable way to make decisions.

If the agent's lifetime is long (in number of steps) compared to the number of states, then the optimal policy will be *repetitive*. For example, a taxi driver aiming to maximize his income will usually adopt a standard set of waiting patterns for times when he does not have a passenger. The **system gain** is defined as the average reward obtained per unit time. It can be shown that after an initial "transient" period, any optimal policy has a constant system gain. This fact can be used to compute optimal policies—for example, telling the taxi driver where to wait at different times of day—using a version of policy iteration.

17.4   DECISION-THEORETIC AGENT DESIGN

In this section, we outline a comprehensive approach to agent design for environments with uncertainty. It ties together belief and decision networks with the techniques for sequential decision problems discussed earlier. It addresses the problem of large state spaces by decomposing the state description into a set of random variables, much as the planning algorithms in Part IV used logical representations to decompose the state space used by search algorithms. We begin by describing the basic approach, which harks back to the sketch of the **utility-based agent** provided in Chapter 2. We then show how sensing works in an uncertain, partially accessible environment. Section 17.5 extends the idea of belief networks to cover environments that change over time, and then Section 17.6 includes decisions, providing a complete agent design.

The decision cycle of a rational agent

DECISION CYCLE

Figure 17.8 repeats the schematic agent design for rational agents first shown in Figure 14.1. At each step, the processing done by the agent is called the **decision cycle**. In this section, we will make components of the cycle more precise. We begin with the first step, that of determining the current state of the world.

---

function DECISION-THEORETIC-AGENT(*percept*) **returns** *action*

    calculate updated probabilities for current state based on
        available evidence including current percept and previous action
    calculate outcome probabilities for actions
        given action descriptions and probabilities of current states
    select *action* with highest expected utility
        given probabilities of outcomes and utility information
    return *action*

Figure 17.8   A decision-theoretic agent (repeat of earlier figure).

STATE VARIABLES

In general, we will assume that we have a set of random variables $\mathbf{X}_t$ that refer to the current state of the world. We will call these the **state variables**. For example, if the agent is a robot moving in the X–Y plane, then we might use X_t and Y_t to refer to the robot's position at time t, and $\dot{X}_t$ and $\dot{Y}_t$ to refer to the velocity. Notice the similarity to the propositional version of situation calculus used in Chapter 6 for the first logical-agent design. This similarity is not a coincidence: probability theory essentially combines propositional logic with uncertainty. As in situation calculus, it is important to distinguish between beliefs about a changing world and changing beliefs about a given world. The former is achieved by having different propositions referring to different times, and the latter by conditioning the probability of a given proposition on additional evidence. Thus, if the percept history up to and including time t is $\mathbf{E}_1, \dots, \mathbf{E}_t$

(where each $\mathbf{E}_i$ may also consist of observations on several random variables), and the previous actions have been $A_1 \ldots A_{t-1}$, then what we are interested in is

$$\mathbf{P}(\mathbf{X}_t | \mathbf{E}_1 \ldots \mathbf{E}_t, A_1 \ldots A_{t-1}),$$

that is, the probability distribution over the current state given all available evidence. We refer to this quantity as $Bel(\mathbf{X}_t)$—the belief about the state at time t, given all evidence up to time t.

This is a rather complicated expression, and direct evaluation is out of the question because it requires conditioning on a large number of variables. As in Chapter 14, we can use conditional independence statements to simplify this expression. The main assumption is that the problem is *Markovian*—the probability distribution for the current state of the world depends only on the previous state and the action taken in it. If X_t is the state of the world at time t and A_t is the action taken at time t, then we have

$$\mathbf{P}(\mathbf{X}_t | \mathbf{X}_1 \ldots \mathbf{X}_{t-1}, A_1 \ldots A_{t-1}) = \mathbf{P}(\mathbf{X}_t | \mathbf{X}_{t-1}, A_{t-1}) \tag{17.5}$$

Whether the Markov property holds depends on which state variables the agent is tracking, and on the details of the environment. For example, in the case of a robot moving in the X–Y plane, the previous position and velocity might well be enough to predict the current position and velocity, given the previous motor command—one can simply use Newton's laws to calculate the new position and velocity. On the other hand, if the robot is battery-powered, then the effect of an action will depend on whether the battery is exhausted. Because this in turn depends on how much power was used by all previous commands, the Markov property is violated. We can restore the Markov property by including $BatteryLevel_t$ as one of the state variables that comprise X_t.

We also assume that each percept depends only on the state at the time. This amounts to the assertion that percepts (E_t) are causally determined by the state of the world:

$$\mathbf{P}(\mathbf{E}_t | \mathbf{X}_1 \ldots \mathbf{X}_t, A_1 \ldots A_{t-1}, \mathbf{E}_1 \ldots \mathbf{E}_{t-1}) = \mathbf{P}(\mathbf{E}_t | \mathbf{X}_t) \tag{17.6}$$

Finally, we assume that a similar equation holds for actions. The action taken depends only on the percepts the agent has received to date:

$$\mathbf{P}(A_{t-1} | A_1 \ldots A_{t-2}, \mathbf{E}_1 \ldots \mathbf{E}_{t-1}) = \mathbf{P}(A_{t-1} | \mathbf{E}_1 \ldots \mathbf{E}_{t-1}) \tag{17.7}$$

This final assertion is valid because of the structure of the agent itself: its only input from the outside is the percept at each time step.

Taken together, Equations (17.5), (17.6), and (17.7) allow us to simplify the calculation of the current state estimate $Bel(\mathbf{X}_t)$. The calculation takes place in two phases:

PREDICTION PHASE
◇ **Prediction phase**: first, we predict the probability distribution over states we *would have expected*, given our knowledge of the previous state and how actions affect states. We call this $\widehat{Bel}$, and calculate it by adding up the probabilities of arriving in a given state at time t for each of the states we could have been in at time $t-1$:

$$\widehat{Bel}(\mathbf{X}_t) = \sum_{\mathbf{X}_{t-1}} \mathbf{P}(\mathbf{X}_t | \mathbf{X}_{t-1} = \mathbf{x}_{t-1}, A_{t-1}) Bel(\mathbf{X}_{t-1} = \mathbf{x}_{t-1}) \tag{17.8}$$

where $\mathbf{x}_{t-1}$ ranges over all possible values of the state variables $\mathbf{X}_{t-1}$.

ESTIMATION PHASE
◇ **Estimation phase**: now we have a distribution over the current state variables, given everything but the most recent observation. The estimation phase updates this using the

percept $\mathbf{E}_t$. Because both the state variables and the percept refer to the same time, this is a simple matter of Bayesian updating, using $\widehat{Bel}(\mathbf{X}_t)$ as the prior:

$$Bel(\mathbf{X}_t) = \alpha \mathbf{P}(\mathbf{E}_t|\mathbf{X}_t)\widehat{Bel}(\mathbf{X}_t) \qquad (17.9)$$

where α is a normalization constant.

Exercise 17.5 asks you to derive these equations from the assumptions listed earlier.

KALMAN FILTERING

It is worth noting that the equations for Bel and $\widehat{Bel}$ are a generalization of the technique known in classical control theory as **Kalman filtering** (Kalman, 1960). Kalman filtering assumes that each state variable is real-valued and distributed according to a Gaussian distribution; that each sensor suffers from unbiased Gaussian noise; that each action can be described as a vector of real values, one for each state variable; and that the new state is a linear function of the previous state and the action. These assumptions, taken together, allow prediction and estimation to be implemented by some simple matrix calculations, even with a large number of state variables. Kalman filtering is universally applied in monitoring and controlling all sorts of dynamical systems, from chemical plants to guided missiles. It has good success even in domains where not all the assumptions are satisfied.

Given a probability distribution over the current state, it is a simple matter to carry out the remaining steps of the decision cycle, which involve projecting forward the possible results of the available actions and choosing the one with maximal expected utility. The belief update equations also allow us to design an agent that keeps around just the current belief vector for the state variables. The complete design is shown in Figure 17.9. Although the formulas look quite complicated, bear in mind that they simply instantiate the basic design given in Figure 17.8. Furthermore, the conditional probabilities appearing in the various expressions are

SENSOR MODEL
ACTION MODEL

exactly what we would expect to see. We have $\mathbf{P}(\mathbf{E}_t|\mathbf{X}_t)$, the **sensor model**, which describes how the environment generates the sensor data; and we have $\mathbf{P}(\mathbf{X}_t|\mathbf{X}_{t-1}, A_{t-1})$, the **action model**, which describes the effects of actions (and similarly for $t, t+1$).[3] These are the same kinds of information that we have used throughout the book to make decisions. The action model generalizes the transition model used earlier for sequential decision problems. The sensor model was not used there, of course, because we assumed an accessible environment in which the percept and the state can be equated.

The following sections describe sensor and action models in more detail, and show how the complete agent design can be implemented directly using the belief and decision network technology described in the previous chapters.

Sensing in uncertain worlds

We begin with the sensor model, which we defined previously as $\mathbf{P}(\mathbf{E}_t|\mathbf{X}_t)$, the probability of a percept given a state of the world. Actually, this is unnecessarily complicated, because it allows the sensor model to vary with time. We will instead assume a **stationary sensor model**:

STATIONARY
SENSOR MODEL

$$\forall t \ \ \mathbf{P}(\mathbf{E}_t|\mathbf{X}_t) = \mathbf{P}(\mathbf{E}|\mathbf{X})$$

---

[3] The notation used to describe the action model might make it look as if it only allows for actions by the agent. In fact, because the actions of other agents are presumably themselves determined by the state variables $\mathbf{X}_{t-1}$, the model can certainly handle multiple agents as is.

---

function DECISION-THEORETIC-AGENT(E_t) **returns** an action
   inputs: E_t, the percept at time t
   static: BN, a belief network with nodes $\mathbf{X}$
       $Bel(X)$, a vector of probabilities, updated over time

$\widehat{Bel}(\mathbf{X}_t) \leftarrow \sum_{\mathbf{X}_{t-1}} \mathbf{P}(\mathbf{X}_t \mid \mathbf{X}_{t-1}=\mathbf{x}_{t-1}, A_{t-1})\, Bel(\mathbf{X}_{t-1}=\mathbf{x}_{t-1})$
$Bel(\mathbf{X}_t) \leftarrow \alpha\, \mathbf{P}(\mathbf{E}_t \mid \mathbf{X}_t)\, \widehat{Bel}(\mathbf{X}_t)$
$action \leftarrow \arg\max_{A_t} \sum_{\mathbf{X}_t} \left[Bel(\mathbf{X}_t=\mathbf{x}_t) \sum_{\mathbf{X}_{t+1}} P(\mathbf{X}_{t+1} = \mathbf{x}_{t+1} \mid \mathbf{X}_t=\mathbf{x}_t, A_t)\, U(\mathbf{x}_{t+1}) \right]$
return $action$

Figure 17.9   Detailed design for a decision-theoretic agent.

---

where $\mathbf{E}$ and $\mathbf{X}$ are random variables ranging over percepts and states, respectively. What this means is that given a state of the world, the chances of the sensor giving a certain reading will be the same today as it was yesterday. This does *not* mean, for example, that the sensor can never break; it just means that we have to include in $\mathbf{X}$ all the variables that are important to the sensor's performance. The advantage of the stationary sensor model is that the fixed model $\mathbf{P}(\mathbf{E}|\mathbf{X})$ can then be used at each time step.

The basic idea of a sensor model can be implemented very simply in a belief network, because the assumption embodied in Equation (17.6) effectively isolates the sensor variables for a given time step from the rest of the network. Figure 17.10(a) shows an abstract belief network fragment with generalized state and sensor variables. The sensor model itself is the conditional probability table associated with the percept node. The direction of the arrow is the crucial element here: the state of the world *causes* the sensor to take on a particular value.[4] The sensor model is therefore an example of the general principle, stated in Chapter 7 and again in Chapter 15, that causal models are to be preferred when possible. If the sensor gives a perfect report of the actual state, then the sensor model—the conditional probability table— will be purely deterministic. Noise and errors in the sensor are reflected in the probabilities of "incorrect" readings. In fact, we have already seen examples of sensor models of this kind: in the burglar-alarm network (Figure 15.1), both *JohnCalls* and *MaryCalls* can be viewed as sensor nodes for the *Alarm* state variable. Their conditional probability tables, shown in Figure 15.2, show how reliable they are as sensors.

The next step is to break apart the generalized state and sensor variables into their components. Typically, each sensor only measures some small aspect of the total state. An example is shown in Figure 17.10(b), where temperature and pressure gauges measure the actual temperature and pressure of some system. Decomposing the overall sensor model in Figure 17.10(a) into its separate components greatly reduces the size of the CPTs, unless the sensors are very badly designed. As an example of how not to couple sensor nodes to state nodes: consider two sensors

---

[4] Of course, the process of *inference* will go the other way: evidence arrives at the sensor node, and is propagated to the state variable. The inference process essentially *inverts* the sensor model. This is basically what makes a Kalman filter simple. If $P(E|X)$ is Gaussian, then $P(X|E)$ is also Gaussian with an identical distribution, so that inversion is trivial.

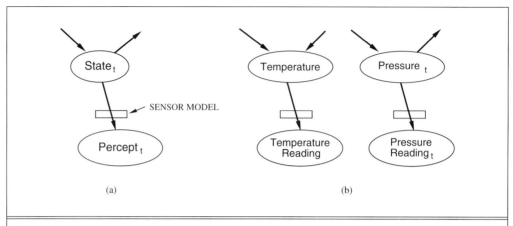

Figure 17.10   (a) Belief network fragment showing the general relationship between state variables and sensor variables. (b) An example with pressure and temperature gauges.

that (somehow) measure *Pressure/Temperature* and *Pressure* × *Temperature*. Each of the two state nodes would have to be connected to both sensor nodes, resulting in large CPTs for the sensor models.

Often, we will have several sensors that are measuring the same state variable. In Figure 17.11, we show an example where two gauges are being used to measure the actual temperature of some object, perhaps a superconductor. *The crucial thing to notice here is that the sensor values are conditionally independent of each other, given the actual value.* The reasoning here is similar to the reasoning for the conditional independence of symptoms given a disease. Although the sensors are not unconditionally independent—in fact, they will usually display approximately the same reading—they are correlated only inasmuch as they depend on the actual temperature. When we have multiple sensors for the same state variables, the resulting inference process is called **sensor fusion** or **data fusion**. To see how important this can be, consider the situation when Gauge 1 reads 13.6°K, while Gauge 2 reads 14.4°K. If each gauge is accurate to within 0.5°K, as represented in the sensor models, then the network will infer that the actual temperature is between 13.9°K and 14.1°K. Integrating the results of multiple sensors can provide greater accuracy than any one sensor on its own. This is true whether the sensors are similar, as in the case of temperature gauges, or very different, as in the case of sonar and infrared distance sensors used in robotics. Detailed sensor models have been built for both sonar and infrared, which have somewhat complementary performance. Sonar has a long range, but is subject to "ghost" images caused by multiple reflections and specularities. Infrared is only accurate over short distances. By using sensor fusion, it is often possible to create an accurate model of the robot's environment in cases where the sensors used separately would be lost.

Anyone with hands-on experience of robotics, computerized process control, or other forms of automatic sensing will readily testify to the fact that sensors fail. When a sensor fails, it does not necessarily send a signal saying, "Oh, by the way, the data I'm about to send you is a load of nonsense." Instead, it simply sends the nonsense. This can be dangerous if taken literally. For example, a robot's sonar distance sensor might start sending "infinity," meaning that no object

SENSOR FUSION

DATA FUSION

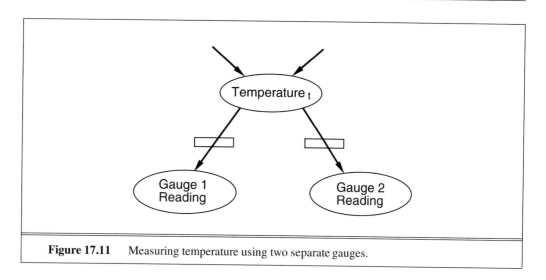

Figure 17.11   Measuring temperature using two separate gauges.

was detected within the sonar's range. This could be because the robot has wandered outside or it could be because the sonar's detector is broken. In the latter case, the robot could start crashing into walls. *In order for the system to handle sensor failure, the sensor model must include the possibility of failure.* For example, in the case of sonar, a sensor model that says that the sensor is accurate to within 10 cm explicitly *disallows* the possibility of failure, and therefore forces the robot to take the sonar reading literally. For any given *actual* distance, the sonar model should allow the possibility that the *observed* distance will be "infinity." Then the robot can handle sensor failure more appropriately. For example, if the robot is in a corridor, its *prediction* will be that the closest object remains about 60 cm away. If the sonar suddenly reports "infinity," then the most likely conclusion is that the sensor has failed, not that the corridor has disappeared. Furthermore, if the robot has more than one distance sensor, the sensor fusion process will automatically discount the readings of the failed sensor.

It is also possible to use more detailed models of sensor failure by incorporating additional state variables representing the condition of the sensor. Figure 17.12 shows a model of a vision-based lane-position sensor. Such sensors are used in autonomous vehicles to keep them in the center of their lane. They also could be used to sound a warning in a human-driven car when it starts to stray off the road. The sensor's accuracy is directly affected by rain and an uneven road surface. Furthermore, rain might also cause the sensor to fail by damaging the electronics, as might a bumpy road. Sensor failure in turn affects the sensor's accuracy. This kind of model is capable of some quite subtle reasoning. For example, if the system believes (perhaps from another sensor's input) that it is raining, then that will alter the sensor accuracy variable, raising the likelihood of larger error in the lane-position sensor. When an unexpected reading occurs, the system will be less likely to assume that the car is out of position. Conversely, a large discrepancy between expected and observed position can increase the system's belief that it is raining! A really serious discrepancy would raise the posterior probability of sensor failure; hence this kind of network can perform "diagnosis" of the sensors. In the next section, we will see how this capability can be extended by reasoning over time.

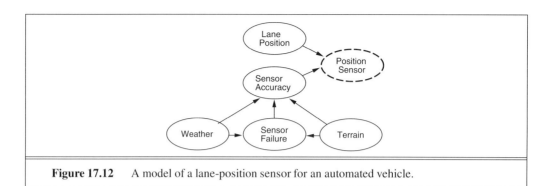

Figure 17.12   A model of a lane-position sensor for an automated vehicle.

17.5   DYNAMIC BELIEF NETWORKS

We now consider the evolution of the state of the environment over time, and how this can be represented in a dynamic belief network. As we said earlier, the evolution of the environment is modelled by the conditional probability distribution $\mathbf{P}(\mathbf{X}_t|\mathbf{X}_{t-1}, A_{t-1})$, which describes how the state depends on the previous state and the action of the agent. As with the sensor model, we make a stationarity assumption: the conditional probabilities are the same for all t. In this section, we will cover the case where the agent is passively monitoring and predicting a changing environment, rather than acting on it. The agent is thus concerned with a sequence of $\mathbf{X}_t$ values, where each one is determined solely by the previous one: $\mathbf{P}(\mathbf{X}_t|\mathbf{X}_{t-1})$. This sequence is called

STATE EVOLUTION
MODEL
a **state evolution model** or **Markov chain**. Monitoring and prediction is important in its own

MARKOV CHAIN
right, and it also makes the explanation simpler. In the next section, we will show how an agent can use the $\mathbf{X}_t$ to make decisions and take action.

In principle, we want to build a belief network with one node for each state and sensor

DYNAMIC BELIEF
NETWORK
variable, for each time step. A network of this kind is called a **dynamic belief network** (DBN). The generic structure of a DBN is shown in Figure 17.13. (In a real network for a specific problem, the state and percept nodes would be replaced by several nodes each, with appropriate connections. Notice also the resemblance to Figure 7.3.) If t is the current time step, then we have have evidence for the percept nodes up to and including time t. The task of the network is then to calculate the probability distribution for the state at time t. One may also want to know how the state will evolve into the future—the probability distributions for $State_{t+1}$ and so on.

PROBABILISTIC
PROJECTION
This task is called **probabilistic projection**. Both tasks can be carried out using the standard algorithms from Chapter 15.

A little thought reveals that although the previous sentence is true, it may not be very useful. A dynamic belief network of the kind shown in Figure 17.13 could be extremely large, so the belief net algorithms could be extremely inefficient. Now we will see the benefit of all the work that went into Equations (17.8) and (17.9) (for $\widehat{Bel}$ and Bel). We can implement the prediction and estimation phases as operations on the belief network. Furthermore, we need only

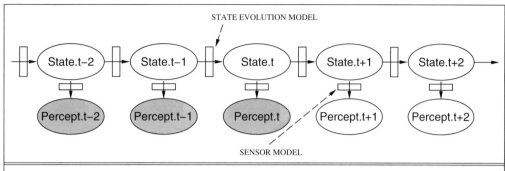

STATE EVOLUTION MODEL

SENSOR MODEL

Figure 17.13   The generic structure of a dynamic belief network. The shaded nodes show the evidence that has been accumulated so far.

SLICES

keep enough network structure to represent *two* time steps (otherwise known as two **slices** of the network). Figure 17.14 shows the prediction-estimation process in operation, a truly beautiful thing. Each cycle of the process works as follows:

$\diamond$ **Prediction**: we begin with a two-slice network; let us call the slices $t-1$ and t. We assume that we have already calculated $Bel(\mathbf{X}_{t-1})$, incorporating all evidence up to and including $\mathbf{E}_{t-1}$. Notice that slice $t-1$ has no connections to previous slices. The state variables in $t-1$ have prior probabilities associated with them (see the next step). We then calculate the belief vector $\widehat{Bel}(\mathbf{X}_t)$, according to Equation (17.8). This is actually the standard belief network updating process applied to evidence $\mathbf{E}_{t-1}$.

ROLLUP

$\diamond$ **Rollup**: now we *remove* slice $t-1$. This requires adding a prior probability table for the state variables at time t. This prior is just $\widehat{Bel}(\mathbf{X}_t)$.

$\diamond$ **Estimation**: now we add the new percept $\mathbf{E}_t$, applying standard belief network updating to calculate $Bel(\mathbf{X}_t)$, the probability distribution over the current state. We then add the slice for $t+1$. The network is now ready for the next cycle.

This process implements the formal algorithm specified in Figure 17.9, using the belief network inference machinery for all the calculations. Notice that, as in the formal algorithm, the percept history is summarized in the belief vector for the current state—a summarization justified by Equation (17.5).

Probabilistic projection is also straightforward. We can take the network after step (c), add slices for future times, and apply a belief network inference algorithm to calculate the posterior probability distributions for the future states, given the current percept. Unlike the update cycle, this might be expensive because it involves inference in a temporally extended network. However, this network has a special property: none of the future nodes has any evidence associated with it. This means that a simple stochastic simulation technique such as logic sampling (see page 455) will work well, because every run can be consistent with the evidence. Given a desired accuracy level for the sampling process, the time complexity will usually be $O(n)$.

As an example of the application of dynamic belief networks, consider again the sensor-failure model shown in Figure 17.12. We can extend this into a DBN (Figure 17.15) by adding state evolution models for state variables *Weather*, *Terrain* and *SensorFailure*, as well as for the

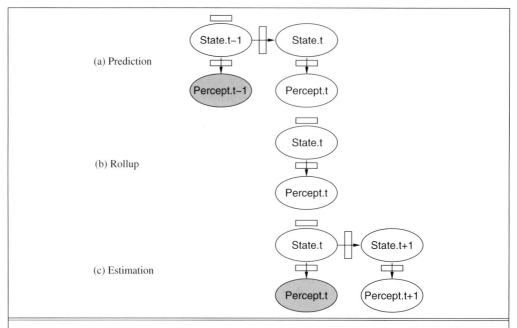

Figure 17.14   The steps in updating a dynamic belief network over time. Each step is described in detail in the text.

principal state variable *LanePosition*. The model of interest here is that for *SensorFailure*. The model is quite simple: basically, once a sensor has broken, it usually stays broken. What happens over time is that as the sensor continues to send nonsense signals, it becomes more and more likely that they are incorrect. This is especially true if there are other sensors through which the network can infer *LanePosition* indirectly. It will even work, however, just using the state evolution model for *LanePosition*, which will usually put limits on how much lateral motion we can expect for a vehicle.

17.6   DYNAMIC DECISION NETWORKS

DYNAMIC DECISION
NETWORKS   All we need in order to convert dynamic belief networks into **dynamic decision networks** (DDNs) is to add utility nodes and decision nodes for actions. Figure 17.16 shows the generic structure of a DDN for a sequential decision problem where the terminal states are three steps ahead. The decision problem involves calculating the value of D_t that maximizes the agent's expected utility over the remaining state sequence.[5] In addition to the decision nodes for the

---

[5] Usually, the final utility will be calculated as a sum of expected rewards $R_t + R_{t+1} \ldots$. We omit the reward nodes in order to simplify the diagram.

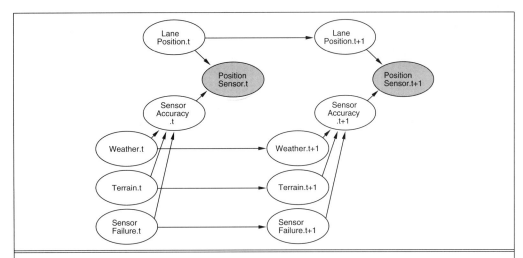

Figure 17.15   A two-slice fragment of a dynamic belief network for continuous monitoring of the lane positioning of an automated vehicle. Evidence variables are shaded.

current and future time steps, notice that the network also contains the previous decision, D_{t-1}, as an evidence node. It is treated as evidence because it has already happened.

The evaluation algorithm for DDNs is essentially the same as that for ordinary decision networks. In the worst case, the DDN calculates the expected utility of each decision sequence by fixing the decision nodes and applying probabilistic inference to calculate the final state. As in our discussion of sequential decision problems earlier in the chapter, we must also be careful to take into account the fact that, for each future decision, the agent does not currently know what information will be available at the time the future decision is made. That is, for decision D_{t+i}, the agent *will* have available percepts $\mathbf{E}_{t+1}, \ldots, \mathbf{E}_{t+i}$; but currently, it does not know what those percepts will be. For example, an autonomous vehicle might be contemplating a lane change at time $t + i$, but it will not know until then if there is another car blocking its path.

In our earlier discussion, we handled this by iteratively computing a **policy** that associates a decision with each *state*. With DDNs, we do not have this option because the states are represented implicitly by the set of state variables. Furthermore, in inaccessible environments, the agent will not know what state it is in anyway. What we must do instead is consider each possible instantiation of the future sensor variables as well as each possible instantiation of the future decision variables. The expected utility of each decision sequence is then the weighted sum of the utilities computed using each possible percept sequence, where the weight is the probability of the percept sequence given the decision sequence. Thus, the DDN provides approximate solutions for partially observable Markov decision problems, where the degree of approximation depends on the amount of lookahead.

The preceding paragraph boils down to this: in evaluating an action, one must consider not only its effect on the environment, but also its effect on the internal state of the agent via the percepts it generates (see also Section 16.6). In still plainer terms: such considerations allow the agent to see the value of (actively) looking before leaping, to hunt for lost keys, and so on.

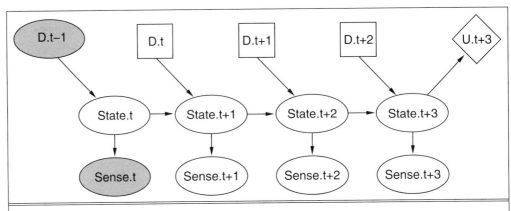

Figure 17.16   The generic structure of a dynamic decision network, showing a sequential decision problem with three steps. Evidence variables are shaded.

Just as we used a limited horizon in game playing and with value iteration and policy iteration, we can limit the extent of forward projection in the DDN in order to reduce complexity. This, combined with a heuristic estimate for the utility of the remaining steps, can provide a reasonable approximation to rational action. There are many other possible approximation techniques, such as using less detailed state variables for states in the distant future; using a greedy heuristic search through the space of decision sequences; assuming "most likely" values for future percept sequences rather than considering all possible values; and so on. There remain many possible techniques for DDN evaluation that are as yet unexplored.

Discussion

All in all, the DDN promises potential solutions to many of the problems that arise as AI systems are moved from static, accessible, and above all *simple* environments to dynamic, inaccessible, complex environments that are closer to the real world.

- They can handle uncertainty correctly, and sometimes efficiently.
- They deal with continuous streams of sensor input.
- They can handle unexpected events because they have no fixed "plan."
- They can handle noisy sensors and sensor failure.
- They can act in order to obtain relevant information.
- They can handle relatively large state spaces because they decompose the state into a set of state variables with sparse connections.
- They exhibit "graceful degradation" under time pressure and in complex environments, using various approximation techniques.

What is missing? The first, and probably the most important, defect of DDNs is that they retain the property of forward search through concrete states that is typical of the search algorithms studied in Part II. In Part IV, we explained how the ability to consider partially ordered, abstract plans using goal-directed search provided a massive increase in problem-solving power, particularly when combined with plan libraries. At present, we do not really know how to extend these methods into the probabilistic domain. A second, related problem is the basically propositional nature of our probabilistic language. It is impossible, *within* the language of probability theory, to state properly beliefs such as "If any car hits a lamp post going over 30 mph, the occupants of the car will be injured with probability 0.6," because probability theory has no quantifiers ("any car") and no functions ("occupants of the car"). What this means in practice is that some of what goes on in DBNs and DDNs is that programs (rather than pure probabilistic inferences) are responsible for choosing which random variables to instantiate and for filling in their conditional probability tables. If we had an appropriate combination of first-order logic with probability, many of these difficulties could be addressed within a well-understood reasoning system. Work on such a language is one of the most important topics in knowledge representation research, and some progress has been made recently (Bacchus, 1990; Bacchus *et al.*, 1992).

Overall, the potential payoff of combining DDN-like techniques with planning methods is enormous. The technical and mathematical problems involved in getting it right are difficult, but it is an important area of current research.

17.7   SUMMARY

This chapter shows how to use knowledge about the world to make decisions even when the outcomes of an action are uncertain and the payoffs will not be reaped until several (or many) actions have passed. The main points are as follows:

- Sequential decision problems in uncertain environments can be solved by calculating a **policy** that associates an optimal decision with every state that the agent might reach.
- **Value iteration** and **policy iteration** are two methods for calculating optimal policies. Both are closely related to the general computational technique of dynamic programming.
- Slightly more complex methods are needed to handle the case where the length of the action sequence is unbounded. We briefly discussed the use of **system gain** and **discounting**.
- State-based methods for sequential decision problems do not scale well to large state spaces. Heuristic techniques using best-first search and a limited horizon seem to mitigate this to some extent, but suffer from local minima.
- Decomposing the state into a set of state variables provides a significant advantage. It also simplifies the handling of inaccessible environments.
- We derived a simple updating cycle for a decision-theoretic agent, using a set of **Markov assumptions**.
- We showed how **dynamic belief networks** can handle sensing and updating over time, and provide a direct implementation of the update cycle.
- We showed how **dynamic decision networks** can solve sequential decision problems, handling many (but not all) of the issues arising for agents in complex, uncertain domains.

BIBLIOGRAPHICAL AND HISTORICAL NOTES

Richard Bellman (1957) initiated the modern approach to sequential decision problems, and proposed the dynamic programming approach in general and the value iteration algorithm in particular. A remarkable Ph.D. thesis by Ron Howard (1960) introduced policy iteration and the idea of system gain for solving infinite-horizon problems. Several additional results were introduced by Bellman and Dreyfus (1962). The analysis of discounting in terms of stationary preferences is due to Koopmans (1972). Bertsekas (1987) provides an authoritative modern text on dynamic programming, which has become one of the most widely used tools for search and optimization problems.

The observation that partially observable Markov decision problems can be transformed into a regular Markov decision problem using the belief states is due to Astrom (1965). The first complete algorithm for exact solution of partially-observable Markov decision problems (POMDPs) was proposed by Edward Sondik (1971) in his Ph.D. thesis. (A later journal paper by Smallwood and Sondik (1973) contains some errors but is more accessible.) Lovejoy (1991) surveys the state of the art in POMDPs. In AI, Cassandra *et al.* (1994) have investigated the application of POMDP algorithms to planning problems.

Several recent papers have attempted to combine dynamic programming algorithms such as policy iteration with planning and search models from AI (Dean *et al.*, 1993; Tash and Russell, 1994). This line of work involves approximating a Markov decision problem using a limited horizon and abstract states, in an effort to overcome the combinatorics of large state spaces. Heuristics based on the value of information can be used to select areas of the state space where a local expansion of the horizon will yield a significant improvement in decision quality. Agents using this approach can tailor their effort to handle time pressure, and generate some interesting behaviors such as using familiar "beaten paths" to find their way around the state space quickly without having to recompute optimal decisions at each point.

Many of the basic ideas for estimating the state of dynamical systems came from the mathematician C. F. Gauss (1809). The prediction–estimation cycle for monitoring environments under uncertainty was proposed by Kalman (Kalman, 1960), building on classified wartime research by Wiener (1942) and Kolmogorov (1941). Kalman filtering, which Kalman derived for linear systems with Gaussian noise, has since become an industry in itself (Gelb, 1974; Bar-Shalom and Fortmann, 1988). Leonard and Durrant-Whyte (1992) describe probabilistic sensor models in detail, with particular attention to the modelling of sonar sensors.

Dynamic belief networks (DBNs) can be viewed as a sparse encoding of a Markov process, and were first used in AI by Dean and Kanazawa (1989), Nicholson (1992), and Kjaerulff (1992). The last work includes a generic extension to the HUGIN belief net system to provide the necessary facilities for dynamic belief network generation and compilation. The development given in this chapter owes a good deal to the book by Dean and Wellman (1991), which provides extensive discussion of the use of DBNs and DDNs (dynamic decision networks) in mobile robots. Huang *et al.* (1994) describe an application of DBNs to the analysis of freeway traffic using computer vision. A notation and an evaluation algorithm for additive DDNs are provided by Tatman and Shachter (1990).

EXERCISES

17.1   For the stochastic version of the world shown in Figure 17.1, calculate which squares can be reached by the action sequence [*Up, Right*], and with what probabilities.

17.2   For a specific environment (which you can make up), construct a utility function on histories that is *not* separable. Explain how the concept of utility on states fails in this case.

17.3   Consider the stochastic version of the environment shown in Figure 17.1.

   a. Implement an environment simulator for this environment, such that the specific geography of the environment is easily altered.

   b. Create a SIMPLE-POLICY-AGENT that uses policy iteration, and measure its performance in the environment simulator from various starting states.

   c. Experiment with increasing the size of the environment. How does the execution time per action vary with the size of the environment?

   d. Analyze the policy iteration algorithm to find its worst-case complexity, assuming that value determination is done using a standard equation-solving method.

   e. Does value iteration terminate if the utility values are required to converge *exactly*?

17.4   For the environment shown in Figure 17.1, find all the threshold values for the cost of a step, such that the optimal policy changes when the threshold is crossed.

17.5   Prove that the calculations in the prediction and estimation phases of the basic decision cycle (Equations (17.8) and (17.9)) do in fact yield the correct value for $Bel(\mathbf{X}_t)$, given assumptions (17.5), (17.6), and (17.7).

17.6   In this exercise, we will consider part of the problem of building a robot that plays Ping-Pong.

   One of the things it will have to do is find out where the ball is and estimate its trajectory. Let us suppose for a moment that we have a vision system that can return an estimated instantaneous (x, y, z) position for the ball. This position estimate for time t_i will be used as an evidence node O_i in a belief network that infers the desired information. The idea is that nodes X_i and V_i in the network represent the ball's instantaneous position and velocity. The trajectory of the ball is followed by having multiple copies of these nodes, one for each time step. In addition to these nodes, we also have nodes for the instantaneous friction force F_i acting on the ball due to air resistance, which depends only on the current velocity. The times $t_1, t_2, t_3, \ldots$ can be assumed to be separated by some small interval δt.

   a. Which of the belief networks in Figure 17.17 correctly (but not necessarily efficiently) represent the preceding information? (You may assume that second-order effects—proportional to δt^2—are ignored.)

   b. Which is the best network?

   c. Which networks can be solved by local propagation algorithms?

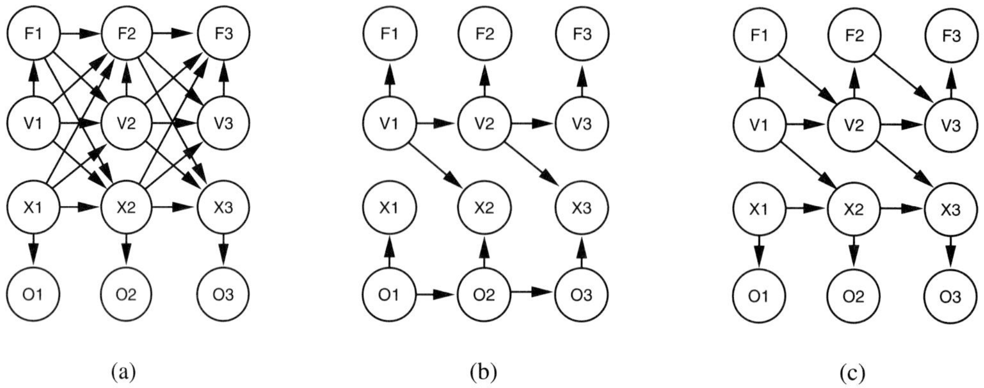

Figure 17.17   Some proposed networks for Ping-Pong tracking.

d. The nodes in the networks shown in the figure refer to past and present times. Explain how the networks can be extended and used to predict the position at any future time.

e. Now consider the vision subsystem, whose job it is to provide observation evidence. Its input is an array of intensity values from the camera image. Assuming that the ball is white, whereas most of the room is darker, explain briefly how to calculate the position of the ball given the array.

f. Does it make more sense to calculate the position in coordinates relative to the robot or relative to the room? Why?

Part VI

LEARNING

So far we have assumed that all the "intelligence" in an agent has been built in by the agent's designer. The agent is then let loose in an environment, and does the best it can given the way it was programmed to act. But this is not necessarily the best approach—for the agent or the designer. Whenever the designer has incomplete knowledge of the environment that the agent will live in, learning is the only way that the agent can acquire what it needs to know. Learning thus provides **autonomy** in the sense defined in Chapter 1. It also provides a good way to build high-performance systems—by giving a learning system experience in the application domain.

The four chapters in this part cover the field of **machine learning**—the subfield of AI concerned with programs that learn from experience. Chapter 18 introduces the basic design for learning agents, and addresses the general problem of learning from examples. Chapter 19 discusses the process of learning in neural networks—collections of simple nonlinear processing elements—and in belief networks. In Chapter 20, we tackle the general problem of improving the behavior of an agent given some feedback as to its performance. Finally, Chapter 21 shows how learning can be improved by using prior knowledge.

18 LEARNING FROM OBSERVATIONS

In which we describe agents that can improve their behavior through diligent study of their own experiences.

The idea behind learning is that percepts should be used not only for acting, but also for improving the agent's ability to act in the future. Learning takes place as a result of the interaction between the agent and the world, and from observation by the agent of its own decision-making processes. Learning can range from trivial memorization of experience, as exhibited by the wumpus agent in Chapter 7, to the creation of entire scientific theories, as exhibited by Albert Einstein. This chapter starts with the design of general learning agents, and describes inductive learning—constructing a description of a function from a set of input/output examples. We then give several algorithms for inductive learning in logical agents and a theoretical analysis that explains why learning works.

18.1 A GENERAL MODEL OF LEARNING AGENTS

A learning agent can be divided into four conceptual components, as shown in Figure 18.1. The most important distinction is between the **learning element**, which is responsible for making improvements, and the **performance element**, which is responsible for selecting external actions. The performance element is what we have previously considered to be the entire agent: it takes in percepts and decides on actions. The learning element takes some knowledge about the learning element and some feedback on how the agent is doing, and determines how the performance element should be modified to (hopefully) do better in the future. The design of the learning element depends very much on the design of the performance element. When trying to design an agent that learns a certain capability, the first question is not "How am I going to get it to learn this?" but "What kind of performance element will my agent need to do this once it has learned how?" For example, the learning algorithms for producing rules for logical systems are quite different from the learning algorithms for producing belief networks. We will see, however, that the *principles* behind the learning algorithms are much the same.

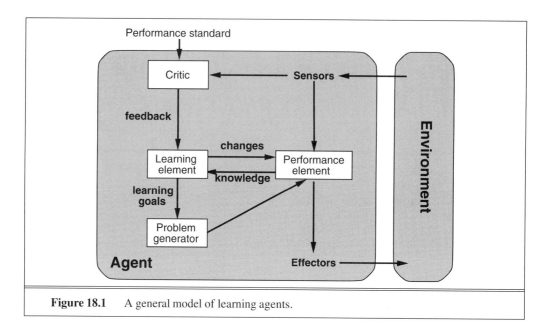

Figure 18.1   A general model of learning agents.

CRITIC

The **critic** is designed to tell the learning element how well the agent is doing. The critic employs a fixed standard of performance. This is necessary because the percepts themselves provide no indication of the agent's success. For example, a chess program may receive a percept indicating that it has checkmated its opponent, but it needs a performance standard to know that this is a good thing; the percept itself does not say so. It is important that the performance standard is a fixed measure that is conceptually outside the agent; otherwise the agent could adjust its performance standards to meet its behavior. In humans, this form of irrationality is called "sour grapes" and is characterized by comments such as "Oh well, never mind, I didn't want that stupid Nobel prize anyway."

PROBLEM
GENERATOR

The last component of the learning agent is the **problem generator**. It is responsible for suggesting actions that will lead to new and informative experiences. The point is that if the performance element had its way, it would keep doing the actions that are best, given what it knows. But if the agent is willing to explore a little, and do some perhaps suboptimal actions in the short run, it might discover much better actions for the long run. The problem generator's job is to suggest these exploratory actions. This is what scientists do when they carry out experiments. Galileo did not think that dropping rocks from the top of a tower in Pisa was valuable in itself; he was not trying to break the rocks, nor to render pedestrians unconscious. His aim was to demonstrate a better theory of the motion of objects.

To make the overall design more concrete, let us return to the automated taxi example. The performance element consists of whatever collection of knowledge and procedures the taxi has for selecting its driving actions (turning, accelerating, braking, honking, and so on). The taxi goes out on the road and drives, using this performance element. The learning element formulates goals, for example, to learn better rules describing the effects of braking and accelerating, to learn the geography of the area, to learn how the taxi behaves on wet roads, and to learn what causes annoyance to other drivers. The critic observes the world and passes information along to the learning element. For example, after the taxi makes a quick left turn across three lanes of traffic, the critic observes the shocking language used by other drivers, the learning element is able to formulate a rule saying this was a bad action, and the performance element is modified by installing the new rule. Occasionally, the problem generator kicks in with a suggestion: try taking 7th Avenue uptown this time, and see if it is faster than the normal route.

SPEEDUP LEARNING

The learning element is also responsible for improving the *efficiency* of the performance element. For example, when asked to make a trip to a new destination, the taxi might take a while to consult its map and plan the best route. But the next time a similar trip is requested, the planning process should be much faster. This is called **speedup learning**, and is dealt with in Chapter 21. In this chapter, we concentrate on the acquisition of knowledge.

Machine learning researchers have come up with a large variety of learning elements. To understand them, it will help to see how their design is affected by the context in which they will operate. The design of the learning element is affected by four major issues:

- Which *components* of the performance element are to be improved.
- What *representation* is used for those components.
- What *feedback* is available.
- What *prior information* is available.

Components of the performance element

We have seen that there are many ways to build the performance element of an agent. The components can include the following:

1. A direct mapping from conditions on the current state to actions.
2. A means to infer relevant properties of the world from the percept sequence.
3. Information about the way the world evolves.
4. Information about the results of possible actions the agent can take.
5. Utility information indicating the desirability of world states.
6. Action-value information indicating the desirability of particular actions in particular states.
7. Goals that describe classes of states whose achievement maximizes the agent's utility.

Each of the components can be learned, given the appropriate feedback. For example, if the agent does an action and then perceives the resulting state of the environment, this information can be used to learn a description of the results of actions (4). If the taxi exerts a certain braking pressure when driving on a wet road, then it will soon find out how much actual deceleration is achieved. Similarly, if the critic can use the performance standard to deduce utility values from the percepts, then the agent can learn a useful representation of its utility function (5). If the taxi receives no tips from passengers who have been thoroughly shaken up during the trip, it can learn a useful component of its overall utility function. In a sense, the performance standard can be seen as defining a set of *distinguished percepts* that will be interpreted as providing direct feedback on the quality of the agent's behavior. Hardwired performance standards such as pain and hunger in animals can be understood in this way.

Representation of the components

Any of these components can be represented using any of the representation schemes in this book. We have seen several examples: deterministic descriptions such as linear weighted polynomials for utility functions in game-playing programs and propositional and first-order logical sentences for all of the components in a logical agent; and probabilistic descriptions such as belief networks for the inferential components of a decision-theoretic agent. Effective learning algorithms have been devised for all of these. The details of the learning algorithm will be different for each representation, but the main idea remains the same.

Available feedback

SUPERVISED
LEARNING

For some components, such as the component for predicting the outcome of an action, the available feedback generally tells the agent what the correct outcome is. That is, the agent predicts that a certain action (braking) will have a certain outcome (stopping in 10 feet), and the environment immediately provides a percept that describes the actual correct outcome (stopping in 15 feet). Any situation in which both the inputs and outputs of a component can be perceived is called **supervised learning**. (Often, the outputs are provided by a friendly teacher.)

REINFORCEMENT
LEARNING

REINFORCEMENT

On the other hand, in learning the condition-action component, the agent receives some evaluation of its action (such as a hefty bill for rear-ending the car in front) but is not told the correct action (to brake more gently and much earlier). This is called **reinforcement learning**; the hefty bill is called a **reinforcement**.[1] The subject is covered in Chapter 20.[2]

UNSUPERVISED
LEARNING

Learning when there is no hint at all about the correct outputs is called **unsupervised learning**. An unsupervised learner can always learn relationships among its percepts using supervised learning methods—that is, it can learn to predict its future percepts given its previous percepts. It cannot learn what to *do* unless it already has a utility function.

Prior knowledge

The majority of learning research in AI, computer science, and psychology has studied the case in which the agent begins with no knowledge at all about what it is trying to learn. It only has access to the examples presented by its experience. Although this is an important special case, it is by no means the general case. Most human learning takes place in the context of a good deal of background knowledge. Some psychologists and linguists claim that even newborn babies exhibit knowledge of the world. Whatever the truth of this claim, there is no doubt that prior knowledge can help enormously in learning. A physicist examining a stack of bubble-chamber photographs may be able to induce a theory positing the existence of a new particle of a certain mass and charge; but an art critic examining the same stack might learn nothing more than that the "artist" must be some sort of abstract expressionist. In Chapter 21, we see several ways in which learning is helped by the use of existing knowledge.

---

[1] The terms **reward** and **punishment** are also used as synonyms for **reinforcement**.

[2] Drawing the line between supervised and reinforcement learning is somewhat arbitrary; reinforcement learning can also be thought of as supervised learning with a less informative feedback signal.

Bringing it all together

Each of the seven components of the performance element can be described mathematically as a **function**: for example, information about the way the world evolves can be described as a function from a world state (the current state) to a world state (the next state or states); a goal can be described as a function from a state to a Boolean value (0 or 1) indicating whether the state satisfies the goal. The key point is that *all learning can be seen as learning the representation of a function.* We can choose which component of the performance element to improve and how it is to be represented. The available feedback may be more or less useful, and we may or may not have any prior knowledge. The underlying problem remains the same.

18.2   INDUCTIVE LEARNING

EXAMPLE

PURE INDUCTIVE
INFERENCE

HYPOTHESIS

In supervised learning, the learning element is given the correct (or approximately correct) value of the function for particular inputs, and changes its representation of the function to try to match the information provided by the feedback. More formally, we say an **example** is a pair $(x, f(x))$, where x is the input and $f(x)$ is the output of the function applied to x. The task of **pure inductive inference** (or **induction**) is this: given a collection of examples of f, return a function h that approximates f. The function h is called a **hypothesis**.

Figure 18.2 shows an example of this from plane geometry. The examples in Figure 18.2(a) are (x, y) points in the plane, where $y = f(x)$, and the task is to find a function $h(x)$ that fits the points well. In Figure 18.2(b) we have a piecewise-linear h function, while in Figure 18.2(c) we have a more complicated h function. Both functions agree with the example points, but differ on the y values they assign to other x inputs. In (d) we have a function that apparently ignores one of the example points, but fits the others with a simple function. The true f is unknown, so there are many choices for h, but without further knowledge, we have no way to prefer (b), (c), or (d). Any preference for one hypothesis over another, beyond mere consistency with the examples, is called a **bias**. Because there are almost always a large number of possible consistent hypotheses, all learning algorithms exhibit some sort of bias. We will see many examples in this and subsequent chapters.

BIAS

To get back to agents, suppose we have a reflex agent[3] that is being taught by a teacher. Figure 18.3 shows that the REFLEX-LEARNING-ELEMENT updates a global variable, *examples*, that holds a list of (*percept, action*) pairs. The percept could be a chess board position, and the action could be the best move as determined by a helpful grandmaster. When the REFLEX-PERFORMANCE-ELEMENT is faced with a percept it has been told about, it chooses the corresponding action. Otherwise, it calls a learning algorithm INDUCE on the examples it has seen so far. INDUCE returns a hypothesis h which the agent uses to choose an action.

There are many variants on this simple scheme. For example, the agent could perform **incremental learning**: rather than applying the learning algorithm to the entire set of examples each time a new prediction is needed, the agent could just try to update its old hypothesis whenever

INCREMENTAL
LEARNING

---

[3] Recall that reflex agents map directly from percepts to actions.

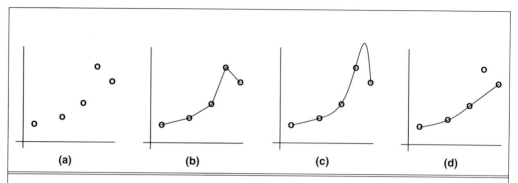

Figure 18.2   In (a) we have some example *(input,output)* pairs. In (b), (c), and (d) we have three hypotheses for functions from which these examples could be drawn.

---

global *examples* ← { }

function REFLEX-PERFORMANCE-ELEMENT(*percept*) **returns** an action

   if (*percept*, *a*) **in** *examples* **then return** *a*
   else
       h ← INDUCE(*examples*)
       return *h*(*percept*)

procedure REFLEX-LEARNING-ELEMENT(*percept*, *action*)
   inputs: *percept*, feedback percept
         action, feedback action

   examples ← *examples* ∪ {(*percept*,*action*)}

Figure 18.3   Skeleton for a simple reflex learning agent. The learning element just stores each example percept/action pair. The performance element either does whatever was done last time for a given percept, or it induces an action from similar percepts. The set of *examples* is a global variable that is shared by the learning and performance elements.

---

a new example arrives. Also, the agent might receive some feedback concerning the quality of the actions it chooses. These variants, and many others, are examined in this part.

    REFLEX-PERFORMANCE-ELEMENT makes no commitment to the way in which the hypothesis is represented. Because of its expressiveness and well-understood semantics, logic has been intensively studied as the target language for learning algorithms. In this chapter, we discuss two approaches to learning logical sentences: **decision tree** methods, which use a restricted representation of logical sentences specifically designed for learning, and the **version-space** approach, which is more general but often rather inefficient. In Chapter 19, we discuss **neural networks**, which are a general representation for nonlinear, numerical functions. The linear weighted polynomials used for game-playing evaluation functions are a special case of neural networks. The design of learning algorithms for **belief networks** is also a very active area of research, and a brief sketch is provided in Section 19.6.

The choice of *representation* for the desired function is probably the most important issue facing the designer of a learning agent. As well as affecting the nature of the learning algorithm, it can affect whether the problem is feasible at all. As with reasoning, in learning there is a fundamental trade-off between *expressiveness*—is the desired function representable in the representation language—and *efficiency*—is the learning problem going to be tractable for a given choice of representation language. If one chooses to learn sentences in a nice, expressive language such as first-order logic, then one will probably have to pay a heavy penalty in terms of both computation time and the number of examples required to learn a good set of sentences.

By "a good set of sentences," we mean a set that not only correctly reflects the experiences the agent has already had, but also one that correctly predicts its future experiences. Therein lies one of the most vexing philosophical problems of all time. How can one possibly know that one's learning algorithm has produced a theory that will correctly predict the future? And if one does not, then how can one say that the algorithm is any good? Certainly, if one cannot say for sure that an algorithm is any good, then one cannot hope to design good learning algorithms! In Section 18.6, we discuss a mathematical approach to the study of induction algorithms that provides tentative answers to these questions, and also sheds considerable light on the complexity of learning different kinds of function representations.

18.3   LEARNING DECISION TREES

Decision tree induction is one of the simplest and yet most successful forms of learning algorithm. It serves as a good introduction to the area of inductive learning, and is easy to implement. We first describe the performance element, and then show how to learn it. Along the way, we will introduce many of the ideas and terms that appear in all areas of inductive learning.

Decision trees as performance elements

DECISION TREE   A **decision tree** takes as input an object or situation described by a set of properties, and outputs a yes/no "decision." Decision trees therefore represent Boolean functions. Functions with a larger range of outputs can also be represented, but for simplicity we will usually stick to the Boolean case. Each internal node in the tree corresponds to a test of the value of one of the properties, and the branches from the node are labelled with the possible values of the test. Each leaf node in the tree specifies the Boolean value to be returned if that leaf is reached.

GOAL PREDICATE   As an example, consider the problem of whether to wait for a table at a restaurant. The aim here is to learn a definition for the **goal predicate**[4] *WillWait*, where the definition is expressed as a

---

4 The term **goal concept** is often used. Unfortunately, the word "concept" has been used in so many different ways in machine learning that we think it best to avoid it for a few years.

decision tree.[5] In setting this up as a learning problem, we first have to decide what properties or *attributes* are available to describe examples in the domain.[6] Suppose we decide on the following list of attributes:

1. *Alternate*: whether there is a suitable alternative restaurant nearby.
2. *Bar*: whether the restaurant has a comfortable bar area to wait in.
3. *Fri/Sat*: true on Fridays and Saturdays.
4. *Hungry*: whether we are hungry.
5. *Patrons*: how many people are in the restaurant (values are *None*, *Some*, and *Full*).
6. *Price*: the restaurant's price range ($, $$, $$$).
7. *Raining*: whether it is raining outside.
8. *Reservation*: whether we made a reservation.
9. *Type*: the kind of restaurant (French, Italian, Thai, or Burger).
10. *WaitEstimate*: the wait estimated by the host (0–10 minutes, 10–30, 30–60, >60).

The decision tree usually used by the first author for this domain is shown in Figure 18.4. Notice that the tree does not use the *Price* and *Type* attributes, considering these to be irrelevant given the data it has seen. Logically, the tree can be expressed as a conjunction of individual implications corresponding to the paths through the tree ending in *Yes* nodes. For example, the path for a restaurant full of patrons, with an estimated wait of 10-30 minutes when the agent is not hungry is expressed by the logical sentence

$$\forall r \; Patrons(r, Full) \wedge WaitEstimate(r, 0\text{-}10) \wedge Hungry(r, N) \Rightarrow WillWait(r)$$

Expressiveness of decision trees

If decision trees correspond to sets of implication sentences, a natural question is whether they can represent any set. The answer is no, because decision trees are implicitly limited to talking about a single object. That is, the decision tree language is essentially propositional, with each attribute test being a proposition. We cannot use decision trees to represent tests that refer to two or more different objects, for example,

$$\exists r_2 \; Nearby(r_2, r) \wedge Price(r, p) \wedge Price(r_2, p_2) \wedge Cheaper(p_2, p)$$

(is there a cheaper restaurant nearby). Obviously, we could add another Boolean attribute with the name *CheaperRestaurantNearby*, but it is intractable to add *all* such attributes.

Decision trees *are* fully expressive within the class of propositional languages, that is, any Boolean function can be written as a decision tree. This can be done trivially by having each row in the truth table for the function correspond to a path in the tree. This would not necessarily be a good way to represent the function, because the truth table is exponentially large in the number of attributes. Clearly, decision trees can represent many functions with much smaller trees.

---

[5] Meanwhile, the automated taxi is learning whether to wait for the passengers in case they give up waiting for a table and want to go on to another restaurant.

[6] One might ask why this isn't the job of the learning program. In fact, it is, but we will not be able to explain how it is done until Chapter 21.

PARITY FUNCTION

MAJORITY FUNCTION

For some kinds of functions, however, this is a real problem. For example, if the function is the **parity function**, which returns 1 if and only if an even number of inputs are 1, then an exponentially large decision tree will be needed. It is also difficult to use a decision tree to represent a **majority function**, which returns 1 if more than half of its inputs are 1.

In other words, decision trees are good for some kinds of functions, and bad for others. Is there any kind of representation that is efficient for all kinds of functions? Unfortunately, the answer is no. We can show this in a very general way. Consider the set of all Boolean functions on n attributes. How many different functions are in this set? This is just the number of different truth tables that we can write down, because the function is defined by its truth table. The truth table has 2^n rows, because each input case is described by n attributes. We can consider the "answer" column of the table as a 2^n bit number that defines the function. No matter what representation we use for functions, some of the functions (almost all of them, in fact) are going to require at least this many bits to represent.

If it takes 2^n bits to define the function, this means that there are 2^{2^n} different functions on n attributes. This is a scary number. For example, with just six Boolean attributes, there are about 2×10^{19} different functions to choose from. We will need some ingenious algorithms to find consistent hypotheses in such a large space.

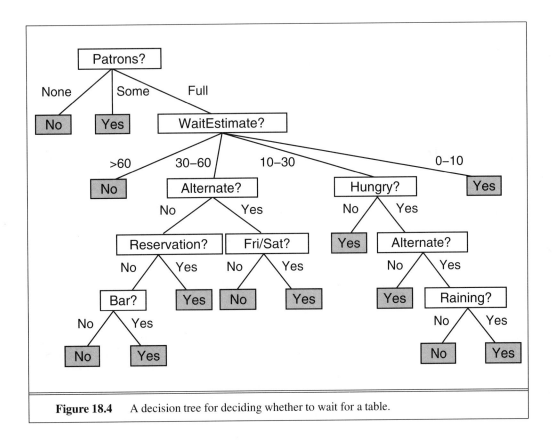

Figure 18.4   A decision tree for deciding whether to wait for a table.

Inducing decision trees from examples

CLASSIFICATION

An **example** is described by the values of the attributes and the value of the goal predicate. We call the value of the goal predicate the **classification** of the example. If the goal predicate is true for some example, we call it a **positive** example; otherwise we call it a **negative** example. A set of examples $X_1, \ldots, X_{12}$ for the restaurant domain is shown in Figure 18.5. The positive examples are ones where the goal *WillWait* is true ($X_1, X_3, \ldots$) and negative examples are ones where it is false ($X_2, X_5, \ldots$). The complete set of examples is called the **training set**.

TRAINING SET

Example	Attributes										Goal
	Alt	*Bar*	*Fri*	*Hun*	*Pat*	*Price*	*Rain*	*Res*	*Type*	*Est*	*WillWait*
X_1	Yes	No	No	Yes	Some	\$\$\$	No	Yes	French	0–10	Yes
X_2	Yes	No	No	Yes	Full	\$	No	No	Thai	30–60	No
X_3	No	Yes	No	No	Some	\$	No	No	Burger	0–10	Yes
X_4	Yes	No	Yes	Yes	Full	\$	No	No	Thai	10–30	Yes
X_5	Yes	No	Yes	No	Full	\$\$\$	No	Yes	French	>60	No
X_6	No	Yes	No	Yes	Some	\$\$	Yes	Yes	Italian	0–10	Yes
X_7	No	Yes	No	No	None	\$	Yes	No	Burger	0–10	No
X_8	No	No	No	Yes	Some	\$\$	Yes	Yes	Thai	0–10	Yes
X_9	No	Yes	Yes	No	Full	\$	Yes	No	Burger	>60	No
X_{10}	Yes	Yes	Yes	Yes	Full	\$\$\$	No	Yes	Italian	10–30	No
X_{11}	No	No	No	No	None	\$	No	No	Thai	0–10	No
X_{12}	Yes	Yes	Yes	Yes	Full	\$	No	No	Burger	30–60	Yes

Figure 18.5   Examples for the restaurant domain.

The problem of finding a decision tree that agrees with the training set might seem difficult, but in fact there is a trivial solution. We could simply construct a decision tree that has one path to a leaf for each example, where the path tests each attribute in turn and follows the value for the example, and the leaf has the classification of the example. When given the same example again,[7] the decision tree will come up with the right classification. Unfortunately, it will not have much to say about any other cases!

The problem with this trivial tree is that it just memorizes the observations. It does not extract any pattern from the examples and so we cannot expect it to be able to extrapolate to examples it has not seen.

Extracting a pattern means being able to describe a large number of cases in a concise way. Rather than just trying to find a decision tree that agrees with the examples, we should try to find a concise one, too. This is an example of a general principle of inductive learning often called **Ockham's razor**:[8] *The most likely hypothesis is the simplest one that is consistent with all observations.* Some people interpret this as meaning "the world is inherently simple." Even if the world is complex, however, Ockham's razor still makes sense. There are far fewer simple

---

[7]   The same example *or an example with the same description*—this distinction is very important and we will return to it in Chapter 21.

[8]   Sometimes spelled "Occam," although the origin of this corruption is obscure.

hypotheses than complex ones, so that there is only a small chance that *any* simple hypothesis that is wildly incorrect will be consistent with all observations. Hence, other things being equal, a simple hypothesis that is consistent with the observations is more likely to be correct than a complex one. We discuss hypothesis quality further in Section 18.6.

Unfortunately, finding the *smallest* decision tree is an intractable problem, but with some simple heuristics, we can do a good job of finding a smallish one. The basic idea behind the DECISION-TREE-LEARNING algorithm is to test the most important attribute first. By "most important," we mean the one that makes the most difference to the classification of an example. This way, we hope to get to the correct classification with a small number of tests, meaning that all paths in the tree will be short and the tree as a whole will be small.

Figure 18.6 shows how the algorithm gets started. We are given 12 training examples, which we classify into positive and negative sets. We then decide which attribute to use as the first test in the tree. Figure 18.6(a) shows that *Patrons* is a fairly important attribute, because if the value is *None* or *Some*, then we are left with example sets for which we can answer definitively (*No* and *Yes*, respectively). (If the value is *Full*, we will need additional tests.) In Figure 18.6(b) we see that *Type* is a poor attribute, because it leaves us with four possible outcomes, each of which has the same number of positive and negative answers. We consider all possible attributes in this way, and choose the most important one as the root test. We leave the details of how importance is measured for Section 18.4, because it does not affect the basic algorithm. For now, assume the most important attribute is *Patrons*.

After the first attribute test splits up the examples, each outcome is a new decision tree learning problem in itself, with fewer examples and one fewer attribute. There are four cases to consider for these recursive problems:

1. If there are some positive and some negative examples, then choose the best attribute to split them. Figure 18.6(c) shows *Hungry* being used to split the remaining examples.

2. If all the remaining examples are positive (or all negative), then we are done: we can answer *Yes* or *No*. Figure 18.6(c) shows examples of this in the *None* and *Some* cases.

3. If there are no examples left, it means that no such example has been observed, and we return a default value calculated from the majority classification at the node's parent.

4. If there are no attributes left, but both positive and negative examples, we have a problem. It means that these examples have exactly the same description, but different classifications. This happens when some of the data are incorrect; we say there is **noise** in the data. It also happens when the attributes do not give enough information to fully describe the situation, or when the domain is truly nondeterministic. One simple way out of the problem is to use a majority vote.

NOISE

We continue to apply the DECISION-TREE-LEARNING algorithm (Figure 18.7) until we get the tree shown in Figure 18.8. The tree is distinctly different from the original tree shown in Figure 18.4, despite the fact that the data were actually generated from an agent using the original tree.

One might conclude that the learning algorithm is not doing a very good job of learning the correct function. This would be the wrong conclusion to draw. The learning algorithm looks at the *examples*, not at the correct function, and in fact, its hypothesis (see Figure 18.8) not only agrees with all the examples, but is considerably simpler than the original tree. The learning algorithm has no reason to include tests for *Raining* and *Reservation*, because it can classify all

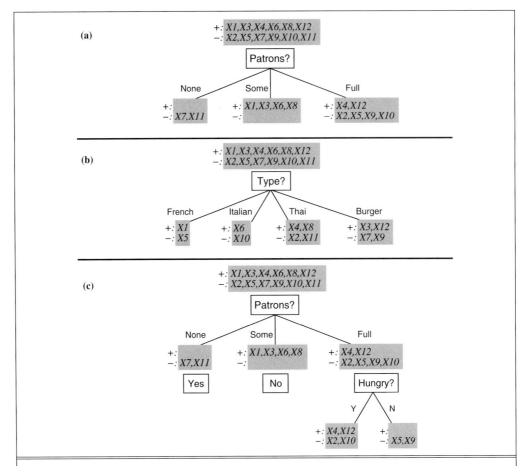

Figure 18.6   Splitting the examples by testing on attributes. In (a), we see that *Patrons* is a good attribute to test first; in (b), we see that *Type* is a poor one; and in (c), we see that *Hungry* is a fairly good second test, given that *Patrons* is the first test.

the examples without them. It has also detected an interesting regularity in the data (namely, that the first author will wait for Thai food on weekends) that was not even suspected. Many hours have been wasted by machine learning researchers trying to debug their learning algorithms when in fact the algorithm was behaving properly all along.

Of course, if we were to gather more examples, we might induce a tree more similar to the original. The tree in Figure 18.8 is bound to make a mistake; for example, it has never seen a case where the wait is 0–10 minutes but the restaurant is full. For a case where *Hungry* is false, the tree says not to wait, but the author would certainly wait. This raises an obvious question: if the algorithm induces a consistent but incorrect tree from the examples, how incorrect will the tree be? The next section shows how to analyze this experimentally.

---

function DECISION-TREE-LEARNING(*examples, attributes, default*) **returns** a decision tree
   inputs: *examples*, set of examples
          attributes, set of attributes
          default, default value for the goal predicate

   if *examples* is empty **then return** *default*
   else if all *examples* have the same classification **then return** the classification
   else if *attributes* is empty **then return** MAJORITY-VALUE(*examples*)
   else
      best ← CHOOSE-ATTRIBUTE(*attributes, examples*)
      tree ← a new decision tree with root test *best*
      for each value v_i of *best* **do**
         examples$_i$ ← {elements of *examples* with *best* = v_i}
         subtree ← DECISION-TREE-LEARNING(*examples$_i$, attributes − best*,
                                 MAJORITY-VALUE(*examples*))
         add a branch to *tree* with label v_i and subtree *subtree*
      end
      return *tree*

Figure 18.7   The decision tree learning algorithm.

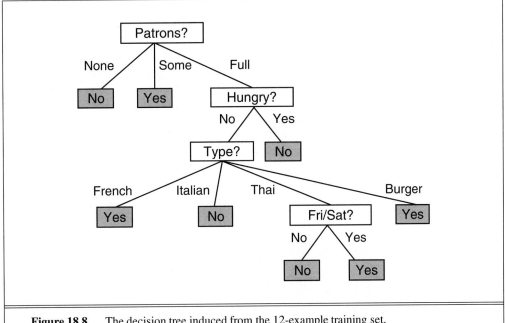

Figure 18.8   The decision tree induced from the 12-example training set.

Assessing the performance of the learning algorithm

A learning algorithm is good if it produces hypotheses that do a good job of predicting the classifications of unseen examples. In Section 18.6, we will see how prediction quality can be estimated in advance. For now, we will look at a methodology for assessing prediction quality after the fact.

Obviously, a prediction is good if it turns out to be true, so we can assess the quality of a hypothesis by checking its predictions against the correct classification once we know it. We do this on a set of examples known as the **test set**. If we train on all our available examples, then we will have to go out and get some more to test on, so often it is more convenient to adopt the following methodology:

1. Collect a large set of examples.
2. Divide it into two disjoint sets: the **training set** and the **test set**.
3. Use the learning algorithm with the training set as examples to generate a hypothesis H.
4. Measure the percentage of examples in the test set that are correctly classified by H.
5. Repeat steps 1 to 4 for different sizes of training sets and different randomly selected training sets of each size.

The result of this is a set of data that can be processed to give the average prediction quality as a function of the size of the training set. This can be plotted on a graph, giving what is called the **learning curve** for the algorithm on the particular domain. The learning curve for DECISION-TREE-LEARNING with the restaurant examples is shown in Figure 18.9. Notice that as the training set grows, the prediction quality increases. (For this reason, such curves are also called **happy graphs**.) This is a good sign that there is indeed some pattern in the data and the learning algorithm is picking it up.

The key idea of the methodology is to keep the training and test data separate, for the same reason that the results of an exam would not be a good measure of quality if the students saw the test beforehand. The methodology of randomly dividing up the examples into training and test sets is fair when each run is independent of the others—in that case, no run can "cheat" and tell the other runs what the right answers are. But there is the problem that you, as the designer of the learning algorithm, can cheat. If you run some examples, notice a pattern, and change either the learning or the performance element, then the runs are no longer independent, and you have effectively passed on information about the test set. In theory, every time you make a change to the algorithm, you should get a new set of examples to work from. In practice, this is too difficult, so people continue to run experiments on tainted sets of examples.

Practical uses of decision tree learning

Decision trees provide a simple representation for propositional knowledge that can be used for decision making and classification of objects. Although decision tree learning cannot generate interesting scientific theories because of its representational restrictions, it has been used in a wide variety of applications. Here we describe just two.

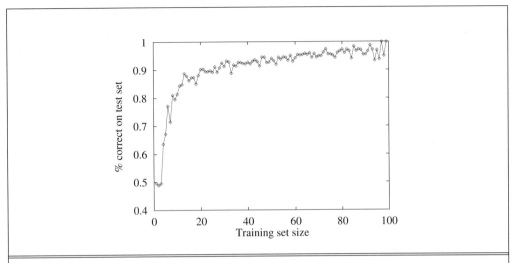

Figure 18.9   A learning curve for the decision tree algorithm on 100 randomly generated examples in the restaurant domain. The graph summarizes 20 trials.

Designing oil platform equipment

In 1986, BP deployed an expert system called GASOIL for designing gas-oil separation systems for offshore oil platforms. Gas-oil separation is done at the wellhead by a very large, complex, and expensive separation system, whose design depends on a number of attributes including the relative proportions of gas, oil, and water, and the flow rate, pressure, density, viscosity, temperature, and susceptibility to waxing. At the time, GASOIL was the largest commercial expert system in the world, containing approximately 2500 rules. Building such a system by hand would have taken roughly 10 person-years. Using decision-tree learning methods applied to a database of existing designs, the system was developed in 100 person-days (Michie, 1986). It is said to outperform human experts and to have saved BP many millions of dollars.

Learning to fly

There are two ways to design an automatic controller for a complex system. One can construct a precise model of the dynamics of the system, and use one of a variety of formal methods (including AI planning methods) to design a controller that has certain guaranteed properties. Alternatively, one can simply learn the correct mapping from the state of the system to the correct action. For very complex systems, such as aircraft and electorates, developing a detailed model may be infeasible, which leaves the second alternative. Sammut *et al.* (1992) adopted this alternative for the task of learning to fly a Cessna on a flight simulator. The data was generated by watching three skilled human pilots performing an assigned flight plan 30 times each. Each time the pilot took an action by setting one of the control variables such as thrust or flaps, a training example was created. In all, 90,000 examples were obtained, each described by 20 state variables and labelled by the action taken. From these examples, a decision tree was extracted using the C4.5 system (Quinlan, 1993a). The decision tree was then converted into C code and inserted into the flight simulator's control loop so that it could fly the plane itself.

The results are surprising: not only does the program learn to fly, it learns to fly somewhat *better* than its teachers. This is because the generalization process cleans up the occasional mistakes made by humans. Such results suggest that machine learning techniques may yield controllers that are more robust than conventional, manually programmed autopilots. For difficult tasks such as flying helicopters carrying heavy loads in high winds, no autopilots are available and very few humans are competent. Such tasks are potentially suitable for systems based on automated learning.

18.4   USING INFORMATION THEORY

This section looks at a mathematical model for choosing the best attribute and at methods for dealing with noise in the data. It can be skipped by those who are not interested in these details.

The scheme used in decision tree learning for selecting attributes is designed to minimize the depth of the final tree. The idea is to pick the attribute that goes as far as possible toward providing an exact classification of the examples. A perfect attribute divides the examples into sets that are all positive or all negative. The *Patrons* attribute is not perfect, but it is fairly good. A really useless attribute such as *Type* leaves the example sets with roughly the same proportion of positive and negative examples as the original set.

All we need, then, is a formal measure of "fairly good" and "really useless" and we can implement the CHOOSE-ATTRIBUTE function of Figure 18.7. The measure should have its maximum value when the attribute is perfect and its minimum value when the attribute is of no

INFORMATION   use at all. One suitable measure is the expected amount of **information** provided by the attribute, where we use the term in the mathematical sense first defined in (Shannon and Weaver, 1949). To understand the notion of information, think about it as providing the answer to a question, for example, whether a coin will come up heads. If one already has a good guess about the answer, then the actual answer is less informative. Suppose you are going to bet $1 on the flip of a coin, and you believe that the coin is rigged so that it will come up heads with probability 0.99. You will bet heads (obviously), and have expected value $0.98 for the bet. That means you would only be willing to pay less than $0.02 for advance information about the actual outcome of the flip. If the coin were fair, your expected value would be zero, and you would be willing to pay up to $1.00 for advance information—the less you know, the more valuable the information.

Information theory uses this same intuition, but instead of measuring the value of information in dollars, it measures information content in **bits**. One bit of information is enough to answer a yes/no question about which one has no idea, such as the flip of a fair coin. In general, if the possible answers v_i have probabilities $P(v_i)$, then the information content I of the actual answer is given by

$$I(P(v_1), \ldots, P(v_n)) = \sum_{i=1}^{n} -P(v_i) \log_2 P(v_i)$$

This is just the average information content of the various events (the $-\log_2 P$ terms) weighted by the probabilities of the events. To check this equation, for the tossing of a fair coin we get

$$I\left(\frac{1}{2}, \frac{1}{2}\right) = -\frac{1}{2}\log_2 \frac{1}{2} - \frac{1}{2}\log_2 \frac{1}{2} = 1\,bit$$

If the coin is loaded to give 99% heads we get $I\,(1/100, 99/100) = 0.08$ bits, and as the probability of heads goes to 1, the information of the actual answer goes to 0.

For decision tree learning, the question that needs answering is: for a given example, what is the correct classification? A correct decision tree will answer this question. An estimate of the probabilities of the possible answers before any of the attributes have been tested is given by the proportions of positive and negative examples in the training set. Suppose the training set contains p positive examples and n negative examples. Then an estimate of the information contained in a correct answer is

$$I\left(\frac{p}{p+n}, \frac{n}{p+n}\right) = -\frac{p}{p+n}\log_2 \frac{p}{p+n} - \frac{n}{p+n}\log_2 \frac{n}{p+n}$$

For the restaurant training set shown in Figure 18.5, we have $p = n = 6$, so we need 1 bit of information.

Now a test on a single attribute A will not usually tell us this much information, but it will give us some of it. We can measure exactly how much by looking at how much information we still need *after* the attribute test. Any attribute A divides the training set E into subsets $E_1, \ldots, E_v$ according to their values for A, where A can have v distinct values. Each subset E_i has p_i positive examples and n_i negative examples, so if we go along that branch we will need an additional $I\,(p_i/(p_i + n_i), n_i/(p_i + n_i))$ bits of information to answer the question. A random example has the ith value for the attribute with probability $(p_i + n_i)/(p + n)$, so on average, after testing attribute A, we will need

$$Remainder(A) = \sum_{i=1}^{v} \frac{p_i + n_i}{p+n} I\left(\frac{p_i}{p_i + n_i}, \frac{n_i}{p_i + n_i}\right)$$

INFORMATION GAIN   bits of information to classify the example. The **information gain** from the attribute test is defined as the difference between the original information requirement and the new requirement:

$$Gain(A) = I\left(\frac{p}{p+n}, \frac{n}{p+n}\right) - Remainder(A)$$

and the heuristic used in the CHOOSE-ATTRIBUTE function is just to choose the attribute with the largest gain.

Looking at the attributes *Patrons* and *Type* and their classifying power, as shown in Figure 18.6, we have

$$Gain(Patrons) = 1 - \left[\frac{2}{12}I(0, 1) + \frac{4}{12}I(1, 0) + \frac{6}{12}I\left(\frac{2}{6}, \frac{4}{6}\right)\right] \approx 0.541 \text{ bits}$$

$$Gain(Type) = 1 - \left[\frac{2}{12}I\left(\frac{1}{2}, \frac{1}{2}\right) + \frac{2}{12}I\left(\frac{1}{2}, \frac{1}{2}\right) + \frac{4}{12}I\left(\frac{2}{4}, \frac{2}{4}\right) + \frac{4}{12}I\left(\frac{2}{4}, \frac{2}{4}\right)\right] = 0 \text{ bits}$$

In fact, *Patrons* has the highest gain of any of the attributes and would be chosen by the decision-tree learning algorithm as the root.

Noise and overfitting

We saw earlier that if there are two or more examples with the same descriptions (in terms of the attributes) but different classifications, then the DECISION-TREE-LEARNING algorithm must fail to find a decision tree consistent with all the examples. The solution we mentioned before is to have each leaf node report either the majority classification for its set of examples or report the estimated probabilities of each classification using the relative frequencies. The former is appropriate for an agent that requires the decision tree to represent a strict logical function, whereas the latter can be used by a decision-theoretic agent.

Unfortunately, this is far from the whole story. It is quite possible, and in fact likely, that even when vital information is missing, the decision tree learning algorithm will find a decision tree that is consistent with all the examples. This is because the algorithm can use the *irrelevant* attributes, if any, to make spurious distinctions among the examples.

Consider the problem of trying to predict the roll of a die. Suppose that experiments are carried out during an extended period of time with various dice, and that the attributes describing each training example are as follows:

1. *Day*: the day on which the die was rolled (Mon, Tue, Wed, Thu).
2. *Month*: the month in which the die was rolled (Jan or Feb).
3. *Color*: the color of the die (Red or Blue).

As long as there are no two examples with identical descriptions, DECISION-TREE-LEARNING will find an exact hypothesis. This will, however, be totally spurious. What we would like is that DECISION-TREE-LEARNING return a single leaf node with probabilities close to 1/6 for each roll, once it has seen enough examples.

Whenever there is a large set of possible hypotheses, one has to be careful not to use the resulting freedom to find meaningless "regularity" in the data. This problem is called **overfitting**. It is a very general phenomenon, and occurs even when the target function is not at all random. It afflicts every kind of learning algorithm, not just decision trees.

A complete mathematical treatment of overfitting is beyond the scope of this book. Here we present a simple technique called **decision tree pruning**. Pruning works by preventing recursive splitting on attributes that are not clearly relevant, even when the data at that node in the tree is not uniformly classified. The question is, how do we detect an irrelevant attribute?

Suppose we split a set of examples using an irrelevant attribute. Generally speaking, we would expect the resulting subsets to have roughly the same proportions of each class as the original set. In this case, the information gain will be close to zero.[9] Thus, the information gain is a good clue to irrelevance. Now the question is, how large a gain should we require in order to split on a particular attribute?

This is exactly the sort of question addressed by classical tests for statistical significance. A significance test begins by assuming that there is no underlying pattern (the so-called **null hypothesis**). Then the actual data are analyzed to calculate the extent to which it deviates from a perfect absence of pattern. If the degree of deviation is statistically unlikely (usually taken to mean a 5% probability or less), then that is considered to be good evidence for the presence of a

OVERFITTING

DECISION TREE
PRUNING

NULL HYPOTHESIS

---

[9] In fact, the gain be will be greater than zero unless the proportions are all exactly the same (see Exercise 18.9).

significant pattern in the data. The probabilities are calculated from standard distributions of the amount of deviation one would expect to see due to random sampling.

In this case, the null hypothesis is that the attribute is irrelevant, and hence the information gain for an infinitely large sample would be zero. We need to calculate the probability that, under the null hypothesis, a sample of size v would exhibit the observed deviation from the expected distribution of positive and negative examples. We can measure the deviation by comparing the actual numbers of positive and negative examples in each subset, p_i and n_i, to the expected numbers $\hat{p}_i$ and $\hat{n}_i$ assuming true irrelevance:

$$\hat{p}_i = p \times \frac{p_i + n_i}{p + n} \qquad\qquad \hat{n}_i = n \times \frac{p_i + n_i}{p + n}$$

A convenient measure of the total deviation is given by

$$D = \sum_{i=1}^{v} \frac{(p_i - \hat{p}_i)^2}{\hat{p}_i} + \frac{(n_i - \hat{n}_i)^2}{\hat{n}_i}$$

Under the null hypothesis, the value of D is distributed according to the χ^2 (chi-squared) distribution with $v - 1$ degrees of freedom. The probability that the attribute is really irrelevant can be calculated with the help of standard χ^2 tables, or with statistical software. Exercise 18.10 asks you to make the appropriate changes to DECISION-TREE-LEARNING to implement this form of pruning, which is known as χ^2 **pruning**.

χ^2 PRUNING

With pruning, noise can be tolerated—classification errors give a linear increase in prediction error, whereas errors in the descriptions of examples (i.e, the wrong output for a given input) have an asymptotic effect that gets worse as the tree shrinks down to smaller sets. Trees constructed with pruning perform significantly better than trees constructed without pruning when the data contain a large amount of noise. The pruned trees are often much more compact, and are therefore easier to understand.

CROSS-VALIDATION

Cross-validation is another technique that eliminates the dangers of overfitting. The basic idea of cross-validation is to try to estimate how well the current hypothesis will predict unseen data. This is done by setting aside some fraction of the known data, and using it to test the prediction performance of a hypothesis induced from the rest of the known data. This can be done repeatedly with different subsets of the data, with the results averaged. Cross-validation can be used in conjunction with any tree-construction method (including pruning) in order to select a tree with good prediction performance.

Broadening the applicability of decision trees

In order to extend decision tree induction to a wider variety of problems, a number of issues must be addressed. We will briefly mention each, suggesting that a full understanding is best obtained by doing the associated exercises:

◇ **Missing data**: In many domains, not all the attribute values will be known for every example. The values may not have been recorded, or they may be too expensive to obtain. This gives rise to two problems. First, given a complete decision tree, how should one classify an object that is missing one of the test attributes? Second, how should one modify the information gain formula when some examples have unknown values for the attribute? These questions are addressed in Exercise 18.11.

⬦ **Multivalued attributes**:When an attribute has a large number of possible values, the information gain measure gives an inappropriate indication of the attribute's usefulness. Consider the extreme case where every example has a different value for the attribute—for instance, if we were to use an attribute *RestaurantName* in the restaurant domain. In such a case, each subset of examples is a singleton and therefore has a unique classification, so the information gain measure would have its highest value for this attribute. However, the attribute may be irrelevant or useless. One possible solution is to use the **gain ratio**, as described in Exercise 18.12.

⬦ **Continuous-valued attributes**: Attributes such as *Height* and *Weight* have a large or infinite set of possible values. They are therefore not well-suited for decision-tree learning in raw form. An obvious way to deal with this problem is to **discretize** the attribute. For example, the *Price* attribute for restaurants was discretized into $, $$, and $$$ values. Normally, such discrete ranges would be defined by hand. A better approach is to preprocess the raw attribute values during the tree-growing process in order to find out which ranges give the most useful information for classification purposes.

A decision-tree learning system for real-world applications must be able to handle all of these problems. Handling continuous-valued variables is especially important, because both physical and financial processes provide numerical data. Several commercial packages have been built that meet these criteria, and they have been used to develop several hundred fielded systems.

18.5   LEARNING GENERAL LOGICAL DESCRIPTIONS

In this section, we examine ways in which more general kinds of logical representations can be learned. In the process, we will construct a general framework for understanding learning algorithms, centered around the idea that inductive learning can be viewed as a process of searching for a good hypothesis in a large space—the **hypothesis space**—defined by the representation language chosen for the task. We will also explain what is going on in logical terms: the logical connections among examples, hypotheses, and the goal. Although this may seem like a lot of extra work at first, it turns out to clarify many of the issues in learning. It enables us to go well beyond the simple capabilities of the decision tree learning algorithm, and allows us to use the full power of logical inference in the service of learning.

HYPOTHESIS SPACE

Hypotheses

The situation is usually this: we start out with a goal predicate, which we will generically call Q. (For example, in the restaurant domain, Q will be *WillWait*.) Q will be a unary predicate, and we are trying to find an equivalent logical expression that we can use to classify examples correctly. Each hypothesis proposes such an expression, which we call a **candidate definition** of the goal predicate. Using C_i to denote the candidate definition, each hypothesis H_i is a sentence of the form $\forall x \; Q(x) \Leftrightarrow C_i(x)$. For example, the decision tree shown in Figure 18.8 expresses the following logical definition (which we will call H_r for future reference):

$$\forall r \; WillWait(r) \Leftrightarrow Patrons(r, Some)$$
$$\lor \; Patrons(r, Full) \land \neg Hungry(r) \land Type(r, French)$$
$$\lor \; Patrons(r, Full) \land \neg Hungry(r) \land Type(r, Thai) \land Fri/Sat(r)$$
$$\lor \; Patrons(r, Full) \land \neg Hungry(r) \land Type(r, Burger)$$

The hypothesis space is then the set of all hypotheses that the learning algorithm is designed to entertain. For example, the DECISION-TREE-LEARNING algorithm can entertain any decision tree hypothesis defined in terms of the attributes provided; its hypothesis space therefore consists of all these decision trees. We will generically use the letter **H** to denote the hypothesis space $\{H_1, \ldots, H_n\}$. Presumably, the learning algorithm believes that one of the hypotheses is correct; that is, it believes the sentence

$$H_1 \lor H_2 \lor H_3 \lor \ldots \lor H_n \tag{18.1}$$

EXTENSION

Each hypothesis predicts that a certain set of examples—namely, those that satisfy its candidate definition—will be examples of the goal predicate. This set is called the **extension** of the predicate. Two hypotheses with different extensions are therefore logically inconsistent with each other, because they disagree on their predictions for at least one example. If they have the same extension, they are logically equivalent.

Examples

Logically speaking, an example is an object to which the goal concept may or may not apply, and that has some logical description. Let us generically call the ith example X_i. Its description will be the sentence $D_i(X_i)$, where D_i can be any logical expression taking a single argument. The classification will be given by a sentence $Q(X_i)$ if the example is positive, and $\neg Q(X_i)$ if the example is negative. For instance, the first example from Figure 18.5 is described by the sentences

$$Alternate(X_1) \land \neg Bar(X_1) \land \neg Fri/Sat(X_1) \land Hungry(X_1) \land \ldots$$

and the classification

$$WillWait(X_1)$$

The complete training set is then just the conjunction of all these sentences. A hypothesis agrees with all the examples if and only if it is logically consistent with the training set; ideally, we would like to find such a hypothesis.

Let us examine this notion of consistency more carefully. Obviously, if hypothesis H_i is consistent with the entire training set, it has to be consistent with each example. What would it mean for it to be inconsistent with an example? This can happen in one of two ways:

FALSE NEGATIVE

- An example can be a **false negative** for the hypothesis, if the hypothesis says it should be negative but in fact it is positive. For instance, the new example X_{13} described by

$$Patrons(X_{13}, Full) \land Wait(X_{13}, 0\text{-}10) \land \neg Hungry(X_{13}) \land \ldots \land WillWait(X_{13})$$

would be a false negative for the hypothesis H_r given earlier. From H_r and the example description, we can deduce both $WillWait(X_{13})$, which is what the example says, and $\neg WillWait(X_{13})$, which is what the hypothesis predicts. The hypothesis and the example are therefore logically inconsistent.

FALSE POSITIVE

- An example can be a **false positive** for the hypothesis, if the hypothesis says it should be positive but in fact it is negative.[10]

If an example is a false positive or false negative for a hypothesis, then the example and the hypothesis are logically inconsistent with each other. Assuming that the example is a correct observation of fact, then the hypothesis can be ruled out. Logically, this is exactly analogous to the resolution rule of inference (see Chapter 9), where the disjunction of hypotheses corresponds to a clause and the example corresponds to a literal that resolves against one of the literals in the clause. An ordinary logical inference system therefore could, in principle, learn from the example by eliminating one or more hypotheses. Suppose, for example, that the example is denoted by the sentence I_1, and the hypothesis space is $H_1 \lor H_2 \lor H_3 \lor H_4$. Then if I_1 is inconsistent with H_2 and H_3, the logical inference system can deduce the new hypothesis space $H_1 \lor H_4$.

We therefore can characterize inductive learning in a logical setting as a process of gradually eliminating hypotheses that are inconsistent with the examples, narrowing down the possibilities. Because the hypothesis space is usually vast (or even infinite in the case of first-order logic), we do not recommend trying to build a learning system using resolution-based theorem proving and a complete enumeration of the hypothesis space. Instead, we will describe two approaches that find logically consistent hypotheses with much less effort.

Current-best-hypothesis search

CURRENT-BEST-
HYPOTHESIS

The idea behind **current-best-hypothesis** search is to maintain a single hypothesis, and to adjust it as new examples arrive in order to maintain consistency. The basic algorithm was described by John Stuart Mill (1843), and may well have appeared even earlier.

Suppose we have some hypothesis such as H_r, of which we have grown quite fond. As long as each new example is consistent, we need do nothing. Then along comes a false negative example, X_{13}. What do we do?

Figure 18.10(a) shows H_r schematically as a region: everything inside the rectangle is part of the extension of H_r. The examples that have actually been seen so far are shown as "+" or "−", and we see that H_r correctly categorizes all the examples as positive or negative examples of *WillWait*. In Figure 18.10(b), a new example (circled) is a false negative: the hypothesis says it should be negative but it is actually positive. The extension of the hypothesis must be increased to

GENERALIZATION

include it. This is called **generalization**; one possible generalization is shown in Figure 18.10(c). Then in Figure 18.10(d), we see a false positive: the hypothesis says the new example (circled) should be positive, but it actually is negative. The extension of the hypothesis must be decreased

SPECIALIZATION

to exclude the example. This is called **specialization**; in Figure 18.10(e) we see one possible specialization of the hypothesis.

---

[10] The terms "false positive" and "false negative" were first used in medicine to describe erroneous results from laboratory tests. A result is a false positive if it indicates that the patient has the disease when in fact no disease is present.

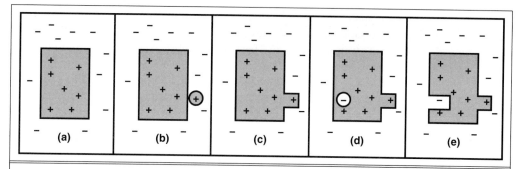

Figure 18.10   (a) A consistent hypothesis. (b) A false negative. (c) The hypothesis is generalized. (d) A false positive. (e) The hypothesis is specialized.

We can now specify the CURRENT-BEST-LEARNING algorithm, shown in Figure 18.11. Notice that each time we consider generalizing or specializing the hypothesis, we must check for consistency with the other examples, because there is no guarantee that an arbitrary increase/decrease in the extension will avoid including/excluding any other negative/positive examples.

---

function CURRENT-BEST-LEARNING(*examples*) **returns** a hypothesis

   $H \leftarrow$ any hypothesis consistent with the first example in *examples*
   for each remaining example in *examples* **do**
      if *e* is false positive for *H* **then**
         $H \leftarrow$ **choose** a specialization of *H* consistent with *examples*
      else if *e* is false negative for *H* **then**
         $H \leftarrow$ **choose** a generalization of *H* consistent with *examples*
      if no consistent specialization/generalization can be found **then fail**
   end
   return *H*

Figure 18.11   The current-best-hypothesis learning algorithm. It searches for a consistent hypothesis and backtracks when no consistent specialization/generalization can be found.

We have defined generalization and specialization as operations that change the *extension* of a hypothesis. Now we need to determine exactly how they can be implemented as syntactic operations that change the candidate definition associated with the hypothesis, so that a program can carry them out. This is done by first noting that generalization and specialization are also *logical* relationships between hypotheses. If hypothesis H_1, with definition C_1, is a generalization of hypothesis H_2 with definition C_2, then we must have

$$\forall x \ \ C_2(x) \ \Rightarrow \ C_1(x)$$

Therefore in order to construct a generalization of H_2, we simply need to find a definition C_1 that is logically implied by C_2. This is easily done. For example, if $C_2(x)$ is *Alternate*(x) $\wedge$

DROPPING
CONDITIONS

Patrons$(x, Some)$, then one possible generalization is given by $C_1(x) \equiv Patrons(x, Some)$. This is called **dropping conditions**. Intuitively, it generates a weaker definition and therefore allows a larger set of positive examples. There are a number of other generalization operations, depending on the language being operated on. Similarly, we can specialize a hypothesis by adding extra conditions to its candidate definition or by removing disjuncts from a disjunctive definition. Let us see how this works on the restaurant example, using the data in Figure 18.5.

- The first example X_1 is positive. *Alternate*(X_1) is true, so let us assume an initial hypothesis

  $H_1: \quad \forall x \; WillWait(x) \; \Leftrightarrow \; Alternate(x)$

- The second example X_2 is negative. H_1 predicts it to be positive, so it is a false positive. Therefore, we need to specialize H_1. This can be done by adding an extra condition that will rule out X_2. One possibility is

  $H_2: \quad \forall x \; WillWait(x) \; \Leftrightarrow \; Alternate(x) \wedge Patrons(x, Some)$

- The third example X_3 is positive. H_2 predicts it to be negative, so it is a false negative. Therefore, we need to generalize H_2. This can be done by dropping the *Alternate* condition, yielding

  $H_3: \quad \forall x \; WillWait(x) \; \Leftrightarrow \; Patrons(x, Some)$

- The fourth example X_4 is positive. H_3 predicts it to be negative, so it is a false negative. We therefore need to generalize H_3. We cannot drop the *Patrons* condition, because that would yield an all-inclusive hypothesis that would be inconsistent with X_2. One possibility is to add a disjunct:

  $H_4: \quad \forall x \; WillWait(x) \; \Leftrightarrow \; Patrons(x, Some) \vee (Patrons(x, Full) \wedge Fri/Sat(x))$

Already, the hypothesis is starting to look reasonable. Obviously, there are other possibilities consistent with the first four examples; here are two of them:

$H'_4: \quad \forall x \; WillWait(x) \; \Leftrightarrow \; \neg WaitEstimate(x, 30\text{-}60)$

$H''_4: \quad \forall x \; WillWait(x) \; \Leftrightarrow \; Patrons(x, Some)$
$\qquad\qquad\qquad \vee (Patrons(x, Full) \wedge WaitEstimate(x, 10\text{-}30))$

The CURRENT-BEST-LEARNING algorithm is described nondeterministically, because at any point, there may be several possible specializations or generalizations that can be applied. The choices that are made will not necessarily lead to the simplest hypothesis, and may lead to an unrecoverable situation where no simple modification of the hypothesis is consistent with all of the data. In such cases, the program must backtrack to a previous choice point.

The CURRENT-BEST-LEARNING algorithm and its variants have been used in a many machine learning systems, starting with Patrick Winston's (1970) "arch-learning" program. With a large number of instances and a large space, however, some difficulties arise:

1. Checking all the previous instances over again for each modification is very expensive.

2. It is difficult to find good search heuristics, and backtracking all over the place can take forever. As we saw earlier, hypothesis space can be a doubly exponentially large place.

Least-commitment search

Backtracking arises because the current-best-hypothesis approach has to *choose* a particular hypothesis as its best guess even though it does not have enough data yet to be sure of the choice. What we can do instead is to keep around all and only those hypotheses that are consistent with all the data so far. Each new instance will either have no effect or will get rid of some of the hypotheses. Recall that the original hypothesis space can be viewed as a disjunctive sentence

$$H_1 \vee H_2 \vee H_3 \ldots \vee H_n$$

As various hypotheses are found to be inconsistent with the examples, this disjunction shrinks, retaining only those hypotheses not ruled out. Assuming that the original hypothesis space does in fact contain the right answer, the reduced disjunction must still contain the right answer because only incorrect hypotheses have been removed. The set of hypotheses remaining is called the **version space**, and the learning algorithm (sketched in Figure 18.12) is called the version space learning algorithm (also the **candidate elimination** algorithm).

VERSION SPACE

CANDIDATE
ELIMINATION

---

function VERSION-SPACE-LEARNING(*examples*) **returns** a version space
   local variables: *V*, the version space: the set of all hypotheses

   V ← the set of all hypotheses
   for each example *e* in *examples* **do**
      if *V* is not empty **then** *V* ← VERSION-SPACE-UPDATE(*V*, *e*)
   end
   return *V*

function VERSION-SPACE-UPDATE(V, e) **returns** an updated version space

   $V \leftarrow \{h \in V : h$ is consistent with $e\}$

Figure 18.12   The version space learning algorithm. It finds a subset of *V* that is consistent with the *examples*.

One important property of this approach is that it is *incremental*: one never has to go back and reexamine the old examples. All remaining hypotheses are guaranteed to be consistent with them anyway. It is also a **least-commitment** algorithm because it makes no arbitrary choices (cf. the partial-order planning algorithm in Chapter 11). But there is an obvious problem. We already said that the hypothesis space is enormous, so how can we possibly write down this enormous disjunction?

The following simple analogy is very helpful. How do you represent all the real numbers between 1 and 2? After all, there is an infinite number of them! The answer is to use an interval representation that just specifies the boundaries of the set: [1,2]. It works because we have an *ordering* on the real numbers.

We also have an ordering on the hypothesis space, namely, generalization/specialization. This is a partial ordering, which means that each boundary will not be a point but rather a set of hypotheses called a **boundary set**. The great thing is that we can represent the entire version

BOUNDARY SET

G-SET
S-SET
space using just two boundary sets: a most general boundary (the **G-set**) and a most specific
boundary (the **S-set**). *Everything in between is guaranteed to be consistent with the examples.*
Before we prove this, let us recap:

- The current version space is the set of hypotheses consistent with all the examples so far.
  It is represented by the S-set and G-set, each of which is a set of hypotheses.
- Every member of the S-set is consistent with all observations so far, and there are no
  consistent hypotheses that are more specific.
- Every member of the G-set is consistent with all observations so far, and there are no
  consistent hypotheses that are more general.

We want the initial version space (before any examples have been seen) to represent all possible
hypotheses. We do this by setting the G-set to contain just *True* (the hypothesis that contains
everything), and the S-set to contain just *False* (the hypothesis whose extension is empty).

Figure 18.13 shows the general structure of the boundary set representation of the version
space. In order to show that the representation is sufficient, we need the following two properties:

1. Every consistent hypothesis (other than those in the boundary sets) is more specific than
   some member of the G-set, and more general than some member of the S-set. (That is,
   there are no "stragglers" left outside.) This follows directly from the definitions of S and
   G. If there were a straggler h, then it would have to be no more specific than any member
   of G, in which case it belongs in G; or no more general than any member of S, in which
   case it belongs in S.
2. Every hypothesis more specific than some member of the G-set and more general than
   some member of the S-set is a consistent hypothesis. (That is, there are no "holes" between
   the boundaries.) Any h between S and G must reject all the negative examples rejected by
   each member of G (because it is more specific), and must accept all the positive examples
   accepted by any member of S (because it is more general). Thus, h must agree with all the
   examples, and therefore cannot be inconsistent. Figure 18.14 shows the situation: there are
   no known examples outside S but inside G, so any hypothesis in the gap must be consistent.

We have therefore shown that *if* S and G are maintained according to their definitions, then they
provide a satisfactory representation of the version space. The only remaining problem is how to
update S and G for a new example (the job of the VERSION-SPACE-UPDATE function). This may
appear rather complicated at first, but from the definitions and with the help of Figure 18.13, it is
not too hard to reconstruct the algorithm.

We need to worry about the members S_i and G_i of the S- and G-sets. For each one, the new
instance may be a false positive or a false negative.

1. False positive for S_i: This means S_i is too general, but there are no consistent specializations
   of S_i (by definition), so we throw it out of the S-set.
2. False negative for S_i: This means S_i is too specific, so we replace it by all its immediate
   generalizations.
3. False positive for G_i: This means G_i is too general, so we replace it by all its immediate
   specializations.
4. False negative for G_i: This means G_i is too specific, but there are no consistent generalizations of G_i (by definition) so we throw it out of the G-set.

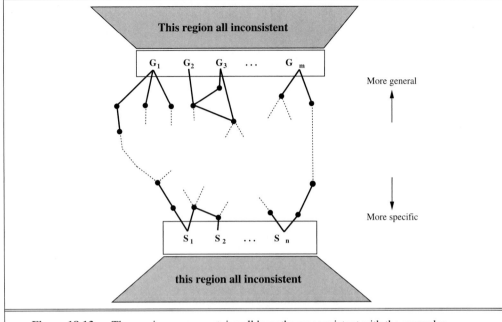

Figure 18.13   The version space contains all hypotheses consistent with the examples.

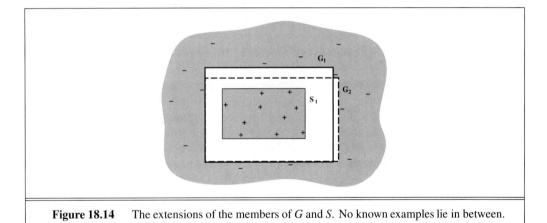

Figure 18.14   The extensions of the members of *G* and *S*. No known examples lie in between.

We continue these operations for each new instance until one of three things happens:

1. We have exactly one concept left in the version space, in which case we return it as the unique hypothesis.

2. The version space *collapses*—either S or G becomes empty, indicating that there are no consistent hypotheses for the training set. This is the same case as the failure of the simple version of the decision tree algorithm.

3. We run out of examples with several hypotheses remaining in the version space. This means the version space represents a disjunction of hypotheses. For any new example, if all the disjuncts agree, then we can return their classification of the example. If they disagree, one possibility is to take the majority vote.

We leave as an exercise the application of the VERSION-SPACE-LEARNING algorithm to the restaurant data.

Discussion

There are two principal drawbacks to the version-space approach:

- If the domain contains noise or insufficient attributes for exact classification, the version space will always collapse.
- If we allow unlimited disjunction in the hypothesis space, the S-set will always contain a single most-specific hypothesis, namely, the disjunction of the descriptions of the positive examples seen to date. Similarly, the G-set will contain just the negation of the disjunction of the descriptions of the negative examples.

GENERALIZATION
HIERARCHY

To date, no completely successful solution has been found for the problem of noise. The problem of disjunction can be addressed by allowing limited forms of disjunction or by including a **generalization hierarchy** of more general predicates. For example, instead of using the disjunction $WaitEstimate(x, 30\text{-}60) \lor WaitEstimate(x, {>}60)$, we might use the single literal $LongWait(x)$. The set of generalization and specialization operations can be easily extended to handle this.

The pure version space algorithm was first applied in the Meta-DENDRAL system, which was designed to learn rules for predicting how molecules would break into pieces in a mass spectrometer (Buchanan and Mitchell, 1978). Meta-DENDRAL was able to generate rules that were sufficiently novel to warrant publication in a journal of analytical chemistry—the first real scientific knowledge generated by a computer program. It was also used in the elegant LEX system (Mitchell *et al.*, 1983), which was able to learn to solve symbolic integration problems by studying its own successes and failures. Although version space methods are probably not practical in most real-world learning problems, mainly because of noise, they provide a good deal of insight into the logical structure of hypothesis space.

18.6   WHY LEARNING WORKS: COMPUTATIONAL LEARNING THEORY

Learning means behaving better as a result of experience. We have shown several algorithms for inductive learning, and explained how they fit into an agent. The main unanswered question was posed in Section 18.2: how can one possibly know that one's learning algorithm has produced a theory that will correctly predict the future? In terms of the definition of inductive learning, how do we know that the hypothesis h is close to the target function f if we don't know what f is?

These questions have been pondered for several centuries, but unless we find some answers, machine learning will, at best, be puzzled by its own success. Fortunately, within the last decade,

COMPUTATIONAL
LEARNING THEORY

answers have begun to emerge. We will focus on the answers provided by **computational learning theory**, a field at the intersection of AI and theoretical computer science.

The underlying principle is the following: any hypothesis that is seriously wrong will almost certainly be "found out" with high probability after a small number of examples, because it will make an incorrect prediction. Thus, any hypothesis that is consistent with a sufficiently large set of training examples is unlikely to be seriously wrong—that is, it must be **Probably Approximately Correct**. **PAC-learning** is the subfield of computational learning theory that is devoted to this idea.

PROBABLY
APPROXIMATELY
CORRECT
PAC-LEARNING

There are some subtleties in the preceding argument. The main question is the connection between the training and the test examples—after all, we want the hypothesis to be approximately correct on the test set, not just on the training set. The key assumption, introduced by Valiant, is that the training and test sets are drawn randomly from the same population of examples using the *same probability distribution*. This is called the **stationarity** assumption. It is much more precise than the usual proposals for justifying induction, which mutter something about "the future being like the past." Without the stationarity assumption, the theory can make no claims at all about the future because there would be no necessary connection between future and past. The stationarity assumption amounts to supposing that the process that selects examples is not malevolent. Obviously, if the training set consisted only of weird examples—two-headed dogs, for instance—then the learning algorithm cannot help but make unsuccessful generalizations about how to recognize dogs.

STATIONARITY

How many examples are needed?

In order to put these insights into practice, we will need some notation:

- Let **X** be the set of all possible examples.
- Let D be the distribution from which examples are drawn.
- Let **H** be the set of possible hypotheses.
- Let m be the number of examples in the training set.

ERROR

Initially, we will assume that the true function f is a member of **H**. Now we can define the **error** of a hypothesis h with respect to the true function f given a distribution D over the examples as the probability that h is different from f on an example:

$$\text{error}(h) = P(h(x) \neq f(x) | x \text{ drawn from } D)$$

This is the same quantity being measured experimentally by the learning curves shown earlier.

A hypothesis h is called **approximately correct** if $\text{error}(h) \leq \epsilon$, where ϵ is a small constant. The plan of attack is to show that after seeing m examples, with high probability, all consistent hypotheses will be approximately correct. One can think of an approximately correct hypothesis as being "close" to the true function in hypothesis space—it lies inside what is called the ϵ-ball around the true function f. Figure 18.15 shows the set of all hypotheses **H**, divided into the ϵ-ball around f and the remainder, which we call **H**$_{\text{bad}}$.

ϵ-BALL

We can calculate the probability that a "seriously wrong" hypothesis $h_b \in$ **H**$_{\text{bad}}$ is consistent with the first m examples as follows. We know that $\text{error}(h_b) > \epsilon$. Thus, the probability that it

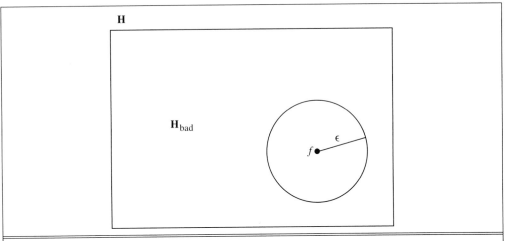

Figure 18.15   Schematic diagram of hypothesis space, showing the "ϵ-ball" around the true function f.

agrees with any given example is $\leq (1 - \epsilon)$. The bound for m examples is

$$P(h_b \text{ agrees with } m \text{ examples}) \leq (1 - \epsilon)^m$$

For $\mathbf{H}_{\text{bad}}$ to contain a consistent hypothesis, at least one of the hypotheses in $\mathbf{H}_{\text{bad}}$ must be consistent. The probability of this occurring is bounded by the sum of the individual probabilities:

$$P(\mathbf{H}_{\text{bad}} \text{ contains a consistent hypothesis}) \leq |\mathbf{H}_{\text{bad}}|(1 - \epsilon)^m$$
$$\leq |\mathbf{H}|(1 - \epsilon)^m$$

We would like to reduce the probability of this event below some small number δ:

$$|\mathbf{H}|(1 - \epsilon)^m \leq \delta$$

We can achieve this if we allow the algorithm to see

$$m \geq \frac{1}{\epsilon}\left(\ln\frac{1}{\delta} + \ln|\mathbf{H}|\right) \tag{18.2}$$

examples. Thus, if a learning algorithm returns a hypothesis that is consistent with this many examples, then with probability at least $1 - \delta$, it has error at most ϵ. In other words, it is probably approximately correct. The number of required examples, as a function of ϵ and δ, is called the
SAMPLE COMPLEXITY **sample complexity** of the hypothesis space.

It appears, then, that the key question is the size of the hypothesis space. As we saw earlier, if $\mathbf{H}$ is the set of all Boolean functions on n attributes, then $|\mathbf{H}| = 2^{2^n}$. Thus, the sample complexity of the space grows as 2^n. Because the number of possible examples is also 2^n, this says that any learning algorithm for the space of all Boolean functions will do no better than a lookup table, if it merely returns a hypothesis that is consistent with all known examples. Another way to see this is to observe that for any unseen example, the hypothesis space will contain as many consistent hypotheses predicting a positive outcome as predict a negative outcome.

The dilemma we face, then, is that unless we restrict the space of functions the algorithm can consider, it will not be able to learn; but if we do restrict the space, we may eliminate the true function altogether. There are two ways to "escape" this dilemma. The first way is to insist that the algorithm returns not just any consistent hypothesis, but preferably the simplest one. The theoretical analysis of such algorithms is beyond the scope of this book, but in most cases, finding the simplest hypothesis is intractable. The second escape, which we pursue here, is to focus on learnable subsets of the entire set of Boolean functions. The idea is that in most cases we do not need the full expressive power of Boolean functions, and can get by with more restricted languages. We now examine one such restricted language in more detail.

Learning decision lists

DECISION LIST

A **decision list** is a logical expression of a restricted form. It consists of a series of tests, each of which is a conjunction of literals. If a test succeeds when applied to an example description, the decision list specifies the value to be returned. If the test fails, processing continues with the next test in the list.[11] Decision lists resemble decision trees, but their overall structure is simpler, whereas the individual tests are more complex. Figure 18.16 shows a decision list that represents the hypothesis H_4 obtained by the earlier CURRENT-BEST-LEARNING algorithm:

$$\forall x \ \ WillWait(x) \ \Leftrightarrow \ Patrons(x, Some) \lor (Patrons(x, Full) \land Fri/Sat(x))$$

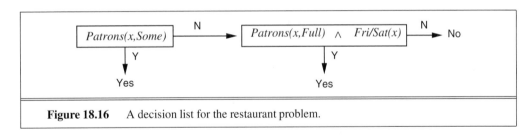

Figure 18.16   A decision list for the restaurant problem.

If we allow tests of arbitrary size, then decision lists can represent any Boolean function (Exercise 18.13). On the other hand, if we restrict the size of each test to at most k literals, then it is possible for the learning algorithm to generalize successfully from a small number of examples. We call this language k-DL. The example in Figure 18.16 is in 2-DL. It is easy to show (Exercise 18.13) that k-DL includes as a subset the language k-DT, the set of all decision trees of depth at most k. It is important to remember that the particular language referred to by k-DL depends on the attributes used to describe the examples. We will use the notation k-DL(n) to denote a k-DL language using n Boolean attributes.

k-DL
k-DT

The first task is to show that k-DL is learnable—that is, any function in k-DL can be accurately approximated after seeing a reasonable number of examples. To do this, we need to calculate the number of hypotheses in the language. Let the language of tests—conjunctions of at most k literals using n attributes—be $Conj(n, k)$. Because a decision list is constructed of tests, and each test can be attached to either a *Yes* or a *No* outcome or can be absent from the decision list, there

---

[11] A decision list is therefore identical in structure to a COND statement in Lisp.

are at most $3^{|Conj(n,k)|}$ distinct sets of component tests. Each of these sets of tests can be in any order, so

$$|k\text{-}\mathrm{DL}(n)| \leq 3^{|Conj(n,k)|}|Conj(n,k)|!$$

The number of conjunctions of k literals from n attributes is given by

$$|Conj(n,k)| = \sum_{i=0}^{k} \binom{2n}{i} = O(n^k)$$

Hence, after some work, we obtain

$$|k\text{-}\mathrm{DL}(n)| = 2^{O(n^k \log_2(n^k))}$$

We can plug this into Equation (18.2) to show that the number of examples needed for PAC-learning a k-DL function is polynomial in n:

$$m \geq \frac{1}{\epsilon}\left(\ln\frac{1}{\delta} + O(n^k \log_2(n^k))\right)$$

Therefore, any algorithm that returns a consistent decision list will PAC-learn a k-DL function in a reasonable number of examples, for small k. The next task is to find an efficient algorithm that returns a consistent decision list. We will use a greedy algorithm called DECISION-LIST-LEARNING that repeatedly finds a test that agrees exactly with some subset of the training set. Once it finds such a test, it adds it to the decision list under construction and removes the corresponding examples. It then constructs the remainder of the decision list using just the remaining examples. This is repeated until there are no examples left. The algorithm is shown in Figure 18.17.

   This algorithm does not specify the method for selecting the next test to add to the decision list. Although the formal results given earlier do not depend on the selection method, it would seem reasonable to prefer small tests that match large sets of uniformly classified examples, so that the overall decision list will be as compact as possible. The simplest strategy is to find the smallest test t that matches any uniformly classified subset, regardless of the size of the subset. Even this approach works quite well. The results for the restaurant data are shown in Figure 18.18, and suggest that learning decision lists is an effective way to make predictions.

---

function DECISION-LIST-LEARNING(*examples*) **returns** a decision list, *No* or failure

    if *examples* is empty **then return** the value *No*
    t ← a test that matches a nonempty subset *examples$_t$* of *examples*
        such that the members of *examples$_t$* are all positive or all negative
    if there is no such *t* **then return** failure
    if the examples in *examples$_t$* are positive **then** o ← *Yes*
    else o ← *No*
    return a decision list with initial test t and outcome o
        and remaining elements given by DECISION-LIST-LEARNING(*examples* − *examples$_t$*)

Figure 18.17   An algorithm for learning decision lists.

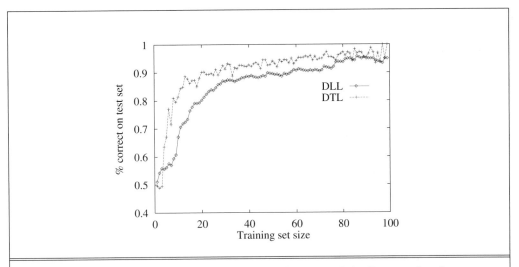

Figure 18.18   Graph showing the predictive performance of the DECISION-LIST-LEARNING algorithm on the restaurant data, as a function of the number of examples seen. The curve for DECISION-TREE-LEARNING is shown for comparison.

Discussion

IDENTIFICATION IN
THE LIMIT

Computational learning theory has generated a new way of looking at the problem of learning. In the early 1960s, the theory of learning focussed on the problem of **identification in the limit**. An identification algorithm must return a hypothesis that exactly matches the true function. The standard approach combines the current-best-hypothesis and version space methods: the current best hypothesis is the first consistent hypothesis in some fixed simplicity ordering of the hypothesis space. As examples arrive, the learner abandons simpler hypotheses as they become inconsistent. Once it reaches the true function, it will never abandon it. Unfortunately, in many hypothesis spaces, the number of examples and the computation time required to reach the true function is enormous. Computational learning theory does not insist that the learning agent find the "one true law" governing its environment, but instead that it find a hypothesis with a certain degree of predictive accuracy. It also brings sharply into focus the trade-off between the expressiveness of the hypothesis language and the complexity of learning.

The results we have shown are worst-case complexity results, and do not necessarily reflect the average-case sample complexity as measured by the learning curves we have shown. An average-case analysis must also make assumptions as to the distribution of examples and the distribution of true functions that the algorithm will have to learn. As these issues become better understood, computational learning theory is providing valuable guidance to machine learning researchers who are interested in predicting or modifying the learning ability of their algorithms. Besides decision lists, results have been obtained for almost all known subclasses of Boolean functions, for neural networks (see Chapter 19) and for sets of first-order logical sentences (see Chapter 21). The results show that the pure inductive learning problem, where the agent begins with no prior knowledge about the target function, is generally very hard. As we show in Chapter 21, the use of prior knowledge to guide inductive learning makes it possible to learn quite large sets of sentences from reasonable numbers of examples, even in a language as expressive as first-order logic.

18.7   SUMMARY

We have seen that all learning can be seen as learning a function, and in this chapter we concentrate on induction: learning a function from example input/output pairs. The main points were as follows:

- Learning in intelligent agents is essential for dealing with unknown environments (i.e., compensating for the designer's lack of omniscience about the agent's environment).

- Learning is also essential for building agents with a reasonable amount of effort (i.e., compensating for the designer's laziness, or lack of time).

- Learning agents can be divided conceptually into a **performance element**, which is responsible for selecting actions, and a **learning element**, which is responsible for modifying the performance element.

- Learning takes many forms, depending on the nature of the performance element, the available feedback, and the available knowledge.

- Learning any particular component of the performance element can be cast as a problem of learning an accurate representation of a **function**.

- Learning a function from examples of its inputs and outputs is called **inductive learning**.

- The difficulty of learning depends on the chosen representation. Functions can be represented by logical sentences, polynomials, belief networks, neural networks, and others.

- Decision trees are an efficient method for learning deterministic Boolean functions.

- Ockham's razor suggests choosing the simplest hypothesis that matches the observed examples. The information gain heuristic allows us to find a simple decision tree.

- The performance of inductive learning algorithms is measured by their learning curve, which shows the prediction accuracy as a function of the number of observed examples.

- We presented two general approaches for learning logical theories. The current-best-hypothesis approach maintains and adjusts a single hypothesis, whereas the version space approach maintains a representation of all consistent hypotheses. Both are vulnerable to noise in the training set.

- Computational learning theory analyses the sample complexity and computational complexity of inductive learning. There is a trade-off between the expressiveness of the hypothesis language and the ease of learning.

BIBLIOGRAPHICAL AND HISTORICAL NOTES

The general architecture for learning systems portrayed in Figure 18.1 is classic in the machine learning literature (Buchanan *et al.*, 1978). The architecture itself, as embodied in programs, goes back at least as far as Arthur Samuel's (1959; 1967) program for playing checkers, which improved its performance through learning. It is described further in Chapter 20.

Claude Shannon was the inventor of information theory (Shannon and Weaver, 1949), which revolutionized the study of communication as well as contributing to the success of decision-tree learning. He also contributed one of the earliest examples of machine learning, a mechanical mouse named Theseus that learned how to travel efficiently through a maze by trial and error. EPAM, the "Elementary Perceiver And Memorizer" (Feigenbaum, 1961), was one of the earliest systems to use decision trees (or **discrimination nets**). EPAM was intended as a cognitive-simulation model of human concept learning. CLS (Hunt *et al.*, 1966) used a heuristic lookahead method to construct decision trees. ID3 (Quinlan, 1979) added the crucial idea of using information content to provide the heuristic function. Quinlan (1986) experimentally investigates the effect of noise on learning and describes a modification of ID3 designed to handle noise. A copy of C4.5, an industrial-strength version of ID3, can be found in Quinlan (1993a).

William of Ockham (c. 1285–1349), the most influential philosopher of his century and a major contributer to medieval epistemology, logic, and metaphysics, is credited with a statement called "Ockham's Razor"—in Latin, *Entia non sunt multiplicanda praeter necessitatem*, and in English, "Entities are not to be multiplied without necessity." Unfortunately, this laudable piece of advice is nowhere to be found in his writings in precisely these words.

The current-best-hypothesis approach has been a mainstay of the philosophy of science, as a model of scientific theory formation, for centuries. In AI, the approach is most closely associated with the work of Patrick Winston, whose Ph.D. thesis (Winston, 1970) addressed the problem of learning descriptions of complex objects. Tom Mitchell (1977; 1982) invented version spaces and the learning algorithm that uses them. They were initially used in the Meta-DENDRAL expert system for chemistry (Buchanan and Mitchell, 1978), and later in Mitchell's (1983) LEX system, which learns to solve calculus problems. The importance of bias in inductive learning was emphasized by Mitchell (1980), who showed that an unbiased algorithm is incapable of learning because its hypothesis space always contains equal numbers of consistent hypotheses that predict Q and $\neg Q$ for any example and for any goal predicate Q.

Historically, the earliest research on the theoretical analysis of learning focused on the problem of "identification in the limit" (Gold, 1967), which involves showing that a learning algorithm will eventually converge on the correct hypothesis once it has seen enough examples. This approach was motivated in part by models of scientific discovery from the philosophy of science (Popper, 1962), but has been applied mainly to the problem of learning grammars from example sentences. Osherson, Stob, and Weinstein (1986) provide a modern and rigorous treatment of the field.

Whereas the identification-in-the-limit approach concentrates on eventual convergence, the study of **Kolmogorov complexity** or **algorithmic complexity**, developed independently by Solomonoff (1964) and Kolmogorov (1965), attempts to provide a formal definition for the notion of simplicity used in Ockham's razor. To escape the problem that simplicity depends on the way

KOLMOGOROV
COMPLEXITY

in which information is represented, it is proposed that simplicity be measured by the length of the shortest program for a universal Turing machine that correctly reproduces the observed data. Although there are many possible universal Turing machines, and hence many possible "shortest" programs, these programs differ in length by at most a constant that is independent of the amount of data. This beautiful insight, which essentially shows that *any* initial representation bias will eventually be overcome by the data itself, is marred only by the undecidability of computing the length of the shortest program. Approximate measures such as the **minimum description length** or MDL (Rissanen, 1984) can be used instead, and have produced excellent results in practice. The recent text by Li and Vitanyi (1993) is the best source for Kolmogorov complexity.

MINIMUM
DESCRIPTION
LENGTH

Computational learning theory in the modern sense, that is, the theory of PAC-learning, was inaugurated by Leslie Valiant (1984), but also has roots in the subfield of statistics called **uniform convergence theory** (Vapnik and Chervonenkis, 1971). Valiant's work brought computational complexity issues into the picture, and emphasized the idea that the learner need find only *approximately* correct hypotheses. With Michael Kearns (1990), Valiant showed that several concept classes cannot be PAC-learned tractably even though sufficient information is available in the examples. Some positive results have been obtained for classes such as decision lists (Rivest, 1987), although most PAC-learning results have been negative.

UNIFORM
CONVERGENCE
THEORY

PAC-learning theory and uniform convergence theory were unified by the "four Germans" (none of whom are actually German): Blumer, Ehrenfeucht, Haussler, and Warmuth (1989). PAC learning is also related to other theoretical approaches through the notion of an **Ockham algorithm**. Such algorithms are capable of finding a consistent hypothesis that achieves a "significant" compression of the data it represents. The four Germans showed that if an Ockham algorithm exists for a given class of concepts, then the class is PAC-learnable (Blumer *et al.*, 1990). Board and Pitt (1992) showed that the implication also goes the other way: if a concept class is PAC-learnable, then there must exist an Ockham algorithm for it.

OCKHAM
ALGORITHM

A large number of important papers on machine learning have been collected in *Readings in Machine Learning* (Shavlik and Dietterich, 1990). The two volumes *Machine Learning 1* (Michalski *et al.*, 1983) and *Machine Learning 2* (Michalski *et al.*, 1986) also contain many important papers as well as huge bibliographies. Weiss and Kulikowski (1991) provide a broad introduction to function-learning methods from machine learning, statistics, and neural networks. The STATLOG project (Michie *et al.*, 1994) is by far the most exhaustive investigation into the comparative performance of learning algorithms. Good current research in machine learning is published in the annual proceedings of the International Conference on Machine Learning, in the journal *Machine Learning*, and in mainstream AI journals. Work in computational learning theory appears in the annual ACM Workshop on Computational Learning Theory (COLT), in *Machine Learning*, and in several theoretical journals.

EXERCISES

18.1   Consider the problem faced by an infant learning to speak and understand a language. Explain how this process fits into the general learning model, identifying each of the components of the model as appropriate.

18.2   Repeat Exercise 18.1 for the case of learning to play tennis (or some other competitive sport with which you are familiar). Is this supervised learning or reinforcement learning?

18.3   Draw a decision tree for the problem of deciding whether or not to move forward at a road intersection given that the light has just turned green.

18.4   We never test the same attribute twice along one path in a decision tree. Why not?

18.5   A good "straw man" learning algorithm is as follows: create a table out of all the training examples. Determine which output occurs most often among the training examples; call it d. Then when given an input that is not in the table, just return d. For inputs that are in the table, return the output associated with it (or the most frequent output, if there is more than one). If the input does not appear in the table, then return d. Implement this algorithm and see how well it does in a sample domain. This should give you an idea of the baseline for the domain—the minimal performance that any algorithm should be able to obtain (although many published algorithms have managed to do worse).

18.6   Look back at Exercise 3.16, which asked you to predict from a sequence of numbers (such as [1,4,9,16]) the function underlying the sequence. What techniques from this chapter are applicable to this problem? How would they allow you to do better than the problem-solving approach of Exercise 3.16?

18.7   In the recursive construction of decision trees, it sometimes occurs that a mixed set of positive and negative examples remains at a leaf node, even after all the attributes have been used. Suppose that we have p positive examples and n negative examples.

  a. Show that the solution used by DECISION-TREE-LEARNING, which picks the majority classification, minimizes the absolute error over the set of examples at the leaf.

CLASS PROBABILITY   **b.** Show that returning the **class probability** $p/(p + n)$ minimizes the sum of squared errors.

18.8   Suppose that a learning algorithm is trying to find a consistent hypothesis when the classifications of examples are actually being generated randomly. There are n Boolean attributes, and examples are drawn uniformly from the set of 2^n possible examples. Calculate the number of examples required before the probability of finding a contradiction in the data reaches 0.5.

18.9   Suppose that an attribute splits the set of examples E into subsets E_i, and that each subset has p_i positive examples and n_i negative examples. Show that unless the ratio $p_i/(p_i + n_i)$ is the same for all i, the attribute has strictly positive information gain.

18.10   Modify DECISION-TREE-LEARNING to include χ^2-pruning. You may wish to consult Quinlan (1986) for details.

18.11   The standard DECISION-TREE-LEARNING algorithm described in the chapter does not handle cases in which some examples have missing attribute values.

  a. First, we need to find a way to classify such examples, given a decision tree that includes tests on the attributes for which values may be missing. Suppose an example X has a missing value for attribute A, and that the decision tree tests for A at a node that X reaches. One way to handle this case is to pretend that the example has *all* possible values for the attribute, but to weight each value according to its frequency among all of the examples that reach that node in the decision tree. The classification algorithm should follow all branches at any node for which a value is missing, and should multiply the weights along each path. Write a modified classification algorithm for decision trees that has this behavior.

b. Now modify the information gain calculation so that in any given collection of examples C at a given node in the tree during the construction process, the examples with missing values for any of the remaining attributes are given "as–if" values according to the frequencies of those values in the set C.

18.12 In the chapter, we noted that attributes with many different possible values can cause problems with the gain measure. Such attributes tend to split the examples into many small classes or even singleton classes, thereby appearing to be highly relevant according to the gain measure. The **gain ratio** criterion selects attributes according to the ratio between their gain and their intrinsic information content, that is, the amount of information contained in the answer to the question, "What is the value of this attribute?" The gain ratio criterion therefore tries to measure how efficiently an attribute provides information on the correct classification of an example. Write a mathematical expression for the information content of an attribute, and implement the gain ratio criterion in DECISION-TREE-LEARNING.

18.13 In this exercise, we will consider the expressiveness of decision lists, as defined in Section 18.6.

a. Show that if the tests can be of any size, decision lists can represent any Boolean function.

b. Show that if the tests can contain at most k literals each, then decision lists can represent any function that can be represented by a decision tree of depth k.

18.14 We have shown how a learning element can improve the performance element. What if we wanted to improve the learning element (or the critic or the problem generator)? Give some examples of this kind of improvement in the taxi domain. Is it possible to represent this kind of learning with our general model of learning agents? How?

19 LEARNING IN NEURAL AND BELIEF NETWORKS

In which we see how to train complex networks of simple computing elements, thereby perhaps shedding some light on the workings of the brain.

This chapter can be viewed in two ways. From a computational viewpoint, it is about a method of representing functions using networks of simple arithmetic computing elements, and about methods for learning such representations from examples. These networks represent functions in much the same way that circuits consisting of simple logic gates represent Boolean functions. Such representations are particularly useful for complex functions with continuous-valued outputs and large numbers of noisy inputs, where the logic-based techniques in Chapter 18 sometimes have difficulty.

From a biological viewpoint, this chapter is about a mathematical model for the operation of the brain. The simple arithmetic computing elements correspond to **neurons**—the cells that perform information processing in the brain—and the network as a whole corresponds to a collection of interconnected neurons. For this reason, the networks are called **neural networks**.[1] NEURAL NETWORKS Besides their useful computational properties, neural networks may offer the best chance of understanding many psychological phenomena that arise from the specific structure and operation of the brain. We will therefore begin the chapter with a brief look at what is known about brains, because this provides much of the motivation for the study of neural networks. In a sense, we thereby depart from our intention, stated in Chapter 1, to concentrate on rational action rather than on imitating humans. These conflicting goals have characterized the study of neural networks ever since the very first paper on the topic by McCulloch and Pitts (1943). Methodologically speaking, the goals can be reconciled by acknowledging the fact that humans (and other animals) *do* think, and use their powers of thought to act quite successfully in complex domains where current computer-based agents would be lost. It is instructive to try to see how they do it.

Section 19.2 then presents the idealized models that are the main subject of study. Simple, single-layer networks called **perceptrons** are covered in Section 19.3, and general multilayer networks in Section 19.4. Section 19.5 illustrates the various uses of neural networks.

---

[1] Other names that have been used for the field include **connectionism**, **parallel distributed processing**, **neural computation**, **adaptive networks**, and **collective computation**. It should be emphasized that these are artificial neural networks; there is no attempt to build computing elements out of animal tissue.

The network theme is continued in Section 19.6, where we discuss methods for learning belief networks from examples. The connection is deeper than the superficial similarity implied by the word "network"—not only do the two fields share some learning methods, but in some cases, it can be shown that neural networks *are* belief networks.

19.1   HOW THE BRAIN WORKS

The exact way in which the brain enables thought is one of the great mysteries of science. It has been appreciated for thousands of years that strong blows to the head can lead to unconsciousness, temporary loss of memory, or even permanent loss of mental capability. This suggests that the brain is somehow involved in thought. It has also long been known that the human brain is somehow different; in about 335 B.C. Aristotle wrote, "Of all the animals, man has the largest brain in proportion to his size."[2] Still, it was not until the middle of the eighteenth century that the brain was widely recognized as the seat of consciousness, and it was not until the late nineteenth century that the functional regions of animal brains began to be mapped out. Before the nineteenth century, candidate locations for the seat of consciousness included the heart, the spleen, and the pineal body, a small appendage of the brain present in all vertebrates.

NEURON
SOMA
DENDRITES

AXON

We do know that the **neuron**, or nerve cell, is the fundamental functional unit of all nervous system tissue, including the brain. Each neuron consists of a cell body, or **soma**, that contains a cell nucleus. Branching out from the cell body are a number of fibers called **dendrites** and a single long fiber called the **axon**. Dendrites branch into a bushy network around the cell, whereas the axon stretches out for a long distance—usually about a centimeter (100 times the diameter of the cell body), and as far as a meter in extreme cases. Eventually, the axon also branches into strands and substrands that connect to the dendrites and cell bodies of other neurons. The

SYNAPSE

connecting junction is called a **synapse**. Each neuron forms synapses with anywhere from a dozen to a hundred thousand other neurons. Figure 19.1 shows the parts of a neuron.

Signals are propagated from neuron to neuron by a complicated electrochemical reaction. Chemical transmitter substances are released from the synapses and enter the dendrite, raising or lowering the electrical potential of the cell body. When the potential reaches a threshold,

ACTION POTENTIAL

an electrical pulse or **action potential** is sent down the axon. The pulse spreads out along the branches of the axon, eventually reaching synapses and releasing transmitters into the bodies of

EXCITATORY
INHIBITORY

other cells. Synapses that increase the potential are called **excitatory**, and those that decrease it are called **inhibitory**. Perhaps the most significant finding is that synaptic connections exhibit

PLASTICITY

plasticity—long-term changes in the strength of connections in response to the pattern of stimulation. Neurons also form new connections with other neurons, and sometimes entire collections of neurons can migrate from one place to another. These mechanisms are thought to form the basis for learning in the brain.

Most information processing goes on in the cerebral cortex, the outer layer of the brain. The basic organizational unit appears to be a barrel-shaped module of tissue about 0.5 mm in

---

[2] Since then, it has been discovered that some species of dolphins and whales have relatively larger brains. The large size of human brains is now thought to be enabled in part by recent improvements in its cooling system.

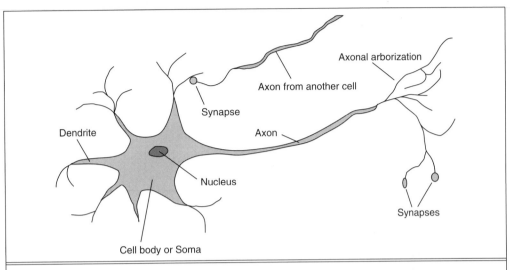

Figure 19.1   The parts of a nerve cell or neuron. In reality, the length of the axon should be about 100 times the diameter of the cell body.

APHASIA

diameter, extending the full depth of the cortex, which is about 4 mm in humans. A module contains about 2000 neurons. It is known that certain areas of the brain have specific functions. In 1861, Pierre Paul Broca was able to demonstrate that the third left frontal convolution of the cerebral cortex is important for speech and language by his studies of patients with **aphasia**—an inability to speak, often brought on by brain damage. This soon led to surgical experiments on animals that mapped out the connection between areas of the cortex and specific motor controls. We now have some data on the mapping between areas of the brain and the parts of the body that they control, or from which they receive sensory input. Such mappings seem to be able to change radically over the course of a few weeks, and some animals seem to have multiple maps. Moreover, we do not fully understand how other areas can take over functions when one area is damaged. There is almost no theory about how an individual memory is stored.

The truly amazing thing is that *a collection of simple cells can lead to thought, action, and consciousness.* Neurobiology is a long way from a complete theory of consciousness, but even if there are some important electrical or chemical processes that have been overlooked, the amazing conclusion is the same: *brains cause minds* (Searle, 1992). The only real alternative theory is mysticism: that there is some mystical realm in which minds operate that is beyond physical science.

Comparing brains with digital computers

Brains and digital computers perform quite different tasks, and have different properties. Figure 19.2 shows that there are more neurons in the typical human brain than there are bits in a typical high-end computer workstation. We can predict that this will not hold true for long, because the human brain is evolving very slowly, whereas computer memories are growing rapidly. In any

	Computer	Human Brain
Computational units	1 CPU, 10^5 gates	10^{11} neurons
Storage units	10^9 bits RAM, 10^{10} bits disk	10^{11} neurons, 10^{14} synapses
Cycle time	10^{-8} sec	10^{-3} sec
Bandwidth	10^9 bits/sec	10^{14} bits/sec
Neuron updates/sec	10^5	10^{14}

Figure 19.2   A crude comparison of the raw computational resources available to computers (*circa* 1994) and brains.

case, the difference in storage capacity is minor compared to the difference in switching speed and in parallelism. Computer chips can execute an instruction in tens of nanoseconds, whereas neurons require milliseconds to fire. Brains more than make up for this, however, because all the neurons and synapses are active simultaneously, whereas most current computers have only one or at most a few CPUs. A neural network running on a serial computer requires hundreds of cycles to decide if a single neuron-like unit will fire, whereas in a real brain, *all* the neurons do this in a single step. Thus, *even though a computer is a million times faster in raw switching speed, the brain ends up being a billion times faster at what it does.* One of the attractions of the neural network approach is the hope that a device could be built that combines the parallelism of the brain with the switching speed of the computer. Full-scale hardware development will depend on finding a family of neural network algorithms that provides a basis for long-term investment.

A brain can perform a complex task—recognize a face, for example—in less than a second, which is only enough time for a few hundred cycles. A serial computer requires billions of cycles to perform the same task less well. Clearly, there *is* an opportunity for massive parallelism here. Neural networks may provide a model for massively parallel computation that is more successful than the approach of "parallelizing" traditional serial algorithms.

Brains are more fault-tolerant than computers. A hardware error that flips a single bit can doom an entire computation, but brain cells die all the time with no ill effect to the overall functioning of the brain. It is true that there are a variety of diseases and traumas that can affect a brain, but for the most part, brains manage to muddle through for 70 or 80 years with no need to replace a memory card, call the manufacturer's service line, or reboot. In addition, brains are constantly faced with novel input, yet manage to do something with it. Computer programs rarely work as well with novel input, unless the programmer has been exceptionally careful. The third attraction of neural networks is **graceful degradation**: they tend to have a gradual rather than sharp drop-off in performance as conditions worsen.

GRACEFUL
DEGRADATION

The final attraction of neural networks is that they are designed to be trained using an inductive learning algorithm. (Contrary to the impression given by the popular media, of course, neural networks are far from being the only AI systems capable of learning.) After the network is initialized, it can be modified to improve its performance on input/output pairs. To the extent that the learning algorithms can be made general and efficient, this increases the value of neural networks as psychological models, and makes them useful tools for creating a wide variety of high-performance applications.

19.2   NEURAL NETWORKS

UNITS

LINKS

WEIGHT

A neural network is composed of a number of nodes, or **units**, connected by **links**. Each link has a numeric **weight** associated with it. Weights are the primary means of long-term storage in neural networks, and learning usually takes place by updating the weights. Some of the units are connected to the external environment, and can be designated as input or output units. The weights are modified so as to try to bring the network's input/output behavior more into line with that of the environment providing the inputs.

ACTIVATION LEVEL

Each unit has a set of input links from other units, a set of output links to other units, a current **activation level**, and a means of computing the activation level at the next step in time, given its inputs and weights. The idea is that each unit does a local computation based on inputs from its neighbors, but without the need for any global control over the set of units as a whole. In practice, most neural network implementations are in software and use synchronous control to update all the units in a fixed sequence.

To build a neural network to perform some task, one must first decide how many units are to be used, what kind of units are appropriate, and how the units are to be connected to form a network. One then initializes the weights of the network, and trains the weights using a learning algorithm applied to a set of training examples for the task.[3] The use of examples also implies that one must decide how to encode the examples in terms of inputs and outputs of the network.

Notation

Neural networks have lots of pieces, and to refer to them we will need to introduce a variety of mathematical notations. For convenience, these are summarized in Figure 19.3.

Simple computing elements

INPUT FUNCTION

ACTIVATION
FUNCTION

Figure 19.4 shows a typical unit. Each unit performs a simple computation: it receives signals from its input links and computes a new activation level that it sends along each of its output links. The computation of the activation level is based on the values of each input signal received from a neighboring node, and the weights on each input link. The computation is split into two components. First is a *linear* component, called the **input function**, in_i, that computes the weighted sum of the unit's input values. Second is a *nonlinear* component called the **activation function**, g, that transforms the weighted sum into the final value that serves as the unit's activation value, a_i. Usually, all units in a network use the same activation function. Exercise 19.3 explains why it is important to have a nonlinear component.

The total weighted input is the sum of the input activations times their respective weights:

$$in_i = \sum_j W_{j,i}a_j = \mathbf{W}_i \cdot \mathbf{a}_i$$

---

[3]   In this chapter, we will assume that all examples are labelled with the correct outputs. In Chapter 20, we will see how to relax this assumption.

Notation	Meaning
a_i	Activation value of unit i (also the output of the unit)
$\mathbf{a}_i$	Vector of activation values for the inputs to unit i
g	Activation function
g'	Derivative of the activation function
Err_i	Error (difference between output and target) for unit i
Err^e	Error for example e
I_i	Activation of a unit i in the input layer
$\mathbf{I}$	Vector of activations of all input units
$\mathbf{I}^e$	Vector of inputs for example e
in_i	Weighted sum of inputs to unit i
N	Total number of units in the network
O	Activation of the single output unit of a perceptron
O_i	Activation of a unit i in the output layer
$\mathbf{O}$	Vector of activations of all units in the output layer
t	Threshold for a step function
T	Target (desired) output for a perceptron
$\mathbf{T}$	Target vector when there are several output units
$\mathbf{T}^e$	Target vector for example e
$W_{j,i}$	Weight on the link from unit j to unit i
W_i	Weight from unit i to the output in a perceptron
$\mathbf{W}_i$	Vector of weights leading into unit i
$\mathbf{W}$	Vector of all weights in the network

Figure 19.3   Neural network notation. Subscripts denote units; superscripts denote examples.

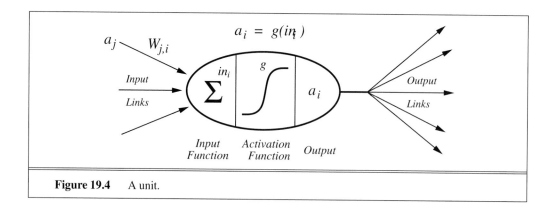

Figure 19.4   A unit.

where the final expression illustrates the use of vector notation. In this notation, the weights on links into node i are denoted by $\mathbf{W}$, the set of input values is called $\mathbf{a}_i$, and the dot product denotes the sum of the pairwise products.

The elementary computation step in each unit computes the new activation value for the unit by applying the activation function, g, to the result of the input function:

$$a_i \leftarrow g(in_i) = g\left(\sum_j W_{j,i}a_j\right)$$

Different models are obtained by using different mathematical functions for g. Three common choices are the step, sign, and sigmoid functions, illustrated in Figure 19.5. The step function has a threshold t such that it outputs a 1 when the input is greater than its threshold, and outputs a 0 otherwise. The biological motivation is that a 1 represents the firing of a pulse down the axon, and a 0 represents no firing. The threshold represents the minimum total weighted input necessary to cause the neuron to fire. Threshold versions of the sign and sigmoid functions can also be defined.

In most cases, we will find it mathematically convenient to replace the threshold with an extra input weight. This allows for a simpler learning element because it need only worry about adjusting weights, rather than adjusting both weights and thresholds. Thus, instead of having a threshold t for each unit, we add an extra input whose activation a_0 is fixed at -1. The extra weight $W_{0,i}$ associated with a_0 serves the function of a threshold at t, provided that $W_{0,i}a_0 = -t$. Then all units can have a fixed threshold at 0. Mathematically, the two representations for thresholds are entirely equivalent:

$$a_i = \text{step}_t\left(\sum_{j=1}^{n} W_{j,i}a_j\right) = \text{step}_0\left(\sum_{j=0}^{n} W_{j,i}a_j\right) \text{ where } W_{0,i} = t \text{ and } a_0 = -1$$

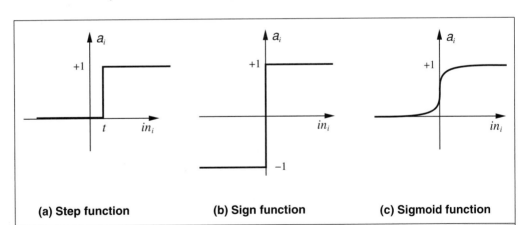

(a) Step function   **(b) Sign function**   **(c) Sigmoid function**

Figure 19.5   Three different activation functions for units.

$$\text{step}_t(x) = \begin{cases} 1, & \text{if } x \geq t \\ 0, & \text{if } x < t \end{cases} \quad \text{sign}(x) = \begin{cases} +1, & \text{if } x \geq 0 \\ -1, & \text{if } x < 0 \end{cases} \quad \text{sigmoid}(x) = \frac{1}{1+e^{-x}}$$

We can get a feel for the operation of individual units by comparing them with logic gates. One of the original motivations for the design of individual units (McCulloch and Pitts, 1943) was their ability to represent basic Boolean functions. Figure 19.6 shows how the Boolean functions *AND*, *OR*, and *NOT* can be represented by units with suitable weights and thresholds. This is important because it means we can use these units to build a network to compute any Boolean function of the inputs.

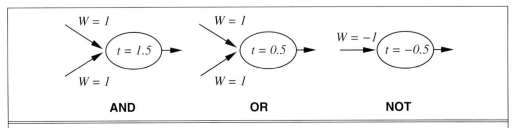

Figure 19.6   Units with a step function for the activation function can act as logic gates, given appropriate thresholds and weights.

Network structures

There are a variety of kinds of network structure, each of which results in very different computational properties. The main distinction to be made is between **feed-forward** and **recurrent** networks. In a feed-forward network, links are unidirectional, and there are no cycles. In a recurrent network, the links can form arbitrary topologies. Technically speaking, a feed-forward network is a directed acyclic graph (DAG). We will usually be dealing with networks that are arranged in layers. In a layered feed-forward network, each unit is linked only to units in the next layer; there are no links between units in the same layer, no links backward to a previous layer, and no links that skip a layer. Figure 19.7 shows a very simple example of a layered feed-forward network. This network has *two* layers; because the input units (square nodes) simply serve to pass activation to the next layer, they are not counted (although some authors would describe this as a three-layer network).

The significance of the lack of cycles is that computation can proceed uniformly from input units to output units. The activation from the previous time step plays no part in the computation, because it is not fed back to an earlier unit. Hence, a feed-forward network simply computes a function of the input values that depends on the weight settings—it has *no internal state* other than the weights themselves. Such networks can implement adaptive versions of simple reflex agents or they can function as components of more complex agents. In this chapter, we will focus on feed-forward networks because they are relatively well-understood.

Obviously, the brain cannot be a feed-forward network, else we would have no short-term memory. Some regions of the brain are largely feed-forward and somewhat layered, but there are rampant back-connections. In our terminology, the brain is a recurrent network. Because activation is fed back to the units that caused it, recurrent networks have internal state stored in the activation levels of the units. This also means that computation can be much less orderly than in feed-forward networks. Recurrent networks can become unstable, or oscillate, or exhibit chaotic behavior. Given some input values, it can take a long time to compute a stable output, and learning is made more difficult. On the other hand, recurrent networks can implement more complex agent designs and can model systems with state. Because recurrent networks require some quite advanced mathematical methods, we can only provide a few pointers here.

HOPFIELD
NETWORKS

Hopfield networks are probably the best-understood class of recurrent networks. They use *bidirectional* connections with *symmetric* weights (i.e., $W_{i,j} = W_{j,i}$); all of the units are both input and output units; the activation function g is the sign function; and the activation levels can

ASSOCIATIVE
MEMORY

only be ± 1. A Hopfield network functions as an **associative memory**—after training on a set of examples, a new stimulus will cause the network to settle into an activation pattern corresponding to the example in the training set that *most closely resembles* the new stimulus. For example, if the training set consists of a set of photographs, and the new stimulus is a small piece of one of the photographs, then the network activation levels will reproduce the photograph from which the piece was taken. Notice that the original photographs are not stored separately in the network; each weight is a partial encoding of all the photographs. One of the most interesting theoretical results is that Hopfield networks can reliably store up to $0.138N$ training examples, where N is the number of units in the network.

BOLTZMANN
MACHINES

Boltzmann machines also use symmetric weights, but include units that are neither input nor output units (cf. the units labelled H_3 and H_4 in Figure 19.7). They also use a *stochastic* activation function, such that the probability of the output being 1 is some function of the total weighted input. Boltzmann machines therefore undergo state transitions that resemble a simulated annealing search for the configuration that best approximates the training set (see Chapter 4). It turns out that Boltzmann machines are formally identical to a special case of belief networks evaluated with a stochastic simulation algorithm (see Section 15.4).

Returning to feed-forward networks, there is one more important distinction to be made. Examine Figure 19.7, which shows the topology of a very simple neural network. On the left are

INPUT UNITS

the **input units**. The activation value of each of these units is determined by the environment. At

OUTPUT UNITS

the right-hand end of the network are four **output units**. In between, the nodes labelled H_3 and

HIDDEN UNITS

H_4 have no direct connection to the outside world. These are called **hidden units**, because they cannot be directly observed by noting the input/output behavior of the network. Some networks,

PERCEPTRONS

called **perceptrons**, have no hidden units. This makes the learning problem much simpler, but it means that perceptrons are very limited in what they can represent. Networks with one or

MULTILAYER
NETWORKS

more layers of hidden units are called **multilayer networks**. With one (sufficiently large) layer of hidden units, it is possible to represent any continuous function of the inputs; with two layers, even discontinuous functions can be represented.

With a fixed structure and fixed activation functions g, the functions representable by a feed-forward network are restricted to have a specific parameterized structure. The weights chosen for the network determine which of these functions is actually represented. For example, the network in Figure 19.7 calculates the following function:

$$
\begin{aligned}
a_5 &= g(W_{3,5}a_3 + W_{4,5}a_4) \\
&= g(W_{3,5}g(W_{1,3}a_1 + W_{2,3}a_2) + W_{4,5}g(W_{1,4}a_1 + W_{2,4}a_2))
\end{aligned}
\tag{19.1}
$$

where g is the activation function, and a_i is the output of node i. Notice that because the activation functions g are nonlinear, the whole network represents a complex nonlinear function. If you

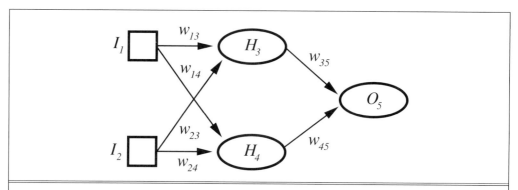

Figure 19.7   A very simple, two-layer, feed-forward network with two inputs, two hidden nodes, and one output node.

NONLINEAR
REGRESSION

think of the weights as parameters or coefficients of this function, then *learning just becomes a process of tuning the parameters to fit the data in the training set*—a process that statisticians call **nonlinear regression**. From the statistical viewpoint, this is what neural networks do.

Optimal network structure

So far we have considered networks with a fixed structure, determined by some outside authority. This is a potential weak point, because the wrong choice of network structure can lead to poor performance. If we choose a network that is too small, then the model will be incapable of representing the desired function. If we choose a network that is too big, it will be able to memorize all the examples by forming a large lookup table, but will not generalize well to inputs that have not been seen before. In other words, like all statistical models, neural networks are subject to **overfitting** when there are too many parameters (i.e., weights) in the model. We saw this in Figure 18.2 (page 530), where the high-parameter models (b) and (c) fit all the data, but may not generalize as well as the low-parameter model (d).

It is known that a feed-forward network with one hidden layer can approximate any continuous function of the inputs, and a network with two hidden layers can approximate any function at all. However, the number of units in each layer may grow exponentially with the number of inputs. As yet, we have no good theory to characterize **NERFs**, or Network Efficiently Representable Functions—functions that can be approximated with a small number of units.

NERFS

We can think of the problem of finding a good network structure as a search problem. One approach that has been used is to use a **genetic algorithm** (Chapter 20) to search the space of network structures. However, this is a very large space, and evaluating a state in the space means running the whole neural network training protocol, so this approach is very CPU-intensive. Therefore, it is more common to see hill-climbing searches that selectively modify an existing network structure. There are two ways to do this: start with a big network and make it smaller, or start with a small one and make it bigger.

The zip code reading network described on page 586 uses an approach called **optimal brain damage** to remove weights from the initial fully-connected model. After the network is initially trained, an information theoretic approach identifies an optimal selection of connections that can be dropped (i.e., the weights are set to zero). The network is then retrained, and if it is performing as well or better, the process is repeated. This process was able to eliminate 3/4 of the weights, and improve overall performance on test data. In addition to removing connections, it is also possible to remove units that are not contributing much to the result.

Several algorithms have been proposed for growing a larger network from a smaller one. The **tiling algorithm** (Mézard and Nadal, 1989) is interesting because it is similar to the decision tree learning algorithm. The idea is to start with a single unit that does its best to produce the correct output on as many of the training examples as possible. Subsequent units are added to take care of the examples that the first unit got wrong. The algorithm adds only as many units as are needed to cover all the examples.

The **cross-validation** techniques of Chapter 18 are useful for deciding when we have found a network of the right size.

19.3   PERCEPTRONS

Layered feed-forward networks were first studied in the late 1950s under the name **perceptrons**. Although networks of all sizes and topologies were considered, the only effective learning element at the time was for single-layered networks, so that is where most of the effort was spent. Today, the name perceptron is used as a synonym for a single-layer, feed-forward network. The left-hand side of Figure 19.8 shows such a perceptron network. Notice that each output unit is independent of the others—each weight only affects one of the outputs. That means that we can limit our study to perceptrons with a single output unit, as in the right-hand side of Figure 19.8, and use several of them to build up a multi-output perceptron. For convenience, we can drop subscripts, denoting the output unit as O and the weight from input unit j to O as W_j. The activation of input unit j is given by I_j. The activation of the output unit is therefore

$$O = Step_0 \left(\sum_j W_j I_j \right) = Step_0(\mathbf{W} \cdot \mathbf{I}) \tag{19.2}$$

where, as discussed earlier, we have assumed an additional weight W_0 to provide a threshold for the step function, with $I_0 = -1$.

What perceptrons can represent

We saw in Figure 19.6 that units can represent the simple Boolean functions AND, OR, and NOT, and that therefore a feed-forward network of units can represent any Boolean function, if we allow for enough layers and units. But what Boolean functions can be represented with a single-layer perceptron?

Some complex Boolean functions can be represented. For example, the **majority function**, which outputs a 1 only if more than half of its n inputs are 1, can be represented by a perceptron with each $W_j = 1$ and threshold $t = n/2$. This would require a decision tree with $O(2^n)$ nodes.

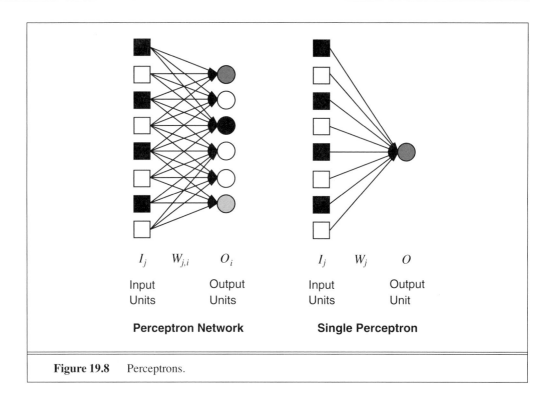

$$I_j \qquad W_{j,i} \qquad O_i \qquad\qquad I_j \qquad W_j \qquad O$$

Input	Output	Input	Output
Units	Units	Units	Unit

Perceptron Network   **Single Perceptron**

Figure 19.8   Perceptrons.

The perceptron, with 1 unit and n weights, gives a much more compact representation of this function. In accordance with Ockham's razor, we would expect the perceptron to do a much better job of learning a majority function, as we will soon see.

Unfortunately, it turns out that perceptrons are severely limited in the Boolean functions they can represent. The problem is that any input I_j can only influence the final output in one direction, no matter what the other input values are. Consider some input vector **a**. Suppose that this vector has $a_j = 0$ and that the vector produces a 0 as output. Furthermore, suppose that when a_j is replaced with 1, the output changes to 1. This implies that W_j must be positive. It also implies that there can be no input vector **b** for which the output is 1 when $b_j = 0$, but the output is 0 when b_j is replaced with 1. Because this limitation applies to each input, the result is a severe limitation in the total number of functions that can be represented. For example, the perceptron is unable to represent the function for deciding whether or not to wait for a table at a restaurant (shown as a decision tree in Figure 18.4).

A little geometry helps make clear what is going on. Figure 19.9 shows three different Boolean functions of two inputs, the AND, OR, and XOR functions. Each function is represented as a two-dimensional plot, based on the values of the two inputs. Black dots indicate a point in the input space where the value of the function is 1, and white dots indicate a point where the value is 0. As we will explain shortly, a perceptron can represent a function only if there is some line that separates all the white dots from the black dots. Such functions are called **linearly separable**. Thus, a perceptron can represent AND and OR, but not XOR.

LINEARLY
SEPARABLE

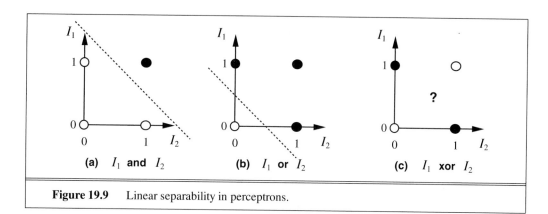

Figure 19.9   Linear separability in perceptrons.

The fact that a perceptron can only represent linearly separable functions follows directly from Equation (19.2), which defines the function computed by a perceptron. A perceptron outputs a 1 only if $\mathbf{W} \cdot \mathbf{I} > 0$. This means that the entire input space is divided in two along a boundary defined by $\mathbf{W} \cdot \mathbf{I} = 0$, that is, a plane in the input space with coefficients given by the weights. With n inputs, the input space is n-dimensional, and linear separability can be rather hard to visualize if n is too large. It is easiest to understand for the case where $n = 2$. In Figure 19.9(a), one possible separating "plane" is the dotted line defined by the equation

$$I_1 = -I_2 + 1.5 \qquad \text{or} \qquad I_1 + I_2 = 1.5$$

The region above the line, where the output is 1, is therefore given by

$$-1.5 + I_1 + I_2 > 0$$

or, in vector notation,

$$\mathbf{W} \cdot \mathbf{I} = \langle 1.5, 1, 1 \rangle \cdot \langle -1, I_1, I_2 \rangle > 0$$

With three inputs, the separating plane can still be visualized. Figure 19.10(a) shows an example in three dimensions. The function we are trying to represent is true if and only if a minority of its three inputs are true. The shaded separating plane is defined by the equation

$$I_1 + I_2 + I_3 = 1.5$$

This time the positive outputs lie below the plane, in the region

$$(-I_1) + (-I_2) + (-I_3) > -1.5$$

Figure 19.10(b) shows a unit to implement the function.

Learning linearly separable functions

As with any performance element, the question of what perceptrons can represent is prior to the question of what they can learn. We have just seen that a function can be represented by a perceptron if and only if it is linearly separable. That is relatively bad news, because there are not many linearly separable functions. The (relatively) good news is that *there is a perceptron algorithm that will learn any linearly separable function, given enough training examples.*

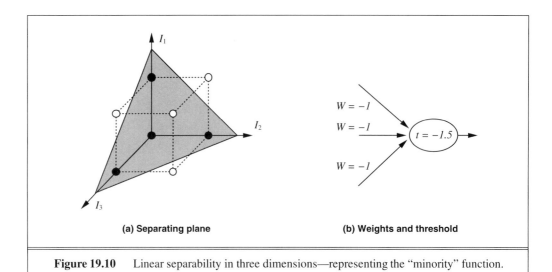

(a) Separating plane   **(b) Weights and threshold**

Figure 19.10   Linear separability in three dimensions—representing the "minority" function.

Most neural network learning algorithms, including the perceptron learning method, follow the current-best-hypothesis (CBH) scheme described in Chapter 18. In this case, the hypothesis is a network, defined by the current values of the weights. The initial network has randomly assigned weights, usually from the range [–0.5,0.5]. The network is then updated to try to make it consistent with the examples. This is done by making small adjustments in the weights to reduce the difference between the observed and predicted values. The main difference from the logical algorithms is the need to repeat the update phase several times for each example in EPOCHS   order to achieve convergence. Typically, the updating process is divided into **epochs**. Each epoch involves updating all the weights for all the examples. The general scheme is shown as NEURAL-NETWORK-LEARNING in Figure 19.11.

For perceptrons, the weight update rule is particularly simple. If the predicted output for the single output unit is O, and the correct output should be T, then the error is given by

$$Err = T - O$$

If the error is positive, then we need to increase O; if it is negative, we need to decrease O. Now each input unit contributes $W_j I_j$ to the total input, so if I_j is positive, an increase in W_j will tend to increase O, and if I_j is negative, an increase in W_j will tend to decrease O. Thus, we can achieve the effect we want with the following rule:

$$W_j \leftarrow W_j + \alpha \times I_j \times Err$$

LEARNING RATE   where the term α is a constant called the **learning rate**. This rule is a slight variant of the
PERCEPTRON
LEARNING RULE   **perceptron learning rule** proposed by Frank Rosenblatt in 1960. Rosenblatt proved that a learning system using the perceptron learning rule will converge to a set of weights that correctly represents the examples, as long as the examples represent a linearly separable function.

The perceptron convergence theorem created a good deal of excitement when it was announced. People were amazed that such a simple procedure could correctly learn any representable function, and there were great hopes that intelligent machines could be built from

---

function NEURAL-NETWORK-LEARNING(*examples*) **returns** *network*

    network ← a network with randomly assigned weights
    repeat
        for each *e* **in** *examples* **do**
            O ← NEURAL-NETWORK-OUTPUT(*network, e*)
            T ← the observed output values from *e*
            update the weights in *network* based on *e*, **O**, and **T**
        end
    until all examples correctly predicted or stopping criterion is reached
    return *network*

Figure 19.11   The generic neural network learning method: adjust the weights until predicted output values **O** and true values **T** agree.

---

perceptrons. It was not until 1969 that Minsky and Papert undertook what should have been the first step: analyzing the class of representable functions. Their book *Perceptrons* (Minsky and Papert, 1969) clearly demonstrated the limits of linearly separable functions.

In retrospect, the perceptron convergence theorem should not have been surprising. The perceptron is doing a **gradient descent** search through weight space (see Chapter 4). It is fairly easy to show that the weight space has no local minima. Provided the learning rate parameter is not so large as to cause "overshooting," the search will converge on the correct weights. In short, perceptron learning is easy because the space of representable functions is simple.

We can examine the learning behavior of perceptrons using the method of constructing learning curves, as described in Chapter 18. There is a slight difference between the example descriptions used for neural networks and those used for other attribute-based methods such as decision trees. In a neural network, all inputs are real numbers in some fixed range, whereas decision trees allow for multivalued attributes with a discrete set of values. For example, the attribute for the number of patrons in the restaurant has values *None*, *Some*, and *Full*. There are two ways to handle this. In a **local encoding**, we use a single input unit and pick an appropriate number of distinct values to correspond to the discrete attribute values. For example, we can use *None* = 0.0, *Some* = 0.5, and *Full* = 1.0. In a **distributed encoding**, we use one input unit for each value of the attribute, turning on the unit that corresponds to the correct value.

Figure 19.12 shows the learning curve for a perceptron on two different problems. On the left, we show the curve for learning the majority function with 11 Boolean inputs (i.e., the function outputs a 1 if 6 or more inputs are 1). As we would expect, the perceptron learns the function quite quickly because the majority function is linearly separable. On the other hand, the decision tree learner makes no progress, because the majority function is very hard (although not impossible) to represent as a decision tree. On the right of the figure, we have the opposite situation. The *WillWait* problem is easily represented as a decision tree, but is not linearly separable. The perceptron algorithm draws the best plane it can through the data, but can manage no more than 65% accuracy.

LOCAL ENCODING

DISTRIBUTED ENCODING

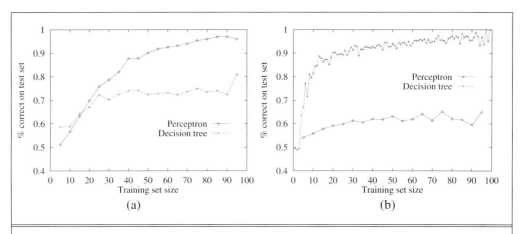

Figure 19.12   Comparing the performance of perceptrons and decision trees. (a) Perceptrons are better at learning the majority function of 11 inputs. (b) Decision trees are better at learning the *WillWait* predicate for the restaurant example.

19.4   MULTILAYER FEED-FORWARD NETWORKS

Rosenblatt and others described multilayer feed-forward networks in the late 1950s, but concentrated their research on single-layer perceptrons. This was mainly because of the difficulty of finding a sensible way to update the weights between the inputs and the hidden units; whereas an error signal can be calculated for the output units, it is harder to see what the error signal should be for the hidden units. When the book *Perceptrons* was published, Minsky and Papert (1969) stated that it was an "important research problem" to investigate multilayer networks more thoroughly, although they speculated that "there is no reason to suppose that any of the virtues [of perceptrons] carry over to the many-layered version." In a sense, they were right. Learning algorithms for multilayer networks are neither efficient nor guaranteed to converge to a global optimum. On the other hand, the results of computational learning theory tell us that learning general functions from examples is an intractable problem in the worst case, regardless of the method, so we should not be too dismayed.

BACK-PROPAGATION   The most popular method for learning in multilayer networks is called **back-propagation**. It was first invented in 1969 by Bryson and Ho, but was more or less ignored until the mid-1980s. The reasons for this may be sociological, but may also have to do with the computational requirements of the algorithm on nontrivial problems.

Back-Propagation Learning

Suppose we want to construct a network for the restaurant problem. We have already seen that a perceptron is inadequate, so we will try a two-layer network. We have ten attributes

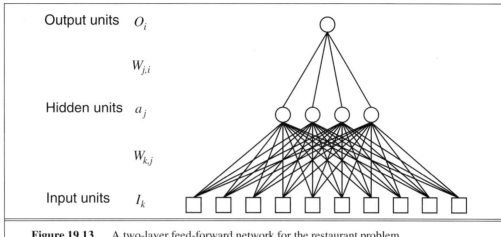

Output units O_i

$W_{j,i}$

Hidden units a_j

$W_{k,j}$

Input units I_k

Figure 19.13   A two-layer feed-forward network for the restaurant problem.

describing each example, so we will need ten input units. How many hidden units are needed? In Figure 19.13, we show a network with four hidden units. This turns out to be about right for this problem. The problem of choosing the right number of hidden units in advance is still not well-understood. We cover what is known on page 572.

Learning in such a network proceeds the same way as for perceptrons: example inputs are presented to the network, and if the network computes an output vector that matches the target, nothing is done. If there is an error (a difference between the output and target), then the weights are adjusted to reduce this error. *The trick is to assess the blame for an error and divide it among the contributing weights.* In perceptrons, this is easy, because there is only one weight between each input and the output. But in multilayer networks, there are many weights connecting each input to an output, and each of these weights contributes to more than one output.

The back-propagation algorithm is a sensible approach to dividing the contribution of each weight. As in the perceptron learning algorithm, we try to minimize the error between each target output and the output actually computed by the network.[4] At the output layer, the weight update rule is very similar to the rule for the perceptron. There are two differences: the activation of the hidden unit a_j is used instead of the input value; and the rule contains a term for the gradient of the activation function. If Err_i is the error $(T_i - O_i)$ at the output node, then the weight update rule for the link from unit j to unit i is

$$W_{j,i} \leftarrow W_{j,i} + \alpha \times a_j \times Err_i \times g'(in_i)$$

where g' is the derivative of the activation function g. We will find it convenient to define a new error term Δ_i, which for output nodes is defined as $\Delta_i = Err_i g'(in_i)$. The update rule then becomes

$$W_{j,i} \leftarrow W_{j,i} + \alpha \times a_j \times \Delta_i \tag{19.3}$$

For updating the connections between the input units and the hidden units, we need to define a quantity analogous to the error term for output nodes. Here is where we do the error back-propagation. The idea is that hidden node j is "responsible" for some fraction of the error Δ_i in

---

[4] Actually, we minimize the square of the error; Section 19.4 explains why, but the result is almost the same.

each of the output nodes to which it connects. Thus, the Δ_i values are divided according to the strength of the connection between the hidden node and the output node, and propagated back to provide the Δ_j values for the hidden layer. The propagation rule for the Δ values is the following:

$$\Delta_j = g'(in_j) \sum_i W_{j,i} \Delta_i \tag{19.4}$$

Now the weight update rule for the weights between the inputs and the hidden layer is almost identical to the update rule for the output layer:

$$W_{k,j} \leftarrow W_{k,j} + \alpha \times I_k \times \Delta_j$$

The detailed algorithm is shown in Figure 19.14. It can be summarized as follows:

- Compute the Δ values for the output units using the observed error.
- Starting with output layer, repeat the following for each layer in the network, until the earliest hidden layer is reached:
  - Propagate the Δ values back to the previous layer.
  - Update the weights between the two layers.

Recall that in computing the observed error for a given example, NEURAL-NETWORK-LEARNING first feeds the example to the network inputs in order to calculate the predicted output values. During this computation, it is a good idea to save some of the intermediate values computed in each unit. In particular, caching the activation gradient $g'(in_i)$ in each unit speeds up the subsequent back-propagation phase enormously.

TRAINING CURVE

Now that we have a learning method for multilayer networks, we can test our claim that adding a hidden layer makes the network more expressive. In Figure 19.15, we show two curves. The first is a **training curve**, which shows the mean squared error on a given training set of 100 restaurant examples during the weight-updating process. This demonstrates that the network does indeed converge to a perfect fit to the training data. The second curve is the standard learning curve for the restaurant data, with one minor exception: the y-axis is no longer the proportion of correct answers on the test set, because sigmoid units do not give 0/1 outputs. Instead, we use the mean squared error on the test set, which happens to coincide with the proportion of correct answers in the 0/1 case. The curve clearly shows that the network is capable of learning in the restaurant domain; indeed, the curve is very similar to that for decision-tree learning, albeit somewhat shallower.

Back-propagation as gradient descent search

ERROR SURFACE

We have given some suggestive reasons why the back-propagation equations are reasonable. It turns out that the equations also can be given a very simple interpretation as a method for performing **gradient descent** in weight space. In this case, the gradient is on the **error surface**: the surface that describes the error on each example as a function of the all the weights in the network. An example error surface is shown in Figure 19.16. The current set of weights defines a point on this surface. At that point, we look at the slope of the surface along the axis formed by each weight. This is known as the *partial derivative* of the surface with respect to each weight—how much the error would change if we made a small change in weight. We then alter

function BACK-PROP-UPDATE(*network, examples,* α) **returns** a network with modified weights
   inputs: *network*, a multilayer network
         examples, a set of input/output pairs
         α, the learning rate

  repeat
    for each *e* **in** *examples* **do**
      / * *Compute the output for this example* * /
      O $\leftarrow$ RUN-NETWORK(*network*, $\mathbf{I}^e$)
      / * *Compute the error and* Δ *for units in the output layer* * /
      $\mathbf{Err}^e \leftarrow \mathbf{T}^e - \mathbf{O}$
      / * *Update the weights leading to the output layer* * /
      $W_{j,i} \leftarrow W_{j,i} + \alpha \times a_j \times Err_i^e \times g'(in_i)$
      for each subsequent layer **in** *network* **do**
        / * *Compute the error at each node* * /
        $\Delta_j \leftarrow g'(in_j) \sum_i W_{j,i} \Delta_i$
        / * *Update the weights leading into the layer* * /
        $W_{k,j} \leftarrow W_{k,j} + \alpha \times I_k \times \Delta_j$
    end
    end
  until *network* has converged
  return *network*

Figure 19.14   The back-propagation algorithm for updating weights in a multilayer network.

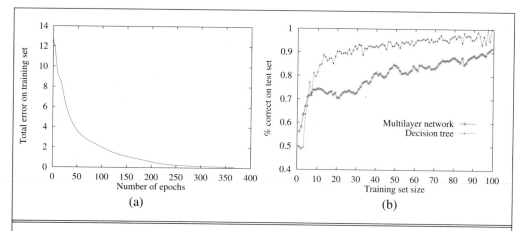

(a)   (b)

Figure 19.15   (a) Training curve showing the gradual reduction in error as weights are modified over several epochs, for a given set of examples in the restaurant domain. (b) Comparative learning curves for a back-propagation and decision-tree learning.

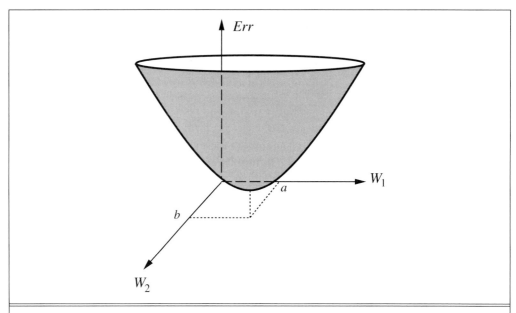

Figure 19.16   An error surface for gradient descent search in weight space. When $w_1 = a$ and $w_2 = b$, the error on the training set is minimized.

the weights in an amount proportional to the slope in each direction. This moves the network as a whole in the direction of steepest descent on the error surface.

   Basically, this is the key: *back-propagation provides a way of dividing the calculation of the gradient among the units, so the change in each weight can be calculated by the unit to which the weight is attached, using only local information.* Like any gradient descent search, back-propagation has problems with efficiency and convergence, as we will discuss shortly. Nonetheless, the decomposition of the learning algorithm is a major step towards parallelizable and biologically plausible learning mechanisms.

   For the mathematically inclined, we will now derive the back-propagation equations from first principles. We begin with the error function itself. Because of its convenient form, we use the sum of squared errors over the output values:

$$E = \frac{1}{2} \sum_i (T_i - O_i)^2$$

The key insight, again, is that the output values O_i are a function of the weights (see Equation (19.1), for example). For a general two-layer network, we can write

$$E(\mathbf{W}) = \frac{1}{2} \sum_i \left(T_i - g \left(\sum_j W_{j,i} a_j \right) \right)^2$$

$$= \frac{1}{2} \sum_i \left(T_i - g \left(\sum_j W_{j,i}\, g \left(\sum_k W_{k,j} I_k \right) \right) \right)^2 \tag{19.5}$$

Notice that although the a_j term in the first line represents a complex expression, it does not depend on $W_{j,i}$. Also, only one of the terms in the summation over i and j depends on a particular $W_{j,i}$, so all the other terms are treated as constants with respect to $W_{j,i}$ and will disappear when differentiated. Hence, when we differentiate the first line with respect to $W_{j,i}$, we obtain

$$\frac{\partial E}{\partial W_{j,i}} = -a_j(T_i - O_i)g'\left(\sum_j W_{j,i}a_j\right)$$

$$= -a_j(T_i - O_i)g'(in_i) = -a_j\Delta_i$$

with Δ_i defined as before. The derivation of the gradient with respect to $W_{k,j}$ is slightly more complex, but has a similar result:

$$\frac{\partial E}{\partial W_{k,j}} = -I_k\Delta_j$$

To obtain the update rules for the weights, we have to remember that the object is to *minimize* the error, so we need to take a small step in the direction *opposite* to the gradient.

There is one minor technical observation to make about these update rules. They require the derivative of the activation function g, so we cannot use the sign or step functions. Back-propagation networks usually use the sigmoid function, or some variant thereof. The sigmoid also has the convenient property that the derivative $g' = g(1 - g)$, so that little extra calculation is needed to find $g'(in_i)$.

Discussion

Let us stand back for a moment from the delightful mathematics and the fascinating biology, and ask whether back-propagation learning in multilayer networks is a good method for machine learning. We can examine the same set of issues that arose in Chapter 18:

◇ **Expressiveness**: Neural networks are clearly an attribute-based representation, and do not have the expressive power of general logical representations. They are well-suited for continuous inputs and outputs, unlike most decision tree systems. The class of multilayer networks *as a whole* can represent any desired function of a set of attributes, but any *particular* network may have too few hidden units. It turns out that $2^n/n$ hidden units are needed to represent all Boolean functions of n inputs. This should not be too surprising. Such a network has $O(2^n)$ weights, and we need at least 2^n bits to specify a Boolean function. In practice, most problems can be solved with many fewer weights. Designing a good topology is, however, a black art.

◇ **Computational efficiency**: Computational efficiency depends on the amount of computation time required to train the network to fit a given set of examples. If there are m examples, and $|\mathbf{W}|$ weights, each epoch takes $O(m|\mathbf{W}|)$ time. However, work in computational learning theory has shown that the worst-case number of epochs can be exponential in n, the number of inputs. In practice, time to convergence is highly variable, and a vast array of techniques have been developed to try to speed up the process using an assortment of tunable parameters. Local minima in the error surface are also a problem. Networks quite often converge to give a constant "yes" or "no" output, whichever is most common in the training set. At the cost of some additional computation, the simulated annealing method (Chapter 4) can be used to assure convergence to a global optimum.

◇ **Generalization**: As we have seen in our experiments on the restaurant data, neural networks can do a good job of generalization. One can say, somewhat circularly, that they will generalize well on functions for which they are well-suited. These seem to be functions in which the interactions between inputs are not too intricate, and for which the output varies smoothly with the input. There is no theorem to be proved here, but it does seem that neural networks have had reasonable success in a number of real-world problems.

◇ **Sensitivity to noise**: Because neural networks are essentially doing nonlinear regression, they are very tolerant of noise in the input data. They simply find the best fit given the constraints of the network topology. On the other hand, it is often useful to have some idea of the degree of certainty of the output values. Neural networks do not provide probability distributions on the output values. For this purpose, belief networks seem more appropriate.

◇ **Transparency**: Neural networks are essentially black boxes. Even if the network does a good job of predicting new cases, many users will still be dissatisfied because they will have no idea *why* a given output value is reasonable. If the output value represents, for example, a decision to perform open heart surgery, then an explanation is clearly in order. With decision trees and other logical representations, the output can be explained as a logical derivation and by appeal to a specific set of cases that supports the decision. This is not currently possible with neural networks.

◇ **Prior knowledge**: As we mentioned in Chapter 18, learning systems can often benefit from prior knowledge that is available to the user or expert. Prior knowledge can mean the difference between learning from a few well-chosen examples and failing to learn anything at all. Unfortunately, because of the lack of transparency, it is quite hard to use one's knowledge to "prime" a network to learn better. Some tailoring of the network topology can be done—for example, when training on visual images it is common to connect only small sets of nearby pixels to any given unit in the first hidden layer. On the other hand, such "rules of thumb" do not constitute a *mechanism* by which previously accumulated knowledge can be used to learn from subsequent experience. It is possible that learning methods for belief networks can overcome this problem (see Section 19.6).

All these considerations suggest that simple feed-forward networks, although very promising as construction tools for learning complex input/output mappings, do not fulfill our needs for a comprehensive theory of learning in their present form. Researchers in AI, psychology, theoretical computer science, statistics, physics, and biology are working hard to overcome the difficulties.

19.5   APPLICATIONS OF NEURAL NETWORKS

In this section, we give just a few examples of the many significant applications of neural networks. In each case, the network design was the result of several months of trial-and-error experimentation by researchers. From these examples, it can be seen that neural networks have wide applicability, but that they cannot magically solve problems without any thought on the part of the network designer. John Denker's remark that "neural networks are the second best way of doing just about anything" may be an exaggeration, but it is true that neural networks provide passable performance on many tasks that would be difficult to solve explicitly with other programming techniques. We encourage the reader to experiment with neural network algorithms to get a feel for what happens when data arrive at an unprepared network.

Pronunciation

Pronunciation of written English text by a computer is a fascinating problem in linguistics, as well as a task with high commercial payoff. It is typically carried by first mapping the text stream to **phonemes**—basic sound elements—and then passing the phonemes to an electronic speech generator. The problem we are concerned with here is learning the mapping from text to phonemes. This is a good task for neural networks because most of the "rules" are only approximately correct. For example, although the letter "k" usually corresponds to the sound [k], the letter "c" is pronounced [k] in *cat* and [s] in *cent*.

The NETtalk program (Sejnowski and Rosenberg, 1987) is a neural network that learns to pronounce written text. The input is a sequence of characters presented in a window that slides through the text. At any time, the input includes the character to be pronounced along with the preceding and following three characters. Each character is actually 29 input units—one for each of the 26 letters, and one each for blanks, periods, and other punctuation. There were 80 hidden units in the version for which results are reported. The output layer consists of features of the sound to be produced: whether it is high or low, voiced or unvoiced, and so on. Sometimes, it takes two or more letters to produce a single sound; in this case, the correct output for the second letter is nothing.

Training consisted of a 1024–word text that had been hand-transcribed into the proper phonemic features. NETtalk learns to perform at 95% accuracy *on the training set* after 50 passes through the training data. One might think that NETtalk should perform at 100% on the text it has trained on. But any program that learns individual words rather than the entire text as a whole will inevitably score less than 100%. The difficulty arises with words like *lead*, which in some cases should be pronounced to rhyme with *bead* and sometimes like *bed*. A program that looks at only a limited window will occasionally get such words wrong.

So much for the ability of the network to reproduce the training data. What about the generalization performance? This is somewhat disappointing. On the test data, NETtalk's accuracy goes down to 78%, a level that is intelligible, but much worse than commercially available programs. Of course, the commercial systems required years of development, whereas NETtalk only required a few dozen hours of training time plus a few months of experimentation with various network designs. However, there are other techniques that require even less development and perform just as well. For example, if we use the input to determine the probability of producing a particular phoneme given the current and previous character and then use a Markov model to find the sequence of phonemes with maximal probability, we do just as well as NETtalk.

NETtalk was perhaps the "flagship" demonstration that converted many scientists, particularly in cognitive psychology, to the cause of neural network research. A post hoc analysis suggests that this was not because it was a particularly successful program, but rather because it provided a good showpiece for the philosophy of neural networks. Its authors also had a flair for the dramatic: they recorded a tape of NETtalk starting out with poor, babbling speech, and then gradually improving to the point where the output is understandable. Unlike conventional speech generators, which use a midrange tenor voice to generate the phonemes, they used a high-pitched generator. The tape gives the unmistakable impression of a child learning to speak.

Handwritten character recognition

In one of the largest applications of neural networks to date, Le Cun *et al.* (1989) have implemented a network designed to read zip codes on hand-addressed envelopes. The system uses a preprocessor that locates and segments the individual digits in the zipcode; the network has to identify the digits themselves. It uses a 16×16 array of pixels as input, *three* hidden layers, and a distributed output encoding with 10 output units for digits 0–9. The hidden layers contained 768, 192, and 30 units, respectively. A fully connected network of this size would contain 200,000 weights, and would be impossible to train. Instead, the network was designed with connections intended to act as **feature detectors**. For example, each unit in the first hidden layer was connected by 25 links to a 5×5 region in the input. Furthermore, the hidden layer was divided into 12 groups of 64 units; within each group of 64 units, each unit used the *same* set of 25 weights. Hence the hidden layer can detect up to 12 distinct features, each of which can occur anywhere in the input image. Overall, the complete network used only 9760 weights.

FEATURE
DETECTORS

The network was trained on 7300 examples, and tested on 2000. One interesting property of a network with distributed output encoding is that it can display confusion over the correct answer by setting two or more output units to a high value. After rejecting about 12% of the test set as marginal, using a confusion threshold, the performance on the remaining cases reached 99%, which was deemed adequate for an automated mail-sorting system. The final network has been implemented in custom VLSI, enabling letters to be sorted at high speed.

Driving

ALVINN (Autonomous Land Vehicle In a Neural Network) (Pomerleau, 1993) is a neural network that has performed quite well in a domain where some other approaches have failed. It learns to steer a vehicle along a single lane on a highway by observing the performance of a human driver. We described the system briefly on page 26, but here we take a look under the hood.

ALVINN is used to control the NavLab vehicles at Carnegie Mellon University. NavLab 1 is a Chevy van, and NavLab 2 is a U.S. Army HMMWV personnel carrier. Both vehicles are specially outfitted with computer-controlled steering, acceleration, and braking. Sensors include color stereo video, scanning laser range finders, radar, and inertial navigation. Researchers ride along in the vehicle and monitor the progress of the computer and the vehicle itself. (Being inside the vehicle is a big incentive to making sure the program does not "crash.")

The signal from the vehicle's video camera is preprocessed to yield an array of pixel values that are connected to a 30×32 grid of input units in a neural network. The output is a layer of 30 units, each corresponding to a steering direction. The output unit with the highest activation is the direction that the vehicle will steer. The network also has a layer of five hidden units that are fully connected to the input and output layers.

ALVINN's job is to compute a function that maps from a single video image of the road in front of it to a steering direction. To learn this function, we need some training data—some image/direction pairs with the correct direction. Fortunately, it is easy to collect this data just by having a human drive the vehicle and recording the image/direction pairs. After collecting about five minutes of training data (and applying the back-propagation algorithm for about ten minutes), ALVINN is ready to drive on its own.

One fine point is worth mentioning. There is a potential problem with the methodology of training based on a human driver: the human is too good. If the human never strays from the proper course then there will be no training examples that show how to recover when you are off course. ALVINN corrects this problem by rotating each video image to create additional views of what the road would look like from a position a little to the right or left.

The results of the training are impressive. ALVINN has driven at speeds up to 70 mph for distances up to 90 miles on public highways near Pittsburgh. It has also driven at normal speeds on single lane dirt roads, paved bike paths, and two lane suburban streets.

ALVINN is unable to drive on a road type for which it has not been trained, and is also not very robust with respect to changes in lighting conditions or the presence of other vehicles. A more general capability is exhibited by the MANIAC system (Jochem *et al.*, 1993). MANIAC is a neural network that has as subnets two or more ALVINN models that have each been trained for a particular type of road. MANIAC takes the output from each subnet and combines them in a second hidden layer. With suitable training, MANIAC can perform well on any of the road types for which the component subnets have been trained.

Some previous autonomous vehicles employed traditional vision algorithms that used various image-processing techniques on the entire scene in order to find the road and then follow it. Such systems achieved top speeds of 3 or 4 mph.[5] Why has ALVINN proven to be successful? There are two reasons. First and foremost, a neural network of this size makes an efficient performance element. Once it has been trained, ALVINN is able to compute a new steering direction from a video image 10 times a second. This is important because it allows for some slack in the system. Individual steering directions can be off by 10% from the ideal as long as the system is able to make a correction in a few tenths of a second. Second, the use of a learning algorithm is more appropriate for this domain than knowledge engineering or straight programming. There is no good existing theory of driving, but it is easy to collect sample input/output pairs of the desired functional mapping. This argues for a learning algorithm, but not necessarily for neural nets. But driving is a continuous, noisy domain in which almost all of the input features contribute some useful information; this means that neural nets are a better choice than, say, decision trees. Of course, ALVINN and MANIAC are pure reflex agents, and cannot execute maneuvers that are much more complex than lane-following, especially in the presence of other traffic. Current research by Pomerleau and other members of the group is aimed at combining ALVINN's low-level expertise with higher-level symbolic knowledge. Hybrid systems of this kind are becoming more common as AI moves into the real (physical) world.

---

[5] A notable exception is the work by Dickmanns and Zapp (1987), whose autonomous vehicle drove several hundred miles at 75 mph using traditional image processing and Kalman filtering to track the lane boundaries.

19.6   BAYESIAN METHODS FOR LEARNING BELIEF NETWORKS

Part V made the case for the importance of probabilistic representations of uncertain knowledge, and presented belief networks as a general and useful performance element based on probability theory. In this section, we discuss the general problem of learning probabilistic knowledge, and the specific problem of learning belief networks. We will see that a Bayesian view of learning is extremely powerful, providing general solutions to the problems of noise, overfitting, and optimal prediction. We will also find striking parallels between belief networks and neural networks in their amenability to local, gradient-descent learning methods. Most of this section is fairly mathematical, although the general lessons can be understood without plunging into the details. It may be helpful at this point to review the material in Chapters 14 and 15.

Bayesian learning

BAYESIAN LEARNING   **Bayesian learning** views the problem of constructing hypotheses from data as a subproblem of the more fundamental problem of making predictions. The idea is to use hypotheses as intermediaries between data and predictions. First, the probability of each hypothesis is estimated, given the data. Predictions are then made from the hypotheses, using the posterior probabilities of the hypotheses to weight the predictions. As a simple example, consider the problem of predicting tomorrow's weather. Suppose the available experts are divided into two camps: some propose model A, and some propose model B. The Bayesian method, rather than choosing between A and B, gives some weight to each based on their likelihood. The likelihood will depend on how much the known data support each of the two models.

Suppose that we have data D and hypotheses $H_1, H_2, \ldots$, and that we are interested in making a prediction concerning an unknown quantity X. Furthermore, suppose that each H_i specifies a complete distribution for X. Then we have

$$\mathbf{P}(X|D) = \sum_i \mathbf{P}(X|D, H_i)\mathbf{P}(H_i|D) = \sum_i \mathbf{P}(X|H_i)\mathbf{P}(H_i|D)$$

This equation describes full Bayesian learning, and may require a calculation of $\mathbf{P}(H_i|D)$ for all H_i. In most cases, this is intractable; it can be shown, however, that there is no better way to make predictions.

The most common approximation is to use a *most probable* hypothesis, that is, an H_i that maximizes $\mathbf{P}(H_i|D)$. This often called a **maximum a posteriori** or MAP hypothesis H_{MAP}:

MAXIMUM A
POSTERIORI

$$\mathbf{P}(X|D) \approx \mathbf{P}(X|H_{\text{MAP}})$$

The problem is now to find H_{MAP}. By applying Bayes' rule, we can rewrite $\mathbf{P}(H_i|D)$ as follows:

$$\mathbf{P}(H_i|D) = \frac{\mathbf{P}(D|H_i)\mathbf{P}(H_i)}{\mathbf{P}(D)}$$

Notice that in comparing hypotheses, $P(D)$ remains fixed. Hence, to find H_{MAP}, we need only maximize the numerator of the fraction.

The first term, $\mathbf{P}(D|H_i)$, represents the probability that this particular data set would have been observed, given H_i as the underlying model of the world. The second term represents the prior probability assigned to the given model. Arguments over the nature and significance of this prior probability distribution, and its relation to preference for simpler hypotheses (Ockham's razor), have raged unchecked in the statistics and learning communities for decades. The only reasonable policy seems to be to assign prior probabilities based on some simplicity measure on hypotheses, such that the prior of the entire hypothesis space adds up to 1. The more we bias the priors towards simpler hypotheses, the more we will be immune to noise and overfitting. Of course, if the priors are *too* biased, then we get underfitting, where the data is largely ignored. There is a careful trade-off to make.

In some cases, a **uniform** prior over belief networks seems to be appropriate, as we shall see. With a uniform prior, we need only choose an H_i that maximizes $\mathbf{P}(D|H_i)$. This is called a **maximum-likelihood** (ML) hypothesis, H_{ML}.

MAXIMUM-
LIKELIHOOD

Belief network learning problems

The learning problem for belief networks comes in several varieties. The structure of the network can be *known* or *unknown*, and the variables in the network can be *observable* or *hidden*.

◇ **Known structure, fully observable**: In this case, the only learnable part is the set of conditional probability tables. These can be estimated directly using the statistics of the set of examples. Some belief network systems incorporate automatic updating of conditional probability table entries to reflect the cases seen.

◇ **Unknown structure, fully observable**: In this case, the problem is to reconstruct the topology of the network. This problem can be cast as a search through the space of structures, guided by the ability of each structure to model the data correctly. Fitting the data to a given structure reduces to the fixed-structure problem, and the MAP or ML probability value can be used as heuristic for hill-climbing or simulated annealing search.

◇ **Known structure, hidden variables**: This case is analogous to neural network learning. We discuss methods for this problem in the next section.

◇ **Unknown structure, hidden variables**: When some variables are sometimes or always unobservable, the prior techniques for recovering structure become difficult to apply, because they essentially require averaging over all possible combinations of values of the unknown variables. At present, no good, general algorithms are known for this problem.

Learning networks with fixed structure

Experience in constructing belief networks for applications has shown that finding the topology of the network is often the easy part. Humans find it easy to say what causes what, but hard to put exact numbers on the links. This is particularly true when some of the variables cannot be observed directly in actual cases. The "known structure, hidden variable" learning problem is therefore of great importance.

One might ask why the problem cannot be reduced to the fully observable case by eliminating the hidden variables using marginalization ("averaging out"). There are two reasons for this. First, it is not necessarily the case that any particular variable is hidden in all the observed cases (although we do not rule this out). Second, networks with hidden variables can be more *compact* than the corresponding fully observable network. Figure 19.17 shows an example. If the underlying domain has significant local structure, then with hidden variables it is possible to take advantage of that structure to find a more concise representation for the joint distribution on the observable variables. This, in turn, makes it possible to learn from fewer examples.

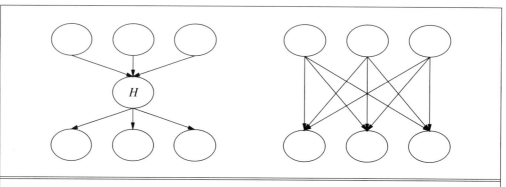

Figure 19.17   A network with a hidden variable (labelled *H*), and the corresponding fully observable network. If the variables are Boolean, then the hidden-variable network requires 17 independent conditional probability values, whereas the fully observable network requires 27.

If we are to approach this problem in Bayesian terms, then the "hypotheses" H_i are the different possible complete assignments to all the conditional probability table (CPT) entries. We will assume that all possible assignments are equally likely a priori, which means that we are looking for a maximum likelihood hypothesis. That is, we wish to find the set of CPT entries that maximizes the probability of the data, $P(D|H_i)$.

The method we will use to do this is quite similar to the gradient descent method for neural networks. We will write the probability of the data as a function of the CPT entries, and then calculate a gradient. As with neural networks, we will find that the gradient can be calculated locally by each node using information that is available in the normal course of belief network calculations. Thus, the CPT entries are analogous to the weights, and $P(D|H_i)$ is (inversely) analogous to the error *E*. Belief network systems equipped with this kind of learning scheme are

called **adaptive probabilistic networks** (APNs).

Suppose we have a training set $\mathbf{D} = \{D_1, \ldots, D_m\}$, where each case D_j consists of an assignment of values to some subset of the variables in the network. We assume that each case is drawn independently from some underlying distribution that we are trying to model. The problem is to adjust the conditional probabilities in the network in order to maximize the likelihood of the data. We will write this likelihood as $P(\mathbf{D})$. The reader should bear in mind that here $P(\cdot)$ is really $P_\mathbf{w}(\cdot)$, that is, the probability according to a joint distribution specified by $\mathbf{w}$, the set of all of the conditional probability values in the network. In order to construct a hill-climbing algorithm to maximize the likelihood, we need to calculate the derivative of the likelihood with respect to each of the conditional probability values w_i in $\mathbf{w}$.

It turns out to be easiest to compute the derivative of the logarithm of the likelihood. Because the log-likelihood is monotonically related to the likelihood itself, a maximum on the log-likelihood surface is also a maximum on the likelihood surface. We calculate the gradient using partial derivatives, varying a single value w_i while keeping the others constant:[6]

$$\frac{\partial \ln P(\mathbf{D})}{\partial w_i} = \frac{\partial \ln \prod_j P(D_j)}{\partial w_i} = \sum_j \frac{\partial \ln P(D_j)}{\partial w_i} = \sum_j \frac{\partial P(D_j)/\partial w_i}{P(D_j)}$$

Hence, we can calculate separately the gradient contribution of each case and sum the results.

Now the aim is to find an expression for the gradient contribution from a single case, such that the contribution can be calculated using only information local to the node with which w_i is associated. Let w_i be a specific entry in the conditional probability table for a node X given its parent variables $\mathbf{U}$. We'll assume that it is the entry for the case $X = x_i$ given $\mathbf{U} = \mathbf{u}_i$:

$$w_i = P(X = x_i \mid \mathbf{U} = \mathbf{u}_i) = P(x_i \mid \mathbf{u}_i)$$

In order to get an expression in terms of local information, we introduce X and $\mathbf{U}$ by averaging over their possible values:

$$\frac{\partial P(D_j)/\partial w_i}{P(D_j)} = \frac{\frac{\partial}{\partial w_i}\left(\sum_{x,\mathbf{u}} P(D_j \mid x, \mathbf{u})P(x, \mathbf{u})\right)}{P(D_j)}$$

$$= \frac{\frac{\partial}{\partial w_i}\left(\sum_{x,\mathbf{u}} P(D_j \mid x, \mathbf{u})P(x \mid \mathbf{u})P(\mathbf{u})\right)}{P(D_j)}$$

For our purposes, the important property of this expression is that w_i appears only in linear form. In fact, w_i appears only in one term in the summation, namely the term for x_i and $\mathbf{u}_i$. For this term, $P(x \mid \mathbf{u})$ is just w_i, hence

$$\frac{\partial P(D_j)/\partial w_i}{P(D_j)} = \frac{P(D_j \mid x_i, \mathbf{u}_i)P(\mathbf{u}_i)}{P(D_j)}$$

Further manipulation reveals that the gradient calculation can "piggyback" on the calculations of posterior probabilities done in the normal course of belief network operation—that is, calculations of the probabilities of network variables given the observed data. To do this, we apply Bayes' theorem to the above equation, yielding

$$\frac{\partial P(D_j)/\partial w_i}{P(D_j)} = \frac{P(x_i, \mathbf{u}_i \mid D_j)P(D_j)P(\mathbf{u}_i)}{P(x_i, \mathbf{u}_i)P(D_j)} = \frac{P(x_i, \mathbf{u}_i \mid D_j)}{P(x_i \mid \mathbf{u}_i)} = \frac{P(x_i, \mathbf{u}_i \mid D_j)}{w_i}$$

In most implementations of belief network inference, the term $P(x_i, \mathbf{u}_i \mid D_j)$ is either computed directly or is easily obtained by summing a small number of table entries. The complete gradient vector is obtained by summing the above expression over the data cases to give the gradient component with respect to each w_i for the likelihood of the entire training set. Thus, the necessary information for calculating the gradient can be derived directly from the normal computations done by belief networks as new evidence is obtained.

Once we have a locally computable expression for the gradient, we can apply the same kinds of hill-climbing or simulated annealing methods as are used for neural networks. Learning with belief networks has the advantage that a human expert can easily provide a structure for the

---

[6] We also need to include the constraint that the conditional probability values for any given conditioning case must remain normalized. A formal analysis shows that the derivative of the constrained system (where the columns sum to one) is equal to the orthogonally projection of the unconstrained derivative onto the constraint surface.

network that reflects the causal structure of the domain. This prior knowledge should help the network to learn much faster from a given set of examples. Moreover, the results of learning are more easily understood, and, because probabilities are produced, the results can be used in making rational decisions.

One can also use the gradient-descent method in association with an algorithm designed to generate the structure of the network. Because such algorithms usually work by evaluating candidate structures for their ability to model the data, one can simply use the gradient descent to find the best fit between any candidate structure and the data.

A comparison of belief networks and neural networks

Given the close similarity between belief networks (particularly the adaptive variety) and neural networks, a detailed comparison is in order. The two formalisms can be compared as representation systems, inference systems, and learning systems.

Both neural networks and belief networks are attribute-based representations. Both handle discrete and continuous inputs, although algorithms for handling continuous variables in belief networks are less developed. The principal difference is that belief networks are localized representations, whereas neural networks are distributed representations. Nodes in belief networks represent propositions with well-defined semantics and well-defined probabilistic relationships to other propositions. Units in neural networks, on the other hand, typically do not represent specific propositions. Even if they did, the calculations carried by the network do not treat propositions in any semantically meaningful way. In practical terms, this means that humans can neither construct nor understand neural network representations. The well-defined semantics of belief networks also means that they can be constructed automatically by programs that manipulate first-order representations.

Another representational difference is that belief network variables have *two* dimensions of "activation"—the range of values for the proposition, and the probability assigned to each of those values. The outputs of a neural network can be viewed as *either* the probability of a Boolean variable, or an exact value for a continuous variable, but neural networks cannot handle both probabilities and multivalued or continuous variables simultaneously.

As inference mechanisms—once they have been trained—feedforward neural networks can execute in linear time, whereas general belief network inference is NP-hard. On closer inspection, this is not as clear an advantage as it might seem, because a neural network would in some cases have to be exponentially larger in order to represent the same input/output mapping as a belief network (else we would be able to solve hard problems in polynomial time). Practically speaking, any neural network that can be trained is small enough so that inference is fast, whereas it is not hard to construct belief networks that take a long time to run. One other important aspect of belief networks is their flexibility, in the sense that at any time any subset of the variables can be treated as inputs, and any other subset as outputs, whereas feedforward neural networks have fixed inputs and outputs.

With respect to learning, a comparison is difficult because adaptive probabilistic networks (APNs) are a very recent development. One can expect the time per iteration of an APN to be slower, because it involves an inference process. On the other hand, a human (or another part of the agent) can provide prior knowledge to the APN learning process in the form of the network structure and/or conditional probability values. Since this reduces the hypothesis space, it should allow the APN to learn from fewer examples. Also, the ability of belief networks to represent propositions locally may mean that they converge faster to a correct representation of a domain that has local structure—that is, in which each proposition is directly affected by only a small number of other propositions.

19.7   SUMMARY

Learning in complex network representations is currently one of the hottest topics in science. It promises to have broad applications in computer science, neurobiology, psychology, and physics. This chapter has presented some of the basic ideas and techniques, and given a flavor of the mathematical underpinnings. The basic points are as follows:

- A **neural network** is a computational model that shares some of the properties of brains: it consists of many simple units working in parallel with no central control. The connections between units have numeric weights that can be modified by the learning element.

- The behavior of a neural network is determined by the connection topology and the nature of the individual units. **Feed-forward** networks, in which the connections form an acyclic graph, are the simplest to analyze. Feed-forward networks implement state-free functions.

- A **perceptron** is a feed-forward network with a single layer of units, and can only represent **linearly separable** functions. If the data are linearly separable, the **perceptron learning rule** can be used to modify the network's weights to fit the data exactly.

- **Multilayer feed-forward** networks can represent any function, given enough units.

- The **back-propagation** learning algorithm works on multilayer feed-forward networks, using gradient descent in weight space to minimize the output error. It converges to a locally optimal solution, and has been used with some success in a variety of applications. As with all hill-climbing techniques, however, there is no guarantee that it will find a global solution. Furthermore, its convergence is often very slow.

- **Bayesian learning** methods can be used to learn representations of probabilistic functions, particularly belief networks. Bayesian learning methods must trade off the prior belief in a hypothesis against its degree of agreement with the observed data.

- There are a variety of learning problems associated with belief networks, depending on whether the structure is fixed or unknown, and whether variables are hidden or observable.

- With a fixed structure and hidden variables, belief network learning has a remarkable similarity to neural network learning. Gradient descent methods can be used, but belief networks also have the advantage of a well-understood semantics for individual nodes. This allows the provision of prior knowledge in order to speed up the learning process.

BIBLIOGRAPHICAL AND HISTORICAL NOTES

McCulloch and Pitts (1943) introduced the fundamental idea of analyzing neural activity via thresholds and weighted sums. Early cybernetics and control theory (Wiener, 1948), based on the notion of negative feedback loops, played a role as a model for learning in neural networks. *The Organization of Behavior* (Hebb, 1949) was influential in promoting the hypothesis that human and animal long-term memory is mediated by permanent alterations in the synapses. *Design for a Brain* (Ashby, 1952) put forth the idea that intelligence could be created by the use of "homeostatic" devices which learn through a kind of exhaustive search.

Minsky and Papert (1988, pp. ix–x) mention a machine built by Marvin Minsky in 1951 that may well be the first actual neural network learning system ever built. Minsky's (1954) doctoral dissertation continued the exploration of neural networks. The aptly-named "Pandemonium" system (Selfridge, 1959; Selfridge and Neisser, 1960) involved a relatively fine-grained distributed control regime reminiscent of neural networks. Cragg and Temperley (1954; 1955) drew parallels between McCulloch–Pitts neural networks and "spin systems" in physics. Caianello (1961) designed a statistical theory of learning in neural networks, drawing on classical statistical mechanics. Von Neumann (1958) provides a comparison between the functioning of the brain and the operation of digital computers. Frank Rosenblatt (1957) invented the modern "perceptron" style of neural network, composed of trainable threshold units.

Similar devices called "adalines" (for "Adaptive Linear") were invented about the same time (Widrow and Hoff, 1960; Widrow, 1962). Hawkins (1961) gives a detailed history of early work in "self-organizing systems" or "neural cybernetics," as these approaches were then called.

Frank Rosenblatt (1960) found the first proof of the perceptron convergence theorem, although it had been foreshadowed by purely mathematical work outside the context of neural networks (Agmon, 1954; Motzkin and Schoenberg, 1954). Two good books on this period of research are *Neurodynamics* (Rosenblatt, 1962) and *Learning Machines* (Nilsson, 1965). Nilsson's book is especially comprehensive and detailed. It has recently been republished as *The Mathematical Foundations of Learning Machines* (Nilsson, 1990) with a new introduction by Terrence Sejnowski and Halbert White.

Most work in neural networks before 1970 focused on the one-layer perceptron type of machine, but there were some exceptions. Widrow designed multilayer machines called "madalines"(Widrow, 1962). Other early multilayer machines are described in (Palmieri and Sanna, 1960; Gamba *et al.*, 1961).

The publication of *Perceptrons* (Minsky and Papert, 1969) marked the end of an era. The authors were severely critical of the unguided experimentation and lack of mathematical rigor that characterized much of the early work on perceptrons. They established the linear separability criterion for tasks that could be accomplished by one-layer perceptrons, thus explaining the failure of the early efforts at solving problems that violated this criterion. Minsky and Papert also gave some results on early multilayer systems. In the Epilogue to the expanded edition of *Perceptrons* (Minsky and Papert, 1988), they forcefully rebut the charge that the publication of the first edition was responsible for the long perceptron winter of the 1970s, arguing that perceptron research had already lost its momentum and that the first edition merely explained this phenomenon. They reaffirm the long-term promise of mathematically sound neural network research, while at the same time criticizing contemporary connectionism circa 1988 for the same lack of rigor that had plagued the early perceptron work.

The papers in (Hinton and Anderson, 1981), based on a conference in San Diego in 1979, can be regarded as marking the renaissance of connectionism. The two-volume "PDP" (Parallel Distributed Processing) anthology (Rumelhart *et al.*, 1986) really put neural networks on the map for many AI researchers, as well as popularizing the back-propagation algorithm. Several advances made this possible. Hopfield (1982) analyzed symmetric networks using statistical mechanics and analogies from physics. The Boltzmann Machine (Hinton and Sejnowski, 1983; Hinton and Sejnowski, 1986) and the analysis of neural networks using the physical theory of magnetic spin glasses (Amit *et al.*, 1985) tightened the links between statistical mechanics and neural network theory—providing not only useful mathematical insights but also *respectability*. The back-propagation technique had been invented quite early (Bryson and Ho, 1969) but it was rediscovered several times (Werbos, 1974; Parker, 1985). Minsky and Papert (1988) criticize the generalized delta rule as a straightforward variant of simple hill-climbing, just as the perceptron learning algorithm had been.

The expressiveness of multilayer networks was investigated by Cybenko (1988; 1989), who showed that two hidden layers are enough to represent any function and a single layer is enough to represent any *continuous* function. These results, although reassuring, are not very exciting when one realizes that they are achieved by allocating a separate collection of units to represent the output value for each small region of the (exponentially large) input space.

The problem of finding a good structure for a multilayer network was addressed using genetic algorithms by Harp et al. (1990) and by Miller et al. (1989). The "optimal brain damage" method for removing useless connections is by LeCun et al. (1989), and Sietsma and Dow (1988) show how to remove useless units. The tiling algorithm for growing larger structures is by Mézard and Nadal (1989). Similar algorithms that grow slightly different topologies were proposed by Marchand *et al.* (1990) and by Frean (1990).

The complexity of neural network learning has been investigated by researchers in computational learning theory. Some of the earliest results were obtained by Judd (1990), who showed that the general problem of finding a set of weights consistent with a set of examples is NP-complete, even under very restrictive assumptions. Avrim Blum and Ron Rivest (1992) proved that training even a *three-node network* is NP-complete! These results suggest that weight space can contain an exponential number of local minima, for otherwise a random-restart hill-climbing algorithm would be able to find a global optimum in polynomial time.

One topic of great current interest in neural network research is the use of specialized parallel hardware, including analog computation. Systems may use analog VLSI (Alspector *et al.*, 1987; Mead, 1989), optoelectronics (Farhat *et al.*, 1985; Peterson *et al.*, 1990), or exotic, fully optical computing technologies such as spatial light modulation (Abu-Mostafa and Psaltis, 1987; Hsu *et al.*, 1988).

Neural networks constitute a large field of study with an abundance of resources available for the inquirer. Probably best available textbook is *Introduction to the Theory of Neural Computation* (Hertz *et al.*, 1991), which emphasizes the connections with statistical mechanics (the authors are physicists). *Self-Organization and Associative Memory* (Kohonen, 1989) provides considerable mathematical background. For biological nervous systems, a very thorough introduction is (Kandel *et al.*, 1991). A good introduction to the detailed functioning of individual neurons is (Miles, 1969). Articles by Cowan and Sharp (1988b; 1988a) present inclusive surveys of the history of neural network research. A very comprehensive bibliography is available in *NeuralSource* (Wasserman and Oetzel, 1990).

The most important conference in the field is the annual NIPS (Neural Information Processing Conference) conference, whose proceedings are published as the series *Advances in Neural Information Processing Systems*, starting with (Touretzky, 1989). Current research also appears in the International Joint Conference on Neural Networks (IJCNN). Major journals for the field include *Neural Computation*; *Neural Networks*; *IEEE Transactions on Neural Networks*; the *International Journal of Neural Systems*; and *Concepts in Neuroscience*.

The topic of learning belief networks has received attention only very recently. For the fixed-structure, fully observable case, Spiegelhalter, Dawid, Lauritzen, and Cowell (Spiegelhalter *et al.*, 1993) provide a thorough analysis of the statistical basis of belief network modification using Dirichlet priors. They also give a heuristic approximation for the hidden-variable case. Pearl (1988, Chapter 8) describes an algorithm for learning polytrees with unknown structure and fully observable variables. Heckerman, Geiger, and Chickering (1994) describe an elegant and effective heuristic algorithm for recovering the structure of general networks in the fully observable case, building on the work of Cooper and Herskovits (1992). For the case of hidden variables and unknown structure, see (Spirtes *et al.*, 1993).

The general problem of recovering distributions from data with missing values and hidden variables is addressed by the EM algorithm (Dempster *et al.*, 1977). The algorithm in the chapter (Russell *et al.*, 1994) can be seen as a variant of EM in which the "maximize" phase is carried out by a gradient-following method. Lauritzen (1991) also considers the application of EM to belief networks. A gradient-following algorithm for learning **sigmoid networks** (belief networks in which each CPT represents the same function as a standard neural-network unit) was proposed by Radford Neal (1991), who went on to show that Boltzmann Machines are a special case of belief networks. Neal was among the first to point out the extremely close connection between neural and belief networks.

EXERCISES

19.1   Construct by hand a neural network that computes the XOR function of two inputs. Make sure to specify what sort of units you are using.

19.2   We know that a simple perceptron cannot represent XOR (or, generally, the parity function of its inputs). Describe what happens to the weights of a four-input, step-function perceptron, beginning with all weights set to 0.1, as examples of the parity function arrive.

19.3   Suppose you had a neural network with linear activation functions. That is, for each unit the output is some constant c times the weighted sum of the inputs.

    a. Assume that the network has one hidden layer. For a given assignment to the weights $\mathbf{W}$, write down equations for the value of the units in the output layer as a function of $\mathbf{W}$ and the input layer **I**, without any explicit mention to the output of the hidden layer. Show that there is a network with no hidden units that computes the same function.

b. Repeat the calculation in part (a), this time for a network with any number of hidden layers. What can you conclude about linear activation functions?

19.4   Consider the following set of examples. Each example has six inputs and one target output:

I_1	1	1	1	1	1	1	1	0	0	0	0	0	0	0
I_2	0	0	0	1	1	0	0	1	1	0	1	0	1	1
I_3	1	1	1	0	1	0	0	1	1	0	0	0	1	1
I_4	0	1	0	0	1	0	0	1	0	1	1	1	0	1
I_5	0	0	1	1	0	1	1	0	1	1	0	0	1	0
I_6	0	0	0	1	0	1	0	1	1	0	1	1	1	0
T	1	1	1	1	1	1	0	1	0	0	0	0	0	0

a. Run the perceptron learning rule on this example set, and show the resulting set of weights.

b. Run the decision tree learning rule, and show the resulting decision tree.

c. Comment on your results.

19.5   Implement a data structure for layered, feed-forward neural networks, remembering to provide the information needed for both forward evaluation and backward propagation. Using this data structure, write a function NEURAL-NETWORK-OUTPUT that takes an example and a network and computes the appropriate output values.

19.6   Suppose that a training set contains only a single example, repeated 100 times. In 80 of the 100 cases, the single output value is 1; in the other 20, it is 0. What will a back-propagation network predict for this example, assuming that it has been trained and reaches a global optimum? (*Hint:* to find the global optimum, differentiate the error function and set to zero.)

19.7   The network in Figure 19.13 has four hidden nodes. This number was chosen somewhat arbitrarily. Run systematic experiments to measure the learning curves for networks with different numbers of hidden nodes. What is the optimal number? Would it be possible to use a cross-validation method to find the best network before the fact?

20 REINFORCEMENT LEARNING

In which we examine how an agent can learn from success and failure, reward and punishment.

20.1 INTRODUCTION

In the previous two chapters, we have studied learning methods that learn from examples. That is, the environment provides input/output pairs, and the task is to learn a function that could have generated those pairs. These supervised learning methods are appropriate when a teacher is providing correct values or when the function's output represents a prediction about the future that can be checked by looking at the percepts in the next time step. In this chapter, we will study how agents can learn in much less generous environments, where the agent receives no examples, and starts with no model of the environment and no utility function.

For example, we know an agent can learn to play chess by supervised learning—by being given examples of game situations along with the best move for that situation. But if there is no friendly teacher providing examples, what can the agent do? By trying random moves, the agent can eventually build a predictive model of its environment: what the board will be like after it makes a given move, and even how the opponent is likely to reply in a given situation. But without some feedback as to what is good and what is bad, the agent will have no grounds for deciding which move to make. Fortunately, the chess-playing agent does receive some feedback, even without a friendly teacher—at the end of the game, the agent perceives whether it has won or lost. This kind of feedback is called a **reward**, or **reinforcement**. In games like chess, the reinforcement is received only at the end of the game. We call this a **terminal state** in the state history sequence. In other environments, the rewards come more frequently—in ping-pong, each point scored can be considered a reward. Sometimes rewards are given by a teacher who says "nice move" or "uh-oh" (but does not say what the best move is).

The task of **reinforcement learning** is to use rewards to learn a successful agent function. This is difficult because the agent is never told what the right actions are, nor which rewards are

REWARD

TERMINAL STATE

due to which actions. A game-playing agent may play flawlessly except for one blunder, and at the end of the game get a single reinforcement that says "you lose." The agent must somehow determine which move was the blunder.

Within our framework of agents as functions from percepts to actions, a reward can be provided by a percept, but the agent must be "hardwired" to recognize that percept as a reward rather than as just another sensory input. Thus, animals seem to be hardwired to recognize pain and hunger as negative rewards, and pleasure and food as positive rewards. Training a dog is made easier by the fact that humans and dogs happen to agree that a low-pitched sound (either a growl or a "bad dog!") is a negative reinforcement. Reinforcement has been carefully studied by animal psychologists for over 60 years.

In many complex domains, reinforcement learning is the only feasible way to train a program to perform at high levels. For example, in game playing, it is very hard for a human to provide accurate and consistent evaluations of large numbers of positions, which would be needed to train an evaluation function directly from examples. Instead, the program can be told when it has won or lost, and can use this information to learn an evaluation function that gives reasonably accurate estimates of the probability of winning from any given position. Similarly, it is extremely difficult to program a robot to juggle; yet given appropriate rewards every time a ball is dropped or caught, the robot can learn to juggle by itself.

In a way, reinforcement learning is a restatement of the entire AI problem. An agent in an environment gets percepts, maps some of them to positive or negative utilities, and then has to decide what action to take. To avoid reconsidering all of AI and to get at the principles of reinforcement learning, we need to consider how the learning task can vary:

- The environment can be accessible or inaccessible. In an accessible environment, states can be identified with percepts, whereas in an inaccessible environment, the agent must maintain some internal state to try to keep track of the environment.

- The agent can begin with knowledge of the environment and the effects of its actions; or it will have to learn this model as well as utility information.

- Rewards can be received only in terminal states, or in any state.

- Rewards can be components of the actual utility (points for a ping-pong agent or dollars for a betting agent) that the agent is trying to maximize, or they can be hints as to the actual utility ("nice move" or "bad dog").

PASSIVE LEARNER
ACTIVE LEARNER
- The agent can be a **passive learner** or an **active learner**. A passive learner simply watches the world going by, and tries to learn the utility of being in various states; an active learner must also act using the learned information, and can use its problem generator to suggest explorations of unknown portions of the environment.

Furthermore, as we saw in Chapter 2, there are several different basic designs for agents. Because the agent will be receiving rewards that relate to utilities, there are two basic designs to consider:

- The agent learns a utility function on states (or state histories) and uses it to select actions that maximize the expected utility of their outcomes.

ACTION-VALUE
Q-LEARNING
- The agent learns an **action-value** function giving the expected utility of taking a given action in a given state. This is called **Q-learning**.

An agent that learns utility functions must also have a model of the environment in order to make decisions, because it must know the states to which its actions will lead. For example, in order to make use of a backgammon evaluation function, a backgammon program must know what its legal moves are *and how they affect the board position*. Only in this way can it apply the utility function to the outcome states. An agent that learns an action-value function, on the other hand, need not have such a model. As long as it knows its legal moves, it can compare their values directly without having to consider their outcomes. Action-value learners therefore can be slightly simpler in design than utility learners. On the other hand, because they do not know where their actions lead, they cannot look ahead; this can seriously restrict their ability to learn, as we shall see.

We first address the problem of learning utility functions, which has been studied in AI since the earliest days of the field. (See the discussion of Samuel's checker player in Chapter 5.) We examine increasingly complex versions of the problem, while keeping initially to simple state-based representations. Section 20.6 discusses the learning of action-value functions, and Section 20.7 discusses how the learner can generalize across states. Throughout this chapter, we will assume that the environment is nondeterministic. At this point the reader may wish to review the basics of decision making in complex, nondeterministic environments, as covered in Chapter 17.

20.2   PASSIVE LEARNING IN A KNOWN ENVIRONMENT

To keep things simple, we start with the case of a passive learning agent using a state-based representation in a known, accessible environment. In passive learning, the environment generates state transitions and the agent perceives them.[1] Consider an agent trying to learn the utilities of the states shown in Figure 20.1(a). We assume, for now, that it is provided with a model M_{ij} giving the probability of a transition from state i to state j, as in Figure 20.1(b). In each **training sequence**, the agent starts in state (1,1) and experiences a sequence of state transitions until it reaches one of the terminal states (4,2) or (4,3), where it receives a reward.[2] A typical set of training sequences might look like this:

$$(1,1)\rightarrow(1,2)\rightarrow(1,3)\rightarrow(1,2)\rightarrow(1,3)\rightarrow(1,2)\rightarrow(1,1)\rightarrow(2,1)\rightarrow(3,1)\rightarrow(4,1)\rightarrow(4,2)\ \underline{-1}$$
$$(1,1)\rightarrow(1,2)\rightarrow(1,3)\rightarrow(2,3)\rightarrow(3,3)\rightarrow(4,3)\ \underline{+1}$$
$$(1,1)\rightarrow(1,2)\rightarrow(1,1)\rightarrow(1,2)\rightarrow(1,1)\rightarrow(2,1)\rightarrow(3,1)\rightarrow(3,2)\rightarrow(4,2)\ \underline{-1}$$
$$(1,1)\rightarrow(1,2)\rightarrow(1,1)\rightarrow(1,2)\rightarrow(1,3)\rightarrow(2,3)\rightarrow(1,3)\rightarrow(2,3)\rightarrow(3,3)\rightarrow(4,3)\ \underline{+1}$$
$$(1,1)\rightarrow(2,1)\rightarrow(3,1)\rightarrow(2,1)\rightarrow(1,1)\rightarrow(1,2)\rightarrow(1,3)\rightarrow(2,3)\rightarrow(3,3)\rightarrow(4,3)\ \underline{+1}$$
$$(1,1)\rightarrow(2,1)\rightarrow(1,1)\rightarrow(1,2)\rightarrow(1,3)\rightarrow(2,3)\rightarrow(3,3)\rightarrow(3,2)\rightarrow(4,2)\ \underline{-1}$$

The object is to use the information about rewards to learn the expected utility $U(i)$ associated with each nonterminal state i. We will make one big simplifying assumption: the utility of a sequence is the sum of the rewards accumulated in the states of the sequence. That is, the utility

TRAINING
SEQUENCE

---

[1]   Another way to think of a passive learner is as an agent with a fixed policy trying to determine its benefits.

[2]   The period from initial state to terminal state is often called an **epoch**.

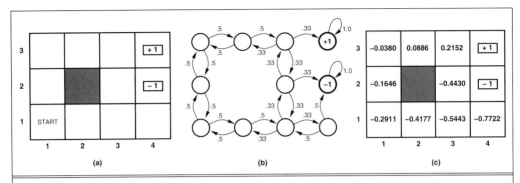

Figure 20.1   (a) A simple stochastic environment. State (1,1) is the start state. (b) Each state transitions to a neighboring state with equal probability among all neighboring states. State (4,2) is terminal with reward –1, and state (4,3) is terminal with reward +1. (c) The exact utility values.

REWARD-TO-GO

function is **additive** in the sense defined on page 502. We define the **reward-to-go** of a state as the sum of the rewards from that state until a terminal state is reached. Given this definition, it is easy to see that *the expected utility of a state is the expected reward-to-go of that state.*

The generic agent design for passive reinforcement learning of utilities is shown in Figure 20.2. The agent keeps an estimate U of the utilities of the states, a table N of counts of how many times each state was seen, and a table M of transition probabilities from state to state. We assume that each percept e is enough to determine the STATE (i.e., the state is accessible), the agent can determine the REWARD component of a percept, and the agent can tell if a percept indicates a TERMINAL? state. In general, an agent can update its current estimated utilities after each observed transition. The key to reinforcement learning lies in the algorithm for updating the utility values given the training sequences. The following subsections discuss three possible approaches to UPDATE.

Naïve updating

ADAPTIVE CONTROL
THEORY

A simple method for updating utility estimates was invented in the late 1950s in the area of **adaptive control theory** by Widrow and Hoff (1960). We will call it the LMS (least mean squares) approach. In essence, it assumes that for each state in a training sequence, the *observed reward-to-go* on that sequence provides direct evidence of the actual expected reward-to-go. Thus, at the end of each sequence, the algorithm calculates the observed reward-to-go for each state and updates the estimated utility for that state accordingly. It can easily be shown (Exercise 20.1) that the LMS approach generates utility estimates that minimize the mean square error with respect to the observed data. When the utility function is represented by a table of values for each state, the update is simply done by maintaining a running average, as shown in Figure 20.3.

If we think of the utility function as a function, rather than just a table, then it is clear that the LMS approach is simply learning the utility function directly from examples. Each example has the state as input and the observed reward-to-go as output. This means that we have reduced reinforcement learning to a standard inductive learning problem, as discussed in Chapter 18. As

---

function PASSIVE-RL-AGENT(*e*) **returns** an action
    static: *U*, a table of utility estimates
            N, a table of frequencies for states
            M, a table of transition probabilities from state to state
            percepts, a percept sequence (initially empty)

    add *e* to *percepts*
    increment *N*[STATE[*e*]]
    U ← UPDATE(*U*, *e*, *percepts*, *M*, *N*)
    if TERMINAL?[*e*] **then** *percepts* ← the empty sequence
    return the action *Observe*

Figure 20.2   Skeleton for a passive reinforcement learning agent that just observes the world and tries to learn the utilities, *U*, of each state. The agent also keeps track of transition frequencies and probabilities. The rest of this section is largely devoted to defining the UPDATE function.

---

function LMS-UPDATE(*U*, *e*, *percepts*, *M*, *N*) **returns** an updated *U*

    if TERMINAL?[*e*] **then**
        reward-to-go ← 0
        for each e_i **in** *percepts* (starting at end) **do**
            reward-to-go ← *reward-to-go* + REWARD[e_i]
            U[STATE[e_i]] ← RUNNING-AVERAGE(*U*[STATE[e_i]], *reward-to-go*, *N*[STATE[e_i]])
    end

Figure 20.3   The update function for least mean square (LMS) updating of utilities.

---

we will show, it is an easy matter to use more powerful kinds of representations for the utility function, such as neural networks. Learning techniques for those representations can be applied directly to the observed data.

    One might think that the LMS approach more or less solves the reinforcement learning problem—or at least, reduces it to one we already know a lot about. In fact, the LMS approach misses a very important aspect of the reinforcement learning problem, namely, the fact that the utilities of states are not independent! The structure of the transitions among the states in fact imposes very strong additional constraints: *The actual utility of a state is constrained to be the probability-weighted average of its successors' utilities, plus its own reward.* By ignoring these constraints, LMS-UPDATE usually ends up converging very slowly on the correct utility values for the problem. Figure 20.4 shows a typical run on the 4×3 environment in Figure 20.1, illustrating both the convergence of the utility estimates and the gradual reduction in the root-mean-square error with respect to the *correct* utility values. It takes the agent well over a thousand training sequences to get close to the correct values.

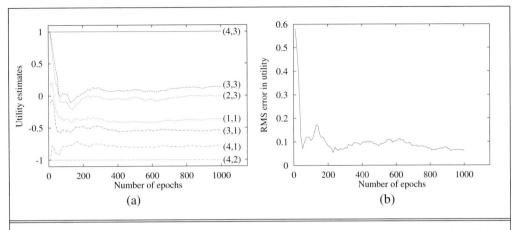

Figure 20.4   The LMS learning curves for the 4×3 world shown in Figure 20.1. (a) The utility estimates of the states over time. (b) The RMS error compared to the correct values.

Adaptive dynamic programming

Programs that use knowledge of the structure of the environment usually learn much faster. In the example in Figure 20.5 (from (Sutton, 1988)), the agent already has a fair amount of experience with the three states on the right, and has learned the values indicated. However, the path followed from the new state reaches an unusually good terminal state. The LMS algorithm will assign a utility estimate of +1 to the new state, whereas it is clear that the new state is much less promising, because it has a transition to a state known to have utility ≈ -0.8, and no other known transitions.

Fortunately, this drawback can be fixed. Consider again the point concerning the constraints on neighboring utilities. Because, for now, we are assuming that the transition probabilities are listed in the known table M_{ij}, the reinforcement learning problem becomes a well-defined sequential decision problem (see Chapter 17) as soon as the agent has observed the rewards for all the states. In our 4×3 environment, this usually happens after a handful of training sequences, at which point the agent can compute the exact utility values for all states. The utilities are computed by solving the set of equations

$$U(i) = R(i) + \sum_{j} M_{ij} U(j) \tag{20.1}$$

where $R(i)$ is the reward associated with being in state i, and M_{ij} is the probability that a transition will occur from state i to state j. This set of equations simply formalizes the basic point made in the previous subsection. Notice that because the agent is passive, no maximization over actions is involved (unlike Equation (17.3)). The process of solving the equations is therefore identical to a single **value determination** phase in the policy iteration algorithm. The exact utilities for the states in the 4×3 world are shown in Figure 20.1(c). Notice how the "safest" squares are those along the top row, away from the negative reward state.

ADAPTIVE DYNAMIC PROGRAMMING
ADP

We will use the term **adaptive dynamic programming** (or **ADP**) to denote any reinforcement learning method that works by solving the utility equations with a dynamic programming algorithm. In terms of its ability to make good use of experience, ADP provides a standard

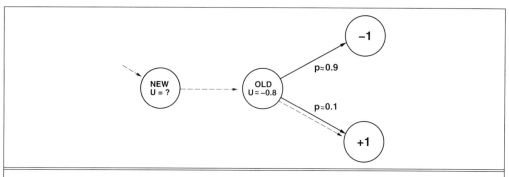

Figure 20.5   An example where LMS does poorly. A new state is reached for the first time, and then follows the path marked by the dashed lines, reaching a terminal state with reward +1.

against which to measure other reinforcement learning algorithms. It is, however, somewhat intractable for large state spaces. In backgammon, for example, it would involve solving roughly 10^{50} equations in 10^{50} unknowns.

Temporal difference learning

It is possible to have (almost) the best of both worlds—that is, one can approximate the constraint equations shown earlier without solving them for all possible states. *The key is to use the observed transitions to adjust the values of the observed states so that they agree with the constraint equations.* Suppose that we observe a transition from state i to state j, where currently $U(i) = -0.5$ and $U(j) = +0.5$. This suggests that we should consider increasing $U(i)$ to make it agree better with its successor. This can be achieved using the following updating rule:

$$U(i) \leftarrow U(i) + \alpha(R(i) + U(j) - U(i)) \tag{20.2}$$

TEMPORAL-
DIFFERENCE

where α is the **learning rate** parameter. Because this update rule uses the difference in utilities between successive states, it is often called the **temporal-difference**, or **TD**, equation.

The basic idea of all temporal-difference methods is to first define the conditions that hold locally when the utility estimates are correct; and then to write an update equation that moves the estimates toward this ideal "equilibrium" equation. In the case of passive learning, the equilibrium is given by Equation (20.1). Now Equation (20.2) does in fact cause the agent to reach the equilibrium given by Equation (20.1), but there is some subtlety involved. First, notice that the update only involves the actual successor, whereas the actual equilibrium conditions involve all possible next states. One might think that this causes an improperly large change in $U(i)$ when a very rare transition occurs; but, in fact, because rare transitions occur only rarely, the *average value* of $U(i)$ will converge to the correct value. Furthermore, if we change α from a fixed parameter to a function that decreases as the number of times a state has been visited increases, then $U(i)$ itself will converge to the correct value (Dayan, 1992). This gives us the algorithm TD-UPDATE, shown in Figure 20.6. Figure 20.7 shows a typical run of the TD learning algorithm on the world in Figure 20.1. Although TD generates noisier values, the RMS error is actually significantly less than that for LMS after 1000 iterations.

function TD-UPDATE(U, e, $percepts$, M, N) **returns** the utility table U

if TERMINAL?[e] **then**
    $U[$STATE$[e]] \leftarrow$ RUNNING-AVERAGE($U[$STATE$[e]]$, REWARD$[e]$, $N[$STATE$[e]]$)
else if $percepts$ contains more than one element **then**
    $e' \leftarrow$ the penultimate element of $percepts$
    $i, j \leftarrow$ STATE$[e']$, STATE$[e]$
    $U[i] \leftarrow U[i] + \alpha(N[i])($REWARD$[e'] + U[j] - U[i])$

Figure 20.6   An algorithm for updating utility estimates using temporal differences.

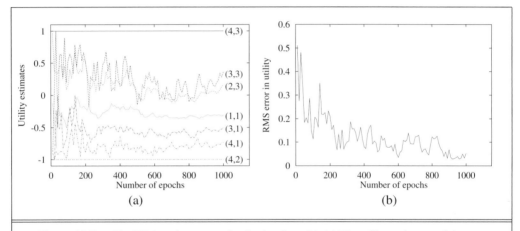

(a)   (b)

Figure 20.7   The TD learning curves for the 4×3 world. (a) The utility estimates of the states over time. (b) The RMS error compared to the correct values.

20.3   PASSIVE LEARNING IN AN UNKNOWN ENVIRONMENT

The previous section dealt with the case in which the environment model M is already known. Notice that of the three approaches, only the dynamic programming method used the model in full. TD uses information about connectedness of states, but only from the current training sequence. (As we mentioned before, all utility-learning methods will use the model during subsequent action selection.) Hence LMS and TD will operate unchanged in an initially unknown environment.

The adaptive dynamic programming approach simply adds a step to PASSIVE-RL-AGENT that updates an estimated model of the environment. Then the estimated model is used as the basis for a dynamic programming phase to calculate the corresponding utility estimates after each observation. As the environment model approaches the correct model, the utility estimates will, of course, converge to the correct utilities. Because the environment model usually changes only slightly with each observation, the dynamic programming phase can use value iteration with the previous utility estimates as initial values and usually converges quite quickly.

The environment model is learned by direct observation of transitions. In an accessible environment, each percept identifies the state, and hence each transition provides a direct input/output example for the transition function represented by M. The transition function is usually stochastic—that is, it specifies a probability for each possible successor rather than a single state. A reinforcement learning agent can use any of the techniques for learning stochastic functions from examples discussed in Chapters 18 and 19. We discuss their application further in Section 20.7.

Continuing with our tabular representation for the environment, we can update the environment model M simply by keeping track of the percentage of times each state transitions to each of its neighbors. Using this simple technique in the 4×3 world from Figure 20.1, we obtain the learning performance shown in Figure 20.8. Notice that the ADP method converges far faster than either LMS or TD learning.

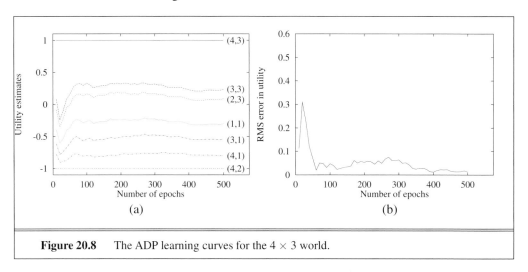

Figure 20.8   The ADP learning curves for the 4×3 world.

The ADP approach and the TD approach are actually closely related. Both try to make local adjustments to the utility estimates in order to make each state "agree" with its successors. One minor difference is that TD adjusts a state to agree with its *observed* successor (Equation (20.2)), whereas ADP adjusts the state to agree with *all* of the successors that might occur given an optimal action choice, weighted by their probabilities (Equation (20.1)). This difference disappears when the effects of TD adjustments are averaged over a large number of transitions, because the frequency of each successor in the set of transitions is approximately proportional to its probability. A more important difference is that whereas TD makes a single adjustment per observed transition, ADP makes as many as it needs to restore consistency between the utility estimates U and the environment model M. Although the observed transition only makes a local change in M, its effects may need to be propagated throughout U. Thus, TD can be viewed as a crude but efficient first approximation to ADP.

Each adjustment made by ADP could be viewed, from the TD point of view, as a result of a "pseudo-experience" generated by simulating the current environment model. It is possible to extend the TD approach to use an environment model to generate several pseudo-experiences— transitions that the TD agent can imagine *might* happen given its current model. For each observed transition, the TD agent can generate a large number of imaginary transitions. In this way, the resulting utility estimates will approximate more and more closely those of ADP—of course, at the expense of increased computation time.

In a similar vein, we can generate more efficient versions of ADP by directly approximating the algorithms for value iteration or policy iteration. Recall that full value iteration can be intractable when the number of states is large. Many of the adjustment steps, however, are extremely tiny. One possible approach to generating reasonably good answers quickly is to bound the number of adjustments made after each observed transition. One can also use a heuristic to rank the possible adjustments so as to carry out only the most significant ones. The **prioritized-sweeping** heuristic prefers to make adjustments to states whose *likely* successors have just undergone a *large* adjustment in their own utility estimates. Using heuristics like this, approximate ADP algorithms usually can learn roughly as fast as full ADP, in terms of the number of training sequences, but can be several orders of magnitude more efficient in terms of computation (see Exercise 20.3). This enables them to handle state spaces that are far too large for full ADP. Approximate ADP algorithms have an additional advantage: in the early stages of learning a new environment, the environment model *M* often will be far from correct, so there is little point in calculating an exact utility function to match it. An approximation algorithm can use a minimum adjustment size that decreases as the environment model becomes more accurate. This eliminates the very long value iterations that can occur early in learning due to large changes in the model.

PRIORITIZED-
SWEEPING

20.4   ACTIVE LEARNING IN AN UNKNOWN ENVIRONMENT

A passive learning agent can be viewed as having a fixed policy, and need not worry about which actions to take. An active agent must consider what actions to take, what their outcomes may be, and how they will affect the rewards received.

The PASSIVE-RL-AGENT model of page 602 needs only minor changes to accommodate actions by the agent:

- The environment model must now incorporate the probabilities of transitions to other states *given a particular action*. We will use M_{ij}^a to denote the probability of reaching state *j* if the action *a* is taken in state *i*.

- The constraints on the utility of each state must now take into account the fact that the agent has a choice of actions. A rational agent will maximize its expected utility, and instead of Equation (20.1) we use Equation (17.3), which we repeat here:

$$U(i) = R(i) + \max_a \sum_j M_{ij}^a U(j) \qquad (20.3)$$

- The agent must now choose an action at each step, and will need a performance element to do so. In the algorithm, this means calling PERFORMANCE-ELEMENT(e) and returning the resulting action. We assume that the model M and the utilities U are shared by the performance element; that is the whole point of learning them.

We now reexamine the dynamic programming and temporal-difference approaches in the light of the first two changes. The question of how the agent should act is covered in Section 20.5.

Because the ADP approach uses the environment model, we will need to change the algorithm for learning the model. Instead of learning the probability M_{ij} of a transition, we will need to learn the probability M_{ij}^a of a transition conditioned on taking an action a. In the explicit tabular representation for M, this simply means accumulating statistics in a three-dimensional table. With an implicit functional representation, as we will soon see, the input to the function will include the action taken. We will assume that a procedure UPDATE-ACTIVE-MODEL takes care of this. Once the model has been updated, then the utility function can be recalculated using a dynamic programming algorithm and then the performance element chooses what to do next. We show the overall design for ACTIVE-ADP-AGENT in Figure 20.9.

An active temporal-difference learning agent that learns utility functions also will need to learn a model in order to use its utility function to make decisions. The model acquisition problem for the TD agent is identical to that for the ADP agent. What of the TD update rule itself? Perhaps surprisingly, the update rule (20.2) remains unchanged. This might seem odd, for the following reason. Suppose the agent takes a step that normally leads to a good destination, but because of nondeterminism in the environment the agent ends up in a catastrophic state. The TD update rule will take this as seriously as if the outcome had been the normal result of the

---

function ACTIVE-ADP-AGENT(e) **returns** an action
    static: U, a table of utility estimates
               M, a table of transition probabilities from state to state for each action
               R, a table of rewards for states
               percepts, a percept sequence (initially empty)
               last-action, the action just executed

    add e to *percepts*
    $R[\text{STATE}[e]] \leftarrow \text{REWARD}[e]$
    $M \leftarrow \text{UPDATE-ACTIVE-MODEL}(M, percepts, last\text{-}action)$
    $U \leftarrow \text{VALUE-ITERATION}(U, M, R)$
    if TERMINAL?[e] **then**
        percepts $\leftarrow$ the empty sequence
    last-action $\leftarrow$ PERFORMANCE-ELEMENT(e)
    return *last-action*

Figure 20.9   Design for an active ADP agent. The agent learns an environment model M by observing the results of its actions, and uses the model to calculate the utility function U using a dynamic programming algorithm (here POLICY-ITERATION could be substituted for VALUE-ITERATION).

action, whereas one might suppose that because the outcome was a fluke, the agent should not worry about it too much. In fact, of course, the unlikely outcome will only occur infrequently in a large set of training sequences; hence in the long run its effects will be weighted proportionally to its probability, as we would hope. Once again, it can be shown that the TD algorithm will converge to the same values as ADP as the number of training sequences tends to infinity.

20.5   EXPLORATION

The only remaining issue to address for active reinforcement learning is the question of what actions the agent should take—that is, what PERFORMANCE-ELEMENT should return. This turns out to be harder than one might imagine.

One might suppose that the correct way for the agent to behave is to choose whichever action has the highest expected utility given the current utility estimates—after all, that is all the agent has to go on. But this overlooks the contribution of action to learning. In essence, an action has two kinds of outcome:[3]

- It gains rewards on the current sequence.
- It affects the percepts received, and hence the ability of the agent to learn—and receive rewards in future sequences.

An agent therefore must make a trade-off between its immediate good—as reflected in its current utility estimates—and its long-term well-being. An agent that simply chooses to maximize its rewards on the current sequence can easily get stuck in a rut. At the other extreme, continually acting to improve one's knowledge is of no use if one never puts that knowledge into practice. In the real world, one constantly has to decide between continuing in a comfortable existence and striking out into the unknown in the hopes of discovering a new and better life.

In order to illustrate the dangers of the two extremes, we will need a suitable environment. We will use the stochastic version of the 4×3 world shown in Figure 17.1. In this world, the agent can attempt to move *North*, *South*, *East*, or *West*; each action achieves the intended effect with probability 0.8, but the rest of the time, the action moves the agent at right angles to the intended direction. As before, we assume a reward of -0.04 (i.e., a cost of 0.04) for each action that doesn't reach a terminal state. The optimal policy and utility values for this world are shown in Figure 17.2, and the object of the learning agent is to converge towards these.

Let us consider two possible approaches that the learning agent might use for choosing what to do. The "wacky" approach acts randomly, in the hope that it will eventually explore the entire environment; and the "greedy" approach acts to maximize its utility using current estimates. As we see from Figure 20.10, the wacky approach succeeds in learning good utility estimates for all the states (top left). Unfortunately, its wacky policy means that it never actually gets better at reaching the positive reward (top right). The greedy agent, on the other hand, often finds a path to the +1 reward along the lower route via (2,1), (3,1), (3,2), and (3,3). Unfortunately, it then sticks to that path, never learning the utilities of the other states (bottom left). This means

---
[3] Notice the direct analogy to the theory of information value in Chapter 16.

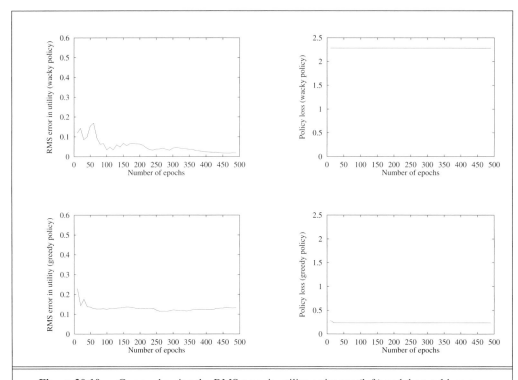

Figure 20.10   Curves showing the RMS error in utility estimates (left) and the total loss associated with the corresponding policy (right), for the wacky (top) and greedy (bottom) approaches to exploration.

that it too fails to achieve perfection (bottom right) because it does not find the optimal route via (1,2), (1,3), and (2,3).

Obviously, we need an approach somewhere between wackiness and greediness. The agent should be more wacky when it has little idea of the environment, and more greedy when it has a model that is close to being correct. Can we be a little more precise than this? Is there an *optimal* exploration policy? It turns out that this question has been studied in depth in the subfield of statistical decision theory that deals with so-called **bandit problems** (see sidebar).

BANDIT PROBLEMS

Although bandit problems are extremely difficult to solve exactly to obtain an *optimal* exploration policy, it is nonetheless possible to come up with a *reasonable* policy that seems to have the desired properties. In a given state, the agent should give some weight to actions that it has not tried very often, while being inclined to avoid actions that are believed to be of low utility. This can be implemented by altering the constraint equation (20.3) so that it assigns a higher utility estimate to relatively unexplored action–state pairs. Essentially, this amounts to an optimistic prior over the possible environments, and causes the agent to behave initially as if there were wonderful rewards scattered all over the place. Let us use $U^+(i)$ to denote the optimistic estimate of the utility (i.e., the expected reward-to-go) of the state i, and let $N(a, i)$ be the number of times action a has been tried in state i. Suppose we are using value iteration

EXPLORATION AND BANDITS

In Las Vegas, a *one-armed bandit* is a slot machine. A gambler can insert a coin, pull the lever, and collect the winnings (if any). An *n*-**armed bandit** has *n* levers. The gambler must choose which lever to play on each successive coin—the one that has paid off best, or maybe one that has not been tried?

The *n*-armed bandit problem is a formal model for real problems in many vitally important areas, such as deciding on the annual budget for AI research and development. Each arm corresponds to an action (such as allocating $20 million for development of new AI textbooks) and the payoff from pulling the arm corresponds to the benefits obtained from taking the action (immense). Exploration, whether it is exploration of a new research field or exploration of a new shopping mall, is risky, expensive, and has uncertain payoffs; on the other hand, failure to explore at all means that one never discovers *any* actions that are worthwhile.

To formulate a bandit problem properly, one must define exactly what is meant by optimal behavior. Most definitions in the literature assume that the aim is to maximize the expected total reward obtained over the agent's lifetime. These definitions require that the expectation be taken over the possible worlds that the agent could be in, as well as over the possible results of each action sequence in any given world. Here, a "world" is defined by the transition model M_{ij}^a. Thus, in order to act optimally, the agent needs a prior distribution over the possible models. The resulting optimization problems are usually wildly intractable. In some cases, however, appropriate independence assumptions enable the problem to be solved in closed form. With a row of real slot machines, for example, the rewards in successive time steps and on different machines can be assumed to be independent. It turns out that the fraction of one's coins invested in a given machine should drop off proportionally to the probability that the machine is in fact the best, given the observed distributions of rewards.

The formal results that have been obtained for optimal exploration policies apply only to the case in which the agent represents the transition model as an explicit table and is not able to generalize across states and actions. For more realistic problems, it is possible to prove only convergence to a correct model and optimal behavior in the limit of infinite experience. This is easily obtained by acting randomly on some fraction of steps, where that fraction decreases appropriately over time.

One can use the theory of *n*-armed bandits to argue for the reasonableness of the selection strategy in genetic algorithms (see Section 20.8). If you consider each arm in an *n*-armed bandit problem to be a possible string of genes, and the investment of a coin in one arm to be the reproduction of those genes, then genetic algorithms allocate coins optimally, given an appropriate set of independence assumptions.

in an ADP learning agent; then we need to rewrite the update equation (i.e., Equation (17.4)) to incorporate the optimistic estimate. The following equation does this:

$$U^+(i) \leftarrow R(i) + \max_a f\left(\sum_j M_{ij}^a U^+(j),\ N(a, i)\right) \tag{20.4}$$

EXPLORATION
FUNCTION

where $f(u, n)$ is called the **exploration function**. It determines how greed (preference for high values of u) is traded off against curiosity (preference for low values of n, i.e., actions that have not been tried often). The function $f(u, n)$ should be increasing in u, and decreasing in n. Obviously, there are many possible functions that fit these conditions. One particularly simple definition is the following:

$$f(u, n) = \begin{cases} R^+ & \text{if } n < N_e \\ u & \text{otherwise} \end{cases}$$

where R^+ is an optimistic estimate of the best possible reward obtainable in any state, and N_e is a fixed parameter. This will have the effect of making the agent try each action-state pair at least N_e times.

The fact that U^+ rather than U appears on the right-hand side of Equation (20.4) is very important. As exploration proceeds, the states and actions near the start state may well be tried a large number of times. If we used U, the nonoptimistic utility estimate, then the agent would soon become disinclined to explore further afield. The use of U^+ means that the benefits of exploration are propagated back from the edges of unexplored regions, so that actions that lead *toward* unexplored regions are weighted more highly, rather than just actions that are themselves unfamiliar. The effect of this exploration policy can be seen clearly in Figure 20.11, which shows a rapid convergence toward optimal performance, unlike that of the wacky or the greedy approaches. A very nearly optimal policy is found after just 18 trials. Notice that the utility estimates themselves do not converge as quickly. This is because the agent stops exploring the unrewarding parts of the state space fairly soon, visiting them only "by accident" thereafter. However, it makes perfect sense for the agent not to care about the exact utilities of states that it knows are undesirable and can be avoided.

20.6   LEARNING AN ACTION-VALUE FUNCTION

An action-value function assigns an expected utility to taking a given action in a given state; as mentioned earlier, such values are also called **Q-values**. We will use the notation $Q(a, i)$ to denote the value of doing action a in state i. Q-values are directly related to utility values by the following equation:

$$U(i) = \max_a Q(a, i) \tag{20.5}$$

Q-values play an important role in reinforcement learning for two reasons: first, like condition-action rules, they suffice for decision making without the use of a model; second, unlike condition-action rules, they can be learned directly from reward feedback.

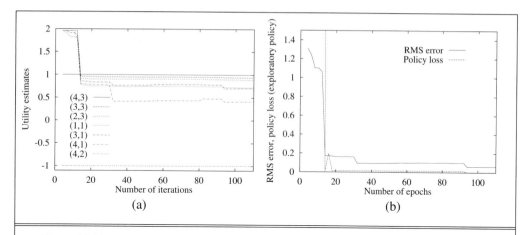

Figure 20.11   Performance of the exploratory ADP agent. using $R^+ = 2$ and $N_e = 5$. (a) Utility estimates for selected states over time. After the initial exploratory phase in which the states get an exploration bonus, the high-valued states quickly reach their correct values. The low-valued states converge slowly because they are seldom visited. (b) The RMS error in utility values and the associated policy loss.

As with utilities, we can write a constraint equation that must hold at equilibrium when the Q-values are correct:

$$Q(a, i) = R(i) + \sum_j M_{ij}^a \max_{a'} Q(a', j) \tag{20.6}$$

As in the ADP learning agent, we can use this equation directly as an update equation for an iteration process that calculates exact Q-values given an estimated model. This does, however, require that a model be learned as well because the equation uses M_{ij}^a. The temporal-difference approach, on the other hand, requires no model. The update equation for TD Q-learning is

$$Q(a, i) \leftarrow Q(a, i) + \alpha(R(i) + \max_{a'} Q(a', j) - Q(a, i)) \tag{20.7}$$

which is calculated after each transition from state i to state j.

The complete agent design for an exploratory Q-learning agent using TD is shown in Figure 20.12. Notice that it uses exactly the same exploration function f as used by the exploratory ADP agent, hence the need to keep statistics on actions taken (the table N). If a simpler exploration policy is used—say, acting randomly on some fraction of steps, where the fraction decreases over time—then we can dispense with the statistics.

Figure 20.13 shows the performance of the Q-learning agent in our 4×3 world. Notice that the utility estimates (derived from the Q-values using Equation (20.5)) take much longer to settle down than they did with the ADP agent. This is because TD does not enforce consistency among values via the model. Although a good policy is found after only 26 trials, it is considerably further from optimality than that found by the ADP agent (Figure 20.11).

Although these experimental results are for just one set of trials on one specific environment, they do raise a general question: is it better to learn a model and a utility function or to learn an action-value function with no model? In other words, what is the best way to represent the

function Q-LEARNING-AGENT(e) **returns** an action
    static: Q, a table of action values
              N, a table of state-action frequencies
              a, the last action taken
              i, the previous state visited
              r, the reward received in state i

    $j \leftarrow$ STATE$[e]$
    if i is non-null **then**
        $N[a,i] \leftarrow N[a,i] + 1$
        $Q[a,i] \leftarrow Q[a,i] + \alpha(r + \max_{a'} Q[a',j] - Q[a,i])$
    if TERMINAL?$[e]$ **then**
        $i \leftarrow$ null
    else
        $i \leftarrow j$
        $r \leftarrow$ REWARD$[e]$
    $a \leftarrow \arg\max_{a'} f(Q[a',j], N[a',j])$
    return a

Figure 20.12   An exploratory Q-learning agent. It is an active learner that learns the value $Q(a, i)$ of each action in each situation. It uses the same exploration function f as the exploratory ADP agent, but avoids having to learn the transition model M_{ij}^a because the Q-value of s state can be related directly to those of its neighbors.

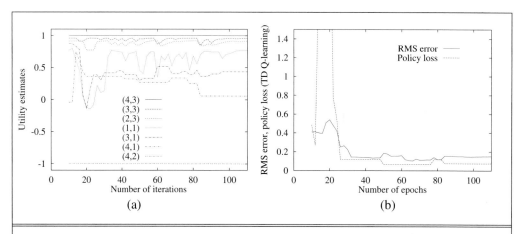

Figure 20.13   Performance of the exploratory TD Q-learning agent. using $R^+ = 2$ and $N_e = 5$. (a) Utility estimates for selected states over time. (b) The RMS error in utility values and the associated policy loss.

agent function? This is an issue at the foundations of artificial intelligence. As we stated in Chapter 1, one of the key historical characteristics of much of AI research is its (often unstated) adherence to the **knowledge-based** approach. This amounts to an assumption that the best way to represent the agent function is to construct an explicit representation of at least some aspects of the environment in which the agent is situated.

Some researchers, both inside and outside AI, have claimed that the availability of model-free methods such as Q-learning means that the knowledge-based approach is unnecessary. There is, however, little to go on but intuition. Our intuition, for what it's worth, is that as the environment becomes more complex, the advantages of a knowledge-based approach become more apparent. This is borne out even in games such as chess, checkers (draughts), and backgammon (see next section), where efforts to learn an evaluation function using a model have met with more success than Q-learning methods. Perhaps one day there will be a deeper theoretical understanding of the advantages of explicit knowledge; but as yet we do not even have a formal definition of the difference between model-based and model-free systems. All we have are some purported examples of each.

20.7   GENERALIZATION IN REINFORCEMENT LEARNING

EXPLICIT
REPRESENTATION

So far we have assumed that all the functions learned by the agents (U, M, R, Q) are represented in tabular form —that is, an **explicit representation** of one output value for each input tuple. Such an approach works reasonably well for small state spaces, but the time to convergence and (for ADP) the time per iteration increase rapidly as the space gets larger. With carefully controlled, approximate ADP methods, it may be possible to handle 10,000 states or more. This suffices for two-dimensional, maze-like environments, but more realistic worlds are out of the question. Chess and backgammon are tiny subsets of the real world, yet their state spaces contain on the order of 10^{50} to 10^{120} states. It would be absurd to suppose that one must visit all these states in order to learn how to play the game!

IMPLICIT
REPRESENTATION

The only way to handle such problems is to use an **implicit representation** of the function—a form that allows one to calculate the output for any input, but that is usually much more compact than the tabular form. For example, an estimated utility function for game playing can be represented as a weighted linear function of a set of board features $f_1, \ldots, f_n$:

$$U(i) = w_1 f_1(i) + w_2 f_2(i) + \cdots + w_n f_n(i)$$

Thus, instead of, say, 10^{120} values, the utility function is characterized by the n weights. A typical chess evaluation function might only have about 10 weights, so this is an *enormous* compression. *The compression achieved by an implicit representation allows the learning agent to generalize from states it has visited to states it has not visited.* That is, the most important aspect of an implicit representation is not that it takes up less space, but that it allows for inductive generalization over input states. For this reason, methods that learn such representations are said

INPUT
GENERALIZATION

to perform **input generalization**. To give you some idea of the power of input generalization: by examining only one in 10^{44} of the possible backgammon states, it is possible to learn a utility function that allows a program to play as well as any human (Tesauro, 1992).

On the flip side, of course, there is the problem that there may be no function in the chosen space of implicit representations that faithfully approximates the true utility function. As in all inductive learning, there is a trade-off between the size of the hypothesis space and the time it takes to learn the function. A larger hypothesis space increases the likelihood that a good approximation can be found, but also means that convergence is likely to be delayed.

Let us now consider exactly how the inductive learning problem should be formulated. We begin by considering how to learn utility and action-value functions, and then move on to learning the transition function for the environment.

In the LMS (least mean squares) approach, the formulation is straightforward. At the end of each training sequence, the LMS algorithm associates a reward-to-go with each state visited along the way. The ⟨*state, reward*⟩ pair can be used directly as a labelled example for any desired inductive learning algorithm. This yields a utility function $U(i)$.

It is also possible for a TD (temporal-difference) approach to apply inductive learning directly, once the U and/or Q tables have been replaced by implicit representations. The values that would be inserted into the tables by the update rules (20.2 and 20.7) can be used instead as labelled examples for a learning algorithm. The agent has to use the learned function on the next update, so the learning algorithm must be incremental.

One can also take advantage of the fact that the TD update rules provide small changes in the value of a given state. This is especially true if the function to be learned is characterized by a vector of weights **w** (as in linear weighted functions and neural networks). Rather than update a single tabulated value of U, as in Equation (20.2), we simply adjust the weights to try to reduce the temporal difference in U between successive states. Suppose that the parameterized utility function is $U_{\mathbf{w}}(i)$. Then after a transition $i \rightarrow j$, we apply the following update rule:

$$\mathbf{w} \leftarrow \mathbf{w} + \alpha[r + U_{\mathbf{w}}(j) - U_{\mathbf{w}}(i)]\nabla \mathbf{w} U_{\mathbf{w}}(i) \tag{20.8}$$

This form of updating performs gradient descent in weight space, trying to minimize the observed local error in the utility estimates. A similar update rule can be used for Q-learning (Exercise 20.9). Because the utility and action-value functions have real-valued outputs, neural networks and other continuous function representations are obvious candidates for the performance element. Decision-tree learning algorithms that provide real-valued output can also be used (see for MODEL TREES example Quinlan's (1993b) **model trees**), but cannot use the gradient descent method.

The formulation of the inductive learning problem for constructing a model of the environment is also very straightforward. Each transition provides the agent with the next state (at least in an accessible environment), so that labelled examples consist of a state-action pair as input and a state as output. It is not so easy, however, to find a suitable implicit representation for the model. In order to be useful for value and policy iteration and for the generation of pseudo-experiences in TD learning, the output state description must be sufficiently detailed to allow prediction of outcomes several steps ahead. Simple parametric forms cannot usually sustain this kind of reasoning. Instead, it may be necessary to learn general action models in the logical form used in Chapters 7 and 11. In a nondeterministic environment, one can use the conditional-probability-table representation of state evolution typical of dynamic belief networks (Section 17.5), in which generalization is achieved by describing the state in terms of a large set of features and using only sparse connections. Although model-based approaches have advantages in terms of their ability to learn value functions quickly, they are currently hampered by a lack of suitable inductive generalization methods for learning the model. It is also not obvious how methods such as value and policy iteration can be applied with a generalized model.

We now turn to examples of large-scale applications of reinforcement learning. We will see that in cases where a utility function (and hence a model) is used, the model is usually taken as given. For example, in learning an evaluation function for backgammon, it is normally assumed that the legal moves, and their effects, are known in advance.

Applications to game-playing

The first significant application of reinforcement learning was also the first significant learning program of any kind—the checker-playing program written by Arthur Samuel (1959; 1967). Samuel first used a weighted linear function for the evaluation of positions, using up to 16 terms at any one time. He applied a version of Equation (20.8) to update the weights. There were some significant differences, however, between his program and current methods. First, he updated the weights using the difference between the current state and the backed-up value generated by full lookahead in the search tree. This works fine, because it amounts to viewing the state space at a different granularity. A second difference was that the program did *not* use any observed rewards! That is, the values of terminal states were ignored. This means that it is quite possible for Samuel's program not to converge, or to converge on a strategy designed to lose rather than win. He managed to avoid this fate by insisting that the weight for material advantage should always be positive. Remarkably, this was sufficient to direct the program into areas of weight space corresponding to good checker play (see Chapter 5).

The TD-gammon system (Tesauro, 1992) forcefully illustrates the potential of reinforcement learning techniques. In earlier work (Tesauro and Sejnowski, 1989), Tesauro tried learning a neural network representation of $Q(a, i)$ directly from examples of moves labelled with relative values by a human expert. This approach proved extremely tedious for the expert. It resulted in a program, called Neurogammon, that was strong by computer standards but not competitive with human grandmasters. The TD-gammon project was an attempt to learn from self-play alone. The only reward signal was given at the end of each game. The evaluation function was represented by a fully connected neural network with a single hidden layer containing 40 nodes. Simply by repeated application of Equation (20.8), TD-gammon learned to play considerably better than Neurogammon, even though the input representation contained just the raw board position with no computed features. This took about 200,000 training games and two weeks of computer time. Although this may seem like a lot of games, it is only a vanishingly small fraction of the state space. When precomputed features were added to the input representation, a network with 80 hidden units was able, after 300,000 training games, to reach a standard of play comparable with the top three human players worldwide.

Application to robot control

CART-POLE

INVERTED
PENDULUM

The setup for the famous **cart-pole** balancing problem, also known as the **inverted pendulum**, is shown in Figure 20.14. The problem is to control the position x of the cart so that the pole stays roughly upright ($\theta \approx \pi/2$), while staying within the limits of the cart track as shown. This problem has been used as a test bed for research in control theory as well as reinforcement

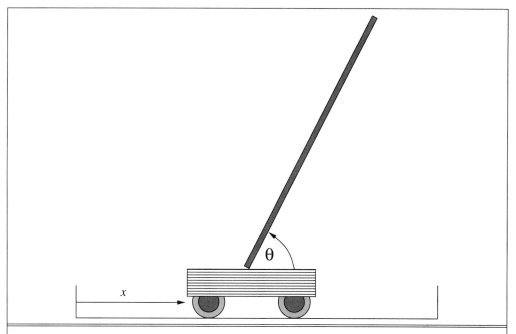

Figure 20.14   Setup for the problem of balancing a long pole on top of a moving cart. The cart can be jerked left or right by a controller that observes x, θ, $\dot{x}$, and $\dot{\theta}$.

BANG-BANG
CONTROL

learning, and over 200 papers have been published on it. The cart-pole problem differs from the problems described earlier in that the state variables x, θ, $\dot{x}$, and $\dot{\theta}$ are continuous. The actions are usually discrete—jerk left or jerk right, the so-called **bang-bang control** regime.

The earliest work on learning for this problem was carried out by Michie and Chambers (1968). Their BOXES algorithm was able to balance the pole for over an hour after only about 30 trials. Moreover, unlike many subsequent systems, BOXES was implemented using a real cart and pole, not a simulation. The algorithm first discretized the four-dimensional state space into boxes, hence the name. It then ran trials until the pole fell over or the cart hit the end of the track. Negative reinforcement was associated with the final action in the final box, and then propagated back through the sequence. It was found that the discretization causes some problems when the apparatus was initialized in a different position from those used in training, suggesting that generalization was not perfect. Improved generalization and faster learning can be obtained using an algorithm that *adaptively* partitions the state space according to the observed variation in the reward.

More recently, neural networks have been used to provide a continuous mapping from the state space to the actions, with slightly better results. The most impressive performance, however, belongs to the control algorithm derived using classical control theory for the *triple* inverted pendulum, in which three poles are balanced one on top of another with torque controls at the joints (Furuta *et al.*, 1984). (One is disappointed, but not surprised, that this algorithm was implemented only in simulation.)

20.8 GENETIC ALGORITHMS AND EVOLUTIONARY PROGRAMMING

Nature has a robust way of evolving successful organisms. The organisms that are ill-suited for an environment die off, whereas the ones that are fit live to reproduce. Offspring are similar to their parents, so each new generation has organisms that are similar to the fit members of the previous generation. If the environment changes slowly, the species can gradually evolve along with it, but a sudden change in the environment is likely to wipe out a species. Occasionally, random mutations occur, and although most of these mean a quick death for the mutated individual, some mutations lead to new successful species. The publication of Darwin's *The Origin of Species on the Basis of Natural Selection* was a major turning point in the history of science.

It turns out that what's good for nature is also good for artificial systems. Figure 20.15 shows the GENETIC-ALGORITHM, which starts with a set of one or more individuals and applies selection and reproduction operators to "evolve" an individual that is successful, as measured by

FITNESS FUNCTION

a **fitness function**. There are several choices for what the individuals are. They can be entire agent functions, in which case the fitness function is a performance measure or reward function, and the analogy to natural selection is greatest. They can be component functions of an agent, in which case the fitness function is the critic. Or they can be anything at all that can be framed as an optimization problem.

Since the evolutionary process learns an agent function based on occasional rewards (offspring) as supplied by the selection function, it can be seen as a form of reinforcement learning. Unlike the algorithms described in the previous sections, however, no attempt is made to learn the relationship between the rewards and the actions taken by the agent or the states of the environment. GENETIC-ALGORITHM simply searches directly in the space of individuals, with the goal of finding one that maximizes the fitness function. The search is parallel because each individual in the population can be seen as a separate search. It is hill climbing because we are making small genetic changes to the individuals and using the best resulting offspring. The key question is how to allocate the searching resources: clearly, we should spend most of our time on the most promising individuals, but if we ignore the low-scoring ones, we risk getting stuck on a local maximum. It can be shown that, under certain assumptions, the genetic algorithm allocates resources in an optimal way (see the discussion of n-armed bandits in, e.g., Goldberg (1989)).

Before we can apply GENETIC-ALGORITHM to a problem, we need to answer the following four questions:

- What is the fitness function?
- How is an individual represented?
- How are individuals selected?
- How do individuals reproduce?

The fitness function depends on the problem, but in any case, it is a function that takes an individual as input and returns a real number as output.

In the "classic" genetic algorithm approach, an individual is represented as a string over a

GENE

finite alphabet. Each element of the string is called a **gene**. In real DNA, the alphabet is AGTC (adenine, guanine, thymine, cytosine), but in genetic algorithms, we usually use the binary alphabet (0,1). Some authors reserve the term "genetic algorithm" for cases where the representation

---

function GENETIC-ALGORITHM(*population*, FITNESS-FN) **returns** an individual
   inputs: *population*, a set of individuals
          FITNESS-FN, a function that measures the fitness of an individual

   repeat
      parents ← SELECTION(*population*, FITNESS-FN)
      population ← REPRODUCTION(*parents*)
   until some individual is fit enough
   return the best individual in *population*, according to FITNESS-FN

Figure 20.15   The genetic algorithm finds a fit individual using simulated evolution.

EVOLUTIONARY
PROGRAMMING

is a bit string, and use the term **evolutionary programming** when the representation is more complicated. Other authors make no distinction, or make a slightly different one.

The selection strategy is usually randomized, with the probability of selection proportional to fitness. That is, if individual X scores twice as high as Y on the fitness function, then X is twice as likely to be selected for reproduction than is Y. Usually, selection is done with replacement, so that a very fit individual will get to reproduce several times.

Reproduction is accomplished by cross-over and mutation. First, all the individuals that have been selected for reproduction are randomly paired. Then for each pair, a cross-over point is randomly chosen. Think of the genes of each parent as being numbered from 1 to N. The

CROSS-OVER

cross-over point is a number in that range; let us say it is 10. That means that one offspring will get genes 1 through 10 from the first parent, and the rest from the second parent. The second offspring will get genes 1 through 10 from the second parent, and the rest from the

MUTATION

first. However, each gene can be altered by random **mutation** to a different value, with small independent probability. Figure 20.16 diagrams the process.

For example, suppose we are trying to learn a decision list representation for the restaurant waiting problem (see page 556). The fitness function in this case is simply the number of examples that an individual is consistent with. The representation is the tricky part. There are ten attributes in the problem, but not all of them are binary. It turns out that we need 5 bits to represent each distinct attribute/value pair:

      $00000 : Alternate(x)$
      $00001 : \neg Alternate(x)$

      $\vdots$

      $10111 : WaitEstimate(x, 0{-}10)$
      $11000 : WaitEstimate(x, 10{-}30)$
      $11001 : WaitEstimate(x, 30{-}60)$
      $11010 : WaitEstimate(x, {>}60)$

We also need one bit for each test to say if the outcome is *Yes* or *No*. Thus, if we want to represent a k-DL with a length of up to t tests, we need a representation with $t(5k + 1)$ bits. We can use the standard selection and reproduction approaches. Mutation can flip an outcome or change an attribute. Cross-over combines the head of one decision list with the tail of another.

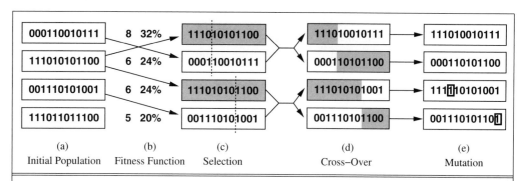

000110010111	8 32%	110‚10101100	111010010111	111010010111
111010101100	6 24%	0001‚10010111	000110101100	000110101100
001110101001	6 24%	111010101100	111010101001	111◻10101001
111011011100	5 20%	001110101001	001110101100	001110101100◻
(a) Initial Population	(b) Fitness Function	(c) Selection	(d) Cross–Over	(e) Mutation

Figure 20.16   The genetic algorithm. In (a), we have an initial population of 4 individuals. They are scored by the fitness function in (b); the top individual scores an 8 and the bottom scores a 5. It works out that the top individual has a 32% chance of being chosen on each selection. In (c), selection has given us two pairs of mates, and the cross-over points (dotted lines) have been chosen. Notice that one individual mates twice; one not at all. In (d), we see the new offspring, generated by cross-over of their parents' genes. Finally, in (e), mutation has changed the two bits surrounded by boxes. This gives us the population for the next generation.

Like neural networks, genetic algorithms are easy to apply to a wide range of problems. The results can be very good on some problems, and rather poor on others. In fact, Denker's remark that "neural networks are the second best way of doing just about anything" has been extended with "and genetic algorithms are the third." But don't be afraid to try a quick implementation of a genetic algorithm on a new problem—just to see if it does work—before investing more time thinking about another approach.

20.9   SUMMARY

This chapter has examined the reinforcement learning problem—how an agent can become proficient in an unknown environment given only its percepts and occasional rewards. Reinforcement learning can be viewed as a microcosm for the entire AI problem, but is studied in a number of simplified settings to facilitate progress. The following major points were made:

- The overall agent design dictates the kind of information that must be learned. The two main designs studied are the model-based design, using a model M and a utility function U, and the model-free approach, using an action-value function Q.

- The utility of a state is the expected sum of rewards received between now and termination of the sequence.

- Utilities can be learned using three approaches.

  1. The LMS (least-mean-square) approach uses the total observed reward-to-go for a given state as direct evidence for learning its utility. LMS uses the model only for the purposes of selecting actions.

2. The ADP (adaptive dynamic programming) approach uses the value or policy iteration algorithm to calculate exact utilities of states given an estimated model. ADP makes optimal use of the local constraints on utilities of states imposed by the neighborhood structure of the environment.

3. The TD (temporal-difference) approach updates utility estimates to match those of successor states, and can be viewed as a simple approximation to the ADP approach that requires no model for the learning process. Using the model to generate pseudo-experiences can, however, result in faster learning.

- Action-value functions, or Q-functions, can be learned by an ADP approach or a TD approach. With TD, Q-learning requires no model in either the learning or action-selection phases. This simplifies the learning problem but potentially restricts the ability to learn in complex environments.

- When the learning agent is responsible for selecting actions while it learns, it must trade off the estimated value of those actions against the potential for learning useful new information. Exact solution of the exploration problem is infeasible, but some simple heuristics do a reasonable job.

- In large state spaces, reinforcement learning algorithms must use an implicit functional representation in order to perform input generalization over states. The temporal-difference signal can be used directly to direct weight changes in parametric representations such as neural networks.

- Combining input generalization with an explicit model has resulted in excellent performance in complex domains.

- Genetic algorithms achieve reinforcement learning by using the reinforcement to increase the proportion of successful functions in a population of programs. They achieve the effect of generalization by mutating and cross-breeding programs with each other.

Because of its potential for eliminating hand coding of control strategies, reinforcement learning continues to be one of the most active areas of machine learning research. Applications in robotics promise to be particularly valuable. As yet, however, there is little understanding of how to extend these methods to the more powerful performance elements described in earlier chapters. Reinforcement learning in *inaccessible* environments is also a topic of current research.

BIBLIOGRAPHICAL AND HISTORICAL NOTES

Arthur Samuel's work (1959) was probably the earliest successful machine learning research. Although this work was informal and had a number of flaws, it contained most of the modern ideas in reinforcement learning, including temporal differencing and input generalization. Around the same time, researchers in adaptive control theory (Widrow and Hoff, 1960), building on work by Hebb (1949), were training simple networks using the LMS rule. (This early connection between neural networks and reinforcement learning may have led to the persistent misperception that the latter is a subfield of the former.) The cart-pole work of Michie and Chambers (1968) can also be seen as a reinforcement learning method with input generalization.

A more recent tradition springs from work at the University of Massachusetts in the early 1980s (Barto *et al.*, 1981). The paper by Sutton (1988) reinvigorated reinforcement learning research in AI, and provides a good historical overview. The Ph.D. theses by Watkins (1989) and Kaelbling (1990) and the survey by Barto *et al.* (1991) also contain good reviews of the field. Watkin's thesis originated Q-learning, and proved its convergence in the limit. Some recent work appears in a special issue of *Machine Learning* (Vol. 8, Nos. 3/4, 1992), with an excellent introduction by Sutton. The presentation in this chapter is heavily influenced by Moore and Atkeson (1993), who make a clear connection between temporal differencing and classical dynamic programming techniques. The latter paper also introduced the idea of prioritized sweeping. An almost identical method was developed independently by Peng and Williams (1993). Bandit problems, which model the problem of exploration, are analyzed in depth by Berry and Fristedt (1985).

Reinforcement learning in games has also undergone a renaissance in recent years. In addition to Tesauro's work, a world-class Othello system was developed by Lee and Mahajan (1988). Reinforcement learning papers are published frequently in the journal *Machine Learning*, and in the International Conferences on Machine Learning.

Genetic algorithms originated in the work of Friedberg (1958), who attempted to produce learning by mutating small FORTRAN programs. Since most mutations to the programs produced inoperative code, little progress was made. John Holland (1975) reinvigorated the field by using bit-string representations of agents such that any possible string represented a functioning agent. John Koza (1992) has championed more complex representations of agents coupled with mutation and mating techniques that pay careful attention to the syntax of the representation language. Current research appears in the annual Conference on Evolutionary Programming.

EXERCISES

20.1   Show that the estimates developed by the LMS-UPDATE algorithm do indeed minimize the mean square error on the training data.

20.2   Implement a passive learning agent in a simple environment, such as that shown in Figure 20.1. For the case of an initially unknown environment model, compare the learning performance of the LMS, TD, and ADP algorithms.

20.3   Starting with the passive ADP agent, modify it to use an approximate ADP algorithm as discussed in the text. Do this in two steps:

  a. Implement a priority queue for adjustments to the utility estimates. Whenever a state is adjusted, all of its predecessors also become candidates for adjustment, and should be added to the queue. The queue is initialized using the state from which the most recent transition took place. Change ADP-UPDATE to allow only a fixed number of adjustments.

  b. Experiment with various heuristics for ordering the priority queue, examining their effect on learning rates and computation time.

20.4   The environments used in the chapter all assume that training sequences are finite. In environments with no clear termination point, the unlimited accumulation of rewards can lead to problems with infinite utilities. To avoid this, a discount factor γ is often used, where $\gamma < 1$. A reward k steps in the future is discounted by a factor of γ^k. For each constraint and update equation in the chapter, explain how to incorporate the discount factor.

20.5   The description of reinforcement learning agents in Section 20.1 uses distinguished terminal states to indicate the end of a training sequence. Explain how this additional complication could be eliminated by modelling the "reset" as a transition like any other. How will this affect the definition of utility?

20.6   Prove formally that Equations (20.1) and (20.3) are consistent with the definition of utility as the expected reward-to-go of a state.

20.7   How can the value determination algorithm be used to calculate the expected loss experienced by an agent using a given set of utility estimates U and an estimated model M, compared to an agent using correct values?

20.8   Adapt the vacuum world (Chapter 2) for reinforcement learning by including rewards for picking up each piece of dirt and for getting home and switching off. Make the world accessible by providing suitable percepts. Now experiment with different reinforcement learning agents. Is input generalization necessary for success?

20.9   Write down the update equation for Q-learning with a parameterized implicit representation. That is, write the counterpart to Equation (20.8).

 20.10   Extend the standard game-playing environment (Chapter 5) to incorporate a reward signal. Put two reinforcement learning agents into the environment (they may of course share the agent program) and have them play against each other. Apply the generalized TD update rule (Equation (20.8)) to update the evaluation function. You may wish to start with a simple linear weighted evaluation function, and a simple game such as tic-tac-toe.

20.11   (Discussion topic.) Is reinforcement learning an appropriate abstract model for human learning? For evolution?

21 KNOWLEDGE IN LEARNING

In which we examine the problem of learning when you already know something.

In all of the approaches to learning described in the previous three chapters, the idea is to construct a program that has the input/output behavior observed in the data. We have seen how this general problem can be solved for simple logical representations, for neural networks, and for belief networks. In each case, the learning methods can be understood as searching a hypothesis space to find a suitable program. The learning methods also made few assumptions, if any, concerning the nature of the correct program. In this chapter, we go beyond these approaches to study PRIOR KNOWLEDGE learning methods that can take advantage of **prior knowledge** about the environment. We also examine learning algorithms that can learn general first-order logical theories. These are essential steps toward a truly autonomous intelligent agent.

21.1 KNOWLEDGE IN LEARNING

We begin by examining the ways in which prior knowledge can get into the act. In order to do this, it will help to have a general *logical* formulation of the learning problem, as opposed to the *function-learning* characterization of pure inductive inference given in Section 18.2. The reason that a logical characterization is helpful is that it provides a very natural way to specify *partial* information about the function to be learned. This is analogous to the distinction between problem solving (which uses a "black-box" functional view of states and goals) and planning (which opens up the black boxes and uses logical descriptions of states and actions).

Recall from Section 18.5 that examples are composed of descriptions and classifications. The object of inductive learning in the logical setting is to find a hypothesis that explains the classifications of the examples, given their descriptions. We can make this logically precise as follows. If we use *Descriptions* to denote the conjunction of all the example descriptions, and *Classifications* to denote the conjunction of all the example classifications, then the *Hypothesis* must satisfy the following property:

$$Hypothesis \wedge Descriptions \models Classifications \tag{21.1}$$

We call this kind of relationship an **entailment constraint**, in which *Hypothesis* is the "unknown." Pure inductive learning means solving this constraint, where *Hypothesis* is drawn from some predefined hypothesis space. For example, if we consider a decision tree as a logical formula (see page 532), then a decision tree that is consistent with all the examples will satisfy Equation (21.1). If we place *no* restrictions on the logical form of the hypothesis, of course, then *Hypothesis = Classifications* also satisfies the constraint. Normally, Ockham's razor tells us to prefer *small*, consistent hypotheses, so we try to do better than simply memorizing the examples.

This simple picture of inductive learning persisted until the early 1980s. The modern approach is to design agents that *already know something* and are trying to learn some more. This may not sound like a terrifically deep insight, but it makes quite a difference to the way in which we write programs. It might also have some relevance to our theories about how science itself works. The general idea is shown schematically in Figure 21.1.

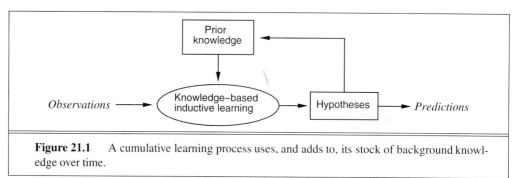

Figure 21.1   A cumulative learning process uses, and adds to, its stock of background knowledge over time.

If we want to build an autonomous learning agent that uses background knowledge, the agent must have some method for obtaining the background knowledge in the first place, in order for it to be used in the new learning episodes. This method must itself be a learning process. The agent's life history will therefore be characterized by *cumulative*, or *incremental*, development. Presumably, the agent could start out with nothing, performing inductions *in vacuo* like a good little pure induction program. But once it has eaten from the Tree of Knowledge, it can no longer pursue such naive speculations, and should use its background knowledge to learn more and more effectively. The question is then how to actually do this.

Some simple examples

Let us consider some commonsense examples of learning with background knowledge. Many apparently rational cases of inferential behavior in the face of observations clearly do not follow the simple principles of pure induction.

- Sometimes one leaps to general conclusions after only one observation. Gary Larson once drew a cartoon in which a bespectacled caveman, Zog, is roasting his lizard on the end of a pointed stick. He is watched by an amazed crowd of his less intellectual contemporaries, who have been using their bare hands to hold their victuals over the fire. This enlightening experience is enough to convince the watchers of a general principle of painless cooking.

- Or consider the case of the traveller to Brazil meeting her first Brazilian. On hearing him speak Portuguese, she immediately concludes that Brazilians speak Portuguese, yet on discovering that his name is Fernando, she does not conclude that all Brazilians are called Fernando. Similar examples appear in science. For example, when a freshman physics student measures the density and conductance of a sample of copper at a particular temperature, she is quite confident in generalizing those values to all pieces of copper. Yet when she measures its mass, she does not even consider the hypothesis that all pieces of copper have that mass. On the other hand, it would be quite reasonable to make such a generalization over all pennies.

- Finally, consider the case of a pharmacologically ignorant but diagnostically sophisticated medical student observing a consulting session between a patient and an expert internist. After a series of questions and answers, the expert tells the patient to take a course of a particular antibiotic. The medical student infers the general rule that that particular antibiotic is effective for a particular type of infection.

These are all cases in which *the use of background knowledge allows much faster learning than one might expect from a pure induction program.*

Some general schemes

In each of the preceding examples, one can appeal to prior knowledge to try to justify the generalizations chosen. We will now look at what kinds of entailment constraints are operating in each of these cases. The constraints will involve the *Background* knowledge, in addition to the *Hypothesis* and the observed *Descriptions* and *Classifications*.

In the case of lizard toasting, the cavemen generalize by *explaining* the success of the pointed stick: it supports the lizard while keeping the hand intact. From this explanation, they can infer a general rule: that any long, thin, rigid, sharp object can be used to toast small, soft-bodied edibles. This kind of generalization process has been called **explanation-based learning**, or **EBL**. Notice that the general rule *follows logically* from the background knowledge possessed by the cavemen. Hence, the entailment constraints satisfied by EBL are the following:

EXPLANATION-BASED LEARNING

$$Hypothesis \wedge Descriptions \models Classifications$$
$$Background \models Hypothesis$$

The first constraint looks the same as Equation (21.1), so EBL was initially thought to be a better way to learn from examples. But because it requires that the background knowledge be sufficient to explain the *Hypothesis*, which in turn explains the observations, the agent does not actually learn anything *factually new* from the instance. The agent *could have* derived the example from what it already knew, although that might have required an unreasonable amount of computation. EBL is now viewed as a method for converting first-principles theories into useful, special-purpose knowledge. We describe algorithms for EBL in Section 21.2.

The situation of our traveller in Brazil is quite different. For she cannot necessarily explain why Fernando speaks the way he does, unless she knows her Papal bulls. But the same generalization would be forthcoming from a traveller entirely ignorant of colonial history. The relevant prior knowledge in this case is that, within any given country, most people tend to speak the same language; on the other hand, Fernando is not assumed to be the name of all Brazilians because this kind of regularity does not hold for names. Similarly, the freshman physics student also would be hard put to explain the particular values that she discovers for the conductance and density of copper. She does know, however, that the material of which an object is composed and its temperature together determine its conductance. In each case, the prior knowledge *Background* concerns the **relevance** of a set of features to the goal predicate. This knowledge, *together with the observations*, allows the agent to infer a new, general rule that explains the observations:

RELEVANCE

$$Hypothesis \wedge Descriptions \models Classifications$$
$$Background \wedge Descriptions \wedge Classifications \models Hypothesis \tag{21.2}$$

RELEVANCE-BASED
LEARNING

We call this kind of generalization **relevance-based learning**, or **RBL** (although the name is not standard). Notice that whereas RBL does make use of the content of the observations, it does not produce hypotheses that go beyond the logical content of the background knowledge and the observations. It is a *deductive* form of learning, and cannot by itself account for the creation of new knowledge starting from scratch. We discuss applications of RBL in Section 21.3.

In the case of the medical student watching the expert, we assume that the student's prior knowledge is sufficient to infer the patient's disease D from the symptoms. This is not, however, enough to explain the fact that the doctor prescribes a particular medicine M. The student needs to propose another rule, namely, that M generally is effective against D. Given this rule, and the student's prior knowledge, the student can now explain why the expert prescribes M in this particular case. We can generalize this example to come up with the entailment constraint:

$$Background \wedge Hypothesis \wedge Descriptions \models Classifications \tag{21.3}$$

KNOWLEDGE-BASED
INDUCTIVE
LEARNING

INDUCTIVE LOGIC
PROGRAMMING

That is, *the background knowledge and the new hypothesis combine to explain the examples.* As with pure inductive learning, the learning algorithm should propose hypotheses that are as simple as possible, consistent with this constraint. Algorithms that satisfy constraint 21.3 are called **knowledge-based inductive learning**, or **KBIL**, algorithms.

KBIL algorithms, which are described in detail in Section 21.4, have been studied mainly in the field of **inductive logic programming** or **ILP**. In ILP systems, prior knowledge plays two key roles in reducing the complexity of learning:

1. Because any hypothesis generated must be consistent with the prior knowledge as well as with the new observations, the effective hypothesis space size is reduced to include only those theories that are consistent with what is already known.

2. For any given set of observations, the size of the hypothesis required to construct an explanation for the observations can be much reduced, because the prior knowledge will be available to help out the new rules in explaining the observations. The smaller the hypothesis, the easier it is to find.

In addition to allowing the use of prior knowledge in induction, ILP systems can formulate hypotheses in general first-order logic, rather than the restricted languages used in Chapter 18. This means that they can learn in environments that cannot be understood by simpler systems.

21.2   EXPLANATION-BASED LEARNING

As we explained in the introduction to this chapter, explanation-based learning is a method for extracting general rules from individual observations. As an example, consider the problem of differentiating and simplifying algebraic expressions (Exercise 10.4). If we differentiate an expression such as X^2 with respect to X, we obtain $2X$. (Notice that we use a capital letter for the arithmetic unknown X, to distinguish it from the logical variable x.) In a logical reasoning system, the goal might be expressed as ASK($Derivative(X^2, X) = d$, KB), with solution $d = 2X$.

We can see this solution "by inspection" because we have many years of practice in solving such problems. A student encountering such problems for the first time, or a program with no experience, will have a much more difficult job. Application of the standard rules of differentiation eventually yields the expression $1 \times (2 \times (X^{(2-1)}))$, and eventually this simplifies to $2X$. In the authors' logic programming implementation, this takes 136 proof steps, of which 99 are on dead-end branches in the proof. After such an experience, we would like the program to solve the same problem much more quickly the next time.

MEMOIZATION

The technique of **memoization** has long been used in computer science to speed up programs by saving the results of computation. The basic idea of memo functions is to accumulate a database of input/output pairs; when the function is called, it first checks the database to see if it can avoid solving the problem from scratch. Explanation-based learning takes this a good deal further, by creating *general* rules that cover an entire class of cases. In the case of differentiation, memoization would remember that the derivative of X^2 with respect to X is $2X$, but would leave the agent to calculate the derivative of Z^2 with respect to Z from scratch. We would like to be able to extract the general rule[1] that for any arithmetic unknown u, the derivative of u^2 with respect to u is $2u$. In logical terms, this is expressed by the rule

$$ArithmeticUnknown(u) \;\Rightarrow\; Derivative(u^2, u) = 2u$$

If the knowledge base contains such a rule, then any new case that is an instance of this rule can be solved immediately.

This is, of course, merely a trivial example of a very general phenomenon. Once something is understood, it can be generalized and reused in other circumstances. It becomes an "obvious" step, and can then be used as a building block in solving still more complex problems. Alfred North Whitehead (1911), co-author with Bertrand Russell of *Principia Mathematica*, wrote that *"Civilization advances by extending the number of important operations that we can do without thinking about them,"* perhaps himself applying EBL to his understanding of events such as Zog's discovery. If you have understood the basic idea of the differentiation example, then your brain is already busily trying to extract the general principles of explanation-based learning from it. Notice that unless you are a good deal smarter than the authors, you hadn't *already* invented EBL before we showed you an example of it. Like the cavemen watching Zog, you (and we) needed an example before we could generate the basic principles. This is because *explaining why* something is a good idea is much easier than coming up with the idea in the first place.

---

[1] Of course, a general rule for u^n can also be produced, but the current example suffices to make the point.

Extracting general rules from examples

The basic idea behind EBL is first to construct an explanation of the observation using prior knowledge, and then to establish a definition of the class of cases for which the same explanation structure can be used. This definition provides the basis for a rule covering all of the cases in the class. The "explanation" can be a logical proof, but more generally it can be any reasoning or problem-solving process whose steps are well-defined. The key is to be able to identify the necessary conditions for those same steps to apply to another case.

We will use for our reasoning system the simple backward-chaining theorem prover described in Chapter 9. The proof tree for $Derivative(X^2, X) = d$ is too large to use as an example, so we will use a somewhat simpler problem to illustrate the generalization method. Suppose our problem is to simplify $1 \times (0 + X)$. The knowledge base includes the following rules:

$$Rewrite(u, v) \wedge Simplify(v, w) \Rightarrow Simplify(u, w)$$
$$Primitive(u) \Rightarrow Simplify(u, u)$$
$$ArithmeticUnknown(u) \Rightarrow Primitive(u)$$
$$Number(u) \Rightarrow Primitive(u)$$
$$Rewrite(1 \times u, u)$$
$$Rewrite(0 + u, u)$$
$$\vdots$$

The proof that the answer is X is shown in the top half of Figure 21.2. The EBL method actually constructs two proof trees simultaneously. The second proof tree uses a *variabilized* goal in which the constants from the original goal are replaced by variables. As the original proof proceeds, the variabilized proof proceeds using *exactly the same rule applications*. This may cause some of the variables to become instantiated. For example, in order to use the rule $Rewrite(1 \times u, u)$, the variable x in the subgoal $Rewrite(x \times (y + z), v)$ must be bound to 1. Similarly, y must be bound to 0 in the subgoal $Rewrite(y + z, v')$ in order to use the rule $Rewrite(0 + u, u)$.

Once we have the generalized proof tree, we take the leaves (with the necessary bindings) and form a general rule for the goal predicate:

$$Rewrite(1 \times (0 + z), 0 + z) \wedge Rewrite(0 + z, z) \wedge ArithmeticUnknown(z)$$
$$\Rightarrow Simplify(1 \times (0 + z), z)$$

Notice that the first two conditions on the left-hand side are true *regardless of the value of z*. We can therefore drop them from the rule, yielding

$$ArithmeticUnknown(z) \Rightarrow Simplify(1 \times (0 + z), z)$$

In general, conditions can be dropped from the final rule if they impose no constraints on the variables on the right-hand side of the rule, because the resulting rule will still be true and will be more efficient. Notice that we cannot drop the condition $ArithmeticUnknown(z)$, because not all possible values of z are arithmetic unknowns. Values other than arithmetic unknowns might require different forms of simplification— for example, if z were 2×3, then the correct simplification of $1 \times (0 + (2 \times 3))$ would be 6 and not 2×3.

To recap, the basic EBL process works as follows:

1. Given an example, construct a proof that the goal predicate applies to the example using the available background knowledge.

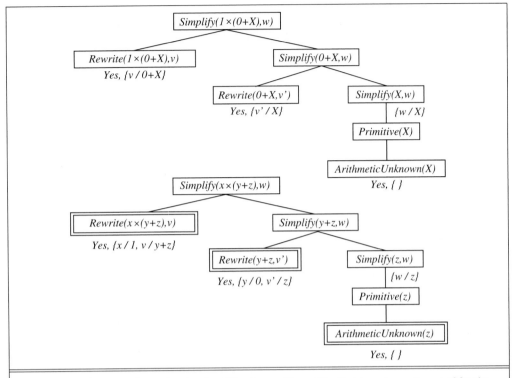

Figure 21.2   Proof trees for the simplification problem. The first tree shows the proof for the original problem instance. The second shows the proof for a problem instance with all constants replaced by variables.

2. In parallel, construct a generalized proof tree for the variabilized goal using the same inference steps as in the original proof.

3. Construct a new rule whose left-hand side consists of the leaves of the proof tree, and whose right-hand side is the variabilized goal (after applying the necessary bindings from the generalized proof).

4. Drop any conditions that are true regardless of the values of the variables in the goal.

Improving efficiency

Examining the generalized proof tree in Figure 21.2, we see that there is more than one generalized rule that can be extracted from the tree. For example, if we terminate, or **prune**, the growth of the right-hand branch in the proof tree when it reaches the *Primitive* step, we get the rule

$$Primitive(z) \ \Rightarrow \ Simplify(1 \times (0 + z), z)$$

This rule is equally valid, but also *more general* than the rule using *ArithmeticUnknown*, because it covers cases where z is a number. We can extract a still more general rule by pruning after the step $Simplify(y + z, w)$, yielding the rule

$$Simplify(y + z, w) \Rightarrow Simplify(1 \times (y + z), w)$$

In general, a rule can be extracted from *any partial subtree* of the generalized proof tree. Now we have a problem: which of these rules do we choose?

The choice of which rule to generate comes down to the question of efficiency. There are three factors involved in the analysis of efficiency gains from EBL:

1. Adding large numbers of rules to a knowledge base can slow down the reasoning process, because the inference mechanism must still check those rules even in cases where they do not yield a solution. In other words, it increases the **branching factor** in the search space.

2. To compensate for this, the derived rules must offer significant increases in speed for the cases that they do cover. This mainly comes about because the derived rules avoid dead ends that would otherwise be taken, as well as shortening the proof itself.

3. Derived rules should also be as general as possible, so that they apply to the largest possible set of cases.

OPERATIONALITY   A common approach to ensuring that derived rules are efficient is to insist on the **operationality** of each subgoal in the rule. A subgoal is operational, roughly speaking, if it is "easy" to solve. For example, the subgoal $Primitive(z)$ is easy to solve, requiring at most two steps, whereas the subgoal $Simplify(y + z, w)$ could lead to an arbitrary amount of inference, depending on the values of y and z. If a test for operationality is carried out at each step in the construction of the generalized proof, then we can prune the rest of a branch as soon as an operational subgoal is found, keeping just the operational subgoal as a conjunct of the new rule.

Unfortunately, there is usually a trade-off between operationality and generality. More specific subgoals are usually easier to solve but cover fewer cases. Also, operationality is a matter of degree; one or two steps is definitely operational, but what about 10, or 100? Finally, the cost of solving a given subgoal depends on what other rules are available in the knowledge base. It can go up or down as more rules are added. Thus, EBL systems really face a very complex optimization problem in trying to maximize the efficiency of a given initial knowledge base. It is sometimes possible to derive a mathematical model of the effect on overall efficiency of adding a given rule, and to use this model to select the best rule to add. The analysis can become very complicated, however, especially when recursive rules are involved. One promising approach is to address the problem of efficiency empirically, simply by adding several rules and seeing which ones are useful and actually speed things up.

 The idea of empirical analysis of efficiency is actually at the heart of EBL. What we have been calling loosely the "efficiency of a given knowledge base" is actually the average-case complexity on a population of problems that the agent will have to solve. *By generalizing from past example problems, EBL makes the knowledge base more efficient for the kind of problems that it is reasonable to expect.* This works as long as the distribution of past examples is roughly the same as for future examples—the same assumption used for PAC-learning in Section 18.6. If the EBL system is carefully engineered, it is possible to obtain very significant improvements on future problems. In a very large Prolog-based natural language system designed for real-time speech-to-speech translation between Swedish and English, Samuelsson and Rayner (1991) report that EBL made the system more than 1200 times faster.

21.3   LEARNING USING RELEVANCE INFORMATION

Our traveller in Brazil seems to be able to make a confident generalization concerning the language spoken by other Brazilians. The inference is sanctioned by her background knowledge, namely, that people in a given country (usually) speak the same language. We can express this in first-order logic as follows:[2]

$$\forall x, y, n, l \quad Nationality(x, n) \land Nationality(y, n) \land Language(x, l) \Rightarrow Language(y, l) \quad (21.4)$$

(Literal translation: "If x and y have a common nationality n and x speaks language l, then y also speaks it.") It is not difficult to show that, given this sentence and the observation

$$Nationality(Fernando, Brazil) \land Language(Fernando, Portuguese)$$

the conclusion

$$\forall x \quad Nationality(x, Brazil) \Rightarrow Language(x, Portuguese)$$

follows logically (see Exercise 21.1).

Sentences such as (21.4) express a strict form of relevance: given nationality, language is fully determined. Put another way: language is a function of nationality. These sentences are called **functional dependencies** or **determinations**. They occur so commonly in certain kinds of applications (e.g., defining database designs) that a special syntax is used to write them. We adopt the notation used by Davies (1985):

$$Nationality(x, n) \succ Language(x, l)$$

As usual, this is simply a syntactic sugaring, but it makes it clear that the determination is really a relationship between the predicates: nationality determines language. The relevant properties determining conductance and density can be expressed similarly:

$$Material(x, m) \land Temperature(x, t) \succ Conductance(x, \rho)$$
$$Material(x, m) \land Temperature(x, t) \succ Density(x, d)$$

The corresponding generalizations follow logically from the determinations and observations.

Determining the hypothesis space

Although the determinations sanction general conclusions concerning all Brazilians, or all pieces of copper at a given temperature, they cannot, of course, yield a general predictive theory for *all* nationalities, or for *all* temperatures and materials, from a single example. Their main effect can be seen as limiting the space of hypotheses that the learning agent need consider. In predicting conductance, for example, one has only to consider material and temperature and can ignore mass, ownership, day of the week, the current president, and so on. Hypotheses can certainly include terms that are in turn determined by material and temperature, such as molecular structure, thermal energy, or free-electron density. *Determinations specify a sufficient basis vocabulary*

---

2   We assume for the sake of simplicity that a person speaks only one language. Clearly, the rule also would have to be amended for countries such as Switzerland or India.

from which to construct hypotheses concerning the target predicate. This statement can be proved by showing that a given determination is logically equivalent to a statement that the correct definition of the target predicate is one of the set of all definitions expressible using the predicates in the left-hand side of the determination.

Intuitively, it is clear that a reduction in the hypothesis space size should make it easier to learn the target predicate. Using the basic results of computational learning theory (Section 18.6), we can quantify the possible gains. First, recall that for Boolean functions, $\log(|\mathbf{H}|)$ examples are required to converge to a reasonable hypothesis, where $|\mathbf{H}|$ is the size of the hypothesis space. If the learner has n Boolean features with which to construct hypotheses, then, in the absence of further restrictions, $|\mathbf{H}| = O(2^{2^n})$, so the number of examples is $O(2^n)$. If the determination contains d predicates in the left-hand side, the learner will require only $O(2^d)$ examples, a reduction of $O(2^{n-d})$. For biased hypothesis spaces, such as a conjunctively biased space, the reduction will be less dramatic but still significant.

Learning and using relevance information

As we stated in the introduction to this chapter, prior knowledge is useful in learning, but it also has to be learned. In order to provide a complete story of relevance-based learning, we must therefore provide a learning algorithm for determinations. The learning algorithm we now present is based on a straightforward attempt to find the simplest determination consistent with the observations. A determination $P \succ Q$ says that if any examples match on P, then they must also match on Q. A determination is therefore consistent with a set of examples if every pair that matches on the predicates on the left-hand side also matches on the target predicate, that is, has the same classification. For example, suppose we have the following examples of conductance measurements on material samples:

Sample	Mass	Temperature	Material	Size	Conductance
S1	12	26	Copper	3	0.59
S1	12	100	Copper	3	0.57
S2	24	26	Copper	6	0.59
S3	12	26	Lead	2	0.05
S3	12	100	Lead	2	0.04
S4	24	26	Lead	4	0.05

The minimal consistent determination is *Material* $\wedge$ *Temperature* $\succ$ *Conductance*. There is a nonminimal but consistent determination, namely, *Mass* $\wedge$ *Size* $\wedge$ *Temperature* $\succ$ *Conductance*. This is consistent with the examples because mass and size determine density, and in our data set, we do not have two different materials with the same density. As usual, we would need a larger sample set in order to eliminate a nearly correct hypothesis.

There are several possible algorithms for finding minimal consistent determinations. The most obvious approach is to conduct a search through the space of determinations, checking all determinations with one predicate, two predicates, and so on, until a consistent determination is found. We will assume a simple attribute-based representation, like that used for decision-tree learning in Chapter 18. A determination d will be represented by the set of attributes on the left-hand side, because the target predicate is assumed fixed. The basic algorithm is outlined in Figure 21.3.

---

function MINIMAL-CONSISTENT-DET(E, A) **returns** a determination
  inputs: E, a set of examples
        A, a set of attributes, of size n

  for $i \leftarrow 0, \ldots, n$ **do**
    for each subset A_i of A of size i **do**
      if CONSISTENT-DET?(A_i, E) **then return** A_i
    end
  end

---

function CONSISTENT-DET?(A, E) **returns** a truth-value
  inputs: A, a set of attributes
        E, a set of examples
  local variables: H, a hash table

  for each example e **in** E **do**
    if some example in H has the same values as e for the attributes A
      but a different classification **then return** *False*
    store the class of e in H, indexed by the values for attributes A of the example e
  end
  return *True*

Figure 21.3   An algorithm for finding a minimal consistent determination.

The time complexity of this algorithm depends on the size of the smallest consistent determination. Suppose this determination has p attributes out of the n total attributes. Then the algorithm will not find it until searching the subsets of A of size p. There are $\binom{n}{p} = O(n^p)$ such subsets, hence the algorithm is exponential in the size of the minimal determination. It turns out that the problem is NP-complete, so we cannot expect to do better in the general case. In most domains, however, there will be sufficient local structure (see Chapter 15 for a definition of locally structured domains) such that p will be small.

Given an algorithm for learning determinations, a learning agent has a way to construct a minimal hypothesis within which to learn the target predicate. We can combine MINIMAL-CONSISTENT-DET with the DECISION-TREE-LEARNING algorithm, for example, in order to create a relevance-based decision-tree learning algorithm RBDTL:

---

function RBDTL(E,A,v) **returns** a decision tree

  return DECISION-TREE-LEARNING(E,MINIMAL-CONSISTENT-DET(E,A),v)

Unlike DECISION-TREE-LEARNING, RBDTL simultaneously learns and uses relevance information in order to minimize its hypothesis space. We expect that RBDTL's learning curve will show
some improvement over the learning curve achieved by DECISION-TREE-LEARNING, and this is
in fact the case. Figure 21.4 shows the learning performance for the two algorithms on randomly
generated data for a function that depends on only 5 of 16 attributes. Obviously, in cases where
all the available attributes are relevant, RBDTL will show no advantage.

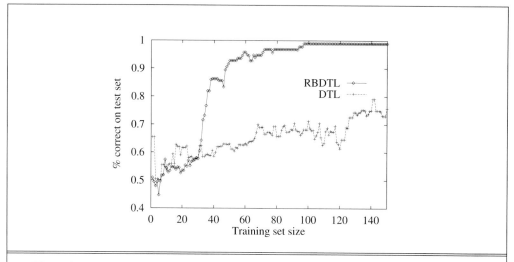

Figure 21.4   A performance comparison RBDTL and DECISION-TREE-LEARNING on randomly
generated data for a target function that depends on only 5 of 16 attributes.

DECLARATIVE BIAS   This section has only scratched the surface of the field of **declarative bias**, which aims to
understand how prior knowledge can be used to identify the appropriate hypothesis space within
which to search for the correct target definition. There are many unanswered questions:

- How can the algorithms be extended to handle noise?

- How can other kinds of prior knowledge be used, besides determinations?

- How can the algorithms be generalized to cover any first-order theory, rather than just an
  attribute-based representation?

Some of these are addressed in the next section.

21.4   INDUCTIVE LOGIC PROGRAMMING

Inductive logic programming (ILP) is one of the newest subfields in AI. It combines inductive
methods with the power of first-order representations, concentrating in particular on the representation of theories as logic programs. Over the last five years, it has become a major part of

the research agenda in machine learning. This has happened for two reasons. First, it offers a rigorous approach to the general KBIL problem mentioned in the introduction. Second, it offers complete algorithms for inducing general, first-order theories from examples, which can therefore learn successfully in domains where attribute-based algorithms fail completely. ILP is a highly technical field, relying on some fairly advanced material from the study of computational logic. We therefore cover only the basic principles of the two major approaches, referring the reader to the literature for more details.[3]

An example

Recall from Equation (21.3) that the general knowledge-based induction problem is to "solve" the entailment constraint

$$Background \land Hypothesis \land Descriptions \models Classifications$$

for the unknown *Hypothesis*, given the *Background* knowledge and examples described by *Descriptions* and *Classifications*. To illustrate this, we will use the problem of learning family relationships from examples. The observations will consist of an extended family tree, described in terms of *Mother*, *Father*, and *Married* relations, and *Male* and *Female* properties. The target predicates will be such things as *Grandparent*, *BrotherInLaw*, and *Ancestor*. We will use the family tree from Exercise 7.6, shown here in Figure 21.5. The example *Descriptions* include facts such as

$$Father(Philip, Charles) \quad Father(Philip, Anne) \qquad \ldots$$
$$Mother(Mum, Margaret) \quad Mother(Mum, Elizabeth) \quad \ldots$$
$$Married(Diana, Charles) \quad Married(Elizabeth, Philip) \ldots$$
$$Male(Philip) \qquad\qquad Male(Charles) \qquad\qquad \ldots$$
$$Female(Beatrice) \qquad\quad Female(Margaret) \qquad \ldots$$

The sentences in *Classifications* depend on the target concept being learned. If Q is *Grandparent*, say, then the sentences in *Classifications* might include the following:

$$Grandparent(Mum, Charles) \quad Grandparent(Elizabeth, Beatrice) \ \ldots$$
$$\neg Grandparent(Mum, Harry) \quad \neg Grandparent(Spencer, Peter)$$

The object of an inductive learning program is to come up with a set of sentences for the *Hypothesis* such that the entailment constraint is satisfied. Suppose, for the moment, that the agent has no background knowledge: *Background* is empty. Then one possible solution for *Hypothesis* is the following:

$$
\begin{aligned}
Grandparent(x, y) \quad\Leftrightarrow\quad & [\exists z \ Mother(x, z) \land Mother(z, y)] \\
\lor\quad & [\exists z \ Mother(x, z) \land Father(z, y)] \\
\lor\quad & [\exists z \ Father(x, z) \land Mother(z, y)] \\
\lor\quad & [\exists z \ Father(x, z) \land Father(z, y)]
\end{aligned}
$$

---

[3] We suggest that it might be appropriate at this point for the reader to refer back to Chapter 9 for some of the underlying concepts, including Horn clauses, conjunctive normal form, unification, and resolution.

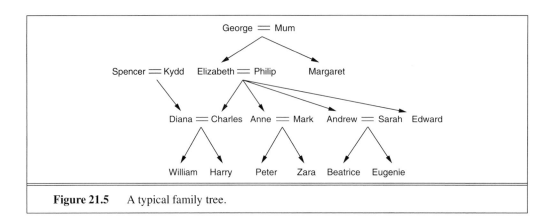

Figure 21.5   A typical family tree.

Notice that an attribute-based learning algorithm such as DECISION-TREE-LEARNING will get nowhere in solving this problem. In order to express *Grandparent* as an attribute (i.e., a unary predicate), we would need to make *pairs* of people into objects:

$Grandparent(\langle Mum, Charles \rangle)\ldots$

Then we get stuck in trying to represent the example descriptions. The only possible attributes are horrible things such as

$FirstElementIsMotherOfElizabeth(\langle Mum, Charles \rangle)$

The definition of *Grandparent* in terms of these attributes simply becomes a large disjunction of specific cases that does not generalize to new examples at all. *Attribute-based learning algorithms are incapable of learning relational predicates.* Thus, one of the principal advantages of ILP algorithms is their applicability to a much wider range of problems.

The reader will certainly have noticed that a little bit of background knowledge would help in the representation of the *Grandparent* definition. For example, if *Background* included the sentence

$Parent(x, y) \Leftrightarrow [Mother(x, y) \vee Father(x, y)]$

then the definition of *Grandparent* would be reduced to

$Grandparent(x, y) \Leftrightarrow [\exists z \ Parent(x, z) \wedge Parent(z, y)]$

This shows how background knowledge can dramatically reduce the size of hypothesis required to explain the observations.

It is also possible for ILP algorithms to *create* new predicates in order to facilitate the expression of explanatory hypotheses. Given the example data shown earlier, it is entirely reasonable to propose an additional predicate, which we would call "*Parent*," in order to simplify the definitions of the target predicates. Algorithms that can generate new predicates are called **constructive induction** algorithms. Clearly, constructive induction is a necessary part of the picture of cumulative learning sketched in the introduction. It has been one of the hardest problems in machine learning, but some ILP techniques provide effective mechanisms for achieving it.

CONSTRUCTIVE
INDUCTION

In the rest of this chapter, we will study the two principal approaches to ILP. The first uses techniques based on inverting a resolution proof, and the second uses a generalization of decision-tree methods.

Inverse resolution

Inverse resolution is based on the observation that if the example *Classifications* follow from *Background* ∧ *Hypothesis* ∧ *Descriptions*, then one must be able to prove this fact by resolution (because resolution is complete). If we can "run the proof backwards," then we can find a *Hypothesis* such that the proof goes through. The key, then, is to find a way to invert the resolution process so that we can run the proof backwards.

Generating inverse proofs

The backward proof process consists of individual backward steps. An ordinary resolution step takes two clauses C_1 and C_2 and resolves them to produce the **resolvent** C. An inverse resolution step takes a resolvent C and produces two clauses C_1 and C_2, such that C is the result of resolving C_1 and C_2; or it takes C and C_1 and produces a suitable C_2.

The early steps in an inverse resolution process are shown in Figure 21.6, where we focus on the positive example *Grandparent(George, Anne)*. The process begins at the end of the proof, that is, at the contradiction, and works backwards. The negated goal clause is ¬*Grandparent(George, Anne)*, which is *Grandparent(George, Anne)* ⇒ *False* in implicative normal form. The first inverse step takes this and the contradictory clause *True* ⇒ *False*, and generates *Grandparent(George, Anne)*. The next step takes this clause and the known clause *Parent(Elizabeth, Anne)*, and generates the clause

$$Parent(Elizabeth, y) \Rightarrow Grandparent(George, y)$$

With one further step, the inverse resolution process will generate the correct hypothesis.

Clearly, inverse resolution involves a search. Each inverse resolution step is nondeterministic, because for any C and C_1, there can be several or even an infinite number of clauses C_2 that satisfy the requirement that when resolved with C_1 it generates C. For example, in-

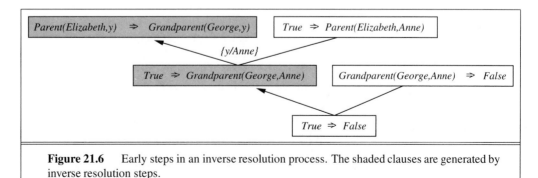

Figure 21.6   Early steps in an inverse resolution process. The shaded clauses are generated by inverse resolution steps.

stead of $Parent(Elizabeth, y) \Rightarrow Grandparent(George, y)$, the inverse resolution step might have generated the following sentences:

$Parent(Elizabeth, Anne) \Rightarrow Grandparent(George, Anne)$
$Parent(z, Anne) \Rightarrow Grandparent(George, Anne)$
$Parent(z, y) \Rightarrow Grandparent(George, y)$
$\vdots$

(See Exercises 21.4 and 21.5.) Furthermore, the clauses C_1 (and perhaps also C_2) that participate in each step can be chosen from the *Background* knowledge, from the example *Descriptions*, from the negated *Classifications*, or from hypothesized clauses that have already been generated in the inverse resolution tree.

An exhaustive search process for inverse resolution would be extremely inefficient. ILP systems use a number of restrictions to make the process more manageable, including the elimination of function symbols, generating only the most specific hypotheses possible, and the use of Horn clauses. One can also consider inverting the *restricted* resolution strategies that were introduced in Chapter 9. With a restricted but complete strategy, such as linear resolution, the inverse resolution process will be more efficient because certain clauses will be ruled out as candidates for C_1 and C_2. Other useful constraints include the fact that all the hypothesized clauses must be consistent with each other, and that each hypothesized clause must agree with the observations. This last criterion would rule out the clause $Parent(z, y) \Rightarrow Grandparent(George, y)$ listed before.

Discovering new predicates and new knowledge

An inverse resolution procedure that inverts a complete resolution strategy is, in principle, a complete algorithm for learning first-order theories. That is, if some unknown *Hypothesis* generates a set of examples, then an inverse resolution procedure can generate *Hypothesis* from the examples. This observation suggests an interesting possibility. Suppose, for example, that the available examples include a variety of trajectories of falling bodies. Would an inverse resolution program be theoretically capable of inferring the law of gravity? The answer is clearly yes, because the law of gravity allows one to explain the examples, given suitable background mathematics. Similarly, one can imagine that electromagnetism, quantum mechanics, and the theory of relativity are also within the scope of ILP programs. However, such imaginings are on a par with the proverbial monkey with a typewriter, at least until we find ways to overcome the very large branching factors and the lack of structure in the search space that characterize current systems.

One thing that inverse resolution systems *will* do for you is invent new predicates. This ability is often seen as somewhat magical, because computers are often thought of as "merely working with what they are given." In fact, new predicates fall directly out of the inverse resolution step. The simplest case arises when hypothesizing two new clauses C_1 and C_2, given a clause C. The resolution of C_1 and C_2 eliminates a literal that the two clauses share, hence it is quite possible that the eliminated literal contained a predicate that does not appear in C. Thus, when working backwards, one possibility is to generate a new predicate from which to reconstruct the missing literal.

Figure 21.7 shows an example in which the new predicate P is generated in the process of learning a definition for *Ancestor*. Once generated, P can be used in later inverse resolution steps. For example, a later step might hypothesize that $Mother(x, y) \Rightarrow P(x, y)$. Thus, the new predicate P has its meaning constrained by the generation of hypotheses that involve it. Another example might lead to the constraint $Father(x, y) \Rightarrow P(x, y)$. In other words, the predicate P is what we usually think of as the *Parent* relationship. As we mentioned earlier, the invention of new predicates can significantly reduce the size of the definition of the goal predicate. Hence, by including the ability to invent new predicates, inverse resolution systems can often solve learning problems that are infeasible with other techniques.

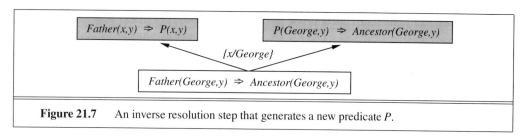

Figure 21.7   An inverse resolution step that generates a new predicate P.

Some of the deepest revolutions in science come from the invention of new predicates and functions—for example, Galileo's invention of acceleration or Joule's invention of thermal energy. Once these terms are available, the discovery of new laws becomes (relatively) easy. The difficult part lies in realizing that some new entity, with a specific relationship to existing entities, will allow an entire body of observations to be explained with a much simpler and more elegant theory than previously existed.

As yet, ILP systems have not been applied to such difficult tasks. It does appear, however, that the ability to use background knowledge provides significant advantages. In several applications, ILP techniques have outperformed knowledge-free methods. For example, in molecular biology, it is useful to have background knowledge about typical molecular bonding patterns, valences of atoms, bond strengths, and so on. Using such knowledge, Stephen Muggleton's GOLEM system has been able to generate high-quality predictions of both protein structure from sequence information (Muggleton *et al.*, 1992) and the therapeutic efficacy of various drugs based on their molecular structures (King *et al.*, 1992). These results, like Meta-DENDRAL's, were considered sufficiently interesting in their own right to be published in leading scientific journals. The differences between GOLEM's and Meta-DENDRAL's performance are that (1) the new domains are much more difficult, and (2) GOLEM is a completely general-purpose program that is able to make use of background knowledge about any domain whatsoever.

Top-down learning methods

The second approach to ILP is essentially a generalization of the techniques of decision-tree learning to the first-order case. Rather than starting from the observations and working backwards, we start with a very general rule and gradually specialize it so that it fits the data. This is essentially what happens in decision-tree learning, where a decision tree is gradually grown until it is consistent with the observations. In the first-order case, we use first-order literals instead of attributes, and the hypothesis is a set of clauses instead of a decision tree. This section describes FOIL (Quinlan, 1990), one of the first programs to use this approach.

Suppose we are trying to learn a definition of the $Grandfather(x, y)$ predicate, using the same family data as before. As with decision-tree learning, we can divide the examples into positive and negative examples. Positive examples are

$$\langle George, Anne \rangle, \ \langle Philip, Peter \rangle, \ \langle Spencer, Harry \rangle, \ \ldots$$

and negative examples are

$$\langle George, Elizabeth \rangle, \ \langle Harry, Zara \rangle, \ \langle Charles, Philip \rangle, \ \ldots$$

Notice that each example is a *pair* of objects, because *Grandfather* is a binary predicate. In all, there are 12 positive examples in the family tree, and 388 negative examples (all the other pairs of people).

FOIL constructs a set of Horn clauses with $Grandfather(x, y)$ as the head, such that the 12 positive examples are classified as instances of the $Grandfather(x, y)$ relationship, whereas the other 388 examples are ruled out because no clause succeeds with those bindings for x and y. We begin with a clause with an empty body:

$$\Rightarrow \ Grandfather(x, y)$$

This classifies every example as positive, so it needs to be specialized. This is done by adding literals one at a time to the left-hand side. Here are three potential additions:

$$Father(x, y) \ \Rightarrow \ Grandfather(x, y)$$
$$Parent(x, z) \ \Rightarrow \ Grandfather(x, y)$$
$$Father(x, z) \ \Rightarrow \ Grandfather(x, y)$$

(Notice that we are assuming that a clause defining *Parent* is already present as part of the background knowledge.) The first of these three incorrectly classifies all of the 12 positive examples as negative, and therefore can be ruled out. The second and third agree with all of the positive examples, but the second is incorrect on a larger fraction of the negative examples—twice as many, in fact, because it allows mothers as well as fathers. Hence, we prefer the third clause.

Now we need to specialize this clause further, to rule out the cases in which x is the father of some z but z is not a parent of y. Adding the single literal $Parent(z, y)$ gives the clause

$$Father(x, z) \wedge Parent(z, y) \ \Rightarrow \ Grandfather(x, y)$$

which correctly classifies all the examples. FOIL will find and choose this literal, thereby solving the learning task.

The preceding example is a very simple illustration of how FOIL operates. A sketch of the complete algorithm is shown in Figure 21.8. Essentially, the algorithm repeatedly constructs a clause, literal by literal, until it agrees with some subset of the positive examples and none of the negative examples. Then the positive examples covered by the clause are removed from the training set, and the process continues until no positive examples remain. The two main components to be explained are NEW-LITERALS, which constructs all possible new literals to add to the clause, and CHOOSE-LITERAL, which selects a literal to add.

---

function FOIL(*examples, target*) **returns** a set of Horn clauses
   inputs: *examples*, set of examples
        target, a literal for the goal predicate
   local variables: *clauses*, set of clauses, initially empty

   while *examples* contains positive examples **do**
      clause ← NEW-CLAUSE(*examples, target*)
      remove examples covered by *clause* from *examples*
      add *clause* to *clauses*
   return *clauses*

---

function NEW-CLAUSE(*examples, target*) **returns** a Horn clause
   local variables: *clause*, a clause with *target* as head and an empty body
               l, a literal to be added to the clause
               extended-examples, a set of examples with values for new variables

   extended-examples ← *examples*
   while *extended-examples* contains negative examples **do**
      l ← CHOOSE-LITERAL(NEW-LITERALS(*clause*), *extended-examples*)
      append *l* to the body of *clause*
      extended-examples ← set of examples created by applying EXTEND-EXAMPLE
         to each example in *extended-examples*
   return *clause*

---

function EXTEND-EXAMPLE(*example, literal*) **returns**
   if *example* satisfies *literal*
      then return the set of examples created by extending *example* with
         each possible constant value for each new variable in *literal*
   else return the empty set

Figure 21.8   Sketch of the FOIL algorithm for learning sets of first-order Horn clauses from examples. NEW-LITERAL and CHOOSE-LITERAL are explained in the text.

NEW-LITERALS takes a clause and constructs all possible "useful" literals that could be added to the clause. Let us use as an example the clause

$$Father(x, z) \Rightarrow Grandfather(x, y)$$

There are three kinds of literals that can be added.

1. Literals using predicates: the literal can be negated or unnegated, any existing predicate (including the goal predicate) can be used, and the arguments must all be variables. Any variables can be used for any argument of the predicate, with one restriction: each literal must include *at least one* variable from an earlier literal or from the head of the clause. Literals such as *Mother*(z, u), *Married*(z, z), ¬*Male*(y), and *Grandfather*(v, x) are allowed, whereas *Married*(u, v) is not. Notice that the use of the predicate from the head of the clause allows FOIL to learn *recursive* definitions.

2. Equality and inequality literals: these relate variables already appearing in the clause. For example, we might add $z \neq x$. These literals can also include user-specified constants. In the family domain, there will not usually be any such "special" constants, whereas in learning arithmetic, we might use 0 and 1, and in list functions, the empty list [ ].

3. Arithmetic comparisons: when dealing with functions of continuous variables, literals such as $x > y$ and $y \leq z$ can be added. As in decision-tree learning, one can also use constant threshold values that are chosen to maximize the discriminatory power of the test.

All this adds up to a very large branching factor in the search space (see Exercise 21.6). Implementations of FOIL may also use type information to restrict the hypothesis space. For example, if the domain included numbers as well as people, type restrictions would prevent NEW-LITERALS from generating literals such as $Parent(x, n)$, where x is a person and n is a number.

CHOOSE-LITERAL uses a heuristic somewhat similar to information gain (see page 541) to decide which literal to add. The exact details are not so important here, particularly as a number of different variations are currently being tried out. One interesting additional feature of FOIL is the use of Ockham's razor to eliminate some hypotheses. If a clause becomes longer (according to some metric) than the total length of the positive examples that the clause explains, that clause is not considered as a potential hypothesis. This technique provides a way to avoid overcomplex clauses that fit noise in the data. For an explanation of the connection between noise and clause length, see Section 19.6.

FOIL and its relatives have been used to learn a wide variety of definitions. One of the most impressive demonstrations (Quinlan and Cameron-Jones, 1993) involved solving a long sequences of exercises on list-processing functions from Bratko's (1986) Prolog textbook. In each case, the program was able to learn a correct definition of the function from a small set of examples, using the previously learned functions as background knowledge.

21.5   SUMMARY

This chapter has investigated various ways in which prior knowledge can help an agent to learn from new experiences.

- The use of prior knowledge in learning leads to a picture of **cumulative learning**, in which learning agents improve their learning ability as they acquire more knowledge.

- Prior knowledge helps learning by eliminating otherwise consistent hypotheses and by "filling in" the explanation of examples, thereby allowing for shorter hypotheses. These contributions improve both the sample complexity and computation complexity of learning.

- Understanding the different logical roles played by prior knowledge, as expressed by **entailment constraints**, helps to define a variety of learning techniques.

- **Explanation-based learning** (EBL) extracts general rules from single examples by *explaining* the examples and generalizing the explanation. It provides a deductive method to turn first-principles knowledge into useful, efficient, special-purpose expertise.

- **Relevance-based learning** (RBL) uses prior knowledge in the form of determinations to identify the relevant attributes, thereby generating a reduced hypothesis space and speeding up learning. RBL also allows deductive generalizations from single examples.

- **Knowledge-based inductive learning** (KBIL) finds inductive hypotheses that explain sets of observations with the help of background knowledge.

- **Inductive logic programming** (ILP) techniques perform KBIL using knowledge expressed in first-order logic. ILP methods can learn relational knowledge that is not expressible in attribute-based systems.

- ILP methods naturally generate new predicates with which concise new theories can be expressed, and show promise as general-purpose scientific theory formation systems.

BIBLIOGRAPHICAL AND HISTORICAL NOTES

The use of prior knowledge in learning from experience has had a surprisingly brief period of intensive study. *Fact, Fiction, and Forecast*, by the philosopher Nelson Goodman (1954), refuted the earlier supposition that induction was simply a matter of seeing enough examples of some universally quantified proposition and then adopting it as a hypothesis. Consider, for

GRUE

example, the hypothesis "All emeralds are grue," where **grue** means "green if observed before time t, but blue if observed thereafter." At any time up to t, we might have observed millions of instances confirming the rule that emeralds are grue, and no disconfirming instances, and yet we are unwilling to adopt the rule. This can only be explained by appeal to the role of relevant prior knowledge in the induction process. Goodman proposes a variety of different kinds of prior knowledge that might be useful, including a version of determinations called **overhypotheses**. Unfortunately, Goodman's work was never taken up in early studies of machine learning.

EBL had its roots in the techniques used by the STRIPS planner (Fikes *et al.*, 1972). When a plan was constructed, a generalized version of it was saved in a plan library and used in later planning as a **macro-operator**. Similar ideas appeared in Anderson's ACT* architecture, under the heading of **knowledge compilation** (Anderson, 1983); and in the SOAR architecture as **chunking** (Laird *et al.*, 1986). **Schema acquisition** (DeJong, 1981), **analytical generalization** (Mitchell, 1982), and **constraint-based generalization** (Minton, 1984) were immediate precursors of the rapid growth of interest in EBL stimulated by the publication of (Mitchell *et al.*, 1986; DeJong and Mooney, 1986). Hirsh (1987) introduced the EBL algorithm described in the text, showing how it could be incorporated directly into a logic programming system. Van Harmelen and Bundy (1988) explain EBL as a variant of the **partial evaluation** method used in program analysis systems (Jones *et al.*, 1993).

More recently, rigorous analysis and experimental work has led to a better understanding of the potential costs and benefits of EBL in terms of problem-solving speed. Minton (1988) showed that without extensive extra work, EBL could easily slow down a program significantly. Tambe *et al.* (1990) found a similar problem with chunking, and proposed a reduction in the expressive power of the rule language in order to minimize the cost of matching rules against working memory. This work bears strong parallels with recent results on the complexity of inference in restricted versions of first-order logic (see Chapter 10). Formal probabilistic analysis of the expected payoff of EBL can be found in (Greiner, 1989; Subramanian and Feldman, 1990). An excellent survey appears in (Dietterich, 1990).

ANALOGICAL
REASONING

Instead of using examples as foci for generalization, one can use them directly to solve new problems in a process known as **analogical reasoning**. This form of reasoning ranges from a form of plausible reasoning based on degree of similarity (Gentner, 1983), through a form of deductive inference based on determinations (Davies and Russell, 1987) but requiring the participation of the example, to a form of "lazy" EBL that tailors the direction of generalization of the old example to fit the needs of the new problem. This latter form of analogical reasoning is found most commonly in **case-based reasoning** (Kolodner, 1993) and **derivational analogy** (Veloso and Carbonell, 1993).

Relevance information in the form of functional dependencies was first developed in the database community, where it is used to structure large sets of attributes into manageable subsets. Functional dependencies were used for analogical reasoning by Carbonell and Collins (1973), and given a more logical flavor by Bobrow and Raphael (1974). Dependencies were independently rediscovered, and given a full logical analysis, by Davies and Russell (Davies, 1985; Davies and Russell, 1987) for the problem of analogical inference. They were used for declarative bias by Russell and Grosof (1987). The equivalence of determinations to a restricted-vocabulary hypothesis space was proved in (Russell, 1988). Learning algorithms for determinations, and the improved performance obtained by RBDTL, were first shown in the FOCUS algorithm in (Al-muallim and Dietterich, 1991). Tadepalli (1993) describes an ingenious algorithm for learning with determinations that shows large improvements in learning speed.

The study of methods for learning first-order logical sentences began with the remarkable Ph.D. thesis by Gordon Plotkin (1971) at Edinburgh. Although Plotkin developed many of the theorems and methods that are in current use in ILP, he was discouraged by some undecidability results for certain subproblems in induction. MIS (Shapiro, 1981) reintroduced the problem of learning logic programs, but was mainly seen as a contribution to the theory of automated debugging. The field was reinvigorated by Muggleton and Buntine (1988), whose CIGOL program incorporated a slightly incomplete version of inverse resolution and was capable of generating new predicates.[4] More recent systems include GOLEM (Muggleton and Cao, 1990), ITOU (Rouveirol and Puget, 1989) and CLINT (De Raedt, 1992). A second thread of ILP research began with Quinlan's FOIL system, described in this chapter (Quinlan, 1990). A formal analysis of ILP methods appears in (Muggleton, 1991), and a large collection of papers in (Muggleton, 1992).

Early complexity results by Haussler (1989) suggested that learning first-order sentences was hopelessly complex. However, with better understanding of the importance of various kinds of syntactic restrictions on clauses, positive results have been obtained even for clauses with recursion (Dzeroski *et al.*, 1992). A recent paper by Kietz and Dzeroski (1994) provides an excellent survey of complexity results in ILP.

DISCOVERY
SYSTEMS

Although ILP now seems to be the dominant approach to constructive induction, it has not been the only approach taken. So-called **discovery systems** aim to model the process of scientific discovery of new concepts, usually by a direct search in the space of concept definitions. Doug Lenat's AM (Automated Mathematician) (Davis and Lenat, 1982) used discovery heuristics

---

[4]   The inverse resolution method also appears in (Russell, 1986), where a complete algorithm is mentioned in a footnote.

expressed as expert system rules to guide its search for concepts and conjectures in elementary number theory. In sharp contrast with most systems designed for mathematical reasoning, AM lacked a concept of proof and could only make conjectures. It rediscovered Goldbach's Conjecture and the Unique Prime Factorization Theorem. AM's architecture was generalized in the EURISKO system (Lenat, 1983) by adding a mechanism capable of rewriting the system's own discovery heuristics. EURISKO was applied in a number of areas other than mathematical discovery, although with less success than AM. The methodology of AM and EURISKO has been controversial (Ritchie and Hanna, 1984; Lenat and Brown, 1984).

Another class of discovery systems aims to operate with real scientific data to find new laws. The systems DALTON, GLAUBER, and STAHL (Langley *et al.*, 1987) are rule-based systems that look for quantitative relationships in experimental data from physical systems; in each case, the system has been able to recapitulate a well-known discovery from the history of science. AUTOCLASS (Cheeseman *et al.*, 1988) takes a more theoretically grounded approach to concept discovery: it uses Bayesian probabilistic reasoning to partition given data into the "most likely" collection of classes. AUTOCLASS has been applied to a number of real-world scientific classification tasks, including the discovery of new types of stars from spectral data and the analysis of protein structure (Hunter and States, 1992).

EXERCISES

21.1 Show, by translating into conjunctive normal form and applying resolution, that the conclusion drawn on page 633 concerning Brazilians is sound.

21.2 For each of the following determinations, write down the logical representation and explain why the determination is true (if it is):

   a. Zip code determines the state (U.S.).

   b. Design and denomination determine the mass of a coin.

   c. For a given program, input determines output.

   d. Climate, food intake, exercise, and metabolism determine weight gain/loss.

   e. Baldness is determined by the baldness (or lack thereof) of one's maternal grandfather.

21.3 Would a probabilistic version of determinations be useful? Suggest a definition.

21.4 Fill in the missing values for the clauses C_1 and/or C_2 in the following sets of clauses, given that C is the resolvent of C_1 and C_2.

   a. $C = \textit{True} \Rightarrow P(A, B)$, $C_1 = P(x, y) \Rightarrow Q(x, y)$, $C_2 =$??.

   b. $C = \textit{True} \Rightarrow P(A, B)$, $C_1 =$??, $C_2 =$??.

   c. $C = P(x, y) \Rightarrow P(x, f(y))$, $C_1 =$??, $C_2 =$??.

If there is more than one possible solution, provide one example of each different kind.

21.5   Suppose one writes a logic program that carries out a resolution inference step. That is, let $Resolve(c_1, c_2, c)$ succeed if c is the result of resolving c_1 and c_2. Normally, $Resolve$ would be used as part of a theorem prover by calling it with c_1 and c_2 instantiated to particular clauses, thereby generating the resolvent c. Now suppose instead that we call it with c instantiated and c_1 and c_2 uninstantiated. Will this succeed in generating the appropriate results of an inverse resolution step? Would you need any special modifications to the logic programming system for this to work?

21.6   Suppose that FOIL is considering adding a literal to a clause using a binary predicate P, and that previous literals (including the head of the clause) contain five different variables.

    a. How many functionally different literals can be generated? Notice that two literals are functionally identical if they differ only in the names of the *new* variables that they contain.

    b. Can you find a general formula for the number of different literals with a predicate of arity r when there are n variables previously used?

    c. Why does FOIL not allow literals that contain no previously used variables?

21.7   Using the data from the family tree in Figure 21.5, or a subset thereof, apply the FOIL algorithm to learn a definition for the *Ancestor* predicate.

Part VII

COMMUNICATING, PERCEIVING, AND ACTING

So far we have been concerned with what happens inside an agent—from the time it receives a percept to the time it decides on an action. In this part, we concentrate on the interface between the agent and the environment. On one end, we have *perception:* vision, hearing, touch, and possibly other senses. On the other end, we have *action:* the movement of a robot arm, for example.

Also covered in this part is *communication*. A group of agents can be more successful—individually and collectively—if they communicate their beliefs and goals to each other. We look most closely at human language and how it can be used as a communication tool.

AGENTS THAT COMMUNICATE

In which we see why agents might want to exchange information-carrying messages with each other, and how they can do so.

It is dusk in the savanna woodlands of Amboseli National Park near the base of Kilimanjaro. A group of vervet monkeys are foraging for food. One vervet lets out a loud barking call and the group responds by scrambling for the trees, neatly avoiding the leopard that the first vervet had seen hiding in the bush. The vervet has successfully communicated with the group.

Communication is such a widespread phenomenon that it is hard to pin down an exact definition. In general, *communication is the intentional exchange of information brought about by the production and perception of signs drawn from a shared system of conventional signs.* Most animals employ a fixed set of signs to represent messages that are important to their survival: food here, predator nearby, approach, withdraw, let's mate. The vervet is unusual in having a variety of calls for different predators: a loud bark for leopards, a short cough for eagles, and a chutter for snakes. They use one kind of grunt in exchanges with dominant members of their own social group, another kind with subordinate members, and yet another with vervets in other social groups.

The leopard alarm (the loud bark) is a conventional sign that both alerts others that there is danger in the bush nearby, and signals the action of escaping to the trees. But consider a vervet that is too far away to hear the call, but can see the others heading for the trees. He too may climb the nearest tree, but he has not participated in communication because he did not perceive any intentionally conveyed signs, but rather used his general powers of perception and reasoning.

Humans use a limited number of conventional signs (smiling, shaking hands) to communicate in much the same way as other animals. Humans have also developed a complex, structured system of signs known as **language** that enables them to communicate most of what they know about the world. Although chimpanzees, dolphins, and other mammals have shown vocabularies of hundreds of signs and some aptitude for stringing them together, humans are the only species that can reliably communicate an unbounded number of qualitatively different messages.[1]

LANGUAGE

---

[1] The bee's tail-wagging dance specifies the distance and angle from the sun at which food can be found, so in one sense the bee can convey an infinite number of messages, but we do not count this as unbounded variation.

Of course, there are other attributes that are uniquely human: no other species wears clothes, creates representational art, or watches four hours of television a day. But when Turing proposed his test (see Section 1.1), he based it on language because language is intimately tied to thinking in a way that, say, clothing is not. In this chapter, we will explain how a communicating agent works and present a simplified version of English that is sufficient to illustrate the workings of the agent's major components.

22.1   COMMUNICATION AS ACTION

SPEECH ACT

One of the actions available to an agent is to produce language. This is called a **speech act**. "Speech" is used in the same sense as in "free speech," not "talking," so typing, skywriting, and using sign language all count as speech acts. English has no neutral word for an agent that produces language, either by speaking or writing or anything else. We will use **speaker**, **hearer**, and **utterance** as generic terms referring to any mode of communication. We will also use the term **words** to refer to any kind of conventional communicative sign.

Why would an agent bother to perform a speech act when it could be doing a "regular" action? Imagine a group of agents are exploring the wumpus world together. The group gains an advantage (collectively and individually) by being able to do the following:

- **Inform** each other about the part of the world each has explored, so that each agent has less exploring to do. This is done by making statements: *There's a breeze here in 3 4.*

- **Query** other agents about particular aspects of the world. This is typically done by asking questions: *Have you smelled the wumpus anywhere?*

- **Answer** questions. This is a kind of informing. *Yes, I smelled the wumpus in 2 5.*

INDIRECT SPEECH ACT

- **Request** or **command** other agents to perform actions: *Please help me carry the gold.* It can be seen as impolite to make a direct requests, so often an **indirect speech act** (a request in the form of a statement or question) is used instead: *I could use some help carrying this* or *Could you help me carry this?*

- **Promise** to do things or **offer** deals: *I'll shoot the wumpus if you let me share the gold.*

- **Acknowledge** requests and offers: *OK.*

- **Share** feelings and experiences with each other: *You know, old chap, when I get in a spot like that, I usually go back to the start and head out in another direction*, or *Man, that wumpus sure needs some deodorant!*

These examples show that speech acts can be quite useful and versatile. Some kinds of speech acts (informing, answering, acknowledging, sharing) have the intended effect of transferring information to the hearer. Others (requesting, commanding, querying, leopard alarm) have the intended effect of making the hearer take some action. A dual purpose of communication is to establish trust and build social ties (just as primates groom each other both to remove fleas and to build relationships). This helps to explain what is communicated in exchanges such as "Hello, how are you? Fine, how are you? Not bad."

THE EVOLUTION OF LANGUAGE

In 1866, the Société de Linguistique de Paris passed a by-law banning all debate on the origin of language. Outside the halls of that body, the debate goes on. One proposal (Chomsky, 1980; Fodor, 1983) is that there is a language module that exists only in the brain of humans. There is now considerable evidence (Dingwell, 1988) that language use is made possible by a large repertoire of different skills that did not develop in isolation of general cognitive capabilities, and that many of the precursors of human language use can be seen in the other primates and in the fossil record.

At least seven researchers claim to have taught primates over 100 words. Koko the gorilla is the vocabulary queen with over a thousand. Although some argue that the researchers become too attached to the animals and attribute abilities to them that are not really there, it seems safe to say that primates can learn words spontaneously (from human trainers or from each other) and can use them to inform others of what they know and what they want. They can produce and understand sentences involving abstract concepts in a limited way, such as referring to objects that are not present. For example, chimpanzees can correctly respond to "get the ball that is outside" or "bring the red ball over to the blue ball." They can even tell lies: a vervet who is losing a fight may give the leopard alarm, causing the fight to be called off while everyone heads for the trees. Some have claimed that such behavior is evidence that animals form models of the world, including models of how other agents act. Unfortunately, present psychological methodologies do not allow us to distinguish between behaviors that are mediated by internal models and those that are merely stimulus-response patterns. Also, although primates clearly learn some rules for ordering words, there appear to be limitations in the way they use syntax to produce unbounded sequences. Despite some impressive accomplishments, no primate has duplicated the explosion of language use that all normal human children accomplish by age four.

Language and thought reinforce each other, but it is not known if humans evolved to use language well because they are smart, or if they are smart because they use language well. One theory (Jerison, 1991) is that human language stems primarily from a need for better cognitive maps of the territory. Canines and other social carnivores rely heavily on scent marking and their olfactory system to decide both where they are and what other animals have been there—just as the wumpus world agents use the presence of a smell or breeze to help map out that world. But the early hominids (monkeys and apes of 30 million years ago) did not have a well enough developed olfactory system to map out the world this way, so they substituted vocal sounds for scent marking. Thus, the rest of this chapter, in Jerison's view, is devoted to the way we humans compensate for our inadequate noses.

The hard part for an agent is to decide *when* a speech act of some kind is called for, and to decide *which* speech act, out of all the possibilities, is the right one. At one level, this is just the familiar **planning** problem—an agent has a set of possible actions to choose from, and must somehow try to choose actions that achieve the goal of communicating some information to another agent. *All the difficulties that make planning hard (see Chapter 12) apply to planning speech acts.* It would be impossibly complex to plan English conversations at the level of individual movements of the mouth and tongue, so we need to plan with several levels of hierarchical abstraction—words, phrases and sentences, at least. Another problem is nondeterminism. Whereas most actions in the wumpus world are deterministic, speech acts are not. Consider the action *Speak("Turn Right!")*. If another agent perceives the words, and if the agent interprets it as a command to turn right, then that agent may do so. Or then again, the agent may ignore the command and choose another action. The nondeterminism means that we will need conditional plans. Instead of planning a conversation from beginning to end, the best we can do is construct a general plan or policy for the conversation, generate the first sentence, stop to perceive the reply, and react to it.

UNDERSTANDING   The problem of understanding speech acts is much like other **understanding** problems, such as image understanding or medical diagnosis. We are given a set of ambiguous inputs, and from them we have to work backwards to decide what state of the world could have created the inputs. Part of the speech act understanding problem is specific to language. We need to know something about the syntax and semantics of a language to determine why another agent performed a given speech act. The understanding problem also includes the more general

PLAN RECOGNITION   problem of **plan recognition**. If we observe an agent turning and moving toward the gold, we can understand the actions by forming a model of the agent's beliefs that says the agent has the goal of getting the gold. A similar kind of mental model building is required to understand the agent who turns toward the gold and says, "I'm going to grab it." Even though there may be other objects nearby, it is fairly clear that "it" refers to the gold.

Part of the understanding problem can be handled by logical reasoning. We will see that logical implications are a good way of describing the ways that words and phrases combine to form larger phrases. Another part of the understanding problem can only be handled by uncertain reasoning techniques. Usually, there will be several states of the world that could all lead to the same speech act, so the understander has to decide which one is more probable.

Now that we have seen how communication fits into our general agent design, we can turn our attention to language itself. As we focus more and more on the way language *actually is*, rather than on the general properties of communication methods, we will find ourselves moving into the realm of natural science—that is, science that works by finding out things about the real world rather than about programs or other artifacts. Natural language understanding is one of the few areas of AI that have this property.

Fundamentals of language

FORMAL LANGUAGES   We distinguish between **formal languages**—the ones like Lisp and first-order logic that are
NATURAL
LANGUAGES   invented and rigidly defined—and **natural languages**—the ones like Chinese, Danish, and English that humans use to talk to one another. Although we are primarily interested in natural

languages, we will make use of all the tools of formal language theory, starting with the Backus–Naur form (BNF) notation, which is described in Appendix B on page 854.

STRINGS

TERMINAL SYMBOLS

A formal language is defined as a set of **strings**, where each string is a sequence of symbols taken from a finite set called the **terminal symbols**. For English, the terminal symbols include words like *a, aardvark, aback, abacus*, and about 400,000 more.

One of the confusing things in working with both formal and natural languages is that there are so many different formalisms and notations for writing grammars (see the Historical Notes section for this chapter). However, most of them are similar in that they are based on

PHRASE STRUCTURE

NOUN PHRASE

the idea of **phrase structure**—that strings are composed of substrings called **phrases**, which come in different categories. For example, the phrases "the wumpus," "the king," and "the agent in the corner" are all examples of the category **noun phrase** (or *NP* for short). There are two reasons for identifying phrases in this way. First, phrases are convenient handles on which we can attach semantics. Second, categorizing phrases helps us to describe the allowable strings of the

VERB PHRASE

SENTENCE

language. We can say that any of the noun phrases can combine with a **verb phrase** (or *VP*) such as "is dead" to form a phrase of category **sentence** (or *S*). Without the intermediate notions of noun phrase and verb phrase, it would be difficult to explain why "the wumpus is dead" is a sentence whereas "wumpus the dead is" is not. Grammatical categories are essentially posited as part of a scientific theory of language that attempts to account for the difference between grammatical and ungrammatical categories. It is theoretically possible, although perhaps unlikely, that in some future theory of the English language, the *NP* and *VP* categories may not exist.

NONTERMINAL
SYMBOLS

REWRITE RULES

Categories such as *NP, VP,* and *S* are called **nonterminal symbols**. In the BNF notation, **rewrite rules** consist of a single nonterminal symbol on the left-hand side, and a sequence of terminals or nonterminals on the right-hand side. The meaning of a rule such as

$$S \rightarrow NP\ VP$$

is that we can take any phrase categorized as a *NP*, append to it any phrase categorized as a *VP*, and the result will be a phrase categorized as an *S*.

The component steps of communication

A typical communication episode, in which speaker *S* wants to convey proposition *P* to hearer *H* using words *W*, is composed of seven processes. Three take place in the speaker:

Intention: *S* wants *H* to believe *P* (where *S* typically believes *P*)
Generation: *S* chooses the words *W* (because they express the meaning *P*)
Synthesis: *S* utters the words *W* (usually addressing them to *H*)

Four take place in the hearer:

Perception: *H* perceives *W'* (ideally *W'* = *W*, but misperception is possible)
Analysis: *H* infers that *W'* has possible meanings $P_1, \ldots, P_n$ (words and
                           phrases can have several meanings)
Disambiguation: *H* infers that *S* intended to convey P_i (where ideally $P_i = P$,
                           but misinterpretation is possible)
Incorporation: *H* decides to believe P_i (or rejects it if it is out of line with
                           what *H* already believes)

GENERATIVE CAPACITY

Grammatical formalisms can be classified by their **generative capacity**: the set of languages they can represent. Chomsky (1957) describes four classes of grammatical formalisms that differ only in the form of the rewrite rules. The classes can be arranged in a hierarchy, where each class can be used to describe all the languages that can be described by a less powerful class, as well as some additional languages. Here we list the hierarchy, most powerful class first:

Recursively enumerable grammars use unrestricted rules: both sides of the rewrite rules can have any number of terminal and nonterminal symbols. These grammars are equivalent to Turing machines in their expressive power.

Context-sensitive grammars are restricted only in that the right-hand side must contain at least as many symbols as the left-hand side. The name context-sensitive comes from the fact that a rule such as $ASB \rightarrow AXB$ says that an S can be rewritten as an X in the context of a preceding A and a following B.

In **context-free grammars** (or **CFG**s), the left-hand side consists of a single nonterminal symbol. Thus, each rule licenses rewriting the nonterminal as the right-hand side in *any* context. CFGs are popular for natural language grammars, although it is now widely accepted that at least some natural languages are not context-free (Pullum, 1991).

Regular grammars are the most restricted class. Every rule has a single nonterminal on the left-hand side, and a terminal symbol optionally followed by a nonterminal on the right-hand side. Regular grammars are equivalent in power to finite-state machines. They are poorly suited for programming languages because, for example, they cannot represent constructs such as balanced opening and closing parentheses.

To give you an idea of which languages can be handled by which classes, the language $a^n b^n$ (a sequence of n copies of a followed by the same number of b) can be generated by a context-free grammar, but not a regular grammar. The language $a^n b^n c^n$ requires a context-sensitive grammar, whereas the language $a^* b^*$ (a sequence of any number of a followed by any number of b) can be described by any of the four classes. A summary of the four classes follows.

Class	Sample Rule	Sample Language
Recursively enumerable	$A\ B \rightarrow C$	any
Context-sensitive	$A\ B \rightarrow B\ A$	$a^n b^n c^n$
Context-free	$S \rightarrow a\ S\ b$	$a^n b^n$
Regular	$S \rightarrow a\ S$	$a^* b^*$

Let us look at these seven processes in the context of the example shown in Figure 22.1.

Intention. Somehow, the speaker decides that there is something that is worth saying to the hearer. This often involves reasoning about the beliefs and goals of the hearer, so that the utterance will have the desired effect. For our example, the speaker has the intention of having the hearer know that the wumpus is no longer alive.

Generation. The speaker uses knowledge about language to decide what to say. In many ways, this is harder than the inverse problem of understanding (i.e., analysis and disambiguation). Generation has not been stressed as much as understanding in AI, mainly because we humans are anxious to talk to machines, but are not as excited about them talking back. For now, we just assume the hearer is able to choose the words "The wumpus is dead."

Synthesis. Most language-based AI systems synthesize typed output on a screen or paper, which is a trivial task. Speech synthesis has been growing in popularity, and some systems are beginning to sound human. In Figure 22.1, we show the agent synthesizing a string of sounds written in the phonetic alphabet defined on page 758: "[thaxwahmpahsihzdeyd]." The details of this notation are unimportant; the point is that the sounds that get synthesized are different from the words that the agent generates. Also note that the words are run together; this is typical of quickly spoken speech.

Perception. When the medium is speech, the perception step is called **speech recognition**; when it is printing, it is called **optical character recognition**. Both have moved from being

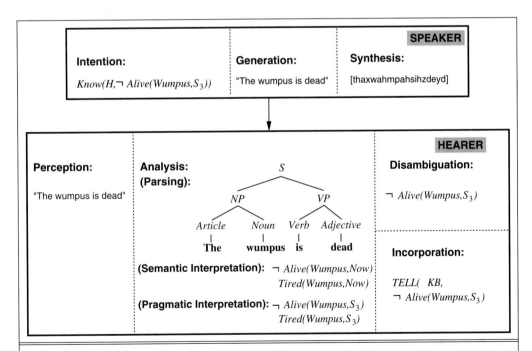

Figure 22.1   Seven processes involved in communication, using the example sentence "The wumpus is dead."

esoteric to being commonplace within the last five years. For the example, let us assume that the hearer perceives the sounds and recovers the spoken words perfectly. (In Chapter 24 we see how this might be done.)

ANALYSIS

Analysis. We divide analysis into two main parts: syntactic interpretation (or parsing) and semantic interpretation. Semantic interpretation includes both understanding the meanings of words and incorporating knowledge of the current situation (also called pragmatic interpretation).

PARSING

The word **parsing** is derived from the Latin phrase *pars orationis*, or "part of speech," and refers to the process of assigning a part of speech (noun, verb, and so on) to each word in a sentence and grouping the words into phrases. One way of displaying the result of a syntactic analysis is with a **parse tree**, as shown in Figure 22.1. A parse tree is a tree in which interior nodes represent phrases, links represent applications of grammar rules, and leaf nodes represent words. If we define the **yield** of a node as the list of all the leaves below the node, in left-to-right order, then we can say that the meaning of a parse tree is that each node with label X asserts that the yield of the node is a phrase of category X.

PARSE TREE

SEMANTIC INTERPRETATION

Semantic interpretation is the process of extracting the meaning of an utterance as an expression in some representation language. In Figure 22.1 we show two possible semantic interpretations: that the wumpus is not alive, and that it is tired (a colloquial meaning of *dead*). Utterances with several possible interpretations are said to be **ambiguous**. We use logic as the representation language, but other representations could be used. **Pragmatic interpretation** is the part of semantic interpretation that takes the current situation into account.[2] In the example, all that pragmatics does is replace the constant *Now* with the constant S_3, which stands for the current situation.

PRAGMATIC INTERPRETATION

DISAMBIGUATION

Disambiguation. Most speakers are not intentionally ambiguous, but most utterances have several legal interpretations. Communication works because the hearer does the work of figuring out which interpretation is the one the speaker probably meant to convey. Notice that this is the first time we have used the word *probably*, and disambiguation is the first process that depends heavily on uncertain reasoning. Analysis generates possible interpretations; if more than one interpretation is found, then disambiguation chooses the one that is best.

INCORPORATION

Incorporation. A totally naive agent might believe everything it hears, but a sophisticated agent treats the words W and the derived interpretation P_i as additional pieces of evidence that get considered along with all other evidence for and against P_i.

Note that it only makes sense to use language when there are agents to communicate with who (a) understand a common language, (b) have a shared context on which to base the conversation, and (c) are at least somewhat rational. Communication does not work when agents are completely irrational, because there is no way to predict how an irrational agent will react to a speech act. Interestingly, communication can work when agents are uncooperative. Even if you believe that another wumpus world explorer would lead you astray in order to get the gold all for itself, you can still communicate to help each other kill the wumpus or perform some other task that is helpful to both agents. Returning to Africa for another example, when an antelope sees a

---

[2] Thus, pragmatic interpretation associates meanings with *utterances* made in specific contexts, whereas the rest of semantic interpretation associates meanings with *strings* in isolation. This is controversial, and other authors draw the line between semantics and pragmatics in different places, or just group them together. Also, some authors use the term **parsing** to encompass all of what we call analysis.

predator at a safe distance, it will **stot**, or leap high into the air. This not only communicates to other antelopes that danger is near, but also communicates to the predator "I see you, and I am healthy enough to run away, so don't even bother chasing me." So even though the two animals are enemies with no common goal, the communication saves both of them from wasting time and energy on a fruitless chase.

Two models of communication

ENCODED MESSAGE

SITUATED LANGUAGE

Our study of communication centers on the way that an agent's beliefs are turned into words and back into beliefs in another agent's knowledge base (or head). There are two ways of looking at the process. The **encoded message** model says that the speaker has a definite proposition P in mind, and encodes the proposition into the words (or signs) W. The hearer then tries to decode the message W to retrieve the original proposition P (cf. Morse code). Under this model, the meaning in the speaker's head, the message that gets transmitted, and the interpretation that the hearer arrives at all ideally carry the same content. When they differ, it is because of noise in the communication channel or an error in encoding or decoding.

Limitations of the encoded message model led to the **situated language** model, which says that the meaning of a message depends on both the words and the **situation** in which the words are uttered. In this model, just as in situation calculus, the encoding and decoding functions take an extra argument representing the current situation. This accounts for the fact that the same words can have very different meanings in different situations. "I am here now" represents one fact when spoken by Peter in Boston on Monday, and quite another fact when spoken by Stuart in Berkeley on Tuesday. More subtly, "You must read this book" is a suggestion when written by a critic in the newspaper, and an assignment when spoken by an instructor to the class. "Diamond" means one thing when the subject is jewelry, and another when the subject is baseball.

The situated language model points out a possible source of communication failure: if the speaker and hearer have different ideas of what the current situation is, then the message may not get through as intended. For example, suppose agents X, Y, and Z are exploring the wumpus world together. X and Y secretly meet and agree that when they smell the wumpus they will both shoot it, and if they see the gold, they will grab it and run, and try to keep Z from sharing it. Now suppose X smells the wumpus, while Y in the adjacent square smells nothing, but sees the gold. X yells "Now!," intending it to mean that now is the time to shoot the wumpus, but Y interprets it as meaning now is the time to grab the gold and run.

22.2   TYPES OF COMMUNICATING AGENTS

In this chapter, we consider agents that communicate in two different ways. First are agents who share a common internal representation language; they can communicate without any external language at all. Then come agents that make no assumptions about each other's internal language, but share a communication language that is a subset of English.

Communicating using Tell and Ask

TELEPATHIC
COMMUNICATION

In this section, we study a form of communication in which agents share the same internal representation language and have direct access to each other's knowledge bases through the TELL and ASK interface. That is, agent A can communicate proposition P to agent B with TELL(KB_B, "P"), just as A would add P to its own knowledge base with TELL(KB_A, "P"). Similarly, agent A can find out if B knows Q with ASK(KB_B, "Q"). We will call this **telepathic communication**. Figure 22.2 shows a schematic diagram in which each agent is modified to have an input/output port to its knowledge base, in addition to the perception and action ports.

Humans are lacking in telepathy powers, so they cannot make use of this kind of communication, but it is feasible to program a group of robots with a common internal representation language and equip them with radio or infrared links to transmit internal representations directly to each other's knowledge bases. Then if agent A wanted to tell agent B that there is a pit in location [2,3], all A would have to do is execute:

$$\text{TELL}(KB_B, \text{``}Pit(P_{A1}) \land At(P_{A1}, [2, 3], S_{A9})\text{''})$$

where S_{A9} is the current situation, and P_{A1} is A's symbol for the pit. For this to work, the agents have to agree not just on the format of the internal representation language, but also on a great many symbols. Some of the symbols are static: they have a fixed denotation that can be easily agreed on ahead of time. Examples are the predicates At and Pit, the constants A and B representing the agents, and the numbering scheme for locations.

Other symbols are dynamic: they are created after the agents start exploring the world. Examples include the constant P_{A1} representing a pit, and S_{A9} representing the current situation. The hard part is synchronizing the use of these dynamic symbols. There are three difficulties:

1. There has to be a naming policy so that A and B do not simultaneously introduce the same symbol to mean different things. We have adopted the policy that each agent includes its own name as part of the subscript to each symbol it introduces.

2. There has to be some way of relating symbols introduced by different agents, so that an agent can tell whether P_{A1} and, say, P_{B2} denote the same pit or not. In part, this is the same problem that a single agent faces. An agent that detects a breeze in two different squares

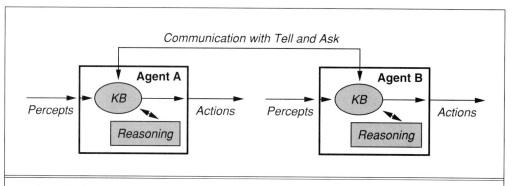

Figure 22.2   Two agents with a shared internal language communicating directly with each other's knowledge bases through TELL and ASK.

might introduce the symbols P_1 and P_2 to denote the two pits that caused the breezes, and must then do some reasoning to decide if $P_1 = P_2$. But the problem is harder for multiple agents because they share fewer symbols to begin with, and thus have less common ground to reason with. In particular, agent B has the problem of deciding how the situation S_{A9} relates to its own situation symbols. This problem can be lessened by minimizing the number of new symbols. For example, A could tell B that there is a pit in [2,3] without introducing any new dynamic symbols with the following action:

$$\text{TELL}(KB_B, \text{``}\exists p, s \ \ Pit(p) \land At(p, [2, 3], s)\text{''})$$

This sentence is weaker than the one containing P_{A1} and S_{A9} because it does not say which pit is in [2,3], nor when it was there, but it turns out that these facts do not really matter for the wumpus world. Note that this sentence is similar to the English sentence "There is a pit in 2,3," which also fails to uniquely identify the pit and the time.

3. The final difficulty is in reconciling the differences between different agents' knowledge bases. If communication is free and instantaneous, then all agents can adopt the policy of broadcasting each new fact to everyone else as soon as they learn it. That way everyone will have all the same knowledge. But in most applications, the bandwidth between agents is limited, and they are often completely out of touch with each other for periods of time. When they come back into contact, they have the problem of deciding what new information is worth communicating, and of discovering what interesting facts the other agent knows.

Another problem with telepathic agents as we have described them is that they are vulnerable to sabotage. Another agent could TELL lies directly into the knowledge base and make our naive telepathic agent believe anything.

Communicating using formal language

Because of the sabotage problem, and because it is infeasible for everyone to have the same internal language, most agents communicate through language rather than through direct access to knowledge bases. Figure 22.3 shows a diagram of this type of communication. Agents can perform actions that produce language, which other agents can perceive. The external communication language can be different from the internal representation language, and the agents can each have different internal languages. They need not agree on any internal symbols at all as long as each one can map reliably from the external language to its own internal symbols.

An external communication language brings with it the problems of generation and analysis, and much of the effort in natural language processing (NLP) has gone into devising algorithms for these two processes. But the hardest part of communication with language is still problem (3) from the previous section: reconciling the differences between different agents' knowledge bases. What agent A says, and how agent B interprets A's statement depends crucially on what A and B already believe (including what they believe about each other's beliefs). This means that agents that have the same internal and external language would have an easy time with generation and analysis, but they would still find it challenging to decide what to say to each other.

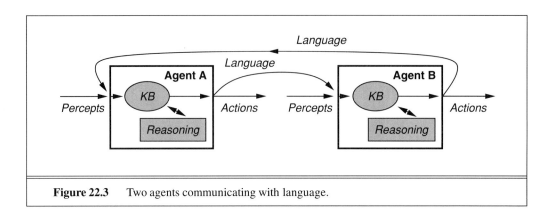

Figure 22.3   Two agents communicating with language.

An agent that communicates

We will now look at an example of communication, in the form of a wumpus world agent that acts as a robot slave that can be commanded by a master. On each turn, the slave describes its percepts in English (actually in a restricted subset), waits for a command from the master, and then interprets the command and executes it. Here is a fragment of a typical dialogue:

ROBOT SLAVE	MASTER
I feel a breeze.	Go to 1 2.
Nothing is here.	Go north.
I feel a breeze and I smell a stench	
and I see a glitter.	Grab it.
⋮	⋮

The agent program is shown in Figure 22.4. The rest of this chapter fills in the missing routines in the agent program. First, Section 22.3 defines the subset of English in which the agents communicate. Then, Section 22.4 shows how to implement the PARSE function to syntactically analyze strings of the language. Section 22.7 shows how to recover the meaning of a string (the function SEMANTICS), and Section 22.8 shows what to do when there are several possible meanings (the function DISAMBIGUATE). The function GENERATE-DESCRIPTION is not covered in depth, but in general much the same knowledge that is used for understanding can also be used for producing language.

22.3   A FORMAL GRAMMAR FOR A SUBSET OF ENGLISH

In this section, we define a formal grammar for a small subset of English that is suitable for making statements about the wumpus world. We will call this language $\mathcal{E}_0$. In defining the language this way, we are implicitly claiming that formal language techniques are appropriate for dealing with natural language. In many ways, they *are* appropriate: natural languages make use

---

function SIMPLE-COMMUNICATING-AGENT(*percept*) **returns** *action*
    static: *KB*, a knowledge base
          t, a counter, initially 0, indicating time

    TELL(*KB*, MAKE-PERCEPT-SENTENCE(*KB, t*))
    words ← SPEECH-PART(*percept*)
    semantics ← DISAMBIGUATE(SEMANTICS(PARSE(*words*)))
    if TYPE[*semantics*] = *Command* **then**
        action ← CONTENTS[*semantics*]
    else if TYPE[*semantics*] = *Statement* **then**
        TELL(*KB*, CONTENTS[*semantics*])
        action ← ASK(*KB*, MAKE-ACTION-QUERY(*percept, t*))
    else if TYPE[*semantics*] = *None* **then**
        action ← ASK(*KB*, MAKE-ACTION-QUERY(*percept, t*))
    description ← GENERATE-DESCRIPTION(*percept*)
    return COMPOUND-ACTION(SAY(*description*), DO(*action*))

Figure 22.4   A communicating agent that accepts commands and statements, and returns a compound action that both describes its percepts and does something else.

of a fixed set of letters (for written language) or sounds (for spoken language) that combine into a relatively fixed set of words. Either level can be considered the symbols of a formal language. The symbols are formed into strings, and it is clear that strings such as "This is a sentence" are part of the English language, and strings such as "A is sentence this" are not. We can come up with a set of grammar rules that cover at least part of English, and compose phrases to form arbitrarily complex sentences.

However, there are ways in which natural languages differ from formal ones. It is hard to characterize a natural language as a set of strings for four reasons. First, not all speakers agree on what is in the language. Some Canadians end sentences with "eh?," some U.S. southerners use "y'all," and one can start arguments in some circles by asking whether "This ain't a sentence" is. Second, the language changes over time—the English of Shakespeare's day is quite different from what we speak today. Third, some utterances that are clearly ungrammatical are nevertheless understandable. Fourth, grammaticality judgments are often graded rather than absolute. That means that there are some sentences that do not sound quite right, but are not clearly wrong, either. The following sentences (for most speakers) range from good to bad:

    To whom did you send the letter?
    Next to whom did you stand?
    Of whom did you meet a friend?
    Of whom did you see the dealer that bought the picture that Vincent painted?

Even if we could agree on exactly which sentences are English and which are not, that would be only a small part of natural language processing. The really hard parts are semantic interpretation and disambiguation. Speech act interpretation (which takes place across the syntactic, semantic, and pragmatic levels) also complicates the picture. In programming languages, every statement is a command, but in natural language the hearer has to determine if an utterance is a command, question, statement, promise, or whatever. Formal language theory provides a framework within which we can address these more difficult problems, but it does not answer them on its own. In the remainder of this section, we define a formal language for our English subset, $\mathcal{E}_0$.

The Lexicon of $\mathcal{E}_0$

LEXICON

The first step in defining a grammar is to define a **lexicon**, or list of allowable vocabulary words. The words are grouped into the categories or parts of speech familiar to dictionary users: nouns, pronouns, and names to denote things, verbs to denote events, adjectives to modify nouns, and adverbs to modify verbs. Categories that may be less familiar to some readers are **articles** (such as *the*), **prepositions** (*in*), and **conjunctions** (*and*).[3] Figure 22.5 shows a small lexicon.

ARTICLES
PREPOSITIONS
CONJUNCTIONS

Each of the categories ends in ... to indicate that there are other words in the category. However, it should be noted that there are two distinct reasons for the missing words. For nouns, verbs, adjectives, and adverbs, it is in principle infeasible to list them all. Not only are there thousands or tens of thousands of members in each class, but new ones are constantly being added. For example, "fax" is now a very common noun and verb, but it was coined only a few years ago. These four categories are called **open classes**. The other categories (pronoun, article, preposition, and conjunction) are called **closed classes**. They have a small number of words (a few to a few dozen) that could in principle be enumerated. Closed classes change over the course of centuries, not months. For example, "thee" and "thou" were commonly used pronouns in the seventeenth century, were on the decline in the nineteenth, and are seen today only in poetry and regional dialects.

OPEN CLASSES
CLOSED CLASSES

The Grammar of $\mathcal{E}_0$

The next step is to combine the words into phrases. We will use five nonterminal symbols to define the different kinds of phrases: sentence (*S*), noun phrase (*NP*), verb phrase (*VP*), prepositional phrase (*PP*), and relative clause (*RelClause*).[4] Figure 22.6 shows a grammar for $\mathcal{E}_0$ with an example for each rewrite rule.

22.4   SYNTACTIC ANALYSIS (PARSING)

PARSE FOREST

There are many algorithms for **parsing**—recovering the phrase structure of an utterance, given a grammar. In Figure 22.7, we give a very simple algorithm that nondeterministically chooses one possible parse tree, if one exists. It treats the list of words as a **parse forest**: an ordered list of parse trees. On each step through the main loop, it finds some subsequence of elements in the

---

[3] The term **conjunction** here means something that joins two phrases together. It addition to *and*, it includes *but, since, while, or,* and *because*. Do not be confused by the fact that *or* is logically a disjunction but syntactically a conjunction.

[4] A relative clause follows and modifies a noun phrase. It consists of a relative pronoun (such as "who" or "that") followed by a verb phrase (and sometimes a whole sentence). An example of a relative clause is *that gave me the gold* in "The agent *that gave me the gold* is in 2,2."

$$
\begin{array}{rcl}
Noun & \rightarrow & \textbf{stench} \mid \textbf{breeze} \mid \textbf{glitter} \mid \textbf{nothing} \\
     &   & \mid \textbf{wumpus} \mid \textbf{pit} \mid \textbf{pits} \mid \textbf{gold} \mid \textbf{east} \mid \ldots \\
Verb & \rightarrow & \textbf{is} \mid \textbf{see} \mid \textbf{smell} \mid \textbf{shoot} \mid \textbf{feel} \mid \textbf{stinks} \\
     &   & \mid \textbf{go} \mid \textbf{grab} \mid \textbf{carry} \mid \textbf{kill} \mid \textbf{turn} \mid \ldots \\
Adjective & \rightarrow & \textbf{right} \mid \textbf{left} \mid \textbf{east} \mid \textbf{south} \mid \textbf{back} \mid \textbf{smelly} \mid \ldots \\
Adverb & \rightarrow & \textbf{here} \mid \textbf{there} \mid \textbf{nearby} \mid \textbf{ahead} \\
       &   & \mid \textbf{right} \mid \textbf{left} \mid \textbf{east} \mid \textbf{south} \mid \textbf{back} \mid \ldots \\
Pronoun & \rightarrow & \textbf{me} \mid \textbf{you} \mid \textbf{I} \mid \textbf{it} \mid \ldots \\
Name & \rightarrow & \textbf{John} \mid \textbf{Mary} \mid \textbf{Boston} \mid \textbf{Aristotle} \mid \ldots \\
Article & \rightarrow & \textbf{the} \mid \textbf{a} \mid \textbf{an} \mid \ldots \\
Preposition & \rightarrow & \textbf{to} \mid \textbf{in} \mid \textbf{on} \mid \textbf{near} \mid \ldots \\
Conjunction & \rightarrow & \textbf{and} \mid \textbf{or} \mid \textbf{but} \mid \ldots \\
Digit & \rightarrow & \textbf{0} \mid \textbf{1} \mid \textbf{2} \mid \textbf{3} \mid \textbf{4} \mid \textbf{5} \mid \textbf{6} \mid \textbf{7} \mid \textbf{8} \mid \textbf{9}
\end{array}
$$

Figure 22.5   The lexicon for $\mathcal{E}_0$.

$S \rightarrow$	$NP\ VP$	I + feel a breeze
$\mid$	$S\ Conjunction\ S$	I feel a breeze + and + I smell a wumpus
$NP \rightarrow$	$Pronoun$	I
$\mid$	$Noun$	pits
$\mid$	$Article\ Noun$	the + wumpus
$\mid$	$Digit\ Digit$	3 4
$\mid$	$NP\ PP$	the wumpus + to the east
$\mid$	$NP\ RelClause$	the wumpus + that is smelly
$VP \rightarrow$	$Verb$	stinks
$\mid$	$VP\ NP$	feel + a breeze
$\mid$	$VP\ Adjective$	is + smelly
$\mid$	$VP\ PP$	turn + to the east
$\mid$	$VP\ Adverb$	go + ahead
$PP \rightarrow$	$Preposition\ NP$	to + the east
$RelClause \rightarrow$	$\textbf{that}\ VP$	that + is smelly

Figure 22.6   The grammar for $\mathcal{E}_0$, with example phrases for each rule.

forest that match the right-hand side of one of the grammar rules. It then replaces the subsequence with a single parse tree whose category is the left-hand side of the rule, and whose children are the nodes in the original subsequence. In Figure 22.8, we show a trace of the execution in parsing the string "the wumpus is dead." Every choice is a good one, so there is no backtracking.

There are many possible parsing algorithms. Some operate top-down, starting with an S and expanding it according to the grammar rules to match the words in the string. Some use a combination of top-down and bottom-up, and some use dynamic programming techniques to avoid the inefficiencies of backtracking. We cover one efficient algorithm for parsing context-free grammars in Section 23.2. But first, we will show how the parsing problem can be interpreted as a logical inference problem, and thus can be handled by general inference algorithms.

---

function BOTTOM-UP-PARSE(*words, grammar*) **returns** a parse tree

    forest ← *words*
    loop do
        if LENGTH(*forest*) = 1 **and** CATEGORY(*forest*[1]) = START(*grammar*) **then**
            return *forest*[1]
        else
            i ← **choose** from {1…LENGTH(*forest*)}
            rule ← **choose** from RULES(*grammar*)
            n ← LENGTH(RULE-RHS(*rule*))
            subsequence ← SUBSEQUENCE(*forest, i, i+n-*1)
            if MATCH(*subsequence*, RULE-RHS(*rule*)) **then**
                forest[*i*…*i+n*-1] ← [MAKE-NODE(RULE-LHS(*rule*), *subsequence*)]
            else fail
    end

Figure 22.7   Nondeterministic bottom-up parsing algorithm for context-free grammars. It picks one parse to return. Each node in a parse tree has two fields: CATEGORY and CHILDREN.

---

forest	*subsequence*	*rule*
The wumpus is dead	The	*Article* → **the**
Article wumpus is dead	wumpus	*Noun* → **wumpus**
Article Noun is dead	*Article Noun*	*NP* → *Article Noun*
NP is dead	is	*Verb* → **is**
NP Verb dead	dead	*Adjective* → **dead**
NP Verb Adjective	*Verb*	*VP* → *Verb*
NP VP Adjective	*VP Adjective*	*VP* → *VP Adjective*
NP VP	*NP VP*	*S* → *NP VP*
S		

Figure 22.8   Trace of BOTTOM-UP-PARSE on the string "The wumpus is dead."

22.5 DEFINITE CLAUSE GRAMMAR (DCG)

There are two problems with BNF. First, we are interested in using language for communication, so we need some way of associating a meaning with each string, and BNF only talks about strings, not meanings. Second, we will want to describe grammars that are context-sensitive, whereas BNF is strictly context-free. In this section, we introduce a formalism that can handle both of these problems.

The idea is to use the full power of first-order logic to talk about strings and their meanings. Each nonterminal symbol becomes a one-place predicate that is true of strings that are phrases of that category. For example, $Noun("stench")$ is a true logical sentence, whereas $Noun("the")$ is false. It is easy to write BNF rules as logical implication sentences in first-order logic:

BNF	**First-Order Logic**
$S \rightarrow NP\ VP$	$NP(s_1) \wedge VP(s_2) \Rightarrow S(Append(s_1, s_2))$
$Noun \rightarrow$ **stench** $\mid \ldots$	$(s = "stench" \vee \ldots) \Rightarrow Noun(s)$

The first of these rules says that if there is a string s_1 that is a noun phrase and a string s_2 that is a verb phrase, then the string formed by appending them together is a sentence. The second rule says that if s is the string "stench" (or one of the other words not shown), then the string s is a noun. A grammar written with logical sentences is called a **logic grammar**. Since unrestricted logical inference is computationally expensive, most logic grammars insist on a restricted format. The most common is **definite clause grammar** or **DCG**, in which every sentence must be a definite clause.[5]

The DCG *formalism* is attractive because it allows us to describe grammars in terms of something we understand well: first-order logic. Unfortunately, it has the disadvantage of being more verbose than BNF notation. We can have the best of both by defining a special DCG *notation* that is an extension of BNF, but retains the well-founded DCG semantics. From now on, when we say "definite clause grammar," we mean a grammar written in this special notation, which is defined as follows:

- The notation $X \rightarrow Y\ Z\ \ldots$ translates as $Y(s_1) \wedge Z(s_2) \wedge \ldots \Rightarrow X(Append(s_1, s_2, \ldots))$.
- The notation $X \rightarrow$ **word** translates as $X(["word"])$.
- The notation $X \rightarrow Y \mid Z \mid \ldots$ translates as $Y'(s) \vee Z'(s) \vee \ldots \Rightarrow X(s)$, where Y' is the translation into logic of the DCG expression Y.

These three rules allow us to translate BNF into definite clauses. We now see how to extend the notation to incorporate grammars that can not be expressed in BNF.

- Nonterminal symbols can be **augmented** with extra arguments. In simple BNF notation, a nonterminal such as NP gets translated as a one-place predicate where the single argument represents a string: $NP(s)$. In the augmented DCG notation, we can write $NP(sem)$, for example, to express "an NP with semantics *sem*." This gets translated into logic as the two-place predicate $NP(sem, s)$.

---

5   A definite clause is a type of Horn clause that, when written as an implication, has exactly one atom in its consequent, and a conjunction of zero or more atoms in its antecedent, for example, $A_1 \wedge A_2 \wedge \ldots \Rightarrow C_1$.

margin notes:

LOGIC GRAMMAR

DEFINITE CLAUSE GRAMMAR

DCG

- A **variable** can appear on the right-hand side of a DCG rule. The variable represents a single symbol in the input string, without saying what it is. We can use this to define the nonterminal category *Double* as the set of strings consisting of a word repeated twice. Here is the definition in both DCG notation and normal first-order logic notation:

DCG	**First-Order Logic**
$Double \rightarrow w \; w$	$(s_1 = [w] \land s_2 = [w]) \Rightarrow Double(Append(s_1, s_2))$

- An arbitrary logical test can appear on the right-hand side of a rule. Such tests are enclosed in curly braces in DCG notation.

As an example using all three extensions, here are rules for *Digit* and *Number* in the grammar of arithmetic (see Appendix B). The nonterminals take an extra argument representing their semantic interpretation:

DCG	**First-Order Logic**
$Digit(sem) \rightarrow sem \; \{0 \le sem \le 9\}$	$(s = [sem]) \Rightarrow Digit(sem, s)$
$Number(sem) \rightarrow Digit(sem)$	$Digit(sem, s) \Rightarrow Number(sem, s)$
$Number(sem) \rightarrow Number(sem_1) \; Digit(sem_2)$	$Number(sem, s_1) \land Digit(sem, s_2)$
$\{sem = 10 \times sem_1 + sem_2\}$	$\land \; sem = 10 \times sem_1 + sem_2 \Rightarrow$
	$Number(sem, Append(s_1, s_2))$

The first rule can be read as "a phrase of category *Digit* and semantic value *sem* can be formed from a symbol *sem* between 0 and 9." The second rule says that a number can consist of a single digit, and has the same semantics as that digit. The third can be read as saying "a number with semantic value *sem* can be formed from a number with semantic value sem_1 followed by a digit with semantic value sem_2, where $sem = 10 \times sem_1 + sem_2$."

There are now five things that can appear on the right-hand side of a rule in DCG notation: an un-augmented nonterminal (*Digit*), an augmented nonterminal (*Digit(sem)*), a variable representing a terminal (*sem*), a constant terminal (**word**), or a logical test ($\{0 \le sem \le 9\}$). The left-hand side must consist of a single nonterminal, with or without augmentation.

22.6 AUGMENTING A GRAMMAR

OVERGENERATES

The simple grammar for $\mathcal{E}_0$ generates many sentences of English, but it also **overgenerates**—generates sentences that are not grammatical—such as "Me smells a stench." There are two problems with this string: it should be "I," not "me," and it should be "smell," not "smells." To fix these problems, we will first determine what the facts of English are, and then see how we can get the grammar to reflect the facts.

CASES

Many languages divide their nouns into different **cases**, depending on their role in the sentence. Those who have taken Latin are familiar with this, but in English there is no notion of case on regular nouns, only on pronouns. We say that pronouns like "I" are in the subjective (or nominative) case, and pronouns like "me" are in the objective (or accusative) case. Many languages have a dative case for words in the indirect object position. Many languages also

AGREEMENT

require **agreement** between the subject and main verb of a sentence. Here, too, the distinctions are minimal in English compared to most languages; all verbs except "be" have only two forms. One form (e.g., "smells") goes with third person singular subjects such as "he" or "the wumpus." The other form (e.g., "smell") goes with all other subjects, such as "I" or "you" or "wumpuses."

Now we are ready to fix our grammar. We will consider noun cases first. The problem is that with the distinctions we have made so far (i.e., the nonterminals we have defined), English is not context-free. It is not the case that any *NP* can combine with a *VP* to form a sentence, for example, the *NP* "I" can, but "me" cannot. If we want to stick with a context-free grammar we will have to introduce new categories such as NP_S and NP_O, to stand for noun phrases in the subjective and objective case, respectively. We would also need to split the category *Pronoun* into the two categories $Pronoun_S$ (which includes "I") and $Pronoun_O$ (which includes "me"). The necessary changes to the grammar are outlined in Figure 22.9. Notice that all the *NP* rules are duplicated,

$$
\begin{aligned}
S &\rightarrow NP_S\ VP \mid \ldots \\
NP_S &\rightarrow Pronoun_S \mid Noun \mid Article\ Noun \\
NP_O &\rightarrow Pronoun_O \mid Noun \mid Article\ Noun \\
VP &\rightarrow VP\ NP_O \mid \ldots \\
PP &\rightarrow Preposition\ NP_O \\
Pronoun_S &\rightarrow \mathbf{I} \mid \mathbf{you} \mid \mathbf{he} \mid \mathbf{she} \mid \ldots \\
Pronoun_O &\rightarrow \mathbf{me} \mid \mathbf{you} \mid \mathbf{him} \mid \mathbf{her} \mid \ldots
\end{aligned}
$$

Figure 22.9   The changes needed in $\mathcal{E}_0$ to handle subjective and objective cases.

once for NP_S and once for NP_O. It would not be too bad if the number of rules doubled once, but it would double again when we changed the grammar to account for subject/verb agreement, and again for the next distinction. Thus, the size of the grammar can grow exponentially with the number of distinctions we need to make.

AUGMENT   An alternative approach is to **augment** the existing rules of the grammar instead of introducing new rules. The result is a concise, compact grammar. We start by parameterizing the categories *NP* and *Pronoun* so that they take a parameter indicating their case. In the rule for *S*, the *NP* must be in the subjective case, whereas in the rules for *VP* and *PP*, the *NP* must be in the objective case. The rule for *NP* takes a variable as its argument. This use of a variable— avoiding a decision where the distinction is not important—is what keeps the size of the rule set manageable. Figure 22.10 shows the augmented grammar, which defines a language we call $\mathcal{E}_1$.

The problem of subject/verb agreement could also be handled with augmentations, but we delay showing this until the next chapter. Instead, we address a slightly harder problem: verb subcategorization.

Verb Subcategorization

The $\mathcal{E}_1$ language is an improvement over $\mathcal{E}_0$, but it still allows ungrammatical sentences. One problem is in the way verb phrases are put together. We want to accept verb phrases like "give me the gold" and "go to 1,2." All these are in $\mathcal{E}_1$, but unfortunately so are "go me the gold"

$$
\begin{aligned}
S &\rightarrow NP(Subjective)\ VP \mid \ldots \\
NP(case) &\rightarrow Pronoun(case) \mid Noun \mid Article\ Noun \mid \ldots \\
VP &\rightarrow VP\ NP(Objective) \mid \ldots \\
PP &\rightarrow Preposition\ NP(Objective) \\
Pronoun(Subjective) &\rightarrow \mathbf{I} \mid \mathbf{you} \mid \mathbf{he} \mid \mathbf{she} \mid \ldots \\
Pronoun(Objective) &\rightarrow \mathbf{me} \mid \mathbf{you} \mid \mathbf{him} \mid \mathbf{her} \mid \ldots
\end{aligned}
$$

Figure 22.10   The grammar of $\mathcal{E}_1$ using augmentations to represent noun cases.

SUBCATEGORIZATION
COMPLEMENTS

and "give to 1,2." To eliminate these, the grammar must state which verbs can be followed by which other categories. We call this the **subcategorization** information for the verb. Each verb has a list of **complements**—obligatory phrases that follow the verb within the verb phrase. So in "Give the gold to me," the *NP* "the gold" and the *PP* "to me" are complements of "give."[6]

SUBCATEGORIZATION
LIST

A **subcategorization list** is a list of complement categories that the verb accepts, so "give" has the subcategorization list [*NP, PP*] in this example. It is possible for a verb to have more than one subcategorization list, just as it is possible for a word to have more than one category, or for a pronoun to have more than one case.[7] In fact, "give" also has the subcategorization list [*NP, NP*], as in "Give me the gold." We can treat this like any other kind of ambiguity. It is also important to know what subcategorization lists a verb does not take. The fact that "give" does not take the list [*PP*] means that "give to me" is not by itself a valid verb phrase. Figure 22.11 gives some examples of verbs and their subcategorization lists, or **subcats** for short.

Verb	Subcats	Example Verb Phrase
give	[*NP, PP*] [*NP, NP*]	give the gold in 3 3 to me give me the gold
smell	[*NP*] [*Adjective*] [*PP*]	smell a wumpus smell awful smell like a wumpus
is	[*Adjective*] [*PP*] [*NP*]	is smelly is in 2 2 is a pit
died	[]	died
believe	[*S*]	believe the smelly wumpus in 2 2 is dead

Figure 22.11   Examples of verbs with their subcategorization frames.

---

6 This is one definition of *complement*, but other authors have different terminology. Some say that the subject of the verb is also a complement. Others say that only the prepositional phrase is a complement, and the noun phrase should be called an **argument**.

7 For example, "you" can be used in either subjective or objective case.

To integrate verb subcategorization into the grammar, we do three things. The first step is to augment the category *VP* to take a subcategorization argument that indicates the complements that are needed to form a complete *VP*. For example, "give" can be made into a complete *VP* by adding [*NP*, *PP*], "give the gold" can be made complete by adding [*PP*], and "give the gold to me" is already complete; its subcategorization list is []. That gives us these rules:

$$VP(subcat) \;\rightarrow\; VP([NP|subcat])\; NP(Objective)$$
$$|\quad VP([Adjective|subcat])\; Adjective$$
$$|\quad VP([PP|subcat])\; PP$$
$$|\quad Verb(subcat)$$

The first line can be read as "A *VP* with a given subcat list, *subcat*, can be formed by a *VP* followed by a *NP* in the objective case, as long as that *VP* has a subcat list that starts with the symbol *NP* and is followed by the elements of the list *subcat*."

The second step is to change the rule for *S* to say that it requires a verb phrase that has all its complements, and thus has a subcat list of []. This means that "He died" is a legal sentence, but "You give" is not. The new rule,

$$S \;\rightarrow\; NP(Subjective)\; VP([])$$

can be read as "A sentence can be composed of a *NP* in the subjective case, followed by a *VP* which has a null subcat list." Figure 22.12 shows a parse tree using this grammar.

The third step is to remember that in addition to complements, verb phrases (and other ADJUNCTS phrases) can also take **adjuncts**, which are phrases that are not licensed by the individual verb but rather may appear in any verb phrase. Phrases representing time and place are adjuncts, because almost any action or event can have a time or place. For example, the adverb "now" in "I smell a wumpus now" and the *PP* "on Tuesday" in "give me the gold on Tuesday" are adjuncts. Here are two rules to allow adjuncts:

$$VP(subcat) \;\rightarrow\; VP(subcat)\; PP$$
$$|\quad VP(subcat)\; Adverb$$

Notice that we now have two rules with *VP PP* on the right-hand side, one as an adjunct and one as a complement. This can lead to ambiguities. For example, "I walked Sunday" is usually interpreted as an intransitive *VP* followed by a time adjunct meaning "I moved myself with my feet on Sunday." But if Sunday is the name of a dog, then Sunday is an *NP* complement, and the meaning is that I took the dog for a walk at some unspecified time.

Generative Capacity of Augmented Grammars

The generative capacity of augmented grammars depends on the number of values for the augmentations. If there is a finite number, then the augmented grammar is equivalent to a RULE SCHEMA context-free grammar. To see this, consider each augmented rule as a **rule schema**, which stands for a set of rules, one for each possible combination of values for the augmented constituents. If we replace each rule schema with the complete set of rules, we end up with a finite (although perhaps exponentially large) set of context-free rules. But in the general case, augmented grammars go

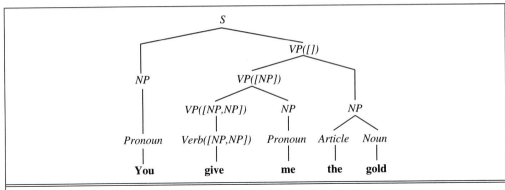

Figure 22.12   Parse tree for "You give me the gold" showing subcategorization of the verb and verb phrase.

beyond context-free. For example, the context-sensitive language $a^n b^n c^n$ can be represented with the following augmented grammar (where ϵ represents the empty string):

$$S(n) \rightarrow A(n) \; B(n) \; C(n)$$
$$A(0) \rightarrow \epsilon \qquad\qquad A(n+1) \rightarrow \boldsymbol{a} \; A(n)$$
$$B(0) \rightarrow \epsilon \qquad\qquad B(n+1) \rightarrow \boldsymbol{b} \; B(n)$$
$$C(0) \rightarrow \epsilon \qquad\qquad C(n+1) \rightarrow \boldsymbol{c} \; C(n)$$

22.7   SEMANTIC INTERPRETATION

Throughout Part III, we gained experience in translating between English and first-order logic. There it was done informally, to get a feeling for what statements of first-order logic mean. Here we will do the same thing in a more carefully controlled way, to define what statements of $\mathcal{E}_1$ mean. Later on we will investigate the meaning of other types of speech acts besides sentences.

Before moving on to natural languages, we will consider the semantics of formal languages. It is easy to deal with meanings of expressions like "$X + Y$" in arithmetic or $X \wedge Y$ in logic because they have a **compositional semantics**. This means that the semantics of any phrase is a function of the semantics of its subphrases; it does not depend on any other phrase before, after, or encompassing the given phrase. So if we know the meaning of X and Y (and +), then we know the meaning of the whole phrase.

Things get more complicated when we go beyond the simple language of arithmetic. For example, the programming language expression "10+10" might have the semantic interpretation 4 when it appears in the larger string "BASE(2); x $\leftarrow$ 10+10." However, we can still salvage a compositional semantics out of this if we say that the semantic function associated with "$x + y$" is to add x and y in the current base. The great advantage of compositional semantics is the same as the advantage of context-free grammars: it lets us handle an infinite grammar with a finite (and often small) set of rules.

COMPOSITIONAL
SEMANTICS

At first glance, natural languages appear to have a noncompositional semantics. In "The batter hit the ball," we expect the semantic interpretation of "batter" to be *one who swings a bat* and of "ball" to be *spherical sporting equipment*. But in "The chef mixed the batter to be served at the ball," we expect the two words to have different meanings. This suggests that the meaning of "batter" and "ball" depends noncompositionally on the surrounding context. However, these semantic interpretations are only the expected, preferred ones, not the only possible ones. It is *possible* that "The batter hit the ball" refers to a cake mixture making a grand appearance at a formal dance. If you work hard enough, you can invent a story where that is the preferred reading. In short, *semantic interpretation alone cannot be certain of the right interpretation of a phrase or sentence.* So we divide the work—semantic interpretation is responsible for combining meanings compositionally to get a set of possible interpretations, and disambiguation is responsible for choosing the best one.

There are other constructions in natural language that pose problems for the compositional approach. The problem of quantifier scope (page 678) is one example. But overall, the compositional approach is the one most favored by modern natural language systems.

Semantics as DCG Augmentations

On page 668 we saw how augmentations could be used to specify the semantics of numbers and digits. In fact, it is not difficult to use the same idea to specify the semantics of the complete language of arithmetic, as we do in Figure 22.13. Figure 22.14 shows the parse tree for $3 + (4 \div 2)$ according to this grammar, with the semantic augmentations. The string is analyzed as $Exp(5)$, an expression whose semantic interpretation is 5.

$Exp(sem) \rightarrow Exp(sem_1) \ Operator(op) \ Exp(sem_2) \ \{sem = Apply(op, sem_1, sem_2)\}$
$Exp(sem) \rightarrow (\ Exp(sem) \ )$
$Exp(sem) \rightarrow Number(sem)$
$Digit(sem) \rightarrow sem \ \{0 \le sem \le 9\}$
$Number(sem) \rightarrow Digit(sem)$
$Number(sem) \rightarrow Number(sem_1) \ Digit(sem_2) \ \{sem = 10 \times sem_1 + sem_2\}$
$Operator(sem) \rightarrow sem \ \{sem \in \{+, -, \div, \times\}\}$

Figure 22.13   A grammar for arithmetic expressions, with semantics.

The semantics of "John loves Mary"

We are now ready to write a grammar with semantics for a very small subset of English. As usual, the first step is to determine what the facts are—what semantic representations we want to associate with what phrases. We will look at the simple sentence "John loves Mary" and associate with it the semantic interpretation $Loves(John, Mary)$. It is trivial to see which parts of the semantic interpretation come from which words in the sentence. The complicated part is

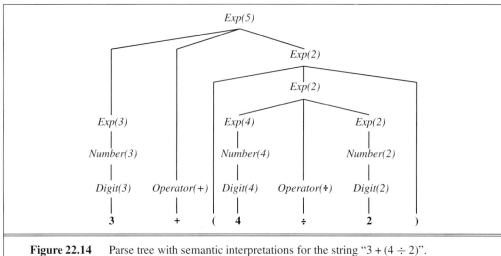

Figure 22.14   Parse tree with semantic interpretations for the string "3 + (4 ÷ 2)".

deciding how the parts fit together, particularly for intermediate phrases such as the *VP* "loves Mary." Note that the semantic interpretation of this phrase is neither a logical term nor a complete logical sentence. Intuitively, "loves Mary" is a description that may or may not apply to a particular person (in this case, it applies to John). This means that "loves Mary" is a **predicate** that, when combined with a term that represents a person (the person doing the loving), yields a complete logical sentence. Using the λ-notation (see page 195), we can represent "loves Mary" as the predicate

$\lambda x\ Loves(x, Mary)$

The *NP* "Mary" can be represented by the logical constant *Mary*. That sets us up to define a rule that says "an *NP* with semantics *obj* followed by a *VP* with semantics *rel* yields a sentence whose semantics is the result of applying the relation *rel* to the object *obj*:"

$S(rel(obj)) \rightarrow NP(obj)\ VP(rel)$

The rule tells us that the semantic interpretation of "John loves Mary" is

$(\lambda x\ Loves(x, Mary))(John)$

which is equivalent to *Loves(John, Mary)*.

The rest of the semantics follows in a straightforward way from the choices we have made so far. Because *VP*s are represented as predicates, it is a good idea to be consistent and represent verbs as predicates as well. The verb "loves" is represented as $\lambda y\ \lambda x\ Loves(x, y)$, the predicate that, when given an argument such as *Mary*, returns the predicate $\lambda x\ Loves(x, Mary)$.

The $VP \rightarrow Verb\ NP$ rule applies the predicate that is the semantic interpretation of the verb to the object that is the semantic interpretation of the *NP* to get the semantic interpretation of the whole *VP*. We end up with the grammar shown in Figure 22.15 and the parse tree shown in Figure 22.16.

$S(rel(obj)) \rightarrow NP(obj) \; VP(rel)$
$VP(rel(obj)) \rightarrow Verb(rel) \; NP(obj)$
$NP(obj) \rightarrow Name(obj)$

$Name(John) \rightarrow$ **John**
$Name(Mary) \rightarrow$ **Mary**
$Verb(\lambda x \; \lambda y \; Loves(x, y)) \rightarrow$ **loves**

Figure 22.15   A grammar that can derive a parse tree and semantic interpretation for "John loves Mary" (and three other sentences).

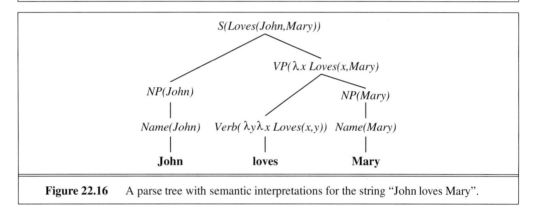

Figure 22.16   A parse tree with semantic interpretations for the string "John loves Mary".

The semantics of $\mathcal{E}_1$

We had no problem with "John loves Mary," but things get more complicated when we consider all of $\mathcal{E}_1$. Immediately we are faced with all the choices of Chapter 8 for our semantic representation; for example, how do we represent time, events, and substances? Our first choice will be to use the event calculus notation of Section 8.4. In this notation, the sentence "Every agent smells a wumpus" can be expressed as:

$$\forall a \; Agent(a) \; \Rightarrow \; \exists w \; Wumpus(w) \wedge \exists e \; e \in Perceive(a, w, Nose) \wedge During(Now, e)$$

We could have used a *Smell* predicate instead of *Perceive*, but we wanted to be able to emphasize the similarities between smelling, hearing, feeling, touching, and seeing.

Our task is to build up our desired representation from the constituents of the sentence. We first break the sentence into *NP* and *VP* phrases, to which we can assign the following semantics:

Every agent $NP(\forall a \; Agent(a) \; \Rightarrow \; \dots)$
smells a wumpus $VP(\exists w \; Wumpus(w) \wedge$
$\exists e \; (e \in Perceive(\dots, w, Nose) \wedge During(Now, e))$

Right away there are two problems. First, the semantics of the entire sentence appears to be the semantics of the *NP* with the semantics of the *VP* filling in the ... part. That means that we cannot form the semantics of the sentence with *rel(obj)*. We could do it with *obj(rel)*, which seems a little odd (at least at first glance). The second problem is that we need to get the variable a as an argument to the relation *Perceive*. In other words, the semantics of the sentence is formed by plugging the semantics of the *VP* into the right argument slot of the *NP*, while also plugging the variable a from the *NP* into the right argument slot of the semantics of the *VP*. It looks as if we need two functional compositions, and promises to be rather confusing. The complexity stems from the fact that the semantic structure is very different from the syntactic structure.

To avoid this confusion, many modern grammars take a different tack. They define an INTERMEDIATE FORM **intermediate form** to mediate between syntax and semantics. The intermediate form has two key properties. First, it is structurally similar to the syntax of the sentence, and thus can be easily constructed through compositional means. Second, it contains enough information so that it can be translated into a regular first-order logical sentence. Because it sits between the syntactic QUASI-LOGICAL FORM and logical forms, it is sometimes called a **quasi-logical form**.[8] In this chapter, we will use a quasi-logical form that includes all of first-order logic and is augmented by lambda expressions QUANTIFIED TERM and one new construction, which we will call a **quantified term**. The quantified term that is the semantic interpretation of "every agent" is written

$$[\forall a\ Agent(a)]$$

This looks like a logical sentence, but it is used in the same way that a logical term is used. In the following example, we see quantified terms as arguments to the relation *Perceive* in the interpretation of "Every agent smells a wumpus":

$$\exists e\ (e \in Perceive([\forall a\ Agent(a)], [\exists w\ Wumpus(w)], Nose) \wedge During(Now, e))$$

We will write our grammar so that it generates this quasi-logical form. In Section 22.7 we will see how to translate this into regular first-order logic.

It can be difficult to write a complex grammar that always comes up with the right semantic interpretation, and everyone has their own way of attacking the problem. We suggest a methodology based on these steps:

1. Decide on the logical or quasi-logical form you want to generate. Write down some example sentences and their corresponding logical forms. One such example sentence is at the top of Figure 22.17.

2. Make one-word-at-a-time modifications to your example sentences, and study the corresponding logical forms. For example, the semantics of "Every agent smelled a wumpus" is the same as our example sentence, except that $During(Now, e)$ is replaced with $After(Now, e)$. This suggests that *During* is part of the semantics of "smells" and *After* is part of the semantics of "smelled." Similarly, changing the word "every" to "an" might result in a change of $\forall$ to $\exists$ in the logical form. This gives you a hint about the semantic interpretation of "an" and "every."

3. Eventually you should be able to write down the basic logical type of each lexical category (noun, verb, and so on), along with some word/logical form pairs. This is motivated in part by example sentences and in part by your intuitions. For example, it seems clear enough that the pronoun "I" should denote the object *Speaker* (which happens to be a fluent, dependent on the situation). Once we decide that one word in a category is of a

---

[8] Some quasi-logical forms have the third property that they can succinctly represent ambiguities that could only be represented in logical form by a long disjunction.

certain semantic type, then we know that everything in the category is of the same type. Otherwise, the compositionality would not work out right. See the middle of Figure 22.17 for types and examples of all the lexical categories.

4. Now consider phrase-at-a-time modifications to your example sentences (e.g., substituting "every stinking wumpus" for "I"). You should be able to determine examples and types for constituent phrases, as in the bottom of Figure 22.17. In Figure 22.18, we see the complete parse tree for a sentence.

5. Once you know the type of each category, it is not too hard to attach semantic interpretation augmentations to the grammar rules. Some of the rules have only one right-hand side constituent and only need to copy up the semantics of that constituent:

$$NP(sem) \rightarrow Pronoun(sem)$$

6. Other times, the right-hand side of a rule will contain a semantic interpretation that is a predicate (or function), and one or more that are objects. To get the semantics of the whole phrase, just apply the relation (or function) to the object(s):

$$S(rel(obj)) \rightarrow NP(obj) \ VP(rel)$$

7. Sometimes the semantics is built up by concatenating the semantics of the constituents, possibly with some connectors wrapped around them:

$$NP([sem_1, sem_2]) \rightarrow Digit(sem_1) \ Digit(sem_2)$$

8. Finally, sometimes you need to take apart one of the constituents before putting the semantics of the whole phrase back together. Here is a complex example:

$$VP(\lambda x \ rel_1(x) \wedge rel_2(\text{EVENT-VAR}(rel_1))) \rightarrow VP(rel_1) \ Adverb(rel_2)$$

The intent here is that the function EVENT-VAR picks out the event variable from the intermediate form expression rel_1. The end result is that a verb phrase such as "saw me yesterday" gets the interpretation:

$$\lambda x \ \exists e \ e \in Sees(x, Speaker) \wedge After(Now, e) \wedge During(e, Yesterday)$$

By following these steps, we arrive at the grammar in Figure 22.19. To actually use this grammar, we would augment it further with the case and subcategorization information that we worked out previously. There is no difficulty in combining such things with semantics, but the grammar is easier to understand when we look at one type of augmentation at a time.

Converting quasi-logical form to logical form

The final step of semantic interpretation is to convert the quasi-logical form into real first-order logic. For our quasi-logical form, that means turning quantified terms into real terms. This is done by a simple rule: For each quantified term $[q \, x \ P(x)]$ within a quasi-logical form QLF, replace the quantified term with x, and replace QLF with $q \, x \ P(x) \ op \ QLF$, where op is $\Rightarrow$ when q is $\forall$, and is $\wedge$ when q is $\exists$ or $\exists!$. For example, the sentence "Every dog has a day" has the quasi-logical form:

$$\exists e \ e \in Has([\forall d \ Dog(d)], [\exists a \ Day(a)], Now)$$

Category	Type	Example	Quasi-Logical Form
S	Sentence	I sleep.	$\exists e \; e \in (Sleep, Speaker)$ $\land During(Now, e)$
Adjective	$object \rightarrow sentence$	smelly	$\lambda x \; Smelly(x)$
Adverb	$event \rightarrow sentence$	today	$\lambda e \; During(e, Today)$
Article	Quantifier	the	$\exists!$
Conjunction	$sentence^2 \rightarrow sentence$	and	$\lambda p, q \; (p \land q)$
Digit	Number	7	7
Noun	$object \rightarrow sentence$	wumpus	$\lambda x \; Wumpus(x)$
Preposition	$object^2 \rightarrow sentence$	in	$\lambda x \; \lambda y \; In(x, y)$
Pronoun	Object	I	$Speaker$
Verb	$object^n \rightarrow sentence$	eats	$\lambda y \; \lambda x \; \exists e \; e \in Eats(x, y)$ $\land During(Now, e)$
NP	Object	a dog	$[\exists d \; Dog(d)]$
PP	$object^2 \rightarrow sentence$	in [2,2]	$\lambda x \; In(x, [2, 2])$
RelClause	$object \rightarrow sentence$	that sees me	$\lambda x \; \exists e \; e \in Sees(x, Speaker)$ $\land During(Now, e)$
VP	$object^n \rightarrow sentence$	sees me	$\lambda x \; \exists e \; e \in Sees(x, Speaker)$ $\land During(Now, e)$

Figure 22.17   Table showing the type of quasi-logical form expression for each syntactic category. The notation $t \rightarrow r$ denotes a function that takes an argument of type t and returns a result of type r.

We did not specify which of the two quantified terms gets pulled out first, so there are actually two possible interpretations:

$$\forall d \; Dog(d) \Rightarrow \exists a \; Day(a) \land \exists e \; e \in Has(d, a, Now)$$
$$\exists a \; Day(a) \land \forall d \; Dog(d) \Rightarrow \exists e \; e \in Has(d, a, Now)$$

The first one says that each dog has his own day, while the second says there is a special day that all dogs share. Choosing between them is a job for disambiguation. Often the left-to-right order of the quantified terms matches the left-to-right order of the quantifiers, but other factors come into play. The advantage of quasi-logical form is that it succinctly represents all the possibilities. The disadvantage is that it doesn't help you choose between them; for that we need the full power of disambiguation using all sources of evidence.

Pragmatic Interpretation

We have shown how an agent can perceive a string of words and use a grammar to derive a set of possible semantic interpretations. Now we address the problem of completing the interpretation by adding information about the current situation, information that is noncompositional and context-dependent.

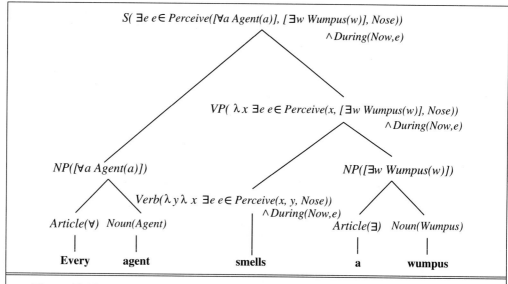

Figure 22.18   Parse tree for the sentence "Every agent smells a wumpus," showing both syntactic structure and semantic interpretations.

INDEXICALS

The most obvious need for pragmatic information is in resolving the meaning of **indexicals**, which are phrases that refer directly to the current situation. For example, in the sentence "I am in Boston today," the interpretation of the indexicals "I" and "today" depend on who uttered the sentence when. We represent indexicals by Skolem constants (such as *Speaker*), which are interpreted as fluents. The hearer who perceives a speech act should also perceive who the speaker is, and use this information to resolve the indexical. For example, the hearer might know $T((Speaker = Agent_B), Now)$.

ANAPHORA

Another important concern is **anaphora**, the occurrence of phrases referring to objects that have been mentioned previously. Consider the passage:

"John was hungry. He entered a restaurant."

To understand that "he" in the second sentence refers to John, we need to have processed the first sentence and used it as part of the situational knowledge in interpreting the second sentence. Anaphoric reference can also be made with definite noun phrases like "the man." In fact, the pattern of reference can be rather complicated, requiring a thorough understanding of the discourse. Consider the following sentence:

"After John proposed to Marsha, they found a preacher and got married. For the honeymoon, they went to Hawaii."

Here the definite noun phrase "the honeymoon" refers to something that was only implicitly alluded to by the verb "married." The pronoun "they" refers to a group that was not explicitly mentioned before: John and Marsha (but *not* the preacher).

When pronouns are used to refer to things within the same sentence, we at least get some help from syntax. For example, in "He saw him in the mirror" the two pronouns must refer to

---

$S(rel(obj)) \rightarrow NP(obj) \, VP(rel)$
$S(conj(sem_1, sem_2)) \rightarrow S(sem_1) \, Conjunction(conj) \, S(sem_2)$

$NP(sem) \rightarrow Pronoun(sem)$
$NP(sem) \rightarrow Name(sem)$
$NP([q \, x \, sem(x)]) \rightarrow Article(q) \, Noun(sem)$
$NP([q \, x \, obj \wedge rel(x)]) \rightarrow NP([q \, x \, obj]) \, PP(rel)$
$NP([q \, x \, obj \wedge rel(x)]) \rightarrow NP([q \, x \, obj]) \, RelClause(rel)$
$NP([sem_1, sem_2]) \rightarrow Digit(sem_1) \, Digit(sem_2)$

/ * VP rules for subcategorization: * /
$VP(sem) \rightarrow Verb(sem)$
$VP(rel(obj)) \rightarrow VP(rel) \, NP(obj)$
$VP(sem_1(sem_2) \rightarrow VP(sem_1) \, Adjective(sem_2)$
$VP(sem_1(sem_2)) \rightarrow VP(sem_1) \, PP(sem_2)$
/ * VP rules for adjuncts: * /
$VP(\lambda x \, sem_1(x) \wedge sem_2(\text{EVENT-VAR}(sem_1))) \rightarrow VP(sem_1) \, PP(sem_2)$
$VP(\lambda x \, sem_1(x) \wedge sem_2(\text{EVENT-VAR}(sem_1))) \rightarrow VP(sem_1) \, Adverb(sem_2)$

$RelClause(sem) \rightarrow \textbf{\textit{that}} \, VP(sem)$

$PP(\lambda x \, rel(x, obj)) \rightarrow Preposition(rel) \, NP(obj)$

Figure 22.19   A grammar for $\mathcal{E}_2$ with semantics.

---

different people, whereas in "He saw himself," they refer to the same person. But most of the time, there are no strict rules on on anaphoric reference. So deciding which reference is the right one is a part of disambiguation, although the disambiguation is certainly guided by pragmatic (i.e., context-dependent) information.

22.8   AMBIGUITY AND DISAMBIGUATION

In the ideal communicative exchange, the speaker has a proposition P in mind and performs a speech act that may have several interpretations, but which in the current situation can best be interpreted as communicating P. The hearer realizes this, and so arrives at P as the interpretation. We say that the hearer has disambiguated or resolved the ambiguity. Occasionally, the hearer may be confused and need to ask for clarification, but it would be tiresome if this happened too often, or if the hearer asked for clarification on the clarification. Unfortunately, there are many ways in which communication can break down. A speaker who does not speak loudly enough will not be heard. But *the biggest problem is that most utterances are ambiguous*. Here are some examples taken from newspaper headlines:

> Squad helps dog bite victim.
> Red-hot star to wed astronomer.
> Helicopter powered by human flies.
> Once-sagging cloth diaper industry saved by full dumps.

and the World War II favorite:

> American pushes bottle up Germans.

LEXICAL AMBIGUITY

The simplest type of ambiguity is **lexical ambiguity**, where a word has more than one meaning. For example, the adjective "hot" can mean warm or spicy or electrified or radioactive or vehement or sexy or popular or stolen. Lexical ambiguity can cut across categories: "back" is an adverb in "go back," an adjective in "back door," a noun in "the back of the room," and a verb in "back up your files."

SYNTACTIC AMBIGUITY

Syntactic ambiguity (also known as **structural ambiguity**) can occur with or without lexical ambiguity. For example, the string "I smelled a wumpus in 2,2" has two parses: one where the propositional phrase modifies the noun, and one where it modifies the verb. The

SEMANTIC AMBIGUITY

syntactic ambiguity leads to a **semantic ambiguity**, because one parse means the wumpus is in 2,2 and the other means that a stench is in 2,2. In this case, getting the wrong interpretation could be a deadly mistake. The lexical ambiguities of the previous paragraph also lead to semantic ambiguities. On the other hand, semantic ambiguity can occur even in phrases with no lexical or syntactic ambiguity. For example, the noun phrase "cat person" can be someone who likes felines or the lead of the movie *Attack of the Cat People*. A "coast road" can be a road that follows the coast, or a road that leads to the coast.

REFERENTIAL AMBIGUITY

One pervasive form of semantic ambiguity is **referential ambiguity**. Anaphoric expressions such as "it" can refer to almost anything. Referential ambiguity occurs because natural languages consist almost entirely of words for categories, not for individual objects. There is no word for *the-apple-I-had-for-lunch-today*, just categories like *apple*.

PRAGMATIC AMBIGUITY

One type of **pragmatic ambiguity** occurs when the speaker and hearer disagree on what the current situation is. If the speaker says "I'll meet you next Friday" thinking that they're talking about the 17th, and the hearer thinks that they are talking about the 24th, then there is miscommunication. The example on page 659 about "Now!" also involves pragmatic ambiguity.

LOCAL AMBIGUITY

Sometimes a phrase or sentence has **local ambiguity**, where a substring can be parsed several ways, but only one of those ways fits into the larger context of the whole string. For example, in the C programming language, the string `*c` means "pointer to `c`" when it appears in the declaration `char *c;` but it means "multiply by `c`" when it appears in the expression `2*c`. In English, "the radio broadcasts" is a noun phrase in "the radio broadcasts inform" and a noun phrase followed by a verb in "the radio broadcasts information." It is possible for a phrase or sentence to be syntactically ambiguous but semantically unambiguous. For example, "S_1 and S_2 and S_3" has two different parses. But they both have the same meaning (at least in $\mathcal{E}_2$), because conjunction is associative.

VAGUE

Natural languages are also **vague**. When we say, "It's hot outside," it says something about the temperature, but it is open to a wide range of interpretation because "hot" is a vague term. To some it might mean the temperature is above $75°F$, and to others it might mean $90°F$.

Finally, there can be ambiguity about what speech act has been performed. A hearer who says, "yes" when asked, "Do you know what time it is?" has successfully interpreted the sentence as if it were question, but most likely it was actually intended as a request for information.

Disambiguation

As we said before, *disambiguation is a question of diagnosis.* The hearer maintains a model of the world and, upon hearing a new speech act, adds the possible interpretations of the speech act to the model as hypotheses. The uncertain reasoning techniques of Part V can then be used to decide which interpretation is best. To do this well, the model must include a lot of information about the world. For example, to correctly resolve the syntactic ambiguity in "Chris saw the Grand Canyon flying to New York," one needs to know that it is more likely that Chris is doing the flying than that the Grand Canyon is. Similarly, to understand "Donald keeps his money in the bank," it helps to know that money is kept in savings institutions more often than in snowbanks.

One also needs a good model of the beliefs of speaker and hearer, in order to decide what the speaker will bother to say. For example, the normal interpretation of the statement "I am not a crook" is that the speaker is not a criminal. This is true even though an alternative interpretation—that the speaker is not a hooked shepherd's staff—has a higher probability of being true. Similarly, "Howard doesn't keep his money in the bank" probably refers to saving institutions, because it would not be worth remarking that he did not keep his money in a snowbank. In general, disambiguation requires the combination of four models:

1. The **world model**: the probability that a fact occurs in the world.
2. The **mental model**: the probability that the speaker forms the intention of communicating this fact to the hearer, given that it occurs.[9] (This combines models of what the speaker believes, what the speaker believes the hearer believes, and so on.)
3. The **language model**: the probability that a certain string of words will be chosen, given that the speaker has the intention of communicating a certain fact.
4. The **acoustic model**: the probability that a particular sequence of sounds will be generated, given that the speaker has chosen a given string of words. This will be taken up when we consider perception in Chapter 24.

The final reason why it is hard to pick the right interpretation is that there may be several right ones. Jokes rely on the fact that the hearer will entertain two interpretations simultaneously. In "She criticized his apartment so he knocked her flat," we have three lexical and one syntactic ambiguity. But the joke would be lost on a hearer who simply accepted the best interpretation and ignored the other. Poetry, advertising, political rhetoric, and murder mysteries are other genres that make use of deliberate ambiguity. Most language understanding programs ignore this possibility, just as many diagnosis systems ignore the possibility of multiple causes.

Context-free grammars do not provide a very useful language model (even when augmentations are included). The problem is that the grammar does not say which strings are more probable than others—it simply divides the strings into two classes: grammatical and agrammatical.

---

[9] We should also consider the possibility that the speaker intends to convey some information given that it did *not* occur, that is, that the speaker is mistaken or lying.

PROBABILISTIC
CONTEXT-FREE
GRAMMAR

The simplest way to provide a probability distribution is to use a **probabilistic context-free grammar** or PCFG.[10] In the PCFG language model, each rewrite rule has a probability associated with it, such that the sum for all rules with the same left-hand side is 1—for example,

$$S \rightarrow NP\ VP \qquad (0.9)$$
$$S \rightarrow S\ Conjunction\ S \qquad (0.1)$$

In the PCFG model, the probability of a string, *P(words)*, is just the sum of the probabilities of its parse trees—one such tree for an unambiguous string, no trees for an ungrammatical string, and several trees for an ambiguous string. The probability of a given tree is the product of the probabilities of all the rules that make up the nodes of the tree.

The problem with PCFGs is that they are context-free. That means that the difference between P("I ate a banana") and P("I ate a bandana") depends only on P("banana") versus P("bandana"), and not on the relation between "ate" and the respective nouns. To get at that kind of relationship, we will need some kind of context-sensitive model. Other probabilistic language models that include context sensitivity have been proposed (see the Historical Notes section). The problem of combining the four models into one is taken up when we discuss speech recognition in Section 24.7.

22.9   A COMMUNICATING AGENT

We have now seen how to go all the way from strings to meanings using syntactic and semantic analysis and disambiguation. The final step is to show how this fits in to an agent that can communicate. We start with the simple wumpus world robot slave described on page 662.

The first step in building the communicating agent is to extend the grammar to accept commands such as "Go east." So far, the language $\mathcal{E}_2$ has only one type of speech act: the statement. We will extend it with commands and acknowledgments to yield the language $\mathcal{E}_3$.

The new words and grammar rules are not complicated. A command can be formed from a *VP*, where the subject is implicitly the hearer. For example, "Go to 2 2" is a command, and it already is a *VP* according to the $\mathcal{E}_2$ grammar. The semantics of the command is derived by applying the semantics of the *VP* to the object *Hearer*. Now that we have several kinds of speech acts, we will identify the kind (i.e, command or statement) as part of the quasi-logical form. Here are the rules for commands and statements:

$$S(Command(rel(Hearer))) \rightarrow VP(rel)$$
$$S(Statement(rel(obj))) \rightarrow NP(obj)\ VP(rel)$$

So the quasi-logical form for "Go to 2 2" is:[11]

$$Command(\exists e\ \ e \in Go(Hearer, [2, 2]))$$

---

[10] PCFGs are also known as stochastic context-free grammars or SCFGs.

[11] Note that the quasi-logical form for a command does not include the time of the event (e.g., *During(Now, e)*). That is because commands are tenseless. We can't tell that by looking at commands with "go," but consider that the correct form of a command is "[you] be good," (using the untensed form "be") not "[you] are good."

Acknowledgments are even simpler—they consist of a single word: "yes" or "OK" to positively acknowledge, and "no" to negatively acknowledge. Here are the rules:

$S(Acknowledge(sem)) \longrightarrow Ack(sem)$
$Ack(True) \longrightarrow \textbf{yes}$
$Ack(True) \longrightarrow \textbf{OK}$
$Ack(False) \longrightarrow \textbf{no}$

It is up to the master (or whoever hears an acknowledgment) to do pragmatic interpretation to realize that "OK," which gets the interpretation $Ack(True)$, means that the agent has agreed to follow out a command (usually the most recent command). The agent program for the robot slave was shown in Figure 22.4 (page 663). But in a sense we do not need a new agent program; all we need to do is use an existing agent (such as a logical planning agent) and give it the goals of understanding the input and responding to it properly.

22.10   SUMMARY

We have seen why it is useful to communicate, and how language can be interpreted by agents in a situation. Natural language processing is difficult for three reasons. First, one has to have a lot of specific knowledge about the words and grammar rules of the language. Second, one must be able to integrate this knowledge with other knowledge about the world. Third, language involves an additional complication that we have not dealt with so far: that there are other agents in the world who have their own beliefs, goals, and plans. This chapter makes the following points in addressing these difficulties:

- Agents send signals to each other to achieve certain purposes: to inform, to warn, to elicit help, to share knowledge, or to promise something. Sending a signal in this way is called a **speech act**. Ultimately, all speech acts are an attempt to get another agent to believe something or do something.

- All animals use some conventional signs to communicate, but humans use language in a more sophisticated way that enables them to communicate much more.

- Formal language theory and **phrase structure** grammars (and in particular, **context-free** grammar) are useful tools for dealing with some aspects of natural language.

- Communication involves three steps by the speaker: the intention to convey an idea, the mental generation of words, and their physical synthesis. The hearer then has four steps: perception, analysis, disambiguation, and incorporation of the meaning.

- The **encoded message** model of communication states that a speaker encodes a representation of a proposition into language, and the hearer then decodes the message to uncover the proposition. The **situated language** model states that the meaning of a message is a function of both the message and the situation in which it occurs.

- It is convenient to **augment** a grammar to handle such problems as subject/verb agreement, pronoun case, and semantics. Definite Clause Grammar (DCG) is an extension of BNF that allows for augmentations.

- There are many algorithms for parsing strings. We showed a simple one. It is also possible to feed DCG rules directly to a logic programming system or theorem prover.
- **Pragmatic** interpretation takes the current situation into account to determine the effect of an utterance in context.
- **Disambiguation** is the process of deciding which of the possible interpretations is the one that the speaker intended to convey.

BIBLIOGRAPHICAL AND HISTORICAL NOTES

The idea of language as action stems from twentieth-century linguistically oriented philosophy (Wittgenstein, 1953; Grice, 1957; Austin, 1962) and particularly from the book *Speech Acts* (Searle, 1969). A precursor to the idea of speech acts was Protagoras's distinction of four types of sentence: prayer, question, answer, and injunction. Hobbs *et al.* (1987) describe a more practical application of the situated model.

Like semantic networks, context-free grammars (also known as phrase structure grammars) are a reinvention of a technique first used by the ancient Indian grammarians (especially Panini, c. 350 B.C.) studying Shastric Sanskrit (Ingerman, 1967). In modern times, they were reinvented by Noam Chomsky for the analysis of English syntax (Chomsky, 1956) and independently by John Backus for the analysis of Algol-60 syntax. Naur (Naur, 1963) extended Backus's notation, and is now credited with the "N" in BNF, which originally stood for "Backus Normal Form."

ATTRIBUTE
GRAMMAR
Knuth (1968) defined a kind of augmented grammar called **attribute grammar**.

There have been many attempts to write formal grammars of natural languages, both in "pure" linguistics and in computational linguistics. The Linguistic String Project at New York University (Sager, 1981) produced a large grammar for the machine parsing of English, using essentially context-free rewrite rules with some restrictions based on subcategorization. A good example of a modern system using unification grammar is the Core Language Engine (Alshawi, 1992). There are several comprehensive but informal grammars of English (Quirk *et al.*, 1985; Huddleston, 1988). Good textbooks on linguistics include Baker (1989) and Chierchia and McConnell-Ginet (1990). McCawley's (1993) text concentrates on logic for linguists. Definite clause grammars were introduced by Colmerauer (1975) and developed and popularized by Pereira and Warren (1980).

Formal semantic interpretation of natural languages originates within philosophy and formal logic and is especially closely related to Alfred Tarski's (1935) work on the semantics of formal languages. Bar-Hillel was the first to consider the problems of pragmatics and propose that they could be handled by formal logic. For example, he introduced C.S. Peirce's (1902) term *indexical* into linguistics (Bar-Hillel, 1954). Richard Montague's essay "English as a formal language" (1970) is a kind of manifesto for the logical analysis of language, but the book by Dowty, Wall, and Peters (1991) and the article by Lewis (1972) are more readable. A complete collection of Montague's contributions has been edited by Thomason (1974). In artificial intelligence, the work of McAllester and Givan (1992) continues the Montagovian tradition, adding many new technical insights.

The idea of an intermediate or quasi-logical form to handle problems such as quantifier scoping goes back to Woods (1978), and is present in many recent systems (Alshawi, 1992; Hwang and Schubert, 1993). Van Lehn (1978) gives a survey of human preferences for quantifier scope disambiguation.

Linguists have dozens of different formalisms; hundreds if you count all the minor modifications and notational variants. We have stuck to a single approach—definite clause grammar with BNF-style notation—but the history of the others is interesting. Sells (1985) offers a good comparison of some current formalisms, but Gerald Gazdar's (1989) analysis is more succinct:

> Here is the history of linguistics in one sentence: once upon a time linguists (i.e., syntacticians) used augmented phrase structure grammars, then they went over to transformational grammars, and then some of them started using augmented phrase structure grammars again, *<space for moral>*. Whilst we are in this careful scholarly mode, let us do the same service for computational linguistics: once upon a time computational linguistics (i.e., builders of parsers) used augmented phrase structure grammars, then they went over to augmented transition networks, and then many of them started using augmented phrase structure grammars again, *<space for moral>*.

We can characterize the different formalisms according to four dichotomies: transformational versus monostratal, unification versus assignment, lexical versus grammatical, and syntactic categories versus semantic categories.

The dominant formalism for the quarter century starting in 1956 was **transformational grammar** (Chomsky, 1957; Chomsky, 1965). In this approach, the commonality in meaning between sentences like "Man bites dog" and "Dog is bitten by man" is captured by a context-free grammar that generates proto-sentences in a canonical form called the **deep structure**. "Man bites dog" and "Dog is bitten by man" would have the same deep structure, but different **surface structure**. A separate set of rules called **transformations** map between deep and surface structure. The fact that there are two distinct levels of analysis and two sets of rules makes transformational grammar a **multistratal** theory. Computational linguists have turned away from transformational grammar, because it is difficult to write parsers that can invert the transformations to recover the deep structure.

TRANSFORMATIONAL
GRAMMAR

DEEP STRUCTURE

SURFACE
STRUCTURE

AUGMENTED
TRANSITION
NETWORK

The **augmented transition network** (ATN) grammars mentioned in the Gazdar quote were invented as a way to go beyond context-free grammar while maintaining a monostratal approach that is computationally tractable. They were invented by Thorne (1968) but are mostly associated with the work of Woods (1970). The rules in an ATN grammar are represented as a directed graph, but one can easily transliterate between transition networks and context-free grammars, so choosing one over the other is mostly a matter of taste. The other big difference is that DCGs are augmented with **unification** assertions, whereas ATNs are augmented with **assignment** statements. This makes DCGs closer to standard first-order logic, but more importantly, it allows a DCG grammar to be processed by a variety of algorithms. Any order of application of the rules will arrive at the same answer, because unification is commutative. Assignment, of course, is not commutative. GPSG or Generalized Phrase Structure Grammar (Gazdar *et al.*, 1985) and HPSG or Head-driven Phrase Structure Grammar (Pollard and Sag, 1994) are two important examples of unification-based grammars. Shieber (1986) surveys them and others.

Since the mid-1980s, there has also been a trend toward putting more information in the lexicon and less in the grammar. For example, rather than having a grammar rule to transform active sentences into passive, many modern grammars place the burden of passives on the lexicon. The grammar would have one or more rules saying a verb phrase can be a verb optionally preceded by an auxiliary verb and followed by complements. The lexical entry for "bitten" would say that it is preceded by a form of the auxiliary verb "be" and followed by a prepositional phrase with the preposition "by."

In the 1970s it was felt that putting this kind of information in the lexicon would be missing an important generality—that most transitive verbs have passive forms.[12] The current view is that if we can account for the way the passives of new verbs are learned, then we have not lost any generalities. Putting the information in the lexicon rather than the grammar is just a kind of compilation—it can make the parser's job easier at run time. LFG or lexical-functional grammar (Bresnan, 1982) was the first major grammar of English and formalism to be highly lexicalized. If we carry lexicalization to an extreme, we end up with **categorial grammar**, in which there can be as few as two grammar rules, or **dependency grammar** (Melćuk and Polguere, 1988), in which there are no phrases, only words. TAG or Tree-Adjoining Grammar (Joshi, 1985) is not strictly lexical, but it is gaining popularity in its lexicalized form (Schabes *et al.*, 1988).

A major barrier to the widespread use of natural language processing is the difficulty of tuning an NLP system to perform well in a new domain, and the amount of specialized training (in linguistics and computer science) needed to do the tuning. One way to lower this barrier is to throw out the specialized terminology and methodology of linguistics and base the system's grammar more directly on the problem domain. This is achieved by replacing abstract syntactic categories with domain-specific semantic categories. Such a grammar is called a **semantic grammar**. For example, an interface to an airline reservation system could have categories like *Location* and *Fly-To* instead of *NP* and *VP*. See Birnbaum and Selfridge (1981) for an implementation of a system based on semantic grammars.

SEMANTIC
GRAMMAR

There are two main drawbacks to semantic grammars. First, they are specific to a particular domain. Very little of the work that goes into building a system can be transferred to a different domain. Second, they make it hard to add syntactic generalizations. Handling constructions such as passive sentences means adding not just one new rule, but one rule for each verb-like category. Getting it right is time-consuming and error-prone. Semantic grammars can be used to get a small application working quickly in a limited domain, but they do not scale up well.

The other approach to knowledge acquisition for NLP is to use machine learning. Gold (1967) set the groundwork for this field, and Fu and Booth (1986a; 1986b) give a tutorial of recent work. Stolcke (1993) gives an algorithm for learning probabilistic context-free grammars, and Black et al. (1992) and Magerman (1993) show how to learn more complex grammars.

Research on language learning by humans is surveyed by Wanner and Gleitman (1982) and by Bloom (1994). Pinker (1989) gives his take on the field. A variety of machine learning experiments have tried to duplicate human language learning (Clark, 1992; Siskind, 1994).

Disambiguation has always been one of the hardest parts of NLP. In part, this is because of a lack of help from other fields. Linguistics considers disambiguation to be largely outside its domain, and literary criticism (Empson, 1953; Hobbs, 1990) is ambiguous about whether

---

[12] It is now known that passivity is a feature of sentences, not verbs. For example, "This bed was slept in by George Washington" is a good sentence, but "The stars were slept under by Fred" is not (even though the two corresponding active sentences are perfectly good).

ambiguity is something to be resolved or to be cherished. Some of the earliest work on disambiguation was Wilks' (1975) theory of **preference semantics**, which tried to find interpretations
that minimize the number of semantic anomalies. Hirst (1987) describes a system with similar
aims that is closer to the compositional semantics described in this chapter. Some problems with
multiple interpretations are addressed by Norvig (1988).

Probabilistic techniques for disambiguation have been predominant in recent years, partly
because of the availability of large corpora of text from which to gather statistics, and partly
because the field is evolving towards a more scientific methodology. Research involving large
corpora of text is described in the special issue of *Computational Linguistics* (Volume 19,
Numbers 1 and 2, 1993) and the book by Garside *et al.* (1987). The statistical approach to
language is covered in a book by Charniak (1993). This subfield started when NLP researchers
noticed the success of probabilistic models in information retrieval (Salton, 1989) and speech
recognition (Rabiner, 1990). This lead to the development of probabilistic models for word
sense disambiguation (Yarowsky, 1992; Resnik, 1993) and eventually to the full parsing task,
as in the work by Church (1988) and by Chitrao and Grishman (1990). Some recent work
casts the disambiguation problem as belief network evaluation (Charniak and Goldman, 1992;
Goldman and Charniak, 1992; Wu, 1993).

The Association for Computational Linguistics (ACL) holds regular conferences; much
current research on natural language processing is published in their proceedings, and in the
ACL's journal *Computational Linguistics. Readings in Natural Language Processing* (Grosz *et
al.*, 1986) is an anthology containing many important papers in the field. The leading textbook
is *Natural Language Understanding* (Allen, 1995). Pereira and Sheiber (1987) and Covington
(1994) offer concise overviews based on implementations in Prolog. The *Encyclopedia of AI*
has many useful articles on the field; see especially "Computational Linguistics" and "Natural
Language Understanding."

EXERCISES

22.1   Outline the major differences between Pascal (or any other computer language with which
you are familiar) and English, and the "understanding" problem in each case. Think about such
things as grammar, syntax, semantics, pragmatics, compositionality, context-dependence, lexical
ambiguity, syntactic ambiguity, reference-finding (including pronouns), background knowledge,
and what it means to "understand" in the first place.

22.2   Which of the following are reasons for introducing a quasi-logical form?

   a. To make it easier to write simple compositional grammar rules.

   b. To extend the expressiveness of the semantic representation language.

   c. To be able to represent quantifier scoping ambiguities (among others) in a succinct form.

   d. To make it easier to do semantic disambiguation.

22.3   Determine what semantic interpretation would be given to the following sentences by the grammar in this chapter:

   a. It is a wumpus.

   b. The wumpus is dead.

   c. The wumpus is in 2,2.

Would it be a good idea to have the semantic interpretation for "It is a wumpus" be simply $\exists x \; Wumpus(x)$? Consider alternative sentences such as "It was a wumpus."

22.4   Augment the grammar from this chapter so that it handles the following:

   a. Pronoun case.

   b. Subject/verb agreement.

   c. Article/noun agreement: "agents" is an *NP* but "agent" is not. In general, only plural nouns can appear without an article.

22.5   This exercise concerns grammars for very simple languages.

   a. Write a context-free grammar for the language $a^n b^n$.

   b. Write a context-free grammar for the palindrome language: the set of all strings whose second half is the reverse of the first half.

   c. Write a context-sensitive grammar for the language $a^n b^n c^n$.

   d. Write a context-sensitive grammar for the duplicate language: the set of all strings whose second half is the same as the first half.

22.6   This exercise continues the example of Section 22.9 by making the slave more intelligent. On each turn, the slave describes its percepts as before, but it also says where it is (e.g., "I am in 1,1") and reports any relevant facts it has deduced about the neighboring squares (e.g., "There is a pit in 1,2" or "2,1 is safe"). You need not do any fancy language generation, but you do have to address the intention problem: deciding which facts are worth mentioning. In addition, you should give your slave a sense of self-preservation. If it is commanded to enter a deadly square, it should politely refuse. If commanded to enter an unsafe square, it can ask for confirmation, but if commanded again, it should obey. Run this slave in the wumpus environment a few times. How mush easier is it to work with this slave than the simple one from Section 22.9?

22.7   Consider the sentence "Someone walked slowly to the supermarket" and the following set of context-free rewrite rules which give the grammatical categories of the words of the sentence:

Pronoun →**someone**	*V* →**walked**
Adv →**slowly**	*Prep* →**to**
Det →**the**	*Noun* →**supermarket**

Which of the following three sets of rewrite rules, when added to the preceding rules, yield context-free grammars that can generate the above sentence?

(A):   *(B):*   *(C):*
$S \rightarrow NP\ VP$ $S \rightarrow NP\ VP$ $S \rightarrow NP\ VP$
$NP \rightarrow Pronoun$ $NP \rightarrow Pronoun$ $NP \rightarrow Pronoun$
$NP \rightarrow Det\ Noun$ $NP \rightarrow Noun$ $NP \rightarrow Det\ NP$
$VP \rightarrow VP\ PP$ $NP \rightarrow Det\ NP$ $VP \rightarrow V\ Adv$
$VP \rightarrow VP\ Adv\ Adv$ $VP \rightarrow V\ Vmod$ $Adv \rightarrow Adv\ Adv$
$VP \rightarrow V$ $Vmod \rightarrow Adv\ Vmod$ $Adv \rightarrow PP$
$PP \rightarrow Prep\ NP$ $Vmod \rightarrow Adv$ $PP \rightarrow Prep\ NP$
$NP \rightarrow Noun$ $Adv \rightarrow PP$ $NP \rightarrow Noun$
                             $PP \rightarrow Prep\ NP$

Write down at least one other English sentence generated by Grammar (B). It should be significantly different from the above sentence, and should be at least six words long. Do not use any of the words from the preceding sentence; instead, add grammatical rules of your own, for instance, *Noun →* **bottle**. Show the parse tree for your sentence.

22.8 This exercise concerns a language we call *Buffalo^n*, which is very much like English except the only word in its lexicon is *buffalo*. (The language is due to Barton, Berwick, and Ristad.) Here are two sentences from the language:

- Buffalo buffalo buffalo Buffalo buffalo.
- Buffalo Buffalo buffalo buffalo buffalo Buffalo buffalo.

In case you don't believe these are sentences, here are two English sentences with corresponding syntactic structure:

- Dallas cattle bewilder Denver cattle.
- Chefs London critics admire cook French food.

Write a grammar for *Buffalo^n*. The lexical categories are adjective, noun, and (transitive) verb, and there should be one grammar rule for sentence, one for verb phrase, and three rules for noun phrase: raw noun, adjective modifier, and reduced relative clause (i.e., a relative clause without the word "that"). Tabulate the number of possible parses for *Buffalo^n* for *n* up to 10.

23 PRACTICAL NATURAL LANGUAGE PROCESSING

In which we see how to scale up from toy domains like the wumpus world to practical systems that perform useful tasks with language.

In Chapter 22, we saw that agents can gain by communicating with each other. We also saw some techniques for interpreting sentences from simple subsets of English. In this chapter, we show how far beyond the wumpus world one can go by elaborating on those techniques. The topics covered are as follows:

◇ **Practical applications**: tasks where natural language has proved useful.
◇ **Discourse processing**: the problem of handling more than one sentence.
◇ **Efficient parsing**: algorithms for parsing and interpreting sentences quickly.
◇ **Scaling up the lexicon**: dealing with unusual and even unknown words.
◇ **Scaling up the grammar**: dealing with complicated syntax.
◇ **Semantic interpretation**: some problems that make semantic interpretation more than just a matter of composing simple functions.
◇ **Disambiguation**: how to choose the right interpretation.

23.1 PRACTICAL APPLICATIONS

We start by surveying successful systems that put natural language to practical use. The successful systems share two properties: they are focused on a particular *domain* rather than allowing discussion of any topic, and they are focused on a particular *task* rather than attempting to understand language completely. We will look at five tasks.

Machine translation

In the early 1960s, there was great hope that computers would be able to translate from one natural language to another, just as Turing's project "translated" coded messages into intelligible

691

German. But by 1966, it became clear that translation requires an understanding of the meaning of the message (and hence detailed knowledge about the world), whereas code breaking depends only on the syntactic properties of the messages.

Although there has been no fundamental breakthrough in machine translation, there has been real progress, to the point that there are now dozens of machine translation systems in everyday use that save money over fully manual techniques. One of the most successful is the TAUM-METEO system, developed by the University of Montreal, which translates weather reports from English to French. It works because the language used in these government weather reports is highly stylized and regular.

In more open domains, the results are less impressive. A representative system is SPANAM (Vasconcellos and León, 1985), which can translate a Spanish passage into English of this quality:

> The extension of the coverage of the health services to the underserved or not served population of the countries of the region was the central goal of the Ten-Year Plan and probably that of greater scope and transcendence. Almost all the countries formulated the purpose of extending the coverage although could be appreciated a diversity of approaches for its attack, which is understandable in view of the different national policies that had acted in the configuration of the health systems of each one of the countries.

This is mostly understandable, but not always grammatical and rarely fluent. Standing on its own, unrestricted machine translation is still inadequate. But when a human translator is given a text like this as an initial guideline, the human is able to work two to four times faster. Sometimes a monolingual human can post-edit the output without having to read the original. This saves money because such editors can be paid less than bilingual translators.

Another possibility is to invest the human effort on pre-editing the original document. If the original document can be made to conform to a restricted subset of English (or whatever the original language is), then it can sometimes be translated without the need for post-editing. This approach is particularly cost-effective when there is a need to translate one document into many languages, as is the case for legal documents in the European Community, or for companies that sell the same product internationally. Restricted languages are sometimes called "Caterpillar English," because Caterpillar was the first firm to try writing their manuals in this form. The first really successful use of this approach was made by Xerox. They defined a language for their maintenance manuals that was simple enough that it could be translated by the SYSTRAN system into all the languages Xerox deals with. As an added benefit, the original English manuals became clearer as well.

There is a substantial start-up cost to any machine translation effort. To achieve broad coverage, translation systems have lexicons of 20,000 to 100,000 words and grammars of 100 to 10,000 rules, the numbers varying greatly depending on the choice of formalism.

Translation is difficult because, in the general case, it requires in-depth understanding of the text, and that requires in-depth understanding of the situation that is being communicated. This is true even for very simple texts—even "texts" of one word. Consider the word "Open" on the door of a store.[1] It communicates the idea that the store is accepting customers at the moment. Now consider the same word "Open" on a large banner outside a newly constructed store. It means that the store is now in daily operation, but readers of this sign would not feel

---

[1]   This example is due to Martin Kay.

misled if the store closed at night without removing the banner. The two signs use the identical word to convey different meanings. In some other languages, the same word or phrase would be used in both cases, but in German, the sign on the door would be "Offen" while the banner would read "Neu Eröffnet."

The problem is that different languages categorize the world differently. A majority of the situations that are covered by the English word "open" are also covered by the German word "offen," but the boundaries of the category differ across languages. In English, we extend the basic meaning of "open" to cover open markets, open questions, and open job offerings. In German, the extensions are different. Job offerings are "freie," not open, but the concepts of loose ice, private firms, and blank checks all use a form of "offen."

To do translation well, a translator (human or machine) must read the original text, understand the situation to which it is referring, and find a corresponding text in the target language that does a good job of describing the same or a similar situation. Often this involves a choice. For example, the English word "you" can be translated into French as either the formal "vous" or the informal "tu." There is just no way that one can refer to the concept of "you" in French without also making a choice of formal or informal. Translators (both machine and human) sometimes find it difficult to make this choice.

Database access

The first major success for natural language processing (NLP) was in the area of database access. Circa 1970, there were many databases on mainframe computers, but they could be accessed only by writing complicated programs in obscure programming languages. The staff in charge of the mainframes could not keep up with all the requests of users who needed to get at this data, and the users understandably did not want to learn how to program their own requests. Natural language interfaces provided a solution to this dilemma.

The first such interface was the LUNAR system, a prototype built by William Woods (1973) and his team for the NASA Manned Spacecraft Center. It enabled a geologist to ask questions about the chemical analysis data of lunar rock and soil samples brought back by the Apollo missions. The system was not put into real operational use, but in one test it successfully answered 78% of queries such as

> What is the average modal plagioclase concentration for lunar samples that contain rubidium?

Fernando Pereira's CHAT system (Pereira, 1983) is at a similar level of complexity. It generates the following answers to questions about a geographical database:

> Q: Which countries are bordered by two seas?
> A: Egypt, Iran, Israel, Saudi Arabia and Turkey
> Q: What are the countries from which a river flows into the Black sea?
> A: Romania, Soviet Union
> Q: What is the total area of countries south of the equator and not in Australasia?
> A: 10,228,000 square miles
> Q: What is the ocean that borders African countries and that borders Asian countries?
> A: Indian Ocean

The advantages of systems like this are obvious. The disadvantage is that the user never knows which wordings of a query will succeed and which are outside the system's competence. For example, CHAT handles "south of the equator" and "with latitude less than zero," but not "in the southern hemisphere." There is no principled reason why this last paraphrase should not work; it just happens that "hemisphere" is not in the dictionary (nor is this sense of "in"). Similarly, the final sample question could not be phrased as "What ocean borders both African countries and Asian?" because the grammar does not allow that kind of conjunction.

Over the last decade, some commercial systems have built up large enough grammars and lexicons to handle a fairly wide variety of inputs. The main challenge for current systems is to follow the context of an interaction. The user should be able to ask a series of questions where some of them implicitly refer to earlier questions or answers:

> What countries are north of the equator?
> How about south?
> Show only the ones outside Australasia.
> What is their total area?

Some systems (e.g., TEAM (Grosz *et al.*, 1987)) handle problems like this to a limited degree. We return to the problem in Section 23.6.

In the 1990s, companies such as Natural Language Inc. and Symantec are still selling database access tools that use natural language, but customers are less likely to make their buying decisions based on the strength of the natural language component than on the graphical user interface or the degree of integration of the database with spreadsheets and word processing. Natural language is not always the most natural way to communicate: sometimes it is easier to point and click with a mouse to express an idea (e.g., "sum *that* column of the spreadsheet").

TEXT
INTERPRETATION

The emphasis in practical NLP has now shifted away from database access to the broad field of **text interpretation**. In part, this is a reflection of a change in the computer industry. In the early 1980s, most online information was stored in databases or spreadsheets. Now the majority of online information is text: email, news, journal articles, reports, books, encyclopedias. Most computer users find there is too much information available, and not enough time to sort through it. Text interpretation programs help to retrieve, categorize, filter, and extract information from text. Text interpretation systems can be split into three types: information retrieval, text categorization, and data extraction.

Information retrieval

In information retrieval (IR), the task is to choose from a set of documents the ones that are relevant to a query. Sometimes a document is represented by a surrogate, such as the title and a list of keywords and/or an abstract. Now that so much text is online, it is more common to use the full text, possibly subdivided into sections that each serve as a separate document for retrieval purposes. The query is normally a list of words typed by the user. In early information retrieval systems, the query was a Boolean combination of keywords. For example, the query "(natural and language) or (computational and linguistics)" would be a reasonable query to find documents related to this chapter. However, users found it difficult to get good results with Boolean queries. When a query finds no documents, for example, it is not clear how to relax the query to find some. Changing an "and" to an "or" is one possibility; adding another disjunction is another, but users found there were too many possibilities and not enough guidance.

VECTOR-SPACE   Most modern IR systems have switched from the Boolean model to a **vector-space** model, in which every list of words (both document and query) is treated as a vector in n-dimensional space, where n is the number of distinct tokens in the document collection. In this model, the query would simply be "natural language computational linguistics," which would be treated as a vector with the value 1 for these four words (or **terms**, as they are called in IR) and the value 0 for all the other terms. Finding documents is then a matter of comparing this vector against a collection of other vectors and reporting the ones that are close. The vector model is more flexible than the Boolean model because the documents can be ranked by their distance to the query, and the closest ones can be reported first.

There are many variations on this model. Some systems are equipped with morphological analyzers that match "linguistic computation" with "computational linguistics." Some allow the query to state that two words must appear near each other to count as a match, and others use a thesaurus to automatically augment the words in the query with their synonyms. Only the most naive systems count all the terms in the vectors equally. Most systems ignore common words like "the" and "a," and many systems weight each term differently. A good way to do this is to give a term a larger weight if it is a good discriminator: if it appears in a small number of documents rather than in many of them.

This model of information retrieval is almost entirely at the word level. It admits a minuscule amount of syntax in that words can be required to be near each other, and allows a similarly tiny role for semantic classes in the form of synonym lists. You might think that IR would perform much better if it used some more sophisticated natural language processing techniques. Many people have thought just that, but surprisingly, none has been able to show a significant improvement on a wide range of IR tasks. It is possible to tune NLP techniques to a particular subject domain, but nobody has been able to successfully apply NLP to an unrestricted range of texts.

The moral is that most of the information in a text is contained in the words. The IR approach does a good job of applying statistical techniques to capture most of this information. It is as if we took all the words in a document, sorted them alphabetically, and then very carefully compared that list to another sorted list. While the sort loses a lot of information about the original document, it often maintains enough to decide if two sorted lists are on similar topics. In contrast, the NLP technology we have today can sometimes pick out additional information—disambiguating words and determining the relations between phrases—but it often fails to recover anything at all. We are just beginning to see hybrid IR/NLP systems that combine the two approaches.

Text categorization

NLP techniques have proven successful in a related task: sorting text into fixed topic categories. There are several commercial services that provide access to news wire stories in this manner. A subscriber can ask for all the news on a particular industry, company, or geographic area, for example. The providers of these services have traditionally used human experts to assign the categories. In the last few years, NLP systems have proven to be just as accurate, correctly categorizing over 90% of the news stories. They are also far faster and more consistent, so there has been a switch from humans to automated systems.

Text categorization is amenable to NLP techniques where IR is not because the categories are fixed, and thus the system builders can spend the time tuning their program to the problem. For example, in a dictionary, the primary definition of the word "crude" is vulgar, but in a large sample of the *Wall Street Journal*, "crude" refers to oil 100% of the time.

Extracting data from text

The task of data extraction is to take on-line text and derive from it some assertions that can be put into a structured database. For example, the SCISOR system (Jacobs and Rau, 1990) is able to take the following Dow Jones News Service story:

> PILLSBURY SURGED 3 3-4 TO 62 IN BIG BOARD COMPOSITE TRADING OF 3.1 MIL-
> LION SHARES AFTER BRITAIN'S GRAND METROPOLITAN RAISED ITS HOSTILE
> TENDER OFFER BY $3 A SHARE TO $63. THE COMPANY PROMPTLY REJECTED
> THE SWEETENED BID, WHICH CAME AFTER THE TWO SIDES COULDN'T AGREE
> TO A HIGHER OFFER ON FRIENDLY TERMS OVER THE WEEKEND.

and generate this template to add to a database:

```
Corp-Takeover-Core:
  Subevent: Increased Offer, Rejected Offer
  Type: Hostile
  Target: Pillsbury
  Suitor: Grand Metropolitan
  Share-Price: 63
  Stock-Exchange: NYSE
  Volume: 3.1M
  Effect-On-Stock: (Up Increment: 3 3-4, To: 62)
```

23.2   EFFICIENT PARSING

Consider the following two sentences:

> Have the students in section 2 of Computer Science 101 take the exam.
> Have the students in section 2 of Computer Science 101 taken the exam?

Even though they share the first ten words, these sentences have very different parses, because the first is a command and the second is a question. A left-to-right parsing algorithm like the one in Section 22.4 that nondeterministically tries to build the right structure would have to guess if the first word is part of a command or a question, and will not be able to tell if the guess is correct until at least the eleventh word, "take/taken." If the algorithm guessed wrong, it will have to backtrack all the way to the first word. This kind of backtracking is inevitable, but if our parsing algorithm is to be efficient, it must avoid reanalyzing "the students in section 2 of Computer Science 101" as an *NP* each time it backtracks.

In this section, we look at efficient parsing algorithms. *At the broadest level, there are three main things we can do improve efficiency:*

1. Don't do twice what you can do once.
2. Don't do once what you can avoid altogether.
3. Don't represent distinctions that you don't need.

To be more specific, we will design a parsing algorithm that does the following:

CHART

1. Once we discover that "the students in section 2 of Computer Science 101" is an *NP*, it is a good idea to record that result in a data structure known as a **chart**. Algorithms that do this are called **chart parsers**. Because we are dealing with context-free grammars, any phrase that was found in the context of one branch of the search space can work just as well in any other branch of the search space. Recording results in the chart is a form of dynamic programming that avoids duplicate work.

2. We will see that our chart-parsing algorithm uses a combination of top-down and bottom-up processing in a way that means it never has to consider certain constituents that could not lead to a complete parse. (This also means it can handle grammars with both left-recursive rules and rules with empty right-hand sides without going into an infinite loop.)

PACKED FOREST

3. The result of our algorithm is a **packed forest** of parse tree constituents rather than an enumeration of all possible trees. We will see later why this is important.

VERTICES

EDGES

The chart is a data structure for representing partial results of the parsing process in such a way that they can be reused later on. The chart for an *n*-word sentence consists of *n* + 1 **vertices** and a number of **edges** that connect vertices. Figure 23.1 shows a chart with 6 vertices (circles), and 3 edges (lines). For example, the edge labelled

$$[0, 5, \ S \rightarrow NP \ VP \ \bullet]$$

means that an *NP* followed by a *VP* combine to make an *S* that spans the string from 0 to 5. The symbol • in an edge separates what has been found so far from what remains to be found.[2] Edges with the • at the end are called **complete edges**. The edge

$$[0, 2, \ S \rightarrow NP \ \bullet \ VP]$$

says that an *NP* spans the string from 0 to 2, and if we could find a *VP* to follow it, then we would have an *S*. Edges like this with the dot before the end are called incomplete edges,[3] and we say that the edge is looking for a *VP*. We have already seen two ways to look at the parsing process. In BOTTOM-UP-PARSE on page 666, we described parsing as a process of building words into trees, backtracking when necessary. With Definite Clause Grammar, we described parsing as a form of logical inference on strings. Backtracking was used when several rules could derive the

---

[2] It is because of the • that edges are often called **dotted rules**. We think this term is a little confusing, because there can be many dotted rules corresponding to the same grammar rule.

[3] Some authors call these **active** edges. In some papers (Earley, 1970), edges are called **states**; the idea is that an incomplete edge marks an intermediate state in the process of finding a complete constituent.

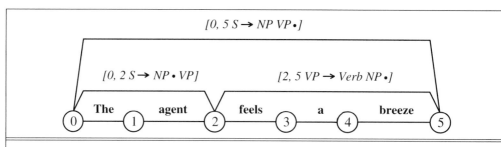

Figure 23.1   Part of the chart for the sentence "The agent feels a breeze." All 6 vertices are shown, but only three of the edges that would make up a complete parse.

same predicate. Now we will see a third approach, chart-parsing. Under this view, the process of parsing an n-word sentence consists of forming a chart with $n + 1$ vertices and adding edges to the chart one at a time, trying to produce a complete edge that spans from vertex 0 to n and is of category S. There is no backtracking; everything that is put in the chart stays there.

There are four ways to add an edge to the chart, and we can give each one a name: The **initializer** adds an edge to indicate that we are looking for the start symbol of the grammar, S, starting at position 0, but that we have not found anything yet. The **predictor** takes an incomplete edge that is looking for an X and adds new incomplete edges that, if completed, would build an X in the right place. The **completer** takes an incomplete edge that is looking for an X and ends at vertex j and a complete edge that begins at j and has X as the left-hand side, and combines them to make a new edge where the X has been found. Finally, the **scanner** is similar to the completer, except that it uses the input words rather than existing complete edges to generate the X. That is, if there is an edge ending at vertex j that is looking for a *Noun*, and if the jth word in the input string has a *Noun* entry in the lexicon, then the scanner will add a new edge that incorporates the word, and goes to vertex $j + 1$.

We will show two versions of chart-parsing algorithms. Figure 23.2 treats the chart as a set of edges and at each step adds one new edge to the set, nondeterministically choosing between the possible additions. This algorithm uses the operator **pick** rather than **choose** to indicate that it has no backtrack points. Any order of choices leads to the same result in the end. The algorithm terminates when none of the four methods can add a new edge. We use a slight trick to start: we add the edge $[0, 0, \ S' \rightarrow \bullet S]$ to the chart, where S is the grammar's start symbol, and S' is a new symbol that we just invented. This edge makes the PREDICTOR add an edge for each grammar rule with S on the left-hand side, which is just what we need to start.

Figures 23.3 and 23.4 show a chart and trace of the algorithm parsing the sentence "I feel it." Thirteen edges (labelled a-m) are recorded in the chart, including five complete edges (shown above the vertices of the chart) and eight incomplete ones (below the vertices). Note the cycle of predictor, scanner, and completer actions. For example, the predictor uses the fact that edge (a) is looking for an S to license the prediction of an *NP* (edge b) and a *Pronoun* (edge c). Then the scanner recognizes that there is a *Pronoun* in the right place (edge d), and the completer combines the incomplete edge b with the complete edge d to yield a new edge, e. Note that the name COMPLETER is misleading in that the edges it produces (like e) are not necessarily complete. We use the name because it has a long history, but a better name might have been EXTENDER.

INITIALIZER
PREDICTOR

COMPLETER

SCANNER

---

function NONDETERMINISTIC-CHART-PARSE(*string, grammar*) **returns** *chart*

    INITIALIZER:
        chart ← [0, 0, S' → • S]
    while new edges can still be added **do**
        edge ← **choose** [i, j, A → α • $B\,\beta$] **in** *chart*
        choose one of the three methods that will succeed:
            PREDICTOR:
                choose (B → γ) **in** RULES[*grammar*]
                add [j, j, B → • γ] to *chart*
            COMPLETER:
                choose [j, k, B → F •] **in** *chart*
                add [i, k, A → αB • β] to *chart*
            SCANNER:
                if *string*[$j + 1$] is of category B **then**
                    add [$j, j + 1$, A → αB • β] to *chart*
    end
    return *chart*

Figure 23.2   Nondeterministic chart parsing algorithm. S is the start symbol and S' is a new nonterminal symbol. The Greek letters match a string of zero or more symbols. The variable *edge* is an edge looking for a B. The predictor adds an edge that will form a B, the completer chooses a complete edge with B on the left-hand side and adds a new edge that is just like *edge* except the dot is advanced past B. The scanner advances the dot if the next word is of category B.

An important feature of our chart-parsing algorithm is that it avoids building some edges that could not possibly be part of an S spanning the whole string. Consider the sentence "The ride the horse gave was wild." Some algorithms would parse "ride the horse" as a *VP*, and then discard it when it is found not to fit into a larger S. But if we assume that the grammar does not allow a *VP* to follow "the," then the chart-parsing algorithm will never predict a *VP* at that point, and thus will avoid wasting time building the *VP* constituent there. Algorithms that have LEFT-CORNER this property are called **left-corner** parsers, because they build up a parse tree that starts with the grammar's start symbol and extends down to the left-most word in the sentence (the left corner). An edge is added to the chart only if it can serve to extend this parse tree. See Figure 23.5 for an example of this.

Our algorithm has the constraint that the edges are added in left-to-right order. That is, if edge [i, j, A → B] is added before [i', j', C → D], then it must be that $j \leq j'$. Figure 23.6 shows a deterministic implementation that obeys this constraint. To get efficiency, we index edges in the chart by their ending vertex number. The notation *chart*[j] means the set of edges that end at vertex j. Additional indexing of edges may lead to further efficiency: the loop in SCANNER could be eliminated if we indexed edges at a vertex by the terminal symbol they are looking for, and the loop in COMPLETER could be eliminated if we indexed the complete edges at a vertex by their left-hand side. The algorithm also indexes rules so that REWRITES-FOR(X, G) returns all rules in G whose left-hand side is X.

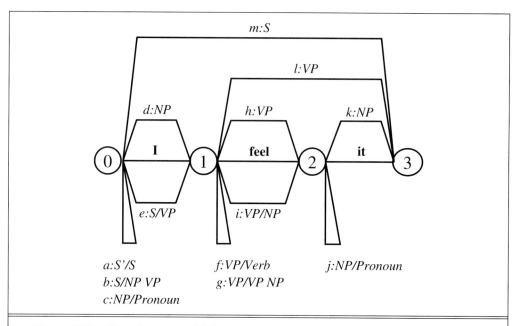

Figure 23.3   Chart for a parse of "$_0$ I $_1$ feel $_2$ it $_3$." The notation *m:S* means that edge *m* has an *S* on the left-hand side, while the notation *f:VP/Verb* means that edge *f* has a *VP* on the left-hand side, but it is looking for a *Verb*. There are 5 complete edges above the vertices, and 8 incomplete edges below.

Edge	Procedure	Derivation
a	INITIALIZER	$[0, 0, \ S' \rightarrow \bullet S]$
b	PREDICTOR(a)	$[0, 0, \ S \rightarrow \bullet NP \ VP]$
c	PREDICTOR(b)	$[0, 0, \ NP \rightarrow \bullet Pronoun]$
d	SCANNER(c)	$[0, 1, \ NP \rightarrow Pronoun\bullet]$
e	COMPLETER(b,d)	$[0, 1, \ S \rightarrow NP \bullet VP]$
f	PREDICTOR(e)	$[1, 1, \ VP \rightarrow \bullet Verb]$
g	PREDICTOR(e)	$[1, 1, \ VP \rightarrow \bullet VP \ NP]$
h	SCANNER(f)	$[1, 2, \ VP \rightarrow Verb\bullet]$
i	COMPLETER(g,h)	$[1, 2, \ VP \rightarrow VP \bullet NP]$
j	PREDICTOR(g)	$[2, 2, \ NP \rightarrow \bullet Pronoun]$
k	SCANNER(j)	$[2, 3, \ NP \rightarrow Pronoun\bullet]$
l	COMPLETER(i,k)	$[1, 3, \ VP \rightarrow VP \ NP\bullet]$
m	COMPLETER(e,l)	$[0, 3, \ S \rightarrow NP \ VP\bullet]$

Figure 23.4   Trace of a parse of "$_0$ I $_1$ feel $_2$ it $_3$." For each edge a-m, we show the procedure used to derive the edge from other edges already in the chart.

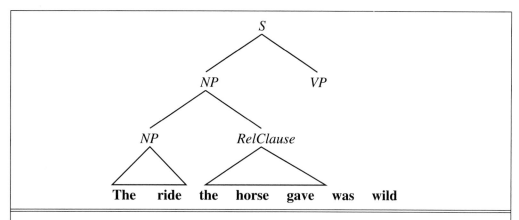

Figure 23.5   A left-corner parsing algorithm avoids predicting a *VP* starting with "ride," but does predict a *VP* starting with "was," because the grammar expects a *VP* following an *NP*. The triangle over "the horse gave" means that the words have a parse as a *RelClause*, but with additional intermediate constituents that are not shown.

Extracting parses from the chart: Packing

When the chart-parsing algorithm finishes, it returns the entire chart, but what we really want is a parse tree (or trees). Depending on how the parser is used, we may want to pick out one or all the parse trees that span the entire input, or we may want to look at some subtrees that do not span the whole input. If we have an augmented grammar, we may only want to look at the semantic augmentation, ignoring the syntactic structure. In any case, we need to be able to extract parses from the chart.

The easiest way to do that is to modify COMPLETER so that when it combines two child edges to produce a parent edge, it stores in the parent edge the list of children that comprise it. Then, when we are done with the parse, we need only look in *chart*[n] for an edge that starts at 0, and recursively look at the children lists to reproduce a complete parse tree. The only complication is deciding what to do about ambiguous parses. To see why this is a problem, let us look at an example. The sentence

       Fall leaves fall and spring leaves spring

is highly ambiguous because each word (except "and") can be either a noun or a verb, and "fall" and "spring" can be adjectives as well. Altogether the sentence has four parses:[4]

       [S [S [NP Fall leaves] fall] and [S [NP spring leaves] spring]
       [S [S [NP Fall leaves] fall] and [S spring [VP leaves spring]]
       [S [S Fall [VP leaves fall]] and [S [NP spring leaves] spring]
       [S [S Fall [VP leaves fall]] and [S spring [VP leaves spring]]

---

4   The parse [S Fall [VP leaves fall]] is equivalent to "Autumn abandons autumn."

---

function CHART-PARSE(*string, grammar*) **returns** *chart*

   chart[0] ← {[0, 0, $S' \rightarrow \bullet S$]}
   for $v \leftarrow$ **from** 1 **to** LENGTH(*string*) **do**
    SCANNER(*v, string*[*v*])
   end
   return *chart*

   procedure ADD-EDGE(*edge*)
      if *edge* in *chart*[END(*edge*)] **then** do nothing
      else
         push *edge* on *chart*[END(*edge*)]
         if COMPLETE?(*edge*) **then** COMPLETER(*edge*)
         else PREDICTOR(*edge*)

   procedure SCANNER(*j, word*)
      for each [$i, j, A \rightarrow \alpha \bullet B \beta$] **in** *chart*[*j*] **do**
        if *word* is of category *B* **then**
            ADD-EDGE([$i, j+1, A \rightarrow \alpha B \bullet \beta$])
      end

   procedure PREDICTOR([$i, j, A \rightarrow \alpha \bullet B \beta$])
      for each ($B \rightarrow \gamma$) **in** REWRITES-FOR(*B, grammar*) **do**
         ADD-EDGE([$j, j, B \rightarrow \bullet \gamma$])
      end

   procedure COMPLETER([$j, k, B \rightarrow \gamma \bullet$])
      for each [$i, j, A \rightarrow \alpha \bullet B' \beta$] **in** *chart*[*j*] **do**
        if $B = B'$ **then**
            ADD-EDGE([$i, k, A \rightarrow \alpha B' \bullet \beta$])
      end

Figure 23.6   Deterministic version of the chart-parsing algorithm. *S* is the start symbol and *S'* is a new nonterminal symbol. The function ADD-EDGE adds an edge to the chart, and either completes it or predicts from it.

The ambiguity can be divided into two independent parts: each of the two subsentences is ambiguous in two ways. If we had a sentence with *n* such subsentences joined by conjunctions, then we would get one big sentence with 2^n parses. (There also would be ambiguity in the way the subsentences conjoin with each other, but that is another story, one that is told quite well by Church and Patil (1982).) An exponential number of parses is a bad thing, and one way to avoid the problem is to represent the parses implicitly. Consider the following representation:

$$[\text{S } [\text{S} \left\{ \begin{array}{l} [\text{NP Fall leaves}] \ [\text{VP fall}] \\ [\text{NP Fall}] \ [\text{VP leaves fall}] \end{array} \right\}] \text{ and } [\text{S} \left\{ \begin{array}{l} [\text{NP spring leaves}] \ [\text{VP spring}] \\ [\text{NP spring}] \ [\text{VP leaves spring}] \end{array} \right\}]]$$

Instead of multiplying out the ambiguity to yield 2^n separate parse trees, we have one big "tree" with ambiguous subparts represented by curly braces. Of course, when *n* = 2, there is not much difference between 2^n and $2n$, but for large n, this representation offers considerable saving. The representation is called a **packed forest**, because it is the equivalent to a set of trees (a forest), but they are efficiently packed into one structure.

To implement the packed forest representation, we modify COMPLETER to keep track of lists of possible children, and we modify ADD-EDGE so that when we go to add an edge that is already in the chart, we merge its list of possible children with the list that is already there.

We end up with a parsing algorithm that is $O(n^3)$ in the worst case (where n is the number of words in the input). This is the best that can be achieved for a context-free grammar. Note that without the packed forest, the algorithm would be exponential in the worst case, because it is possible for a sentence to have $O(2^n)$ different parse trees. In practice, one can expect a good implementation of the algorithm to parse on the order of 100 words per second, with variation depending on the complexity of the grammar and the input.

23.3   SCALING UP THE LEXICON

In Chapter 22, the input was a sequence of words. In real text-understanding systems, the input is a sequence of characters from which the words must be extracted. Most systems follow a four-step process of tokenization, morphological analysis, dictionary lookup, and error recovery.

TOKENIZATION

Tokenization is the process of dividing the input into distinct tokens—words and punctuation marks. In Japanese, this is difficult because there are no spaces between words. Languages like English are easier, but not trivial. A hyphen at the end of the line may be an inter- or intraword dash. In some types of text, font changes, underlines, superscripts, and other control sequences must be accounted for. Tokenization routines are designed to be fast, with the idea that as long as they are consistent in breaking up the input text into tokens, any problems can always be handled at some later stage of processing.

MORPHOLOGICAL ANALYSIS

Morphological analysis is the process of describing a word in terms of the prefixes, suffixes, and root forms that comprise it. There are three ways that words can be composed:

INFLECTIONAL MORPHOLOGY

$\diamond$ **Inflectional morphology** reflects the changes to a word that are needed in a particular grammatical context. For example, most nouns take the suffix "s" when they are plural.

DERIVATIONAL MORPHOLOGY

$\diamond$ **Derivational morphology** derives a new word from another word that is usually of a different category. For example, the noun "shortness" is derived from the adjective "short" together with the suffix "ness."

COMPOUNDING

$\diamond$ **Compounding** takes two words and puts them together. For example, "bookkeeper" is a compound of "book" and "keeper." (The noun "keeper" is in turn derived from the verb "keep" by derivational morphology.)

Even in a morphologically simple language like English, there can be morphological ambiguities. "Walks" can be either a plural noun or a third-person singular verb. "Unionizable" can be analyzed as "un-ion-izable" or "union-izable," and "untieable" can be "un-(tie-able)" or "(un-tie)-able." Many languages make more use of morphology than English. In German, it is not uncommon to see words like "Lebensversicherungsgesellschaftsangestellter" (life insurance company employee). Languages such as Finish, Turkish, Inuit, and Yupik have recursive morphological rules that can generate an infinite number of infinitely long words.

DICTIONARY LOOKUP **Dictionary lookup** is performed on every token (except for special ones such as punctuation). It may be more efficient to store morphologically complex words like "walked" in the dictionary, or it may be better to do morphological analysis first: a morphological rule applies to the input and says that we strip off the "ed" and look up "walk." If we find that it is a verb that is not marked as being irregular, then the rule says that "walked" is the past tense of the root verb. Either way, the task of dictionary lookup is to find a word in the dictionary and return its definition. Thus, any implementation of the *table* abstract data type can serve as a dictionary. Good choices include hash tables, binary trees, b-trees, and tries. The choice depends in part on if there is room to fit the dictionary in primary storage, or if it resides in a file.

ERROR RECOVERY **Error recovery** is undertaken when a word is not found in the dictionary. There are at least four types of error recovery. First, morphological rules can guess at the word's syntactic class: "smarply" is not in the dictionary, but it is probably an adverb. Second, capitalization is a clue that a word (or sequence of words) is a proper name. Third, other specialized formats denote dates, times, social security numbers, and so forth. These are often domain-dependent.

Finally, spelling correction routines can be used to find a word in the dictionary that is close to the input word. There are two popular models of "closeness" between words. In the letter-based model, an error consists of inserting or deleting a single letter, transposing two adjacent letters, or replacing one letter with another. Thus, a 10-letter word is one error away from 555 other words: 10 deletions, 9 swaps, 10×25 replacements, and 11×26 insertions. Exercise 23.11 discusses the implications of this for dictionary implementation. This model is good for correcting slips of the finger, where one key on the keyboard is hit instead of another.

In the sound-based model, words are translated into a canonical form that preserves most of information needed to pronounce the word, but abstracts away some of the details. For example, the word "attention" might be translated into the sequence [a,T,a,N,SH,a,N], where "a" stands for any vowel. The idea is that words such as "attension" and "atennshun" translate to the same sequence. If no other word in the dictionary translates to the same sequence, then we can unambiguously correct the spelling error. Note that the letter-based approach would work just as well for "attension," but not for "atennshun," which is 5 errors away from "attention."

Practical NLP systems have lexicons with from 10,000 to 100,000 root word forms. Building a lexicon of this size is a big investment in time and money, and one that dictionary publishers and companies with NLP programs have not been willing to share. An exception is Wordnet, a freely available dictionary of roughly 100,000 words produced by a group at Princeton led by George Miller. Figure 23.7 gives some of the information on the word "ride" in Wordnet.

As useful as dictionaries like Wordnet are, they do not provide all the lexical information you would like. The two missing pieces are frequency information and semantic restrictions. Frequency information tells us that the teasing sense of ride is unusual, while the other senses are common, or that the female swan sense of "pen" is very rare, while the other senses are common. Semantic restrictions tell us that the direct object of the first sense of ride is a horse, camel, or similar animal, while the direct object of the second kind is a means of conveyance such as a car, bus, skateboard, or airplane. Some frequency information and semantic restrictions can be captured with the help of a large **corpus** of text.

```
Noun: ride
    => mechanical device (device based on mechanical principles)
Noun: drive, ride
    => journey (the act of traveling)
Verb: ride, ride an animal (of animals)
    => travel, go, move, change location, locomote
    *> Somebody rides
    *> Somebody rides something
Verb: ride, travel in a conveyance
    => travel, go, move, change location, locomote
    OP walk, go on foot, foot, leg it, hoof, hoof it
    *> Somebody rides
    *> Somebody rides something
Verb: tease, cod, tantalize, bait, taunt, twit, rally, ride
    => mock, bemock, treat with contempt
    *> Somebody rides somebody
Other words containing "ride":
  rider, joyride, ride piggyback, ride the bench,
  phencyclidine hydrochloride ...
```

Figure 23.7   Part of Wordnet's information for "ride." Wordnet distinguishes two noun and three verb senses, and lists the superclass of each sense. (The user has the option of following superclass links all the way up or down the tree.) There is also one opposite listed (OP), many superclass relations (=>), and for each verb, a list of subcategorization frames (*>). Finally, a few of the other entries with "ride" are listed to give an idea of the breadth of coverage. Note that expressions like "ride piggyback" are included in addition to individual words. You can get Wordnet by anonymous ftp from clarity.princeton.edu.

23.4   SCALING UP THE GRAMMAR

Figure 23.8 shows two examples of real-life language. These examples contrast with our simple $\mathcal{E}_2$ language in many ways. In tokenization, we have to deal with hyphenation (e.g., smal- lest), unusual punctuation conventions (e.g., fnctl()), and formatting (the unindented DESCRIP-TION indicating a section header). Lexically, we have novel words like cmd and FD_CLOEXEC. Syntactically, we have an odd sort of conjunction (read/write); apposition of two noun phrases (the argument fd); the "greater than or equal to" construction, which can be treated either as an idiom or an unusual disjunction of post-nominal modifiers; and the fact that "the same file pointer" is the object of "shares," even though there are a dozen words between them. And then there is the 67-word alleged sentence, which is actually a convoluted subordinate clause at best.

   To make any sense at all out of these real-life examples requires much more sophistication at every step of the language interpretation process. In this section, we extend $\mathcal{E}_2$ to yield $\mathcal{E}_3$, a language that covers much more, but still has a long way to go.

```
DESCRIPTION
    fcntl() performs a variety of functions on open descriptors.
    The  argument   fd   is an open descriptor used by cmd as fol-
    lows:
    F_DUPFD Returns a new descriptor, which the the smal-
            lest  value greater than or equal to arg.  It
            refers to the same  object   as   the   original
            descriptor,  and  has  the   same   access mode
            (read,  write  or   read/write).    The    new
            descriptor   shares  descriptor   status   flags
            with fd, and if the object was   a   file,   the
            same   file   pointer.   It   is also associated
            with a FD_CLOEXEC (close-on-exec) flag set to
            remain open across execve(2V) system calls.
```

"And since I was not informed—as a matter of fact, since I did not know that there were
excess funds until we, ourselves, in that checkup after the whole thing blew up, and that
was, if you'll remember, that was the incident in which the attorney general came to me and
told me that he had seen a memo that indicated that there were no more funds."

Figure 23.8   Two examples of real-life language: one from the UNIX manual entry for `fcntl`,
and one from a statement made by Ronald Reagan, printed in the May 4, 1987, *Roll Call*.

Nominal compounds and apposition

Technical text is full of nominal compounds: strings of nouns such as "POSTSCRIPT language
code input file." The first thing we have to do to handle nominal compounds is realize that we
are dealing with nouns, not *NP*s. It is not the case that "the input" and "the file" combine to form
"the input the file." Rather, we have two nouns combining to form a larger unit that still can
combine with an article to form a *NP*. We will call the larger unit a noun[5] and thus will need a
rule of the form:

$$Noun \rightarrow Noun\ Noun$$

For our example compound, the parse that leads to a semantically sensible interpretation is

$$[_{Noun}\ [_{Noun}\ [_{Noun}\ \text{POSTSCRIPT language}]\ \text{code}]\ [_{Noun}\ \text{input file}]]$$

The hardest part about nominal compounds is specifying the semantics. Our example can be
paraphrased as "a file that is used for input and that consists of code written in a language
named POSTSCRIPT." Clearly, there is a wide variety in the meaning associated with a nominal
compound. We will use the generic relation *NN* to stand for any of the semantic relations that

---

[5] Some grammars introduce intermediate categories between noun and *NP*.

Example Nominal Compound	Relation	Semantic Rule
input file	*UsedFor*	$\forall x, y \ UsedFor(y, x) \ \Rightarrow \ NN(x, y)$
code file	*ConsistsOf*	$\forall x, y \ ConsistsOf(y, x) \ \Rightarrow \ NN(x, y)$
language code	*WrittenIn*	$\forall x, y \ WrittenIn(y, x) \ \Rightarrow \ NN(x, y)$
POSTSCRIPT language	*Named*	$\forall x, y \ Named(y, x) \ \Rightarrow \ NN(x, y)$
basketball shoes	*UsedFor*	$\forall x, y \ UsedFor(y, x) \ \Rightarrow \ NN(x, y)$
baby shoes	*UsedBy*	$\forall x, y \ UsedBy(y, x) \ \Rightarrow \ NN(x, y)$
alligator shoes	*MadeOf*	$\forall x, y \ MadeOf(y, x) \ \Rightarrow \ NN(x, y)$
designer shoes	*MadeBy*	$\forall x, y \ MadeBy(y, x) \ \Rightarrow \ NN(x, y)$
brake shoes	*PartOf*	$\forall x, y \ PartOf(y, x) \ \Rightarrow \ NN(x, y)$

Figure 23.9   Nominal compounds and the corresponding semantic relationships.

can hold between two nouns in a nominal compound. We can then write logical rules that say, for example, that when a *UsedFor* relation holds between two objects, we can infer that a *NN* relation holds. Some examples are shown in Figure 23.9.

We would like a noun phrase like "every file input" to get the semantic interpretation:

$$[\forall f \ \exists i \ Input(i) \land File(f) \land NN(i, f)]$$

Given what we have already decided about representing the semantics of *NP*s and articles, we can get this if we arrange for the semantics of the nominal compound "file input" to be

$$\lambda f \ \exists i \ Input(i) \land File(f) \land NN(i, f)$$

And we can get that with the rule

$$Noun(\lambda y \ \exists x \ sem_1(x) \land sem_2(y) \land NN(x, y)) \rightarrow Noun(sem_1) \ Noun(sem_2)$$

APPOSITION

Another complication is that two noun phrases (not two *Noun*s) can be concatenated together in a construction called **apposition**, in which both noun phrases refer to the same thing. Two examples are "[$_{NP}$ the argument] [$_{NP}$ fd]" and "[$_{NP}$ the language] [$_{NP}$ POSTSCRIPT]." In these examples, the second *NP* is a name, but it need not always be. In "[$_{NP}$ David McDonald] [$_{NP}$ the CMU grad] wrote about nominal compounds" we are using "the CMU grad" to distinguish this David McDonald from the other one.[6] A simplified rule for apposition is

$$NP([q \, x \ sem_1 \land sem_2]) \rightarrow NP([q \, x \ sem_1]) \ NP([q \, x \ sem_2])$$

Adjective Phrases

In $\mathcal{E}_2$, adjectives were only allowed as complements to a verb, as in "the wumpus is *smelly*." But of course adjectives also appear as modifiers before a noun, as in "a *smelly* wumpus." The semantics of a phrase like this can be formed by a conjunction of the semantics contributed by the adjective and by the noun:

$$\exists w \ Smelly(w) \land Wumpus(w)$$

---

[6] This is called a **restrictive** apposition because it restricts the set of possible references. Nonrestrictive appositions just add new information. They are often set off by commas or dashes, as in "Tarzan, lord of the jungle."

This is called **intersective semantics**, because the meaning of "smelly wumpus" is the intersection of smelly things and things that are wumpuses. Both nouns and adjectives are represented by predicates that define categories; this was the first scheme for representing categories shown in Section 8.4. If all adjectives had intersective semantics, it would be easy to handle them. We would add a rule for *Noun*, saying it can be composed of an *Adjective* and another *Noun*:

$$Noun(\lambda x \ sem_1(x) \wedge sem_2(x)) \rightarrow Adjective(sem_1) \ Noun(sem_2)$$

Unfortunately, the semantic relation between adjective and noun is often more complicated than just intersection. For example:

- A "red book" has a red cover, but not red pages or lettering. A "red pen" has red ink or a red body. In general, color adjectives refer to a major, salient, visible part of the object.
- "Red hair" is orangish, not red. This implies that the modification is dependent on both the noun and the adjective.
- A "red herring" is an irrelevant distraction, not a fish nor something red. In this case, the phrase has an idiomatic meaning that is completely independent of its parts.
- A "small moon" is bigger than a "large molecule" and is clearly not the intersection of small things and things that are moons.
- A "mere child" is the same as a child: you cannot take a group of children and separate them into the children and the mere children. The adjective "mere" refers to the speaker's attitude about the noun, and not to actual properties of the noun at all.
- In "alleged murderer," the adjective again says something about the attitude of some person (not necessarily the speaker), but the phrase makes no commitment as to whether the referent actually is a murderer.
- "Real leather" is no different from "leather," but the adjective is used when the listener might expect artificial leather.
- A "fake gun" is not a gun at all. Its appearance is similar to a gun's, but it lacks the functional properties.

These kinds of semantic relations can be handled by reifying the categories that were formerly represented as predicates. This is the second scheme for representing categories in Section 8.4. For example, instead of the predicate *Gun*, we will use the object *Guns* to represent the class of all guns. Then "a gun" is represented by $\exists g \ (g \in Guns)$ and "a fake gun" is $\exists g \ (g \in Fake(Guns))$.

Determiners

DETERMINER

In Chapter 22, we showed how articles such as "a" and "the" can be part of noun phrases. Articles are just one type of the more general class of **determiner**, which we abbreviate as *Det*. Determiners can become quite complicated, as in "[$_{Det}$ my brother's neighbor's] dog" and "[$_{Det}$ all but three of her many] good friends." For our $\mathcal{E}_3$ language, we allow only one new kind of determiner, a number, as in "three dogs." We will use the quasi-logical form $[3 \ x \ Dog(x)]$ to represent this. This gives us the following grammar rules:

$$Det(q) \rightarrow Article(q)$$
$$Det(q) \rightarrow Number(q)$$
$$NP([q \ x \ noun(x)]) \rightarrow Det(q) \ Noun(noun)$$

So far, the rules are simple, and the mapping from strings to quasi-logical form is easy. The hard part is translating from quasi-logical form to logical form. Here are two examples of the logical form we would like to end up with:

> Three women carried a piano.
> $\exists s \ Cardinality(s) = 3 \wedge \forall w \ ((w \in s \ \Rightarrow \ Woman(w))$
> $\wedge \exists p \ Piano(p) \wedge \exists e \ (e \in Carry_1(s, p, Past)))$
> *(There is a set of 3 women; this set carried the piano.)*

> Three women carried a baby.
> $\exists s \ Cardinality(s) = 3 \wedge \forall w \ ((w \in s \ \Rightarrow \ Woman(w))$
> $\wedge \exists b \ Baby(b) \wedge \exists e \ (e \in Carry_2(w, p, Past)))$
> *(There is a set of 3 women; each woman in the set carried a baby.)*

These examples are ambiguous. In the most likely interpretations, it is the set of women, s, who are carrying the piano together in the first example, whereas in the second example, each woman is separately carrying a different baby. The subscripts on *Carry* indicate different senses. To account for these two different interpretations, we will have to make the rule for translating $[3 \ w \ Woman(w)]$ capable of equating either the variable denoting the set (s) or the variable denoting the elements of the set (w) with the variable representing the subject of the verb phrase.

Noun phrases revisited

Now we look at the rules for noun phrases. The rule for pronouns is unchanged from Chapter 22, and the old rule for *Article* plus *Noun* could be updated simply by changing *Article* to *Det* and including case information and agreement in person and number, yielding the following rule:

> $NP(case, Person(3), number, [q \ x \ sem(x)]) \rightarrow Det(number, q) \ Noun(number, sem)$

We stick to the convention that the semantics is always the last argument. The *case* variable is unbound, indicating that the *NP* can be used in either the subjective or objective case. The *number* variable can take on the values *Singular* or *Plural*, and the rule says that the *Det* and *Noun* must have the same number. For example, "a dog" and "those dogs" are grammatical because they agree in number, but "a dogs" and "those dog" are ungrammatical because they disagree. Note that some determiners (like "the") and some nouns (like "sheep") can be either singular or plural.

Besides playing a role inside the noun phrase, the *number* variable is also important externally: in the $S \rightarrow NP \ VP$ rule, the subject noun phrase must agree with the verb phrase in *number* and *person*. All nouns are in the third person, which we have denoted *Person(3)*. Pronouns have more variety; the pronoun "you," for example, is in the second person and "I" is in the third. Verbs are also marked for person and number. For example, the verb "am" is *Singular* and *Person(1)*, and therefore "I am" is grammatical, while "you am" is not. Here is a rule that enforces subject/verb agreement:

> $S(rel(obj)) \rightarrow NP(Subject, person, number, obj) \ VP(person, number, rel)$

It is also possible to form a noun phrase from a noun with no determiner. There are several ways to do this. One is with a name, such as "John" or "Berkeley." There are several choices for the semantics of names. The simplest choice is to represent "John" with the constant *John*. Then the representation of "John slept" is $\exists e \ \ e \in Sleep(John, Past)$. But this simple approach does not work in a world with more than one thing called John. A better representation is therefore $\exists e, x \ \ e \in Sleep([\exists ! \, x \, Name(x) = John], Past)$. Here are rules that derive that representation:

$$NP(case, Person(3), number, [\exists ! \, x \, Name(x) = name]) \rightarrow Name(number, name)$$
$$Name(Singular, John) \rightarrow \textbf{\textit{John}}$$

A noun also needs no determiner if it is a mass noun (e.g., "water") or a generic plural (e.g., "Dogs like bones"). We leave these rules as exercises.

Clausal complements

In $\mathcal{E}_2$, all the verbs took only noun phrases and prepositional phrases as complements. But some verbs accept clauses (i.e., sentences or certain types of verb phrases) as complements. For example, in "I believe [he has left]," the object of "believe" is a sentence, and in "I want [to go there]," the object of want is an infinitive verb phrase. We can handle this with the same subcategorization mechanism we have been using (here shown without the other augmentations):

$$VP(subcat) \rightarrow VP([S|subcat]) \ S$$
$$VP(subcat) \rightarrow VP([VP|subcat]) \ VP$$

$$Verb([S]) \rightarrow \textbf{\textit{believe}}$$
$$Verb([VP]) \rightarrow \textbf{\textit{want}}$$

Relative clauses

The grammar of $\mathcal{E}_2$ allows relative clauses such as "the person [that saw me]," in which the relative clause consists of the word "that" followed by a *VP*, and the interpretation is that the head noun phrase (the person) is the subject of the embedded *VP*. In English, it is also possible to have relative clauses such as "the person [that I saw ␣]," in which a sentence follows the word "that," but the sentence is missing an object. The ␣ symbol, which we call a **gap**[7] indicates the place where the head noun phrase (the person) logically would appear to complete the sentence. We say that the head noun phrase is the **filler** of the gap. In this example, the gap is in the direct object position, but it could be nested farther into the relative clause. For example, it could be the object of a preposition (e.g., "the person [that I looked [$_{PP}$ at ␣]]") or the object of a deeply nested clause:

the person [that [$_S$ you said [$_S$ you thought [$_S$ I gave the book to ␣]]]]

So far, all the syntactic relationships we have seen have been at a single level in the parse tree. The filler–gap relationship is called a **long-distance dependency** because it reaches down a potentially unbounded number of nodes into the parse tree. The subscripts (*i*) on parse nodes are used to show that there is an identity relationship—that the recipient of the book giving is the same as "the person" that is the head noun phrase:

[the person]$_i$ [that [$_S$ you said [$_S$ you thought [$_S$ I gave the book to ␣$_i$]]]]

---

[7] The gap is called a **trace** in some theories.

To represent filler–gap relationships, we augment most of the category predicates with a *gap* argument. This argument says what is missing from the phrase. For example, the sentence "I saw him" has no gaps, which we represent as *S(Gap(None))*. The phrases "␣saw him" and "I saw ␣" are both represented as *S(Gap(NP))*.

To define relative clauses, all we have to do is say that an *NP* can be modified by following it with a relative clause, and that a relative clause consists of a relative pronoun followed by a sentence that contains an *NP* gap. This allows us to handle both "the person that I saw ␣" and "the person that ␣saw him." Here are the rules with all other augmentations removed:

$NP(gap) \rightarrow NP(gap)$ *RelClause*
RelClause $\rightarrow$ *Pronoun(Relative) S(Gap(NP))*}

We also have to say that the empty string, ϵ, comprises an *NP* with an *NP* gap in it:

$NP(Gap(NP)) \rightarrow \epsilon$

The rest of the grammar has to cooperate by passing the *gap* argument along; for example:

$S(Gap(Concat(g_1, g_2))) \rightarrow NP(Gap(g_1))$ $VP(Gap(g_2))$

Here $Concat(g_1, g_2)$ means g_1 and g_2 together. If g_1 and g_2 are both *Gap(None)*, then the *S* as a whole has no gap. But if, say, g_1 is *Gap(NP)* and g_2 is *Gap(None)*, then the *S* has an *NP* gap.

Questions

In English, there are two main types of questions:

◇ **Yes/No**: Did you see that?

◇ **Wh (gapped)**: What did you see ␣?

A yes/no question, as the name implies, expects a yes or no as answer. It is just like a declarative sentence, except that it has an auxiliary verb that appears before the subject *NP*. We call this **subject-aux inversion** and use the category *Sinv* to denote a sentence that has it. If there are several auxiliary verbs, only the first one comes before the subject: "Should you have been seeing that?" Thus, the grammar rules covering simple yes/no sentences are as follows:

SUBJECT-AUX
INVERSION

$S \rightarrow$ *Question*
Question $\rightarrow$ *Sinv*
Sinv $\rightarrow$ *Aux NP VP*

Wh questions (pronounced "double-U H") expect a noun phrase as an answer. In the simplest case, they start with an interrogative pronoun (who, what, when, where, why, how), which is followed by a gapped *Sinv*:

Question $\rightarrow$ *Pronoun(Interrogative) Sinv(Gap(NP))*

There are also some less common question constructions, as these examples show:

◇ **Echo**: You saw *what*?

◇ **Raising intonation**: You see something?

◇ **Yes/No with "be"**: Is it safe?

◇ **Wh subject**: What is the frequency, Kenneth?

◇ **Wh NP**: [What book] did you read ⊔?
◇ **Wh PP**: [With what] did you see it ⊔?
◇ **Wh PP**: [Whence] did he come ⊔?

Echo questions can also be answered with a noun phrase, but they are normally used rhetorically to express the speaker's amazement at what was just said. For example, "I saw a 30-foot-high purple cow" is answered by "You saw *what*?" Sentences with normal declarative structure can be made into questions with the use of raising intonation at the end of the sentence. This is uncommon in written text. The verb "to be" is the only verb that can stand by itself (without another verb) in an inverted yes/no question. That is, we can say "Is it safe?" but not "Seems it safe?" or "Did they it?" In some dialects, "have" can be used, as in "Have you the time?" or "Have you any wool?" Finally, it is possible to have an *Sinv* with a prepositional phrase gap by prefacing it with a prepositional wh phrase like "from where" or "whence."

Handling agrammatical strings

No matter how thorough the grammar, there will always be strings that fall outside it. It doesn't much matter if this happens because the string is a mistake or because the grammar is missing something. Either way, the speaker is trying to communicate something and the system must process it in some way. Thus, it is the hearer's job to interpret a string somehow, even if it is not completely grammatical. For example, if a character in a mystery novel suddenly keels over but manages to gasp "Poison—Butler—Martini," most people would be able to come up with a good interpretation of these dying words: the butler is the agent of the poisoning action of which the speaker is the victim and the martini is the instrument. We arrive at this interpretation by considering the possible semantic relations that could link each component together, and choosing the best one. It would not do to say "I'm sorry, that's not a grammatical sentence; could you please rephrase it?"

23.5   AMBIGUITY

In this chapter, we have extended the range of syntactic constructions and semantic representations that we can handle. This helps us cover a wider range of language, but it also makes the job of disambiguation harder, because there are more possibilities to choose from. *Finding the right interpretation involves reasoning with uncertainty* using the evidence provided by lexical, syntactic, semantic, and pragmatic sources.

Historically, most approaches to the disambiguation problem have been based on logical inference with no quantitative measures of certainty. In the last few years, the trend has been toward quantitative probabilistic models such as belief networks and hidden Markov models.

Belief networks provide an answer to one hard part of the problem—how to combine evidence from different sources. But we are still left with two more problems: deciding what evidence to put into the network, and deciding what to do with the answers that come back. We start by looking at several sources of evidence. *It is important to distinguish between sources of evidence and sources of ambiguity.* It is quite possible that a syntactic ambiguity is resolved by semantic evidence. For example, in "I ate spaghetti and meatballs and salad," there is a syntactic ambiguity (is it [$_{NP}$ spaghetti and meatballs] or [$_{NP}$ meatballs and salad]?) that is resolved by nonsyntactic evidence: that spaghetti and meatballs is a common dish, whereas meatballs and salad is not.

Syntactic evidence

Modifiers such as adverbs and prepositional phrases cause a lot of ambiguity, because they can attach to several different heads. For example, in

> Lee asked Kim to tell Toby to leave on Saturday.

the adverb "Saturday" can modify the asking, the telling, or the leaving. Psychological studies show that in the absence of other evidence, there is a preference to attach such modifiers to the most recent constituent (in this case, the leaving). So this is a syntactic ambiguity that can be resolved by syntactic evidence.

Lexical evidence

Many words are ambiguous, but not all senses of a word are equally likely. When asked what the word "pen" means, most people will say first that it is a writing instrument. However, it has two other fairly common senses meaning an enclosure for animals and a penitentiary. The senses meaning a female swan and the internal shell of a squid are more obscure, known mostly to specialists in biology (or specialists in ambiguity). As another example, consider the following:

> Lee positioned the dress on the rack.
> Kim wanted the dress on the rack.

Here "on the rack" is best interpreted as modifying the verb in the first sentence and the dress in the second. That is, Lee is putting the dress on the rack (not moving a dress that is on the rack), and Kim wants to have a dress that is on the rack (and does not want the dress to be on the rack). In both cases, either interpretation is semantically plausible. So this is a syntactic ambiguity that is resolved by lexical evidence—by the preference of the verb for one subcategorization.

Semantic evidence

The a priori probability of a word sense is usually less important than the conditional probability in a given context. Consider the following:

> ball, diamond, bat, base

Even without any syntactic structure to speak of, it is easy to pick out the baseball senses of each of these words as being the intended interpretation. This is true even though the a priori probability for "diamond" favors the jewel interpretation. So this is a case of lexical ambiguity resolved by semantic evidence.

As another example, here are five sentences, along with the most likely interpretation of the relation represented by the word "with." Each of the sentences has a lexical ambiguity ("with" has several senses) and a syntactic ambiguity (the *PP* can attach to either "spaghetti" or "ate"), but each is resolved by semantic evidence.

Sentence	Relation
I ate spaghetti with meatballs.	(ingredient of spaghetti)
I ate spaghetti with salad.	(side dish of spaghetti)
I ate spaghetti with abandon.	(manner of eating)
I ate spaghetti with a fork.	(instrument of eating)
I ate spaghetti with a friend.	(accompanier of eating)

It is certainly *possible* to use meatballs as a utensil with which to eat spaghetti, but it is unlikely (not to mention messy), so we prefer interpretations that refer to more likely events. Of course, likeliness of events or situations is not the only factor. In Chapter 22, we saw that the right interpretation of "I am not a crook" is not the most likely situation. It is perfectly coherent to use language to talk about unlikely or even impossible situations: "I ran a mile in one minute" or "This square is a triangle."

Metonymy

METONYMY

A **metonymy** is a figure of speech in which one object is used to stand for another. When we hear "Chrysler announced a new model," we do not interpret it as saying that companies can talk; rather we understand that a spokesperson representing the company made the announcement. Metonymy is common in many kinds of text, and often goes unnoticed by human readers. Unfortunately, our grammar as it is written is not so facile. To handle the semantics of metonymy properly, we need to introduce a whole new level of ambiguity. We do this by providing two objects for the semantic interpretation of every phrase in the sentence: one for the object that the phrase literally refers to (Chrysler), and one for the metonymic reference (the spokesperson). We then have to say that there is a relation between the two. In our current grammar, "Chrysler announced" gets interpreted as

$$\exists x, e \; Chrysler(x) \land e \in Announce(x, Past)$$

We need to change that to

$$\exists m, x, e \; Chrysler(x) \land Metonymy(m, x) \land e \in Announce(m, Past)$$

This gives a representation for the problem, but not a solution. The next step is to define what kinds of metonymy can occur, that is, to define constraints on the *Metonymy* relation. The simplest case is when there is no metonymy at all—the literal object x and the metonymic object m are identical:

$$\forall m, x \; (m = x) \; \Rightarrow \; Metonymy(m, x)$$

For the Chrysler example, a reasonable generalization is that an organization can be used to stand for a spokesperson of that organization:

$$\forall m, x \; Organization(x) \land Spokesperson(m, x) \; \Rightarrow \; Metonymy(m, x)$$

Other metonymies include the author for the works (I read Shakespeare) or more generally the producer for the product (I drive a Honda) and the part for the whole (The Red Sox need a strong arm). Other examples of metonymy, such as "The ham sandwich on Table 4 wants another beer," are somewhat harder to classify.

Metaphor

METAPHOR
A **metaphor** is a figure of speech in which a phrase with one literal meaning is used to suggest a different meaning by way of an analogy. Most people think of metaphor as a tool used by poets that does not play a large role in everyday text. However, there are a number of basic metaphors that are so common that we do not even recognize them as such. One such metaphor is the idea that *more is up*. This metaphor allows us to say that prices have risen, climbed, or skyrocketed, that the temperature has dipped or fallen, that one's confidence has plummeted, or that a celebrity's popularity has jumped or soared.

There are two ways to approach metaphors like this. One is to compile all knowledge of the metaphor into the lexicon—to add new senses of the words rise, fall, climb, and so on, that describe them as dealing with quantities on any scale rather than just altitude. This approach suffices for many applications, but it does not capture the generative character of the metaphor that allows humans to use new instances such as "nose-dive" without fear of misunderstanding. The second approach is to include explicit knowledge of common metaphors and use them to interpret new uses as they are read. For example, suppose the system knows the "more is up" metaphor. That is, it knows that logical expressions that refer to a point on a vertical scale can be interpreted as being about corresponding points on a quantity scale. Then the expression "sales are high" would get a literal interpretation along the lines of *Altitude(Sales, High)*, which could be interpreted metaphorically as *Quantity(Sales, Much)*.

23.6   DISCOURSE UNDERSTANDING

DISCOURSE
TEXT
In the technical sense, a **discourse** or **text** is any string of language, usually one that is more than one sentence long. Novels, weather reports, textbooks, conversations, and almost all nontrivial uses of language are discourses. So far we have largely ignored the problems of discourse, preferring to dissect language into individual sentences that can be studied *in vitro*. In this section, we study sentences in their native habitat.

To produce discourse, a speaker must go through the standard steps of intention, generation, and synthesis. Discourse understanding includes perception, analysis (and thus syntactic, semantic, and pragmatic interpretation), disambiguation, and incorporation. The hearer's state of knowledge plays a crucial part in arriving at an understanding—two agents with different knowledge may well understand the same text differently. Discourse understanding can be modelled crudely by the following equation:

$$KB' = \text{DISCOURSE-UNDERSTANDING}(text, KB)$$

where *KB* is the hearer's knowledge base, and *KB'* is the hearer's knowledge base after incorporating the text. The difference between *KB* and *KB'* is the hearer's **understanding** of the text. At least six types of knowledge come into play in arriving at an understanding:

1. General knowledge about the world.
2. General knowledge about the structure of coherent discourse.
3. General knowledge about syntax and semantics.
4. Specific knowledge about the situation being discussed.
5. Specific knowledge about the beliefs of the characters.
6. Specific knowledge about the beliefs of the speaker.

Let us look at an example discourse:

> John went to a fancy restaurant.
> He was pleased and gave the waiter a big tip.
> He spent $50.

A proper understanding of this discourse would include the fact that John ate a fancy meal at the restaurant, that the waiter was employed by the restaurant, and that John paid some of the $50 to the waiter and most of it to the restaurant. We'll call this understanding (a). All the inferences seem obvious, but to get them right we need to know a lot and apply the knowledge in just the right way. To understand why this is hard, we give an alternative understanding (b):

> John ducked into a fancy restaurant to ask directions. He was pleased that they were able to help him. Back on the street, John bumped into a man that he had met at a party the other night. All John could remember was that the man was a waiter at another restaurant and that he was interested in getting a new radio. John gave the man a tip that there was a great sale going on at the stereo store down the block. The man spent $50 on a radio.

This is a situation that could conceivably be described by our three-sentence discourse. It is far-fetched for two reasons: First, the situation in (a) has a higher a priori probability—people go to restaurants to eat more often than to ask for directions. Second, the situation in (a) is more probable given the text. A rational speaker would not expect a hearer to extract understanding (b) from the discourse. To see why (a) is better, let us look at it piece by piece:

- John ate a fancy meal at the restaurant.
  To get this requires going beyond disambiguation and into incorporation. There is certainly no part of the discourse that mentions the eating explicitly, but it still should be part of the updated knowledge base that the hearer comes away with. To get it, the hearer has to know that restaurants serve meals, and thus that a reason for going to a restaurant is to eat. The hearer also knows that fancy restaurants serve fancy meals, and that $50 is a typical price for such a meal, and that paying and leaving a tip are typically done after eating a restaurant meal. Besides this general knowledge about the world, it also helps if the hearer knows that discourses are commonly structured so that they describe some steps of a plan for a character, but leave out steps that can be easily inferred from the other steps. From this, the hearer can infer from the first sentence that John has adopted the eat-at-restaurant plan, and that the eat-meal step probably occurred even if it was not mentioned.

- The waiter was employed by the restaurant.

  Again, this is a mixture of general world knowledge—that restaurants employ waiters—and knowledge about discourse conventions—that the definite article "the" is used for objects that have been mentioned before, or at least have been implicitly alluded to; in this case, by the eat-at-restaurant plan.

- John paid some of the $50 to the waiter and most of it to the restaurant.

  This is another example of identifying a step in a currently active plan that matches a sentence in the text, and unifying them to arrive at the interpretation that "He" is John, and that the recipients of the deal are the restaurant and waiter.

The structure of coherent discourse

In logic, conjunction is commutative, so there is no difference between $P \wedge Q \wedge R$ and $R \wedge P \wedge Q$. But this is certainly not true of natural languages. Consider the following two discourses, which contain the same sentences in different order:

Discourse (A)	Discourse (B)
I visited Paris.	I visited Paris.
I bought you some expensive cologne.	Then I flew home.
Then I flew home.	I went to Kmart.
I went to Kmart.	I bought you some expensive cologne.
I bought some underwear.	I bought some underwear.

In (A), the preferred interpretation is that the cologne comes from Paris, whereas in (B) it comes from Kmart. Both discourses have a sequential structure in which the sentences that come later in the discourse also occur later in time. But there is more to the understanding of these discourses than just temporal ordering. In (A), we understand that a (or the) reason for going to Kmart was to buy the underwear. Similarly, we understand that visiting Paris enabled the speaker to buy cologne there, but that was not necessarily the purpose of the trip.

SEGMENTS

COHERENCE
RELATION

We need a theory of how discourses are put together. We will say that discourses are composed of **segments**, where a segment can be a clause, a complete sentence, or a group of several consecutive sentences. There are several theories built on the idea that each segment of the discourse is related to the previous one by a **coherence relation** that determines the role that each segment plays in the unfolding discourse. For example, the coherence relation between the first two sentences of (A) is one of **enablement**. *Coherence relations serve to bind the discourse together.* A speaker knows that she can extend a discourse by adding a sentence that stands in a coherence relation to the existing text, and the hearer knows that in addition to interpreting and disambiguating each sentence, he is supposed to recover the coherence relations that bind the segments together. This means that the hearer of a discourse is doing more work than the hearer in Chapter 22, who only had to worry about interpreting and disambiguating a single sentence. But it also means that the hearer of a discourse has some help, because the coherence relations constrain the possible meanings of each sentence. So even though the individual sentences may have many possible meanings, the discourse as a whole will have few meanings (preferably one).

We present the theory by Hobbs (1990), which starts with the observation that the speaker does four things in putting together a discourse:

- The speaker wants to convey a message.
- The speaker has a motivation or goal in doing this.
- The speaker wants to make it easy for the hearer to understand.
- The speaker must link the new information to what the hearer already knows.

A sentence is a coherent extension of a discourse if it can be interpreted by the hearer as being in service of one of these four points. Let us look at some examples of each of the four as they appear in the following discourse:

(1) A funny thing happened yesterday.
(2) John went to a fancy restaurant.
(3) He ordered the duck.
(4) The bill came to $50.
(5) John got a shock when the waiter came to collect the bill.
(6) He realized he didn't have a cent on him.
(7) He had left his wallet at home.
(8) The waiter said it was all right to pay later.
(9) He was very embarrassed by his forgetfulness.

Sentence (1) describes what the speaker wants to talk about—a funny thing. It is a meta-comment, an evaluation by the speaker of what the coming message holds. Once the speaker has made it clear that she has the goal of describing this, it is coherent to add (2), which starts to describe the funny thing. The coherence relation between (1) and (2) is that uttering (2) is part of the speaker's plan that was implicitly alluded to by (1). More formally, we can say that two adjacent discourse segments S_i and S_j stand in the **evaluation** coherence relation, if from S_i we can infer that S_j is a step in the speaker's plan for achieving some discourse goal.

Sentences (3) and (4) are coherent because they can be interpreted as steps in John's plan of eating a meal. Sentences (2) and (3) stand in the enablement coherence relation, and (3) and (4) are in the **causal** relation. Both relations arise from the speaker's goal of conveying a message about the world. Thus, we see that understanding discourse involves two levels of **plan recognition**—recognizing the speaker's plans and the characters' plans.

Sentences (5) and (6) overlap in their content: the shock *is* the realization, but it is described in a different way. We say that (5) and (6) stand in the **elaboration** relation. This is an example of the speaker making it easier for the hearer by lessening the amount of inference the hearer has to make. Sentence (6) could well have been left out of the discourse, but then the jump from (5) to (7) would have been a little harder to make. Note that once we recognize that (6) is an elaboration of (5), we can infer that "he" in (6) refers to John. Without the coherence relation, we might be tempted to assume that "he" refers to the waiter, who was mentioned more recently.

The relation between (6) and (7) is one of **explanation**: the reason John didn't have a cent on him is because he left his wallet at home. This is one case where a sentence that appears later in the discourse actually occurs earlier in the real world. This is an example of the speaker linking a new explanation to the hearer's existing knowledge.

Sentence (9) stands in a causal relation with the discourse segment comprised of (5) and (6). Recognizing this allows us to interpret "he" in (9) as John, not the waiter.

There have been several catalogs of coherence relations. Mann and Thompson (1983) give a more elaborate one that includes solutionhood, evidence, justification, motivation, reason, sequence, enablement, elaboration, restatement, condition, circumstance, cause, concession, background, and thesis–antithesis.

ATTENTION

The theory of Grosz and Sidner (1986) also accounts for where the speaker and hearer's **attention** is focused during the discourse. Their theory includes a pushdown stack of focus spaces. Certain utterances cause the focus to shift by pushing or popping elements off the stack. For example, in Discourse (A), the sentence "I visited Paris" causes a new focus to be pushed on the stack. Within that focus, the speaker can use definite descriptions to refer to, say, "the museums" or "the cafes." The sentence "Then I flew home" would cause the focus on Paris to be popped from the stack; from that point on, the speaker would need to use an indefinite description such as "the cafe I went to in Paris" rather than a simple definite description. There is also a more specific notion of local focus that affects the interpretation of pronouns.

23.7   SUMMARY

In this chapter, we have seen what can be done with state-of-the-art natural language processing, and what is involved in getting there. The main points were as follows:

- Natural language processing techniques make it practical to develop programs that make queries to a database, extract information from texts, retrieve relevant documents from a collection, translate from one language to another, or recognize spoken words. In all these areas, there exist programs that are useful, but there are no programs that do a thorough job in an open-ended domain.

- It is possible to parse sentences efficiently using an algorithm that is careful to save its work, avoid unnecessary work, and pack the results into a forest rather than an exhaustive list of trees.

- In recent years, there has been a shift of emphasis from the grammar to the lexicon. Building a lexicon is a difficult task.

- Natural languages have a huge variety of syntactic forms. Nobody has yet captured them all, but we can extend the simple grammar of the last chapter to give more complete coverage of English sentences.

- Choosing the right interpretation of a sentence in the situation in which it was uttered requires evidence from many sources, including syntactic, lexical, and semantic.

- Most of the interesting language comes in connected discourse rather than in isolated sentences. Coherence relations constrain how a discourse is put together, and thus constrain the possible interpretations it has.

BIBLIOGRAPHICAL AND HISTORICAL NOTES

Locke and Booth (1955) present the very early protohistory of machine translation, and capture the enthusiasm of the early days. Later disillusionment with machine translation is described by Bar-Hillel (1960); Lindsay (1963) also points out some of the obstacles to machine translation having to do with the interaction between syntax and semantics, and the need for world knowledge. Quinlan and O'Brien (1992) describe TAUM-METEO. Voorhees (1993) reports some recent applications based on Wordnet.

One problem with the prototype natural language interfaces we describe—LUNAR (Woods, 1972), CHAT (Pereira, 1983), and TEAM (Grosz *et al.*, 1987), is that they are necessarily incomplete. In the mid-1980s, several companies invested the effort to build serious natural language database access programs. Artificial Intelligence Corporation's INTELLECT (Harris, 1984) is one of the best known. With a decade of tuning it performs better than a prototype, but still has the difficult problem of revealing to the user its range of competence. The NL-MENU system (Tennant *et al.*, 1983) mitigates this problem by using a mode of interaction in which the user builds a query by selecting words and phrases from a series of on-screen menus instead of typing. In other words, the system reveals what it is capable of accepting rather than attempting to handle anything the user throws at it.

The fundamental advances in efficient, general parsing methods were made in the late 1960s, with a few twists since then (Kasami, 1965; Younger, 1967; Earley, 1970; Graham *et al.*, 1980). Maxwell and Kaplan (1993) show how chart parsing with non-context-free grammars can be made efficient in the average case. Church and Patil (1982) introduce some refinements in the resolution of syntactic ambiguity. A number of researchers have attempted to use quantitative measures of the goodness of syntactic and semantic fit in parsing and semantic interpretation. This can either be done within a basically deductive framework (Hobbs *et al.*, 1993) or within the framework of Bayesian belief network reasoning (Charniak and Goldman, 1992; Wu, 1993).

Nunberg (1979) gives an outline of a computational model of metonymy. Lakoff and Johnson (1980) give an engaging analysis and catalog of common metaphors in English. Ortony (1979) presents a collection of articles on metaphor; Helman (1988) focuses on analogical reasoning, but also contains a number of articles about the phenomenon of metaphor. Martin (1990) presents a computational approach to metaphor interpretation.

Kukich (1992) surveys the literature on spelling correction.

Hobbs (1990) outlines the theory of discourse coherence on which this chapter's exposition is based. Mann and Thompson (1983) give a similar catalog of coherence relations. Grimes (1975) lays the groundwork for much of this work. Grosz and Sidner (1986) present a theory of discourse coherence based on shifting focus of attention. Joshi, Webber, and Sag (1981) collect important early work in the field. Webber presents a model of the interacting constraints of syntax and discourse on what can be said at any point in the discourse (1983) and of the way verb tense interacts with discourse (1988). The idea of tracking the characters' goals and plans as a means of understanding stories was first studied by Wilensky (Wilensky, 1983). A plan-based model of speech acts was suggested first by Cohen and Perrault (1979). Cohen, Morgan, and Pollack (1990) collect more recent work in this area.

EXERCISES

23.1   Read the following text once for understanding and remember as much of it as you can. There will be a test later.

> The procedure is actually quite simple. First you arrange things into different groups. Of course, one pile may be sufficient depending on how much there is to do. If you have to go somewhere else due to lack of facilities that is the next step, otherwise you are pretty well set. It is important not to overdo things. That is, it is better to do too few things at once than too many. In the short run this may not seem important but complications can easily arise. A mistake is expensive as well. At first the whole procedure will seem complicated. Soon, however, it will become just another facet of life. It is difficult to foresee any end to the necessity for this task in the immediate future, but then one can never tell. After the procedure is completed one arranges the material into different groups again. Then they can be put into their appropriate places. Eventually they will be used once more and the whole cycle will have to be repeated. However, this is part of life.

23.2   Describe how a simple pseudo-natural-language (template-based) explanation facility can be built for a vanilla, backward-chaining, logical reasoning system. The explanation facility should be written as a program WHY that generates an explanation after ASK has answered a question from the user. The explanation should consist of a description of the premises and inference method used to reach the conclusion; the user should be able to further query the premises to see how they were derived.

23.3   Without looking back at Exercise 23.1, answer the following questions:

- What are the four steps that are mentioned?
- What step is left out?
- What is "the material" that is mentioned in the text?
- What kind of mistake would be expensive?
- Is it better to do too few or too many?
- Why?

23.4   Open any book or magazine to a random page and write down the first 20 nominal compounds you find. Characterize the semantic relations (e.g., made-of, used-for, etc.).

23.5   Open any book or magazine to a random page and copy down the first 10 sentences. How many of them are in $\mathcal{E}_3$? Show the parses of the sentences that are, and explain what went wrong for the sentences that are not.

23.6   Work out the grammar rules for possessive noun phrases. There are three parts to this. (a) Write a rule of the form $Det \rightarrow NP(Case(Possessive))$. (b) Make sure this rule combines with the $NP \rightarrow Det\ Noun$ rule to produce the right semantics. (c) Write a rule that builds a possessive

NP using the *'s* ending. You will first have to decide if *'s* attaches to a noun or *NP*. To help you do this, consider at least the following examples:

> the Queen of England's speech
> the attorney general's decision
> the man I saw yesterday's name
> the man and woman's house
> Russell and Norvig's text

23.7   Collect some examples of time expressions, such as "two o'clock," "midnight," and "12:46." Also think up some examples that are ungrammatical, such as "thirteen o'clock" or "half past two fifteen." Write a grammar for the time language.

23.8   In this exercise, you will write rules for noun phrases consisting of a noun with no determiner. Consider these examples:

> **a**. Dogs like bones.
>
> **b**. I ate rice.
>
> **c**. Gold is valuable.
>
> **d**. I saw some gold in 2,2.
>
> **e**. I saw gold in 2,2.

Write down the semantics for each of these sentences. Then use that to write down lexical entries for "gold" and "rice," and to write a rule (or rules) of the form *NP* → *Noun*.

23.9   We said that $\exists e,x \ e \in Sleep(John, Past) \wedge Name(x) = John$ was a plausible interpretation for "John slept." But it is not quite right, because it blurs the distinction between "John slept" and "Some person named John slept." The point is that the former sentence presupposes that speaker and hearer agree on which John is being talked about. Write grammar and lexical rules that will distinguish the two examples.

23.10   Write grammar rules for the category *Adjp*, or adjective phrase, using reified categories. Show how to derive $\exists g \ (g \in Fake(Guns)$ as the semantics of "a fake gun." An adjective phrase can be either a lone adjective (*big*), a conjunction (*big and dumb*), or an adjective phrase modified by an adjective or adverb (*light green* or *very dumb*).

23.11   One way to define the task of spelling correction is this: given a misspelled word and a dictionary of correctly spelled words, find the word(s) in the dictionary that can be transformed into the misspelled word in one insertion, deletion, substitution, or transposition. Given a dictionary of *w* words and a misspelled word that is *k* letters long, give the average case time complexity of spelling correction for a dictionary implemented as (a) a hash table, (b) a b-tree, and (c) a trie.

23.12   We forgot to mention that the title of the text in Exercise 23.1 is "Washing Clothes." Go back and reread the text, and answer the questions in Exercise 23.3. Did you do better this time? Bransford and Johnson (1973) used this text in a better-controlled experiment and found that the title helped significantly. What does this tell you about discourse comprehension?

23.13   Implement a version of the chart-parsing algorithm that returns a packed tree of all edges that span the entire input.

23.14   Implement a version of the chart-parsing algorithm that returns a packed tree for the longest leftmost edge, and then if that edge does not span the whole input, continues the parse from the end of that edge. Show why you will need to call PREDICT before continuing. The final result is a list of packed trees such that the list as a whole spans the input.

PERCEPTION

In which we connect the computer to the raw, unwashed world.

24.1 INTRODUCTION

Perception provides agents with information about the world they inhabit. Perception is initiated by **sensors**. A sensor is anything that can change the computational state of the agent in response to a change in the state of the world. It could be as simple as a one-bit sensor that detects whether a switch is on or off, or as complex as the retina of the human eye, which contains more than a hundred million photosensitive elements.

There are a variety of sensory modalities that are available to artificial agents. Those they share with humans include vision, hearing, and touch. In this chapter, our focus will be on vision, because this is by far the most useful sense for dealing with the physical world. Hearing in the context of speech recognition is also covered briefly in Section 24.7. Touch, or **tactile sensing**, is discussed in Chapter 25, where we examine its use in dextrous manipulation by robots.

We will not have all that much to say about the design of sensors themselves. The main focus will be on the processing of the raw information that they provide. The basic approach taken is to first understand how sensory stimuli are created by the world, and then to ask the following question: *if sensory stimuli are produced in such and such a way by the world, then what must the world have been like to produce this particular stimulus?* We can write a crude mathematical analogue of this question. Let the sensory stimulus be S, and let W be the world (where W will include the agent itself). If the function f describes the way in which the world generates sensory stimuli, then we have

$$S = f(W)$$

Now, our question is: given f and S, what can be said about W? A straightforward approach would try to calculate what the world is like by inverting the equation for generating the stimulus:

$$W = f^{-1}(S)$$

724

Unfortunately, f does not have a proper inverse. For one thing, we cannot see around corners, so we cannot recover all aspects of the current world state from the stimulus. Moreover, even the part we *can* see is enormously ambiguous. A key aspect of the study of perception is to understand what additional information can be brought to bear to resolve ambiguity.

A second, and perhaps more important, drawback of the straightforward approach is that it is trying to solve too difficult a problem. In many cases, the agent does not *need* to know everything about the world. Sometimes, just one or two predicates are needed—such as "Is there any obstacle in front of me?" or "Is that an electrical outlet over there?"

In order to understand what sorts of processing we will need to do, let us look at some of the possible uses for vision:

MANIPULATION   ◇ **Manipulation**: grasping, insertion, and so on, need local shape information and feedback ("getting closer, too far to the right, ...) for motor control.

NAVIGATION   ◇ **Navigation**: finding clear paths, avoiding obstacles, and calculating one's current velocity and orientation.

OBJECT
RECOGNITION   ◇ **Object recognition**: a useful skill for distinguishing between tasty mice and dangerous carnivores; edible and inedible objects; close relations and strangers; ordinary vehicles, Volvos. and police cars.

None of these applications requires the extraction of complete descriptions of the environment.

This chapter is organized as follows. In Section 24.2, we study the process of image formation. We cover both the geometry of the process, which dictates where a given point will be imaged, and the photometry of the process, which dictates how bright the point will appear. Section 24.3 treats the basic image-processing operations commonly used in early vision. They set the stage for later analysis that extracts the information needed for tasks such as manipulation, navigation, and recognition. In Section 24.4, we study various cues in the image that can be harnessed to this end, including motion, stereopsis, texture, shading, and contour. Section 24.5 discusses the information needed for visually guided manipulation and navigation, and Section 24.6 covers various approaches to object recognition. Finally, Section 24.7 addresses the problem of perception in the context of speech recognition, thereby helping to pinpoint the issues that arise in perception in general.

24.2   IMAGE FORMATION

SCENE
IMAGE   Vision works by gathering light scattered from objects in the **scene** and creating a 2-D **image**. In order to use this image to obtain information about the scene, we have to understand the geometry of the process.

Pinhole camera

PINHOLE CAMERA   The simplest way to form an image is to use a **pinhole camera** (Figure 24.1). Let P be a point in the scene, with coordinates (X, Y, Z), and P' be its image on the image plane, with coordinates

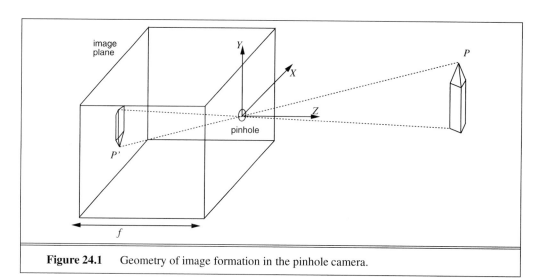

Figure 24.1   Geometry of image formation in the pinhole camera.

(x, y, z). If f is the distance from the pinhole O to the image plane, then by similar triangles, we can derive the following equations:

$$\frac{-x}{f} = \frac{X}{Z}, \frac{-y}{f} = \frac{Y}{Z} \quad \Rightarrow \quad x = \frac{-fX}{Z}, \; y = \frac{-fY}{Z}$$

Note that the image is *inverted*, both left–right and up–down, compared to the scene as indicated in the equations by the negative signs. These equations define an image formation process known PERSPECTIVE PROJECTION as **perspective projection**.

Equivalently, we can model the perspective projection process with the projection plane being at a distance f in *front* of the pinhole. This device of imagining a projection surface in front was first recommended to painters in the Italian Renaissance by Alberti in 1435 as a technique for constructing geometrically accurate depictions of a three-dimensional scene. For our purposes, the main advantage of this model is that it avoids lateral inversion and thereby eliminates the negative signs in the perspective projection equations.

Under perspective projection, parallel lines appear to converge to a point on the horizon—think of railway tracks. Let us see why this must be so. We know from vector calculus that an arbitrary point P_λ on the line passing through (X_0, Y_0, Z_0) in the direction (U, V, W) is given by $(X_0 + \lambda U, Y_0 + \lambda V, Z_0 + \lambda W)$, with λ varying between $+\infty$ and $-\infty$. The projection of P_λ on the image plane is given by

$$\left(f \frac{X_0 + \lambda U}{Z_0 + \lambda W}, f \frac{Y_0 + \lambda V}{Z_0 + \lambda W} \right)$$

As $\lambda \to \infty$ or $\lambda \to -\infty$, this becomes $p_\infty = (fU/W, fV/W)$ if $W \neq 0$. We call p_∞ the **vanishing** VANISHING POINT **point** associated with the family of straight lines with direction (U, V, W). It does *not* depend on the point (X_0, Y_0, Z_0) through which the straight line in the scene passes, only on the direction.

If the object is relatively shallow compared to its distance from the camera, we can ap-SCALED ORTHOGRAPHIC PROJECTION proximate perspective projection by **scaled orthographic projection**. The idea is the following. If the depth Z of points on the object varies in some range $Z_0 \pm \Delta Z$, with $\Delta Z \ll Z_0$, then the perspective scaling factor f/Z can be approximated by a constant $s = f/Z_0$. The equations for projection from the scene coordinates (X, Y, Z) to the image plane become $x = sX$ and $y = sY$. Note that scaled orthographic projection is an approximation valid only for parts of the scene with not much internal depth variation. It should not be used to study properties "in the large." An example to convince you of the need for caution: under orthographic projection, parallel lines stay parallel instead of converging to a vanishing point!

Lens systems

LENS

Vertebrate eyes and real cameras use a **lens**. A lens is much wider than a pinhole, enabling it to let in more light. This is paid for by the fact that not all the scene can be in sharp focus at the same time. The image of an object at distance Z in the scene is produced at a fixed distance from the lens Z', where the relation between Z and Z' is given by the lens equation

$$\frac{1}{Z} + \frac{1}{Z'} = \frac{1}{f}$$

where f is the focal length of the lens. Given a certain choice of image distance Z'_0 between the nodal point of the lens and the image plane, scene points with depths in a range around Z_0, where Z_0 is the corresponding object distance, will be imaged in reasonably sharp focus. This range of

DEPTH OF FIELD

depths in the scene is referred to as the **depth of field**.

Note that because the object distance Z is typically much greater than the image distance Z' or f, we often make the following approximation:

$$\frac{1}{Z} + \frac{1}{Z'} \approx \frac{1}{Z'} \quad \Rightarrow \quad \frac{1}{Z'} \approx \frac{1}{f}$$

Thus, the image distance $Z' \approx f$. We can therefore continue to use the pinhole camera perspective projection equations to describe the geometry of image formation in a lens system.

In order to focus objects at different distances Z, the lens in the eye (see Figure 24.2) changes shape, whereas the lens in a camera moves in the Z-direction.

The image plane is coated with photosensitive material:

- Silver halides on photographic film.
- Rhodopsin and variants in the retina.
- Silicon circuits in the CCD (charge-coupled device) camera. Each site in a CCD integrates the electrons released by photon absorption for a fixed time period.

PIXELS

In the eye and CCD camera, the image plane is subdivided into **pixels**: typically 512×512 (0.25×10^6) in the CCD camera, arranged in a rectangular grid; 120×10^6 rods and 6×10^6 cones in the eye, arranged in a hexagonal mosaic.

In both cases, we can model the signal detected in the image plane by the variation in image brightness over time: $I(x, y, t)$. Figure 24.3 shows a digitized image of a stapler on a desk, and Figure 24.4 shows an array of image brightness values associated with a 12×12 block of pixels extracted from the stapler image. A computer program trying to interpret the image would have to start from such a representation.

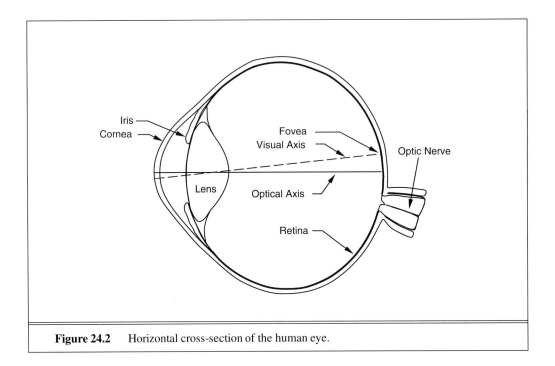

Figure 24.2   Horizontal cross-section of the human eye.

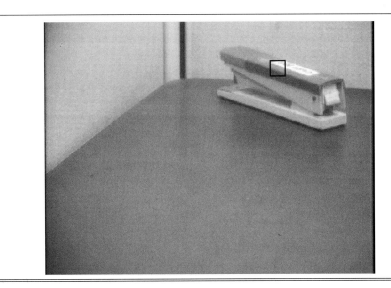

Figure 24.3   A photograph of a stapler on a table. The outlined box has been magnified and displayed in Figure 24.4.

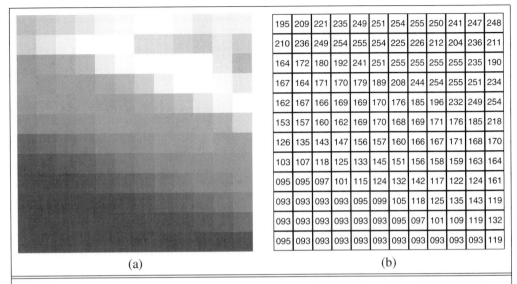

195	209	221	235	249	251	254	255	250	241	247	248
210	236	249	254	255	254	225	226	212	204	236	211
164	172	180	192	241	251	255	255	255	255	235	190
167	164	171	170	179	189	208	244	254	255	251	234
162	167	166	169	169	170	176	185	196	232	249	254
153	157	160	162	169	170	168	169	171	176	185	218
126	135	143	147	156	157	160	166	167	171	168	170
103	107	118	125	133	145	151	156	158	159	163	164
095	095	097	101	115	124	132	142	117	122	124	161
093	093	093	093	095	099	105	118	125	135	143	119
093	093	093	093	093	093	095	097	101	109	119	132
095	093	093	093	093	093	093	093	093	093	093	119

(a)   (b)

Figure 24.4   (a) Magnified view of a 12 × 12 block of pixels from Figure 24.3.   (b) The associated image brightness values.

Photometry of image formation

The brightness of a pixel p in the image is proportional to the amount of light directed toward the camera by the surface patch S_p that projects to pixel p. This in turn depends on the reflectance properties of S_p, the position and distribution of the light sources. There is also a dependence on the reflectance properties of the rest of the scene because other scene surfaces can serve as indirect light sources by reflecting light received by them onto S_p.

The light reflected from an object is characterized as being either diffusely or specularly reflected. Diffusely reflected light is light that has penetrated below the surface of an object, been absorbed, and then re-emitted. The surface appears equally bright to an observer in any direction. Lambert's cosine law is used to describe the reflection of light from a perfectly diffusing or **Lambertian** surface. The intensity E of light reflected from a perfect diffuser is given by

LAMBERTIAN

$$E = \rho E_0 \cos \theta$$

where E_0 is the intensity of the light source; ρ is the albedo, which varies from 0 (for perfectly black surfaces) to 1 (for pure white surfaces); and θ is the angle between the light direction and the surface normal.

Specularly reflected light is reflected from the outer surface of the object. Here the energy of reflected light is concentrated primarily in a particular direction—the one where the reflected ray is in the same plane as the incident ray and satisfies the condition that the angle of reflection is equal to the angle of incidence. This is the behavior of a perfect mirror.

In real life, surfaces exhibit a combination of diffuse and specular properties. Modelling this on the computer is the bread and butter of computer graphics. Rendering realistic images is usually done by ray tracing, which aims to simulate the physical process of light originating from light sources and being reflected and rereflected multiple times. The shape-from-shading problem in computer vision is aimed at inverting the process, that is, starting from the "rendered" image and figuring out the layout of the three-dimensional scene that gave rise to it. We will talk about this in more depth in Section 24.4.

Spectrophotometry of image formation

We have been talking of image intensity $I(x, y, t)$, merrily ignoring the fact that visible light comes in a range of wavelengths—ranging from 400 nm on the violet end of the spectrum to 700 nm on the red end. Given that there is a continuum of wavelengths, what does it mean that we have three primary colors? The explanation is that color is quite literally in the eye of the beholder. There are three different cone types in the eye with three different spectral sensitivity curves $R_k(\lambda)$. The output of the kth cone at location (x, y) at time t then is $I_k(x, y, t) = \int I(x, y, t, \lambda) R_k(\lambda) \, d\lambda$. The infinite dimensional wavelength space has been projected to a three-dimensional color space. This means that we ought to think of I as a three-dimensional vector at (x, y, t). Because the eye maps many different frequency spectra into the same color sensation, we should expect that there
METAMERS   exist **metamers**—different light spectra that appear the same to a human.

24.3   IMAGE-PROCESSING OPERATIONS FOR EARLY VISION

Figure 24.5 shows an image of a scene containing a stapler resting on a table as well as the
EDGES   **edges** detected on this image. Edges are curves in the image plane across which there is a "significant" change in image brightness. The ultimate goal of edge detection is the construction of an idealized line drawing such as Figure 24.6. The motivation is that edge contours in the image correspond to important scene contours. In the example, we have depth discontinuities, labelled 1; surface-orientation discontinuities, labelled 2; a reflectance discontinuity, labelled 3; and an illumination discontinuity (shadow), labelled 4.

As you can see, there is a big difference between the output of an edge detector as shown in Figure 24.5(b) and an ideal line drawing. Typically, there are missing contours (such as the top edge of the stapler), as well as noise contours that do not correspond to anything of significance in the scene. Later stages of processing based on edges have to take these errors into account.

How do we detect edges in an image? Consider the profile of image brightness along a 1-D cross-section perpendicular to an edge, for example, the one between the left edge of the table and the wall. It looks something like what is shown in Figure 24.7(a). The location of the edge corresponds to $x = 50$.

Because edges correspond to locations in images where the brightness undergoes a sharp change, a naive idea would be to differentiate the image and look for places where the magnitude of the derivative $I'(x)$ is large. Well, that almost works. In Figure 24.7(b) we see that although there is a peak at $x = 50$, there are also subsidiary peaks at other locations (e.g., $x = 75$) that could potentially be mistaken as true edges. These arise because of the presence of noise in the
SMOOTHING   image. We get much better results by combining the differentiation operation with **smoothing**.

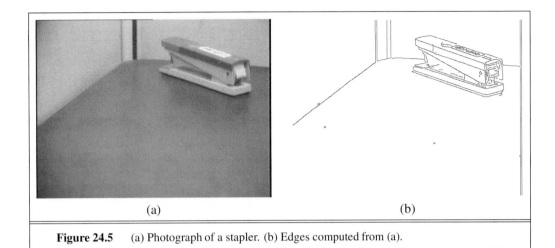

(a)   (b)

Figure 24.5   (a) Photograph of a stapler. (b) Edges computed from (a).

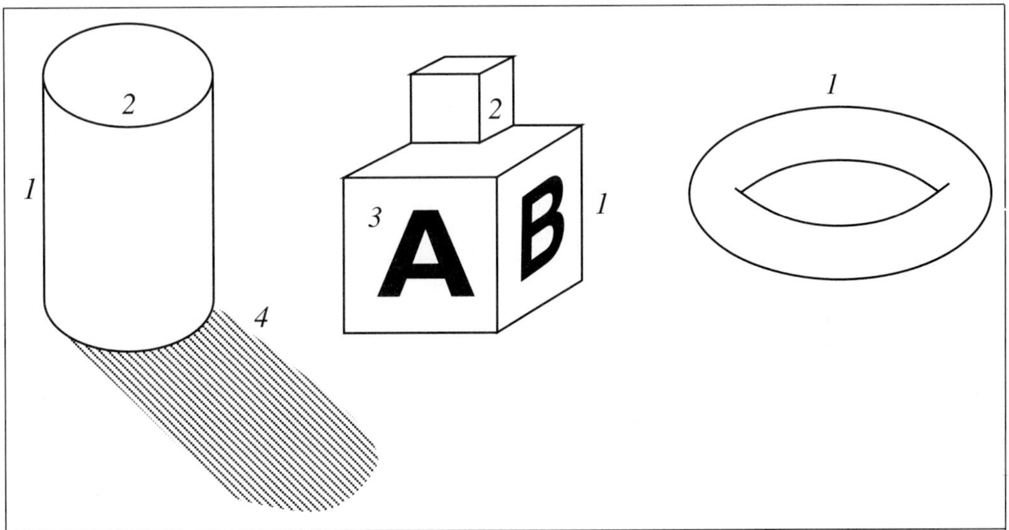

Figure 24.6   Different kinds of edges: (1) depth discontinuities; (2) surface orientation discontinuities; (3) reflectance discontinuities; (4) illumination discontinuities (shadows).

The result is Figure 24.7(c), in which the central peak at $x = 50$ remains and the subsidiary peaks are much diminished. This allows one to find the edges without getting confused by the noise.

CONVOLUTION   To understand these ideas better, we need the mathematical concept of **convolution**. Many useful image-processing operations such as smoothing and differentiation can be performed by convolving the image with suitable functions.

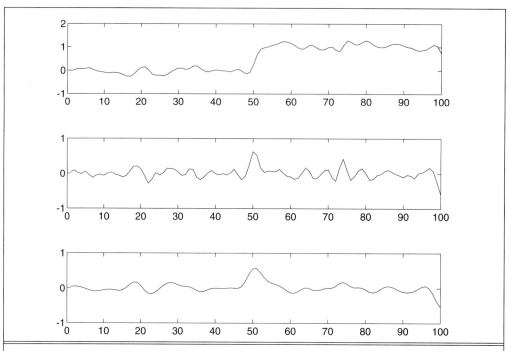

Figure 24.7 (a) Intensity profile $I(x)$ along a 1-D section across a step edge. (b) Its derivative $I'(x)$. (c) The result of the convolution $R(x) = I * G'_\sigma$. Looking for large values in this function is a good way to find edges in (a).

Convolution with linear filters

The result of convolving two functions f and g is the new function h, denoted as $h = f * g$, which is defined by

$$h(x) = \int_{-\infty}^{+\infty} f(u)\, g(x - u)\, du \quad \text{and} \quad h(x) = \sum_{u=-\infty}^{+\infty} f(u)\, g(x - u)$$

for continuous and discrete domains respectively. Typically, the functions f and g that we work with take nonzero values only in some finite interval, so the summation can be easily performed on a computer.

The generalization to functions defined on two dimensions (such as images) is straightforward. We replace the 1-D integrals (or sums) by 2-D integrals (or sums). The result of convolving two functions f and g is the new function h, denoted as $h = f * g$, which is defined by

$$h(x, y) = \int_{-\infty}^{+\infty} \int_{-\infty}^{+\infty} f(u, v)\, g(x - u, y - v)\, du\, dv$$

or if we take the domains of the two functions to be discrete

$$h(x, y) = \sum_{-\infty}^{+\infty} \sum_{-\infty}^{+\infty} f(u, v)\, g(x - u, y - v)$$

Edge detection

Let us go back to our 1-D example in Figure 24.7. We want to make the notion of image smoothing more precise. One standard form of smoothing is to convolve the image with a Gaussian function

$$G_\sigma(x) = \frac{1}{\sqrt{2\pi}\sigma} e^{-x^2/2\sigma^2}$$

Now it can be shown that for any functions f and g, $f * g' = (f * g)'$, so smoothing the image by convolving with a Gaussian G_σ and then differentiating is equivalent to convolving the image with $G'_\sigma(x)$, the first derivative of a Gaussian:

$$G'_\sigma(x) = \frac{-x}{\sqrt{2\pi}\sigma^3} e^{-x^2/2\sigma^2}$$

So, we have a simple algorithm for 1-D edge detection:

1. Convolve the image I with G'_σ to obtain R.
2. Find the absolute value of R.
3. Mark those peaks in $||R||$ that are above some prespecified threshold T_n. The threshold is chosen to eliminate spurious peaks due to noise.

In two dimensions, we need to cope with the fact that the edge may be at any angle θ. To detect vertical edges, we have an obvious strategy: convolve with $G'_\sigma(x)G_\sigma(y)$. In the y-direction, the effect is just to smooth (because of the Gaussian convolution), and in the x-direction, the effect is that of differentiation accompanied with smoothing. The algorithm for detecting vertical edges then is as follows:

1. Convolve the image $I(x, y)$ with $f_V(x, y) = G'_\sigma(x)G_\sigma(y)$ to obtain $R_V(x, y)$.
2. Find the absolute value of $R_V(x, y)$.
3. Mark those peaks in $||R_V||(x, y)$ that are above some prespecified threshold T_n.

In order to detect an edge at an arbitrary orientation, we need to convolve the image with two filters $f_V = G'_\sigma(x)G_\sigma(y)$ and $f_H = G'_\sigma(y)G_\sigma(x)$, which is just f_V rotated by $90°$. The algorithm for detecting edges at arbitrary orientations is

1. Convolve the image $I(x, y)$ with $f_V(x, y)$ and $f_H(x, y)$ to obtain $R_V(x, y)$ and $R_H(x, y)$, respectively. Define $R(x, y) = R_V^2(x, y) + R_H^2(x, y)$
2. Find the absolute value of $R(x, y)$.
3. Mark those peaks in $||R||(x, y)$ that are above some prespecified threshold T_n.

Once we have marked edge pixels by this algorithm, the next stage is to link those pixels that belong to the same edge curves. This can be done by assuming that any two neighboring pixels that are both edge pixels with consistent orientations must belong to the same edge curve.

We have just outlined the basic procedure used in the Canny edge detector (Canny, 1986), which is a standard algorithm widely used for detecting edges in images.

24.4   EXTRACTING 3-D INFORMATION USING VISION

We need to extract 3-D information for performing certain tasks such as manipulation, navigation, and recognition. There are three aspects of this:

1. Segmentation of the scene into distinct objects.
2. Determining the position and orientation of each object relative to the observer.
3. Determining the shape of each object.

SEGMENTATION

Segmentation of the image is a key step towards organizing the array of image pixels into regions that would correspond to semantically meaningful entities in the scene. For recognition, we would like to know what features belong together so that one could compare them with stored models; to grasp an object, one needs to know what belongs together as an object.

Edge detection, as discussed in the last section, is a useful first step toward image and scene segmentation, but not adequate by itself. This is because of two reasons: (a) some fraction of the edge curves that correspond to surface boundaries may be low contrast and not get detected; (b) many of the edge curves that are detected may correspond to noise, surface markings, or shadows. Segmentation is best viewed as part of extraction of 3-D information about the scene.

POSE

Determining the position and orientation of an object relative to the observer (the so-called **pose** of the object) is most important for manipulation and navigation tasks. To move around in a grocery store, one needs to know the locations of the obstacles, so that one can plan a path avoiding them. If one wants to pick up and grasp an object, one needs to know its position relative to the hand so that an appropriate trajectory of moves could be generated. Manipulation and navigation actions typically are done in a control loop setting—the sensory information provides feedback to modify the motion of the robot, or the robot arm. In fact, often we may be interested more in relative change of position.

Let us specify position and orientation in mathematical terms. The position of a point P in the scene is characterized by three numbers, the (X, Y, Z) coordinates of P in a coordinate frame with its origin at the pinhole and the Z-axis along the optical axis (Figure 24.1). What we have available is the perspective projection of the point in the image (x, y). This specifies the ray from the pinhole along which P lies; what we do not know is the distance. The term "orientation" could be used in two senses:

1. The orientation of the object as a whole. This can be specified in terms of a three-dimensional rotation relating its coordinate frame to that of the camera.
2. The orientation of the surface of the object at P. This can be specified by a vector **n** that specifies the direction of the unit surface normal vector, which is locally perpendicular to the surface. Often we express the surface orientation using the variables **slant** and **tilt**.

SLANT

TILT

Slant is the angle between the Z-axis and **n**. Tilt is the angle between the X-axis and the projection of **n** on the image plane.

SHAPE

When the camera moves relative to an object, both the object's distance and its orientation change. What is preserved is the **shape** of the object. If the object is a cube, that fact is not changed when the object moves. Geometers have been attempting to formalize shape for centuries—the basic concept being that shape is what remains unchanged under some group of transformations, for example, combinations of rotations and translations. The difficulty lies in finding a representation of global shape that is general enough to deal with the wide variety of objects in the real world— not just simple forms like cylinders, cones, and spheres—and yet can be recovered easily from the visual input. The problem of characterizing the *local* shape of a surface is much better understood. Essentially, this can be done in terms of curvature—how does the surface normal change as one moves in different directions on the surface. For a plane, there is no change at all. For a cylinder, if one moves parallel to the axis there is no change, but in the perpendicular direction, the surface normal rotates at a rate inversely proportional to the radius of the cylinder. And so on. All this is studied in the subject of differential geometry.

The shape of an object is relevant for some manipulation tasks, for example, deciding where to grasp an object. But its most significant role is in object recognition, where geometric shape along with color and texture provide the most significant cues to enable us to identify objects, classify what is in the image as an example of some class one has seen before, and so on.

The fundamental question is the following: Given the fact that during perspective projection, all points in the 3-D world along a ray from the pinhole have been projected to the same point in the image, how do we recover 3-D information? There are a number of cues available in the visual stimulus for this, including **motion**, **binocular stereopsis**, **texture**, **shading**, and **contour**. Each of these cues relies on background assumptions about physical scenes in order to provide unambiguous interpretations. We discuss each of these cues in the following subsections.

Motion

OPTICAL FLOW

If the camera moves relative to the three-dimensional scene, the resulting apparent motion in the image is called **optical flow**. This describes the direction and speed of motion of features *in the image* as a result of relative motion between the viewer and the scene. In Figure 24.8, we show two frames from a video of a rotating Rubik's cube. Figure 24.9 shows the optical flow vectors computed from these images. The optical flow encodes useful information about scene structure. For example, when viewed from a moving car, distant objects have much slower apparent motion than close objects; thus, the rate of apparent motion can tell us something about distance.

The optical flow vector field can be represented by its components $v_x(x, y)$ in the x-direction and $v_y(x, y)$ in the y-direction. To measure optical flow, we need to find corresponding points between one time frame and the next. We exploit the fact that image patches around corresponding points have similar intensity patterns. Consider a block of pixels centered at pixel p, (x_0, y_0) at time t_0. This block of pixels is to be compared with pixel blocks centered at various candidate pixels q_i at $(x_0 + D_x, y_0 + D_y)$ at time $t_0 + D_t$. One possible measure of similarity is the **sum of squared differences** (SSD):

SUM OF SQUARED DIFFERENCES

$$SSD(D_x, D_y) = \sum_{(x,y)} (I(x, y, t) - I(x + D_x, y + D_y, t + D_t))^2$$

Here (x, y) range over pixels in the block centered at (x_0, y_0). We find the (D_x, D_y) that minimizes the SSD. The optical flow at (x_0, y_0) is then $(v_x, v_y) = (D_x/D_t, D_y/D_t)$. Alternatively, one can maximize the **cross-correlation**:

CROSS-CORRELATION

$$Correlation(D_x, D_y) = \sum_{(x,y)} I(x, y, t)I(x + D_x, y + D_y, t + D_t)$$

Figure 24.8   (a) A Rubik's cube on a rotating turntable.   (b) The same cube, shown 19/30 seconds later. (Image courtesy of Richard Szeliski.)

Cross-correlation works best when there is texture in the scene, resulting in windows containing significant brightness variation among the pixels. If one is looking at a uniform white wall, then the cross-correlation is going to be nearly the same for the different candidate matches q, and the algorithm is reduced to making a blind guess.

EGOMOTION

Suppose that the viewer has translational velocity $\mathbf{T}$ and angular velocity $\boldsymbol{\omega}$ (which thus describe the **egomotion**). One can derive an equation relating the viewer velocities, the optical flow, and the positions of objects in the scene. In fact, assuming $f = 1$,

$$v_x(x, y) = \left[-\frac{T_x}{Z(x, y)} - \omega_y + \omega_z y \right] - x \left[-\frac{T_z}{Z(x, y)} - \omega_x y + \omega_y x \right]$$

$$v_y(x, y) = \left[-\frac{T_y}{Z(x, y)} - \omega_z x + \omega_x \right] - y \left[-\frac{T_z}{Z(x, y)} - \omega_x y + \omega_y x \right]$$

where $Z(x, y)$ gives the z-coordinate of the scene point corresponding to the image point at (x, y).

One can get a good intuition by considering the case of pure translation. In that case, the flow field becomes

$$v_x(x, y) = \frac{-T_x + xT_z}{Z(x, y)}, \qquad v_y(x, y) = \frac{-T_y + yT_z}{Z(x, y)}$$

FOCUS OF
EXPANSION

One can observe some interesting properties. Both components of the optical flow, $v_x(x, y)$ and $v_y(x, y)$, are zero at the point $x = T_x/T_z, y = T_y/T_z$. This point is called the **focus of expansion** of the flow field. Suppose we change the origin in the x–y plane to lie at the focus of expansion; then the expressions for optical flow take on a particularly simple form. Let (x', y') be the new coordinates defined by $x' = x - T_x/T_z, y' = y - T_y/T_z$. Then

$$v_x(x', y') = \frac{x' T_z}{Z(x', y')}, \qquad v_y(x', y') = \frac{y' T_z}{Z(x', y')}$$

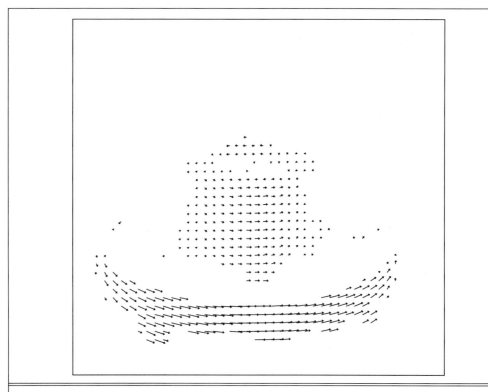

Figure 24.9   Flow vectors calculated by comparing the two images in Figure 24.8. (Courtesy of Joe Weber and Jitendra Malik.)

This equation has some interesting applications. Suppose you are a fly trying to land on wall, and you want to know the time to contact at the current velocity. This time is given by Z/T_z. Note that although the instantaneous optical flow field cannot provide either the distance Z or the velocity component T_z, it can provide the ratio of the two, and can therefore be used to control the landing approach. Experiments with real flies show that this is exactly what they use.

To recover depth, one should make use of multiple frames. If the camera is looking at a rigid body, the shape does not change from frame to frame and thus we are able to better deal with the inherently noisy optical flow measurements. Results from one such approach due to Tomasi and Kanade (1992) are shown in Figures 24.10 and 24.11.

Binocular stereopsis

The idea here is rather similar to motion parallax, except that instead of using images over time, we use two (or more) images separated in space, such as are provided by the forward-facing eyes of humans. Because a given feature in the scene will be in a different place relative to the z-axis of each image plane, if we superpose the two images, there will be a **disparity** in the location of

DISPARITY

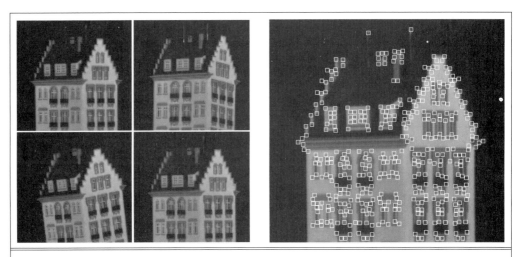

Figure 24.10   (a) Four frames from a video sequence in which the camera is moved and rotated relative to the object. (b) The first frame of the sequence, annotated with small boxes highlighting the features found by the feature detector. (Courtesy of Carlo Tomasi.)

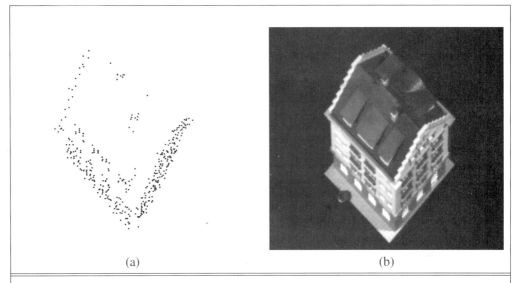

(a)   (b)

Figure 24.11   (a) 3-D reconstruction of the locations of the image features in Figure 24.10, shown from above. (b) The real house, taken from the same position.

the image feature in the two images. You can see this clearly in Figure 24.12, where the nearest point of the pyramid is shifted to the left in the right image and to the right in the left image.

Let us work out the geometrical relationship between disparity and depth. First, we will consider the case when both the eyes (or cameras) are looking forward with their optical axes

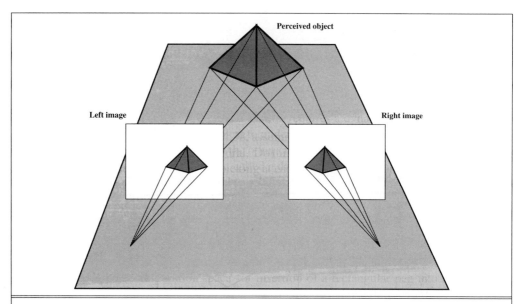

Figure 24.12   The idea of stereopsis: different camera positions result in slightly different 2-D views of the same 3-D scene.

parallel. The relationship of the right camera to the left camera is then just translation along the *x*-axis by an amount *b*, the baseline. We can use the optical flow equations from the previous section to compute the horizontal and vertical disparity as $H = v_x \Delta t$, $V = v_y \Delta t$, given that $T_x = b/\Delta t$ and $T_y = T_z = 0$. The rotational parameters ω_x, ω_y, and ω_z are zero. One obtains $H = b/Z$, $V = 0$. In words, the horizontal disparity is equal to the ratio of the baseline to the depth, and the vertical disparity is zero.

This is, of course, the simplest viewing geometry (relationship between the two cameras) that we could consider. Under normal viewing conditions, humans **fixate**; that is, there is some point in the scene at which the optical axes of the two eyes intersect. Figure 24.13 shows two eyes fixated at a point P_0, which is at a distance Z from the midpoint of the eyes. For convenience, we will compute the *angular* disparity, measured in radians. The disparity at the point of fixation P_0 is zero. For some other point P in the scene that is δZ further away, we can compute the angular displacements of the left and right images of P, which we will call P_L and P_R. If each of these is displaced by an angle $\delta\theta/2$ relative to P_0, then the displacement between P_L and P_R, which is the disparity of P, is just $\delta\theta$. From simple geometry, we have

$$\frac{\delta\theta}{\delta Z} = \frac{-b}{Z^2}$$

In humans, *b* (the **baseline**) is about 6 cm. Suppose that Z is about 100 cm. The smallest detectable $\delta\theta$ (corresponding to the pixel size) is about 5 seconds of arc, or 2.42×10^{-5} radians, giving a δZ of about 0.4 mm. For $Z = 30$ cm (1 ft), we get the impressively small value $\delta Z = 0.036$ mm. Stating this in words, at a distance of 30 cm, humans can discriminate depths that differ by as little as 0.036 mm, enabling us to thread needles and the like.

FIXATE

BASELINE

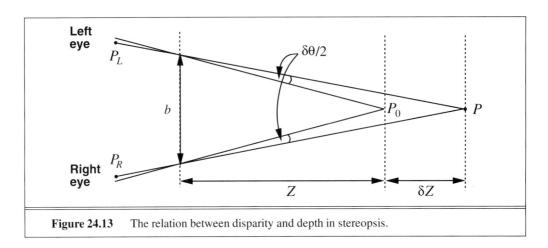

Figure 24.13   The relation between disparity and depth in stereopsis.

Note that unlike the case of motion, we have assumed that we know the viewing geometry, or the relative orientation between the eyes. This is often a reasonable assumption. In the case of the eyes, the brain has commanded a particular state of the ocular muscles to move the eyes, and hence the positions of the eyes relative to the head are known. Similarly, in a binocular camera system, one knows the relative configuration.

Knowledge of the viewing geometry is very useful in trying to measure disparity. As in the case of optical flow, we can try to find corresponding points between the left and right images by maximizing some measure of similarity. However, one does not have to search in a two-dimensional region. Corresponding points must always lie along **epipolar lines** in the images (see Figure 24.14). These lines correspond to the intersections of an epipolar plane (the plane through a point in the scene and the nodal points of the two eyes) with the left and right image planes. Exploiting this epipolar constraint reduces an initially two-dimensional search to a one-dimensional one. Obviously determination of the epipolar lines requires a knowledge of the viewing geometry.

EPIPOLAR LINES

A simple-minded approach for finding disparity would be to search along epipolar lines looking to maximize the cross-correlation, just as in the case of optical flow. Given a point p_i in the left view, its corresponding point q_i in the right view is obtained by searching along the associated epipolar line in the other view. For each of the possible matches q, the cross-correlation between windows centered at p_i and q is computed. The corresponding point is declared to be the pixel q_i for which the cross-correlation is maximized.

One can do better by exploiting some additional constraints:

1. Uniqueness: a point in one image can correspond to at most one point in the other image. We say at most one, because it is possible that the point may be occluded in the other view.

2. Piecewise continuity of surfaces in the scene: the fact the world is usually piecewise continuous means that nearby points in the scene have nearby values of depth, and consequently of disparity, except across object boundaries and occlusions.

An example of a system that exploits these multiple constraints is the work of Belhumeur (1993). Belhumeur's results for an oblique view of a box (Figure 24.15) are shown in Figure 24.16. His

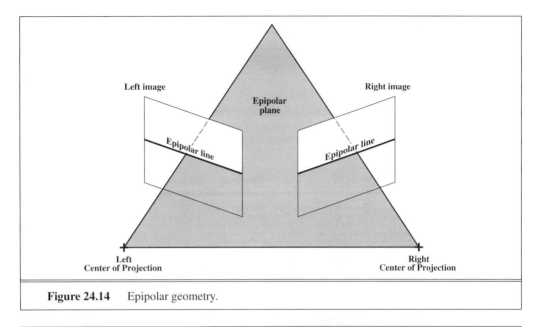

Figure 24.14   Epipolar geometry.

| (a) | (b) |

Figure 24.15   The figure shows an image of a Q-tips box standing on end with a long vertical crease protruding toward the camera. Behind the box is a flat surface.

algorithm uses the ordering constraint and deals with depth discontinuities where the windows at corresponding points in the image are not sampling corresponding patches in the scene. Because of occlusion in one of the views, there is a strip seen only in one eye. Note also the use of stereopsis for scene segmentation as demonstrated in Figure 24.16(c).

A standard criticism of area-based matching approaches is that they are susceptible to errors when corresponding patches in the two images do not look similar. This can happen for a variety of reasons: (1) the surface reflectance function has an appreciable specular component,

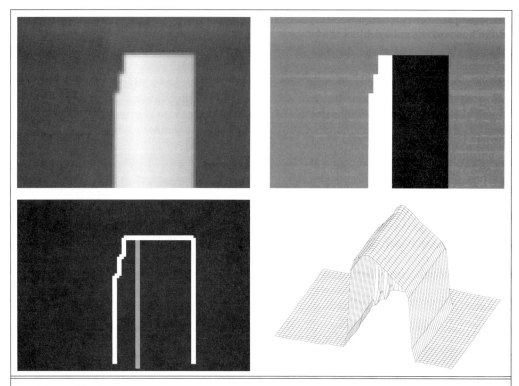

Figure 24.16   Results from processing the Q-tips stereo pair. (a) Image of depth. (b) Image of smoothed slope. (c) Object boundaries (white) and surface creases (gray). (d) Wire frame of depth. (Images courtesy of Peter Belhumeur.)

so the brightness of a point in the scene is a function of viewpoint; (2) there is a differing amount of foreshortening in the two views, because the patch makes different angles to the optical axes in the two views.

Another family of approaches is based on first finding edges and then looking for matches. Edges are deemed compatible if they are near enough in orientation and have the same sign of contrast across the edge. Corresponding edges are usually assumed to obey the same left-to-right ordering in each image, which allows one to restrict the number of possible matches and lends itself to efficient algorithms based on **dynamic programming**. With any edge-based approach, however, the resulting depth information is sparse, because it is available only at edge locations. Thus, a further step is needed to interpolate depth across surfaces in the scene.

Texture gradients

TEXTURE

Texture in everyday language is a property of surfaces associated with the tactile quality they suggest (texture has the same root as textile). In computational vision, it refers to a closely related concept, that of a spatially repeating pattern on a surface that can be sensed visually. Examples include the pattern of windows on a building, the stitches on a sweater, the spots on a leopard's skin, blades of grass on a lawn, pebbles on a beach or a crowd of people in a stadium. Sometimes the arrangement is quite periodic, as in the stitches on a sweater; in other instances, as in pebbles on a beach the regularity is only in a statistical sense—the density of pebbles is roughly the same on different parts of the beach.

TEXELS

What we just said is true *in the scene*. In the image, the apparent size, shape, spacing, and so on, of the texture elements (the **texels**) do indeed vary, as illustrated in Figure 24.17. The tiles are identical in the scene. There are two main causes for this variation in the projected size and shape of the tiles:

1. Varying distances of the different texels from the camera. Recall that under perspective projection, distant objects appear smaller. The scaling factor is $1/Z$.

2. Varying foreshortening of the different texels. This is related to the orientation of the texel relative to the line of sight from the camera. If the texel is perpendicular to the line of sight, there is no foreshortening. The magnitude of the foreshortening effect is proportional to $\cos \sigma$, where σ is the slant of the plane of the texel.

After some mathematical analysis (Garding, 1992), one can compute expressions for the rate of change of various image texel features, such as area, foreshortening, and density. These **texture gradients** are functions of the surface shape as well as its slant and tilt with respect to the viewer.

TEXTURE
GRADIENTS

To recover shape from texture, one can use a two-step process: (a) measure the texture gradients; (b) estimate the surface shape, slant, and tilt that would give rise to the measured texture gradients. We show the results of an algorithm developed by Malik and Rosenholtz(1994) in Figures 24.17 and 24.18.

Shading

Shading—variation in the intensity of light received from different portions of a surface in the scene—is determined by scene geometry and reflectance properties of the surfaces. In computer graphics, the objective is to determine the image brightness $I(x, y)$ given the scene geometry and reflectance properties. In computer vision, our hope might be to invert the process, that is, recover the scene geometry and reflectance properties given the image brightness $I(x, y)$. This has proved difficult to do in anything but the simplest cases.

Let us start with an example of a situation where we can in fact solve for shape from shading. Consider a Lambertian surface illuminated by a distant point light source. We will assume that the surface is distant enough from the camera so that we could use orthographic projection as an approximation to perspective projection. The image brightness is

$$I(x, y) = k\mathbf{n}(x, y).\mathbf{s}$$

where k is a scaling constant, $\mathbf{n}$ is the unit surface normal vector, and $\mathbf{s}$ is the unit vector in the direction of the light source. Because $\mathbf{n}$ and $\mathbf{s}$ are unit vectors, their dot product is just the cosine of the angle between them. Surface shape is captured in the variation of the surface normal $\mathbf{n}$ along the surface. Let us assume that k and $\mathbf{s}$ are known. Our problem then is to recover the surface normal $\mathbf{n}(x, y)$ given the image intensity $I(x, y)$.

Figure 24.17   A scene illustrating texture gradient. Assuming that the real texture is uniform allows recovery of the surface orientation. The computed surface orientation is indicated by overlaying a white circle and pointer, transformed as if the circle were painted on the surface at that point. (Image courtesy of Jitendra Malik and Ruth Rosenholtz.)

Figure 24.18   Recovery of shape from texture for a curved surface.

The first observation to make is that the problem of determining **n**, given the brightness I at a given pixel (x, y), is underdetermined locally. We can compute the angle that **n** makes with the light source vector, but that only constrains it to lie on a certain cone of directions with axis **s** and apex angle $\theta = \cos^{-1}(I/k)$. To proceed further, note that **n** cannot vary arbitrarily from pixel to pixel. It corresponds to the normal vector of a smooth surface patch and consequently must also vary in a smooth fashion—the technical term for the constraint is **integrability**. Several different techniques have been developed to exploit this insight. One technique is simply to rewrite **n** in terms of the partial derivatives Z_x and Z_y of the depth $Z(x, y)$. This results in a partial differential equation for Z that can be solved to yield the depth $Z(x, y)$, given appropriate boundary conditions.

One can generalize the approach somewhat. It is not necessary for the surface to be Lambertian nor for the light source to be a point source. As long as one is able to determine the **reflectance map** $R(\mathbf{n})$, which specifies the brightness of a surface patch as a function of its surface normal **n**, essentially the same kind of techniques can be used.

The real difficulty comes in dealing with interreflections. If we consider a typical indoor scene, such as the objects inside an office, surfaces are illuminated not only by the light sources, but also by the light reflected from other surfaces in the scene that effectively serve as secondary light sources. These mutual illumination effects are quite significant. The reflectance map formalism completely fails in this situation—image brightness depends not just on the surface normal, but also on the complex spatial relationships among the different surfaces in the scene.

Humans clearly do get some perception of shape from shading, so this remains an interesting problem in spite of all these difficulties.

Contour

When we look at a line drawing, such as Figure 24.19, we get a vivid perception of 3-D shape and layout. How? After all, we saw earlier that there is an infinity of scene configurations that can give rise to the same line drawing. Note that we get even a perception of surface slant and tilt. It could be due to a combination of high-level knowledge about typical shapes as well as some low-level constraints.

We will consider the qualitative knowledge available from a line drawing. As discussed earlier, lines in a drawing can have multiple significances (see Figure 24.6 and the accompanying text). The task of determining the actual significance of each line in an image is called **line labelling**, and was one of the first tasks studied in computer vision. For now, let us deal with a simplified model of the world where the objects have no surface marks and where the lines due to illumination discontinuities like shadow edges and specularities have been removed in some preprocessing step, enabling us to limit our attention to line drawings where each line corresponds either to a depth or orientation discontinuity.

Each line then can be classified as either the projection of a **limb** (the locus of points on the surface where the line of sight is tangent to the surface) or as an **edge** (a surface normal discontinuity). Additionally, each edge can be classified as a convex, concave, or occluding edge. For occluding edges and limbs, we would like to determine which of the two surfaces bordering the curve in the line drawing is nearer in the scene. These inferences can be represented by giving each line one of 6 possible **line labels** as illustrated in Figure 24.20.

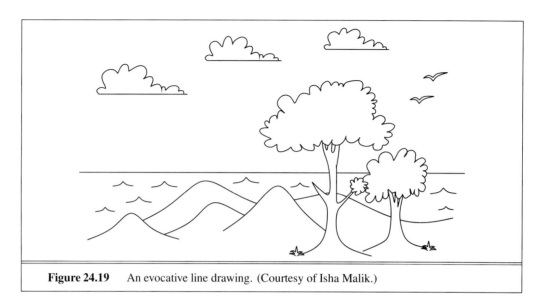

Figure 24.19   An evocative line drawing. (Courtesy of Isha Malik.)

1. "+" and "−" labels represent convex and concave edges, respectively. These are associated with surface normal discontinuities where both surfaces that meet along the edge are visible.

2. A "←" or a "→" represents an occluding convex edge. When viewed from the camera, both surface patches that meet along the edge lie on the same side, one occluding the other. As one moves in the direction of the arrow, these surfaces are to the right.

3. A "←←" or a "→→" represents a limb. Here the surface curves smoothly around to occlude itself. As one moves in the direction of the twin arrows, the surface lies to the right. The line of sight is tangential to the surface for all points on the limb. Limbs move on the surface of the object as the viewpoint changes.

Of the 6^n combinatorially possible label assignments to the n lines in a drawing, only a small number are physically possible. The determination of these label assignments is the line labelling problem. Note that the problem only makes sense if the label is the same all the way along a line. This is not always true, because the label can change along a line for images of curved objects. In this section, we will deal only with polyhedral objects, so this is not a concern.

Huffman (1971) and Clowes (1971) independently attempted the first systematic approach to polyhedral scene analysis. Huffman and Clowes limited their analysis to scenes with opaque **trihedral** solids—objects in which exactly three plane surfaces come together at each vertex. For scenes with multiple objects, they also ruled out object alignments that would result in a violation of the trihedral assumption, such as two cubes sharing a common edge. **Cracks**, that is, "edges" across which the tangent planes are continuous, were also not permitted. For the trihedral world, Huffman and Clowes made an exhaustive listing of all the different vertex types and the different ways in which they could be viewed under general viewpoint. The general viewpoint condition essentially ensures that if there is a small movement of the eye, none of the junctions changes character. For example, this condition implies that if three lines intersect in the image, the corresponding edges in the scene must also intersect.

TRIHEDRAL

CRACKS

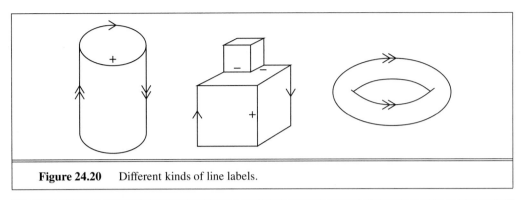

Figure 24.20   Different kinds of line labels.

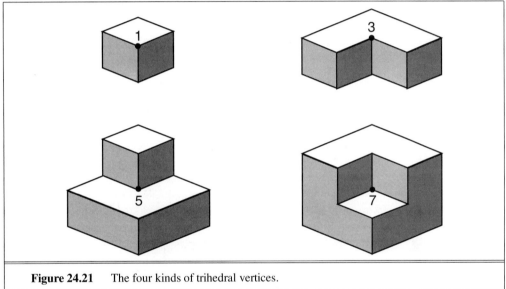

Figure 24.21   The four kinds of trihedral vertices.

OCTANTS

The four ways in which three plane surfaces can come together at a vertex are shown in Figure 24.21. These cases have been constructed by taking a cube and dividing it into eight **octants**. We want to generate the different possible trihedral vertices at the center of the cube by filling in various octants. The vertex labeled 1 corresponds to 1 filled octant, 3 to 3 filled octants, and so on. Readers should convince themselves that these are indeed *all* the possibilities. For example, if one fills two octants in a cube, one cannot construct a valid trihedral vertex at the center. Note also that these four cases correspond to different combinations of convex and concave edges that meet at the vertex.

The three edges meeting at the vertex partition the surrounding space into eight octants. A vertex can be viewed from any of the octants not occupied by solid material. Moving the viewpoint within a single octant does not result in a picture with different junction types. The vertex labeled 1 in Figure 24.21 can be viewed from any of the remaining seven octants to give the junction labels in Figure 24.22.

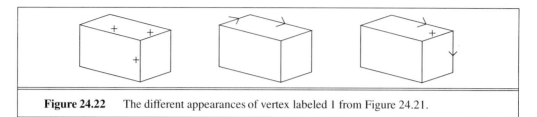

Figure 24.22   The different appearances of vertex labeled 1 from Figure 24.21.

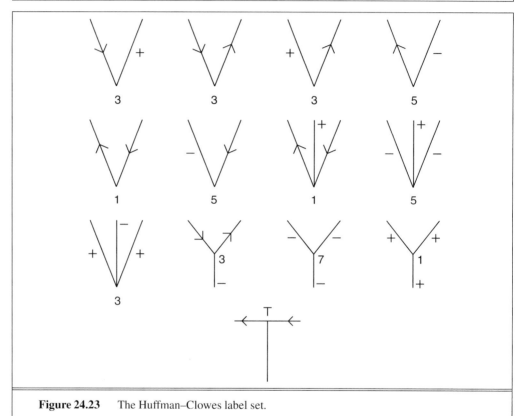

Figure 24.23   The Huffman–Clowes label set.

An exhaustive listing of the different ways each vertex can be viewed results in the possibilities shown in Figure 24.23. We get four different junction types which can be distinguished in the image: L-, Y-, arrow, and T-junctions. L-junctions correspond to two visible edges. Y- and arrow junctions correspond to a triple of edges—in a Y-junction none of the three angles is greater than π. T-junctions are associated with occlusion. When a nearer, opaque surface blocks the view of a more distant edge, one obtains a continuous edge meeting a half edge. The four T-junction labels correspond to the occlusion of four different types of edges.

When using this junction dictionary to find a labeling for the line drawing, the problem is to determine which junction interpretations are globally consistent. Consistency is forced by the rule that each line in the picture must be assigned one and only one label along its entire length.

Waltz (1975) proposed an algorithm for this problem (actually for an augmented version with shadows, cracks, and separably concave edges) that was one of the first applications of constraint satisfaction in AI (see Chapter 3). In the terminology of CSPs, the variables are the junctions, the values are labellings for the junctions, and the constraints are that each line has a single label. Although Kirousis and Papadimitriou (1988) have shown that the line-labelling problem for trihedral scenes is NP-complete, standard CSP algorithms perform well in practice.

Although the Huffman–Clowes–Waltz labeling scheme was limited to trihedral objects, subsequent work by Mackworth(1973) and Sugihara (1984) resulted in a generalization for arbitrary polyhedra and work by Malik (1987) for piecewise smooth curved objects.

24.5   USING VISION FOR MANIPULATION AND NAVIGATION

One of the principal uses of vision is to provide information for manipulating objects—picking them up, grasping, twirling, and so on—as well as navigating in a scene while avoiding obstacles.

The capability to use vision for these purposes is present in the most primitive of animal visual systems. Perhaps the evolutionary origin of the vision sense can be traced back to the presence of a photosensitive spot on one end of an organism that enabled it to orient itself toward (or away from) the light. Flies use vision based on optic flow to control their landing responses.

Mobile robots moving around in an environment need to know where the obstacles are, where free space corridors are available, and so on. More on this in Chapter 25.

Let us study the use of vision in driving in detail. Consider the tasks for the driver of the car in the bottom left corner of Figure 24.24.

1. Keep moving at a reasonable speed v_0.

2. Lateral control—ensure that the vehicle remains securely within its lane, that is, keep $d_l = d_r$.

3. Longitudinal control—ensure that there is a safe distance d_2 between it and the vehicle in front of it.

4. Monitor vehicles in neighboring lanes (at distances d_1 and d_3) and be prepared for appropriate maneuvers if one of them decides to change lanes.

The problem for the driver is to generate appropriate steering, actuation or braking actions to best accomplish these tasks. Focusing specifically on lateral and longitudinal control, what information is needed for these tasks?

For lateral control, one needs to maintain a representation of the position and orientation of the car relative to the lane. The view of the road from a camera mounted on a car is shown in Figure 24.25. We detect edges corresponding to the lane marker segments and then fit smooth curves to these. The parameters of these curves carry information about the lateral position of the car, the direction it is pointing relative to the lane, and the curvature of the lane. This information, along with the dynamics of the car, is all that is needed by the steering control system. Note also that because from every frame to the next frame there is only a small change in the position

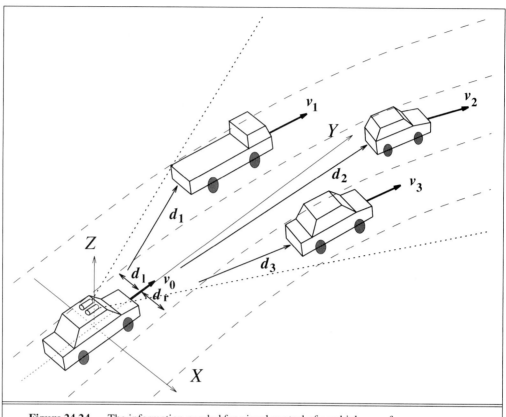

Figure 24.24   The information needed for visual control of a vehicle on a freeway.

of the projection of the lane in the image, one knows *where* to look for the lane markers in the image—in the figure, this is indicated by showing the search windows.

For longitudinal control, one needs to know distances to the vehicles in front. This can be accomplished using binocular stereopsis or optical flow. Both these approaches can be simplified by exploiting the domain constraints derived from the fact that one is driving on a planar surface. Using these techniques, Dickmanns and Zapp (1987) have demonstrated visually controlled car driving on freeways at high speeds. Pomerleau (1993) achieved similar performance using a neural network approach (see discussion on page 586).

The driving example makes one point very clear: *for a specific task, one does not need to recover all the information that in principle can be recovered from an image.* One does not need to recover the exact shape of every vehicle, solve for shape-from-texture on the grass surface adjacent to the freeway, and so on. The needs of the task require only certain kinds of information and one can gain considerable computational speed and robustness by recovering only that information and fully exploiting the domain constraints. Our purpose in discussing the general approaches in the previous section was that they form the basic theory, which one can specialize for the needs of particular tasks.

Figure 24.25   Image of a road taken from a camera inside the car.

24.6   OBJECT REPRESENTATION AND RECOGNITION

The object recognition problem can be defined as follows. Given

1. a scene consisting of one or more objects chosen from a collection of objects $O_1, O_2, \ldots, O_n$ known a priori, and

2. an image of the scene taken from an unknown viewer position and orientation,

determine the following:

1. Which of the objects $O_1, O_2, \ldots, O_n$ are present in the scene.

2. For each such object, determine its position and orientation relative to the viewer.

Obviously, this determination requires prior storage of suitable descriptions of the objects.

This problem is clearly of considerable industrial importance. For example, in an assembly process, the robot has to identify the different components and compute their positions and orientations in order to generate a grasping or pick-and-place strategy. In addition to the engineering standpoint, the problem is of great scientific interest. Humans have the impressive ability to recognize thousands of objects almost instantaneously even when the objects are partially occluded or presented in highly simplified line drawings.

The two fundamental issues that any object recognition scheme must address are the representation of the models and the matching of models to images.

First, let us consider the representation problem. The two most popular representations of 3-D objects in computer vision have been polyhedral approximations and generalized cylinders. Polyhedral descriptions are general, but they get painfully long if a high accuracy is desired in modeling curved objects. They are also very cumbersome for users to input. **Generalized** **cylinders** (Figure 24.26) provide compact descriptions for a wide class of objects and have been used in a number of object recognition systems.

GENERALIZED
CYLINDERS

A generalized cylinder is defined by a planar cross section, an axis (which may be curved), and a sweeping rule which describes how the cross section changes along the axis. Many shapes can be built up using generalized cylinders as parts. Generalized cylinders are not always ideal for representing arbitrary objects; the object may have to be decomposed into many parts, each of which is a generalized cylinder. In such situations, there can be many alternative decompositions into parts with each part describable as a generalized cylinder in several ways. This leads to difficulties at matching time. In general, the problem of effective shape representation for curved objects is largely unsolved.

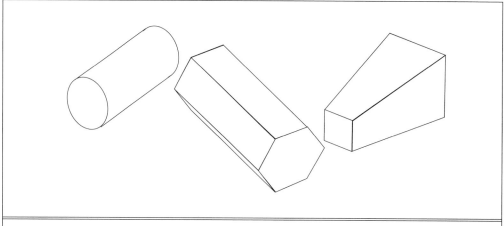

Figure 24.26   Some examples of generalized cylinders. Each of these shapes has a principal axis and a planar cross-section whose dimensions may vary along the axis.

The alignment method

We will consider one particular version of the problem in greater detail—we are asked to identify a three-dimensional object from its projection on the image plane. For convenience, the projection process is modelled as a scaled orthographic projection. We do not know the pose of the object—its position and orientation with respect to the camera.

The object is represented by a set of m features or distinguished points $\mu_1, \mu_2, \ldots, \mu_m$ in three-dimensional space—perhaps vertices for a polyhedral object. These are measured in some coordinate system natural for the object. The points are then subjected to an unknown 3-D rotation $\mathbf{R}$, followed by translation by unknown amount $\mathbf{t}$ and projection to give rise to image feature points $p_1, p_2, \ldots, p_n$ on the image plane. In general, $n \neq m$ because some model points may be occluded. The feature detector in the image also may miss true features and mark false ones due to noise. We can express this as

$$p_i = \Pi(\mathbf{R}\mu_i + \mathbf{t})$$

for 3-D model point μ_i and corresponding image point p_i. Here Π denotes perspective projection or one of its approximations such as scaled orthographic projection. We can summarize this by the equation $p_i = Q\mu_i$ where Q is the (unknown) transformation that brings the model points in alignment with the image. Assuming the object is rigid, the transformation Q is the *same* for all the model points.

One can solve for Q given the 3-D coordinates of three model points and their 2-D projections. The intuition is as follows: one can write down equations relating the coordinates of p_i to those of μ_i. In these equations, the unknown quantities correspond to the parameters of the rotation matrix $\mathbf{R}$ and the translation vector $\mathbf{t}$. If we have sufficiently many equations, we ought to be able to solve for Q. We will not give any proof here, but merely state the following result (Huttenlocher and Ullman, 1990):

> Given three noncollinear points μ_1, μ_2, and μ_3 in the model, and their projections on the image plane, p_1, p_2, and p_3 under scaled orthographic projection, there exist exactly two transformations from the three-dimensional model coordinate frame to a two-dimensional image coordinate frame.

These transformations are related by a reflection around the image plane and can be computed by a simple closed-form solution. We will just assume that there exists a function FIND-TRANSFORM, as shown in Figure 24.27.

If we could identify the corresponding model features for three features in the image, we could compute Q, the pose of the object. The problem is that we do not know these correspondences. The solution is to operate in a generate-and-test paradigm. We have to guess an initial correspondence of an image triplet with a model triplet and use the function FIND-TRANSFORM to hypothesize Q. If the guessed correspondence was correct, then Q will be correct, and when applied to the remaining model points will result in prediction of the image points. If the guessed correspondence was incorrect, then Q will be incorrect, and when applied to the remaining model points would not predict the image points.

---

function FIND-TRANSFORM($p_1, p_2, p_3, \mu_1, \mu_2, \mu_3$) **returns** a transform Q such that
$$Q(\mu_1) = p_1$$
$$Q(\mu_2) = p_2$$
$$Q(\mu_3) = p_3$$

inputs: p_1, p_2, p_3, image feature points
μ_1, μ_2, μ_3, model feature points

Figure 24.27   The definition of the transformation-finding process. We omit the algorithm (Huttenlocher and Ullman, 1990).

function ALIGN(*Image feature points, Model feature points*) **returns** a solution or failure

> **loop do**
> > **choose** an untried triplet p_{i_1}, p_{i_2}, p_{i_3} from image
> > **if** no untried triplets left **then return** failure
> > **while** there are still untried model triplets left **do**
> > > **choose** an untried triplet μ_{j_1}, μ_{j_2}, μ_{j_3} from model
> > > $Q \leftarrow$ FIND-TRANSFORM(p_{i_1}, p_{i_2}, p_{i_3}, μ_{j_1}, μ_{j_2}, μ_{j_3})
> > > **if** projection according to Q explains image **then**
> > > > **return** (success, Q)
> >
> > **end**
>
> **end**

Figure 24.28   An informal description of the alignment algorithm.

This is the basis of the algorithm ALIGN, which seeks to find the pose for a given model and return failure otherwise (see Figure 24.28). The worst-case time complexity of the algorithm is proportional to the number of combinations of model triplets and image triplets—this gives the number of times Q has to be computed—times the cost of verification. This gives $\binom{n}{3}\binom{m}{3}$ times the cost of verification. The cost of verification is $m \log n$, as we must predict the image position of each of m model points, and find the distance to the nearest image point, a $\log n$ operation if the image points are arranged in an appropriate data structure. Thus, the worst-case complexity of the alignment algorithm is $O(m^4 n^3 \log n)$, where m and n are the number of model and image points, respectively.

One can lower the time complexity by a number of ideas. One simple technique is to hypothesize matches only between pairs of image and model points. Given two image points and the edges at these points, a third virtual point can be constructed by extending the edges and finding the intersection. This lowers the complexity to $O(m^3 n^2 \log n)$. Techniques based on using pose clustering in combination with randomization (Olson, 1994) can be used to bring the complexity down to $O(mn^3)$. Results from the application of this algorithm to the stapler image are shown in Figure 24.29.

Using projective invariants

Alignment using outline geometry and recognition is considered successful if outline geometry in an image can be explained as a perspective projection of the geometric model of the object. A disadvantage is that this involves trying each model in the model library, resulting in a recognition complexity proportional to the number of models in the library.

GEOMETRIC
INVARIANTS
          A solution is provided by using **geometric invariants** as the shape representation. These shape descriptors are *viewpoint invariant*, that is, they have the same value measured on the object or measured from a perspective image of the object, and are unaffected by object pose. The simplest example of a projective invariant is the "cross-ratio" of four points on a line, illustrated

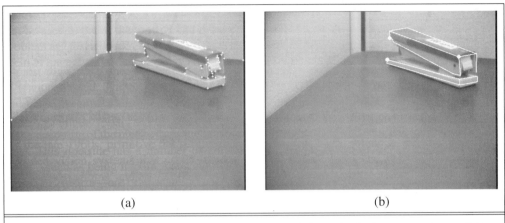

(a)   (b)

Figure 24.29   (a) Corners found in the stapler image. (b) Hypothesized reconstruction overlaid on the original image. (Courtesy of Clark Olson.)

in Figure 24.30. Under perspective projection, the ratios of distances are not preserved—think of the spacing of sleepers on an image of a receding railway track. The spacing is constant in the world, but decreases with distance from the camera in an image. However, the ratio of ratio of distances on a line is preserved, that is, it is the same measured on the object or in the image.

INDEX FUNCTIONS   Invariants are significant in vision because they can be used as **index functions**, so that a value measured in an image directly indexes a model in the library. To take a simple example, suppose there are three models $\{A, B, C\}$ in the library, each with a corresponding and distinct invariant value $\{I(A), I(B), I(C)\}$. Recognition proceeds as follows: After edge detection and grouping, invariants are measured from image curves. If a value $I = I(B)$ is measured, then there is evidence that object B is present. It is not necessary to consider objects A and C any further. It may be that for a large model base, all invariants are not distinct (i.e., several models may share invariant values). Consequently, when an invariant measured in the image corresponds to a value in the library, a recognition hypothesis is generated. Recognition hypotheses corresponding to the same object are merged if compatible. The hypotheses are *verified* by back projecting the outline as in the alignment method. An example of object recognition using invariants is given in Figure 24.31.

Another advantage of invariant shape representation is that models can be acquired directly from images. It is not necessary to make measurements on the actual object, because the shape descriptors have the same value when measured in any image. This simplifies and facilitates automation of model acquisition. It is particularly useful in applications such as recognition from satellite images.

Although the two approaches to object recognition that we have described are useful in practice, it should be noted that we are far away from human competence. The generation of sufficiently rich and descriptive representations from images, segmentation and grouping to identify those features that belong together, and the matching of these to object models are difficult research problems under active investigation.

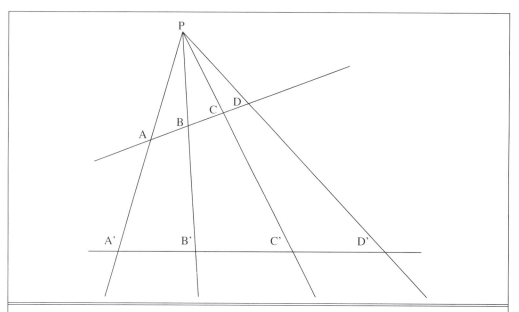

Figure 24.30   Invariance of the cross-ratio: AC.BD/AB.CD = A′C′.B′D′/A′B′.C′D′. Exercise 24.7 asks you to verify this fact.

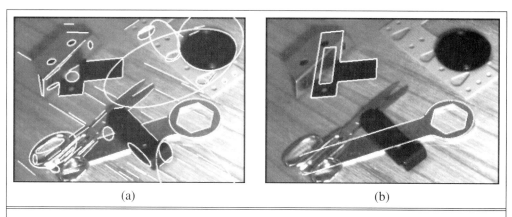

(a)   (b)

Figure 24.31   (a) A scene containing a number of objects, two of which also appear in the model library. These are recognized using invariants based on lines and conics. The image shows 100 fitted lines and 27 fitted conics superimposed in white. Invariants are formed from combinations of lines and conics, and the values index into a model library. In this case, there are 35 models in the library. Note that many lines are caused by texture, and that some of the conics correspond to edge data over only a small section. (b) The two objects from the library are recognized correctly. The lock striker plate is matched with a single invariant and 50.9% edge match, and the spanner with three invariants and 70.7% edge match. Courtesy of Andrew Zisserman.

24.7 SPEECH RECOGNITION

SPEECH
RECOGNITION

In this section, we turn from vision to another type of percept—speech. Speech is the dominant modality for communication between humans, and promises to be important for communication between humans and machines, if it can just be made a little more reliable. **Speech recognition** is the task of mapping from a digitally encoded acoustic signal to a string of words. **Speech understanding** is the task of mapping from the acoustic signal all the way to an interpretation of the meaning of the utterance. A speech understanding system must answer three questions:

1. What speech sounds did the speaker utter?

2. What words did the speaker intend to express with those speech sounds?

3. What meaning did the speaker intend to express with those words?

PHONES

To answer question 1, we have to first decide what a speech sound is. It turns out that all human languages use a limited repertoire of about 40 or 50 sounds, called **phones**. Roughly speaking, a phone is the sound that corresponds to a single vowel or consonant, but there are some complications: combinations of letters such as "th" and "ng" produce single phones, and some letters produce different phones in different contexts (for example, the "a" in *rat* and *rate*. Figure 24.32 lists all the phones in English with an example of each. Once we know what the possible sounds are, we need to characterize them in terms of features that we can pick out of the acoustic signal, such as the frequency or amplitude of the sound waves.

HOMOPHONES

SEGMENTATION

Question 2 is conceptually much simpler. You can think of it as looking up words in a dictionary that is arranged by pronunciation. We get a sequence of three phones, *[k]*, *[æ]*, and *[t]*, and find in the dictionary that this is the pronunciation for the word "cat." Two things make this difficult. The first is the existence of **homophones**, different words that sound the same, like "two" and "too."[1] The second is **segmentation**, the problem of deciding where one word ends and the next begins. Anyone who has tried to learn a foreign language will appreciate this problem; at first all the words seem to run together. Gradually, one learns to pick out words from the jumble of sounds. In this case, first impressions are correct; a spectrographic analysis shows that in fluent speech, the words really *do* run together with no silence between them. We learn to identify word boundaries despite the lack of silence.

Question 3 we already know how to answer—use the parsing and analysis algorithms described in Chapter 22. Some speech understanding systems extract the most likely string of words and pass them directly to an analyzer. Other systems have a more complex control structure that considers multiple possible word interpretations so that understanding can be achieved even if some individual words are not recognized correctly.

We will shortly define a model that answers questions 1 and 2, but first we will explain a little about how the speech signal is represented.

---

[1] It is also true that one word can be pronounced several ways—you say tow-may-tow and I say tow-mah-tow. This makes it more tedious to construct the pronunciation dictionary, but it does not make it any harder to look up a word.

Vowels		Consonants B-N		Consonants P-Z	
Phone	Example	Phone	Example	Phone	Example
[iy]	b**eat**	[b]	**b**et	[p]	**p**et
[ih]	b**i**t	[ch]	**Ch**et	[r]	**r**at
[ey]	b**e**t	[d]	**d**ebt	[s]	**s**et
[æ]	b**a**t	[f]	**f**at	[sh]	**sh**oe
[ah]	b**u**t	[g]	**g**et	[t]	**t**en
[ao]	b**ough**t	[hh]	**h**at	[th]	**th**ick
[ow]	b**oa**t	[hv]	**h**igh	[dh]	**th**at
[uh]	b**oo**k	[jh]	**j**et	[dx]	but**t**er
[ux]	b**eau**ty	[k]	**k**ick	[v]	**v**et
[er]	B**er**t	[l]	**l**et	[w]	**w**et
[ay]	b**uy**	[el]	bott**le**	[wh]	**wh**ich
[oy]	b**oy**	[m]	**m**et	[y]	**y**et
[axr]	din**er**	[em]	bott**om**	[z]	**z**oo
[aw]	d**ow**n	[n]	**n**et	[zh]	mea**s**ure
[ax]	**a**bout	[en]	butt**on**		
[ix]	ros**e**s	[ng]	si**ng**		
[aa]	c**o**t	[eng]	Wash**ing**ton	[-]	*(silence)*

Figure 24.32   The DARPA phonetic alphabet, listing all the phones used in English. There are several alternative notations, including an International Phonetic Alphabet (IPA), which contains the phones in all known languages.

Signal processing

Sound is an analog energy source. When a sound wave strikes a microphone, it is converted to an electrical current, which can be passed to an analog-to-digital converter to yield a stream of bits representing the sound. We have two choices in deciding how many bits to keep. First, the **sampling rate** is the frequency with which we look at the signal. For speech, a sampling rate between 8 and 16 KHz (i.e., 8 to 16,000 times per second) is typical. Telephones deliver only about 3 KHz. Second, the **quantization factor** determines the precision to which the energy at each sampling point is recorded. Speech recognizers typically keep 8 to 12 bits. That means that a low-end system, sampling at 8 KHz with 8-bit quantization, would require nearly half a megabyte per minute of speech. This is a lot of information to manipulate, and worse, it leaves us very far from our goal of discovering the phones that make up the signal.

The first step in coming up with a better representation for the signal is to group the samples together into larger blocks called **frames**. This makes it possible to analyze the whole frame for the appearance of speech phenomena such as a rise or drop in frequency, or a sudden onset or cessation of energy. A frame length of about 10 msecs (i.e., 80 samples at 8 KHz) seems to be long enough so that most such phenomena can be detected and that few short-duration phenomena will be missed. Within each frame, we represent what is happening with a vector of **features**. For example, we might want to characterize the amount of energy at each of several frequency ranges.

SAMPLING RATE

QUANTIZATION FACTOR

FRAMES

FEATURES

Other important features include overall energy in a frame, and the difference from the previous frame. Picking out features from a speech signal is like listening to an orchestra and saying "here the French horns are playing loud and the violins are playing softly." Breaking the sound down into components like this is much more useful than leaving it as a single undifferentiated sound source. Figure 24.33 shows frames with a vector of three features. Note that the frames overlap; this prevents us from losing information if an important acoustic event just happens to fall on a frame boundary.

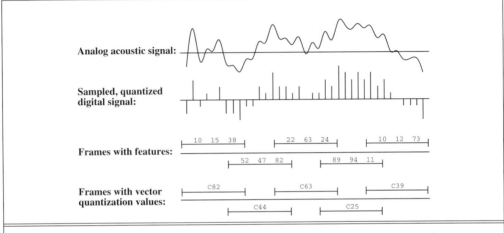

Figure 24.33   Translating the acoustic signal into a sequence of vector quantization values. (Don't try to figure out the numbers; they were assigned arbitrarily.)

VECTOR
QUANTIZATION

The final step in many speech signal processing systems is **vector quantization**. If there are n features in a frame, we can think of this as an n-dimensional space containing many points. Vector quantization divides this n-dimensional space into, say, 256 regions labelled C1 through C256. Each frame can then be represented with a single label rather than a vector of n numbers. So we end up with just one byte per frame, which is about a 100-fold improvement over the original half megabyte per minute. Of course, some information is lost in going from a feature vector to a label that summarizes a whole neighborhood around the vector, but there are automated methods for choosing an optimal quantization of the feature vector space so that little or no inaccuracy is introduced (Jelinek, 1990).

There are two points to this whole exercise. First, we end up with a representation of the speech signal that is compact. But more importantly, we have a representation that is likely to encode features of the signal that will be useful for word recognition. A given speech sound can be pronounced so many ways: loud or soft, fast or slow, high-pitched or low, against a background of silence or noise, and by any of millions of different speakers each with different accents and vocal tracts. Signal processing hopes to capture enough of the important features so that the commonalities that define the sound can be picked out from this backdrop of variation. (The dual problem, **speaker identification**, requires one to focus on the variation instead of the commonalities in order to decide who is speaking.

Defining the overall speech recognition model

Speech recognition is the diagnostic task of recovering the words that produce a given acoustic signal. It is a classic example of reasoning with uncertainty. We are uncertain about how well the microphones (and digitization hardware) have captured the actual sounds, we are uncertain about which phones would give rise to the signal, and we are uncertain about which words would give rise to the phones. As is often the case, the diagnostic task can best be approached with a causal model—the words cause the signal. We can break this into components with Bayes' rule:

$$P(words|signal) = \frac{P(words)P(signal|words)}{P(signal)}$$

Given a *signal*, our task is to find the sequence of *words* that maximizes $P(words|signal)$. Of the three components on the right-hand side, $P(signal)$ is a normalizing constant that we can ignore. $P(words)$ is known as the **language model**. It is what tells us, when we are not sure if we heard "bad boy" or "pad boy" that the former is more likely. Finally, $P(signal|words)$ is the **acoustic model**. It is what tells us that "cat" is very likely to be pronounced *[kæt]*.

LANGUAGE MODEL

ACOUSTIC MODEL

The language model: P(words)

In *Take the Money and Run*, a bank teller interprets Woody Allen's sloppily written hold-up note as saying "I have a gub." A better language model would have enabled the teller to determine that the string "I have a gun" has a much higher prior probability of being on a hold-up note. That makes "gun" a better interpretation even if $P(signal|gub)$ is a little higher than $P(signal|gun)$. The language model should also tell us that "I have a gun" is a much more probable utterance than "gun a have I."

At first glance, the language model task seems daunting. We have to assign a probability to each of the (possibly infinite) number of strings. Context-free grammars are no help for this task, but probabilistic context-free grammars (PCFGs) are promising. Unfortunately, as we saw in Chapter 22, PCFGs aren't very good at representing contextual effects. In this section, we approach the problem using the standard strategy of defining the probability of a complex event as a product of probabilities of simpler events. Using the notation $w_1 \cdots w_n$ to denote a string of n words and w_i to denote the ith word of the string, we can write an expression for the probability of a string as follows:[2]

$$\begin{aligned} P(w_1 \cdots w_n) &= P(w_1)\,P(w_2|w_1)\,P(w_3|w_1w_2)\,\cdots\,P(w_n|w_1 \cdots w_{n-1}) \\ &= \textstyle\prod_{i=1}^{n} P(w_i|w_1 \cdots w_{i-1}) \end{aligned}$$

Most of these terms are quite complex and difficult to estimate or compute, and they have no obvious relation to CFGs or PCFGs. Fortunately, we can approximate this formula with something simpler and still capture a large part of the language model. One simple, popular, and effective approach is the **bigram** model. This model approximates $P(w_i|w_1 \cdots w_{i-1})$ with $P(w_i|w_{i-1})$. In other words, it says that the probability of any given word is determined solely by the previous word in the string. The probability of a complete string is given by

BIGRAM

$$P(w_1 \cdots w_n) = P(w_1)\,P(w_2|w_1)\,P(w_3|w_2)\,\cdots\,P(w_n|w_{n-1}) = \textstyle\prod_{i=1}^{n} P(w_i|w_{i-1})$$

---

[2]   Actually, it would be better if all the probabilities were conditioned on the situation. Few speech recognizers do this, however, because it is difficult to formalize what counts as a situation.

Word	Unigram count	Previous words									
		OF	IN	IS	ON	TO	FROM	THAT	WITH	LINE	VISION
THE	367	179	143	44	44	65	35	30	17	0	0
ON	69	0	0	1	0	0	0	0	0	0	0
OF	281	0	0	2	0	1	0	3	0	4	0
TO	212	0	0	19	0	0	0	0	0	0	1
IS	175	0	0	0	0	0	0	13	0	1	3
A	153	36	36	33	23	21	14	3	15	0	0
THAT	124	0	3	18	0	1	0	0	0	0	0
WE	105	0	0	0	1	0	0	12	0	0	0
LINE	17	1	0	0	0	1	0	0	0	0	0
VISION	13	3	0	0	1	0	1	0	0	0	0

Figure 24.34   A partial table of unigram and bigram counts for the words in this chapter. The word "the" appears 367 times in all (out of 17613 total words), the bigram "of the" appeared 179 times (or about 1%), and the bigram "in the" appeared 143 times. It turns out these are the only two bigrams that occur more than 100 times.

A big advantage of the bigram model is that it is easy to train the model by counting the number of times each word pair occurs in a representative corpus of strings and using the counts to estimate the probabilities. For example, if "a" appears 10,000 times in the training corpus and it is followed by "gun" 37 times, then $\hat{P}(gun_i|a_{i-1}) = 37/10,000$, where by $\hat{P}$ we mean the estimated probability. After such training one would expect "I have" and "a gun" to have relatively high estimated probabilities, while "I has" and "an gun" would have low probabilities. One problem is that the training corpus would probably not contain "gub" at all and more importantly, it would be missing many valid English words as well, so these words would be assigned an estimated probability of zero. Therefore, it is customary to set aside a small portion of the probability distribution for words that do not appear in the training corpus. Figure 24.34 shows some bigram counts derived from the words in this chapter.

TRIGRAM   It is possible to go to a **trigram** model that provides values for $P(w_i|w_{i-1}w_{i-2})$. This is a more powerful language model, capable of determining that "ate a banana" is more likely than "ate a bandana." The problem is that there are so many more parameters in trigram models that it is hard to get enough training data to come up with accurate probability estimates. A good compromise is to use a model that consists of a weighted sum of the trigram, bigram, and unigram (i.e., word frequency) models. The model is defined by the following formula (with $c_1 + c_2 + c_3 = 1$):

$$P(w_1 \cdots w_n) = c_1 P(w_i) + c_2 P(w_i|w_{i-1}) + c_3 P(w_i|w_{i-1}w_{i-2})$$

Bigram or trigram models are not as sophisticated as PCFGs, but they account for local context-sensitive effects better, and manage to capture some local syntax. For example, the fact that the word pairs "I has" and "man have" get low scores is reflective of subject-verb agreement. The problem is that these relationships can only be detected locally: "the man have" gets a low score, but "the man over there have" is not penalized.

The acoustic model: P(signal|words)

The acoustic model is responsible for saying what sounds will be produced when a given string of words is uttered. We divide the model into two parts. First, we show how each word is described as a sequence of phones, and then we show how each phone relates to the vector quantization values extracted from the acoustic signal.

Some words have very simple pronunciation models. The word "cat," for example, is always pronounced with the three phones [k æ t]. There are, however, two sources of phonetic variation. First, different dialects have different pronunciations. The top of Figure 24.35 gives an example of this: for "tomato," you say [tow mey tow] and I say [tow maa tow]. The alternative pronunciations are specified as a **Markov model**. In general, a Markov model is a way of describing a process that goes through a series of states. The model describes all the possible paths through the state space and assigns a probability to each one. The probability of transitioning from the current state to another one depends only on the current state, not on any prior part of the path. (This is the Markov property mentioned in Chapter 17.)

MARKOV MODEL

The top of Figure 24.35 is a Markov model with seven states (circles), each corresponding to the production of a phone. The arrows denote allowable transitions between states, and each transition has a probability associated with it.[3] There are only two possible paths through the model, one corresponding to the phone sequence [t ow m ey t ow] and the other to [t ow m aa t ow]. The probability of a path is the product of the probabilities on the arcs that make up the path. In this case, most of the arc probabilities are 1 and we have

$$P([towmeytow]|\text{``tomato''}) = P([towmaatow]|\text{``tomato''}) = 0.5$$

The second source of phonetic variation is **coarticulation**. Remember that speech sounds are produced by moving the tongue and jaw and forcing air through the vocal tract. When the speaker is talking slowly and deliberately, there is time to place the tongue in just the right spot before producing a phone. But when the speaker is talking quickly (or sometimes even at a normal pace), the movements slur together. For example, the [t] phone is produced with the tongue at the top of the mouth, whereas the [ow] has the tongue near the bottom. When spoken quickly, the tongue often goes to an intermediate position, and we get [tah] rather than [tow]. The bottom half of Figure 24.35 gives a more complicated pronunciation model for "tomato" that takes this coarticulation effect into account. In this model there are four distinct paths and we have

COARTICULATION

$$P([towmeytow]|\text{``tomato''}) = P([towmaatow]|\text{``tomato''}) = 0.1$$
$$P([tahmeytow]|\text{``tomato''}) = P([tahmaatow]|\text{``tomato''}) = 0.4$$

Similar models would be constructed for every word we want to be able to recognize. Now if the speech signal were a list of phones, then we would be done with the acoustic model. We could take a given input signal (e.g., [towmeytow]) and compute $P(signal|words)$ for various word strings (e.g., "tomato," "toe may tow," and so on). We could then combine these with $P(words)$ values taken from the language model to arrive at the *words* that maximize $P(words|signal)$.

Unfortunately, signal processing does not give us a string of phones. So all we can do so far is maximize $P(words|phones)$. Figure 24.36 shows how we can compute $P(signal|phone)$ using a model called a **hidden Markov model** or **HMM**. The model is for a particular phone,

HIDDEN MARKOV
MODEL

HMM

---

[3] Arcs with probability 1 are unlabelled in Figure 24.35. The 0.5 numbers are estimates based on the two authors' preferred pronunciations.

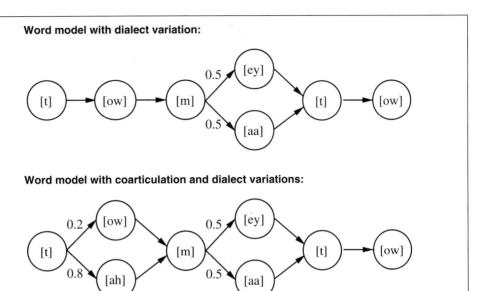

Figure 24.35   Two pronunciation models of the word "tomato." The top one accounts for dialect differences. The bottom one does that and also accounts for a coarticulation effect.

[m], but all phones will have models with similar topology. A hidden Markov model is just like a regular Markov model in that it describes a process that goes through a sequence of states. The difference is that in a regular Markov model, the output is a sequence of state names, and because each state has a unique name, the output uniquely determines the path through the model. In a hidden Markov model, each state has a probability distribution of possible outputs, and the same output can appear in more than one state.[4] HMMs are called hidden models because the true state of the model is hidden from the observer. In general, when you see that an HMM outputs some symbol, you can't be sure what state the symbol came from.

Suppose our speech signal is processed to yield the sequence of vector quantization values [C1,C4,C6]. From the HMM in Figure 24.36, we can compute the probability that this sequence was generated by the phone [m] as follows. First, we note that there is only one path through the model that could possibly generate this sequence: the path from Onset to Mid to End, where the output labels from the three states are C1, C4, and C6, respectively. By looking at the probabilities on the transition arcs, we see that the probability of this path is $0.7 \times 0.1 \times 0.6$ (these are the values on the three horizontal arrows in the middle of the Figure 24.36). Next, we look at the output probabilities for these states to see that the probability of [C1,C4,C6] given this path is $0.5 \times 0.7 \times 0.5$ (these are the values for $P(C1|Onset)$, $P(C4|Mid)$ and $P(C6|End)$, respectively). So the probability of [C1,C4,C6] given the [m] model is

$$P([C1, C4, C6]|[m]) = (0.7 \times 0.1 \times 0.6) \times (0.5 \times 0.7 \times 0.5) = 0.00735$$

---

[4]   Note that this means that the "tomato" models in Figure 24.35 are actually hidden Markov models, because the same output (e.g., [t]) appears on more than one state.

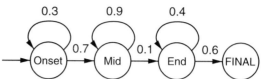

Output probabilities for the phone HMM:

Onset:	Mid:	End:
C1: 0.5	C3: 0.2	C4: 0.1
C2: 0.2	C4: 0.7	C6: 0.5
C3: 0.3	C5: 0.1	C7: 0.4

Figure 24.36   An HMM for the phone [m]. Each state has several possible outputs, each with its own probability.

We could repeat the calculation for all the other phone models to see which one is the most probable source of the speech signal.

Actually, most phones have a duration of 50-100 milliseconds, or 5-10 frames at 10 msec/frame. So the [C1,C4,C6] sequence is unusually quick. Suppose we have a more typical speaker who generates the sequence [C1,C1,C4,C4,C6,C6] while producing the phone. It turns out there are two paths through the model that generate this sequence. In one of them both C4s come from the Mid state (note the arcs that loop back), and in the other the second C4 comes from the End state. We calculate the probability that this sequence came from the [m] model in the same way: take the sum over all possible paths of the probability of the path times the probability that the path generates the sequence.

$$P([C1, C1, C4, C4, C6, C6]|[m]) =$$
$$(0.3 \times 0.7 \times 0.9 \times 0.1 \times 0.4 \times 0.6) \times (0.5 \times 0.5 \times 0.7 \times 0.7 \times 0.5 \times 0.5) +$$
$$(0.3 \times 0.7 \times 0.1 \times 0.4 \times 0.4 \times 0.6) \times (0.5 \times 0.5 \times 0.7 \times 0.1 \times 0.5 \times 0.5)$$
$$= 0.0001477$$

We see that the loops in the phone model allow the model to represent both fast and slow speech, a very important source of variation. The multiple vector quantization values on each state represent other sources of variation. Altogether, this makes for a fairly powerful model. The hard part is getting good probability values for all the parameters. Fortunately, there are ways of acquiring these numbers from data, as we shall see.

Putting the models together

We have described three models. The language bigram model gives us $P(word_i|word_{i-1})$. The word pronunciation HMM gives us $P(phones|word)$. The phone HMM gives us $P(signal|phone)$. If we want to compute $P(words|signal)$, we will need to combine these models in some way. One approach is to combine them all into one big HMM. The bigram model can be thought of as an HMM in which every state corresponds to a word and every word has a transition arc to every other word. Now replace each word-state with the appropriate word model, yielding a bigger model in which each state corresponds to a phone. Finally, replace each phone-state with the appropriate phone model, yielding an even bigger model in which each state corresponds to a distribution of vector quantization values.

Some speech recognition systems complicate the picture by dealing with coarticulation effects at either the word/word or phone/phone level. For example, we could use one phone model for [ow] when it follows a [t] and a different model for [ow] when it follows a [g]. There are many trade-offs to be made—a more complex model can handle subtle effects, but it will be harder to train. Regardless of the details, we end up with one big HMM that can be used to compute $P(words|signal)$.

The search algorithm

From a theoretical point of view, we have just what we asked for: a model that computes $P(words|signal)$. All we have to do is enumerate all the possible word strings, and we can assign a probability to each one. Practically, of course, this is infeasible, because there are too many candidate word strings. Fortunately, there is a better way.

VITERBI ALGORITHM   The **Viterbi algorithm** takes an HMM model and an output sequence, $[C_1, C_2, \ldots, C_n]$, and returns the most probable path through the HMM that outputs the sequence. It also returns the probability for the path. Think of it as an iterative algorithm that first finds *all* the paths that output the first symbol, C_1. Then, for each of those paths it finds the most probable path that outputs the rest of the sequence, given that we have chosen a particular path for C_1. So far this doesn't sound very promising. If the length of the sequence is n and there are M different states in the model, then this algorithm would seem to be at least $O(M^n)$.

The key point of the Viterbi algorithm is to use the Markov property to make it more efficient. The Markov property says that the most probable path for the rest of any sequence can depend only on the state in which it starts, not on anything else about the path that got there. That means we need not look at all possible paths that lead to a certain state; for each state, we only need to keep track of the *most probable* path that ends in that state. Thus, the Viterbi algorithm is an instance of **dynamic programming**.

Figure 24.37 shows the algorithm working on the HMM from Figure 24.36 and the output sequence [C1,C3,C4,C6]. Each column represents one iteration of the algorithm. In the leftmost column, we see that there is only one way to generate the sequence [C1], with the path [Onset]. The oval labelled "Onset 0.5" means that the path ends in the Onset state and has probability 0.5. The arc leading into the oval has the label "1.0; 0.5," which means that the probability of making this transition is 1.0, and the probability of outputting a C1, given that the transition is made, is 0.5. In the second column, we consider all the possible continuations of the paths in the first column that could lead to the output [C1,C3]. There are two such paths, one ending in the Onset state and one in the Mid state. In the third column, it gets more interesting. There are two paths that lead to the Mid state, one from Onset and the other from Mid. The bold arrow indicates that the path from Mid is more probable (it has probability 0.0441), so that is the only one we have to remember. The path [Onset,Onset,Mid] has a lower probability, 0.022, so it is discarded. We continue in this fashion until we reach the FINAL state, with probability 0.0013. By tracing backwards and following the bold arrows whenever there is a choice, we see that the most probable path is [Onset,Onset,Mid,End,Final]. The Viterbi algorithm is $O(bMn)$, where b is the branching factor (the number of arcs out of any state). If the model is fully connected, then $b = M$, and the algorithm is $O(M^2n)$, which is still quite an improvement over $O(M^n)$.

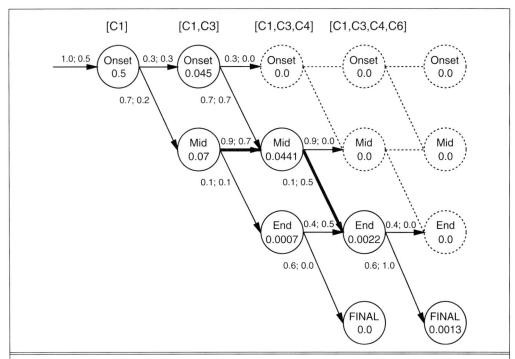

Figure 24.37   A diagram of the Viterbi algorithm computing the most probable path (and its probability) for the output [C1,C3,C4,C6] on the HMM from Figure 24.36.

Training the model

The HMM approach is used in speech recognition for two reasons. First, it is a reasonably good performance element—we saw that the Viterbi algorithm is linear in the length of the input. More importantly, HMMs can be learned directly from a training set of [signal,words] pairs. This is important because it is far too difficult to determine all the parameters by hand. There are other approaches that make better performance elements than HMMs, but they require the training data to be labelled on a phone-by-phone basis rather than a sentence-by-sentence basis, and that too is a difficult task. The standard algorithm for training an HMM is called the Baum–Welch or forward-backward algorithm. Rabiner (1990) gives a tutorial on this and other HMM algorithms.

The best current speech recognition systems recognize from about 80% to 98% of the words correctly, depending on the quality of the signal, the allowable language, the length of each input, and the variation in speakers. Speech recognition is easy when there is a good microphone, a small vocabulary, a strong language model that predicts what words can come next, a limit of one-word utterances (or a requirement for pauses between words), and when the system can be trained specifically for a single speaker. The systems are not as accurate over phone lines, when there is noise in the room, when there is a large vocabulary with no restrictions, when the words of an utterance run together, and when the speaker is new to the system.

24.8   SUMMARY

Although perception appears to be an effortless activity for humans, it requires a significant amount of sophisticated computation. This chapter studies vision as the prime example of perceptual information processing. The goal of vision is to extract information needed for tasks such as manipulation, navigation, and object recognition. We also looked at speech recognition.

- The process of **image formation** is well-understood in its geometric and physical aspects. Given a description of a 3-D scene, we can easily produce a picture of it from some arbitrary camera position (the graphics problem). Inverting the process by going from an image to a description of the scene is difficult.

- To extract the visual information necessary for the tasks of manipulation, navigation, and recognition, intermediate representations have to be constructed. **Image-processing** algorithms extract primitive elements from the image, such as edges and regions.

- In the image, there exist multiple cues that enable one to obtain 3-D information about the scene. These include motion, stereopsis, texture, shading, and contour analysis. Each of these cues relies on background assumptions about physical scenes in order to provide unambiguous interpretations.

- Object recognition in its full generality is a very hard problem. We discussed two relatively simple techniques—alignment and indexing using geometric invariants—that provide robust recognition in restricted contexts.

- Speech recognition is a problem in diagnosis. It can be solved with a language model and an acoustic model. Current emphasis is on systems that do well both as a performance element and a learning element.

BIBLIOGRAPHICAL AND HISTORICAL NOTES

Systematic attempts to understand human vision can be traced back to ancient times. Euclid (ca. 300 B.C.) wrote about natural perspective, the mapping that associates with each point P in the three-dimensional world the direction of the ray OP joining the center of projection O to the point *P*. He was well aware of the notion of motion parallax. The mathematical understanding of perspective projection, this time in the context of projection onto planar surfaces, had its next significant advance in the fifteenth century in Renaissance Italy. Brunelleschi (1413) is usually credited with creating the first paintings based on geometrically correct projection of the three-dimensional scene. In 1435, Alberti codified the rules and inspired generations of artists whose artistic achievements amaze us to this day (Kemp, 1990). Particularly notable in their development of the science of perspective, as it was called in those days, were Leonardo Da Vinci and Albrecht Dürer. Leonardo's late fifteenth century descriptions of the interplay of light and shade (chiaroscuro), umbra and penumbra regions of shadows, and aerial perspective are still worth reading in translation (Kemp, 1989).

Although perspective was known to the Greeks, they were curiously confused by the role of the eyes in vision. Aristotle thought of the eyes as devices emitting rays, rather in the manner of modern laser range finders. This mistaken view was laid to rest by the work of Arab scientists, such as Alhazen in the tenth century. The development of various kinds of cameras followed. These consisted of rooms (*camera* is Latin for chamber) where light would be let in through a small hole in one wall to cast an image of the scene outside on the opposite wall. Of course, in all these cameras, the image was inverted, which caused no end of confusion. If the eye was to be thought of as such an imaging device, how do we see right side up? This exercised the greatest brains of the era (including Leonardo). It took the work of Kepler and Descartes to settle the question. Descartes placed an eye from which the opaque cuticle had been removed in a hole in a window shutter. This resulted in an inverted image being formed on a piece of paper laid out on the retina. While the retinal image is indeed inverted, this need not cause a problem if the brain interprets the image the right way. In modern jargon, one just has to access the data structure appropriately.

The next major advances in the understanding of vision took place in the nineteenth century. The work of Helmholtz and Wundt, described in Chapter 1, established psychophysical experimentation as a rigorous scientific discipline. Through the work of Young, Maxwell, and Helmholtz, a trichromatic theory of color vision was established. That humans can see depth if the images presented to the left and right eyes are slightly different was demonstrated by Wheatstone's (1838) invention of the stereoscope. The device immediately became very popular in parlors and salons throughout Europe. The essential concept of binocular stereopsis, that two images of a scene taken from slightly different viewpoints carry information sufficient to obtain a 3-D reconstruction of the scene, was exploited in the field of photogrammetry. Key mathematical results were obtained—Kruppa (1913) proved that given two views of five distinct points, one could reconstruct the rotation and translation between the two camera positions as well as the depth of the scene (up to a scale factor). Although the geometry of stereopsis had been understood for a long time, the correspondence problem in photogrammetry used to be solved by humans trying to match up corresponding points. The amazing ability of humans in solving the correspondence problem was illustrated by Julesz's invention of the random dot stereogram (Julesz, 1971). Both in computer vision and in photogrammetry, much effort was devoted to solving this problem in the 1970s and 1980s.

The second half of the nineteenth century was a major foundational period for the psychophysical study of human vision. In the first half of the twentieth century the most significant research results in vision were obtained by the Gestalt school of psychology led by Max

Wertheimer. With the slogan "The whole is greater than the sum of the parts," they laid primary emphasis on grouping processes, both of contours and regions. Constructing computational models of these processes remains a difficult problem to this day.

The period after World War 2 was marked by renewed activity. Most significant was the work of J. J. Gibson (1950; 1979), who pointed out the importance of optical flow as well as texture gradients in the estimation of environmental variables such as surface slant and tilt. He reemphasized the importance of the stimulus and how rich it was. Gibson, Olum, and Rosenblatt (1955) pointed out that the optical flow field contained enough information to determine the egomotion of the observer relative to the environment. In the computational vision community, work in this area and the (mathematically equivalent) area of structure from motion developed mainly in the 1980s, following the seminal works of Koenderink and van Doorn (1975), Ullman (1979), and Longuet-Higgins (1981). Faugeras (1993) presents a comprehensive account of our understanding in this area. In the 1990s, with the increase in computer speed and storage, the importance of motion sequence analysis from digital video is growing rapidly.

In computational vision, major early works in shape from texture are due to Bajscy and Liebermann (1976) and Stevens (1981). Whereas this work was for planar surfaces, a comprehensive analysis for curved surfaces is due to Garding (1992) and Malik and Rosenholtz (1994).

In the computational vision community, shape from shading was first studied by Berthold Horn (1970). Horn and Brooks (1989) present an extensive survey of the main papers in the area. This framework made a number of simplifying assumptions, the most critical of which was ignoring the effect of mutual illumination. The importance of mutual illumination has been well-appreciated in the computer graphics community, where ray tracing and radiosity have been developed precisely to take mutual illumination into account. A theoretical and empirical critique may be found in Forsyth and Zisserman (1991).

In the area of shape from contour, after the key initial contributions of Huffman (1971) and Clowes (1971), Mackworth (1973) and Sugihara (1984) completed the analysis for polyhedral objects. Malik (1987) developed a labeling scheme for piecewise smooth curved objects. Understanding the visual events in the projection of smooth curved objects requires an interplay of differential geometry and singularity theory. The best study is Koenderink's (1990) *Solid Shape*.

In the area of three-dimensional object recognition, the seminal work was Roberts's (1963) thesis at MIT. It is often considered to be the first PhD thesis in computer vision and introduced several key ideas including edge detection and model-based matching. The idea of alignment, first introduced by Roberts, resurfaced in the 1980s in the work of Lowe (1987) and Huttenlocher and Ullman (1990). Generalized cylinders were introduced by Binford in 1971, and were used extensively by Brooks in the ACRONYM system (Brooks, 1981). Geometrical invariants were studied extensively in the late nineteenth century by English and German mathematicians. Their use in object recognition is surveyed by Mundy and Zisserman (1992), Excellent results have been achieved even in cluttered scenes (Rothwell *et al.*, 1993).

A word about the research methodology used in computer vision. The early development of the subject, like that of rest of AI, was mostly through Ph.D. theses that consisted largely of descriptions of implemented systems. The work lacked significant contact with the literature on human vision and photogrammetry, in which many of the same problems had been studied. David Marr played a major role in connecting computer vision to the traditional areas of biological vision—psychophysics and neurobiology. His main work, *Vision* (Marr, 1982), was published posthumously. That book conveys the excitement of working in vision better than any written since, despite the fact that many of the specific hypotheses and models proposed by Marr have not stood the test of time.

Under Marr's influence, reconstruction of the three-dimensional scene from various cues became the dominant ideology of the day. This of course proved to be a difficult problem, and it was inevitable that people would question whether it was really necessary. The old ideas of Gibson—active vision and affordances—came back. The most solid proof that reconstruction was not necessary for many (or most) tasks came from the work of Dickmanns in Germany, who demonstrated robust driving using a control system perspective (Dickmanns and Zapp, 1987). As a general philosophy, active vision was advocated by Ruzena Bajcsy (1988) and John Aloimonos (1988). A number of papers are collected in a special issue of *CVGIP* (Aloimonos, 1992). In the 1990s, the dominant perspective is that of vision as a set of processes aimed at extracting information for manipulation, navigation, and recognition.

Eye, Brain and Vision by David Hubel (1988) and *Perception* by Irvin Rock (1984) provide excellent introductions to the field of biological vision. *A Guided Tour of Computer Vision* (Nalwa, 1993) is a good general introduction to computer vision; *Robot Vision* (Horn, 1986) and *Three-Dimensional Computer Vision* (Faugeras, 1993) cover more advanced topics. Two of the main journals for computer vision are the IEEE *Transactions on Pattern Analysis and Machine Intelligence* and the *International Journal of Computer Vision*. Computer vision conferences include ICCV (International Conference on Computer Vision), CVPR (Computer Vision and Pattern Recognition), and ECCV (European Conference on Computer Vision).

The hidden Markov model was first used to model language by Markov himself in a letter-sequence analysis of the text of *Eugene Onegin* (Markov, 1913). Early development of algorithms for inferring Markov models from data was carried by Baum and Petrie (1966). These were applied to speech by Baker (1975) and Jelinek (1976). In 1971, the Defense Advanced Research Projects Agency (DARPA) of the United States Department of Defense, in cooperation with a number of research centers, set out a five-year plan for speech recognition research. The two most significant systems to emerge from this massive effort were HEARSAY-II (Erman *et al.*, 1980) and HARPY (Lowerre and Reddy, 1980). HARPY was the only system that clearly met the rigorous specifications of the five-year plan. It used a highly compiled network representation for all possible meaningful sequences of speech elements. HEARSAY-II, however, has had a greater
BLACKBOARD influence on other research because of its use of the **blackboard architecture**. HEARSAY-II was
ARCHITECTURE designed as an expert system with a number of more or less independent, modular **knowledge sources** which communicated via a common **blackboard** from which they could write and read. Because this representation was less compiled and more modular than HARPY's, HEARSAY-II was much easier to comprehend and modify, but was not fast enough to meet the DARPA criteria.

A good introduction to speech recognition is given by Rabiner and Juang (1993). Waibel and Lee (1990) collect important papers in the area, including some tutorial ones. Lee (1989) describes a complete modern speech recognition system. The presentation in this chapter drew on the survey by Kay, Gawron, and Norvig (1994), and on an unpublished manuscript by Dan Jurafsky. Speech recognition research is published in *Computer Speech and Language* and the IEEE *Transactions on Acoustics, Speech, and Signal Processing*, and at the DARPA Workshops on Speech and Natural Language Processing.

EXERCISES

24.1 In the shadow of a tree with a dense, leafy canopy, one sees a number of light spots. Surprisingly, they all appear to be circular. Why? After all, the gaps between the leaves through which the sun shines through are not likely to be circular.

24.2 Label the line drawing in Figure 24.38, assuming that the outside edges have been labelled as occluding and that all vertices are trihedral. Do this by a backtracking algorithm that examines the vertices in the order A, B, C, and D, picking at each stage a choice consistent with previously labelled junctions and edges. Now try the vertices in the order B, D, A, and C.

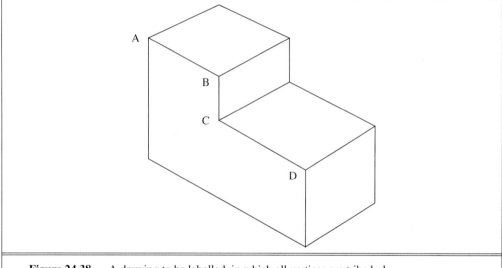

Figure 24.38   A drawing to be labelled, in which all vertices are trihedral.

24.3 Consider an infinitely long cylinder of radius r oriented with its axis along the y-axis. The cylinder has a Lambertian surface and is viewed by a camera along the positive z-axis. What will you expect to see in the image of the cylinder if the cylinder is illuminated by a point source at infinity located on the positive x-axis. Explain your answer by drawing the isobrightness contours in the projected image. Are the contours of equal brightness uniformly spaced?

24.4 Edges in an image can correspond to a variety of scene events. Consider the photograph on the cover of your book and assume that it is a picture of a real 3-D scene. Identify a set of ten different brightness edges in the image, and for each, decide whether it corresponds to a discontinuity in (a) depth, (b) surface normal, (c) reflectance, or (d) illumination.

24.5 Show that convolution with a given function f commutes with differentiation, that is,

$$(f * g)' = f * g'$$

24.6   A stereo system is being contemplated for terrain mapping. It will consist of two CCD cameras, each having 512×512 pixels on a 10 cm $\times$ 10 cm square sensor. The lenses to be used have focal length 16 cm, and focus is fixed at infinity. For corresponding points (u_1, v_1) in the left image and (u_2, v_2) in the right image, $v_1 = v_2$ as the x-axes in the two image planes are parallel to the epipolar lines. The optical axes of the two cameras are parallel. The baseline between the cameras is 1 meter.

   a. If the nearest range to be measured is 16 meters, what is the largest disparity that will occur (in pixels)?

   b. What is the range resolution, due to the pixel spacing, at 16 meters?

   c. What range corresponds to a disparity of one pixel?

24.7   In Figure 24.30, physically measure the cross ratio of the points $ABCD$ as well as of the points $A'B'C'D'$. Are they equal?

24.8   We wish to use the alignment algorithm in an industrial situation where flat parts are moving along a conveyor belt and being photographed by a camera vertically above the conveyor belt. The pose of the part is specified by three variables, one for the rotation and two for the 2-D position. This simplifies the problem and the function FIND-TRANSFORM needs only two pairs of corresponding image and model features to determine the pose. Determine the worst-case complexity of the alignment procedure in this context.

24.9   Read this chapter from the beginning until you find ten examples of homophones. Does the status of a word as a homophone depend on the accent of the speaker?

24.10   Calculate the most probable path through the HMM in Figure 24.36 for the output sequence [C1,C2,C3,C4,C4,C6,C7]. Also give its probability.

24.11   Some sports announcers have been known to celebrate a score with the drawn out pronunciation [g ow ow ow ow ow ow el]. Draw a word HMM for "goal" such that the most probable path has a sequence of four [ow]s, but any number greater than 1 is possible.

24.12   The Viterbi algorithm finds the most probable sequence of phones corresponding to the speech signal. Under the assumption that some words can be pronounced with more than one sequence of phones, explain why the Viterbi algorithm only computes an approximation to $P(words|signal)$.

25 ROBOTICS

In which agents are endowed with physical effectors with which to do mischief.

25.1 INTRODUCTION

ROBOT

The Robot Institute of America defines a **robot** as *a programmable, multifunction manipulator designed to move material, parts, tools, or specific devices through variable programmed motions for the performance of a variety of tasks.* This definition is not very demanding; a conveyer belt with a two-speed switch would arguably satisfy it.

We will define **robot** simply as *an active, artificial agent whose environment is the physical world.* The *active* part rules out rocks, the *artificial* part rules out animals, and the *physical* part rules out pure software agents or **softbots**, whose environment consists of computer file systems, databases and networks. We will be concerned primarily with **autonomous robots**, those that make decisions on their own, guided by the feedback they get from their physical sensors.

AUTONOMOUS ROBOTS

Most of the design of an autonomous robot is the same as the design of any autonomous agent. To some extent, we could take a generic planning agent (Chapter 11) or decision-making agent (Chapter 16), equip it with wheels, grippers, and a camera, point it out the door, and wish it good luck. Unfortunately, unless we pointed it at an exceptionally benign environment, it would not fare very well. The real world, in general, is very demanding. We can see this by considering the five properties of environments from page 46:

- The real world is **inaccessible**. Sensors are imperfect, and in any case can only perceive stimuli that are near the agent.
- The real world is **nondeterministic**, at least from the robot's point of view. Wheels slip, batteries run down, and parts break, so you never know if an action is going to work. That means a robot needs to deal with uncertainty (Part V).
- The real world is **nonepisodic**—the effects of an action change over time. So a robot has to handle sequential decision problems (Chapter 17) and learning (Part VI).

- The real world is **dynamic**. Therefore, a robot has to know when it is worth deliberating and when it is better to act immediately.
- The real world is **continuous**, in that states and actions are drawn from a continuum of physical configurations and motions. Because this makes it impossible to enumerate the set of possible actions, many of the search and planning algorithms described in earlier chapters will need to be modified.

We could go on about the unique properties of robotics, but instead we will refer you to Exercise 25.1. It does not require any additional reading, it will give you an instant and visceral appreciation of the problems of robotics (and their possible solutions), and it can be amusing.

This chapter has three main points. First, we look at the tasks that robots perform (Section 25.2) and the special effectors and sensors they use (Section 25.3). Second, we step away from robots *per se* and look at agent architectures for inaccessible, nondeterministic, nonepisodic, dynamic domains (Section 25.4). Third, we look at the specific problem of selecting actions in a continuous state space (Sections 25.5 and 25.6). The algorithms rely on a level of computational geometry that is more suited for a specialized advanced text, so we only give qualitative descriptions of the problems and solutions.

25.2   TASKS: WHAT ARE ROBOTS GOOD FOR?

While humans do a wide variety of things using more or less the same body, robot designs vary widely depending on the task for which they are intended. In this section, we survey some of the tasks, and in the next section, we look at the available parts (effectors and sensors) that make up a robot's body.

Manufacturing and materials handling

Manufacturing is seen as the traditional domain of the robot. The repetitive tasks on a production line are natural targets for automation, and so in 1954 George Devol patented the programmable robot arm, based on the same technology—punch cards—that was used in the Jacquard loom 150 years earlier. By 1985, there were about 180,000 robots in production lines around the world, with Japan, the United States, and France accounting for 150,000 of them. The automotive and microelectronics industries are major consumers of robots. However, most robots in use today are very limited in their abilities to sense and adapt. *Autonomous* robots are still struggling for acceptance. The reasons for this are historical, cultural, and technological. Manufacturing existed and burgeoned long before robots appeared, and many tricks were developed for solving manufacturing problems without intelligence. And it is still true that simple machines are the best solution for simple tasks.

Material handling is another traditional domain for robots. Material handling is the storage, transport, and delivery of material, which can range in size from silicon chips to diesel trucks. The robots used for material handling likewise vary from table-top manipulators to gantry cranes, and include many types of AGV (autonomous guided vehicles, typically golf-cart sized four-wheeled vehicles that are used to ferry containers around a warehouse). Handling odd-shaped parts is simplified by placing each part in a cradle or *pallet* that has a base of fixed shape. Bar codes on the pallets make it easy to identify and inventory the parts. But these techniques falter when applied to food packaging and handling, an area likely to see rapid growth in the future. The large variety of forms, weights, textures, and firmnesses in familiar foods make this task a challenge for future research.

Robots have recently been making their mark in the construction industry. Large prototype robots have been built that can move a one-ton object with an accuracy of 2.5 mm in a workspace of radius 10 m. Sheep shearing is another impressive application. Australia boasts a population of 140 million sheep, and several industrial and academic development groups have deployed automated sheep shearers. Because sheep come in different sizes, some kind of sensing (vision or mechanical probing) is needed to get an idea of the right overall shearing pattern. Tactile feedback is used to follow the contours of the animal without injuring it.

Gofer robots

MOBOTS

Mobile robots (**mobots**) are also becoming widely useful. Two primary applications are as couriers in buildings, especially hospitals, and as security guards. One company has sold over 3000 "mailmobiles." These robots respond to requests from a computer terminal and carry documents or supplies to a destination somewhere else in the building. The robot negotiates hallways and elevators, and avoids collision with other obstacles such as humans and furniture. The robot is appropriate for this task because it has high availability (it can work 24 hours a day), high reliability so that supplies are not lost or misplaced, and its progress can be monitored to allow preparation for its arrival, or detection of failure.

We have seen (page 586) that autonomous vehicles are already cruising our highways, and AUVs (autonomous underwater vehicles) are cruising the seas. It is far less expensive to send a robot to the bottom of the ocean than a manned submarine. Furthermore, a robot can stay down for months at a time, making scientific observations, reporting on enemy submarine traffic, or fixing problems in transoceanic cables.

Hazardous environments

Mobile robots are an important technology for reducing risk to human life in hazardous environments. During the cleanup of the Chernobyl disaster, several Lunokhod lunar explorer robots were converted to remote-controlled cleaning vehicles. In Japan and France, robots are used for routine maintenance of nuclear plants. Crisis management is now being taken seriously as a technological challenge in the United States. Robots can reduce risk to humans in unstable buildings after earthquakes, near fire or toxic fumes, and in radioactive environments. They can also be used for routine tasks in dangerous situations including toxic waste cleanup, deep sea recovery, exploration, mining, and manipulation of biologically hazardous materials. A human operator is often available to guide the robot, but it also needs autonomy to recognize and respond to hazards to its own and others' well-being.

Autonomy is also essential in remote environments (such as the surface of Mars) where communication delays are too long to allow human guidance. A robot for hazardous environments should be able to negotiate very rough ground without falling or tipping over.[1] It should have sensing modalities that work with no light present. It should above all avoid doing harm to humans who may be present but unconscious or disabled in its environment. Achieving this level of autonomy along with reliability is a challenge for robotics. But the return is very great, and this area of research is bound to continue its growth.

Telepresence and virtual reality

As computers spread from scientific/business applications to a consumer technology, telepresence and virtual reality continue to captivate the public imagination. The idea of staying in one's home and being able to sense exotic environments, either real (telepresence) or imaginary (virtual reality) is indeed compelling, and is a driving force behind some major moves in the computer and entertainment industries. Among the possible environments to which one might connect, there are many important applications. Today, New York City police use teleoperated robots to answer many of the city's estimated 9000 yearly bomb scares. Architects and customers can walk through or fly over a building before it is built.[2] Oceanographers can collect samples with a deep-sea submersible off the Pacific coast without leaving their offices. Medical specialists can examine patients hundreds of miles away. Surgeons can practice new techniques on virtual organ models. Or they can operate with miniature implements through a catheter inserted in a tiny incision.[3]

Much of the research in telepresence and virtual reality fall in the robotics category. Robotics researchers have for many years been studying, designing, and improving anthropomorphic hands. They have also built exoskeletons and gloves that provide both control and sensory feedback for those hands. Tactile sensing research opens the possibility of a true remote sense of touch. Realistic virtual environments require object models with a full set of physical attributes. Simulation requires algorithms that accurately factor in those attributes, including inertia, friction, elasticity, plasticity, color, texture, and sound. There remains much work to do to fully exploit the possibilities of remote and virtual presence.

Augmentation of human abilities

A precursor to telepresence involves putting a human inside a large, strong robot. In 1969, General Electric built the Quadrupedal Walking Machine, an 11-foot, 3000-pound robot with a control harness in which a human operator was strapped. Project leader Ralph Mosher remarked that the man-machine relationship "is so close that the experienced operator begins to feel as if those mechanical legs are his own. You imagine that you are actually crawling along the ground

---

[1] The robot DANTE-II caused embarrassment to its sponsors when it tipped over while exploring a volcano in July, 1994.

[2] The cover of this book shows a tiny model of Soda Hall, the computer science building at Berkeley. The model was used for walkthroughs prior to actual construction.

[3] The first medical telepresence system was deployed in 1971, under NASA sponsorship. A mobile van parked at the Papago Indian Reservation near Tucson, Arizona, allowed patients to be diagnosed remotely.

on all fours—but with incredible strength." A futuristic full-body exoskeleton of this kind was worn by Ripley (Sigourney Weaver) in the final confrontation of the movie "Aliens."

No less fascinating is the attempt to duplicate lost human effectors. When an arm or leg is amputated, the muscles in the stump still respond to signals from the brain, generating myoelectric currents. Prosthetic limbs can pick up these signals and amplify them to flex joints and move artificial fingers. Some prosthetics even have electrocutaneous feedback that gives a sense of touch. There has also been work in giving humans artificial sensors. A Japanese MITI project, for example, built a prototype robot guide dog for the blind. It uses ultrasound to make sure that its master stays in a safe area as they walk along together. Artificial retinas and cochleas, mostly based on analog VLSI, are the subject of intensive research at present.

25.3   Parts: What Are Robots Made Of?

LINKS

JOINTS

END EFFECTORS

Robots are distinguished from each other by the effectors and sensors with which they are equipped. For example, a mobile robot requires some kind of legs or wheels, and a teleoperated robot needs a camera. We will assume that a robot has some sort of rigid body, with rigid **links** that can move about. Links meet each other at **joints**, which allow motion. For example, on a human the upper arm and forearm are links, and the shoulder and elbow are joints. The palm is a link, and fingers and thumb have three links. Wrists and finger joints are joints. Robots need not be so anthropomorphic; a wheel is a perfectly good link. Attached to the final links of the robot are **end effectors**, which the robot uses to interact with the world. End effectors may be suction cups, squeeze grippers, screwdrivers, welding guns, or paint sprayers, to name a few. Some robots have special connectors on the last link that allow them to quickly remove one end effector and attach another. The well-equipped robot also has one or more sensors, perhaps including cameras, infrared sensors, radar, sonar, and accelerometers.

Effectors: Tools for action

EFFECTOR

ACTUATOR

DEGREE OF FREEDOM

An **effector** is any device that affects the environment, under the control of the robot. To have an impact on the physical world, an effector must be equipped with an **actuator** that converts software commands into physical motion. The actuators themselves are typically electric motors or hydraulic or pneumatic cylinders. For simplicity, we will assume that each actuator determines a single motion or **degree of freedom**. For example, an automatic phonograph turntable has three degrees of freedom. It can spin the turntable, it can raise and lower the stylus arm, and it can move the arm laterally to the first track. A side effect of the motion of the turntable is that one or more vinyl recordings rotate as well. This motion, assuming the stylus has been lowered into a recording groove, leads to a useful and musical product.

LOCOMOTION

MANIPULATION

Effectors are used in two main ways: to change the position of the robot within its environment (**locomotion**), and to move other objects in the environment (**manipulation**). A third use, to change the shape or other physical properties of objects, is more in the realm of mechanical engineering than robotics, so we will not cover it.

Locomotion

The vast majority of land animals use legs for locomotion. Legged locomotion turns out to be very difficult for robots, and is used only in special circumstances. The most obvious application is motion in rough terrain with large obstacles. The Ambler robot (Simmons *et al.*, 1992), for example, is a six-legged robot, about 30 feet tall, capable of negotiating obstacles more than 6 feet in diameter. The Ambler, unlike most animals, is a **statically stable** walker. That is, it can pause at any stage during its gait without tumbling over. Statically stable walking is very slow and energy-inefficient, and the quest for faster, more efficient legged machines has led to a series of **dynamically stable** hopping robots (Raibert, 1986), which would crash if forced to pause, but do well as long as they keep moving. These robots use rhythmic motion of four, two, or even a single leg to to control the locomotion of the body in three dimensions. They do not have enough legs in contact with the ground to be stable statically, and will fall if their hopping motion stops. They are dynamically stable because corrections to leg motion keep the body upright when it is bumped or when the ground is uneven. The control of legged machines is too complex a subject to discuss here, except to remark on its difficulty and to marvel at recent successes—for example, the one-legged robot shown in Figure 25.1 can "run" in any direction, hop over small obstacles, and even somersault.

Despite the anthropomorphic attractions of legged locomotion, wheel or tread locomotion is still the most practical for most environments. Wheels and treads are simpler to build, are more efficient than legs, and provide static support. They are also easier to control, although they are not without subtle problems of their own. Consider the car-like robot of Figure 25.2. We know from experience that without obstructions, we can drive a car to any position, and leave it pointing in any direction that we choose. Thus, the car has three degrees of freedom, two for its x–y position, and one for its direction. But there are only two actuators, namely, driving and steering. And for small motions, the car seems to have only two degrees of freedom, because we can move it in the direction it points, or rotate it slightly, but we cannot move it sideways.

It is important here to draw the distinction between what the actuators actually do, namely, turning or steering the wheels, and what these motions do to the environment. In this case, the side effect of the wheel motion is to move the car to any point in a three-dimensional space. Because the number of *controllable* degrees of freedom is only two, which is less than the total degrees of freedom (three), this is a **nonholonomic** robot. In general, a nonholonomic robot has fewer controllable degrees of freedom than total degrees of freedom. As a rule, the larger the gap between controllable and total degrees of freedom, the harder it is to control the robot. A car with a trailer has four total degrees of freedom but only two controllable ones, and takes considerable skill to drive in reverse. If the number of total and controllable degrees freedom of the system is the same, the robot is **holonomic**.

It is possible to build truly holonomic mobile robots, but at the cost of high mechanical complexity. It is necessary to design the wheels or treads so that motion in the driving direction is controlled, but sideways motion is free. Holonomic drives usually replace the tire or tread with a series of rollers lined up with the drive direction. Although these designs make life easier for the control architect, the common designs of nonholonomic mobile robots (Figures 25.2 and 25.3) are not that difficult to control, and their mechanical simplicity makes them the best choice in most situations. The main distinction to be made between different designs is whether the robot

STATICALLY STABLE

DYNAMICALLY STABLE

NONHOLONOMIC

HOLONOMIC

Figure 25.1   Raibert's dynamically stable hopping robot in motion. (© 1986. MIT Leg Laboratory. All rights reserved.)

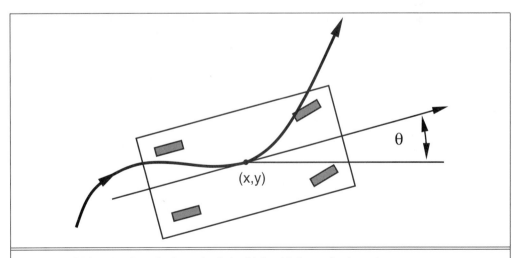

Figure 25.2   Motion of a four-wheeled vehicle with front-wheel steering.

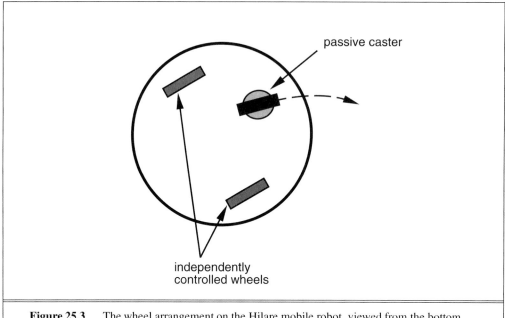

passive caster

independently
controlled wheels

Figure 25.3   The wheel arrangement on the Hilare mobile robot, viewed from the bottom.

has a minimum turning radius or can turn on the spot. If the latter is true, then it is always possible
to move from configuration A to B by turning on the spot toward B, moving to B in a straight
line, and rotating on the spot to the orientation of B. If there is a turning-radius constraint, or if
one would like to move without slowing down too much (which generates the same constraint),
a special path planner is needed. It can be shown that the shortest path in such cases consists of
straight-line segments joining segments of circles with the minimum radius.

Sometimes the robot's design makes the control of locomotion very difficult. Reversing a
wheeled vehicle with several trailers is beyond the capability of most humans; hence some large
fire engines are fitted with a second steering wheel for the back wheels to make it easier. Fire
engines have only a single trailer, but two-trailer examples can be seen at any modern airport.
When leaving a gate, most aircraft are driven by a nose-wheel tender. The nose-wheel tender
(the car) drives a long link attached to the nose wheel (first trailer). The aircraft itself forms the
second trailer. This combination must be backed out of the gate each time an aircraft departs,
and the only control is the steering of the tender. Fortunately, the much greater length of the
aircraft makes it insensitive to small motions of the tender and link, and the control problem is
tractable for an experienced driver. Recent advances in control theory have resulted in algorithms
for automatically steering vehicles with any number of trailers of any size.

Manipulation

MANIPULATORS   We return now to **manipulators**, effectors that move objects in the environment. The ancestors of
robot manipulators were teleoperated mechanisms that allowed humans to manipulate hazardous

KINEMATICS

materials, and that mimicked the geometry of a human arm. Early robots as a rule followed this precedent, and have anthropomorphic kinematics. Broadly defined, **kinematics** is the study of the correspondence between the actuator motions in a mechanism, and the resulting motion of its various parts.

ROTARY

PRISMATIC

Most manipulators allow for either **rotary** motion (rotation around a fixed hub) or **prismatic** motion (linear movement, as with a piston inside a cylinder). Figure 25.4 shows the Stanford Manipulator, used in several early experiments in robotics. A nearly anthropomorphic design is the Unimation PUMA shown in Figure 25.5. This design has six rotary joints arranged sequentially. The shorthand description of its kinematic configuration is "RRRRRR," ("6R" for short) listing joint types from base to tip. A free body in space has six degrees of freedom (three for x–y–z position, three for orientation), so six is the minimum number of joints a robot requires in order to be able to get the last link into an arbitrary position and orientation.

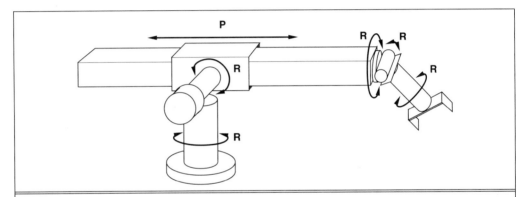

Figure 25.4   The Stanford Manipulator, an early robot arm with five rotary (R) and one prismatic (P) joints, for a total of six degrees of freedom.

In case this total of six degrees of freedom for a free body is not intuitively obvious, imagine the body is a tennis ball. The center of the ball can be described with three position coordinates. Now suppose that the ball is resting on a table with its center fixed. You can still rotate the ball without moving its center. Paint a dot anywhere on the surface of the ball, you can rotate the ball so that the dot touches the table-top. This takes two degrees of freedom, because the dot can be specified with latitude and longitude. With the center fixed and the dot touching the table-top, you can still rotate the ball about a vertical axis. This is the third and last degree of rotational freedom. (In an airplane or boat, the three types of rotation are called pitch, yaw, and roll.)

At the end of the manipulator is the robot's **end effector**, which interacts directly with objects in the world. It may be a screwdriver or other tool, a welding gun, paint sprayer, or a gripper. Grippers vary enormously in complexity. Two- and three-fingered grippers perform most tasks in manufacturing. The mechanical simplicity of these grippers makes them reliable and easy to control, both important attributes for manufacturing.

At the other end of the complexity spectrum are anthropomorphic hands. The Utah-MIT hand shown in Figure 25.6 faithfully replicates most of the kinematics of a human hand, less one finger. A human hand has a very large number of degrees of freedom (see Exercise 25.4).

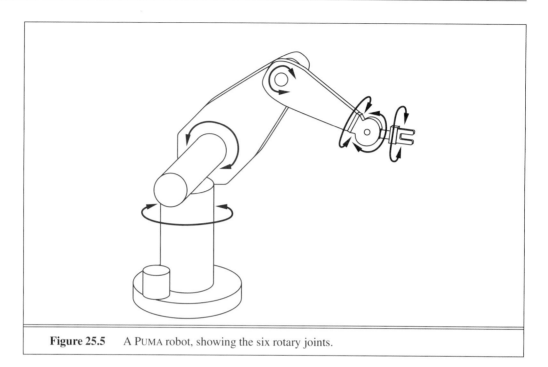

Figure 25.5   A PUMA robot, showing the six rotary joints.

Ultimately, the effectors are driven by electrical (or other) signals. Some effectors only accept on/off signals, some accept scalar values (e.g., turn right 3°), and some robot development environments provide higher level subroutine libraries or have complete languages for specifying actions that can be turned into primitive signals.

Sensors: Tools for perception

Chapter 24 covered the general principles of perception, using vision as the main example. In this section, we describe the other kinds of sensors that provide percepts for a robot.

Proprioception

Like humans, robots have a **proprioceptive**[4] sense that tells them where their joints are. **Encoders** fitted to the joints provide very accurate data about joint angle or extension. If the output of the encoder is fed back to the control mechanism during motion, the robot can have much greater positioning accuracy than humans. For a manipulator, this typically translates to around a few mils (thousandths of an inch) of accuracy in its end-effector position. In contrast, humans can manage only a centimeter or two. To test this for yourself, place your finger at one end of a ruler (or some other object whose length is familiar). Then with your eyes closed try to touch the other

---

[4] The word **proprioceptive** is derived from the same source as **proprietary**, and thus means "perception of privately owned (i.e., internal) stimuli."

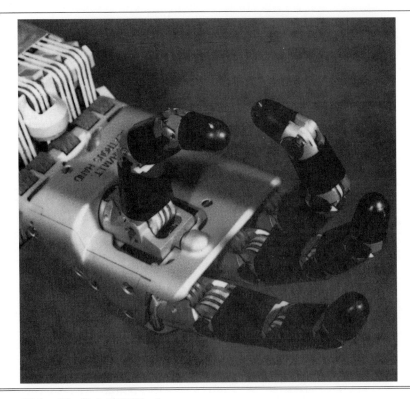

Figure 25.6   The Utah–MIT Hand.

REPEATABILITY   end. You should do better after a few tries, which shows that your positioning **repeatability** is better than your accuracy. The same is usually true for robots.

ODOMETRY   Mobots can measure their change in position using **odometry**, based on sensors that measure wheel rotation (or, in the case of stepper motors that rotate a fixed angle per step, the number of steps). Unfortunately, because of slippage as the robot moves, the position error from wheel motion deteriorates as the robot moves, and may be several percent of the distance travelled. Orientation can be measured more reliably, using a magnetic compass or a gyroscope system. Accelerometers can measure the change in velocity.

Force sensing

Even though robots can sense and control the positions of their joints much more accurately than humans, there are still many tasks that cannot be carried out using only position sensing. Consider, for example, the task of scraping paint off a windowpane using a razor blade. To get all the paint requires positioning accuracy of about a micron in the direction perpendicular to the glass. An error of a millimeter would cause the robot to either miss the paint altogether or break the glass. Obviously, humans are not doing this using position control alone. This and many other tasks involving contact, such as writing, opening doors, and assembling automobiles, require accurate control of *forces*. Force can be regulated to some extent by controlling electric motor current, but accurate control requires a **force sensor**. These sensors are usually placed between the manipulator and end effector and can sense forces and torques in six directions. Using force control, a robot can move along a surface while maintaining contact with a fixed pressure. Such motions are called **compliant motions**, and are extremely important in many robotic applications.

Tactile sensing

Picking up a paper coffee cup or manipulating a tiny screw requires more than proprioception. The force applied to the cup must be just enough to stop it from slipping, but not enough to crush it. Manipulating the screw requires information about exactly where it lies against the fingers that it contacts. In both cases, **tactile sensing** (or touch sensing) can provide the needed information. Tactile sensing is the robotic version of the human sense of touch. A robot's tactile sensor uses an elastic material and a sensing scheme that measures the distortion of the material under contact. The sensor may give data at an array of points on the elastic surface, producing the analogue of a camera image, but of deformation rather than light intensity. By understanding the physics of the deformation process, it is possible to derive algorithms that are analogous to vision algorithms, and can compute position information for the objects that the sensor touches. Tactile sensors can also sense vibration, which helps to detect the impending escape of the coffee cup from the holder's grasp. Human beings use this scheme with a very fast servo loop[5] to detect slip and control the grasping force to near the minimum needed to prevent slip.

Sonar

Sonar is SOund NAvigation and Ranging. Sonar provides useful information about objects very close to the robot and is often used for fast emergency collision avoidance. It is sometimes used to map the robot's environment over a larger area. In the latter case, an array of a dozen or more sonar sensors is fitted around the perimeter of the robot, each pointing in a different direction. Each sensor ideally measures the distance to the nearest obstacle in the direction it is pointing.

Sonar works by measuring the time of flight for a sound pulse generated by the sensor to reach an object and be reflected back. The pulse or "chirp" is typically about 50 kHz. This is more than twice the upper limit for humans of 20 kHz. Sound at that frequency has a wavelength of about 7 mm. The speed of sound is about 330 m/second, so the round-trip time delay for an object 1 m away is about 6×10^{-3} seconds. Sonar has been very effective for obstacle avoidance and tracking a nearby target, such as another mobile robot. But although it should be possible to measure the time delay very accurately, sonar has rarely been able to produce reliable and precise data for mapping. The first problem is beam width. Rather than a narrow beam of sound, a typical sensor produces a conical beam with $10°$ or more of spread. The second problem comes from the relatively long (7 mm) wavelength of the sonar sound. Objects that are very smooth

---

[5] A servomechanism is a device for controlling a large amount of power with a small amount of power. A servo loop uses feedback to regulate the power.

relative to this wavelength look shiny or "specular" to the sensor. Such objects reflect sound like a perfect mirror. Sound will only be received back from patches of surface that are at right angles to the beam. Objects with flat surfaces and sharp edges reflect very little sound in most directions. (The same observation is used to design radar-eluding stealth aircraft and ships.) After being reflected from the surface, the sound may yet strike a rough surface and be reflected back to the sensor. The time delay will correspond not to a physical object, but to a "ghost," which may mysteriously disappear when the robot moves.

As discussed in Chapter 17, noisy sensors can be handled by first constructing a probabilistic model of the sensor, and then using Bayesian updating to integrate the information obtained over time as the robot moves around. Eventually, reasonably accurate maps can be built up, and ghost images can be eliminated.

Camera data

Human and animal vision systems remain the envy of all machine-vision researchers. Chapter 24 provides an introduction to the state of the art in machine vision, which is still some way from handling complex outdoor scenes and general object recognition. Fortunately, for a robot's purposes, something simpler than a general vision system will usually suffice. If the set of tasks the robot needs to perform is limited, then vision need only supply the information relevant to those tasks. Special-purpose robots can also take advantage of so-called **domain constraints** that can be assumed to apply in restricted environments. For example, in a building (as opposed to a forest), flat surfaces can be assumed to be vertical or horizontal, and objects are supported on a flat ground plane.

DOMAIN CONSTRAINTS

In some cases, one can also modify the environment itself to make the robot's task easier. One simple way of doing this, widely used in warehousing tasks, is to put bar-code stickers in various locations that the robot can read and use to get an exact position fix. Slightly more drastic is the use of **structured light sensors**, which project their own light source onto objects to simplify the problem of shape determination. Imagine a vertical light stripe cast as shown in Figure 25.7. When this stripe cuts an object, it produces a contour whose 3-D shape is easily inferred by triangulation from any vantage point not in the plane of the stripe. A camera placed in the same *horizontal* plane as the source needs only to locate the stripe within each horizontal scan line. This is a simple image-processing task and easily done in hardware.

STRUCTURED LIGHT SENSORS

By moving the stripe, or by using several rasters of stripes at different spacings, it is possible to produce a very dense three-dimensional map of the object in a short space of time. A number of devices are available now that include a laser source, stripe control, camera, and all the image processing needed to compute a map of distances to points in the image. From the user's point of view, these **laser range finders** really are depth sensors, providing a depth image that updates rapidly, perhaps several times a second.

LASER RANGE FINDERS

For model-based recognition, some very simple light-beam sensors have been used recently. These sensors provide a small number of very accurate measurements of object geometry. When models are known, these measurements suffice to compute the object's identity and position. In Figure 25.8, two examples are shown, a **cross-beam sensor** and a **parallel-beam sensor**.

CROSS-BEAM SENSOR
PARALLEL-BEAM SENSOR

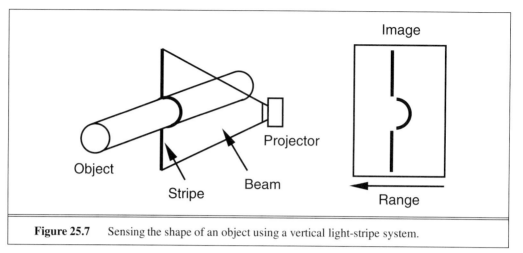

Figure 25.7   Sensing the shape of an object using a vertical light-stripe system.

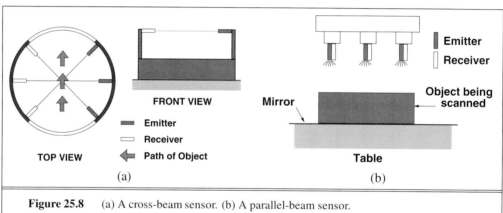

Figure 25.8   (a) A cross-beam sensor. (b) A parallel-beam sensor.

25.4   ARCHITECTURES

In this section, we step back from the nuts and bolts of robots and look at the overall control mechanism. *The **architecture** of a robot defines how the job of generating actions from percepts is organized.* We will largely be concerned with autonomous mobile robots in dynamic environments, for which the need for a sophisticated control architecture is clear.

The design of robot architectures is essentially the same agent design problem that we discussed in Chapter 2. We saw in the introduction to the current chapter that the environment for mobile robots is toward the difficult end as environments go. Furthermore, the perceptual input available to a robot is often voluminous; nevertheless, the robot needs to react quickly in some situations. In the following subsections, we briefly describe a variety of architectures, ranging from fully deliberative to fully reflex. There is no accepted theory of architecture design that can be used to prove that one design is better than another. Many theoreticians deride the entire problem as "just a bunch of boxes and arrows." Nonetheless, many superficially different designs seem to have incorporated the same set of features for dealing with the real world.

Classical architecture

By the late 1960s, primitive but serviceable tools for intelligent robots were available. These included vision systems that could locate simple polyhedral objects; two-dimensional path-planning algorithms; and resolution theorem provers that could construct simple, symbolic plans using situation calculus. From these tools, together with a collection of wheels, motors and sensors, emerged Shakey, the forerunner of many intelligent robot projects.

The first version of Shakey, appearing in 1969, demonstrated the importance of experimental research in bringing to light unsuspected difficulties. The researchers found that general-purpose resolution theorem-provers were too inefficient to find nontrivial plans, that integrating geometric and symbolic representations of the world was extremely difficult, and that plans don't work. This last discovery came about because Shakey was designed to execute plans without monitoring their success or failure. Because of wheel slippage, measurement errors and so on, almost all plans of any length failed at some point during execution.

The second version of Shakey incorporated several improvements. First, most of the detailed work of finding paths and moving objects was moved from the general problem-solving level down into special-purpose programs called **intermediate-level actions** (ILAs). These actions in fact consisted of complex routines of **low-level actions** (LLAs) for controlling the physical robot, and included some error detection and recovery capabilities. For example, one ILA called NAVTO could move the robot from one place to another within a room by calling the A* algorithm to plan a path and then calling LLAs to execute the path, doing some path corrections along the way. The LLAs were also responsible for updating the internal model of the world state, which was stored in first-order logic. Motion errors were explicitly modelled, so that as the robot moved, its uncertainty about its location increased. Once the uncertainty exceeded a threshold for safe navigation, the LLA would call on the vision subsystem to provide a new position fix. The key contribution of the ILA/LLA system, then, was to provide a relatively clean and reliable set of actions for the planning system.

MACRO-OPERATORS

The planning system used the STRIPS algorithm, essentially a theorem-prover specially designed for efficient generation of action sequences. STRIPS also introduced the idea of compiling the results of planning into generalized **macro-operators**, so that future problem-solving could be more efficient (see Section 21.2). The entire system was controlled by PLANEX, which accepted goals from the user, called STRIPS to generate plans, then executed them by calling the specified ILAs. The execution mechanism was a simple version of the methods described in Chapter 12. PLANEX kept track of the current world state, comparing it to the preconditions of each subsequence in the original plan. After each action completed, PLANEX would execute the shortest plan subsequence that led to a goal and whose preconditions were satisfied. In this way, actions that failed would be retried, and fortunate accidents would lead to reduced effort. If no subsequence was applicable, PLANEX could call STRIPS to make a new plan.

The basic elements of Shakey's design—specialized components for low-level control and geometric reasoning, a centralized world model for planning, compilation to increase speed, and execution monitoring to handle unexpected problems—are repeated in many modern systems. Improvements in the symbolic planning and execution monitoring components are discussed in depth in Part IV. Compilation, or explanation-based learning, has been used extensively in two robot architectures: Robo-SOAR (Laird *et al.*, 1991) and THEO (Mitchell, 1990). Computation times for simple tasks can be reduced from several minutes to less than a second in some cases. In both of these architectures, compilation is invoked whenever a problem is solved for which no ready-made solution was available. In this way, the robot gradually becomes competent and efficient in routine tasks, while still being able to fall back on general-purpose reasoning when faced with unexpected circumstances.

Much of the research in robotics since Shakey was switched off has been at the level of ILAs and LLAs. Shakey was able to move on a flat floor, and could push large objects around with difficulty. Modern robots can twirl pencils in their fingers, screw in screws and perform high-precision surgery with greater accuracy than human experts. Sections 25.5 and 25.6 describe some of the theoretical advances in geometric reasoning and sensor integration that have made such achievements possible. Hilare II (Giralt *et al.*, 1991) is probably the most comprehensive modern example of a robot architecture in the classical tradition that makes use of advanced geometric methods.

Situated automata

SITUATED AUTOMATA

Since the mid-1980s, a significant minority of AI and robotics researchers have begun to question the "classical" view of intelligent agent design based on representation and manipulation of explicit knowledge. In robotics, *the principal drawback of the classical view is that explicit reasoning about the effects of low-level actions is too expensive to generate real-time behavior.* We have seen that compilation can alleviate this to some extent. Researchers working on **situated automata** have taken this idea one step further, by eliminating explicit deliberation from their robot designs altogether.

A situated automaton is essentially a finite-state machine whose inputs are provided by sensors connected to the environment, and whose outputs are connected to effectors. Situated automata provide a very efficient implementation of reflex agents with state. There have been two main strands in the development of such robots. The first approach involves generating the automaton by an offline compilation process, starting with an explicit representation. The second approach involves a manual design process based on a decomposition according to the various behaviors that the robot needs to exhibit.

The compilation approach, pioneered by Stan Rosenschein, (Rosenschein, 1985; Kaelbling and Rosenschein, 1990) distinguishes between the use of explicit knowledge representation by human designers (what he calls the "grand strategy") and the use of explicit knowledge within the agent architecture (the "grand tactic"). Through a careful logical analysis of the relationship between perception, action, and knowledge, Rosenschein was able to design a compiler that generates finite state machines whose internal states can be *proved* to correspond to certain logical propositions about the environment, provided that the initial state and the correct laws

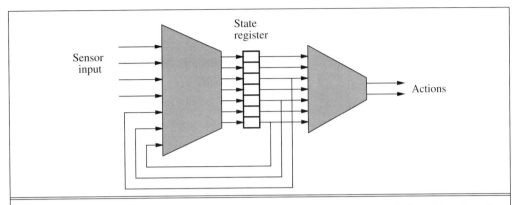

Figure 25.9   The basic structure of Rosenschein's situated automaton design. The shaded region on the left represents a Boolean circuit for updating the current state registers. The shaded region to the right represents a circuit for selecting actions based on the current state.

of "physics" are given to the compiler. Thus, the robot "knows" a set of propositions about the environment, even though it has no explicit representation of the propositions.

Rosenschein's basic design is shown in Figure 25.9. It relies on a theorem to the effect that *any* finite-state machine can be implemented as a state register together with a feedforward circuit that updates the state based on the sensor inputs and the current state, and another circuit that calculates the output given the state register. Because all the computation is carried out by fixed-depth, feedforward circuits, the execution time for each decision cycle is vanishingly small. Flakey, a robot based on situated automata theory, was able to navigate the halls of SRI, run errands, and even ask questions, all without the benefit of explicit representations.

Rodney Brooks (1986) has advocated an approach to robot design that he calls **behavior-based robotics**. The idea is that the overall agent design can be decomposed, not into functional components such as perception, learning, and planning, but into behaviors such as obstacle avoidance, wall-following, and exploration. Each behavioral module accesses the sensor inputs independently to extract just the information it needs, and sends its own signals to the effectors. Behaviors are arranged into a prioritized hierarchy in which higher level behaviors can access the internal state of lower level behaviors and can modify or override their outputs. Figure 25.10 shows a hierarchy of behaviors proposed for a mobile robot by Brooks (1986).

BEHAVIOR-BASED
ROBOTICS

The main aim of behavior-based robotics is to eliminate the reliance on a centralized, complete representation of the world state, which seems to be the most expensive aspect of the classical architecture. Internal state is needed only to keep track of those aspects of the world state that are inaccessible to the sensors and are required for action selection in each behavior. For tasks in which the appropriate action is largely determined by the sensor inputs, the slogan "The world is its own model" is quite appropriate. In some cases, only a few bits of internal state are needed even for quite complex tasks such as collecting empty soft drink cans. Similar results have been found in Rosenschein's designs, in which the state register can be surprisingly small.

Behavior-based robotics has been quite successful in demonstrating that many basic competences in the physical world can be achieved using simple, inexpensive mechanisms. At

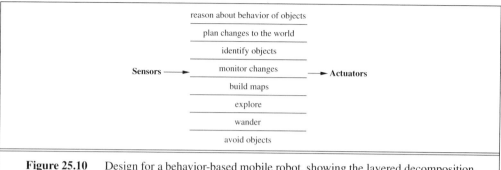

Figure 25.10   Design for a behavior-based mobile robot, showing the layered decomposition.

present, however, it is difficult to see how the design methodology can scale up to more complex tasks. Even for the task "Find an empty cup and bring it back to the starting location," the robot must form an internal representation that corresponds to a map in the classical architecture. Furthermore, the behavior-based approach requires the design of a new controller for each task, whereas classical robots are **taskable**: they can be assigned a goal and can carry out a plan to achieve it. In many ways, behavior-based designs resemble the ILA and LLA levels in Shakey, which are "nonclassical" components of an overall classical architecture.

Rosenschein's situated automata fall somewhere in between. The process of generating the automaton can be completely automated, so that if the the compiler is included in the robot's software, the robot can be given a task and can compile its own situated automaton. The automaton can then be executed in software. Comparing this approach with the explanation-based learning method used in SOAR and THEO, we see that the situated automaton is compiled prior to execution and must handle all possible situations that can arise, whereas the explanation-based learning approach generates efficient rules for handling the types of situations that actually arise during execution. In simple domains, the situated-automaton approach is feasible and probably more efficient, whereas in very complex domains, especially those with recursive structure, the complete automaton becomes too large or even infinite in size.

25.5   CONFIGURATION SPACES: A FRAMEWORK FOR ANALYSIS

Recall from Chapter 3 that the main element in analyzing a problem is the **state space**,[6] which describes all the possible configurations of the environment. In robotics, the environment includes the body of the robot itself. The main distinction between the problems discussed in Chapter 3 and those in robotics is that robotics usually involves *continuous* state spaces. Both the configuration of the robot's body and the locations of objects in physical space are defined by real-valued

---

[6] There is a source of confusion here because the term "state space" is used in the robotics and control literature to include the robot's state parameters and certain of their derivatives. Enough derivatives are included that the robot's motion can be predicted from its dynamics and control equations. For simplicity, we assume here that derivatives of state parameters are excluded.

coordinates. It is therefore impossible to apply standard search algorithms in any straightforward way because the numbers of states and actions are infinite. *Much of the work in robot planning has dealt with ways to tame these continuous state spaces.*

Suppose that we have a robot with k degrees of freedom. Then the state or configuration of the robot can be described with k real values $q_1, \ldots, q_k$. For the PUMA robot, this would be a list of six joint angles $\theta_1, \ldots, \theta_6$. The k values can be considered as a point p in a k-dimensional space called the **configuration space** of the robot. We use $\mathcal{C}$ to refer to the configuration space of the robot itself. This description is convenient because it lets us describe the complex three-dimensional shape of the robot with a single k-dimensional point. In other words, from the six joint angles, we can determine the exact shape of the entire PUMA robot. This works because the individual robot links are rigid—they rotate when the joint angles change, but they do not change size or shape.

Configuration space can be used to determine if there is a path by which a robot can move from one position to another. Consider the problem of getting the PUMA hand to replace a spark plug in a car. We have to find a path through three-dimensional physical space that will lead the hand to the right spot, without bumping into anything. But that is not enough—we need to make sure that the other links of the robot do not bump into anything either. This is a difficult problem to visualize in physical space, but it is easy to visualize in configuration space. We start by considering the points in $\mathcal{C}$ for which any part of the robot bumps into something. This set of points is called the **configuration space obstacle**, or $\mathcal{O}$. The set difference $\mathcal{C} - \mathcal{O}$ is called free space, or $\mathcal{F}$, and is the set of configurations in which the robot can move safely. (Note that we also have to worry about the robot bumping into itself, or over-twisting power and data cables that pass through its joints. For these reasons, there are upper and lower limits on the joint angles of most robots, and corresponding bounds on the size of configuration space.)

Assume we have an initial point c_1 and a destination point c_2 in configuration space. The robot can safely move between the corresponding points in physical space *if and only if* there is a continuous path between c_1 and c_2 that lies entirely in $\mathcal{F}$. This idea is illustrated in Figure 25.11. A two-link robot is shown at the left of the figure, and its two-dimensional configuration space at the right. The configuration obstacle is the shaded region, and configurations c_1 and c_2 are shown in both domains, with a safe path drawn in $\mathcal{C}$ between them. Even in this simple example, the advantage of searching for a safe path in $\mathcal{C}$ is clear.

We humans have it much easier than the PUMA, because our shoulder joint has three degrees of freedom, while the PUMA's only has two. That gives the human arm seven degrees of freedom overall, one more than is needed to reach any point. This extra or **redundant** degree of freedom allows the arm to clear obstacles while keeping the hand in one spot, a wonderful facility that helped our ancestors climb around in trees, and helps us change spark plugs.

We should emphasize that configuration space and free space are mathematical tools for designing and analyzing motion-planning algorithms. The algorithms themselves need not explicitly construct or search a configuration space; nonetheless, any motion-planning method or control mechanism can be interpreted as seeking a safe path in $\mathcal{F}$. Configuration-space analysis can be used to establish whether or not a given mechanism is complete and correct, and can be used to analyze the complexity of the underlying problems.

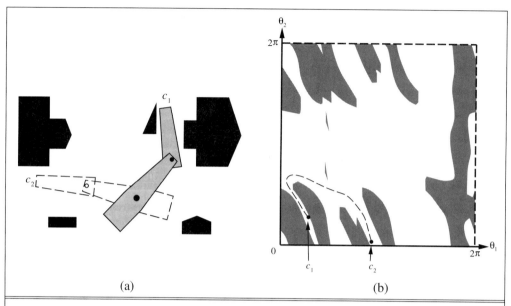

Figure 25.11   (a) A workspace with a rotary two-link arm. The goal is to move from configuration c_1 to configuration c_2. (b) The corresponding configuration space, showing the free space and a path that achieves the goal.

Generalized configuration space

GENERALIZED
CONFIGURATION
SPACE

ASSEMBLY
PLANNING

The term **generalized configuration space** has been applied to systems where the state of other objects is included as part of the configuration. The other objects may be movable, and their shapes may vary. Shape variation occurs in objects such as scissors or staplers that have mechanical joints, and in deformable objects like string and paper. Generalized configuration spaces are especially useful in understanding tasks such as **assembly planning** in which the robot must move a set of objects into some desired arrangement.

Let $\mathcal{E}$ denote the space of all possible configurations of all possible objects in the world, other than the robot. If a given configuration can be defined by a finite set of parameters $\alpha_1, \ldots, \alpha_m$, then $\mathcal{E}$ will be an m-dimensional space. This will not work for objects like string and paper, whose shapes are not describable with finitely many parameters. These objects represent a considerable challenge for geometric modelling at this stage. But we can use $\mathcal{E}$ as a conceptual tool even in those cases.

Now consider $\mathcal{W} = \mathcal{C} \times \mathcal{E}$. $\mathcal{W}$ is the space of all possible configurations of the world, both robot and obstacles. In the two-link robot $\mathcal{C}$ described earlier, there was no variation in the object shapes, so $\mathcal{E}$ was a single point and $\mathcal{W}$ and $\mathcal{C}$ were equivalent.

If all of the objects in the environment are robots under central control, then the situation is really the same as before. In this setting, it is best to cluster all the degrees of freedom of the robots together to create a single super-robot. The generalized configuration space is the space of all joint angles for all robots. Illegal configurations now include those where two robots overlap in space. The planning problem again reduces to finding a safe path for a point in the generalized free space $\mathcal{F}$.

If the other objects are not robots but are nonetheless movable, the problem is very much harder. Unfortunately, this is also the most interesting case, because usually we would like a robot to move inanimate things around. We can still construct a generalized configuration space, and eliminate configurations where the robot overlaps an object, or two objects overlap. But even if we find a path between two configurations c_1 and c_2 in generalized $\mathcal{F}$, we may not be able to execute it. The problem is that an unrestricted path in $\mathcal{W}$ will usually describe motion of objects through midair without any help from the robot. We can partially address this problem by restricting $\mathcal{W}$ to comprise configurations where objects are either held by the robot or are supported by another object against gravity.

But legal paths in this $\mathcal{W}$ can still describe object motions without robot aid, such as spontaneous sliding on a tabletop, which should be illegal. There is no easy solution to this problem. We simply cannot think of $\mathcal{W}$ as a benign sea in which we can navigate freely. Instead, we must follow certain shipping lanes, between which we transfer only at special configurations. Although generalized $\mathcal{W}$ has many degrees of freedom, ($k + m$ degrees using the notation above), only k of these are actually controllable. Most of the time, we are changing only the robot configuration $q_1, \ldots, q_k$, and the object configurations $\alpha_1, \ldots, \alpha_m$ stay fixed. Sometimes though, if the robot is grasping an object, we can change both the robot and the objects configuration. We are still moving in a k-dimensional subset of $\mathcal{W}$, but no longer one involving only the q (robot) coordinates. So we are in a $(k + m)$-dimensional sea with steerage only along two types of k-dimensional lanes. Motions where the robot moves freely are called **transit paths**, and those where the robot moves an object are called **transfer paths**.

TRANSIT PATHS

TRANSFER PATHS

FOLIATION

The navigable $\mathcal{W}$ in this case is called a **foliation**, suggesting an abundance of small randomly oriented sheets, but it is really more like a book. Each page of the book is a slightly different free space for the robot, defined by slightly different positions for the movable objects. Look again at Figure 25.12. On the left half of the figure, one of the objects has an arrow attached, indicating possible motion. The variable b is a coordinate measuring the object's displacement. The $\mathcal{W}$ for the system is now three-dimensional, and b is the new coordinate. For b fixed, a slice through the $\mathcal{W}$ describes the allowable motions of the robot with the obstacles fixed, and looks like the $\mathcal{C}$ in the right half of the figure. Imagine constructing the $\mathcal{C}$ for many different values of b, printing the results on separate pages, sorting them by b coordinate, and assembling the pages into a book. Transit motion is possible within any page of the book, on which the object positions are fixed, but not between pages. Transfer motions, in which an object is moving (or being moved), form a kind of spine for the book, and allow motion between pages.

The difficulty of planning for movable objects is real: the towers of Hanoi problem[7] is a special case of it. The number of motions needed to move n Hanoi disks is exponential in n, implying that planning for movable objects requires time that grows at least exponentially with the dimension of $\mathcal{W}$. At this time, there are no proved upper bounds for general planning with n movable objects. Robot planners usually make some strong assumptions to avoid tackling this problem head-on. One can do any of the following:

---

[7] The towers of Hanoi problem is to move a set of n disks of different sizes from one peg to another, using a third peg for temporary storage. Disks are moved one at a time, and a larger disk cannot rest on a smaller one.

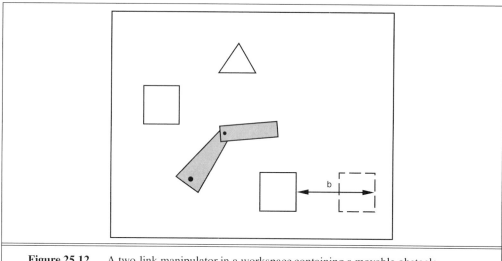

Figure 25.12   A two-link manipulator in a workspace containing a movable obstacle.

1. Partition $\mathcal{W}$ into finitely many states—a form of **abstraction** (see Section 12.2). The planning problem then reduces to a logical planning problem of the kind addressed in Part IV. For example, the blocks world involves a partition of block configurations into those in which one block is "on another," and those in which it is "on the table." The exact locations of the blocks are ignored. The partitioning must be done carefully, because it involves a considerable loss of generality. In the blocks world case, one can no longer construct plans involving blocks that are leaning, or in which two or more blocks perch on another, or in which block positions are important (as in building a wall). Obviously, the appropriate partition depends on the goal, but as yet no general method for constructing partitions has been devised.

2. Plan object motions first and then plan for the robot. This could be called the classical approach to assembly planning. We first restrict the object motions so that all the objects move as two rigid subgroups, one representing the main assembly, and the other a sub-assembly that is being added to it. A single robot then has a good chance to be able to perform that step, and a separate planning phase generates the robot's motion.

   Planning object motions also can be abstracted into discrete actions such as "screw part A onto part B." Many early assembly planners used this kind of representation, and are therefore able to use standard partial-order planning algorithms. They support a variety of constraints on the order of assembly steps, but questions of geometric feasibility are usually handled by separate geometric algorithms, or in some cases by the user.

   Recently though, a very elegant method was described that plans a geometrically feasible assembly sequence and runs in time *polynomial* in n (Wilson and Schweikard, 1992). This scheme necessarily does not generate all possible sequences, because there are exponentially many. But a user can reject certain of the subassemblies it has chosen, and it will generate another feasible sequence just as fast that satisfies the user's strictures.

3. Restrict object motions. Here one chooses a parameterized family of basic motions, and searches for a sequence of such motions that will solve the planning problem. The best-known example of this is the "LMT" approach[8] (Lozano-Pérez *et al.*, 1984). One must be careful about the choice of motions, because the problem will be intractable if they are too general, but unsolvable if they are too restrictive. LMT suggests the use of compliant motions, which produce straight-line motions in free space, but which follow the boundaries of configuration space when needed. LMT also explicitly models uncertainty in control and sensing. So the result of an LMT basic motion is not a single trajectory, but an envelope of possible trajectories that grows with time. LMT is described more fully in Section 25.6.

Recognizable Sets

Configuration space is a useful tool for understanding constraints induced by object shape. We have so far tacitly assumed that robot planning problems are all of the form "How do I get from here to there in $\mathcal{W}$?" But the reality is that most robots have poor knowledge of where they are in $\mathcal{W}$. The robot has reasonably good knowledge of its own state (although often not accurately enough for precision work), but its knowledge of other objects comes second hand from sensors like sonar, laser range finders, and computer vision. Some objects simply may not be visible from the robot's current vantage point, so their uncertainty is enormous. Rather than a point in configuration space, our planner must start with a probability cloud, or an envelope of possible configurations. We call such an envelope a **recognizable set**.[9]

RECOGNIZABLE SET

ABSTRACT SENSOR

It will be useful to formalize this notion. An **abstract sensor** σ is a function from the true world state $\mathcal{W}$ to the space of possible sensor values. A recognizable set is a set $\sigma^{-1}(s)$ of all world states in which the robot would receive the sensor reading s.[10]

If the sensor is perfect, that is, if it always produces the same sensor values in the same world state, the sets $\sigma^{-1}(s)$ form a **partition** of $\mathcal{W}$. Distinct recognizable sets do not overlap, and their union is all of $\mathcal{W}$. Unfortunately, because of noise, and because the chosen $\mathcal{W}$ often does not incorporate all of the factors that can affect sensor readings, the value returned by the sensor may not be a unique function of the state. To allow for this, we can treat σ as a relation rather than a function. The relation is true of a state and a sensor reading if the sensor reading *could possibly* be returned in that world state. It still makes sense to define recognizable sets as $\sigma^{-1}(s)$, where we now take this to mean the set of states in which the sensor could return the value s. Now it no longer holds that distinct recognizable sets are disjoint, although their union is still all of $\mathcal{W}$.

Recognizable sets simplify the problem of planning with uncertainty. A robot will always be in a recognizable set, because it will always have sensor readings available. The robot may also use memories of earlier sensor readings, but this is equivalent to a virtual sensor that provides both current and past readings. The (virtual) sensor readings determine uniquely which

---

[8] LMT is named after the three authors.

[9] **Recognizable sets** are to continuous domains what multiple state sets are to discrete problems (see Chapter 3).

[10] Notice the close analogy with the idea of **possible worlds** introduced in the context of modal logic in Chapter 8. A recognizable set is essentially the set of possible worlds given what the robot knows about the world.

recognizable set $\sigma^{-1}(s_0)$ the robot is in. From there, the planner can determine where the robot might move next, given a motion command with uncertainty, and what the next sensor reading s_1 could be. Thinking of recognizable sets as states of the robot, the motion command caused a nondeterministic transition from the state $\sigma^{-1}(s_0)$ to one of the states $\sigma^{-1}(s_1)$. Although there are infinitely many such states with a continuous sensor, it is still possible to represent the possible transitions, and to find a correct plan if one exists. Unfortunately, the complexity of doing this is extremely high—in fact, doubly exponential in the number of plan steps (Canny and Reif, 1987).

25.6   NAVIGATION AND MOTION PLANNING

We now turn to the question of how to move around successfully. Given our analysis of robotics problems as motion in configuration spaces, we will begin with algorithms that handle $\mathcal{C}$ directly. These algorithms usually assume that an exact description of the space is available, so they cannot be used where there is significant sensor error and motion error. In some cases, no description of the space is available until the robot actually starts moving around in it.

We can identify five major classes of algorithms, and arrange them roughly in order of the amount of information required at planning time and execution time:

◇ **Cell decomposition** methods break continuous space into a finite number of cells, yielding a discrete search problem.

◇ **Skeletonization** methods compute a one-dimensional "skeleton" of the configuration space, yielding an equivalent graph search problem.

◇ **Bounded-error planning** methods assume bounds on sensor and actuator uncertainty, and in some cases can compute plans that are guaranteed to succeed even in the face of severe actuator error.

◇ **Landmark-based navigation** methods assume that there are some regions in which the robot's location can be pinpointed using landmarks, whereas outside those regions it may have only orientation information.

◇ **Online algorithms** assume that the environment is completely unknown initially, although most assume some form of accurate position sensor.

As always, we are interested in establishing some of of the properties of these algorithms, including their soundness, completeness, and complexity. When we talk about the complexity of a planning method, we must keep in mind both offline costs (before execution) and the online cost of execution.

Cell decomposition

Recalling that motion planning for a robot reduces to navigating a point in free space $\mathcal{F}$, the basic idea of **cell decomposition** is easy to state:

1. Divide $\mathcal{F}$ into simple, connected regions called "cells." This is the cell decomposition.

2. Determine which cells are adjacent to which others, and construct an "adjacency graph." The vertices of this graph are cells, and edges join cells that abut each other.

3. Determine which cells the start and goal configurations lie in, and search for a path in the adjacency graph between these cells.

4. From the sequence of cells found at the last step, compute a path within each cell from a point of the boundary with the previous cell to a boundary point meeting the next cell.

The last step presupposes an easy method for navigating within cells. The cells are usually geometrically "simple," so that this step is easy. For example, one could use rectangular cells, and then it is possible to join any two points in the cell with a straight-line path (this property is shared by all convex cells). The difficulty is that the cells must be constructed in configuration space, and $\mathcal{F}$ typically has complex, curved boundaries (see Figure 25.12).

Because of the difficulty of the $\mathcal{F}$-boundary, the first approaches to cell decomposition did not represent it exactly. Approximate subdivisions were used, using either boxes or rectangular strips. A strip approximation to the configuration space of the 2-link robot is shown in Figure 25.13. The start and goal configurations are visible as points, and the cells joining them from step 3 above are shaded. Finally, an explicit path from start to goal is constructed by joining the midpoint (centroid) of each strip with the midpoints of the boundaries with neighboring cells.

This approach must be conservative if it is to produce a collision-free path. The strips must be entirely in free space or a path found inside them might cross a $\mathcal{C}$-boundary and cause a collision. So there will be some "wasted" wedges of free space at the ends of the strips. This is not usually a problem, but in very tight situations, there might be no path except through those wedges. To find this path, thinner strips would have to be used. This raises a general issue for approximate cell decomposition: choosing the resolution of the decomposition. This is sometimes done adaptively by the algorithm, by choosing smaller cells in "tight" parts of free space. Or there might be a natural "safety clearance" below which it is inadvisable to move. To be concrete about this, suppose that we are able to control our robot's motion to within 1 cm. If we cannot find a safe path with cells at 1 cm resolution, a path through cells at a finer resolution would take the robot closer than 1 cm to the obstacles. Because that conflicts with our desire for a sensible path, there is no point in performing that more expensive search.

The approach just described is sound but not complete. It produces a safe path, but may not always find one if one exists. With some small changes, we could instead have produced a planner that is complete but not sound. If we were reckless rather than conservative, we could have declared all partially free cells as being free. If there were any safe path, it would then pass entirely through free cells, and our planner would be guaranteed to find it. As you can imagine though, given the unforgiving nature of steel and aluminum during collisions, incorrect plans are not very useful.

An alternative to approximate algorithms is exact cell decomposition. An exact decomposition divides free space into cells that exactly fill it. These cells necessarily have complex shapes, because some of their boundaries are also boundaries of $\mathcal{F}$. Such a decomposition is shown in Figure 25.14. This decomposition looks rather like a coarse strip decomposition, but there are two important differences. The first is that the cells have curved top and bottom ends, so there are no gaps of free space outside the decomposition. We call these cells cylinders. The

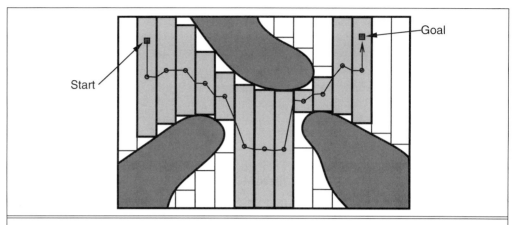

Figure 25.13   A vertical strip cell decomposition of the configuration space for a two-link robot. The obstacles are dark blobs, the cells are rectangles, and the solution is contained within the grey rectangles.

second difference is that the width of the cylinders is not fixed, but determined by the geometry of the environment. This is a key aspect of the exact method. To be useful for planning, the cell shapes must be kept simple. Otherwise, we could declare all of free space as a single cell. This does not help because there is no simple way to move around in such a cell. The cells in the cylindrical decomposition are easy to move in, because their left and right boundaries are straight lines (although sometimes of zero length).

To construct a cylindrical decomposition of a two-dimensional set, we first find **critical points** of the boundary. These are the points where the boundary curve is vertical. Equivalently, imagine sweeping a vertical line from left to right across Figure 25.14. At every instant, the line can be divided into segments that lie in free space or in the obstacle. Critical points are exactly those points where segments split or join as the line moves. As the line moves within a cylindrical cell, there are no splitting or joining events, and this makes it easy to plan paths within the cell. For example, to move from the left boundary to the right boundary of a cylindrical cell, we could use this sweeping line. A single segment of the line would always lie in this cell, and its midpoint would give us the path we want.

Skeletonization methods

SKELETONIZATION

SKELETON

Rather than producing a decomposition into a finite number of discrete chunks of space, **skeletonization** methods collapse the configuration space into a one-dimensional subset, or **skeleton**. They simplify the task of navigating in a high-dimensional space by requiring paths to lie along the skeleton. The skeleton is essentially a web with a finite number of vertices, and paths within the skeleton can be computed using graph search methods. If the start and goal points do not lie on the skeleton, short path segments are computed joining them to the nearest point on it. Skeletonization methods are generally simpler than cell decomposition, because they provide a

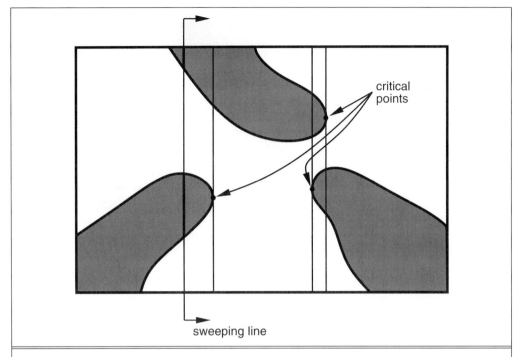

critical
points

sweeping line

Figure 25.14   A cylindrical cell decomposition of the configuration space for a two-link robot.
There are three critical points indicated by dots, and nine cylinders.

"minimal" description of free space. They avoid an explicit description of the boundary of free
space, and this can provide considerable time savings. There is only one kind of data structure
needed to describe skeleton curves, and this helps simplify implementation.

To be complete for motion planning, skeletonization methods must satisfy two properties:

1. If $\mathcal{S}$ is a skeleton of free space $\mathcal{F}$, then $\mathcal{S}$ should have a single connected piece within each
   connected region of $\mathcal{F}$.

2. For any point p in $\mathcal{F}$, it should be "easy" to compute a path from p to the skeleton.

The second condition is rather vague, but it will become clearer from the examples of skeletonization methods coming up. The condition is crucial, because otherwise we could construct a
skeleton that consisted of a single point in each connected region of $\mathcal{F}$. Such a skeleton would be
a procrastination of the planning problem, rather than a solution of it. There are many types of
skeletonization methods in two dimensions. These include visibility graphs, Voronoi diagrams,
and roadmaps. We briefly describe each in turn.

VISIBILITY GRAPH   The **visibility graph** for a polygonal configuration space $\mathcal{C}$ consists of edges joining all
pairs of vertices that can see each other. That is, there is an unobstructed straight line joining those
vertices. It is shown in Figure 25.15. To see that the visibility graph is complete for planning,
we need only observe that the *shortest* path between two points with polygonal obstacles lies
entirely on the visibility graph, except for its first and last segment (see Exercise 25.7).

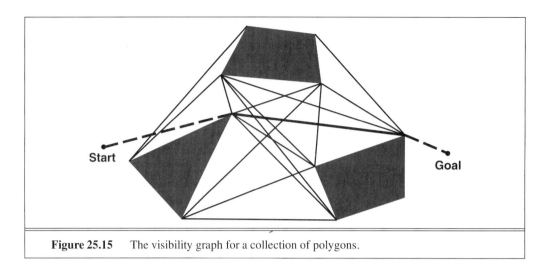

Figure 25.15   The visibility graph for a collection of polygons.

The **Voronoi diagram** of a polygonal free space $\mathcal{F}$ is shown in Figure 25.16. You can understand the diagram as follows. For each point in free space, compute its distance to the nearest obstacle. Plot that distance on Figure 25.16 as a height coming out of the page. The height of the terrain is zero at the boundary with the obstacles and increases as you move away from them. The bounding rectangle of this $\mathcal{C}$ also counts as an obstacle. The terrain has sharp ridges at points that are equidistant from two or more obstacles. The Voronoi diagram consists of those sharp ridge points. Algorithms that find paths on this skeleton are complete, because the existence of a path in $\mathcal{F}$ implies the existence of one on the Voronoi diagram. However, the path in the Voronoi diagram is not in general the shortest path.

The most efficient complete method for motion planning is based on **roadmaps**. A roadmap is a skeleton consisting of two types of curves: **silhouette curves** (also known as "freeways") and **linking curves** (also known as "bridges"). The idea behind roadmaps is to make the search for a path simpler by limiting it to travel on a few freeways and connecting bridges rather than an infinite space of points. Figure 25.17 shows a roadmap for a three-dimensional torus. The complexity of computing a roadmap is $O(n^k \log n)$ for a robot with k degrees of freedom. Here, n is the size of the $\mathcal{C}$ description, which is taken to be the number of equations in the formula describing $\mathcal{F}$.

There are two versions of roadmaps. The first has been called the **silhouette method** because it uses curves that define the visible silhouette of the free-space boundary. The roadmap shown in Figure 25.17 is of this type. To define it, we first choose two directions in $\mathcal{C}$, and think of them as coordinate axes. Call them X and Y. The roadmap is defined as follows:

- Silhouette curves are local extrema in Y of slices in X. That is, take a slice through $\mathcal{F}$ by setting $X = c$ for some constant c. The cross-section of $\mathcal{F}$ will have several connected pieces. Every piece is either unbounded, or will have at least one point where the Y-coordinate is locally maximized, and one where it is locally minimized. With some technical tricks, we can make sure that all the pieces are bounded. If we then compute all the local maxima and minima of $\mathcal{F}$ in Y, we are guaranteed to get at least one point

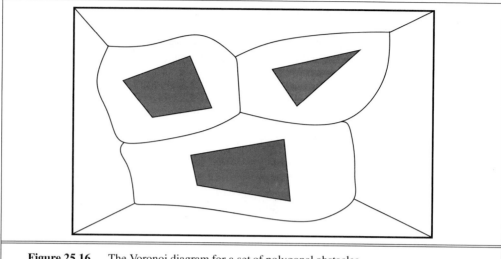

Figure 25.16   The Voronoi diagram for a set of polygonal obstacles.

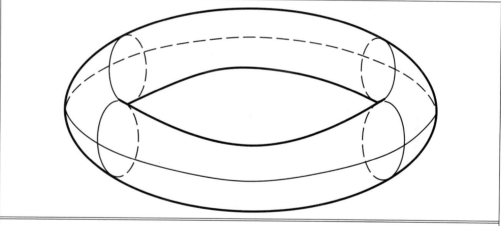

Figure 25.17   A roadmap of a torus, showing one horizontal freeway and four vertical bridges.

in every connected piece of $\mathcal{F}$'s cross section. See Figure 25.17. To get silhouette curves from these extremal points, we simply allow c to vary, and follow the extremal points in Y as the plane $X = c$ moves through $\mathcal{F}$.

- Linking curves join **critical points** to silhouette curves. Critical points are points where the cross section $X = c$ changes abruptly as c varies. By referring to Figure 25.17, the reader will find two critical points where the cross-section changes. If the critical point has X-coordinate c_0, then for $X < c_0$, the cross-section is an hourglass-shaped curve. For $X > c_0$ side, the hourglass has pinched off into two circles. We will call a slice $X = c$ containing a critical point a "critical slice." Linking curves can be defined several ways, but the easiest is to define a linking curve as the roadmap of a critical slice. Because roadmaps are defined in terms of linking curves, this is a circular definition. But because the linking curve is a roadmap of a slice that has one less dimension, the recursive construction is well-defined and terminates after a number of steps that equals the dimension of $\mathcal{C}$.

One disadvantage of this definition is that it gives curves on the boundary of free space. This is undesirable from both efficiency and safety perspectives. A slightly better definition borrows some ideas from Voronoi diagrams. Instead of using extremals in Y to define the silhouette curves, it uses *extremals of distance from obstacles in slices $X = c$*. This sounds like the same definition as the Voronoi diagram, but there are slight differences in two dimensions, and major differences in more than two. The definition of linking curves also changes. They still link critical points to silhouette curves, but this time, linking curves are computed by moving away from a critical point along curves that follow the direction of maximum increase of the distance function. In other words, start from a critical point, and hill-climb in configuration space to a local maximum of the distance function. That point lies on a silhouette curve under the new definition. This kind of roadmap is exemplified in Figure 25.18.

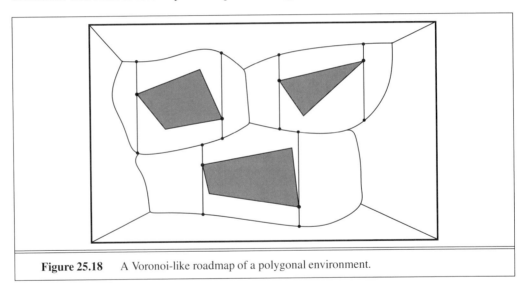

Figure 25.18   A Voronoi-like roadmap of a polygonal environment.

Fine-motion planning

Fine-motion planning (FMP) is about planning small, precise motions for assembly. At the distance scales appropriate for FMP, the environment is not precisely known. Furthermore, the robot is unable to measure or control its position accurately. Dealing with these uncertainties is the principal concern of FMP. Like online algorithms, fine-motion plans are strategies or policies that make use of sensing or environment shape to determine the robot's path at run time. However, whereas online algorithms assume nothing about the environment, partial knowledge is available to the fine-motion planner. This knowledge includes explicit models of the uncertainties in sensing, control, and environment shape. A fine-motion planner does most of its work offline, generating a strategy that should work in all situations consistent with its models.

A fine-motion plan consists of a series of **guarded motions**. Each guarded motion consists of (1) a motion command and (2) a termination condition, which is a predicate on the robot's sensor values, and returns true to indicate the end of the guarded move. The motion commands are typically **compliant motions** that allow the robot to slide if the motion command would cause collision with an obstacle. Compliant motion requires a dynamic model such as a spring or damper. The spring model is the simplest to understand. Rather than moving the robot itself, imagine moving one end of a spring with the other end attached to the robot. The damper model is similar but instead of a spring, a device called a damper is attached to the robot. Whereas the spring gives a reaction force proportional to relative displacement of its endpoints, the damper gives a reaction force proportional to relative velocity. Both allow the robot to slide on a surface so long as the commanded velocity is not directly into the surface. (In reality, there will be some friction between robot and obstacle, and the robot will not move even if the commanded velocity is close to right angles with the surface.)

As an example, Figure 25.19 shows a 2-D configuration space with a narrow vertical hole. It could be the configuration space for insertion of a rectangular peg into a hole that is slightly larger. The motion commands are constant velocities. The termination conditions are contact with a surface. To model uncertainty in control, we assume that instead of moving at the commanded velocity, the robot's actual motion lies in the cone C_v about it. The figure shows what would happen if we commanded a velocity straight down from the start region s. Because of the uncertainty in velocity, the robot could move anywhere in the conical envelope, possibly going into the hole, but more likely landing to one side of it. Because the robot would not then know which side of the hole it was on, it would not know which way to move.

A more sensible strategy is shown in Figures 25.20 and 25.21. In Figure 25.20, the robot deliberately moves to one side of the hole. The motion command is shown in the figure, and the termination test is contact with any surface. In Figure 25.21, a motion command is given that causes the robot to slide along the surface and into the hole. This assumes we use a compliant motion command. Because all possible velocities in the motion envelope are to the right, the robot will slide to the right whenever it is in contact with a horizontal surface. It will slide down the right-hand vertical edge of the hole when it touches it, because all possible velocities are down relative to a vertical surface. It will keep moving until it reaches the bottom of the hole, because that is its termination condition. In spite of the control uncertainty, all possible trajectories of the robot terminate in contact with the bottom of the hole. (That is, unless friction or irregularities in the surface causes the robot to stick in one place.)

As one might imagine, the problem of *constructing* fine-motion plans is not trivial; in fact, it is a good deal harder than planning with exact motions. One can either choose a fixed number of discrete values for each motion or use the environment geometry to choose directions that give qualitatively different behavior. A fine-motion planner takes as input the configuration-space description, the angle of the velocity uncertainty cone, and a specification of what sensing is possible for termination (surface contact in this case). It should produce a multistep conditional plan or policy that is guaranteed to succeed, if such a plan exists.

We did not include uncertainty in the environment in our example, but there is one elegant way to do it. If the variation can be described in terms of parameters, those parameters can

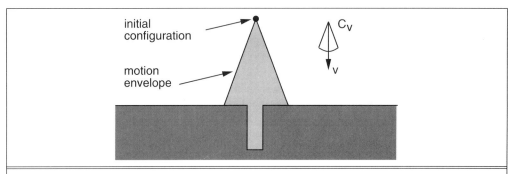

Figure 25.19   A 2-D environment, velocity uncertainty cone, and envelope of possible robot motions. The intended velocity is *v*, but with uncertainty the actual velocity could be anywhere in C_v, resulting in a final configuration somewhere in the motion envelope, which means we wouldn't know if we hit the hole or not.

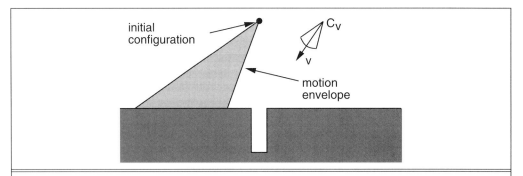

Figure 25.20   The first motion command and the resulting envelope of possible robot motions. No matter what the error, we know the final configuration will be to the left of the hole.

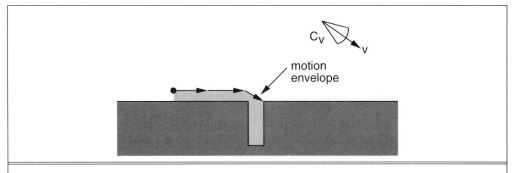

Figure 25.21   The second motion command and the envelope of possible motions. Even with error, we will eventually get into the hole.

be added as degrees of freedom to the configuration space. In the last example, if the depth and width of the hole were uncertain, we could add them as two degrees of freedom to the configuration space. It is impossible to move the robot in these directions in $\mathcal{C}$ or to sense its position directly. But both those restrictions can be incorporated when describing this problem as an FMP problem by appropriately specifying control and sensor uncertainties. This gives a complex, four-dimensional planning problem, but exactly the same planning techniques can be applied. Notice that unlike the decision-theoretic methods in Chapter 17, this kind of approach results in plans designed for the worst case outcome, rather than maximizing the expected quality of the plan. Worst-case plans are only optimal in the decision-theoretic sense if failure during execution is much worse than any of the other costs involved in execution.

Unfortunately, the complexity of fine-motion planning is extremely high. It grows exponentially not only with the dimension of configuration space, but also with the number of steps in the plan. FMP as described earlier also involves some tenuous assumptions about control and sensor uncertainty, uncertainty in environment shape, and capabilities of the run-time system. On the other hand, the FMP methodology can be applied to mobile robot navigation, and its assumptions seem more reasonable there. We will see some examples of this in the next section.

Landmark-based navigation

In the last two sections, we saw motion planning extended to include run-time decisions based on sensing. The sensors were assumed to be simple position or contact sensors, and to provide uniform accuracy across the environment. More complex sensors, such as vision and sonar, have very different attributes. It is much more difficult to model these sensors in a reasonable way, but we will present a couple of recent approaches.

LANDMARKS

In the first, called the **landmark model** of sensing, we assume that the environment contains easily recognizable, unique **landmarks**. A landmark is modeled as a point with a surrounding circular **field of influence**. Within the field of influence, the robot is able to know its position exactly. If the robot is outside all the fields of influence, it has no direct position information. This model might seem unrealistic at first, but it is good model for landmarks such as bar codes. Bar codes, like the ones on supermarket items, are sometimes used as landmarks for mobile robots in indoor environments. They are placed in strategic locations on walls, a few feet above the floor. They have unique codes enabling each to be distinguished. As long as the robot is close enough to recognize a bar code, it can get a good estimate of distance from that landmark. Getting good angular data is harder, but some estimate can be computed. Beyond the range of recognition of the code, the robot cannot get any information from it.

The robot's control is assumed to be imperfect. When it is commanded to move in a direction v, we assume the actual motion lies in a cone of paths centered on v. This is the same uncertainty model that we used in the last section. It is a very reasonable one for mobile robots. If the robot has a gyroscope or magnetic compass, the errors in its motion will be offsets in direction from the commanded motion. This is exactly what the uncertainty cone models.

An environment with landmarks is shown in Figure 25.22. This environment is known at planning time, but not the robot's position. We assume though that the robot lies somewhere inside a region (rectangular in the figure) that we do know. We plan a strategy for the robot by working backwards from the goal. Figure 25.22 shows a commanded velocity v, and the **backprojection** of the goal region with respect to v. If the robot starts anywhere in the backprojection and moves with commanded velocity v, it will definitely reach the goal disk. Notice that the backprojection intersects a landmark D_1. Because D_1 is the field of influence of a landmark, the robot has perfect position sensing inside D_1. So if it reaches any part of D_1, it can move reliably to the part of D_1 that intersects the backprojection of the goal. From there it can move in direction v to the goal.

This means that the robot can reach the goal from a region R if it can move reliably from R straight to the goal or if it can move reliably from R to disk D_1. Continuing to work backwards, Figure 25.23 shows a backprojection of the union of the goal and D_1 relative to velocity command u. This new backprojection contains the start region S. This gives us a guaranteed strategy for reaching the goal. The execution of this strategy would be (1) move in direction u to D_1 and then (2) move in direction v to the goal.

As for fine-motion planning, we must choose these velocities by searching all possibilities. Fortunately, in this case, we do not have an exponential blowup with the number of plan steps. This is because the backprojections all have the same form, namely, they are backprojections of unions of disks. This gives a polynomial bound on the number of qualitatively different motion command directions. By using this observation, it is possible to plan in time that is polynomial in the number of disks. The plan itself will have at most n steps if there are n landmarks, because no landmark need be visited more than once. This planning method is both sound and complete.

Online algorithms

Most robot applications have to deal with some amount of uncertainty about the environment. Even robots used for manufacturing, which may have complete geometric models of robot and environment, have to perform high-precision tasks such as assembly. Assembly may require motions of a thousandth of an inch or less, and at this scale, models are far from accurate. *When the environment is poorly known, it is impossible to plan a path for the robot that will be collision-free and reach a goal under all circumstances.*

ONLINE ALGORITHM

Instead, one can try to produce a **conditional plan** (in the language of Chapter 13) or **policy** (in the language of Chapter 17) that will make decisions at run time. In some cases, it is possible to compute such a plan with no knowledge of the environment at all. This avoids the need for an offline planning stage, and all choices are made at run time. We will call such an algorithm an **online algorithm**. Online algorithms need to be simple, because they must make choices in real time. For that reason, they cannot "remember" much about their environment.

Despite their simplicity, online algorithms have been found that are both complete and "efficient." Efficiency for online algorithms can be defined in different ways. Because it depends on the environment, it must depend on measures of the environment's complexity. In Figure 25.24 we see a two-dimensional environment with start and goals points. The environment is not known to the robot when it begins, and it cannot "see" anything. It can only sense a boundary when it runs into it. The robot is equipped with a position sensor, and it knows where the goal is. Here is one complete online strategy:

1. Let l be the straight line joining the initial position of the robot with its goal position. The robot begins to move toward the goal along l.

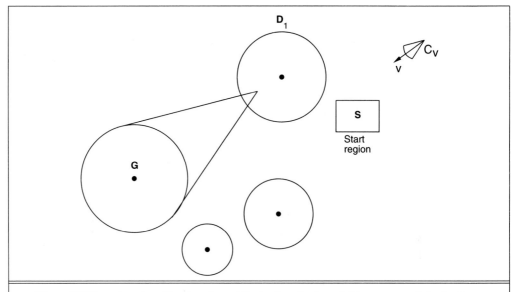

Figure 25.22   A series of landmarks and the backprojection of G for commanded velocity v.

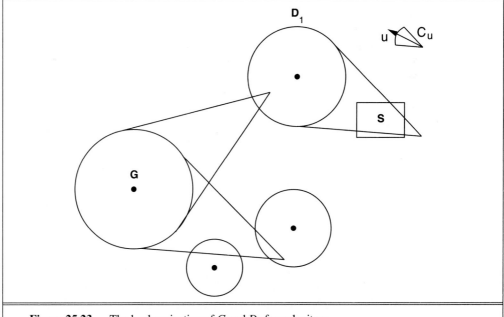

Figure 25.23   The backprojection of G and D_1 for velocity u.

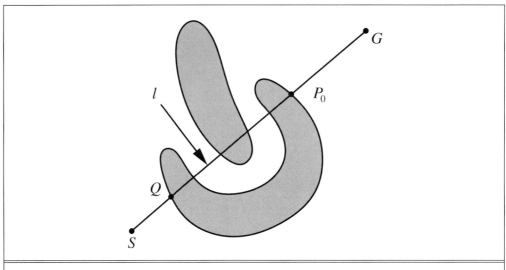

Figure 25.24   A two-dimensional environment, robot, and goal.

2. If the robot encounters an obstacle before it reaches the goal, it stops and records its current position Q. The robot then walks around the obstacle clockwise (the direction is not important) back to Q. During this walk, the robot records points where it crosses the line l, and how far it has walked to reach them. After the walk, let P_0 be the closest such point to the goal.

3. The robot then walks around the obstacle from Q to P_0. Because it knows how far it walked to reach P_0, it can decide whether it will get to P_0 faster by going clockwise or counterclockwise. Once it reaches P_0, it starts moving toward the goal along l, and continues until it reaches another obstacle (in which case, it executes step 2 again) or until it reaches the goal.

COMPETITIVE RATIO

Online algorithms such as this are usually very fast in terms of computation time, but almost always give up any guarantee of finding the shortest path. Their efficiency is often measured using a **competitive ratio**. In the case of robot motion, one typically uses the worst-case ratio between the actual length of the path found, and the shortest path. For example, the preceding algorithm has a competitive ratio of at most $1 + 1.5B/|l|$, where B is the sum of the lengths of all the obstacle boundaries and $|l|$ is the length of the line l from start to goal.

It is fairly easy to see that this ratio can be very bad in some cases. For example, if an enormous obstacle protrudes just a teeny bit into the straight-line path, and the robot happens to start walking around it the wrong way, then the ratio can be unbounded. For some special cases, there are algorithms with competitive ratios bounded by a constant (Exercise 25.12), but there are some environments for which no algorithm has a finite competitive ratio. Fortunately for humans, these do not occur often in practice.

25.7 SUMMARY

Robotics is a challenging field for two reasons. First, it requires hardware (sensors and effectors) that actually work, a real challenge for mechanical engineering. Second, robots have to work in the physical world, which is more complex than most of the simulated software worlds that we have used for our examples in other chapters. Some robots finesse this problem by operating in a restricted environment. But modern autonomous robots with sophisticated sensors and effectors provide a challenging testbed for determining what it takes to build an intelligent agent.

- In general, the physical world is inaccessible, nondeterministic, nonepisodic, and dynamic.
- Robots have made an economic impact in many industries, and show promise for exploring hazardous and remote environments.
- Robots consist of a body with rigid **links** connected to each other by **joints**. The movement of the links is characterized by the degrees of freedom of the joints.
- Robots can have sensors of various types, including vision, force sensing, tactile (touch) sensing, sonar, and a sense of where their own body parts are.
- In a dynamic world, it is important to be able to take action quickly. Robots are designed with this in mind.
- The problem of moving a complex-shaped object (i.e., the robot and anything it is carrying) through a space with complex-shaped obstacles is a difficult one. The mathematical notion of a **configuration space** provides a framework for analysis.
- **Cell decomposition** and **skeletonization** methods can be used to navigate through the configuration space. Both reduce a high-dimensional, continuous space to a discrete graph-search problem.
- Some aspects of the world, such as the exact location of a bolt in the robot's hand, will always be unknown. **Fine-motion planning** deals with this uncertainty by creating a sensor-based plan that will work regardless of the exact initial conditions.
- Uncertainty applies to sensors at the large scale as well. In the **landmark model**, a robot uses certain well-known landmarks in the environment to determine where it is, even in the face of uncertainty.
- If a map of the environment is not available, then the robot will have to plan its navigation as it goes. **Online algorithms** do this. They do not always choose the shortest route, but we can analyze how far off they will be.

BIBLIOGRAPHICAL AND HISTORICAL NOTES

The word **robot** was popularized by Czech playwright Karel Capek in his 1921 play *R.U.R.* (Rossum's Universal Robots). The theme of the play—the dehumanization of mankind in a technological society—appealed to audiences in war-torn Europe and the United States. The robots, which were grown chemically rather than constructed mechanically, end up resenting their masters and decide to take over. It appears (Glanc, 1978) that it was actually Capek's brother, Josef, who first combined the Czech words "robota" (obligatory work) and "robotnik" (serf) to yield "robot" in his 1917 short story *Opilec*.

Reichardt (1978) surveys the history and future of robots, grouping them into four categories: (1) strictly mythological, fictional, or fraudulent; (2) working, but nonelectronic; (3) controlled by very special-purpose electronic or electromechanical hardware; (4) controlled by general-purpose computers. Brief accounts of early robots of all four kinds are given by Raphael(1976), McCorduck (1979), and Heppenheimer (1985); more detailed treatments are given by Cohen (1966) and Chapuis and Droz (1958). The most famous classical instances of the first type are Talos (supposedly designed and built by Hephaistos, the Greek god of metallurgy) and the Golem of Prague. Perhaps the first impressive example of the second type was Jacques Vaucanson's mechanical duck, unveiled in 1738. An early instance of the third type is Torres y Quevedo's electromechanical automaton for playing the chess endgame of king and rook vs. king, described in Chapter 5. In the 1890s, Nikola Tesla built some experimental vehicles that were teleoperated (or remote controlled) via radio. Grey Walter's "turtle," built in 1948, could be considered the first modern type three robot.

In the late 1950s, George Engelberger and George Devol developed the first useful industrial robots, starting with type three, and moving on to type four. Engelberger founded Unimation to market them, and earned the title "father of robotics." His *Robotics in Practice* (1980) is a good survey of the early days of industrial robots. In the mid-1980s, there was a surge of interest in the field, largely funded by automotive companies. Reality did not live up to expectations, and there was a major shakeout in the robotics industry in the late 1980s. Perhaps in reaction to this shakeout, Engelberger's *Robotics in Service* (1989) is much more sanguine about the imminent practicality of type four robots in industrial settings.

Type four robots can be further divided into mobile robots (or mobots) and static manipulators, originally called **hand-eye machines**. The first modern mobile robot was the "Hopkins Beast," built in the early 1960s at Johns Hopkins University. It had pattern-recognition hardware and could recognize the cover plate of a standard AC power outlet. It was capable of searching for outlets, plugging itself in, and then recharging its batteries! Still, the Beast had a limited repertoire of skills. The first general-purpose mobot was "Shakey," developed at SRI International from 1966 through 1972 (Nilsson, 1984).

The first major effort at creating a hand-eye machine was Heinrich Ernst's MH-1, described in his MIT Ph.D. thesis (Ernst, 1961) and in a retrospective by Taylor (1989). The Machine Intelligence project at Edinburgh (Michie, 1972) also demonstrated an impressive early system for vision-based assembly called FREDDY.

Robotics engages virtually every component and subfield of AI. Some areas of AI were originally driven primarily by the demands of robotics, although they have since become separate areas of study. The main two are computer vision (and other forms of perception) and planning. The Shakey robot project at SRI, in particular, was seminal in the development of the techniques of planning. There are also several problem areas that are unique to robotics. Planning in continuous state spaces is usually restricted to robotics. Sensor and motion errors are taken much more seriously in robotics, although they are also studied for military applications. Also, quite apart from perception and planning, it is far from trivial simply to describe the motions

HAND-EYE
MACHINES

one wishes a robot arm (for instance) to undertake, and then design physical devices and control systems to carry out the motions described. The mechanics and control of multilink robot arms are among the most complex problems studied in applied mathematics today.

Robot Manipulators: Mathematics, Programming, and Control (Paul, 1981) is a classic guide to the basics of robot arm design. Yoshikawa (1990) provides a more up-to-date text in this area. Latombe (1991) presents a good specialized textbook on motion planning. The robot motion planning problem, stated in the most natural way, is PSPACE-hard (Reif, 1979) (see page 853 for a description of PSPACE). Canny (1988) gives a book-length treatment of the computational complexity of robot motion planning, dealing with a number of ways of stating the problem. The major conference for robotics is the *IEEE International Conference on Robotics and Automation*. Robotics journals include *IEEE Robotics and Automation*, the *International Journal of Robotics Research*, and *Robotics and Autonomous Systems*.

EXERCISES

25.1   (This exercise was first devised by Michael Genesereth and Nils Nilsson.) Humans are so adept at basic tasks such as picking up cups or stacking blocks that they often forget what it was like to try such things as newborn babies. The idea of this exercise is to make explicit some of the difficulties involved, in a very direct manner. As you solve these difficulties, you should find yourself recapitulating the last 20 years of developments in robotics.

First, pick a task. The task should not be too difficult! (For example, making a column from three cereal boxes standing on end takes over an hour.) Set up the initial environment. Then, build a robot out of four other humans as follows:

⬦ **Brain**: the job of the Brain is to come up with a plan to achieve the goal, and to direct the hands in the execution of the plan. The Brain receives input from the Eyes, but *cannot see the scene directly*.

⬦ **Eyes**: the Eyes' job is to report a brief description of the scene to the Brain. The Eyes should stand a few feet away from the working environment, and can provide qualitative descriptions (such as "There is a red box standing on top of a green box, which is on its side") or quantitative descriptions ("The green box is about two feet to the left of the blue cylinder"). Eyes can also answer questions from the Brain such as, "Is there a gap between the Left Hand and the red box?" The Eyes *should not know what the goal is*.

⬦ **Hands** (Left and Right): one person plays each Hand. The two Hands stand next to each other; the Left Hand uses only his or her left hand, and the Right Hand only his or her right hand. The Hands execute only simple commands from the Brain—for example, "Left Hand, move two inches forward." They cannot execute commands other than motions; for example, "Pick up the box" is not something a Hand can do. To discourage cheating, you might want to have the hands wear gloves, or have them operate tongs. As well as being ignorant of the goal, the Hands must be *blindfolded*. The only sensory capability they have is the ability to tell when their path is blocked by an immovable obstacle such as a table or the other Hand. In such cases, they can beep to inform the Brain of the difficulty.

We have given only the most basic protocol. As the task unfolds, you may find that more complex protocols are needed in order to make any progress. What you learn about robotics will depend very much on the task chosen and on how closely you stick to the protocols.

25.2   Design and sketch a mobile robot for an office environment. Your robot should be able to perform typical office tasks like retrieving files, books, journals, and mail, and photocopying. What types of arm/hand did you choose? Consider carefully the trade-off between flexibility and custom design for those tasks. What kinds of sensing did you choose?

25.3   Consider the problem of designing a robot that will keep an office building tidy by periodically collecting and emptying bins and picking up empty cans and paper cups.

  a. Describe an appropriate physical design for the robot.

  b. Define a suitable performance evaluation measure.

  c. Propose an overall architecture for the robot agent. Mitchell (1990) and Brooks (1989) describe two different approaches to the problem.

25.4   Calculate the number of degrees of freedom of your hand, with the forearm fixed.

25.5   Consider the arm of a record player as a two-link robot. Let θ_1 measure the elevation of the arm, and θ_2 measure its horizontal rotation. Sketch the configuration space of this robot with θ_1 and θ_2 axes. Include the configuration space obstacles for the platter and spindle.

25.6   Draw the cylindrical cell decomposition for the environment in Figure 25.25. With n boards in such an arrangement, how many regions would there be in the cell decomposition?

25.7   If you have not done them already, do Exercises 4.13 to 4.15. Also answer the following:

  a. Prove rigorously that shortest paths in two dimensions with convex polygonal obstacles lie on the visibility graph.

  b. Does this result hold in three dimensions? If so, prove it. If not, provide a counterexample.

  c. Can you suggest (and prove) a result for the shortest paths in two dimensions with *curved* obstacles?

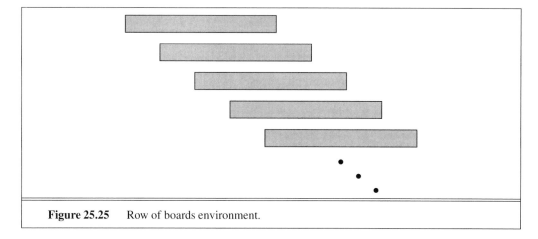

Figure 25.25   Row of boards environment.

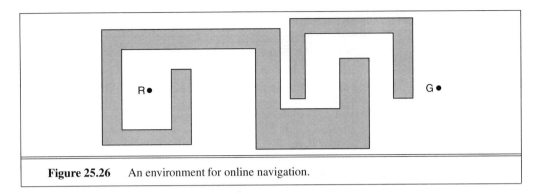

Figure 25.26   An environment for online navigation.

d. Can the two-dimensional path-planning problem be solved using Voronoi diagrams instead of visibility graphs? Explain the modifications that would be needed to the overall system.

25.8   Suppose a robot can see two point landmarks L_1 and L_2, and that it measures the angle between them as $17°$. What is the shape of the recognizable set corresponding to this sensor reading? What is the shape of the recognizable set if the angle measurement has an uncertainty of $\pm 1°$? Sketch this situation.

25.9   For the environment in Figure 25.26, sketch the path taken by the robot in executing the online navigation strategy. This strategy always completely circumnavigates any obstacle it encounters, which is often unnecessary. Try to think of another strategy that will travel less distance around some obstacles. Make sure your strategy will not get stuck in cycles. Your strategy will probably have a worse worst-case bound than the one presented in this chapter, but should be faster in typical cases.

25.10   Implement a general environment in which to exercise the online navigation algorithm, such that arbitrary obstacles can be placed in the environment. Construct a specific environment corresponding to Figure 25.26. Then implement an agent that incorporates the online algorithm, and show that it works.

25.11   Explain how to approach the problem of online navigation for a cylindrical robot of significant diameter. Does the point-robot algorithm need to be modified? What happens when the robot is heading down a passageway that becomes too narrow to get through?

25.12   We stated in our discussion of online algorithms that some special classes of environments are amenable to online algorithms with constant competitive ratios. An example is shown in Figure 25.27, which shows a robot on the bank of a river. We assume that the robot has an exact position sensor. The robot is trying to find the bridge, which it knows is somewhere nearby, but is not sure how far and in which direction. Unfortunately, there is a thick fog and the robot cannot see the bridge unless it stumbles right onto it.

a. Describe an online algorithm for the robot that is guaranteed to find the bridge after a finite search, no matter where the bridge is.

b. Calculate the total distance traversed by the robot using your algorithm, and compute its competitive ratio.

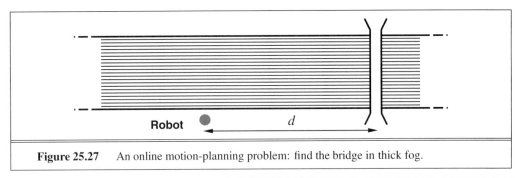

Figure 25.27   An online motion-planning problem: find the bridge in thick fog.

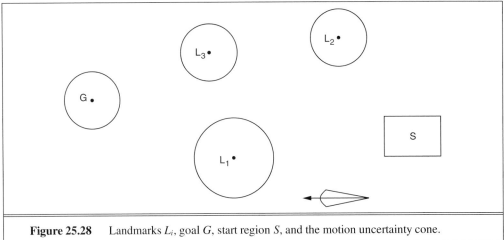

Figure 25.28   Landmarks L_i, goal G, start region S, and the motion uncertainty cone.

25.13   For the environment and motion uncertainty cone shown in Figure 25.28, find a navigation strategy that is guaranteed to reach the goal G.

25.14   Here are the three laws of robotics from the science fiction book *I, Robot* (Asimov, 1950):

> 1. A robot may not injure a human being or through inaction allow a human being to come to harm.
> 2. A robot must obey the orders given to it by human beings except where such orders would conflict with the first law.
> 3. A robot must protect its own existence as long as such protection does not conflict with the first or second law.

So far, only a few attempts have been made to build such safeguards into robotic software (Weld and Etzioni, 1994).

> **a**. How would you design a robot to obey these laws? What type of architecture would be best? What aspects of the laws are hard to obey?
>
> **b**. Are the laws sensible? That is, if it were possible to build a sophisticated robot, would you want it to be governed by them? Can you think of a better set of laws?

Part VIII

CONCLUSIONS

In this part we summarize what has come before, and give our views of what the future of AI is likely to hold. We also delve into the philosophical foundations of AI, which have been quietly assumed in the previous parts.

26 PHILOSOPHICAL FOUNDATIONS

In which we consider what it means to think and to be conscious, and whether artifacts could ever do such things.

26.1 THE BIG QUESTIONS

As we mentioned in Chapter 1, philosophers have been around for much longer than computers, and have been trying to resolve many of the same questions that AI and cognitive science claim to address: How *can* minds work, how *do* human minds work, and can nonhumans have minds? For most of the book we have concentrated on getting AI to work at all, but in this chapter, we address the big questions.

Sometimes the questions have led philosophers and AI researchers to square off in heated debate. More often, the philosophers have debated each other. Some philosophers have sided with the computational approach provided by artificial intelligence, partly because it has the tools and the inclination to give detailed, causal explanations of intelligent behavior:[1]

> It is rather as if philosophers were to proclaim themselves expert explainers of the methods of a stage magician, and then, when we ask them to explain how the magician does the sawing-the-lady-in-half trick, they explain that it is really quite obvious: the magician doesn't really saw her in half; he simply makes it appear that he does. "But how does he do *that*?" we ask. "Not our department," say the philosophers. (Dennett, 1984)

> ... among philosophers of science one finds an assumption that machines can do everything that people can do, followed by an attempt to interpret what this bodes for the philosophy of mind; while among moralists and theologians one finds a last-ditch retrenchment to such highly sophisticated behavior as moral choice, love and creative discovery, claimed to be beyond the scope of any machine. (Dreyfus, 1972)

---

[1] At a recent meeting of the American Philosophical Association, it was put to us by one philosopher, who may prefer to remain nameless, that "Philosophy has already capitulated to AI."

817

Other philosophers have openly derided the efforts of AI researchers and, by implication, their philosophical fellow travellers:

> Artificial intelligence *pursued within the cult of computationalism* stands not even a ghost of a chance of producing durable results ... it is time to divert the efforts of AI researchers—and the considerable monies made available for their support—into avenues other than the computational approach. (Sayre, 1993)

> After fifty years of effort, however, it is clear to all but a few diehards that this attempt to produce general intelligence has failed. (Dreyfus, 1992)

The nature of philosophy is such that clear disagreements can continue to exist unresolved for many years. If there were any simple experiment that could resolve the disagreements, the issues would not be of philosophical interest.

We will begin in Section 26.2 by looking at those areas of philosophical investigation in which AI and philosophy are on the same team, so to speak—the "how to" questions concerning the basic capabilities of perception, learning, and reasoning. This will help to clarify the concepts used later.

In Section 26.3, we look at the question "Can machines be made to act *as if* they were intelligent?" The assertion that they can is called the **weak AI** position. Arguments against weak AI make one of these three claims:

WEAK AI

- There are things that computers cannot do, no matter how we program them.

- Certain ways of designing intelligent programs are bound to fail in the long run.

- The task of *constructing* the appropriate programs is infeasible.

The arguments can be, and sometimes have been, refuted by exhibiting a program with the supposedly unattainable capabilities. On the other hand, by making AI researchers think more carefully about their unstated assumptions, the arguments have contributed to a more robust methodology for AI.

STRONG AI

In Section 26.4, we take on the real bone of contention: the **strong AI** position, which claims that machines that act intelligently have real, conscious minds. Debates about strong AI bring up some of the most difficult conceptual problems in philosophy.

Note that one could legitimately believe in strong AI but not weak AI. It is perfectly consistent to believe that it is infeasible to build machines that act intelligently, but to be willing to grant such a machine full consciousness if it could in fact ever be built.

We will try to present the arguments in their simplest forms, while preserving the lunges and parries that characterize philosophical debates. We do not have space to do them full justice, and we encourage the reader to consult the original sources. A caution: one of the most important things to keep in mind when reading the contributions to a philosophical debate is that what often appears to be an attempt to refute some proposition (such as "computers understand English") is actually an attempt to refute a particular *justification* for the proposition, or an attempt to show that the proposition is merely possible rather than logically necessary. Thus, many of the debates are not what they may seem at first, but there is still plenty to argue about.

26.2 FOUNDATIONS OF REASONING AND PERCEPTION

PHYSICALISM

MATERIALISM

BIOLOGICAL
NATURALISM

Almost all parties to the AI debate share a certain amount of common ground regarding the relation of brain and mind. The common ground goes under various names—**physicalism**, **materialism**, and **biological naturalism** among others —but it can be reduced to the characteristically pithy remark by John Searle: *"Brains cause minds."* Intelligence and mental phenomena are products of the operation of the physical system of neurons and their associated cells and support structures.

This doctrine has a number of corollaries. Perhaps the most important is that mental states—such as being in pain, knowing that one is riding a horse, or believing that Vienna is the capital of Austria—are brain states. This does not commit one to very much, other than to avoid speculation about nonphysical processes beyond the ken of science. The next step is to abstract away from specific brain states. One must allow that different brain states can correspond to the same mental state, provided they are of the *same type*. Various authors have various positions on what one means by *type* in this case. Almost everyone believes that if one takes a brain and replaces some of the carbon atoms by a new set of carbon atoms,[2] the mental state will not be affected. This is a good thing because real brains are continually replacing their atoms through metabolic processes, and yet this in itself does not seem to cause major mental upheavals.

FUNCTIONALISM

Functionalism, on the other hand, proposes a much looser definition of "same type," based on identity of the functional properties of the components of the brain—that is, their input/output specifications. In the neural version of functionalism,[3] what matters is the input/output properties of the neurons, not their physical properties. Because the same input/output properties can be realized by many different physical devices, including silicon devices, functionalism naturally leads to the belief that AI systems with the appropriate structure might have real mental states.

HOMUNCULI

Now we begin to explain *how* it is that brains cause minds. Some of the earliest forms of explanation involved what are now called **homunculi**—a Latin term meaning "miniature men." For example, when it was found that a small image of the world was formed on the retina by the lens, some early philosophers proposed that vision was achieved by a subsystem of the brain—a homunculus—that looked at this image and reported what it saw.[4] Unfortunately, one then has

INFINITE REGRESS

to explain how it is that the homunculus can see. An **infinite regress** begins when one proposes that the homunculus sees by means of a smaller homunculus inside his head.

Modern proponents of rule-based models of human behavior have been accused of falling into the same infinite regress trap. The objection goes as follows: every use of a logical rule (such as "all men are mortal") must itself be governed by a rule (such as Modus Ponens). The application of a rule such as Modus Ponens must in turn be governed by another rule, and so on *ad infinitum*. Therefore, intelligent behavior cannot be produced by following rules. Now this argument has a certain superficial plausibility, particularly if we note that the forward-chaining application of inference rules such as Modus Ponens indeed can be viewed as itself an application

---

[2] Perhaps even atoms of a different isotope of carbon, as is sometimes done in brain-scanning experiments.

[3] There are other versions of functionalism that make the decomposition at different points. In general, there is a wide range of choices in what counts as a component.

[4] Proponents of this theory were excited by the discovery of the pineal gland, which in many mammals looks superficially like an eye. Closer examination of course revealed that it has no powers of vision.

of Modus Ponens at a higher level. Clearly, however, logical systems do manage to work without infinite regress. This is because at some point, the rule application process is *fixed*; for example, in Prolog, the process of left-to-right, depth-first chaining applies to all inferences. Although this process *could* be implemented by a meta-Prolog interpreter, there is no need because it is not subject to alteration. This means that it can be implemented directly by a physical process, based on the actual operation of the laws of physics, rather than the application of rules representing those laws. The physical implementation of the reasoning system serves as the base case that terminates the regress before it becomes infinite. There is therefore no in-principle philosophical difficulty in seeing how a machine can operate as a reasoning system to achieve intelligent behavior. There is a practical difficulty: the system designer must show both that the rules will lead to the right inferences, and that the reasoning system (the fixed, physical instantiation) correctly implements the metalevel reasoning rules.

So much for intelligent behavior, at least for now. What about mental states? How do we explain their possession by humans, and do machines have them? We will first consider propositional attitudes, which are also known as **intentional states**. These are states, such as believing, knowing, desiring, fearing, and so on, that refer to some aspect of the external world. For example, the belief that Vienna is the capital of Austria is a belief *about* a particular city and its status (or if you prefer, a belief about a proposition which is in turn about a city). The question is, when can one say that a given entity has such a belief?

One approach is to adopt what Daniel Dennett (1971) has called the **intentional stance** toward the entity. On this view, ascribing beliefs or desires to entities is no more than a calcula-tional device that allows one to predict the entity's behavior. For example, a thermostat can be said to desire that room temperature be maintained in a certain range, and to believe that the room is currently too cold and that switching on the heat increases the room temperature (McCarthy and Hayes, 1969). It is then reasonable to ascribe intentional states when that provides the most succinct explanatory model for the entity's behavior. As mentioned in Chapter 1, this is similar to ascribing pressure to a volume of gas. However, the thermostat's "belief" that the room is too cold is not identical to the corresponding belief held by a person. The thermostat's sensors only allow it to distinguish three states in the world, which we might call *Hot*, *OK*, and *Cold*. It can have no conception of a room, nor of heat for that matter. "The room is too cold" is simply a way of naming the proposition in which the thermostat is said to believe.

The "intentional stance" view has the advantage of being based solely on the entity's behavior and not on any supposed internal structures that might constitute "beliefs." This is also a disadvantage, because any given behavior can be implemented in many different ways. The intentional stance cannot distinguish among the implementations. For some implementations, there are no structures that might even be candidates for representations of the ascribed beliefs or desires. For example, if a chess program is implemented as an enormous lookup table, then it does not seem reasonable to suppose that the program *actually* believes that it is going to capture the opponent's queen; whereas a human with identical chess behavior might well have such a belief. The question of *actual* intentional states is still a real one.

The intentional stance allows us to avoid paradoxes and clashes of intuition (such as being forced to say that thermostats have beliefs). This makes us all feel more comfortable, but it is not necessarily the right scientific approach. Intuitions can change, and paradoxes can be resolved. The hypothesis that the earth revolves around the sun was once called "the Copernican paradox"

INTENTIONAL STATES

INTENTIONAL STANCE

precisely because it clashed with the intuitions afforded by the folk cosmology of the time. We may find out that our current folk psychology is so far off base that it is giving us similar kinds of faulty intuitions.

CORRESPONDENCE
THEORY

The **correspondence theory** of belief goes somewhat further toward a realistic account. According to this theory, an internal structure in an agent is a reasonable candidate for a representation of a proposition if the following conditions hold:

1. The structure is formed when sensory evidence for the truth of the proposition is obtained.
2. The structure ceases to exist when sensory evidence for the proposition's falsehood is obtained.
3. The structure plays the appropriate causal role in the selection of actions.

Thus, the internal structure acts as a "flag" that correlates with the external proposition.

GROUNDING

The correspondence theory contains the crucial element of **grounding**—the agent's beliefs are grounded in its sensory experience of the world. Grounding is often viewed as essential to the possession of intentional states. For example, before an agent can be said to be dying for a hamburger, it must have some direct experience of hamburgers, or at least of related comestibles. It is not enough that its knowledge base contain the sentence *DyingFor*(*Me, Hamburger*). However, if the sentence gets there "in the right way"—that is, through experience of hamburgers and so

CAUSAL SEMANTICS

on —then we say it has the appropriate **causal semantics**. It has meaning relating to hamburgers because of its connection to actual hamburger experiences.

WIDE CONTENT

There are two views on the sense in which an internal representation has actual meaning. The first view, called **wide content**, has it that the internal representation *intrinsically* refers to some aspect of the outside world; that is, there is some connection between the internal representation and the external world that exists by the nature of the representation. For example, the internal state corresponding to the belief that "This hamburger is delicious" intrinsically refers to the particular hamburger that it is "about." The second view, called **narrow content**, says that

NARROW CONTENT

no such connection exists. The "hamburgery" aspect of the belief is an intrinsic aspect of the belief *as experienced by the agent.*

BRAIN IN A VAT

We can distinguish between the two views by considering one of the favorite devices of philosophers: the **brain in a vat**. Imagine, if you will, that your brain was removed from your body at birth and placed in a marvellously engineered vat. The vat sustains your brain, allowing it to grow and develop. At the same time, electronic signals are fed to your brain from a computer simulation of an entirely fictitious world, and motor signals from your brain are intercepted and used to modify the simulation as appropriate. The brain in a vat has been wheeled out many times to resolve questions in philosophy. Its role here is to show that wide content is not consistent with physicalism. The brain in the vat can be in an identical state to the brain of someone eating a hamburger; yet in one case, the hamburger exists; in the other, it does not. Even in the former case, then, the belief only refers to the actual hamburger in the eyes of a third party who has independent access to the internals of the brain and to the external world containing the hamburger. The brain by itself does not refer to the hamburger.

QUALIA

The narrow-content view goes beyond the simple correspondence theory. The belief that a hamburger is delicious has a certain intrinsic nature—there is something that it is like to have this belief. Now we get into the realm of **qualia**, or intrinsic experiences (from the Latin word meaning, roughly, "such things"). The correspondence theory can account for the verbal or discriminatory behaviors associated with the beliefs "the light is red" or "the light is green," for example. But it cannot distinguish between the experiences of red and green—what it is like to see red as opposed to what it is like to see green. It does seem that there is a real question here, but it is not one that seems likely to yield to a behavioral analysis. If the intrinsic experiences arising from exposure to red and green lights were somehow switched, it seems reasonable to suppose that we would still behave the same way at traffic lights, but it also seems reasonable to say that our lives would be in some way different. This final aspect of intentional states—their "felt quality" if you like—is by far the most problematic. It brings up the question of consciousness, which, as we will see, is very ticklish indeed.

26.3   ON THE POSSIBILITY OF ACHIEVING INTELLIGENT BEHAVIOR

One of the most basic philosophical questions for AI is "Can machines think?" We will not attempt to answer this question directly, because it is not clearly defined. To see why, consider the following questions:

- Can machines fly?
- Can machines swim?

Most people would agree that the answer to the first question is yes, airplanes can fly, but the answer to the second is no; boats and submarines do move through the water, but we do not normally call that swimming. However, neither the questions nor the answers have any impact at all on the working lives of aeronautic and naval engineers. The answers have very little to do with the design or capabilities of airplanes and submarines, and much more to do with the way we have chosen to use words. The word "swim" has come to mean "to move along in the water by movements of the limbs or other body parts," whereas the word "fly" has no such limitation on the means of locomotion.

To complicate matters, words can be used metaphorically, so when we say a computer (or an engine, or the economy) is running well, we mean it is operating smoothly, not that it is propelling itself with its legs in an admirable fashion. Similarly, a person who says, "My modem doesn't work because the computer thinks it is a 2400-baud line" is probably using "thinks" metaphorically, and may still maintain that computers do not *literally* think.

The practical possibility of "thinking machines" has been with us only for about 40 years, not long enough for speakers of English to settle on an agreed meaning for the word "think." In the early days of the debate, some philosophers thought that the question of thinking machines could be settled by means of linguistic analysis of the kind hinted at earlier. If we define "think" to mean something like "make decisions or deliberations by means of an organic, natural brain," then we must conclude that computers cannot think. Ultimately, the linguistic community will come to a decision that suits its need to communicate clearly,[5] but the decision will not tell us much about the capabilities of machines.

---

[5] Wittgenstein said that we should "look at the word 'to think' as a tool."

Alan Turing, in his famous paper "Computing Machinery and Intelligence" (Turing, 1950), suggested that instead of asking "Can machines think?" we should instead ask if they can pass a behavioral test (which has come to be called the Turing Test) for intelligence. He conjectured that by the year 2000, a computer with a storage of 10^9 units could be programmed well enough to have a conversation with an interrogator for 5 minutes and have a 30% chance of fooling the interrogator into thinking it was human. Although we would certainly not claim that anything like general, human-level intelligence will be achieved by that time, his conjecture may not be that far off the truth. Turing also examined a wide variety of possible objections to the possibility of intelligent machines, including virtually all of those that have been raised in the 44 years since his paper appeared.

Some of the objections can be overcome quite easily. For example, Lady Ada Lovelace, commenting on Babbage's Analytical Engine, says, "It has no pretensions to *originate* anything. It can do *whatever we know how to order it* to perform." This objection, that computers can only do what they are told to do and are therefore not capable of creativity, is commonly encountered even today. It is refuted simply by noting that one of the things we can tell them to do is to learn from their experience. For example, Samuel's checker-playing program performed very poorly with its original programming. However, it was able to learn, over the course of a few days of self-play, to play checkers far better than Samuel himself (see Chapter 20). One can try to preserve Lady Lovelace's objection by maintaining that the program's ability to learn originated in Samuel, and so too did its checker-playing ability. But then one would also be led to say that Samuel's creativity originated in his parents, and theirs originated in their parents, and so on.

The "argument from disability" takes the form of a claim, usually unsupported, to the effect that "a machine can never do X." As examples of X, Turing lists the following:

> Be kind, resourceful, beautiful, friendly, have initiative, have a sense of humor, tell right from wrong, make mistakes, fall in love, enjoy strawberries and cream, make someone fall in love with it, learn from experience, use words properly, be the subject of its own thought, have as much diversity of behavior as man, do something really new.

Although some of these abilities concern the consciousness of machines, which we discuss at length in what follows, many concern behavioral properties (see Exercise 26.1). Turing suggests that scepticism of this nature arises from experience of machines as devices for carrying out repetitive tasks requiring little sensory and no reasoning ability. He points to the fact that in the late 1940s, the general population found it difficult to believe that machines could find numerical solutions of equations or predict ballistic trajectories. Even today, however, many technically literate people do not believe that machines can learn.

The supposed inability to make mistakes presents an interesting problem when considering the Turing Test. Certainly, instantaneous and correct answers to long division problems would be a giveaway, and some attempt to simulate human fallibility would be required.[6] But this is not a mistake in the normal sense, because the program is doing exactly what its designer intended. Something more akin to human mistakes will arise when intractable problems are involved. For example, given only a small amount of time to find a chess move, the computer must essentially guess that its move is correct. Similarly, a program that is trying to induce hypotheses from

---

[6] In recent Turing Test competitions, the winning programs are those that type their answers back slowly and irregularly, with occasional corrections and spelling mistakes. A Markov model of typing speed and accuracy is sufficient.

a small amount of data is bound to make mistakes when using such hypotheses for prediction. When unavoidably irrational behavior on the part of the computer matches corresponding failings of humans, this provides evidence that similar mechanisms are in operation. Rational behavior, on the other hand, provides much weaker constraints on mechanisms.

What Turing calls the mathematical objection concerns the proven inability of computers to answer certain questions. We discuss this in-principle barrier to intelligence in Section 26.3. In-practice objections center on the so-called "argument from informality," which claims that intelligent behavior cannot be captured by formal rules. We discuss this category of objections in Section 26.3. The final, and most interesting, objection claims that even if computers behave as intelligently as humans, they still will not *be* intelligent. Although AI cannot do much more than make machines behave intelligently, we still have some fun discussing the issue in Section 26.4.

The mathematical objection

It is well-known, partly through the work of Turing himself (Turing, 1936) as well as that of Gödel (1931), that certain questions cannot be answered correctly by any formal system. An

HALTING PROBLEM

example is the **halting problem**: will the execution of a program P eventually halt, or will it run forever? Turing proved that for any algorithm H that purports to solve halting problems there will always be a program P_i such that H will not be able to answer the halting problem correctly. Turing therefore acknowledges that for any particular machine that is being subjected to the Turing Test, the interrogator can formulate a halting problem that the machine cannot answer correctly.

Philosophers such as Lucas (1961) have claimed that this limitation makes machines inferior to humans, who can always "step outside" the limiting logic to see whether the problem in question is true or not. Lucas bases his argument not on the halting problem but on Gödel's incompleteness theorem (see Chapter 9). Briefly, for any non-trivial formal system F (a formal language, and a set of axioms and inference rules), it is possible to construct a so-called "Gödel sentence" $G(F)$ with the following properties:

- $G(F)$ is a sentence of F, but cannot be proved within F.
- If F is consistent, then $G(F)$ is true.

Lucas claims that because a computer is a formal system, in a sense that can be made precise, then there are sentences whose truth it cannot establish—namely, its own Gödel sentences. A human, on the other hand, can establish the truth of these sentences by applying Gödel's theorem to the formal system that describes the computer and its program.

Lucas's point is essentially the same as the potential objection raised by Turing himself, and can be refuted in the same way. We admit that there is a strong intuition that human mathematicians can switch from one formalism to another until they find one that solves the problem they are faced with. But there is no reason why we could not have the same intuition about a computer that was programmed to try thousands of different formalisms (and to invent new formalisms) in an attempt to solve the halting or Gödel problem. If we accept that the brain is a deterministic physical device operating according to normal physical laws, then it is just as much a formal system as the computer (although a harder one to analyze), and thus has the same limitations as computers. If you believe there are nondeterministic aspects of the world that keep the brain from being a formal system, then we can build a computer that incorporates analog devices to achieve the same nondeterminism (for example, using a Geiger counter to seed a random number generator).

In practical terms, the limitations of formal systems are not going to be of much help to the interrogator in the Turing Test anyway. First of all, descriptions of the halting problems for either humans or sufficiently intelligent computers are going to be far too large to talk about. Even if they were small enough, the interrogator does not know the details of the computer it is talking to, and thus has no way of posing the right halting problem. And even if the interrogator made a lucky guess, the computer could just wait a few minutes (or weeks) and then reply "It looks like it doesn't halt, but I'm not sure—it's pretty complicated." Presumably that would be a good imitation of a typical human reply.

Another way of stating the refutation argument, in a form appropriate to Lucas's version, is that a human being cannot show the consistency of a formal system that describes the operation of his or her brain or of a large computer, and cannot therefore establish the truth of the corresponding Gödel sentence. Therefore, humans have the same limitations that formal systems have.

In a more recent revival of the mathematical objection, the mathematician Roger Penrose has written a reasonably controversial book on AI, provocatively entitled *The Emperor's New Mind*,[7] which purports to overcome these objections to Lucas. Penrose argues that, at least when we consider the mental faculties that mathematicians use to generate new mathematical propositions and their proofs, the claim that *F* is complex cannot hold up. This is because when a new result is found, it is usually a simple matter for one mathematician to communicate it to another, and to provide convincing evidence by means of a series of simple steps. He begins by assuming that this universal facility for mathematics *is* algorithmic, and tries to show a contradiction:

> Now this putative "universal" system, or algorithm, cannot ever be known as the one that we mathematicians use to decide truth. For if it were, we would construct its Gödel proposition and *know that to be a mathematical truth also*. Thus, we are driven to the conclusion that the algorithm that mathematicians use to decide mathematical truth is so complicated or obscure that its very validity can never be known to us. (Penrose, 1990, p. 654).

And because mathematical truths are in fact simple to see, at least step by step, mathematical "insight" cannot be algorithmic. We can paraphrase the argument as follows:

1. Mathematics is simple, and includes the "Gödelisation" process, which is also simple.
2. Hence the "validity of mathematics" is easily seen.
3. Thus, if mathematics were a formal system, its Gödel sentence would easily be seen to be true by mathematicians.
4. Hence mathematical insight cannot be algorithmic.

In an entertaining series of replies appearing in the journal *Behavioral and Brain Sciences*, a number of mathematicians including George Boolos (1990) and Martin Davis (1990) point out an obvious flaw in the first two steps. Mathematics has a long history of inconsistencies, the most famous of which is Frege's *Basic Laws of Arithmetic*, shown inconsistent by Russell's paradox

---

[7] Penrose (1990) strenuously denies that the obvious analogy to the tale of the Emperor's New Clothes was intended in any way to suggest that AI is not all it claims to be.

in 1902. Almost every major figure in the history of logic has at one time or another published an inconsistent set of axioms. Even today, there is some doubt as to whether the principal axiomatization of set theory known as ZFC (the Zermelo-Fraenkel axioms plus the Axiom of Choice) is consistent, even though it is used widely as the basis for most of mathematics. Penrose replies as follows:

> I am not asserting that, in any particular case of a formal system F, we need necessarily be able to "see" that $G(F)$ is true, but I am asserting that the "Gödelian insight" that enables one to pass from F to $G(F)$ is just as good a mathematical procedure for deriving new truths from old as are any other procedures in mathematics. This insight is not contained within the rules of F itself, however. Thus, F does not encapsulate all the insights available to mathematicians. The insights that *are* available to mathematicians are not formalizable. (Penrose, 1990, p. 694).

Penrose does not say why he thinks the "Gödelian insight" is not formalizable, and it appears that in fact it has been formalized. In his Ph.D. thesis, Natarajan Shankar (1986) used the Boyer–Moore theorem prover BMTP to derive Gödel's theorem from a set of basic axioms, in much the same way that Gödel himself did.[8] The thesis was intended mainly to demonstrate the power of automatic theorem provers, in particular the capability of BMTP to develop and apply lemmata. But it shows, as Robert Wilensky (1990) has pointed out, that one needs to be careful to distinguish between the formal system that is doing the proving—in this case, a computer programmed with the BMTP—and the formal system within which the proof is carried out, namely, an axiomatization of arithmetic and of sentences in that axiomatization. Just like a mathematician, a good automated theorem prover can apply Gödelisation to the particular formal system that it is working on; but it can no more establish the consistency of its own program and hardware than a mathematician can establish the consistency of his or her own brain. We therefore seem to be back where we started, with the refutation of the "mathematical objection" that Turing himself raised.

Penrose naturally maintains that in some way, mathematicians' use of insight remains nonalgorithmic. Perhaps the most interesting aspect of his book is the conclusion he draws from this. After providing a valuable discussion of the relevance of physics to the brain, he deduces that nothing in our current physical understanding of its operation would suggest that it has nonalgorithmic aspects—that is, the simulation of its operation by a computer, as described earlier, would in principle be possible according to modern physics. Rather than accepting the conclusion that perhaps the brain is, after all, algorithmic in this sense, he prefers to believe that modern physics must be wrong. In particular, the brain must use physical principles not yet discovered, but probably relating to the interaction between quantum theory and gravity, that must also be nonalgorithmic in character.

The argument from informality

One of the most influential and persistent criticisms of AI as an enterprise was raised by Turing as the "argument from informality of behavior." Essentially, this is the claim that human behavior

---

[8] Ammon's SHUNYATA system (1993) even appears to have developed by itself the diagonalization technique used by Gödel and developed originally by Cantor.

is far too complex to be captured by any simple set of rules; and because computers can do no more than follow a set of rules, they cannot generate behavior as intelligent as that of humans.

The principal proponent of this view has been the philosopher Hubert Dreyfus, who has produced a series of powerful critiques of artificial intelligence: *What Computers Can't Do* (1972; 1979), *What Computers Still Can't Do* (1992), and, with his brother Stuart, *Mind Over Machine* (1986). Terry Winograd, whose PhD thesis (Winograd, 1972) on natural language understanding is criticized fiercely by Dreyfus (1979), has also expressed views similar to those of Dreyfus in his recent work (Winograd and Flores, 1986).

The position they criticize came to be called "Good Old-Fashioned AI," or GOFAI, a term coined by Haugeland (1985). GOFAI is supposed to claim that all intelligent behavior can be captured by a system that reasons logically from a set of facts and rules describing the domain. It therefore corresponds to the simplest logical agent described in Chapter 6. Dreyfus claims that

> when Minsky or Turing claims that man can be understood as a Turing machine, they must mean that a digital computer can reproduce human behavior . . . by *processing data representing facts about the world using logical operations* that can be reduced to matching, classifying and Boolean operations. (Dreyfus, 1972, p. 192)

It is important to point out, before continuing with the argument, that AI and GOFAI are not the same thing. In fact, it is not clear whether any substantial section of the field has ever adhered to GOFAI in this extreme form, although the phrase "facts and rules" did appear in Turing's two-sentence speculation concerning how systems might be programmed to pass the Turing Test.[9] One only has to read the preceding chapters to see that the scope of AI includes far more than logical inference. However, we shall see that Dreyfus' criticisms of GOFAI make for interesting reading and raise issues that are of interest for all of AI.

Whether or not anyone adheres to GOFAI, it has indeed been a working hypothesis of most AI research that the knowledge-based approach to intelligent system design has a major role to play. Hubert Dreyfus has argued that this presumption is based in a long tradition of **rationalism** going back to Plato (see Section 1.2). He cites Leibniz as providing a clear statement of the goals of the modern "expert systems" industry:

> The most important observations and turns of skill in all sorts of trades and professions are as yet unwritten . . . We can also write up this practice, since it is at bottom just another theory.

Furthermore, he claims that the presumption is wrong; that competence can be achieved without explicit reasoning or rule following. The Dreyfus critique therefore is not addressed against computers *per se*, but against one particular way of programming them. It is reasonable to suppose, however, that a book called *What First-Order Logical Rule-Based Systems Can't Do* might have had less impact.

Dreyfus's first target is the supposition that early successes of GOFAI justify optimism that the methodology will succeed in scaling up to human-level intelligence. Many AI programs in the 1960s and early 1970s operated in **microworlds**—small, circumscribed domains such as the Blocks World. In microworlds, the totality of the situation can be captured by a small number of facts. At the time, many AI researchers were well aware that success in microworlds could be achieved without facing up to a major challenge in the real world: the vast amount of

---

9 Significantly, Turing also said that he expected AI to be achieved by a learning machine, not a preprogrammed store.

potentially relevant information that could be brought to bear on any given problem. As we saw in Chapter 22, disambiguation of natural language seems to require access to this background knowledge. Dreyfus gives as an example the text fragment

> Mary saw a dog in the window. She wanted it.

This example was used originally by Lenat (Lenat and Feigenbaum, 1991) to illustrate the commonsense knowledge needed to disambiguate the "it" in the second sentence. Presumably, "it" refers to the dog rather than the window. If the second sentence had been "She smashed it" or "She pressed her nose up against it," the interpretation would be different. To generate these different interpretations in the different contexts, an AI system would need a fair amount of knowledge about dogs, windows, and so on. The project of finding, encoding, and using such knowledge has been discussed since the early days of AI, and Lenat's CYC project (Lenat and Guha, 1990) is probably the most well-publicized undertaking in this area.

The position that Dreyfus adopts, however, is that this general commonsense knowledge is not explicitly represented or manipulated in human performance. It constitutes the "holistic context" or "Background" within which humans operate. He gives the example of appropriate social behavior in giving and receiving gifts: "Normally one simply responds in the appropriate circumstances by giving an appropriate gift." One apparently has "a direct sense of how things are done and what to expect." The same claim is made in the context of chess playing: "A mere chess master might need to figure out what to do, but a grandmaster just sees the board as demanding a certain move." Apparently, the "right response just pops into his or her head."

Dreyfus seems at first to be making a claim that might appear somewhat irrelevant to the weak AI program: that if humans are sometimes not conscious of their reasoning processes, then on those occasions no reasoning is occurring. The obvious AI reply would be to distinguish PHENOMENOLOGY between **phenomenology**—how things, including our own reasoning, appear to our conscious experience—and causation. AI is required to find a causal explanation of intelligence. One might well claim that knowledge of chess—the legal moves and so on—is being used, but perhaps not at a conscious level. As yet, AI does not claim to have a theory that can distinguish between conscious and unconscious deliberations, so the phenomenological aspects of decision-making are unlikely to falsify any particular approach to AI.

Another approach might be to propose that the grandmaster's supposed ability to see the right move immediately derives from a partial situation-action mapping used by a reflex agent with internal state. The mapping might be learned directly (see Chapter 20) or perhaps compiled from more explicit knowledge (see Chapter 21). And as discussed in Chapter 2, situation-action mappings have significant advantages in terms of efficiency. On the other hand, even a grandmaster sometimes needs to use his or her knowledge of the legal moves to deal with unfamiliar situations, to find a way out of a trap, or to ensure that a mating attack is unavoidable.

Dreyfus's position is actually more subtle than a simple appeal to magical intuition. *Mind Over Matter* (Dreyfus and Dreyfus, 1986) proposes a five-stage process of acquiring expertise, beginning with rule-based processing (of the sort proposed in AI) and ending with the ability to select correct responses instantaneously:

> We have seen that computers do indeed reason things out rather like inexperienced persons, but only with greater human experience comes know-how, a far superior, holistic, intuitive way of approaching problems that cannot be imitated by rule-following computers.

Dreyfus's first proposal for how this "know-how" operates is that humans solve problems by analogy, using a vast "case library" from which somehow the most relevant precedents are extracted. He proposed "some sort of holographic memory" as a potential mechanism. He later suggests neural networks as a possible implementation for the final "know-how" phase.

Now he reaches what is perhaps the inevitable destination of the weak-AI critic: he ends up effectively as an AI researcher, because he cannot avoid the question "If AI mechanisms cannot work, what mechanism do you propose instead for human performance?" His answer, that humans use some sort of learning method, is not new to AI. Since the very early experiments of Samuel and Friedberg, researchers have proposed using machine learning as a method of achieving higher levels of performance and avoiding the difficulties of hand coding. The question is, what is the target representation for the learning process? Dreyfus chooses neural networks because they can achieve intelligence, to some degree, *without explicit representation of symbolic knowledge.*[10] He claims, however, that there is no reason to suppose that real intelligence can be achieved without a brain-sized network; nor would we understand the results of training such a network.

Dreyfus's natural pessimism also leads him to make two useful observations on the difficulty of a naive scheme to construct intelligence by training a large network with appropriate examples:

1. Good generalization from examples cannot be achieved without a good deal of background knowledge; as yet, no one has any idea how to incorporate background knowledge into the neural network learning process.

2. Neural network learning is a form of **supervised** learning (see Chapter 18), requiring the prior identification of relevant inputs and correct outputs. Therefore, it cannot operate autonomously without the help of a human trainer.

The first objection was also raised in Chapter 18, and in Chapter 21, we saw several ways in which background knowledge indeed can improve a system's ability to generalize. Those techniques, however, relied on the availability of knowledge in explicit form, something that Dreyfus denies strenuously. In our view, this is a good reason for a serious redesign of current models of neural processing so that they *can* take advantage of previously learned knowledge. There has been some progress in this direction. The second objection leads directly to the need for **reinforcement learning** (Chapter 20), in which the learning system receives occasional positive or negative rewards, rather than being told the correct action in every instance. Given enough experience, a reinforcement learning agent can induce a utility function on situations, or alternatively a mapping from situation-action pairs to expected values. For example, by winning and losing games a chess-playing agent can gradually learn which sorts of positions are promising or dangerous. Reinforcement learning is currently very popular in neural network systems.

Dreyfus correctly points out that the major problem associated with reinforcement learning is how to generalize from particular situations to more general classes of situations—the general problem of inductive learning. One can take heart from the observation that reinforcement learning reduces to ordinary inductive learning, for which we already have some well-developed techniques. There are, of course, problems yet to be solved with inductive learning, including problem 1, mentioned earlier, concerning how to use background knowledge to improve learning. Dreyfus also brings up the problem of learning in the context of a large number of potentially

---

[10] In fact, many neural network researchers are proud that their networks seem to learn distinct, higher-level "features" of the input space and to combine them in approximately logical ways.

relevant features. One possible solution is to stick to a small finite set of features, and add new ones when needed. But according to him, "There is no known way of adding new features should the current set prove inadequate to account for the learned facts." As we saw in Chapter 21, there are well-principled ways to generate new features for inductive learning.

Another difficult problem in reinforcement learning arises when the available perceptual inputs do not completely characterize the situation. In such cases, the agent must develop additional internal state variables, in terms of which output mappings can be learned. Dreyfus claims that "Since no one knows how to incorporate internal states appropriately, a breakthrough will be necessary." Again, this is a tricky problem, but one on which some progress has been made (see Chapter 20).

The final problem to which Dreyfus refers in *What Computers Still Can't Do* is that of controlling the acquisition of sensory data. He notes that the brain is able to direct its sensors to seek relevant information and to process it to extract aspects relevant to the current situation. He says (page xliv), "Currently, no details of this mechanism are understood or even hypothesized in a way that could guide AI research." Yet the field of active vision, underpinned by the theory of information value (Chapter 16), is concerned with exactly this problem, and already robots incorporate the theoretical results obtained.

Dreyfus seems willing to grant that success in overcoming these obstacles would constitute the kind of real progress in AI that he believes to be impossible. In our view, the fact that AI has managed to reduce the problem of producing human-level intelligence to a set of relatively well-defined technical problems seems to be progress in itself. Furthermore, these are problems that are clearly soluble in principle, and for which partial solutions are already emerging. In summary, we have seen that the life of a weak-AI critic is not an easy one. Claims that "*X* is impossible for computers" (e.g., *X* might be beating a chess master) tend to be overtaken by actual events. They also open the critic to the requirement of suggesting a mechanism by which humans do *X*; this forces them, essentially, to become AI researchers. On the other hand, perceptive criticism from outside the field can be very useful. Many of the issues Dreyfus has focused on—background commonsense knowledge, the qualification problem, uncertainty, learning, compiled forms of decision making, the importance of considering situated agents rather than disembodied inference engines—are now widely accepted as important aspects of intelligent agent design.

26.4   INTENTIONALITY AND CONSCIOUSNESS

Many critics have objected to the Turing Test, stating that it is not enough to see how a machine acts; we also need to know what internal "mental" states it has. This is a valid and useful criticism; certainly in trying to understand any computer program or mechanical device it is helpful to know about its internal workings as well as its external behavior. Again, the objection was foreseen by Turing. He cites a speech by a Professor Jefferson:

> Not until a machine could write a sonnet or compose a concerto because of thoughts and emotions felt, and not by the chance fall of symbols, could we agree that machine equals brain—that is, not only write it but know that it had written it.

Jefferson's key point is consciousness: *the machine has to be aware of its own mental state and actions.* Others focus on intentionality, that is, the "aboutness" (or lack thereof) of the machine's purported beliefs, desires, intentions, and so on.

Turing's response to the objection is interesting. He could have presented reasons why machines can in fact be conscious. But instead he maintains that the question is just as ill-defined as asking "can machines think," and in any case, why should we insist on a higher standard for machines than we do for humans? After all, in ordinary life we never have *any* evidence about the internal mental states of other humans, so we cannot know that anyone else is conscious. Nevertheless, "instead of arguing continually over this point, it is usual to have the polite convention that everyone thinks," as Turing puts it.

Turing argues that Jefferson would be willing to extend the polite convention to machines if only he had experience with ones that act intelligently, as in the following dialog, which has become such a part of AI's oral tradition that we simply have to include it:

> HUMAN: In the first line of your sonnet which reads 'shall I compare thee to a summer's day,' would not a 'spring day' do as well or better?
> MACHINE: It wouldn't scan.
> HUMAN: How about 'a winter's day'. That would scan all right.
> MACHINE: Yes, but nobody wants to be compared to a winter's day.
> HUMAN: Would you say Mr. Pickwick reminded you of Christmas?
> MACHINE: In a way.
> HUMAN: Yet Christmas is a winter's day, and I do not think Mr. Pickwick would mind the comparison.
> MACHINE: I don't think you're serious. By a winter's day one means a typical winter's day, rather than a special one like Christmas.

Jefferson's objection is still an important one, because it points out the difficulty of establishing any objective test for consciousness, where by "objective" we mean a test that can be carried out with consistent results by any sufficiently competent third party. Turing also concedes that the question of consciousness is not easily dismissed: "I do not wish to give the impression that I think there is no mystery about consciousness ... But I do not think these mysteries necessarily need to be solved before we can answer the question with which we are concerned in this paper," namely, "Can machines think?"

Although many, including Jefferson, have claimed that thinking necessarily involves consciousness, the issue is most commonly associated with the work of the philosopher John Searle. We will now discuss two thought experiments that, Searle claims, refute the thesis of strong AI.

The Chinese Room

We begin with the Chinese Room argument (Searle, 1980). The idea is to describe a hypothetical system that is clearly running a program and passes the Turing Test, but that equally clearly (according to Searle) does not understand anything of its inputs and outputs. The conclusion will be that running the appropriate program (i.e., having the right outputs) is not a *sufficient* condition for being a mind.

The system consists of a human, who understands only English, equipped with a rule book, written in English, and various stacks of paper, some blank, some with indecipherable inscriptions. (The human therefore plays the role of the CPU, the rule book is the program, and the stacks of paper are the storage device.) The system is inside a room with a small opening to the outside. Through the opening appear slips of paper with indecipherable symbols. The human finds matching symbols in the rule book, and follows the instructions. The instructions may include writing symbols on new slips of paper, finding symbols in the stacks, rearranging the stacks, and so on. Eventually, the instructions will cause one or more symbols to be transcribed onto a piece of paper that is handed through the opening to the outside world.

So far, so good. But from the outside, we see a system that is taking input in the form of Chinese sentences and generating answers in Chinese that are as obviously "intelligent" as those in the conversation imagined by Turing.[11] Searle then argues as follows: the person in the room does not understand Chinese (given); the rule book and the stacks of paper, being just pieces of paper, do not understand Chinese; therefore there is no understanding of Chinese going on. *Hence, According to Searle, running the right program does not necessarily generate understanding.*

Like Turing, Searle considered and attempted to rebuff a number of replies to his argument. First, we will consider the so-called Robot Reply (due to Jerry Fodor (1980) among others), which turns out to be a red herring, although an interesting one. The Robot Reply is that although the symbols manipulated by the Chinese Room may not have real meaning to the room itself (e.g., nothing in the room has any experience of acupuncture, with respect to which the symbol for it might have any meaning), a fully equipped robot would not be subject to the same limitations. Its internal symbols would have meaning to it by virtue of its direct experience of the world. Searle's reply is to put the Chinese Room inside the robot's "head": the sensors are redesigned to generate Chinese symbols instead of streams of bits, and the effectors redesigned to accept Chinese symbols as control inputs. Then we are back where we started. The Robot Reply is a red herring because the causal semantics of the symbols is not the real issue. Even the original Chinese Room needs some causal semantics, in order to be able to answer questions such as "How many questions have I asked so far?" Conversely, the outputs of human sensors, for example, along the optic nerve or the auditory nerve, might as well be in Chinese (see the earlier discussion of wide and narrow content). Not even Searle would argue that connecting artificial sensors to these nerves would remove consciousness from the brain involved.[12]

Several commentators, including John McCarthy and Robert Wilensky, propose what Searle calls the Systems Reply. This gets to the point. The objection is that although one can ask if the human in the room understands Chinese, this is analogous to asking if the CPU can take cube roots. In both cases, the answer is no, and in both cases, according to the Systems Reply, the entire system *does* have the capacity in question. Certainly, if one asks the Chinese Room whether it understands Chinese, the answer would be affirmative (in fluent Chinese). Searle's response is to reiterate the point that the understanding is not in the human, and cannot be in the paper, so there cannot be any understanding. He further suggests that one could imagine the human memorizing the rule book and the contents of all the stacks of paper, so that there would

---

[11] The fact that the stacks of paper might well be larger than the entire planet, and the generation of answers would take millions of years, has no bearing on the *logical* structure of the argument. One aim of philosophical training is to develop a finely honed sense of which objections are germane and which are not.

[12] This is a good thing, because artificial inner ears are at the prototype stage (Watson, 1991), and artificial retinas, with associated image processing, are rapidly becoming feasible (Campbell *et al.*, 1991).

be nothing to have understanding *except* the human; and again, when one asks the human (in English), the reply will be in the negative.

Now we are down to the real issues. The shift from paper to memorization is a red herring, because both forms are simply physical instantiations of a running program. The real claim made by Searle has the following form:

1. Certain kinds of objects are incapable of conscious understanding (of Chinese).

2. The human, paper, and rule book are objects of this kind.

3. If each of a set of objects is incapable of conscious understanding, then any system constructed from the objects is incapable of conscious understanding

4. Therefore there is no conscious understanding in the Chinese room.

While the first two steps are on firm ground,[13] the third is not. Searle just assumes it is true without giving any support for it. But notice that if you do believe it, and if you believe that humans are composed of molecules, then either you must believe that humans are incapable of conscious understanding, or you must believe that individual molecules are capable.

It is important to see that the rebuttal of Searle's argument lies in rejecting the third step, and not in making any claims about the room. You can believe that the room is not conscious (or you can be undecided about the room's consciousness) and still legitimately reject Searle's argument as invalid.

EMERGENT
PROPERTY

Searle's (1992) more recent position, described in his book *The Rediscovery of the Mind*, is that consciousness is an **emergent property** of appropriately arranged systems of neurons in the same way that solidity is an emergent property of appropriately arranged collections of molecules, none of which are solid by themselves.

Now most supporters of strong AI would also say that consciousness is an emergent property of systems of neurons (or electronic components, or whatever). The question is, which properties of neurons are *essential* to consciousness, and which are merely incidental? In a solid, what counts are the forces that molecules exert on each other, and the way in which those forces change with distance. The solid would still be solid if we replaced each molecule with a tiny computer connected to electromagnetic force field generators. As yet, we do not know which properties of neurons are important—the functional properties associated with information processing or the intrinsic properties of the biological molecules. The Chinese Room argument therefore can be reduced to the empirical claim that *the only physical medium that can support consciousness is the neural medium.* The only empirical evidence for this empirical claim is that other media do not resemble neurons in their intrinsic physical properties. Searle (1992) admits that it is *possible* that other media, including silicon, might support consciousness, but he would claim that in such cases, the system would be conscious *by virtue of the physical properties of the medium* and not by virtue of the program it was running.

To reiterate, the aim of the Chinese Room argument is to refute strong AI—the claim that running the right sort of program necessarily generates consciousness. It does this by exhibiting an apparently intelligent system running the right sort of program that is, according to Searle, *demonstrably* unconscious. He tried to demonstrate this with the argument that unconscious parts

---

[13] Searle never explicitly says what kinds of objects are incapable of consciousness. Books and papers for sure, but he wants us to generalize this to computers but not brains without saying exactly what the generalization is.

cannot lead to a conscious whole, an argument that we have tried to show is invalid. Having failed to *prove* that the room is unconscious, Searle then appeals to intuition: just look at the room; what's there to be conscious? While this approach gains some supporters, intuitions can be misleading. It is by no means intuitive that a hunk of brain can support consciousness while an equally large hunk of liver cannot. Furthermore, when Searle admits that materials other than neurons could in principle support consciousness, he weakens his argument even further, for two reasons: first, one has only Searle's intuitions (or one's own) to say that the Chinese room is not conscious, and second, even if we decide the room is not conscious, that tells us nothing about whether a program running on some other physical media might be conscious.

Searle describes his position as "biological naturalism." The physical nature of the system is important, and not its computational description. He even goes so far as to allow the logical possibility that the brain is actually implementing an AI program of the traditional sort. But even if that program turned out to be an exact copy of some existing AI program, moving it to a different machine would destroy consciousness. The distinction between the intrinsic properties (those inherent in its specific physical makeup) and functional properties (the input/output specification) of a neuron is thus crucial.

One way to get at the distinction between intrinsic and functional properties is to look at other artifacts. In 1848, artificial urea was synthesized for the first time, by Wöhler. This was important because it proved that organic and inorganic chemistry could be united, a question that had been hotly debated. Once the synthesis was accomplished, chemists agreed that artificial urea *was* urea, because it had all the right physical properties. Similarly, artificial sweeteners are undeniably sweeteners, and artificial insemination (the other AI) is undeniably insemination. On the other hand, artificial flowers are not flowers, and Daniel Dennett points out that artificial Chateau Latour wine would not be Chateau Latour wine, even if it was chemically indistinguishable, simply because it was not made in the right place in the right way. Similarly, an artificial Picasso painting is not a Picasso painting, no matter what it looks like.

Searle is interested in the notion of *simulations* as well as in artifacts. He claims that AI programs can at best be simulations of intelligence, and such simulations imply no intrinsic properties. The following quote is representative:

> No one supposes that a computer simulation of a storm will leave us all wet . . . Why on earth would anyone in his right mind suppose a computer simulation of mental processes actually had mental processes? (Searle, 1980, pp. 37–38)

While it is easy to agree that computer simulations of storms do not make us wet, it is not clear how to carry this analogy over to computer simulations of mental processes. After all, a Hollywood simulation of a storm using sprinklers and wind machines *does* make the actors wet. A computer simulation of multiplication *does* result in a product—in fact a computer simulation of multiplication *is* multiplication. Searle achieves his rhetorical effect by choosing examples carefully. It would not have been as convincing to say "Why on earth would anyone in his right mind suppose that a computer simulation of a video game actually is a game?," but it would have the same logical force as his original quote.

To help decide whether intelligence is more like Chateau Latour and Picasso or more like urea and multiplication, we turn to another thought experiment.

The Brain Prosthesis Experiment

The Brain Prosthesis Experiment was touched on by Searle (1980), but is most commonly associated with the work of Hans Moravec (1988). It goes like this. Suppose we have developed neurophysiology to the point where the input/output behavior and connectivity of all the neurons in the brain are perfectly understood. Furthermore, suppose that we can build microscopic electronic devices that mimic this behavior and can be smoothly interfaced to neural tissue. Lastly, suppose that some miraculous surgical technique can replace individual neurons with the corresponding electronic devices without interrupting the operation of the brain as a whole. The experiment consists of gradually replacing all the neurons with electronic devices, and then reversing the process to return the subject to his or her normal biological state.

We are concerned with both the external behavior and the internal experience of the subject, during and after the operation. By the definition of the experiment, the subject's external behavior must remain unchanged compared to what would be observed if the operation were not carried out.[14] Now although the presence or absence of consciousness cannot be easily ascertained by a third party, the subject of the experiment ought at least to be able to record any changes in his or her own conscious experience. Apparently, there is a direct clash of intuitions as to what would happen. Moravec, a robotics researcher, is convinced his consciousness would remain unaffected. He adopts the **functionalist** viewpoint, according to which the input/output behavior of neurons is their only significant property. Searle, on the other hand, is equally convinced his consciousness would vanish:

> You find, to your total amazement, that you are indeed losing control of your external behavior. You find, for example, that when doctors test your vision, you hear them say "We are holding up a red object in front of you; please tell us what you see." You want to cry out "I can't see anything. I'm going totally blind." But you hear your voice saying in a way that is completely out of your control, "I see a red object in front of me." ... [Y]our conscious experience slowly shrinks to nothing, while your externally observable behavior remains the same. (Searle, 1992)

But one can do more than argue from intuition. First, note that in order for the external behavior to remain the same while the subject gradually becomes unconscious, it must be the case that the subject's volition is removed instantaneously and totally, otherwise the shrinking of awareness would be reflected in external behavior—"Help, I'm shrinking!" or words to that effect. This instantaneous removal of volition as a result of gradual neuron-at-a-time replacement seems an unlikely claim to have to make.

Second, consider what happens if we do ask the subject questions concerning his or her conscious experience during the period when no real neurons remain. By the conditions of the experiment, we will get responses such as "I feel fine. I must say I'm a bit surprised because I believed the Chinese Room argument." Or we might poke the subject with a pointed stick, and observe the response, "Ouch, that hurt." Now, in the normal course of affairs, the sceptic can dismiss such outputs from AI programs as mere contrivances. Certainly, it is easy enough to use a rule such as "If sensor 12 reads 'High' then print 'Ouch.'" But the point here is that because we have replicated the functional properties of a normal human brain, we assume that the electronic brain contains no such contrivances. Then we must have an explanation of the manifestations of

---

[14] One can imagine using an identical "control" subject who is given a placebo operation, so that the two behaviors can be compared.

"consciousness" produced by the electronic brain that appeals only to the functional properties of the neurons. *And this explanation must also apply to the real brain, which has the same functional properties.* There are, it seems, only two possible conclusions:

1. The causal mechanisms involved in consciousness that generate these kinds of outputs in normal brains are still operating in the electronic version, which is therefore "conscious."

2. The conscious mental events in the normal brain have no causal connection to the subject's behavior, and are missing from the electronic brain.

EPIPHENOMENAL Although we cannot rule out the second possibility, it reduces consciousness to what philosophers call an **epiphenomenal** role—something that happens but casts no shadow, as it were, on the observable world. Furthermore, if consciousness is indeed epiphenomenal, then the brain must contain a second, unconscious mechanism that is responsible for the "Ouch."

Third, consider the situation after the operation has been reversed and the subject has a normal brain. Once again, the subject's external behavior must be as if the operation had not occurred. In particular, we should be able to ask, "What was it like during the operation? Do you remember the pointed stick?" The subject must have accurate memories of the actual nature of his or her conscious experiences, including the qualia, despite the fact that according to Searle there were no such experiences.

Searle might reply that we have not specified the experimental conditions properly. If the real neurons are, say, put into suspended animation between the time they are extracted and the time they are replaced in the brain, then of course they will not "remember" the experiences during the operation. To deal with this, we simply need to make sure that the neurons' state is updated, by some means, to reflect the internal state of the artificial neurons they are replacing. If the supposed "nonfunctional" aspects of the real neurons then result in functionally different behavior from that observed with artificial neurons still in place, then we have a simple *reductio ad absurdum*, because that would mean that the artificial neurons are not functionally equivalent to the real neurons. (Exercise 26.4 addresses a rebuttal to this argument.)

Patricia Churchland (1986) points out that the functionalist arguments that operate at the level of the neuron can also operate at the level of any larger functional unit—a clump of neurons, a mental module, a lobe, a hemisphere, or the whole brain. That means that if you accept that the brain prosthesis experiment shows that the replacement brain is conscious, then you should also believe that consciousness is maintained when the entire brain is replaced by a circuit that maps from inputs to outputs via a huge lookup table. This is disconcerting to many people (including Turing himself) who have the intuition that lookup tables are not conscious.

Discussion

We have seen that the subject of consciousness is problematic. Simple intuitions seem to lead to conflicting answers if we propose different experimental situations. But what is clear is that *if* there is an empirical question concerning the presence or absence of consciousness in appropriately programmed computers, then like any empirical question it can only be settled by experiment. Unfortunately, it is not clear what sort of experiment could settle the question, nor what sort of scientific theory could explain the results. Scientific theories are designed to account for objective phenomena; in fact Popper (1962) has characterized all physical laws as theories that, ultimately, allow one to conclude the existence of particles in certain space-time locations. How would we view a theory that allowed one to infer pains, for example, from premises of the ordinary physical kind? It seems that it would be at best a *description* ("When a voltage is applied to such-and-such neuron, the subject will feel pain") rather than an *explanation*. An explanatory theory should, among other things, be able to explain why it is *pain* that the subject experiences when a given neuron is stimulated, rather than, say, the smell of bacon sandwiches.

It is also hard to imagine how a better understanding of neurophysiology could help. Suppose, for example, that (1) we could train a subject to record all his or her conscious thoughts without interrupting them too much; (2) neuroscientists discovered a system of neurons whose activity patterns could be decoded and understood;[15] and (3) the decoded activity patterns corresponded exactly to the recorded conscious thoughts. Although we might claim to have located the "seat of consciousness," it seems we would still be no better off in our understanding of why these patterns of activity actually constitute consciousness.

The problem seems to be that consciousness, as we currently (fail to) understand it, is not understandable by the normal means available to science.

> No one can rule out a major intellectual revolution that would give us a new—and at present unimaginable—concept of reduction, according to which consciousness would be reducible. (Searle, 1992, p. 124).

If consciousness is indeed irreducible, that would suggest that there can be no explanations in nonsubjective terms of why red is the sort of sensation it is and not some other sort, or why pain is like pain and not like the smell of bacon sandwiches.

One final (but not necessarily conclusive) argument can be made concerning the evolutionary origin of consciousness. Both sides of the debate agree that simple animals containing only a few neurons do not possess consciousness. In such animals, neurons fulfill a purely functional role by allowing simple adaptive and discriminative behaviors. Yet the basic design and construction of neurons in primitive animals is almost identical to the design of neurons in higher animals. Given this observation, the proponent of consciousness as an intrinsic neural phenomenon must argue that neurons, which evidently evolved for purely functional purposes, just happen by chance to have exactly the properties required to generate consciousness. The functionalist, on the other hand, can argue that consciousness necessarily emerges when systems reach the kind of functional complexity needed to sustain complex behavior.

26.5   SUMMARY

We have presented some of the main philosophical issues in AI. These were divided into questions concerning its technical feasibility (weak AI), and questions concerning its relevance and explanatory power with respect to the mind (strong AI). We concluded, although by no means conclusively, that the arguments against weak AI are needlessly pessimistic and have often mischaracterized the content of AI theories. Arguments against strong AI are inconclusive; although

---

[15] It is not clear if this really makes sense, but the idea is to grant neuroscience as much success as we can imagine.

they fail to prove its impossibility, it is equally difficult to prove its correctness. Fortunately, few mainstream AI researchers, if any, believe that anything significant hinges on the outcome of the debate given the field's present stage of development. Even Searle himself recommends that his arguments not stand in the way of continued research on AI as traditionally conceived.

Like genetic engineering and nuclear power, artificial intelligence has its fair share of critics concerned about its possible misuses. We will discuss these concerns in the next chapter. But unlike other fields, artificial intelligence has generated a thriving industry devoted to proving its impossibility. This second batch of critics has raised some important issues concerning the basic aims, claims, and assumptions of the field. Every AI scientist and practitioner should be aware of these issues, because they directly affect the social milieu in which AI research is carried out and in which AI techniques are applied. Although general societal awareness should be part of the education of every scientist, it is especially important for AI because the nature of the field seems to arouse scepticism and even hostility in a significant portion of the population. There persists an incredible degree of misunderstanding of the basic claims and content of the field, and, like it or not, these misunderstandings have a significant effect on the field itself.

BIBLIOGRAPHICAL AND HISTORICAL NOTES

The nature of the mind has been a standard topic of philosophical theorizing from ancient times to the present. In the *Phaedo*, Plato specifically considered and rejected the idea that the mind could be an "attunement" or pattern of organization of the parts of the body, a viewpoint that approximates the functionalist viewpoint in modern philosophy of mind. He decided instead that the mind had to be an immortal, immaterial soul, separable from the body and different in substance—the viewpoint of dualism. Aristotle distinguished a variety of souls (Greek $\psi\upsilon\chi'\eta$) in living things, some of which, at least, he described in a functionalist manner. (See Nussbaum (1978) for more on Aristotle's functionalism.) Aristotle also conceived of deliberation about what action to take in a way reminiscent of the modern situated agent approach (the last part of this extract also appears on the cover of the book):

> But how does it happen that thinking is sometimes accompanied by action and sometimes not, sometimes by motion, and sometimes not? It looks as if almost the same thing happens as in the case of reasoning and making inferences about unchanging objects. But in that case the end is a speculative proposition . . . whereas here the the conclusion which results from the two premises is an action. . . . I need covering; a cloak is a covering. I need a cloak. What I need, I have to make; I need a cloak. I have to make a cloak. And the conclusion, the "I have to make a cloak," is an action. (Nussbaum, 1978, p. 40)

Descartes is notorious for his dualistic view of the human mind, but ironically his historical influence was toward mechanism and physicalism. He explicitly conceived of animals as automata, and his spirited defense of this viewpoint actually had the effect of making it easier to conceive of humans as automata as well, even though he himself did not take this step. The book *L'Homme Machine* or *Man a Machine* (La Mettrie, 1748) did explicitly argue that humans are automata.

Twentieth-century analytic philosophy has typically accepted physicalism (often in the form of the brain-state "identity theory" (Place, 1956; Armstrong, 1968), which asserts that mental states are identical with brain states), but has been much more divided on functionalism, the machine analogy for the human mind, and the question of whether machines can literally think. A number of early philosophical responses to Turing's (1950) "Computing Machinery and Intelligence," for example, Scriven (1953), attempted to deny that it was even *meaningful* to say that machines could think, on the ground that such an assertion violated the meanings of the relevant terms. Scriven, at least, had retracted this view by 1963; see his addendum to a reprint of his article (Anderson, 1964). In general, later philosophical responses to AI have at least granted the meaningfulness of the question, although some might answer it vehemently in the negative.

Following the classification used by Block (1980), we can distinguish varieties of functionalism. *Functional specification theory* (Lewis, 1966; Lewis, 1980) is a variant of brain-state identity theory that selects the brain states that are to be identified with mental states on the basis of their functional role. *Functional state identity theory* (Putnam, 1960; Putnam, 1967) is more closely based on a machine analogy. It identifies mental states not with *physical* brain states but with abstract computational states of the brain conceived expressly as a computing device. These abstract states are supposed to be independent of the specific physical composition of the brain, leading some to charge that functional state identity theory is a form of dualism!

Both the brain-state identity theory and the various forms of functionalism have come under attack from authors who claim that they do not account for the *qualia* or "what it's like" aspect of mental states (Nagel, 1974). Searle has focused instead on the alleged inability of functionalism to account for intentionality (Searle, 1980; Searle, 1984; Searle, 1992). Churchland and Churchland (1982) rebut both these types of criticism.

Functionalism is the philosophy of mind most naturally suggested by AI, and critiques of functionalism often take the form of critiques of AI (as in the case of Searle). Other critics of AI, most notably Dreyfus, have focused specifically on the assumptions and research methods of AI itself, rather than its general philosophical implications. Even philosophers who are functionalists are not always sanguine about the prospects of AI as a practical enterprise (Fodor, 1983). Despite Searle's "strong"/"weak" terminology, it is possible for a philosopher to believe that human intellectual capabilities could in principle be duplicated by duplicating their functional structure alone (and thus to support "strong AI") while also believing that as a practical matter neither GOFAI nor any other human endeavor is likely to discover that functional structure in the foreseeable future (and thus to oppose "weak AI"). In fact, this seems to be a relatively common viewpoint among philosophers.

Not all philosophers are critical of GOFAI, however; some are, in fact, ardent advocates and even practitioners. Zenon Pylyshyn (1984) has argued that cognition can best be understood through a computational model, not only in principle but also as a way of conducting research at present, and has specifically rebutted Dreyfus's criticisms of the computational model of human cognition (Pylyshyn, 1974). Gilbert Harman (1983), in analyzing belief revision, makes connections with AI research on truth maintenance systems. Michael Bratman has applied his "belief-desire-intention" model of human psychology (Bratman, 1987) to AI research on planning (Bratman, 1992). At the extreme end of strong AI, Aaron Sloman (1978, p. xiii) has even described as "racialist" Joseph Weizenbaum's view (Weizenbaum, 1976) that hypothetical intelligent machines should not be regarded as persons.

ELIMINATIVE
MATERIALISM
Eliminative materialism (Rorty, 1965; Churchland, 1979) differs from all other prominent theories in the philosophy of mind, in that it does not attempt to give an account of why our "folk psychology" or commonsense ideas about the mind are true, but instead rejects them as false and attempts to replace them with a purely scientific theory of the mind. In principle, this scientific theory could be given by classical AI, but in practice, eliminative materialists tend to lean on neuroscience and neural network research instead (Churchland, 1986), on the grounds that classical AI, especially "knowledge representation" research of the kind described in Chapter 8, tends to rely on the truth of folk psychology. Although the "intentional stance" viewpoint (Dennett, 1971) could be interpreted as functionalist, it should probably instead be regarded as a form of eliminative materialism, in that taking the "intentional stance" is not supposed to reflect any objective property of the agent toward whom the stance is taken. It should also be noted that it is possible to be an eliminative materialist about some aspects of mentality while analyzing others in some other way. For instance, Dennett (1978a) is much more strongly eliminativist about qualia than about intentionality.

The *Encyclopedia of Philosophy* (1967) is an impressively authoritative source. General collections of articles on philosophy of mind, including functionalism and other viewpoints related to AI, are *Materialism and the Mind-Body Problem* (Rosenthal, 1971) and *Readings in the Philosophy of Psychology*, volume 1 (Block, 1980). Biro and Shahan (1982) present a collection devoted to the pros and cons of functionalism. Anthologies of articles dealing more specifically with the relation between philosophy and AI include *Minds and Machines* (Anderson, 1964), *Philosophical Perspectives in Artificial Intelligence* (Ringle, 1979), *Mind Design* (Haugeland, 1981), and *The Philosophy of Artificial Intelligence* (Boden, 1990). There are several general introductions to the philosophical "AI question" (Boden, 1977; Haugeland, 1985; Copeland, 1993). *The Behavioral and Brain Sciences*, abbreviated *BBS*, is a major journal devoted to philosophical questions (and high-level, abstract scientific questions) about AI and neuroscience. A *BBS* article includes occasionally amusing peer commentary from a large number of critics and a rebuttal by the author of the main article.

EXERCISES

26.1   Go through Turing's list of alleged "disabilities" of machines, identifying which have been shown to be achievable, which are achievable in principle by a program, and which are still problematic because they require conscious mental states.

26.2   Does a refutation of the Chinese Room argument necessarily prove that appropriately programmed computers are conscious?

26.3   Suppose we ask the Chinese Room to prove that John Searle is not a conscious being. After a while, it comes up with a learned paper that looks remarkably like Searle's paper, but switches "computer" and "human" throughout, along with all the corresponding terms. The claim would be that if Searle's argument is a refutation of the possibility of conscious machines, then the Chinese Room's argument is a refutation of the possibility of conscious humans. Then, provided we agree that humans are conscious, this refutes Searle's argument by *reductio ad absurdum*. Is this a sound argument? What might Searle's response be?

26.4   In the Brain Prosthesis argument, it is important to be able to restore the subject's brain to normal, such that its external behavior is as it would have been if the operation had not taken place. Can the sceptic reasonably object that this would require updating those neurophysiological properties of the neurons relating to conscious experience, as distinct from those involved in the functional behavior of the neurons?

26.5   Find and analyze an account in the popular media of one or more of the arguments to the effect that AI is impossible.

26.6   Under the correspondence theory, what kinds of propositions can be represented by a logical agent? A reflex (condition-action) agent?

26.7   Attempt to write definitions of the terms "intelligence," "thinking," and "consciousness." Suggest some possible objections to your definitions.

27 AI: PRESENT AND FUTURE

In which we take stock of where we are and where we are going, this being a good thing to do before continuing.

27.1 HAVE WE SUCCEEDED YET?

In Part I, we proposed a unified view of AI as intelligent agent design. We showed that the design problem depends on the percepts and actions available to the agent, the goals that the agent's behavior should satisfy, and the nature of the environment. A variety of different agent designs are possible, ranging from reflex agents to fully deliberative, knowledge-based agents. Moreover, the components of these designs can have a number of different instantiations—for example, logical, probabilistic, or "neural." The intervening chapters presented the principles by which these components operate.

In areas such as game playing, logical inference and theorem proving, planning, and medical diagnosis, we have seen systems based on rigorous theoretical principles that can perform as well as, or better than, human experts. In other areas, such as learning, vision, robotics, and natural language understanding, rapid improvements in performance are occurring through the application of better analytical methods and improvements in our understanding of the underlying problems. Continued research will bear fruit in the form of better capabilities in all of these areas.

Enthralled by the technical details, however, one can sometimes lose sight of the big picture. We need an antidote for this tendency. *We will consider therefore whether we have the tools with which to build a complete, general-purpose intelligent agent.* This will also help to reveal a number of gaps in our current understanding.

Let us begin with the question of the agent architecture. We discussed some general principles and types in Chapter 2, and some specific architectures in Chapter 25. One key aspect of a general architecture is the ability to incorporate a variety of types of decision making, ranging from knowledge-based deliberation to reflex responses. Reflex responses are needed for situations in which time is of the essence, whereas knowledge-based deliberation allows the agent to take into account more information, to plan ahead, to handle situations in which no immediate response is available, and to produce better responses tailored specifically for the current situation. Compilation processes such as explanation-based learning (Chapter 21) continually convert declarative information at the deliberative level into more efficient representations, eventually reaching the reflex level (Figure 27.1). Architectures such as SOAR (Laird *et al.*, 1987) and THEO (Mitchell, 1990) have exactly this structure. Every time they solve a problem by explicit deliberation, they save away a generalized version of the solution for use by the reflex component.

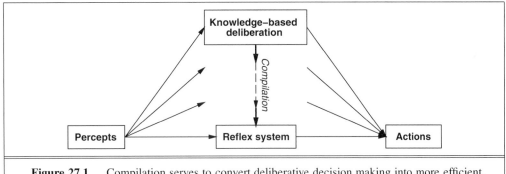

Figure 27.1   Compilation serves to convert deliberative decision making into more efficient, reflexive mechanisms.

As we saw in Part V, uncertainty is an inevitable problem in the real world. We also saw how uncertain knowledge is one possible response to the fact that exactly correct rules in realistic environments are usually very complex, and hence unusable. Unfortunately, there are clear gaps in our understanding of how to incorporate uncertain reasoning into general-purpose agent architectures. First, very little work has been done on compilation of uncertain reasoning and decision making. Second, we need more expressive languages for uncertain knowledge— a first-order probabilistic logic. Third, we need much better mechanisms for planning under uncertainty. Current algorithms, such as policy iteration (Chapter 17), are really more analogous to the simple search algorithms of Part II than to the powerful planning methods of Part IV. The latter methods incorporate partial ordering, goal directedness, and abstraction in order to handle very complex domains. *AI is only just beginning to come to grips with the problem of integrating techniques from the logical and probabilistic worlds* (Hanks *et al.*, 1994).

Agents in real environments also need ways to control their own deliberations. They must be able to cease deliberation when action is demanded, and they must be able to use the available time for deliberation to execute the most profitable computations. For example, a taxi-driving agent that sees an accident ahead should decide either to brake or to take avoiding action in a split second rather than in half an hour. It should also spend that split second thinking about the most important questions, such as whether the lanes to the left and right are clear and whether there is a large truck close behind, rather than worrying about wear and tear on the tires or where to pick up the next passenger. These issues are usually studied under the heading of **real-**

REAL-TIME AI   **time AI**. As AI systems move into more complex domains, all problems will become real-time because the agent will never have long enough to solve the decision problem exactly (see also Section 27.2). This issue came up in our discussion of game-playing systems in Chapter 5, where we described alpha-beta pruning to eliminate irrelevant deliberations and depth limits to ensure timely play. Clearly, there is a pressing need for methods that work in more general decision-making situations. Two promising techniques have emerged in recent years. The first involves the use of **anytime algorithms** (Dean and Boddy, 1988). An anytime algorithm is an algorithm whose output quality improves gradually over time, so that it has a reasonable decision ready whenever it is interrupted. Such algorithms are controlled by a metalevel decision procedure that decides whether further computation is worthwhile. Iterative deepening search in game playing provides a simple example of an anytime algorithm. More complex systems, composed of many such algorithms working together, can also be constructed (Zilberstein, 1993).

ANYTIME
ALGORITHMS

The second technique is **decision-theoretic metareasoning** (Russell and Wefald, 1991). This method applies the theory of information value (Chapter 16) to select computations. The value of a computation depends on both its cost (in terms of delaying action) and its benefits (in terms of improved decision quality). Metareasoning techniques can be used to design better search algorithms, and automatically guarantee that the algorithms have the anytime property. Metareasoning is expensive, of course, and compilation methods can be applied to generate more efficient implementations. The application of anytime and metareasoning methods to general decision-making architectures has not yet been investigated in any depth.

DECISION-
THEORETIC
METAREASONING

The final architectural component for a general intelligent agent is the learning mechanism, or mechanisms. As the architecture becomes more complicated, the number of niches for learning increases. As we saw in Part VI, however, the same methods for inductive learning, reinforcement learning, and compilation can be used for all of the learning tasks in an agent. The learning methods do depend on the representations chosen, of course. Methods for attribute-based logical and neural representations are well understood, and methods for first-order logical representations and probabilistic representations are catching up fast. As new representations, such as first-order probabilistic logics, are developed, new learning algorithms will have to be developed to accompany them. We also will need to find a way to integrate inductive methods into the agent architecture in the same way that compilation methods are integrated into architectures such as SOAR and THEO.

An agent architecture is an empty shell without knowledge to fill it. Some have proposed that the necessary knowledge can be acquired through a training process, starting virtually from scratch. To avoid recapitulating the entire intellectual history of the human race, the training process also might include direct instruction and knowledge acquisition from sources such as encyclopedias and television programs. Although such methods might avoid the need for knowledge representation and ontological engineering work, they currently seem impractical. For the foreseeable future, useful knowledge-based systems will require some work by human knowledge engineers. Robust natural language systems, for example, may require very broad knowledge bases. Further work on general-purpose ontologies, as sketched in Chapter 8, is clearly needed. The CYC project (Lenat and Guha, 1990) is a brave effort in this direction, but many open problems remain and we have little experience in *using* large knowledge bases.

To sum up: by looking at current systems and how they would need to be extended, we can identify a variety of research questions whose answers would take us further toward general-purpose intelligent systems. This incremental approach is useful, provided we are fairly confident that we have a reasonable starting point. In the next section, we look at the AI problem from first principles to see whether this is in fact the case.

27.2 WHAT EXACTLY ARE WE TRYING TO DO?

Even before the beginning of artificial intelligence, philosophers, control theorists, and economists sought a satisfactory definition of rational action. This is needed to underpin theories of ethics, inductive learning, reasoning, optimal control, decision making, and economic modelling. *It has also been our goal in this book to show how to design agents that act rationally.* Initially, we presented no formal definition of rational action. Later chapters presented logical and decision-theoretic definitions together with specific designs for achieving them. The role of such definitions in AI is clear: if we define some desirable property P, then we ought in principle to be able to design a system that provably possesses property P. Theory meets practice when our systems exhibit P in reality. Furthermore, that they exhibit P in reality should be something that we actually care about. In a sense, the choice of what P to study determines the nature of the field. Therefore, we need to look carefully at what exactly we are trying to do.

There are a number of possible choices for P. Here are three:

PERFECT
RATIONALITY

⬦ **Perfect rationality**: the classical notion of rationality in decision theory. A perfectly rational agent acts at every instant in such a way as to maximize its expected utility, given the information it has acquired from the environment. In Chapter 1, we warned that

> achieving perfect rationality—always doing the right thing—is just not possible in complicated environments. The computational demands are just too high. However, for most of the book, we will adopt the working hypothesis that understanding perfect decision making is a good place to start.

Because perfect rational agents do not exist for nontrivial environments, perfect rationality is not a suitable candidate for P.

CALCULATIVE
RATIONALITY

⬦ **Calculative rationality**: the notion of rationality that we have used implicitly in designing logical and decision-theoretic agents. A calculatively rational agent *eventually* returns what *would have been* the rational choice at the beginning of its deliberation. This is an interesting property for a system to exhibit because it constitutes an "in-principle" capacity to do the right thing. Calculative rationality is sometimes of limited value, because the actual behavior exhibited by such systems can be rather irrational. For example, a calculatively rational chess program may choose the right move, but may take 10^{50} times too long to do so. In practice, AI system designers are forced to compromise on decision quality to obtain reasonable overall performance, yet the theoretical basis of calculative rationality does not provide for such compromises.

BOUNDED
OPTIMALITY

⬦ **Bounded optimality** (BO): a bounded optimal agent behaves as well as possible *given its computational resources*. That is, the expected utility of the agent program for a bounded optimal agent is at least as high as the expected utility of any other agent program running on the same machine.

Of these three possibilities, choosing P to be "bounded optimality" seems to offer the best hope for a strong theoretical foundation for AI. Clearly, a BO agent is of real, practical interest because its behavior is the best that can be obtained. Equally clearly, BO programs exist for any given task, machine, and environment. Obviously, *finding* the BO program is the trick; AI as the study of bounded optimality is feasible in principle, but no one said it was easy! One obvious difficulty is that the designer may not have a probability distribution over the kinds of environments in which the agent is expected to operate, and so may not be able to ascertain the bounded optimality of a given design. In such cases, however, a suitably designed learning agent should be able to adapt to the initially unknown environment; analytical results on the bounded optimality of learning agents can be obtained using computational learning theory (Chapter 18). One crucial open question is to what extent bounded optimal systems can be *composed* from bounded optimal subsystems, thereby providing a hierarchical design methodology.

Although bounded optimality is a very general specification, it is no more general than the definition of calculative rationality on which much of past AI work has been based. The important thing is that by including resource constraints from the beginning, questions of efficiency and decision quality can be handled within the theory rather than by *ad hoc* system design. The two approaches only coincide if BO agents look *something like* calculatively rational agents with various efficiency improvements added on. Real environments are *far* more complex than anything that can be handled by a pure calculatively rational agent, however, so this would quite a radical assumption.

As yet, little is known about bounded optimality. It is possible to construct bounded optimal programs for very simple machines and for somewhat restricted kinds of environments (Etzioni, 1989; Russell and Subramanian, 1993), but as yet we have no idea what BO programs are like for large, general-purpose computers in complex environments. If there is to be a constructive theory of bounded optimality, we have to hope that the design of bounded optimal programs does not depend too strongly on the details of the computer being used. It would make scientific research very difficult if adding a few kilobytes of memory to a machine with 100 megabytes made a significant difference to the design of the BO program and to its performance in the environment. One way to make sure this cannot happen is to be slightly more relaxed about the criteria for bounded optimality. By analogy with asymptotic complexity (Appendix A), we can define **asymptotic bounded optimality** (ABO) as follows (Russell and Subramanian, 1993). Suppose a program P is bounded optimal for a machine M in a class of environments $\mathbf{E}$ (the complexity of environments in $\mathbf{E}$ is unbounded). Then program P' is ABO for M in $\mathbf{E}$ if it can outperform P by running on a machine kM that is k times faster (or larger). Unless k were enormous, we would be happy with a program that was ABO for a nontrivial environment on a nontrivial architecture. There would be little point in putting enormous effort into finding BO rather than ABO programs, because the size and speed of available machines tends to increase by a constant factor in a fixed amount of time anyway.

We can hazard a guess that BO or ABO programs for powerful computers in complex environments will not necessarily have a simple, elegant structure. We have already seen that general-purpose intelligence requires some reflex capability and some deliberative capability, a variety of forms of knowledge and decision making, learning and compilation mechanisms for all of those forms, methods for controlling reasoning, and a large store of domain-specific knowledge. A bounded optimal agent must adapt to the environment in which it finds itself, so that eventually its internal organization may reflect optimizations that are specific to the particular environment. This is only to be expected, and is similar to the way in which racing cars restricted by weight and horsepower have evolved into extremely complex designs. We suspect that a science of artificial intelligence based on bounded optimality will involve a good deal of study of

ASYMPTOTIC
BOUNDED
OPTIMALITY

the processes that allow an agent program to converge to bounded optimality, and perhaps less concentration on the details of the messy programs that result.

In summary, the concept of bounded optimality is proposed as a formal task for artificial intelligence research that is both well-defined and feasible. Bounded optimality specifies optimal *programs* rather than optimal *actions*. Actions are, after all, generated by programs, and it is over programs that designers have control.

This move from prescribing actions to prescribing programs is not unique to AI. Philosophy has also seen a gradual evolution in the definition of rationality. There has been a shift from consideration of **act utilitarianism**—the rationality of individual acts—to **rule utilitarianism**, or the rationality of general policies for acting. A philosophical proposal generally consistent with the notion of bounded optimality can be found in the "Moral First Aid Manual" (Dennett, 1986). Dennett explicitly discusses the idea of reaching equilibrium within the space of feasible configurations of decision procedures. He uses as an example the Ph.D. admissions procedure of a philosophy department. He concludes, as do we, that the best configuration may be neither elegant nor illuminating. The existence of such a configuration and the process of reaching it are the main points of interest.

Another area to undergo the same transition is **game theory**, a branch of economics initiated in the same book—*Theory of Games and Economic Behavior* (Von Neumann and Morgenstern, 1944)—that began the widespread study of decision theory. Game theory studies decision problems in which the utility of a given action depends not only on chance events in the environment but also on the actions of other agents. The standard scenario involves a set of agents who make their decisions simultaneously, without knowledge of the decisions of the other agents. The **Prisoner's Dilemma** is a famous example, in which each of two crime suspects can "collaborate" (refuse to implicate his or her partner) or "defect" (spill the beans in return for a free pardon). If the suspects collaborate, they will only be convicted of a minor offense, a one-year sentence. If they both defect, both receive a four-year sentence. If one defects and the other does not, the defector goes free whereas the other receives the maximum sentence of ten years. Considered from the point of view of either player separately, the best plan is to defect, because this gives better results whatever the other agent does. Unfortunately for the suspects (but not for the police), this results in both suspects spilling the beans and receiving a four-year sentence, whereas if they had collaborated, they would both have received lighter sentences. Even more disturbing is the fact that defection also occurs when the game has a finite number of rounds. (This can easily be proved by working backwards from the last round.) Recently, however, there has been a shift from consideration of optimal decisions in games to a consideration of optimal decision-making programs. This leads to different results because it limits the ability of each agent to do unlimited simulation of the other, who is also doing unlimited simulation of the first, and so on. Even the requirement of computability makes a significant difference (Megiddo and Wigderson, 1986). Bounds on the complexity of players have also become a topic of intense interest. Neyman's theorem (Neyman, 1985), recently proved by Papadimitriou and Yannakakis (1994), shows that a collaborative equilibrium exists if each agent is a finite automaton with a number of states that is less than exponential in the number of rounds. This is essentially a bounded optimality result, where the bound is on space rather than speed of computation. Again, the bounded optimal program for the automaton is rather messy, but its existence and properties are what counts.

27.3   WHAT IF WE DO SUCCEED?

In David Lodge's *Small World*, a novel about the academic world of literary criticism, the protagonist causes consternation by asking a panel of eminent but contradictory literary theorists the following question: *"What if you were right?"* None of the theorists seems to have considered this question before, perhaps because debating unfalsifiable theories is an end in itself. Similar confusion can sometimes be evoked by asking AI researchers, "What if you succeed?" AI is fascinating, and intelligent computers are clearly more useful than unintelligent computers, so why worry?

To the extent that AI has already succeeded in finding uses within society, we are now facing some of the real issues. In the litigious atmosphere that prevails in the United States, it is hardly surprising that legal liability needs to be discussed. When a physician relies on the judgment of a medical expert system for a diagnosis, who is at fault if the diagnosis is wrong? Fortunately, due in part to the growing influence of decision-theoretic methods in medicine, it is now accepted that negligence cannot be shown if the physician performs medical procedures that have high *expected* utility, even if the *actual* utility is catastrophic. The question should therefore be, "Who is at fault if the diagnosis is unreasonable?" So far, courts have held that medical expert systems play the same role as medical textbooks and reference books; physicians are responsible for understanding the reasoning behind any decision and for using their own judgment in deciding whether or not to accept the system's recommendations. In designing medical expert systems as agents, therefore, the actions should not be thought of as directly affecting the patient but as influencing the physician's behavior. If expert systems become reliably more accurate than human diagnosticians, doctors may be legally liable if they *fail* to use the recommendations of an expert system.

Similar issues are beginning to arise regarding the use of intelligent agents on the "information highway." Some progress has been made in incorporating constraints into intelligent agents so that they cannot damage the files of other users (Weld and Etzioni, 1994). Also problematic is the fact that network services already involve monetary transactions. If those monetary transactions are made "on one's behalf" by an intelligent agent, is one liable for the debts incurred? Would it be possible for an intelligent agent to have assets itself and to perform electronic trades on its own behalf? Could it own stocks and bonds in the same way that corporations own stocks and bonds? So far, these questions do not seem to be well understood. To our knowledge, no program has been granted legal status as an individual for the purposes of financial transactions; at present, it seems unreasonable to do so. Programs are also not considered to be "drivers" for the purposes of enforcing traffic regulations on real highways. In California law, at least, there do not seem to be any legal sanctions to prevent an automated vehicle from exceeding the speed limits, although the designer of the vehicle's control mechanism would be liable in the case of accident. As with human reproductive technology, the law has yet to catch up with the new developments. These topics, among others, are covered in journals such as *AI and Society, Law, Computers and Artificial Intelligence*, and *Artificial Intelligence and Law*.

Looking further into the future, one can anticipate questions that have been the subject of innumerable works of science fiction, most notably those of Asimov (1942). If we grant that machines will achieve high levels of intelligent behavior and will communicate with humans as apparent equals, then these questions are unavoidable. Should (or will) intelligent machines have rights? How should intelligent machines interact with humans? What might happen if intelligent machines decide to work against the best interests of human beings? What if they succeed?

In *Computer Power and Human Reason*, Joseph Weizenbaum (the author of the ELIZA program) has argued that the effect of intelligent machines on human society will be such that continued work on artificial intelligence is perhaps unethical. One of Weizenbaum's principal arguments is that AI research makes possible the idea that humans are automata—an idea that results in a loss of autonomy or even of humanity. (We note that the idea has been around much longer than AI. See *L'Homme Machine* (La Mettrie, 1748).) One can perhaps group such concerns with the general concern that any technology can be misused to the detriment of humanity. Arguments over the desirability of a given technology must weigh the benefits and risks, and put the onus on researchers to ensure that policy makers and the public have the best possible information with which to reach a decision. On the other hand, AI raises deeper questions than, say, nuclear weapons technology. No one, to our knowledge, has suggested that reducing the planet to a cinder is better than preserving human civilization. Futurists such as Edward Fredkin and Hans Moravec have, however, suggested that once the human race has fulfilled its destiny in bringing into existence entities of higher (and perhaps unlimited) intelligence, its own preservation may seem less important. Something to think about, anyway.

Looking on the bright side, success in AI would provide great opportunities for improving the material circumstances of human life. Whether it would improve the quality of life is an open question. Will intelligent automation give people more fulfilling work and more relaxing leisure time? Or will the pressures of competing in a nanosecond-paced world lead to more stress? Will children gain from instant access to intelligent tutors, multimedia online encyclopedias, and global communication, or will they play ever more realistic war games? Will intelligent machines extend the power of the individual, or of centralized governments and corporations? Science fiction authors seem to favor dystopian futures over utopian ones, probably because they make for more interesting plots. In reality, however, the trends seem not to be too terribly negative.

A COMPLEXITY ANALYSIS AND O() NOTATION

A

Computer scientists are often faced with the task of comparing two algorithms to see which runs faster or takes less memory. There are two approaches to this task. The first is **benchmarking**—running the two algorithms on a computer and measuring which is faster (or which uses less memory). Ultimately, this is what really matters, but a benchmark can be unsatisfactory because it is so specific: it measures the performance of a particular program written in a particular language running on a particular computer with a particular compiler and particular input data. From the single result that the benchmark provides, it can be difficult to predict how well the algorithm would do on a different compiler, computer, or data set. A useful variant of benchmarking is to count the number of operations performed of a particular kind: for example, in testing a numerical sorting algorithm we might count the number of "greater-than" tests.

A.1 ASYMPTOTIC ANALYSIS

ANALYSIS OF ALGORITHMS

The second approach relies on a mathematical **analysis of algorithms**, independent of the particular implementation and input. We will discuss the approach with the following example, a program to compute the sum of a sequence of numbers:

```
function SUMMATION(sequence) returns a number
    sum ← 0
    for i ← 1 to LENGTH(sequence)
        sum ← sum + sequence[i]
    end
    return sum
```

The first step in the analysis is to abstract over the input, to find some parameter or parameters that characterize the size of the input. In this example, the input can be characterized by the length of the sequence, which we will call n. The second step is to abstract over the implementation, to find some measure that reflects the running time of the algorithm, but is not tied to a particular compiler or computer. For the SUMMATION program, this could be just the number of lines of code executed. Or it could be more detailed, measuring the number of additions, assignments, array references, and branches executed by the algorithm. Either way gives us a characterization of the total number of steps taken by the algorithm, as a function of the size of the input. We will call this $T(n)$. With the simpler measure, we have $T(n) = 2n + 2$ for our example.

If all programs were as simple as SUMMATION, analysis of algorithms would be a trivial field. But two problems make it more complicated. First, it is rare to find a parameter like n that completely characterizes the number of steps taken by an algorithm. Instead, the best we can usually do is compute the worst case $T_{worst}(n)$ or the average case $T_{avg}(n)$. Computing an average means that the analyst must assume some distribution of inputs.

The second problem is that algorithms tend to resist exact analysis. In that case, it is necessary to fall back on an approximation. We say that the SUMMATION algorithm is $O(n)$, meaning that its measure is at most a constant times n, with the possible exception of a few small values of n. More formally,

$$T(n) \text{ is } O(f(n)) \text{ if } T(n) \leq kf(n) \text{ for some } k, \text{ for all } n > n_0$$

ASYMPTOTIC
ANALYSIS

The $O()$ notation gives us what is called an **asymptotic analysis**. We can say without question that as n asymptotically approaches infinity, an $O(n)$ algorithm is better than an $O(n^2)$ algorithm. A single benchmark figure could not substantiate such a claim.

The $O()$ notation abstracts over constant factors, which makes it easier to use than the $T()$ notation, but less precise. For example, an $O(n^2)$ algorithm will always be worse than an $O(n)$ in the long run, but if the two algorithms are $T(n^2 + 1)$ and $T(100n + 1000)$, then the $O(n^2)$ algorithm is actually better for $n \leq 110$.

Despite this drawback, asymptotic analysis is the most widely used tool for analyzing algorithms. It is precisely because the analysis abstracts both over the exact number of operations (by ignoring the constant factor, k) and the exact content of the input (by only considering its size, n) that the analysis becomes mathematically feasible. The $O()$ notation is a good compromise between precision and ease of analysis.

A.2   INHERENTLY HARD PROBLEMS

COMPLEXITY
ANALYSIS

Analysis of algorithms and the $O()$ notation allow us to talk about the efficiency of a particular algorithm. However, they have nothing to say about whether or not there could be a better algorithm for the problem at hand. The field of **complexity analysis** analyzes problems rather than algorithms. The first gross division is between problems that can be solved in polynomial time and those that cannot be solved in polynomial time, no matter what algorithm is used. The class of polynomial problems is called P. These are sometimes called "easy" problems, because the class contains those problems with running times like $O(\log n)$ and $O(n)$. But it also contains those with $O(n^{1000})$, so the name "easy" should not be taken too literally.

Another important class of problems is NP, the class of nondeterministic polynomial problems. A problem is in this class if there is some algorithm that can guess a solution and then verify whether or not the guess is correct in polynomial time. The idea is that if you either have an exponentially large number of processors so that you can try all the guesses at once, or you are very lucky and always guess right the first time, then the NP problems become P problems.

One of the big open questions in computer science is whether the class NP is equivalent to the class P when one does not have the luxury of an infinite number of processors or omniscient guessing. Most computer scientists are convinced that $P \neq NP$, that NP problems are inherently hard and only have exponential time algorithms. But this has never been proven.

NP-COMPLETE

Those who are interested in deciding if $P = NP$ look at a subclass of NP called the **NP-complete** problems. The word complete is used here in the sense of "most extreme," and thus refers to the hardest problems in the class NP. It has been proven that either all the NP-complete problems are in P or none of them is. This makes the class theoretically interesting, but the class is also of practical interest because many important problems are known to be NP-complete. An example is the satisfiability problem: given a logical expression (see Chapter 6), is there an assignment of truth values to the variables of the expression that make it true?

Also studied is the class of PSPACE problems, those that require a polynomial amount of space, even on a nondeterministic machine. It is generally believed that *PSPACE*-hard problems are worse than NP-complete, although it could turn out that NP = PSPACE, just as it could turn out that P = NP.

BIBLIOGRAPHICAL AND HISTORICAL NOTES

The $O()$ notation so widely used in computer science today was first introduced in the context of number theory by the German mathematician P. G. H. Bachmann (1894). The concept of NP-completeness was invented by Cook (1971), and the modern method for establishing a reduction from one problem to another is due to Karp (1972). Cook and Karp have both won the Turing award, the highest honor in computer science, for their work.

Classic works on the analysis and design of algorithms include those by Knuth (1973) and Aho, Hopcroft, and Ullman (1974); more recent contributions are by Tarjan (1983) and Cormen, Leiserson, and Rivest (1990). These books place an emphasis on designing and analyzing algorithms to solve tractable problems. For the theory of NP-completeness and other forms of intractability, the best introduction is by Garey and Johnson (1979). In addition to the underlying theory, Garey and Johnson provide examples that convey very forcefully why computer scientists are unanimous in drawing the line between tractable and intractable problems at the border between polynomial and exponential time complexity. They also provide a voluminous catalog of problems that are known to be NP-complete or otherwise intractable.

B NOTES ON LANGUAGES AND ALGORITHMS

B.1 DEFINING LANGUAGES WITH BACKUS–NAUR FORM (BNF)

In this book, we define several languages, including the languages of propositional logic (page 166), first-order logic (page 187), and a subset of English (page 670). A formal language is defined as a set of strings where each string is a sequence of symbols. All the languages we are interested in consist of an infinite set of strings, so we need a concise way to characterize the set. We do that with a **grammar**. We have chosen to write our grammars in a formalism called **Backus–Naur form**, or **BNF**. There are four components to a BNF grammar:

- A set of **terminal symbols**. These are the symbols or words that make up the strings of the language. They could be letters (**A, B, C, ...**) or words (**a, aardvark, abacus, ...**) for English. For the language of arithmetic, the set of symbols is

$$\{0, 1, 2, 3, 4, 5, 6, 7, 8, 9, +, -, \div, \times, (,)\}$$

- A set of **nonterminal symbols** that categorize subphrases of the language. For example, the nonterminal symbol *NounPhrase* in English denotes an infinite set of strings including "you" and "the big slobbery dog."

- A **start symbol**, which is the nonterminal symbol that denotes the complete strings of the language. In English, this is *Sentence*; for arithmetic, it might be *Exp*.

- A set of **rewrite rules** or **productions** of the form *LHS* → *RHS*, where *LHS* is a nonterminal, and *RHS* is a sequence of zero or more symbols (either terminal or nonterminal).

A rewrite rule of the form

> *Digit* → **7**

means that anytime we see the string consisting of the lone symbol 7, we can categorize it as a *Digit*. A rule of the form

> *Sentence* → *NounPhrase VerbPhrase*

means that whenever we have two strings categorized as a *NounPhrase* and a *VerbPhrase*, we can append them together and categorize the result as a *Sentence*. As an abbreviation, the symbol |

can be used to separate alternative right-hand sides. Here is a BNF grammar for simple arithmetic expressions:

$$Exp \quad \rightarrow \; Exp \; Operator \; Exp$$
$$| \; (\; Exp \;)$$
$$| \; Number$$

$$Number \quad \rightarrow \; Digit$$
$$| \; Number \; Digit$$

$$Digit \quad \rightarrow \; \mathbf{0} \; | \; \mathbf{1} \; | \; \mathbf{2} \; | \; \mathbf{3} \; | \; \mathbf{4} \; | \; \mathbf{5} \; | \; \mathbf{6} \; | \; \mathbf{7} \; | \; \mathbf{8} \; | \; \mathbf{9}$$
$$Operator \; \rightarrow \; \mathbf{+} \; | \; \mathbf{-} \; | \; \mathbf{\div} \; | \; \mathbf{\times}$$

We cover languages and grammars in more detail in Chapter 22. Be aware that other books use slightly different notations for BNF; for example, you might see $\langle Digit \rangle$ instead of *Digit* for a nonterminal; 'word' instead of **word** for a terminal; or : : = instead of $\rightarrow$ in a rule.

B.2   DESCRIBING ALGORITHMS WITH PSEUDO-CODE

In this book, we define over 100 algorithms. Rather than picking a programming language (and risking that readers who are unfamiliar with the language will be lost), we have chosen to describe the algorithms in pseudo-code. Most of it should be familiar to users of languages like Pascal, C, or Common Lisp, but in some places we use mathematical formulas or ordinary English to describe parts that would otherwise be more cumbersome. There are a few idiosyncrasies that should be remarked on.

Nondeterminism

It is the nature of AI that we are often faced with making a decision before we know enough to make the right choice. So our algorithms have to make a choice, but keep track of the alternatives in case the choice does not succeed. The clearest way to describe such algorithms without bogging them down with bookkeeping details is with the primitives **choose** and **fail**.

The idea is that when we call **choose**(*a,b,c*), the algorithm will return either *a*, *b*, or *c* as the value of the **choose** expression. But it will also save the other two on an agenda of pending choices. The algorithm continues; if it terminates normally then all is done, and we forget about the agenda. But if a **fail** statement is encountered, then a pending choice is taken off the agenda, and control is resumed *at the point in the algorithm where that choice was saved*. Algorithms

NONDETERMINISTIC
ALGORITHMS

that make use of **choose** are called **nondeterministic algorithms**.

You can think of a nondeterministic algorithm as a search through the space of possible choices. As such, any of the search algorithms from Chapters 3 or 4 can be used. The beauty of the nondeterministic algorithm is that the search strategy can be specified separately from the main algorithm.

Another way to think of nondeterministic algorithms is to imagine an **oracle** that magically advises the algorithm to make the correct choice at every choice point. If such an oracle could be found, the algorithm would be deterministic; it would never need to backtrack. You can think of the agenda as a slower means of simulating the advice of the oracle.

Nondeterministic algorithms are often clearer than deterministic versions, but unfortunately only a few programming languages support nondeterminism directly—Prolog and ICON are probably the best known. **choose** and **fail** can be implemented in SCHEME in about 15 lines of code, using the function `call-with-current-continuation`.

Here is an example of a nondeterministic function: the function call INTEGER(*start*) returns an integer greater than or equal to *start*, chosen nondeterministically.

---

function INTEGER(*start*) **returns** an integer
   return choose(*start*, INTEGER(*start* + 1))

It is important to understand what the code fragment PRINT(INTEGER (0)); **fail** will do. First, it will print some integer, although we cannot say which one without knowing what control strategy is used by **choose**. Then **fail** will return control to one of the choice points in one of the recursive calls to INTEGER. Eventually, a different integer will be chosen and printed, and then **fail** will be executed again. The result is an infinite loop, with a single integer printed each time.

We sometimes use the term **pick** to mean a choice that is not a backtracking point. For example, an algorithm to sum the elements of a set is to initialize the total to 0, pick an element from the set and add it to the total, and continue until there are no more elements to pick. There is no need to backtrack, because any order of picking will get the job done.

Static variables

We use the keyword **static** to say that a variable is given an initial value the first time a function is called and retains that value (or the value given to it by a subsequent assignment statement) on all subsequent calls to the function. Thus, static variables are like global variables in that they outlive a single call to their function, but they are only accessible within the function. The agent programs in the book use static variables for "memory." Programs with static variables can be implemented as "objects" in object-oriented languages such as C++ and Smalltalk. In functional languages, they can be implemented easily by executing lambda-expressions within an environment in which the required variables are defined.

Functions as values

Functions and procedures have capitalized names and variables have lower case italic names. So most of the time, a function call looks like SOME-FUNCTION(*variable*). However, we allow the value of a variable to be a function; for example, if the value of *variable* is the square root function, then *variable*(9) returns 3.

B.3   THE CODE REPOSITORY

The pseudo-code in the book is meant to be easy to read and understand, but it is not easy to run on a computer. To fix this problem, we have provided a repository of working code. Most of the algorithms in the book are implemented, as well as a set of basic tools not covered in the book. Currently, the algorithms are all written in Lisp, although we may add other languages in the future. If you are reading this book as part of a course, your instructor will probably retrieve the code for you. If not, send an electronic mail message to

```
aima-request@cs.berkeley.edu
```

with the word "help" in the subject line or in the body. You will receive a return message with instructions on how to get the code. (We don't print the instructions here because they are subject to frequent change.) You can also order the code on a floppy disk by writing to Prentice-Hall Inc., Englewood Cliffs, NJ, 07632. Finally, a good deal of information about the book, including the code, can be obtained from the World-Wide Web at the URL

```
http://www.cs.berkeley.edu/~russell/aima.html
```

B.4   COMMENTS

If you have any comments on the book, any typos you have noticed, or any suggestions on how it can be improved, we would like to hear from you. Please send a message to

```
aima-bug@cs.berkeley.edu
```

or write to us in care of Prentice-Hall.

Bibliography

Aarup, M., Arentoft, M. M., Parrod, Y., Stader, J., and Stokes, I. (1994). OPTIMUM-AIV: A knowledge-based planning and scheduling system for spacecraft AIV. In Fox, M. and Zweben, M., editors, *Knowledge Based Scheduling*. Morgan Kaufmann, San Mateo, California.

Abu-Mostafa, Y. S. and Psaltis, D. (1987). Optical neural computers. *Scientific American*, 256:88–95.

Acharya, A., Tambe, M., and Gupta, A. (1992). Implementation of production systems on message-passing computers. *IEEE Transactions on Parallel and Distributed Systems*, 3(4):477–487.

Adelson-Velsky, G. M., Arlazarov, V. L., Bitman, A. R., Zhivotovsky, A. A., and Uskov, A. V. (1970). Programming a computer to play chess. *Russian Mathematical Surveys*, 25:221–262.

Adelson-Velsky, G. M., Arlazarov, V. L., and Donskoy, M. V. (1975). Some methods of controlling the tree search in chess programs. *Artificial Intelligence*, 6(4):361–371.

Agmon, S. (1954). The relaxation method for linear inequalities. *Canadian Journal of Mathematics*, 6(3):382–392.

Agre, P. E. and Chapman, D. (1987). Pengi: an implementation of a theory of activity. In *Proceedings of the Tenth International Joint Conference on Artificial Intelligence (IJCAI-87)*, pages 268–272, Milan, Italy. Morgan Kaufmann.

Aho, A. V., Hopcroft, J. E., and Ullman, J. D. (1974). *The Design and Analysis of Computer Algorithms*. Addison-Wesley, Reading, Massachusetts.

Ait-Kaci, H. (1991). *Warren's Abstract Machine: A Tutorial Reconstruction*. MIT Press, Cambridge, Massachusetts.

Ait-Kaci, H. and Nasr, R. (1986). LOGIN: a logic programming language with built-in inheritance. *Journal of Logic Programming*, 3(3):185–215.

Ait-Kaci, H. and Podelski, A. (1993). Towards a meaning of LIFE. *Journal of Logic Programming*, 16(3-4):195–234.

Allais, M. (1953). Le comportement de l'homme rationnel devant le risque: Critique des postulats et axiomes de l'école américaine. *Econometrica*, 21:503–546.

Allen, J. F. (1983). Maintaining knowledge about temporal intervals. *Communications of the Association for Computing Machinery*, 26(11):832–843.

Allen, J. F. (1984). Towards a general theory of action and time. *Artificial Intelligence*, 23:123–154.

Allen, J. F. (1991). Time and time again: the many ways to represent time. *International Journal of Intelligent Systems*, 6:341–355.

Allen, J. F. (1995). *Natural Language Understanding*. Benjamin/Cummings, Redwood City, California.

Allen, J. F., Hendler, J., and Tate, A., editors (1990). *Readings in Planning*. Morgan Kaufmann, San Mateo, California.

Almuallim, H. and Dietterich, T. G. (1991). Learning with many irrelevant features. In *Proceedings of the Ninth National Conference on Artificial Intelligence (AAAI-91)*, volume 2, pages 547–552, Anaheim, California. AAAI Press.

Aloimonos, J., Weiss, I., and Bandyopadhyay, A. (1988). Active vision. *International Journal of Computer Vision*, 1:333–356.

Aloimonos, Y. (1992). Special issue on purposive, qualitative, active vision. *CVGIP: Image Understanding*, 56(1).

Alshawi, H., editor (1992). *The Core Language Engine*. MIT Press, Cambridge, Massachusetts.

Alspector, J., Allen, R. B., Hu, V., and Satyanarayana, S. (1987). Stochastic learning networks and their electronic implementation. In Anderson, D. Z., editor, *Neural Information Processing Systems, Denver 1987*, pages 9–21, Denver, Colorado. American Institute of Physics.

Alterman, R. (1988). Adaptive planning. *Cognitive Science*, 12:393–422.

Amarel, S. (1968). On representations of problems of reasoning about actions. In Michie, D., editor, *Machine Intelligence 3*, volume 3, pages 131–171. Elsevier/North-Holland, Amsterdam, London, New York.

Ambros-Ingerson, J. and Steel, S. (1988). Integrating planning, execution and monitoring. In *Proceedings of the Seventh National Conference on Artificial Intelligence (AAAI-88)*, pages 735–740, St. Paul, Minnesota. Morgan Kaufmann.

Amit, D., Gutfreund, H., and Sompolinsky, H. (1985). Spin-glass models of neural networks. *Physical Review*, A 32:1007–1018.

Ammon, K. (1993). An automatic proof of Gödel's incompleteness theorem. *Artificial Intelligence*, 61(2):291–306.

Andersen, S. K., Olesen, K. G., Jensen, F. V., and Jensen, F. (1989). HUGIN—a shell for building Bayesian belief universes for expert systems. In *Proceedings of the Eleventh International Joint Conference on Artificial Intelligence (IJCAI-89)*, volume 2, pages 1080–1085, Detroit, Michigan. Morgan Kaufmann.

Anderson, A. R., editor (1964). *Minds and Machines*. Prentice-Hall, Englewood Cliffs, New Jersey.

Anderson, J. (1980). *Cognitive Psychology and its Implications*. W. H. Freeman, New York.

Anderson, J. A. and Rosenfeld, E., editors (1988). *Neurocomputing: Foundations of Research*. MIT Press, Cambridge, Massachusetts.

Anderson, J. R. (1983). *The Architecture of Cognition*. Harvard University Press, Cambridge, Massachusetts.

Armstrong, D. M. (1968). *A Materialist Theory of the Mind*. Routledge and Kegan Paul, London.

Arnauld, A. (1662). *La logique, ou l'art de penser*. Chez Charles Savreux, au pied de la Tour de Nostre Dame, Paris. Usually referred to as the *Port-Royal Logic*; translated into English as Arnauld (1964).

Arnauld, A. (1964). *The Art of Thinking*. Bobbs-Merrill, Indianapolis, Indiana. Translation of Arnauld (1662), usually referred to as the *Port-Royal Logic*.

Ashby, W. R. (1952). *Design for a Brain*. Wiley, New York.

Asimov, I. (1942). Runaround. *Astounding Science Fiction*.

Asimov, I. (1950). *I, Robot*. Doubleday, Garden City, New York.

Astrom, K. J. (1965). Optimal control of Markov decision processes with incomplete state estimation. *J. Math. Anal. Applic.*, 10:174–205.

Austin, J. L. (1962). *How To Do Things with Words*. Harvard University Press, Cambridge, Massachusetts.

Bacchus, F. (1990). *Representing and Reasoning with Probabilistic Knowledge*. MIT Press, Cambridge, Massachusetts.

Bacchus, F., Grove, A., Halpern, J. Y., and Koller, D. (1992). From statistics to beliefs. In *Proceedings of the Tenth National Conference on Artificial Intelligence (AAAI-92)*, pages 602–608, San Jose, California. AAAI Press.

Bach, E. (1986). The algebra of events. *Linguistics and Philosophy*, 9:5–16.

Bachmann, P. G. H. (1894). *Die analytische Zahlentheorie*. B. G. Teubner, Leipzig.

Bain, M. and Muggleton, S. H. (1991). Non-monotonic learning. In Hayes, J. E., Michie, D., and Tyugu, E., editors, *Machine Intelligence 12*, pages 105–119. Oxford University Press, Oxford.

Bajcsy, R. (1988). Active perception. *Proceedings of the IEEE*, 76(8):996–1005.

Bajcsy, R. and Lieberman, L. (1976). Texture gradient as a depth cue. *Computer Graphics and Image Processing*, 5(1):52–67.

Baker, C. L. (1989). *English Syntax*. MIT Press, Cambridge, Massachusetts.

Baker, J. (1975). The Dragon system—an overview. *IEEE Transactions on Acoustics, Speech, and Signal Processing*, 23.

Ballard, B. W. (1983). The *-minimax search procedure for trees containing chance nodes. *Artificial Intelligence*, 21(3):327–350.

Bar-Hillel, Y. (1954). Indexical expressions. *Mind*, 63:359–379.

Bar-Hillel, Y. (1960). The present status of automatic translation of languages. In Alt, F. L., editor, *Advances in Computers*. Academic Press, New York.

Bar-Shalom, Y. and Fortmann, T. E. (1988). *Tracking and Data Association*. Academic Press, New York.

Barr, A., Cohen, P. R., and Feigenbaum, E. A., editors (1989). *The Handbook of Artificial Intelligence*, volume 4. Addison-Wesley, Reading, Massachusetts.

Barr, A. and Feigenbaum, E. A., editors (1981). *The Handbook of Artificial Intelligence*, volume 1. HeurisTech Press and William Kaufmann, Stanford, California and Los Altos, California. First of four volumes; other volumes published separately (Barr and Feigenbaum, 1982; Cohen and Feigenbaum, 1982; Barr *et al.*, 1989).

Barr, A. and Feigenbaum, E. A., editors (1982). *The Handbook of Artificial Intelligence*, volume 2. HeurisTech Press and William Kaufmann, Stanford, California and Los Altos, California.

Barrett, A., Golden, K., Penberthy, J. S., and Weld, D. S. (1993). UCPOP user's manual (version 2.0). Technical Report 93-09-06, Department of Computer Science and Engineering, University of Washington.

Barrett, R., Ramsay, A., and Sloman, A. (1985). *POP-11: A Practical Language for Artificial Intelligence*. Ellis Horwood, Chichester, England.

Barstow, D. R. (1979). *Knowledge-Based Program Construction*. Elsevier/North-Holland, Amsterdam, London, New York.

Barto, A. G., Bradtke, S. J., and Singh, S. P. (1991). Real-time learning and control using asynchronous dynamic programming. Technical Report TR-91-57, University of Massachusetts Computer Science Department, Amherst, Massachusetts.

Barto, A. G., Sutton, R. S., and Brouwer, P. S. (1981). Associative search network: a reinforcement learning associative memory. *Biological Cybernetics*, 40(3):201–211.

Barwise, J. (1993). Everyday reasoning and logical inference. *Behavioral and Brain Sciences*, 16(2):337–338.

Barwise, J. and Etchemendy, J. (1993). *The Language of First-Order Logic: Including the Macintosh Program Tarski's World 4.0*. Center for the Study of Language and Information (CSLI), Stanford, California, third revised and expanded edition.

Baum, L. E. and Petrie, T. (1966). Statistical inference for probabilistic functions of finite state Markov chains. *Annals of Mathematical Statistics*, 41.

Bayes, T. (1763). An essay towards solving a problem in the doctrine of chances. *Philosophical Transactions of the Royal Society of London*, 53:370–418.

Beal, D. F. (1980). An analysis of minimax. In Clarke, M. R. B., editor, *Advances in Computer Chess 2*, pages 103–109. Edinburgh University Press, Edinburgh, Scotland.

Beck, H. W., Gala, S. K., and Navathe, S. B. (1989). Classification as a query processing technique in the CANDIDE semantic data model. In *Proceedings Fifth International Conference on Data Engineering*, pages 572–581, Los Angeles, California. IEEE Computer Society Press.

Belhumeur, P. N. (1993). A binocular stereo algorithm for reconstructing sloping, creased, and broken surfaces in the presence of half-occlusion. In *Proceedings of the 4th International Conference on Computer Vision*, Berlin. IEEE Computer Society Press.

Bell, C. and Tate, A. (1985). Using temporal constraints to restrict search in a planner. In *Proceedings of the Third Alvey IKBS SIG Workshop*, Sunningdale, Oxfordshire.

Bell, J. L. and Machover, M. (1977). *A Course in Mathematical Logic*. Elsevier/North-Holland, Amsterdam, London, New York.

Bellman, R. E. (1957). *Dynamic Programming*. Princeton University Press, Princeton, New Jersey.

Bellman, R. E. (1978). *An Introduction to Artificial Intelligence: Can Computers Think?* Boyd & Fraser Publishing Company, San Francisco.

Bellman, R. E. and Dreyfus, S. E. (1962). *Applied Dynamic Programming*. Princeton University Press, Princeton, New Jersey.

Berlekamp, E. R., Conway, J. H., and Guy, R. K. (1982). *Winning Ways, For Your Mathematical Plays*. Academic Press, New York.

Berliner, H. J. (1977). BKG—A program that plays backgammon. Technical report, Computer Science Department, Carnegie-Mellon University, Pittsburgh, Pennsylvania.

Berliner, H. J. (1979). The B* tree search algorithm: A best-first proof procedure. *Artificial Intelligence*, 12(1):23–40.

Berliner, H. J. (1980a). Backgammon computer program beats world champion. *Artificial Intelligence*, 14:205–220.

Berliner, H. J. (1980b). Computer backgammon. *Scientific American*, 249(6):64–72.

Berliner, H. J. (1989). Hitech chess: From master to senior master with no hardware change. In *MIV-89: Proceedings of the International Workshop on Industrial Applications of Machine Intelligence and Vision (Seiken Symposium)*, pages 12–21.

Berliner, H. J. and Ebeling, C. (1989). Pattern knowledge and search: The SUPREM architecture. *Artificial Intelligence*, 38(2):161–198.

Berliner, H. J. and Goetsch, G. (1984). A quantitative study of search methods and the effect of constraint satisfaction. Technical Report CMU-CS-84-187, Computer Science Department, Carnegie-Mellon University, Pittsburgh, Pennsylvania.

Bernoulli, D. (1738). Specimen theoriae novae de mensura sortis. *Proceedings of the St. Petersburg Imperial Academy of Sciences*, 5. Translated into English as Bernoulli (1954).

Bernoulli, D. (1954). Exposition of a new theory of the measurement of risk. *Econometrica*, 22:123–136. Translation of Bernoulli (1738) by Louise Sommer.

Bernstein, A. and Roberts, M. (1958). Computer vs. chess player. *Scientific American*, 198(6):96–105.

Bernstein, A., Roberts, M., Arbuckle, T., and Belsky, M. S. (1958). A chess playing program for the IBM 704. In *Proceedings of the 1958 Western Joint Computer Conference*, pages 157–159, Los Angeles.

Berry, D. A. and Fristedt, B. (1985). *Bandit Problems: Sequential Allocation of Experiments*. Chapman and Hall, London.

Bertsekas, D. P. (1987). *Dynamic Programming: Deterministic and Stochastic Models*. Prentice-Hall, Englewood Cliffs, New Jersey.

Beth, E. W. (1955). Semantic entailment and formal derivability. *Mededelingen van de Koninklijke Nederlandse Akademie van Wetenschappen, Afdeling Letterkunde, N.R.*, 18(13):309–342.

Bibel, W. (1981). On matrices with connections. *Journal of the Association for Computing Machinery*, 28(4):633–645.

Bibel, W. (1986). A deductive solution for plan generation. *New Generation Computing*, 4(2):115–132.

Birnbaum, L. and Selfridge, M. (1981). Conceptual analysis of natural language. In Schank, R. and Riesbeck, C., editors, *Inside Computer Understanding*. Lawrence Erlbaum.

Biro, J. I. and Shahan, R. W., editors (1982). *Mind, Brain and Function: Essays in the Philosophy of Mind*. University of Oklahoma Press, Norman, Oklahoma.

Birtwistle, G., Dahl, O.-J., Myrhaug, B., and Nygaard, K. (1973). *Simula Begin*. Studentlitteratur (Lund) and Auerbach, New York.

Bitner, J. R. and Reingold, E. M. (1975). Backtrack programming techniques. *Communications of the Association for Computing Machinery*, 18(11):651–656.

Black, E., Jelinek, F., Lafferty, J., Magerman, D., Mercer, R., and Roukos, S. (1992). Towards history-based grammars: using richer models for probabilistic parsing. In Marcus, M., editor, *Fifth DARPA Workshop on Speech and Natural Language*, Arden Conference Center, Harriman, New York.

Block, N., editor (1980). *Readings in Philosophy of Psychology*, volume 1. Harvard University Press, Cambridge, Massachusetts.

Bloom, P. (1994). *Language Acquisition: Core Readings*. MIT Press.

Blum, A. L. and Rivest, R. L. (1992). Training a 3-node neural network is NP-complete. *Neural Networks*, 5(1):117–127.

Blumer, A., Ehrenfeucht, A., Haussler, D., and Warmuth, M. K. (1989). Learnability and the Vapnik-Chervonenkis dimension. *Journal of the Association for Computing Machinery*, 36(4):929–965.

Blumer, A., Ehrenfeucht, A., Haussler, D., and Warmuth, M. K. (1990). Occam's razor. In Shavlik, J. W. and Dietterich, T. G., editors, *Readings in Machine Learning*, pages 201–204. Morgan Kaufmann.

Board, R. and Pitt, L. (1992). On the necessity of Occam algorithms. *Theoretical Computer Science*, 100(1):157–184.

Bobrow, D. G. (1967). Natural language input for a computer problem solving system. In Minsky, M. L., editor, *Semantic Information Processing*, pages 133–215. MIT Press, Cambridge, Massachusetts.

Bobrow, D. G. and Raphael, B. (1974). New programming languages for artificial intelligence research. *Computing Surveys*, 6(3):153–174.

Boden, M. A. (1977). *Artificial Intelligence and Natural Man*. Basic Books, New York.

Boden, M. A., editor (1990). *The Philosophy of Artificial Intelligence*. Oxford University Press, Oxford.

Boole, G. (1847). *The Mathematical Analysis of Logic: Being an Essay towards a Calculus of Deductive Reasoning*. Macmillan, Barclay, and Macmillan, Cambridge.

Boolos, G. S. (1990). On "seeing" the truth of the Gödel sentence. *Behavioral and Brain Sciences*, 13(4):655–656. Peer commentary on Penrose (1990).

Boolos, G. S. and Jeffrey, R. C. (1989). *Computability and Logic*. Cambridge University Press, Cambridge, third edition.

Borgida, A., Brachman, R. J., McGuinness, D. L., and Alperin Resnick, L. (1989). CLASSIC: a structural data model for objects. *SIGMOD Record*, 18(2):58–67.

Boyer, R. S. (1971). *Locking: A Restriction of Resolution*. PhD thesis, University of Texas, Austin, Texas.

Boyer, R. S. and Moore, J. S. (1972). The sharing of structure in theorem-proving programs. In Meltzer, B. and Michie, D., editors, *Machine Intelligence 7*, pages 101–116. Edinburgh University Press, Edinburgh, Scotland.

Boyer, R. S. and Moore, J. S. (1979). *A Computational Logic*. Academic Press, New York.

Boyer, R. S. and Moore, J. S. (1984). Proof checking the RSA public key encryption algorithm. *American Mathematical Monthly*, 91(3):181–189.

Brachman, R. J. (1979). On the epistemological status of semantic networks. In Findler, N. V., editor, *Associative Networks: Representation and Use of Knowledge by Computers*, pages 3–50. Academic Press, New York.

Brachman, R. J., Fikes, R. E., and Levesque, H. J. (1983). Krypton: A functional approach to knowledge representation. *Computer*, 16(10):67–73.

Brachman, R. J. and Levesque, H. J., editors (1985). *Readings in Knowledge Representation*. Morgan Kaufmann, San Mateo, California.

Bransford, J. and Johnson, M. K. (1973). Consideration of some problems in comprehension. In Chase, W. G., editor, *Visual Information Processing*. Academic Press, New York.

Bratko, I. (1986). *Prolog Programming for Artificial Intelligence*. Addison-Wesley, Reading, Massachusetts, first edition.

Bratko, I. (1990). *Prolog Programming for Artificial Intelligence*. Addison-Wesley, Reading, Massachusetts, second edition.

Bratman, M. E. (1987). *Intention, Plans, and Practical Reason*. Harvard University Press, Cambridge, Massachusetts.

Bratman, M. E. (1992). Planning and the stability of intention. *Minds and Machines*, 2(1):1–16.

Brelaz, D. (1979). New methods to color the vertices of a graph. *Communications of the Association for Computing Machinery*, 22(4):251–256.

Bresnan, J. (1982). *The Mental Representation of Grammatical Relations*. MIT Press, Cambridge, Massachusetts.

Briggs, R. (1985). Knowledge representation in Sanskrit and artificial intelligence. *AI Magazine*, 6(1):32–39.

Brooks, R. A. (1981). Symbolic reasoning among 3-D models and 2-D images. *Artificial Intelligence*, 17:285–348.

Brooks, R. A. (1986). A robust layered control system for a mobile robot. *IEEE Journal of Robotics and Automation*, 2:14–23.

Brooks, R. A. (1989). Engineering approach to building complete, intelligent beings. *Proceedings of the SPIE—The International Society for Optical Engineering*, 1002:618–625.

Brudno, A. L. (1963). Bounds and valuations for shortening the scanning of variations. *Problems of Cybernetics*, 10:225–241.

Bryson, A. E. and Ho, Y.-C. (1969). *Applied Optimal Control*. Blaisdell, New York.

Buchanan, B. G. and Mitchell, T. M. (1978). Model-directed learning of production rules. In Waterman, D. A. and Hayes-Roth, F., editors, *Pattern-Directed Inference Systems*, pages 297–312. Academic Press, New York.

Buchanan, B. G., Mitchell, T. M., Smith, R. G., and Johnson, C. R. (1978). Models of learning systems. In *Encyclopedia of Computer Science and Technology*, volume 11. Dekker.

Buchanan, B. G. and Shortliffe, E. H., editors (1984). *Rule-Based Expert Systems: The MYCIN Experiments of the Stanford Heuristic Programming Project*. Addison-Wesley, Reading, Massachusetts.

Buchanan, B. G., Sutherland, G. L., and Feigenbaum, E. A. (1969). Heuristic DENDRAL: a program for generating explanatory hypotheses in organic chemistry. In Meltzer, B., Michie, D., and Swann, M., editors, *Machine Intelligence 4*, pages 209–254. Edinburgh University Press, Edinburgh, Scotland.

Buchler, J., editor (1955). *Philosophical Writings of Peirce*. Dover, New York.

Bundy, A. (1983). *The Computer Modelling of Mathematical Reasoning*. Academic Press, New York.

Bunt, H. C. (1985). The formal representation of (quasi-) continuous concepts. In Hobbs, J. R. and Moore, R. C., editors, *Formal Theories of the Commonsense World*, chapter 2, pages 37–70. Ablex, Norwood, New Jersey.

Burstall, R. M. (1974). Program proving as hand simulation with a little induction. In *Information Processing '74*, pages 308–312. Elsevier/North-Holland, Amsterdam, London, New York.

Burstall, R. M. and Darlington, J. (1977). A transformation system for developing recursive programs. *Journal of the Association for Computing Machinery*, 24(1):44–67.

Bylander, T. (1992). Complexity results for serial decomposability. In *Proceedings of the Tenth National Conference on Artificial Intelligence (AAAI-92)*, pages 729–734, San Jose, California. AAAI Press.

Caianello, E. R. (1961). Outline of a theory of thought and thinking machines. *Journal of Theoretical Biology*, 1:204–235.

Campbell, P. K., Johnes, K. E., Huber, R. J., Horch, K. W., and Normann, R. A. (1991). A silicon-based, 3-dimensional neural interface: manufacturing processes for an intracortical electrode array. *IEEE Transactions on Biomedical Engineering*, 38(8):758–768.

Canny, J. (1986). A computational approach to edge detection. *IEEE Transactions on Pattern Analysis and Machine Intelligence (PAMI)*, 8:679–698.

Canny, J. and Reif, J. (1987). New lower bound techniques for robot motion planning problems. In *IEEE FOCS*, pages 39–48.

Canny, J. F. (1988). *The Complexity of Robot Motion Planning*. MIT Press, Cambridge, Massachusetts.

Carbonell, J. R. and Collins, A. M. (1973). Natural semantics in artificial intelligence. In *Proceedings of the Third International Joint Conference on Artificial Intelligence (IJCAI-73)*, Stanford, California. IJCAII.

Carnap, R. (1948). On the application of inductive logic. *Philosophy and Phenomenological Research*, 8:133–148.

Carnap, R. (1950). *Logical Foundations of Probability*. University of Chicago Press, Chicago, Illinois.

Cassandra, A. R., Kaelbling, L. P., and Littman, M. L. (1994). Acting optimally in partially observable stochastic domains. In *Proceedings of the Twelfth National Conference on Artificial Intelligence (AAAI-94)*, pages 1023–1028, Seattle, Washington. AAAI Press.

Chakrabarti, P. P., Ghose, S., Acharya, A., and de Sarkar, S. C. (1989). Heuristic search in restricted memory. *Artificial Intelligence*, 41(2):197–122.

Chang, C.-L. and Lee, R. C.-T. (1973). *Symbolic Logic and Mechanical Theorem Proving*. Academic Press, New York.

Chapman, D. (1987). Planning for conjunctive goals. *Artificial Intelligence*, 32(3):333–377.

Chapuis, A. and Droz, E. (1958). *Automata: A Historical and Technological Study*. Editions du Griffon, Neufchatel, Switzerland.

Charniak, E. (1972). *Toward a Model of Children's Story Comprehension*. PhD thesis, Massachusetts Institute of Technology.

Charniak, E. (1993). *Statistical Language Learning*. MIT Press.

Charniak, E. and Goldman, R. P. (1992). A Bayesian model of plan recognition. *Artificial Intelligence*, 64(1):53–79.

Charniak, E. and McDermott, D. (1985). *Introduction to Artificial Intelligence*. Addison-Wesley, Reading, Massachusetts.

Charniak, E., Riesbeck, C., McDermott, D., and Meehan, J. (1987). *Artificial Intelligence Programming*. Lawrence Erlbaum Associates, Potomac, Maryland, second edition.

Cheeseman, P. (1985). In defense of probability. In *Proceedings of the Ninth International Joint Conference on Artificial Intelligence (IJCAI-85)*, pages 1002–1009, Los Angeles, California. Morgan Kaufmann.

Cheeseman, P. (1988). An inquiry into computer understanding. *Computational Intelligence*, 4(1):58–66.

Cheeseman, P., Self, M., Kelly, J., and Stutz, J. (1988). Bayesian classification. In *Proceedings of the Seventh National Conference on Artificial Intelligence (AAAI-88)*, volume 2, pages 607–611, St. Paul, Minnesota. Morgan Kaufmann.

Chellas, B. F. (1980). *Modal Logic: An Introduction*. Cambridge University Press, Cambridge.

Cherniak, C. (1986). *Minimal Rationality*. MIT Press, Cambridge, Massachusetts.

Chierchia, G. and McConnell-Ginet, S. (1990). *Meaning and Grammar*. MIT Press.

Chitrao, M. and Grishman, R. (1990). Statistical parsing of messages. In *Proceedings of DARPA Speech and Natural Language Processing*. Morgan Kaufman: New York.

Chomsky, N. (1956). Three models for the description of language. *IRE Transactions on Information Theory*, 2(3):113–124.

Chomsky, N. (1957). *Syntactic Structures*. Mouton, The Hague and Paris.

Chomsky, N. (1965). *Aspects of the Theory of Syntax*. MIT Press, Cambridge, Massachusetts.

Chomsky, N. (1980). Rules and representations. *The Behavioral and Brain Sciences*, 3:1–61.

Chung, K. L. (1979). *Elementary Probability Theory with Stochastic Processes*. Springer-Verlag, Berlin, third edition.

Church, A. (1936). A note on the Entscheidungsproblem. *Journal of Symbolic Logic*, 1:40–41 and 101–102.

Church, A. (1941). *The Calculi of Lambda-Conversion*. Princeton University Press, Princeton, New Jersey.

Church, K. (1988). A stochastic parts program and noun phrase parser for unrestricted texts. In *Proceedings of the Second Conference on Applied Natural Language Processing*, Austin, Texas.

Church, K. and Patil, R. (1982). Coping with syntactic ambiguity or how to put the block in the box on the table. *American Journal of Computational Linguistics*, 8(3–4):139–149.

Churchland, P. M. (1979). *Scientific Realism and the Plasticity of Mind*. Cambridge University Press, Cambridge.

Churchland, P. M. and Churchland, P. S. (1982). Functionalism, qualia, and intentionality. In Biro, J. I. and Shahan, R. W., editors, *Mind, Brain and Function: Essays in the Philosophy of Mind*, pages 121–145. University of Oklahoma Press, Norman, Oklahoma.

Churchland, P. S. (1986). *Neurophilosophy: Toward a Unified Science of the Mind-Brain*. MIT Press, Cambridge, Massachusetts.

Clark, K. L. (1978). Negation as failure. In Gallaire, H. and Minker, J., editors, *Logic and Data Bases*, pages 293–322. Plenum, New York.

Clark, K. L. and Gregory, S. (1986). PARLOG: parallel programming in logic. *ACM Transactions on Programming Languages*, 8:1–49.

Clark, R. (1992). The selection of syntactic knowledge. *Language Acquisition*, 2(2):83–149.

Clarke, M. R. B., editor (1977). *Advances in Computer Chess 1*. Edinburgh University Press, Edinburgh, Scotland.

Clocksin, W. F. and Mellish, C. S. (1987). *Programming in Prolog*. Springer-Verlag, Berlin, third revised and extended edition.

Clowes, M. B. (1971). On seeing things. *Artificial Intelligence*, 2(1):79–116.

Cobham, A. (1964). The intrinsic computational difficulty of functions. In Bar-Hillel, Y., editor, *Proceedings of the 1964 International Congress for Logic, Methodology, and Philosophy of Science*, pages 24–30. Elsevier/North-Holland.

Cohen, J. (1966). *Human Robots in Myth and Science*. Allen and Unwin, London.

Cohen, J. (1988). A view of the origins and development of PROLOG. *Communications of the Association for Computing Machinery*, 31:26–36.

Cohen, P., Morgan, J., and Pollack, M. (1990). *Intentions in Communication*. MIT Press.

Cohen, P. and Perrault, C. R. (1979). Elements of a plan-based theory of speech acts. *Cognitive Science*, 3(3):177–212.

Cohen, P. R. and Feigenbaum, E. A., editors (1982). *The Handbook of Artificial Intelligence*, volume 3. HeurisTech Press and William Kaufmann, Stanford, California and Los Altos, California.

Colmerauer, A. (1975). Les grammaires de métamorphose. Technical report, Groupe d'Intelligence Artificielle, Université de Marseille-Luminy. Translated into English as Colmerauer (1978).

Colmerauer, A. (1978). Metamorphosis grammars. In Bolc, L., editor, *Natural Language Communication with Computers*. Springer-Verlag, Berlin. English translation of Colmerauer (1975).

Colmerauer, A. (1985). Prolog in 10 figures. *Communications of the Association for Computing Machinery*, 28(12):1296–1310.

Colmerauer, A. (1990). Prolog III as it actually is. In Warren, D. H. D. and Szeredi, P., editors, *Logic Programming: Proceedings of the Seventh International Conference*, page 766, Jerusalem. MIT Press.

Colmerauer, A., Kanoui, H., Pasero, R., and Roussel, P. (1973). Un système de communication homme-machine en français. Rapport, Groupe d'Intelligence Artificielle, Université d'Aix-Marseille II.

Colomb, R. M. (1991). Enhancing unification in PROLOG through clause indexing. *Journal of Logic Programming*, 10(1):23–44.

Condon, E. U., Tawney, G. L., and Derr, W. A. (1940). Machine to play game of Nim. U.S. Patent 2,215,544, United States Patent Office, Washington, D.C.

Condon, J. H. and Thompson, K. (1982). Belle chess hardware. In Clarke, M. R. B., editor, *Advances in Computer Chess 3*, pages 45–54. Pergamon, New York.

Cook, S. A. (1971). The complexity of theorem-proving procedures. In *Proceedings of the 3rd Annual ACM Symposium on Theory of Computing*, pages 151–158, New York.

Cooper, G. and Herskovits, E. (1992). A Bayesian method for the induction of probabilistic networks from data. *Machine Learning*, 9:309–347.

Cooper, G. F. (1990). The computational complexity of probabilistic inference using Bayesian belief networks. *Artificial Intelligence*, 42:393–405.

Copeland, J. (1993). *Artificial Intelligence: A Philosophical Introduction*. Blackwell, Oxford.

Cormen, T. H., Leiserson, C. E., and Rivest, R. R. (1990). *Introduction to Algorithms*. MIT Press, Cambridge, Massachusetts.

Covington, M. A. (1994). *Natural Language Processing for Prolog Programmers*. Prentice-Hall, Englewood Cliffs, New Jersey.

Cowan, J. D. and Sharp, D. H. (1988a). Neural nets. *Quarterly Reviews of Biophysics*, 21:365–427.

Cowan, J. D. and Sharp, D. H. (1988b). Neural nets and artificial intelligence. *Daedalus*, 117:85–121.

Cox, R. T. (1946). Probability, frequency, and reasonable expectation. *American Journal of Physics*, 14(1):1–13.

Cragg, B. G. and Temperley, H. N. V. (1954). The organization of neurones: A cooperative analogy. *EEG and Clinical Neurophysiology*, 6:85–92.

Cragg, B. G. and Temperley, H. N. V. (1955). Memory: The analogy with ferromagnetic hysteresis. *Brain*, 78(II):304–316.

Craik, K. J. W. (1943). *The Nature of Explanation*. Cambridge University Press, Cambridge.

Crevier, D. (1993). *AI: The Tumultuous History of the Search for Artificial Intelligence*. Basic Books, New York.

Crockett, L. (1994). *The Turing Test and the Frame Problem: AI's Mistaken Understanding of Intelligence*. Ablex, Norwood, New Jersey.

Cullingford, R. E. (1981). Integrating knowledge sources for computer 'understanding' tasks. *IEEE Transactions on Systems, Man and Cybernetics*, SMC-11.

Currie, K. W. and Tate, A. (1991). O-Plan: the Open Planning Architecture. *Artificial Intelligence*, 52(1):49–86.

Curry, H. B. and Feys, R. (1958). *Combinatory Logic*, volume 1. Elsevier/North-Holland, Amsterdam, London, New York.

Cybenko, G. (1988). Continuous valued neural networks with two hidden layers are sufficient. Technical report, Department of Computer Science, Tufts University, Medford, Massachusetts.

Cybenko, G. (1989). Approximation by superpositions of a sigmoidal function. *Mathematics of Controls, Signals, and Systems*, 2:303–314.

Dagum, P. and Luby, M. (1993). Approximating probabilistic inference in Bayesian belief networks is NP-hard. *Artificial Intelligence*, 60(1):141–153.

Dahl, O.-J., Myrhaug, B., and Nygaard, K. (1970). (Simula 67) common base language. Technical Report N. S-22, Norsk Regnesentral (Norwegian Computing Center), Oslo.

Dantzig, G. B. (1960). On the significance of solving linear programming problems with some integer variables. *Econometrica*, 28:30–44.

Darwiche, A. Y. and Ginsberg, M. L. (1992). A symbolic generalization of probability theory. In *Proceedings of the Tenth National Conference on Artificial Intelligence (AAAI-92)*, pages 622–627, San Jose, California. AAAI Press.

Davidson, D. (1980). *Essays on Actions and Events*. Oxford University Press, Oxford.

Davies, T. (1985). Analogy. Informal Note IN-CSLI-85-4, Center for the Study of Language and Information (CSLI), Stanford, California.

Davies, T. R. and Russell, S. J. (1987). A logical approach to reasoning by analogy. In *Proceedings of the Tenth International Joint Conference on Artificial Intelligence (IJCAI-87)*, volume 1, pages 264–270, Milan, Italy. Morgan Kaufmann.

Davis, E. (1986). *Representing and Acquiring Geographic Knowledge*. Pitman and Morgan Kaufmann, London and San Mateo, California.

Davis, E. (1990). *Representations of Commonsense Knowledge*. Morgan Kaufmann, San Mateo, California.

Davis, M. (1957). A computer program for Presburger's algorithm. In Robinson, A., editor, *Proving Theorems, (as Done by Man, Logician, or Machine)*, pages 215–233, Cornell University, Ithaca, New York. Communications Research Division, Institute for Defense Analysis. Summaries of Talks Presented at the 1957 Summer Institute for Symbolic Logic. Second edition; publication date is 1960.

Davis, M. and Putnam, H. (1960). A computing procedure for quantification theory. *Journal of the Association for Computing Machinery*, 7(3):201–215.

Davis, R. (1980). Meta-rules: reasoning about control. *Artificial Intelligence*, 15(3):179–222.

Davis, R. and Lenat, D. B. (1982). *Knowledge-Based Systems in Artificial Intelligence*. McGraw-Hill, New York.

Dayan, P. (1992). The convergence of TDλ for general λ. *Machine Learning*, 8(3–4):341–362.

de Dombal, F. T., Leaper, D. J., Horrocks, J. C., and Staniland, J. R. (1974). Human and computer-aided diagnosis of abdominal pain: Further report with emphasis on performance of clinicians. *British Medical Journal*, 1:376–380.

de Dombal, F. T., Staniland, J. R., and Clamp, S. E. (1981). Geographical variation in disease presentation. *Medical Decision Making*, 1:59–69.

de Finetti, B. (1937a). Foresight: Its logical laws, its subjective sources. In Kyburg, H. E. and Smokler, H. E., editors, *Studies in Subjective Probability*, pages 55–118. Krieger, New York.

de Finetti, B. (1937b). La prévision: Ses lois logiques, ses sources subjectives. *Ann. Inst. Poincaré*, 7:1–68. Translated into English as De-Finetti (1937a).

de Groot, A. D. (1946). *Het Denken van den Schaker*. Elsevier/North-Holland, Amsterdam, London, New York. Translated as DeGroot (1978).

de Groot, A. D. (1978). *Thought and Choice in Chess*. Mouton, The Hague and Paris, second edition.

de Kleer, J. (1975). Qualitative and quantitative knowledge in classical mechanics. Technical Report AI-TR-352, MIT Artificial Intelligence Laboratory.

de Kleer, J. (1986). An assumption-based TMS. *Artificial Intelligence*, 28(2):127–162.

de Kleer, J. (1986a). Extending the ATMS. *Artificial Intelligence*, 28(2):163–196.

de Kleer, J. (1986b). Problem solving with the ATMS. *Artificial Intelligence*, 28(2):197–224.

de Kleer, J. and Brown, J. S. (1985). A qualitative physics based on confluences. In Hobbs, J. R. and Moore, R. C., editors, *Formal Theories of the Commonsense World*, chapter 4, pages 109–183. Ablex, Norwood, New Jersey.

de Kleer, J., Doyle, J., Steele, G. L., and Sussman, G. J. (1977). AMORD: explicit control of reasoning. *SIGPLAN Notices*, 12(8):116–125.

De Morgan, A. (1864). On the syllogism IV and on the logic of relations. *Cambridge Philosophical Transactions*, x:331–358.

De Raedt, L. (1992). *Interactive Theory Revision: An Inductive Logic Programming Approach*. Academic Press, New York.

Dean, T. and Boddy, M. (1988). An analysis of time-dependent planning. In *Proceedings of the Seventh National Conference on Artificial Intelligence (AAAI-88)*, pages 49–54, St. Paul, Minnesota. Morgan Kaufmann.

Dean, T., Firby, J., and Miller, D. (1990). Hierarchical planning involving deadlines, travel time, and resources. *Computational Intelligence*, 6(1).

Dean, T., Kaelbling, L. P., Kirman, J., and Nicholson, A. (1993). Planning with deadlines in stochastic domains. In *Proceedings of the Eleventh National Conference on Artificial Intelligence (AAAI-93)*, pages 574–579, Washington, D.C. AAAI Press.

Dean, T. and Kanazawa, K. (1989). A model for reasoning about persistence and causation. *Computational Intelligence*, 5(3):142–150.

Dean, T. L. and Wellman, M. P. (1991). *Planning and Control*. Morgan Kaufmann, San Mateo, California.

Debreu, G. (1960). Topological methods in cardinal utility theory. In Arrow, K. J., Karlin, S., and Suppes, P., editors, *Mathematical Methods in the Social Sciences, 1959*. Stanford University Press, Stanford, California.

Dechter, R. and Pearl, J. (1985). Generalized best-first search strategies and the optimality of A*. *Journal of the Association for Computing Machinery*, 32(3):505–536.

DeGroot, M. H. (1970). *Optimal Statistical Decisions*. McGraw-Hill, New York.

DeGroot, M. H. (1989). *Probability and Statistics*. Addison-Wesley, Reading, Massachusetts, second edition. Reprinted with corrections.

DeJong, G. (1981). Generalizations based on explanations. In *Proceedings of the Seventh International Joint Conference on Artificial Intelligence (IJCAI-81)*, pages 67–69, Vancouver, British Columbia. Morgan Kaufmann.

DeJong, G. and Mooney, R. (1986). Explanation-based learning: An alternative view. *Machine Learning*, 1:145–176.

Dempster, A., Laird, N., and Rubin, D. (1977). Maximum likelihood from incomplete data via the EM algorithm. *Journal of the Royal Statistical Society*, 39 (Series B):1–38.

Dempster, A. P. (1968). A generalization of Bayesian inference. *Journal of the Royal Statistical Society*, 30 (Series B):205–247.

Dennett, D. C. (1969). *Content and Consciousness*. Routledge and Kegan Paul, London.

Dennett, D. C. (1971). Intentional systems. *The Journal of Philosophy*, 68(4):87–106.

Dennett, D. C. (1978a). *Brainstorms: Philosophical Essays on Mind and Psychology*. MIT Press, Cambridge, Massachusetts, first edition.

Dennett, D. C. (1978b). Why you can't make a computer that feels pain. *Synthese*, 38(3).

Dennett, D. C. (1984). Cognitive wheels: the frame problem of AI. In Hookway, C., editor, *Minds, Machines, and Evolution: Philosophical Studies*, pages 129–151. Cambridge University Press, Cambridge.

Dennett, D. C. (1986). The moral first aid manual. Tanner lectures on human values, University of Michigan.

Deo, N. and Pang, C. (1982). Shortest path algorithms: Taxonomy and annotation. Technical Report CS-80-057, Computer Science Department, Washington State University.

Descotte, Y. and Latombe, J. C. (1985). Making compromises among antagonist constraints in a planner. *Artificial Intelligence*, 27:183–217.

Devanbu, P., Brachman, R. J., Selfridge, P. G., and Ballard, B. W. (1991). LaSSIE: a knowledge-based software information system. *Communications of the Association for Computing Machinery*, 34(5):34–49.

Dickmanns, E. D. and Zapp, A. (1987). Autonomous high speed road vehicle guidance by computer vision. In Isermann, R., editor, *Automatic Control—World Congress, 1987: Selected Papers from the 10th Triennial World Congress of the International Federation of Automatic Control*, pages 221–226, Munich, Germany. Pergamon.

Dietterich, T. G. (1990). Machine learning. *Annual Review of Computer Science*, 4.

Dijkstra, E. W. (1959). A note on two problems in connexion with graphs. *Numerische Mathematik*, 1:269–271.

Dincbas, M. and LePape, J.-P. (1984). Metacontrol of logic programs in METALOG. In *Proceedings of the International Conference on Fifth-Generation Computer Systems*, Tokyo. Elsevier/North-Holland.

Dingwell, W. O. (1988). The evolution of human communicative behavior. In Newmeyer, F. J., editor, *Linguistics: The Cambridge Survey, Vol. III*, pages 274–313. Cambridge University Press.

Doran, J. and Michie, D. (1966). Experiments with the graph traverser program. *Proceedings of the Royal Society of London*, 294, Series A:235–259.

Dowty, D., Wall, R., and Peters, S. (1991). *Introduction to Montague Semantics*. D. Reidel, Dordrecht, The Netherlands.

Doyle, J. (1979). A truth maintenance system. *Artificial Intelligence*, 12(3):231–272. Reprinted in Webber and Nilsson (1981).

Doyle, J. (1980). A model for deliberation, action, and introspection. Technical Report AI-TR-581, Artificial Intelligence Laboratory, Massachusetts Institute of Technology, Cambridge, Massachusetts. Republished PhD dissertation.

Doyle, J. (1983). What is rational psychology? Toward a modern mental philosophy. *AI Magazine*, 4(3):50–53.

Doyle, J. and Patil, R. S. (1991). Two theses of knowledge representation: language restrictions, taxonomic classification, and the utility of representation services. *Artificial Intelligence*, 48(3):261–297.

Drabble, B. (1990). Mission scheduling for spacecraft: Diaries of T-SCHED. In *Expert Planning Systems*, pages 76–81. Institute of Electrical Engineers.

Draper, D., Hanks, S., and Weld, D. (1994). Probabilistic planning with information gathering and contingent execution. In *Proceedings 2nd AIPS*, San Mateo, California. Morgan Kaufmann.

Dreyfus, H. L. (1972). *What Computers Can't Do: A Critique of Artificial Reason*. Harper and Row, New York, first edition.

Dreyfus, H. L. (1979). *What Computers Can't Do: The Limits of Artificial Intelligence*. Harper and Row, New York, revised edition.

Dreyfus, H. L. (1992). *What Computers Still Can't Do: A Critique of Artificial Reason*. MIT Press, Cambridge, Massachusetts.

Dreyfus, H. L. and Dreyfus, S. E. (1986). *Mind over Machine: The Power of Human Intuition and Expertise in the Era of the Computer*. Blackwell, Oxford. With Tom Athanasiou.

Dreyfus, S. E. (1969). An appraisal of some shortest-paths algorithms. *Operations Research*, 17:395–412.

Dubois, D. and Prade, H. (1994). A survey of belief revision and updating rules in various uncertainty models. *International Journal of Intelligent Systems*, 9(1):61–100.

Duda, R., Gaschnig, J., and Hart, P. (1979). Model design in the Prospector consultant system for mineral exploration. In Michie, D., editor, *Expert Systems in the Microelectronic Age*, pages 153–167. Edinburgh University Press, Edinburgh, Scotland.

Dyer, M. (1983). *In-Depth Understanding*. MIT Press, Cambridge, Massachusetts.

Dzeroski, S., Muggleton, S., and Russell, S. J. (1992). PAC-learnability of determinate logic programs. In *Proceedings of the Fifth Annual ACM Workshop on Computational Learning Theory (COLT-92)*, Pittsburgh, Pennsylvania. ACM Press.

Earley, J. (1970). An efficient context-free parsing algorithm. *Communications of the Association for Computing Machinery*, 13(2):94–102.

Ebeling, C. (1987). *All the Right Moves*. MIT Press, Cambridge, Massachusetts.

Edmonds, J. (1962). Covers and packings in a family of sets. *Bulletin of the American Mathematical Society*, 68:494–499.

Edmonds, J. (1965). Paths, trees, and flowers. *Canadian Journal of Mathematics*, 17:449–467.

Edwards, P., editor (1967). *The Encyclopedia of Philosophy*. Macmillan, London.

Elkan, C. (1992). Reasoning about action in first-order logic. In *Proceedings of the Conference of the Canadian Society for Computational Studies of Intelligence*, Vancouver, British Columbia.

Elkan, C. (1993). The paradoxical success of fuzzy logic. In *Proceedings of the Eleventh National Conference on Artificial Intelligence (AAAI-93)*, pages 698–703, Washington, D.C. AAAI Press.

Empson, W. (1953). *Seven Types of Ambiguity*. New Directions.

Enderton, H. B. (1972). *A Mathematical Introduction to Logic*. Academic Press, New York.

Engelberger, J. F. (1980). *Robotics in Practice*. Amacom, New York.

Engelberger, J. F. (1989). *Robotics in Service*. MIT Press, Cambridge, Massachusetts.

Erman, L. D., Hayes-Roth, F., Lesser, V. R., and Reddy, D. R. (1980). The HEARSAY-II speech-understanding system: Integrating knowledge to resolve uncertainty. *Computing Surveys*, 12(2):213–253. Reprinted in Webber and Nilsson (1981).

Ernst, H. A. (1961). *MH-1, a Computer-Operated Mechanical Hand*. PhD thesis, Massachusetts Institute of Technology, Cambridge, Massachusetts.

Erol, K., Hendler, J., and Nau, D. S. (1994). HTN planning: complexity and expressivity. In *Proceedings of the Twelfth National Conference on Artificial Intelligence (AAAI-94)*, Seattle, Washington. AAAI Press.

Etzioni, O. (1989). Tractable decision-analytic control. In *Proc. of 1st International Conference on Knowledge Representation and Reasoning*, pages 114–125, Toronto, Ontario.

Etzioni, O., Hanks, S., Weld, D., Draper, D., Lesh, N., and Williamson, M. (1992). An approach to planning with incomplete information. In *Proceedings of the 3rd International Conference on Principles of Knowledge Representation and Reasoning*.

Evans, T. G. (1968). A program for the solution of a class of geometric-analogy intelligence-test questions. In Minsky, M. L., editor, *Semantic Information Processing*, pages 271–353. MIT Press, Cambridge, Massachusetts.

Fahlman, S. E. (1974). A planning system for robot construction tasks. *Artificial Intelligence*, 5(1):1–49.

Fahlman, S. E. (1979). *NETL: A System for Representing and Using Real-World Knowledge*. MIT Press, Cambridge, Massachusetts.

Farhat, N. H., Psaltis, D., Prata, A., and Paek, E. (1985). Optical implementation of the Hopfield model. *Applied Optics*, 24:1469–1475. Reprinted in Anderson and Rosenfeld (1988).

Faugeras, O. (1993). *Three-Dimensional Computer Vision: A Geometric Viewpoint*. MIT Press, Cambridge, Massachusetts.

Feigenbaum, E. and Shrobe, H. (1993). The Japanese national fifth generation project: introduction, survey, and evaluation. *Future Generation Computer Systems*, 9(2):105–117.

Feigenbaum, E. A. (1961). The simulation of verbal learning behavior. *Proceedings of the Western Joint Computer Conference*, 19:121–131. Reprinted in (Feigenbaum and Feldman, 1963, pp. 297–309).

Feigenbaum, E. A., Buchanan, B. G., and Lederberg, J. (1971). On generality and problem solving: A case study using the DENDRAL program. In Meltzer, B. and Michie, D., editors, *Machine Intelligence 6*, pages 165–190. Edinburgh University Press, Edinburgh, Scotland.

Feigenbaum, E. A. and Feldman, J., editors (1963). *Computers and Thought*. McGraw-Hill, New York.

Feldman, J. A. and Sproull, R. F. (1977). Decision theory and artificial intelligence II: The hungry monkey. Technical report, Computer Science Department, University of Rochester.

Feldman, J. A. and Yakimovsky, Y. (1974). Decision theory and artificial intelligence I: Semantics-based region analyzer. *Artificial Intelligence*, 5(4):349–371.

Fikes, R. E., Hart, P. E., and Nilsson, N. J. (1972). Learning and executing generalized robot plans. *Artificial Intelligence*, 3(4):251–288.

Fikes, R. E. and Nilsson, N. J. (1971). STRIPS: a new approach to the application of theorem proving to problem solving. *Artificial Intelligence*, 2(3–4):189–208.

Fikes, R. E. and Nilsson, N. J. (1993). STRIPS, a retrospective. *Artificial Intelligence*, 59(1–2):227–232.

Findlay, J. N. (1941). Time: A treatment of some puzzles. *Australasian Journal of Psychology and Philosophy*, 19(3):216–235.

Fischer, M. J. and Ladner, R. E. (1977). Propositional modal logic of programs. In *Proceedings of the 9th ACM Symposium on the Theory of Computing*, pages 286–294.

Fisher, R. A. (1922). On the mathematical foundations of theoretical statistics. *Philosophical Transactions of the Royal Society of London*, Series A 222:309–368.

Floyd, R. W. (1962a). Algorithm 96: Ancestor. *Communications of the Association for Computing Machinery*, 5:344–345.

Floyd, R. W. (1962b). Algorithm 97: Shortest path. *Communications of the Association for Computing Machinery*, 5:345.

Fodor, J. A. (1980). Searle on what only brains can do. *Behavioral and Brain Sciences*, 3:431–432. Peer commentary on Searle (1980).

Fodor, J. A. (1983). *The Modularity of Mind: An Essay on Faculty Psychology*. MIT Press, Cambridge, Massachusetts.

Forbus, K. D. (1985). The role of qualitative dynamics in naive physics. In Hobbs, J. R. and Moore, R. C., editors, *Formal Theories of the Commonsense World*, chapter 5, pages 185–226. Ablex, Norwood, New Jersey.

Forbus, K. D. and de Kleer, J. (1993). *Building Problem Solvers*. MIT Press, Cambridge, Massachusetts.

Forsyth, D. and Zisserman, A. (1991). Reflections on shading. *IEEE Transactions on Pattern Analysis and Machine Intelligence (PAMI)*, 13(7):671–679.

Fox, M. S. (1990). Constraint-guided scheduling: a short history of research at CMU. *Computers in Industry*, 14(1–3):79–88.

Fox, M. S., Allen, B., and Strohm, G. (1981). Job shop scheduling: an investigation in constraint-based reasoning. In *Proceedings of the Seventh International Joint Conference on Artificial Intelligence (IJCAI-81)*, Vancouver, British Columbia. Morgan Kaufmann.

Fox, M. S. and Smith, S. F. (1984). Isis: a knowledge-based system for factory scheduling. *Expert Systems*, 1(1):25–49.

Frean, M. (1990). The upstart algorithm: A method for constructing and training feedforward neural networks. *Neural Computation*, 2:198–209.

Frege, G. (1879). *Begriffsschrift, eine der arithmetischen nachgebildete Formelsprache des reinen Denkens*. Halle, Berlin. Reprinted in English translation in van Heijenoort (1967).

Friedberg, R., Dunham, B., and North, T. (1959). A learning machine: Part II. *IBM Journal of Research and Development*, 3(3):282–287.

Friedberg, R. M. (1958). A learning machine: Part I. *IBM Journal*, 2:2–13.

Fu, K.-S. and Booth, T. L. (1986a). Grammatical inference: Introduction and survey—part I. *IEEE Transactions on Pattern Analysis and Machine Intelligence*, PAMI-8(3):343–359. Reprinted from *IEEE Trans. on Systems, Man, and Cybernetics*, Vol. SMC-5, No. 1, January 1975.

Fu, K.-S. and Booth, T. L. (1986b). Grammatical inference: Introduction and survey—part II. *IEEE Transactions on Pattern Analysis and Machine Intelligence*, PAMI-8(3):360–375. Reprinted from IEEE Trans. on Systems, Man, and Cybernetics, Vol. SMC-5, No. 4, January 1975.

Fuchs, J. J., Gasquet, A., Olalainty, B., and Currie, K. W. (1990). PlanERS-1: An expert planning system for generating spacecraft mission plans. In *First International Conference on Expert Planning Systems*, pages 70–75, Brighton, United Kingdom. Institute of Electrical Engineers.

Fung, R. and Chang, K. C. (1989). Weighting and integrating evidence for stochastic simulation in Bayesian networks. In *Proceedings of the Fifth Conference on Uncertainty in Artificial Intelligence (UAI-89)*, Windsor, Ontario. Morgan Kaufmann.

Furukawa, K. (1992). Summary of basic research activities of the FGCS project. In *Fifth Generation Computer Systems 1992*, volume 1, pages 20–32, Tokyo. IOS Press.

Furuta, K., Ochiai, T., and Ono, N. (1984). Attitude control of a triple inverted pendulum. *International Journal of Control*, 39(6):1351–1365.

Gabbay, D. M. (1991). Abduction in labelled deductive systems: A conceptual abstract. In Kruse, R. and Siegel, P., editors, *Symbolic and Quantitative Approaches to Uncertainty: Proceedings of European Conference ECSQAU*, pages 3–11. Springer-Verlag.

Gallaire, H. and Minker, J., editors (1978). *Logic and Databases*. Plenum, New York.

Gallier, J. H. (1986). *Logic for Computer Science: Foundations of Automatic Theorem Proving*. Harper and Row, New York.

Gamba, A., Gamberini, L., Palmieri, G., and Sanna, R. (1961). Further experiments with PAPA. *Nuovo Cimento Supplemento*, 20(2):221–231.

Garding, J. (1992). Shape from texture for smooth curved surfaces in perspective projection. *Journal of Mathematical Imaging and Vision*, 2(4):327–350.

Gardner, M. (1968). *Logic Machines, Diagrams and Boolean Algebra*. Dover, New York.

Garey, M. R. and Johnson, D. S. (1979). *Computers and Intractability*. W. H. Freeman, New York.

Garside, R., Leech, F., and Sampson, G., editors (1987). *The Computational Analysis of English*. Longman.

Gaschnig, J. (1979). Performance measurement and analysis of certain search algorithms. Technical Report CMU-CS-79-124, Computer Science Department, Carnegie-Mellon University.

Gauss, K. F. (1809). *Theoria Motus Corporum Coelestium in Sectionibus Conicis Solem Ambientium*. Sumtibus F. Perthes et I. H. Besser, Hamburg.

Gazdar, G. (1989). COMIT $\Rightarrow^*$ PATR. In Wilks, Y., editor, *Theoretical Issues in Natural Language Processing*, Potomac, Maryland. Lawrence Erlbaum Associates.

Gazdar, G., Klein, E., Pullum, G., and Sag, I. (1985). *Generalized Phrase Structure Grammar*. Blackwell, Oxford.

Geffner, H. (1992). *Default Reasoning: Causal and Conditional Theories*. MIT Press, Cambridge, Massachusetts.

Gelb, A. (1974). *Applied Optimal Estimation*. MIT Press, Cambridge, Massachusetts.

Gelernter, H. (1959). Realization of a geometry-theorem proving machine. In *Proceedings of an International Conference on Information Processing*, pages 273–282, Paris. UNESCO House.

Gelernter, H., Hansen, J. R., and Gerberich, C. L. (1960). A FORTRAN-compiled list processing language. *Journal of the Association for Computing Machinery*, 7(2):87–101.

Gelfond, M. and Lifschitz, V. (1988). Compiling circumscriptive theories into logic programs. In Reinfrank, M., de Kleer, J., Ginsberg, M. L., and Sandewall, E., editors, *Non-Monotonic Reasoning: 2nd International Workshop Proceedings*, pages 74–99, Grassau, Germany. Springer-Verlag.

Gelfond, M. and Lifschitz, V. (1991). Classical negation in logic programs and disjunctive databases. *New Generation Computing*, 9(3–4):365–385.

Genesereth, M. R. (1984). The use of design descriptions in automated diagnosis. *Artificial Intelligence*, 24(1–3):411–436.

Genesereth, M. R. and Ketchpel, S. P. (1994). Software agents. *Communications of the Association for Computing Machinery*, 37(7).

Genesereth, M. R. and Nilsson, N. J. (1987). *Logical Foundations of Artificial Intelligence*. Morgan Kaufmann, San Mateo, California.

Genesereth, M. R. and Smith, D. (1981). Meta-level architecture. Memo HPP-81-6, Computer Science Department, Stanford University, Stanford, California.

Gentner, D. (1983). Structure mapping: A theoretical framework for analogy. *Cognitive Science*, 7:155–170.

Gentzen, G. (1934). Untersuchungen über das logische Schliessen. *Mathematische Zeitschrift*, 39:176–210, 405–431.

Georgeff, M. P. and Lansky, A. L., editors (1986). *Reasoning about Actions and Plans: Proceedings of the 1986 Workshop*, Timberline, Oregon. Morgan Kaufmann.

Gibson, J. J. (1950). *The Perception of the Visual World*. Houghton Mifflin, Boston, Massachusetts.

Gibson, J. J. (1979). *The Ecological Approach to Visual Perception*. Houghton Mifflin, Boston, Massachusetts.

Gibson, J. J., Olum, P., and Rosenblatt, F. (1955). Parallax and perspective during aircraft landings. *American Journal of Psychology*, 68:372–385.

Gilmore, P. C. (1960). A proof method for quantification theory: Its justification and realization. *IBM Journal of Research and Development*, 4:28–35.

Ginsberg, M. (1993). *Essentials of Artificial Intelligence*. Morgan Kaufmann, San Mateo, California.

Ginsberg, M. L., editor (1987). *Readings in Nonmonotonic Reasoning*. Morgan Kaufmann, San Mateo, California.

Ginsberg, M. L. (1989). Universal planning: An (almost) universally bad idea. *AI Magazine*, 10(4):40–44.

Giralt, G., Alami, R., Chatila, R., and Freedman, P. (1991). Remote operated autonomous robots. In *Intelligent Robotics: Proceedings of the International Symposium*, volume 1571, pages 416–427, Bangalore, India. International Society for Optical Engineering (SPIE).

Glanc, A. (1978). On the etymology of the word "robot". *SIGART Newsletter*, 67:12.

Glover, F. (1989). Tabu search: 1. *ORSA Journal on Computing*, 1(3):190–206.

Gödel, K. (1930). *Über die Vollständigkeit des Logikkalküls*. PhD thesis, University of Vienna.

Gödel, K. (1931). Über formal unentscheidbare Sätze der Principia mathematica und verwandter Systeme I. *Monatshefte für Mathematik und Physik*, 38:173–198.

Gold, E. M. (1967). Language identification in the limit. *Information and Control*, 10:447–474.

Goldberg, D. E. (1989). *Genetic Algorithms in Search, Optimization and Machine Learning*. Addison-Wesley, Reading, Massachusetts.

Goldman, R. P. and Charniak, E. (1992). Probabilistic text understanding. *Statistics and Computing*, 2(2):105–114.

Goldszmidt, M., Morris, P., and Pearl, J. (1990). A maximum entropy approach to nonmonotonic reasoning. In *Proceedings of the Eighth National Conference on Artificial Intelligence (AAAI-90)*, volume 2, pages 646–652, Boston, Massachusetts. MIT Press.

Good, I. J. (1950). Contribution to the discussion of Eliot Slater's "Statistics for the chess computer and the factor of mobility". In *Symposium on Information Theory*, page 199, London. Ministry of Supply.

Good, I. J. (1961). A causal calculus. *British Journal of the Philosophy of Science*, 11:305–318. Reprinted in Good (1983).

Good, I. J. (1983). *Good Thinking: The Foundations of Probability and Its Applications*. University of Minnesota Press, Minneapolis, Minnesota.

Goodman, N. (1954). *Fact, Fiction and Forecast*. University of London Press, London, first edition.

Goodman, N. (1977). *The Structure of Appearance*. D. Reidel, Dordrecht, The Netherlands, third edition.

Gorry, G. A. (1968). Strategies for computer-aided diagnosis. *Mathematical Biosciences*, 2(3–4):293–318.

Gorry, G. A., Kassirer, J. P., Essig, A., and Schwartz, W. B. (1973). Decision analysis as the basis for computer-aided management of acute renal failure. *American Journal of Medicine*, 55:473–484.

Gould, S. J. (1994). This view of life. *Natural History*, 8:10–17.

Graham, S. L., Harrison, M. A., and Ruzzo, W. L. (1980). An improved context-free recognizer. *ACM Transactions on Programming Languages and Systems*, 2(3):415–462.

Grayson, C. J. (1960). Decisions under uncertainty: Drilling decisions by oil and gas operators. Technical report, Division of Research, Harvard Business School, Boston.

Green, C. (1969a). Application of theorem proving to problem solving. In *Proceedings of the First International Joint Conference on Artificial Intelligence (IJCAI-69)*, pages 219–239, Washington, D.C. IJCAII.

Green, C. (1969b). Theorem-proving by resolution as a basis for question-answering systems. In Meltzer, B., Michie, D., and Swann, M., editors, *Machine Intelligence 4*, pages 183–205. Edinburgh University Press, Edinburgh, Scotland.

Greenblatt, R. D., Eastlake, D. E., and Crocker, S. D. (1967). The Greenblatt chess program. In *Proceedings of the Fall Joint Computer Conference*, pages 801–810.

Greiner, R. (1989). Towards a formal analysis of EBL. In *Proceedings of the Sixth International Machine Learning Workshop*, Ithaca, NY. Morgan Kaufmann.

Grice, H. P. (1957). Meaning. *Philosophical Review*, 66:377–388.

Grimes, J. (1975). *The Thread of Discourse*. Moulton.

Grosz, B., Appelt, D., Martin, P., and Pereira, F. (1987). Team: An experiment in the design of transportable natural-language interfaces. *Artificial Intelligence*, 32(2):173–244.

Grosz, B. J. and Sidner, C. L. (1986). Attention, intentions, and the structure of discourse. *Computational Linguistics*, 12(3):175–204.

Grosz, B. J., Sparck Jones, K., and Webber, B. L., editors (1986). *Readings in Natural Language Processing*. Morgan Kaufmann, San Mateo, California.

Gu, J. (1989). *Parallel Algorithms and Architectures for Very Fast AI Search*. PhD thesis, University of Utah.

Guard, J., Oglesby, F., Bennett, J., and Settle, L. (1969). Semi-automated mathematics. *Journal of the Association for Computing Machinery*, 16:49–62.

Haas, A. (1986). A syntactic theory of belief and action. *Artificial Intelligence*, 28(3):245–292.

Hacking, I. (1975). *The Emergence of Probability*. Cambridge University Press, Cambridge.

Hald, A. (1990). *A History of Probability and Statistics and Their Applications Before 1750*. Wiley, New York.

Halpern, J. Y. (1987). Using reasoning about knowledge to analyze distributed systems. In Traub, J. F., Grosz, B. J., Lampson, B. W., and Nilsson, N. J., editors, *Annual review of computer science*, volume 2, pages 37–68. Annual Reviews, Palo Alto.

Hamming, R. W. (1991). *The Art of Probability for Scientists and Engineers*. Addison-Wesley, Reading, Massachusetts.

Hammond, K. (1989). *Case-Based Planning: Viewing Planning as a Memory Task*. Academic Press, New York.

Hanks, S., Russell, S., and Wellman, M., editors (1994). *Proceedings of the AAAI Spring Symposium on Decision-Theoretic Planning*, Stanford, California.

Hanski, I. and Cambefort, Y., editors (1991). *Dung Beetle Ecology*. Princeton University Press, Princeton, New Jersey.

Hansson, O. and Mayer, A. (1989). Heuristic search as evidential reasoning. In *Proceedings of the Fifth Workshop on Uncertainty in Artificial Intelligence*, Windsor, Ontario. Morgan Kaufmann.

Haralick, R. and Elliot, G. (1980). Increasing tree search efficiency for constraint-satisfaction problems. *Artificial Intelligence*, 14(3):263–313.

Harel, D. (1984). Dynamic logic. In Gabbay, D. and Guenthner, F., editors, *Handbook of Philosophical Logic*, volume 2, pages 497–604. D. Reidel, Dordrecht, The Netherlands.

Harkness, K. and Battell, J. S. (1947). This made chess history. *Chess Review*.

Harman, G. H. (1983). *Change in View: Principles of Reasoning*. MIT Press, Cambridge, Massachusetts.

Harp, S. A., Samad, T., and Guha, A. (1990). Designing application-specific neural networks using the genetic algorithm. In Touretzky, D. S., editor, *Advances in Neural Information Processing Systems II*, pages 447–454. Morgan Kaufmann, San Mateo, California.

Harris, L. R. (1984). Experience with INTELLECT: Artificial intelligence technology transfer. *AI Magazine*, 5(2, Summer):43–55.

Hart, P. E., Nilsson, N. J., and Raphael, B. (1968). A formal basis for the heuristic determination of minimum cost paths. *IEEE Transactions on Systems Science and Cybernetics*, SSC-4(2):100–107.

Hart, P. E., Nilsson, N. J., and Raphael, B. (1972). Correction to "A formal basis for the heuristic determination of minimum cost paths". *SIGART Newsletter*, 37:28–29.

Hart, T. P. and Edwards, D. J. (1961). The tree prune (TP) algorithm. Artificial Intelligence Project Memo 30, Massachusetts Institute of Technology, Cambridge, Massachusetts.

Haugeland, J., editor (1981). *Mind Design*. MIT Press, Cambridge, Massachusetts.

Haugeland, J., editor (1985). *Artificial Intelligence: The Very Idea*. MIT Press, Cambridge, Massachusetts.

Haussler, D. (1989). Learning conjunctive concepts in structural domains. *Machine Learning*, 4(1):7–40.

Hawkins, J. (1961). Self-organizing systems: A review and commentary. *Proceedings of the IRE*, 49(1):31–48.

Hayes, J. E. and Levy, D. N. L. (1976). *The World Computer Chess Championship: Stockholm 1974*. Edinburgh University Press, Edinburgh, Scotland.

Hayes, P. J. (1973). Computation and deduction. In *Proceedings of the Second Symposium on Mathematical Foundations of Computer Science*, Czechoslovakia. Czechoslovakian Academy of Science.

Hayes, P. J. (1978). The naive physics manifesto. In Michie, D., editor, *Expert Systems in the Microelectronic Age*. Edinburgh University Press, Edinburgh, Scotland.

Hayes, P. J. (1979). The logic of frames. In Metzing, D., editor, *Frame Conceptions and Text Understanding*, pages 46–61. de Gruyter, Berlin.

Hayes, P. J. (1985a). Naive physics I: ontology for liquids. In Hobbs, J. R. and Moore, R. C., editors, *Formal Theories of the Commonsense World*, chapter 3, pages 71–107. Ablex, Norwood, New Jersey.

Hayes, P. J. (1985b). The second naive physics manifesto. In Hobbs, J. R. and Moore, R. C., editors, *Formal Theories of the Commonsense World*, chapter 1, pages 1–36. Ablex, Norwood, New Jersey.

Hazan, M. (1973). *The Classic Italian Cookbook*. Ballantine.

Hebb, D. O. (1949). *The Organization of Behavior*. Wiley, New York.

Heckerman, D. (1986). Probabilistic interpretation for MYCIN's certainty factors. In Kanal, L. N. and Lemmer, J. F., editors, *Uncertainty in Artificial Intelligence*, pages 167–196. Elsevier/North-Holland, Amsterdam, London, New York.

Heckerman, D. (1991). *Probabilistic Similarity Networks*. MIT Press, Cambridge, Massachusetts.

Heckerman, D., Geiger, D., and Chickering, M. (1994). Learning Bayesian networks: The combination of knowledge and statistical data. Technical Report MSR-TR-94-09, Microsoft Research, Redmond, Washington.

Held, M. and Karp, R. M. (1970). The traveling salesman problem and minimum spanning trees. *Operations Research*, 18:1138–1162.

Helman, D. H., editor (1988). *Analogical Reasoning: Perspectives of Artificial Intelligence, Cognitive Science, and Philosophy*. Kluwer, Dordrecht, The Netherlands.

Hendrix, G. G. (1975). Expanding the utility of semantic networks through partitioning. In *Proceedings of the Fourth International Joint Conference on Artificial Intelligence (IJCAI-75)*, pages 115–121, Tbilisi, Georgia. IJCAII.

Henrion, M. (1988). Propagation of uncertainty in Bayesian networks by probabilistic logic sampling. In Lemmer, J. F. and Kanal, L. N., editors, *Uncertainty in Artificial Intelligence 2*, pages 149–163. Elsevier/North-Holland, Amsterdam, London, New York.

Heppenheimer, T. A. (1985). Man makes man. In Minsky, M., editor, *Robotics*, pages 28–69. Doubleday, Garden City, New York.

Herbrand, J. (1930). *Recherches sur la Théorie de la Démonstration*. PhD thesis, University of Paris.

Hertz, J., Krogh, A., and Palmer, R. G. (1991). *Introduction to the Theory of Neural Computation*. Addison-Wesley, Reading, Massachusetts.

Hewitt, C. (1969). PLANNER: a language for proving theorems in robots. In *Proceedings of the First International Joint Conference on Artificial Intelligence (IJCAI-69)*, pages 295–301, Washington, D.C. IJCAII.

Hintikka, J. (1962). *Knowledge and Belief*. Cornell University Press, Ithaca, New York.

Hinton, G. E. and Anderson, J. A. (1981). *Parallel Models of Associative Memory*. Lawrence Erlbaum Associates, Potomac, Maryland.

Hinton, G. E. and Sejnowski, T. (1983). Optimal perceptual inference. In *Proceedings of the IEEE Computer Society Conference on Computer Vision and Pattern Recognition*, pages 448–453, Washington, D.C. IEEE Computer Society Press.

Hinton, G. E. and Sejnowski, T. J. (1986). Learning and relearning in Boltzmann machines. In Rumelhart, D. E. and McClelland, J. L., editors, *Parallel Distributed Processing*, chapter 7, pages 282–317. MIT Press, Cambridge, Massachusetts.

Hirsh, H. (1987). Explanation-based generalization in a logic programming environment. In *Proceedings of the Tenth International Joint Conference on Artificial Intelligence (IJCAI-87)*, Milan, Italy. Morgan Kaufmann.

Hirst, G. (1987). *Semantic Interpretation Against Ambiguity*. Cambridge University Press.

Hobbs, J. R. (1985). Ontological promiscuity. In *Proceedings, 23rd Annual Meeting of the Association for Computational Linguistics*, pages 61–69, Chicago, Illinois.

Hobbs, J. R. (1986). Overview of the TACITUS project. *Computational Linguistics*, 12(3):220–222.

Hobbs, J. R. (1990). *Literature and Cognition*. CSLI Press, Stanford, California.

Hobbs, J. R., Blenko, T., Croft, B., Hager, G., Kautz, H. A., Kube, P., and Shoham, Y. (1985). Commonsense summer: Final report. Technical Report CSLI-85-35, Center for the Study of Language and Information (CSLI), Stanford, California.

Hobbs, J. R., Croft, W., Davies, T., Edwards, D. D., and Laws, K. I. (1987). Commonsense metaphysics and lexical semantics. *Computational Linguistics*, 13(3–4):241–250.

Hobbs, J. R. and Moore, R. C., editors (1985). *Formal Theories of the Commonsense World*. Ablex, Norwood, New Jersey.

Hobbs, J. R., Stickel, M., Appelt, D., and Martin, P. (1990). Interpretation as abduction. Technical Note 499, SRI International, Menlo Park, California.

Hobbs, J. R., Stickel, M. E., Appelt, D. E., and Martin, P. (1993). Interpretation as abduction. *Artificial Intelligence*, 63(1–2):69–142.

Holland, J. H. (1975). *Adaption in Natural and Artificial Systems*. University of Michigan Press.

Hopfield, J. J. (1982). Neurons with graded response have collective computational properties like those of two-state neurons. *Proceedings of the National Academy of Sciences (USA)*, 79:2554–2558.

Horn, A. (1951). On sentences which are true of direct unions of algebras. *Journal of Symbolic Logic*, 16:14–21.

Horn, B. K. P. (1970). Shape from shading: a method for obtaining the shape of a smooth opaque object from one view. Technical Report 232, MIT Artificial Intelligence Laboratory, Cambridge, Massachusetts.

Horn, B. K. P. (1986). *Robot Vision*. MIT Press, Cambridge, Massachusetts.

Horn, B. K. P. and Brooks, M. J. (1989). *Shape from Shading*. MIT Press, Cambridge, Massachusetts.

Horvitz, E. J., Breese, J. S., and Henrion, M. (1988). Decision theory in expert systems and artificial intelligence. *International Journal of Approximate Reasoning*, 2:247–302.

Horvitz, E. J. and Heckerman, D. (1986). The inconsistent use of measures of certainty in artificial intelligence research. In Kanal, L. N. and Lemmer, J. F., editors, *Uncertainty in Artificial Intelligence*, pages 137–151. Elsevier/North-Holland, Amsterdam, London, New York.

Horvitz, E. J., Heckerman, D. E., and Langlotz, C. P. (1986). A framework for comparing alternative formalisms for plausible reasoning. In *Proceedings of the Fifth National Conference on Artificial Intelligence (AAAI-86)*, volume 1, pages 210–214, Philadelphia, Pennsylvania. Morgan Kaufmann.

Horvitz, E. J., Suermondt, H. J., and Cooper, G. F. (1989). Bounded conditioning: Flexible inference for decisions under scarce resources. In *Proceedings of the Fifth Conference on Uncertainty in Artificial Intelligence (UAI-89)*, pages 182–193, Windsor, Ontario. Morgan Kaufmann.

Howard, R. A. (1960). *Dynamic Programming and Markov Processes*. MIT Press, Cambridge, Massachusetts.

Howard, R. A. (1966). Information value theory. *IEEE Transactions on Systems Science and Cybernetics*, SSC-2:22–26.

Howard, R. A. (1977). Risk preference. In Howard, R. A. and Matheson, J. E., editors, *Readings in Decision Analysis*, pages 429–465. Decision Analysis Group, SRI International, Menlo Park, California.

Howard, R. A. (1989). Microrisks for medical decision analysis. *International Journal of Technology Assessment in Health Care*, 5:357–370.

Howard, R. A. and Matheson, J. E. (1984). Influence diagrams. In Howard, R. A. and Matheson, J. E., editors, *Readings on the Principles and Applications of Decision Analysis*, pages 721–762. Strategic Decisions Group, Menlo Park, California. Article dates from 1981.

Hsu, F.-H., Anantharaman, T. S., Campbell, M. S., and Nowatzyk, A. (1990). A grandmaster chess machine. *Scientific American*, 263(4):44–50.

Hsu, K., Brady, D., and Psaltis, D. (1988). Experimental demonstration of optical neural computers. In Anderson, D. Z., editor, *Neural Information*

Processing Systems, Denver 1987, pages 377–386, Denver, Colorado. American Institute of Physics.

Huang, T., Koller, D., Malik, J., Ogasawara, G., Rao, B., Russell, S., and Weber, J. (1994). Automatic symbolic traffic scene analysis using belief networks. In *Proceedings of the Twelfth National Conference on Artificial Intelligence (AAAI-94)*, pages 966–972, Seattle, Washington. AAAI Press.

Hubel, D. H. (1988). *Eye, Brain, and Vision*. W. H. Freeman, New York.

Huddleston, R. D. (1988). *English Grammar: An Outline*. Cambridge University Press, Cambridge.

Huffman, D. A. (1971). Impossible objects as nonsense sentences. In Meltzer, B. and Michie, D., editors, *Machine Intelligence 6*, pages 295–324. Edinburgh University Press, Edinburgh, Scotland.

Hughes, G. E. and Cresswell, M. J. (1968). *An Introduction to Modal Logic*. Methuen, London.

Hughes, G. E. and Cresswell, M. J. (1984). *A Companion to Modal Logic*. Methuen, London.

Hume, D. (1978). *A Treatise of Human Nature*. Oxford University Press, Oxford, second edition. Edited by L. A. Selby-Bigge and P. H. Nidditch.

Hunt, E. B., Marin, J., and Stone, P. T. (1966). *Experiments in Induction*. Academic Press, New York.

Hunter, G. (1971). *Metalogic: An Introduction to the Metatheory of Standard First-Order Logic*. University of California Press, Berkeley and Los Angeles.

Hunter, L. and States, D. J. (1992). Bayesian classification of protein structure. *IEEE Expert*, 7(4):67–75.

Huttenlocher, D. P. and Ullman, S. (1990). Recognizing solid objects by alignment with an image. *International Journal of Computer Vision*, 5(2):195–212.

Huygens, C. (1657). Ratiociniis in ludo aleae. In van Schooten, F., editor, *Exercitionum Mathematicorum*. Elsevirii, Amsterdam.

Hwang, C. H. and Schubert, L. K. (1993). EL: a formal, yet natural, comprehensive knowledge representation. In *Proceedings of the Eleventh National Conference on Artificial Intelligence (AAAI-93)*, pages 676–682, Washington, D.C. AAAI Press.

Hyatt, R. M., Gower, A. E., and Nelson, H. L. (1986). Cray Blitz. In Beal, D. F., editor, *Advances in Computer Chess 4*, pages 8–18. Pergamon, New York.

Ingerman, P. Z. (1967). Panini-Backus form suggested. *Communications of the Association for Computing Machinery*, 10(3):137.

Jackson, P. (1986). *Introduction to Expert Systems*. Addison-Wesley, Reading, Massachusetts.

Jacobs, P. and Rau, L. (1990). Scisor: A system for extracting information from on-line news. *Communications of the ACM*, 33(11):88–97.

Jaffar, J. and Lassez, J.-L. (1987). Constraint logic programming. In *Proceedings of the Fourteenth ACM Conference on Principles of Programming Languages*, Munich. Association for Computing Machinery.

Jaffar, J., Michaylov, S., Stuckey, P. J., and Yap, R. H. C. (1992a). The CLP(R) language and system. *ACM Transactions on Programming Languages and Systems*, 14(3):339–395.

Jaffar, J., Stuckey, P. J., Michaylov, S., and Yap, R. H. C. (1992b). An abstract machine for CLP(R). *SIGPLAN Notices*, 27(7):128–139.

Jáskowski, S. (1934). On the rules of suppositions in formal logic. *Studia Logica*, 1.

Jeffrey, R. C. (1983). *The Logic of Decision*. University of Chicago Press, Chicago, Illinois, second edition.

Jelinek, F. (1976). Continuous speech recognition by statistical methods. *Proceedings of the IEEE*, 64(4):532–556.

Jelinek, F. (1990). Self-organizing language modeling for speech recognition. In Waibel, A. and Lee, K.-F., editors, *Readings in Speech Recognition*, pages 450–506. Morgan Kaufmann.

Jensen, F. V., Lauritzen, S. L., and Olesen, K. G. (1990). Bayesian updating in causal probabilistic networks by local computations. *Computational Statistics Quarterly*, 5(4):269–282.

Jerison, H. J. (1991). *Brain Size and the Evolution of Mind*. American Museum of Natural History, New York.

Jochem, T., Pomerleau, D., and Thorpe, C. (1993). Maniac: A next generation neurally based autonomous road follower. In *Proceedings of the International Conference on Intelligent Autonomous Systems: IAS–3*.

Johnson, W. W. and Story, W. E. (1879). Notes on the "15" puzzle. *American Journal of Mathematics*, 2:397–404.

Johnson-Laird, P. N. (1988). *The Computer and the Mind: An Introduction to Cognitive Science*. Harvard University Press, Cambridge, Massachusetts.

Johnston, M. D. and Adorf, H.-M. (1992). Scheduling with neural networks: the case of the Hubble space telescope. *Computers & Operations Research*, 19(3–4):209–240.

Jones, N. D., Gomard, C. K., and Sestoft, P. (1993). *Partial Evaluation and Automatic Program Generation*. Prentice-Hall, Englewood Cliffs, New Jersey.

Joshi, A. (1985). Tree-adjoining grammars: How much context sensitivity is required to provide reasonable structural descriptions. In Dowty, D., Karttunen, L., and Zwicky, A., editors, *Natural Language Parsing*. Cambridge University Press.

Joshi, A., Webber, B., and Sag, I. (1981). *Elements of Discourse Understanding*. Cambridge University Press.

Judd, J. S. (1990). *Neural Network Design and the Complexity of Learning*. MIT Press, Cambridge, Massachusetts.

Julesz, B. (1971). *Foundations of Cyclopean Perception*. University of Chicago Press, Chicago, Illinois.

Kaelbling, L. P. (1990). Learning functions in *k*-DNF from reinforcement. In *Machine Learning: Proceedings of the Seventh International Conference*, pages 162–169, Austin, Texas. Morgan Kaufmann.

Kaelbling, L. P. and Rosenschein, S. J. (1990). Action and planning in embedded agents. *Robotics and Autonomous Systems*, 6(1–2):35–48.

Kahneman, D., Slovic, P., and Tversky, A., editors (1982). *Judgment under Uncertainty: Heuristics and Biases*. Cambridge University Press, Cambridge.

Kaindl, H. (1990). Tree searching algorithms. In Marsland, A. T. and Schaeffer, J., editors, *Computers, Chess, and Cognition*, pages 133–158. Springer-Verlag, Berlin.

Kaindl, H. and Khorsand, A. (1994). Memory-bounded bidirectional search. In *Proceedings of the Twelfth National Conference on Artificial Intelligence (AAAI-94)*, pages 1359–1364, Seattle, Washington. AAAI Press.

Kalman, R. E. (1960). A new approach to linear filtering and prediction problems. *Journal of Basic Engineering*, pages 35–46.

Kambhampati, S. and Nau, D. S. (1993). On the nature and role of modal truth criteria in planning. Technical Report ISR-TR-93-30, University of Maryland, Institute for Systems Research.

Kanal, L. N. and Kumar, V. (1988). *Search in Artificial Intelligence*. Springer-Verlag, Berlin.

Kanal, L. N. and Lemmer, J. F., editors (1986). *Uncertainty in Artificial Intelligence*. Elsevier/North-Holland, Amsterdam, London, New York.

Kandel, E. R., Schwartz, J. H., and Jessell, T. M., editors (1991). *Principles of Neural Science*. Elsevier/North-Holland, Amsterdam, London, New York, third edition.

Kaplan, D. and Montague, R. (1960). A paradox regained. *Notre Dame Journal of Formal Logic*, 1(3):79–90. Reprinted in Thomason (1974).

Karger, D. R., Koller, D., and Phillips, S. J. (1993). Finding the hidden path: time bounds for all-pairs shortest paths. *SIAM Journal on Computing*, 22(6):1199–1217.

Karp, R. M. (1972). Reducibility among combinatorial problems. In Miller, R. E. and Thatcher, J. W., editors, *Complexity of Computer Computations*, pages 85–103. Plenum, New York.

Kasami, T. (1965). An efficient recognition and syntax analysis algorithm for context-free languages. Technical Report AFCRL-65-758, Air Force Cambridge Research Laboratory, Bedford, Massachusetts.

Kautz, H. A. and Selman, B. (1991). Hard problems for simple default logics. *Artificial Intelligence*, 49(1–3):243–279.

Kay, M., Gawron, J. M., and Norvig, P. (1994). *Verbmobil: A Translation System for Face-To-Face Dialog*. CSLI Press, Stanford, California.

Kearns, M. J. (1990). *The Computational Complexity of Machine Learning*. MIT Press, Cambridge, Massachusetts.

Keeney, R. L. (1974). Multiplicative utility functions. *Operations Research*, 22:22–34.

Keeney, R. L. and Raiffa, H. (1976). *Decisions with Multiple Objectives: Preferences and Value Trade-offs*. Wiley, New York.

Kemp, M., editor (1989). *Leonardo on Painting: An Anthology of Writings*. Yale University Press, New Haven, Connecticut.

Kemp, M. (1990). *The Science of Art: Optical Themes in Western Art from Brunelleschi to Seurat*. Yale University Press, New Haven, Connecticut.

Keynes, J. M. (1921). *A Treatise on Probability*. Macmillan, London.

Kierulf, A., Chen, K., and Nievergelt, J. (1990). Smart Game Board and Go Explorer: A study in software and knowledge engineering. *Communications of the Association for Computing Machinery*, 33(2):152–167.

Kietz, J.-U. and Dzeroski, S. (1994). Inductive logic programming and learnability. *SIGART Bulletin*, 5(1):22–32.

Kim, J. H. (1983). *CONVINCE: A Conversational Inference Consolidation Engine*. PhD thesis, Department of Computer Science, University of California at Los Angeles.

Kim, J. H. and Pearl, J. (1983). A computational model for combined causal and diagnostic reasoning in inference systems. In *Proceedings of the Eighth International Joint Conference on Artificial Intelligence (IJCAI-83)*, pages 190–193, Karlsruhe, Germany. Morgan Kaufmann.

Kim, J. H. and Pearl, J. (1987). CONVINCE: A conversational inference consolidation engine. *IEEE Transactions on Systems, Man, and Cybernetics*, 17(2):120–132.

King, R. D., Muggleton, S., Lewis, R. A., and Sternberg, M. J. E. (1992). Drug design by machine learning: the use of inductive logic programming to model the structure activity relationships of trimethoprim analogues binding to dihydrofolate reductase. *Proceedings of the National Academy of Sciences of the United States of America*, 89(23):11322–11326.

King, S., Motet, S., Thoméré, J., and Arlabosse, F. (1993). A visual surveillance system for incident detection. In *AAAI 93 Workshop on AI in Intelligent Vehicle Highway Systems*, pages 30–36, Washington, D.C.

Kirkpatrick, S., Gelatt, C. D., and Vecchi, M. P. (1983). Optimization by simulated annealing. *Science*, 220:671–680.

Kirkpatrick, S. and Selman, B. (1994). Critical behavior in the satisfiability of random Boolean expressions. *Science*, 264(5163):1297–1301.

Kirousis, L. M. and Papadimitriou, C. H. (1988). The complexity of recognizing polyhedral scenes. *Journal of Computer and System Sciences*, 37(1):14–38.

Kister, J., Stein, P., Ulam, S., Walden, W., and Wells, M. (1957). Experiments in chess. *Journal of the Association for Computing Machinery*, 4:174–177.

Kjaerulff, U. (1992). A computational scheme for reasoning in dynamic probabilistic networks. In *Proceedings of the Eighth Conference on Uncertainty in Artificial Intelligence*, pages 121–129.

Knight, K. (1989). Unification: A multidisciplinary survey. *ACM Computing Surveys*, 21(1):93–121.

Knoblock, C. A. (1990). Learning abstraction hierarchies for problem solving. In *Proceedings of the Eighth National Conference on Artificial Intelligence (AAAI-90)*, volume 2, pages 923–928, Boston, Massachusetts. MIT Press.

Knuth, D. (1968). Semantics for context-free languages. *Mathematical Systems Theory 2*, pages 127–145.

Knuth, D. E. (1973). *The Art of Computer Programming*, volume 2: Fundamental Algorithms. Addison-Wesley, Reading, Massachusetts, second edition.

Knuth, D. E. and Bendix, P. B. (1970). Simple word problems in universal algebras. In Leech, J., editor, *Computational Problems in Abstract Algebra*, pages 263–267. Pergamon, New York.

Knuth, D. E. and Moore, R. W. (1975). An analysis of alpha-beta pruning. *Artificial Intelligence*, 6(4):293–326.

Koenderink, J. J. (1990). *Solid Shape*. MIT Press, Cambridge, Massachusetts.

Koenderink, J. J. and van Doorn, A. J. (1975). Invariant properties of the motion parallax field due to the movement of rigid bodies relative to an observer. *Optica Acta*, 22(9):773–791.

Kohn, W. (1991). Declarative control architecture. *Communications of the Association for Computing Machinery*, 34(8):65–79.

Kohonen, T. (1989). *Self-Organization and Associative Memory*. Springer-Verlag, Berlin, third edition.

Koller, D., Weber, J., Huang, T., Malik, J., Ogasawara, G., Rao, B., and Russell, S. (1994). Towards robust automatic traffic scene analysis in real-time. In *Proceedings of the International Conference on Pattern Recognition*, Israel.

Kolmogorov, A. N. (1941). Interpolation und extrapolation von stationaren zufalligen folgen. *Bulletin of the Academy of Sciences of the USSR*, Ser. Math. 5:3–14.

Kolmogorov, A. N. (1950). *Foundations of the Theory of Probability*. Chelsea, New York. English translation of Kolmogorov (1950).

Kolmogorov, A. N. (1963). On tables of random numbers. *Sankhya, the Indian Journal of Statistics*, Series A 25.

Kolmogorov, A. N. (1965). Three approaches to the quantitative definition of information. *Problems in Information Transmission*, 1(1):1–7.

Kolodner, J. (1983). Reconstructive memory: A computer model. *Cognitive Science*, 7:281–328.

Kolodner, J. (1993). *Case-Based Reasoning*. Morgan Kaufmann, San Mateo, California.

Konolige, K. (1982). A first order formalization of knowledge and action for a multi-agent planning system. In Hayes, J. E., Michie, D., and Pao, Y.-H., editors, *Machine Intelligence 10*. Ellis Horwood, Chichester, England.

Koopmans, T. C. (1972). Representation of preference orderings over time. In McGuire, C. B. and Radner, R., editors, *Decision and Organization*. Elsevier/North-Holland, Amsterdam, London, New York.

Korf, R. E. (1985a). Depth-first iterative-deepening: an optimal admissible tree search. *Artificial Intelligence*, 27(1):97–109.

Korf, R. E. (1985b). Iterative-deepening A*: An optimal admissible tree search. In *Proceedings of the Ninth International Joint Conference on Artificial Intelligence (IJCAI-85)*, pages 1034–1036, Los Angeles, California. Morgan Kaufmann.

Korf, R. E. (1988). Optimal path finding algorithms. In Kanal, L. N. and Kumar, V., editors, *Search in Artificial Intelligence*, chapter 7, pages 223–267. Springer-Verlag, Berlin.

Korf, R. E. (1993). Linear-space best-first search. *Artificial Intelligence*, 62(1):41–78.

Kotok, A. (1962). A chess playing program for the IBM 7090. AI Project Memo 41, MIT Computation Center, Cambridge, Massachusetts.

Kowalski, R. (1974). Predicate logic as a programming language. In *Proceedings of the IFIP-74 Congress*, pages 569–574. Elsevier/North-Holland.

Kowalski, R. (1979a). Algorithm = logic + control. *Communications of the Association for Computing Machinery*, 22:424–436.

Kowalski, R. (1979b). *Logic for Problem Solving*. Elsevier/North-Holland, Amsterdam, London, New York.

Kowalski, R. (1988). The early years of logic programming. *Communications of the Association for Computing Machinery*, 31:38–43.

Kowalski, R. and Sergot, M. (1986). A logic-based calculus of events. *New Generation Computing*, 4(1):67–95.

Koza, J. R. (1992). *Genetic Programming: On the Programming of Computers by Means of Natural Selection*. MIT Press, Cambridge, Massachusetts.

Kripke, S. A. (1963). Semantical considerations on modal logic. *Acta Philosophica Fennica*, 16:83–94.

Kruppa, E. (1913). Zur Ermittlung eines Objecktes aus zwei Perspektiven mit innerer Orientierung. *Sitz.-Ber. Akad. Wiss., Wien, Math. Naturw., Kl. Abt. IIa*, 122:1939–1948.

Kuehner, D. (1971). A note on the relation between resolution and Maslov's inverse method. DCL Memo 36, University of Edinburgh.

Kukich, K. (1992). Techniques for automatically correcting words in text. *ACM Computing Surveys*, 24(4):377–439.

Kumar, V. (1991). A general heuristic bottom-up procedure for searching AND/OR graphs. *Information Sciences*, 56(1–3):39–57.

Kumar, V. and Kanal, L. N. (1983). A general branch and bound formulation for understanding and synthesizing and/or tree search procedures. *Artificial Intelligence*, 21:179–198.

Kumar, V. and Kanal, L. N. (1988). The CDP: A unifying formulation for heuristic search, dynamic programming, and branch-and-bound. In Kanal, L. N. and Kumar, V., editors, *Search in Artificial Intelligence*, chapter 1, pages 1–27. Springer-Verlag, Berlin.

Kumar, V., Nau, D. S., and Kanal, L. N. (1988). A general branch-and-bound formulation for AND/OR graph and game tree search. In Kanal, L. N. and Kumar, V., editors, *Search in Artificial Intelligence*, chapter 3, pages 91–130. Springer-Verlag, Berlin.

Kurzweil, R. (1990). *The Age of Intelligent Machines*. MIT Press, Cambridge, Massachusetts.

Kyburg, H. E. (1977). Randomness and the right reference class. *The Journal of Philosophy*, 74(9):501–521.

Kyburg, H. E. (1983). The reference class. *Philosophy of Science*, 50:374–397.

La Mettrie, J. O. d. (1748). *L'homme machine*. E. Luzac, Leyde. Translated into English as La Mettrie (1912).

La Mettrie, J. O. d. (1912). *Man a Machine*. Open Court, La Salle, Illinois. English translation of La Mettrie (1748).

Ladkin, P. (1986a). Primitives and units for time specification. In *Proceedings of the Fifth National Conference on Artificial Intelligence (AAAI-86)*, volume 1, pages 354–359, Philadelphia, Pennsylvania. Morgan Kaufmann.

Ladkin, P. (1986b). Time representation: a taxonomy of interval relations. In *Proceedings of the Fifth National Conference on Artificial Intelligence (AAAI-86)*, volume 1, pages 360–366, Philadelphia, Pennsylvania. Morgan Kaufmann.

Laird, J. E., Newell, A., and Rosenbloom, P. S. (1987). SOAR: an architecture for general intelligence. *Artificial Intelligence*, 33(1):1–64.

Laird, J. E., Rosenbloom, P. S., and Newell, A. (1986). Chunking in Soar: the anatomy of a general learning mechanism. *Machine Learning*, 1:11–46.

Laird, J. E., Yager, E. S., Hucka, M., and Tuck, M. (1991). Robo-Soar: an integration of external interaction, planning, and learning using Soar. *Robotics and Autonomous Systems*, 8(1–2):113–129.

Lakoff, G. (1987). *Women, Fire, and Dangerous Things: What Categories Reveal About the Mind*. University of Chicago Press, Chicago, Illinois.

Lakoff, G. and Johnson, M. (1980). *Metaphors We Live By*. University of Chicago Press, Chicago, Illinois.

Langley, P., Simon, H. A., Bradshaw, G. L., and Zytkow, J. M. (1987). *Scientific Discovery: Computational Explorations of the Creative Processes*. MIT Press, Cambridge, Massachusetts.

Lassez, J.-L., Maher, M. J., and Marriott, K. (1988). Unification revisited. In Minker, J., editor, *Foundations of Deductive Databases and Logic Programming*, pages 587–625. Morgan Kaufmann, San Mateo, California.

Latombe, J.-C. (1991). *Robot Motion Planning*. Kluwer, Dordrecht, The Netherlands.

Lauritzen, S. L. (1991). The EM algorithm for graphical association models with missing data. Technical Report TR-91-05, Department of Statistics, Aalborg University.

Lauritzen, S. L. and Spiegelhalter, D. J. (1988). Local computations with probabilities on graphical structures and their application to expert systems. *Journal of the Royal Statistical Society*, B 50(2):157–224.

Lauritzen, S. L. and Wermuth, N. (1989). Graphical models for associations between variables, some of which are qualitative and some quantitative. *Annals of Statistics*, 17:31–57.

Lawler, E. L. and Wood, D. E. (1966). Branch-and-bound methods: A survey. *Operations Research*, 14(4):699–719.

Le Cun, Y., Jackel, L. D., Boser, B., and Denker, J. S. (1989). Handwritten digit recognition: applications of neural network chips and automatic learning. *IEEE Communications Magazine*, 27(11):41–46.

Lee, K.-F. (1989). *Automatic Speech Recognition: The Development of the SPHINX System*. Kluwer, Dordrecht, The Netherlands.

Lee, K.-F. and Mahajan, S. (1988). A pattern classification approach to evaluation function learning. *Artificial Intelligence*, 36(1):1–26.

Lefkovitz, D. (1960). A strategic pattern recognition program for the game Go. Technical Note 60-243, Wright Air Development Division, University of Pennsylvania, The Moore School of Electrical Engineering.

Lenat, D. B. (1983). EURISKO: a program that learns new heuristics and domain concepts: the nature of heuristics, III: program design and results. *Artificial Intelligence*, 21(1–2):61–98.

Lenat, D. B. and Brown, J. S. (1984). Why AM and EURISKO appear to work. *Artificial Intelligence*, 23(3):269–294.

Lenat, D. B. and Feigenbaum, E. A. (1991). On the thresholds of knowledge. *Artificial Intelligence*, 47(1–3):185–250.

Lenat, D. B. and Guha, R. V. (1990). *Building Large Knowledge-Based Systems: Representation and Inference in the CYC Project*. Addison-Wesley, Reading, Massachusetts.

Leonard, H. S. and Goodman, N. (1940). The calculus of individuals and its uses. *Journal of Symbolic Logic*, 5(2):45–55.

Leonard, J. J. and Durrant-Whyte, H. F. (1992). *Directed sonar sensing for mobile robot navigation*. Kluwer, Dordrecht, The Netherlands.

Leśniewski, S. (1916). Podstawy ogólnej teorii mnogości. Moscow.

Levesque, H. J. and Brachman, R. J. (1987). Expressiveness and tractability in knowledge representation and reasoning. *Computational Intelligence*, 3(2):78–93.

Levy, D. N. L. (1983). *Computer Gamesmanship: The Complete Guide to Creating and Structuring Intelligent Games Programs*. Simon and Schuster, New York.

Levy, D. N. L., editor (1988a). *Computer Chess Compendium*. Springer-Verlag, Berlin.

Levy, D. N. L., editor (1988b). *Computer Games*. Springer-Verlag, Berlin. Two volumes.

Lewis, D. K. (1966). An argument for the identity theory. *The Journal of Philosophy*, 63(1):17–25.

Lewis, D. K. (1972). General semantics. In Davidson, D. and Harman, G., editors, *Semantics of Natural Language*, pages 169–218. D. Reidel, Dordrecht, The Netherlands.

Lewis, D. K. (1980). Mad pain and Martian pain. In Block, N., editor, *Readings in Philosophy of Psychology*, volume 1, pages 216–222. Harvard University Press, Cambridge, Massachusetts.

Li, M. and Vitanyi, P. M. B. (1993). *An Introduction to Kolmogorov Complexity and Its Applications*. Springer-Verlag, Berlin.

Lifschitz, V. (1986). On the semantics of STRIPS. In Georgeff, M. P. and Lansky, A. L., editors, *Reasoning about Actions and Plans: Proceedings of the 1986 Workshop*, pages 1–9, Timberline, Oregon. Morgan Kaufmann.

Lifschitz, V. (1989). Between circumscription and autoepistemic logic. In Brachman, R. J. and Levesque, H. J., editors, *Proceedings of the First International Conference on Principles of Knowledge Representation and Reasoning*, pages 235–244, Toronto, Ontario. Morgan Kaufmann.

Lighthill, J. (1973). Artificial intelligence: A general survey. In Lighthill, J., Sutherland, N. S., Needham, R. M., Longuet-Higgins, H. C., and Michie, D., editors, *Artificial Intelligence: A Paper Symposium*. Science Research Council of Great Britain, London.

Lin, S. (1965). Computer solutions of the travelling salesman problem. *Bell Systems Technical Journal*, 44(10):2245–2269.

Linden, T. A. (1991). Representing software designs as partially developed plans. In Lowry, M. R. and McCartney, R. D., editors, *Automating Software Design*, pages 603–625. MIT Press, Cambridge, Massachusetts.

Lindsay, R. K. (1963). Inferential memory as the basis of machines which understand natural language. In Feigenbaum, E. A. and Feldman, J., editors, *Computers and Thought*, pages 217–236. McGraw-Hill, New York.

Lindsay, R. K., Buchanan, B. G., Feigenbaum, E. A., and Lederberg, J. (1980). *Applications of Artificial Intelligence for Organic Chemistry: The DENDRAL Project*. McGraw-Hill, New York.

Lloyd, J. W. (1987). *Foundations of Logic Programming*. Springer-Verlag, Berlin.

Locke, W. N. and Booth, A. D. (1955). *Machine Translation of Languages: Fourteen Essays*. MIT Press, Cambridge, Massachusetts.

Longuet-Higgins, H. C. (1981). A computer algorithm for reconstructing a scene from two projections. *Nature*, 293:133–135.

Lovejoy, W. S. (1991). A survey of algorithmic methods for partially observed Markov decision processes. *Annals of Operations Research*, 28(1–4):47–66.

Loveland, D. W. (1968). Mechanical theorem proving by model elimination. *Journal of the Association for Computing Machinery*, 15(2):236–251.

Loveland, D. W. (1984). Automated theorem-proving: A quarter-century review. *Contemporary Mathematics*, 29:1–45.

Lowe, D. G. (1987). Three-dimensional object recognition from single two-dimensional images. *Artificial Intelligence*, 31:355–395.

Löwenheim, L. (1915). Über möglichkeiten im Relativkalkül. *Mathematische Annalen*, 76:447–470. Reprinted in English translation in van Heijenoort (1967).

Lowerre, B. T. and Reddy, R. (1980). The HARPY speech recognition system. In Lea, W. A., editor, *Trends in Speech Recognition*, chapter 15. Prentice-Hall, Englewood Cliffs, New Jersey.

Lowry, M. R. and McCartney, R. D. (1991). *Automating Software Design*. MIT Press, Cambridge, Massachusetts.

Loyd, S. (1959). *Mathematical Puzzles of Sam Loyd: Selected and Edited by Martin Gardner*. Dover, New York.

Lozano-Pérez, T., Mason, M., and Taylor, R. (1984). Automatic synthesis of fine-motion strategies for robots. *International Journal of Robotics Research*, 3(1):3–24.

Lucas, J. R. (1961). Minds, machines, and Gödel. *Philosophy*, 36.

Luger, G. F. and Stubblefield, W. A. (1993). *Artificial Intelligence: Structures and Strategies for Complex Problem Solving*. Benjamin/Cummings, Redwood City, California, second edition.

Mackworth, A. K. (1973). Interpreting pictures of polyhedral scenes. *Artificial Intelligence*, 4:121–137.

Maes, P., Darrell, T., Blumberg, B., and Pentland, A. (1994). ALIVE: Artificial Life Interactive Video Environment. In *Proceedings of the Twelfth National Conference on Artificial Intelligence (AAAI-94)*, page 1506, Seattle, Washington. AAAI Press.

Magerman, D. (1993). *Natural Language Parsing as Statistical Pattern Recognition*. PhD thesis, Stanford University.

Mahanti, A. and Daniels, C. J. (1993). A SIMD approach to parallel heuristic search. *Artificial Intelligence*, 60(2):243–282.

Malik, J. (1987). Interpreting line drawings of curved objects. *International Journal of Computer Vision*, 1(1):73–103.

Malik, J. and Rosenholtz, R. (1994). Recovering surface curvature and orientation from texture distortion: a least squares algorithm and sensitivity analysis. In Eklundh, J.-O., editor, *Proceedings of the Third European Conf. on Computer Vision*, pages 353–364, Stockholm. Springer-Verlag. Published as Lecture Notes in Computer Science 800.

Manin, Y. I. (1977). *A Course in Mathematical Logic*. Springer-Verlag, Berlin.

Mann, W. C. and Thompson, S. A. (1983). Relational propositions in discourse. Technical Report RR-83-115, Information Sciences Institute.

Manna, Z. and Waldinger, R. (1971). Toward automatic program synthesis. *Communications of the Association for Computing Machinery*, 14(3):151–165.

Manna, Z. and Waldinger, R. (1985). *The Logical Basis for Computer Programming: Volume 1: Deductive Reasoning*. Addison-Wesley, Reading, Massachusetts.

Manna, Z. and Waldinger, R. (1986). Special relations in automated deduction. *Journal of the Association for Computing Machinery*, 33(1):1–59.

Manna, Z. and Waldinger, R. (1992). Fundamentals of deductive program synthesis. *IEEE Transactions on Software Engineering*, 18(8):674–704.

Marchand, M., Golea, M., and Ruján, P. (1990). A convergence theorem for sequential learning in two-layer perceptrons. *Europhysics Letters*, 11:487–492.

Markov, A. A. (1913). An example of statistical investigation in the text of "Eugene Onegin" illustrating coupling of "tests" in chains. *Proceedings of the Academy of Sciences of St. Petersburg*, 7.

Marr, D. (1982). *Vision: A Computational Investigation into the Human Representation and Processing of Visual Information*. W. H. Freeman, New York.

Marsland, A. T. and Schaeffer, J., editors (1990). *Computers, Chess, and Cognition*. Springer-Verlag, Berlin.

Martelli, A. and Montanari, U. (1973). Additive AND/OR graphs. In *Proceedings of the Third International Joint Conference on Artificial Intelligence (IJCAI-73)*, pages 1–11, Stanford, California. IJCAII.

Martelli, A. and Montanari, U. (1976). Unification in linear time and space: A structured presentation. Internal Report B 76-16, Istituto di Elaborazione della Informazione, Pisa, Italy.

Martelli, A. and Montanari, U. (1978). Optimizing decision trees through heuristically guided search. *Communications of the Association for Computing Machinery*, 21:1025–1039.

Martin, C. D. (1993). The myth of the awesome thinking machine. *Communications of the Association for Computing Machinery*, 36(4):120–133.

Martin, J. H. (1990). *A Computational Model of Metaphor Interpretation*. Academic Press.

Maslov, S. Y. (1964). An inverse method for establishing deducibility in classical predicate calculus. *Doklady Akademii nauk SSSR*, 159:17–20.

Maslov, S. Y. (1967). An inverse method for establishing deducibility of nonprenex formulas of the predicate calculus. *Doklady Akademii nauk SSSR*, 172:22–25.

Maslov, S. Y. (1971). Relationship between tactics of the inverse method and the resolution method. *Seminars in Mathematics, V. A. Steklov Mathematical Institute, Leningrad, Consultants Bureau, New York-London*, 16:69–73.

Mason, M. T. (1993). Kicking the sensing habit. *AI Magazine*, 14(1):58–59.

Mates, B. (1953). *Stoic Logic*. University of California Press, Berkeley and Los Angeles.

Maxwell, J. and Kaplan, R. (1993). The interface between phrasal and functional constraints. *Computational Linguistics*, 19(4):571–590.

Mays, E., Apte, C., Griesmer, J., and Kastner, J. (1987). Organizing knowledge in a complex financial domain. *IEEE Expert*, 2(3):61–70.

McAllester, D. and Rosenblitt, D. (1991). Systematic nonlinear planning. In *Proceedings of the Ninth National Conference on Artificial Intelligence (AAAI-91)*, volume 2, pages 634–639, Anaheim, California. AAAI Press.

McAllester, D. A. (1980). An outlook on truth maintenance. AI Memo 551, MIT AI Laboratory, Cambridge, Massachusetts.

McAllester, D. A. (1988). Conspiracy numbers for min-max search. *Artificial Intelligence*, 35(3):287–310.

McAllester, D. A. (1989). *Ontic: A Knowledge Representation System for Mathematics*. MIT Press, Cambridge, Massachusetts.

McAllester, D. A. and Givan, R. (1992). Natural language syntax and first-order inference. *Artificial Intelligence*, 56(1):1–20.

McCarthy, J. (1958). Programs with common sense. In *Proceedings of the Symposium on Mechanisation of Thought Processes*, volume 1, pages 77–84, London. Her Majesty's Stationery Office.

McCarthy, J. (1963). Situations, actions, and causal laws. Memo 2, Stanford University Artificial Intelligence Project, Stanford, California. Reprinted as part of McCarthy (1968).

McCarthy, J. (1968). Programs with common sense. In Minsky, M. L., editor, *Semantic Information Processing*, pages 403–418. MIT Press, Cambridge, Massachusetts.

McCarthy, J. (1977). Epistemological problems in artificial intelligence. In *Proceedings of the Fifth International Joint Conference on Artificial Intelligence (IJCAI-77)*, Cambridge, Massachusetts. IJCAII.

McCarthy, J. (1978). History of LISP. In Wexelblat, R. L., editor, *History of Programming Languages: Proceedings of the ACM SIGPLAN Conference*, pages 173–197. Academic Press. Published in 1981; 1978 is date of conference.

McCarthy, J. (1980). Circumscription: a form of non-monotonic reasoning. *Artificial Intelligence*, 13(1–2):27–39.

McCarthy, J. and Hayes, P. J. (1969). Some philosophical problems from the standpoint of artificial intelligence. In Meltzer, B., Michie, D., and Swann, M., editors, *Machine Intelligence 4*, pages 463–502. Edinburgh University Press, Edinburgh, Scotland.

McCawley, J. D. (1993). *Everything That Linguists Have Always Wanted to Know About Logic But Were Ashamed to Ask*. University of Chicago Press, Chicago, Illinois, second edition.

McCorduck, P. (1979). *Machines Who Think: A Personal Inquiry into the History and Prospects of Artificial Intelligence*. W. H. Freeman, New York.

McCulloch, W. S. and Pitts, W. (1943). A logical calculus of the ideas immanent in nervous activity. *Bulletin of Mathematical Biophysics*, 5:115–137.

McCune, W. W. (1992). Automated discovery of new axiomatizations of the left group and right group calculi. *Journal of Automated Reasoning*, 9(1):1–24.

McDermott, D. (1976). Artificial intelligence meets natural stupidity. *SIGART Newsletter*, 57.

McDermott, D. (1978a). Planning and acting. *Cognitive Science*, 2(2):71–109.

McDermott, D. (1978b). Tarskian semantics, or, no notation without denotation! *Cognitive Science*, 2(3).

McDermott, D. (1987). A critique of pure reason. *Computational Intelligence*, 3(3):151–237. Includes responses by a number of commentators and final rebuttal by the author.

McDermott, D. (1991). Regression planning. *International Journal of Intelligent Systems*, 6:357–416.

McDermott, D. and Doyle, J. (1980). Non-monotonic logic I. *Artificial Intelligence*, 13(1–2):41–72.

McDermott, J. (1982). R1: A rule-based configurer of computer systems. *Artificial Intelligence*, 19(1):39–88.

Mead, C. (1989). *Analog VLSI and Neural Systems*. Addison-Wesley, Reading, Massachusetts.

Megiddo, N. and Wigderson, A. (1986). On play by means of computing machines. In Halpern, J. Y., editor, *Theoretical Aspects of Reasoning about Knowledge: Proceedings of the 1986 Conference (TARK-86)*, pages 259–274, Monterey, California. IBM and AAAI, Morgan Kaufmann.

Melćuk, I. A. and Polguere, A. (1988). A formal lexicon in the meaning-text theory (or how to do lexica with words). *Computational Linguistics*, 13(3–4):261–275.

Mero, L. (1984). A heuristic search algorithm with modifiable estimate. *Artificial Intelligence*, 23(1):13–27.

Metropolis, N., Rosenbluth, A., Rosenbluth, M., Teller, A., and Teller, E. (1953). Equations of state calculations by fast computing machines. *Journal of Chemical Physics*, 21:1087–1091.

Mézard, M. and Nadal, J.-P. (1989). Learning in feedforward layered networks: The tiling algorithm. *Journal of Physics*, 22:2191–2204.

Michalski, R. S., Carbonell, J. G., and Mitchell, T. M., editors (1983). *Machine Learning: An Artificial Intelligence Approach*, volume 1. Morgan Kaufmann, San Mateo, California.

Michalski, R. S., Carbonell, J. G., and Mitchell, T. M., editors (1986). *Machine Learning: An Artificial Intelligence Approach*, volume 2. Morgan Kaufmann, San Mateo, California.

Michie, D. (1966). Game-playing and game-learning automata. In Fox, L., editor, *Advances in Programming and Non-Numerical Computation*, pages 183–200. Pergamon, New York.

Michie, D. (1972). Machine intelligence at Edinburgh. *Management Informatics*, 2(1):7–12.

Michie, D. (1982). The state of the art in machine learning. In *Introductory Readings in Expert Systems*, pages 209–229. Gordon and Breach, New York.

Michie, D. (1986). Current developments in expert systems. In *Proc. 2nd Australian Conference on Applications of Expert Systems*, pages 163–182, Sydney, Australia.

Michie, D. and Chambers, R. A. (1968). BOXES: An experiment in adaptive control. In Dale, E. and Michie, D., editors, *Machine Intelligence 2*, pages 125–133. Elsevier/North-Holland, Amsterdam, London, New York.

Michie, D., Spiegelhalter, D. J., and Taylor, C. C., editors (1994). *Machine Learning, Neural and Statistical Classification*. Ellis Horwood, Chichester, England.

Miles, F. A. (1969). *Excitable Cells*. William Heinemann Medical Books, London.

Mill, J. S. (1843). *A System of Logic, Ratiocinative and Inductive: Being a Connected View of the Principles of Evidence, and Methods of Scientific Investigation*. J. W. Parker, London.

Mill, J. S. (1863). *Utilitarianism*. Parker, Son and Bourn, London.

Miller, A. C., Merkhofer, M. M., Howard, R. A., Matheson, J. E., and Rice, T. R. (1976). Development of automated aids for decision analysis. Technical report, SRI International, Menlo Park, California.

Miller, G. F., Todd, P. M., and Hegde, S. U. (1989). Designing neural networks using genetic algorithms. In Schaffer, J. D., editor, *Proceedings of the Third International Conference on Genetic Algorithms*, pages 379–384, Arlington, Virginia. Morgan Kaufmann.

Milne, A. A. (1926). *Winnie-the-Pooh*. Methuen, London. With decorations by Ernest H. Shepard.

Minker, J., editor (1988). *Foundations of Deductive Databases and Logic Programming*. Morgan Kaufmann, San Mateo, California.

Minsky, M. L. (1954). *Neural Nets and the Brain-Model Problem*. PhD thesis, Princeton University.

Minsky, M. L., editor (1968). *Semantic Information Processing*. MIT Press, Cambridge, Massachusetts.

Minsky, M. L. (1975). A framework for representing knowledge. In Winston, P. H., editor, *The Psychology of Computer Vision*, pages 211–277. McGraw-Hill, New York. Originally appeared as an MIT Artificial Intelligence Laboratory memo; the present version is abridged, but is the most widely cited. Another, later abridged version appeared in Haugeland (1981).

Minsky, M. L. and Papert, S. (1969). *Perceptrons: An Introduction to Computational Geometry*. MIT Press, Cambridge, Massachusetts, first edition.

Minsky, M. L. and Papert, S. (1988). *Perceptrons: An Introduction to Computational Geometry*. MIT Press, Cambridge, Massachusetts, expanded edition.

Minton, S. (1984). Constraint-based generalization: Learning game-playing plans from single examples. In *Proceedings of the National Conference on Artificial Intelligence (AAAI-84)*, pages 251–254, Austin, TX. Morgan Kaufmann.

Minton, S. (1988). Quantitative results concerning the utility of explanation- based learning. In *Proceedings of the Seventh National Conference on Artificial Intelligence (AAAI-88)*, St. Paul, Minnesota. Morgan Kaufmann.

Minton, S., Johnston, M. D., Philips, A. B., and Laird, P. (1992). Minimizing conflicts: a heuristic repair method for constraint satisfaction and scheduling problems. *Artificial Intelligence*, 58(1–3):161–205.

Mitchell, T., Keller, R., and Kedar-Cabelli, S. (1986). Explanation-based generalization: A unifying view. *Machine Learning*, 1:47–80.

Mitchell, T. M. (1977). Version spaces: a candidate elimination approach to rule learning. In *Proceedings of the Fifth International Joint Conference on Artificial Intelligence (IJCAI-77)*, pages 305–310, Cambridge, Massachusetts. IJCAII.

Mitchell, T. M. (1980). The need for biases in learning generalizations. Technical Report CBM-TR-117, Department of Computer Science, Rutgers University, New Brunswick, New Jersey.

Mitchell, T. M. (1982). Generalization as search. *Artificial Intelligence*, 18(2):203–226.

Mitchell, T. M. (1990). Becoming increasingly reactive (mobile robots). In *Proceedings of the Eighth National Conference on Artificial Intelligence (AAAI-90)*, volume 2, pages 1051–1058, Boston, Massachusetts. MIT Press.

Mitchell, T. M., Utgoff, P. E., and Banerji, R. (1983). Learning by experimentation: acquiring and refining problem-solving heuristics. In Michalski, R. S., Carbonell, J. G., and Mitchell, T. M., editors, *Machine Learning: An Artificial Intelligence Approach*, pages 163–190. Morgan Kaufmann, San Mateo, California.

Montague, R. (1970). English as a formal language. In *Linguaggi nella Società e nella Tecnica*, pages 189–224. Edizioni di Comunità, Milan. Reprinted in (Thomason, 1974, pp. 188–221).

Montague, R. (1973). The proper treatment of quantification in ordinary English. In Hintikka, K. J. J., Moravcsik, J. M. E., and Suppes, P., editors, *Approaches to Natural Language*. D. Reidel, Dordrecht, The Netherlands.

Moore, A. W. and Atkeson, C. G. (1993). Prioritized sweeping—reinforcement learning with less data and less time. *Machine Learning*, 13:103–130.

Moore, J. and Newell, A. (1973). How can Merlin understand? In Gregg, L., editor, *Knowledge and Cognition*. Lawrence Erlbaum Associates, Potomac, Maryland.

Moore, R. C. (1980). Reasoning about knowledge and action. Artificial Intelligence Center Technical Note 191, SRI International, Menlo Park, California.

Moore, R. C. (1985a). A formal theory of knowledge and action. In Hobbs, J. R. and Moore, R. C., editors, *Formal Theories of the Commonsense World*, pages 319–358. Ablex, Norwood, New Jersey.

Moore, R. C. (1985b). Semantical considerations on nonmonotonic logic. *Artificial Intelligence*, 25(1):75–94.

Moore, R. C. (1993). Autoepistemic logic revisited. *Artificial Intelligence*, 59(1–2):27–30.

Moravec, H. (1988). *Mind Children: The Future of Robot and Human Intelligence*. Harvard University Press, Cambridge, Massachusetts.

Morgenstern, L. (1987). Knowledge preconditions for actions and plans. In *Proceedings of the Tenth International Joint Conference on Artificial Intelligence (IJCAI-87)*, pages 867–874, Milan, Italy. Morgan Kaufmann.

Morrison, P. and Morrison, E., editors (1961). *Charles Babbage and His Calculating Engines: Selected Writings by Charles Babbage and Others*. Dover, New York.

Mostow, J. and Prieditis, A. E. (1989). Discovering admissible heuristics by abstracting and optimizing: a transformational approach. In *Proceedings of the Eleventh International Joint Conference on Artificial Intelligence (IJCAI-89)*, volume 1, pages 701–707, Detroit, Michigan. Morgan Kaufmann.

Motzkin, T. S. and Schoenberg, I. J. (1954). The relaxation method for linear inequalities. *Canadian Journal of Mathematics*, 6(3):393–404.

Mourelatos, A. P. D. (1978). Events, processes, and states. *Linguistics and Philosophy*, 2:415–434.

Moussouris, J., Holloway, J., and Greenblatt, R. (1979). CHEOPS: A chess-oriented processing system. In Hayes, J. E., Michie, D., and Mikulich, L. I., editors, *Machine Intelligence 9*, pages 351–360. Ellis Horwood, Chichester, England.

Muggleton, S. (1991). Inductive logic programming. *New Generation Computing*, 8:295–318.

Muggleton, S. (1992). *Inductive Logic Programming*. Academic Press, New York.

Muggleton, S. and Buntine, W. (1988). Machine invention of first-order predicates by inverting resolution. In *MLC-88*.

Muggleton, S. and Cao, F. (1990). Efficient induction of logic programs. In *Proceedings of the Workshop on Algorithmic Learning Theory*, Tokyo.

Muggleton, S., King, R. D., and Sternberg, M. J. E. (1992). Protein secondary structure prediction using logic-based machine learning. *Protein Engineering*, 5(7):647–657.

Mundy, J. and Zisserman, A., editors (1992). *Geometric Invariance in Computer Vision*. MIT Press, Cambridge, Massachusetts.

Nagel, T. (1974). What is it like to be a bat? *Philosophical Review*, 83:435–450.

Nalwa, V. S. (1993). *A Guided Tour of Computer Vision*. Addison-Wesley, Reading, Massachusetts.

Nau, D. S. (1980). Pathology on game trees: A summary of results. In *Proceedings of the First Annual National Conference on Artificial Intelligence (AAAI-80)*, pages 102–104, Stanford, California. AAAI.

Nau, D. S. (1983). Pathology on game trees revisited, and an alternative to minimaxing. *Artificial Intelligence*, 21(1–2):221–244.

Nau, D. S., Kumar, V., and Kanal, L. N. (1984). General branch and bound, and its relation to A* and AO*. *Artificial Intelligence*, 23:29–58.

Naur, P. (1963). Revised report on the algorithmic language Algol 60. *Communications of the Association for Computing Machinery*, 6(1):1–17.

Neal, R. M. (1991). Connectionist learning of belief networks. *Artificial Intelligence*, 56:71–113.

Neapolitan, R. E. (1990). *Probabilistic Reasoning in Expert Systems: Theory and Algorithms*. Wiley, New York.

Netto, E. (1901). *Lehrbuch der Combinatorik*. B. G. Teubner, Leipzig.

Newell, A. (1982). The knowledge level. *Artificial Intelligence*, 18(1):82–127.

Newell, A. (1990). *Unified Theories of Cognition*. Harvard University Press, Cambridge, Massachusetts.

Newell, A. and Ernst, G. (1965). The search for generality. In Kalenich, W. A., editor, *Information Processing 1965: Proceedings of IFIP Congress 1965*, volume 1, pages 17–24. Spartan.

Newell, A. and Shaw, J. C. (1957). Programming the logic theory machine. In *Proceedings of the 1957 Western Joint Computer Conference*, pages 230–240. IRE.

Newell, A., Shaw, J. C., and Simon, H. A. (1957). Empirical explorations with the logic theory machine. *Proceedings of the Western Joint Computer Conference*, 15:218–239. Reprinted in Feigenbaum and Feldman (1963).

Newell, A., Shaw, J. C., and Simon, H. A. (1958). Chess playing programs and the problem of complexity. *IBM Journal of Research and Development*, 4(2):320–335. Reprinted in Feigenbaum and Feldman (1963).

Newell, A. and Simon, H. A. (1961). GPS, a program that simulates human thought. In Billing, H., editor, *Lernende Automaten*, pages 109–124. R. Oldenbourg, Munich, Germany. Reprinted in (Feigenbaum and Feldman, 1963, pp. 279–293).

Newell, A. and Simon, H. A. (1972). *Human Problem Solving*. Prentice-Hall, Englewood Cliffs, New Jersey.

Neyman, A. (1985). Bounded complexity justifies cooperation in the finitely repeated prisoners' dilemma. *Economics Letters*, 19:227–229.

Nicholson, A. E. and Brady, J. M. (1992). The data association problem when monitoring robot vehicles using dynamic belief networks. In *ECAI 92: 10th European Conference on Artificial Intelligence Proceedings*, pages 689–693, Vienna, Austria. Wiley.

Nilsson, N. J. (1965). *Learning Machines: Foundations of Trainable Pattern-Classifying Systems*. McGraw-Hill, New York.

Nilsson, N. J. (1971). *Problem-Solving Methods in Artificial Intelligence*. McGraw-Hill, New York.

Nilsson, N. J. (1980). *Principles of Artificial Intelligence*. Morgan Kaufmann, San Mateo, California.

Nilsson, N. J. (1984). Shakey the robot. Technical Note 323, SRI International, Menlo Park, California.

Nilsson, N. J. (1990). *The Mathematical Foundations of Learning Machines*. Morgan Kaufmann, San Mateo, California. Introduction by Terrence J. Sejnowski and Halbert White.

Nitta, K., Taki, K., and Ichiyoshi, N. (1992). Experimental parallel inference software. In *Fifth Generation Computer Systems 1992*, volume 1, pages 166–190, Tokyo. IOS Press.

Norvig, P. (1988). Multiple simultaneous interpretations of ambiguous sentences. In *Proceedings of the 10th Annual Conference of the Cognitive Science Society*.

Norvig, P. (1992). *Paradigms of Artificial Intelligence Programming: Case Studies in Common Lisp*. Morgan Kaufmann, San Mateo, California.

Nowick, S. M., Dean, M. E., Dill, D. L., and Horowitz, M. (1993). The design of a high-performance cache controller: a case study in asynchronous synthesis. *Integration: The VLSI Journal*, 15(3):241–262.

Nunberg, G. (1979). The non-uniqueness of semantic solutions: Polysemy. *Language and Philosophy*, 3(2):143–184.

Nussbaum, M. C. (1978). *Aristotle's* De Motu Animalium. Princeton University Press, Princeton, New Jersey.

O'Keefe, R. (1990). *The Craft of Prolog*. MIT Press, Cambridge, Massachusetts.

Olawsky, D. and Gini, M. (1990). Deferred planning and sensor use. In Sycara, K. P., editor, *Proceedings, DARPA Workshop on Innovative Approaches to Planning, Scheduling, and Control*, San Diego, California. Defense Advanced Research Projects Agency (DARPA), Morgan Kaufmann.

Olesen, K. G. (1993). Causal probabilistic networks with both discrete and continuous variables. *IEEE Transactions on Pattern Analysis and Machine Intelligence (PAMI)*, 15(3):275–279.

Oliver, R. M. and Smith, J. Q., editors (1990). *Influence Diagrams, Belief Nets and Decision Analysis*. Wiley, New York.

Olson, C. F. (1994). Time and space efficient pose clustering. In *Proceedings of the IEEE Conference on Computer Vision and Pattern Recognition*, pages 251–258, Seattle, Washington.

Ortony, A., editor (1979). *Metaphor and Thought*. Cambridge University Press, Cambridge.

Osherson, D. N., Stob, M., and Weinstein, S. (1986). *Systems That Learn: An Introduction to Learning Theory for Cognitive and Computer Scientists.* MIT Press, Cambridge, Massachusetts.

Paige, R. and Henglein, F. (1987). Mechanical translation of set theoretic problem specifications into efficient RAM code—a case study. *Journal of Symbolic Computation*, 4:207–232.

Palay, A. J. (1985). *Searching with Probabilities.* Pitman, London.

Palmieri, G. and Sanna, R. (1960). Automatic probabilistic programmer/analyzer for pattern recognition. *Methodos*, 12(48):331–357.

Papadimitriou, C. H. and Yannakakis, M. (1994). On complexity as bounded rationality. In *Symposium on Theory of Computation (STOC-94)*.

Parker, D. B. (1985). Learning logic. Technical Report TR-47, Center for Computational Research in Economics and Management Science, Massachusetts Institute of Technology, Cambridge, Massachusetts.

Partridge, D. (1991). *A New Guide to Artificial Intelligence.* Ablex, Norwood, New Jersey.

Paterson, M. S. and Wegman, M. N. (1978). Linear unification. *Journal of Computer and System Sciences*, 16:158–167.

Patrick, B. G., Almulla, M., and Newborn, M. M. (1992). An upper bound on the time complexity of iterative-deepening-A*. *Annals of Mathematics and Artificial Intelligence*, 5(2–4):265–278.

Paul, R. P. (1981). *Robot Manipulators: Mathematics, Programming, and Control.* MIT Press, Cambridge, Massachusetts.

Peano, G. (1889). *Arithmetices principia, nova methodo exposita.* Fratres Bocca, Turin.

Pearl, J. (1982a). Reverend Bayes on inference engines: A distributed hierarchical approach. In *Proceedings of the National Conference on Artificial Intelligence (AAAI-82)*, pages 133–136, Pittsburgh, Pennsylvania. Morgan Kaufmann.

Pearl, J. (1982b). The solution for the branching factor of the alpha-beta pruning algorithm and its optimality. *Communications of the Association for Computing Machinery*, 25(8):559–564.

Pearl, J. (1984). *Heuristics: Intelligent Search Strategies for Computer Problem Solving.* Addison-Wesley, Reading, Massachusetts.

Pearl, J. (1986). Fusion, propagation, and structuring in belief networks. *Artificial Intelligence*, 29:241–288.

Pearl, J. (1987). Evidential reasoning using stochastic simulation of causal models. *Artificial Intelligence*, 32:247–257.

Pearl, J. (1988). *Probabilistic Reasoning in Intelligent Systems: Networks of Plausible Inference.* Morgan Kaufmann, San Mateo, California.

Pednault, E. P. D. (1986). Formulating multiagent, dynamic-world problems in the classical planning framework. In Georgeff, M. P. and Lansky, A. L., editors, *Reasoning about Actions and Plans: Proceedings of the 1986 Workshop*, pages 47–82, Timberline, Oregon. Morgan Kaufmann.

Peirce, C. S. (1870). Description of a notation for the logic of relatives, resulting from an amplification of the conceptions of Boole's calculus of logic. *Memoirs of the American academy of arts and sciences*, 9:317–378.

Peirce, C. S. (1883). A theory of probable inference. Note B. The logic of relatives. In *Studies in logic by members of the Johns Hopkins University*, pages 187–203, Boston.

Peirce, C. S. (1902). Logic as semiotic: the theory of signs. Unpublished manuscript; reprinted in (Buchler, 1955, pp. 98–119).

Penberthy, J. S. and Weld, D. S. (1992). UCPOP: A sound, complete, partial order planner for ADL. In *Proceedings of KR-92*, pages 103–114.

Peng, J. and Williams, R. J. (1993). Efficient learning and planning within the Dyna framework. *Adaptive Behavior*, 2:437–454.

Penrose, R. (1990). The emperor's new mind: concerning computers, minds, and the laws of physics. *Behavioral and Brain Sciences*, 13(4):643–654.

Peot, M. and Smith, D. (1992). Conditional nonlinear planning. In Hendler, J., editor, *Proceedings of the First International Conference on AI Planning Systems*, pages 189–197, College Park, Maryland. Morgan Kaufmann.

Pereira, F. (1983). Logic for natural language analysis. Technical Note 275, SRI International.

Pereira, F. C. N. and Shieber, S. M. (1987). *Prolog and Natural-Language Analysis*. Center for the Study of Language and Information (CSLI), Stanford, California.

Pereira, F. C. N. and Warren, D. H. D. (1980). Definite clause grammars for language analysis: a survey of the formalism and a comparison with augmented transition networks. *Artificial Intelligence*, 13:231–278.

Peterson, C., Redfield, S., Keeler, J. D., and Hartman, E. (1990). An optoelectronic architecture for multilayer learning in a single photorefractive crystal. *Neural Computation*, 2:25–34.

Pinker, S. (1989). *Learnability and Cognition*. MIT Press, Cambridge, MA.

Place, U. T. (1956). Is consciousness a brain process? *British Journal of Psychology*, 47:44–50.

Plotkin, G. D. (1971). *Automatic Methods of Inductive Inference*. PhD thesis, Edinburgh University.

Pnueli, A. (1977). The temporal logic of programs. In *Proceedings of the 18th IEEE Symposium on the Foundations of Computer Science (FOCS-77)*, pages 46–57, Providence, Rhode Island. IEEE, IEEE Computer Society Press.

Pohl, I. (1969). Bi-directional and heuristic search in path problems. Technical Report 104, SLAC (Stanford Linear Accelerator Center, Stanford, California.

Pohl, I. (1970). First results on the effect of error in heuristic search. In Meltzer, B. and Michie, D., editors, *Machine Intelligence 5*, pages 219–236. Elsevier/North-Holland, Amsterdam, London, New York.

Pohl, I. (1971). Bi-directional search. In Meltzer, B. and Michie, D., editors, *Machine Intelligence 6*, pages 127–140. Edinburgh University Press, Edinburgh, Scotland.

Pohl, I. (1973). The avoidance of (relative) catastrophe, heuristic competence, genuine dynamic weighting and computational issues in heuristic problem solving. In *Proceedings of the Third International Joint Conference on Artificial Intelligence (IJCAI-73)*, pages 20–23, Stanford, California. IJCAII.

Pohl, I. (1977). Practical and theoretical considerations in heuristic search algorithms. In Elcock, E. W. and Michie, D., editors, *Machine Intelligence 8*, pages 55–72. Ellis Horwood, Chichester, England.

Pollard, C. and Sag, I. A. (1994). *Head-Driven Phrase Structure Grammar*. University of Chicago Press, Chicago, Illinois.

Pólya, G. (1957). *How to Solve It: A New Aspect of Mathematical Method*. Doubleday, Garden City, New York, second edition.

Pomerleau, D. A. (1993). *Neural Network Perception for Mobile Robot Guidance*. Kluwer, Dordrecht, The Netherlands.

Popper, K. R. (1959). *The Logic of Scientific Discovery*. Basic Books, New York.

Popper, K. R. (1962). *Conjectures and Refutations: The Growth of Scientific Knowledge*. Basic Books, New York.

Post, E. L. (1921). Introduction to a general theory of elementary propositions. *American Journal of Mathematics*, 43:163–185.

Pradhan, M., Provan, G. M., Middleton, B., and Henrion, M. (1994). Knowledge engineering for large belief networks. In *Proceedings of Uncertainty in Artificial Intelligence*, Seattle, Washington. Morgan Kaufmann.

Pratt, V. R. (1976). Semantical considerations on Floyd-Hoare logic. In *Proceedings of the 17th IEEE Symposium on the Foundations of Computer Science*, pages 109–121.

Prawitz, D. (1960). An improved proof procedure. *Theoria*, 26:102–139.

Prawitz, D. (1965). *Natural Deduction: A Proof Theoretical Study*. Almquist and Wiksell, Stockholm.

Prieditis, A. E. (1993). Machine discovery of effective admissible heuristics. *Machine Learning*, 12(1–3):117–141.

Prinz, D. G. (1952). Robot chess. *Research*, 5:261–266.

Prior, A. N. (1967). *Past, Present, and Future*. Oxford University Press, Oxford.

Pullum, G. K. (1991). *The Great Eskimo Vocabulary Hoax (and Other Irreverent Essays on the Study of Language)*. University of Chicago Press, Chicago, Illinois.

Purdom, P. (1983). Search rearrangement backtracking and polynomial average time. *Artificial Intelligence*, 21:117–133.

Putnam, H. (1960). Minds and machines. In Hook, S., editor, *Dimensions of Mind*, pages 138–164. Macmillan, London.

Putnam, H. (1963). 'Degree of confirmation' and inductive logic. In Schilpp, P. A., editor, *The Philosophy of Rudolf Carnap*. Open Court, La Salle, Illinois.

Putnam, H. (1967). The nature of mental states. In Capitan, W. H. and Merrill, D. D., editors, *Art, Mind, and Religion*, pages 37–48. University of Pittsburgh Press, Pittsburgh, Pennsylvania.Original title was "Psychological predicates"; title changed in later reprints at the request of the author.

Pylyshyn, Z. W. (1974). Minds, machines and phenomenology: Some reflections on Dreyfus' "What Computers Can't Do". *International Journal of Cognitive Psychology*, 3(1):57–77.

Pylyshyn, Z. W. (1984). *Computation and Cognition: Toward a Foundation for Cognitive Science*. MIT Press, Cambridge, Massachusetts.

Quillian, M. R. (1961). A design for an understanding machine. Paper presented at a colloquium: Semantic Problems in Natural Language, King's College, Cambridge, England.

Quillian, M. R. (1968). Semantic memory. In Minsky, M. L., editor, *Semantic Information Processing*, pages 216–270. MIT Press, Cambridge, Massachusetts.

Quine, W. V. (1953). Two dogmas of empiricism. In *From a Logical Point of View*, pages 20–46. Harper and Row, New York.

Quine, W. V. (1960). *Word and Object*. MIT Press, Cambridge, Massachusetts.

Quine, W. V. (1982). *Methods of Logic*. Harvard University Press, Cambridge, Massachusetts, fourth edition.

Quinlan, E. and O'Brien, S. (1992). Sublanguage: characteristics and selection guidelines for MT. In *AI and Cognitive Science '92: Proceedings of Annual Irish Conference on Artificial Intelligence and Cognitive Science '92*, pages 342–345, Limerick, Ireland. Springer-Verlag.

Quinlan, J. R. (1979). Discovering rules from large collections of examples: a case study. In Michie, D., editor, *Expert Systems in the Microelectronic Age*. Edinburgh University Press, Edinburgh, Scotland.

Quinlan, J. R. (1986). Induction of decision trees. *Machine Learning*, 1:81–106.

Quinlan, J. R. (1990). Learning logical definitions from relations. *Machine Learning*, 5(3):239–266.

Quinlan, J. R. (1993a). *C4.5: Programs for Machine Learning*. Morgan Kaufmann, San Mateo, California.

Quinlan, J. R. (1993b). Combining instance-based and model-based learning. In *Proceedings of the Tenth International Conference on Machine Learning*, pages 236–243, Amherst, Massachusetts. Morgan Kaufmann.

Quinlan, J. R. and Cameron-Jones, R. M. (1993). FOIL: a midterm report. In Brazdil, P. B., editor, *European Conference on Machine Learning Proceedings (ECML-93)*, pages 3–20, Vienna. Springer-Verlag.

Quirk, R., Greenbaum, S., Leech, G., and Svartvik, J. (1985). *A Comprehensive Grammar of the English Language*. Longman, New York.

Rabiner, L. R. (1990). A tutorial on hidden Markov models and selected applications in speech recognition. *Proceedings of the IEEE*. Reprinted in Waibel and Lee (1990).

Rabiner, L. R. and Juang, B.-H. (1993). *Fundamentals of Speech Recognition*. Prentice-Hall.

Raibert, M. H. (1986). *Legged Robots That Balance*. MIT Press, Cambridge, Massachusetts.

Ramsey, F. P. (1931). Truth and probability. In Braithwaite, R. B., editor, *The Foundations of Mathematics and Other Logical Essays*. Harcourt Brace Jovanovich, New York.

Raphael, B. (1968). SIR: Semantic information retrieval. In Minsky, M. L., editor, *Semantic Information Processing*, pages 33–134. MIT Press, Cambridge, Massachusetts.

Raphael, B. (1976). *The Thinking Computer: Mind Inside Matter*. W. H. Freeman, New York.

Ratner, D. and Warmuth, M. (1986). Finding a shortest solution for the $n \times n$ extension of the 15-puzzle is intractable. In *Proceedings of the Fifth National Conference on Artificial Intelligence (AAAI-86)*, volume 1, pages 168–172, Philadelphia, Pennsylvania. Morgan Kaufmann.

Reichardt, J. (1978). *Robots: Fact, Fiction, and Prediction*. Penguin Books, New York.

Reichenbach, H. (1949). *The Theory of Probability: An Inquiry into the Logical and Mathematical Foundations of the Calculus of Probability*. University of California Press, Berkeley and Los Angeles, second edition.

Reif, J. H. (1979). Complexity of the mover's problem and generalizations. In *Proceedings of the 20th IEEE Symposium on Foundations of Computer Science*, pages 421–427, San Juan, Puerto Rico. IEEE, IEEE Computer Society Press.

Reiter, R. (1980). A logic for default reasoning. *Artificial Intelligence*, 13(1–2):81–132.

Reiter, R. (1991). The frame problem in the situation calculus: a simple solution (sometimes) and a completeness result for goal regression. In Lifschitz, V., editor, *Artificial Intelligence and Mathematical Theory of Computation: Papers in Honor of John McCarthy*, pages 359–380. Academic Press, New York.

Reitman, W. and Wilcox, B. (1979). The structure and performance of the INTERIM.2 Go program. In *Proceedings of the Sixth International Joint Conference on Artificial Intelligence (IJCAI-79)*, pages 711–719, Tokyo. IJCAII.

Remus, H. (1962). Simulation of a learning machine for playing Go. In *Proceedings IFIP Congress*, pages 428–432. Elsevier/North-Holland.

Rényi, A. (1970). *Probability Theory*. Elsevier/North-Holland, Amsterdam, London, New York.

Rescher, N. and Urquhart, A. (1971). *Temporal Logic*. Springer-Verlag, Berlin.

Resnik, P. (1993). Semantic classes and syntactic ambiguity. *Proceedings of the ARPA Workshop on Human Language Technology*, Princeton, New Jersey.

Rich, E. and Knight, K. (1991). *Artificial Intelligence*. McGraw-Hill, New York, second edition.

Rieger, C. (1976). An organization of knowledge for problem solving and language comprehension. *Artificial Intelligence*, 7:89–127.

Ringle, M. (1979). *Philosophical Perspectives in Artificial Intelligence*. Humanities Press, Atlantic Highlands, New Jersey.

Rissanen, J. (1984). Universal coding, information, prediction, and estimation. *IEEE Transactions on Information Theory*, IT-30(4):629–636.

Ritchie, G. D. and Hanna, F. K. (1984). AM: a case study in AI methodology. *Artificial Intelligence*, 23(3):249–268.

Rivest, R. L. (1987). Learning decision lists. *Machine Learning*, 2(3):229–246.

Roach, J. W., Sundararajan, R., and Watson, L. T. (1990). Replacing unification by constraint satisfaction to improve logic program expressiveness. *Journal of Automated Reasoning*, 6(1):51–75.

Roberts, D. D. (1973). *The Existential Graphs of Charles S. Peirce*. Mouton, The Hague and Paris.

Roberts, L. G. (1963). Machine perception of three-dimensional solids. Technical Report 315, MIT Lincoln Laboratory. Ph.D. dissertation.

Robinson, J. A. (1965). A machine-oriented logic based on the resolution principle. *Journal of the Association for Computing Machinery*, 12:23–41.

Rock, I. (1984). *Perception*. W. H. Freeman, New York.

Rorty, R. (1965). Mind-body identity, privacy, and categories. *Review of Metaphysics*, 19(1):24–54.

Rosenblatt, F. (1957). The perceptron: A perceiving and recognizing automaton. Report 85-460-1, Project PARA, Cornell Aeronautical Laboratory, Ithaca, New York.

Rosenblatt, F. (1960). On the convergence of reinforcement procedures in simple perceptrons. Report VG-1196-G-4, Cornell Aeronautical Laboratory, Ithaca, New York.

Rosenblatt, F. (1962). *Principles of Neurodynamics*. Spartan, Chicago.

Rosenschein, J. S. and Genesereth, M. R. (1987). Communication and cooperation among logic-based agents. In Friesen, O. and Golshani, F., editors, *Sixth Annual International Phoenix Conference on Computers and Communications: 1987 Conference Proceedings*, pages 594–600. IEEE Computer Society Press.

Rosenschein, S. J. (1985). Formal theories of knowledge in AI and robotics. *New Generation Computing*, 3(4):345–357.

Rosenthal, D. M., editor (1971). *Materialism and the Mind-Body Problem*. Prentice-Hall, Englewood Cliffs, New Jersey.

Ross, S. M. (1988). *A First Course in Probability*. Macmillan, London, third edition.

Rothwell, C. A., Zisserman, A., Mundy, J. L., and Forsyth, D. A. (1993). Efficient model library access by projectively invariant indexing functions. In *Proceedings 1992 IEEE Computer Society Conference on Computer Vision and Pattern Recognition*, pages 109–114, Champaign, Illinois. IEEE Computer Society Press.

Roussel, P. (1975). Prolog: Manuel de référence et d'utilisation. Technical report, Groupe d'Intelligence Artificielle, Université d'Aix-Marseille.

Rouveirol, C. and Puget, J.-F. (1989). A simple and general solution for inverting resolution. In *Proceedings of the European Working Session on Learning*, pages 201–210, Porto, Portugal. Pitman.

Rowe, N. C. (1988). *Artificial intelligence through Prolog*. Prentice-Hall, Englewood Cliffs, New Jersey.

Rumelhart, D. E., Hinton, G. E., and Williams, R. J. (1986). Learning internal representations by error propagation. In Rumelhart, D. E. and McClelland, J. L., editors, *Parallel Distributed Processing*, volume 1, chapter 8, pages 318–362. MIT Press, Cambridge, Massachusetts.

Rumelhart, D. E. and McClelland, J. L., editors (1986). *Parallel Distributed Processing*. MIT Press, Cambridge, Massachusetts. In two volumes.

Ruspini, E. H., Lowrance, J. D., and Strat, T. M. (1992). Understanding evidential reasoning. *International Journal of Approximate Reasoning*, 6(3):401–424.

Russell, J. G. B. (1990). Is screening for abdominal aortic aneurysm worthwhile? *Clinical Radiology*, 41:182–184.

Russell, S. J. (1985). The compleat guide to MRS. Report STAN-CS-85-1080, Computer Science Department, Stanford University.

Russell, S. J. (1986). Preliminary steps toward the automation of induction. In *Proceedings of the Fifth National Conference on Artificial Intelligence (AAAI-86)*, Philadelphia, Pennsylvania. Morgan Kaufmann.

Russell, S. J. (1988). Tree-structured bias. In *Proceedings of the Seventh National Conference on Artificial Intelligence (AAAI-88)*, volume 2, pages 641–645, St. Paul, Minnesota. Morgan Kaufmann.

Russell, S. J. (1992). Efficient memory-bounded search methods. In *ECAI 92: 10th European Conference on Artificial Intelligence Proceedings*, pages 1–5, Vienna, Austria. Wiley.

Russell, S. J., Binder, J., and Koller, D. (1994). Adaptive probabilistic networks. Technical Report UCB/CSD-94-824, Computer Science Division, University of California at Berkeley.

Russell, S. J. and Grosof, B. (1987). A declarative approach to bias in concept learning. In *Proceedings of the Sixth National Conference on Artificial Intelligence (AAAI-87)*, Seattle, Washington. Morgan Kaufmann.

Russell, S. J. and Subramanian, D. (1993). Provably bounded optimal agents. In *Proceedings of the Thirteenth International Joint Conference on Artificial Intelligence (IJCAI-93)*, Chambery, France. Morgan Kaufmann.

Russell, S. J. and Wefald, E. H. (1989). On optimal game-tree search using rational meta-reasoning. In *Proceedings of the Eleventh International Joint Conference on Artificial Intelligence (IJCAI-89)*, pages 334–340, Detroit, Michigan. Morgan Kaufmann.

Russell, S. J. and Wefald, E. H. (1991). *Do the Right Thing: Studies in Limited Rationality*. MIT Press, Cambridge, Massachusetts.

Ryder, J. L. (1971). Heuristic analysis of large trees as generated in the game of Go. Memo AIM-155, Stanford Artificial Intelligence Project, Computer Science Department, Stanford University, Stanford, California.

Sacerdoti, E. D. (1974). Planning in a hierarchy of abstraction spaces. *Artificial Intelligence*, 5(2):115–135.

Sacerdoti, E. D. (1975). The nonlinear nature of plans. In *Proceedings of the Fourth International Joint Conference on Artificial Intelligence (IJCAI-75)*, pages 206–214, Tbilisi, Georgia. IJCAII.

Sacerdoti, E. D. (1977). *A Structure for Plans and Behavior*. Elsevier/North-Holland, Amsterdam, London, New York.

Sacerdoti, E. D., Fikes, R. E., Reboh, R., Sagalow-icz, D., Waldinger, R. J., and Wilber, B. M. (1976). QLISP—a language for the interactive development of complex systems. In *Proceedings of the AFIPS National Computer Conference*, pages 349–356.

Sachs, J. S. (1967). Recognition memory for syntactic and semantic aspects of connected discourse. *Perception and Psychophysics*, 2:437–442.

Sacks, E. and Joskowicz, L. (1993). Automated modeling and kinematic simulation of mechanisms. *Computer Aided Design*, 25(2):106–118.

Sager, N. (1981). *Natural Language Information Processing: A Computer Grammar of English and Its Applications*. Addison-Wesley, Reading, Massachusetts.

Salton, G. (1989). *Automatic Text Processing*. Addison-Wesley.

Sammut, C., Hurst, S., Kedzier, D., and Michie, D. (1992). Learning to fly. In *Proceedings of the Ninth International Conference on Machine Learning*, Aberdeen. Morgan Kaufmann.

Samuel, A. L. (1959). Some studies in machine learning using the game of checkers. *IBM Journal of Research and Development*, 3(3):210–229.

Samuel, A. L. (1967). Some studies in machine learning using the game of checkers II—Recent progress. *IBM Journal of Research and Development*, 11(6):601–617.

Samuelsson, C. and Rayner, M. (1991). Quantitative evaluation of explanation-based learning as an optimization tool for a large-scale natural language system. In *Proceedings of the Twelfth International Joint Conference on Artificial Intelligence (IJCAI-91)*, pages 609–615, Sydney. Morgan Kaufmann.

Saraswat, V. A. (1993). *Concurrent constraint programming*. MIT Press, Cambridge, Massachusetts.

Savage, L. J. (1954). *The Foundations of Statistics*. Wiley, New York.

Sayre, K. (1993). Three more flaws in the computational model. Paper presented at the APA (Central Division) Annual Conference, Chicago, Illinois.

Schabes, Y., Abeille, A., and Joshi, A. K. (1988). Parsing strategies with 'lexicalized' grammars: application to tree adjoining grammars. In Vargha, D., editor, *Proceedings of the 12th International Conference on Computational Linguistics (COLING)*, volume 2, pages 578–583, Budapest, Hungary. John von Neumann Society for Computer Science.

Schaeffer, J., Culberson, J., Treloar, N., and Knight, B. (1992). A world championship caliber checkers program. *Artificial Intelligence*, 53(2–3):273–289.

Schalkoff, R. J. (1990). *Artificial Intelligence: An Engineering Approach*. McGraw-Hill, New York.

Schank, R. C. and Abelson, R. P. (1977). *Scripts, Plans, Goals, and Understanding*. Lawrence Erlbaum Associates, Potomac, Maryland.

Schank, R. C. and Riesbeck, C. K. (1981). *Inside Computer Understanding: Five Programs Plus Miniatures*. Lawrence Erlbaum Associates, Potomac, Maryland.

Scherl, R. B. and Levesque, H. J. (1993). The frame problem and knowledge-producing actions. In *Proceedings of the Eleventh National Conference on Artificial Intelligence (AAAI-93)*, pages 689–695, Washington, D.C. AAAI Press.

Schmolze, J. G. and Lipkis, T. A. (1983). Classification in the KL-ONE representation system. In *Proceedings of the Eighth International Joint Conference on Artificial Intelligence (IJCAI-83)*, Karlsruhe, Germany. Morgan Kaufmann.

Schofield, P. D. A. (1967). Complete solution of the eight puzzle. In Dale, E. and Michie, D., editors, *Machine Intelligence 2*, pages 125–133. Elsevier/North-Holland, Amsterdam, London, New York.

Schönfinkel, M. (1924). Über die Bausteine der mathematischen Logik. *Mathematische Annalen*, 92:305–316. Translated into English and republished as "On the building blocks of mathematical logic" in (van Heijenoort, 1967, pp. 355–366).

Schoppers, M. J. (1987). Universal plans for reactive robots in unpredictable environments. In *Proceedings of the Tenth International Joint Conference on Artificial Intelligence (IJCAI-87)*, pages 1039–1046, Milan, Italy. Morgan Kaufmann.

Schoppers, M. J. (1989). In defense of reaction plans as caches. *AI Magazine*, 10(4):51–60.

Schröder, E. (1877). *Der Operationskreis des Logikkalküls*. B. G. Teubner, Leipzig.

Schwuttke, U. M. (1992). Artificial intelligence for real-time monitoring and control. In *Proceedings of the IEEE International Symposium on Industrial Electronics*, volume 1, pages 290–294, Xian, China.

Scriven, M. (1953). The mechanical concept of mind. *Mind*, 62:230–240.

Searle, J. R. (1969). *Speech Acts: An Essay in the Philosophy of Language*. Cambridge University Press, Cambridge.

Searle, J. R. (1980). Minds, brains, and programs. *Behavioral and Brain Sciences*, 3:417–457.

Searle, J. R. (1984). *Minds, Brains and Science*. Harvard University Press, Cambridge, Massachusetts.

Searle, J. R. (1992). *The Rediscovery of the Mind*. MIT Press, Cambridge, Massachusetts.

Sejnowski, T. J. and Rosenberg, C. R. (1987). Parallel networks that learn to pronounce English text. *Complex Systems*, 1:145–168.

Selfridge, O. G. (1959). Pandemonium: A paradigm for learning. In Blake, D. V. and Uttley, A. M., editors, *Proceedings of the Symposium on Mechanization of Thought Processes*, pages 511–529, Teddington, United Kingdom. National Physical Laboratory, Her Majesty's Stationery Office.

Selfridge, O. G. and Neisser, U. (1960). Pattern recognition by machine. *Scientific American*, 203:60–68. Reprinted in Feigenbaum and Feldman (1963).

Sells, P. (1985). *Lectures on Contemporary Syntactic Theories: An Introduction to Government-Binding Theory, Generalized Phrase Structure Grammar, and Lexical-Functional Grammar*. Center for the Study of Language and Information (CSLI), Stanford, California.

Selman, B., Levesque, H., and Mitchell, D. (1992). A new method for solving hard satisfiability problems. In *Proceedings of the Tenth National Conference on Artificial Intelligence (AAAI-92)*, pages 440–446, San Jose, California. AAAI Press.

Selman, B. and Levesque, H. J. (1993). The complexity of path-based defeasible inheritance. *Artificial Intelligence*, 62(2):303–339.

Shachter, R. D. (1986). Evaluating influence diagrams. *Operations Research*, 34:871–882.

Shachter, R. D., D'Ambrosio, B., and Del Favero, B. A. (1990). Symbolic probabilistic inference in belief networks. In *Proceedings of the Eighth National Conference on Artificial Intelligence (AAAI-90)*, pages 126–131, Boston, Massachusetts. MIT Press.

Shachter, R. D. and Peot, M. A. (1989). Simulation approaches to general probabilistic inference on belief networks. In *Proceedings of the Fifth Conference on Uncertainty in Artificial Intelligence (UAI-89)*, Windsor, Ontario. Morgan Kaufmann.

Shachter, R. S. and Kenley, C. R. (1989). Gaussian influence diagrams. *Management Science*, 35(5):527–550.

Shafer, G. (1976). *A Mathematical Theory of Evidence*. Princeton University Press, Princeton, New Jersey.

Shafer, G. and Pearl, J., editors (1990). *Readings in Uncertain Reasoning*. Morgan Kaufmann, San Mateo, California.

Shankar, N. (1986). *Proof-Checking Metamathematics*. PhD thesis, Computer Science Department, University of Texas at Austin.

Shannon, C. E. (1950). Programming a computer for playing chess. *Philosophical Magazine*, 41(4):256–275.

Shannon, C. E. and Weaver, W. (1949). *The Mathematical Theory of Communication*. University of Illinois Press, Urbana.

Shapiro, E. (1981). An algorithm that infers theories from facts. In *Proceedings of the Seventh International Joint Conference on Artificial Intelligence (IJCAI-81)*, Vancouver, British Columbia. Morgan Kaufmann.

Shapiro, E. Y. (1983). A subset of Concurrent Prolog and its interpreter. ICOT Technical Report TR-003, Institute for New Generation Computing Technology, Tokyo.

Shapiro, S. C. (1979). The SNePS semantic network processing system. In Findler, N. V., editor, *Associative Networks: Representation and Use of Knowledge by Computers*, pages 179–203. Academic Press, New York.

Shapiro, S. C. (1992). *Encyclopedia of Artificial Intelligence*. Wiley, New York, second edition. Two volumes.

Sharples, M., Hogg, D., Hutchinson, C., Torrance, S., and Young, D. (1989). *Computers and Thought: A Practical Introduction to Artificial Intelligence*. MIT Press, Cambridge, Massachusetts.

Shavlik, J. and Dietterich, T., editors (1990). *Readings in Machine Learning*. Morgan Kaufmann, San Mateo, California.

Shenoy, P. P. (1989). A valuation-based language for expert systems. *International Journal of Approximate Reasoning*, 3(5):383–411.

Shieber, S. M. (1986). *An Introduction to Unification-Based Approaches to Grammar*. Center for the Study of Language and Information (CSLI), Stanford, California.

Shirayanagi, K. (1990). Knowledge representation and its refinement in Go programs. In Marsland, A. T. and Schaeffer, J., editors, *Computers, Chess, and Cognition*, pages 287–300. Springer-Verlag, Berlin.

Shoham, Y. (1987). Temporal logics in AI: semantical and ontological considerations. *Artificial Intelligence*, 33(1):89–104.

Shoham, Y. (1988). *Reasoning about Change: Time and Causation from the Standpoint of Artificial Intelligence*. MIT Press, Cambridge, Massachusetts.

Shoham, Y. and McDermott, D. (1988). Problems in formal temporal reasoning. *Artificial Intelligence*, 36(1):49–61.

Shortliffe, E. H. (1976). *Computer-Based Medical Consultations: MYCIN*. Elsevier/North-Holland, Amsterdam, London, New York.

Shwe, M. and Cooper, G. (1991). An empirical analysis of likelihood-weighting simulation on a large, multiply connected medical belief network. *Computers and Biomedical Research*, 1991(5):453–475.

Siekmann, J. and Wrightson, G., editors (1983). *Automation of Reasoning*. Springer-Verlag, Berlin. Two volumes.

Sietsma, J. and Dow, R. J. F. (1988). Neural net pruning—why and how. In *IEEE International Conference on Neural Networks*, pages 325–333, San Diego. IEEE.

Siklossy, L. and Dreussi, J. (1973). An efficient robot planner which generates its own procedures. In *Proceedings of the Third International Joint Conference on Artificial Intelligence (IJCAI-73)*, pages 423–430, Stanford, California. IJCAII.

Simmons, R., Krotkov, E., Whittaker, W., and Albrecht, B. (1992). Progress towards robotic exploration of extreme terrain. *Applied Intelligence: The*

International Journal of Artificial Intelligence, Neural Networks, and Complex Problem-Solving Technologies, 2(2):163–180.

Simon, H. A. (1958). Rational choice and the structure of the environment. In *Models of Bounded Rationality*, volume 2. MIT Press, Cambridge, Massachusetts.

Simon, H. A. (1963). Experiments with a heuristic compiler. *Journal of the Association for Computing Machinery*, 10:493–506.

Simon, H. A. (1981). *The Sciences of the Artificial*. MIT Press, Cambridge, Massachusetts, second edition.

Simon, H. A. and Newell, A. (1958). Heuristic problem solving: The next advance in operations research. *Operations Research*, 6:1–10. Based on a talk given in 1957.

Simon, H. A. and Newell, A. (1961). Computer simulation of human thinking and problem solving. *Datamation*, pages 35–37.

Siskind, J. M. (1994). Lexical acquisition in the presence of noise and homonymy. In *Proceedings of AAAI-94*.

Skinner, B. F. (1953). *Science and Human Behavior*. Macmillan, London.

Skolem, T. (1920). Logisch-kombinatorische Untersuchungen über die Erfüllbarkeit oder Beweisbarkeit mathematischer Sätze nebst einem Theoreme über die dichte Mengen. *Videnskapsselskapets skrifter, I. Matematisk-naturvidenskabelig klasse*, 4.

Skolem, T. (1928). Über die mathematische Logik. *Norsk matematisk tidsskrift*, 10:125–142.

Slagle, J. R. (1963a). A heuristic program that solves symbolic integration problems in freshman calculus. *Journal of the Association for Computing Machinery*, 10(4). Reprinted in Feigenbaum and Feldman (1963).

Slagle, J. R. (1963b). Game trees, *m* & *n* minimaxing, and the *m* & *n* alpha-beta procedure. Artificial Intelligence Group Report 3, University of California, Lawrence Radiation Laboratory, Livermore, California.

Slagle, J. R. (1971). *Artificial Intelligence: The Heuristic Programming Approach*. McGraw-Hill, New York.

Slagle, J. R. and Dixon, J. K. (1969). Experiments with some programs that search game trees. *Journal of the Association for Computing Machinery*, 16(2):189–207.

Slate, D. J. and Atkin, L. R. (1977). CHESS 4.5—The Northwestern University chess program. In Frey, P. W., editor, *Chess Skill in Man and Machine*, pages 82–118. Springer-Verlag, Berlin.

Slater, E. (1950). Statistics for the chess computer and the factor of mobility. In *Symposium on Information Theory*, pages 150–152, London. Ministry of Supply.

Sloman, A. (1978). *The Computer Revolution in Philosophy*. Harvester Press, Hassocks, Sussex.

Sloman, A. (1985). POPLOG, a multi-purpose multi-language program development environment. In *Artificial Intelligence—Industrial and Commercial Applications. First International Conference*, pages 45–63, London. Queensdale.

Smallwood, R. D. and Sondik, E. J. (1973). The optimal control of partially observable Markov processes over a finite horizon. *Operations Research*, 21:1071–1088.

Smith, D. E. (1989). Controlling backward inference. *Artificial Intelligence*, 39(2):145–208.

Smith, D. E., Genesereth, M. R., and Ginsberg, M. L. (1986). Controlling recursive inference. *Artificial Intelligence*, 30(3):343–389.

Smith, D. R. (1990). KIDS: a semiautomatic program development system. *IEEE Transactions on Software Engineering*, 16(9):1024–1043.

Soderland, S. and Weld, D. (1991). Evaluating nonlinear planning. Technical Report TR-91-02-03, University of Washington Department of Computer Science and Engineering, Seattle, Washington.

Solomonoff, R. J. (1964). A formal theory of inductive inference. *Information and Control*, 7:1–22, 224–254.

Sondik, E. J. (1971). *The Optimal Control of Partially Observable Markov Decision Processes*. PhD thesis, Stanford University, Stanford, California.

Spiegelhalter, D., Dawid, P., Lauritzen, S., and Cowell, R. (1993). Bayesian analysis in expert systems. *Statistical Science*, 8:219–282.

Spiegelhalter, D. J. (1986). Probabilistic reasoning in predictive expert systems. In Kanal, L. N. and Lemmer, J. F., editors, *Uncertainty in Artificial Intelligence*, pages 47–67. Elsevier/North-Holland, Amsterdam, London, New York.

Spirtes, P., Glymour, C., and Scheines, R. (1993). *Causation, prediction, and search*. Springer-Verlag, Berlin.

Srivas, M. and Bickford, M. (1990). Formal verification of a pipelined microprocessor. *IEEE Software*, 7(5):52–64.

Steele, G. (1990). *Common LISP: The Language*. Digital Press, Bedford, Massachusetts, second edition.

Stefik, M. J. (1981a). Planning and meta-planning. *Artificial Intelligence*, 16:141–169.

Stefik, M. J. (1981b). Planning with constraints. *Artificial Intelligence*, 16:111–140.

Sterling, L. and Shapiro, E. (1986). *The Art of Prolog*. MIT Press, Cambridge, Massachusetts.

Stevens, K. A. (1981). The information content of texture gradients. *Biological Cybernetics*, 42:95–105.

Stickel, M. E. (1985). Automated deduction by theory resolution. *Journal of Automated Reasoning*, 1(4):333–355.

Stickel, M. E. (1988). A Prolog Technology Theorem Prover: implementation by an extended Prolog compiler. *Journal of Automated Reasoning*, 4:353–380.

Stockman, G. (1979). A minimax algorithm better than alpha-beta? *Artificial Intelligence*, 12(2):179–196.

Stolcke, A. (1993). An efficient probabilistic context-free parsing algorithm that computes prefix probabilities. Report TR-93-065, ICSI, Berkeley.

Stone, H. S. and Stone, J. (1986). Efficient search techniques: an empirical study of the *n*-queens problem. Technical Report RC 12057, IBM Thomas J. Watson Research Center, Yorktown Heights, New York.

Stonebraker, M. (1992). The integration of rule systems and database systems. *IEEE Transactions on Knowledge and Data Engineering*, 4(5):415–423.

Strachey, C. S. (1952). Logical or non-mathematical programmes. In *Proceedings of the Association for Computing Machinery (ACM)*, pages 46–49, Ontario, Canada.

Subramanian, D. (1993). Artificial intelligence and conceptual design. In *Proceedings of the Thirteenth International Joint Conference on Artificial Intelligence (IJCAI-93)*, pages 800–809, Chambery, France. Morgan Kaufmann.

Subramanian, D. and Feldman, R. (1990). The utility of EBL in recursive domain theories. In *Proceedings of the Eighth National Conference on Artificial Intelligence (AAAI-90)*, volume 2, pages 942–949, Boston, Massachusetts. MIT Press.

Subramanian, D. and Wang, E. (1994). Constraint-based kinematic synthesis. In *Proceedings of the International Conference on Qualitative Reasoning*. AAAI Press.

Sugihara, K. (1984). A necessary and sufficient condition for a picture to represent a polyhedral scene. *IEEE Transactions on Pattern Analysis and Machine Intelligence (PAMI)*, 6(5):578–586.

Sussman, G. J. (1975). *A Computer Model of Skill Acquisition*. Elsevier/North-Holland, Amsterdam, London, New York.

Sussman, G. J. and McDermott, D. V. (1972). From PLANNER to CONNIVER—a genetic approach. In *Proceedings of the 1972 AFIPS Joint Computer Conference*, pages 1171–1179.

Sussman, G. J. and Winograd, T. (1970). MICRO-PLANNER Reference Manual. AI Memo 203, MIT AI Lab, Cambridge, Massachusetts.

Sutton, R. S. (1988). Learning to predict by the methods of temporal differences. *Machine Learning*, 3:9–44.

Swade, D. D. (1993). Redeeming Charles Babbage's mechanical computer. *Scientific American*, 268(2):86–91.

Tadepalli, P. (1993). Learning from queries and examples with tree-structured bias. In *Proceedings of the Tenth International Conference on Machine Learning*, Amherst, Massachusetts. Morgan Kaufmann.

Tait, P. G. (1880). Note on the theory of the "15 puzzle". *Proceedings of the Royal Society of Edinburgh*, 10:664–665.

Taki, K. (1992). Parallel inference machine PIM. In *Fifth Generation Computer Systems 1992*, volume 1, pages 50–72, Tokyo. IOS Press.

Tambe, M., Newell, A., and Rosenbloom, P. S. (1990). The problem of expensive chunks and its solution by restricting expressiveness. *Machine Learning*, 5:299–348.

Tanimoto, S. (1990). *The Elements of Artificial Intelligence Using Common LISP*. Computer Science Press, Rockville, Maryland.

Tarjan, R. E. (1983). *Data Structures and Network Algorithms*. CBMS-NSF Regional Conference Series in Applied Mathematics. SIAM (Society for Industrial and Applied Mathematics, Philadelphia, Pennsylvania.

Tarski, A. (1935). Die Wahrheitsbegriff in den formalisierten Sprachen. *Studia Philosophica*, 1:261–405.

Tarski, A. (1956). *Logic, Semantics, Metamathematics: Papers from 1923 to 1938*. Oxford University Press, Oxford.

Tash, J. K. and Russell, S. J. (1994). Control strategies for a stochastic planner. In *Proceedings of the Twelfth National Conference on Artificial Intelligence (AAAI-94)*, Seattle, Washington. AAAI Press.

Tate, A. (1975a). Interacting goals and their use. In *Proceedings of the Fourth International Joint Conference on Artificial Intelligence (IJCAI-75)*, pages 215–218, Tbilisi, Georgia. IJCAII.

Tate, A. (1975b). *Using Goal Structure to Direct Search in a Problem Solver*. PhD thesis, University of Edinburgh, Edinburgh, Scotland.

Tate, A. (1977). Generating project networks. In *Proceedings of the Fifth International Joint Conference on Artificial Intelligence (IJCAI-77)*, pages 888–893, Cambridge, Massachusetts. IJCAII.

Tate, A. and Whiter, A. M. (1984). Planning with multiple resource constraints and an application to a naval planning problem. In *Proceedings of the First Conference on AI Applications*, pages 410–416, Denver, Colorado.

Tatman, J. A. and Shachter, R. D. (1990). Dynamic programming and influence diagrams. *IEEE Transactions on Systems, Man and Cybernetics*, 20(2):365–379.

Taylor, R. J. (1989). Review of ernst (1961). In Khatib, O., Craig, J. J., and Lozano-Pérez, T., editors, *The Robotics Review 1*, pages 121–127. MIT Press, Cambridge, Massachusetts.

Tenenberg, J. (1988). Abstraction in planning. Technical Report TR250, University of Rochester, Rochester, New York.

Tennant, H. R., Ross, K. M., Saenz, R. M., and Thompson, C. W. (1983). Menu-based natural language understanding. In *21st Annual Meeting of the Association for Computational Linguistics: Proceedings of the Conference*, pages 151–158, Cambridge, Massachusetts.

Tesauro, G. (1992). Practical issues in temporal difference learning. *Machine Learning*, 8(3–4):257–277.

Tesauro, G. and Sejnowski, T. J. (1989). A parallel network that learns to play backgammon. *Artificial Intelligence*, 39(3):357–390.

Thomason, R. H., editor (1974). *Formal Philosophy: Selected Papers of Richard Montague*. Yale University Press, New Haven, Connecticut.

Thorne, J., Bratley, P., and Dewar, H. (1968). The syntactic analysis of English by machine. In Michie, D., editor, *Machine Intelligence 3*, pages 281–310. Elsevier/North-Holland, Amsterdam, London, New York.

Todd, B. S., Stamper, R., and Macpherson, P. (1993). A probabilistic rule-based expert system. *International Journal of Bio-Medical Computing*, 33(2):129–148.

Tomasi, C. and Kanade, T. (1992). Shape and motion from image streams under orthography: a factorization method. *International Journal of Computer Vision*, 9:137–154.

Touretzky, D. S. (1986). *The Mathematics of Inheritance Systems*. Pitman and Morgan Kaufmann, London and San Mateo, California.

Touretzky, D. S., editor (1989). *Advances in Neural Information Processing Systems 1*. Morgan Kaufmann, San Mateo, California.

Turing, A. M. (1936). On computable numbers, with an application to the Entscheidungsproblem. *Proceedings of the London Mathematical Society, 2nd series*, 42:230–265. Correction published in Vol. 43, pages 544–546.

Turing, A. M. (1950). Computing machinery and intelligence. *Mind*, 59:433—460.

Turing, A. M., Strachey, C., Bates, M. A., and Bowden, B. V. (1953). Digital computers applied to games. In Bowden, B. V., editor, *Faster Than Thought*, pages 286–310. Pitman, London. Turing is believed to be sole author of the section of this paper that deals with chess.

Tversky, A. and Kahneman, D. (1982). Causal schemata in judgements under uncertainty. In Kahneman, D., Slovic, P., and Tversky, A., editors, *Judgement Under Uncertainty: Heuristics and Biases*. Cambridge University Press, Cambridge.

Ueda, K. (1985). Guarded Horn clauses. ICOT Technical Report TR-103, Institute for New Generation Computing Technology, Tokyo.

Ullman, J. D. (1989). *Principles of Database and Knowledge-Base Bystems*. Computer Science Press, Rockville, Maryland.

Ullman, S. (1979). *The Interpretation of Visual Motion*. MIT Press, Cambridge, Massachusetts.

Valiant, L. (1984). A theory of the learnable. *Communications of the Association for Computing Machinery*, 27:1134–1142.

van Benthem, J. (1983). *The Logic of Time*. D. Reidel, Dordrecht, The Netherlands.

van Benthem, J. (1985). *A Manual of Intensional Logic*. Center for the Study of Language and Information (CSLI), Stanford, California.

van Harmelen, F. and Bundy, A. (1988). Explanation-based generalisation = partial evaluation. *Artificial Intelligence*, 36(3):401–412.

van Heijenoort, J., editor (1967). *From Frege to Gödel: A Source Book in Mathematical Logic, 1879–1931*. Harvard University Press, Cambridge, Massachusetts.

Van Roy, P. L. (1990). Can logic programming execute as fast as imperative programming? Report UCB/CSD 90/600, Computer Science Division, University of California, Berkeley. Ph.D. dissertation.

VanLehn, K. (1978). Determining the scope of English quantifiers. Technical Report AI-TR-483, MIT AI Lab.

Vapnik, V. N. and Chervonenkis, A. Y. (1971). On the uniform convergence of relative frequencies of events to their probabilities. *Theory of Probability and Its Applications*, 16:264–280.

Vasconcellos, M. and León, M. (1985). SPANAM and ENGSPAN: machine translation at the Pan American Health Organization. *Computational Linguistics*, 11(2–3):122–136.

Veloso, M. and Carbonell, J. (1993). Derivational analogy in PRODIGY: automating case acquisition, storage, and utilization. *Machine Learning*, 10:249–278.

Vendler, Z. (1967). *Linguistics and Philosophy*. Cornell University Press, Ithaca, New York.

Vendler, Z. (1968). *Adjectives and Nominalizations*. Mouton, The Hague and Paris.

Vere, S. A. (1983). Planning in time: windows and durations for activities and goals. *IEEE Transactions on Pattern Analysis and Machine Intelligence (PAMI)*, 5:246–267.

von Mises, R. (1928). *Wahrscheinlichkeit, Statistik und Wahrheit*. J. Springer, Berlin. Translated into English as von Mises (1957).

von Mises, R. (1957). *Probability, Statistics, and Truth*. Allen and Unwin, London.

Von Neumann, J. (1958). *The Computer and the Brain*. Yale University Press, New Haven, Connecticut.

Von Neumann, J. and Morgenstern, O. (1944). *Theory of games and economic behavior*. Princeton University Press, Princeton, New Jersey, first edition.

von Winterfeldt, D. and Edwards, W. (1986). *Decision Analysis and Behavioral Research*. Cambridge University Press, Cambridge.

Voorhees, E. M. (1993). Using WordNet to disambiguate word senses for text retrieval. In *Sixteenth Annual International ACM SIGIR Conference on Research and Development in Information Retrieval*, pages 171–80, Pittsburgh, Pennsylvania. Association for Computing Machinery.

Waibel, A. and Lee, K.-F. (1990). *Readings in Speech Recognition*. Morgan Kaufmann, San Mateo, California.

Waldinger, R. (1975). Achieving several goals simultaneously. In Elcock, E. W. and Michie, D., editors, *Machine Intelligence 8*, pages 94–138. Ellis Horwood, Chichester, England.

Waltz, D. (1975). Understanding line drawings of scenes with shadows. In Winston, P. H., editor,

The Psychology of Computer Vision. McGraw-Hill, New York.

Wand, M. (1980). Continuation-based program transformation strategies. *Journal of the ACM*, 27(1):174–180.

Wang, H. (1960). Toward mechanical mathematics. *IBM Journal of Research and Development*, 4:2–22.

Wanner, E. and Gleitman, L., editors (1982). *Language Acquisition: The State of the Art*. Cambridge University Press.

Warren, D. H. D. (1974). WARPLAN: a system for generating plans. Department of Computational Logic Memo 76, University of Edinburgh, Edinburgh, Scotland.

Warren, D. H. D. (1976). Generating conditional plans and programs. In *Proceedings of the AISB Summer Conference*, pages 344–354.

Warren, D. H. D. (1983). An abstract Prolog instruction set. Technical Note 309, SRI International, Menlo Park, California.

Warren, D. H. D., Pereira, L. M., and Pereira, F. (1977). PROLOG: The language and its implementation compared with LISP. *SIGPLAN Notices*, 12(8):109–115.

Wasserman, P. D. and Oetzel, R. M., editors (1990). *NeuralSource: The Bibliographic Guide to Artificial Neural Networks*. Van Nostrand Reinhold, New York.

Watkins, C. J. (1989). *Models of Delayed Reinforcement Learning*. PhD thesis, Psychology Department, Cambridge University, Cambridge, United Kingdom.

Watson, C. S. (1991). Speech-perception aids for hearing-impaired people: current status and needed research. *Journal of the Acoustical Society of America*, 90(2):637–685.

Webber, B. L. (1983). So what can we talk about now. In Brady, M. and Berwick, R., editors, *Computational Models of Discourse*. MIT Press. Reprinted in Grosz *et al.* (1986).

Webber, B. L. (1988). Tense as discourse anaphora. *Computational Linguistics*, 14(2):61–73.

Webber, B. L. and Nilsson, N. J. (1981). *Readings in Artificial Intelligence*. Morgan Kaufmann, San Mateo, California.

Weiss, S. M. and Kulikowski, C. A. (1991). *Computer Systems That Learn: Classification and Prediction Methods from Statistics, Neural Nets, Machine Learning, and Expert Systems*. Morgan Kaufmann, San Mateo, California.

Weizenbaum, J. (1965). ELIZA—a computer program for the study of natural language communication between man and machine. *Communications of the Association for Computing Machinery*, 9(1):36–45.

Weizenbaum, J. (1976). *Computer Power and Human Reason*. W. H. Freeman, New York.

Weld, D. and Etzioni, O. (1994). The first law of robotics: A call to arms. In *Proceedings of the Twelfth National Conference on Artificial Intelligence (AAAI-94)*, Seattle, Washington. AAAI Press.

Weld, D. S. (1994). An introduction to least commitment planning. *AI Magazine*. To appear.

Weld, D. S. and de Kleer, J. (1990). *Readings in Qualitative Reasoning about Physical Systems*. Morgan Kaufmann, San Mateo, California.

Wellman, M. and Doyle, J. (1992). Modular utility representation for decision-theoretic planning. In *Proceedings, First International Conference on AI Planning Systems*, College Park, Maryland. Morgan Kaufmann.

Wellman, M. P. (1985). Reasoning about preference models. Technical Report MIT/LCS/TR-340, Laboratory for Computer Science, MIT, Cambridge, Massachusetts. M.S. thesis.

Wellman, M. P. (1988). *Formulation of Trade-offs in Planning under Uncertainty*. PhD thesis, Massachusetts Institute of Technology, Cambridge, Massachusetts.

Wellman, M. P. (1990). Fundamental concepts of qualitative probabilistic networks. *Artificial Intelligence*, 44(3):257–303.

Werbos, P. (1974). *Beyond Regression: New Tools for Prediction and Analysis in the Behavioral Sciences*. PhD thesis, Harvard University, Cambridge, Massachusetts.

Wheatstone, C. (1838). On some remarkable, and hitherto unresolved, phenomena of binocular vision. *Philosophical Transactions of the Royal Society of London*, 2:371–394.

Whitehead, A. N. (1911). *An Introduction to Mathematics*. Williams and Northgate, London.

Whitehead, A. N. and Russell, B. (1910). *Principia Mathematica*. Cambridge University Press, Cambridge.

Whorf, B. (1956). *Language, Thought, and Reality*. MIT Press, Cambridge, Massachusetts.

Widrow, B. (1962). Generalization and information storage in networks of adaline "neurons". In Yovits, M. C., Jacobi, G. T., and Goldstein, G. D., editors, *Self-Organizing Systems 1962*, pages 435–461, Chicago, Illinois. Spartan.

Widrow, B. and Hoff, M. E. (1960). Adaptive switching circuits. In *1960 IRE WESCON Convention Record*, pages 96–104, New York.

Wiener, N. (1942). The extrapolation, interpolation, and smoothing of stationary time series. OSRD 370, Report to the Services 19, Research Project DIC-6037, MIT.

Wiener, N. (1948). *Cybernetics*. Wiley, New York.

Wilensky, R. (1983). *Planning and Understanding*. Addison-Wesley.

Wilensky, R. (1990). Computability, consciousness, and algorithms. *Behavioral and Brain Sciences*, 13(4):690–691. Peer commentary on Penrose (1990).

Wilkins, D. E. (1980). Using patterns and plans in chess. *Artificial Intelligence*, 14(2):165–203.

Wilkins, D. E. (1986). Hierarchical planning: definition and implementation. In *ECAI '86: Seventh European Conference on Artificial Intelligence*, volume 1, pages 466–478, Brighton, United Kingdom.

Wilkins, D. E. (1988). *Practical Planning: Extending the AI Planning Paradigm*. Morgan Kaufmann, San Mateo, California.

Wilkins, D. E. (1990). Can AI planners solve practical problems? *Computational Intelligence*, 6(4):232–246.

Wilks, Y. (1975). An intelligent analyzer and understander of English. *Communications of the ACM*, 18(5):264–274. Reprinted in Grosz *et al.* (1986).

Wilson, R. H. and Schweikard, A. (1992). Assembling polyhedra with single translations. In *IEEE Conference on Robotics and Automation*, pages 2392–2397.

Winograd, S. and Cowan, J. D. (1963). *Reliable Computation in the Presence of Noise*. MIT Press, Cambridge, Massachusetts.

Winograd, T. (1972). Understanding natural language. *Cognitive Psychology*, 3(1). Reprinted as a book by Academic Press.

Winograd, T. and Flores, F. (1986). *Understanding Computers and Cognition*. Ablex, Norwood, New Jersey.

Winston, P. H. (1970). Learning structural descriptions from examples. Technical Report MAC-TR-76, Department of Electrical Engineering and Computer Science, Massachusetts Institute of Technology, Cambridge, Massachusetts. PhD dissertation.

Winston, P. H. (1992). *Artificial Intelligence*. Addison-Wesley, Reading, Massachusetts, third edition.

Wittgenstein, L. (1922). *Tractatus Logico-Philosophicus*. Routledge and Kegan Paul, London, second edition. Reprinted 1971, edited by D. F. Pears and B. F. McGuinness. This edition of the English translation also contains Wittgenstein's original German text on facing pages, as well as Bertrand Russell's introduction to the 1922 edition.

Wittgenstein, L. (1953). *Philosophical Investigations*. Macmillan, London.

Woehr, J. (1994). Lotfi visions, part 2. *Dr. Dobbs Journal*, 217.

Wojciechowski, W. S. and Wojcik, A. S. (1983). Automated design of multiple-valued logic circuits by automated theorem proving techniques. *IEEE Transactions on Computers*, C-32(9):785–798.

Wojcik, A. S. (1983). Formal design verification of digital systems. In *ACM IEEE 20th Design Automation Conference Proceedings*, pages 228–234, Miami Beach, Florida. IEEE.

Woods, W. (1972). Progress in natural language understanding: An application to lunar geology. In *AFIPS Conference Proceedings*, Vol. 42.

Woods, W. (1978). Semantics and quantification in natural language question answering. In *Advances in Computers*. Academic Press. Reprinted in Grosz *et al.* (1986).

Woods, W. A. (1970). Transition network grammars for natural language analysis. *Communications of the Association for Computing Machinery*, 13(10):591–606.

Woods, W. A. (1973). Progress in natural language understanding: An application to lunar geology. In *AFIPS Conference Proceedings*, volume 42, pages 441–450.

Woods, W. A. (1975). What's in a link: Foundations for semantic networks. In Bobrow, D. G. and Collins, A. M., editors, *Representation and Understanding: Studies in Cognitive Science*, pages 35–82. Academic Press, New York.

Wos, L., Carson, D., and Robinson, G. (1964). The unit preference strategy in theorem proving. In *Proceedings of the Fall Joint Computer Conference*, pages 615–621.

Wos, L., Carson, D., and Robinson, G. (1965). Efficiency and completeness of the set-of-support strategy in theorem proving. *Journal of the Association for Computing Machinery*, 12:536–541.

Wos, L., Overbeek, R., Lusk, E., and Boyle, J. (1992). *Automated Reasoning: Introduction and Applications*. McGraw-Hill, New York, second edition.

Wos, L., Robinson, G., Carson, D., and Shalla, L. (1967). The concept of demodulation in theorem proving. *Journal of the Association for Computing Machinery*, 14:698–704.

Wos, L. and Robinson, G. A. (1968). Paramodulation and set of support. In *Proceedings of the IRIA Symposium on Automatic Demonstration*, pages 276–310. Springer-Verlag.

Wos, L. and Winker, S. (1983). Open questions solved with the assistance of AURA. In Bledsoe, W. W. and Loveland, D. W., editors, *Automated Theorem Proving: After 25 Years: Proceedings of the Special Session of the 89th Annual Meeting of the American Mathematical Society*, pages 71–88, Denver, Colorado. American Mathematical Society.

Wright, S. (1921). Correlation and causation. *Journal of Agricultural Research*, 20:557–585.

Wright, S. (1934). The method of path coefficients. *Annals of Mathematical Statistics*, 5:161–215.

Wu, D. (1993). Estimating probability distributions over hypotheses with variable unification. In *Proceedings of the Thirteenth International Joint Conference on Artificial Intelligence (IJCAI-93)*, pages 790–795, Chambery, France. Morgan Kaufmann.

Yang, Q. (1990). Formalizing planning knowledge for hierarchical planning. *Computational Intelligence*, 6:12–24.

Yarowsky, D. (1992). Word-sense disambiguation using statistical models of Roget's categories trained on large corpora. In *Proceedings of COLING-92*, pages 454–460, Nantes, France.

Yip, K. M.-K. (1991). *KAM: A System for Intelligently Guiding Numerical Experimentation by Computer*. MIT Press, Cambridge, Massachusetts.

Yoshikawa, T. (1990). *Foundations of Robotics: Analysis and Control*. MIT Press, Cambridge, Massachusetts.

Younger, D. H. (1967). Recognition and parsing of context-free languages in time n^3. *Information and Control*, 10(2):189–208.

Zadeh, L. A. (1965). Fuzzy sets. *Information and Control*, 8:338–353.

Zadeh, L. A. (1978). Fuzzy sets as a basis for a theory of possibility. *Fuzzy Sets and Systems*, 1:3–28.

Zermelo, E. (1976). An application of set theory to the theory of chess-playing. *Firbush News*, 6:37–42.

English translation of German paper given at the 5th International Congress of Mathematics, Cambridge, England, in 1912.

Zilberstein, S. (1993). *Operational Rationality through Compilation of Anytime Algorithms*. PhD thesis, University of California, Berkeley, California.

Zimmermann, H.-J. (1991). *Fuzzy Set Theory—And Its Applications*. Kluwer, Dordrecht, The Netherlands, second revised edition.

Zobrist, A. L. (1970). *Feature Extraction and Representation for Pattern Recognition and the Game of Go*. PhD thesis, University of Wisconsin.

Zue, V., Seneff, S., Polifroni, J., Phillips, M., Pao, C., Goddeau, D., Glass, J., and Brill, E. (1994). Pegasus: A spoken language interface for on-line air travel planning. In *ARPA Workshop on Human Language Technology*.

Zuse, K. (1945). The Plankalkül. Report 175, Gesellschaft für Mathematik und Datenverarbeitung, Bonn. Technical report version republished in 1989.

Index

Page numbers in **bold** are definitions of terms and algorithms; page numbers in *italics* are references to the bibliography.